ENCYCLOPEDIA OF

U.S. Campaigns, Elections, and Electoral Behavior

★ ★ ★

(Volume 2)

ENCYCLOPEDIA OF

U.S. Campaigns, Elections, and Electoral Behavior

★ ★ ★

KENNETH F. WARREN
GENERAL EDITOR

SAGE

Los Angeles • London • New Delhi • Singapore

A SAGE Reference Publication

For information:

SAGE Publications, Inc.
2455 Teller Road
Thousand Oaks, California 91320
E-mail: order@sagepub.com

SAGE Publications Ltd.
1 Oliver's Yard
55 City Road
London EC1Y 1SP
United Kingdom

SAGE Publications India Pvt. Ltd.
B 1/I 1 Mohan Cooperative Industrial Area
Mathura Road, New Delhi 110 044
India

SAGE Publications Asia-Pacific Pte. Ltd.
33 Pekin Street #02-01
Far East Square
Singapore 048763

Library of Congress Cataloging-in-Publication Data

Encyclopedia of U.S. campaigns, elections, and electoral behavior / Kenneth F. Warren, general editor.
    p. cm. — (A Sage reference publication)
Includes bibliographical references and index.
ISBN 978-1-4129-5489-1 (cloth)
  1. Political campaigns-- United States --Encyclopedias. 2. Elections-- United States --Encyclopedias. I. Warren, Kenneth F., 1943-

JK2281.E53 2008
324.973003--dc22   2007050207

This book is printed on acid-free paper.
08 09 10 11 12 10 9 8 7 6 5 4 3 2 1

Photo credits are on page I–54

GOLSON BOOKS, LTD.

President and Editor	J. Geoffrey Golson
Creative Director	Mary Jo Scibetta
Managing Editor	Susan Moskowitz
Copyeditor	Mary Le Rouge
Layout Editor	Oona Patrick
Proofreader	Deborah Green
Indexer	J S Editorial

SAGE REFERENCE

Vice President and Publisher	Rolf Janke
Project Editor	Tracy Buyan
Cover Production	Janet Foulger
Marketing Manager	Amberlyn Erzinger
Editorial Assistant	Michele Thompson
Reference Systems Manager	Leticia Gutierrez

ENCYCLOPEDIA OF

U.S. Campaigns, Elections, and Electoral Behavior

CONTENTS

List of Articles

Nader, Ralph (1934–)

PRIOR TO THE 2000 presidential contest, most Americans knew Ralph Nader better as a crusading consumer and environmental activist. While his candidacies had little effect on the outcomes of the 1996 and 2004 presidential elections, his candidacy in 2000 probably changed the outcome of that election. An Arab-American born in Winsted, Connecticut, Nader graduated from Princeton University in 1955 with a double major in economics and Far Eastern Studies, and from Harvard Law School in 1958. After achieving national recognition in 1965, with the publication of the path-breaking exposé *Unsafe at Any Speed*, Nader went on to publish numerous books on environmental, consumer, and government reform issues; mobilized hundreds of young activists to work as "Nader's Raiders" in Washington, D.C.; and founded nonprofit organizations such as the Capitol Hill News Service and the state Public Interest Research Groups (PIRGs).

In the 1996 presidential election, Nader's name appeared on a handful of state ballots as the nominee of the Green Party. With a miniscule campaign budget, Nader won less than one percent of the national popular vote and had no practical effect on the outcome of the election. However, the Nader campaign did strengthen the national Green Party organization.

In 2000, the national Green Party was prepared to formally nominate Nader as its presidential candidate. In addition to the post-materialist issues common to the green movement around the planet, Nader's vigorous 2000 campaign endorsed a moratorium on capital punishment, legalization of gay marriage, legalization of marijuana, and rejection of standardized testing in education. Winning 2.5 percent of the national popular vote, electoral support for the Green Party ticket varied widely across the 47 states and the District of Columbia where it appeared on the ballot. Nader did not appear on the ballot in Oklahoma, South Dakota, and South Carolina. He won an impressive 10.1 percent of the vote in Alaska, but only 0.8 percent of the vote in Indiana and Mississippi. In addition to Alaska, Nader received more than five percent of the vote in Colorado, Hawaii, Maine, Massachusetts, Minnesota, Montana, Oregon, Rhode Island, Vermont, and the District of Columbia.

However, it was in Florida, where voters gave Nader 97,488 votes or 1.6 percent of the vote, that his candidacy probably changed the outcome of the 2000 election. The debacle in Florida presented a variety of election system pathologies so profound that they tended to obscure the fact that if the votes received by Nader had gone to Democratic presidential nominee Al Gore they would have been sufficient for Gore to win the state and the presidency. Gore received only 537 votes fewer

In the 2000 presidential election, Florida voters gave Ralph Nader 97,488 votes, likely altering the outcome of the race.

than Republican nominee George W. Bush. Nader ran for president again in 2004, but this time as an Independent with the endorsement, but not the nomination, of the national Green Party. As in 1996, Nader received less than one percent of the popular vote and had no effect on the outcome of the election.

In February 2008, Nader announced he was joining the 2008 presidential race as an Independent, citing public displeasure with the Democratic and Republican parties.

SEE ALSO: Green Party; Presidential Election of 2000; Third Parties.

BIBLIOGRAPHY. P.R. Abramson, J.H. Aldrich, and D.W. Rohde, *Change and Continuity in the 2000 and 2002 Elections* (CQ Press, 2003); Ralph Nader, "Acceptance Statement of Ralph Nader," *Synthesis/Regeneration* (Fall, 2000); Gerald M. Pomper, "The 2000 Presidential Election: Why Gore Lost," *Political Science Quarterly* (Summer, 2001); Daniel Solnit, "The Green Party and the Nader Campaign," *Synthesis/Regeneration* (Spring 1996).

JOHN HICKMAN
BERRY COLLEGE

National Debt

FROM THE INCEPTION of the United States, the possibility of maintaining a national debt of the federal government on behalf of the American people, owed to domestic and foreign lenders, has been a divisive subject among both politicians and the people. Once that debt was created, so too was the question of how and when to pay it back. It has been a rallying point for voters, it has provided statistics frequently cited by politicians to condemn incumbent administrations, and it has proved a salient consideration in most economic policies.

The nation has carried a debt since its inception, when loans taken during the Revolutionary War accumulated to some $75 million. Rather than being paid down, the debt continued to grow—a source of great frustration for the Anti-Federalists and Democratic-Republicans. They opposed the Federalist Party, which was sympathetic to bankers, northeastern industrialists, and other monied interests, and, in particular, Alexander Hamilton, the first secretary of the treasury and an outspoken proponent of maintaining a national debt.

ORIGINS

Under Hamilton's secretariat, a number of changes were made to the American economy as it had existed under the Articles of Confederation, all of which would have permanent effects on the character of the federal government. To begin with, the United States took over the accumulated debts of its individual states, which may have seemed a reasonable concession in exchange for the powers it assumed from those states, but the greater the national debt, the more money would eventually have to flow upwards to the federal government in order to pay it off.

Hamilton's federalism was deeply suspect to his opponents, who feared a return to monarchy. Hamilton had openly campaigned for an American monarchy before the adoption of the Constitution, and had made overtures to European princes in the hopes that Congress would approve his plan. As Washington's secretary of the treasury, the recommendation to assume the state debt of $25 million was one of his first actions, and it drew sharp criticism from Speaker of the House James Madison and Secretary of State Thomas Jefferson. Hamilton proposed that the bulk of the creditors of those state debts be encouraged to invest in new short-term federal bonds, which would provide some source of revenue for the federal government. He further outlined a plan of customs, excise taxes, tariffs, and rapid development of a manufacturing base in order to help generate the monies to pay off the nation's debts. The plan appealed to the Federalist Party's constituency in the northeast, but not to the agrarian south, better represented by Jefferson and Madison.

Hamilton's suggestions, his Four Pillars, passed into law, upholding not only the national debt, but a national bank that his opponents disdained just as strongly. Though the Federalist Party would not survive its opposition to the War of 1812, Hamilton won many of its early major battles, and few of the victories have ever been undone. The national debt steadily grew. The debt and the national bank were so viciously opposed by Andrew Jackson that when he was finally elected president in 1828, (after a four-year campaign; he felt he was cheated out of the election in 1824), he proceeded to begin to pay off the debt. He succeeded briefly in paying it off completely, though the Panic of 1837 soon followed. Since then, the debt has always existed in some amount; Congress sets a debt ceiling (when it exceeds this ceiling, non-essential branches of government are shut down in order to slow spending), but this ceiling is routinely raised without controversy or incident in order to prevent such occurrences.

The Civil War drove the size of the debt up to what must have seemed like irreversible heights. Less than $100 million before Lincoln's election, the debt rose to nearly $3 billion by the war's end, and never came down significantly. By this time, other economic concerns were on the table: the free silver debate, the ramifications of the Industrial Revolution and labor disputes, and westward and overseas expansion.

WORLD WAR II AND THE COLD WAR

World War I caused another rapid debt increase, and in 1920, it was nearly 10 times what it had been during Reconstruction. Roosevelt's New Deal in the wake of the Great Depression, and the military buildup in preparation for World War II, saw another spike. Though the government spending of the New Deal has often been blamed by the right wing for accounting for a large portion of the national debt, it was in no small part the revolution in military technology during World War II, including the invention of the nuclear bomb, that led to a steady increase during and immediately following the war.

With the Cold War, a military had to be kept at the ready even with no war to fight, and new weapons were constantly developed even with no battlefield to use them on. Nuclear weapons were stockpiled in extraordinary numbers, and they cost a good deal more than weaponry of the past, not only in their manufacture, but also in the industry of nuclear secrets. During this time, the United States continued to lend money to individuals and foreign powers, and so quickly became the world's leading creditor nation, somewhat offsetting the implications of the national debt.

REAGANOMICS

Ronald Reagan was elected in 1980 on a platform emphasizing both the economy (flagging in the 1970s, thanks to two energy crises and the combination of inflation and stagnant growth the press nicknamed *stagflation*) and the national defense against the Soviet Union. Inflation and unemployment were soaring when Reagan took office, but slowed down quickly, whether thanks to his new policies or those instituted by Jimmy Carter, who preceeded him, that had not yet had time to take effect.

Those new policies depended on universal tax cuts in order to increase the amount of spending money active in the economy. The scope of Reaganomics approached or exceeded the scope of the New Deal, preserving the financial and banking safeguards of that era, but otherwise implementing wide-scale deregulation. Reagan succeeded in stemming the tide of inflation and unemployment, but when the Democrat-controlled Congress refused to approve his wide-reaching spending cuts and his defense-driven administration ratcheted up its military spending, the result was a skyrocketing national budget.

Unlike Hamilton, Reagan did not seek debt, the national debt was plenty big enough when he arrived in Washington, but under his presidency it rose from $700 billion to $3 trillion in eight years. He admitted his disappointment, and implemented small tax increases to offset the cuts he had made when he first arrived in office, but spending continued perforce as the military build-up matched that of the Soviet Union.

The debt rose again under the presidency of George W. Bush, after a slight decrease during Bill Clinton's presidency. Though not rising nearly as sharply as under Reagan, by the end of Bush's second term, the debt was expected to equal about two-thirds of the Gross Domestic Product.

SEE ALSO: Anti-Federalists; Conservatism; Defense; Democratic-Republican Party; Economy; Federalist Party; Government Spending; Limited Government; Taxes.

BIBLIOGRAPHY. M.J. Boskin, *Reagan and the U.S. Economy: The Successes, Failures, and Unfinished Agenda* (ICEG, 1987); Ron Chernow, *Alexander Hamilton* (Penguin, 2004); J.J. Ellis, *Founding Brothers: The Revolutionary Generation* (Vintage, 2002); Bray Hammond, *Banks and Politics in America: From the Revolution to the Civil War* (Princeton University Press, 1991); Richard Hofstadter, *The American Political Tradition and the Men Who Made It* (Vintage, 1989); Stephen Knott, *Alexander Hamilton and the Persistence of Myth* (University Press of Kansas, 2002); R.B. Latner, *The Presidency of Andrew Jackson: White House Politics 1820–1937* (University of Georgia, 1982); W.A. Niskanen, *Reaganomics: An Insider's Account of The Policies and The People* (Oxford University Press, 1988); J.T. Patterson, *Restless Giant: The United States from Watergate to Bush vs Gore* (Oxford University Press, 2007); R.V. Remini, *Andrew Jackson and the Bank War: A Study in the Growth of Presidential Power* (W.W. Norton, 1967); M.N. Rothbard, *A History of Money and Banking in the United States: The Colonial Era to World War II* (Ludwig Von Mises, 2002); Peter Temin, *The Jacksonian Economy* (W.W. Norton, 1969)

BILL KTE'PI
INDEPENDENT SCHOLAR

National Labor Reform Party

THE NATIONAL LABOR Reform Party was a short-lived social and political action movement in the years after the American Civil War. Beginning as a labor federation, it eventually turned to electoral politics. Its goal was to improve working conditions through legislation and employer-employee arbitration, rather than strikes and collective bargaining.

The National Labor Union (NLU) was founded in 1866, at a convention of 77 delegates held in Baltimore, Maryland. This was the first attempt to form a national labor federation in the United States. The National Labor Union brought together labor unions, farmers, and "eight hour leaguers" to pressure Congress to pass a law mandating an eight-hour workday and help create new labor unions around the country. The group also called for excluding Chinese workers from the United States and for the abolition of convict labor. The NLU believed that owners and workers had common interests, and that arbitration was more effective than strikes. The NLU also called for the creation of a "labor party" as an alternative to the Republican and Democratic Parties.

During its existence as a labor federation, the NLU membership may have reached as many as 650,000 in construction unions, unions of other skilled employees, and groups of farmers and unskilled workers. William Sylvis, a founder of the Iron Molder's International Union, became its first president. Sylvis also edited and wrote many articles for the *Workingman's Advocate*, the newspaper of the NLU.

In 1868, Congress approved a law limiting the workday for federal government employees to eight hours, providing the NLU with what appeared to be a major legislative victory. However, many federal agencies reduced employees' wages to reflect the shortened workday. Following Sylvis's death in July 1869, a conflict developed between unionists who supported the NLU remaining a labor federation and those who wished to see it become a national political party.

In 1871, the National Labor Union decided to shift its emphasis to electoral politics and organize a National Labor Reform Party. In February 1872, the party opened its convention in Columbus, Ohio. In its platform, the Party declared, "It is the duty of the Government to establish a just distribution of capital and labor by providing a purely national circulating medium based on the faith and resources of the nation." The platform also called for the free distribution of government lands to landless settlers; that the eight-hour day be extended to employees of federal government contractors; for the introduction of the merit system in federal government employment; and for limiting the president to one four-year term.

The convention nominated David Davis, U.S. Supreme Court Justice from Illinois, as its presidential candidate. Joel Parker, the Democratic Governor of New Jersey, was nominated for vice president. However, Davis withdrew as the party's candidate when he did not receive the nomination of the Liberal Republican Party, leaving the party without a presidential candidate. After holding a final convention in 1873, the National Labor Union and the Labor Reform Party collapsed. Many of its members moved to the Knights of Labor, which had been formed in Philadelphia in 1869.

SEE ALSO: Democratic Party; Eight-Hour Day; Immigration; Labor Vote; Liberal Republican Party; Presidential Election of 1872; Third Parties.

BIBLIOGRAPHY. P.S. Foner, *History of the Labor Movement in the United States* (International Publishers, 1947); J. Grossman, *William Sylvis, a Pioneer of American Labor: A Study of the Labor Movement During the Era of the Civil War* (Octagon Books, 1973); C. Todes, *William Sylvis and the National Labor Union* (International Publishers, 1942).

JEFFREY KRAUS
WAGNER COLLEGE

National Republican Party

THE NATIONAL REPUBLICAN Party was a political party that existed 1829–33, first opposing President Andrew Jackson. The National Republican Party was a faction of the Democratic-Republican Party, which had been the dominant political party in the United States since the election of 1800. By the 1820s, the party was no longer functioning as a national party, and the presidential election of 1824 saw the emergence of four "Republican" candidates: John Quincy Adams, Henry Clay, William H. Crawford, and Andrew Jackson. As no candidate received a majority of the electoral vote, the House of Representatives decided the election. Although Jackson received a plurality of the electoral votes, he was denied the presidency as the House elected John Quincy Adams president. Following this election, the supporters of Andrew Jackson would eventually become the Democratic Party. Adams's followers were known as the National Republicans.

Henry Clay, who had become secretary of state under Adams after agreeing to throw his support to him in the House of Representatives (an agreement that Jackson's supporters labeled a "corrupt bargain"), cobbled together a national network of supporters that became the National Republicans. The party supported Clay's American System, which he, along with John C. Calhoun, championed in the years after the War of 1812. Around 1815 the term *National Republican* was first used to describe Jeffersonians who supported Clay's plans. The system called for protective tariffs that would make imported goods more expensive than domestic products, the continuation of the Second Bank of the United States, and the financing by the federal government of "internal improvements" that would improve transportation and promote economic development. Clay believed that his plan would promoted the economic development of the nation, and would foster national unity. This placed him in conflict with Jackson and his followers, who rejected using the national government to promote economic development.

In 1828, Jackson defeated Adams, becoming the seventh president of the United States. The coalition that had supported Adams became a formal party. During the 1828 campaign, they established a campaign newspaper called *We the People*. The party's supporters included businessmen, farmers, and laborers who supported Clay's program of high tariffs, internal improvements, and a national bank. Geographically, the party's base was New England, the Mid-Atlantic, Kentucky, Ohio, and Louisiana. However, their unpopularity in the south made it difficult for the party to compete with Jackson. Among the leading figures of the party were Adams, Clay, Senator Daniel Webster of Massachusetts, and Senator John M. Clayton of Delaware.

In 1830, the party formally took on the name National Republicans, and opposed the Jackson-backed Indian Removal Act, which called for the relocation of Native American tribes from the southeastern states to west of the Mississippi River. Their opposition to this legislation made the National Republicans unpopular throughout much of the south, because they deemed it immoral legislation and an attempt by Jackson to expand slavery westward. They also condemned Jackson for his veto of the Maysville Road Bill, which would have appropriated $150,000 for a 60-mile road between Maysville and Lexington, an extension of the Cumberland Road and National Roads. They saw this action as an attack on the American System.

In December 1831, the party held a convention in Baltimore, Maryland, where it nominated Henry Clay to oppose Jackson in the 1832 election. John Sergeant of Pennsylvania (who was legal counsel for the Second Bank of the United States) was nominated for vice president. The major issue in the 1832 election was Jackson's veto of legislation that would have extended the bank's charter. The charter was not due to expire until 1836. Nicholas Biddle, the bank's president, decided to seek an extension of the bank's charter four years prior to its expiration. Clay was able to secure passage in both houses of Congress, but Jackson vetoed the law, asserting that primarily foreign nations and a small number of wealthy Americans owned the bank's stock. This appeal to the common man aided Jackson in the election; he defeated Clay, 219 electoral votes to 49 (18 electoral votes were cast for other candidates).

By 1834, a new party emerged from the National Republicans, Anti-Masons (a third party of the era), supporters of the Second Bank of the United States, disillusioned supporters of Andrew Jackson, and former Federalists. The new party claimed that Jackson governed as "King Andrew I," and called itself the Whigs—after the British political party that had opposed the power of the monarchy. By this time, the National Republican Party had ceased to exist.

SEE ALSO: Anti-Masonic Party; Presidential Election of 1828; Presidential Election of 1832; Whig Party.

BIBLIOGRAPHY. E.M. Carroll, *Origins of the Whig Party* (Duke University Press, 1925); D.W. Howe, *The Political Culture of the American Whigs* (University of Chicago Press, 1979); R.V. Remini, *John Quincy Adams* (Times Books, 2002); P.E. Teed, *John Quincy Adams: Yankee President* (Nova Science Publishers, 2006); H.L. Watson, *Andrew Jackson v. Henry Clay: Democracy and Development in Antebellum America* (Bedford/St. Martin's, 1998).

JEFFREY KRAUS
WAGNER COLLEGE

Nebraska

NATIVE AMERICAN TRIBES settled Nebraska, the western part of which is dominated by the Great Plains, long before intrepid white settlers first inhabited it during the early 19th century. It was called the Nebraska Territory in 1854, as a result of the Kansas-Nebraska Act, a political move by which Kansas was expected to become a slave state, and Nebraska a free state. The capital was initially at Omaha, but was moved to Lancaster, renamed Lincoln after President Abraham Lincoln. Nebraska gained statehood in 1867 as the 37th state, with David Butler, a Republican, elected as the first governor.

David Butler, born in Indiana, had been nominated for an Indiana state senate seat in 1856, then moved to Pawnee City, Nebraska. He was elected state senator in 1863, and governor in 1866. He won a second two-year term, entrenching the Republican Party in power, although Butler himself was removed from office before the end of his term. Although the Republicans tended to dominate in the state, Nebraska generally elected moderate Republicans or, at times, moderate Democrats, showing itself to be a politically progressive state. The state also had a long tradition of support for civil rights.

In the 1890 gubernatorial election, the incumbent John Milton Thayer believed he had won, but victory was awarded to James E. Boyd, the first Democrat to be elected as a governor. Boyd was sworn in as governor in January 1891, but Thayer appealed and in May, Boyd had to stand down and Thayer returned as governor. However, Boyd succeeded him in 1892. In the 1894 gubernatorial election, Silas A. Holcomb ran for the Democratic Party and the Populist Party on a fusion ticket. He was elected, as was his successor, William A. Poynter, also on a fusion ticket.

Control of the state then returned to the Republican Party, until 1909 when Ashton C. Shallenberger was elected as the governor. He was former member of the U.S. House of Representatives and after his term as governor he returned to being a congressman, remaining in House of Representatives from 1915 through 1935. In 1918, Nebraska voted in favor of Prohibition, making it the 37th state to support the 18th Amendment to the U.S. Constitution.

One of the major political figures in the first part of the 20th century was George Norris, who served in the U.S. House of Representatives 1903–13, and as a U.S. Senator 1913–43. Of Dutch descent, in 1911 he had helped establish the National Progressive Republican League, becoming its vice president. Norris then supported Robert La Follette, Sr. in the 1912 U.S. presidential election, and then transferred his support to Theodore Roosevelt.

Remaining a progressive Republican, Norris urged that Nebraska have a unicameral legislative body, which was finally introduced in 1934. As a result, Nebraska remains the only state with a unicameral legislature, with its members all known as senators. One other aspect of Nebraska politics that differs from most other states is that, although many candidates in elections have party affiliations, technically they all stand as Independent candidates: no party name appears on the ballot. Norris spent his last years in the state legislature as an Independent.

The man who won the 1930 gubernatorial elections for Nebraska was Charles W. Bryan, governor 1923–25, and the younger brother of the U.S. Democratic Party presidential candidate William Jennings Bryan. Charles Bryan was the Democratic Party's vice presidential candidate in the 1924 elections. In 1926 and again in 1928 he ran for governor without success. By this time, although most of the governors and other elected state politicians were Republicans, enough were Democrats, to ensure a healthy two-party system. The first governor to win three consecutive terms was Dwight P. Griswold, who was governor 1941–47. Val Peterson, who succeeded him, also won three consecutive terms.

In September 1960, Democrat governor Ralph G. Brooks died in office, and was succeeded by Dwight W. Burney, who served as acting governor until the inauguration of Democrat Frank B. Morrison. In the U.S. presidential elections that year, Richard M. Nixon carried the state with 380,533 votes (62.1 percent) to John F. Kennedy's 232,542 votes (37.9 percent). Following the assassination of John F. Kennedy, Morrison was summoned to the White House as the Democratic Party, under Lyndon B. Johnson, decided on what policy course to follow. In Nebraska, there was a change in the electoral laws for gubernatorial elections. A referendum passed in 1962, and went into effect in 1966, ensuring that a governor could serve a maximum of two consecutive terms. The same limit applying to the office of lieutenant governor, who was to be elected on the same ticket as the governor.

The 1964 U.S. presidential election resulted in victory for Lyndon B. Johnson, who received 307,307 votes (52.6 percent) to Barry Goldwater's 276,847 votes (47.4 percent); and in the 1968 presidential election, Richard M. Nixon carried the state with 321,163 votes (59.8 percent), to 170,784 votes (31.8 percent) for Hubert H. Humphrey, and 44,904 votes (8.4 percent) for George Wallace. In 1970, J. James Exon won the gubernatorial election, and was one of the major political figures to have never lost an election. He was elected governor in 1970, re-elected in 1974, and then elected to the U.S. Senate in 1978, and re-elected in 1984 and 1990. With the exception of George Norris, who designed the unicameral legislature of Nebraska, Exon is the only other Nebraskan politician to win five consecutive statewide elections.

In 2004, George W. Bush won the state with 65.9 percent of the overall vote, defeating John Kerry by a 33 percent margin, making Nebraska the fourth safest Republican state in the Union. Only Thurston County, which included within it two Native American reservations, voted for John Kerry. Of Nebraska's two U.S. senators in 2007, Republican Chuck Hagel is a moderate member of his party, and Democrat Ben Nelson is conservative in his political views.

SEE ALSO: Populist Party; Prohibitionist Party; Red States.

BIBLIOGRAPHY. R.W. Cherny, *Populism, Progressivism and the Transformation of Nebraska Politics 1885–1915* (University of Nebraska Press, 1981); E.G. Curtis, "John Milton Thayer," *Nebraska History* (v.29, 1948); Duane Hutchinson, *Exon: Biography of a Governor* (Foundation Books, 1973); Richard Lowitt, *George W. Norris, The Making of a Progressive, 1861–1912* (Syracuse University Press, 1963); Richard Lowitt, *George W. Norris; The Persistence of a Progressive, 1913–1933* (University of Illinois Press, 1971); Richard Lowitt, *George W. Norris: The Triumph of a Progressive, 1933–1944* (University of Illinois Press, 1978); F.C. Luebke, *Immigrants and Politics: The Germans of Nebraska 1880–1900* (University of Nebraska Press, 1969); Robert Miewald, *Nebraska Government and Politics* (University of Nebraska Press, 1984); Frank Morrison, *My Journey through the Twentieth Century* (Media Productions and Marketing, 2001); J.F. Pedersen and K.D. Wald, *Shall the People Rule? A History of the Democratic Party in Nebraska Politics* (Jacob North, Inc., 1972); B.F. Schaffner, Gerald Wright, and Matthew Streb, "Teams Without Uniforms: The Nonpartisan Ballot in State and Local Elections," *Political Research Quarterly* (v.54/1, 2001).

JUSTIN CORFIELD
GEELONG GRAMMAR SCHOOL, AUSTRALIA

Negative Campaigning

NEGATIVE CAMPAIGNING IS the employment of strategies and tactics throughout an election cycle that inhibit the open and fair presentation of competing policy options and the conduct of reasonable debate. Tactics of campaign negativity are limited only by the ingenuity of those political actors who seek to implement them. Moreover, definitions of campaign negativity are subjective. A negative campaign is one that may encompass: Personal and professional vindictiveness; attempts to defeat opponents through smear, innuendo, false inferences, and distortions; and unethical tactics designed to derail opponents' campaigns and to mislead the public.

A positive campaign is not necessarily a polite and genteel encounter. Hard-hitting criticism and even attack can serve useful purposes in a vibrant democracy, because a meaningful exchange of policy ideas is necessary. If people are sufficiently passionate, they are normally granted some latitude in frankly expressing their point of view. Revelations of wrongdoing on the part of an opponent are important, and they can serve an essential and positive public purpose. Trenchant attacks on an opponent's policies and visions often serve the public interest by clarifying choices.

The principal opportunities for negative campaigning occur through major campaign events: Speeches and debates, campaign advertisements, news media, current affairs and talk shows, press releases, and through campaign networks such as push polls and popular internet sites. While the impact of negative campaigning is uncertain, it is widely acknowledged to be a detriment to democracy and therefore in need of reform.

HISTORY

The politics of smear campaigns have a long and dishonorable tradition, all the way back to the first contested American presidential election in 1800. While frank criticism of one's opponents is anticipated, and attacks play well with partisan crowds, speeches and debates that become personally vindictive and deliberately distort the message of an opponent cross the line into negative campaigning.

A smear campaign entails the deliberate attempt to undermine the reputation of an opponent in the eyes of the public. Obscure information on a party or a candidate can be removed from its appropriate context, and twisted to promote a misleading line. Such attacks can be very personal and hard-hitting, and candidates who are thinking of running for office often have to reflect upon what events or circumstances in their past life might come back to haunt them.

Prior to the age of radio and television, it was possible for candidates to make unsubstantiated accusations and unfounded attacks to a particular audience and by the time opponents had discovered what had been said or published, the election was over and it was too late to respond. In an age of rapid communication, political actors have to exercise greater caution. Thus, contemporary negative campaigns are

more likely to distort through the presentation of decontextualized information and invitation to false inferences, rather than through simple falsification. Moreover, contemporary campaigns, notably those backed by substantial financial contributions, are able to employ a dual-track process. The most direct attacks are disassociated from the name or reputation of the candidate or party who stand to benefit from the attack, leaving them to deliver the more positive message, while others engage in mudslinging.

In contemporary American federal election campaigns, a great deal of negativity can be generated through the channeling of campaign spending into the hands of organizations not directly regulated by the Federal Elections Commission, through the unregulated use of viral websites such as blogs, and through techniques such as push polling that may spread personal rumors and even outright lies about an opponent via networks of telephone calling.

In the United States, negative campaigning has been influenced by a series of campaign finance reforms beginning with the Federal Election Campaign Act in 1971. The unintended consequence of tightening regulations on parties and candidates was to promote the proliferation of unregulated politics by single issue or special interest campaigns throughout the 1980s and 1990s. The 2002 Bipartisan Campaign Reform Act and subsequent decisions by the Supreme Court restricted soft money expenditures and increased disclosure regulations. In so doing, these measures limited unidentified and anonymous smear campaigns that engage in drive-by attacks. American campaign reformers wishing to reduce negative campaigning further advocate for greater public money for campaigns and free airtime for political advertisements to diminish the power of unregulated money.

POLITICAL ADVERTISING

The largest single expense throughout each election cycle is that of political advertising. In the United States and Canada, approximately two-thirds of all campaign spending is devoted to electronic media alone. It is through the genre of the television spot, also available via the internet, that the contemporary political campaign is most powerfully concentrated. The first televised advertisements began in the 1950s as somewhat tedious, if clearly informative, 30-minute recitals of political platforms. The 1960s saw them condense into five-minute backgrounders. By the 1970s, they had been reduced to one-minute slots, and today most political advertisements are usually 30-second, highly produced and polished impression pieces. Such time constraints do not allow for much discussion of the issues, even though the advertisements may transmit powerful impressions. Contemporary campaign advertisements are not normally designed to discuss specific issues and ideas, but to convey an image and general issues, at most. If they mention issues at all, such references are predominantly vague and consensual in nature.

According to Kathleen Hall Jamieson, political advertisements fall into three principal categories: Advocacy advertisements that simply promote a party or leader; contrast advertisements that explain the policies of the parties or the qualities of the leaders side by side; and attack advertisements that are largely restricted to criticism of the other party or leader. Advocacy advertisements tend to avoid negativity, and contrast advertisements employ negativity in the context of a hard-hitting series of differentiations, if at all. It is pure attack advertisements that most routinely express negativity. A dominant research finding is that attack advertisements make many viewers uncomfortable. Regardless of this, campaign strategists wish to know how well they actually work.

DO ATTACK ADVERTISEMENTS WORK?

Voting publics in liberal democracies have grown up with television advertising, and many of these people are discriminating media consumers. Contemporary trends in tracking political views demonstrate a widespread decline in public trust of governments and leaders, combined with growing levels of personal political efficacy.

In this cultural climate of wariness, cynicism, and media savvy, it is difficult to explain people's faith in most political advertisements and their continued willingness to be persuaded. In fact, people's engagement with political advertisements today is negotiated and qualified, rather than merely absorbent. People are reluctant to buy anything from anyone, even while they are happy to be seduced by the right combination of charm and appeal. Viewers groan with derision at the tired stereotypes in advertisements that attempt to sell politicians or pizza. Even as they groan, however, they perceive and they store a memory, which can later be retrieved. If viewers are able to recall the image, then the advertisers have done their job of setting their agenda, at least in a preliminary manner.

The most successful advertisements tap into our deepest needs and articulate our voices in ways we have not thought about before. They appear to speak to us and for us, and, therefore, with us. Political advertisements work most effectively when they attach new information to attitudes, impressions, and emotions already active within the audience, rather than when they attempt to preach something entirely new. Research by Kathleen Hall Jamieson and her colleagues reveals that in their appeal to viewers' rationality and sense of fairness, contrast advertisements are often the most successful genre of election advertisements and tend to be more persuasive than purely negative advertisements.

However, hard-hitting advertisements that specifically criticize or attack an opponent can also be highly effective under certain circumstances. Early research on negative political advertising points to generic evidence that negativity in advertising is usually more striking, more credible, and more memorable than positive expressiveness. Negative and hostile attacks arouse fear and anger, emotions that tend to narrow and limit critical capacities, and people seem to retain negative information better than positive information. Attack advertisements were found to work best with people who lack political information and interest.

Advertisements work most effectively if they are verifiable, if the source is trusted more than the target, if they are based on genuine issue concerns, and to the extent that they are not personally vindictive. They work best when they are visually and acoustically striking, attention-grabbing, and entertaining; employ signs, symbols, and icons that relate to the viewer's political experiences; recall related political themes and perspectives that resonate with the viewer; and motivate the viewer in some way to translate the core message into appropriate political action.

Attack advertisements work most effectively when they successfully invite what Jamieson refers to as unwarranted inferences. In other words, successful attack advertisements are able to engage viewers in a political game of bait and switch. This process works by encouraging viewers to come to conclusions that, while not superficially apparent or even logical, are read into the visual text of the attack advertisement according to the pre-existing stereotypes and ideological assumptions of the viewer. It helps if they come wrapped in a compelling and familiar narrative. So-called reality television or tabloid television effects are highly persuasive, because the evidence appears to be immediately present and available, requiring no further explanation. Images are said to speak for themselves. The grainy image on tape, the doom-laden voice-over, the shaky hand-held camera, the stark and alarming music, and other techniques enhance the believability of an advertisement. Humor can be effective, particularly when satire focuses on an opponent's hypocrisy. Among the more successful attack advertisements have been those that employ a narrative frame to relate a story that reveals an unwelcome, yet credible, truth about an opponent who has something important to hide.

Attack advertisements tend to be most effective when opponents are targeted before they have a chance to define themselves in the public mind. Given the dangers and opportunities associated with such timing, any candidate with a skeleton in the closet will be well advised to generate positive biographical and advocacy advertisements early in the campaign, and might even put together an inoculation advertisement or public appearance that minimizes any damage done by negative information prior to its release. If a candidate misses such opportunities and is confronted with a credible attack from an opponent, then at the very least, there must be an immediate and robust counterattack.

The degree to which a counterattack is necessary or appropriate requires further analysis. A tit-for-tat strategy is unlikely to succeed and might do more harm than good. It is always possible that an attack advertisement can simply boomerang, causing more damage to the originator than to the intended target. A vexatious personal assault on a candidate or the candidate's family might induce sympathy for the target candidate, anger at the unpleasantness of the source of the attack, or elements of both. Double impairment occurs when both victim and perpetrator suffer from the diffuse disgust or repulsion that occurs throughout the course of a negative campaign. While empirical evidence is mixed, for at least some of the people, some of the time, negativity in campaigns leads to disaffection and disengagement.

CONSEQUENCES

While most citizens would agree that negative campaigning is unpleasant, and while it deflects attention from the serious debates of the day, it is also regarded as a sad reality of contemporary election campaigning. There is widespread concern that negative campaigning is associated with declining voter turnout and increasing voter cynicism. However, causal relationships are not at all well established, and there is persuasive empirical evidence that negativity is less effective than earlier commentators believed. A number of politicians have recently pledged to take the high road in their campaigning, but the results have been mixed. The challenge is that those who wish to succeed must always remain alert to what the opposition is planning. With the best will in the world, unless there is a great deal of trust on all sides, suspicion can trigger a pre-emptive attack.

In their bid to go positive, politicians have been assisted to the extent that public policies limit the impact of under-regulated sources of financial backing, as well as the range of opportunities available to smear behind a shield of anonymity. A series of further public policy reforms would promote political equity, balance, the full and frank exchange of ideas, disclosure, and access to the media. Media enterprises that have adopted public-interest standards of news reportage, going beyond standard stereotypes, winner and loser coverage, and the amplification of attack and negativity, have further contributed to the enhancement of positive campaigning. Further innovations could establish forums for adequate and dignified political debate, ensuring right of reply, demanding proof, and revealing lies, distortions, and hypocrisy.

The target of negative campaigning is the voting public. To the extent that they refuse negativity and insist to each other, to their leaders, and to the media that the affairs of the polity must occupy the center stage of serious and sustained debate, the discourses of electoral campaigning will improve.

SEE ALSO: Advertising, Campaign; Demagogues in Political Campaigns; Democratic "Rules of the Game"; Fairness Doctrine; Scandals, Presidential Elections.

BIBLIOGRAPHY. Stephen Ansolabehere and Shanto Iyengar, *Going Negative: How Attack Ads Shrink and Polarize the Electorate* (Free Press, 1995); K.H. Jamieson, *Dirty Politics: Deception, Distraction, and Democracy* (Oxford University Press, 1992); Katherine H. Jamieson, *Everything You Think You Know About Politics…And Why You're Wrong* (Basic Books, 2000); R.R. Lau and G.M. Pomper, *Negative Campaigning: An Analysis of U.S. Senate Elections* (Rowman and Littlefield, 2004); David Mark,

Going Dirty: The Art of Negative Campaigning (Rowman and Littlefield, 2006); D.P. Redlawsk, ed., *Feeling Politics: Emotion in Political Information Processing* (Palgrave Macmillan, 2006).

PAUL WINGFIELD NESBITT-LARKING, PH.D.
HURON UNIVERSITY COLLEGE, CANADA

Nevada

THE FIRST EUROPEANS reached the area that became Nevada in the 17th century, when Father Kino led some expeditions through the region. It was claimed by the Spanish and was a part of the Viceroyalty of New Spain. When Mexico gained its independence, the region became a part of Mexico. The Mexican-American War from 1846 till 1848, was ended with the Guadalupe-Hidalgo Treaty whereby the region was ceded to the United States. The area had already been surveyed by John Frémont of the U.S. Army Topographical Corps, later the first Republican presidential candidate. The U.S. Congress formed the Utah territory on August 14, 1850, which included Nevada. The Nevada Territory was established on March 2, 1861. This occurred two years after the discovery of gold and silver at the Comstock Lode.

Nevada itself was granted statehood on October 31, 1864, eight days before the 1864 presidential election, which helped Abraham Lincoln get re-elected. By this time, there were substantial numbers of miners living in the state, and Henry G. Blasdel, a Republican from Indiana, was elected as the first governor. He was re-elected in 1866, serving until 1870. The second governor, Lewis R. Bradley, a Democrat from Virginia, was elected in 1870, and also served two terms, losing when he ran again in 1878.

With a healthy two-party system, the third governor, John Henry Kinkead, was a Republican from Pennsylvania (who went on to be the district governor of Alaska), the fourth governor, Jewett W. Adams, was a Democrat from Vermont; and the fifth governor, Charles Clark Stevenson, was a Republican from New York. What followed was a period of Republican rule, with the election of Frank Bell in 1889. Bell, a Republican, born in Toronto, Canada, was Nevada's first foreign-born governor. He had been a telegraph operator and was the man who telegraphed the state constitution to Washington, D.C., in 1864.

THE PURITY OF ELECTIONS ACT

In the 1890s, the Silver Party was formed in Nevada. It supported a platform of bimetallism, whereby the currency was defined by both gold and silver. Aligned with the Populist Party, it urged for the passing of the Purity of Elections Act of 1895, a state statute that aimed to reduce the influence of money-politics on the state, and erode the influence of the Southern Pacific Railroad Company, which was said to have exerted extraordinary control on the state legislature.

The act had the support of the outgoing governor, the Republican Roswell K. Colcord, as well as the Silver Party, and came just before the election of John E. Jones of the Silver Party as governor in the 1895 elections. However, there have been doubts about the public impact of the Purity of Elections Act, indicating that either the role of the Southern Pacific Railroad Company was overestimated, or that it had been able to hide its actions. Jones died in office on April 10, 1896, after only a year, and the Prussian-born Reinhold Sadler succeeded him.

In 1903, John Sparks of the Silver-Democratic Party was elected governor. Born in Mississippi, he had moved to Texas during the American Civil War, drove cattle into Nevada, where he became a prominent stud breeder, entered politics as his businesses started failing, and died in office during his second term. His successor, Denver S. Dickerson, completed his term, after which the office of governor was shared between the Republicans and the Democrats; eight of the subsequent governors were Republicans, and nine were Democrats. The first of these governors to be born in Nevada was Emmet D. Boyle, governor 1915–23; of the 28 governors of Nevada 1864–2007, only seven were born in Nevada.

LAS VEGAS

Mining had been the traditional backbone of the Nevada economy along with gambling, which had become common in mining towns across the state, until it was declared illegal in 1909. The re-legalization of gambling on March 19, 1931, was to have a dramatic effect on the state. Similarly, liberal divorce laws resulted in Reno becoming the place where many Americans from all over the country came for divorces. This all coincided with the start of work on the Hoover Dam, constructed near Las Vegas, and it was not long before the casinos in Las Vegas easily surpassed those in Reno. The comple-

The re-legalization of gambling on March 19, 1931, had a dramatic effect on the state of Nevada. It coincided with the start of work on the Hoover Dam, and led to the concentration of a majority of the state's population in Clark County.

tion of the Hoover Dam also provided enough water and electricity for Las Vegas. Soon Clark County, which included Las Vegas, had the majority of the state's population. It was not long before gangsters started controlling many of the gambling venues in Las Vegas, but they failed to have much of an impact on state politics.

Atmospheric tests of nuclear weapons took place in Nevada 1951–62, with people from Las Vegas often watching the explosions from their houses. Subsequent tests were carried out underground 1962–92. Surprisingly, the tests remained relatively popular in Nevada, although the level of nuclear waste has been questioned in recent years.

PAUL LAXALT

The 1964 presidential election saw Lyndon Johnson win the state by 58.5 percent. Walter S. Baring, Jr., the Democratic Party incumbent, won the congressional seat by 63.2 percent. Baring was an accomplished campaigner,

having won his first election, a seat in the Nevada state legislature, in 1936. However, in the senate race, Democratic incumbent Howard Cannon defeated Republican Lieutenant Governor Paul Laxalt by just 84 votes, with the victory declared only after a recount.

Laxalt was the son of a Basque shepherd who, along with his wife, had opened a restaurant in Carson City, the capital of Nevada. After losing the 1964 election, Laxalt ran in the 1966 gubernatorial election and defeated incumbent Grant Sawyer, serving until 1970. During that time, he became close friends with Ronald Reagan, governor of the neighboring state of California. Four years later, Laxalt ran for the U.S. Senate and managed to defeat Nevada's Lieutenant Governor Harry Reid by fewer than 600 votes. Laxalt remained as senator until 1987, and was a close adviser of Reagan, as the national chairman of the Reagan presidential campaigns in 1976, 1980, and 1984, and general chairman of the Republican Party 1983–87. It was during that time that Laxalt rose to international notice when he played an important role in a foreign presidential election.

Laxalt had served in the Philippines during World War II and long cherished his connection with the country. In 1985, President Ferdinand Marcos, a close friend of Ronald Reagan, was involved in an openly fraudulent election, in which he was declared the winner by his own party. Marcos's opponent, Cory Aquino, had herself sworn in as president in a rival ceremony timed to coincide with that of Marcos's.

Marcos was anxious to know what the American government's attitude was to the event, and unable to speak to Reagan, spoke to Laxalt, who told the longtime Filipino president that he should "cut and cut cleanly." Laxalt later commented that there was a very long pause on the telephone line, after which Marcos remarked how sorry he was by what he clearly viewed as betrayal by the U.S. government; 16 hours later he left the country, averting the possibility of civil war.

RECENT ELECTIONS

Richard Bryan, a Democrat, was elected governor in the 1982 election, in which Robert Joseph "Bob" Miller was re-elected as the Clark County district attorney, the first Clark County district attorney to be re-elected. Bryan was governor 1983–89 and followed Laxalt's career path, elected as a U.S. Senator, and serving two terms in Washington, D.C. He was followed as governor by Robert Miller, who in turn was followed by Republican Kenneth Carroll "Kenny" Guinn, who quickly earned a reputation as a moderate and was re-elected in 2002 with 68 percent of the vote, to Joe Neal of the Democratic Party, who gained only 22 percent.

In the next elections, held in 2006, Guinn refused to endorse the Republican candidate Jim Gibbons, who had been a member of the Nevada state assembly for four years and then spent 10 years in the U.S. House of Representatives. Gibbons had interrupted his time in the Nevada state assembly to serve as a flight leader in the Gulf War, winning a Distinguished Flying Cross.

The 2006 gubernatorial elections in Nevada were described as "contentious, ugly and negative" with Gibbons dubbing his opponent, Dina Titus, the minority leader in the Nevada state senate, as "Dina Taxes." Titus managed to win Clark County, with Gibbons winning every other county in the state, the final voting figures giving Gibbons victory with 279,998 votes (47.9 percent) to 255,684 (43.9 percent) for Titus.

SEE ALSO: Populist Party.

BIBLIOGRAPHY. M.W. Bowers, *The Sagebrush State: Nevada's History, Government and Politics* (University of Nevada Press, 1996); Eleanore Bushnell, "The 1964 Election in Nevada," *Western Political Quarterly* (v.18/2, 1965); D.W. Driggs, "The 1970 Election in Nevada," *Western Political Quarterly* (v.24/2, 1971); D.W. Driggs and L.E. Goodall, *Nevada Politics and Government: Conservatism in Open Society* (University of Nevada Press, 1996); M.E. Glass, *Silver and Politics in Nevada: 1892–1902* (University of Nevada Press, 1970); Jon Ralston, *The Anointed One: An Inside Look at Nevada Politics* (Huntington, 2000); E.R. Rusco, "Campaign Finance Reform in the Silver Era: A Puzzle," *Nevada Historical Society Quarterly* (v.38/3–4, 1995); A.C. Titus, *Bombs in the Backyard: Atomic Testing and American Politics* (University of Nevada Press, 1987).

JUSTIN CORFIELD
GEELONG GRAMMAR SCHOOL, AUSTRALIA

New Hampshire

NEW HAMPSHIRE WAS inhabited by Algonquian tribes before the arrival of the Europeans who first explored the region around 1600, and established the first settlement in 1623. In 1679, it became a Royal Province, and was then one of the 13 states that were involved in the American War of Independence, being the first state to declare its independence. Since independence, New Hampshire and its neighbor Vermont have been the only two states in the Union that have held gubernatorial elections every two years. New Hampshire has no term limit on the office of governor.

The first elected president of the state of New Hampshire, as the position was initially styled, was Meshech Weare, who had been elected to represent the town of Hampton Falls in the assembly and was three times elected speaker of the state House of Representatives. In 1776 when New Hampshire became the first American state to adopt a formal written constitution, Weare became head of the executive during the Revolutionary War, and in 1785 John Langdon took over from him. Langdon was to serve again 1788–89, and 1805–09.

Beginning in 1786, the elections were for the office which was titled the president of the state of New Hampshire, but in 1791 this was amended to governor.

EARLY PARTY AFFILIATIONS

Until 1828, the Democratic-Republicans and the Federalists competed in elections, with most victories being relatively narrow. The most popular politician during this period was Federalist John Taylor Gilman, a shipbuilder, who won five consecutive gubernatorial elections, but lost two subsequent elections. In 1812, the results of the gubernatorial elections were so close that the final choice was sent to the state legislature to declare the final result. William Plumer, longtime New Hampshire politician, was declared to have won the election. Plumer remained governor until 1819. In the following year he was the one member of the presidential election college to vote against James Monroe, the last of nine occasions he was a presidential elector.

After 1816, the Federalists had been too weak in the state to run a candidate in the gubernatorial elections. When Samuel Bell, the incumbent governor, decided to move to the U.S. Senate in 1822, part of the Democratic-Republican Party decided to endorse Samuel Dinsmoor from Keene as their candidate, with the Federalists throwing their support behind Levi Woodbury, also Democratic-Republican, who won the election. In the 1832 election, Bell, still a member of the U.S. Senate, and Levi Woodbury, by then the secretary of the Navy, were able to get the state to strongly support Andrew Jackson.

All but one of the governors of New Hampshire were Democrats 1829–55, the exception being Anthony Colby, a Whig. In 1855, Ralph Metcalf of the Know-Nothing Party was elected as governor in a four-way race against two Democratic Party candidates, and a Whig candidate. In the next election, held in the following year, the race was so close that once again the state house of representatives was asked to decide, and voted to re-elect Metcalf. In 1857, with tension over the issue of slavery, William Haile, a merchant from Hinsdale, and a member of the newly-formed Republican Party, was elected governor. Some historians have claimed that the Republican Party was founded in New Hampshire, dating it back to a meeting held in Exeter, New Hampshire, in 1853.

Haile was succeeded by Ichabod Goodwin, who was elected in 1859. In the following year, New Hampshire voted heavily for Abraham Lincoln, who received 37,519 votes (56.9 percent), with Stephen Douglas getting 25,887 votes (39.3 percent), John Breckinridge, 2,125 votes (3.2 percent), and John Bell only 412 votes (0.6 percent). Goodwin's support for the Union when the Civil War started was evidenced by his borrowing money in his own name to equip two regiments in May 1861, an action affirmed by the state legislature when it came into session in June.

LATER ELECTIONS

From then until 1913, the Republicans won every gubernatorial election except two, with James A. Weston, the Mayor of Manchester, elected for two non-consecutive terms. Samuel D. Felker from the Democrats was governor 1913–15, with only five subsequent Democratic governors (of the 28 who have served), including the 2002, two term governor, John Lynch. The Labor Reform Party of New Hampshire managed to get 10.6 percent of the popular vote in the state elections in 1870, making it the most successful third party in the state until 1912. However, in the state legislature it failed to get any of its policies adopted, and, by the late 1870s, many of its supporters had turned to the Greenback Party essentially to cast protest votes.

New Hampshire had long been regarded as strongly Republican until it supported Bill Clinton in 1992; it had supported three Democratic Party candidates: Woodrow Wilson, Franklin D. Roosevelt, and Lyndon B. Johnson. In 1996, it again supported Clinton in his re-election, switched to George W. Bush in 2000, but voted for John Kerry (with 50.2 percent of the vote) in 2004, being the only state to vote Republican in 2000 and Democratic in 2004.

With Democratic Governor John Lynch re-elected with 74 percent of the vote, and both the U.S. congressional seats won by the Democrats in the 2006 midterm elections, the Democrats also did well in state elections. They gained a majority on the executive council, and also were able to take control of both houses of the state legislature for the first time since 1911.

POLITICAL ROLE OF THE STATE

New Hampshire is one of the most politically aware states in the country, with 400 members in the state general assembly, one for every 3,200 citizens. New Hampshire was the only state in the Union to hold a referendum on membership in the United Nations. It was held with citizens in their annual town meetings in the spring of

1945. Citizens were asked to endorse or oppose joining, and voted 20 to one in favor of joining.

The political role of New Hampshire is most obvious through the New Hampshire primaries, wherein the state has had the first Democratic Party and Republican Party primary in the election cycle since 1952. Drawing more attention than any other primary, it often creates a momentum that allows candidates to gain enough notice to get them campaign financing, which could propel them to the presidential election itself.

In addition to this, in Dixville Notch in Coos County, and at Hart's Location in Carroll County, a very small number of residents vote just after midnight on the day of the primary to ensure that they are the first to vote. Their results are declared early. This is because New Hampshire state law allows the counting in a town where all registered citizens vote. The same then happens in presidential elections. A state law in 1977 ensured that New Hampshire would always be the first state to hold its primaries. They were originally held in March, but were brought forward in 1996 to February 20, in 2000 to February 1, and in 2004 to January 27, to prevent other states voting first.

In the 1960 U.S. presidential election, the people of Hart's Location voted so quickly that the ballots from the 12 registered voters could be counted first and the results announced before most of the rest of the people in the country had voted. Overall, in the 1960 U.S. presidential election, Richard M. Nixon carried the state with 157,989 votes (53.4 percent) to 137,772 votes (46.6 percent) for John F. Kennedy. During the 1964 Republican primaries, New Hampshire played an important role by not endorsing then favorite Nelson Rockefeller, and overwhelmingly supporting Henry Cabot Lodge, who was U.S. ambassador to Vietnam at the time, and whose name was not on the ballot. In the 1964 U.S. presidential election, Lyndon B. Johnson easily carried the state with 182,065 votes (63.6 percent) against Barry Goldwater's 104,029 votes (36.4 percent).

The New Hampshire primaries in 1968 saw Lyndon Johnson getting only 49 percent (as a "write-in candidate") over Eugene McCarthy whose anti-war platform resulted in 42 percent, but more delegates than the incumbent president. McCarthy's performance led to Robert Kennedy deciding to stand in the primary campaign, during which he was assassinated. Richard M. Nixon comfortably carried the state in the 1968 U.S. presidential election, with 154,903 votes (52.1 percent), against 130,589 votes (43.9 percent) for Hubert H.

Humphrey, and 11,173 votes (3.8 percent) for George Wallace. In 1992, Bill Clinton became the first person elected president who had not won his party's primary in New Hampshire; George W. Bush also did this in 2000 when John McCain won the state, but Bush won the nomination, and the subsequent election.

SEE ALSO: Democratic-Republican Party; Federalist Party; New Hampshire Primary; Nomination Process, Presidential; Presidential Primaries.

BIBLIOGRAPHY. Charles Brereton, *First Primary: Presidential Politics in New Hampshire* (Union Leader, 1987); V.J. Capowski, "The Era of Good Feelings in New Hampshire: The Gubernatorial Campaigns of Levi Woodbury, 1823–24," *Historical New Hampshire* (v.21/4, 1966); J.R. Churgin, *From Truman to Johnson: New Hampshire's Impact on American Politics* (Yeshiva University Press, 1972); P.A. Grant, Jr., "The Bank Controversy and New Hampshire Politics, 1834–1835," *Historical New Hampshire* (v.23/3, 1968); G.B. McKinney, "The Politics of Protest: The Labor Reform and Greenback Parties in New Hampshire," *Historical New Hampshire* (v.36/2–3, 1981); G.F. Moncrief and J.A. Thompson, "Electoral Structure and State Legislative Representation: A Research Note," *Journal of Politics* (v.54/1, 1992); G.R. Orren, *Media and Momentum: the New Hampshire Primary and Nomination Politics* (Chatham House Publishing, 1987); J.P. Reid, *Controlling the Law: Legal Politics in Early National New Hampshire* (Northern Illinois University Press, 2004); Lex Renda, *Running on the Record: Civil War-era Politics in New Hampshire* (University of Virginia Press, 1997); D.J. Scala, *Stormy Weather: The New Hampshire Primary and Presidential Politics* (Palgrave Macmillan, 2003); L.K. Shapiro, *Tax Policy and Voting Behavior in Statewide Elections: The 1992 New Hampshire Gubernatorial Race*, thesis (Johns Hopkins University, 1995); E.P. Veblen, *The Manchester Union Leader in New Hampshire Elections* (University Press of New England, 1975).

JUSTIN CORFIELD
GEELONG GRAMMAR SCHOOL, AUSTRALIA

New Hampshire Primary

THE NEW HAMPSHIRE Primary has, since the 1950s, become a key early test for candidates seeking their party's presidential nomination. The "first in the nation" status of the event has attracted media coverage and given victorious candidates momentum as they head into Super Tuesday and subsequent primaries and caucuses. In 1913, the general court (state legislature) voted to create a primary for the purpose of selecting delegates to the Democratic and Republican National Conventions. Up to that time, delegates had been selected through town caucuses, which would send delegates to state conventions that would select delegates to the national conventions. The 1913 law allowed candidates for delegate to be listed on a statewide ballot. Candidates could pledge to support specific candidates or could appear on the ballot as "uncommitted" delegates. Primaries were to be held on the same day as the town meeting day, the second Tuesday in March.

When the first primary was held in 1916 (the Democratic primary was won by President Woodrow Wilson's delegates, who were unopposed, and the Republican Primary was won by a slate of uncommitted delegates), Indiana had already held its primary, and Minnesota held its primary on the same day as New Hampshire. In 1920, Indiana moved its primary election to May, and Minnesota discontinued their primary, which established New Hampshire's as the first in the nation.

In 1920, delegates supporting General Leonard Wood (the former chief of staff of the Army and a New Hampshire native) won the primary, but were not nominated (the Republicans nominated Warren G. Harding), and in 1924, President Calvin Coolidge's delegates won the primary without opposition. For the next 20 years, slates of unpledged delegates won the state's primary elections. By the 1940s, interest in the primary had declined; voter turnout was eight percent in 1944 and 27 percent in 1948, despite a vigorous Republican Primary where delegates supporting former Minnesota Governor Harold Stassen defeated a slate pledged to New York Governor Thomas E. Dewey (who would win the nomination).

In 1949, in order to encourage more voters to come to the polls, voters were allowed to state their preferences for presidential and vice presidential candidates. Candidates would be placed on the ballot if petitions containing the signatures of 50 voters from each of the state's two congressional districts were submitted on their behalf. The candidate's name would be placed on the ballot, unless they asked to have it withdrawn. As the votes would have no bearing on delegate selection, the primary was described as a "beauty contest." Delegates would continue to be elected apart from this beauty contest, but would

now have to be approved by the candidate to whom they were pledged. The law also allowed for candidates for delegate to seek election as a "favorable" delegate, which would not require the candidate's approval.

In the first beauty contest held in 1952, Dwight Eisenhower defeated Robert Taft in the Republican Primary, and Estes Kefauver defeated President Harry Truman, causing Truman to withdraw from the race. In 1968, President Lyndon Johnson decided not to seek re-election after defeating anti-war candidate Eugene McCarthy, 49 to 42 percent.

NOMINATION PROCESS REFORM

In 1968, the Democratic National Convention passed a motion to establish a commission to reform the party's candidate selection process. In 1969, the 28-member Commission on Party Structure and Delegate Selection was established. Senator George McGovern was named the chair of this Reform Commission (he would be succeeded by Minnesota Congressman Don Fraser). The commission's recommendations were intended to open access to the presidential nomination process and insure representation at the convention of women, minorities, and young people. The most important recommendation of the Commission was that Democratic primaries and caucuses should determine the party's presidential candidate. This resulted in convention delegate selection being shifted from party leaders to voters in primaries and caucuses.

This made the New Hampshire Primary even more significant, as the event now sets the stage for the rest of the process. Candidates who do poorly in New Hampshire often have to drop out, as fundraising becomes more difficult and media attention begins to shift to other candidates. Candidates who do well in New Hampshire are able to raise additional campaign contributions and attract media attention for subsequent primaries and caucuses. This has magnified the importance of the primary. The significance of the New Hampshire Primary, and the Iowa Caucus that precedes it, have been challenged in recent years by those who contend that the states are not representative of the nation's ethnic and racial diversity.

In 1971, the state legislature increased the signature requirement from 50 to 500 in each congressional district and also required a $500 filing fee. In 1976, 391 candidates filed to run as delegates or alternates. The following year, the legislature voted to eliminate the separate delegate filings. The law specified that any candidate receiving 10 percent of their party's primary vote would be allotted a proportion of the delegates from the state at the national convention.

FIRST IN THE NATION

Since 1977, New Hampshire law has stated that its primary will be the first in the nation. It states that, "the presidential primary election shall be held on the second Tuesday in March or on a Tuesday selected by the secretary of state which is seven days or more immediately preceding the date on which any other state shall hold a similar election, whichever is earlier, of each year when a president of the United States is to be elected or the year previous." As a result, the date of the primary has been moved up as other states have moved their primaries up, in order to gain more influence in the candidate selection process.

Historically, the primary has been held in early March. In 1996, the primary took place on February 20; in 2000, February 1; in 2004 January 27; and January 22 in 2008. "Front-loading" of primaries and caucuses keeps forcing New Hampshire, in order to preserve its first primary status, to schedule its primary earlier and earlier.

While candidates historically have spent much time in New Hampshire prior to the primary, victory does not always insure nomination. Pat Buchanan (1996) and John McCain (2000) both won in New Hampshire, but did not win the Republican Party nomination. Gary Hart (1984) and Paul Tsongas (1992) won in New Hampshire, but they were not the Democratic nominees. However, until 1992, no candidate had become president without winning New Hampshire. Since then, Bill Clinton (1992) and George W. Bush (2000) became president after losing in New Hampshire. In Clinton's case, his third-place finish exceeded expectations, allowing him to declare himself the Comeback Kid, and continue his campaign that, up to that point in time, had been shaken by rumors of his extramarital affairs.

For many years, one of the most influential figures in the primary was William Loeb, who was the publisher of the Manchester *Union Leader* 1946–81. For many years, the *Union Leader* was the dominant newspaper in the state, and Loeb used his editorial pages to support his favored candidates and excoriate those he opposed. He is best known for his role in the publication of what became known as "the Canuck Letter" during the 1972 primary. The letter, which appeared two weeks before the primary in the paper's letters to the editor section on February 24, 1972, suggested that Senator Edmund Muskie, the front-runner for the Democratic Party nomination, was prejudiced against French-Canadians, who constituted a significant voting block in the state.

On March 4, 1972 (three days before the primary), Muskie delivered a speech in front of the newspaper's offices, denouncing Loeb as a liar. Press accounts at the time reported that Muskie cried during the speech, causing many Democratic voters to question Muskie's toughness, and many defected to other Democratic candidates. While Muskie would win the primary, 46 to 37 percent over Senator McGovern, he would soon be out of the race.

New Hampshire Presidential Primary Winners 1952–2004		
	Democrats	**Republicans**
1952	C. Estes Kefauver	Dwight D. Eisenhower
1956	C. Estes Kefauver	Dwight D. Eisenhower
1960	John F. Kennedy	Richard M. Nixon
1964	Lyndon B. Johnson	Henry Cabot Lodge
1968	Lyndon B. Johnson	Richard M. Nixon
1972	Edmund S. Muskie	Richard M. Nixon
1976	James E. Carter, Jr.	Gerald R. Ford
1980	James E. Carter, Jr.	Ronald W. Reagan
1984	Gary W. Hart	Ronald W. Reagan
1988	Michael S. Dukakis	George H.W. Bush
1992	Paul E. Tsongas	George H.W. Bush
1996	William J. Clinton	Patrick J. Buchanan
2000	Albert A. Gore, Jr.	John S. McCain
2004	John F. Kerry	George W. Bush

ELIGIBILITY

In 1983, the legislature eliminated the petition requirement, replacing it with a filing fee of $1,000 for presidential candidates. This made it easier for fringe candidates to get on the primary ballot: 67 candidates filed in 1992 and 45 in 1996. In 1996, New Hampshire allowed Election Day registration for the first time in the primary. More than 26,000 new voters participated, with 74 percent of registered Republicans turning out to vote and 45 percent of the Democrats (even though President Clinton had no opposition).

Any person who is qualified under the U.S. Constitution and is a registered Republican or Democrat may file to be a candidate in the New Hampshire Presidential Primary. Candidates file their declaration of candidacy between the first Monday and the third Friday in November with the New Hampshire Secretary of State's office. A person who is otherwise qualified to run for president, who is unable to pay the required $1,000 filing fee by reason of indigence may, after proving such indigence, have their name placed on the primary ballot by filing with the secretary of state 10 primary petitions from each county of the state signed by registered voters of the party.

Each person who files for president shall file with the secretary of state, prior to the primary, the names and addresses in alphabetical order of the delegates and their alternates, who shall represent the candidate at the national convention. Delegates and alternates file a certificate with the secretary of state indicating their willingness to serve as delegates or alternates. While Republicans and Democrats can only vote in their party primary, Independent voters can vote in either party primary. Often overlooked is the vice presidential primary that has been held in New Hampshire since 1952.

IMPACT

Critics of the primary contend that too much attention is paid to the primary given that New Hampshire is not a reflection of the nation at large. Supporters of the primary respond that no state is reflective of the entire nation, and that New Hampshire is a first step in the presidential selection process. They also argue that it allows unknown, under-funded candidates to have a chance to win the election. Because New Hampshire is an exercise in grassroots politics, where candidates meet ordinary voters in their living rooms, these candidates have the chance to meet with activists and generate support that allows them to build organizations that allow them to do well in the primary. Further, they contend that New Hampshire residents are engaged voters.

The primary has a number of impacts upon the state. According to the New Hampshire Department of State, "Analysis of 2000 primary coverage shows that up to 22 million people received positive messages about New Hampshire, and the percentage of stories that actually recommended New Hampshire as a place to visit reached up to 14 million people around the world." State officials estimate that 130 new firms and 2,600 jobs will

eventually be located in New Hampshire as a result of positive coverage of the state during the 2000 primary season. The total economic impact of the 1996 primary was $210 million; in 2000, it was $306 million.

During the 2004 election, there were groups within the Democratic Party that called for a new primary schedule that would end New Hampshire's first-in-the-nation status. The 2004 Democratic National Convention passed a resolution calling for the creation of a Commission on Presidential Nomination Timing and Scheduling. The Commission, chaired by former Labor Secretary Alexis Herman and Congressman David Price of North Carolina, recommended that one or two caucuses be added between Iowa and New Hampshire, and that one or two primaries be added after New Hampshire and prior to February 8, 2008. However, despite challenges to New Hampshire's first-in-the-nation presidential primary status, New Hampshire held the nation's first primary for the 2008 election on January 8, 2008, just five days after the Iowa Caucus.

SEE ALSO: New Hampshire; Nomination Process, Presidential; Presidential Primaries.

BIBLIOGRAPHY. Charles Brereton, *First in the Nation: New Hampshire and the Premier Presidential Primary* (Peter E. Randall, 1987); Dayton Duncan, *Grass Roots: One Year in the Life of the New Hampshire Primary* (Viking, 1991); New Hampshire Department of State, www.sos.nh.gov (cited August 2007); G.R. Orren and Nelson W. Polsby, eds., *Media and Momentum: the New Hampshire Primary and Nomination Politics* (Chatham House Publishers, 1987); N.A. Palmer, *The New Hampshire Primary and the American Electoral Process* (Praeger, 1997); B.J. Rudell, *Only in New Hampshire: My Journey on the Campaign Trail* (Plaideswede Pub., 2003); D.J. Scala, *Stormy Weather: The New Hampshire Primary and Presidential Politics* (Palgrave Macmillan, 2003).

JEFFREY KRAUS
WAGNER COLLEGE

New Jersey

NEW JERSEY WAS long home to Native Americans from the Lenni-Lenape and other tribes. When the Dutch claimed early New Jersey, they established the colony of New Netherland, which covered modern-day New York and New Jersey. In 1664, the region was taken over by the English, and the colony was subsequently named New Jersey, because the island of Jersey had remained loyal to the Crown during the English Civil War and the subsequent rule by Cromwell.

New Jersey adopted its 1776 constitution two days before the Second Continental Congress declared American independence from the British Crown. This constitution allowed all inhabitants of the state who were "of full age" and worth £50 in "proclamation money" to vote, an act that enfranchised many African Americans, spinsters, and widows, but excluded married women who were not able to hold property in their own right. In the early elections many candidates ridiculed their opponents for having to rely on the votes of women.

On December 18, 1787, New Jersey was the third state to ratify the U.S. Constitution, and was the first state to ratify the Bill of Rights. After independence, the Federalists remained strong in New Jersey until 1801, when Joseph Bloomfield of the Democratic-Republican Party was elected as governor. With the success of Thomas Jefferson as U.S. president, New Jersey voters re-elected Bloomfield many times, later electing him to the U.S. House of Representatives. After the short governorships of Aaron Ogden of the Federalists, and William Sanford Pennington and Mahlon Dickerson of the Democratic-Republicans, each serving one term, Isaac Halstead Williamson of the Federalists was elected as governor by the legislature, holding office 1817–29, being the most successful politician for the Democratic Party in the state during that period.

A major influence on New Jersey politics during this period was the role played in presidential elections by New York. The outcome of many of the elections in the early 19th century decided by the votes of New York and New Jersey, which the Federalists needed to win if they stood any chance of winning the presidency. In 1844, a second New Jersey State Constitution was introduced that removed the right to vote from African Americans and women. It also enshrined the direct election of governors, previously elected by the state legislature.

The first gubernatorial election in the state saw Charles C. Stratton, a member of the Whig Party, elected as governor, and New Jersey remained largely Democratic until 1896. The only exception was in the run-up to the American Civil War, with the state electing William A. Newell in 1856. Newell, a physician, was from the newly established Republican Party and had completed three terms in the U.S. House of Representatives before he was elected governor. He was later governor of the Washington Territory. In 1859, New Jersey elected Republican Charles S. Olden as its governor. In the 1860 U.S. presidential election, New Jersey was one of only two states (Missouri being the other) that voted for Stephen Douglas for the presidency, with Douglas getting 62,869 votes (51.9 percent) to Abraham Lincoln's 58,346 votes (48.1 percent), a victory which had resulted from John Breckinridge and John Bell having a partial fusion ticket with Douglas.

When Olden's term as governor ended in 1863, his successor, was Democrat Joel Parker. In the 1864 U.S. presidential election, which took place during the American Civil War, Democrat George B. McClellan from New Jersey carried the state, one of only three states that he won. McClellan went on to be elected governor of the state in 1877, serving 1878–81. Although Marcus L. Ward, a Republican, was elected governor in 1865, when his term ended in 1869, the Democrats won the state until 1896 when the Republicans held the governorship from then until 1910.

THE 20TH CENTURY
In 1911, Democrat Woodrow Wilson was elected governor, holding office until 1913, when he was elected U.S. president. In 1916, Republican Walter Evans Edge was elected as governor, serving 1917–19, and again 1944–47. The 1919 gubernatorial elections saw Democrat Edward I. Edwards elected as governor, managing to defeat Newton Bugbee of the Republican Party by 52 percent to 48 percent. Edwards had to build an urban coalition to get elected, as the Republicans won most of the rural seats in the state, controlled the state legislature, and managed to override many of the governor's vetoes.

With governors not allowed to run for consecutive terms in New Jersey at that time, Edwards, had considered trying to get the Democratic Party nomination for the presidency in 1920, but instead ran for and was elected to the U.S. Senate, campaigning against Prohibition. After Edwards's term in office, George Sebastian Silzer, another Democrat, was elected governor. He was followed by Arthur Harry Moore, who was to serve three non-consecutive terms as governor of New Jersey, with Republican governors holding office throughout the 1930s except for 1932–35 when Moore served his second term.

In 1928, there was controversy in New Jersey in the run-up to the U.S. presidential election, with the state legislature having to oust Thomas A. McDonald as superintendent of the Hudson County Election Bureau after charges of fraud were made. The gubernatorial election held at the end of the year saw the Republican candidate Morgan Foster Larson elected, (who was succeeded by Arthur Harry Moore in his second term as governor).

In the 1940 state gubernatorial election, which came at the same time as the U.S. presidential election, many people decided not to vote for Wendell Wilkie for the presidency, supported Franklin D. Roosevelt, but voted Republican in the elections for the U.S. senatorial, U.S. congressional, and state legislature races. However, in the gubernatorial elections, the Republicans were split between support for Frank Hague who controlled the state legislature, and Hagueism, his political creed, and their candidate Robert Hendrickson. This allowed the Democratic Party's candidate, Charles Edison, to win the election by 57,000 votes.

In 1947, New Jersey adopted a new constitution that allowed governors to be elected for consecutive terms; the first governor elected was Alfred E. Driscoll of the Republican Party. After he had achieved seven years in office, Robert B. Meyner, of the Democrats, was elected for two terms, 1954–62. In the 1960 U.S. presidential election, John F. Kennedy just carried the state with 1,385,415 votes (49.9 percent) to 1,363,324 votes (49.2 percent) for Richard M. Nixon, and 24,372 votes for other candidates. In 1961, Richard J. Hughes, another Democrat, was elected governor, also serving two terms.

Vice President Lyndon B. Johnson became president when John F. Kennedy was assassinated in office. In the 1964 U.S. presidential election, Lyndon Johnson easily carried the state with 1,867,671 votes (65.6 percent) against Barry Goldwater's 963,843 votes (33.9 percent). Richard M. Nixon carried the state comfortably in the 1968 U.S. presidential election, with 1,325,467 votes (46.1 percent), against 1,264,206 votes (44 percent) for Hubert H. Humphrey and 262,187 votes (9.1 percent) for George Wallace, with 23,536 votes for minor candidates, Fred Halstead of the Socialist Worker Party getting 8,668 votes, and Hennings Blomen of the Socialist-Labor Party getting 6,784 votes.

In 1969, Republican William T. Cahill, who had served in the U.S. House of Representatives since 1959,

was elected governor, serving one term, and was succeeded by Brendan Byrne, a Democrat, who served two terms. With Ronald Reagan dominating U.S. politics from his election as president in 1980, in 1981 Republican Thomas Kean was elected governor, and re-elected in 1985. However, New Jersey swung to the Democrats in the following gubernatorial election, electing James Florio, the first Italian American to be governor of New Jersey. Christine Todd Whitman, a Republican, an author, and the first woman to be elected governor of the state, succeeded him. She served two terms, and was appointed the administrator of the Environmental Protection Agency by George W. Bush.

From 2002 through 2008, all three governors have been Democrats, with Jon Corzine, an American with family from the Netherlands, being elected governor in 2004, and being sworn into office on January 17, 2006. New Jersey is now seen as leaning to the Democratic Party in federal elections, with Democratic Party candidates having won every U.S. Senate race in the state since 1980, with only Massachusetts and Hawaii having elected Democrats for a longer period. This is despite easy victories for the Republicans in close presidential elections held in 1948, 1968, and 1976, and largely because of New Jersey's support for Bill

Woodrow Wilson, governor of New Jersey from 1911 to 1913, at home with his wife and three daughters in 1912.

Clinton in the 1990s, and for John F. Kerry who defeated George W. Bush in the state by a margin of six percent.

In the presidential elections of 1960, 1968, and 1992, New Jersey was a swing state. This has led to extensive studies of politics in the state that show the Democrats maintaining strongholds in urban areas, especially in Newark, Jersey City, Trenton, and Princeton, and holding Essex County and Hudson County, the most urban of the counties in the state. By contrast, the Republicans have tended to rely on support from rural parts of the state.

SEE ALSO: Democratic-Republican Party; Federalist Party; Socialist-Labor Party.

BIBLIOGRAPHY. Thomas Fleming, *Mysteries of My Father: An Irish-American Memoir—a Glimpse of Hague Era Politics in Jersey City, New Jersey* (John Wiley & Sons, 2005); T.L. Purvis, *Proprietors, Patronage and Paper Money: Legislative Politics in New Jersey 1703–1776* (Rutgers University Press, 1986); Alan Rosenthal and John Blydenburgh, *Politics in New Jersey* (Rutgers University Press, 1975); B.G. Salmore and S.A. Salmore, *New Jersey Politics and Government: Suburban Politics Comes of Age* (University of Nebraska Press, 1993); Alan Shank, *New Jersey Reapportionment Politics: Strategies and Tactics in the Legislative Process* (Farleigh Dickinson University Press, 1969); W.E. Stickle III, "Edward I. Edwards and the Urban Coalition of 1919," *New Jersey History* (v.90/2, 1972).

JUSTIN CORFIELD
GEELONG GRAMMAR SCHOOL, AUSTRALIA

New Mexico

MEMBERS OF THE Clovis culture originally inhabited New Mexico, and the first European contact occurred when Spanish explorers led by Francisco de Coronado traversed the region in 1540–42. By this time, the Native Americans there were the Navajo, the Apache, and the Ute. It was not until 1598 that the first permanent European settlement was established, and the Spanish administered the region until Mexico's independence, whereupon it became a part of Mexico. At the end of the Mexican-American War, the area was ceded to the United States.

After the American Civil War, settlers started to move to New Mexico and very soon there were tensions with the Navajo and then the Apaches. In 1876, Lew Wallace

A surveying outfit in New Mexico in October 1912. New Mexico was admitted into the Union in January 1912.

(the author of the book *Ben Hur*) who was a prominent member of the Republican committee that recounted the Florida votes in the 1876 presidential election, in which Rutherford B. Hayes narrowly defeated Samuel J. Tilden, was nominated as governor of New Mexico Territory for the part he had played in giving Hayes the victory. However, the nomination took two years to approve, and Wallace only became governor after his predecessor Samuel Axtell was suspended by the secretary of the interior for misconduct.

STATEHOOD AND THE 20TH CENTURY

On January 6, 1912, New Mexico was admitted as the 47th state in the Union. The neighboring state of Arizona was admitted on February 14, ensuring that all parts of the U.S. mainland were parts of the Union. The first governor of New Mexico was William C. McDonald who was born in New York, who moved to New Mexico in 1881, where he became a rancher, and a member of the New Mexico legislature 1891–92. The first senators were Thomas Benton Catron, a former boxer; and Albert Bacon Fall who, nine years later, became U.S. secretary of the interior, the first New Mexican to hold a U.S. cabinet position, until he was forced from office in the Teapot Dome Scandal. The second governor, Ezequiel C. de Baca, born in Las Vegas, New Mexico, was elected in 1916, but died in office the following year; Washington E. Lindsey, the lieutenant governor, became the third governor, filling his unexpired term.

The fourth governor of New Mexico was Octaviano Ambrosio Larrazolo, who was born in Mexico, at age 11 years moved to Arizona, and to El Paso, Texas, as a teacher before training as a lawyer. He moved to Las Vegas in New Mexico and established a law practice, running three times as the Democratic Party candidate for delegate to Congress from the New Mexico Territory. In 1911, he changed his political stance, joining the Republican Party, and was the first Hispanic to be elected as governor of the state of New Mexico, serving for two years before being elected to the New Mexico House of Representatives.

In 1930, businessman Arthur Seligman, a Democrat, born in New Mexico, was elected governor. He was re-elected in 1932, and died in office. His successor was Lieutenant Governor Andrew W. Hockenhull, who remains the only lieutenant governor to become governor owing to the death of his predecessor. He died in 1974, aged 97, making him the longest surviving former governor of New Mexico.

In the 1934 Senate elections, Republican Senator Bronson Cutting, opposed by the Republican Old Guard, challenged Democratic Congressman Dennis Chavez, who had been endorsed by Franklin D. Roosevelt. With the Old Guard of the Republican Party refusing to vote for Cutting, and the left wing of the Democrats not supporting Chavez, it was Cutting who managed to win support of the Hispanic Roman Catholics, although Chavez was Catholic.

Hockenhull's successor, another Democrat, was Clyde K. Tingley, who was born in Ohio, moving to New Mexico just before it gained statehood. He was the first governor of New Mexico to win two consecutive terms in office, and, in 1938, resurrected the New Mexico State Fair. He was elected chairman of the Albuquerque City Commission (later re-designated as mayor of Albuquerque). The 1938 gubernatorial election saw a near unknown, John E. Miles, originally from Tennessee, elected although the New Mexico Democratic Party was opposed to many of Roosevelt's New Deal policies. Pennsylvania-born John J. Dempsey, former undersecretary of the interior, served as governor of New Mexico from January 1, 1943, until January 1, 1947, failing to win the Democratic Party nomination for the New Mexico senate seat in 1946, but later managing to win a seat in the U.S. House of Representatives.

In 1950, Edwin L. Mecham, a Republican, was elected for his first term as governor of New Mexico, serving 1951–55, 1957–59, and for a third time in 1961–62, before winning a seat in the U.S. Senate 1962–64. The nephew of Merritt C. Mecham, who had been governor in 1921–23,

he was the son of a judge, and was the second governor to have been born in New Mexico. His successor was John F. Simms, Jr., a Democratic member of the New Mexico House of Representatives 1947–49, who was elected governor of New Mexico in 1954 at the age of 38, making him the youngest governor to be elected in the state.

In 1964, the Democrats won all the federal and state positions in the election, except for 12 seats in the state legislature that were won by Republicans. Although worry about a rising state deficit may have caused Democratic dominance, the main reasons have been proven to be worries about Barry Goldwater, the Republican Party's candidate, and the fear of right-wing extremism inherent in his supporters. David F. Cargo's election in 1966 was notable for the fact that Cargo, aged 37, was one of the youngest elected governors in the United States. A liberal Republican, he drew Nelson Rockefeller supporters, who had been disenchanted with the policy platform of Barry Goldwater. Re-elected in 1968, Cardo did not seek a third term in 1970, after which the gubernatorial term was increased from two to four years. In the 1970 election, Republican businessman Pete V. Domenici of Albuquerque narrowly lost to Democrat Bruce King, who polled 148,935 votes (51.3 percent) against 134,640 (46.4 percent) for Domenici, the remainder of the votes going to a minor candidate. Domenici then moved to the U.S. Senate.

The 1974 gubernatorial election saw Jerry Apodaca, a Democrat, elected governor. From a Mexican background, he appealed to many "Anglo" Democrats who rallied to support him. In 1978, Bruce King, another Democrat, won the gubernatorial election, starting his second non-consecutive term, were in King was blamed for mishandling the New Mexico State Penitentiary Riot in February 2–3, 1974.

RECENT ELECTIONS

In 1990, Bruce King won the gubernatorial election, returning for his third non-consecutive term. Republican Gary E. Johnson succeeded him in 1994. Democrat Bill Richardson succeeded Johnson, assuming office on January 1, 2003. He had previously been U.S. ambassador to the United Nations, taking over from Madeleine Albright, and then U.S. secretary of energy. In January 2007, he announced that he would be running in the 2008 presidential election.

In the 24 presidential elections in which New Mexico has participated, on 13 occasions it has voted Republican, and in the remaining 11 it has voted for the Democrats, supporting Woodrow Wilson, Franklin D. Roosevelt, Harry S. Truman, John F. Kennedy, Lyndon B. Johnson, and Bill Clinton. With the exception of 2000, when it voted for Al Gore, it has always voted for the candidate who was declared the winner in the presidential elections. The votes were often close, with Kennedy defeating Nixon in 1960 by 156,027 votes (50.2 percent) to Nixon's 153,733 votes (49.4 percent). Four years later, Johnson's victory was decisive, getting 194,017 votes (59.2 percent) to Barry Goldwater's 131,838 votes (40.2 percent). Nixon comfortably won in 1968 with 169,692 votes (51.8 percent) to Hubert H. Humphrey's 130,081 votes (39.7 percent) and Wallace's 25,737 votes (7.9 percent).

According Thomas M. Carsey, the victors in campaigns tend to win as a result of their championing of specific causes and issues, with large blocs of voters keen to ally themselves with a candidate who supports their special interests. In New Mexico, given the large Hispanic population, this prevalence remains slightly lower than the other nearby states. Of the 26 governors, six were born in New Mexico, including the two who had three non-consecutive terms.

SEE ALSO: Bellwether States; Hispanic Vote.

BIBLIOGRAPHY. T.M. Carsey, "Gubernatorial Electoral Coalitions in the Great Plains," *Great Plains Research* (v.7/1, 1997); A.S. Hill, "The 1964 Election in New Mexico," *Western Political Quarterly* (v.18/2, 1965); Marc Simmons, *New Mexico: An Interpretive History* (University of New Mexico Press, 1988); L.S. Theisen, "A 'Fair Count' in Florida: General Lew Wallace and the Contested Presidential Election of 1876," *Hayes Historical Journal* (v.2/1, 1978); M.E. Vigil, "Jerry Apodaca and the 1974 Gubernatorial Election in New Mexico: An Analysis," *Aztlan* (v.9, 1978); P.T. Wolf, "The 1970 Election in New Mexico," *Western Political Quarterly* (v.24/2, 1971); P.T. Wolf, W.H. Pickens, and G.L. Seligmann, Jr., "[Cutting vs. Chavez, 1934]," *New Mexico Historical Review* (v.47/4, 1972).

JUSTIN CORFIELD
GEELONG GRAMMAR SCHOOL, AUSTRALIA

New York

NEW YORK WAS the largest state in population from the 1810 census until the 1970 census and was one of the most important states politically until recently. Although only third in population after Virginia and Pennsylvania at ratification of the Constitution, and tied for third with Massachusetts in 1800, New York took the lead in 1810 and, within a few decades, had one in six seats in the House of Representatives. This primacy diminished as the rest of the country grew, but New York remained the largest state until the late 1960s when California surpassed it. It is now the third most populous state, after California and Texas, with Florida not far behind.

Even as New York State's dominance declined beginning in the mid-19th century, New York City's primacy grew. The prominence of having the country's largest city is perhaps the only thing left that keeps New York politics in the national spotlight. New York was the biggest prize in the era when it was both the largest state and a politically competitive one, but in the current period, New York has become utterly unimportant in national politics because it is reliably Democratic in national politics and less important by dint of its numbers.

New York has produced seven presidents: Martin Van Buren, Millard Fillmore, Chester Alan Arthur, Grover Cleveland, Theodore Roosevelt, Franklin D. Roosevelt, and Richard M. Nixon. New York has also produced a large number of unsuccessful presidential candidates, including George Clinton, Horatio Seymour, Samuel J. Tilden, Charles Evans Hughes, Alfred E. Smith, Thomas E. Dewey, W. Averell Harriman, and Nelson A. Rockefeller. Senator Hillary Rodham Clinton is a candidate for the Democratic presidential nomination in 2008.

NEW YORK GOVERNORS

The governorship of New York has been competitive politically for nearly all of the state's existence, except for the period of one-party Democratic dominance following the evaporation of the Federalist Party in the early 19th century. The New York governorship remained competitive following the formation of the Republican Party in the 1850s, and was not wholly dominated by that party as were the governorships of many other northern states.

The governorship of New York practically entails a national audience. Many nationally prominent men have served as governor of New York, including George Clinton, John Jay, Daniel Tompkins, DeWitt Clinton, Martin Van Buren, William H. Seward, Samuel J. Tilden, Hamilton Fish, Grover Cleveland, Levi P. Morton, Theodore

Roosevelt, Charles Evans Hughes, Alfred E. Smith, Franklin D. Roosevelt, Thomas E. Dewey, W. Averell Harriman, Nelson A. Rockefeller, and Mario M. Cuomo. The pinnacle of domination of American politics by New York governors may have been the 1944 presidential race between former New York Governor Franklin D. Roosevelt, the Democratic incumbent, and current Republican New York Governor Thomas E. Dewey. In the early 21st century, the Democratic Party holds an edge in gubernatorial elections in New York, but not a decisive one.

THE MULTIPARTY SYSTEM

The state's unique multiparty system has occasionally produced a third-party victory. The American Labor Party was created in 1936, so that New York City voters who wanted to support the city's popular Republican mayor, Fiorello LaGuardia, would not then vote the straight Republican ticket. The party also ran President Franklin D. Roosevelt as its candidate to maximize the number of left-leaning voters to bring in the rest of its left-leaning slate. The Liberal Party was formed to do the same thing, but eschew the radical left, which was dominant in the American Labor Party.

The Conservative Party of New York State was formed as something of a reaction to the Liberal Party's success. Ordinarily, these two parties piggyback on the two major parties by endorsing their respective candidates, as does the Right To Life Party. However, occasionally these elections backfire. For example, in 1980, Jacob Javits, one of the U.S. Senate's most liberal Republicans, was defeated in the Republican primary by Alfonse D'Amato. Ordinarily, this would have been the end of Javits's political career. However, on the same day, he also won the Liberal primary. Thus, he was on the ballot in the general election, and D'Amato benefited by the left-of-center vote being split between Javits and Democratic candidate Elizabeth Holtzman (whom Javits had beaten in the Liberal primary). Thus, he narrowly beat Holtzman 45 to 44 percent, with Javits taking 11 percent. In a two-person contest, Holtzman almost certainly would have won.

The multiparty system brought about a different result in 1969, when liberal Republican John Lindsay lost the Republican primary for mayor of New York City. He was re-elected as the Liberal Party candidate. A similar situation happened in 1970, when the Republican appointed to fill the term of the late Robert F. Kennedy, Charles Goodell, was challenged by James L. Buckley, brother of conservative guru William F. Buckley. Buckley won the conservative primary and was able to win the general election with 38 percent of the vote. Some allege that the Republican Party tries to avoid running candidates who are not acceptable to the Conservative Party in order to keep the vote splits that elected Buckley and Javits from recurring. Thus, the right wing in New York has institutionalized its influence through the operation of the Conservative Party.

NEW YORK SENATORS

New York appointments to the U.S. Senate during the period of legislative election were very heavily partisan. The early period was dominated by Federalists, then by Democrats. Between the formation of the Republican Party and the direct election of senators, the state appointed only four Democrats. One critical juncture for New York and the Stalwart Republican faction in the Senate came in 1881. The Stalwarts were a group of Republicans who opposed the changes in presidential patronage that President James A. Garfield proposed.

Stalwart Republican senators Roscoe Conkling and Thomas C. Platt resigned in a dispute with Garfield. They hoped to demonstrate to the president that the state legislature would back them up by re-electing them to the Senate. However, after dozens of ballots, the legislature elected other Republicans to fill the vacancies. (Garfield was assassinated later that year by a disgruntled patronage seeker and New Yorker Chester A. Arthur ascended to the presidency.) So prominent was Conkling in this era that two men born at this time were named for him and became senators themselves: Roscoe Conkling Patterson and Roscoe Conkling McCullough. Platt was later elected to two more terms in the Senate by the legislature.

In the era of direct election, instituted by the Seventeenth Amendment, New York has had several long-serving senators who became prominent nationally: Robert F. Wagner served 1927–49; Jacob Javits 1957–81; Daniel Patrick Moynihan 1977–2001; and Alfonse D'Amato 1981–99. Until recently, the partisanship of the electorate in Senate elections was competitive and fairly balanced, but in recent years, Democrats have acquired a pronounced advantage. Both of New York's Democratic U.S. Senators, facing their first re-election

stems in part from New York City's place as the center of American business and cultural life and the relative ease with which people move to and from there. Both were accused by their opponents of carpetbagging, and after election, both used the post to launch presidential campaigns. Both were only able to reach the Senate through the acquiescence of the Democratic Party to the incredible clout both had in the party by the time they decided to run.

Except for a few years around the Republican peak ascendancy in the 1890s, New York City has been overwhelmingly loyal to the Democratic Party in House elections. Until recently, upstate New York had been resoundingly Republican almost since the party's founding. For decades in the 19th and 20th centuries, the city and upstate pursued completely different political ends in House elections. They have converged somewhat in recent times. In the current era, New York overwhelmingly elects Democrats to the U.S. House of Representatives. In 2006, the state elected 23 Democrats and only six Republicans. This change precedes the post-2000 redistricting. In 2000, under the previous apportionment, the state elected 19 Democrats and 12 Republicans. At that time, the upstate delegation was predominantly Republican. Unless the 2006 election was a fluke, upstate New York is becoming as strongly Democratic as the New York metropolitan area has traditionally been.

PRESIDENTIAL ELECTIONS

In presidential politics, New York supported the winner in nearly every election through 1984. Before 1988, the only times it supported the loser were 1812, 1856, 1868, 1876, 1916, 1948, and 1968, and of those, all but 1856 (the first Republican presidential campaign by John C. Fremont) and 1968 (when the state supported Hubert Humphrey) featured losing candidates from New York (DeWitt Clinton, Horatio Seymour, Samuel Tilden, Charles Evans Hughes, and Thomas Dewey, respectively). Part of this tendency to support the winner was because New York was the largest state with the most electoral votes, so it was difficult for anyone to win without winning New York.

Since 1988, New York has become inexorably a Democratic state in presidential elections. The Republicans barely run a presidential campaign in the state anymore (and in response, neither do the Democrats). While New Yorkers for most of their history were

Fiorello LaGuardia, the popular mayor of New York City, examines a 300-pound halibut at the Fulton Market in 1939.

bids in the mid-2000s, attracted only a moderate threat from Republican challengers.

New York has several times been used by people from outside the state to serve in the Senate. The first instance was the election of Robert F. Kennedy in 1964. The second was the election of Hillary Rodham Clinton in 2000. Neither had a nexus to claim New York as their home state prior to these elections: Kennedy was serving from Massachusetts as attorney general of the United States at the time he began his campaign; Clinton was First Lady of the United States and had claimed Arkansas, where she had lived and practiced law from 1974 until her husband became president in 2003, as her home. This undoubtedly eagerly courted by both parties, having had a considerable sway in the outcome, they now find themselves irrelevant, their influence lost to voters in places such as New Mexico and Ohio where the outcome of national elections is more in doubt.

THE CITY AND THE STATE

An important cleavage in New York politics has been between the New York metropolitan area and upstate New York. As of the 2000 census, 69 percent of the state's population live in the New York metropolitan area; 42 percent of the state's population is in New York City alone. This is a typical cleavage that emerges in other states with a large metropolitan area (such as Illinois and Massachusetts). However, in the case of New York, unlike some of the others, the suburban area sides more uniformly with the city than with the rural part of the state. While downstate interests in Illinois can often get the Chicago suburbs to align with them against the city, this happens less frequently in New York politics. Part of the reason is perhaps the isolation of some of the suburban population (such as Long Island) from the rest of the state.

New York has a number of large cities in its upstate, including Albany (the capital), Syracuse, Rochester, and Buffalo. There is occasional interest in a secessionist movement to form a new state for upstate New York, although it is difficult to gauge whether this is a serious movement or one calculated only to garner more benefits for upstate New York from the state government. The constant strain between the city and upstate, although not as pronounced in national politics, often makes governance of the state a challenge because upstate residents and city residents are in perpetual opposition.

SEE ALSO: Federalist Party; Rural Vote; Urban Vote.

BIBLIOGRAPHY. S.F. Liebschutz and R.W. Bailey, *New York Politics and Government: Competition and Compassion* (University of Nebraska Press, 1998); E.V. Schneier and J.B. Murtaugh, *New York Politics: A Tale of Two States* (M.E. Sharpe, 2001); J.M. Stonecash, ed., *Governing New York State* (State University of New York Press, 2001); R.B. Ward, *New York State Government: What It Does, How It Works* (Rockefeller Institute Press, 2006).

TONY L. HILL
MASSACHUSETTS INSTITUTE OF TECHNOLOGY

Nineteenth Amendment

THE 19TH CENTURY witnessed the rise of women in prominent, even dominant, positions within the abolitionist and temperance movements throughout the United States. However, interest in women's suffrage did not begin to grow until 1848, during a gathering of women in Seneca Falls, New York, organized by Lucretia Coffin Mott and Elizabeth Cady Stanton. The women passed resolutions by a large margin endorsing equal rights for women in the areas of marriage, education, religion, and employment, but endorsed women's suffrage by just a slim majority of votes. Divisions among the women over the tactics to be used, and whether or not the vote should be the key issue within the women's movement, hindered the suffrage movement. In addition, there was a general lack of enthusiasm for women's suffrage among prominent women of the time. Author Edith Wharton believed that women had the necessary skills to get what they wanted without resorting to the ballot box.

After the conference, Stanton worked with Susan Brownell Anthony to form the National Women's Suffrage Association (NWSA). The NWSA took a more radical approach than the American Woman Suffrage Association (AWSA) by accepting only women as members, working only for the right to vote, and denouncing the Fifteenth Amendment for only enfranchising African-American men. The two organizations bitterly opposed one another until they merged under the leadership of Susan Brownell Anthony in 1890.

Alice Paul further split the suffrage movement early in the 20th century with the establishment of the politically militant National Women's Party (NWP). Paul was dissatisfied with the lack of progress and split with other suffragists over the tactics to be used to draw attention to the cause. Paul supported adopting the more radical and aggressive tactics being used in Great Britain by their suffrage movement. Paul viewed the movement of women into factories in support of the American war effort during World War I as patriotic and did not want to wait, as others in the movement counseled, for the end of the war to push their cause. Other suffragists, and their supporters, pointed to the growing number of states granting suffrage and the adoption of party platforms in 1916 by the Democrats and Republicans supporting women's suffrage, although neither party offered a timetable or

A National Woman's Party member works to convince an unidentified man to support the cause of women's suffrage in January 1913, while other Party supporters distribute handbills advertising the Inaugural Suffrage Parade of March 3, 1913.

thought the issue should be addressed before the conclusion of the war.

Paul and the NWP conducted hunger strikes and picketed the White House to draw attention to their cause, tactics that were used by British suffragettes. In July 1917, a number of NWP members attempted to storm the White House and were arrested and placed in the local workhouse. Tensions were further heightened when the women first refused the pardons offered by President Wilson. The women accepted the pardons only after speaking with the attorney general.

Wilson gave his administration's support for women's suffrage in January 1918. Congress passed the legislation on June 4, 1919, and submitted it to the states for ratification. The first two sections of the amendment read: "The right of citizens of the United States to vote shall not be denied or abridged by the United States or any State on account of sex. The Congress shall have power to enforce this article by appropriate legislation." The Nineteenth Amendment was ratified on August 26, 1920, in time to permit women to vote for the first time in a presidential election in the 1920 election of Warren G. Harding.

SEE ALSO: Fifteenth Amendment; Gender and Voting Behavior; Gender Gap.

BIBLIOGRAPHY. Eleanor Clift, *Founding Sisters and the Nineteenth Amendment* (John Wiley & Sons, 2003); D.G. Felder, *A Century of Women: The Most Influential Events in Twentieth-Century Women's History* (Carol Publishing Group, 1999); Jeff Hill, *Women's Suffrage* (Omnigraphics, 2006); Paul Johnson, *A History of the American People* (Weidenfeld & Nicolson, 1997).

ABBE ALLEN DEBOLT M.A., M.A., M.S.S.
COLUMBUS STATE COMMUNITY COLLEGE

Nomination Process, Presidential

WINNING THE PRESIDENCY requires a majority in the Electoral College, but the U.S. Constitution does not dictate whom electors of the various states should consider. Since George Washington's presidency, informal coalitions and, later, political parties coordinated their efforts by nominating candidates for the general election. The nominating process has evolved over time, becoming less centralized, more participatory, and, arguably, more democratic. The matter of nominations was not an issue for George Washington, who was selected by unanimous acclamation. After Washington, however, factions emerged to contest the election.

Presidential nominations were made by the congressional king caucus, in which factions of legislators in the nation's capitol nominated candidates and coordinated campaign efforts in their respective states. The congressional caucus, however, was problematic for several reasons. One, it violated the constitutional principle of separation of powers, as legislators determined who could become president. Two, the system created a void in geographic areas represented by a legislator of the other party. This system collapsed in 1824, when different factions in Congress nominated four candidates in different sections of the country, none of whom gained a majority in the Electoral College.

CONVENTIONS AND PRIMARIES

Starting with the 1832 election, political parties have held national conventions to nominate presidential candidates. For over a century, these conventions featured party bosses meeting to negotiate over the nominee, policy agendas, and the spoils of government in the event of victory. Nominations during the caucus-convention system were controlled by state and local party bosses who held sway because they controlled the local caucuses or meetings used to select delegates to state conventions, which in turn selected delegates to the national conventions. Though national in scope, the power was decentralized among the largely autonomous state and local political party organizations. Nominating candidates required building coalitions among the party organizations divided into factions along sectional lines.

The caucus-convention system shifted to a mixed caucus-primary convention system in the early 1900s.

Starting in 1912, a few states began holding presidential primaries in which partisans could vote on their party's presidential nominee. Most of these primaries were advisory rather than binding, however, and the selection of most convention delegates continued to be controlled by party establishments at the state and local levels. Still, over time, nonbinding preference primaries began to weigh heavily in the decisions of party bosses, who needed to nominate candidates with mass appeal if they were going to win the general election. By the 1960s, it had become possible for a candidate to actively seek the nomination using primaries to demonstrate their popular support (for example, Kennedy in 1960) or even seize control of the nominating apparatus in the various states by coordinating activists to send candidate-loyal delegates to the conventions (for example, Goldwater in 1964). Power over nominations during this period started to gravitate from party elites to party activists.

REFORM

After a divisive and violent convention in 1968, the Democratic Party initiated a series of commissions, beginning with the McGovern-Fraser Committee in 1970, to reform the nomination process. The reforms were intended to make the process more open and participatory and to nominate candidates more representative of party constituencies. Both political parties now use binding presidential primaries and open caucuses to select delegates to the national nominating conventions. The majority of convention delegates are selected in state presidential primaries in which most voters are party identifiers (though some states allow any registered voter to participate). The reformed nomination process shifted control of the nomination from party bosses and insiders to party activists, campaign contributors, and voters in the presidential primaries.

In the post-McGovern-Fraser Committee era, candidates run candidate-centered campaigns of mass appeal for the support of millions of primary voters across the country. They seek nominations by raising funds, assembling their own campaign organizations, and using the media to appeal to party constituencies and aligned groups. The growing importance of resources to finance nomination campaigns, combined with an increasingly condensed primary schedule, has increased the pre-primary campaign, during which candidates build networks of fundraisers and organizational supporters. The candidates most able to compete for the nomination are those who secure endorsements from politicians and organizations aligned with the parties; raise large sums of money; build national; professional campaign organizations; attract national news coverage; and become well-known to party activists and identifiers.

The earliest caucus and primary, traditionally Iowa and New Hampshire, attract the most competition and media coverage and have a disproportionate impact on the nominations. Though these states are often criticized for being unrepresentative of voters nationally, the voters in these states tend to be better informed about the candidates as a result of the intensive retail and wholesale campaigning. Candidates who do better than expected in these early caucuses and primaries tend to receive a boost in their fundraising, media exposure, and public support as they move into the subsequent primaries. Candidates who do not fare well, often find that their fundraising and media exposure decline, and some of these candidates deciding to drop out of the race after Iowa or New Hampshire. Because the majority of convention delegates are selected in the primaries, the nominees are known months in advance of the national conventions. The conventions have now become well-orchestrated events used by the parties to kick-off the general election campaign.

The selection of the nominee matters greatly for the policy or ideological direction and image of a political party, so the presidential nominations of the two major political parties are also competitions among leaders and activists to determine the direction of the parties. Contemporary presidential nominations thus attract substantial attention and involvement by party elites, activists, and advocacy groups aligned with the political parties. Activists and groups influence nominations through their support for candidates before and during the caucuses and primaries. The mass media also became more important in the nomination process, as journalists advance or hinder the cause of particular candidates by giving them more or less coverage, labeling candidates with more or less favorable terms, paying attention to certain issues and not others, and, finally, by setting expectations for and critiquing candidate performance.

SEE ALSO: Caucuses; Conventions; Iowa Caucus; National Nominating Party; New Hampshire Primary; Presidential Primaries.

BIBLIOGRAPHY. Larry Bartels, *Presidential Primaries and the Dynamics of Public Choice* (Princeton University Press, 1988); J.W. Ceaser, *Presidential Selection: Theory and Development* (Princeton University Press, 1979); Richard Herrera, "The Crosswinds of Change: Sources of Change in Democratic and Republican Parties," *Political Research Quarterly* (v.48, 1995); W.H. Keech and D.R. Matthews, *The Party's Choice* (Brookings, 1976); Barbara Norrander, "Field Essay: Presidential Nomination Politics in the Post-Reform Era," *Political Research Quarterly* (v.49, 1996).

WAYNE P. STEGER
DEPAUL UNIVERSITY

Nonpartisan Election

A NONPARTISAN ELECTION is an election where the candidates do not have a formal political party affiliation. In a nonpartisan election system, candidates do not run in party nominating elections (primaries) and the ballot does not indicate a party affiliation. Instead, all candidates' names appear on the ballot. In most instances, if no candidate receives a majority of the vote, a run-off election will be held where the top two vote-getters will appear on the ballot. Supporters of nonpartisan elections frequently seek to limit the power of political parties. By making the elections nonpartisan, they hope to reduce the influence that political party leaders have over elections. They contend that eliminating party labels will encourage qualified people from outside politics, and candidates who are not part of the party machine, to run for public office.

Nonpartisan elections were part of the package of municipal reforms, which included at-large elections, off-year elections, the secret ballot, the short ballot, council-manager, and commission forms of municipal government that were advocated by Progressive reformers during the late-19th and early-20th centuries. In 1909, Boston, Massachusetts became the first major American city to adopt nonpartisan elections. The reforms were part of a larger reform agenda, which was a reaction to the excesses of the Industrial Revolution. Political reforms were directed against the corrupt governments that were dominated by political party machines. Muckraking journalists exposed the abuses of the party bosses and the elected officials they placed in office. The reformers intended to reduce corruption and political patronage, create more choices for the voters, and limit the power of party leaders by stripping them of their ability to decide who ran for public office in municipal elections.

Nonpartisan elections are held in many municipalities, including Atlanta, Boston, Chicago (where they were introduced in 1995), Dallas, Denver, Detroit, Houston, Los Angeles, Phoenix, San Antonio, San Diego, San Francisco, and Seattle. Today, 41 of the 50 largest cities in the United States with an elected mayor utilize nonpartisan elections. They are also often used to elect school board members and, in some states, judges. The Nebraska State Legislature is the only state legislature that is elected on a nonpartisan basis.

In most nonpartisan elections, there is a requirement that the winner receive a majority of the vote. If no candidate secures a majority, a run-off election will be held between the top two vote-getters. Such run-offs avoid the problem of candidates being elected with a small percentage of the votes cast, and allow voters to focus on the two remaining candidates. In some nonpartisan elections, the party affiliation of the candidates is well known; in other cases, political parties are not involved in the election and voters make their selections without giving much consideration to partisan politics. There are instances where civic organizations have influence over the results of nonpartisan elections. While political parties may still have an influence over the election by endorsing candidates and working on their behalf, they no longer control access to the ballot.

Proponents of nonpartisan elections argue that they increase the number of people who participate in the election of officeholders. They also argue that removing party designations from the ballot will encourage voters to focus on campaign issues, rather than party labels. However, studies of jurisdictions that have switched from partisan to nonpartisan elections, and comparisons of paired jurisdictions with similar political characteristics other than partisan elections, generally show lower voter participation under nonpartisan elections. Research also indicates that this decrease in participation is concentrated among less educated and less affluent voters. It has also been contended that ethnicity/race and incumbency replace party affiliation as cues for voters in nonpartisan elections, and that nonpartisan elec-

tions result in the under-representation of minorities in local legislative bodies.

SEE ALSO: Election Laws, State and Local Elections; Machine Politics and Political Bosses.

BIBLIOGRAPHY. W.P. Collins, "Race as a Salient Factor in Nonpartisan Elections," *Western Political Quarterly* (v.33/3, 1980); W.D. Hawley, *Nonpartisan Elections and the Case for Party Politics* (John Wiley and Sons, 1973); N.P. Lovrich, Jr., C.H. Sheldon, and Erik Wasmann, "The Racial Factor in Nonpartisan Judicial Elections: A Research Note," *Western Political Quarterly* (v.41/4, 1988); B.F. Schaffner, Matthew Streb, and Gerald Wright, "Teams Without Uniforms: The Nonpartisan Ballot in State and Local Elections," *Political Research Quarterly* (v.54/1, 2001); Susan Welch and Timothy Bledsoe, "The Partisan Consequences of Nonpartisan Elections and the Changing Nature of Urban Politics," *American Journal of Political Science* (v.30, 1986).

JEFFREY KRAUS
WAGNER COLLEGE

Nonvoters

VOTER TURNOUT IN consolidated democracies is generally determined by three factors: The provisions for suffrage as outlined in the constitution, electoral rules that govern the voting process, and individual voter characteristics. Nonvoters are therefore those individuals who do not participate in elections because they either do not legally have the right to vote, they face institutional barriers such as voter registration that make it more difficult to vote, or they share certain demographic and psychological characteristics that make it less likely they will vote.

Although the composition of the electorate has generally expanded in democracies worldwide as more populations have been granted suffrage, a large number of nonvoters remain due to various physical, social, and psychological obstacles to voting. In addition, the United States continues to have a relatively high proportion of the electorate that is comprised of nonvoters, especially compared to other advanced democracies.

In early democracies, nonvoters were the norm, comprising well over the majority of individuals living under representative government. In the first 50 years after the founding of the United States, nonvoters consisted of all persons except white property-holding males. It was not until 1840 that all states in the union extended suffrage to property-less white males. Women continued to be nonvoters in the United States until 1920, when the ratification of the Nineteenth Amendment to the Constitution provided adult females with the franchise. African Americans fully became voters through a combination of the Twenty-Fourth Amendment in 1964, various Supreme Court decisions, and the Voting Rights Act of 1965. Together, these provisions swept away barriers such as the poll tax and literacy tests that had effectively barred African Americans in the south from voting.

Today in the United States, nonvoters are legally defined at the federal level as individuals under the age of 18 (as per the Twenty-Sixth Amendment), convicted felons, and non-citizens. At the state level, there are different rules that define voter eligibility, with some states repealing restrictions for convicted felons and legal immigrant non-citizens.

As in the United States, women and ethnic minorities worldwide have a history of being legally constrained to nonvoter status. Women first became voters in New Zealand in 1893 and Australia in 1902. By 1919, much of Europe had provided women with the franchise; however, women were nonvoters for longer in some European countries, including the Czech Republic (1920), Portugal (1931), Spain (1931), France (1944), Italy (1945), Greece (1952), and Switzerland (1971). Among developing areas, Azerbaijan (1920) and Georgia (1920) were the first to allow women to vote, while Ecuador (1929) was the first country in Latin America to enact women's suffrage. Today, women are still considered nonvoters in Saudi Arabia, and only gained suffrage in Kuwait in 2005.

Certain ethnic groups have also been prevented from entering the electorate. Like African Americans, African minorities around the world have been notoriously restricted to nonvoter status, such as in Colombia, the Dominican Republic, Venezuela, and South Africa. Until recently, indigenous populations were excluded from the electorate in Latin American countries such as Ecuador, Honduras, Paraguay, and Peru, either through formal definitions of suffrage or with the use of literacy tests. Other historic examples of nonvoting ethnic minorities are the Hmong in Laos, the Roma in

Greece, and Serbs in Croatia, many of whom still face restrictions on voting.

ELECTORAL RULES AND NONVOTERS

Although most adults living in democracies now have the legal right to vote, many choose not to vote regularly, a self-selecting process that places those individuals in the category of nonvoters. Certain electoral rules create barriers to the voting process, requiring more knowledge and effort on the part of the voter, and make it more difficult for even eligible citizens to participate in elections. One such rule is requiring voters to be registered. When registration is the responsibility of the individual and is not done automatically by the government, more citizens are nonvoters.

In addition, when elections are held more frequently, there is a higher burden placed on the voter, and a higher likelihood that voters will not cast ballots in all electoral contests. Whether or not elections are held on a holiday or a weekend also affects whether an individual participates, because on a weekday most adults must find time before or after work to get to the polls. The electoral system, whether a country uses single-member districts versus more proportional methods of allocating legislative seats, also appears to affect a citizen's potential to vote. Finally, approximately 32 countries have compulsory voting, where voters are required to show up at the polls or they face punitive measures such as fines or community service. There are generally fewer nonvoters when citizens are sanctioned for failing to participate in elections.

From a comparative perspective, the United States has a proportionally large amount of its electorate who are consistently nonvoters. Nearly 47 percent of the voting age population in the United States were nonvoters in the 1990s. By comparison, Australia had the smallest percentage (six percent) of nonvoters, followed by Iceland, Italy, Sweden, Luxembourg and Belgium, where nonvoters were less than 15 percent of their voting age population. Of 24 industrialized democracies, only Switzerland had a larger proportion (54 percent) of nonvoters than the United States.

The large number of nonvoting Americans is not surprising, given the fact that in every industrialized democracy except the United States and France, registration is automatic. In most of them (save the United States, Denmark, Great Britain, and Canada) Election Day is on a weekend or holiday, and the majority (except for the United States and Britain) have some form of proportional representation.

Although nonvoters are clearly affected by voting rules, they also typically share a number of individual characteristics, such as similar socioeconomic, demographic, and psychological traits. In the United States, nonvoters generally have lower levels of education and smaller family incomes, and work in service jobs or labor-intensive occupations. In addition, nonvoters tend to be younger citizens, with the majority of nonvoters under the age of 30. After decades of being nonvoters, women in the United States are now slightly more likely to vote than men, making it impossible to classify nonvoters in terms of gender. Finally, nonvoters are likely to be those individuals who do not identify with a political party, who feel as though their vote has little effect on government, who have very little interest in politics, and who distrust government.

SEE ALSO: Age and Voting Behavior; Educational Level and Voting Behavior; Gender and Voting Behavior; Income and Voting Behavior; Occupation and Voting Behavior; Psychological Reasons for Voting and Nonvoting; Race and Voting Behavior.

BIBLIOGRAPHY. André Blais and R.K. Carty, "Does Proportional Representation Foster Voter Turnout?" *European Journal of Political Research* (March 1990); M.M. Conway, *Political Participation in the United States* (CQ Press, 2000); Benjamin Highton, "Easy Registration and Voter Turnout," *Journal of Politics* (May 1997); R.W. Jackman and R.A. Miller, "Voter Turnout in the Industrial Democracies in the 1980s," *Comparative Political Studies* (Winter 1995); Stanley Kelley, Jr., R.E. Ayres, and W.G. Bowen, "Registration and Voting: Putting First Things First," *American Political Science Review* (June 1967); *Minorities at Risk Project* (Center for International Development and Conflict Management, 2005); F.F. Piven and Richard Cloward, *Why Americans Don't Vote* (Pantheon, 1988); G.B. Powell, Jr., "American Voter Turnout in Comparative Perspective," *American Political Science Review* (March 1986); F.O. Ramirez, Yasemin Soysal, and Suzanne Shanahan, "The Changing Logic of Political Citizenship: Cross-National Acquisition of Women's Suffrage Rights, 1890 to 1990," *American Sociological Review* (October 1997); S.J. Rosenstone, "Economic Adversity and Voter Turnout," *American Journal of Political Science* (February 1982).

KARLEEN JONES
UNIVERSITY OF IOWA

North Carolina

BEFORE THE ARRIVAL of Europeans, North Carolina was occupied by a many of Native American tribes, including the Cherokee and the Tuscarora. It was the second territory in North America that the British tried to colonize, with its state capital Raleigh taking its name from Sir Walter Raleigh, the Elizabethan English adventurer who established two colonies on the coast in the late 1580s. The name of the state was given in 1712 in memory of the late King Charles I of England, using the Latin word for Charles.

In 1776, North Carolina was the first of the colonies to instruct its delegates to vote for independence from the British Crown, with Richard Caswell elected as the first governor of the state. He wrote the first North Carolina Constitution and was re-elected in April 1777, stepping down in 1780, as the constitution allowed only three non-consecutive terms. He was later speaker of the senate in North Carolina. Abner Nash, the second governor, was elected by the legislature at a time when North Carolina was a battlefield in the Revolutionary War. The third governor, also appointed, was Thomas Burke, a doctor who had originally been born in Ireland. The fourth governor, Alexander Martin, was elected by the North Carolina general assembly in 1782, and after he stood down as governor in 1784, he returned to the North Carolina Senate where he served until 1788, and was then elected to the U.S. Senate 1793–99.

Richard Caswell then returned to the position of governor, followed by Samuel Johnston, a Federalist, the first governor who had a political party affiliation. Alexander Martin succeeded him as an Anti-Federalist, returning to the governorship for a second term. His successor was Richard Dobbs Spaight, the first governor to be born in North Carolina, and the only one to be killed from injuries sustained in a duel.

Federalists and Anti-Federalists battled in successive elections until 1802, when James Turner, a longtime politician, was elected as a Democratic-Republican. Turner served for three one-year terms, the constitutional limit, before being elected to a seat in the U.S. Senate, with the Democratic-Republicans dominating the North Carolina political scene until 1828. This period was characterized by many of the governors serving the maximum three years in office, with Benjamin Williams doing so on two occasions.

Gabriel Holmes, who was governor 1821–24, was effectively an Independent, although he is generally regarded as affiliated with the Democratic-Republican Party; his successor Hutching Gordon Burton was also an Independent, but was associated with the Federalist Party, and later with the National Republican Party. In December 1828, John Owen became the first Democratic Party governor of North Carolina, after narrowly defeating Richard Dobbs Spaight, Jr., with the vote being 96 to 92.

In 1830, David Lowry Swain of the National Republican Party was elected at the age of 29—at that time the youngest governor in state history, and the first to become affiliated with the Whig Party. One of his tasks was to push through the ratification of the North Carolina Constitution. In 1835, Richard Dobbs Spaight, Jr., was elected for the Democrats, the first governor who was the son of a previous governor. Spaight was the last governor to be elected by the state legislature; the new constitution called for the governor to be elected by the people.

The first popularly elected governor was Edward Bishop Dudley of the Whig Party. He was succeeded by three more Whig governors, the second of whom, William Alexander Graham, won the 1844 gubernatorial elections with a policy of founding a national bank and a protectionist tariff. In the U.S. presidential election in the same year, James K. Polk campaigned on a policy of westward expansion, and managed to get many votes for the Democrats from the traditionally Whig western part of North Carolina, with the Whigs still carrying the state narrowly. Also, William W. Holden, editor of the Raleigh *North Carolina Standard,* was able to misrepresent Whig attitudes in the 1848 and 1850 elections and influence the election results.

THE CIVIL WAR AND RECONSTRUCTION

In 1850, David Settle Reid of the Democratic Party was elected governor on his second attempt. He had lost the 1848 election to Charles Manly by 854 votes, he won in 1850 by 2,853 votes. As governor Reid campaigned for "free suffrage," which would allow people who were eligible to vote for the North Carolina House of Commons to also be able to vote for the North Carolina Senate—there was a 50-acre freehold requirement for a person to vote for the senate.

In 1854 Thomas Bragg was elected governor of North Carolina, and served until 1859. He then won a seat in the U.S. Senate, serving from 1859 until the start of the Civil War in 1861, when he was expelled from Congress for supporting the Confederacy, of which he became the attorney general. In the 1858 gubernatorial election, John Willis Ellis was elected, easily defeating Duncan K. McRae, a Democrat who had gained the support of the remnants of the Whig Party. In 1860, Ellis easily defeated John Pool of the "Opposition Party," largely members of the former Whig Party; Pool later became a Republican Party senator.

One of the major issues in this election was whether to tax slaves as persons or as property according to their value, with poor whites favoring the latter policy. The political problem was that the large planters represented only a small percentage of voters, but made up a large proportion of the legislators, using their power regularly to block changes in the tax laws, that were unfavorable to them. Within a few years, the issue that so savagely split voters in 1860 became irrelevant with the freeing of the slaves at the end of the Civil War.

In the 1860 U.S. presidential election, North Carolina narrowly voted for Southern Democrat John Breckinridge, who received 48,845 votes (50.5 percent) against John Bell of the Constitutional Union who received 45,129 votes (46.7 percent), with Stephen Douglas of the northern Democrats receiving 2,737 votes (2.8 percent), Abraham Lincoln was not on the ballot in North Carolina. North Carolina seceded from the Union in May 1861, and joined the Confederate States of America. When John W. Ellis died in office, Henry Toole Clark, from an elite planter family, succeeded him as the state's chief executive, mobilizing tens of thousands of soldiers for the war effort. On September 8, 1862, Zebulon Baird Vance became governor, after winning the gubernatorial elections for the Conservative Party, a state coalition party of Democrats and Whigs. He remained governor until Union forces captured him in May 1865, William W. Holden of the National Union became the provisional governor.

On November 9, 1865, a special election was held in North Carolina, with Jonathan Worth, the winner, from the Conservative Party, being sworn in as governor on December 15, 1865. Holden then returned as the Republican Governor, with two more Republican governors presiding over the Reconstruction period ending in 1877. Their wasn't another Republican governor elected until 1897–1901, and after that, not until 1973.

THE AFRICAN-AMERICAN VOTE

During the 1890s, there were a series of bitter state elections held in North Carolina, with Democratic Party candidates assured of victory. In 1892, the Republicans in North Carolina tried to unite their party with some of the leaders wanting to prevent African Americans from having a major role in their party, yet realizing that they would never be able to gain control of the governorship or the legislature without African Americans voting in large numbers. Seeing the dilemma, the Democrats savagely attacked the Republicans for becoming too reliant on African-American votes, leading to some African Americans voting for Populist candidates, or even Democrats.

In the 1896 state elections, the Republicans had Daniel L. Russell, Jr., running in the gubernatorial election, which, in itself, was an issue that split Republican voters. Russell advocated a fusion of the Republican and Populist parties, and African Americans were not keen on supporting Russell who, as a teenager, was a captain in the Confederate Army during the Civil War. In the elections held on November 3, 1896, Russell managed to get elected for one four-year term with 153,787 votes (46.5 percent) to 145,266 votes for Cyrus B. Watson for the Democrats, 31,143 for the Populist candidate William A. Guthrie, and 809 for other candidates. In 1900, Democrat Charles Brantley Aycock was elected as governor, with the Democrats winning all gubernatorial elections in the state until 1972.

THE 20TH CENTURY

In U.S. presidential elections during the 20th century, North Carolina has mainly voted Democratic. The 1908 gubernatorial election saw the Republican Party's support fade with African Americans angry at their treatment, and the loss of their votes was not compensated for by any real increase in support from whites. In 1908, Jonathan Elwood Cox, a furniture manufacturer, led an inept campaign for the gubernatorial elections, losing to Democrat William Walton Kitchin.

In 1928 presidential election the state switched its support to a Republican, Herbert Hoover. This was mainly in opposition to Democrat Alfred E. Smith, who was a Roman Catholic. The 1928 swing away from the Democrats surprised many political observers who had not foreseen the importance of Smith's Roman Catholicism as an issue. In 1932, the state swung back to the Democrats under Franklin D. Roosevelt, and, in 1936, the Works Progress Administration (WPA) was to play a major role in the campaign. Although North Carolina was such a strong Democratic Party state, the patronage of the WPA tended to benefit particular factions within the Democrats, who used it to their advantage.

In the 1960 U.S. presidential election, the issue of John F. Kennedy's Roman Catholicism was not as important as it had been for Al Smith in 1928. Kennedy won the state for the Democrats with 713,318 votes to 655,648 votes for Richard M. Nixon. In 1964, the state voted for Democrat Lyndon B. Johnson, who received 800,139 votes to Barry Goldwater's 624,844 votes.

North Carolina started a swing back to voting for Republican presidents once again in 1968 and 1972, with supporting Richard M. Nixon. In 1968, George Wallace had hoped to win the state, but Richard M. Nixon won it by 627,192 votes (39.5 percent) to Wallace's 496,188 votes (31.3 percent) and Hubert H. Humphrey's 464,113 votes (29.2 percent).

JESSE HELMS

North Carolina voted for Nixon in 1972, and in the same year, in their gubernatorial elections, elected James Eubert Holshouser who, at the age of 38, was the youngest governor of North Carolina in the 20th century. Holshouser was a moderate Republican and in the 1976 Republican Party primary, he supported Gerald Ford, with North Carolina's senator Jesse Helms supporting Ronald Reagan. In the gubernatorial election in the same year Jesse Helms, a senator since 1973, led the opposition to the Democrat, James B. Hunt, Jr., who was elected governor, and held office until 1985.

During this time, Republican Jesse Helms emerged as one of the major forces in North Carolina politics, as U.S. Senator 1973–2003, and chair of the U.S. Senate Committee on Foreign Relations 1995–2001. Helms was always controversial, even supporting Argentina during the Falklands War, with Great Britain, in 1982. In the following year, he opposed the Martin Luther King, Jr Holiday Bill on the basis that King allegedly had Communist associates and had allegedly committed adultery.

However, in 1984, Jim Hunt, the outgoing Democratic governor, challenged Jesse Helms for the U.S. Senate seat for North Carolina, with the most expensive senate election campaign up to that point. Helms won with 1,156,768 votes (51.7 percent) versus Hunt, who received 1,070,488 votes (47.8 percent). In the 1990 re-election campaign, Helms used television commercials that were critical of the stance taken by his opponent, Harvey Gantt, on affirmative action, urging white voters to support him. Helms won with 1,087,221 votes (52.5 percent) to Gantt's 981,573 votes (47.4 percent). In 1996, Helms received 1,345,833 votes (52.6 percent) to Gantt's 1,173,875 votes (45.9 percent). Republican James G. Martin held the governorship 1985–93, with Hunt being re-elected in 1992, and serving until 2001, when Mike Easley, another Democrat, became the governor.

SEE ALSO: Anti-Federalists; Democratic-Republican Party; Federalist Party; Southern Democratic Party; Whig Party.

BIBLIOGRAPHY. J.M. Beeby, "'Equal Rights to All and Special Privileges to None': Grass-Roots Populism in North Carolina," *North Carolina Historical Review* (v.78/2, 2001); D.C. Butts, "The 'Irrepressible Conflict': Slave Taxation and North Carolina's Gubernatorial Election of 1860," *North Carolina Historical Review* (v.58/2, 1981); J.J. Crow, "'Fusion, Confusion, and Negroism': Schisms among Negro Republicans in the North Carolina Election of 1896," *North Carolina Historical Review* (v.53/4, 1976); T.E. Jeffrey, "'Free Suffrage' Revisited: Party Politics and Constitutional Reform in Antebellum North Carolina," *North Carolina Historical Review* (v.59/1, 1982); R.E. Marcello, "The Politics of Relief: the North Carolina WPA and the Tar Heel Elections of 1936," *North Carolina Historical Review* (v.68/1, 1991); R.A. Strickland and M.L. Whicker, "Comparing the Wilder and Gantt Campaigns: A Model for Black Candidate Success in Statewide Elections," *PS: Political Science & Politics* (v.25/3, 1992); B.G. Walton, "Elections to the United States Senate in North Carolina, 1835–1861," *North Carolina Historical Review* (v.53/2, 1976); M.R. Williams, "William A. Graham and the Election of 1844: A Study in North Carolina Politics," *North Carolina Historical Review* (v.45/1, 1968).

JUSTIN CORFIELD
GEELONG GRAMMAR SCHOOL, AUSTRALIA

North Dakota

EUROPEANS FIRST EXPLORED the area that became the state of North Dakota in the 18th century, with the Lewis and Clark expedition passing through it 1804–05. The first settlement founded by the Hudson's Bay Trading Company followed soon afterward, with the fur-trapping business and trade by riverboat. In 1861, the Dakota Territory was delineated, covering what is now both North Dakota and South Dakota. From the 1870s, the population of the area grew, and on November 2, 1889, North Dakota and South Dakota were admitted into the Union as separate states.

The first governor, Republican John Miller, had moved to the area in 1878, purchasing land in the Red River Valley. Miller had then taken part in the constitutional convention held at Bismarck on July 4, 1889, and was persuaded to run for governor. Although he had no political experience, he was a firm governor and resisted attempts to cajole or bribe him. Declining to serve another term as governor, he returned to agriculture and Andrew H. Burke, also a Republican, was elected as the second governor. He had been orphaned at the age of 4, worked on the farm of his adoptive parents, and enlisted as a drummer boy in the Civil War, managing to save up enough to go back to school. He and his wife migrated to North Dakota in 1880, bringing with them $65. Burke then ended up as a bank manager before being elected governor. In 1892, the electorate of North Dakota participated for the first time in the presidential elections.

By this time money politics had emerged in North Dakota, and Alex McKenzie became a political boss and a representative of railroads and other large corporations. While McKenzie tried to control the state politics, the voters chose Eli C.D. Shortridge as their governor in 1892. He was an Independent, but also a Populist who used his two years in office to enlarge the state capitol and enhance the executive mansion, being the first governor to live there. The fourth governor, Roger Allin, had moved to Canada from England when he was 4 and then migrated to the Dakota Territory in 1881. In the following year, he was elected as a justice of the peace. The former state auditor, Frank A. Briggs, succeeded him at the age of 38. His successor, Joseph M. Devine, aged 36, was the youngest person to be elected governor of North Dakota.

In 1912, Louis B. Hanna was elected governor of North Dakota, having represented the state in the U.S. House of Representatives since 1909. He was the first governor of Norwegian heritage, although he was born in Pennsylvania. Since then, five more governors have been Norwegian-Americans. Two, Ragnvald A. Nestos (governor 1921–25) and John Moses (governor 1939–45) were born in Norway, with three others, Ole H. Olson, Fred George Aandahl, and Allen I. Olsen, born in the United States, the first in Wisconsin, and the other two in North Dakota. In the 1976, 1980, and 1984 elections when Walter Mondale, also of Norwegian ancestry and from the neighboring state of Minnesota, twice ran as the Democratic Party's vice presidential candidate, and then as the presidential candidate, North Dakota voted Republican.

THE DEMOCRATIC-NPL PARTY

During the governorship of Louis Hanna, from the mid-1910s, Progressive politics became a factor in North Dakota, with the formation of the Non-Partisan League (NPL), and with its Progressive candidates, who ran against Republicans in the primaries with reform agendas and socialist programs. From its base in Minnesota, the NPL brought together farming interests, and, in 1916, Lynn Frazier managed to win the North Dakota gubernatorial election with 79 percent of the votes. However, in the subsequent election in 1918, even though he did not win, Stephen Joseph Doyle managed to run a campaign that helped to break the control of the NPL, which threatened to end the two-party system in the state.

The major change in state politics in the 1920s was demographic, with the emergence of state politicians who had been born in North Dakota. The first of these to become governor, born in Grand Forks in what was then still the Dakota Territory, was Walter J. Maddock, who became governor after his predecessor, Arthur G. Sorlie, died in office in August 1928. Maddock was ran in the elections later that year, losing to George Shafer, also born in the Dakota Territory. It was not until the election of Fred George Aandahl in 1944 that the state had a governor who had been born in North Dakota after it had become a state. Apart from Allin in the early days of statehood, and the two born in Norway, the only other foreign-born governor was Walter Welford, who became governor in 1935, at the age of 66—the oldest man to be elected governor of the state. Since Aandahl's election in 1944, all of the governors of North Dakota have been born in the state.

Welford was not, however, elected governor. In the 1930s, North Dakota politics were in turmoil for years, with William Langer removed from office for soliciting political contributions from federal employees. He was sentenced to 18 months in prison and fined $10,000, but after three more trials was acquitted of all charges. Nevertheless, his removal had necessitated Ole H. Olson, the lieutenant governor, to serve out Langer's term. In 1934, Thomas H. Moodie received the Democratic nomination for governor and defeated Lydia Langer, the wife of William Langer (who was not allowed to run for office).

Moodie, the first Democratic Party governor since John Burke 1907–13, and only the second in the state's history, was sworn in on January 7, 1935. However, he was removed from office on February 16, 1935, when it was found that he had voted in a 1932 municipal election in Minnesota. To be eligible for governor, he needed to have lived for five consecutive years in North Dakota before an election. When the state supreme court removed him from office, Welford, the Republican lieutenant governor, became governor. In 1936, he defeated Langer in the Republican Party primary, but Langer decided to run as an Independent. He won, but is still regarded as a Republican governor, as he had been during his first term.

By the 1950s, the NPL had become the North Dakota establishment, and saw the formation, in 1956, of the Democratic-NPL Party. Since then, the Republicans have controlled the state legislature, with the Democratic-NPL holding many of the federal seats. In 2008, both U.S. senators from North Dakota, Kent Conrad and Byron Dorgon, as well as the congressman, Earl Pomeroy, are from the Democratic-NPL. By 1965, there were serious concerns about the apportionment of legislature seats in 1931. By the 1950s, small towns were heavily over-represented, leading to calls to have the boundaries changed, which eventually took place. To help alleviate such problems, in the 1980s, multimember districts were established.

SEE ALSO: Nonpartisan Election; South Dakota.

BIBLIOGRAPHY. "Dakotatensis" (pseudonym), "Representation of City and Country," *North Dakota Quarterly* (v.33/1, 1965); G.F. Moncrief and J.A. Thompson, "Electoral Structure and State Legislative Representation: A Research Note," *Journal of Politics* (v.54/1, 1992); E.B. Robinson, *History of North Dakota* (University of Nebraska Press, 1966); R.H. Watrel, *Sectionalism, Coalitions, and Local-National Politics: A Geographical History of Presidential and Gubernatorial Elections in North Dakota, 1889–2000*, thesis (University of Nebraska, 2001); Richard Whaley, "The Other Side of the Mountain: Stephen Joseph Doyle and Opposition to the NPL in 1918," *North Dakota Quarterly* (v.56/4, 1988).

JUSTIN CORFIELD
GEELONG GRAMMAR SCHOOL, AUSTRALIA

Northern Democrats

EARLY IN ITS history, the Democratic Party became divided on the issue of slavery. Most southern Democrats wanted it preserved and most northern Democrats wanted it abolished. When the Democratic Party failed to take a strong abolitionist stand, the Free Soil Party split away from it in 1848. They were composed mostly of expansionist northern Democrats who wanted to expedite the acquisition of the western lands, and outlaw slavery in these new territories, as it was in the northern states. The Free Soilers had little effect on presidential elections, however, in 1848, two senators and 14 congressional representatives were elected from the party.

When the influential Democratic Illinois Senator Stephen Douglas sponsored the 1854 Kansas-Nebraska Act, a law that would allow the settlers of those two territories to self-govern and choose in the matter of slavery, the issue became even more contentious. The Free Soil Party dissolved around the same time, and many of their members joined the northern Democrats who were joining the Republican Party. The remaining Northern Democrats faced frequent accusations from Republicans of being "doughfaces"—pliable, spineless politicians who appeased the southern Slave Power, even though they were not a part of it.

COPPERHEADS AND BOURBON DEMOCRATS

By 1860, the party was in such disarray that it was unable to centralize enough to support a single candidate. Instead, the Southern Democrats nominated Vice President John Breckinridge for president, while the Northern Democrats supported Stephen Douglas. Breckinridge won the 11 slave states. Douglas came in second in the popular vote, but took less than five percent of the electoral vote. With the Democrats split, Republican Abraham Lincoln beat them both, and the Civil War began.

During the war, the only Southern Democrats remaining with the United States were those from the states that had rejected secession: Missouri, Kentucky, Maryland, and Delaware. The Northern Democrats fought over the matter of the war. War Democrats stood with Lincoln, while the Copperheads (sometimes called Butternuts, also a term for a Confederate soldier) sought an immediate peace treaty with the seceding states, and an end to the military draft. The Copperheads blamed the Republicans, and the abolitionists for causing the war, accusing them of inciting the southern states in

to seceding. Copperheads were often been accused of treason, in encouraging soldiers to desert, even directly helping Confederates, but such accusations were mostly made by their political opponents, and fit the vicious and vituperative rhetoric of the day.

As the war waxed on, lasting longer than many first thought, Copperheads fared well in state and local elections where the Democrats had an existing power base, and especially in the border states, which were often settled by former southerners who maintained family and cultural ties to the Confederate states. The 1864 presidential election could have been a significant one for the Democrats: the war had taken a serious toll, and the Republicans showed early signs that they expected a harsh battle to re-elect Lincoln. But infighting ruined the Democrats' chances, as the War Democrats and Copperheads were unable to come to terms. In the end, the pro-war General George McClellan was nominated to run for president, with a party platform that called for the nation to sue for peace. General McClellan was quite clear that he had no intention of doing so. The mixed message brought the Democrats 45 percent of the popular vote, but less than a tenth of the electoral votes. Lincoln was re-elected.

After the war, the Northern Democrats in particular saw a significant loss in their influence: while the southern party was blamed for the war, they at least had the support of the returning southern electorate. Over time, the so-called Bourbon Democrats coalesced around Grover Cleveland, who was elected president in 1884. The Bourbon Democrats, allied with the Redeemer Democrats in the south, represented the business interests of the north and the midwestern cities, earning support from the banks and the railroads while campaigning for a gold standard in the increasingly volatile post-Reconstruction debate over currency.

Though they fought bureaucratic corruption, they had no interest in the sweeping reforms of the more progressive factions of the party. The Northern Democrats remained Bourbon in outlook despite the widespread popularity of anti-gold William Jennings Bryan. Because so much power was consolidated in the northeastern strongholds of Bourbon Democrat sentiment, Bryan found he had no support from Democratic newspapers, even after he won the nomination for the 1896 presidential election.

As the 20th century got underway, the Democratic Party in the north became the party of the working class voters, and especially of Catholics. The party worked for reforms, electing erudite academic Woodrow Wilson in 1912, and re-electing him in 1916. Large business interests were increasingly swayed to the Republican Party. The activists of the Civil Rights Movement and other 20th century reform movements were drawn from the ranks of the Northern Democrats.

SEE ALSO: Catholic Vote; Civil Rights; Civil War and Realignment; Conventions, National Nominating Party; Democratic Party; Free Soil Party; Party Platforms; Southern Democratic Party.

BIBLIOGRAPHY. Jean Baker, *Affairs of Party: The Political Culture of Northern Democrats in the Mid-Nineteenth Century* (Fordham University Press, 1998); D.B. Craig, *After Wilson: The Struggle For the Democratic Party* (University of North Carolina, 1993); H.S. Merrill, *Bourbon Democracy in the Middle West* (University of Washington Press, 1969); J.H. Silbey, *A Respectable Minority: The Democratic Party in the Civil War Era* (W.W. Norton, 1977).

Bill Kte'pi
Independent Scholar

Occupation and Voting Behavior

ONE OF THE easiest ways to classify voters is by occupation. A person's occupation will normally not change much during their lifetime. (Unlike changing jobs, which are often in the same occupation.) A voter's occupation will also determine their income level and lifestyle. General classifications are blue collar and white collar. Blue-collar work is normally defined as an occupation requiring manual labor, while white-collar occupations do not require manual labor. These classifications are easy to determine and have been used to create generalizations about both groups and about how they will vote and what types of candidates they will support. This assumes that the voter identifies with these groups. Researchers have shown that upward of one quarter of voters categorize themselves incorrectly. It is often supposed that blue-collar workers are Democrats and that white-collar workers are Republicans. While always the case, there is a tendency for this to be true.

Also important to a voter is unemployment, both past and future—nothing gets a voter's attention like an issue that will affect their ability to make a living. Unemployment tends to increase voters' desire to have the government guarantee jobs for workers. This increased desire is more pronounced among blue-collar workers, but exists in both groups. Anxiety over unemployment is not limited to voters who have lost a job, or are in danger of losing a job, but can also affect those living in a region burdened with unemployment. In an area that has suffered from job losses, the issue tends to remain important to voters for years after the crisis has passed. These voters tend to be supportive of government intervention to ensure full employment. When comparing blue-collar and white-collar workers, researchers have determined that blue-collar workers, as a group, are more supportive of government intervention than white-collar employees. However, as unemployment rises, both groups tend to be more supportive of government intervention in the economy to reduce unemployment.

REGIONAL FACTORS

In addition, the area a voter lives in can affect his or her attitudes on unemployment and the economy. In rural areas, any type of economic problem tends to indirectly affect more people than it would in an urban area. In rural areas, if the farmers are having problems it will be felt by everyone, so other voters in the area tend to be sensitive to the same issues as farmers. In urban areas, economic classes are more insulated from each other and the problems of blue-collar workers tend to not have an effect on white-collar workers in the same area.

Among various occupations, farmers are the most likely to not vote in an election and are also more likely to switch party affiliation when they do vote. Farmers are also more likely to vote a split ticket. Among urban voters, participation seems to be related to social class: White-collar and professional workers are more likely to vote than blue-collar workers. However, those same white-collar and professional workers are more likely to switch party affiliation than a blue-collar voter.

One region where occupation was not very important until recently is the American south. For most of its history, its voters have been predominantly Democratic. Only since the 1950s has the number of Republicans grown significantly, although the south still tends to be more Democratic than Republican. More change came with the Twenty-Fourth Amendment, passed in 1964, which officially put an end to the Poll Tax that had been used to restrict the poor, especially in southern states, from voting.

While other voters in farming areas are attuned to farm issues, farmers themselves are among the least likely to vote.

PARTICIPATION

A number of studies, along with the U.S. Census, have shown that a person's occupation also affects the likelihood that the person will vote. Those voters who have lower incomes, or are unemployed, along with blue-collar workers, are the least likely to vote in an election. Studies from the 1970s show that of those in this group who were eligible to vote, the majority were not even registered to vote. The studies also show that 40 percent of the unemployed are not registered to vote, and that altogether 50 percent of the unemployed fail to vote. This is in comparison to voters with jobs, where only 26 percent were not registered and only 34 percent did not vote.

White-collar workers tend to be more involved in voting than any other category of voter. Studies have found that for every two white-collar workers who are registered or voted, only one blue-collar voter did likewise. The ratio is even worse when compared to workers in service industries or farming. The U.S. Census report on the 1970 election found a two to one ratio in voter turnout when comparing voters with jobs and those who were unemployed. It also found that 71 percent of the voters with a family income of at least $15,000 voted in the election, while only 44 percent of the voters from families with incomes of $5,000 or less voted. Because of these trends, elected officials tend to better represent more affluent voters, since they are the ones casting votes.

AFFILIATION

There are often general differences in the people who support each of the two major parties. Those who support the Republicans tend to have higher incomes and higher status at their jobs. Union members, and organized labor in general, often tend to be Democrats. The policies of Franklin D. Roosevelt strengthened this connection between the Democratic Party and organized labor.

Another factor that is often thought to be important is the voter's mobility within their social class. The belief is that upwardly mobile voters will tend to move toward the Republican Party whereas those who are downwardly mobile in social class will tend to associate with the Democratic Party. However, this link has never been conclusively proven. There is evidence to suggest that very few voters are actually either upwardly or downwardly mobile in their social class. Among those who are mobile, there appears to be little political difference between the two groups. In addition, upward mobility seems to be similar across all occupations.

In American politics, unlike European, social class plays a very small role. Even as the gap between the poor and the rich has widened since the 1980s, social class has limited impact on voter behavior. This attitude is supported by politicians, who rarely use class differences as an issue.

Given the common belief that Democrats tend to be holders of lower (blue-collar) status jobs while white-collar workers, as well as those in the middle- and upper-classes, tend to be Republican. While there is some truth in this it is important to realize that occupation and social status are not the only factors determining voter behavior.

SOCIAL FACTORS

A voter's occupation will also determine with whom he or she associates. These associates will expose the voter to their political ideas, influencing the behavior of the voter. The people who make up this group can be customers, fellow employees, or others of the same occupation. Each of these groups may have the same political ideas or very different ideas. This includes the possibility of contact with people who the voter might not normally associate with.

It has been noted by researchers that white-collar voters in jobs that require them to associate with large groups of blue-collar workers tend be less likely to vote Republican than voters in the same group without exposure to blue-collar workers. By the same token, research shows that voters who have clerical jobs that require them to work with customers who have higher-status occupations tend to vote Republican more often than voters in similar clerical positions who are only exposed to blue-collar customers. The voter might also have a job that requires him or her to interact with the government directly, which can affect political outlook.

While a voter's economic status, including occupation, has been one of the best ways of gauging voting behavior, it now appears that values are taking the place of economic status. During the mid-1990s, working-class whites deserted the Democratic Party while affluent suburbanites deserted the Republican Party. This signaled a change in previous notions about a correlation between a voter's economic status and party affiliation, and made the use of economic status to predict voter behavior less successful.

SEE ALSO: Age and Voting Behavior; Cross-Pressures, Sociopolitical; Education Level and Voting Behavior; Electoral Behavior; Gender and Voting Behavior; High and Low Stimulus Elections; Income and Voting Behavior; Independent Voters; Martial Status and Voting Behavior; Race and Voting Behavior; Religion and Voting Behavior; Social Groups and Electoral Behavior; Split Ticket Voting; Suburban Vote; Voter Self-Interest.

BIBLIOGRAPHY. Angus Campbell, Philip E. Converse, Warren E. Miller, and Donald Stokes, *The American Voter* (University of Chicago Press, 1960); Angus Campbell, Philip E. Converse, Warren E. Miller, Donald E. Stokes, *Elections and the Political Order* (John Wiley and Sons, 1966); William J. Crotty, *Political Reform and the American Experiment* (Thomas Y. Crowell, 1977); William H. Flanigan and Nancy H. Zingale, *Political Behavior of the American Electorate, 11th Edition* (Congressional Quarterly, 2006); Paul McCaffrey, ed., *The United States Election System* (W.H. Wilson Company, 2004); Norman H. Nie, Sidney Verba, and John R. Petrocik, *The Changing American Voter* (Harvard University Press, 1979); Gerald Pomper, *Voters' Choice: Varieties of American Electoral Behavior* (Dodd, Mead & Company, 1975).

DALLACE W. UNGER, JR.
INDEPENDENT SCHOLAR

Ohio

NATIVE AMERICANS FROM the powerful Iroquois confederation inhabited Ohio before the arrival of European explorers. Initially, the French set up trading posts, which they ceded to Britain at the Treaty of Paris in 1763. In the second Treaty of Paris 20 years later, the British ceded all claims to Ohio to the United States, and the area that included Ohio was formed into the Northwest Territory. In 1801, with Ohio's population at 45,000, it embarked on the road to statehood, and on February 19, 1803, President Thomas Jefferson signed an act of Congress that approved the newly written Ohio Constitution. Curiously, Ohio was never formally admitted as the 17th state of the Union, with the oversight being discovered in

1953. In that year, the formal date of Ohio gaining statehood was set at March 1, 1803.

The first governor of Ohio was Edward Tiffin, who was born in Britain, although his exact place of birth is not known. He emigrated with his parents and became a doctor in Charles Town, Virginia (now West Virginia), before heading west in 1798. Tiffin was elected unopposed, and easily won election for his second term. He then resigned the governorship to take up a seat he had won in the U.S. Senate, serving only two years, and resigning when his wife died. He then was elected to a seat in the Ohio House of Representatives. Tiffin was from the Democratic-Republican Party, as were the next eight governors, one of whom served two nonconsecutive terms.

There were some problems with the early gubernatorial elections in Ohio, with Return Jonathan Meigs, Jr., winning the 1807 election, but disqualified for not meeting the residency requirements. Thomas Kirker took the position, and then Samuel H. Huntington, a nephew and adopted son of Samuel Huntington, the first president of the Continental Congress, served as governor. Meigs, when he was disqualified, had served in the U.S. Senate, and in 1810 he was elected governor, serving until 1814.

The seventh governor of the state, Ethan Allen Brown, born in Darien, Connecticut, on July 4, 1776, had been elected to the Ohio Supreme Court in 1810, re-elected in 1817, and in 1818 won the gubernatorial election. He was governor for four years, and then served in the U.S. Senate, and a diplomatic post in Brazil. One of the major political figures in the 1820s was Robert Skinner, a Methodist newspaperman from Virginia, whose papers were dominant in Dayton, Ohio. He supported particular candidates on local issues, and managed to get his candidates elected to 19 of the 28 seats on the Dayton Town Council.

In the 1830 gubernatorial elections, Duncan McArthur was elected as governor. He was from the National Republican Party, having made a fortune from land speculation, and then serving two short stints in the U.S. House of Representatives. His successor, Robert Lucas, was chair of the Democratic National Convention in 1832, the first convention held by the Democratic Party. He was the 12th governor of Ohio, and then served as a territorial governor of Iowa.

Joseph Vance, a Whig, won election as governor, but was defeated in the 1838 gubernatorial elections by Democrat Joshua Giddings, supported by a Democratic majority in both houses of the state legislature. The reason for Vance's defeat was supposedly the anger of abolitionists when Vance extradited a Methodist minister who had been active in helping escaped slaves to Kentucky. Recent studies of that election suggest that even though abolitionists such as Gamaliel Bailey controlled important newspapers, the main strength of the Democrats was largely in the Western Reserve. Over the next 20 years, the Democratic Party and the Whig Party candidates fought each other in gubernatorial elections, with both achieving some success.

The 1853 election campaign was particularly notable because the Whigs and the Free Soilers (people against the expansion of slavery) tried to form a fusion ticket of their candidates who also supported the prohibition of alcohol measures, introduced in 1851. With the Whigs keen on prohibition, and the Free Soilers going along with the measure, but concentrating on anti-slavery measures, the Democrats fought a bitter campaign on the basis of civil liberties.

THE CIVIL WAR ERA

In 1856, with the issue of slavery looming, Salmon Portland Chase was elected governor of Ohio. The major issue during the election campaign was slavery, which was seen as a moral question by many people in the state. A lawyer, Chase had defended escaped slaves who had been captured in Ohio, and made a name for himself with his vehement opposition to slavery. Initially entering politics as a Whig, he was elected to the Cincinnati city council, but abandoned the party in 1841, and led the Liberal Party. However, in 1846 he was forced into an alliance with the Van Buren Democrats from New York to establish the Free Soil Party, before going on to help found the Republican Party. Chase sought the Republican nomination for the presidency in 1860, but managed to get only 49 votes, then put his support behind Abraham Lincoln.

In the 1860 U.S. presidential election, Ohio voted heavily for Lincoln, who gained 231,709 votes (52.3 percent) to Stephen Douglas who received 187,421 votes (42.3 percent), with John Bell of the Constitutional Union on 12,194 votes (2.8 percent), and John Breckinridge of the Southern Democrats, with 11,406 votes (2.6 percent). This victory gave Lincoln 23 Electoral College seats, the largest block outside New York (35) and Pennsylvania (27).

With Chase first a senator, and then Lincoln's secretary of the treasury, William Dennison, Jr., was elected as governor, defeating Rufus P. Ranney. Dennison only served one term. He was succeeded by David Tod, also of the Republican Party, who had lost the 1843 and 1845 gubernatorial elections, and was elected in 1861, serving 1862–64. In the 1863 gubernatorial election, Clement L. Vallandigham, a Democrat who supported peace, gained the ire of many soldiers who voted 18 to one against him. This was particularly important because during the American Civil War, Ohio was crucial for the transportation of Union soldiers and supplies, with the state contributing more soldiers per capita than any other northern state. John Brough was elected, and the next four governors were all Republicans. In the gubernatorial elections of 1865, Democratic Party racists made great political capital over the role played by African-American voters and measures were introduced two years later to limit African-American participation in the electoral system.

THE MOTHER OF PRESIDENTS
William Allen winning the gubernatorial elections broke the Republican primacy in Ohio in 1873. Thereafter, of the next 34 governors, 14 were Democrats, and the remainder were Republicans, earning Ohio the reputation as a swing state. Between the Civil War and the election of Warren Harding in 1920, seven U.S. presidents were born in Ohio: Ulysses S. Grant, Rutherford B. Hayes, James Garfield, Benjamin Harrison, William McKinley, William Howard Taft, and Warren Harding. This gave rise to Ohio becoming known as the Mother of Presidents, with only Virginia having had more presidents born within its borders.

William Henry Harrison, although born in Virginia, settled in Ohio, as did his grandson Benjamin Harrison. Of the eight presidents who regarded Ohio as their home state, seven were Republicans, and the other was a Whig. During the American Civil War, generals Grant, Sherman, and Sheridan were all from Ohio; and when Harding was elected in 1920, there were six men from Ohio on the U.S. Supreme Court, of whom two had been chief justice.

THE 20TH CENTURY
Most of the governors of Ohio served either one or two terms, having less impact on the state than governors in other states. However, Ohio politics dramatically changed in 1912, when a constitutional convention was held, chaired by Charles B. Galbreath. He was a Progressive, and wanted to introduce the Jeffersonian concept by which laws should be reviewed each generation. The issue of whether or not the laws should be reviewed then appeared on state ballots every 20 years: in 1932, 1952, 1972, and 1992.

In the early 20th century, Warren Harding emerged as a major political force. As a leading member of the local Republican Party, Harding sought the gubernatorial nomination from the party in 1910, but lost out to the incumbent Democrat Governor Judson Harmon, who was able to get the support of the liberal electorate. Harmon then tried to achieve national recognition for his activities in Ohio, in the hope of running in the U.S. presidential elections. However, this did not happen. In 1920, Harding, with support from the 13 northwestern counties of Ohio, launched a bid for the Republican nomination, and won the eventual presidential election, becoming the 29th president of the United States. In addition to supporting Harding for the presidency, Ohio also elected a Republican, Harry L. Davis, as governor.

By the 1930s, there was intense political rivalry between Martin L. Davey, a Democrat, who was elected governor in 1934, and re-elected in 1936, and John W. Bricker, who had the firm support of the 13 northwestern counties of Ohio that had voted for Harding in 1920. In the 1940 gubernatorial election, President Franklin D. Roosevelt did not support Davey's re-election bid as the incumbent governor was, by then, tainted by scandals. The campaign saw Davey try to smear Bricker with a number of personal attacks. The result was a landslide in favor of Bricker, who then was re-elected twice, serving as governor for six years.

When Bricker announced his retirement, the Democrats endorsed Frank J. Lausche as their candidate, and he was elected for one term, later returning for another four terms 1949–57. One of the longest-serving governors of Ohio, Lausche was from a Slovenian family, and had held many offices including mayor of Cincinnati. He campaigned calling himself a "Democrat with a small D," appealing to moderates to support him. In the 1948 U.S. presidential election, Ohio helped ensure victory for Harry S. Truman, who defeated Thomas Dewey, who had won the state four years earlier.

In the 1960 U.S. presidential election, Richard M. Nixon carried the state with 2,217,611 (53.3 percent) to John F. Kennedy's 1,944,248 votes (46.7 percent), a result that annoyed Kennedy immensely as he had campaigned six times in the state. During his visits, Kennedy had shaken so many hands that his right hand had swollen by the end of the campaign and he held up an inflamed hand claiming "Ohio did that to me." In the gubernatorial election held at the same time, Michael V. DiSalle, a Democrat, was elected as governor.

In 1962, James A. Rhodes, a Republican, was elected governor, being re-elected in the next three elections, even though Ohio swung to the Democrats at a federal level, showing clear evidence of ticket-splitting. In the 1964 U.S. presidential election, Lyndon B. Johnson easily carried the state with 1,786,422 votes (76.2 percent) to Barry Goldwater's 549,727 votes (23.4 percent). In the 1968 U.S. presidential election, Richard M. Nixon carried the state with only 1,469,218 votes (63 percent), to 766,844 votes (32.9 percent) for Hubert H. Humphrey and 87,088 votes (3.7 percent) for George Wallace.

James A. Rhodes, who had been elected governor of Ohio in 1962, served as governor 1963–71, and then 1975–83, making him, by many years, the longest serving governor in the history of the state, winning seven gubernatorial elections. Rhodes was the governor in 1970 when the Ohio National Guard opened fire on students demonstrating at Kent State University, with four students shot dead and nine others wounded.

In the 1976 U.S. presidential election, Jimmy Carter narrowly carried the state, defeating the incumbent Republican president, Gerald Ford. Astronaut John Glenn announced in 1964 that he was going to stand against Senator Stephen M. Young in the Democratic Party primary. However, after suffering from a concussion, he was forced to withdraw, but was nominated in 1970, losing the primary to Howard Metzenbaum who went on to lose the senatorial election to Robert Taft, Jr. In 1974. Glenn fought Howard Metzenbaum in the primary, with Glenn winning after a bitter contest. He was elected senator for Ohio in 1974, and remained in the U.S. Senate until 1999.

In the 1990 Ohio gubernatorial election, George Voinovich was elected for the Republicans. The first Serbian-American to be elected as a U.S. governor, he served until 1998, when he ran for a seat in the U.S. Senate, was elected, and was re-elected in 2004. Voinovich's Lieutenant Governor, Nancy P. Hollister, then became the first female governor of Ohio. Robert A. Taft II was elected governor in 1998, serving two terms.

Ohio voted for Bill Clinton in 1992 and 1996, but voted for George W. Bush in 2000 and in 2004. In the 2004 U.S. presidential election, there was controversy about the role played by the state in the defeat of John Kerry, although Kerry chose not to dispute Bush's victory in that state. In 2006, Democrat Ted Strickland was elected governor, taking office on January 8, 2007.

SEE ALSO: Free Soil Party; Slavery; Southern Democratic Party; Whig Party.

BIBLIOGRAPHY. Lawrence Baum, "Explaining the Vote in Judicial Elections: The 1984 Ohio Supreme Court Elections," *Western Political Quarterly* (v.40/2, 1987); A.G. Carey, "The Second Party System Collapses: The 1853 Maine Law Campaign In Ohio," *Ohio History* (v.100, Summer-Autumn 1991); M.F. Curtin and J.B. Bell, *The Ohio Politics Almanac* (Kent State University Press, 1996); R.F. Kennedy, Jr., "Was the 2004 Election Stolen?" *Rolling Stone Magazine* (June 2006); Carl Lieberman, *Government Politics and Public Policy in Ohio* (Midwest Press, Inc., 1995); Emil Pocock, "Popular Roots of Jacksonian Democracy: The Case of Dayton, Ohio, 1815–30," *Journal of the Early Republic* (v.9/4, 1989); Bernard Sternsher, "The Harding and Bricker Revolutions: Party Systems and Voter Behavior in Northwest Ohio, 1860–1982," *Northwest Ohio Quarterly* (v.59/3, 1987); Bernard Sternsher, "The Glenn Revolution: Voter Behavior in Northwest Ohio, 1970–1988," *Northwest Ohio Quarterly* (v.62/3–4, 1990); F.P. Vazzano, "The Feud Renewed: Martin Davey, John Bricker and the Ohio Campaign of 1940," *Ohio History* (v.105, Winter-Summer, 1996); V.L. Volpe, "The Ohio Election of 1838: A Study in the Historical Method?" *Ohio History* (v.95, Summer-Autumn 1986); K.J. Winkle, Robert Fogel, and Stephan Thernstrom, *The Politics of Community: Migration and Politics in Antebellum Ohio* (Cambridge University Press, 1988).

JUSTIN CORFIELD
GEELONG GRAMMAR SCHOOL, AUSTRALIA

Oklahoma

NATIVE AMERICAN TRIBES occupied Oklahoma for many centuries before Francisco Vásquez de Coronado traveled through the region in the early 16th century.

Oklahoma's early history as "Indian Territory," to which Native Americans were forced to move from eastern states, complicated its admission to the Union. The engraving depicts a settlement in Oklahoma Indian Territory.

The area eventually became part of the Mississippi Purchase of 1803. In 1830, the Indian Removal Act signed by President Andrew Jackson resulted in many Native American tribes east of the Mississippi River being forcibly relocated to land in Oklahoma, where they were resettled. The Trail of Tears expulsion resulted in many deaths, and the Native Americans were left with poor agricultural land. After the American Civil War, even more Indian tribes were moved to Oklahoma, and in the 1870s numbers of white settlers started taking over unassigned land. The population in Oklahoma grew steadily, and the Curtis Act of 1898 abolished tribal jurisdiction in the Indian Territory, as Oklahoma was then known.

STATEHOOD

There was considerable debate about statehood for Oklahoma, with four possible plans being raised. The one that was eventually accepted allowed for one state, covering both the land purchased for the Native Americans, and the area opened for general settlement. There were serious suggestions for two states, parts being admitted piecemeal, and also no statehood for the Indian Territory. The debate mainly concerned the view that if Oklahoma were admitted as a single state, there would be a clear Democratic majority. However, if there were two states, it was likely that the Republicans might get support from the non–Native American state. However, eventually the Republican Party of the Oklahoma territory announced that it favored Oklahoma entering the Union as a single state, assuring statehood. In 1907, Oklahoma gained statehood and was admitted to the Union. Since its creation, Oklahoma has been a predominantly Democratic state, with no Republican governors elected until 1962; only three of its 24 governors have been Republican.

The first elected governor, Charles N. Haskell, was born in Ohio and orphaned at the age of three. He had become a successful lawyer and businessman, moving to Muskogee, and had been active in the campaign for statehood. On March 26, 1907, he held a large banquet in Tulsa, and the gathered members of the Democratic Party were urged to choose him over Thomas Doyle of Perry and Lee Cruce of Ardmore.

The primary campaign was hard-fought, with Haskell trying to make up ground for entering the campaign late, making 88 speeches in 45 days and traveling to nearly every county. Haskell won the primary with a majority of over 4,000 votes, and then had to face Frank Frantz, the Republican governor of the Oklahoma Territory. As the election was going to be close, the Republican presidential nominee, William Howard Taft, and the Democratic Party nominee, William Jennings Bryan, both visited the state, with Taft speaking out against the proposed Oklahoma state constitution. However, in the gubernatorial election on September 17, 1907, Haskell won, and the state constitution was also approved, apparently as a reaction against what was seen as interference by Taft. Oklahoma was declared a state on November 16, 1907, and five minutes later, Haskell was inaugurated as its first governor.

20TH CENTURY UPHEAVALS

After one term in office, Lee Cruce, one of the men whom Haskell had defeated in the Oklahoma Democratic primary four years earlier, succeeded Haskell. Unfortunately for Cruce, he did not have majority control over the state legislature, which Haskell had during his term. The third governor, Robert Lee Williams, had played an important part in the drafting of the state constitution, and had managed to defeat John Fields of the Republican Party.

In 1910, the Socialist Party of America appeared on the political scene, and became a major force in Oklahoma, although not in any other state. The result was that the 1918 gubernatorial election was a three-horse race, with James B.A. Robertson running for the Democrats, Horace G. McKeever for the Republicans, and Patrick Nagle for the Socialists. However, the Socialists did poorly owing to the Green Corn Rebellion in the previous year, when poor farmers staged a rural uprising believing that they had the support of the Industrial Workers of the World (IWW).

Robertson's term as governor coincided with the Tulsa Race Riot of 1921, a riot unparalleled in the history of the state, which left some 300 dead, 800 badly injured, and 10,000 homeless. With Robertson not seeking re-election, John C. Walton was successful in getting the Democratic Party's nomination, and spent the election campaign traveling around remote parts of the state giving lively and colorful speeches. He represented the radical wing of the Democratic Party, and had the support of many people in the Oklahoma legislature, which included many progressive members.

Walton promised during the campaign to hold a massive barbecue and square dance to celebrate his victory if he won, and this took place from January 1, 1923, until his inauguration on January 9—125,000 people assembled for the barbecue. However, Walton was not in office for long; in November 1923 he was impeached and removed from office after charges, including the illegal collection of campaign funds, abuse of gubernatorial pardons, "padding the public payroll," and "general incompetence," were leveled against him.

Martin E. Trapp, who succeeded Walton, saw himself as an "acting governor," Henry S. Johnston was elected in 1926, taking office in January 1927. The 1926 election campaign was notable because Johnston, although he had been associated with the Ku Klux Klan, did not seem to get their support during the campaign, downplaying the Klan as a political issue. Johnston, who won the gubernatorial election and ended up being impeached, ousted Trapp in the Democratic Party primaries. William Judson Holloway, and William Henry David "Alfalfa Bill" Murray succeeded him. Born in Texas, Murray had started in politics in 1902 as a political operative for Palmer S. Moseley, a gubernatorial candidate soon after statehood was achieved. Murray won the gubernatorial election with a majority of over 100,000, the largest ever achieved in the state. He had to deal with the problems of the Great Depression, in particular the Dust Bowl, which badly affected many farmers on marginal land in Oklahoma (the Okies) with up to 15 percent of the population of the state moving to California.

In 1934, Ernest Whitworth Marland was elected governor with his avowed policy of starting a Little New Deal. He faced a hostile Oklahoma legislature, but managed during his governorship to create some 90,000 jobs. In the 1936 congressional election, Lyle Boren gained a seat in the U.S. Congress; in a speech to the U.S. House of Representatives in 1940, he memorably declared that John Steinbeck's *The Grapes of Wrath* was a "lying, filthy, dirty manuscript."

Marland left office followed by Leon C. Phillips, elected in 1938. Phillips served one term, as did the next six governors. One of them, Johnston Murray, governor 1951–55, was the son of former governor William H. Murray. The 1954 gubernatorial election started with 16 Democratic Party candidates, and even five Republican candidates. This led to a series of campaigns for the primaries that involved the revelations of many scandals, and to ensure an orderly campaign it was eventually necessary to declare martial law in five of the state's counties.

The campaign teams of two Democrat hopefuls, William O. Coe and Willie Murray (wife of then governor Johnston Murray) both embarked on personal attacks on front runner Raymond D. Gary, who won the primary, and then the general election. Gary's successor, J. Howard Edmondson, was elected in 1958 with the largest majority ever given to any gubernatorial candidate in Oklahoma. Part of his victory was attributed to his promise to enforce the state prohibition laws introduced when Oklahoma gained statehood in 1907; he would first hold a referendum within 90 days of his election to allow the voters of the state to decide on the future of prohibition. However, that was never tested as that election saw Edmondson made governor again. George Nigh was elected lieutenant governor at the age of 31, making him the youngest lieutenant governor in any state of the Union.

Two years later, in the 1960 U.S. presidential election, Richard M. Nixon won the state with 533,039 votes (59 percent), to John F. Kennedy's 370,111 votes (41 percent). In January 1963, U.S. Senator Robert S. Kerr died, and the governor, Edmondson, resigned to fill Kerr's remaining senate term. This allowed George Nigh, the lieutenant governor, to complete Edmondson's unexpired term.

The 1962 gubernatorial election in Oklahoma saw Henry Bellmon elected governor—the first Republican to hold the office of governor of Oklahoma. In the 1964 U.S. presidential election, Lyndon B. Johnson won the state with 519,834 votes (55.7 percent) to Barry Goldwater's 412,665 votes (44.3 percent). With Bellmon not able to stand for consecutive terms as governor, the Republican Party chose Dewey F. Bartlett as their candidate in the gubernatorial election, which he won.

The 1968 U.S. presidential election saw Richard M. Nixon carry the state with 449,697 votes (47.4 percent) to Hubert H. Humphrey's 306,658 votes (32.3 percent) and George Wallace's 191,731 votes (20.3 percent). At this time, Oklahoma ended the restriction on re-election, and Bartlett became the first governor to run for a second consecutive term. Facing him was David Hall, who won the Democratic Party primary (he had come in third in the primary four years earlier). The race between Bartlett and Hall was the closest gubernatorial election ever in Oklahoma, and Hall was only confirmed the winner after a recount. In 1974, Hall sought re-election, but only gained 27 percent of the Democratic Party vote in the primary, pushed into third place by Clem McSpadden, a congressman, and David L. Boren, a university professor, who won the election and became governor in January 1975.

Boren, the son of former Oklahoma congressman Lyle Boren, went on to serve in the U.S. Senate where, despite being a Democrat, he became a strong supporter of the foreign policy of Ronald Reagan and George H.W. Bush. When he stood down in 1978, George Nigh, who had already served as governor, was elected to two terms, the first governor to do so. His successor was another ex-governor, Henry Bellmon, and after one term, the Democratic candidate David Walters won the gubernatorial election. His successor, Frank Keating, a Republican, was sworn in as governor three months before Oklahoma City gained international attention in the aftermath of the Oklahoma City bombing in 1995. Keating served two terms, and was succeeded by Brad Henry, a Democrat, who was elected in 2003.

SEE ALSO: Bryan, William Jennings; Ku Klux Klan; Racial Justice; Socialist Party.

BIBLIOGRAPHY. Kenneth Biggs, *Oklahoma Politics: A History* (University of Oklahoma Press, 1982); D.C. Boles, "Effect of the Ku Klux Klan on the Oklahoma Gubernatorial Election of 1926," *Chronicles of Oklahoma* (v.55/4, 1977–78); Garin Burbank, *When Farmers Voted Red: The Gospel of Socialism in the Oklahoma Countryside 1910–1924* (Greenwood Press, 1977); C.W. Ellinger, "The Drive for Statehood in Oklahoma, 1889–1906," *Chronicles of Oklahoma* (v.41/1, 1963); B.L. Hanson, "Oklahoma's Experience with Direct Legislation," *Southwestern Social Science Quarterly* (v.47/3, 1966); S.A. Kirkpatrick, *The Legislative Practice in Oklahoma: Policy Making, People & Politics* (University of Oklahoma Press, 1978); V.T. Lyon, "The

Repeal of Prohibition: The End of Oklahoma's Noble Experiment," *Chronicles of Oklahoma* (v.76/4, 1998–99); J.C. Milligan and L.D. Norris, "The Aroma of Politics: Raymond Gary and the Election of 1954," *Chronicles of Oklahoma* (v.66/1, 1988); D.R. Morgan, R.E. England, and G.G. Humphreys, *Oklahoma Politics and Policies: Governing the Sooner State* (University of Nebraska Press, 1991); W.W. Rogers, "'I Want You All to Come': John C. Walton and America's Greatest Barbecue," *Chronicles of Oklahoma* (v.75/1, 1997); S.H. Schrems, *Who's Rocking the Cradle? Women Pioneers of Oklahoma Politics from Socialism to the KKK* (Horse Creek Publications, 2004).

JUSTIN CORFIELD
GEELONG GRAMMAR SCHOOL, AUSTRALIA

Oregon

NATIVE AMERICANS LIVED in Oregon for at least 15,000 years. In 1779, Captain James Cook explored the coast, and, in 1805–06, the Lewis and Clark Expedition traveled through Oregon. Astoria, named after New York financier John Jacob Astor, was the first permanent white settlement. However, the area was contested by the British who wanted to control the fur trade in that region, an issue that was finally resolved in 1846 with the Oregon Treaty. On February 14, 1859, statehood was granted, and Oregon was admitted to the Union.

The first elected governor, John Whiteaker, from Indiana, had joined the California Gold Rush in 1849, ending up in Oregon, where he became active in the Democratic Party. He won the gubernatorial election by a large majority, gaining a margin of 1,138 votes, and was inaugurated on July 8, 1858, before the granting of statehood.

In the 1860 U.S. presidential election, Oregon voted narrowly for Abraham Lincoln, giving him 5,329 votes (36.1 percent) to 5,075 votes (34.4 percent) for John Breckinridge and 4,136 votes (28 percent) for Stephen Douglas. John Bell of the Constitutional Union Party finished in a distant fourth place, with 218 votes (1.5 percent). Whiteaker was a supporter of slavery, and the percentage vote for John Breckinridge was the second highest of the states that were neither southern nor border states, and the only northern state that Breckinridge nearly won.

With the outbreak of the American Civil War in 1862, Republican candidate Addison C. Gibbs, from New York, was elected governor and raised soldiers from Oregon to serve in the war. In 1866, another Republican, George L. Woods, was elected governor. He remained in office until 1871, when La Fayette Grover, a Democrat, was elected governor; he resigned in 1877 to take a seat in the U.S. Senate, and his unexpired term was filled by Stephen F. Chadwick.

THE ELECTION OF 1876

The 1876 U.S. presidential election resulted in the closest result ever in the Electoral College, with Oregon's vote decisive in the outcome. Although the statewide vote clearly supported Republican Party candidate Rutherford B. Hayes, La Fayette Grover, the governor of Oregon, claimed that one of the electors in the Electoral College, John W. Watts, was constitutionally ineligible to vote, as he had been an "elected or appointed official." Grover then replaced Watts with Democratic elector C.A. Cronin. If this had been successful, it would have given Samuel Tilden of the Democrats 185 votes in the Electoral College, to 184 for the Republicans. However, when a 15-member electoral commission awarded all three of Oregon's votes to Hayes, he won by 185 votes to 184, becoming the 19th president of the United States.

One of the legal counsels who had challenged the legality of Watts sitting in the Electoral College, William Wallace Thayer, was elected governor in 1878, but declined to run again in 1882 gubernatorial election. Zenas Ferry Moody succeeded him; originally from Massachusetts, he had established a store and transport company in Oregon. The next governor, Sylvester Pennoyer, was from the Democratic-Populist Party. As governor 1887–95, he endorsed many populist policies, and refusing to help Chinese-Americans, who were subject to some attacks during his governorship. In 1902, Oregon approved an initiative and referendum process that allowed ordinary citizens to bring legislation to parliament, making it the first state to introduce such laws.

THE 20TH CENTURY

Oregon saw a number of Republican and Democratic Party governors holding office throughout the first half of the 20th century, with Julius L. Meier elected in 1930 as an Independent. Meier, from a Jewish family, managed to gain 135,608 votes (54.5 percent) as

Democrat Ted Kulongoski was elected governor of Oregon in the 2002 election, winning by a narrow margin.

an Independent candidate, easily defeating his nearest rival, Edward F. Bailey of the Democrats, who gained only 62,434 votes.

Charles H. Martin, who initially supported U.S. President Franklin D. Roosevelt, but came to criticize him, succeeded Meier as governor. He did not win the Democratic Party nomination in 1938 for the gubernatorial election, however, was won by Charles A. Sprague. Sprague claimed to have progressive views; he was editor of the *Washington State Journal* and *Ritzville Times* during World War I, and had support from the German-American community. However, as the newspapers in Oregon started to take a more anti-German stance, Sprague became critical of Germans during his election campaign, and endorsed anti-Japanese xenophobia, supporting the interning of all Japanese-Americans following the bombing of Pearl Harbor, although after the war, he did try to reestablish the rights of Japanese-Americans.

Sprague was succeeded in office by Earl W. Snell, who challenged Sprague in the Republican Party primary and won, with much financial backing from the automobile

dealers' association. He went on to win the gubernatorial election with 78 percent of the vote, taking office on January 11, 1943. Snell was a moderate Republican, and was succeeded by four more Republican governors. In 1956, Robert D. Holmes was elected the first Democratic governor since Charles H. Martin. In 1958, Mark Hatfield, a Republican, was elected governor.

Two years later in the U.S. presidential election, Richard M. Nixon carried the state with 408,060 votes (52.6 percent) to John F. Kennedy's 367,402 votes (47.4 percent). The 1964 U.S. presidential election was closely fought in Oregon where, in the Republican Party Primary, Nelson Rockefeller defeated Henry Cabot Lodge with 94,198 votes to 79,169 votes. Barry Goldwater came in third (50,105 votes), only narrowly pushing Richard M. Nixon into fourth place. However, Rockefeller's support may have been because he outspent Goldwater four times over. In the election, Lyndon B. Johnson received 501,017 votes (63.9 percent), to 282,779 votes (36.1 percent) for Barry Goldwater. In the 1968 U.S. presidential election, Richard M. Nixon carried the state with 408,433 votes (49.8 percent), to Hubert H. Humphrey's 358,865 votes (43.8 percent), and George Wallace's 49,683 votes (6.1 percent).

Tom McCall was governor of Oregon 1967–75, and Robert W. Straub, a Democrat and environmentalist, succeeded him 1975–79. Straub had lost races to Tom McCall in 1966 and 1970, but in 1974, McCall was ineligible to run, allowing Straub to win with the largest margin ever recorded in an Oregon gubernatorial election. The man who lost that election, Victor George Atiyeh, an Arab American and a Republican, was elected in 1978, and served 1979–87. Neil Goldschmidt, a Democrat, was governor 1987–91, followed by Barbara Roberts, another Democrat, and the first woman to be elected governor of Oregon. Democrat John Kitzhaber, a medical doctor, succeeded her, serving two consecutive terms. In 2003, Ted Kulongoski was elected governor for the Democrats.

SEE ALSO: Constitutional Union Party; Presidential Election of 1876; Slavery.

BIBLIOGRAPHY. D.G. Balmer, "The 1964 Election in Oregon," *Western Political Quarterly* (v.18/2, 1965); J.E. Henrickson, *Joe Lane of Oregon—Machine Politics and the Sectional Crisis, 1849–1861* (Yale University Press, 1967); E.K. MacColl, *The Shaping of a City: Business and Politics in Portland, Oregon, 1885–1915* (Georgian Press Co., 1976); T.L. Mason, *Governing Oregon: An*

Inside Look at Politics in One American State (Kendall Hunt Publishing Co., 1994); F.J. McKay, "Charles Sprague's Internal Wars: Civil Liberties Challenges of an Editor and Governor," *Oregon Historical Quarterly* (v.96/4, 1995–1996); T.H. White, *The Making of the President 1964* (Jonathan Cape, 1965); L.H. Zeigler and B.L. Smith, "The 1970 Election in Oregon," *Western Political Quarterly* (v.24/2, 1971).

JUSTIN CORFIELD
GEELONG GRAMMAR SCHOOL, AUSTRALIA

Pack Journalism

PACK JOURNALISM IS a term coined by Timothy Crouse to describe the phenomenon of news reporters following political candidates or a story in a "pack," providing similar coverage of the story. It has become a pejorative term that suggests that, instead of checking facts, reporters follow what other reporters are saying and writing, reflecting laziness on the part of the media and fear of getting the story "wrong." By reporting what others are reporting, the critics of pack journalism argue, the media limits public knowledge. Further, they argue, when journalists rely on "official sources," their reports often support the political status quo. Pack journalism occurs because reporters often depend on the same sources of information when reporting a story. They also spend a great deal of time around one another and because they are aware of what each reporter is reporting, eventually a consensus emerges over what the story is about.

The term emerged from the 1972 presidential campaign. Timothy Crouse wrote *The Boys on the Bus* (1973), which was an expansion of a series of articles about the press covering the election that he wrote for *Rolling Stone* magazine. The most significant aspect of Crouse's analysis was that the press not only covered the news, but also was part of the news. Crouse suggests that sometimes the pack may get the story wrong because

of their isolation. Of the reporters covering Senator George S. McGovern, a group who came to believe that McGovern might win, Crouse wrote:

> The reporters attached to George McGovern had a very limited usefulness as political observers, by and large, for what they knew best was not the American electorate but the tiny community of the press plane, a totally abnormal world that combined the incestuousness of a New England hamlet with the giddiness of a mid-ocean gala and the physical rigors of the long march.

Crouse explained the phenomenon of pack journalism as follows:

> They all fed off the same pool report, the same daily handout, the same speech by the candidate; the whole pack was isolated in the same mobile village. After a while, they began to believe the same rumors, subscribe to the same theories, and write the same stories.

Critics of pack journalism argue that incorrect facts are repeated often enough so that they are believed to be true. During the 2000 presidential campaign, a reporter for the *Washington Times* claimed that New Hampshire officials friendly to Vice President Al Gore had released, at the vice president's request, four billion gallons of water from a dam into the drought-stricken Connecticut River in order to allow Gore to paddle down the river in a photo opportunity. The story reported that the cost of this event was $7 million. The story was repeated by a number of major media outlets. The facts, later revealed but not extensively reported, were that 500 million gallons (which would have been released later the day of the vice president's visit) were released at virtually no cost as the water passed through hydroelectric turbines and generated electrical power that was sold to consumers.

In response to the emergence of the pack, campaigns have attempted to manage the coverage of their campaigns, as well as that of their opponents, by providing their interpretation of events. Spin doctors attempt to convince reporters of their interpretation of events. Knowing that news organizations have, as a cost-cutting measure, reduced or eliminated their research (or fact-checking) operations, campaign press secretaries and political operatives attempt to influence the reporting of political campaigns by providing "credible" information to reporters. Often, spin attempts to discredit opponents so that a candidate appears to have more credibility.

SEE ALSO: Horse Race, Media Coverage of; Issue Coverage by the Media; Media, Control by Campaign Organizations; Media, Role in Campaigns; Media Polls.

BIBLIOGRAPHY. Timothy Crouse, *The Boys on the Bus* (Random House, 1973); Alan Partington, *The Linguistics of Political Argument: The Spin Doctor and the Wolf Pack at the White House* (Routledge, 2003).

JEFFREY KRAUS
WAGNER COLLEGE

Panama Canal

THE PANAMA CANAL was a failed French project led by Ferdinand de Lesseps in the 1880s. In 1903, the United States entered the doomed enterprise and finished the canal. With U.S. interference, the Republic of Panama seceded from Columbia. The United States controlled the Panama Canal for most of the 20th century, and intervened occasionally in the Republic of Panama. The Panama Canal was a campaign issue in at least three countries: France, the United States, and Panama.

In the 1880s the Republican system in France was still unstable. De Lesseps, the aging father of the Suez Canal project, engaged in the much more demanding Panama Canal project. He wanted to finance it with small private shareholders. As the project got into technical and financial trouble, he and his bankers started a large bribing operation, financing friendly newspapers and buying the support of over 100 French parliamentarians.

The canal company soon went bankrupt, but the scandal broke only in 1892, when the anti-Semitic and anti-democratic newspaper *La Libre Parole* published the story. The Panama corruption scandal became the defining political theme in the French 1893 campaign. Many important parliamentarians lost their seats. Public confidence in the Republic and the parliamentary system fell to an all-time low in modern French history. Although the corruption was a legitimate campaign issue, it was a vehicle for anti-Semitic and anti-democratic propaganda, soon to be replaced by the Dreyfus affair as a French campaign topic in the 1890s and in the early 20th century.

The Panama Canal issue entered U.S. politics in 1880, when it was still a French-led operation and President Rutherford B. Hayes confirmed the Monroe Doctrine concerning the envisaged canal. U.S. politics remained firm on this during the 1880s, and assured European governments that the United States would only tolerate the construction as a private enterprise under Ferdinand de Lesseps, but not as a project run by European governments. When the French-led enterprise collapsed, U.S. diplomacy paved the way for American involvement. But, in the United States there was still a dispute about whether Panama would be the right location.

At the same time as the failed French Panama Canal project, the United States had its own collapsed canal enterprise in Nicaragua. The Nicaragua Canal, for most of the 1890s, seemed to be the winning project. But finally, the Panama Canal project succeeded with the Spooner Act in 1902. In the Panama-Nicaragua decision, the threat of volcanoes in Nicaragua was highly exaggerated. The Panama Canal is the most visible symbolic of the presidency of Theodore Roosevelt, when the United States discovered the importance of the link between the Atlantic and the Pacific—which became the Panama Canal—and when the United States became a world power.

The canal was also a political issue in Central America: Before the secession of the Republic of Panama, it

West Indian laborers toiling on the French-led Ferdinand de Lesseps Panama Canal project. The canal, completed by the United States, has been a factor in campaigns in at least three countries over three centuries.

was a political issue in Columbia. The canal was the lifeline of the Republic of Panama; therefore all election campaigns dealt with the issue. The canal was the generator of income for the Republic of Panama, and it was the cause of its long instability and U.S. intervention. In 1989, the United States invaded Panama to oust Manuel Noriega, the strongman of Panama and a leading drug dealer. The Republic of Panama is much more stable now; however, the canal remains a campaign topic, especially in the 2006 Panama Canal expansion referendum, in which expansion was decided by nearly 77 percent.

SEE ALSO: Corruption and Democratic Elections; Defense; Expansionism; Foreign Policy; Military Hero; Presidential Election of 1904; War and Peace.

BIBLIOGRAPHY. David McCullough, *The Path Between Seas: The Creation of the Panama Canal, 1870–1914* (Pocket Books, 2004); Jean-Yves Mollier, *Le Scandale de Panama* (Fayard, 1991); Matthew Parker, *Panama Fever, The Battle to Build the Canal* (Hutchinson, 2007); Panama Canal Authority, www.pancanal.com (cited August 2007).

OLIVER BENJAMIN HEMMERLE
CHEMNITZ UNIVERSITY

Participatory Democracy

ORIGINALLY FORMULATED BY the philosopher Jean-Jacques Rousseau in the 18th century, the concept of participatory democracy is a normative theory of political communication that expands the role of the individual in the processes of governing by creating more opportunities for substantive participation. In its purest form, participatory democracy enables individuals to govern themselves in all matters and contribute to every decision affecting their daily lives. By these standards, however, some would argue that a truly participatory democracy has yet to come into existence. However, democratic theorists have suggested that with the internet, dramatic transformations in democratic processes are both possible and logical. Updated treatments of the more participatory and deliberative variants of democratic theory use terms such as *cyber-governance*, *open-source government*, and *e-democracy* to shed light on the possibility of participatory democracy as a replacement for, or an addendum to, the institutionalized systems of voting. Recent innovations in "e-voting" in Switzerland, for example, may be the first of many technological innovations that will redefine democratic participation.

All democracy is participatory to some degree, but participatory democratic theory is different in that it requires that the entire populace play an active role at each stage of the rulemaking process. The etymological roots of participatory democracy draw from Latin *partis* (part) and *capere* (take), as well as from Greek *demos* (people) and *kratein* (to rule); together they suggest "taking part in rule by the people." But the participatory democracy that Rousseau wrote of and which was revived by the New Left during the political and intellectual turmoil of the 1960s, is a theory of democracy that disperses authority and puts decision-making powers more directly in the hands of ordinary people; thus contributing to the legitimacy of the government. Participatory theory suggests that greater involvement in decision-making instills a deeper sense of belonging and responsibility because the group redefines self-interest in terms of collective benefits, as opposed to what benefits the loudest, the best organized, or the most articulate.

Furthermore, it is believed that direct participation in governance will stimulate participants to be more attentive to politics, and that this drive to acquire information will broaden individual horizons to include the political problems, viewpoints, and potential solutions they would never have been exposed to otherwise. By bringing together disparate segments of society, participatory democracies seek the common good by utilizing the collective wisdom of the whole.

Participatory theorists have challenged the assumed superiority of representative systems of democracy, because these systems do not recognize political participation as a fundamental value in itself. In representative democracies, citizens are usually relegated to a legitimizing function once per year, when they are asked to confirm or reject the work done by their current representatives. The electorate occasionally holds representatives accountable for their body of work, but in large part citizens in representative democracies are not governing themselves, rather, they are selecting people to govern for them. This division of labor in representative democracies has alienated most people from the decision-making processes that govern many aspects of their daily lives.

Participatory democracies, on the other hand, require greater levels of sacrifice and involvement from their citizenry than do representative democracies. The reality in most Western democracies today, however, is that most voters have little interest in participating, and even less interest in becoming informed participants. In addition, voters are not asked to deliberate before they choose a candidate, nor are they substantively involved in framing the debate, setting the agenda, or suggesting the potential solutions to a society's particular political problems. In contrast, by eliminating the barrier between those who govern and those who are governed, and by encouraging processes that focus on group discovery, deliberation, and consensus-based decision-making, participatory democracies augment the legitimacy of a governing body. Thus, participatory democracy can be seen as a form of layperson protest against expert knowledge. A participatory institution differs from a representative one in that authority is decentralized, whereby the ability to make many decisions devolves from the top toward the people who are most likely to be affected by those decisions.

One of the most prominent obstacles to greater acceptance of participatory democracy has been the issue of scale; gathering together a large population for the purpose of deciding all matters affecting those people would be difficult. In the 4th century B.C.E., Aristotle argued that the ideal republic was small enough that a man could walk across it in a single day, thus making certain regular participation in the assembly by all citizens. Early democratic institutions, such as the city-states of Aristotle's day and the town meetings of post-colonial New England, succeeded because of their relatively small size. But maintaining the manageability of these groups came with a heavy price and threatened the very core of their democratic nature. In ancient Athens, for example, which is usually considered one of the first democracies and also one of the "purest," approximately one in eight people had citizen status and could participate in the governing process. Similar exclusionary practices were followed in most New England town meetings of the 18th and 19th century, where women, slaves, and non-property owners were barred from the governing process.

Modern participatory institutions have thus far been most effective at operating at relatively small scales, such as neighborhoods, villages, school districts, or watersheds. These small-scale organizations require repeated interaction among a group of individuals that can have the effect of sustaining the mutual values of trust, equality, and reciprocity.

SEE ALSO: Direct Democracy; Representative Democracy.

BIBLIOGRAPHY. Peter Bachrach and Aryeh Botwinick, *Power and Empowerment: A Radical Theory of Participatory Democracy* (Temple University Press, 1992); B.R. Barber, *Strong Democracy: Participatory Politics for a New Age* (University of California Press, 2004); T.E. Cook and P.M. Morgan, *Participatory Democracy* (Canfield Press, 1971).

TIMOTHY B. HURST
COLORADO STATE UNIVERSITY

Partisanship

PARTISANSHIP HAS BECOME the single most important concept in the study of political behavior. Partisanship is a relatively stable and meaningful force that is developed early in life and serves as a guide for organizing political thought. It refers to an attachment or identification with a political party. This identification, again, affects political attitudes and behavior, leading to the second definition: partisanship as voting behavior. Election outcomes are important; the partisan choices voters make, therefore, may be more important than their identification, although identification and behavior are very closely related. Partisanship is also a cognitive tool. Like ideologies, partisanship can ease the intellectual navigation of the political world. Partisanship can also be described in its collective form, the partisan leaning of the nation.

The most widely-accepted use of partisanship as a concept is as a psychological attachment or identification. In this way, partisanship is considered a long-term, stable force that exerts a powerful influence over many aspects of political behavior, including voting and issue positions. As traditionally measured, partisanship has two components. Direction refers to which party an individual identifies with: Democrat or Republican. Absence of direction, or the lack of a preference for one party or the other, manifests itself in Independent identification. Intensity describes how strongly an individual is attached to the party label. The standard measure is either a five- or seven-point scale. In the seven-point version, the continuum ranges from strong Democrat, to weak Democrat, to Independents who lean toward the Democratic Party; in the middle of the scale are pure Independents, then Independents who lean toward the Republican Party, weak Republicans, and strong Republicans.

Demographic characteristics as well as upbringing are the main determinants of partisan identification. The nature of the political world can and does affect partisanship, but once a partisan attachment is formed, it becomes one of the most stable political forces within the individual. Looking first at upbringing, parental party identification very often can lead to similar identification among offspring. Specifically, the more intense the identification of the parents and the more consistent they are in their identification, that is, both parents identify with the same party, the more likely an individual is to share that partisan identity.

Age is also an important factor in partisanship, although age itself can be very misleading. Empirical evidence shows that there are few characteristics inherent in a particular number of years since birth that would lead someone to identify more closely with a party. What is important is an individual's birth year and when the individual came of age, politically speaking. Those coming of age in the 1920s or 1980s, for example, tend to be Republican. Coming of age from the 1930s through the mid-1960s has been closely linked to Democratic identification.

Race is another very important determinant of partisanship. As with voting behavior, there are clear differences between whites and minorities, with African Americans even more distinguishable in their partisanship than other minority groups. Whites tend to be split in their identification, with neither party nor Independent identification holding a majority of individuals. Racial minorities tend to identify more strongly as Democrats, with African Americans the most consistent in their Democratic identification. Research on partisan realignments illustrates a regional realignment occurring throughout the late 1960s until today. Specifically, Republican identification in the south has vastly increased as the Democratic Party has become more liberal. An overwhelmingly Republican citizenry has replaced the solid Democratic south, especially among southern whites.

Religion is another demographic characteristic that affects partisan identification. Members of certain religions display tendencies to identify with particular political parties. Members of most religions, except Protestants and particular Evangelicals, tend to identify as Democrats. This is especially true of Jews and Catholics. Protestants and Evangelicals tend to hold strong Republican identifications. Religion also carries with it religiosity, which also affects partisan identification. Religiosity, a general sense of how important religion and religious teachings are to the individual, is typically measured by the frequency of attendance at religious services. As religiosity increases, there is an increased likelihood of Republican identification, especially among Christians. Socioeconomic status and income also help determine individual partisanship. As income and social class increase, there are stronger tendencies for Republican identification.

A final concept concerning how demographic characteristics determine partisan identification is the cross-pressures hypothesis. Different characteristics point individuals in specific partisan directions. African Americans are more likely to be Democrats. Protestants are more likely to be Republicans. However, an African-American Protestant's political leanings would be difficult to classify. The answer lies in how these characteristics relate to one another. The cross-pressures hypothesis states that individuals who have characteristics pulling them in different partisan directions will have less partisan intensity. The African-American Protestant might be a Democrat, but would probably be a weaker Democrat than an African-American atheist. Conversely, where characteristics point in the same partisan direction, higher intensity is expected. For example, it is very likely that a white, upper-class Protestant is a strong Republican.

OTHER CLASSIFICATIONS

Some would argue that in the realm of politics, it is outcomes that are most important. Partisanship can also be measured as an action or behavior. Specifically, how an individual expresses his or her partisan preferences in an electoral setting. The behavioral manifestation of partisanship is by no means separate from identification, given the strong effects of identification on behavior. While voting is an individual action, the behavioral aspect of partisanship is more often used in reference to aggregate partisanship.

Partisanship as an identification may also serve another purpose. Associating strongly with a political party may provide individuals a means of analyzing political information without devoting the time or mental energy needed to becoming fully informed on a wide range of issues. Using partisanship in this manner has been referred to as rational ignorance. An individual who identifies strongly with a party does so for many reasons. The factors that contribute to strong partisanship would also lead the individual to have political preferences consistent with the stated preferences of the party. People, therefore, could devote the time to become fully informed about an issue and find that they arrive at the same position they would have without obtaining information and relying only on the partisan cue. The idea of partisan cues, or brand names, is also useful for weak partisans and Independents. Candidate identification with a party label can provide these voters with an efficient means of evaluating the candidate's likely positions on many issues; they only need to know where the party stands.

AN AGGREGATE PHENOMENON

In addition to serving important individual-level functions, partisanship can also be considered on an aggregate or national-level. Partisanship at the national level refers to the partisan balance in the public. There are several different ways in which the national partisan balance is measured. The most popular is the proportion of Democratic identifiers among all partisan identifiers. For survey results, the number of Democratic respondents would be divided by the sum of Democratic and Republican identifiers. Unlike partisanship at the individual level, aggregate partisanship is far less stable. Aggregate partisanship is not a long-term national predisposition, and moves with the national economy and evaluations of the president.

While aggregate partisanship is a cumulative identification, it can also be measured in terms of aggregate behavior. In the literature on electoral realignments scholars often use the percent of the popular vote received by presidential candidates as a collective measure of partisanship. As opposed to identification, aggregate partisan behavior appears more stable, but is subject to rapid, dramatic changes. These periods of change are called partisan realignments and they define the party systems that have existed in the United States since the ratification of the Constitution. The United States has had at least five party systems. The first occurred from the founding of the nation until around 1828 and witnessed the birth of parties. The second, often referred to as Jacksonian Democracy, lasted until 1860 and saw the decline of the Whigs and strong identification with the Democratic Party.

From 1860 until 1896 there was a third party system that was defined by strong Republican Party dominance. Republican strength continued in the fourth period (1896–1932), although there was a change in the Republican Party as it encompassed elements of Progressivism. The final party system that realignment researchers agrees on is the New Deal period, in which the Democratic Party controlled national politics beginning with the election of Franklin Roosevelt in 1932.

After this fifth party system, there is some debate about if partisanship has realigned again or undergone other changes. Some scholars point to 1968 as the end of the New Deal period and the beginning of dealignment, in which there is a significant increase in Independent identification. Realignment is typically described as a national phenomenon, but some consider the developments in the south over the past 40 years a significant regional realignment. What has made examining national partisanship so difficult in terms of party systems is that in recent history, neither party has truly dominated national politics. By 2004, there were roughly equal numbers of Republican and Democrat identifiers in the public. This equalizing of partisanship defied the traditional concept of a party system and contributed to very close national elections.

SEE ALSO: Determinants of Vote Choice; Electoral Behavior.

BIBLIOGRAPHY. J.H. Aldrich, *Why Parties? The Origin and Transformation of Political Parties in America* (University of Chicago Press, 1995); Angus Campbell et al., *The American Voter* (University of Chicago Press, 1960); W.H. Flanigan and N.H. Zingale, *Political Behavior of the American Electorate* (CQ Press, 2006); V.O. Key, Jr., "A Theory of Critical Elections," *Journal of Politics* (v.17/1, 1955); M.B. MacKuen, R.S. Erikson, and J.A. Stimson, "Macropartisanship," *American Political Science Review* (v.83/4, 1989).

ANDREW H. SIDMAN
JOHN JAY COLLEGE, CITY UNIVERSITY OF NEW YORK

Party Image

THE IMAGE OF a political party consists of the impressions that people have of a party, along with the emotional affect (favorable or unfavorable feelings) about the party. In the simplest sense, party images are the adjectives that people think of when describing a political party, such as liberal/conservative, extreme/moderate, and disorganized/weak. Party images are important because they contribute to the selective convergence of the vote choices of large numbers of people who are making independent, discrete decisions based on their beliefs and interpretation of political information.

Political party images result from interactions among the images projected by the visible members of a political party, especially its elite officeholders; characterizations of the party in the media; and the biases of the people exposed to information about the political party. Because political parties are coalitional in nature, there are multiple messages and images conveyed to the public by party leaders and candidates. The image of a given party is also influenced by the countervailing messages of opposing party leaders and candidates. The media tend to reinforce and magnify party images by selecting stories and sources for interviews that fit popular stereotypes of the parties—often interviewing activists or party elites who hold relatively more ideologically extreme views compared to rank-and-file partisans or the public.

Individuals paying attention to and interpreting political information communicated during campaigns ultimately hold the images of the political parties. An individual's attention to and interpretation of political information is influenced by their unique set of beliefs, values, and attitudes formed through their socialization and life experiences. Since an individual's social group affiliations tend to affect the development of their politically relevant beliefs, values, and attitudes, so party images vary with the social group affiliations of individuals, including race, ethnicity, gender, class, and socioeconomic identification. People with greater interest in politics tend to have better developed cognitive schema (networks of associated ideas stored in long-term memory) for interpreting new political information, pay more attention to political information, retain more information, and thus tend to develop the most articulate party images. People with higher levels of education tend to form images of the political parties with broad, philosophical content (for example, incorporating liberal-conservative orientation). Newspaper readers are more likely than television viewers to have well-formed images of political parties.

Perhaps more important, voters with relatively well-developed cognitive schema interpret fragments of information in ways that are consistent with their existing beliefs. As a result, most voters' perceptions are affected by their party loyalties, ideological orientations, and deep-seated political attitudes relevant to the processing of newly-encountered information. For example, Republican and Democratic voters tend to pay attention to and incorporate information favorable to their party, while ignoring or distorting information that is unfavorable to their party.

Voters with relatively weak existing political predispositions (for example, nonpartisans and ideological moderates) tend to have less articulate images of the party, and are relatively more receptive to (and therefore more affected by) the messages and information communicated during a campaign. People lacking a clear image of the political parties often fail to exhibit consistent policy differences based on their party identification. Nonpartisan voters are more likely to form impressions that incorporate both favorable and unfavorable information about both political parties, resulting in greater ambivalence toward the parties.

Unlike candidate images, political party images contain more policy content. While people generally cannot recall the details of policy, they usually can recall if they had a favorable or unfavorable impression of a party when cued to think about a particular issue. The favorability of the impression depends, in part, on the degree to which a party's policies are compatible with a person's existing beliefs and ideas about politics. Such impressions relate to the "ownership" of different issues by the major political parties—when a particular party is perceived by large numbers of people as being better able to "handle" an issue. The images of the political parties have different policy dimensions corresponding

to issue ownership patterns. Images of the Republican Party have generally had more foreign policy content, whereas images of the Democratic Party have generally had more domestic policy content.

SEE ALSO: Candidate Image; Cognitive Dissonance; Issue Ownership Theory.

BIBLIOGRAPHY. A.H. Miller and B.E. Gronbeck, eds., *Presidential Campaigns and American Self Images* (Westview Press, 1994); Dan Nimmo, "Political Image-Makers and the Mass Media," *American Academy of Political and Social Sciences* (v.427, 1976); J.R. Petrocik, "Issue Ownership in Presidential Elections, with a 1980 Case Study," *American Journal of Political Science* (v.40, 1996); Arthur Sanders, "The Meaning of Party Images," *Western Political Quarterly* (v.41, 1988); Roberta Sigel, "Effects of Partisanship on Perceptions of Political Candidates," *Public Opinion Quarterly* (v.28, 1964).

WAYNE P. STEGER
DEPAUL UNIVERSITY

Party Platforms

A POLITICAL PARTY'S statement of policy positions is called a party platform. These documents serve as a public declaration of the beliefs and principles a party stands for, and they can inform voters about what policies the party and its candidates will advocate. Adopting a platform is the second major responsibility of the delegates to a party's national convention, second only to selecting the presidential nominee. Although the relevance of a party's platform to its future governing actions or even its campaign promises has been disputed (candidates are not bound to their party's platform statements), the platform remains an important tool for synthesizing a party's positions on a variety of issues and for educating voters.

Platforms are composed of planks that represent different issue areas of concern to party activists. The range of issues covered in platforms has greatly expanded since the first party platforms. Modern platforms have been long documents; the 2004 Republican platform was more than 40,000 words, and the 2000 Democratic platform was nearly 25,000 words. Early platforms were more concise statements of the party's principles and goals. The 1840 Democratic platform was just over 500 words long, and the 1856 Republican platform was less than 1,000 words. The issues covered in platforms represent what party leaders believe to be the most important policy debates of the presidential election year. The platforms of the 1850s and 1860s dealt with slavery and the Civil War; those of the 1930s proposed solutions to economic strife; and the platforms of 2004 focused on preventing future terrorist attacks and the resolution of the war in Iraq.

Delegates to the party's national convention adopt the platform, giving the document the distinction of having the approval of the party's highest plenary body. In the Democratic and Republican parties, convention delegates come from each state (and territory) and are elected through the state party's primary or caucus system. Each of these state delegations selects representatives to serve as members of the Platform Committee, which is an official committee of each national convention (along with the Rules and Credentials committees). Elected party leaders often chair the platform committees. Senate Majority Leader Bill Frist chaired the Republican Platform Committee in 2004, and Democrats chose Congresswoman Stephanie Tubbs Jones, Governor Tom Vilsack, and Los Angeles City Councilman Antonio Villaraigosa to be the co-chairs of its committee.

State parties often draft their own state platforms, and the representatives they send to the national Platform Committee might advocate for specific planks that appear in the state platform. A small platform drafting committee, which is typically composed of leading policymakers and important interest group representatives, composes a draft platform to send to the full Platform Committee. In 2004, the Platform Drafting Committee for the Democratic Party held hearings in different locations across the country to solicit input on the party's platform from various interests. The full Platform Committee approves the draft national platform, and sends it to the convention floor for a vote by the full convention.

A series of reforms to the delegate selection process that originated in the Democratic Party after fights over minority representation at the 1964 and 1968 conventions had consequences for nominating conventions and platform writing in both parties. Instead of state and local party bosses controlling the composition of convention delegations, and thereby controlling the process of drafting and adopting the platform, delegates are now selected in both major parties through a primary or caucus system in each state, with some slots reserved in both parties for elected officials and party leaders.

Another change that came with the post-1968 reforms was that delegates were more formally committed to a presidential candidate (although still not officially bound to a candidate in most cases), reducing the likelihood of a brokered convention, where a nominee could be decided at the convention instead of through the system of primaries and caucuses. The selection of the party's nominee before the summer nominating conventions has given the presidential campaigns an important role in the process of drafting and adopting the platform. The scope and length of modern platforms could also be attributed to the democratization of the delegate selection process.

HISTORY

The first official party platform in American politics was adopted at the Democratic National Convention in Baltimore in 1840. By 1844, and in every presidential election year since then, the major parties, as well as several minor parties and some splinter factions of the major parties, have drafted and adopted platforms. These platforms provide a concise history of the important issues of presidential campaigns. Although public fights over platform planks are rare in modern campaigns, the platform committee was once a public forum for debate within a party.

In 1860, the country's division over slavery is evident in the four party platforms, including one by a faction that separated from the Democratic Party. In 1932, the Republicans fought over whether to advocate the repeal of Prohibition in their platform. Democrats divided again in 1948, over advocating civil rights advances in its platform, and J. Strom Thurmond led a walkout of southern Democrats to form the Dixiecrats, which wrote its own platform under the name of the States' Rights Democratic Party.

The skirmishes inside and outside the 1968 Democratic National Convention in Chicago had their roots in the party's division over the Vietnam War, and these differences were fought over in the platform deliberations. Party activists and the Democratic presidential candidates were at odds with the Johnson administration over how to address the war in the party's platform. President Johnson was ultimately able to control the platform that year, but he could not contain the frustration of the delegates and other activists who felt that their views were not represented. One lesson of the Democrats' disastrous 1968 convention is that public platform fights do not bode well for the party's presidential candidate.

Because presidential nominees are now known long before the national conventions gather, and since modern, televised conventions are designed to show party unity rather than discord, the presidential campaigns make sure that there are few opportunities for fights over the party's platform. However, even with the unifying force of a presidential campaign, platform fights can still erupt. One example is the fight over abortion at the 1996 Republican convention in San Diego, when pro-choice delegates unsuccessfully attempted to soften the party's stance on abortion. The media coverage of that convention focused on the platform fight.

RELEVANCE IN MODERN CAMPAIGNS

Some contend that party platforms, like the nominating conventions themselves, are meaningless in the era of modern presidential campaigns, because candidates are not bound to uphold the platform. Critics argue that platforms are either too general, in a party's attempt to capture the greatest number of supporters; or they are too extreme, in an attempt to appease the party's radical factions. Whether written to appeal to the largest number of voters or to rally the party faithful, platform strategies reveal something about the time in which they are written and the motivations of the presidential campaigns affiliated with them. Since state primaries and caucuses now determine the party's nominees rather than the nominating conventions, adopting the national platform might be the most important thing that convention delegates do.

A more accurate criticism of party platforms might be that modern platforms lack importance because they are not widely read even by party activists, much less by the undecided voters. Media coverage of the platform process is limited unless there is a fight to cover, and as there have been few public platform fights at recent conventions there is very little coverage of the party platforms. Nevertheless, researchers have found that platform pledges tend to be good indicators of future policy positions. These findings suggest that party platforms would be a reliable source of information for undecided voters, if they seek them out.

SEE ALSO: Campaigns, Presidential; Conventions, National Nominating Party; Delegates, Convention; Issue Coverage by the Media; Political Parties in American Elections; Presidential Elections; Presidential Primaries; Two-Party System; Undecided Voters.

BIBLIOGRAPHY. J.F. Bibby and B.F. Schaffner, *Politics, Parties, and Elections in America* (Wadsworth, 2007); Ian Budge and R.I. Hofferbert, "Mandates and Policy Outputs: U.S. Party Platforms and Federal Expenditures," *American Political Science Review* (v.84, 1990); J.W. Davis, *National Conventions in an Age of Party Reform* (Greenwood Press, 1983); Paul Herrnson, ed., *Guide to Political Campaigns in America* (CQ Press, 1995).

ALICIA KOLAR PREVOST
AMERICAN UNIVERSITY

Patriotism

IN ITS BROADEST sense, patriotism means nothing more than a positive appreciation of one's country. No serious candidate would run on an anti-patriotic platform; more often, patriotism is defined by the candidate's platform to coincide with his or her ideals, or the opponent is accused (if not in so many words) of being less patriotic, even un-American. Wartime brings out patriotism in the form of loyalty and reluctance to change horses midstream: No incumbent president seeking re-election has lost during a major American war, despite the fact that many of those wars were unpopular. Opposition to the War of 1812 essentially destroyed the Federalist Party by the next election. The Mexican-American War attracted vituperative criticism, but when President James Polk retired after his single term in office, General Zachary Taylor was elected, his part in the victory over Mexico praised by the very same factions that had opposed the war. During the Civil War, the Democrats were unable to organize effectively enough to turn anti-war sentiments into votes.

Even during the Vietnam and Iraq wars, wars unpopular enough to turn many Americans into single-issue voters, presidents Johnson and Bush were re-elected. In these latter two cases, the notion that it was unpatriotic to oppose the war was popular. The bumper sticker slogan "My country, right or wrong" was a patriotic badge during Vietnam among those who felt that the anti-war protesters and other opponents of the established status quo went too far in their criticism or their methods. During the Iraq War, this sentiment was rephrased in the "Support the troops" rhetoric, which suggests that it is possible to oppose the war, or to regret it and consider it a necessary evil, but that patriotism demands that Americans support their troops abroad.

The military records of American presidents underline the connection between patriotism and the military: 31 of the 43 presidents served in the military (though controversy has surrounded George W. Bush's military record, and Abraham Lincoln dismissed his own brief service career as insignificant). Of the 12 others, William Howard Taft served as secretary of war, Franklin Roosevelt served as secretary of the Navy (and attempted to resign so that he could serve in the Navy when World War I started), and Herbert Hoover's entrance into public life began with humanitarian efforts and food distribution during World War I.

Patriotism, nationalism, and cultural chauvinism can all overlap, and from somewhere in that mix came the notion of manifest destiny: the idea that the United States had a destiny (perhaps divinely ordained) to pursue its expansion westward to the Pacific Coast, civilizing and Americanizing all that was in its path. Though the idea, in some form or another, predated the United States itself, the phrase was coined by the Jacksonian Democrats in the 1840s, in support of the rapid annexation of western territories such as Oregon. The Whigs and Republicans opposed the idea, seeking a more contained nation, one that would not further dilute the northeast industrial population.

The association of expansion with American destiny, of acquisition with American identity, made the slavery debate even more important in that era and its prohibition (or lack thereof) in territories and newly created states. It likewise became important in the 1890s, as the Census Bureau declared the frontier closed (meaning simply that there was no frontier left unsettled) and expansionists, mostly Republicans and imperialists this time, eyed lands beyond the continent.

In both eras, expansionists appealed to patriotic feelings: if America and American-ness, is good, then it is good to spread it. Isolationists, by contrast, espoused an "America first" approach: Rather than trifle in international affairs, whether in the form of expansion, war, or foreign aid, American concerns should be as limited as possible to the domestic. National pride should be expressed through national activity: The American poor should be the object of concern, not the foreign poor, and the federal government should tend to those matters for which the states created it, not act as a power broker on the global stage. To one degree or another, this was the common American sentiment from the Revolutionary era through World War II, but the two world wars of the 20th century and the expansion of Communism helped to end popular isolationism.

Throughout the Cold War, patriotic appeals were a commonplace feature in political rhetoric, especially where foreign and military policy were concerned. The Cold War pitted Communism against capitalism. But, China and Western Europe notwithstanding, it was more often described as a United States vs. Soviet Union conflict, with "American" and "Soviet" elevated from nationality to ideology.

When Americans fought to make the world safe for democracy, it was American-style democracy they had in mind, even if the regimes they installed or protected rarely resembled their own. When the Japanese government was reshaped in the aftermath of World War II, when advisors were dispatched to south Vietnam and the putatively democratic states throughout Central and south America, it was the American federal government that was used as an ideal, a role model. European democracies were not condemned, but the United States positioned itself as first and foremost among democracies; it likewise took the lead in such international freedom-protecting initiatives as the war in Vietnam and the liberation of Kuwait.

From time to time, Americans have been accused of being unpatriotic or un-American because of a perceived loyalty to some entity other than, and outside of, the United States. Catholics, who did not arrive in the United States in significant numbers until the immigration waves of the 19th century, and who were therefore generally part of the alien ethnic groups that nationalists found untrustworthy, were long considered suspect because they were presumed to answer to the Pope, whose orders could potentially countermand those of the American government.

In the 20th century, Communists came under fire, all Communists being assumed to answer to the Communist states, or even directly to the Kremlin. Before World War II, this was a response to the aggressive expansion of the Communist states, and to the Soviet Union's sponsorship of Communist groups in so many other countries; after the war, as the Cold War began, "Communist" was essentially treated as a synonym for "Soviet agent," and the House Un-American Activities Commission acted accordingly.

Politicians are often accused of abusing patriotic appeals in order to shield themselves from criticism, "wrapping themselves in the American flag." Even the development of the Patriot missile and the adoption of the Uniting and Strengthening America by Providing Appropriate Tools Required to Intercept and Obstruct Terrorism (USA PATRIOT ACT) speaks to borrowing the word and notion for political aims. The Patriot missile was developed in the 1970s and deployed in the middle of Ronald Reagan's presidency; the name reinforces the post-détente notion of a strong defense (and a strong offense) as a cornerstone of patriotism.

The USA Patriot Act was far more controversial, though it passed with little debate or even discussion 45 days after 9/11. The Patriot Act dramatically expanded the powers of the federal government, especially in intelligence gathering and the treatment of immigrants and non-resident aliens. The objective of the Patriot Act was to better equip the government to combat terrorism, which for the purposes of the act included domestic terrorism as well as that engaged in by foreign groups.

Though the name is justified by its lengthy acronym, it also serves to make the act critic-proof; rallying the electorate against "the patriot act" is a good deal more difficult than directing its ire against "the enhanced powers of surveillance and abridged civil liberties act." In the months following 9/11, even those politicians who would have normally opposed the administration supported many of its actions, just as many congresspersons supported the war in Iraq and later claimed, though not in so many words, to be going with the flow.

SEE ALSO: Anti-Communism; Expansionism; Isolationism; Presidential Election of 2004; Vietnam.

BIBLIOGRAPHY. David Caute, *The Great Fear: The Anti-Communist Purge Under Truman and Eisenhower* (Simon and Schuster, 1978); David Cole and J.X. Dempsey, *Terrorism and the Constitution: Sacrificing Liberties in the Name of National Security* (W.W. Norton, 2002); Thomas Doherty, *Cold War, Cool Medium: Television, McCarthyism, and American Culture* (Columbia University Press, 2005); S.W. Hayes and Christopher Morris, eds., *Manifest Destiny and Empire: American Antebellum Expansionism* (Texas A&M University Press, 1997); Stanley Mailman, et al., *USA PATRIOT Act of 2001: An Analysis* (Matthew Bender, 2002); Anders Stephanson, *Manifest Destiny: American Expansionism and the Empire of Right* (Hill and Wang, 1995).

BILL KTE'PI
INDEPENDENT SCHOLAR

Patronage System

A PATRONAGE SYSTEM, or a system that selects public officials on a political basis, rather than job-related factors, was present through much of the 18th century, until politicians and citizens realized the negative consequences it produced. In this system, office winners were allowed to place their political allies and those who supported them in a political campaign into government positions, often producing chaos as supporters of the previous administration were ousted. Since Andrew Jackson's election in 1828, and until the end of the 1800s, patronage was largely practiced in the national government. In the beginning, the idea was accepted among politicians and citizens, but as time passed, people became dissatisfied. Great political strides were made to do away with the patronage system, and gradually they succeeded in mostly eliminating it in the national government. Patronage still exists in government, but today merit-based hiring standards are widely used.

The patronage system allows politicians to distribute public jobs for political support, rather than using objective selection standards such as merit, examination, or job-related competence. This system allows politicians of both parties to use taxes to indirectly pay people who supported or worked on their campaign and to raise money to help finance campaigns. The patronage system emerged out of Andrew Jackson's election in 1828. Andrew Jackson began to reward political supporters by giving them public office, starting what is known as the Second Party System. Other presidents used patronage, such as Abraham Lincoln to support the war effort and the Republican Party, and Thomas Jefferson, who attempted to keep the Federalists from being public officials. However, Jackson is largely credited with its beginning. In 183, patronage became commonly known as the spoils system when Senator William Marcy of New York criticized Jackson in a debate with Senator Henry Clay for seeing nothing wrong with "to the victor belong the spoils."

Citizens and politicians supported the spoils system in the beginning. Jackson strongly upheld the egalitarianism philosophy by stating that the spoils system would encourage the common person to participate in politics, would make politicians more accountable when their appointees did a bad job, and would deal with corruption because he contended that serving for long periods of time in an official position corrupts individuals. In addition, people supported the minor role the federal government played in the process. In the 1840s, the patronage system was at an all-time high in state, local, and the federal government. However, as time went on, citizens and politicians became dissatisfied with it, especially in the years following the Civil War.

The spoils system had several problems. First, Jackson had attempted to make the sample of political appointees more representative of the population as a whole, but had little success due to the limited number of qualified appointees, most of whom were well-to-do and upper-class. This led people to begin viewing election practices as corrupt. In addition, this led to the perception that politics and administration were intertwined and incompetent. Second, there was chaos after the administration changed and the old supporters had to be replaced by the new ones. Finally, there were conflicts over presidential and congressional appointments that ultimately led to the 1869 impeachment trial of Andrew Johnson.

In the 1880s, corruption and favoritism in hiring became more widespread and people and politicians such as Teddy Roosevelt strongly advocated reform. One notable group that wanted reform was the Mugwumps. This group was comprised mostly of Republicans who jumped parties out of lack of support for James Blaine, favoring Civil Service advocate Grover Cleveland. The Mugwumps contended that people should be hired on merit and not on partisan loyalty or political connections.

However, it was not until July 2, 1881, when President James Garfield was assassinated by discouraged office-seeker Charles Guiteau, that the need for reform became evident. On January 16, 1883, the Civil Service Reform or Pendleton Act (ch. 27, 22 Stat. 403), sponsored by Ohio Senator George Pendleton during the Chester Arthur presidency, passed. This created the U.S. Civil Service, which made merit, qualifications, and job-related competence the basis of hiring for national jobs. This act also created the U.S. Civil Service Commission to oversee the merit system. In 1939, reform expanded with the Hatch Act, which banned federal employees from solicitation and campaigning. Remnants of patronage are still seen in the federal government, especially in positions of higher power, including the staff of the White House, government boards, and heads of agencies, but not nearly to the same extent as in the 1800s.

The patronage system was also present in state and local governments. The Pendleton and Hatch Acts applied to the national government, but excluded other governments. Patronage persisted, especially with large city machine politics, or unofficial behind-the-scene political systems. Some of the most notable examples are Tammany Hall from the 1790s to the 1960s in New York City, or Chicago from the 1950s through the 1970s. In Chicago, Richard Daley used the political machines to become easily and persistently re-elected. In Tammany Hall, the political machine was used to solidify support for the Democratic Party through nominations and patronage in local government hiring practices. The patronage system in the United States has been undermined severely by a series of U.S. Supreme Court decisions, most notably *Elrod v. Burns* (1976); *Branti v. Finkel* (1980); and *Rutan v. Republican Party of Illinois* (1990). These decisions have mostly limited patronage to only top-level policy positions of "trust" (for example, top advisors, cabinet, and commission-level appointees) above Civil Service positions at all levels of government.

SEE ALSO: Corruption and Democratic Elections; Machine Politics and Political Bosses; Presidential Election of 1828; Presidential Election of 1960; Tammany Hall; Tweed, William.

BIBLIOGRAPHY. Frederick Mosher, *Democracy and the Public Service* (Oxford University Press, 1968); Morris Fiorina et al., *America's New Democracy* (Longman/Penguin Academics, 2006).

JOSHUA MITCHELL
SOUTHERN ILLINOIS UNIVERSITY

Pendergast, Tom (1873–1945)

ONE OF MISSOURI'S most powerful politicians during the first decades of the 20th century, Thomas Joseph "Boss Tom" Pendergast helped launch the political career of future president Harry S. Truman, but ultimately went to prison for corruption.

Pendergast was born into a large Catholic family in St. Joseph, Missouri. As a young man, he moved to Kansas City, where he worked in a saloon owned by his older brother James. James won a seat as a Democratic alderman in Kansas City and when he retired in 1910 he made sure that his brother Tom followed him onto the council. The younger Pendergast immediately began consolidating his political strength by any means necessary, and proved to be a ruthlessly effective organizer.

He soon controlled Kansas City and became a political force within Missouri's Democratic Party. With the Pendergast machine pulling the strings, Kansas City was wide open, with large sums of cash routinely changing hands in exchange for political favors and jobs. "Boss Tom" did business from an unassuming two-story building downtown where he chose candidates for local and state offices. He also ran a growing business empire that included real estate, a hotel, and a concrete company that prospered as a result of lucrative government contracts. He controlled a variety of gambling operations, and, during Prohibition, profited from speakeasies and the distribution of illegal alcohol. Though notoriously corrupt, Pendergast also had a reputation for efficiently distributing essential items such as food, clothing, and heating fuel to the city's poor.

Pendergast first backed Harry Truman in a successful bid for a district judgeship during the 1920s, beginning a relationship that would later be scrutinized when Truman achieved high office. With "Boss Tom's" backing, Truman won election to the U.S. Senate in 1934, prompting many of the future president's critics to claim that he was actually going to Washington to represent "the State of Pendergast." Once in the Senate, Truman did not behave as many expected. He cooperated with the Pendergast machine in Missouri on routine patronage issues, but did not get involved with the illegal financial dealings and general corruption that eventually brought Pendergast down.

After years of rough-and-tumble conduct that often turned violent and sometimes deadly, the Pendergast machine drew attention from federal authorities in the late 1930s, and the organization began to crumble. After a highly publicized trial, "Boss Tom" was convicted of income tax evasion in 1939. He served 15 months in prison and received a parole on the condition that he refrain from any involvement in politics. No longer a

political power broker, Pendergast retired after his release. He died on January 26, 1945, and Harry Truman raised eyebrows as vice president by unapologetically attending his former patron's funeral.

SEE ALSO: Machine Politics and Political Bosses; Missouri; Presidential Election of 1948.

BIBLIOGRAPHY. R.H. Ferrell, *Truman and Pendergast* (University of Missouri Press, 1999); L.H. Larsen and N.J. Hulston, Pendergast! (University of Missouri Press, 1997).

BEN WYNNE
GAINESVILLE STATE COLLEGE

Pennsylvania

ACCORDING TO THE 2000 census, Pennsylvania had 12,281,054 residents living in its 67 counties. The commonwealth's Bureau of Commissions, Elections, and Legislation reported that the state had 7,770,472 registered voters as of April 2004. One of out every three registered voters (33 percent) lived in Philadelphia, Bucks, Chester, Delaware, or Montgomery counties, while approximately one of out every five registered voters (19.1 percent) lived in Allegheny, Beaver, Butler, Washington, or Westmoreland counties. Thus, the two largest urban centers in the commonwealth account for more than 50 percent of all registered voters. However, 48 of the commonwealth's counties are considered rural, meaning their population density is less than the statewide average.

This geographic dispersion of voters is at the heart of a legendary comment made by Democratic political consultant James Carville during the 1991 Senate contest between Democrat Harris Wofford and former Republican governor Richard Thornburgh. Carville assessed the political landscape in Pennsylvania as "Pittsburgh, Philadelphia, and Alabama in between." However, the state's electoral politics may confound observers because of its individualistic political culture and unprecedented levels of partisan competition.

In his classic work, Daniel Elazar evaluated the political culture in each state as individualistic, moralistic, or traditionalistic. He classified Pennsylvania as an individualistic political culture, an environment that views politics as a business and emphasizes minimum interference from government into the private affairs of its citizens. According to Elazar, public officials are expected to serve those who have supported them in order to remain in power, thus creating a class of individuals who view politics as their profession or career.

The party bosses in the latter part of the 19th century exemplify this model. From the days of the Civil War until 1934, the Republican Party controlled politics in Pennsylvania. With the rise of the New Deal and the increased urbanization of the regions surrounding Philadelphia and Pittsburgh, the Democratic Party gained strength. The increase in Democratic voters in the urban areas challenged the long-time Republican traditions, particularly in the rural regions.

These changes over time have positioned Pennsylvania as the state with the highest level of partisan competition, according to researchers Samuel Patterson and Gregory Caldeira. As of 2004, the Democratic Party held a slight edge in voter registrations with 3,706,112 registered voters as compared to the Republican Party's 3,220,496. The largest third parties in Pennsylvania are the Libertarian Party, with 30,853 registered voters as of April 2004, and the Green Party, with 12,315 registered voters. The individualistic political culture, coupled with the extraordinary level of partisan competition, make Pennsylvania's patterns of electoral behavior difficult to predict. Outcomes vary in national and state elections.

NATIONAL ELECTIONS

Pennsylvania has been one of the leading prizes in the Electoral College since the nation's creation. The value of the prize, however, has declined since 1960, as the Commonwealth's population growth kept up with other states. In the presidential election of 1960, the state had 32 electoral votes; following the 1960 census, Pennsylvania lost three electoral votes. The next three consecutive censuses each resulted in a loss of two electoral votes, reducing the Commonwealth to 21 electoral votes following the 2000 Census.

Even with its declining importance, presidential candidates devote significant attention to campaigning in the Keystone State, as it is considered one of the swing states. Since 1992, the swing vote has favored the Democratic candidate for president, placing Pennsylvania on the map as a blue state. Despite its strong support for Democratic presidential candidates, Pennsylvanians have consistently elected Republicans to the U.S. Senate. Over the last 50 years, Pennsylvanians have elected only three Democrats to the U.S. Senate (Joseph Clark, 1957–69; Harris Wofford, 1991–95; and Robert P. Casey, Jr., 2007–present). Republican Arlen Specter is currently serving his fifth term, making him the longest serving Senator from Pennsylvania. Representatives in the U.S. House from Pennsylvania reflect their districts, with those from the greater Philadelphia and Pittsburgh regions being predominantly members of the Democratic Party, while the representatives from rural central Pennsylvania are overwhelmingly Republicans. Following the 2006 midterm elections, Pennsylvania is represented by 11 Democratic and eight Republican representatives.

STATE ELECTIONS

Just as ticket splitting in national elections has occurred, this division of the electorate is evident in statewide elections as well. With the ratification of the Commonwealth's fifth state constitution in 1968, the state's elected officers, including the governor, can now seek second terms. Since the constitutional change, every incumbent governor has sought an additional term and an eight-year cycle for the governor's office has emerged.

According to the National Conference of State Legislatures, the Pennsylvania General Assembly is a full-time legislative body, resembling the U.S. Congress and requiring its 253 members to work the equivalent of 80 percent or more of a full-time job. As of March 2007, members of the general assembly earned $73,613 per year, ranking the Commonwealth among the top five in salary in the United States. The professionalization of the legislature, combined with the high salary, has produced low levels of turnover among the members and, thus, partisan control, particularly in the Pennsylvania House, often hinges on the outcomes of a handful of elections.

The 2006 state legislative elections will be considered historic not only for the shift of partisan control to the Democratic Party for the first time in 12 years, but also for the heightened scrutiny of legislators' decisions. In the early morning hours of July 7, 2005, the Pennsylvania General Assembly passed its 2005–06 budget; lurking in the budget was a pay increase for state legislators and judges, increasing salaries between 16 and 34 percent. Citizens groups began campaigning for a repeal of the legislative pay increase and the defeat of legislators who supported the pay raise. Political commentators noted that citizen resentment of the pay raise would diminish

Pennsylvania was a prize in the Electoral College from the start, but population decline recently cut its votes to 21.

by the 2006 elections, citing three previous pay raises in 1983, 1987, and 1995 and election outcomes where at least 98 percent of incumbents who voted for the pay raise won their re-election bids.

The pressure of citizen groups persisted and their efforts were further fueled by public comments from Chief Justice of the Pennsylvania Supreme Court, Ralph Cappy, who praised the legislature and governor for their courage in the face of public outrage. Newspapers across the Commonwealth were flooded with responses to the perceived arrogance of the members of the general assembly and the Chief Justice. The legislature repealed the pay raise on November 2, 2005, but the damage was already done. Less than a week later, voters ousted State Supreme Court Justice Russell Nigro, who was running in a retention election, by a margin of 51 percent to 49 percent; he was the first Pennsylvania supreme court justice not to be retained since the implementation of retention elections in 1969. The fallout from the legislative pay raise continued in the 2006 primary elections, with

losses for Republican Bob Jubelirer, president pro tempore of the Pennsylvania Senate, and Republican David "Chip" Brightbill, senate majority leader. By the time the 2006 election cycle concluded, approximately 20 percent of the legislative seats were held by newly-elected members and control of the house shifted to the Democratic Party with the election of Democrat Barbara McIlvaine Smith in a Republican district by a margin of 28 votes.

Pennsylvania uses partisan elections to select the members of its judicial branch. Judges, from the Court of Common Pleas (the trial courts in Pennsylvania) to the state Supreme Court, are elected to serve 10-year terms. At the conclusion of the term, a retention election occurs. Contests for open seats on Pennsylvania's statewide courts, the Supreme Court, the commonwealth court, and the Superior Court, draw large numbers of contenders heading into the primary elections and significant contributions from inside and outside the Commonwealth. Partisan competition for the seats on the state's appellate courts is keen, as is seen in the recent elections for the Pennsylvania Supreme Court.

In the 2001 supreme court contest, Republican Mike Eakin defeated Democrat Kate Ford Elliott, giving Republicans control of the court for the first time since 1971. In the 2003 election, partisan control of the supreme court returned to the Democratic Party when Democrat Max Baer prevailed over Republican Joan Orie Melvin in another bitterly contested election. In both the 2001 and 2003 races, candidates raised more than $1 million to finance their statewide campaigns.

WOMEN AND MINORITIES

Women and minorities have faced significant challenges in achieving national office in Pennsylvania. Pennsylvania has never elected a woman or a minority candidate to the U.S. Senate; Democrat Lynn Yeakel was the last woman to run as a major party candidate, in 1992. Only three women have been elected to serve in the U.S. House from Pennsylvania: Marjorie Margolies Mezvinsky (Democrat, 1993–95), Melissa Hart (Republican, 2001–07), and Allyson Schwartz (Democrat, 2005–present). Four African Americans have represented Pennsylvania in the U.S. House: Robert Nix, Sr. (Democrat, 1958–79); William H. Gray, III (Democrat, 1979–91); Lucien Blackwell (Democrat, 1991–95), and Chaka Fattah (Democrat, 1995–present).

At the state level, neither of the major political parties has selected a woman to run for governor. Catherine

Baker Knoll was elected to serve as the commonwealth's lieutenant governor on the Democratic ticket with Ed Rendell in 2002. Republican Lynn Swann was the first African American to be a major party nominee for governor in 2006. Women and minorities have faced significant challenges in winning seats in the Pennsylvania General Assembly as well. Pennsylvania is ranked 44th in the number of women serving in its state legislature, with 14.6 percent of the seats held by women. African Americans hold approximately seven percent of the seats in the Pennsylvania General Assembly, placing the commonwealth 20th in this national ranking.

SEE ALSO: Gender Gap; Rural Vote; Urban Vote.

BIBLIOGRAPHY. Carrie Budoff, "Democrats Statewide Ride Big Turnout Wave," *Philadelphia Inquirer* (November 6, 2003); Center for the American Woman and Politics, Eagleton Institute of Politics, Rutgers University, "Women in State Legislatures 2007" (April 2007); Center for Rural Pennsylvania, www.ruralpa.org (cited August 2007); Jason DeParle, "G.O.P. Conservatives Topple Veteran State Lawmakers in Pennsylvania," *New York Times* (May 18, 2006); D.J. Elazar, *American Federalism: A View from the States* (Thomas Crowell, 1966); Thomas Fitzgerald and Amy Worden, "Is Pennsylvania Becoming True Blue," *Philadelphia Inquirer* (November 13, 2006); Asher Hawkins, "Cappy Key Figure in Judicial Pay Increase," *Legal Intelligencer* (July 13, 2005); C.A. Johnson, "Political Culture in American States: Elazar's Formulation Examined," *American Journal of Political Science* (August 1976); National Conference of State Legislatures, www.ncsl.org (cited August 2007); S.C. Patterson and G.A. Caldeira, "The Etiology of Partisan Competition," *American Political Science Review* (September 1984); Dennis Roddy, "Eakin Leads G.O.P. Sweep of Pennsylvania Supreme Court Seats," *Pittsburgh Post-Gazette* (November 7, 2001); Elizabeth Schehr, ed., *The Pennsylvania Manual* (Department of General Services, 2005).

Sara A. Grove
Chatham University, Pittsburgh, Pennsylvania

People's Party

AMID THE AGRARIAN strife of the late 19th century, the People's Party (also known as the Populist Party) had its origins in the Alliance movement designed to protect farmers from the ravages of corporate-run industrial capitalism. The Gilded Age witnessed many economic downturns and depressions, known at the time as panics. Almost like clockwork, the nation suffered economic calamity every decade: 1873, 1883, and the worst shock of the 19th century, the panic of 1893.

Farmers, in desperation due to falling prices for crops, high prices for land, and gouging by the railroads that delivered their crops to market, banded together in alliances to survive. These maladies were the result of overproduction and world competition. The most notable of the alliances, the northern, southern, and colored organizations, grew in strength of numbers as the 19th century waned. The strongest of the alliance organizations was the Southern Alliance. A series of conferences in St. Louis, Ocala, and Cincinnati helped to organize a new political party. In Cincinnati, Ohio, in May 1892, the delegates formed the People's Party.

The party ran its first presidential candidate in the election of 1892. The party met in Omaha, Nebraska, and the delegates adopted a militant platform based on the common producer rhetoric of the time. The platform called for government ownership of the railroads, communication, and transportation networks, a flexible national currency, the free and unlimited coinage of silver at a ratio of 16:1, and a graduated income tax. Resolutions not part of the original platform called for a redistribution of land held by the railroads and aliens, the Australian (secret ballot) in elections, limits on immigration to protect American labor, the abolition of Pinkerton strike breakers, and the institution of the initiative and referendum. The platform included resolutions demanding a single term for the president and vice president, opposition to government subsidies for private corporations, and a promise to boycott manufacturers that persecuted labor.

Former Union General James Baird Weaver of Iowa was nominated for president and former Confederate General James G. Field of Virginia was nominated for vice president. The People's Party fared well in their first national election, but not well enough to defeat Grover Cleveland, who regained the White House after losing to Benjamin Harrison in 1888. The People's Party won 22 electoral votes, carried five states, and earned close to nine percent of the popular vote.

In the election campaign of 1896, the People's Party adopted much the same platform as in 1892, but the Democrats had adopted most of their agenda, including a plank in support of free silver. The People's Party endorsed William Jennings Bryan and nominated Thomas Watson of Georgia for vice president in hopes that Bryan would dump industrialist Arthur Sewall of Maine, but Bryan refused. Bryan's defeat in the election of 1896, the "battle of the standards," one of the most exciting in American history, ended the People's Party's dream of running the national government. The People's Party achieved many congressional and state successes, but with the decline of agrarian political power, so went the fortunes of the People's Party. Despite the end of their run at the dawn of the 20th century, many of the Populists lived to see the fulfillment of many of their cherished ideas, such as the graduated income tax, the secret ballot in elections, and the direct election of U.S. senators.

SEE ALSO: Bryan, William Jennings; Presidential Election of 1892; Presidential Election of 1896.

BIBLIOGRAPHY. D.R.B. Ross, *The Emergence of Modern America: 1865–1900* (Thomas Y. Crowell Company, 1970); E.H. Roseboom, *A History of Presidential Elections from George Washington to Richard M. Nixon: The Definitive Account of Our National Conventions, Campaigns, and Elections* (Macmillan, 1970); A.M. Schlesinger, ed., *History of U.S. Political Parties* (Chelsea House, 1973).

JAMES BAUGESS
COLUMBUS STATE COMMUNITY COLLEGE

Period Effect

THE PERIOD EFFECT refers to change within, or influence upon, political behavior that can be ascribed to generational difference, not simply age differences. Age differences would account for a difference of opinion on tax law between a young man and his grandfather, but not for the changes of the Civil Rights Movement or the Progressive Era. While the generation effect may describe differences in outlook that are carried across time by an age cohort, the period effect describes a change or influence that remains true across age, gender, ethnic, and other boundaries, at a particular point in time. Civil Rights workers and Progressive reformers, for example, included people from all walks of life, though, of course some demographics were better represented than oth-

ers. This is sometimes also called a situational effect, especially when the situation is easy to describe, such as the prosperity of the 1920s, the troubles of the subsequent Great Depression, or the problems facing the south during Reconstruction.

The presence of a period effect does not mean that everyone will be affected the same way, or that all groups will be affected equally. As a cause of a general trend, it is more analogous to the effect of a book dropped on someone's dinner plate: the steak may be essentially unscathed, mashed potatoes will be spattered, but lose none of their integrity, a delicate pastry will be ruined, and the plate itself may break, while the silverware simply shifts position. Everything is affected, but the nature of the effect is a product of the interplay of factors rather than a blanket change. In the Progressive Era, for instance, some conservative groups dug in their heels and asserted their conservatism to greater degree (such as the Baptist fundamentalists and the Conservative Jews) as a response to the reformist movements in their environment. Even in doing so, they changed; the silverware shifted position.

There are some clear examples of period effects in American political history: the Civil War, Reconstruction, the Great Depression, and World War II. They were all events that affected every American's way of life, as well as the fundamental behavior of American government. Other period effects are not tied to specific events, and were not necessarily consciously noted by voters: the Progressive Era instilled a spirit of reform so pervasive that not all reformers wanted to reform in the same direction, as nativist anti-immigrant groups and socialist political parties, secularizing churches and fundamentalist seminaries, rose up simultaneously. The Cold War could be described as having a period effect, or perhaps, more accurately, as encompassing several of them: the tensions of the 1950s and 1980s, and the activism of the 1960s.

A realignment election is an election (or series of elections) that is part of a dramatic shift in politics, such as the 1896 election of William McKinley amidst the prevailing spirit of populism and reform among his opponents, the advent of the New Deal Era with the election of Franklin Delano Roosevelt in 1932, and the Democrats' loss of southern loyalty because of their support of the Civil Rights Movement (a shift that began at the Democratic National Convention in 1948 became a fact by 1968). Realignment elections are expected to occur every 36 years in American history. The period effect is similar to the German concept of the *zeitgeist*, the "spirit of the age." Steam Engine Time is also sometimes heard, referring to the simultaneous and independent development of a steam engine by inventors unaware of each other, invoking the idea that the conditions of the time, the resources and scientific climate, were simply conducive to the invention of a steam engine.

SEE ALSO: Cross-Pressures, Sociopolitical; Currency; Dealignment; Focus Groups; Generation Effect; Realignment.

BIBLIOGRAPHY. P.E. Converse, *Cohort-Analyzing Party Identification* (University of Michigan, 1976); N.E. Cutler and V.L. Bengston, "Age and Political Alienation: Maturation, Generation, and Period Effects," *Annals of the American Academy of Political and Social Science* (September 1974); Lewis Gould, *America in the Progressive Era, 1890–1914* (Longman, 2000).

BILL KTE'PI
INDEPENDENT SCHOLAR

Perot, Ross (1930–)

HENRY ROSS PEROT was a presidential candidate in 1992 and 1996, and founded the Reform Party, a third party that emerged from his 1992 Independent candidacy. Perot first came to public attention in 1969, when President Richard Nixon asked him to help get aid to American prisoners of war (POWs) being held in North Vietnam. Perot chartered two Braniff jets and sent them to Hanoi with 30 tons of Christmas presents and medical supplies for the POWs. Most of the supplies were not allowed off the plane, but Perot's effort did attract public attention to the poor treatment that American POWs were receiving in North Vietnam, North Vietnamese captors began to treat POWs better in response to world opinion.

In 1979, the Iranian government imprisoned two of Perot's employees, Paul Chiapparone and Bill Gaylord, over a contractual dispute. Perot assembled a commando team of employees from his company EDS (Electronic Data Systems) led by a retired U.S. Army Special Forces Officer, Arthur D. "Bull" Simons, to free the men. Simons and his group, concluding that they could not free the men from the maximum security prison where they were being held, waited for support-

ers of the Ayatollah Khomeni to attack the prison. This attack freed all 10,000 inmates, and the commando team was able to retrieve Chiapparone and Gaylord, and get them out of Iran.

During the late 1970s and 1980s, Perot began working on a number of public policy problems in Texas. In 1979, he was appointed head of the Texas War on Drugs Committee by Republican Governor Bill Clements. In 1983, he was appointed by Democratic Governor Mark White to lead an effort to reform public education in the state. One of the better-known Perot-initiated reforms was the "No Pass, No Play" rule, which required students to have passing grades in order to participate in high school sports. From 1981 to 1983, Perot served on President Ronald Reagan's Foreign Intelligence Advisory Board. In the late 1980s, Perot started speaking out on national issues. Perot opposed the first Persian Gulf War (1990–91), urging members of Congress to oppose the resolution authorizing American involvement.

On February 20, 1992, Perot appeared on CNN's *Larry King Live* show, and announced that he would run for president if his supporters could get his name

Perot received 18.9 percent of the popular vote in 1992—more than any third-party candidate since 1912.

on the ballot in all 50 states. Perot also laid out a number of policy positions: he favored balancing the federal budget, was pro-choice on abortion, favored expanding the war on drugs, opposed gun control, and proposed "expanding democracy" by initiating "electronic town halls." By June 1992, Perot was actually leading President George H.W. Bush and Arkansas Governor Bill Clinton in a number of national surveys. Perot hired two nationally prominent political operatives: Democrat Hamilton Jordan (who managed Jimmy Carter's presidential campaigns) and Republican Ed Rollins (the national campaign director of President Ronald Reagan's 1984 re-election campaign).

Perot's standing in the polls invited greater scrutiny. The Wall Street Journal reported that Perot had often used private investigators to obtain negative information about business rivals. Stories began appearing that suggested that Perot had received special favors from the Nixon administration. Questions were raised about his management style, which some characterized as authoritarian. He was also criticized for his July 11, 1992, appearance at the National Association for the Advancement of Colored People (NAACP) National Convention, when he addressed the audience at one point as "you people." Days later, Rollins resigned.

On July 16, 1992, citing what he called the "revitalization" of the Democratic Party, Perot announced that he would not run for president even if his supporters succeeded in getting him on the ballot in all 50 states. However, while Perot indicated that he would no longer be a candidate, the effort to place Perot on the ballot in all 50 states continued. By September, Perot had qualified for the ballot in all 50 states and he began to suggest that his decision to leave the race might have been a mistake. On October 1, 1992, Perot announced that he would re-enter the race, selecting retired Vice Admiral James Stockdale, a former Vietnam POW, as his running mate. He claimed that his earlier departure from the campaign was because he believed that Republican political operatives would disrupt his daughter's wedding, although he did not explain how or why.

Perot focused his efforts on 16 states, spending more than $65 million of his own money. One of the distinctive features of his campaign was his purchase of 30-minute primetime blocks of time on the major television networks to present his proposals, which were noted for his extensive use of pie charts. The tone of his campaign was anti-Washington. In addition to emphasizing the need

for a balanced budget, Perot also proposed an increase in the gasoline tax and changes in Social Security in order to reduce the deficit. Perot participated in the general election debates with Bush and Clinton, becoming the only third-party candidate to be permitted to participate in televised debates with the Democratic and Republican Party candidates since they began.

Perot received 18.9 percent of the popular vote, which gave him the highest popular vote percentage of a third-party candidate since 1912, when Theodore Roosevelt polled 27 percent of the popular vote. Unlike Roosevelt, Perot did not carry any states (and did not, therefore, win any electoral votes), and finished second in Maine (ahead of Bush) and Utah (ahead of Clinton). There are some political analysts who believe that Perot might have done even better and perhaps even have carried some states if he had not withdrawn in July and returned in October. Perot's actions contributed to the perception held by some that he was erratic. Nevertheless, he appealed to many voters disillusioned with the existing two-party system.

Perot's vote total in 1992 entitled him to receive federal funding if he decided to seek the presidency again in 1996. Perot became a prominent opponent of the North American Free Trade Agreement (NAFTA), arguing that the agreement would lead to the further outsourcing of American industrial jobs. In 1994, Perot endorsed the House Republicans' Contract With America, and urged support for Republican congressional candidates in the 1994 midterm elections.

In 1995, Perot founded the Reform Party, and said the party would run candidates in every state. Initially, it was not clear that Perot intended to run for president again in 1996. Richard Lamm, the former Democratic Governor of Colorado, announced that he would be a candidate for the Reform Party nomination. Perot did decide to run, and defeated Lamm in the Reform Party primary to secure the party's nomination. Lamm's supporters claimed that Perot's supporters, who controlled the party organization, had rigged the contest by not sending ballots to Lamm supporters. Lamm refused to endorse Perot.

Unlike in 1992, Perot did not self-finance his 1996 campaign, accepting contributions and taking the federal funds that were available to him (but not to his party) because of his 1992 performance. Also, he was not permitted to join in the debates with President Clinton and Republican candidate Robert Dole, because his low poll numbers disqualified him as a serious candidate. In the general election, Perot received eight percent of the popular vote. While Perot remained involved with the Reform Party after the 1996 election, he did not support Jesse Ventura's successful 1998 Reform Party candidacy for governor of Minnesota. In the years that followed, Perot withdrew from the party's activities and declined to run for a third time in 2000. In an appearance on Larry King's show shortly before the 2000 general election, he endorsed George W. Bush for president.

SEE ALSO: Presidential Election of 1992; Presidential Election of 1996; Third Parties.

BIBLIOGRAPHY. T.M. Defrank et al., *Quest for the Presidency* (Texas A&M University Press, 1994); H.R. Perot, *United We Stand: How We Can Take Back Our Country* (Hyperion Books, 1992); Ronald Rapoport and Walter Stone, *Three's a Crowd: The Dynamic of Third Parties, Ross Perot and Republican Resurgence* (University of Michigan Press, 2005).

JEFFREY KRAUS
WAGNER COLLEGE

Plunkitt, George Washington (1842–1924)

GEORGE WASHINGTON PLUNKITT was a New York City politician, immortalized by William L. Riordan as "Plunkitt of Tammany Hall," who admitted to practicing "honest graft" as an operative in the Democratic political machine that dominated New York City politics in the last half of the 19th century and the early part of the 20th century. Plunkitt, who was of Irish ancestry, left school at the age of 11 and went to work in a butcher shop. As a young man, he decided he would make politics his profession.

A Democrat, Plunkitt served one term in the New York State Assembly (1869–70). In 1870, he served simultaneously as a state assemblyman, a New York City alderman, a police magistrate, and a county supervisor. He returned to elective office as a state senator, 1884–87; returned to the state senate a second time 1892–93, and was re-elected, serving 1899–1904. However, his real notoriety comes from his years as part of Tammany Hall. Known as the "sage of Tam-

many Hall" for more than 60 years, Plunkitt was a Tammany operative. He served as a "sachem" of the hall, a trustee of the Society of Tammany, and a Democratic District Leader for more than 40 years. In 1905, Plunkitt agreed to a series of interviews with Riordan, a newspaper reporter who published the interviews as "Very Plain Talks on Very Practical Politics." Most of the interviews were conducted at Plunkitt's "office," which was the shoeshine stand in the basement of the New York County courthouse.

Plunkitt enriched himself by engaging in what he called "honest graft." This often involved using inside information to purchase land that he knew would be needed for government projects. He would purchase the land from the owners and then resell the property to the government at an inflated price. He distinguished this from "dishonest graft," which, from his perspective, would have meant buying the land and then using one's influence to have a government project built on the land. Plunkitt was critical of dishonest graft, stating, "The politician who steals is worse than a thief. He is a fool. With grand opportunities all around for a man with political pull, there's no excuse for stealin' a cent."

Plunkitt was an advocate of the machine politics of his day: the appointment of loyal party men to positions in government and the award of government contracts to party supporters. He believed that the machine politics of the organization had improved New York City. As he told Riordan,

Look at the bosses of Tammany Hall in the last 20 years. What magnificent men! To them New York City owes pretty much all it is today. John Kelly, Richard Croker, and Charles F. Murphy—what names in American history compare with them, except Washington's and Lincoln's?

Plunkitt defended the machine because he saw it as a friend of the poor. Tammany operatives would help the poor directly, by providing them loans and helping them find jobs, while progressive reformers would talk about improving the general conditions of the poor and, from Plunkitt's perspective, do nothing to address their immediate needs.

Plunkitt opposed the introduction of the merit system in public employment that was part of the urban reform agenda of the early 20th century. He believed it not only threatened Tammany, but the stability of the government, which he believed was based on patronage.

However, he thought such reforms would be short-lived. As he explained to Riordan:

> I see a vision. I see the civil service monster lyin' flat on the ground. I see the Democratic Party standin' over it with foot on its neck and wearin' the crown of victory. I see Thomas Jefferson lookin' out from a cloud and sayin', 'Give him another sockdologer: finish him.' And I see millions of men wavin' their hats and singin', Glory Hallelujah.

Plunkitt died a millionaire on November 19, 1924. As he told Riordan 20 years before his death, his epitaph would be: "George W. Plunkitt: He Seen His Opportunities, and He Took 'Em."

SEE ALSO: Machine Politics and Political Bosses; Patronage System; Tammany Hall.

BIBLIOGRAPHY. W.L. Riordan, *Plunkitt of Tammany: A Series of Very Plain Talks on Very Practical Politics* ([1905] St. Martin's Press, 1993).

JEFFREY KRAUS
WAGNER COLLEGE

Pluralist Politics

PLURALISM REFERS TO politics as a process by which people form or join groups that reflect their interests. The groups, in turn, compete for political influence, both in election campaigns and outside the electoral process. Pluralistic models of politics generally hold that political attention and involvement are selective. People who are interested in environmental issues will pay attention to them and mobilize when they want to draw attention to an environmental problem or to influence an upcoming environmental decision. When another issue, such as antipoverty policy, gains prominence, a largely different slate of people and groups will take the field, and most environmentalists will continue their focus on environmental causes or become politically dormant.

According to pluralists, political power is quite widely (but not necessarily equally) dispersed, and somewhat unstable; people who are politically irrelevant today may be influential tomorrow if they mobilize on an issue of concern to them. At any given time, political information, activity, and influence are likely to be unevenly distributed, but the distribution varies from issue to issue and changes over time. Consequently, sensible officials who value re-election will try to anticipate public reactions to governmental decisions and positions taken in campaigns. People who are inattentive and inactive at the time of an action may become attentive and active later and, as a result, affect an official or candidate's career. Pluralistic politics have a number of implications for campaigns and elections.

One of the most important linkages noted between pluralist politics and the electoral process in the political parties literature, is scholars' observation that political groups were an important component of many political parties. In this view, political parties are often coalitions of smaller groups, some of which have different priorities from one another, or even altogether different interests. A group's relationship with a political party may change over time, from strong support to opposition or vice versa, and one test of party and campaign leadership is the ability to keep different groups together, whether during a single campaign or over a longer time period. Group affiliations may influence a political party's public image, as in the case of a party regarded as friendly to working-class people, wealthy people, farmers, or racial minorities.

Pluralist politics may assist candidates and political parties by calling attention to issues or problems, but the result can also create complications. When a group criticizes officials in office, an action that may duplicate somewhat the watchdog role of the opposition party, the result may be helpful to the party that is out of power or a candidate who is challenging an incumbent. If a group runs attack ads against one candidate, other candidates in the race may benefit from the damage inflicted, while appearing to be above the fray. When a group praises the actions of politicians in office, the result may be helpful for incumbents. However, groups may sometimes raise issues that create division in one or more parties, and may divert attention from issues that some candidates or parties want to emphasize.

Political groups may assist campaigns in a wide variety of ways, including contributing money to campaigns, or spending money "independently" to praise or criticize a candidate, and providing volunteer labor for campaigns to distributing information through group newsletters and websites. A group may give a candidate a forum to gain publicity and may also give the candidate background information and analysis on one or more issues. Groups may draft proposals and then try to find candidates or officeholders who are willing to endorse them.

As James Madison observed, larger, more diverse societies are likely to produce a larger number of groups, other things being equal. The presence of large numbers of groups competing for power and influence may help to foster more competitive elections, in part because no single party or political movement is likely to be able to contain all of them for very long. Beyond some point, however, increasing numbers of political groups may make political decision-making more difficult. Candidates and officials may find that no matter what position they take, so many groups may criticize them that political survival becomes almost impossible and very few proposals can make it through the policymaking process. By contrast, small, homogeneous jurisdictions, such as many of America's small towns and less populous counties, are unlikely to have very many groups competing for power and, consequently, may often fail to provide competitive elections, although a number of other factors may contribute to that phenomenon.

For people who find politics confusing, or who are unwilling to devote large amounts of time and effort to learning about the various candidates running in a given election, political groups can provide cues that simplify voting decisions. Many groups publish ratings of public officials and candidates in terms of their positions on issues of interest to group members. Many groups also endorse or at least praise, some candidates and officeholders, and denounce others. The information shortcuts provided by those groups may be especially helpful when party cues are not available, as is the case in nonpartisan elections, party primaries, and referenda. In addition, people whose political interests are usually confined to one or a few issues can often find one or more groups that evaluate candidates largely or entirely in terms of those few issues. Groups may assist candidates and/or parties that want to direct specialized campaign appeals to people who are particularly interested in a given issue, such as gun control.

THE COMPATIBILITY VIEW
Some discussions of pluralistic politics and its emphasis on political groups regard it as compatible with, and even a supplement to, models of democracy that emphasize political parties and elections. Other observ-

ers see a degree of tension, or even incompatibility. One element of the compatibility view is that not all issues can be anticipated during the course of election campaigns, and in the modern era, not all issues can be discussed thoroughly during campaigns without placing an unreasonable burden on voters.

In addition, an issue that seemed unimportant to many voters during the campaign and election may gain importance after the ballots have been counted. In cases like these, elections alone may not be enough to make government respond to public sentiments. People can gravitate to groups that share their views, and the groups can convey public sentiments to public officials. If a country has many political groups, as is the case in the United States, those groups (taken together) may be able to communicate relatively specific positions on a much larger number of issues than could two political parties. Public officials need flexibility to respond to this additional public input and to accommodate conflicting viewpoints.

Pluralism also provides for communication of the strength of people's feelings. In elections, each vote within a given race is counted relatively equally (with some important exceptions, such as presidential elections). People who feel more strongly about a particular viewpoint are not allowed to cast additional votes (although they may register their strong feelings by volunteering to work for a candidate or party, making campaign contributions, and so forth). With pluralistic politics, however, someone who feels very strongly about a particular issue can join several political groups involved in the issue, volunteer to work on their behalf, and communicate directly with officials.

A SUPPLEMENT FOR ELECTORAL POLITICS
In a related vein, pluralism calls attention to the fact that some political issues are not amenable to majority rule because no single viewpoint on the issue is held by a majority. In some cases, people who have no opinion or are otherwise undecided may outnumber the people with settled opinions. Political systems still need to make decisions on those issues, however, and political interest groups enable numerical minorities to register their views and give officials incentives to respond. An important assumption in this linkage process is that group leaders are in step with the opinions of rank and file members; which is not always the case. People may join a group for a variety of reasons and may not be well

informed regarding the activities of group leaders. Pluralistic politics provides a valuable supplement for electoral politics when people want to influence the actions of public bureaucracies. Career administrators are somewhat insulated from electoral outcomes, but their actions still influence public policies in many ways.

Career administrators also recognize that support from political groups can be very helpful when agencies need a budget approved or protection from unfriendly elected officials. That support is only likely to appear if agencies respond to those groups, however. Critics complain that those relationships can mean commitments made during election campaigns are undercut by relatively concealed interest group–agency relationships.

CRITICISMS

One of the most important criticisms of pluralistic politics is that it is biased in favor of people of higher socioeconomic status. People of higher social class are more likely to belong to political groups and are more likely to be active in the groups to which they belong. In addition, business groups are over-represented among the ranks of interest groups, and there are relatively few groups speaking for the poor, the poorly educated, or the homeless. The distribution of political resources needed for group influence—resources such as money, information, organization, and convenient access to officials—is also biased in favor of upper-class interests. Although the extent of bias is subject to dispute, its existence is widely recognized.

In a related vein, some critics charge that pluralism paints an inaccurate picture of the distribution of political power. Some analysts contend that power is much more concentrated in a small number of people and that ordinary people have virtually no influence on important societal decisions, in part because leaders often conceal information or mislead the public. In addition, many important decisions are not made in the political arena, but in corporate boardrooms or in social networks among powerful people.

SEE ALSO: Issue Salience and Voting Behavior; Plurality Vote; Two-Party System.

BIBLIOGRAPHY. Robert Dahl, *Democracy and Its Critics* (Yale University Press, 1989); E. Pendleton Herring, *The Politics of Democracy* (Rinehart and Company, 1940); G.W. Domhoff, *Who Rules America Now?* (Touchstone, 1983); Theodore Lowi, *The End of Liberalism* (Norton, 1979); E.E. Schattschneider, *Party Government* (Holt, Rinehart, and Winston, 1942); Kay Schlozman and John Tierney, *Organized Interests and American Democracy* (Harper and Row, 1986); David Truman, *The Governmental Process* (Knopf, 1951); Sidney Verba and Norman Nie, *Participation in America* (Harper and Row, 1972).

DAVID NICE
WASHINGTON STATE UNIVERSITY
ANDREW THOMAS
WASHINGTON STATE UNIVERSITY

Plurality Vote

PLURALITY IS THE most widespread winner-take-all (or majoritarian) electoral formula. The working of plurality is straightforward: the candidate (or, in some cases, the candidates) who receives the most votes wins the election. Plurality is typically used in single-member districts, and in most cases is employed for legislative elections. Among the advantages of plurality are more direct links between voters and their representatives, more decisive elections, and enhanced governmental accountability. Important drawbacks of plurality are the under-representation of minorities and third parties, disproportional results, and the fact that a party or a candidate can win an election with fewer votes than the opposing party or candidate.

Advocates of plurality argue that in countries such as the United States or Britain, which use single-member district plurality elections for their national legislatures, the system provides more democratic accountability than in countries using proportional representation. However, the logic behind this claim is different in each of the two cases. In the United States, where representatives are more responsive toward their constituents, elections provide citizens with an opportunity to judge individually the performance of each incumbent.

In Britain, plurality elections, combined with a parliamentary system, lead to a two-party system and single-party governments. In this case, voters see legislative elections less as an opportunity to make a judgment about the performance of their representative, and more as a chance to choose the government. Accordingly, a vote for a Labour or a Conservative candidate is mostly the expression of the voter's wish to ensure a majority for one party or the other, and, by doing so, to see their preferred party forming the government.

In parliamentary systems using proportional representation, the governmental majority is typically backed by a majority of popular votes. In parliamentary systems using single-member district plurality, this is seldom the case. In Britain, for example, the last time a party won a majority of votes was in 1935. However, proponents of plurality argue that the efficiency of single-party government is worth the cost of having a government backed by only a plurality of voters. Nonetheless, critics point out that even this is by no means assured, that is, the party that wins the most seats is not always the party that wins the most votes. In Britain, this happened in 1951 and then again in 1974. In New Zealand, this happened in both the 1978 and the 1981 parliamentary elections, the Labour Party won more votes than the incumbent National Party. However, the National Party won a majority of seats on both occasions. Such occurrences raise questions, not only about the fairness of this kind of electoral system, but also about the claims that plurality ensures governmental accountability.

A similar phenomenon, a candidate with less than a plurality of votes winning the election, occurred four times in the history of presidential elections in the United States: in 1824, 1876, 1888, and 2000. However, the election of the U.S. president is indirect, via the Electoral College, and a counter-argument is that the institutional framework of the United States did not assign any particular significance to the popular vote; rather, it was designed in such a way as to ensure that the candidate winning enough support across a number of states would be able to translate this into a majority of votes in the Electoral College.

A more serious problem is when plurality fails to encourage candidates to moderate their positions. If candidates position themselves along a liberal-conservative ideological continuum, the expectation is that only moderate candidates have a chance to win. But there are significant historical examples when this expectation failed to materialize, such as Chile's 1970 presidential election, when the leftist Salvador Allende was elected with only 36.6 percent of the popular vote. This eventually led to a military coup and the breakdown of Chilean democracy. Papua New Guinea provides a further example of how plurality can have perverse effects in a polity fragmented along ethnic and linguistic lines. Unlike ideology, ethnicity is not a matter of degree, and Papua New Guinea's switch to plurality for its parliamentary elections after 1975 led to a significant increase in electoral violence and further fragmentation, rather than consolidation, of its party system. For instance, in the 1997 parliamentary election, 62 of 107 seats in the legislature were won with less than 20 percent of the vote, and 15 of these were won with less than 10 percent.

SEE ALSO: Electoral College; Majority Rule; Two-Party System; Voting Methods; Winner-Take-All System.

BIBLIOGRAPHY. Pippa Norris, "Part I: Introduction," *Electoral Engineering: Voting Rules and Political Behavior* (Cambridge University Press, 2004); Andrew Reynolds and Ben Reilly, eds., *The International IDEA Handbook of Electoral System Design* (International Institute for Democracy and Electoral Assistance, 1997).

FLORIN FESNIC
UNIVERSITY OF BUCHAREST

Political Action Committee

A POLITICAL ACTION COMMITTEE (PAC) is an organization that raises and contributes money to, or spends money in support of, candidates or political parties. The term PAC does not appear in federal law; rather, these organizations are officially known as "separate and segregated funds" because money raised and spent must be kept separate from the general treasury of the sponsoring organization, such as a union or corporation.

Labor unions pioneered the use of PACs, but individual corporations, professional and trade groups (such as the American Medical Association or National Association or Manufacturers), and ideological or single-issue interest groups, such as the National Rifle Association, have formed PACs. Also, in recent years, members of Congress with party leadership aspirations have begun to raise and distribute money to assist their fellow partisans in election campaigns using so-called leadership PACs. Despite some public concerns about PACs, these organizations play an important role in financing congressional candidates.

The regulation of political expenditures led to the creation of PACs, and PAC activities are themselves heavily regulated. Federal election codes govern PACs active in federal elections, and state election codes govern PACs active in state elections. States vary greatly in the extent to which they regulate PACs. At the federal level, limitations placed on the ability of labor unions to fund candidates directly out of their treasuries originated during World War II (the Smith Connally Act of 1943) and were reinforced in the Taft Hartley Act of 1947. These regulations led the Committee on Industrial Organization (CIO) to create the first PACs in the 1940s to support the election of Franklin Roosevelt in 1944. Until the 1970s, labor dominated the PAC system. Like unions, corporations were banned from making political contributions directly from their treasuries (since the passage of the Tillman Act in 1907), yet individual corporations did not use PACs widely until the 1970s, when laws limited the ability of wealthy individuals to contribute large amounts of money to candidates.

The legality of labor and corporate PACs was ambiguous until the passage of the Federal Election Campaign Act (FECA) in 1971, which established the right of these organizations and others to form PACs, and created the Federal Election Commission (FEC) to oversee the new campaign finance regulations. FECA's PAC provisions, its limitations on individual contributions, and FEC administrative decisions clarifying the process of corporate PAC formation, led to the increased use of PACs by corporations. In the mid-1970s, few corporations sponsored PACs, but by the late 1980s over 1,800 did.

The 1974 amendments to FECA placed financial limits on the amount of money that PACs can donate to different entitiesThese were not changed by the 2002 McCain-Feingold campaign finance reform legislation (that is, the Bipartisan Campaign Finance Reform Act or BCRA) and remained in effect as of 2007. The limitations are $5,000 per candidate per election cycle, $5,000 to state parties or other PACs, and $15,000 to national party committees per calendar year, with no limit on the total amount of contributions to all candidates, PACs, and parties.

PACs are an important source of money for congressional candidates, but are generally not as important for presidential candidates. According to the Center for Responsive Politics (CRP), in the 2006 election cycle, PACs contributed approximately $298 million to House and $71 million to Senate candidates, providing 34 percent and 13 percent for each chamber's candidates, respectively. Since McCain-Feingold outlawed organized interests' ability to contribute unregulated soft money to the parties, and placed stricter limitations on independent expenditures, PACs remain a very important means for organized interests to influence elections.

According to Federal Election Commission data, as of 2006 there were 1,968 corporate, 1,089 Trade/Membership/Health (T/M/H), 346 labor union, and 200 nonconnected PACs. Because many trade and membership groups represent business, business interests numerically dominate the PAC system and they also contribute the large majority of PAC money to candidates. According to the Center for Responsive Politics, 10 of the 20 largest PACs represented business interests (including the four largest), and 10 represented organized labor. The Center for Responsive Politics also reports that of the approximately $369 million contributed by PACs in the 2006 election cycle, $59 million came from organized labor, $60 million came from ideological or single issue groups, with most of the rest and from business interests.

Party leaders use leadership PACs to distribute funds to vulnerable incumbents and challengers of their own party to increase their influence within the party. As there is no official definition in the federal code for a leadership PAC, estimating their numbers is difficult; the FEC estimates that approximately 256 leadership PACs were registered for the 2006 election cycle. These PACs have existed for many years, but became more common in the late 1990s. Most congressional party leaders have formed them, as have many presidential hopefuls. According to the Center for Responsive Politics, in the 2006 election cycle, leadership PACs contributed approximately $41 million to federal candidates.

PACs are sometimes controversial with the public because they are often viewed as instruments of wealthy special interests. Political scientists have extensively studied PAC contributions and have found that they are generally a weak influence on roll call voting compared to factors like party and ideology, but that they can influence congressional behavior significantly. Despite public disapproval of PACs, the McCain-Feingold law did not place any new limits on PACs, and these organizations are firmly established in law and political practice in the United States.

SEE ALSO: Campaign Finance, Politics of; Campaign Reforms; Federal Election Commission; Fundraising, Federal

Campaigns; McCain-Feingold Campaign Finance Reform; Special Interests.

BIBLIOGRAPHY. Center for Responsive Politics, www.opensecrets.org (cited August 2007); Federal Election Commission, www.fec.gov (cited August 2007); Thomas Gais, *Improper Influence: Campaign Finance Law, Political Interest Groups, and the Problem of Equality* (University of Michigan Press, 2001); F.J. Sorauf, *What Price PACs?* (Twentieth Century Fund, 1984); Christopher Witko, "PACs, Issue Context and Congressional Decision Making," *Political Research Quarterly* (v.59/2, 2006).

CHRIS WITKO
SAINT LOUIS UNIVERSITY

Political Alienation

POLITICAL ALIENATION IS the sense of estrangement, repulsion, or disaffection that political actors experience to the extent that they regard the political system, regime, or government as distant and unresponsive. The societal causes of political alienation are established in the political sociology of Rousseau, Hegel, and Marx. Marx explains how workers under capitalism come to be isolated from their own humanity, from each other, and to lose their autonomy and sense of purposeful agency. For Marx, who was writing before the era of mass democracy, the political system served to reinforce economic alienation through force and fraud.

Melvin Seeman presents a psychosocial typology of alienation that comprises a cluster of interrelated characteristics: powerlessness, meaninglessness, normlessness, social isolation, and self-estrangement. Facets of political alienation include low levels of trust and political efficacy, cynicism, a sense of rootlessness or anomie, despair, hostility, disaffection, loneliness and isolation, and feelings of apathy or pointlessness. The consequences of political alienation fall into two broad categories: apathetic withdrawal and angry criticism. Those who become apathetic tend to seek a parochial status in political life in which they avoid engagement with the political system, limiting their political participation, grudgingly dealing with political authority, and attempting, as much as possible, to evade political life. If questioned on political matters, such agents might express sentiments of deference to those in authority or vague lack of interest. The apathetic are unlikely to vote or to respond to cues for political involvement.

Those who are angered are more inclined to engage in counter-organizations of various kinds. They may join marginal and/or extreme oppositional organizations in order to express their point of view. Forms of protest focus on acts designed to gain the greatest media exposure, to cause the greatest disruption, and to reveal most glaringly the shortcomings of the sociopolitical establishment. Protest rallies, acts of civil disobedience, the destruction of public property, and even occasionally acts of violence are among the tools employed by those whose political alienation has led them to protest. In electoral terms, angry critics are likely to vote for the more marginal and extreme parties, or not to vote at all and invest their energies in interest group or protest group activity instead.

While political alienation can be a manifestation of a psychological characteristic, it is more likely to be associated with the membership of an individual in a certain social category. Thus, alienation is not always a matter of irrational withdrawal or hostility, but can be the anticipated response of those who genuinely believe that the political system has nothing of interest to offer them, and cannot be made to work in their interests.

SEE ALSO: Nonvoters; Political Cynicism; Protest Voting; Voter Alienation; Voter Apathy.

BIBLIOGRAPHY. Melvin Seeman, "Alienation Studies," *Annual Review of Sociology* (v.1, 1975).

PAUL WINGFIELD NESBITT-LARKING, PHD
HURON UNIVERSITY COLLEGE, CANADA

Political Base

THE TERM *political base* often refers to the group of voters who are most likely to support a candidate within their own party because the candidate holds the same philosophical and political views as both the party to which they belong and themselves. In elections at the local, state, and legislative level, base voters are more likely to support the nominee from within their own party simply because the dynamics of local and legislative politics relies on the majority, and base voting allows attainment of this majority.

The Republican Party's base is typically strongest in the west and the south. Specific demographics pertaining to the Republican base are as follows:

Race: Predominately white; African Americans are not traditionally known to congregate within the Republican Party (only about 15 percent in 2004), while Hispanics and Asians are on the rise (Hispanics 35 percent in 2004; Asians 44 percent in 2004).

Income: Overwhelmingly, the Republican political base is comprised of those with average to above average incomes. In 2006, voters with incomes over $50,000 were 49 percent Republican, while those under that income level were 38 percent Republican. In 2004 George W. Bush won 55 percent of the vote from the richest 20 percent.

Education: Those with an education only at the bachelor's level have been identified as part of the Republican base. The more educated voters become, the greater the tendency to lean toward the liberal ideology.

Age: Republican political ideology is strong among older Americans, indicating that political views grow more conservative with age.

Family Status: The Republican base is dependent on married families with children living at home.

Military: The military has traditionally been conservative, and, as a whole, is a strong supporter of Republican values and ideology.

Sexual Orientation: The Republican base overwhelmingly identifies as heterosexual.

Religion: Religion has always played a major role in both political parties, and prior to 1960, there was a major chasm between parties, with the south being primarily Jewish, Catholic, and Protestant Democrat, and the Northern Protestants primarily Republican. In the 21st century, it is based more on religiosity. Those who attend church more frequently are Republican; Protestant Evangelicals are overwhelmingly Republicans.

The Democratic base is usually thought of as being "liberals"—not in the classic sense, but as it pertains to social liberalism. The Democratic Party is the nation's largest political party with 72 million Americans registered as Democrats in 2004. Specific demographics about the base of the Democratic Party are as follows:

Race: African Americans traditionally belong to the Democratic Party; especially following the New Deal policies of the 1930s and the 1965 Voting Rights Act. Blacks make up 50 percent of the Democratic vote in the south.

Income: Among Democrats, 41 percent had household incomes exceeding $75,000. The working poor overwhelmingly support the values of the Democratic Party.

Education: Democrats have majorities among those with post-graduate studies and full-time faculty (85 percent) indicating that as voters become more educated, the greater the tendency toward liberal ideology. Democrats also find a strong base among those with limited educational attainment.

Age: Democrats do slightly better among younger Americans.

Family Status: The Democratic base is mostly comprised of unmarried and divorced women.

Military: While the military is comprised mostly of Republicans, 43 percent of enlisted personnel identify as Democrats as do 34 percent of officers.

Sexual Orientation: The vast majority of homosexuals find themselves aligned with the Democrat Party (up to 70 percent).

Religion: Religion has always played a major role in both political parties. Jews continue to vote 70–80 percent for the Democratic Party while African American churches such as African-Methodist-Episcopalian (AME) and National Baptists overwhelmingly support Democratic positions. Catholics split between the Republican and Democrat Parties about 50–50. Mainline traditional Protestants make up about 45 percent of the Democratic base, and Protestant Evangelicals are about 20–25 percent registered Democrats.

A political base is very important in establishing public opinion related to performance and competency. The political base is also the key electorate that presidential primary candidates target as they seek their respective party's nomination. As the field is whittled down to just two candidates, one representing each party, the race to the middle begins to solidify the political base and appeal to those who have moderate ideological beliefs.

SEE ALSO: Blue States; Democratic Party; Red States; Right-Wing Candidates; Republican Party.

BIBLIOGRAPHY. Russell J. Dalton, *Democratic Challenges, Democratic Choices: The Erosion of Political Support in Advanced Industrial Democracies* (Oxford University Press, 2007).

RONALD ERIC MATTHEWS, JR.
MOUNT UNION COLLEGE

Political Cartoons

POLITICAL CARTOONS FEATURE a predominantly visual representation of a contemporary event or issue. Cartoon images typically simplify issues into an image in a single panel, and they encapsulate complex ideas with icons and symbols. Political cartoons have often played the role of critic, and track political campaign events, as do other mass media. The impact of political cartoons is not necessarily a direct effect on persuading a reader on a vote choice, but rather on stimulating discussion and possible debate on issues and candidates.

Political cartoons in the United States date back to Benjamin Franklin's image in 1754, "Join or Die," in the *Pennsylvania Gazette*. The woodcut image contained a snake cut into eight pieces, representing eight early colonial governments, and was based on the superstition that a snake that was cut in two would come back to life if the pieces were rejoined by sunset. Thomas Nast was a famous cartoonist for *Harper's Weekly* in the 1870s, and was best known for attacking William "Boss" Tweed and bringing attention to the corruption of Tammany Hall, the political machine led by Tweed that ran New York.

While political cartoons are published on a daily basis in most U.S. newspapers, politics are frequently the focus of cartoon images, as are campaigns and elections, during local, state, and, particularly, national elections for president. To the extent that politics are a primary focus of current events, they are equally a primary focus of political cartoon images. Similar to news stories and other opinion-based coverage, political cartoons track political campaigns through all stages from candidate announcement, to Election Day, to Inauguration Day.

Although politicians and candidates are the focus of critique in political cartoon images during election cycles, there have been some contemporary instances of more positive relationships between politicians and cartoonists. For example, while running for re-election in 1996, Bill Clinton invited *Atlanta Journal Constitution* cartoonist Mike Luckovich aboard Air Force One, and the two took turns drawing cartoon images of each other. In 2004, both the Republican National Committee and the Democratic National Committee featured political cartoons around the time of their respective party conventions.

A REAL CHORE.

The G. O. P.—Well, I've Got That Panama Canal to Dig.
The Dem. Donk.—That's Nothin'! I Got to Dig Up an Issue.

The July 2, 1904, Cleveland Journal *ran this cartoon while most New York papers panned the Republican, Roosevelt, who won.*

The number of full-time political cartoonists has declined from more than 200 in the 1980s, to fewer than 100 in the early 2000s, partly because of technological developments, media ownership, and syndication. Technology permitted cartoonists' work to arrive for publication sooner than traditional delivery methods, so that images can now be sent instantaneously over the internet to numerous newspapers. Newspaper chains may feature the same cartoonists in a number of papers, and some newspapers have abandoned having their own political cartoonists and feature only syndicated editorial cartoons.

Political cartoons do not follow the principles of objectivity expected in news stories, but express opinions oftent parallel newspaper editorial and opinion columns. While some cartoons rely on considerable text to convey the opinion, many cartoons feature almost entirely visual messages. Given the brief time newspaper readers may pause to read a political cartoon, an image that is visually-based and easily understood and interpreted by a reader has a greater likelihood of capturing attention and being remembered.

Most cartoonists have autonomy from the editorial board and the newspaper's publisher, so the commentary reflected in the cartoons is not representative of a broader department's opinion. Political cartoon images reflect only the personal perspective or opinion of the cartoonist, although some cartoonists have been censored or removed due to highly controversial cartoons or themes that were contrary to the publisher's opinions. To be featured in a political cartoon is to be the subject of satire, if not to be attacked directly. Candidate's words or actions are often used against them in political cartoons, with the context for the event often changed to make light of it. If a political cartoonist favors or supports a political candidate, that candidate may be absent from cartoons, rather than the focus of the visual critique. Political cartoons also often feature voter dissatisfaction with candidates, as well as their disinterest in politics, in general, or with the events of the campaign themselves.

Exaggeration is often used in the visual satires of political cartoons, in particular of a person's physical attributes. Features of a politician's face are a common focus for exaggeration, and most physical portrayals in political cartoons are unflattering. For example, Jimmy Carter's smile was the highlight of cartoon images during his presidential campaign in 1976, and Richard Nixon's nose was often the focus of exaggeration in cartoon images during his presidency. Relative size between candidates is common in political cartoon images, as the frontrunner in an election is featured as a considerably larger or taller character than less serious contenders.

Campaigns and elections are featured in political cartoon images often through the use of allusions, references to literature, film, television, or mythology. Another common reference in cartoon images of political campaigns is the sport or battle of the election, with opposing candidates facing off in a boxing ring for imagery of a political debate, or on opposite political sports teams. The sporting nature of political campaigns is highlighted in editorial cartoons about elections, with winners and losers being featured at the end of a campaign race.

Similar to political editorials, political cartoons stimulate discussion and debate among readers. They have not been found, however, to directly shape a voter's opinions independent of other sources of opinion and information. They have the potential to keep an issue alive in individual readers, as an event is encapsulated in a humorous visual image. They may spark discussion among readers and be shared with others who might appreciate their humor; they may also lead to debate of political issues or candidates' tactics during a political campaign. In these ways, political cartoons have the potential to stimulate discussion and debate by presenting a humorous, yet critical, visual argument.

The greatest effect political cartoons have had is raising a response from those featured in an unflattering way in the images. On rare occasions, political cartoonists face lawsuits from those featured in their images, but cartoons are typically considered protected speech in the form of satire. As the popularity of late-night comedians' discussion of politics has grown, it is useful to remember that similar themes of satire were reflected in political cartoons long before many current late-night programs were first aired on television.

SEE ALSO: Candidate Image; Media, Role in Campaigns; Political Editorials.

BIBLIOGRAPHY. J.L. Edwards, *Political Cartoons in the 1988 Presidential Campaign: Image, Metaphor, and Narrative* (Garland Publishing, 1997); Stephen Hess and Sandy Northrup, *Drawn & Quartered: The History of American Political Cartoons* (Elliott & Clark Publishing, 1996); PS Symposium, "The State of the Editorial Cartoon," *Political Science and Politics* (April 2007).

JOAN L. CONNERS
RANDOLPH-MACON COLLEGE

Political Climate

POLITICAL CLIMATE DESCRIBES the current environment and past history of a political situation, such as an election. Knowledge about the political climate allows a better understanding of campaigns, elections, and electoral behavior. The political climate incorporates the past issues or debates relevant to the current political scene. It can play an important role in influencing voter opinion because it incorporates the existing relevant issues and how they are evolving within society, which politicians may base their policy decisions on, as was the case in the 2006 elections. Also, political climates always change with time. Therefore, past issues are liable to come back, or issues may be settled and never return, but many times new issues are found.

One example of an evolving issue for the 2008 election is global warming. Because many Americans believe global warming will be a major factor in their choice for president in 2008, presidential candidates are making campaign promises regarding the topic. This is in sharp contrast to past elections in which global warming was of low priority compared to issues such as Social Security or terrorism. The political climate of global warming has become an increasingly important issue and this shift in focus to global warming shows how political climates are always changing.

Political climates play an important role in elections because they determine how voters feel. Although the entry into the 21st century has seen more money pour into campaigns than ever before, there is a belief that the increased spending was not the only reason that the 2006 elections that resulted in a power shift. It is possible that the political climate was of great influence in the government's switch between parties in power in Congress. The history of the issue is that there was decreasing support of the current Republican government and so the setting called for a change. Many voted for Democrats to prove their dissatisfaction with the conservative government. Thus, the political climate during the 2006 elections caused a switch in party power with the Democratic Party taking control of the House of Representatives and the Senate.

Reading the political climate allows a candidate to understand the historical and current territory of his or her potential constituency or potential office. Understanding of the environment takes into account the constituent members' party affiliation, stance on issues, and feelings toward the current officeholder. In understanding the political climate of a situation, candidates are able to better collaborate with their potential constituents and work to form policy that benefits all stakeholders.

SEE ALSO: Campaign Strategies; Cross-Pressures, Sociopolitical; Political Culture.

BIBLIOGRAPHY: Rex Nutting, "Political Climate Changing on Global Warming," *Market Watch* (May 2007).

MICHELLE PARILO
HARVARD UNIVERSITY

Political Clubs

TRADITIONAL POLITICAL CLUBS are eroding away from the political landscape, replaced by special interest groups, chat-rooms, and political blogs. Yet, these political entities have a rich history in the American political climate. Political clubs have been replaced with interest groups and Political Action Committees (PACs). They are voluntary organizations traditionally found in urban settings. Because of the population density of large metropolitan areas, individuals congregate with people who share similar interests and goals.

With the compactness of communities and the voluntary involvement of participants, political clubs are usually homogeneous in race and ethnicity. Political clubs traditionally have a physical presence in their communities. They meet in clubhouses, clubrooms, libraries, churches, or campaign headquarters. They are formal in nature, and have constitutions, bylaws, officers, and regular meetings. Many provide social activities for the general public and their members, and they work for the election of public and political leaders.

Political clubs in most cases perform very specific tasks related to their locality. They typically represent a specific political party or group and work to uphold a certain political ideology. Some examples of political clubs are: the New Democratic Club, the Patrick Henry Conservation Club, the Bronx-Pelham Reform Democratic Club, and the Independent Democrats of Flatbush.

One of the initial concerns of those who studied political clubs during the time in which they thrived has become reality: if the social component of the political club vanishes, so, too, will the club. While political clubs are popular on college campuses during elections, for the most part they are vanishing from the political arena. While Robert Putnam argues that social capital and civic engagement are also vanishing from the American landscape, technology and the internet are becoming more important. As political clubs no longer occupy physical spaces in small tight-knit communities, they are far-reaching, across a digital medium, and their impact in the election process cannot be underestimated.

Consider the following quasi-political club, MoveOn.org/Civic Action. MoveOn.org/Civic Action is one of the leading political clubs in the country. Formerly known as MoveOn.org, it is a 501(c)(4) non-profit organization. It primarily focuses on education and advocacy of national issues.

Joining MoveOn.org/Civic Action is MoveOn.org/Political Action, a federal PAC (formerly known as MoveOn.org/PAC). This organization mobilizes people across the country to fight battles in Congress and help elect candidates. Both organizations are entirely funded by individuals. MoveOn.org/Political Action, one of the largest PACs in the country, works to involve the electorate in the democratic process. It has conducted campaigns from dealing with the Supreme Court to working against right-wing political ideology. MoveOn.org/Political Action brings hundreds of thousands of small donors together to elect candidates who will represent the American people.

This organization provides individuals, who normally have little political power, an opportunity to aggregate their contributions with others to gain a greater voice in the political process, and brings people together to take stands on the most important issues facing our country. Through 2004, MoveOn.org/Political Action raised approximately $11 million for 81 candidates from over 300,000 donors. In 2005, MoveOn.org/Political Action grew to 3.3 million members, and 125,000 members contributed $9 million to progressive candidates and campaigns, with an average donation of $45.

While political clubs of the past are quickly fading from their respective communities, they are being replaced by organizations such as MoveOn.org. More sophisticated political clubs are providing greater opportunities for people to engage in participatory democracy.

SEE ALSO: Participatory Democracy; Political Action Committee; Political Socialization; Special Interests; Technology.

BIBLIOGRAPHY. Norman Adler and B.D. Blank, *Political Clubs in New York* (Praeger Press, 1975); Moveon.org, www.moveon.org (cited August 2007); Robert D. Putnam, *Bowling Alone: The Collapse and Revival of American Community* (Simon & Schuster, 2001).

RONALD ERIC MATTHEWS, JR.
MOUNT UNION COLLEGE

Political Culture

POLITICAL CULTURE IS the phrase used to describe and summarize the political knowledge, beliefs, emo-

Some propose that Western affluence since the 1960s has shifted values toward lifestyle concerns and self-expression.

tions, and values of a people. Political cultures emerge as people interpret, communicate, and symbolize their political experiences. Characteristically measured at the individual level, using survey instruments and interviews, political culture is, nonetheless, a collective concept that attempts to describe an entire social entity, such as a nation, a polity, or a minority. Political cultures are reproduced, but also sometimes modified and changed through everyday interactions as people agree and disagree about basic political issues, notably the distribution and uses of valued resources and the making of those rules by which they are to be governed. Political cultures are woven into the daily practices of citizens and assimilated in a commonsense manner.

Political Culture first appeared in Gabriel Almond's 1956 article, "Comparative Political Systems," published in the *Journal of Politics*. Almond and his colleague, Sidney Verba, attempted to map political cultures among the citizens of England, Mexico, Germany, Italy, and the United States in their book, *The Civic Culture* (1965). On the basis of analyses of their survey data, Almond and Verba generated portraits of the distinctive political cultures in each country. They attempted to identify common cultural characteristics that might explain why some political systems were more stable than others. Among their findings was the conclusion that stable democracies are grounded in participative democratic political cultures, exhibiting high levels of both political trust and subjective political competence among the citizenry.

Almond and Verba's work inspired a generation of political scientists who adopted their methodology in the study of political culture throughout the 1960s and 1970s. However, despite its widespread success, the approach also attracted its critics. Prominent among the criticisms were: that in its assumption of the civic perfection of the United States, the political culture approach provided a partial and distorted image of political values, beliefs, and attitudes in other countries; that there were serious methodological flaws inherent in attempting to capture something as deep and holistic as political culture merely through adding up a series of quick responses to questions by individuals; and, that in the increasingly conflict-ridden years of the 1960s and early 1970s, the approach could offer little to explain mass discontent, institutional paralysis, sudden change, or socioeconomic breakdown.

Recent refinements of the concept have adopted a more dynamic reading of political cultures as ongoing events, rather than fixed states of affairs. Citizens appear to be growing in their reflexive capacity to undertake political cultural change through their concerted actions. Political cultural analysts now employ a broader range of methodologies than the survey-based quantitative studies by Almond and Verba. Contemporary approaches to political culture also incorporate conceptualizations of the nature and scope of political life that are broader than those of the earlier generation of scholars. Contemporary cultural theorists have built upon the earlier assumptions of political cultural researchers that political cultures set limits to political structures. While they agree with Almond and Verba that political cultures do shape and condition political institutions and organizations, they also argue that political cultures are reproduced through the historical workings of those very political structures. The ongoing interaction of cultures and structures is so dynamic that it is often difficult to distinguish between them.

While political cultures are slow to change, they do evolve. Patterns of political socialization modify a political culture. Ronald Inglehart's modernization thesis illustrates this process of modification. According to Inglehart, the generation that grew up in the 1960s in the west is the first generation to take for granted material affluence and adequate security. This prompted them to shift in their cultural values from economic security and stability of employment toward lifestyle concerns, such as environmental integrity and gender equity. The impact of this period effect has continued as successive generations have declined in concern for material well-being and security. In the most recent versions of this thesis, Inglehart and his colleagues have generated political cultural data from around the world to show that levels of socioeconomic development condition patterns of cultural values, and in the most developed regions, affluence and security condition a set of postmodern values of self-expression and lifestyle. In a controversial extension of this analysis, Inglehart argues that postmodern values are more likely to underpin support for stable democracy than are the modernist-materialist or traditionalist values found elsewhere in the world.

SEE ALSO: Life-Cycle Effect; Period Effect; Political Ideology and Voting; Political Socialization; Trust in Government.

BIBLIOGRAPHY. Gabriel Almond and Sidney Verba, *The Civic Culture: Political Attitudes and Democracy in Five Nations, An Analytic Study* (Little Brown, 1965); Ronald Inglehart and Christian Welzel, *Modernization, Cultural Change, and Democracy: The Human Development Sequence* (Cambridge University Press, 2005).

PAUL WINGFIELD NESBITT-LARKING, PhD
HURON UNIVERSITY COLLEGE, CANADA

Political Cynicism

POLITICAL CYNICISM IS the belief that the government—whether democratic or not—does not serve the public good, but rather serves the interests of the governing elites. This belief can take different forms, varying in scope and depth. At its most general level, it can be defined as a lack of trust in government. Political cynicism can have profound effects—electoral and otherwise. While political cynicism has recently become more popular, it is not, by any means, a new idea, as it can be traced back to the writings of Plato.

Political cynicism can be either local or universal in scope. While a local cynic believes that his or her own government does not care about its people, a universal cynic holds that all governments are in place for the purpose of furthering the interests of those in power.

Political cynicism also varies in depth. Deep or ardent cynics consistently hold that the government is self-interested and cares nothing for the public; therefore they believe the government does not keep its promises and cannot be trusted. Milder cynics share this lack of trust in government, but are not necessarily critical of the government's motives; rather, they usually point to specific failures of the government or its lack of adequate resources.

Regardless of the truth of political cynicism's claims about government, it is important in its effect on voting behavior, specifically, and its effect on democracy, in general. Since the 1960s, political cynicism in the United States has increased, as more voters have come to see the government as self-interested and untrustworthy. This trend has been blamed for the concurrent decline in voter turnout, as those who are more cynical toward government are naturally less likely to vote. More broadly, this rise in cynicism has aroused concern for the quality and sustainability of American democracy, as deeper political cynics see democratic legitimacy as a myth propagated to deceive the public into consenting to be governed. V.I. Lenin, a notable political cynic, considered an election a chance for the oppressed to choose between oppressors. A politically cynical population thus is not only less likely to vote, but also less accepting of government and its laws.

Despite its recent upsurge in public attention, political cynicism is not a new idea. One of the earliest philosophical statements of it is found in Plato's *Republic*, in which the character Thrasymachus argues that justice is defined by the strong to serve their interests, and that terming it as justice manipulates the weak into obedience.

SEE ALSO: Political Legitimacy and Democracy; Psychological Reasons for Voting and Nonvoting; Trust in Government.

BIBLIOGRAPHY. E.M. Berman, "Dealing with Cynical Citizens," *Public Administration Review* (v.57/2, 1997); V.I. Lenin, "State and Revolution," in J. Somerville and R. Santoni, eds., *Social and Political Philosophy* (Anchor Books, 1963); Stephen Nathanson, *Should We Consent to Be Governed?: A Short Introduction to Political Philosophy* (Wadsworth, 1992); Plato, *The Republic*, trans. by Richard W. Sterling and William C. Scott (Norton, 1985).

BENJAMIN DARR
UNIVERSITY OF IOWA

Political Districts

A GEOGRAPHICAL AREA that encompasses some section of a country's population, a political district can serve many purposes. In addition to electoral constituencies, political districts can define the borders of local government, as well as areas of judicial jurisdiction. The boundaries of electoral districts may or may not be dependent on other political boundaries within a country.

In the United States, the Senate electoral districts are defined directly by state borders. The same borders constrain the boundaries for congressional districts; but within a state, those congressional districts can be drawn in any form at the discretion of the state legislature. In fact, the legislatures sometimes take so much freedom in drawing district boundaries that the boundaries weave through partisan areas in order to maximize vote counts in those areas, a process referred to as gerrymandering. Other political districts in the United States overlap with local government areas, such as counties, cities, townships, and school districts. Wide variation is seen in the way other national legislative electoral districts are drawn in other countries, and whether they are directly related to the local-level constituencies.

Observation of electoral districts across countries shows a variation in size from small, local precincts to large, statewide constituencies. The number of officials elected from a particular constituency varies, based on the electoral system. For example, the United States and the United Kingdom use the plurality system to elect the one candidate who receives the greatest number of votes within the district; this is referred to as a single-member district. These districts tend to be relatively small, given the population of the country, because only one member is elected to the legislature from each district.

By contrast, multi-member districts produce more than one member for the legislature, generally through some form of proportional representation. Most multi-member districts have a magnitude of two to five elected members, but an extreme example of multi-member district size is the Netherlands, where the legislative election is conducted in one nation-wide district with a district magnitude of 150. Proportional representation generally increases the number of constituents represented by a particular district because more members are elected from each district.

There are several advantages in the use of single versus multi-member districts. Single-member districts have a clear relationship between the voters and their representatives, a benefit for constituency service and identity. This relationship translates into accountability in the next electoral cycle, because the single representative can be held responsible in each election. Single-member districts can also ensure geographic representation. However, there are several problems with single-member districts. Minority parties within the district are completely denied representation. This problem is especially acute when the majority party has a strong enough hold on the district that the minority party has no foreseeable chance of winning an election. Single-member districts also tend to promote repeated incumbent re-election, as well as clientelistic politics, more problematic aspects of the single representative accountability issue. Furthermore, the effects of gerrymandering are more likely, as districts must be continually redistricted, generally in a partisan manner.

Multi-member districts are preferred in most European countries, largely because of their ability to translate constituent preferences more accurately to the national legislature. This means the candidates available for election are more diverse than those in single-member systems, and represent a broader cross-section of societal views. Multi-member districts are also more flexible regarding numbers of electors assigned to each district (and to the legislature as a whole), which also means boundaries need not be redrawn after each census.

However, while multi-member districts are supposed to increase the ability for multiple parties to gain political office (this ability depends greatly on the particular voting system that is in place), analysts believe multi-member districts also tend to dilute the relationship between constituents and their elected officials, as well as decrease the ability to hold those representatives accountable. The reverse of the single-member constituencies, the greater the number of elected officials present in a single district, and the more complex the party system in place in the legislature, the more difficult it may be for electors to determine who should be held accountable for unfavorable outcomes.

An increasing number of states have adopted mixed-member electoral systems in an attempt to maximize the benefits and minimize the problems inherent in single- and multi-member districts. Mixed-member electoral systems use larger districts based on regional or national boundaries, and proportional representation to elect one portion of the legislature, and plurality in small, single-member districts to elect the other portion of the legislature. Thus, in mixed-member systems, voters have two votes, one in the national or regional electoral district and one in the local single-member district. While the precise method for seat distribution varies across countries and generally relies on the form of proportional representation that is chosen, the hope is that mixed-member systems, and the use of different levels of electoral districts, will maximize both representation and accountability in these countries.

LOCAL GOVERNMENT

Local government districts generally refer to governmental units below the regional level of a country, which have some jurisdiction over a certain geographical area. In small countries, the districts may instead be the regional governments themselves. While the definition of district varies from country to country, there are two main categories of districts found across the world: those that contain several municipalities, and those that subdivide a municipality.

The most common type of local governmental district is an administrative division of a state or region, which geographically contains several cities, towns, and/or villages. Although there is some variety in the way these areas are defined, they generally follow a pattern similar to that of counties in the United States, with limited jurisdiction within the municipalities themselves. Countries as diverse as Germany, Colombia, Iraq, and Serbia use districts as administrative steps between regions and municipalities. The duties of these divisions vary greatly; throughout most of the United Kingdom, districts provide many of the services that municipalities provide in the United States, such as tax collection and urban planning, while most Canadian districts have little power and are truly geographical in nature.

Another definition of district in local government refers to the subdivision of a municipality into smaller administrative units. For example, in South Korea each large city is divided into smaller districts, which have power equal to that of smaller towns and villages. Similarly, in Belgium, instead of maintaining a centralized government, Antwerp is divided into nine districts, each with an elected council. In the United States and many other countries, special districts with elected members also exist within and across municipalities. The most common district of this type is the school district, from which a board is elected and funding for the local schools is determined. These districts largely overlap municipalities, but also extend into unincorporated areas in order to provide education for students who live in the country. Other special districts include community college districts, park districts, public works or environmental districts, fire protection districts, and mass transit districts, all of which have some form of elected officials and tax collection to support the services they provide, but are technically independent of the municipalities that they overlap.

One additional special district in the United States is the District of Columbia, the federal district where the central government lies. As such, the U.S. Congress has ultimate authority over the district, but most of that authority has been delegated to the municipal level. Some other countries, such as Japan and South Korea, have special cities that are similar to the District of Columbia, insofar as those cities are not under state or regional authority. However, the District of Columbia differs from these cities because of its direct link to the federal government.

JUDICIAL DISTRICTS

In the United States, the federal and state courts also have judicial districts. These are geographical areas where the state or federal government has the power to preside over legal matters that happen within that area or involve residents of that area. Federal districts have the added power to determine matters involving federal questions or problems arising between parties from more than one state judicial district.

Congress defines the boundaries of federal judicial districts, with at least one district in each state. A U.S. attorney and a main administrative office in Washington, D.C., oversee these trial courts of the U.S. federal courts system. (Divisions of the U.S. courts of appeals are not referred to as districts.) These districts have administrative subdivisions, called circuits. Additionally, state legislatures define the state judicial district boundaries, which are generally divided further for administrative purposes.

SEE ALSO: Multiparty System; Plurality Vote; Proportional Representation; Two-Party System; Winner-Take-All System.

BIBLIOGRAPHY. Gary Cox, *Making Votes Count: Strategic Coordination in the World's Electoral Systems* (Cambridge University Press, 2002); M.S. Shugart and M.P. Wattenberg, *Mixed-Member Electoral Systems: The Best of Both Worlds?* (Oxford University Press, 2005); Rein Taagepera and M.S. Shugart, *Seats and Votes: The Effects and Determinants of Electoral Systems* (Yale University Press, 1991).

FAON GRANDINETTI
UNIVERSITY OF ILLINOIS AT URBANA-CHAMPAIGN

Political Editorials

IN ADDITION TO campaign coverage during an election, news media in the United States also publish editorials regarding the campaign and candidates. Many of these editorials comment on a particular campaign event or single issue, or perhaps just one candidate. One of the most prominent political editorials a newspaper may publish in an election period is the political endorsement, in which they offer their recommendation on which candidate, or which side of a ballot issue or amendment should be supported. The process of political endorsement is taken quite seriously by a news organization, and while some newspapers regularly make and publish endorsements, other newspapers do not, either because of non-endorsement policies, or their lack of support for any single candidate. While most voters are not persuaded by a single endorsement, such a recommendation by a trusted source in local or state elections may be influential.

Political endorsements by newspapers have been a tradition in American politics since the early 1800s. Today's process of developing a news media political endorsement is a rigorous one. In state level or local elections, members of the editorial board of a newspaper meet with and interview each major party candidate for the elected seat, and, occasionally, third-party candidates as well. The board then discusses their perceptions and recommendations for endorsement, and often confers with the newspaper publisher as well in its decision. One or two members of the editorial board will draft the endorsement and then revise it based on input from other members.

In presidential elections, the news media in states involved in early primaries, such as New Hampshire, privately interview each of the candidates for the party nomination for president. News media in states with primaries later in the spring election cycle often do not get to meet privately with each of the candidates, but may still meet to review candidate information and reach an endorsement decision.

While this pattern is typical for most news organizations, there are different approaches taken by some newspapers. In newspaper chains such as Scripps Howard, the editors of the individual papers and the company's executives may meet with presidential candidates together; the more than 20 newspapers in that chain then publish the same endorsement. There are also occasions when an editorial board publishes an "unendorsement" editorial if it concludes that none of the candidates running are suitable for the position.

Political endorsements for candidates are usually published a few days prior to Election Day. The greatest amount of information and issues can be considered for an endorsement at such a late stage of the race, and voter interest is also at its peak just prior to Election Day. Endorsements typically recommend to readers who to vote for and reasons why, based on candidate issues as well as character. Once published, the endorsed candidate will often incorporate that endorsement into his or her campaign message in campaign speeches or political advertising.

Many newspapers no longer publish political endorsements. Compared to traditional editorials, they are very time-consuming for editorial boards. Some newspapers offer local endorsements, or ballot issue endorsements rather than candidate endorsements. Even those that do not officially endorse a candidate continue to publish editorials discussing the campaign issues. Newspapers in some U.S. cities have gone so far as to have nonendorsement policies. Such papers may publish editorials discussing the issues in the campaign, but do not endorse candidates for any race.

Some news organizations have ceased endorsements out of public concern about media bias. Endorsements may be seen as a contradiction to a newspaper's objectivity, although newsrooms and editorial departments are separate from each other in news organizations. News organizations have concerns that readers will see an endorsement as a signal for the type of coverage a candidate will receive, and then may question a newspaper's objectivity.

In local or state elections, once an endorsement is made by a news organization, access to the non-endorsed candidate can become more difficult for reporters of that newspaper. Candidates may be concerned about receiving fair coverage and attention from a news organization endorsing their opponents and be less willing to be available for interviews with reporters. Beyond the potential concern of influence between editorial departments and newsrooms, some also raise concerns about the influence between the editorial departments and the advertising sales division of newspapers. Some news organizations have also found that paid advertising sponsored by the candidate not endorsed by the newspaper declined, while others found advertising from the endorsed candidate increased to reinforce the endorsement message. Given that endorsements are published less than one week prior to Election Day for most newspapers, there is little time available for candidates to change their advertisement purchases in response to the political endorsement.

INFLUENCE

At the presidential level, endorsements are unlikely to sway voters in the mix of messages among campaign coverage, political advertising, stump speeches, and online communication. A 2004 study by the Pew Research Center for the People and the Press found that 83 percent of respondents said political endorsements by their local news media made no difference in their voting decisions. At the national level, non-media sources of endorsements, such as those from influential organizations or prominent politicians, were seen as being more influential on voters than news endorsements. Rather than changing voters' minds, political endorsements serve to reinforce voters' decisions. Political endorsements have more impact in a primary election when many candidates are in contention for the nomination and voters may not be able to distinguish well between them than in the general election.

In state and local races, however, media political endorsements offer candidates a way to get their name out to potential voters. In many local races, campaign budgets cannot cover advertising costs, so local media attention, especially favorable attention in an endorsement, can be influential. In the absence of other significant information about a candidate, an endorsement from a local newspaper the readers trust on other editorial issues will be influential. Voters have been known to go so far as to cut out the recommendations from newspapers and bring them into the voting booths with them, especially in states with numerous races and ballot issues in one election.

Some editors believe they have a responsibility to publish an endorsement, regardless of any effect of that endorsement on voters, as they are sharing knowledge with citizens that may be used to make their choice on Election Day. For last-minute or undecided voters, that information and the endorser recommendation may be sufficient to influence a vote choice. In close races, that potential influence might mean the difference between one candidate's victory and another's defeat. The impact of endorsements may also vary from election to election, as well as across different types of voters. While political endorsements from news media may influence some voters, their primary purpose is to stimulate discussion and to define issues for readers. This public discourse about politics and upcoming election decisions is the main purpose and effect of political endorsements, rather than to persuade potential voters.

SEE ALSO: Endorsements in Campaigns; Media, Role in Campaigns; Political Cartoons.

BIBLIOGRAPHY. Pew Research Center for the People and the Press, "Cable and Internet Loom Large in Fragmented Political News Universe," www.people-press.org (January 11, 2004); Kenneth Rystrom, "The Impact of Newspaper Endorsements," *Newspaper Research Journal* (v.7/2, 1986).

JOAN L. CONNERS
RANDOLPH-MACON COLLEGE

Political Elites

POWER CANNOT BE evenly distributed in any but the smallest of political societies. This uneven distribution leads to the creation of elites, or relatively small groups of people who have a disproportionate level of influence and power over political outcomes. In modern society, these groups generally have more money and education than non-elites do. The groups are also relatively immobile; it is very difficult to become a part of the elite if not born into the group. There is a lasting divide between opinions of elites in society: Those who believe elite rule is good for society, because elites are better educated and better able to determine what is best politically; and those who believe political

power should not be concentrated in a small group of people, but that the people as a whole will make the best decisions.

Following from this debate, a main concern of democracy is whether the political elites are actually elite; in other words, whether those with the most power have the knowledge, education, and capabilities necessary to lead society in a positive direction. This line of thought questions if democratically elected officials really represent the best interests of the people, or if they are instead selfish actors interested mainly in self-promotion. This concern is greatest in established democracies where the most highly-educated members of society do not generally run for office.

Historical views of political elites have been diverse. Plato explained in his *Republic* that ordinary residents were not fit to govern, and, thus, political (and philosophical) elites should have complete control over the governing of society. Aristotle's rebuttal in *Politics* calls for political debate to strengthen society, but that debate remains focused on only a small portion of the population, those who are by definition not concerned with the mundane necessities of life. Even some modern political philosophers such as Thomas Hobbes believed that elite rule was the only reasonable way to keep peace in a society. These philosophers promoted elite rule for a variety of reasons, but all agreed that the general population is incapable of the level of interest or intelligence necessary to maintain peaceful and just societies.

The goal of populism was to defend common people against self-promoting elites. However, this idea was not new to political philosophers or to politicians. In his *Discourse on the First Ten Books of Titus Livy*, Niccoló Machiavelli explained that the common citizenry needed to have the power to offset the elites in order to prevent corruption and maintain the functioning of the republic. Of the U.S. founding fathers, Thomas Jefferson, especially, believed that elite rule could take away the people's inalienable rights, and saw the Federalist movement as a road toward a new elite rule in the United States that would parallel the one that remained in England. This continuing mistrust of political elites in the United States is most evident today in low voter turnout caused by voter apathy. The Libertarian Party also represents these anti-elite ideals.

Philosopher Robert Michels developed the "iron law of oligarchy" to explain why even the most democratic states revert to oligarchic rule. He explained that the tendency for all organizations to focus on efficiency, delegation, and bureaucratization lead every society to place power in the hands of a few.

SEE ALSO: Anti-Federalists; Federalist Party; Interest in Politics; Libertarian Party; Populists and Populist Movements.

BIBLIOGRAPHY. Mattei Dogan, ed., *Political Mistrust and the Discrediting of Politicians* (Brill, 2005); Robert Michels, *Political Parties: A Sociological Study of the Oligarchical Tendencies of Modern Democracy* (Free Press, 1915); C.W. Mills, *The Power Elite* (Oxford University Press, 1960).

FAON GRANDINETTI
UNIVERSITY OF ILLINOIS AT URBANA–CHAMPAIGN

Political Ephemera

DURING U.S. PRESIDENTIAL election campaigns, as with other election campaigns, vast amounts of ephemera are generated, with many people keen to complete collections either relating to one specific election, one particular person or party, or a range of material covering a number of elections. Generally, material is divided into paper ephemera, such as leaflets and posters; buttons and badges; and "political cloth," which includes flags and banners. Before the advent of large-scale television advertising, and prior to the introduction of the Federal Campaign Act of 1971, political ephemera was much more common than it is today. One of the major problems that has arisen in connection with political ephemera is that much of it is produced relatively cheaply, making copying easy. For this reason, the U.S. Hobby Protection Act of 1973 requires than any imitation "political items" have to be marked permanently with the date of manufacture, and that any imitation "coins and other numismatic items" are to be marked clearly with the word "copy."

Traditionally, the most common form of election ephemera were leaflets that were given out during election campaigns. Some for the 1840 presidential election, showing William Harrison's log cabin, survive, as do many from the famous 1860 election campaign. Although these leaflets were printed in large numbers, sometimes with hundreds of thousands of copies, and were freely distributed, most were thrown away,

making them rare and therefore collectable. With the introduction of the secret ballot after 1888, some people collected ballot papers, although this is illegal in some jurisdictions.

It was not long before buttons became popular in elections, and this later gave way to badges. These were round, and initially were made with a brass base, the remainder being enameled, with a clip attached. These were later replaced by a printed design on a tin badge. It would either have a picture, or caricature of the candidate, and/or a short slogan, such as "I Like Ike," referring to Dwight D. Eisenhower. Delegates to party conventions or party primaries, members of the political party, or campaign canvassers would wear these to show their allegiance to individual candidates. At the primaries and conventions, many people traditionally wore hats or boaters, again demonstrating allegiance to particular candidates, but more commonly also showing support for "tickets," indicating their support for one person for the presidential nomination, and another for the vice presidential nomination. There were also election posters, some for public billboards, and smaller ones for shop windows, front gardens of homes, and for cars, buses, or the sides of vans.

A metal token, likely from Abraham Lincoln's 1864 re-election campaign; it may have hung from a ribbon.

With the increasing use of the automobile beginning in the middle of the 20th century, bumper stickers became common—their first use recorded in 1945 when some were made by Gill Studios, Kansas. These were self-adhesive stickers affixed to the back, and sometimes the front, or side, of a car. Many of these carried the same message as the badges, but more often contained a phrase that might be support for a candidate, or opposition to another candidate. There would often be an attempt at wit in these bumper stickers. Novelist Jeffrey Archer, in his fictional book *The Prodigal Daughter* (1982), has two characters arguing over a bumper sticker "Au + H2O = 1964" showing support for Barry Goldwater in the 1964 U.S. presidential election. The University of Texas Library maintains a large collection of these bumper stickers.

Other campaign ephemera have been produced, such as music sheets, hand-painted banners, flags, medallions, parasols, lanterns, fans, and even, during the late 19th and early 20th century, gentlemen's white collars. There have also been instances of handkerchiefs, pictorial envelopes, crockery, trays, and telephone directories. There has even been the printing of mock currency, with one celebrating George H.W. Bush's dislike of broccoli. However, there are now severe restrictions on this in the United States. The use of designs incorporating the elephant for the GOP, the Republican Party, and the donkey by the Democrats are also common, with Richard Nixon collecting model elephants; and Newt Gingrich bringing zoo elephants to Washington, D.C., when the Republicans won control of Congress in November 1994. For George W. Bush's inauguration ball, Stetsons and cowboy boots representing Texas were in vogue.

The last area of presidential ephemera involves autographs and signatures of candidates. Most have press offices that issue signed photographs. However, with the number of requests, many of these are produced using auto-pens, whereby a pen is instructed by a computer to make a signature, and in some cases a greeting such as "To John Smith." There are, however, a number of political candidates and civic leaders who choose to personally sign all their signed photographs. With many people collecting autographs of presidents, often specializing in the time the president was in office, some autographs are exceptionally hard to come by, such as those made while William Harrison was in office. The earliest presidents from whom signed photographs exist are Martin Van Buren and John Tyler, with pho-

tographs being available for all presidents from Millard Fillmore onward. Autographed letters by George Washington, Thomas Jefferson, and Abraham Lincoln tend to get the highest prices when offered for sale. Handwritten letters that have been signed by Lyndon B. Johnson and Richard M. Nixon are also extremely valuable, as few have survived.

SEE ALSO: Presidential Elections.

BIBLIOGRAPHY. Herbert Collins, *Thread of History: Americana Recorded on Cloth—1775 to the Present* (Smithsonian Institution, 1979); Charles Hamilton, *The Book of Autographs* (Simon & Schuster, 1978); Maurice Rickards, *Encyclopedia of Ephemera* (British Library, 2000); Ken Sequin, *The Graphic Art of the Enamel Badge* (Thames & Hudson, 1999); F.R. Setchfield, *The Official Badge Collector's Guide from the 1890s to the 1980s* (Harlow, 1986); Edmund Sullivan, *Collecting Political Americana* (Christopher, 1991).

JUSTIN CORFIELD
GEELONG GRAMMAR SCHOOL, AUSTRALIA

Political Ideology and Voting

POLITICAL IDEOLOGIES CAN be understood as worldviews or belief systems that provide individuals with a particular way of understanding their social experience and their place in it. Furthermore, political ideologies help individuals to structure their ideas about how society should be organized. Conservatism, liberalism, communism, socialism, and fascism can be considered classic examples of some of the most influential political ideologies. Additionally, this way of approaching political ideologies poses some important challenges to the contention that this is an era characterized by the "end of political ideologies."

In representative regimes, elections—especially when they can be considered as free and fair—are the crucial moment when citizens choose their government, and key mechanisms for renewing political legitimacy and enforcing political accountability. Governments will try to obtain a new mandate and voters have the opportunity to hold them accountable either by maintaining them in office or replacing them with a new political party or party coalition. Accordingly, studies of voting behavior address why and how people choose to vote for particular parties or candidates. Voting behavior is heavily shaped by the political attitudes, policy preferences, and partisan loyalties of individuals, as well as by the political and institutional context of the electoral process. Finally, when voters take into consideration their own policy preferences and concerns, and approach incumbent and challenger candidates on the basis of an evaluation of their past performance and current promises, the role of electoral processes as effective mechanisms of political legitimacy and accountability is increased.

Political ideologies are of particular interest for the study of voting and voting behavior because they can play a critical role in influencing voters' political attitudes, policy preferences, government assessments, and partisan loyalties, and, therefore, influence not only individual voting behavior, but also which parties win and lose elections. In order to clarify the extent to which this is the case in contemporary democratic regimes, it is necessary to consider some of the most important current voting behavior trends.

With scientific public opinion polling, it was possible to discover that during the 1950s and 1960s—particularly in western European countries and the United States—party identification and voting behavior trends were very stable. This was mainly due to the fact that voting behavior during that time was more the expression of loyalty for a particular political party and less an act of choice. Specifically, in the case of western European countries, voters tended to be strongly identified with a political party that explicitly represented the interests of their class or social group (social cleavages fashioned political attitudes and behavior). However, starting in the late 1960s and early 1970s, most established democracies started to experience a significant process of partisan dealignment (the weakening of the previous close ties among voters, social groups, and political parties). This, in turn, led to higher levels of voting volatility, more frequent unexpected electoral outcomes, more sophisticated individual voting decisions (such as tactical voting and ticket-splitting), and even a considerable number of voters deciding how to vote closer to Election Day.

These declines in party identification and in cleavage politics forced scholars to address what was replacing party and social group loyalties as the main determinants of individual voting behavior. Many of these

societies were able to find a successful resolution to past and long-standing conflicts, which explains, for example, why class identities become less relevant. At the same time, almost all these societies experienced the rise of several relatively new interests, concerns, and issues that became extremely relevant for both formal and informal political participation (such as gender, minority, religious, and ecological issues). This gives the impression of societies fragmented along many lines of competing interests, rather than a few lines of social cleavages. Therefore, some of the previously key long-term predispositions (social and class cleavages and party identification) lost centrality vis-à-vis more short-term influences (such as the state of the economy and other specific issues, party and leader images, and electoral campaigns).

Political ideologies based on class or social group cleavages are no longer among the strongest determinants of party identification and voting behavior in current democratic regimes. Voters in some countries are splitting along new political ideological lines (such as a religious or secular cleavage). There is also evidence that in several countries some traditional political ideological dimensions still have a considerable effect on individual voting preferences (such as egalitarian vs. free-market orientations). Current political ideologies are much less all-encompassing political phenomena, because they are not clearly related to the expectations and demands of a particular or traditional class or social group.

SEE ALSO: Dealignment; Determinants of Vote Choice; Electoral Behavior; Single-Issue Voting; Social Groups and Electoral Behavior; Realignment; Religion and Voting Behavior.

BIBLIOGRAPHY. M.P. Fiorina, *Retrospective Voting in American National Elections* (Yale University Press, 1981); M.N. Franklin, "Voting Behavior," *Encyclopedia of Democracy* (CQ Press, 1995); M.N. Franklin, T.T. Mackie, and Henry Valen, eds., *Electoral Change: Responses to Evolving Social and Attitudinal Structures in Western Countries* (Cambridge University Press, 1992); Lawrence LeDuc, R.G. Niemi and Pippa Norris, eds., *Comparing Democracies 2: New Challenges in the Study of Elections and Voting* (SAGE Publications, 2002); David McLellan, *Ideologies* (Taylor and Francis Group, 1995).

JORGE ARAGÓN
SAINT LOUIS UNIVERSITY

Political Legitimacy and Democracy

THE STABILITY AND functioning of any kind of political regime—including democratic or representative ones—relies on the combination of the capacity of rulers and government officials to use coercion and to develop political legitimacy. Political legitimacy can be described as people's recognition and acceptance of the validity of the rules of their entire political system and the decisions of their rulers. Accordingly, two things can be expected from political systems that have higher levels of political legitimacy. These political systems will be more resilient in periods of crisis, and rulers and authorities will enjoy a fundamental condition needed to formulate and implement policies in an effective manner. They will be able to make decisions and commit resources without needing to obtain approval from the ruled and without resorting to coercion for every decision. The issue of political legitimacy can therefore be considered of utmost importance in politics and political analysis.

Most of the essential features of democratic systems, such as the recognition of all citizens as political equals and the right of citizens to self-rule (mainly through the election of their rulers), make this relationship very complex and significant. Furthermore, given the worldwide legitimacy of democracy as a form of political regime and the spread of representative governments around the world, in contrast with an apparent crisis of democratic legitimacy, it is critical to consider the relationship between democracy and legitimacy.

Democratic legitimacy has frequently been defined as citizen's orientation toward the main principles of the political regime or political system. Democracy, and not a particular administration, needs to be perceived as the best form of government. The main problem with this definition is that it does not recognize that other objects of political legitimacy can be equally significant for the functioning of a democratic regime. A persistently negative perception of the performance of democratic authorities and institutions can erode the legitimacy of democracy. Democratic legitimacy is a multidimensional phenomenon. There are at least five dimensions of political legitimacy: support for the political community; support for the core regime principles, norms, and procedures; assessment of the regime performance; support for the regime institutions; and support for the authorities.

Addressing the sources of political legitimacy or the development of democratic legitimacy poses additional challenges. In a democratic regime with a considerable level of legitimacy, citizens have developed a commitment to democracy that is not dependent on the performance of a particular administration. This is largely the situation in established or consolidated democracies where democracy has been practiced for a long time and because these democratic regimes have demonstrated an important capacity to find solutions to the problems of the society. Thus, the performance of democratic governments is one of the most powerful factors for the development of democratic legitimacy.

Moreover, to avoid a decline in political legitimacy, democratic governments need to convince their citizens that they are receiving something in return for their compliance. This is easier to achieve in established democracies. On the contrary, new democracies frequently face more challenges in their development of legitimacy because they lack a record of past achievements and have serious limitations when formulating and implementing effective public policies. Finally, the economic performance of democratic governments is highly valued by citizens; however, these citizens also expect their democratic governments to provide public order and security, an unbiased and effective rule of law, and free and fair elections.

There is also a tendency to contend that what really matters is the democratic commitment of political elites. However, as several historical and recent cases in both developed and developing countries have shown, the strategic calculations of political elites are often shaped by the distribution of political and regime preferences at the popular level. Hence, the lack of support for democratic legitimacy among ordinary citizens, especially during periods of societal crisis, can be a powerful factor behind a process of democratic regression or democratic breakdown.

Both established and new democracies are suffering a decline in some of the key aspects of democratic legitimacy among ordinary citizens. In established democracies, the erosion of democratic legitimacy seems to be constrained to democratic institutions and authorities. In the case of several new democracies, not only is democratic legitimacy itself a much more volatile phenomenon, but its erosion affects some of the main democratic principles and procedures, and sometimes, the entire democratic regime. One likely reason for this is profound citizen dissatisfaction with the economic and political performance of democratic administrations in recently established democratic regimes. However, what both established and new democracies share, is that despite the democratic assertion that the people are the ultimate source of political authority, citizens are not exercising much of this power. At the same time, because the democratic project has been mostly state-centered, both established and new democracies suffer from the fact that the capacities of their states have diminished in recent decades and that much occurs outside the realm of the state.

SEE ALSO: Political Alienation; Political Culture; Political Ideology and Voting; Popular Sovereignty, Doctrine of; Representative Democracy.

BIBLIOGRAPHY. Margaret Canovan, *The People* (Polity Press, 2005); Bernard Crick, *In Defense of Politics* (University of Chicago Press, 1993); R.J. Dalton, *Democratic Challenges, Democratic Choices: The Erosion of Political Support in Advanced Industrial Democracies* (Oxford University Press, 2004); J.S. Dryzek, *Democracy in Capitalist Times: Ideals, Limits, and Struggles* (Oxford University Press, 1996); David Easton, "A Reassessment of the Concept of Political Support," *British Journal of Political Science* (v.5/4, 1975); S.M. Lipset, *Political Man: The Social Bases of Politics* (Johns Hopkins University Press, 1981); Pippa Norris, ed., *Critical Citizens: Global Support for Democratic Government* (Oxford University Press, 1999); S.J. Pharr and R.D. Putnam, eds., *Disaffected Democracies: What's Troubling the Trilateral Countries?* (Princeton University Press, 2000).

JORGE ARAGÓN
SAINT LOUIS UNIVERSITY

Political Parties in American Elections

POLITICAL PARTIES ARE the foundation for the entire electoral government within American elections. They not only control the mechanisms for nomination into public offices, they also serve as important forces in recruiting members, acquiring resources, setting agendas, and organizing party processes. Edmund Burke, the

English political economist and theorist, defined them as "a body of men united, for promoting by their joint endeavors the national interest, upon some particular principal in which they are all agreed." Noted modern political scientist Frank J. Sorauf defines them as:

> any political organization that elects a state committee and officer of a state committee ... which the party has registered members and that nominated candidates for offices to be decided at general elections.

THE TRIPARTITE SYSTEM

American political parties are said to be part of a "tripod" or "tripartite system." The three components are defined as the "party in the electorate," which is made up of people who attach themselves to a party by voting for its candidates or policies; the "party as an organization," which refers to the formal machinery of the party, including the national and state committees, the regulations or rules of the state or national party, and national and state conventions; and the "party in the government," or those who hold office under the party label.

The party in the electorate is mainly a categorical group, meaning it lacks an active group, has little to no interaction among its members, and does not have an orderly set of relationships. Party loyalty and party identification are the characteristics of the party in the electorate. Its members are those who identify with that party, in other words, those who self-identify either as Democrat or Republican. Those who identify with one party or the other are divided into six groups; strong Democrats, weak Democrats, Independents, weak Republicans, strong Republicans, and other. The party in the electorate provides the party organization with electoral support; they help the party organization acquire loyal voters so that they can focus on other issues of the campaign. This sector of the political party serves as a pool of potential activists for the organization as well as a source of funds for party operation.

The party as an organization speaks on behalf of the party and helps to recruit candidates for public office. Increasingly, the party organization has become a source of resources for campaigns, as well as material of labor and expertise. This component of the political party does much of the party planning. It has an efficient set of relationships that is networked throughout the entire party; this sector is also in charge of mobilizing the party. The party organization speaks on behalf of the party, presides over the party, and is legally accountable for the party's actions. The organization acts as the party middleman: its primary role is coordinating between the other components. It is obedient and dependent on the other sectors of the party. It must also provide endless encouragement and support for the party electorate.

The members of this organization consist mainly of party officials, leaders, members, and activists. This organization acts as the device that holds together the precincts, wards, cities, countries, congressional districts, and state (including state legislature) within the party. The focus of both the private and public parts of this organization is to compete with the opposing party's organization for manpower, knowledge, and money. They also focus on incentives for the men and women who work for the party and their organizations, and renewing loyalty and support for their party's membership.

The party in government increasingly challenges elections, controls the party image and reputation, and takes on the important role of policymaking and governing. It does this without much constraint or even contribution from the party organization. The party in government provides the action behind the promises the party may make to it to its members. The party in government works collectively with the other sectors to elect partisans to office, but its agenda often diverges from that of the more ideological actors in the party as an organization.

Officeholders have their own agenda, and the ability of public officials of the same party to enact the programs of their party is, in the American system, often a convergence of circumstance and convenience rather than a carefully planned coordination of interest. They seek the office, its concrete rewards, and its subtle satisfactions, as well as the opportunity to make public decisions and govern the public. Political scientists believe that this part of the political party is responsible for articulating the policy programs that candidates pledged to enact while running for office, and that this should be their main objective. The party in government is obligated to organize and make decisions for the majority of the public.

Each of the three sectors of a political party plays different roles in both local and state affairs. Locally, they form committees to delegate policy and gain support for their party and candidate. The committee members make up the city, town, village, legislative, county and congressional district committees or they elect delegates who do. The smallest building block is most often the county committee. The county elects several public officials who control the county courthouse and other county legislation, their county committee delegates together form the state committee. These county committees do more than provide a simple party structure; they control the party's activity and its internal development, by stating the party's operational standards. These local county committees are stronger than the state committees because of the loyalty and support that they get from the grassroots level of the communities.

At the state level, parties reveal a different agenda and role in the government. Some states leave the makeup of the committee up to the party, but the main differences lie in the ways the committee members are chosen and the party unit from which they choose them. The activities of this party are often outlined by strict rules. They are in charge of calling and organizing party conventions, drafting party platforms, supervising party spending and campaign funds, selecting a presidential elector for the party, and sending representatives to both the national committees and the national convention. This level of the organization does not get much say in terms of setting actual policy, but the power they wield in terms of making rules for the party and its organizational needs is extensive.

OBJECTIVES

American political parties, on the whole, have two main organizational objectives: candidate recruitment and fundraising. It is important for political parties to have a strong candidate recruitment process; but it is hard for the parties to recruit because of the lack of incentives for their members. The state party organization often takes a part in the recruitment process by generating open party assemblies; the election of party officials during primaries tend to encourage self-recruitment at the expense of party initiates, and, of course, this limits party control. The party creates strong party goals and creates awareness of their party to catch the attention of potential party members.

Several factors make up the casual recruitment system of the party. There have to be common goals, motives, and ideas about who the party would like to recruit. There also have to be incentives for potential members of the party, for example the values of patronage and impact of their employment levels. Lastly, there have to be contacts, opportunities, and incentives for potential candidates.

Money is important because the party needs such resources to campaign for its candidates. It is shown that presidential candidates are allowed by the Federal Election Commission (FEC) to spend up to two cents times the national voting population. House candidates, the national and state parties each may spend $10,000 plus an inflation adjustment, and the national and state parties can each spend $20,000 or two cents times the state's voting population. The party needs cash to pay for the information, skills, and manpower necessary for winning elections. There are roughly five sources for candidate finance: individual contributors, Political Action Committees, political parties, the candidates themselves, and public funding. Individual contributors are the top contributors to campaigns. The candidate or party organization acquires most of its money from individual contributors; there is a distinct plan of action to raise this money. For example, the party is active in personal solicitation, mail solicitation, fundraising dinners, other types of parties or campaign-related trips, and pure patronage.

Political Action Committees (also known as PACs) are groups that are not connected with a specific party or candidate, but that are usually tied to an interest group. These committees focus on raising money to influence the outcome of an election. PACs normally support issues; they spend their money in two main ways: in support of a candidate, and in opposition to the election of a candidate.

While political parties themselves give money to specific candidates, this money is not the only money available, but it is helpful in those districts where a race is close. The next contributors are the candidates themselves, these resources can be helpful except when a voter, believing that a candidate does not need money, is reluctant to contribute to their campaign. Lastly is public funding, which is only available to a presidential nominee, who must follow strict guidelines and limitations with these funds. Money is vital to a political party; there are so many needs and uses for it. Individual contributors on the grassroots level raise most of the party money; these contributors are supporters from the local level.

SEE ALSO: Party Image; Party Platforms; Two-Party System.

BIBLIOGRAPHY. L.J. Sabato and B. Larson, *The Party's Just Begun* (Longman, 2002); F.J. Sorauf, *Party Politics in America* (Little, Brown and Company, 1984); J.K. White and D.M. Shea, *New Party Politics* (Bedford/St. Martin's, 2000).

R. Bruce Anderson
Baker University

Political Socialization

POLITICAL SOCIALIZATION IS the learning and internalization of information, beliefs, values, and sentiments that are available in the polity surrounding the individual. Through the internalization of cultural principles, the individual learns politically relevant knowledge and values and is thereby equipped to reproduce the political culture through subsequent behavior. Because political cultures change, not all socialization results in the complete reproduction of political cultural values. To a greater or lesser extent, socialized agents may amend, modify, reinterpret, or reject the cultural cues to which they are exposed. Those engaged in political socialization may experience role confusion or role ambiguity resulting from their exposure to competing role models.

While political socialization during childhood is primary, it is a process that continues throughout a person's life, and the impact of the social environment is constantly in play. A pattern of political socialization is more likely to endure if it is established and continues in a time of relative political stability. Conversely, times of sociopolitical upheaval may well prompt turbulence in political socialization. The historical record is replete with instances of large groups of people undertaking a deliberate re-evaluation of dominant cultural or ideological forces during a relatively short period of time.

The process of acquisition incorporates many sociopsychological steps. In the context of the immediate family, children learn both though imitation, notably that which is rewarded, and through identification, which is a more developed process of internalizing the ideas and values of significant others. Political learning can be indirect, such as learning a generic sense of trust in authority figures, or a sense of autonomy and creativity in one's own agency. Political learning becomes more direct as the child grows in the more elementary forms of political knowledge. Reproducing political consent is the principal effect of political socialization. Beginning in early childhood, political socialization consists of those natural practices through which people impart knowledge, emotional reaction, values, and opinions about political matters to those within their sphere of influence. Routine patterns of political socialization in liberal democracies encourage political participation and the expectation that citizens mobilize at election time.

Socialization is never entirely a one-way process, and it does not always go smoothly. Although it is concentrated in the early years of a person's life, it is never entirely complete. It is possible to think of the process of socialization as one of induction or even indoctrination, in which the agencies of socialization, such as parents, school, peers, and media, tell the person being socialized what to believe. While agents of socialization can exert a great deal of influence, they are never entirely successful. The person being socialized can always talk back, disagree, refuse the message, or even socialize the socializer. Cultural communication, even between unequals, is mutual.

Although what is learned early in life may not persist, a great deal of the deeper learning of dispositions and values can be regarded as durable, if not entirely continuous. Learning specific information or political reasoning and political choice does emerge later. While early studies in political socialization concentrated on children in the elementary school system, later studies came to regard the high school and young adult years as more critical to political formation. If the young child has learned some basic indirect tools for political involvement, and as an adolescent has acquired some elementary political information and values, it is entry into adulthood that is most relevant to political learning.

If the basic ideological frames thrashed out in early adulthood persist through adulthood, adult events including marriage, parenthood, careers, and property ownership influence the subsequent development of political learning. In the context of a general decline in partisan loyalty across liberal democracies, the transmission of political party identification from generation to generation has weakened, resulting in the enhanced impact of adult political socialization, as manifested in patterns of voter volatility.

While any sociodemographic variable, such as sex, race, class, and religion, influence it, political socialization can be studied in specific age groups in the population. An understanding of age-specific inputs from the broader political culture helps to explain the complexity of political orientations. Major cultural experiences, known as period effects, notably if they are transformative and experienced in the early years, can exert a culture shift of socialization, diminishing older ways.

Cohort effects occur when a major change in political culture socializes only one generation. It remains culturally distinct from its predecessors and successors, and its impact gradually diminishes as its numbers decline through death. Life-cycle effects are patterns of socialization that routinely condition political learning in different ways for different age groups. The impact of political socialization in periods, cohorts, and through life cycles is evident in the level and the nature of political involvement.

SEE ALSO: Efficacy, Political; Period Effect; Political Culture; Psychological Reasons for Voting and Nonvoting; Trust in Government; Voter Knowledge/Ignorance.

BIBLIOGRAPHY. D.O. Sears, Leonie Huddy, and Robert Jervis, eds., *Oxford Handbook of Political Psychology* (Oxford University Press, 2003); Orit Ichilov, ed., *Political Socialization, Citizenship Education, and Democracy* (Teachers College Press, 1990).

PAUL WINGFIELD NESBITT-LARKING, PH.D.
HURON UNIVERSITY COLLEGE

Political Theorists

POLITICAL THEORISTS POWERFULLY shape the fundamentals of American society and its elections. On the importance of theory, many state constitutions warn: "a frequent recurrence to fundamental principles is essential to the security of individual right and the perpetuity of free government." (Washington State Const. Art. I, § 32.) However, because voters and policymakers often do not consider "first principles," changes in the form and content of democratic elections are often controlled by at least two other factors. These factors are unexamined assumptions about democracy and its core values of liberty and equality, as well as the spillover of non-democratic values or principles that are nevertheless applied to democratic elections.

THE ORIGINS OF ELECTIONS

Classical liberalism, which focuses on the individual rights of people, is grounded in a notion of a social contract. In social contract theory, humans are understood as originating within a state of nature, in which no person has natural authority over another because they are all identically equal and free in their natural rights. Thus, a social contract based on some form of consent is logically necessary to overcome the absence of any natural authority to create an artificial governmental authority.

As applied in the American Revolution of 1776, elements of the social contract theories of John Locke, Jean-Jacques Rousseau, and Adam Smith were used by Thomas Jefferson in crafting the Declaration of Independence. Jefferson and the Continental Congress declared it self-evident (and therefore without need to be proven) that everyone is:

> … created equal, that they are endowed by their Creator with certain unalienable Rights, that among these are Life, Liberty and the pursuit of Happiness.—That to secure these rights, Governments are instituted among Men, deriving their just powers from the consent of the governed,—That whenever any Form of Government becomes destructive of these ends, it is the Right of the People to alter or to abolish it, and to institute new Government, laying its foundation on such principles and organizing its powers in such form, as to them shall seem most likely to effect their Safety and Happiness.

Though Jefferson was not Christian but Deist, he shared the belief that people are created in the image of God, and equal before God. By making secular political institutions and religious teachings parallel in their sources of power, he literally shifted God's power from blessing the "divine right" of kings to instead blessing people, the ones with souls, and now the ones with ballots for self-government. Democratic ideas were reinforced in a way that made powerful sense to many. In asserting that entering into a social contract does not do away with natural rights, Jefferson rejected both John Locke and Thomas Hobbes's views to the contrary.

Jefferson also demoted the property-based conceptions of John Locke and Adam Smith by substituting the pursuit of happiness as an inalienable right, instead of "property" as it was in the pre-existing formulation of "life, liberty and property." Thus, property is not strictly inalienable. Though subject to protection under the Constitution, property is alienable with due process. The key to the social contract and overthrowing the "divine right" of ruling kings was the "consent of governed" necessary for legitimate government power. Also from Paragraph 2 of the Declaration of Independence, recognized as inalienable is the right to "alter or abolish" the government providing "new guards for their future security." This is accomplished via peaceful elections, or via the method of 1776.

Consistent with the downfall of the king's divine rights and the elevation of the people, the Declaration further identifies the purpose of governments, and obliges them "to secure these Rights." This turned the government into the servant of the people, not the other way around. The intellectual ferment stoked by Thomas Paine and others turned the world of rights on its head, empowered all individuals, and reoriented power so that people would control all of the branches of government, through elections or on juries.

As a political set of principles, founders hoped the Constitution to be constant for all time and for the entire world. The expression of liberty and equality and popular sovereignty can only fully take place in republics and democracies via elections to transfer power, and via juries with the power to change the status quo in both civil and criminal matters. Such revolutionary transformation could not be implemented in a single revolution.

Thomas Jefferson encouraged other rebellions and the reinvigoration of fundamental revolutionary debate they inspire. His election to the presidency in 1800 is often seen as a second American revolution, vindicating a more democratic vision of America. Later, President Abraham Lincoln expanded the commitment to democracy and famously declared that the dead at Gettysburg sacrificed so that government "of the people, by the people and for the people" shall not perish from the earth. Elections continued throughout the Civil War, despite 620,000 deaths.

Some revolutionary leaders were disappointed in conservatism when the Revolution ended, and some feminist and progressive scholars critique the American Revolution strongly for not fully achieving its ideals. But liberty, equality, and democracy were nevertheless clearly fixed as the nation's highest ideals, and thereafter paid dividends throughout American history by guiding further reforms such as the abolition of slavery.

Hard-fought expansions of voting rights over the centuries can be seen as the result of struggling for what Republican Barbara Jordan said Americans want, "An America as good as its promise." Democracy, originally unpopular because it was understood as only direct democracy without constitutional or inalienable rights, has changed in meaning over time to include those rights. With this shift and universal suffrage, democracy is now nearly universally popular.

THE NATURE OF DEMOCRACY

Democracy contains the Greek words *demos*, meaning "the people," and *kratein*, meaning "to rule." Joined together as *democracy*, the meaning is "rule by the people." A republic, which is often used to describe the United States, is a representative democracy instead of a direct democracy. Montesquieu contrasted democracy with aristocracy, "When the body of the people is possessed of the supreme power, it is called a democracy. When the supreme power is lodged in the hands of a part of the people, it is then an aristocracy." Thus, restrictions on suffrage or voting rights logically create aristocracy. In addition, republics recognize certain inalienable rights no one can change, as well as constitutional rights that are difficult for majorities to change.

Citizens are not at all times the rulers in a democracy. As Montesquieu explained, citizens in a republic or representative democracy alternate between acting as a sovereign (or ruler), and acting as subject (the ruled). Thomas Jefferson noted in the margin of Montesquieu's "The Spirit of Laws" it is "by their votes [that] the people exercise their sovereignty." When not acting as voters, people are subject to the rule of law. The people, then, are both rulers and ruled. Elections are purely procedural mechanisms by which power is transferred from its sole legitimate source (the people) to the government. Provided the election meets basic tests for fairness, it can be said to fairly measure the voice and the will of the people and to establish the consent of the governed.

However, the various procedural rules of the election must be met for this to happen, especially because the elections themselves do not and cannot offer substantive guarantees that the "right" side will win. Elections are a procedure related to obtaining consent for the transfer of power. Low voter turnout in the United States can be seen as refusing to give consent. In exercising their voting liberty, voters are governed by principles of equality such as one person, one vote. If the community is constituted properly overall, that is, if the voters come together on the correct date, in the proper manner, and without proof of improprieties in the casting or counting of votes, or other disqualifying circumstances such as illegal voting or ballot box stuffing, the tabulated results are (after a short period of time in which to contest the election) the final irrevocable will of the people.

Today, new theories such as communitarianism stress the community or group roots and goals of freedom and equality and the community function of elections. Consistent with this general vision of public protection, Thomas Jefferson spoke of the elective franchise as "the ark of our safety." Thomas Paine said the right to vote was the right that protected all other rights, without which a person is rendered a slave.

In summary, elections are the core process for a hoped-for peaceful transfer of power in societies with people free to change their leaders. They delegate their sovereign power to representatives, so that they may enjoy "domestic tranquility" and the "pursuit of happiness" while returning occasionally to governance via elections. While not perfect, democracy's unique strength is continually re-evaluating if the powers that be are the powers that ought to be.

OTHER PURPOSES OF ELECTIONS

Ultimately, the election procedures do not guarantee some objectively wise outcome. If a process were controlled in such a manner as to guarantee that, it would not involve full freedom, as freedom must include mistakes. In addition to social contract theory, other justifications for elections have been offered such as their educational function, the fact that the public knows best if they are being served well or not, and the practical value of elections as a method of intervention in politics when vital interests of citizens are threatened.

These secondary justifications, or even secondary critiques, can neither support nor threaten democracy if the Declaration's principles are correct. Because law is a form of force (it is "the will of the tyrant"), it can only be legitimized via consent of the people, which requires something akin to elections. Law needs the spirit of justice and the recognition of rights for its force to be ennobled. Thus, democracy or republicanism are to be corrected via amendment and/or public education, or, as the conservative Alexander Hamilton put it in Federalist Paper #59, the cure for republican ills was more republicanism.

In early America, it was argued that electors should be sufficiently independent to guarantee the survival of liberty. This justification led in a few colonies to only landowning white males being deemed sufficiently independent of mind. Other colonies allowed most all adult white males to vote. Unjust limitations on suffrage in these early days not only be seen as discrimination, but as the inappropriateness of management of who exercises the sovereign power of the vote, even for allegedly well-intended reasons such as concern about voters' independence or education. Although the founders fully expected suffrage rights for African Americans within their lifetimes, it was much more challenging. The rights of women took even longer to be properly appreciated; their alleged dependence formed one of the improper excuses for denying the ballot.

THE DANGERS OF POWER

Montesquieu, the most quoted writer in the revolutionary era, stated that it has

"... eternally been observed that any man who has power is led to abuse it; he continues until he finds limits. ... So that one cannot abuse power, power must check power by the arrangement of things."

From this and other sources such as the governance systems of the Iroquois nation and Greek city-states, and theorists such as Edmund Burke, came notions of checks and balances, three-branches of government, and awareness of danger in concentrated power. Democratic institutions can also be seen as conflict-solving institutions.

However, contested elections have also throughout history been occasions for intimidation, election fraud, violence, and, often, even death, specifically because of the high stakes and passions of elections, and the conflicts of interest of government officials who run them. In the late 19th century, the secret ballot or Australian ballot was instituted specifically in response to the high incidence of open violence and trouble on election days. The pressures on elections did not disappear, but instead moved locations.

Montesquieu wrote, "The corruption of each government almost always begins with that of its principles" so officials are sworn to uphold the Constitution. Founders believed that if a republic is small, a foreign force destroys it; but if it is large, it is destroyed by an internal vice, so they believed moral political principles neces-

sary to republicanism's survival. Ultimately, democracy is based upon values that are considered a higher priority than the lure of possibly attaining wiser policy by specialized bureaucrats. It was the undemocratic Plato, and not those who inspired 1776, who measured the quality of a government by the wisdom of its "philosopher king."

THE MECHANICS OF ELECTIONS

Primarily via state law, with some federal laws for federal elections, the mechanics of elections are further specified. In recent years, ballots have been non-transparently or secretly counted on new electronic and proprietary voting systems never directly approved by the people or even their representatives. Yet, the means and mechanisms of voting are equally fundamental, as Montesquieu wrote:

it is as important to regulate in a republic, in what manner, by whom, to whom, and concerning what suffrages are to be given, as it is in a monarchy to know who is the prince ... .

Especially since the Help America Vote Act in 2002, the United States has fundamentally shifted methods of suffrage to secret vote counting that takes place on computerized optical scanning machines. Today, citizens debate the loss of citizen control over elections during the most critical phase of counting, together with the implications of claims of private ownership of the heart of democracy. Election results have become inherently debatable as to accuracy, and partisans are both engaged and enraged.

Theories regarding conflicts of interest on the part of government officials counting the votes that determine the government's very power, concerns about the inherent lack of checks and balances, and reminders of the first principles of popular sovereignty are once again contested as applied to elections, with an uncertain, but important end result. Because rights and votes are the source of all power, democracy's elections are contested on every level.

THE FUTURE OF ELECTIONS IN DEMOCRACY

Today, democracy is increasingly recognized as a habit of the heart, or a deeply-rooted set of beliefs and practices that encourage individual civic initiative and an active public. The work of citizen activism is ever necessary to support the public virtues. French political theorist Alexis de Tocqueville was all too aware of American democracy's shortcomings; such as the dangers of equality, the ignorance of public officials, and the tendency toward conformism. Yet he also recognized America's voluntarism had great power. Perhaps more than any other book, the democratic spirit is well described in *Democracy in America*, even though it was written in the 1850s.

During other periods, Jefferson, Lincoln, the Iroquois, Tecumseh, slave rebels, Frederick Douglass, feminists like Susan B. Anthony and Elizabeth Cady Stanton, abolitionists like David Walker and William Lloyd Garrison, and civil rights leaders including Martin Luther King, Jr., have all added to the contested rise of democracy, and often cited the Declaration of Independence and founding principles along the way.

Lincoln picked up the theme that genuine democracy could exist only in a free labor society, yet increasingly the private power of contract regulates lives, as does election management that is outsourced from the control of the people to private corporations. Private law or contract is now the most common system in the world, and the laws created thereby need not be fair or support liberty or equality to be enforceable in courts.

Montesquieu's philosophy that "government should be set up so that no man need be afraid of another" is an echo of the fundamentals of freedom. Freedom is still deemed as it was by the founders, to be perfected in citizenship, but perpetually threatened by corruption, with government figuring paradoxically as the guarantor of freedom, yet also the principal source of corruption because of bribery, the corruptions of power, patronage, factions, wars, established churches, and the promotion of corporate interests.

Surviving republican values are described by Thorsten Veblen in *The Theory of the Leisure Class* and include avoiding luxury and ostentation. Other values include those of John Adams, who identified republicanism as "a government, in which all men, ... the first citizen and the last, are equally subject to the laws," which is known in shorthand as "the rule of law." John Adams also wrote,

> "... public Virtue is the only Foundation of Republics. There must be a positive Passion for the public good, the public Interest, ... or there can be no Republican Government, nor any real Liberty: and this public Passion must be Superiour .... Men must be ... happy to sacrifice ... when they stand in Competition with the Rights of Society."

Echoing today's debates, the more conservative John Adams (along with the more liberal Thomas Jefferson)

worried about corporations and banks, writing that "the Spirit of Commerce ... is incompatible with that purity of Heart, and Greatness of soul which is necessary for an happy Republic." Concentrated private power also offends structural values of direct control by the people and the decentralization and dispersal of power that are part of the federalist-republican structures set forth by James Madison and others at the Constitutional Convention of 1787.

Separate state election authorities are also threatened by calls for uniformity. First Amendment rulings deregulating corporate expenditure of money on "issue ads" institutionalize the distorting effects of wealth on political equality principles such as one-person/one-vote. While the principles and rights that founded the United States still have broad-based public support, the inherent freedom of public debate (or lack of exposure to these ideas) leads to either evolution or devolution in those values. For example, business values of "efficiency" or social values of "trust" are often advanced in connection with the reform of elections and voting. This contrasts with the three branch government, because separation of powers and checks and balances are based on a certain type of inefficiency, redundancy, and distrust, especially of power.

In the final analysis, self-governing peoples have freedom to adjust their values. But procedures must be perceived as fair, or else the system itself neither claims legitimacy nor functions properly. Thus, the procedures must be policed by courts and citizens. Ultimately, the "experiments" in freedom of 1776 and 1789 rest on Greek and Enlightenment ideals of the perfectibility of humans, with education and continual discourse as keys to long-term success. Whether democracy's values remain vibrant or are replaced or supplemented by business or other values rests, in large measure, on the consent of the governed and the public virtue to act as responsible sovereigns. The tools of democracy are the citizens' legacy, but freedom can neither compel their use nor force the march of democracy.

SEE ALSO: Direct Democracy; Election Types; Majority Rule; Popular Sovereignty, Doctrine of; Suffrage; Voting; Voting, Obstacles to; Voting Methods.

BIBLIOGRAPHY. Thom Hartmann, *What Would Jefferson Do?* (Harmony Publishers, 2004); Thomas Jefferson, "Declaration of Independence," www.archives.gov (cited August 2007);

Montesquieu, "Spirit of Laws" [1748] in P.B. Kurland and Ralph Lerner, eds., *The Founders' Constitution* (Chicago University Press, 2000); Washington State Constitution, Article I Declaration of Rights, www.courts.wa.gov (cited August 2007).

PAUL R. LEHTO
ATTORNEY AT LAW

Polling

ON JULY 26, 1824, the United States entered the world of pre-election polling when the *Harrisburg Pennsylvanian* conducted a straw poll in two Delaware cities to determine voter preference in the upcoming presidential election. Presidential straw polls began to proliferate in 1896, as other newspapers and journals attempted to get a lead on the competition by publishing interesting copy that included forecasting the future. The science and art of political polling came into its own in the 1930s and 1940s with the work of George Gallup, Elmo Roper, Archibald Crossley, and Mervin Field. These were the first and most significant efforts to collect national and state random samples, not the crude efforts at straw polling that had been predominant.

A typical poll, conducted face-to-face in sampling points all across the United States, normally took weeks to complete. Pollsters had to hire and train field workers, develop samples with maps and pins, and mail questionnaires and completed interviews. There were no personal computers, and no telephone calls because too many areas and households did not have access to telephony. Results were hardly as timely as today's overnight findings that allow for rapid-fire discussions and talking-head punditry on a just-in-time basis.

Since the 1960s, the number of practitioners has grown exponentially and has followed two separate tracks: the partisan pollsters and the public polls. The partisan pollsters conduct most of their work in private trying to probe the depths of public tastes, values, character, and behavior, all in an attempt to see what drives voter decisions, what can move people, and how candidates can best communicate their story to voters. Some of the best work done is Democrats Peter Hart, Mark Mellman, Doug Schoen, and Marc Penn, along with Republicans such as Richard Wirthlin, Robert Teeter, Frank Luntz, and Neil Newhouse.

Success in molding and shaping political campaigns allows these polling gurus to find enormous success as strategic and communications consultants in the corporate world. The private poll allows the campaign team to develop a blueprint that can define the candidate's image, the strategic blueprint, the overall message, what to emphasize and what to play down, even what clothes to wear, how best to market the candidate's spouse, even what family matters will be a problem. Early benchmark polls can feature as many as 120 questions.

The private pollster can be a philosopher-king if correct. In 1996, Pat Caddell, who launched his career in 1972 when he offered to do polling for George McGovern very cheaply, moved into this higher status when he outlined, through very good post-Watergate polling, the image of the "Georgia peanut farmer who will never tell a lie" for Jimmy Carter in 1975 and 1976. However, Caddell seemed to lose much of his magic when he advised Carter to fire his cabinet and deliver the president's famously disastrous "American malaise" speech in the late 1970s.

Public pollsters use the same skills, but their focus is on sharing their results with media. The major national news media began this process in the 1960s to ensure that candidates were not able to misrepresent, or even create fictional polling results to the general public and possible contributors. Despite occasional complaints about "poll-ution," the constant reporting of many public polls in the news media, Americans want to feel connected to their world and to know where they stand in relative to other citizens. Without public polling, candidates could easily manipulate private findings to show they are doing better than they really are. Thus, the major national news networks and daily newspapers all sponsor political polls, both to determine the public's views on issues, as well as their preferences in upcoming major presidential horse races. Too often, these polls, especially when conducted early in a presidential cycle, are misunderstood as predictive tools when, in reality, they are merely occasional barometric readings to see where the public stands at the moment.

Pre-election political polls have been very accurate over the years. While some critics have wondered about the overall reliability of these polls, this has been due to the sheer (and growing) number of pre-election polls in the public domain and the failure to understand the realities and limitations of polls. Both the occasional observer and the political professionals have been critical of polling, but its popularity remains strong and the key question, however, is why public pre-election polls are very close to the final election outcomes. This is due to effective pollsters, despite some differences in methodologies, following basic principles that work.

SAMPLING

Probability sampling is the basis for all survey research. The basic principle is that a randomly selected, small percentage of a population can represent the attitudes, opinions, or projected behavior of all of the people, if the sample is selected correctly. A good sample will reproduce the characteristics of interest in the population, as closely as possible, such that each sampled unit will represent the characteristics of a known number of units in the population.

Some definitions are necessary to make the notion of a good sample more precise. Target population refers to the complete collection of observations needed for study. Defining the target population is an important and often difficult part of the study. For example, in a political poll, the target population could be all adults eligible to vote, all registered voters, or all persons who voted in the last election. The choice of target population will profoundly affect the statistics that result.

Sampled population is the collection of all possible observation units that might have been chosen in a sample; the population from which the sample was taken. Sampling units are the units actually sampled. They can be individuals, households, or schools, depending on the topic of interest. Sampling frame is the list of the sampling units. The sampling frame might be, for telephone surveys, a list of all residential telephone numbers in the city; for personal interviews, a list all street addresses; for an agricultural survey, a list of all farms or a map of areas containing farms.

In an ideal survey, the sampled population will be identical to the target population, but this ideal is rarely met. In public opinion research, the sampled population is usually smaller than the target population. For instance, public opinion polls are often taken to measure a candidate's chances to win the next election. The target population is persons who will vote in the next election; the sampled population is often persons who can be reached by telephone and say that they are likely to vote in the next election. Few national polls in the United States include Alaska or Hawaii or persons in hospitals, dormitories, or jails; they are not part of the sampling frame or the sampled population.

SAMPLE SIZE AND SAMPLE ERROR

Sample size is usually decided by the precision required, the number of interviewers and telephones available, the cost and timeline of the survey, the size and number of subgroups of interest, and the homogeneity of the population. The actual number of people who need to be interviewed for a given sample is, to some degree, less important than the soundness of the fundamental equal probability of selection principle. There is some gain in sampling accuracy that comes from increasing sample size. However, once the survey sample gets to a size of 500 or more, there are fewer and fewer accuracy gains that come from increasing the sample size. For a nationwide poll, pollsters generally use sample sizes of between 1,000 and 1,500 because they provide accuracy without the increased economic cost of larger and larger samples.

The margin of error given in polls is an expression of sampling error, the error that results from taking one sample instead of examining the whole population. Contrary to popular belief, the error attached to a sample depends on the sample size, not on the size of the population from which the sample is drawn. A simple random sample of 400 has an error of + 5.0 while a simple random sample of 700 has an error of + 4.0. Within a sample size of 1,000 national adults, the results are accurate within a margin of error of plus or minus three percent. Thus, if in a given poll President George W. Bush's approval rating is 38 percent, the margin of error indicates that the true rating is very likely to be between 35 and 41 percent. Apart from sampling errors, errors can also come from selection bias and inaccuracy of responses that are examples of non-sampling errors. These errors cannot be attributed to the sample-to-sample variability. Instead, they may come from bad question wording, poor interviewing, non-response problems, or mistakes in data processing.

QUESTIONNAIRE DESIGN

Questionnaire design is as important as the other technical aspects of data collection such as sampling. If not done properly, question wording and question order may easily become the sources of bias and error, especially in public opinion research. Writing a clear, unbiased question takes great care and discipline, as well as extensive knowledge about public opinion. Understanding how questions have been asked is as vital as the sample size in determining a poll's accuracy. Thus, for example, questions need to offer choice to respondents. Pollsters get a much different response if they simply ask "Do you support…?" or "Do you agree?" than if they pose whether respondents support or oppose, agree or disagree. People who definitely do not know, or are not paying attention often try to give the socially acceptable answer. Questions also need to be symmetrical. When asking which statement best describes a person's true feelings, they must be approximately similar in length. Good question wording tries to associate each position or statement with a value so that pollsters can learn what really moves voters (or will move them under certain circumstances), rather simply trying to determine what they would choose on an obscure issue.

ONLINE POLLING

Nearly all political polling is conducted by telephone, but some polling companies are developing internet-based sampling methods. While access to the internet at home has not reached the same level as those having a telephone, nearly three in four adult Americans and approximately nine in 10 likely voters have such access. For the base of likely voters, the actual representation is very close to universality for internet penetration. With a large and growing number of people, especially those under 35, opting out of landlines for cell phones, telephone surveys may not reach this group as efficiently and accurately. The internet, however, provides a useful alternative. In addition, one of the fastest growing segments of the population on the internet is minorities, a group that is always underrepresented in telephone surveys.

There is increasing evidence that pollsters have arrived at a point where the internet can be used accurately and efficiently for public opinion research. Harris Interactive has been conducting nationwide online political polls since the late 1990s. Zogby Interactive, an offshoot of Zogby International, launched online state polls in 2004. More research and development are required, but results suggest that the internet may overtake the telephone poll in the very near future. Using the internet for polling is not new in the corporate and academic worlds, but critics remain skeptical of its validity for politics. Nonetheless, more pollsters are joining Harris Interactive and Zogby International in search of perfecting a methodology to replace over-dependence on the telephone.

INTERNATIONAL ELECTIONS

The campaign poll has spread to all corners of the world. The polling process itself is evidence of a readiness for democracy. In nations where democratic elections are routine, the partisan pollsters are just as active and involved as they are in the United States. One feature that dominates elections in most other democracies, including France, Canada, Mexico, and Brazil, is a government-mandated embargo for published polling results in the closing the days of an election. In areas like the Middle East, where elections are still not the norm, there has been a dramatic growth in political polling on issues, values, and public needs, indicating a growing readiness by the public to have its voice heard.

POLLING CONTROVERSIES

In recent years, political polling has generated numerous controversies. In the disputed election of 2000, which was ultimately resolved in the U.S. Supreme Court, the problem had less to do with the conduct of the polls and more with how they were reported. The major television networks, led first by NBC News, raced ahead of the competition to declare a victory for Vice President Al Gore over Governor George W. Bush, shortly after seven o'clock on election night. The other networks followed suit, but later all retracted because the projection was based on incomplete data from the state of Florida. Well into the night, Fox News decided to call the election for Bush, though Florida was too close to call. The other networks, clearly preferring to be first over being accurate, locked in step. Another retraction followed.

Unlike in 2000, where the exit polls showed an election too close to call, but the media made the mistake of calling them anyway, the 2002 exit polls were forced to shut down in the mid-afternoon because of faulty data collection. A new consortium and a new exit polling team, although reformed for the 2004 elections, made numerous mistakes. News media subscribers rely on exit poll data that comes in three waves: early afternoon, mid-afternoon, and mid-evening. Historically, the first wave of data has been reliable enough to set the stage for election night coverage. The trends have normally been clear. In 2004, the early wave of data was heavily in favor of Senator John Kerry, especially in battleground states he needed to win. On this basis, even the Bush family was photographed in the late afternoon looking despondent. Kerry lost the state of Ohio despite exit polls showing him winning. Exit polling and political polling in general received a black eye from the experience.

Those who directed the exit polls blamed the fiasco on the dubious charge that conservatives were less willing to be interviewed by pollsters, and that an under-representation of rural precinct sampling points existed. The latter charge had some merit, while the former was preposterous. Others who have reviewed the data and process add that interviewers were not adequately trained and that as many as 30 percent of actual voters voted before Election Day. The traditional Election Day exit intercept interview may not be relevant when a growing number of voters have already voted.

Another major controversy revolves around the concept of "probability sampling"; that is, everyone in the population to be polled must have the same chance of being selected as everyone else. Today, the polling industry reports an average response rate of six to 16 percent. For everyone actually reached by telephone, only one in eight to one in 16 fully competed the interviews; a dramatic shift since the mid-1980s when response rates were around 65 percent. Back then, answering machines were still a novelty, call screening technologies were non-existent, not as many households had two wage earners, and telemarketing was not as pervasive as it is today.

In addition to these problems for the industry, there is now a federal Do Not Call Registry composed of millions who have signed a form stating that they are not to be called by telemarketers. Although survey research is not covered by this prohibition, the very presence of the registry has emboldened people to reject outside calls. Perhaps more ominous for pollsters is the proliferation of cell phones. By early 2007, studies showed that nearly one in three adults 18–29 years old had cell phones, but no landlines.

State laws prohibit pollsters and telemarketers from calling cell-phone numbers and as this number of cell-phone users grows even larger (increasing from 12 percent of 18–24 year olds in 2004), it will mean even greater difficulty for pollsters to obtain an adequate representation of the youngest voters. These factors will require even further creativity by polling practitioners, much the same kind of creativity as existed in the late 1960s and early 1970s when the shift was made from slow face-to-face techniques to telephone polling.

SEE ALSO: Election Verification Exit Poll; Exit Poll; Polling and Election Studies Organizations; Presidential Election of 2000; Zogby, John.

BIBLIOGRAPHY. Gallup Organization, www.gallup.com (cited September 2007); Harris Interactive, www.harris-interactive.com (cited September 2007); Ipsos Group, www.ipsos-na.com (cited September 2007); Zogby International, www.zogby.com (cited September 2007).

JOHN ZOGBY
PRESIDENT & CEO, ZOGBY INTERNATIONAL

Polling and Election Studies Organizations

ALTHOUGH POLITICAL POLLING has been around in one form or another since the early 19th century, scientific polling, the type of polling that is now the standard, has only been in use since the 1930s. Today, there are a number of organizations that determine the attitudes of voters on a variety of issues using similar sampling techniques.

Polling has become a vital tool not only for political campaigning, but also for policy making, because polls help to provide politicians with a direction. For policymakers, knowing the strength of constituents' views will determine how much flexibility they have on an issue. If the public is not closely following an issue, a policymaker will have more freedom to act than when the public is deeply committed. Yet, even for those issues with which the public is concerned, if polling data indicate other issues are more important, then, once again, the policymaker has more flexibility.

For candidates, polling helps direct the right message to the right audience. Good polling allows the candidate to determine his or her own supporters, who there is less need to target unless their support is weak; the opponent's supporters, who it is counterproductive to target; and the undecided, who with a properly directed message, can be influenced. Polling data help to better target messages to undecided voters by determining the issues most important to them, as well as the types of policy options they will respond to.

POLLING HISTORY

Efforts to gauge voters' views on specific candidates and issues have been around since the early 19th century. In 1824, newspapers in Harrisburg, Pennsylvania, and Raleigh, North Carolina, used straw polls to determine the strength of that year's presidential candidates. *The Harrisburg Pennsylvanian* declared Andrew Jackson the winner with 335 votes, John Quincy Adams came in second with 169 votes, followed by Henry Clay with 19, and William H. Crawford with nine. The straw poll itself was unscientific and the process would be constantly refined in future years.

Beginning in 1916, a magazine, *The Literary Digest*, asked voters what they thought of specific candidates. By mailing out ballots to as many as 20 million people, identified from car registrations and phone directories, it was able to correctly determine the outcome of every presidential election for two decades. However, George Gallup began to doubt the validity of the magazine's polling. After examining U.S. voting patterns since 1836, he sent out a small number of forms to a scientifically selected group of people. Based on those results he correctly predicted the outcome of the 1934 congressional elections. He used those results to challenge *The Literary Digest*.

As a way to get newspapers to use his polling data, he guaranteed them he would correctly predict the winner of the 1936 presidential election, and would refund their money if he were wrong. Using their different polling methods *The Literary Digest* predicted that Republican Alf Landon would win with 57 percent of the vote. Gallup concluded that Democrat Franklin Roosevelt would be elected with 54 percent of the vote. Gallup proved to be correct as Roosevelt won with 61 percent of the vote.

It was later determined that *The Literary Digest* was wrong because even though it sent out millions of polls, they were sent to the wrong people. By using phone directories and car registrations, the people who responded were concentrated in the upper and upper-middle class, those most likely to vote Republican, thereby skewing the magazine's results in the Republican's favor. Gallup's smaller, but more scientific, sample included voters from the lower classes as well, and enabled him to get a more complete picture of the election.

While the outcome of the 1936 election resulted in *The Literary Digest* poll disappearing, George Gallup, and his contemporaries Archibald Crossley and Elmo Roper, had their own share of problems. The 1948 presidential election almost marked the end of their endeavors as all three predicted that Republican Thomas C. Dewey would defeat Democrat Harry S. Truman. Consequently, they stopped polling several weeks before the election, and missed seeing third-party voters shifting their support to Truman. They also noted problems with how they developed their samples; the quota method that Gallup originally used created biases because the pollsters selected who they wanted to ask, eliminating randomness. Gallup decided to not only change the way he got his sample in the future, but also to poll much longer.

POLLING ORGANIZATIONS

The corrections made after the 1948 elections not only reinforced the validity of scientific polling, but also led to the proliferation of polling organizations. Some of the best known include the Gallup Organization, founded in 1935 by George Gallup as the American Institute of Public Opinion. It published a weekly newspaper column called "America Speaks," which reported on the public's opinion of various contemporary issues based on Gallup's polling. It began political polling at this time too. It became the Gallup Organization, Inc., in 1958, and in 1988, the Gallup family sold its interests to the Selection Research Institute.

Another of the country's longest running public opinion polls, Harris Interactive's *The Harris Poll* is a weekly column, begun in 1963, that surveys individuals on numerous subjects including politics, foreign affairs, and economic issues. Another polling organization is the Ipsos Group, which, through its Ipsos Public Affairs unit, conducts a variety of public opinion polling in the U.S. and abroad for the Associated Press. With its experienced campaign and political polling personnel it also performs opinion research for a variety of other clients.

The Annenberg Public Policy Center organizes the National Annenberg Election Survey, which examines the qualities the American public wants in a presidential candidate, as well as their views on different issues. The survey done in 2004, which had almost 100,000 respondents, became the largest such academic poll ever conducted.

Known from 1990–95 as the Times Mirror Center for the People and the Press, the Pew Research Center for the People and the Press is now sponsored by The Pew Charitable Trusts. The Center does opinion research on public views of political and public policy issues and is also recognized for its work examining trends in political attitudes. Its work breaks U.S. voters into groups and then looks at the attitudes and values that drive those groups' actions.

METHODOLOGY

In order to be useful, polling data must be impartial and scientifically valid. In order to accomplish this, the different polling organizations use a standard set of polling techniques to ensure as representative a sampling as possible. However, there are still issues involving how questions are asked and how results are weighted that may lead to varying results from different polls.

Because it is too expensive and too time-consuming to ask every person about a particular issue, pollsters sample people from different groups within the larger population and assume that others within that larger population would have answered the same way as those in the sample. Consequently, the first key to conducting a poll is to clearly identify the population being targeted. Once that is done an accurate sample of that population can be selected based on its different characteristics.

After the population has been identified, the size of the sample must also be determined. Polls are generally done with 1,000 people because it has been shown statistically that the margin of sampling error is plus or minus three percent with that sample size. This means that if the same poll were given 100 times, the results of 95 of those polls would have the same results within three percentage points, i.e., the true view of the public lies in a range of three percent above or below the poll numbers. While it is possible to reduce error by asking more people (with 5,000 people, the margin of error would be plus or minus one percent) the additional time and expense for doing so is usually not worth it.

The key to getting such accuracy within such a small sample is randomness. Of the 1,000 people sampled, everyone within the target population must have an equal chance of being selected for the poll. For instance, national polls are now conducted by phone because enough Americans have them that every household has an equally likely chance of being selected. They are conducted one of two ways: registration-based sampling (RBS), in which lists of individuals are compiled and contacted using voter registrations, although this has the disadvantage of missing unlisted phone numbers as well as those who have moved; and random digit dialing (RDD), in which samples of area codes are established and random numbers are used to create the telephone numbers that are called. RDD allows for a broader geographical reach and also captures unlisted numbers. However, using phone numbers does exclude a certain portion of the population: those without landlines because of cost or a commitment to cell phones, as well as hospital patients, college students in dorms, and military personnel on bases, among others. There are also those people who are contacted but decline to participate.

Selecting households at random is not enough. Adults living within the contacted household must still have an equally likely chance of being polled. To accomplish this, interviewers will ask the age, gender, and birthdate of the adults in the home and then ask to speak to one of them in order to preserve the randomness. A further problem is people who are not home. Instead of moving on to the next call, the number will be moved to a recontact list and several more attempts will be made to contact them.

There are a number of other factors other than randomness that can account for the range of survey results. One is the questions themselves. Not only can the wording create a certain attitude in the mind of the person being questioned, but the order that the questions are asked in can subconsciously encourage a person to answer in a specific way in order to maintain consistency with previous answers. By presenting options exactly as they will appear on the ballot or wording questions the same way year after year it is possible to minimize these types of problems.

Weighing the results of the survey can also be problematic. Using U.S. census data, polling organizations have a highly detailed picture of the target population. Having this information makes it possible to adjust polling results to reflect portions of the population that otherwise would have been missed. Weighting frequently involves likely voters, as the biggest problem pollsters have is people who claim they will vote, but then fail to do so. Asking individuals if they voted in previous elections or if they know where their voting location is can be helpful, but narrowing the gap between those likely to vote and those who actually do is still difficult.

Finally, it must be understood that polls are simply a view of public attitudes at a particular point in time. As things move forward and events occur, individual attitudes change. To get an accurate sense of trends ,polls must be conducted over an extended period of time.

SEE ALSO: Campaign Strategies; Candidate Image; Canvassing Voters in Campaigns; Crossley, Archibald; Electoral Behavior; Focus Groups; Gallup, George; Harris, Lou; Internet Polls; Issue Framing; Issue Salience and Voting Behavior; Media Polls; Party Image; Polling; Polls, Pre-Election; Presidential Approval Ratings; Push Polls; Roper, Elmo; Targeting Strategies; Voter Expectations; Zogby, John.

BIBLIOGRAPHY. American Association for Public Opinion Research, "Margin of Sampling Error," 2006–2007, www.aapor.org (cited September 2007); Annenberg Public Policy Center of the University of Pennsylvania, "National Annenberg Election Survey (NAES)," 2006, www.annenbergpublicpolicycenter.org (cited September 2007); F. Christopher Arterton, "Public-Opinion Polling," *Issues of Democracy,* October 2000, usinfo.state.gov (cited September 2007); Rebekah Bowser, "Opinion Polls," *Statistics and Polling Useless? Not To A Social Scientist,* May 2, 1996, www.cwrl.utexas.edu (cited September 2007); Michael D. Cohen, "Public Opinion Polling: Answering Common Criticisms," *Campaigns & Elections* (v.24/9, September 2003); Gallup Organization, "George Gallup 1901–84," 2007, www.gallup.com (cited September 2007); Harris Interactive, "About the Harris Poll," www.harrisinteractive.com (cited September 2007); Ipsos Group, "Ipsos Public Affairs U.S.," 2007, www.ipsos-na.com (cited September 2007); Byung-Kwan Lee, "Public Opinion Poll," *Gallup Poll,* 1999, www.ciadvertising.org (cited September 2007); Frank Newport, Lydia Saad, and David Moore, "How Are Polls Conducted?," *Where America Stands,* (John Wiley & Sons, Inc., 1997); Pew Research Center for the People and the Press, "About the Center," people-press.org (cited September 2007); Ben Wattenberg, David Moore , George Gallup, Jr., and Alec Gallup, "George Gallup and the Scientific Opinion Poll" (Panel Discussion), *FMC Program Segments 1930–1960,* www.pbs.org (cited September 2007); John Zogby, "Answers," *Frequently Asked Questions,* 2007, www.zogby.com (cited September 2007); John Zogby, "Watch the Polls: They Have An Important Message," *About Zogby,* 2007, www.zogby.com (cited September 2007); Cliff Zukin, "Sources of Variation in Published Election Polling: A Primer," October 2004, www.aapor.org (cited September 2007).

JAY B. FISHER
UNIVERSITY OF PITTSBURGH

Polling Place

A POLLING PLACE is the building or facility where voters go to vote on Election Day. In the United States, one polling place is normally assigned for each voting precinct, and voters are directed to a specific polling place based on the location of their residence. In some states, polling places are printed with their street address on voter identification (ID) cards. In the states where only the voter's precinct is printed on the voter ID card, the polling location for each precinct is usually published in newspapers before the election. Voters may locate their precincts and polling locations by asking the local election officials in charge. Many states now provide polling location finder services on the internet, as well.

In most states, the local governing body, such as a county commission, or the local election authority, such as a county board of elections, is in charge of establishing election precinct boundaries within the local electoral unit. Normally, election codes designate that the precinct boundaries be drawn so that the precincts are compact, contiguous, and convenient for voters, with the boundaries not crossing state, county, township, or any electoral district boundaries. Some states define the minimum (typically 50 and up) and/or the maximum (for example, 1,000 in California, and 5,000 in Texas) number of voters to be served by a single polling place.

Typically, the local election authority is in charge of choosing a suitable polling site in each precinct. Preferred facilities are government-owned buildings, such as the city or township hall, but various other public locations are utilized in most states (for example, schools, post offices, banks, or churches). Some states allow the use of mobile homes in parking lots, while others allow the building of a new facility if none are available. Most states prohibit the use of establishments that sell alcoholic beverages.

Change of polling places is normally kept to a minimum in order to avoid Election Day confusion; however, polling places that could not meet the accessibility requirements set by the Americans with Disabilities Act of 1990 may have had to be replaced.

On Election Day, polling places are staffed by election judges, and are kept open between specified hours designated in each state. Federal law requires the display of the national flag in or near every polling place on Election Day (36 U.S.C. 174). Other materials that may be required to be posted at the polling place include: the voter's bill of rights, voting instructions, and sample ballots. Only certain people are permitted at polls during elections. A typical list includes: voters for the purpose of voting, minor children accompanying voters, assistants for voters with disabilities, election officers, election sheriffs, poll watchers, and news media representatives. Some states allow teachers and students into the polls for educational purposes. In most states, observer qualification is limited to those selected by political parties, some even require them to be registered voters in the county, while California allows any interested citizen to observe elections.

In the 19th century, the area surrounding a voting place was a vulgar and chaotic space filled with mobs hired by political parties to physically intimidate supporters of the opposing parties. Only those men who had enough courage to make their way to the voting place could cast a ballot. Since then, restraint clauses have been adopted in most states to ensure order in and around the polls and to secure the secrecy of voting. In Minnesota, no one except an election official or an individual who is waiting to register or to vote is allowed to stand within 100 feet of the entrance to a polling place. New York bans electioneering within a 100-foot radius from the entrance, while Rhode Island prohibits individuals from conducting voter opinion polls (exit polls) within 50 feet of the entrance.

Inside the polling place, the voting area is often separated from the area where election officers are stationed by a guard rail, so that only persons admitted inside can approach within five feet of any voting booth. In Indiana, only six voters may be admitted to the polls at one time, and voters may not converse with any person except election officials. Notwithstanding these regulations, illegal intimidation and harassment of eligible voters outside the polls has been and still is experienced, typically in areas with large ethnic or racial minority populations.

Long lines of waiting voters stretching outside and around polling places were widely reported after the 2000 and 2004 elections, became the symbol of inefficient and problematic administration of elections in the United States. In the background was the shortage of election judges, combined with unfamiliarity, on the side of both voters and election officers, with new, high-tech voting machines.

SEE ALSO: Election Boards; Election Judges; Election Laws, State and Local Elections; Vote by Mail; Voter Turnout; Voter Qualifications; Voting, Obstacles to.

BIBLIOGRAPHY. R.F. Bensel, *The American Ballot Box in the Mid-Nineteenth Century* (Cambridge University Press, 2004).

KAORI SHOJI
COLUMBIA UNIVERSITY

Polls, Pre-Election

PRE-ELECTION POLLING IS a scientific effort to estimate what the entire electorate thinks about candidates and/or issues by asking some members of the electorate (a sample) for their opinions. The presumption is that such a sample, if properly drawn, will yield findings that are representative of the big picture. Pre-election polling has become more important in American politics, because the news media often report on polls (and use such polls to determine the extent of their coverage of campaigns and candidates) and political campaigns rely on their pre-election polling to develop campaign messages and political strategy.

Scientific pre-election polls did not exist until the 1930s. Prior to that time, pre-election polling took the form of non-scientific straw polls. Unlike scientific polling, there is no effort to obtain a representative sample of the larger population in a straw poll. Such straw polls date back to the 1820s. In 1824, a straw poll taken in Wilmington, Pennsylvania, found Andrew Jackson to be the people's choice. Straw polls would become increasingly popular throughout the remainder of the 19th, and first few decades of the 20th, centuries.

In 1888, the term *dark horse* was used for the first time by the *Boston Journal* newspaper to describe a candidate other than one of the leading contenders who emerges to win an election. This would eventually become known as horse race journalism. During the early 1900s, a number of newspapers started conducting straw polls. These included the *New York Herald, Cincinnati Enquirer, Columbus Dispatch, Chicago Tribune, Omaha World Herald,* and *Des Moines Tribune.*

In 1932, George Gallup, an executive with an advertising agency, conducted a public opinion poll for his mother-in-law, who was running as a Democrat for the secretary of state in Iowa. Gallup used techniques he had developed while working on his Ph.D., and his mother-in-law was elected. The following year, Gallup decided to experiment with scientific polling by applying many of the methods of market research to politics. Gallup had examined voting records in the United States dating back to 1836, and sent out questionnaires to a sample of voters in each state. When he came within one percent of the actual results of the 1934 mid-term congressional elections, Gallup decided to establish the American Institute of Public Opinion to poll for the 1936 presidential election. In 1935, the Institute started a syndicated newspaper column, "America Speaks," which reported on how Americans felt about the issues of the day by conducting polls.

As Gallup continued with his experiment, the *Literary Digest,* a general interest magazine that had published the result of their presidential straw polls since 1916 (when they correctly predicted that Woodrow Wilson would be re-elected), carried out their straw poll. This poll, based on responses from more than two million people, predicted that Republican Alf Landon would defeat President Franklin D. Roosevelt in a landslide. The straw poll predicted that Landon would receive 57 percent of the popular vote. The actual result was the complete opposite: Roosevelt carried 46 of the 48 states in the union (Landon won Maine and Vermont). This poll was inaccurate because *Literary Digest* drew its sample by taking names from telephone directories and automobile registration lists. Given that the nation was in the throes of the Great Depression, and that people who could afford cars or phones were very wealthy, the *Literary Digest* sample was not representative of the larger electorate. As a result of this failure, the *Literary Digest* lost credibility and, by 1938, the Funk and Wagnalls Company had sold the magazine to *Time Magazine,* which absorbed it.

At the same time that the *Literary Digest* was erroneously predicting a Landon landslide, Gallup correctly predicted the Roosevelt landslide. Gallup's sample of about 3,000 voters, who were personally interviewed by members of Gallup's staff, was more representative of the larger electorate. Elmo Roper, who ran the Fortune Survey for *Fortune* magazine, and Archibald Crossley reached similar conclusions. Crossley predicted that Roosevelt would receive 61.7 percent (Roosevelt received 62.5 percent). Gallup, Roper, and Crossley's correct predictions of the outcome gave scientific survey research credibility. In his 1940 book, *The Pulse of Democracy,* Gallup predicted that polling would give a voice to the views of the common man. During the 1940s, a number of state polls were established: Joe Belden's Texas Poll (1940); the *Des Moine Register*'s Iowa Poll (1943), the *Minneapolis Tribune*'s Minnesota Poll (1944), and Mervin Field's California Poll (1947).

CHANGES IN METHODOLOGY

In 1948, scientific polling experienced a setback when both major pollsters incorrectly predicted that Thomas E. Dewey would win the election in a landslide. This led to changes in methodology suggested by the Social Science Research Council in 1949. The council concluded that the pollsters had failed because of their reliance on quota sampling (where representative percentages of voters from different groups are surveyed), their failure to accurately assess the behavior of undecided voters (whom they assumed would follow the same patterns of those voters who had already made up their minds), and because they ignored shifts in public opinion caused by campaign developments. The council's report called for pollsters to use probability sampling, regarded as a more accurate sampling technique. In probability sampling, every member of the larger universe has an equal chance of being selected for the survey. Pollsters also started taking surveys closer to Election Day, in order to better track undecided voters and to detect shifts in public opinion.

In 1960, a number of news media outlets commissioned polls for the presidential election. CBS News/ *New York Times,* NBC News/Associated Press, ABC News/Harris Poll, the *Washington Post, Los Angeles Times,* and *Time Magazine* all sponsored polls. This was also the first presidential election where a campaign used a pollster; the Kennedy campaign used polls to plot strategy. While initially at the periphery of campaigns, by the 1970s pollsters were becoming key members of campaign teams. In 1976, Jimmy Carter's pollster, Patrick Caddell, was a key member of Carter's inner circle. Today, campaign pollsters often have a role that extends beyond conducting and interpreting polls, often playing major roles in the development of campaign strategy.

A controversy related to pre-election polling is the push poll. Some political operatives have used push polls to spread negative information about an opponent in the guise of a poll. In push polling, the real intent is not to measure public opinion. Rather, the intent is to deliver a message to the poll's respondents (who are not randomly selected but often part of a voting bloc that may be undecided about a race or supporters of the candidate who is being targeted) that will undermine support for the opposing candidate. The first acknowledged instance of push polling was during the 1996 presidential election cycle, when political operatives working for Senator Robert Dole admitted to having engaged in this tactic against the senator's opponents during the primaries.

METHODOLOGICAL PROBLEMS

While sampling error is one problem of polling, it is by no means the only methodological issue that has been identified. Another potential problem is non-response bias. Because there are individuals who refuse to answer questions or cannot be contacted, the issue of whether the characteristics of those willing to respond are different from those who do not participate may arise. Polls also are impacted by response bias, which occurs when respondents do not respond truthfully.

One of the more common reasons for response bias is that respondents do not want to be perceived as holding unacceptable views. For example, in pre-election polling in the 1989 New York City mayoral election, many white respondents indicated that they planned to vote for David Dinkins, an African American, when they were intending to vote for Rudolph Giuliani, because they did want to be perceived as racist. Other problems are related to the questions asked. These problems include the way questions are phrased, which may influence responses; the way questions are sequenced, which may affect the way subsequent questions are answered; and poorly-worded questions that may lead to incorrect conclusions.

INFLUENCE

An important consequence of pre-election polls is that they can influence voting behavior. The bandwagon effect occurs when polling prompts voters to vote for the candidate who appears to be winning. Sometimes, the opposite phenomenon occurs when voters vote for the underdog out of sympathy. The media also use polls in horse race reporting, which focuses on poll results and ignores issues. An increasing number of news stories in each election cycle report poll results while ignoring campaign issues. This influences their coverage of candidates, as certain candidates are anointed as front-runners, and given substantial coverage, while other candidates are ignored. Although survey research is scientific, it can never be 100 percent accurate. However, given the low cost, relative accuracy, and technological improvements that have made polling easier, pre-election polling has become important to the media and campaigns alike.

SEE ALSO: Bandwagon Effect; Crossley, Archibald; Dark Horse Candidate; Electoral Behavior; Field, Mervin; Gallup, George; Harris, Lou; Horse Race, Media Coverage of; Media Polls; Mitofsky, Warren; Push Polls; Roper, Elmo; Undecided Voters; Zogby, John.

BIBLIOGRAPHY. Herbert Asher, *Polling and the Public: What Every Citizen Should Know* (CQ Press, 1998); Irving Crespi, *Public Opinion, Polls, and Democracy* (Westview Press, 1989); G.H. Gallup and Saul Forbes Rae, *The Pulse of Democracy: The Public Opinion Poll and How It Works* (Simon and Schuster, 1940); P.J. Lavrakas, *Election Polls, the News Media, and Democracy* (Chatham House Publishers, 2000); D.W. Moore, *The Superpollsters: How They Measure and Manipulate Public Opinion In America* (Four Walls, Eight Windows, 1995); Frederick Mosteller, *The Pre-election Polls of 1948* (Social Science Research Council, 1949).

JEFFREY KRAUS
WAGNER COLLEGE

Poll Tax

POLL TAX IS a term most often associated with basing the right to vote on a person's status and location of residence. This was not the original intention of the tax. English in origin, the term *poll* means "head" and it came to be associated with a per-person tax. However, America, as the new nation struggled to establish voter fairness within its Constitution, saw the poll tax erect unnecessary barriers to voter participation. Georgia introduced the poll tax in 1871 to establish which citizens were permitted to vote. Following Georgia's lead, every other former Confederate state invoked a poll tax by 1904. The annual tax of $1–2 was often too much for many poor African-American and white sharecroppers, who usually exchanged their survival for services rendered. It is estimated that the Georgia poll tax reduced overall voter turnout by almost one third, and African-American turnout by about one half.

The Supreme Court ruled in 1937 that the poll tax was a legitimate tool for states to raise revenue. The court went on to explain that the Nineteenth Amendment of the Constitution regulated voting practices, not taxation. Challenges to the poll tax were based on the assertion that the tax was being used to disenfranchise voters, not to collect revenue. Such claims were bolstered by the fact that none of the Confederate states that used the poll tax prosecuted individuals for failure to pay the tax. Furthermore, since the Fifteenth Amendment prohibited outright disenfranchisement on the basis of race or prior enslavement, early challenges to the tax

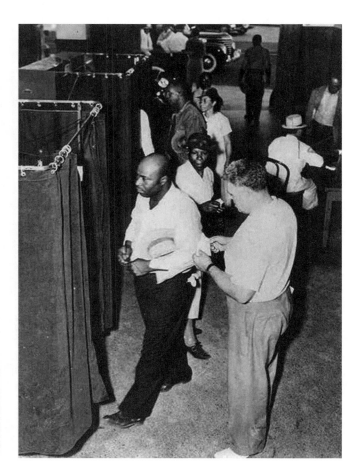

Georgia's former poll tax reduced overall turnout by about one third, and African-American turnout by about one half.

were expected to be successful. These challenges failed, and the poll tax effectively made it difficult for African Americans, Native Americans, and whites of non-British descent to exercise their right to vote.

It took a unique constitutional amendment to prohibit the use of poll taxes in federal elections. The Twenty-Fourth Amendment was introduced in 1962, and ratified in 1964, making the application of poll taxes in federal elections a violation of civil rights. Shortly thereafter, the Voting Rights Act of 1965 prohibited the use of poll taxes in state elections. States persisted in their wish to use poll taxes, but the U.S. Supreme Court in *Harper v. Virginia State Board of Education* (1966) declared poll taxes in any elections to be a violation of the Fourteenth Amendment's equal protection clause.

Even with these legal protections in place, creative politicians in the 21st century are trying to reintroduce a form of poll tax to stamp out voter fraud. Georgia proposed the passage of a voter-identification law in 2005. With this legislation, Georgians who do not have government-issued identification could only vote by securing a special digital identification card from the Department of Motor Vehicles (DMV), $20 for five years, the duration of one federal election cycle. This law replaced the process Georgians used in the past, where one of 17 types of identification showing a person's name and address could be parlayed to gain access to the local voting booth. However, it was revealed that there were no DMV offices in the City of Atlanta, and only 58 of the state's 159 counties had DMV offices, a fact that opponents claim is just another barrier to voter participation. Further debate will be focused on what opponents call an unfair $10 per year poll tax, versus the proponents' claim to stamp out voter fraud.

SEE ALSO: African-American Vote; Election Laws, Federal Elections; Georgia; Nineteenth Amendment; Twenty-Fourth Amendment; Voter Disenfranchisement.

BIBLIOGRAPHY. "Georgia's New Poll Tax," *New York Times* (September 12, 2005); J.M. Kousser, *The Shaping of Southern Politics: Suffrage Restriction and the Establishment of the One-Party South, 1880–1910* (Yale University Press, 1974).

ROBERT KARL KOSLOWSKY
INDEPENDENT SCHOLAR

Popular Sovereignty, Doctrine of

THE DOCTRINE OF popular sovereignty is a political term that implies that the power of the state rests with the people, who have supreme power. In the preamble to the U.S. Constitution, the doctrine is conveyed with the words: "We the people of the United States ... do ordain and establish this Constitution for the United States of America."

The doctrine is also conveyed in three of the seven articles in the Constitution. In Article 1, the representatives to Congress must be "elected by the people." Article 5 allows for amendments to fundamental law by elected officials of the populace. The final Article grants the people the power to appoint their own representatives to the ratification conventions, which required nine of the original 12 states' approval.

SQUATTER SOVEREIGNTY

As it is not identified with the government, but rather with the entire commonwealth, popular sovereignty is fundamentally distinct from territorial sovereignty. A phrase coined by Stephen A. Douglas in 1854 for use by settlers of newly discovered territories, popular sovereignty, also known as squatter sovereignty, is mostly identified with the battle over American slavery. It held that whoever resided on a territory should have ultimate authority. It was applied as an alternative to issuing a federal mandate that would have outlawed slavery, allowing for the decision to be a locally accepted and enforced at the state level.

The Civil War was held off by the Compromise of 1850 and the enactment of the Kansas-Nebraska Act (1854). Paradoxically, Douglas claimed that *Scott v. Sanford* (1857) protected popular sovereignty, although today it is considered to be the worst U.S. Supreme Court decision ever rendered.

Like any political concept or symbol, popular sovereignty has been manipulated for the benefit of private interests. Historically, it was used as a way of appeasing southern, pro-slavery states into not being forced to join the Union. But as a workable compromise, it is viewed largely as a failure because of the devastating violence that ensued in Bleeding Kansas. The idea worked against pro-slavery voters, hurt the reputation of Douglas, divided the Democratic Party, and ultimately helped Abraham Lincoln assume the presidency.

THEORETICAL BASIS

The theoretical basis of the doctrine lies in the dignity and freedom of the individual to secure their fundamental rights. It is not synonymous with democracy, because it can be the founding of other more authoritarian forms of government. As a principle of government, it holds that the origin and power of government resides with the consent of the governed. Its basis is liberal and democratic. It is attached to the social contract theories of Thomas Hobbes, John Locke, and Jean-Jacques Rousseau. It arose largely in response to the Divine Right of Kings doctrine, arguing that the right of the people to govern themselves was decreed by God. Rule is acted out by those who are viewed as having the knowledge needed to govern in the best interest of the people.

Popular sovereignty is one of the most important principles establishing protections against the corruption of those in political power, because any branch or agency derives its authority from the people. Only in a very small community is direct rule by all citizens a likely possibility. All other forms of popular government must rely upon representative systems, unless the demographics of the state are small enough to make direct political involvement possible. Government by the people operates according to majority rule in determining the outcome of elections or passing laws. Abraham Lincoln articulated it best in saying that "government for the people must be government of the people and by the people."

SEE ALSO: Expansionism; Majority Rule; Presidential Election of 1860; Slavery.

BIBLIOGRAPHY. Vernon Bogdanor, *The Blackwell Encyclopedia of Political Institutions* (Basil Blackwell Publishing, 1987); P.H. Collin, *Dictionary of Politics and Government* (Bloomsbury Publishing, 2004); David Miller et al., *The Blackwell Encyclopaedia of Political Thought* (Oxford University Press, 1987); E.S. Morgan, *Inventing the People: The Rise of Popular Sovereignty in England and America* (Norton Publishing, 1988); J.C. Plano et al., *Political Science Dictionary* (Dryden Press, 1973); Geoffrey Roberts and Alistair Edwards, *A New Dictionary of Political Analysis* (Stoughton, 1991); Roger Scruton, *A Dictionary of Political Thought* (Harper and Row, 1982).

MYRON MOSES JACKSON
SOUTHERN ILLINOIS UNIVERSITY

Populists and Populist Movements

THE ORIGINS OF American populism, and the first manifestations of populist movements, can be found in the various regional farmer revolts of the 1880s. The National Farmers Alliance, and other alliance organizations, such as the Southern Alliance and the Colored Farmers Alliance, emerged to lead campaigns against the oppressive economic circumstances that affected American agriculture following the Civil War.

In the midst of a deflationary spiral, crop prices fell steadily, and farmer debt increased at crippling rates. This initial political unrest occurred at a time of rising corporate capitalism and industrial expansion, which concentrated power in the hands of the few. The growth of major special interest political influence on both the Democratic and Republican parties resulted. This was also an era of emergent finance capitalism and banking interests that controlled loans, credit, and the money supply. Control of finance placed major pressures on the economy and on people's livelihoods.

The alliance movement rapidly expanded with the agricultural crisis, and occurred in the midst of America's late-19th-century transformation into a major industrial power. Drawing hundreds of thousands of members, the alliances hoped to forge a political force that could challenge the existing political parties and change the course of American development. They hoped to benefit the producing classes. These advocates opposed capitalist elites, whose concentrated wealth and power controlled the nation's destiny from Wall Street.

The drive toward consolidation led to the formation of the People's Party or Populist Party in the early 1890s, through mergers between the various alliances and groups such as the Knights of Labor. The movement entered the national stage in the election of 1892, when their presidential nominee, James B. Weaver, polled well over one million votes. Agrarian interests and farming needs dominated party goals, which shaped a platform that called for a nationalization of transportation and communication, opposition to the gold standard, unlimited coinage of silver, an expanded currency supply, a flexible system of credit free from the control of national banking interests, and the direct election of senators.

With their growing influence, the populists searched for a merger of their interests with the free silver elements within the Democratic Party. This led to an amalgamation with the Democratic Party in time for the 1896 election. William Jennings Bryan was nominated for the presidency and the Democratic Party adopted many populist policies for its platform. However, Bryan suffered a narrow loss by a margin of 600,000 votes to William McKinley's Republicans. Many populists continued to support the Democrats in 1900, but after this election defeat certain prominent populists, like Thomas E. Watson, chose, in 1904 and 1908, to run for the presidency under the separate Populist Party banner. By 1908, the party had clearly lost its momentum as the Republicans consolidated their political dominance and as America moved toward greater urbanization. Nevertheless, the populist movement did achieve control of a number of governorships and had a degree of congressional success.

An unfortunate offshoot of the populist movement, particularly in the south, was its association with racism as it competed for votes with a racist and segregationist Democratic Party. This tarnished the movement and led to charges that grassroots populism was typified by simple-minded prescriptions for national salvation and an array of racist, nativist, anti-Semitic, and anti-Catholic diatribes. The image that emerged was that of the populist as a demagogic rabble-rouser who exploited people's fears and anxieties for political gain. Huey Long of Louisiana adopted many of these populist approaches during the 1930s, producing a degree of notoriety and success within the south.

Populism was originally seen as a movement in defense of the common citizen who faced unfair advantages because political power rested with elites. These powerful foes were entrenched in the fabric of American life and controlled politics, society, and the economy. By making use of their numbers and a righteous cause, the populists could slay the dragon and fight injustice. Populism saw itself as a mass political movement against banks and the capitalists who resisted populism's simple solutions for a better, fairer America.

The populist movement of the late 19th and early 20th centuries fell outside of mainstream politics and generally relied on a set solution based on an inflationary monetary system that could correct, through a single stroke, the concentration of wealth and power. With its direct action approach, mass participation, fiery lectures, and barnstorming appeals, populism reflected many of the attributes of an evangelical crusade. What the movement lacked was a serious philosophical or ideological core that tied it to either right or left European political traditions. Populism was reformist and not revolutionary, and was clearly egalitarian in its desires. It did animate its supporters and intimidated its opponents with its highly-toned, excitable rhetoric that preached a common reckoning to balance American political life.

Populism played on existing social fears, putting the movement into a narrow and parochial light. At times, populism seemed an irrational, backward-looking force, tied more to the extreme right than to the left, and one that stood against progress. This characteristic led many to see populism as a vulgar negative to be disdained and rejected in the context of modern politics. Yet, recent scholars have given more depth and value to the movement and have placed populism in the broad grouping of reform movements whose ideas influenced debate and even became absorbed at later stages in the political programs of mainstream parties.

Although the Populist Party lost its appeal during the Progressive era, there have been various examples of other types of populism periodically emerging during the 20th century, both in America and abroad. These populist revivals generally appear as third-party challenges to the main political parties and often lack a coherent or sustainable ideological approach. Appeals are variously made to both the left and the right. The most successful third-party challenge was Ross Perot's 1992 presidential campaign, which had populist overtones, and drew 18 percent of the national vote, perhaps splitting the Republicans more than the Democrats.

Populism spans the political spectrum and calls for various aspects of direct democracy. In some local and state arenas, there are campaigns for consumer issues, environmental, and regional concerns. This fragmentation reflects the nature of modern populism as a brand. Its appeal lacks a national focus and is far removed from its origins in agrarian protest. Elements of the religious right and other far-right groups, as well as progressives tired of Washington and the major political parties, still embrace the general populist ideal as a method to challenge the establishment.

SEE ALSO: Farm Issues in Campaigns; People's Party; Perot, Ross; Third Parties.

BIBLIOGRAPHY. Lawrence Goodwyn, *The Populist Moment: A Short History of the Agrarian Revolt in America* (Oxford University Press, 1978); John Lukacs, *Democracy and Populism: Fear and Hatred* (R.R. Donnelley and Sons, 2005); R.C. McMath, *American Populism: A Social History, 1877–1898* (Hill and Wang, 1992); W.T.K. Nugent, *The Tolerant Populists: Kansas Populism and Nativism* (University of Chicago Press, 1963); G.B. Tindall, ed., *A Populist Reader* (Harper and Row Publishers, 1966).

THEODORE W. EVERSOLE, PH.D.
INDEPENDENT SCHOLAR

Presidential Approval Ratings

ONE OF THE most important determinants of who wins a presidential election is citizens' evaluation of the job the president is doing. Presidential approval ratings not only have a significant effect on the electoral prospects of incumbent presidents, but have also been shown to affect the fortunes of successor candidates in open seat presidential elections. Evaluations of the president are also a national factor that contribute to congressional election outcomes. Frequently, public opinion about the president cannot be divorced from evaluations of the president's party.

Approval ratings are derived from public opinion polls. Many polling organizations and media outlets routinely survey the American public regarding their opinions of presidential performance. Approval ratings are different from favorability, which is another type of presidential evaluation. Approval ratings range from general job approval, to approval of specific policy domains such as the economy or foreign policy. Usually, presidential approval ratings refer to the general job approval rating of the president. Approval ratings polls ask whether the respondent approves or disapproves of the job the president is doing. They are essentially an aggregate, or national, phenomenon and are usually reported as survey marginals. The most common reporting of presidential approval ratings comes in the form of the percentage of respondents who approve of the job the president is doing.

The nation's evaluations of the president have strong effects on the outcomes of presidential elections. Approval ratings are a significant predictor of the national popular vote the president can expect to receive when running for re-election. Even in successor elections, in which the incumbent president chooses not to or is ineligible to run, evaluations of the president can have serious implications for the candidate from the president's party. Approval ratings are often used as a predictor of the outcomes of presidential elections in forecasting models. These models typically include very few variables, which indicates the importance of approval ratings as a contributor to election outcomes.

There is some debate over whether presidential approval has the same effect on successor candidates for the presidency as for incumbent presidents. Candidates such as Richard Nixon in 1960, or Al Gore in 2000, are examples of successor candidates who did not capitalize on the approval of their would-be predecessors. However, at least some of the feelings about the outgoing administration are transferred to that party's candidate in the next election. Evaluations of the president can also have an impact on congressional elections. How the public views the president can determine how the public evaluates the party. A more approving public should elect more candidates from the president's party. Presidential approval, or disapproval, is also cited as a cause of the frequent losses suffered by the president's party in midterm elections. After their initial election, presidents usually undergo a brief honeymoon period in which the public approves of the president's work. By the end of the second year, much of this increased support has fallen off and this shift in presidential job approval leads to a loss of seats for the president's party in Congress.

The most common types of policy domain approval occur in economic and foreign policy. Approval in these general domains has been studied consistently since the late 1970s, with the questions appearing in polls almost monthly throughout the 1990s. There are other policy-specific approval questions, but these change with the nature of the times. For example, there were approval ratings of Johnson and Nixon's handling of the Vietnam War. Likewise, approval ratings exist for George W. Bush in his handling of the war in Iraq. As the state of the political world changes, however, these questions become obsolete. The most important question that needs to be answered regarding policy-specific approval ratings is what relationship they have to job approval ratings. It can be very difficult to determine, for example, if individuals base their policy-specific approval on if the gen-

eral approval of the job the president is doing, or if they base their general approval on the president's handling of specific policy domains. It is likely that people engage in both types of evaluations, making causal relationships difficult to establish.

Some researchers have demonstrated that the relationships among economic, foreign policy, and general job approval ratings tend to be equal over time, but these relationships are subject to change. Economic and foreign policy approval has exerted a roughly equal influence over job approval since the Carter administration, until the aftermath of 9/11, when the relationship between foreign policy and job approval became much stronger. The electorate seems to be making more connections between Bush's job performance and his handling of foreign policy than his handling of the economy. With respect to the vote, how the president is performing in all arenas contributes most to election outcomes. It is only since 2001 that foreign policy approval alone has come to define general evaluations of the president.

SEE ALSO: Economy; Election Outcome Forecasting Models; Foreign Policy; Gallup, George; Polling; Polls, Pre-Election.

BIBLIOGRAPHY. J.E. Cohen, "The Polls: Policy Specific Presidential Approval, Part 1," *Presidential Studies Quarterly* (v.32/3, 2005); R.S. Erikson, M.B. MacKuen, and J.A. Stimson, *The Macro Polity* (Cambridge University Press, 2002); Morris Fiorina, *Retrospective Voting in American National Elections* (Yale University Press, 1981); M.B. MacKuen, R.S. Erikson, and J.A. Stimson, "Macropartisanship," *American Political Science Review* (v.83/4, 1989); Michael Nickelsburg and Helmut Norpoth, "Commander-in-Chief or Chief Economist? The President in the Eye of the Public," *Electoral Studies* (v.19/2, 2000).

ANDREW H. SIDMAN
JOHN JAY COLLEGE, CITY UNIVERSITY OF NEW YORK

Presidential Campaign Party Caucuses

THE NOMINATION OF presidential candidates in the United States is based on a system of primaries, caucuses, and conventions that are held in each state. The Democratic and Republican National Committees set rules for these presidential nominating contests that will determine the presidential nominees who will compete in the general election. However, within this framework of rules established by the national parties, the nominating system differs state by state. The state legislature or state political party determines the type of nominating contest a state will hold. Caucuses were the first type of nominating system used in the United States, and although they are no longer the most common since they were replaced by primaries in most states in the 1900s, they are still fiercely advocated in some states and can serve an important purpose for fledgling presidential campaigns.

Caucuses are typically more involved and require a greater commitment of time than a primary election. In a primary, voters simply cast a secret ballot for their preferred candidate. A caucus, however, often involves participants spending several hours discussing issues, candidates, and local party matters, and it requires them to publicly declare their preference for a candidate. Instead of casting ballots, caucus-goers might declare their preference by standing with a group of fellow supporters to be counted. Under Democratic Party rules, a candidate must receive the support of at least 15 percent of the caucus-goers to be considered viable and be awarded a delegate, who will move on to the next tier of the caucus system. The supporters of candidates who are not viable can be courted by other candidate groups. In Iowa in 2004, supporters of Dennis Kucinich might have been persuaded by supporters of Howard Dean to caucus with them so that Dean would achieve viability. It is typical for a state caucus system to begin with precinct caucuses, the first tier of the state's nominating process. Precinct caucuses are followed by county, congressional district, and state conventions at which delegates to the national convention are selected.

Although direct election primaries are the most popular form of determining presidential preference in a state, caucuses are used in about 20 states, and in several states caucuses have a long and proud tradition. Iowa's precinct caucuses might be the most well known because of their prominent position in the calendar, but several states, including Minnesota, Nevada, and North Dakota, have proudly used caucuses for many years. Other states, including Colorado in 2004, have switched to a caucus system because of a lack of state funding to administer a primary. Another group of states uses a caucus system because the state primary violates national party rules. This is the case in Michigan, where the state primary violates the rules for presidential nominations because a voter does not have to state a party preference. In 2004, 18 states and the District of Columbia used a caucus system for at least one major party for determining presidential preference and the allocation of convention delegates.

Caucuses are the oldest method of selecting presidential nominees in the United States. Before political parties played a decisive role in determining nominees, congressional caucuses composed of members of Congress of the same party met to decide the party's nominee. The congressional caucus, in use until 1824 and called King Caucus by its critics, was considered undemocratic because it selected nominees with no input from the public. After Andrew Jackson's narrow loss to John Quincy Adams in 1824, which was aided by Adams's congressional colleagues when no candidate received a majority of the electoral votes and the election was thrown to the House of Representatives, Jackson sought to derail the power of the congressional caucus and give political party activists a role in the selection of nominees. The result was the adoption of party conventions, which were the dominant method of choosing party nominees from the 1830s through the 1900s. The Progressive era ushered in further changes to the nominating process, including a move in many states to direct primaries to involve the largest number of voters. Still, tradition in some states and circumstances in others have kept the caucus system in use.

CRITICISMS

One enduring criticism of using a caucus system for presidential nominations is that they generate low voter turnout. In the 2004 Iowa precinct caucuses, even though the Democratic primary was considered to be very competitive and received considerable attention from candidates and the media, the turnout of registered Democrats was estimated to be less than 10 percent. Critics argue that the time commitment of several hours required to participate in a caucus makes it inconvenient for people who work evenings, parents who require childcare, and people who are generally too busy. Supporters argue that, while turnout is low, those who do turn out are informed voters who have often had direct contact with campaign staff or candidates. Advocates also contend that caucus systems provide an opportunity for lesser-known presidential candidates to gain traction, especially the small caucus states that hold their contests early in the nominating calendar, such as Iowa.

SEE ALSO: Campaigns, Presidential; Conventions, National Nominating Party; Delegates, Convention; Democratic National Committee; Democratic Party; Iowa Caucus; Presidential Primaries; Primaries, State and Local Elections; Republican National Committee; Republican Party.

BIBLIOGRAPHY. J.F. Bibby and B.F. Schaffner, *Politics, Parties, and Elections in America* (Wadsworth, 2007); E.H. Buell, Jr., and W.G. Mayer, eds., *Enduring Controversies in Presidential Nominating Politics* (University of Pittsburgh, 2004); Rhodes Cook, *Race for the Presidency 2004* (CQ Press, 2004) P.S. Herrnson, ed., *Guide to Political Campaigns in America* (CQ Press, 2005); Michael McDonald, "2004 Presidential Primary Turnout Rates," elections.gmu.edu (cited August 2007); The Green Papers, "2004 State by State Summary: 2004 Presidential Primaries, Caucuses, and Conventions," www.thegreenpapers.com (cited August 2007).

ALICIA KOLAR PREVOST
AMERICAN UNIVERSITY

Presidential Debates

PRESIDENTIAL DEBATES HAVE occurred between the two major party candidates during every presidential election year since 1976. Only once in the last 30 years has a third-party candidate participated in the presidential debates with the two major parties. That Independent candidate was Ross Perot in 1992. Additionally, there has been one vice presidential debate every presidential election year since 1984. Presidential debates are important to American democracy, in that they increase issue salience in the minds of American voters and they provide a forum to compare and contrast the major candidates before the presidential election. The debates are also effective campaign strategies that showcase the communication abilities of the presidential candidates, essential for the modern president.

Debates allow for voters who watch to be informed about the candidates' stances on issues that are affect-ing the nation. The debates also allow voters to become better informed about lesser-known candidates, as this forum provides an opportunity for viewers to understand the distinctions between the candidates and compare the candidates communication skills. Voters can become more confident of their vote choice by viewing the debates.

THE FIRST PRESIDENTIAL DEBATES
The first presidential primary debate was May 17, 1948, between two Republican candidates, Thomas Dewey and Harold Stassen. At that time, Thomas Dewey was the governor of New York and Harold Stassen was the former governor of Minnesota. The debate took place in Portland, Oregon, just prior to the Oregon Republican primary, and was approximately one hour long. Dewey and Stassen debated on outlawing the Communist Party in the United States; it was the first presidential debate to cover only one topic. Dewey went on to win the Oregon primary and, eventually, the Republican presidential nomination. Stassen unsuccessfully competed for the Republican nomination eight more times from 1952–92.

Eight years later, on May 21, 1956, the second presidential primary debate occurred between former Illinois governor Adlai Stevenson and U.S. Senator from Tennessee Estes Kefauver. Stevenson and Kefauver were competing for the Democratic presidential nomination. The debate took place in Miami, Florida, shortly before the Florida Democratic presidential primary. The moderator for this debate was Quincy Howe from ABC News. The issues debated included both foreign and domestic policies. After this debate, Stevenson went on to win the Florida primary, and, eventually the Democratic presidential nomination. Kefauver was nominated and ran as Stevenson's running mate for their unsuccessful 1956 presidential bid.

SIGNIFICANT PRESIDENTIAL DEBATES
The most famous presidential debate occurred on September 26, 1960, in Chicago, Illinois, between Vice President Richard Nixon and Massachusetts Senator John F. Kennedy. This was the first national television viewers. The moderator for this debate was Howard K. Smith from CBS News.

The debate included questions on presidential leadership, farm surpluses, the federal debt, teachers' salaries, divided government, and Communism in the United

The first televised presidential debates, between Vice President Richard Nixon and Massachusetts Senator John F. Kennedy, had an audience of over 60 million television viewers in the fall of 1960.

States. It was also the first of the Great Debates between Nixon and Kennedy.

Nixon and Kennedy again debated on October 7, 1960, in Washington, D.C., with Frank McGee from NBC as the moderator; issues ranged from Civil Rights to the Cold War. The third Nixon and Kennedy debate was on October 13, 1960, with Bill Shadel from ABC as the moderator. This debate used an unusual method of a split screen with Nixon in an ABC studio in Los Angeles and Kennedy in an ABC studio in New York. The issues in the debate included Communism, labor unions, economic growth, gold, and American prestige. The final debate between Nixon and Kennedy was on October 21, 1960, in New York City with Quincy Howe from ABC as the moderator. The issues included Cuba, Communism, presidential appointments, nuclear testing, and American prestige. Each of these four debates between Nixon and Kennedy had over 60 million viewers. Kennedy went on to win the presidential election that year, just a few weeks after the last debate. However, 1960–76 there was a hiatus in the

general presidential debates, either because of the federal communication laws requiring equal times for all candidates, and/or because of the refusal of the candidates to debate. Then in 1976, changes in the law and the willingness of the candidates to debate allowed for the general presidential debates to resume.

During the 1976 presidential election, there were three presidential debates between President Gerald Ford and the former governor of Georgia, Jimmy Carter. There was also a vice presidential debate between Kansas Senator Bob Dole (Republican) and Minnesota Senator Walter Mondale (Democrat). The first Ford-Carter debate occurred on September 23, 1976, in Philadelphia, Pennsylvania. The moderator for this debate was Edwin Newman from the *Baltimore Sun*. The issues covered included topics such as unemployment, tax cuts, balanced budgets, the federal deficit, presidential pardons, bureaucratic discretion, the size of the federal government, and divided government. The second debate was on October 6, 1976, in San Francisco, California, with

Pauline Frederick from National Public Radio as the moderator. The issues covered both foreign and defense topics. The third debate was on October 22, 1976, in Williamsburg, Virginia, with Barbara Walters from ABC as the moderator. The topics in this debate included issues such as presidential leadership, conduct during campaigns, Watergate, the environment, urban reconstruction, gun control, and Supreme Court appointments.

The first-ever vice presidential debate occurred on October 15, 1976, between Dole and Mondale in Houston, Texas, with James Hoge from the *Chicago Sun Times* as the moderator. The issues included domestic and foreign policies, such as the economy and defense. Since 1976, formal presidential debates have been held at least twice every four years. Since 1984, one vice-presidential debate has occurred every presidential election year.

The largest recorded viewing audience for a presidential debate in the last 30 years was on October 28, 1980, between President Jimmy Carter and former California governor Ronald Reagan, with approximately 80.6 million viewers. The topics in this debate included defense, racial issues, terrorism, alternative energy sources, and social security. Reagan went on to win the presidential election just one week after this debate. In 1988. the Commission on Presidential Debates assumed control over the sponsorship of the presidential debates, which had been sponsored by the League of Women Voters from 1976–84.

The 1992 presidential debates were the first to include three candidates. The three candidates were President George H.W. Bush, Arkansas Governor Bill Clinton, and businessman Ross Perot. Their first debate was on October 11, 1992, in Saint Louis, Missouri, with Jim Lehrer of Public Television as the moderator. The second debate was on October 15, 1992, in Richmond, Virginia, with Carole Simpson from ABC as the moderator. The third debate occurred on October 19, 1992, in East Lansing, Michigan, with Jim Lehrer again the moderator. The vice presidential debate included Vice President Dan Quayle, Tennessee Senator Al Gore (Clinton's running mate), and retired Admiral James Stockdale (Perot's running mate) on October 13, 1992, with Hal Bruno from ABC as the moderator.

THE PRE-DEBATE DEBATES
Before participating in a presidential debate, both candidates have to agree to every aspect of the debate. This includes, but is not limited to, the format, style, staging, questioners, and length. Each part of the debate is critical because it can provide an advantage or disadvantage to the candidates in front of the voters.

For example, in 1976 Carter's campaign was worried about Ford's height, which was three and a half inches taller than Carter and could provide an advantage for Ford, as voters prefer taller presidents. Ford's campaign, on the other hand, worried about Ford's thinning hair. The compromise was that Carter's podium would be shortened by a couple of inches to make the images of the two candidates more equal in height and the backdrop color would mask Ford's thinning hair.

THE FUTURE OF PRESIDENTIAL DEBATES
Presidential debates have almost become institutionalized in American politics, with the average number of presidential debates increasing over time since 1976. The debates provide valuable information to voters about both the candidates' positions and their communication skills. Television has provided the medium for millions of Americans to view the presidential debates and make more informed decisions when they vote.

As long as the candidates can agree on all parts of the debate beforehand, there seems to be no reason why this practice will not continue well into the future. Candidates have an incentive to agree to debate in some format because they do not want to risk appearing afraid to debate their opponent on television. Vice presidential debates have considerably fewer viewers; however, these debates have occurred regularly since 1984 and are becoming institutionalized as a practice in American elections.

Third-party candidates have fewer chances to join presidential debates, especially if the two major party candidates do not agree to debate them. Unless it becomes in the interest of both parties to have a third-party candidate debate, as it was in 1992 with Ross Perot, it will be very difficult for third-party candidates to become a part of the presidential debates. Even though third parties have debated each other in presidential election years, the fate of third parties in receiving national coverage or joining the two major party candidates in presidential debates is uncertain. It is also unclear how much effect debates have on American elections and voter behavior. However, it is argued that presidential debates increase the information available to the voters, which is an important element for a thriving democracy.

SEE ALSO: Campaign Strategies; Divided Government and Electoral Behavior; Perot, Ross; Presidential Elections; Third Parties.

BIBLIOGRAPHY. Commission on Presidential Debates, www.debates.org (cited August 2007); S.A. Hellweg, Michael Pfau, and S.R. Brydon, *Televised Presidential Debates: Advocacy in Contemporary America* (Praeger Publishers, 1992); Sidney Kraus, *Televised Presidential Debates and Public Policy* (Lawrence Erlbaum Associates, 2000); Alan Schroeder, *Presidential Debates: Forty Years of High-Risk TV* (Columbia University Press, 2000).

JONATHAN DAY
UNIVERSITY OF IOWA

Presidential Election of 1789

THE PRESIDENTIAL ELECTION of 1789 was the first presidential election in the history of the United States. For the first time, Article II of the Constitution was put into action as each state selected presidential and vice presidential electors to cast their votes in the Electoral College. As outlined in the Constitution, the candidate who received the majority of the votes would be sworn in as president, while the candidate receiving the second highest number of electoral votes would be declared vice president.

As these processes and institutions, which to this point had been merely theoretical, were put into practice, it was clear that there were some problems with the system. These would be considered once the new government was in place and changes would be made to ensure a fairer and smoother system of federal elections. Ultimately, George Washington was unanimously selected as the first president of the United States. John Adams, who received the second most electoral votes, 34 compared to Washington's 69, was elected as the first vice president.

SELECTION OF ELECTORS

Electors, responsible for casting votes for president and vice president in the Electoral College, were chosen, as per the Constitution, by each state as determined by its legislature. This meant that there were many different methods by which electors were chosen across the country. These methods included popular election by either the district or on a general ticket, legislative appointment by either joint or contemporaneous vote, or a variety of mixed systems that combined these methods.

Although each state had all of these choices, Congress, in setting an extremely short and strict time restriction on the establishment of the electoral system within each state, seemed to have believed that the states would have chosen their legislatures as the decision makers in determining who would represent the state as presidential and vice presidential electors. As this was not the case in many states, they had to work quickly in order to ensure that their electors were in place before the deadline was reached, as many of the processes involved in their chosen systems of elector selection were lengthy.

Of the 13 states, only 10 cast electoral votes in the 1789 election; North Carolina, Rhode Island, and New York did not participate. North Carolina and Rhode Island had not yet ratified the U.S. Constitution and were, therefore, ineligible to participate in the election. New York was unable to meet the deadline set by the Continental Congress for the appointment of its required number electors, which would have allowed it to cast its votes in the Electoral College.

ELECTORAL PROCESS

This was the first time that Article II of the Constitution, regulating the election of president and vice president of the United States, would be tested. The Article declares that the president and vice president are to be elected in a single election, with electors being allowed to cast two votes, each which must be used on two different candidates. Electors were allowed to use one of their votes on a candidate from their home state, but they were required to use their other vote on a candidate from another state to ensure that they were not merely voting for those candidates who lived within their home states. The candidate who received the majority of the electoral votes became president. The individual who finished second in number of electoral votes was declared vice president. Using this system, there was the potential for a tie between two candidates, in which case it was the House of Representatives' responsibility to make the decision.

Later, the wisdom of this system came into question in the elections of 1796 and 1800. In 1796, it was seen that this system of election could result in two candidates from opposing parties elected to the presidency and the vice presidency. It was potentially difficult to run a government with a divided executive branch. In the 1800 election, it was discovered that if Electoral College members followed their parties' tickets, a tie could result between two candidates who were the most popular on both tickets. Furthermore, the House of Representatives, the entity responsible for remedying such a situation, also had the potential of reaching a stalemate when attempting to make this decision. Therefore in 1804, in an effort to solve this problem, the Twelfth Amendment was ratified, requiring electors to vote once for president and once for vice president in separate elections.

THE ELECTION OF PRESIDENT AND VICE PRESIDENT

When the section of the Constitution establishing the powers of the presidency was written, the delegates had George Washington in mind to fill the position. They created a presidency, although checked by the separation of powers, with a great deal of authority to ensure that the individual in this position would be able to have a fair amount of control in the running of the country and would be able to steer it in the right direction in times of peace and, more importantly, during times of crisis. They believed that George Washington was the only individual at the time who would be able to ensure the continued success of the fledging nation.

As determined by the Continental Congress, the states were to choose their electors and vote by the beginning of February 1789. Therefore, on February 4, 1789, 10 of the 13 states convened their electors. Of the 69 electors who voted, all cast their vote for George Washington for president. However, this decision was not official until these ballots were opened and read before the combined House and Senate by the president of the Senate. Since it was determined that the new government would begin in March 1789, it was at this point that the members of the first Congress were expected to be in New York (which had been chosen as the seat of government) for the official announcement of who would be president and vice president.

However, by March 1789, a quorum had not been convened. It was not until the first week of April that there were enough representatives and senators in the state to open the ballots and count the votes. Finally, it was officially determined that George Washington was president. Nevertheless, the new government would not commence with its new chief executive at this point. Washington had been waiting for word of the decision in his home in Mount Vernon, Virginia, and, because of the poor communication within the United States at the time, it took an entire week for him to get the news that he had been elected and another week for him to arrive in New York for his inauguration. On April 30, 1789, George Washington was sworn in as the first president of the United States.

While the choice for president was obvious, the individual who should fill the vice presidential position was less clear. The fact that there was a possibility of a tie, which would leave it up to the House of Representatives to choose the next president, or the fact that there could be an accident in which the person intended to be vice president was voted into the office of president, worried a number of individuals. This was especially true for Alexander Hamilton, the leader of the Federalists. He was motivated by his great personal dislike of John Adams, who was running against Washington and, out of the field of candidates, was the one most likely to have a chance of causing an upset. Hamilton feared that, by a quirk of fate, Adams would be elected president. Therefore, he worked behind the scenes to ensure that votes for Adams were cast for other candidates who had little chance of winning either position. As a result of Hamilton's efforts, John Adams received the second highest number of electoral votes (34) and was declared the first vice president of the United States.

SEE ALSO: Anti-Federalists; Electoral College; Electors; Federalist Party.

BIBLIOGRAPHY. Gordon DenBoer et al., eds., *The Documentary History of the First Federal Elections 1788–1790* (University of Wisconsin Press, 1989); C.C. Euchner and J.A. Maltese, *Selecting the President: From 1789 to 1996* (CQ Press, 1997); M.J. Heale, *The Presidential Quest: Candidates and Images in American Political Culture, 1787–1852* (Longman Group Ltd., 1982); Reginald Horsman, *The New Republic: The United States of America 1789–1815* (Pearson Education Ltd., 2000); R.P. McCormick, *The Presidential Game: The Origins of American Presidential Politics* (Oxford University Press, 1982); S.M. Milkis and Michael Nelson, *The American Presidency: Origins and Development, 1776–1998* (CQ Press, 1999); A.M. Schlesinger, Jr., and F.L. Israel, eds., *History of*

American Presidential Elections 1789–2001 (Chelsea House Publishers, 2001).

RACHEL YFF
UNIVERSITY OF FLORIDA

Presidential Election of 1792

THE SECOND PRESIDENTIAL election in U.S. history led to the re-election of George Washington and John Adams as president and vice president, respectively. The Electoral College elected President Washington again, giving him all 132 of the electors' votes. John Adams, as in 1789, received the second most votes cast in the Electoral College, a total of 77.

Unlike the presidential election of 1789, political factions played more of a role. This was the first time a partisan battle for political office was seen between factions who desired to see the United States follow very different courses. Washington almost did not run for a second term, but was convinced by James Madison, Alexander Hamilton, and Thomas Jefferson that he was necessary for the country's continued growth and that he was the only man who could unite the warring factions that existed within the country.

SELECTION OF ELECTORS AND ELECTORAL PROCESS

In March 1792, Congress passed the Act of 1792 that established the manner in which electors were chosen for positions in the Electoral College. State legislatures were given the duty of ensuring all electors were appointed by the first Wednesday in December. The states were given 34 days prior to this date to choose these electors by whichever means their state legislatures deemed appropriate. The most popular method of elector selection at this time was appointment. However, some states used different methods to obtain electors to represent their state, such as popular election by district or by a general ticket. Other states used mixed systems that combined different elements of elector selection systems to create their own unique way of appointing their electors.

The act also stated that after the votes were cast, they were to be sent to the president of the Senate, whose responsibility it was to open and read these ballots before a quorum of Congress. The votes were to be read on the second Wednesday in February. This solved the problems faced in the 1789 election with states having to rush to get their electors selected and some not being able to meet the deadline.

This was the first election in U.S. history in which all of the original 13 states, as well as the two new additions, Kentucky and Vermont, were eligible to cast their votes in the Electoral College. In the first presidential election of 1789, North Carolina, Rhode Island, and New York were all unable to have electors cast votes because the first two states had yet to ratify the Constitution, and New York was not able to submit the appropriate number of electors by the deadline set by the Continental Congress.

As in the 1789 presidential election, the process of electing the president and vice president was established in Article II of the Constitution. Each elector was allowed to cast two votes in a single election for president and vice president. One vote was allowed to be cast for a candidate from the elector's home state, however, the other vote had to be cast for an individual who hailed from a different state to ensure favoritism based on a shared home state did not taint the elections. The candidate with the majority of the votes was declared president, while the candidate with the second most votes was declared vice president.

THE BATTLE FOR THE VICE PRESIDENCY

President Washington was even more popular than he was in 1789, both among his loyal supporters and those who opposed what the Federalists stood for. By incorporating the Bill of Rights into the Constitution, President Washington was able to appease many of the Anti-Federalist's concerns. By bringing men of differing beliefs into his administration, for example, Thomas Jefferson, he was able to gain their loyalty to both himself and to the new Constitution. However, despite President Washington's efforts, the country would not remain united in its beliefs, as became clear in the 1792 election. Nevertheless, all of these factions agreed that President George Washington should again be elected to office. Therefore, President Washington was unanimously elected to his second term in office receiving all 132 votes cast in the Electoral College. While it was clear that the position of president was still considered by the voters and the Congress to be only properly filled by one man, the vice president position was considered relatively open. It was in the race to determine who would be vice president that the competitive election was born in the United States.

Vice President Adams faced a much greater contest in his bid for re-election than President Washington. The opposition to Federalist Adams becoming vice president for a second term came from the Democratic-Republicans, with Thomas Jefferson at the helm. This battle for the vice presidency would be only the first step in the ever-widening gulf between the Federalists and Democratic-Republicans. The Federalists believed in a strong national government, which was a leading force with regard to the economy of the country. Their leader, Alexander Hamilton, had been able to create certain measures since the 1789 election as treasury secretary. He was able to create a national bank, institute an excise tax, and arrange for the assumption of debt in both the state and national arenas.

The Democratic-Republicans did not believe that the national government should be as strong as it was; rather, the several states should have a great deal more input in the ruling of the country. These individuals were strongly opposed to Alexander Hamilton's economic measures, believing that the institution of such measures proved what these Democratic-Republicans had always feared, that the U.S. government, would not move toward democracy but would turn in the opposite direction and end up being controlled by a minority of the wealthy who cared little for those they were supposed to serve.

While this was the beginning of division within the government and among its intellectual and political leaders, formal political parties had not yet been created. However, people did place themselves under either Hamiltonian or Jeffersonian ideology depending on their viewpoints. A larger cleavage was beginning in the country.

BIRTH OF THE NOMINATION PROCESS

Although Thomas Jefferson was interested in the vice presidential position, the Democratic-Republicans decided not to put their leader in the running, choosing George Clinton instead to be the Democratic-Republican candidate for vice president. This is considered the first big step toward the nomination process of candidates for political office seen in the 21st century. The choice of George Clinton over Thomas Jefferson was strategic. Jefferson and President Washington were both from the state of Virginia.

As it was clear, if given a choice, electors would vote for President Washington over Jefferson, and because of the restriction of only being able to vote for one candidate from one's home state, Jefferson would lose out on a large block of support. Therefore, the choice of George Clinton was made. However, the Democratic-Republicans were not to change the administration established in 1789 as President Washington received all 132 electoral votes, John Adams received 77, and Clinton received only 50.

USE OF THE MEDIA

This election was the first to show the power of the printed word. Newspapers, when they became involved in the campaign, supporting either the Hamiltonian or Jeffersonian ideology. Newspapers were rapidly being established across the country, based on certain ideologies. Their articles, editorials, and readership reflected these choices. Established newspapers were used to attack their ideological opposition and to write supportive articles about the particular faction that represented their beliefs. Both the *National Gazette* and the *Gazette of the United States* played major roles in the dissemination of Hamiltonian and Jeffersonian ideology.

SEE ALSO: Anti-Federalists; Democratic-Republican Party; Electoral College; Electors; Federalist Party; Media, Role in Campaigns; Presidential Election of 1789.

BIBLIOGRAPHY. Gordon DenBoer et al., eds., *The Documentary History of the First Federal Elections 1788–1790* (University of Wisconsin Press, 1989); C.C. Euchner and John Anthony Maltese, *Selecting the President: From 1789 to 1996* (CQ Press, 1997); M.J. Heale, *The Presidential Quest: Candidates and Images in American Political Culture, 1787–1852* (Longman Group Ltd., 1982); Reginald Horsman, *The New Republic: The United States of America 1789–1815* (Pearson Education Ltd., 2000); R.P. McCormick, *The Presidential Game: The Origins of American Presidential Politics* (Oxford University Press, 1982); S.M. Milkis and Michael Nelson, *The American Presidency: Origins and Development, 1776–1998* (CQ Press, 1999); A.M. Schlesinger, Jr., and F.L. Israel, eds., *History of American Presidential Elections 1789–2001* (Chelsea House Publishers, 2001).

RACHEL YFF
UNIVERSITY OF FLORIDA

Presidential Election of 1796

IN 1796, THE United States would conduct, for the first time in its brief history, a contested presidential election involving candidates from two political parties. George Washington, elected without opposition in 1788 and 1792, announced his retirement on September 17, 1796, beginning what both John and Abigail Adams knew would be a bitter and contentious campaign and election. Unlike modern campaigns, both candidates remained on the sidelines and at their private residences, John Adams at Peacefield and Thomas Jefferson at Monticello. Unlike modern presidential campaigns, proxies conducted 18th and 19th century presidential campaigns while the presidential candidates remained on the sidelines throughout the campaign.

Adams, like Washington, viewed political parties with suspicion and thought their rise was a detriment to the political system of the United States. Adams reluctantly associated with the Federalist Party; the party that most approximated his own political views, after the existence of political parties became a foregone conclusion. Early in 1796, his letters home indicate indecisiveness on running for president; and whether he should seek one or two terms in office. Thomas Jefferson, upon retiring from the Washington cabinet, had stated that his public life was over; he did not wish to seek elective office. However, early in 1796, Jefferson indicated to his political ally, James Madison, that he might consider seeking the presidency.

The Federalist ticket was comprised of Adams from Massachusetts for president and Thomas Pinckney of South Carolina as the vice president; while the Democratic-Republican ticket was Jefferson of Virginia for president and Aaron Burr of New York for vice president. However, a victory by the presidential nominee did not assure victory by the vice presidential nominee of the same party. The vice president would be the candidate, whether the presidential or vice presidential nominee from either party, who came in second place in the number of Electoral College votes.

It was assumed by the fall of 1796 that Adams had 49 of the 70 needed electoral votes safely in his pocket, while Jefferson was credited with 42 electoral votes. The tickets for both parties achieved a regional balance. This balance was considered a necessity as it was assumed that the New England states would support Adams and the south would support Jefferson, making the votes of the middle states the decisive factor in determining the winner of the election.

The Electoral College consisted of 136 electors in 16 states; in nine of the 16 states the electors were chosen by the state legislatures. Adams and Jefferson were both active in the Revolutionary Era serving in the Continental Congress, on the committee that drafted the Declaration of Independence, and representing the United States during the Revolutionary War in France. Later, they both served in the cabinet of George Washington: Adams as the nation's first vice president, and Jefferson as the first secretary of state. While holding different political views, they considered each other friends. The rise of political parties and the viciousness of the elections in 1796 and 1800 would bring an end to their friendship, until it was resurrected years later in retirement at the urging of their mutual friend Benjamin Rusk.

The Republican press pronounced Adams a shameless monarchist who, if elected, would introduce the principle of hereditary succession in anticipation of being succeeded by his eldest son, John Quincy Adams, (later to be elected the sixth president in 1824). To reinforce his alleged preference for the monarchy and to poke fun at his stature, the *Aurora* newspaper referred to Adams as His Rotundity and declared him unfit for the position. The same Republican papers referred to Jefferson as a friend of the people and that hereditary succession was not an issue with Jefferson as he had no sons to position. The Federalist papers returned the fire by calling Jefferson an atheist and a coward for fleeing Monticello in advance of a British cavalry unit in 1781, while reminding voters of Adams' service during the American Revolution and his ability to follow Washington.

The viciousness of the attacks reached such a crescendo that even Washington was attacked. The revolutionary firebrand, Thomas Paine, wrote a letter from Paris calling Washington a hypocrite and impostor for his support of the Jay Treaty published in the *Aurora*. Paine, and many Americans, were disappointed with the Jay Treaty of 1795 that failed to achieve a British guarantee to stop seizing American seamen and opened only the British ports in the West Indies to American ships. Paine, an avid supporter of the French Revolution, had campaigned for another war against Great Britain. Adams, knowing that America was in no position to fight another war with Britain, stood with Washington

The 1789 election results showed sectional divide: John Adams won nearly every northern elector, but only two from the South.

in supporting the treaty as it moved through Congress in the spring of 1796.

Into this swirling political caldron came Alexander Hamilton, the former secretary of the treasury and a member of the Federalist Party. Although Hamilton had left the cabinet and returned to private life in New York, he viewed himself as the power behind the throne. Behind the scenes, Hamilton urged the electors to support Thomas Pinckney. This gambit was conducted to keep Jefferson from being elected John Adams' vice president. This situation was possible because each elector was to vote for two persons for the presidency. However, it was strongly suspected that Hamilton preferred Pinckney's election as president. A less astute and less powerful President Pinckney could be maneuvered and controlled by Hamilton. Elbridge Gerry, a presidential elector for Massachusetts and an old friend and political ally of John Adams, confirmed the rumors regarding Hamilton's political maneuverings later in 1796. John and Abigail Adams would never again trust or respect Alexander Hamilton. Abigail, in private moments,

referred to Hamilton as Cassius and John said Hamilton was the worst hypocrite in the United States.

While the final electoral count would not be announced until February, Adams left Peacefield for Philadelphia in late November, fully expecting to lose to Jefferson. This expectation began to change in December when the rumor circulated throughout Congress that Adams had been elected president with Thomas Jefferson as vice president. The rumor seemed to be confirmed by positive talk of an Adams presidency by Republican members of Congress and by the *Aurora*.

Jefferson received word of Adams's probable election from James Madison, who urged Jefferson to accept the vice presidency for the good of the country. Jefferson expressed neither surprise nor dismay over the election of Adams, and saw logic to it as Adams had been his senior throughout his political life. A few days after Christmas, Jefferson drafted a letter to Adams congratulating him on his victory, offering his support, and reminding Adams of his respect and long friendship. Unfortunately, this letter, which would have had a profound impact on their personal relationship and the conduct of government for the next four years, never reached Adams. Prior to sending the letter to Adams, Jefferson shared it with James Madison. Madison viewed the letter as a terrible political blunder. There was no need to remind Adams of their long association and friendship; he was already aware of it. Jefferson could be sacrificing his own political future if the Adams presidency turned out to be a disaster and this letter and Jefferson's support of Adams became public. The letter was never sent, and remained in Madison's possession.

The final tally of electors was 71 for Adams, 68 for Jefferson, 59 for Pinckney, 30 for Aaron Burr, with the remaining 48 electoral votes going to other candidates. The results illustrated the sectional divide that began to emerge during the Continental Congress and would have devastating consequences less than seven decades later. Adams won every elector in the north, except for Pennsylvania, and only two electors from the south. The statistics were even worse for Jefferson, who did not win a single northern elector. In the end, the election of 1796 set the stage for an even more brutal presidential contest in 1800, when the two primary candidates would face each other once again.

SEE ALSO: Democratic-Republican Party; Federalist Party; Presidential Election of 1792.

BIBLIOGRAPHY. John Ellis, *Founding Brothers* (Alfred A. Knopf, 2000); John Ferling, *Adams vs. Jefferson: The Tumultuous Election of 1800* (Oxford University Press, 2004); Paul Johnson, *A History of the American People* (Weidenfeld & Nicolson, 1997); David McCullough, *John Adams* (Simon & Schuster, 2001); Lynne Withey, *Dearest Friend: A Life of Abigail Adams* (Touchstone, 1981).

ABBE ALLEN DEBOLT
COLUMBUS STATE COMMUNITY COLLEGE

Presidential Election of 1800

THE PRESIDENTIAL ELECTION of 1800 set up a rematch of the 1796 presidential election between John Adams (Federalist) and Thomas Jefferson (Democratic-Republican) and for the only time in history featured a contest between the sitting president and vice president. In their private correspondence with each other and other family members, both John and Abigail Adams voiced their belief early in 1800 that John would lose the election and the desire to return home.

The previous four years had been marked by rising tensions between the two men and their respective parties regarding foreign policy issues. Fear over the impact of the French Revolution and the rise of a radical government in Paris after the revolution led to hostilities once again between Great Britain and France. The European conflict led to actions by both Britain and France that were viewed as hostile and negative by the American people and government. American support for their former ally, France, dissipated with the Reign of Terror, the XYZ affair, and hostile actions by the new French government.

By 1798, there was wide support for declaring war against France, an act that Adams viewed as ruinous for the country. Instead, Congress passed the Alien and Sedition Acts of 1798 that increased the residency requirement from five to 14 years for citizenship, granted the president the right to expel dangerous foreigners, and made malicious writings against the government or president a crime punishable by fine and imprisonment. The prosecutions of well-known Republicans for Sedition created martyrs for the Democratic-Republican press and a campaign issue for Jefferson.

After six days and 36 ballots, the House finally decided the election of 1800 in favor of Thomas Jefferson.

The ugly temper of the campaign was established early in 1800 with the publication, by James Callender, of a series of essays entitled *The Prospect Before Us* that referred to Adams as a "repulsive pedant" and a "gross hypocrite," and speculated as to what type of madness had led the electorate to vote him into office. Callender was a well-known Democratic-Republican propagandist based in Richmond, Virginia, whose work was approved by Thomas Jefferson. Callender's sensational pamphlet led to his arrest and conviction under the Alien and Sedition Acts and created another martyr for the Democratic-Republican cause. The Democratic-Republican press labeled Adams a Tory, an aristocrat who was against the common people, and some went so far as to call Adams insane. The irony of calling a farmer's son an aristocrat was magnified when the same press referred to the plantation and slave-owning Thomas Jefferson as man of the people who would protect their liberties.

As he had in 1796, Alexander Hamilton and his fellow High Federalists worked against the re-election of their own candidate. Hamilton had concluded that both Adams and Jefferson would be disastrous for the country, and he worked to have Charles Cotesworth Pinckney elected instead. In a letter-writing campaign begun in May, Hamilton portrayed Adams as unfit to be president and prophesized ruin for the Federalist Party if Adams were re-elected. However, unlike 1796, Hamilton's actions against Adams were conducted publicly. At the end of October, Hamilton published a pamphlet entitled *A Letter from Alexander Hamilton, Concerning the Public Conduct and Character of John Adams, Esq., president of the United States* in New York that referred to Adams' weak character, his temper, poor relations with his own cabinet, and his foreign policy concerning France as reasons for Federalists to vote for Pinckney rather than Adams.

Federalist Noah Webster responded by attacking Hamilton for his lack of loyalty and for his ambition to be the "American Caesar." Abigail Adams in letters to John expressed her own opinion of Hamilton by referring to him as Cassius (alluding to a Roman senator and friend of Julius Caesar who plotted against, and participated in, the assassination of Caesar), or as another Bonaparte. Republicans rejoiced over the infighting within the Federalist Party. James Madison believed that the Hamilton pamphlet had swung the election in favor of Jefferson, an assessment of the impact of the pamphlet shared by John Adams. However, in the end Adams thought the pamphlet would do even greater harm to Hamilton by insuring the election of Jefferson and damaging Hamilton's reputation within his own party.

Federalist pamphlets and newspapers challenged Jefferson's loyalty by saying he was more French than American. His devotion to the Constitution was called into question due to his support for states' rights over the federal government. He was called a coward in reference to his behavior while governor of Virginia during the Revolutionary War. Jefferson was portrayed as an immoral, godless man who cohabited with slave women. The now widowed Martha Washington even referred to Jefferson as "detestable." A Democratic-Republican newspaper claimed that a Jefferson win would result in the country being overrun by European immigrants and a civil war. While their parties, supporters, and newspapers viciously attacked their character and policies; the candidates remained silent.

In November 1800, John Adams become the first president to take up residence in the unfinished White

House, then referred to as the President's House, and to speak at the opening of Congress when it convened for the first time in the (also unfinished) Capitol. The electors convened on December 3, the same day that John and Abigail Adams would learn of the tragic death of their son Charles. The final electoral count from 16 states gave Jefferson 73 votes, Aaron Burr 73, Adams 65, Pinckney 64, and another Federalist, John Jay, one. Despite the unpopularity of the Alien and Sedition Acts and the attacks from both Republicans and High Federalists, the election was much closer than anticipated. The tie between the Democratic-Republican candidates Thomas Jefferson and Aaron Burr threw the final election decision to the House of Representatives.

RESOLVING THE DEADLOCK
Tension over the deadlocked election rose quickly in the new Capitol once Burr refused to give way to Jefferson. Stories circulated throughout the city of a potential deal between Burr and the Federalist members of the House. Alexander Hamilton, faced with the fact that his work in favor of Pinckney had failed, decided to throw his support to Jefferson. Adams, long a supporter of the separation of powers as a necessary foundation of republican government, refused to make his preference known to the Federalist members of the House. Adams revealed his preference for Jefferson only in his private correspondence with Abigail. In their letters, both John and Abigail Adams speak of Jefferson's abilities and their view that Jefferson is less "dangerous" than Burr.

The Congress met in a joint session on February 11 to officially open the ballots. Once the official balloting ended and the deadlock was declared, the House went into session to begin their own balloting. In the end, it took six days and 36 ballots before the House decided the election in favor of Thomas Jefferson. The decisive vote was cast by a Federalist representative from Delaware, James A. Bayard, who decided to switch and vote in favor of Jefferson.

Thomas Jefferson was inaugurated as the third president of the United States on March 4, 1801. John Adams was not present at the inauguration, having left for Baltimore on the first morning stagecoach hours earlier. Critics have portrayed Adams's "sudden" departure as the last act of an ill-tempered old man. However, Adams had expressed to Billy Shaw his desire to make it to Baltimore in one day. This could only be achieved by leaving on the first stage of the day. Four years earlier,

George Washington, in his famous Farewell Address, had warned against the effects of foreign alliances and the rise of party politics. John Adams, to his own ruin, agreed with Washington's views regarding party politics and had remained neutral throughout his presidency. He would be the last president to attempt this policy.

SEE ALSO: Democratic-Republican Party; Federalist Party.

BIBLIOGRAPHY. John Ellis, *Founding Brothers* (Alfred A. Knopf, 2000); John Ferling, *Adams vs. Jefferson: The Tumultuous Election of 1800* (Oxford University Press, 2004); *Paul Johnson, A History of the American People* (Weidenfeld & Nicolson, 1997); David McCullough, *John Adams* (Simon & Schuster, 2001); Lynne Withey, *Dearest Friend: A Life of Abigail Adams* (Touchstone, 1981).

ABBE ALLEN DEBOLT
COLUMBUS STATE COMMUNITY COLLEGE

Presidential Election of 1804

IN THE U.S. presidential election of 1804, Thomas Jefferson was elected for his second term. The election was the first held after the ratification of the 12th Amendment to the U.S. Constitution allowed the election of both the president and the vice president. Before then, the candidate who received the most votes in the Electoral College was declared president, and the one with the second largest number of votes was declared vice president. The Amendment resolved many of the problems that Alexander Hamilton had seen in earlier presidential elections.

In 1800, Thomas Jefferson narrowly won the presidential election, but during his first four years as president, he become popular. He tried to ensure that his presidency represented a great change from English politics, and, in 1802, the Federalists lost seats in the U.S. congressional elections. On February 19, 1803, Ohio was admitted to the Union as the 17th state, during a period of great prosperity. U.S. merchants increased their trade after the Treaty of Amiens in March 1802, during the brief lull in the Napoleonic Wars. With Jefferson's successful negotiation of the Louisiana Purchase, which came into effect with the signing of a treaty on May 2, 1803, the United States doubled in size. The Tripolitan-

American War was also relatively successful, although pursued with little vigor by the United States.

The Federalists were keen to prevent Thomas Jefferson's election to a second term, and planned to get Vice President Aaron Burr elected as governor of New York. Some Federalists then believed that New York, and also New Jersey, might join the New England states in forming an independent confederacy. However, the leading Federalists, Alexander Hamilton and Rufus King, opposed this, setting the scene for a tense election campaign. Hamilton managed to prevent Burr being elected by disseminating derogatory comments about the vice president. On February 25, 1804, the Democratic-Republican Party held its congressional caucus and nominated Thomas Jefferson for a second term as president. They were anxious to avoid having Burr as his running mate, and turned to George Clinton, a New York rival of Burr, who had won the gubernatorial elections for New York State. Clinton was extremely popular in New York, serving a total of 21 years as governor, 1777–95, and again 1801–04.

The death of Mary Eppes (née Jefferson), the president's younger surviving daughter, on April 17 at Monticello, Jefferson's home, resulted in Thomas Jefferson suffering much grief, and overshadowed the first part of the election campaign. However, during the campaign, Aaron Burr killed Alexander Hamilton in a duel. Burr had challenged Hamilton to the duel over the derogatory comments the latter had made that had prevented Burr's election as governor of New York. After the duel on July 11, at Weehawken, New Jersey, arrest warrants were issued for the apprehension of Burr as duels were illegal. Burr also became involved in a conspiracy with a colleague, General James Wilkinson, possibly to invade Mexico to establish an independent government there, or lead a secessionist movement in the West. This crisis overshadowed the presidential election campaign.

The Federalists chose Charles Cotesworth Pinckney of South Carolina to run against Jefferson, and U.S. Senator Rufus King of New York became the Federalist vice presidential candidate. Pinckney was an aide to General George Washington during the American War of Independence, briefly, as had Aaron Burr. He had also been appointed minister to France in 1796, a post held by Jefferson until seven years earlier. In 1800, he had been a vice presidential candidate for the Federalists. King had been ambassador to the Court of St. James (England) 1796–1803. Both Pinckney and King campaigned against Jefferson, but neither was able to get much support. However, it quickly became apparent that King would be unpopular in the southern states; in 1785 he had introduced a resolution that would prohibit slavery in the newly created North-West Territory, which two years later was included in the Ordinance of 1787. Much of the electioneering was done through the newspapers columns. Some of the allegations first made in 1800 that Jefferson was an atheist resurfaced. However, there was a swell of public opinion in favor of Jefferson because of the rising level of prosperity in the country, and some still saw the Federalists as too Anglophile.

With 176 seats in the Electoral College, the winner needed 89 seats, and well before the election, it became clear that Jefferson and Clinton would win. Jefferson was guaranteed 24 seats from Virginia, 20 seats from Pennsylvania, and 19 votes from New York. In six states (Connecticut, Delaware, Georgia, New York, South Carolina, and Vermont) the state legislature appointed the members of the Electoral College, respectively three for Delaware, six for Georgia, 19 for New York, 10 for South Carolina, and six for Vermont. In Kentucky, Maryland, North Carolina, and Tennessee, the states were divided into electoral districts with one elector chosen from each district. In most of the rest of the states (New Hampshire, New Jersey, Ohio, Pennsylvania, Rhode Island, and Virginia) the electors were chosen by all the voters in the state, with the person winning getting the entire electoral college vote for that state. In Massachusetts, there was an amalgam of systems with two electors chosen by a statewide vote (as were the U.S. senators), and one elector chosen in each congressional district.

Jefferson and Clinton won 162 Electoral College seats, with 104,110 (72.8 percent) of the popular vote for the 11 states that voted. By contrast, Pinckney and King managed only 14 Electoral College seats: nine seats from Connecticut, three from Delaware, and two from Maryland (of the total of 11 electoral college seats for the state). They also managed only 38,919 of the popular vote (27.2 percent). The biggest surprise was how poorly the Federalists did in the New England heartland, and that Pinckney did not even carry his home state. Henry Adams (1838–1918) was later to comment in his *History of the United States (1889–1891)*, "rarely was a presidential election better calculated to turn the head of a president, and never was a president elected who felt more keenly the pleasure of his personal triumph." Adams went on to describe Jefferson as being "the idol of four fifths of the nation."

SEE ALSO: Democratic-Republican Party; Federalist Party.

BIBLIOGRAPHY. Seth Hinshaw, *Ohio Elects the President: Our State's Role in Presidential Elections 1804–1996* (Book Masters, 2000); R.G. Hoxie, "Alexander Hamilton and the Electoral System Revisited," *Presidential Studies Quarterly* (v.18/4, 1988); Henry James, *History of the United States* (New York, 1889–91); M.D. Peterson, ed., *Thomas Jefferson: A Reference Biography* (Scribner, 1986).

JUSTIN CORFIELD
GEELONG GRAMMAR SCHOOL, AUSTRALIA

Presidential Election of 1808

IN THE PRESIDENTIAL election of 1808 James Madison of the Democratic-Republican Party was elected president, defeating Federalist candidate Charles Cotesworth Pinckney. George Clinton was elected vice president, in one of only two instances when a new president was elected and the incumbent vice president was re-elected; the other occasion was the re-election of John C. Calhoun in 1828.

With Thomas Jefferson about to retire, on January 23, 1808, the caucus of the Democratic-Republicans chose Secretary of State James Madison of Virginia as their candidate. Attempts to block this were led by John Randolph of Roanoke, Virginia, later its governor, but these failed, although Randolph's preferred candidate, James Monroe, did appear on the ballot in some states. Madison's family were longtime residents of Virginia, and James Madison himself had served in the House of Delegates, the Virginia State Assembly, and then in the Continental Congress. Madison named George Clinton, the vice president, as his running mate, and the Federalists decided on Charles Cotesworth Pinckney and Rufus King as their presidential and vice presidential candidates, the same candidates that they had chosen in 1804.

James Madison faced two major problems in getting elected. The first was that there were a number of Democratic-Republicans who disliked him, and had wanted Clinton to be their candidate. Most were from New York, with a few from New Jersey, and the Federalists had hoped to capitalize on this by renominating Rufus King for the vice presidency. However, Madison also had a problem over the Embargo Act of 1807, which had been introduced by Jefferson, although Madison had opposed it. Congress had passed the Embargo Act on December 22, 1807, and it ended U.S. foreign trade by banning any U.S. exports by land or sea, and refused access to specified articles manufactured in Britain. The result was that any U.S. ships that were not already overseas, or could not escape and be sold, had to remain in port or carry U.S. goods to other U.S. ports. The reason for this severe measure by Jefferson and Madison was to keep the United States out of the Napoleonic Wars. With the French and the British issuing decrees banning trade with their enemies, any U.S. ships involved in trade were liable to be attacked by one side or the

other. The effect of the Embargo Act was felt in the New England ports of Newburyport and New Haven, which declined quickly. Some U.S. merchants with ships in the Mediterranean continued to rely on British protection, and they made fortunes from this state of affairs. Others, whose shops were in the French West Indies, found their vessels requisitioned by the French, with Napoleon proclaiming that he wanted to help Jefferson enforce the Embargo Act.

The result of the Embargo Act, in electoral terms, was that Madison lost significant support in New England. He relied on the popularity of Thomas Jefferson, which he hoped would ensure that the south and the Mid-Atlantic states supported him. In 1808, the number of Electoral College seats remained the same (176), as in the previous presidential election, although in the end one elector from Kentucky did not vote. In order to ensure his election, the winning candidate needed 89 votes.

The manner in which the Electoral College seats were chosen remained almost the same as 1804. Each state wanted a more powerful impact in the Electoral College, and 13 of the 17 states allocated their Electoral College seats in a single block. In Connecticut, Delaware, Georgia, New York, South Carolina, and Vermont, the state legislature appointed the electors, with Massachusetts also adopting this system. In New Hampshire, New Jersey, Ohio, Pennsylvania, Rhode Island, and Virginia, the electors were chosen by a statewide vote, and in Kentucky, Maryland, North Carolina, and Tennessee, the state was divided into electoral districts, with one elector chosen per district by the voters.

Madison believed that he could rely on the legislatures of Georgia and South Carolina to support him, bringing with them six and 10 votes, respectively. He also believed he could easily win the state of Virginia, with its 24 seats, and also secure the 20 seats from Pennsylvania. This would give him 60 seats. He expected the support of Ohio, with its three electors, and New York with its 19 electors. George Clinton, his vice presidential running mate, was very popular in the state, and had the support of the state legislature). With the support of the majority of the 14 seats in North Carolina, seven from Kentucky and five from Tennessee, there would be an easy victory for Madison and Clinton.

For Pinckney, the only way to gain victory was to broaden his appeal. He was assured of the 19 votes from Massachusetts, nine from Connecticut, seven from

Anger in New England over the Embargo Act meant James Madison (above) had to rely on popularity in the south.

New Hampshire and four from Rhode Island, the states worst hit by the Embargo Act. This would give him 39 seats. Although he believed he would win New Jersey and Vermont, with eight and six electors respectively, he would need to gain the support of New York with its 19 seats to stand any hope of winning. This was the reason the Federalists supported Rufus King as their vice presidential candidate.

King began his political career in Massachusetts, where he was born. A strong supporter of central government, he had managed to get much support in Massachusetts for the U.S. Constitution, but his opposition to the expansion of slavery alienated support for him in the south. He moved to New York in 1788, and after a year in the State Assembly, was one of the first U.S. senators elected, becoming the unofficial Federalist leader in Congress. He then served as ambassador to the Court of St. James (England), before running in the 1804 presidential election. He hoped that his popularity in New York might be able to sway the legislature in their choice of Electoral College members.

The election occured in the states that held elections during November, and although James Madison was comfortably elected, it was not the landslide that took place four years previously. For the 10 states that voted, Madison received 124,732 votes (64.7 percent), to Pinckney's 62,431 votes (32.4 percent), with James Monroe picking up 4,848 votes (2.5 percent), and 680 votes cast for un-pledged electors.

Pinckney did much better than his attempt in 1804: 47 Electoral College seats, as compared with 14 in his earlier bid. As expected, he swept much of New England, gaining Connecticut, Delaware, New Hampshire, and Massachusetts. He also managed to take three districts in North Carolina, and two in Maryland. The major upset when the Electoral College met and voted on December 7, 1808, was that six electors who were supposed to vote for Madison, having been nominated by the state legislature for that purpose, decided to cast their votes for Clinton.

In the vote for the vice president, Clinton received 113 votes, with nine voting for John Langdon, a merchant and former U.S. senator from New Hampshire. Of the six "faithless" electors who voted for Clinton, three voted for Madison as vice president, with the other three casting their votes for James Monroe. All 47 electors who supported Pinckney voted for Rufus King for vice president.

SEE ALSO: Democratic-Republican Party; Federalist Party: Presidential Election of 1808.

BIBLIOGRAPHY. D.A. Carson, "Quiddism and the Reluctant Candidacy of James Monroe in the Election of 1808," *Mid-America* (v.70/2, 1988); J.N. Rakove, *James Madison and the Creation of the American Republic* (Scott, Foresman/Little, Brown Higher Education, 1990).

JUSTIN CORFIELD
GEELONG GRAMMAR SCHOOL, AUSTRALIA

Presidential Election of 1812

THE PRESIDENTIAL ELECTION of 1812 resulted in the re-election of James Madison. It was contested in the shadow of the War of 1812 with several battles fought along the U.S.-Canadian border, and other engagements at sea. James Madison capitalized on his leadership of the United States during a period of tension with the British and the French. Both the British and the French seized U.S. ships in their aims to ensure a blockade of their enemy's lands. There was also worry over the British support for Native Americans in the north and south of the United States, with the British building fortifications in what the Americans believed was U.S. territory, although the British contested this, by occasionally pressing U.S. seamen to work in the British navy.

On May 18, the Democratic-Republican congressional-nominating caucus nominated James Madison as their candidate for the upcoming presidential elections. The vice presidency had been vacant since the death of George Clinton on April 20, and Governor Elbridge Gerry of Massachusetts was nominated. He was famous in electoral politics for his manipulation of the voting system; the term *gerrymander* was coined to describe the actions of Governor Gerry and similar schemes all over the world. It was first used in Britain (as jerrymander) in 1859 and in the United States (as gerrymander) nine years later.

A rival section of the Democratic-Republicans disliked the choice of Madison, and had revolved around George Clinton. Most of their members were from New York, and they formed a caucus in New York. On May 29, they nominated the former U.S. senator and then mayor of New York City, DeWitt Clinton, as their candidate. The nephew of George Clinton, he was an important civic leader in New York, not only as its lieutenant governor, mayor of New York City 1803–07, 1809–10, and again from 1811, but also a patron of the New York Orphan Asylum and the New York City Hospital. On the political front, DeWitt Clinton was pushing for what at the time was described as "practical republicanism," with merchants arguing that commerce was just as important as agricultural production in the healthy economy of the country, and that there should be much greater diversity in the U.S. economic makeup.

DECLARATION OF WAR

On June 12, 1812, the United States declared war on the British and in June, U.S. soldiers launched a poorly-planned attack into Canada, with the British responding by attacking Fort Mackinac, which they captured on July 17. On August 15, the British attacked Fort Dearborn (on the site of modern-day Chicago), where Indians massacred the U.S. garrison after they had surrendered. On the following day, the settlement of Detroit surrendered to a smaller British force under General Sir Isaac Brock.

These reverses had significant implications for the presidential election campaign, and the war became the major issue of the campaign. Political figures such as John Randolph of Roanoke, Virginia, led an antiwar movement against Madison, and argued for peace with the British. The Battle of Queenston on October 13 focused many people's minds more closely on the war. The New York militiamen watched the British defeat their fellow countrymen, but were unable to do anything as the fighting took place on the north bank of the Niagara River, and the militia could not serve outside their state.

THE CAMPAIGN

Essentially, the campaign rested on whether Madison could win the mid-Atlantic states. He was confident that he would win the states in the south, which now included Louisiana, granted statehood on April 30, 1812. In Connecticut, Delaware, Georgia, New York, South Carolina, and Vermont, the state legislatures still allocated their state's Electoral College seats, a system followed for the first time by Louisiana, New Jersey, and North Carolina (the latter largely to prevent the state's

electors being split as they had been in 1804). In New Hampshire, Ohio, Pennsylvania, Rhode Island, and Virginia, the voters decided on their state's allocation of electors, with the winner getting all the Electoral College seats of the state. Kentucky, Maryland, and Tennessee continued to divide their states into electoral districts, which could result in the votes of the state being split, as happened again in the case of Maryland. Massachusetts abandoned the appointment of electors by the state legislature and returned to the system it had used prior to the 1808 election, with two electors chosen from a statewide voters list (as was the case for U.S. senators), and one elector from each congressional district, to mirror the election of members to the U.S. House of Representatives.

The total number of seats in the Electoral College was 218, with 110 votes needed to win, although when the Electoral College met, one voter from Ohio did not vote, and voter apathy in the state led to a low voter turnout. The increase in the size of the Electoral College reflected a rise in the U.S. population, especially in Kentucky, Ohio, Pennsylvania, and New York. The strategy to be followed by Madison was to maintain his support in the south, and to win at the polls in Virginia and Pennsylvania, to get both of their 25 Electoral College seats. With support from the legislatures of Georgia, Louisiana, North Carolina, and South Carolina, he would get their respective six, three, 15, and 11 Electoral College seats. This would give Madison a total of 85 seats. In Kentucky and Tennessee, Madison hoped to win most of their Electoral College seats. He also hoped to make an impact in Massachusetts, through the choice of Gerry Ingersoll as his running mate. This would leave DeWitt Clinton with New York and possibly New Jersey, respectively 29 and eight seats, and the Federalists with the seats for New England.

The Federalists recognized that the three candidates would see Madison's opponents split in Kentucky and Tennessee, delivering Madison a second term. After fierce debates, the Federalist nominating caucus, meeting in New York City, finally decided that the only way to prevent Madison being re-elected was to support DeWitt Clinton. They picked Jared Ingersoll of Pennsylvania, a former Pennsylvania attorney general, and former U.S. attorney for Pennsylvania, as the vice presidential running mate. The hope was that Ingersoll might to snatch enough votes from Madison to give the Clinton-

Ingersoll ticket a majority in Pennsylvania, and the victory. With Clinton desperate to win, his election campaigning was tailored to the views of each state. In the northeast, where the war with the British was becoming increasingly unpopular, Clinton issued pamphlets and made speeches against the war, and was proclaimed by supportive newspapers as an anti-war candidate. By contrast in the south and the West, he urged that the United States should take a tough line on the war and was able to gain much support.

When the election was finally held, and the Electoral College met on December 2, James Madison won a clear majority, with 128 seats in the Electoral College, against DeWitt Clinton with 89 votes. Although Clinton lost, he managed to carry many more states than the anti-Madison forces had in 1808. He took New York and New Jersey, and won 132,781 votes (47.6 percent), to Madison's 140,431 votes (50.4 percent), with Rufus King, a Federalist who was technically not a candidate, getting 5,574 votes. In the voting for the vice president, all of Madison's electors voted for Elbridge Gerry, as did three from Massachusetts (Gerry's home state), who had voted for Clinton for president. In the end, Gerry received 131 votes to Ingersoll's 86 votes, and was duly declared vice president.

SEE ALSO: Democratic-Republican Party; Federalist Party.

BIBLIOGRAPHY. J.N. Rakove, *James Madison and the Creation of the American Republic* (Scott, Foresman/Little, Brown Higher Education, 1990); S.E. Siry, "The Sectional Politics of 'Practical Republicanism': De Witt Clinton's Presidential Bid, 1810–1812," *Journal of the Early Republic* (v.5/4, 1985); M.F. Wehtje, "Opposition in Virginia to the War of 1812," *Virginia Magazine of History and Biography* (v.78/1, 1970).

JUSTIN CORFIELD
GEELONG GRAMMAR SCHOOL, AUSTRALIA

Presidential Election of 1816

IN THE 1816 U.S. presidential election, James Madison completed his second term as president, and the Federalist Party was in disarray. Madison had been secretary of state to Thomas Jefferson, and had succeeded him, with James Monroe, Madison's secretary of state, running for president for the Democratic-Republicans, and was elected by a large majority, but not without controversy.

The War of 1812 ended with the British being driven out of the United States, although not with the U.S. forces being victorious, despite having won the final battle at New Orleans. This had strengthened the position of James Madison, and weakened the Federalists who had argued against the war, and some had talked of secession by New England. James Monroe, the secretary of state, was from Virginia and on March 4, 1816, was nominated by the Democratic-Republicans as their candidate for the upcoming U.S. presidential elections. The caucus chose New York Governor Daniel D. Tompkins. Tompkins was made commander-in-chief of the New York Militia in the War of 1812, after the catastrophe at Queenston, and was an opponent of slavery. Thompson later introduced a law in 1817 that abolished slavery in New York. The choice of Tompkins shows the importance of New York in the electoral politics of the United States in the early-19th century. With Monroe holding Virginia, his home state, and all the states south of Virginia, support from New York would ensure his victory.

The number of seats in the Electoral College in 1816 had expanded to 221 because Congress had, on April 19, 1816, passed an enabling act for the Territory of Indiana. This allowed the territory to hold a constitutional convention that would lead to the formation of a state government and admission into the Union. On June 29, Indiana adopted a state constitution and on December 11, the U.S. Congress passed a joint resolution granting Indiana statehood, a series of events that led to the presidential election results being challenged.

With the total number of seats in the Electoral College now at 221, there were nine states where the state legislatures appointed the state's electors: Connecticut, Delaware, Georgia, Indiana, Louisiana, New York, South Carolina, Vermont, with Massachusetts changing its system again and returning to the system used there in 1808, also having its legislature appointing electors. In New Hampshire, New Jersey, North Carolina, Ohio, Pennsylvania, Rhode Island, and Virginia, the electors were chosen by all the voters in the state, the winner getting the entire Electoral College seats of the state. Kentucky, Maryland, and Tennessee continued with their system by which they divided their

The 1816 election saw controversy over the new state of Indiana's votes, but James Monroe's win was soon confirmed.

two presidential elections. In the states that held state-wide elections, the results were often easy to forecast. Monroe would carry North Carolina, Pennsylvania, and Virginia, giving him, respectively, 15, 25, and 25 seats. Thus, he was assured of 116 votes, with another possible 29 from New York, giving him an easy victory. Even allowing for the loss of all of New England, Monroe's victory was assured. King faced the same problems he had in 1804 and 1808. Despite the Federalist stronghold in New England, if a Federalist candidate could not win New York and Pennsylvania, there was no hope of winning the overall election.

In the voting in November, Monroe won 76,592 votes (68.2 percent) from the 10 states with a popular vote, and Rufus King received 34,740 votes (34 percent), with 1,038 votes (0.9 percent) going to unpledged voters. When the Electoral College met on December 4, 183 electors voted for Monroe, and 34 for King. Only three states voted for King: Connecticut, Massachusetts, and Delaware. In the state of Maryland, with each electoral district choosing an elector, two of the 11 districts were won by Federalist electors, with both cast blank votes. Another elector from Maryland and one from neighboring Delaware, also refrained from voting.

In the vote for the vice president, Daniel D. Tompkins managed to hold all of Monroe's electors; those for Rufus King were split, as each of the states that voted for King had chosen a different vice presidential running-mate. Massachusetts supported John Eager Howard from Maryland, a former Maryland senator, and later governor. The vote from Connecticut was split with five votes for James Ross from Pennsylvania, and four for Chief Justice John Marshall of Virginia. The three Delaware electors voted for Robert Goodloe Harper of Maryland.

After the election, on February 12, 1817, the U.S. Senate and the U.S. House of Representatives met in joint session to count the electoral votes for the president and the vice president, and to confirm the result announced on December 4. The votes of the electors of each state were counted in the order in which the states had been admitted to the Union. All went smoothly, until the time came to count the votes from Indiana. At that point, John W. Taylor, a member of the House of Representatives for New York, objected. He claimed that as the casting of the ballots of the Electoral College took place on December 4, 1816, when Indiana was not formally admitted to the Union until December 11, it

states into electoral districts, which would result in the votes of the state being split.

The Federalists were initially unable to find a candidate, and eventually agreed on Rufus King, who had been twice defeated as a vice presidential candidate. Although he had added some votes in 1816 without being a proper candidate, there was little chance of King winning, but more a matter of how large the protest vote by the Federalists and their supporters would be. The Democratic-Republicans led by Monroe could once again count on the state legislatures of Georgia, Louisiana, and South Carolina supporting them, giving them, respectively, eight, three, and 11 seats. It was also likely that the 29 seats from New York would go to Monroe. Even though King was from the state, apart from the 1812 election when DeWitt Clinton had stood, the state had not supported King in the previous was not a state at the time of the meeting of the Electoral College, and was only the Territory of Indiana. Thus, he argued that the votes cast for Indiana were void. However, members of the House of Representatives defined statehood as when the state constitution and state government were formally established in Indiana. There was an Indiana member of the House of Representatives elected before December 11, and two senators from Indiana, also elected before December 11, all who had been formally seated in, respectively, the House of Representatives and the Senate. At that point Representative Samuel D. Ingham from Pennsylvania moved that the question be postponed indefinitely. The House of Representatives agreed by a massive vote, the Senate was brought back to the joint session, and the votes from Indiana were counted. On March 4, 1817, James Monroe was inaugurated as the fifth president of the United States.

SEE ALSO: Democratic-Republican Party; Federalist Party.

BIBLIOGRAPHY. Harry Ammon, *James Monroe: The Quest for National Identity* (McGraw-Hill, 1971); N.E. Cunningham, *The Presidency of James Monroe* (University of Kansas Press, 1996).

JUSTIN CORFIELD
GEELONG GRAMMAR SCHOOL, AUSTRALIA

Presidential Election of 1820

IN THE U.S. presidential election of 1820, James Monroe, the incumbent president, and Daniel D. Tompkins, the incumbent vice president, ran unopposed. This had happened before in 1789 and 1792, when George Washington was elected without any serious opposition. In 1820, there was little world tension, the Democratic-Republican Party was in control of much of the country, the Federalist Party had collapsed, and there was no new opposition party. The period was to become known in U.S. history as the Era of Good Feeling. There were a number of new states that had been admitted to the Union since the 1816 U.S. presidential election: Mississippi (1817), Illinois (1818), Alabama (1819), Missouri (1820), and Maine (1820), although there were some problems with Missouri's statehood and, hence, the

validity of its Electoral College votes, as had been the case with Indiana in 1816. As Monroe and Tompkins were effectively unopposed, there was little in the way of an election campaign.

The system of choosing electors still varied considerably. There were now 235 electors, with Delaware, Georgia, Indiana, Louisiana, New York, South Carolina, and Vermont, leaving the choice of electors to the state legislature, with Alabama and Missouri opting to follow the same system. In New Hampshire, New Jersey, North Carolina, Ohio, Pennsylvania, Rhode Island, and Virginia, the electors were chosen by all the voters in the state, the winner receiving the Electoral College seats. Connecticut had moved from choice by the state legislature to a statewide vote, and Mississippi also decided to have a statewide vote, the first newly admitted state to opt for a direct statewide vote for many years. Kentucky, Maryland, and Tennessee continued to divide their states into electoral districts, which could result in the votes of the state being split; Illinois also adopted this system. Massachusetts and Maine (which had been a part of Massachusetts until the Missouri Compromise of 1820), abandoned the choice by the state legislature, returning to the original system of having two electors chosen by voters statewide (as for the U.S. senate), and the remainder chosen by congressional districts.

In the November election, with people in 15 of the 24 states voting, James Monroe received 87,343 votes (80.6 percent), 17,465 people (16.1 percent) voted for Federalist electors; 1,893 people voted for DeWitt Clinton, and 1,658 voters chose unpledged electors. When the Electoral College met on December 6, there were only 232 electors; three electors, one from Mississippi, one from Pennsylvania, and one from Tennessee had died and had not been replaced by the time the college met. It was the last time that William Floyd, from Mastic, Long Island, served on the Electoral College, having been a member of the eight previous Electoral Colleges. The vote was not, however, unanimous. Monroe won with 231 votes, with a single elector, William Plumer, casting a vote for John Quincy Adams, then the secretary of state.

It is not certain why William Plumer voted as he did. He had been born in Newburyport, Massachusetts, and when he was nine years old, his family had moved to New Hampshire. Studying law, he was elected to the state legislature on many occasions, becoming speaker of the state house in 1791 and 1797. A friend of Thomas Jefferson, he was a member of the U.S. Senate from 1802 until 1807, and then became active in the Democratic-Republican Party before being elected as governor of New Hampshire after an acrimonious election campaign. With the vote so close, the state legislature eventually opted for Plumer. After ending his term in 1819, Plumer became a presidential elector. It has been suggested that Plumer voted for Adams to ensure that George Washington would be the only U.S. president who was the unanimous choice of an Electoral College, but it has also been suggested that Plumer, at the end of his political career, preferred Adams to Monroe, and voted as he did as a matter of principle.

When it came to the vote for vice president, Daniel D. Tompkins won with 215 votes. Richard Stockton, a Federalist from New Jersey, received eight votes, Daniel Rodney, a Federalist from Delaware received four votes, and one elector voted for Robert Goodloe Harper, a Federalist from Maryland. In addition, William Plumer voted for Richard Rush, a Democratic-Republican from Pennsylvania, for the vice presidency, giving him one vote.

An intense debate ensued over whether or not the Electoral College votes of Missouri should be counted. This largely centered on the Missouri Compromise of 1820. Missouri had wanted to be admitted to the Union from 1817, but with the number of slave and free states evenly balanced, the admission of Missouri would have tipped the balance in favor of the slave states, giving the slave states a majority, albeit a small one, in the U.S. senate. James Tallmadge, a congressman from New York, had tried to introduce an amendment by which no new slaves would be allowed into Missouri and all those there would be freed when they turned 25 years old.

The statesman Henry Clay negotiated a compromise by which Missouri entered the Union as a slave state, and Maine broke off from Massachusetts and became a free state, thus mainaining the same number of free states and slave states. Slavery would not be allowed north of the latitude of 36°30'. On March 6, 1820, the U.S. Congress passed a law directing Missouri to hold a convention to form a constitution and a state government, which had taken place by the time of the presidential election in November 1820. Some politicians claimed that some provisions of the Missouri constitution violated the U.S. Constitution.

After intense debate over whether or not Missouri was allowed to send presidential electors to the Electoral College in December 1820, on February 13, 1821, the U.S. Senate passed a resolution that stated that even if Missouri was declared not to be a state, this would not affect the final results. Tallying the Electoral College votes in the Senate, the president of the U.S. Senate announces the voting figures twice, once including Missouri, and once excluding it.

On the following day the House of Representatives counted the Electoral College votes, and when the votes from Missouri were mentioned, Representative Arthur Livermore from New Hampshire claimed that Missouri was not a state and its votes should not be counted. John Floyd, a congressman from Virginia, stated that Missouri's votes should be counted. After shouting from both sides, the results were declared twice, including Missouri, and excluding it, both with James Monroe elected as president and Daniel D. Tompkins as vice president.

SEE ALSO: Democratic-Republican Party; Federalist Party; Missouri; Slavery.

BIBLIOGRAPHY. Harry Ammon, *James Monroe: The Quest for National Identity* (McGraw-Hill, 1971); T.R. Bayles, "William Floyd, The Signer," *Long Island Forum* (v.35/5, 1972); N.E. Cunningham, *The Presidency of James Monroe* (University of Kansas Press, 1996); W.A. Robinson, "William Plumer," *Dictionary of American Biography* (Charles Scribner's Sons, 1935); A.S. Wait, "The Life, Character and Public Services of Governor William Plumer," *Proceedings of the New Hampshire Historical Society* (v.3, 1902).

JUSTIN CORFIELD
GEELONG GRAMMAR SCHOOL, AUSTRALIA

Presidential Election of 1824

THE 1824 ELECTION featured four candidates representing different wings of the Democratic-Republican Party. The Federalist Party had ceased to effectively exist as a national electoral force, and had not yet been replaced. The election also featured as much electoral drama after the votes were cast in prior years. Unlike the first post-election presidential campaign in 1800 between Thomas Jefferson and Aaron Burr, which led to the ratification of the Twelfth Amendment, this election did not require multiple ballots in the House of Representatives.

THE CANDIDATES

Andrew Jackson, a military hero for his service during the War of 1812 and the Battle of New Orleans, as well as his battles against Native Americans, was in his second stint as Senator from Tennessee. He had previously served as a representative and territorial governor of Florida, though he had resigned from each of his positions. He was known as a man of the people, but was not universally popular. His iron-fisted rule of his troops caused many political leaders to view his military service as indicative that he did not possess the temperament to exercise civilian power. In fact, during his prosecution of the Seminole Wars, he drew rebuke from the House of Representatives, including Speaker Henry Clay, who took a dim view of Jackson's "penchant for shooting wayward militiamen and soldiers with as much zeal as his British and Indian enemies and hoped that the populace would seek a more refined leader as president." Fellow Democrat Thomas Jefferson said that he did not believe Jackson possessed the proper disposition for civilian leadership. Jackson was, however, admired for having brought himself out of poverty.

John Quincy Adams, in contrast, had been brought up in high society. He was son of the former president, and the sitting secretary of state under President James Monroe. In his younger days, he had studied in Europe, and had a much more cosmopolitan lifestyle than did any of his opponents, or almost any American at that time. He did not have a charming personality to match his immense talents. His wife stated her displeasure with the manner in which he acted toward others who did not possess his intellectual aptitude. Adams acknowledged that his personality lagged behind his other abilities, citing statements from his political and personal opponents, but he did not believe he could change. Professionally, he had been a successful proponent of U.S. interests throughout his career. Among other things, he had a hand in negotiating the Treaty of Ghent to end the War of 1812, and had negotiated from Spain the cession of Florida, which included a westward expansion. His personality defects, though, seemed to overshadow his positive traits.

Presidential candidate John Quincy Adams received 84 electoral votes in the 1824 election.

William Crawford was the sitting secretary of the treasury and the choice of the Democratic-Republican Party leadership. He had received overwhelming support at the sparsely attended party caucus. Due to a paralytic stroke suffered in September 1823, Crawford was unable to campaign for the presidency, and by the time of the election, was not expected to win. Henry Clay was the sitting speaker of the House from Kentucky. A lawyer first elected to the House in 1812, he became speaker during his first term and had used his position appointing committee chair to consolidate his power and gain more effective control of the body. John C. Calhoun, who would serve as vice president under both Adams and Jackson, once a contender, but when he realized that the number of viable candidates made it unlikely that any of them would achieve an electoral majority, he dropped out of the race and threw his support to Jackson.

ELECTION RESULTS

There was no dispute over the vote count. Jackson had the most electoral votes (99), followed by Adams (84),

Crawford (41), and Clay (37). In addition to his plurality in the Electoral College, Jackson also won a significant popular margin (though not a majority). However, this result is somewhat misleading; not every state chose electors by popular vote. Six of the 24 states chose via the state legislature, including New York with its 36 electoral votes. Under the Twelfth Amendment, because there was no majority in the electoral vote, the House of Representatives was to choose the president from among the top three electoral vote getters. This placed Clay in a position of power; though he was not among the top three, as speaker of the House he could exercise considerable influence over who among Adams, Jackson, and Crawford would become president.

CLAY'S DECISION

Clay had fundamental political disagreements with Crawford. Specifically, Crawford, known as an Old Republican, had a strong state-centered view of the federal system and was in favor of a narrow reading of the Constitution as it pertained to delegated powers. Clay, a relative nationalist, favored a broader interpretation of the powers of the central government at the expense of the powers of the states. Additionally, Crawford's health was such that it was speculated that he might not survive a four-year term (he actually lived until 1834). Jackson's exercise of his authority as military commander, combined with Clay's fear of the military threat to democratic rule, and his assessment of his capacity for civilian leadership based on his performance in previous political roles, ruled out the possibility that Clay might support Jackson.

This left Adams as the only possibility, being the least of all evils. Clay also had problems with Adams; he disagreed with Adams's policies and conduct during the negotiations of the Treaty of Ghent, where Adams seemed willing to favor the fishing and mercantile interests of New England over those of the west (including Clay's Kentucky). However, these concerns subsided with the passage of time, while Clay's problems with Jackson had not.

THE "CORRUPT BARGAIN"

Clay's support was not dispositive of the issue, however. The House voted by state delegation: each state had one vote, regardless of if it was New York's 34 representatives, or Rhode Island's two. Thirteen states was the required majority. According to the votes cast, Jackson had the

support of 11 states and Adams seven. This is merely suggestive, however, as representatives were (and are) not bound by the votes of their constituents in deciding a presidential election placed in their hands, although some announced that they would follow the wishes of their constituents.

Jackson remained away from Washington and was somewhat aloof to the process, while Adams actively lobbied for his case. Through some careful negotiations with congressional leaders, including promises of appointing political opponents to various executive positions, Adams was able to secure a majority of the states. Most important among these promised appointments was that of Henry Clay as secretary of state. Although others had recorded in June, and again in October, Clay's preference for Adams over Jackson, this appointment gave credence to the rumors that there was a "corrupt bargain" between the two. Unlike Jefferson in 1800, Adams won in the first round of House balloting.

IMPACT ON FUTURE ELECTIONS

The events that led to Adams's election, as well as his actions shortly after (including the Clay appointment, and naming Federalists to other posts) led to his overwhelming defeat four years later. In retrospect, one wonders why Adams would offer, and Clay would accept, the position. Clay certainly had the credentials to serve as secretary of state, but there was the appearance of impropriety.

For his part, Clay later said that because he had supported Adams in the House election, he would of course agree to serve under him. Adams's other political blunders included taking a nationalist position by advocating for federally-funded public works. This created a coalition against him that favored strict constructionism of the Constitution and states' rights; the coalition included John C. Calhoun, his vice president. The 1828 campaign began in the early days of the Adams administration. Campaigning on his having had the White House stolen from him four years earlier, Jackson won majorities in both the popular and electoral votes in 1828. The 1824 election was the last in which the procedures of the Twelfth Amendment have been invoked and the House determined the presidency.

SEE ALSO: Democratic-Republican Party; Electoral College; Military Hero; National Republican Party; Political Legitimacy and Democracy; Presidential Election of 1828; Realignment; Twelfth Amendment.

BIBLIOGRAPHY. Richard Brookhiser, *Alexander Hamilton, American* (Free Press, 1999); Donald Cole, *The Presidency of Andrew Jackson* (University Press of Kansas, 1993); Jonathan Daniels, *Ordeal of Ambition: Jefferson, Hamilton, Burr* (Doubleday, 1970); Mary Hargreaves, *The Presidency of John Quincy Adams* (University Press of Kansas, 1985).

SCOTT MARKOWITZ
UNIVERSITY OF FLORIDA

Presidential Election of 1828

THE ELECTION OF 1828 was a rematch of the 1824 presidential election, pitting Andrew Jackson against John Quincy Adams. Jackson's campaign brought party organization to new levels by taking the campaign to the common man. This election was also the first time that the parties brought questions about the candidates' behavior into the campaign. Jackson's campaign portrayed Jackson as a common man and Adams as an elitist.

Jackson won the election, which had the highest percentage of voter turnout of any presidential election to that point. In 1824, although Jackson had the largest number of electoral votes of any candidate, he lost the election to Adams. The reason for this was that none of the four candidates had a majority of the electoral votes, thus forcing the election into the hands of Congress, which selected Adams. Although it was never proven, Jackson claimed that Congress voted for Adams because of a deal with Henry Clay, who had placed fourth in the election. Rumors of the "corrupt deal" only intensified when Adams appointed Clay secretary of state. Jackson and his supporters believed that Jackson had been cheated out of the presidency, and almost immediately set about campaigning for the 1828 election.

Both candidates left public campaigning to others. Adams did so in keeping with the tradition set by George Washington. Jackson campaigned in private, making no public appearances in support of his quest to be president. The campaign became more about the personalities of the candidates than about the issues.

Adams's views on the issues were known as he was the current president, and in the case of Jackson, he and his people avoided talking about them. But even if the issues of substance had been discussed, there was not a big difference between the stances of the two candidates. The Jacksonians used the "corrupt bargain" of the 1824 election as a symbol of how the aristocrats had taken control of the government away from the common man. When Adams purchased an ivory chess set and a billiard table with his own money for the White House, he was attacked for spending public money on luxuries and gambling. Efforts by his people to set the record straight were ignored. The Jacksonians insisted that Adams was a monarchist who did not trust the people to rule themselves and believed that government should be in the hands of the few.

Adams's supporters fought back, pointing to Jackson's inexperience in politics and what they called his reckless lifestyle. Pointing to his involvement in duels,

In 1828, more than 1 million votes were cast, the highest turnout of any presidential election up to that time.

gambling, brawls, and his well-known bad temper, they said that these were not qualities of a president.

In particular, they criticized Jackson's ordering executions during the War of 1812. Six militiamen led a group of soldiers who deserted their unit (during a time of war), claiming that their enlistments were up. While most of the soldiers were fined and dishonorably discharged, the leaders were executed. Adams's advocates used the story to portray Jackson as a murderer who had no compassion for the soldiers. Like so many of the events during this election, only some of the facts were used to construct a story that made Jackson look bad. Jackson's reputation as the hero of the Battle of New Orleans during the War of 1812 was hard to overcome. One way to attack Jackson was to try to get him to lose his temper in public. Jackson resented the attacks on his character, especially on his war record, and refused to give in to this tactic.

The attacks that most angered Jackson involved his opponents calling into question his wife and mother's marital statuses. Stories had circulated for most of Jackson's life about whether or not his mother had been married to his father. More upsetting to him were stories questioning the legitimacy of his marriage because of the timing of his wife's divorce from her first husband. Jackson had always been protective of his wife, and when she passed away in December 1828, he said the slander directed at her was the cause of her death.

The election also brought about a split in the one existing party. There was only one party after the demise of the Federalist Party, the Democratic-Republican party. Jackson had originally been a member of that party, but split off during the campaign. Initially called the Friends of Jackson, the Democratic-Republicans became the Democratic Party. Adams's party, sometimes called the Coalitionists, eventually became the National Republicans.

Jackson's skills included organization and the party gave him an outlet for his organizational ability. National committees were formed that could coordinate the state committees. These committees could then pass information among themselves. Of more importance was the ability of these parties to organize and mobilize voters for their respective candidates. In Jackson's party, a key member was Martin Van Buren, a believer in the patronage, or spoils, system. One of Jackson's promises was to remove men from appointed offices who had received their posts against what his campaign claimed was the will of the people. Instead, he would appoint people to these offices because they had supported his campaign, thus starting the patronage system of rewarding supporters with government jobs.

The election drew the highest voter turnout of any presidential election up to this time. In 1824, fewer than 360,000 voters turned out (which was about 27 percent of eligible voters) while in 1828, more than a million voters turned out (about 57 percent). Up to this point the best turnout had been 42 percent. By 1828, 22 of the 24 states selected their electors by popular vote, rather than by the state legislatures.

In the states where the popular vote determined who the elector would vote for, there was not universal agreement on the methods. Some states used the winner-takes-all system, while others allowed for a split in the electors. In 1828, there were only two candidates and Jackson won by a large margin in the electoral vote (178 to 83), although the popular vote was closer (647,286 to 508,064). Most of Jackson's support came from the west and the south. To Jackson's supporters, the election was a triumph of the common man over the aristocrat and a return to democratic principles.

SEE ALSO: Democratic-Republican Party; Electoral College; National Republican Party; Patronage System; Presidential Election of 1824.

BIBLIOGRAPHY. G.C. Altschuler and S.M. Blumin, *Rude Republic: Americans and Their Politics in the Nineteenth Century* (Princeton University Press, 2000); P.F. Boller, Jr., *Presidential Campaigns: From George Washington to George W. Bush* (Oxford University Press, 2004); H.W. Brands, *Andrew Jackson: His Life and Times* (Doubleday, 2005); L.S. Maisel and K.Z. Buckley, *Parties and Elections in America: The Electoral Process* (Rowman & Littlefield Publishers, 2005); J.L. Roark et al., *The American Promise: A History of the United States* (Bedford/St. Martin's, 2005).

DALLACE W. UNGER, JR.
INDEPENDENT SCHOLAR

Presidential Election of 1832

THE ELECTION OF 1832 centered on the existence of the Second Bank of the United States. Andrew Jackson, the Democratic-Republican candidate running for re-election, was a vocal opponent of the bank and took a strong stand against it. His primary opponent, Henry Clay (the candidate of the National Republican Party), believed that the issue would bring about Jackson's defeat. In the end, the voters would side with Jackson on the issue and Jackson would take his election as a mandate from the voters to destroy the bank. This election was the first where the candidates were chosen by national convention. It was also the first election with three parties running candidates.

Senator Clay, along with Senator Daniel Webster, believed that they could turn the people of the United States against Jackson by forcing a fight over the charter of the U.S. Bank. Everyone knew that Jackson hated banks, especially the U.S. Bank, and therefore would veto any attempt to renew its charter (which was not scheduled for renewal until 1836). In 1832, Clay's bill to re-charter the bank early came before Jackson for his signature. As expected, Jackson vetoed the charter. Clay knew Jackson would veto the bill and expected the people to turn against him because of it. Instead, Jackson explained his veto in terms of class struggle, saying that the profits from the bank went to foreigners and monopolists. Jackson said that the Bank favored the rich at the expense of common men such as farmers and laborers. The banking issue marked the first time a presidential candidate took a stand on a social issue during an election.

The bank president, Nicholas Biddle, found Jackson's appeal to the masses of the common people dangerous. Biddle believed that he could show everyone how crazy Jackson's reasoning was, so he had copies of Jackson's explanation printed and distributed. Instead of turning the people against Jackson, it actually rallied them for Jackson. The citizens agreed with Jackson's reasoning and believed that the bank was their enemy.

Biddle continued to work against Jackson's election. He provided money to newspapers and congressmen who opposed Jackson. Jackson's supporters told voters they needed to be careful of Biddle and other supporters of the bank because they were only interested in money and power. The National Republicans fought back by saying that it was actually Jackson who was trying to oppress the people, and not the bank. They called him King Andrew I. In return, the Democrats attacked Biddle, calling him an emperor and a czar. Jackson not

only hated the bank, but also the use of paper money. He believed that the only money that should be used was hard money or specie (gold and silver), and he paid for purchases with it. Jackson's supporters refered to gold as Jackson money.

The National Republicans also attacked Jackson's character, as they had in the campaign of 1828. They brought up stories about his bad temper and his early life, and added stories that his health was failing. After Jackson had surgery to remove a bullet from an old wound, the National Republicans started circulating (true) stories about how he had received the wound in a shootout. The Democrats fought back by digging up a story about Clay and the wound he received during a fight. The National Republicans also attacked Jackson's use of the spoils system, where he removed men from appointed offices who did not support him, replacing them with men who had supported his campaign. The Democratic Party was still much better at organizing than the National Republican party. Although the National Republicans made extensive use of cartoons in various media, this was no match for the parades, clubs, meetings, and other public activities used by the Democrats.

THE FIRST NATIONAL CONVENTIONS
The election of 1832 was also the first time the parties used national conventions to select their candidates. All three parties held their conventions in Baltimore, Maryland. The first party to have its convention, which was also the first national convention ever held, was the Anti-Masonic party in September 1831. They opposed secret societies and nominated William Wirt, the Maryland attorney general, as their candidate.

The next convention was of the National Republicans, who met in December of that year. Their choice for president was Henry Clay, the unanimous choice of the states (17 of 24) that were represented. The Democratic Republicans met in May 1832, and one of the convention's issues was to decide what name they should go by. It took them several ballots to decide to go with Democratic Party. Their choice of a presidential candidate was much easier: Jackson. The convention also adopted a few rules that would govern how their convention operated for the next 100 years. The choice of Jackson's running mate, Martin Van Buren, also took several ballots. Jackson's support came from a wide variety of sources, but, overall, tended to be mostly ordinary men (farmers, laborers, and small merchants) who wanted to control their future and the government that presided over them. Clay's support tended to come from the upper classes, or from people who hated Jackson. Jackson's broader-based support would carry him to victory.

Jackson won the election with 55 percent of the popular vote, and 219 of the 286 electoral votes. Clay finished second with a little over 37 percent of the popular vote, and only 49 electoral votes. William Wirt, the Anti-Masonic candidate, won less than eight percent of the popular vote and seven electoral votes. By this time, in every state except South Carolina, electors were chosen by popular vote and paper ballots had replaced voice voting. Also, as the number of polling places increased, it was easier for men in more remote areas to vote. Most states had also removed property requirements for white males to be eligible to vote. Voter participation was just over 55 percent.

When Jackson won the election, he took the victory as a mandate from the people to continue his war on the bank. Jackson believed that his power came not just from the Constitution, but also from the people who had elected him. This scared those who believed that the president's power came solely from the Constitution. With his mandate from the people, Jackson continued his war on the U.S. Bank and eventually destroyed it, which contributed to the economic crash of 1837.

SEE ALSO: Anti-Masonic Party; Conventions, National Nominating Party; Democratic-Republican Party; Electoral College; National Republican Party; Presidential Election of 1828.

BIBLIOGRAPHY. G.C. Altschuler and S.M. Blumin, *Rude Republic: Americans and Their Politics in the Nineteenth Century* (Princeton University Press, 2000); P.F. Boller, Jr., *Presidential Campaigns: From George Washington to George W. Bush* (Oxford University Press, 2004); H.W. Brands, *Andrew Jackson: His Life and Times* (Doubleday, 2005); S.R. Gammon, Jr., *The Presidential Campaign of 1832* (Da Capo Press, 1969); L.S. Maisel and K.Z. Buckley, *Parties and Elections in America: The Electoral Process* (Rowman & Littlefield Publishers, 2005); J.L. Roark et al., *The American Promise: A History of the United States* (Bedford/St. Martin's, 2005).

DALLACE W. UNGER, JR.
INDEPENDENT SCHOLAR

Presidential Election of 1836

IN THE ELECTION of 1836, the Whig Party (formerly the National Republican Party) again tried to defeat the Andrew Jackson's Democrat Party in a presidential election. Unlike the previous two elections, Jackson had decided not to run again. Instead, the Democrats ran Martin Van Buren (Jackson's vice president), while the Whigs ran three different candidates because they could not come to a consensus. At this point, the Whig party was made up of groups that were anti-Jackson, but not necessarily friendly to each other. In the end, this cost them the election.

Although Jackson had decided not to run, he had not given up control of the Democratic Party. Thus, in 1835, when the party held its national convention in Baltimore, Jackson made it clear that he thought that Van Buren should be their candidate for president. The convention complied with Jackson's wishes and picked Van Buren as their candidate. Van Buren promised the convention that he would continue the work that Jackson had started during his two terms as president.

While the choice of a presidential candidate was easy, who to pick for vice president proved more difficult. It was thought that someone from the western United States would be a good choice. The final choice was Richard Mentor Johnson from Kentucky. He had fought in the War of 1812, avoided the Bank War, and made friends in the east among the working class. However, most southerners disliked him because he had a mulatto mistress with whom he had two daughters. The convention came under attack from its enemies because some states were not represented, including Tennessee. When it was determined that more votes to support what Jackson wanted were needed, a man from Tennessee was found and pressed into service as the Tennessee delegation. He, of course, voted as he was told, including supporting Johnson for vice president.

The Whig party, began in 1834, replaced the National Republican Party. They took their name from the English Whig Party that fought against the abuses by the English monarchy and the American Whigs of the Revolutionary War period. Many National Republicans had taken to calling Jackson King Andrew, and found it easy to use this association in their fight against Jackson. The party was made up of various anti-Jackson groups. In some cases, the various groups disliked each other almost as much as they disliked Jackson. The

Whigs did not hold a national convention, and instead of trying to find one candidate they could all agree on, they picked three different candidates, each with strong regional support. The idea was not to win the election, but to keep Van Buren from gaining a majority of the Electoral College. This would then send the top three candidates before the House of Representatives, who would get to pick the president. The Whigs figured they could more easily unite the party in the House than in the general election.

The three Whig candidates were Senator Daniel Webster, Senator Hugh L. White, and William Henry Harrison. Webster, from Massachusetts, had strong support in New England and with the Anti-Masonic Party; White, from Tennessee, supported states' rights and had support in the south; Harrison, a general during the War of 1812 and against the Native Americans, had strong support in the west and from the anti-Indian vote. Harrison ended up being the strongest of the three candidates.

Because Van Buren was the vice president and, therefore, sat in the Senate, the Whigs did everything they could to make him look bad in the Senate. From causing tie votes so that he had to vote on issues (the vice president only voted to break tie votes in the Senate), to causing commotions in the audience. They tried to embarrass him and force his hand on issues. They even went so far as to claim that Van Buren was nothing but a politician. They called him a dandy and a snob, and likened him to an English aristocrat. Some even said that the only reason you could tell Van Buren was a man was because of his whiskers. None of this fazed Van Buren, who had made a name for himself as a backroom politician. He was not a popular public figure, but he knew how to get things done behind the scenes and was an organizer. It was Van Buren who was responsible for many of the techniques the Democratic Party started using in the early 1830s to gain, and keep, the loyalty of its members.

The Democrats also indulged in attacks on their opponents. Given their support among the common people, they painted their opponents as elitist or self-serving. They called Webster a Federalist, and said White was a self-serving politician who had turned away from Jackson in order to further his own career, and called Harrison a failure as a general. But in general, they had trouble defending Van Buren; instead, they relied on party history and talking about the accomplishments of Jackson, Thomas Jefferson, and James Madison. They

Martin Van Buren, unfazed by personal attacks during his campaign, went on to win in 1836.

harkened back to the Democratic-Republican Party and the party's support of states' rights, strict interpretation of the Constitution, and protection of the Union. The Democrat's message was simple: a victory by their opponents was dangerous. They were said to be anti-democratic and not really interested in letting the people participate in their government.

The biggest advantage the Democrats had was the party organization they had been building over the previous 10 years. It was an organization that could work on the local level to raise money, distribute information, hold rallies, set up speakers, get support from newspapers, organize parades, and, most importantly, get the voters out to support the Democratic candidates. Although the Whigs were not as proficient as the Democrats at organizing local support, they were making headway, which would prove beneficial in the election of 1840. When all the votes had been cast, just over 57 percent of the eligible voters cast ballots. Of the votes cast, just over 50 percent of votes were for Van Buren, with 170 of the 294 electoral votes. The closest Whig was Harrison, with 39 percent of the popular vote and 73 electoral votes. The Whig tactic of trying to force the election into the House of Representatives had failed and Van Buren was elected president.

SEE ALSO: Anti-Masonic Party; Conventions, National Nominating Party; Democratic Party; Electoral College; Whig Party.

BIBLIOGRAPHY. P.F. Boller, Jr., *Presidential Campaigns: From George Washington to George W. Bush* (Oxford University Press, 2004); D.B. Cole, *Martin Van Buren and the American Political System* (Princeton University Press, 1984); L.S. Maisel and K.Z. Buckley, *Parties and Elections in America: The Electoral Process* (Rowman & Littlefield Publishers, 2005); J.L. Roark et al., *The American Promise: A History of the United States* (Bedford/St. Martin's, 2005); J.H. Silbey, *Martin Van Buren and the Emergence of American Popular Politics* (Rowman & Littlefield Publishers, 2002).

DALLACE W. UNGER, JR.
INDEPENDENT SCHOLAR

Presidential Election of 1840

AT THE END of Martin Van Buren's tumultuous first term as president of the United States, the divergent Whig Party reemerged under a unified party platform to engage in one of the most memorable campaigning spectacles ever seen in American politics. This was due, in part, to increased suffrage rights for white male voters and newfangled party organization, as well as a multitude of colorful, politically-charged negative advertisements propagated by the competitors, especially from the campaign of Whig Party candidate William Henry Harrison. Ending an era of lukewarm public interest in voting, the presidential election of 1840 garnered a staggering 80 percent voter turnout, soliciting nearly 2.5 million voters. The result of the election was a landslide Electoral College victory for the Whigs over incumbent Van Buren, despite a close popular vote.

Martin Van Buren was groomed for the presidency by his revered predecessor, Andrew Jackson, and took office after a decisive victory against an unorganized

Whig Party in the presidential election of 1836. Van Buren's tenure as the eighth president of the United States oversaw the Panic of 1837, one of the most severe financial crises in the history of the United States to that point, which had ghastly effects on his presidency and his bid for re-election in 1840. The Panic's ensuing unemployment, bank and business closures, and economic depression were largely attributable to Van Buren's predecessor Andrew Jackson's refusal to renew the charter of the Second Bank of the United States, as well as his Specie Circular executive order, which required payment for public lands in "hard money," such as gold or silver.

Van Buren inherited the consequences of Jackson's policies just weeks after taking office, but vowed to continue his predecessor's vision of American fiscal policy. Many believed that Van Buren's unwillingness to involve the government in the resuscitation of the economy was a major factor in prolonging the Panic's duration. As such, the economic depression became a central focus in the presidential election of 1840 and a major motivating force in uniting the Whig Party.

The Whig Party, after nearly obtaining a House majority in 1837, inferred that they had enough political clout to run a single candidate for the presidency in 1840, rather than running several sectional Whig candidates to muddle the Electoral College. The desire to run a single candidate and aim for a win brought together the party faithful. The three Whig candidates who emerged for the party's nomination were Winfield Scott of Virginia, Henry Clay of Kentucky, and William Henry Harrison of Ohio.

The Whig's 1839 national convention was held in Harrisburg, Pennsylvania, and marked a new precedent in American political history as the first such delegation to be called by a central party group. The Whigs also restricted the number of delegates from each state to its allotment of presidential electors, rather than allowing all of the states' electors to vote individually (and possibly tipping the scale by their attendance). At the nominating convention, political maneuvering by shrewd Whig politicians in attendance shifted the nomination in favor of Harrison over Henry Clay, who was portrayed as a candidate who could not defeat Van Buren in the general election. Clay indignantly declined an invitation to run as Harrison's vice presidential candidate on the party ticket after conceding the Whig nomination. John Tyler, a Virginian and close friend of Clay, was chosen as the vice presidential candidate instead. A ratifying convention was later held in Baltimore, Maryland, at the same time and in the same city as the Democratic gathering.

THE WHIG STRATEGY

Andrew Jackson's vivacious election campaign against John Quincy Adams in 1828 painted him as a charismatic man of the people. Nostalgically referred to as Old Hickory, Jackson keenly utilized this manipulation of imagery to galvanize crowds while on the campaign trail. The Whigs took this cue from Jacksonian campaigning, but went further, astutely using the press's influence and manipulating folk culture to create a larger-than-life hero out of Whig candidate Harrison. Instead of Old Hickory or Old Kinderhook (as Van Buren was nicknamed, leading to the use of the vernacular term O.K.), the image of Old Tippecanoe emerged, playing on Harrison's victory at the Battle of Tippecanoe in the War of 1812. The "man of the people" theme was revitalized for a presidential candidate, despite Harrison's wealthy upbringing.

Harrison's political background consisted of service as the first governor of the Indiana Territory, tenure as a member of the U.S. House of Representatives and Senate, and a stint as the U.S. minister to Colombia. He was by no means the decorated war hero that Andrew Jackson was, yet the Whig Party, utilizing Jackson's campaign forte, turned Harrison into a war-trodden folk hero through selective imagery. The slogan that is most identifiable with the election of 1840 was "Tippecanoe and Tyler Too!" the battle cry of Whig supporters. Folk songs, chants, and cartoons incorporated the slogan and invited lay people into the political foray as purveyors of the new oral traditions.

The common man image was continued through advertisements claiming Harrison's fondness for hard cider, coupled it with images of rustic log cabins. The shaped the public perception of Harrison as a common man, someone who could appear at a local tavern to share a few pints, rather than indulge in luxurious excess as Martin Van Buren had been accused of doing. In fact, the imagery was so indicative of Harrison's campaign that it was labeled The Log Cabin Campaign of 1840. The Old Tippecanoe spiel intrigued many inexperienced, new voters and the Whigs were aware of their burgeoning presence. The Whigs shrewdly tailored their message to new voters who had recently obtained suffrage, thereby acclimating them into the Whig political arena before the Democrats could exercise their influence.

In addition to the Whigs' utilization of songs, advertising, and influence on folk culture, the Whigs decided to personally attack the character and competence of incumbent Martin Van Buren, labeling him Martin Van Ruin and lamenting his supposed fondness of luxury during the Panic of 1837 (for which he was blamed). Building on their repertoire of cheerful songs and chants about Whig fortitude, the Whigs lambasted Van Buren by attributing the economic disparity solely to his incompetence and lavish tastes. Cries of "Van is a used up man!" among other insidious chants filled Whig rallies and advertisements. Van Buren and the Democrats dismissed the Whigs' claims as fraudulent and tried to fight back with chastising songs and advertisements of their own, but they simply did not carry the force or influence that the Whigs commanded. As the dust set-

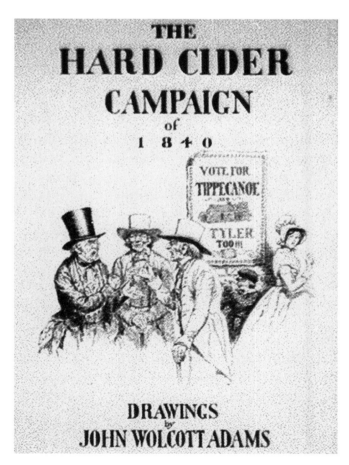

The colorful election of 1840 brought nearly 2.5 million voters to the polls—an 80 percent voter turnout rate.

tled in the presidential election of 1840, one fact was clear: The methods of negative campaigning, mobilization of organized political activity, and increased public interest in such a dirty campaign would reshape subsequent presidential elections in the years to come.

VOTER TURNOUT

After the demise of the Federalist Party and gradual cessation of the Democratic-Republicans, the second party system emerged in the 1820s, ushering in a new era of organized political factions: the Whigs, led by Henry Clay, and the Democrats, led by Andrew Jackson. This resurgence of political party allegiances allowed for greater individual involvement in politics, campaigning, and most importantly, voting. Additionally, new legislation allotted greater voting rights for white males in America, despite denying suffrage to freed slaves and women. Increased suffrage rights and political organization led to a dramatic increase in voter participation in 1840, fueled by the Harrison campaign's relentless negative campaigning against Van Buren and the manipulation of folk culture through media outlets and public conventions.

The combination of these factors garnered an unprecedented 80.2 percent voter turnout, up from 58 percent in 1836, and 27 percent in 1824. Harrison acquired 53 percent (1,275,016) of the popular vote to Van Buren's 46.75 percent (1,129,102), with .25 percent (7,069) going to Liberty Party candidate James Birney. Despite the relative closeness of the popular vote, Harrison handily defeated Van Buren in the Electoral College, with 234 electoral votes (19 states) to Van Buren's 60 electoral votes (seven states).

SEE ALSO: Advertising, Campaign; Campaigns, Presidential; Landslides, Election; Presidential Election of 1828; Presidential Election of 1836; Negative Campaigning; Voter Turnout; Whig Party.

BIBLIOGRAPHY. W.J. Cooper, M.F. Holt, and John McCardell, eds., *A Master's Due: Essays in Honor of David Herbert Donald* (Louisiana State University Press, 1985); R.P. Formisano, "The New Political History and the Election of 1840," *Journal of Interdisciplinary History* (v.23/4, 1993); J.G. Gasaway, "Tippecanoe and the Party Press Too: Mass Communication, Politics, Culture, and the Fabled Presidential Election of 1840," dissertation, (University of Illinois, Urbana-Champaign, 1998); A.M. Schlesinger, Jr., ed., *History of American Presidential Elections 1789– 1968* (McGraw-Hill, 1971).

TREVOR J. BLANK
INDIANA UNIVERSITY

Presidential Election of 1844

THE ELECTION OF 1844 challenged the ability of the two parties to secure a national coalition. The debate over the annexation of Texas and the protective tariff forced the candidates to articulate region-specific messages designed to garner support across sections. In addition, the emergence of the Liberty Party and nativist sentiment influenced the electoral strategy of the two major party candidates. In the early stages of William Henry Harrison's presidency, congressional Whigs, led by Henry Clay of Kentucky, wanted to enact a legislative agenda addressing core Whig issues.

The highlights of the legislative package called for a new national bank charter, the distribution of the proceeds from public land sales throughout the states, internal improvements, and a protective tariff. Almost immediately, Harrison took ill and died, forcing Vice President John Tyler to assume the presidency. Tyler was not as sympathetic to the Whig legislation. His opposition caused Whigs to resign from his cabinet and to formally drop him from the party. Tyler filled the vacant cabinet slots with conservative Democrats and supporters of states' rights.

ANNEXATION OF TEXAS

The debate over whether the United States should annex Texas greatly exacerbated tensions in the Democratic Party, more than in the Whig Party. A latent pro-Texas faction existed in the Democratic Party. As a proponent and visionary of the two-party system in the United States, Martin Van Buren feared the formation of parties along sectional issues, which he believed would split the Union. The annexation of Texas threatened this arrangement. Van Buren worked to articulate party policies that would appeal across sections, and sought to keep this issue out of the 1844 campaign. The Texas issue gained momentum, primarily because Tyler needed an issue on which to stake his campaign. Tyler and John C. Calhoun effectively framed the issue as one of survival for slavery. The United States needed to acquire the Texas territory in order to protect slavery from British interference. Van Buren was principally opposed to the preemptive use of force. He attempted to satisfy the pro-Texas and anti-Texas factions of the party by carving out a moderate position, voicing support for annexation if the next Senate voted for it.

NATIONAL CONVENTIONS

In May of 1844, the Whig national convention met in Baltimore. Clay easily received the nomination for president. Theodore Frelinghuysen (New Jersey) was chosen as his running mate. The Democrats' candidate selection process was beset with intra-party antagonisms. Van Buren's desire to return to the White House met resistance due to questions of his electability, his alliance with hard-money men, and his association with Andrew Jackson's economic policies. Also, many presidential aspirants feared another Van Buren term would endanger their chances of attaining the high office. This group included James Buchanan (Pennsylvania), Calhoun (South Carolina), and Lewis Cass (Michigan). Van Buren still had a strong chance of securing the nomination primarily due to the inability of the anti-Van Buren Democrats to coalesce around a single challenger.

The Democratic national nominating convention also convened in Baltimore in May. By this time, the question of the annexation of Texas had taken center stage. Van Buren's stance on this issue put him at odds with many of the southern and western Democrats, who saw the annexation of Texas as necessary to safeguard the legality of slavery in the United States. Mindful of his supporters in his home state of New York, the growing abolition sentiment there and in other northern areas, Van Buren staked out a moderate position in hopes of maintaining the north-south coalition he had successfully cultivated for so long.

The adoption of the two-thirds rule, requiring a nominee to garner the vote of at least two-thirds of the convention delegates, upset the pro–Van Buren faction. Van Buren could get the nomination with a simple majority vote of the state delegations, but probably could not garner two-thirds of the votes. The anti–Van Buren forces successfully convinced the convention to adopt this rule, which had been in practice in the 1832 and 1836 conventions. With 266 votes needed to win the nomination (compared to the 134 that constituted a majority), Van Buren received 146 votes on the first bal-

James Polk won an extremely close election in 1844, defeating Henry Clay by only 1.4 percent of the popular vote.

lot. On subsequent ballots, Van Buren's total declined in favor of his chief rival, Cass. Realizing that their chances were bleak, Van Buren and his supporters looked for another candidate. As a result, James Knox Polk (Tennessee) was selected as the Democratic nominee for president on the ninth ballot. George M. Dallas (Pennsylvania) served as his running mate.

PLATFORMS

The Whig national platform briefly stated its support of core party principles, such as the protective tariff, and distribution of proceeds from public land sales, but devoted the remainder of its resolutions to endorsing the ticket. The New York State platform also endorsed those core principles and its national and state tickets, but included lengthy resolutions opposing the annexation of Texas. The Democratic national platform offered more detail in support of its core principles: opposition to a protective tariff, internal improvements, and a national bank. Regarding slavery, the platform stated the party's belief that the Constitution prohibited congressional interference "with or control [of] the domestic institutions of the several States." Lastly, the platform briefly mentioned the right of the United States to the Oregon Territory and to Texas. Like the Whig's New York state platform, the Democratic state platform reaffirmed support for core party principles. The main difference was that no mention of slavery or the annexation of Texas appeared in the Democratic document.

THE PROTECTIVE TARIFF

The tariff debate had existed since the nation's founding. Northern industrial interests favored a high tariff on imports to provide revenue as well as protection for domestic industries. Southern plantation interests argued against a high tariff for fear of reciprocal tariffs, which would adversely affect their ability to sell their goods overseas. The Whigs were associated with the former position, and the Democrats the latter. In 1844, Democratic strategists calculated that the south would support Polk based on Texas, but would need to articulate a position on the tariff to win Pennsylvania to enhance their electoral chances. In a letter to John Kane of Philadelphia, Polk shrewdly articulated a tariff position that appealed to Pennsylvanians without alienating his southern supporters. Polk reaffirmed his support for a tariff to generate revenue, but also one that would "afford reasonable incidental protection."

The arrival of the Liberty Party and the American Party (also known as the Know-Nothing Party) on the political scene undercut Clay's chances in the election. The Liberty Party forced Clay to address slavery. Abolitionist sentiment had been growing in New York, Ohio, and other northern regions. The Liberty Party formed to voice this concern and nominated James G. Birney as its presidential candidate. Clay completely mishandled attacks from the Democrats and abolitionists on his slavery stance. Through a series of letters published in the press, Clay obfuscated his position, undercutting his credibility on this issue. In the south, Clay "modified" his position on Texas by stating that he no longer adamantly opposed annexation; in the north, Clay tried to avoid aligning himself too closely with either side.

The American Party, formed in 1843 in New York City, soon spread to Philadelphia. This nativist organization espoused anti-Catholic and anti-immigrant beliefs.

Historically, the Democrats have been more welcoming to immigrants. The Whigs tried to strike up an alliance with the nativists in Philadelphia, which backfired when the nativist campaign frightened immigrants in New York City and Philadelphia, increasing registration and turnout. Clay lost Pennsylvania.

The Democrats won an extremely close election. James Polk defeated Henry Clay by 1.4 percent of the popular vote, and 170 to 105 of the electoral vote. In 15 of the 26 states, the winner had a lead of less than eight percent. Furthermore, Polk fared extremely well in the south, losing only North Carolina, Tennessee, and Clay's home state of Kentucky.

SEE ALSO: Conventions, National Nominating Party; Democratic Party; Presidential Election of 1840; Presidential Election of 1848; Whig Party.

BIBLIOGRAPHY. Lee Benson, *The Concept of Jacksonian Democracy: New York as a Test Case* (Princeton University Press, 1961); CQ Press, www.cqpress.com (cited August 2007); M.F. Holt, *The Rise of the American Whig Party: Jacksonian Politics and the Onset of the Civil War* (Oxford University Press, 1999); J.L. Moore, J.P. Preimesberger, and D.R. Tarr, *Guide to U.S. Elections* (CQ Press, 2001); A.M. Schlesinger, Jr., *History of American Presidential Elections* (Chelsea House Publishers, 1971).

ADAM SILVER
BOSTON UNIVERSITY

Presidential Election of 1848

THE ELECTION OF 1848 can be characterized as the first to feature a candidate-centered campaign. Smarting from their defeat in the 1844 election, the Whig Party chose not to articulate any substantive positions in their official platform. Rather, the party focused attention on their nominee, General Zachary Taylor, and crafted messages to appeal to the different regional interests.

At the same time, the Democrats needed to choose a new nominee. Upon his election in 1844, James Polk stated his intention to serve a single term. In 1848, the parties' responses to the Wilmot Proviso and the treaty concluding the war with Mexico significantly impacted the election. Moreover, the inception of the Free Soil Party drastically altered the campaign in the north.

THE WILMOT PROVISO & THE TREATY OF GUADALUPE HIDALGO

David Wilmot (Pennsylvania) introduced legislation stating that slavery should be prohibited in all territory acquired as a result of the war with Mexico. Although this legislation never became law, it fostered a schism within the Democratic Party, most notably in New York. Lewis Cass (Michigan) offered a path to Democratic unity. In December 1847, Cass penned a letter to A.O.P. Nicholson of Tennessee, addressing the questions raised by the Wilmot Proviso. He stated that the people residing in each official U.S. territory should possess the authority to decide for themselves whether they wanted to legalize slavery in their domain. In articulating the rational for popular sovereignty, Cass mended Democratic fences and paved the way for his nomination at the 1848 national convention.

The United States treaty concluding the war with Mexico in February 1848 was called the Treaty of Guadalupe Hidalgo. The United States acquired California, New Mexico, what would become Nevada, Utah, and Arizona, and parts of Colorado and Wyoming. Furthermore, in 1846, the United States settled a dispute with Great Britain over the Oregon Territory. The countries used the 49th parallel as the dividing line: Below it, the United States carved out Washington, and above it, Britain received British Columbia.

THE NATIONAL CONVENTIONS

The Wilmot Proviso, the territorial agreement with Great Britain, and the Treaty of Guadalupe Hidalgo all created dissension among the national Democrats. northern Democrats harbored concerns that the northwest territorial acquisitions did not match the growth in the southwest. They wanted the two regions to keep pace balancing slave and free territories. Furthermore, growing anti-slavery sentiment in the north pushed the debate over the extension of slavery to the forefront.

The divisiveness of this issue crystallized in the schism of the New York State Democrats. Barnburners consisting of Martin Van Buren supporters who favored reforms and opposed the extension of slavery. Hunkers were conservatives with ties to traditional and southern Democrats. Cass's endorsement of popular sovereignty unified the majority of the national Democrats, but not the Barnburners. The Democrats convened in May in Baltimore and selected Cass as the party nominee on the 4th ballot. William O. Butler was nominated for the vice

presidency. Cass not only hailed from Michigan, but boasted a great deal of support from Ohio. Butler represented the state of Kentucky on the national ticket.

The Whig convention met in June in Philadelphia. On the 4th ballot, the Whigs selected General Zachary Taylor as their nominee. Millard Fillmore completed the ticket as the vice presidential nominee. Taylor fit the Whig desire to run a national candidate who appealed across regions and parties. Because Taylor was from Louisiana and Fillmore from New York, the Whigs, like their main opponent, presented a balanced ticket for the upcoming campaign.

NATIONAL PLATFORMS

Although party leaders articulate policy positions and proposals to their constituents throughout campaigns in various newspapers, other publications, and speeches, platforms are unique in that they represent the official

The Whigs won another election when Taylor defeated Cass by less than five percent of the popular vote.

party positions in the ongoing campaign. The Democratic national platform echoed many of the sentiments expressed in the 1844 platform. The Democrats emphasized their belief that the federal government "is one of limited powers," and their opposition to a national bank, internal improvements, and a protective tariff. In addition, the Democrats expressed their support for the war with Mexico and their presidential nominee. However, out of nine planks and 13 additional resolutions, only one resolution mentioned slavery. The seventh resolution merely endorsed the principle of popular sovereignty. Congress lacks the constitutional authority "to interfere with or control the domestic institutions of the several States, and that such States are the sole and proper judges of everything appertaining to their own affairs, not prohibited by the Constitution."

In contrast, the Whigs did not draft a platform of principles. The Whig platform of 1848 simply espoused why Taylor deserved the support of the electorate. There are only vague references to core party policies, such as protection, the national bank, and internal improvements. The absence of any mention of slavery in the platform highlights Whig campaign strategy. Strategists intended to avoid any divisive issues, nationally in favor of running regional campaigns and messages. For example, the Whigs countered Democratic questions of Taylor's stance on slavery by producing documents depicting Taylor's favorable stance toward slavery in the south, while repeatedly stating his opposition to the expansion of slavery in the north. In addition, they turned their focus away from specific issues in favor of playing on the party's steadfast ideological principles.

Taylor lacked party credentials in the sense that he was not popularly associated as an ardent Whig. Beginning in 1846, Taylor campaigned and accepted nominations from small groups of Democrats, nativists, and Whigs in hopes of cultivating broad support for a run at the Whig nomination. This lack of partisan pedigree hurt his standing with the Whig faithful. A letter written to his brother-in-law, Captain John Allison, only ended up creating more anxiety among party stalwarts. Taylor stated that while he was a Whig, he was not "an ultra Whig." Furthermore, Taylor pledged not to abuse the presidential veto while in office, which could be construed as an endorsement of popular sovereignty and non-interference in the expansion of slavery. The need to assuage Whig partisan anxiety forced Taylor to write a second letter to Allison in September. He clarified his

earlier "ultra Whig" statement as simply iterating basic Whig anti-party sentiment. In office, Taylor would not be ardently partisan. The second letter produced the desired effect.

The Barnburner faction of the New York Democrats joined with the anti-slavery Whigs, former members of the Liberty Party, and other sympathetic northerners to form the Free Soil Party in August 1848. Martin Van Buren and Charles F. Adams were selected as the presidential and vice presidential nominees. Unlike Taylor's vague statements about slavery and Cass's endorsement of popular sovereignty, the Free Soilers presented an unambiguous slogan of "Free Soil, Free Speech, Free Labor, and Free Men."

THE CAMPAIGN

Louisiana and Georgia voted Democratic in 1844, but Taylor was from Baton Rouge and the Whigs developed a strong organization in Georgia. These two facts bolstered Whig chances in these states. New York and Pennsylvania also seemed attainable for the Whigs. New York was widely expected to go Whig due to a split in the Democratic vote between Cass and Van Buren. The Democratic vote also could split in Pennsylvania due to Wilmot's popularity. In addition, the Whigs reaffirmed their alliance with the growing nativist constituency in the state. Ohio supported Clay in 1844, but Cass had a great deal of support, and the anti-slavery vote was expected to divide between the Whigs and Free Soilers.

The Whigs won another close 19th century election. Taylor defeated Cass by less than five percent of the popular vote, and 163 to 127 of the electoral vote. Van Buren received slightly more than 10 percent of the popular vote. Taylor realized the Whig strategy in garnering a national, not sectional, victory. He won eight southern states (11 electoral votes) and seven free states (25 electoral votes). In addition, Taylor exceeded Clay's total from 1844. Finally, five states switched parties after 1844: Georgia, Louisiana, New York, and Pennsylvania went Whig; and Ohio went Democratic. The Free Soil Party only affected the outcome of the vote in New York.

SEE ALSO: Conventions, National Nominating Party; Democratic Party; Free Soil Party; Popular Sovereignty; Presidential Election of 1844; Presidential Election of 1852; Whig Party.

BIBLIOGRAPHY. CQ Press, www.cqpress.com (cited August 2007); M.F. Holt, *The Rise of the American Whig Party: Jackso-*

nian Politics and the Onset of the Civil War (Oxford University Press, 1999); J.L. Moore, J.P.Preimesberger, and D.R. Tarr, eds., *Guide to U.S. Elections* (CQ Press, 2001); K.H. Porter and D.B. Johnson, eds., *National Party Platforms, 1840–1960* (University of Illinois Press, 1961); A.M. Schlesinger, Jr., *History of American Presidential Elections* (Chelsea House Publishers, 1971).

ADAM SILVER
BOSTON UNIVERSITY

Presidential Election of 1852

1852 WAS THE last election in which the Whig Party fielded a presidential candidate. General Winfield Scott's lopsided defeat at the hands of Franklin Pierce ultimately spelled the end of the Whig Party as a competitive opposition party to the Democrats. Initially, the oncoming campaign bode well for the Whigs. Although the Democrats always held an organizational advantage, by this time the Whigs also possessed a viable political organization. Perhaps more importantly, the Whigs controlled the White House. However, the fallout from the war with Mexico, manifested in the Compromise of 1850, fostered divisions in the Whig Party during the 1852 campaign.

In addition, growing anti-slavery sentiment and nativism undercut Whig strength in the north. The Compromise of 1850 caused intra-party strife for the Democrats as well. But, by the time the convention met in June, the party had been able to reach a consensus to at least mute sectional differences over this issue.

THE COMPROMISE OF 1850

As a result of the war with Mexico, the United States acquired California, New Mexico, the eventual states of Utah, Arizona, and Nevada, and parts of Colorado and Wyoming. A debate ensued over the extension of slavery. In December 1847, Lewis Cass, the future Democratic nominee, articulated the policy of popular sovereignty: territorial residents should have the authority to decide whether or not to permit slavery in their domain. However, as California broached statehood, this question generated intense debate and intra-party strife. Congressional moderates attempted to mute sectional antagonisms by drafting a compromise, broken up over five bills. The Compromise of 1850 initially overrode the 36°30' latitude division of the Missouri Compromise. The origi-

nal agreement stated that all territory north of this line would be free and all territory south of it would be slave. The new agreement would admit California as a free state (based on popular sovereignty), carve New Mexico and Utah out of Texas, prohibit slave trade, but maintain the legality of slavery in Washington, D.C., and strengthen the Fugitive Slave Law. This latter point was intended to mollify southern interests by reaffirming and enhancing federal enforcement of the existing law.

The Compromise did not have the desired effect. Southerners split into Unionist and States' Rights camps, regardless of party, based on their support or opposition to the legislation. Congress also divided along moderate and radical lines. In the Senate, southern Whigs and northern Democrats seemed to be more moderate than northern Whigs and southern Democrats. The House divided more clearly along sectional lines: southerners exhibited greater unity than northerners.

President Taylor opposed the Compromise measures. Although Taylor owned slaves and believed that the Constitution prevented Congress from interfering with slavery in the states where it was currently legal, he adamantly opposed the extension of slavery into new western territories. However, the unexpected death of Taylor a few days after an Independence Day celebration in 1850 altered the fortunes of this legislation. Vice President Millard Fillmore assumed the presidency upon Taylor's death and voiced his support for the compromise.

THE NATIONAL CONVENTIONS

By the time the Democrats convened their national convention at Baltimore in June, party leaders had reduced intra-party friction over the Compromise. In fact, supporters of the compromise engineered a strong push for the party to adopt the Compromise as the policy of the Democrats and the final settlement of the slavery question. The convention adopted the two-thirds rule, requiring a successful nominee to garner the vote of two-thirds of the convention delegates. Franklin Pierce of New Hampshire floated his name as a Compromise candidate if the convention could not strongly support one aspirant. Finally, on the 49th ballot, Pierce beat out Lewis Cass (Michigan), James Buchanan (Pennsylvania), William Marcy (New York), and Stephen Douglas (Illinois) to receive the nomination. William R. King of Alabama was chosen as the vice presidential nominee to balance the ticket.

The popular vote was close, but Franklin Pierce trounced Scott in the Electoral College in 1852.

The Whigs also convened in Baltimore in June. The Whigs faced internal conflict primarily over the Fugitive Slave Law. The southern wing of the party held reservations about the younger party faction from the north, led by the New Yorkers William Seward and Thurlow Weed, which began to align itself with the increasing Free Soil sentiment. Seward hoped to counter dissension between eastern and western Whigs over the tariff and internal improvements by cultivating a new alliance on a moderate anti-slavery platform. Moreover, party leaders recognized the need to develop a strategy to counter growing nativist support in the north. A Whig-Nativist alliance enabled Taylor to win Pennsylvania in 1848, but by 1852, nativists threatened to undercut Whig electoral chances. Unlike the Democrats, Whig convention rules required a presidential aspirant merely to receive the support of a majority of the delegates to secure the nomination.

General Winfield Scott won the nomination on the 53rd ballot. Southerners disapproved of Scott because he was widely believed to be beholden to the northern faction of the party led by Seward and Weed. However, once he received the nomination, Scott mollified southerners and angered northerners by endorsing the eighth resolution of the national platform, which stated Whig support for the Compromise measures and the Fugitive Slave Law.

NATIONAL PLATFORMS

The Democratic national platform echoed many of the sentiments expressed in the 1844 and 1848 platforms, especially those reaffirming their belief in federal government "of limited powers" and opposition to a national bank, internal improvements, and a protective tariff. However, the 1852 platform contained three resolutions addressing slavery compared to only one resolution in 1848. As in 1848, the Democrats endorsed the principles of popular sovereignty and non-interference by Congress. But, in 1852, the platform included a plank forcefully supporting the Fugitive Slave Law. Although some party leaders advocated for a plank designating the Compromise as the final statement on slavery, a resolution merely asserts the party's willingness to "resist all attempts at renewing, in congress or out of it, the agitation of the slavery question."

The Whig platform contained resolutions expressing core party policies, such as protection and internal improvements. In addition, while the party recognized the "limited" nature of the government, it ultimately endorsed expansive federal power through the necessary and proper clause. The eighth resolution confirmed the Whigs' support for the Compromise and, specifically, for the Fugitive Slave Law. The eighth resolution and Scott's emphatic support of it caused anti-slavery Whigs to bolt the party and align with Free Soil supporters. The Whig/Free Soil ticket included John P. Hale of New Hampshire and George Washington Julian of Indiana for president and vice president, respectively. Without the celebrity of Martin Van Buren as its standard bearer, the Free Soil Party did not fare as well in the 1852 election as it did in 1848. Hale received only 4.9 percent of the popular vote. The slogan of "Free Soil, Free Speech, Free Labor, and Free Men" appealed to anti-slavery northerners and siphoned votes from the Whig nominee.

In the end, Pierce trounced Scott in the Electoral College, accelerating the demise of the American Whig Party. Pierce won all but four states: Massachusetts,

Vermont, Utah, and Kentucky. However, the popular vote was much closer. Pierce defeated the combination of Scott, Hale, and Webster (who had recently died) by only 1.6 percent. Nevertheless, this was the last election in which the Whigs fielded a presidential candidate. The agitation of the slavery question in the Kansas-Nebraska Act of 1854, and the confluence of ethno-cultural issues, particularly nativism, overwhelmed the Whigs. By 1856, most former Whigs joined either the newly-formed Republican and Know-Nothing parties, or moderate Democratic organizations.

SEE ALSO: Conventions, National Nominating Party; Democratic Party; Presidential Election of 1848; Presidential Election of 1856; Whig Party.

BIBLIOGRAPHY. CQ Press, www.cqpress.com (cited August 2007); W.E. Gienapp, *The Origins of the Republican Party, 1852–1856* (Oxford University Press, 1987); M.F. Holt, *The Rise of the American Whig Party: Jacksonian Politics and the Onset of the Civil War* (Oxford University Press, 1999); J.L. Moore, J.P.Preimesberger, and D.R. Tarr, eds., *Guide to U.S. Elections* (CQ Press, 2001); A.M. Schlesinger, Jr., *History of American Presidential Elections* (Chelsea House Publishers, 1971).

ADAM SILVER
BOSTON UNIVERSITY

Presidential Election of 1856

THE 1856 PRESIDENTIAL election campaign differed dramatically from the previous antebellum campaigns in its sectional focus. In previous elections, from roughly the mid-1830s through 1852, the two major parties attempted to secure a national victory. They promoted core party principles, but tweaked them to recognize regional concerns. However, the introduction of the Kansas-Nebraska Act, in 1854, revitalized the slavery issue, altering the political landscape.

The new Republican Party, formed out of the demise of the Whigs, hoped to gain the White House by running a campaign in the north. The Democratic Party, recognizing its base lay in the south, concentrated campaign efforts there, while making forays into the north, and more importantly, the West. The nativist American Party affected campaign strategy as well.

THE KANSAS-NEBRASKA ACT (1854)

The 1852 election garnered a huge victory for the Democratic Party, with Franklin Pierce in the White House and a 2:1 majority in the Congress. The deaths of well-known leaders Henry Clay and Daniel Webster, and the lopsided defeat of General Winfield Scott, severely hampered the Whigs' ability to foment an effective opposition to the Democrats. Furthermore, the Compromise of 1850, which allowed the admission of California as a free state and provided for federal enforcement of the Fugitive Slave law, appeared to settle the slavery issue.

Stephen Douglas (Illinois) introduced the Kansas-Nebraska Act in January of 1854. The legislation divided the Nebraska Territory in two, to Kansas and Nebraska. Each territory could enter the Union as either free or slave based on popular sovereignty. The act also specifically repealed the 36°30' north latitude component of the Missouri Compromise, which prohibited slavery in all areas north of this line and allowed for slavery all areas south. The last component re-agitated the slavery question because anti-slavery forces believed that it refocused the goal of the bill from westward development to the expansion of slavery. The prospect of opening up new lands to slavery undercut the finality of the slavery question. Moreover, the act helped appease pro-slavery groups, who felt betrayed by the Compromise of 1850 because the northern states refused to enforce the Fugitive Slave Law.

The Democrats experienced a three-way schism: anti-Nebraska, or Independent Democrats; southern and pro-slavery factions who maintained a semblance of support in the north; and northern Democrats looking to mend the rift. The Independent Democrats issued an appeal to the nation asserting that the act was a blatant attempt to spread slavery. The Whigs split between a traditional party faction consisting of northeastern commercial interests and almost all the southern Whigs, known as Silver Greys, and a northern anti-slavery faction, known as Conscience Whigs or Woolly Heads.

The American Party complicated matters even further. This party grew out of the increasing nativist anti-Catholic, anti-immigrant sentiment predominant in northern industrial areas. Although the "American Party" moniker was officially adopted in 1853, the party was informally referred to as the "Know-Nothings" due to their reputation for secrecy. The Silver Grey Whigs, led by Millard Fillmore, attempted to gain control of the Know-Nothings and shift its goals from a nativist anti-Catholic organization to an anti-Democratic, pro-Union one. Conscience Whigs, and a coalition of anti-slavery, anti-Nebraska, religious fanatics, pro-temperance, and disgruntled members of the Democrats and Know-Nothings helped to form the Republican Party in 1854.

ELECTION OF 1854 AND BLEEDING KANSAS

The 1854 midterm elections resulted in a resounding defeat for the Democrats in the north, and their losing the majority in the House. The Kansas-Nebraska Act opened up the slavery debate. While the Know-Nothings tried to mute the issue, instead focusing on anti-Catholicism and anti-immigration, the Republicans made slavery the center of their campaign. In addition to a pathway to economic development between the east and west, Kansas's location caused it be the focus of the renewed battle between northern and southern anti- and pro-slavery forces.

The popular sovereignty component of the act sparked immigration to the territory by both factions. The First Territorial legislature adopted a pro-slavery constitution. Citing fraud, anti-slavery forces adopted a free-state constitution in Topeka. As a result, Kansas boasted two competing governments. Violence erupted between the two groups, almost to the point of civil war within the territory. President Pierce recognized the pro-slavery government in Lecompton, while the free-state governments set up in Lawrence and Topeka. Tensions ran high in the U.S. Congress, too. The infamous caning of Senator Charles Sumner of Massachusetts occurred at this time. On the Senate floor, Sumner attacked Pierce and his Kansas policy, and Senator Andrew Pickens Butler of South Carolina. Sumner's speech angered Butler's nephew, Representative Preston Brooks, who caned Sumner into unconsciousness in the Senate chamber.

THE NATIONAL CONVENTIONS

The American Party convened in February in Philadelphia. A split over slavery resulted in the anti-slavery faction walking out; they eventually joined the Republicans. As a result, the main convention consisted of a mostly southern body. Millard Fillmore (New York), the former Whig, received the presidential nomination; and Andrew J. Donelson, the vice presidential nomination. The Democrats met in June in Cincinnati. The re-agitation of slavery split the party. Leaders sought to appease northerners to prevent them from leaving the party. As Pierce and Douglas's stances on slavery made them unacceptable to the north, Buchanan, hailing from Pennsylvania, emerged as the compromise candidate. He received the nomination on the 17th ballot. John C. Breckinridge (Kentucky) became his running mate.

The Republicans met in June in Philadelphia. Delegates from all free states, and four of the border slave states, attended. The party chose John C. Fremont (South Carolina) as its first presidential nominee, and W.L. Dayton (New Jersey) as the vice presidential nominee. Some delegates believed that Simon Cameron of Pennsylvania should have been nominated as Fremont's running mate to offset Buchanan's popularity in his home state. In comparison to the more staid and polished Fillmore and Buchanan, Fremont was younger, more brash, and passionate. Old Line Whigs attempted to influence the campaign and maybe even resurrect the party by holding a convention in September in Baltimore. The convention endorsed Fillmore and reflected his attempt to shift the Americans toward an anti-sectional, pro-Union party.

NATIONAL PLATFORMS

The American Party platform articulated anti-Catholic and anti-immigrant stances. With regard to slavery, the Americans resolved in favor of popular sovereignty and the noninterference of Congress in the affairs of the states. Finally, the party endorsed Fillmore's support for the Union. The Whig platform of 1856 exclusively focused on the perpetuation of the Union and the endorsement of Fillmore; it did not mention any nativist sentiment. The Democratic platform echoed many of the sentiments expressed in previous platforms: especially those reaffirming their belief in a federal government "of limited powers," opposition to a national bank, internal improvements, and a protective tariff. However, this platform included statements opposing nativism, and devoted a great deal of attention to slavery. The Democrats endorsed the principles of popular sovereignty, noninterference by Congress in the domestic matters of the states, enforcement of the Fugitive Slave Law, and that the Compromise measures of 1850 settled the slavery question. Finally, they condemned the sectional (Republican) party for fomenting disunion by its rejection of the Compromise measures and agitating sectional division. The Republican platform countered the non-interference doctrine by asserting federal authority over the territories, especially in regard to the prohibition of slavery and polygamy.

The Republicans demanded the admission of Kansas under the Topeka Constitution and the prohibition of the extension of slavery into any new territory. Finally, they attributed criminality to the Pierce Administration based on its Kansas policy, and promised to bring all perpetrators to justice.

THE CAMPAIGN

The Democrats framed the campaign as one between union and disunion. They charged the Republicans with fomenting sectional disunion based on their inflammatory rhetoric regarding slavery and federal authority. The Democrats made a valiant attempt to secure a national victory: Buchanan articulated a moderate position in the north, claiming he would find an equitable solution to the problem, maintain the Union, and admit Kansas as a free state; in the south, he promised to end the violence in Kansas and defeat the sectional Republicans. The Republicans did not run a ticket in the south, conceding the region to Buchanan, who they believed would carry it anyway. The campaign trumpeted its youthful candidate and image. In contrast to its rivals, who were old and corrupt, the Republicans represented change and new energy.

Buchanan defeated his opponents by garnering 174 electoral votes to Fremont's 114 and Fillmore's eight. Buchanan got 45.3 percent of the popular vote, Fremont 33.1 percent, and Fillmore 22 percent. Fremont won all but five of the 16 northern states, and did not receive a vote in the south, which went for Buchanan, as did Pennsylvania. New England overwhelmingly supported Fremont. Fillmore won one state: Maryland. The Republican support came predominantly from densely populated urban areas, while the Democrats fared well in rural areas. The Americans influenced the race by forcing Democrats, Republicans, and former Whigs to address nativist sentiment, especially in the Mid-Atlantic region. The Republicans' strong showing in the north generated concern among Democrats who feared that a strong sectional, anti-slavery party could one day control the south.

SEE ALSO: American Party; Conventions, National Nominating Party; Democratic Party; Presidential Election of 1852; Presidential Election of 1860; Republican Party; Whig Party.

BIBLIOGRAPHY. Tyler Anbinder, *Nativism & Slavery: The Northern Know Nothings & the Politics of the 1850s* (Oxford University Press, 1992); CQ Press, www.cqpress.com (cited August 2007); Eric Foner, *Free Soil, Free Labor, Free Men: The Ideology of the Republican Party before the Civil War* (Oxford University Press, 1995); W.E. Gienapp, *The Origins of the Republican Party, 1852–1856* (Oxford University Press, 1987); J.L. Moore, J.P.Preimesberger, and D.R. Tarr, *Guide to U.S. Elections* (CQ Press, 2001); K.H. Porter and D.B. Johnson, eds., *National Party Platforms, 1840–1960* (University of Illinois Press, 1961); A.M. Schlesinger, Jr., *History of American Presidential Elections* (Chelsea House Publishers, 1971).

ADAM SILVER
BOSTON UNIVERSITY

Presidential Election of 1860

THE ELECTION OF 1860 was one of the most bitterly-contested elections in American history and occurred with the backdrop of the impending Civil War. During this tense period, divisions were apparent in American culture, people, and political parties. Ultimately, John Bell of the Constitutional Union Party, John C. Breckinridge of the Southern Democratic Party, Stephen Douglas of the Northern Democratic Party, and Abraham Lincoln of the Republican Party threw themselves into the cauldron of the times and vied for the American presidency. Lincoln was the winner as he gathered enough electoral votes from the northern states. His divisive victory was a prelude to the serious north-south divisions that would lead to the American Civil War.

BACKGROUND ISSUES

The dominant issues facing the candidates were states' rights and the institution of slavery. The question of states' rights plagued the country from its conception. State representatives of the 1787 Constitutional Convention spent five months agreeing on the details of the newly formed United States, and the power structure of each state in the overall union was a major focal point of their discussions. Slavery, the interlinked issue, was also seriously debated seven decades earlier. Ultimately, a compromise was agreed upon, in which the Constitution would allow the importation of slaves into the United States until 1808. However, there was no clear agreement on when slavery would be outlawed altogether. These arguments would fester, and a series of confrontations and compromises dominated the national landscape. In 1820, the Missouri Compromise outlawed slavery north of latitude 36°30' within the Louisiana Purchase territory. This Compromise would perilously stand for the next three decades.

As the United States continued to expand and people moved out west in search of land and riches, the question of slavery in these newly-formed territories plagued the government. Kansas and Nebraska were two territories, in particular, that faced the slavery question with fervor. During the 1850s, the plans for a transcontinental railroad were taking shape and the need for settlement in these territories was vital. Stephen Douglas, the highly-respected senator from Illinois, realized the only possible way southern lawmakers would allow the formation of these two territories was to allow the citizens in the territories to decide the question of slavery.

Douglas's Kansas-Nebraska Act ultimately eliminated the Missouri Compromise and, if voters so decided, would allow slavery north of the original regulations. In 1857, under the Dred Scott Decision, the Supreme Court decided that the newly-formed governments of the territories, as well as the federal government, did not have the constitutional right to ban slavery in the territories. This question of slavery in the territories ultimately led to a serious showdown between pro-slavery and anti-slavery forces in Kansas and Nebraska. Violence between the two groups broke out in the two territories and the territorial conflict was considered a precursor for the upcoming Civil War.

DEMOCRATIC PARTY SPLITS
The first major public split in the political sphere occurred within the Democrats. The party's nominating convention met in April 1860 in Charleston, South Carolina and many realized that a serious political confrontation would be unavoidable. Stephen Douglas was viewed as the favorite for the Democrats, but his stance on slavery put off scores of southerners. The major issue was the question of a federal slave code in the Democratic Party platform. Southern Democrats desired an endorsement of slavery in the new American territories, while northern Democrats vehemently disagreed.

The Democratic Party was torn apart after two days of turmoil and the realization that no candidate would receive the two-thirds majority for nomination. Stephen Douglas and his fellow northern Democrats left the convention without a clear consensus. Ultimately, the northern and southern Democrats decided to hold two separate conventions. Illinois Senator Stephen Douglas received the northern Democratic nomination, and Herschel Johnson of Georgia accepted the party's vice presidential nomination. Vice President John C. Breckinridge from Kentucky received the Southern Democratic nomination, and Senator Joseph Lane from Oregon received the party's vice presidential nomination.

REPUBLICAN PARTY CONVENTION
The Republican Party's convention was not as divisive an affair. Longtime Republican Party stalwart, William Seward, came into the convention with high hopes for a nomination, but Abraham Lincoln, a well-known lawyer and former congressman from Illinois, undid his dreams. Lincoln came onto the national stage during the Illinois state elections two years earlier. At the time, he was running against Democratic candidate Stephen Douglas. During his acceptance speech for the Republican senatorial nomination, Lincoln delivered his famous "House Divided" oratory in which he expounded on his beliefs that the country could not go on much longer being half slave and half free. During the senatorial campaign, which included a series of debates with Stephen Douglas, Lincoln used his law skills to craft a firm outline of his views and created connections with many leading Republicans.

Although Lincoln did not garner enough votes to win the senatorial race, he began to attract a following from Republican circles. In 1860, Lincoln delivered another famous speech at Cooper Union College in New York. The speech outlined beliefs that he would continue to espouse throughout the campaign. He did not believe that slavery should be extended into the new American territories and he disagreed with the institution of slavery. After the third ballot of the convention, Lincoln had secured enough votes to be granted the Republican Party's nomination. The party's vice presidential nominee was Hannibal Hamlin of Maine.

CONSTITUTIONAL UNION PARTY
The fourth presidential candidate in the 1860 election was Constitutional Union Party candidate John Bell. He, like many other moderate southerners of the party, was a former Whig Party member. The Constitutional Unionists believed in upholding the words and principles of the Constitution and the union of the states. Their stance was to maintain the status quo and not touch the slavery question.

This engraving depicts Abraham Lincoln's inaugural address as President in front of the Capitol in Washington on March 4, 1861, after one of the most bitterly-contested elections in American history.

CAMPAIGNING

Because of the divisive times, the campaigns were essentially split between the north and south. The Republicans and northern Democrats campaigned in the north, while the Southern Democrats and Constitutional Unionists focused on the southern states. Each respective party realized that a campaign in enemy territory would lead to tension and probable violence and overall would be a fruitless effort. As was the custom of the times, after the candidates were chosen, each party sent its leading party members to campaign for the party's elected representative. William Seward quickly recovered from his convention defeat and went barnstorming around the northern states in support of Lincoln. Many of the Republican rallies included a procession by the Wide Awakes, a young Republican group that wore caps and capes, and carried torches. Salmon Chase,

Edward Bates, and other influential Republicans also campaigned in support of Lincoln. The "fire eater," William Yancey, was the primary spokesman for the Southern Democratic candidate, John Breckinridge. During numerous speaking engagements in the north, Yancey warned northerners that a vote for Abraham Lincoln would result in the southern states seceding from the union. The main spokesman for the Constitutional Unionists, John J. Crittendon of Kentucky, warned voters of the same outcome.

Stephen Douglas decided to campaign for himself in both northern and southern states. He faced criticism from many for his personal campaigning, but as the months continued it became clear that Douglas was campaigning for more than personal gain. He realized the dire times in the United States and he saw for himself the hostility and tension the country faced. Douglas's firm beliefs in the authority of the president and the negative effects of a possible secession were displayed throughout his campaign.

Throughout the months before the November election, the Republicans were victorious in local elections in Maine and Vermont. In October, Republicans won the critical state elections in Pennsylvania and Indiana. Victory for Abraham Lincoln seemed definite. Even as he faced almost certain defeat, Douglas continued to preach the disastrous effects of secession. Toward the end of his failing campaign, Douglas traveled from city to city with the sole intention of preserving the union.

ELECTION RESULTS

On November 1860, Abraham Lincoln proved victorious in the presidential election. He garnered 1,766,452 popular votes and won 173 electoral votes. Douglas had a very commendable second place finish with 1,376,957 votes, but due to the strict north-south division, won only 12 electoral votes. The 849,781 votes cast for John Breckinridge won him 72 electoral votes. John Bell received 588,879 popular votes and won 39 electoral votes. Lincoln was the victor in all the northern states with the exception of New Jersey, while Breckinridge won all the southern states, except for Tennessee.

For Lincoln, the victorious feeling was surely fleeting. As he prepared to take office, many southern state leaders were speaking of secession from the union; the talk turned into reality over the coming months. Within six months of the presidential election, the United States was fighting the Civil War. The turbulent election of 1860 was ultimately the precursor for the deadliest domestic conflict the United States has ever faced.

SEE ALSO: Constitutional Union Party; Expansionism; Northern Democrats; Republican Party; Slavery; Southern Democratic Party; War and Peace.

BIBLIOGRAPHY. D.K. Goodwin, *Team of Rivals: The Political Genius of Abraham Lincoln* (Simon & Schuster, 2005); Harp Week, Explore History, "1860: Lincoln v. Douglas v. Breckinridge v. Bell," www.elections.harpweek.com (cited May 2007); A.M. Schlesinger, Jr. and F.L. Israel, eds., *History of American Presidential Elections 1789–2001* (Chelsea House Publishers, 2002).

GAVIN WILK
INDEPENDENT SCHOLAR

Presidential Election of 1864

IN 1864, THE American Civil War was over three years old, and the chances of Abraham Lincoln winning re-election did not appear to be good. The war was dragging on, the Union armies seemed unable to make any progress, and the casualties continued to mount. Lincoln's enemies felt that they could do a better job of bringing the war to an end. The Democrats nominated General George B. McClellan and the Radical Republicans nominated General John C. Frémont to oppose Lincoln. In the fall of 1864, the military situation changed in favor of the Union, which helped Lincoln win re-election.

The major issue of the election was the conduct of the Civil War. After over three years of horrendous casualties the war was, seemingly, nowhere near to a conclusion. The government had resorted to conscription to fill the depleted ranks of the army, the writ of habeas corpus had been suspended, taxes and inflation were high. The voters of the north were disillusioned with Lincoln and his administration. By June of 1864, General U.S. Grant was still unable to capture Richmond, Virginia (the capital of the Confederate States of America) and General William T. Sherman was bogged down outside of Atlanta, Georgia. It looked like the Confederacy might be able to survive the war if Lincoln was defeated in the election.

The mainstream Republican Party joined with the War Democrats to re-nominate Lincoln as their candidate. As his running mate, they chose Andrew Jackson from Tennessee, who was a very strong pro-Union politician, a Democrat, and the governor of occupied Tennessee. The alliance of the two parties also adopted the name the "Union Party." Their platform was the ending of slavery by a constitutional amendment and the restoration of the Union.

Within the Republican Party, there were those who believed that Lincoln was the cause of the war's continuance. There were also those who believed that the president should only serve one term, especially because the last president to only serve one term was Andrew Jackson. Lincoln's opponents also disagreed with him over his plan, announced in December 1863, to take it easy on the southern states when the war was over. The Radical Republicans, as they were called, advocated a much harsher peace and a new president. In their search for a candidate, they approached Treasury Secretary Salmon P. Chase, and General Grant. Grant turned them down immediately because he felt that it was important to the war effort for Lincoln to remain president. As for Chase, information showed up in the press concerning the idea of his run for the presidency, creating a huge backlash against the idea, and Chase was forced to remove his name from consideration and apologize to Lincoln. The Radical Republicans finally settled on Frémont as their candidate. Frémont was nominated at their convention in May in Cleveland, Ohio. The party ended up calling themselves the Radical Democrats.

The remainder of the Democratic Party met in Chicago, Illinois, in August. To them, the war had been lost and needed resolution, and the Union needed restoration by any means necessary. As their candidate, they chose McClellan, who had commanded the Union armies earlier in the war, but had been relieved of command by Lincoln because he refused (in Lincoln's opinion) to prosecute the war vigorously enough. No friend of Lincoln's, McClellan accepted the nomination. McClellan did not support emancipation or believe that it should be a goal of the war. However, he also disagreed with his party that the war was lost. As with the Republicans, he felt that the Union had to be restored.

Lincoln's chances of re-election did not look good; even Lincoln did not believe he could win. Many urged Lincoln to suspend the election of 1864. Never before had a country held a general election during a civil war. Lincoln felt that not holding the election was the same as losing the war, and he was not willing to do that. He believed that giving the people a say in how their government was to be run was more important than winning the war.

The Republicans categorized anyone who opposed them as a coward, a Copperhead (Southern sympathizer), disloyal, a traitor, or a defeatist. They attacked McClellan on his record as Commander of the Union armies, pointing out that he had not defeated the Confederacy when he was in command. With the war continuing, it was easy to place the blame for the lack of victory on Lincoln. Yet, Lincoln held firm to his goal of restoring the Union, with slavery abolished.

Lincoln's opponents attacked him on the fact that the war was not over. At its start, almost everyone believed the war would be over in 90 days. Lincoln was ridiculed as backward, a buffoon, lacking in the qualities of a true statesman, a boor, and a backwoods lawyer. His running mate, Johnson, was said to be no

better. The fact that Johnson was from Tennessee (a state that had seceded from the Union) did not help, even though Johnson had supported the Union since the beginning of the war.

Everything changed in September and October. In September, Atlanta fell to Sherman and General Philip Sheridan defeated, and then destroyed, the Confederate army in the Shenandoah Valley of Virginia, while Grant was making headway around Petersburg, Virginia. With these victories, the war appeared to be coming to an end, and Lincoln's opponents suddenly changed their strategies. Frémont withdrew from the race and the Radical Republicans threw their support to Lincoln. The talk focused on how the election would send a message to the south that they were not going to be able to win the war. For the Democrats, it was especially hard to convince the people that the war was lost with Sherman's capture of Atlanta. In order to support his efforts to win the election, Lincoln had some soldiers sent home to vote. There were even cases of entire regiments being sent home to vote. Other states allowed their soldiers to vote in the field.

When the votes were all counted, Lincoln won the popular vote with 55 percent to McClellan's 45 percent. In the Electoral College, it was not even close. Lincoln received 212 votes to McClellan's 21. Lincoln took every state except Kentucky, New Jersey, and Delaware. Lincoln took the vote as a sign that the voters wanted him to continue working toward his goal of restoring the Union, with slavery abolished. Many of the House and Senate elections also went to the Republicans, strengthening their control of Congress. In the House of Representatives, the Republicans went from holding 55 to 78 percent of the seats, and in the Senate from 72 to 80 percent. Although many people had expected the election to be accompanied by violence, it was peaceful. In the military, there was a sense of relief that the people had supported the government and they could get back to work. In the south, there was disappointment that Lincoln had not been turned out, and their prospects looked even worse than before the election.

SEE ALSO: Civil War and Realignment; Democratic Party; Military Vote; Patriotism; Republican Party.

BIBLIOGRAPHY. Paul F. Boller, Jr., *Presidential Campaigns: From George Washington to George W. Bush* (Oxford University Press, 2004); D.D. Jackson, *Twenty Million Yankees* (Time-

Life Books, 1985); J.L. Roark et al., *The American Promise: A History of the United States* (Bedford/St. Martin's, 2005); S.W. Sears, *George B. McClellan: The Young Napoleon* (Ticknor & Field, 1988); J.C. Waugh, *Reelecting Lincoln: The Battle for the 1864 Presidency* (Crown Publishing, 1997).

DALLACE W. UNGER, JR.
INDEPENDENT SCHOLAR

Presidential Election of 1868

THE 1868 ELECTION, the first post-War election for the presidency, reflected the lingering battles between a Radical Republican Congress and a Democratic president. Conducted in the wake of the passage of Reconstruction measures and the impeachment of President Johnson, the election centered on a Democratic Party whose southern base was still petitioning to return to the Union, and a Republican Party attempting to solidify its electoral majority in the postbellum United States.

In the wake of the war, Congress split between Republican/Unionists on the one side, and conservative Republicans, and War, Peace, and Southern Democrats on the other. The Radical Republican/Unionists wanted to enfranchise the newly emancipated African-American population in order to enhance their electoral success. Therefore, the party wanted to enact strict Reconstruction measures designed to enforce and protect the franchise of the freed population. In order to be readmitted into the Union, former Confederate states had to draft new state constitutions that reflected the altered landscape; essentially the removal of the slavery issue.

President Johnson, a Democrat and former vice president to Abraham Lincoln, extended a conciliatory hand to the former Confederacy. While he believed in the necessity of some reconstruction measures, he opposed stern intervention. Unfortunately for President Johnson, a split within his party over this issue hindered his ability to pursue his agenda and strengthen the Democratic Party after the war.

THE CIVIL RIGHTS ACT OF 1866
President Johnson garnered the ire of the Radical Republicans in Congress when he vetoed the Civil Rights Act of 1866. Congress created the Freedmen's Bureau during the last year of the Civil War to provide for emanci-

pated slaves and protect them from oppressive measures. Unfortunately, the Freedmen's Bureau lacked adequate resources and local southern governments refused to enforce statutes passed toward the end of the war that were designed to safeguard the rights of free African Americans in the Confederacy. The Republicans in Congress passed the Civil Rights Act to help secure compliance with these statutes and to counter the "black codes" enacted by southern states to discriminate against the African-American population. The Act granted citizenship to all native-born individuals, regardless of race and previous servitude. Furthermore, the legislation sought to guarantee to African Americans the same rights under the law as whites. President Johnson vetoed this legislation, partly on the grounds of representation. He questioned the validity of the legislation because it passed through Congress without the approval of the affected states; the aftermath of the war prevented their representation. Congress overrode Johnson's veto.

Increased violence in the south and race riots in New Orleans and Memphis provided support for the Radicals' demand for the federal protection, of freedmen, and contributed to the Radical Republicans securing a congressional majority in the midterm election. The election results enabled Radicals in Congress to establish a military presence in the former Confederacy. Congress also asserted its control over the south by requiring the states to ratify the Fourteenth Amendment prior to being readmitted into the Union.

TENURE OF OFFICE ACT AND IMPEACHMENT
In an attempt to assert some authority over the executive branch, Congress passed the Tenure of Office Act in 1867. The act amended the "advise and consent" component of the Constitution, which provides for senatorial approval for presidential nominees to the cabinet, federal judiciary, and ambassadors. Under this law, the president must seek senatorial approval prior to dismissing cabinet members or ambassadors. Congress overrode a presidential veto to enact this bill as well. President Johnson, looking to test congressional resolve, found the perfect case in the form of his Secretary of War, Edwin Stanton.

Secretary Stanton heeded Congress's request to help enforce the Civil Rights Act. President Johnson opposed the reconstruction measures and threatened to remove Stanton if he continued to enforce the law. When Stanton refused, Johnson removed him when

Congress was not in session. Congress complained that this violated the Tenure of Office Act, and returned Stanton to office. Johnson fired him again in February of 1868, but Stanton barricaded himself in his office with a military guard. In response, the House drew up articles of impeachment. The Senate tried Johnson, but fell one vote short of convicting him.

NATIONAL CONVENTIONS & PLATFORMS

The Republicans convened in Chicago in May. Although Johnson originally asked General Ulysses S. Grant to replace Stanton, Grant refused and shrewdly distanced himself from the president. Grant easily won the Republican nomination. The fight in the convention occurred over the vice presidential nominee. Schuyler Colfax (Indiana) beat out Benjamin F. Wade (Ohio) on the sixth ballot.

The Democrats met in New York City on July 4. This was the first national convention for the Democrats since the Civil War. A battle over of the presidential nomination ensued between George H. Pendleton (Ohio) and President Johnson. Because Johnson's bastion of support came from the south, and he faced strong opposition from the north, he withdrew his name. Pendleton's candidacy faltered, as did those of subsequent aspirants General Winfield Scott Hancock (Pennsylvania) and Thomas H. Hendricks (Indiana). Finally, the convention coalesced around Horatio Seymour, the former Governor of New York, who accepted the nomination, reluctantly. Francis P. Blair, Jr. (Missouri) won the nomination for vice president on the first ballot.

The Republican platform asserted the party's support for the Reconstruction measures and for the suffrage rights of all men, regardless of race. However, the platform resolved to give states jurisdiction over suffrage, "while the question of suffrage in all the loyal States properly belongs to the people of those States." Resolutions also condemned the Johnson Administration and renewed calls for his impeachment. Furthermore, the Republicans called for the provision of pensions for war veterans and their families and included a plank encouraging immigration from other nations. Finally, the platform addressed financial matters that would divide the parties internally and externally for most of the remainder of the 19th century. The Republicans adopted a "hard" money stance, opposing the use of paper money or "greenbacks," in circulation during the war, to pay off war debts.

The Democratic platform differed markedly from the Republican platform. The Democrats claimed that the war settled the slavery issue and secession; they called for amnesty and the "immediate restoration of all the States to their rights in the Union, under the Constitution." The platform rejected the Reconstruction measures and called for the repeal of "all political instrumentalities designed to secure negro supremacy." Resolutions called for state regulation of the elective franchise, as well as commending Johnson's administration. With regard to monetary policy, the Democrats seemed to adopt a "soft" approach, as advocated by Pendleton. The Ohio Idea would enable the payment of war bonds and debts with greenbacks. This policy was more beneficial to the south, and this plank was at odds with the hard money supporter, Seymour.

The Republicans held a financial advantage in the campaign. Their pro-business positions and railroad grants provided them with ample support from the wealthier members of society. Furthermore, they were in a much better position after the war. Grant kept his distance during the campaign, staying home in Illinois. Moreover, he chose not to articulate specific issue positions, but to allow the party to run on its platform.

Another component of the Republican campaign strategy included the waving of the bloody shirt to remind people of the Democratic allegiance to the Confederacy. For their part, the Democrats aggressively invoked race during the campaign. The party continually informed voters that the Republican Reconstruction policies would effectively make African Americans superior to whites.

RESULTS

In an election where almost 81 percent of the eligible voting population turned out to vote, Grant defeated Seymour by about five percent of the popular vote: Grant received 52.7 percent and Seymour received 47.3 percent. The margin in the Electoral College was far greater, 218 to 80. The Republicans won 26 of the 34 states that took part in the election. Ultimately, Grant benefited from Radical Republican sentiment in the north and the newly-enfranchised African-American population in the south. The election results enabled the Republicans to fend off moderate Democrats and continue their Reconstruction policies in the south until the deal that decided the election of 1876.

SEE ALSO: Conventions, National Nominating Party; Democratic Party; Presidential Election of 1864; Presidential Election of 1872; Republican Party.

BIBLIOGRAPHY. CQ Press www.cqpress.com (cited August 2007); J.L. Moore, J.P. Preimesberger, and D.R. Tarr, eds., *Guide to U.S. Elections* (CQ Press, 2001); K.H. Porter and D.B. Johnson, eds., *National Party Platforms, 1840–1960* (University of Illinois Press, 1961); Jules Witcover, *Party of the People: A History of the Democrats* (Random House, 2003).

ADAM SILVER
BOSTON UNIVERSITY

Presidential Election of 1872

MUCH OF ULYSSES S. GRANT'S first term in office was a disaster. The popular war hero had been seen as the key to reuniting the nation after the chaos of the Civil War and Lincoln's assassination. Grant symbolized a return to order in a fractured political system and a nation still reeling from the effects of civil war. Grant also brought with him the freedmen's hope that freedom would not be a temporary condition. However, Grant's presidency would dash their hope.

Grant's first term in office was defined by ignorance and incompetence, as well as a completely deferential attitude toward Congress. Although this was understandable after the attempted impeachment of Andrew Johnson. Despite this, Grant stood by as an idle observer as the old Whig theory of legislative supremacy began to reassert itself in American politics. This abdication of constitutional power had important consequences for his presidency. Grant chose friendship over competence in filling administrative positions, which resulted in his administration suffering from numerous abuses of the patronage system, as well as stunning examples of corruption. From the Whiskey Ring and Crédit Mobilier scandals, to the infamous Black Friday gold speculation scheme, the stench of corruption pervaded his term of office.

Grant fared little better in pursuing his limited policy agenda. His support of a new tariff in 1870 alienated many reformers in his party. He engaged in an ill-advised attempt to annex the Dominican Republic, and his appointments to the judiciary handed down rulings that legalized paper money, which angered the deflationists in his party. He also gave in to pressure to put the brakes on attempts at civil service reform, a decision that perpetuated his already corrupt image. Moreover, Grant's failings as a party leader could not have come at a worse time for the Republicans. The growing distance from the issues of the Civil War (anti-slavery and unionism) meant that party ties were rapidly weakening, and fissures were beginning to emerge in the Republican coalition. The election of 1872 would test if the Republican Party could remain unified in the post–Civil War era.

Despite all these failings, Grant's popularity heading into the election remained high and Republicans felt optimistic that he would be re-elected. The path to victory, however, would prove daunting. Heading into the party conventions, the Republicans divided over the rampant corruption in government, as well as the direction of Reconstruction efforts in the south.

Stalwart Republicans, such as Roscoe Conkling of New York, believed that Reconstruction was a worn-out issue. Rather than seeing the idealistic goals of Radical Reconstruction succeed, which would likely cost the party its dominance in American politics, the Stalwarts attempted to move the party away from ideological politics toward an emphasis on organization and control of the political system. While principled politics certainly had their place, the Stalwarts reasoned that one could not bring about change without first winning elections.

This is not to say that the Stalwarts abandoned all principles, as the Republican platform made clear. Though largely self-congratulatory, it also called for strict enforcement of the Reconstruction Amendments, full political and civil rights for the freedmen, civil service reform, and amnesty for southern secessionists. But how much of this was a commitment to progress and how much was political posturing remained an open question. By the end of the convention, though, these Stalwarts, who comprised the dominant wing of the Republican Party, would continue to support Grant in the election, though with Henry Wilson replacing Schuyler Colfax as vice president.

THE LIBERAL REPUBLICAN PARTY

Those who did not agree with the Stalwart eschewal of principles attempted to form a coalition under the label of Liberal Republicans. Many of these Liberals were members of the old guard who had cut their teeth in the ideological battles over slavery and the Civil

War. Such men were, both literally and figuratively, a dying breed and were quickly being pushed aside by the younger party men who were devoted to organizational politics.

Taken as a whole, the Liberal Republicans represented an odd amalgamation of principles and personalities. Some of the Liberal Republicans, like Charles Sumner, were former Radical Republicans who had become disillusioned with the Republican Party's perceived abandonment of the goal of seeking full equality for the freedmen in society. Other members, like Lyman Trumbull, were former Democrats (and later conservative Republican) who wanted to see an immediate end to Reconstruction in the south. Still others, like Charles Schurz, were primarily interested in civil service reform to end the corruption that was plaguing the government.

The Liberal platform tried to straddle all of these competing interests. It accepted the Reconstruction Amendments, but seemed to oppose further intrusion by the national government in local and state affairs by condemning the growth of centralized power. It glorified the heroism of Union soldiers, but demanded immediate amnesty for Confederates. Moreover, the greater part of the platform was devoted to support for civil service reform, reducing the national debt, the return of specie payments, and the imposition of a one-term limit for the presidency. How these disparate personalities and positions in the Liberal Republican Party would have remained united in politics, had the party been successful, was never clear.

In the end, the Liberal Republicans nominated Horace Greeley as their candidate, with Benjamin Gratz Brown nominated for vice president. Greeley was a strange choice for the party, but in some ways was very appropriate given the eclectic issues and principles coalescing under the Liberal banner. He was best known as the founder of the *New York Tribune*, which grew to be one of the leading papers in the nation. Although the paper was strongly pro-Republican, Greeley was known as a political eccentric who romanced a multitude of different ideologies. He was also known for his quick temper and brusque demeanor, and did not take to dissent from his views on politics kindly. These were not traits that would serve him, or his party, well during the campaign.

What allowed the Liberal Republicans to appear viable in the election was the inability of the Democratic Party to unify on a policy program or to take advantage of the missteps made by Grant and the Republicans. The

Democrats continued to be internally divided between Purists who wanted the party to stay true to its pre–Civil War principles, and New Departure Democrats who advocated an acceptance of the outcome of the war and doing whatever was required to win elections, even if that meant abandoning older party principles. With neither side willing to compromise, the Democrats nominated the Greeley/Brown ticket. This was especially odd given that Greeley had been one of the founders of the Republican Party in 1854.

Thus, as the campaign for the presidency got underway, the Republican Party marshaled their support behind Grant, a former Democrat, and the Democratic Party fell in line behind Greeley, a former Republican. The political world had turned upside down. Adding to the novelty of the campaign was the addition of the Equal Rights Party, which nominated the first woman, Victoria Woodhull, for the presidency and named as her running mate the abolitionist Frederick Douglass, though the party was never a factor in the campaign.

The general election campaign was hard-fought and nasty. Opponents attacked Grant for being a tyrant; Greeley was attacked as being a traitor, a charge reinforced by the decision of the Democrats to nominate him as their own candidate. But the Liberal Republican Party's inability to organize at the grassroots level and the ticket's lack of experience and numerous character flaws quickly doomed the party's efforts. Greeley frequently appeared as intemperate and self-righteous to voters, and Brown committed numerous blunders due to his drinking, in one instance attempting to butter a watermelon at a campaign picnic.

Given the insurmountable hurdles facing the Liberal Republicans, the outcome of the election was no surprise. Grant and Wilson captured 286 electoral votes, losing only six states. The victory was overwhelming and complete for the Republicans, and devastating for Greeley. Soon after the election he suffered both the death of his wife and loss of control over his paper. By the end of November he became ill and died soon after. His party quickly met the same fate.

SEE ALSO: Liberal Republican Party; Presidential Elections; Reconstruction; Scandals, Presidential Elections; Third Parties.

BIBLIOGRAPHY. Josiah Bunting and Arthur Schlesinger, Jr., *Ulysses S. Grant* (Times Books, 2004); A.M. Schlesinger, Jr., ed., *History of American Presidential Elections* (Chelsea House Publishers, 1985); A.L. Slap, *The Doom of Reconstruction: The Liberal Republicans in the Civil War Era* (Fordham University Press, 2006); R.C. Williams, *Horace Greeley: Champion of American Freedom* (New York University Press, 2006).

ERIC C. SANDS
BERRY COLLEGE

Presidential Election of 1876

THE 1876 PRESIDENTIAL election remains one of the most controversial in American history. A revitalized Democratic Party nominated Governor Samuel Tilden of New York, known as "Whispering Sammy" because of his soft political demeanor, and campaigned on the issues of political corruption, the end of Reconstruction in the south, and Republican responsibility for a severe economic depression that hit the nation in 1875. The Republicans, after initially courting former Speaker of the House James G. Blaine, finally settled on Governor Rutherford B. Hayes of Ohio as their nominee, and continued a campaign strategy of "waving the bloody shirt," which meant encouraging the American people to "vote as they shot" during the Civil War. This was a campaign tactic that was losing its punch, however, and 1876 would mark the last time that the Republicans would use the sectional conflict as a campaign theme.

But the issues of the 1876 election largely took a back seat to the means and methods used by the two parties in their attempts to win. While fraud and treachery were hardly new tactics used by parties in American politics, the 1876 battle was *sui generis* in how transparent the corruption was. The party organizations made it clear that they were willing to go to any lengths to reap the spoils of victory, whether that meant bribery and ballot stuffing, or intimidation, kidnapping, and murder. For these reasons, the election result was immediately questioned.

By the evening of November 7, things did not look good for the Republicans. The election returns seemed to be going solidly toward Tilden and the Democrats. With 185 electoral votes needed to win, some estimates gave Tilden as many as 209 votes. Many newspapers had even declared Tilden the winner. But, the Republicans were not ready to concede. As party leaders began to scrutinize the returns, a plan was quickly hatched. If the Republicans could find a way of holding the states of South Carolina, Florida, and Louisiana, Hayes would win the election. These three states were still "unreconstructed," meaning that they were still under the control of the so-called carpetbagger governments. The significance of this was that Republicans in these states controlled the canvassing boards that reviewed the election returns. Thus, all the Republicans had to do was find cause to disqualify enough Democratic votes to give the three states to Hayes.

Given the amount of fraud and corruption perpetrated by both parties, it did not require much effort by the Republican canvassing boards to throw out significant numbers of Democratic votes. Democrats protested fiercely, complaining that every challenge to Democratic votes was being upheld but, despite overwhelming evidence of similar fraud in Republican districts, the canvassing boards never disqualified Republican votes. While these Democratic criticisms certainly had merit, the unsurprising result was that the electoral votes of the three states were given to Hayes. This did not mean, however, that the election fight ended.

As the Republicans in the contested states prepared to send the electoral certificates to Washington, the Democrats concocted their own plan to challenge the results. Ignoring the contested electoral votes in South Carolina, Florida, and Louisiana, Tilden still led Hayes in the election by a margin of 184–163. This meant that the Democrats only needed one electoral vote to break their way for Tilden to be elected. And the Democrats felt confident that they could get that vote in Washington. Accordingly, the Democrats dispatched rival electoral certificates to the capitol, declaring that the Republican certificates were illegitimate. Immediately the eyes of the nation turned to Washington to see how the dispute would be resolved.

Most members of Congress looked to the Constitution as a way of deciding the issue, but it did not provide much guidance. The Twelfth Amendment stated that the electors of each state would send the certificates of their decision "to the seat of the Government of the United States, directed to the President of the Senate," and that "the President of the Senate shall, in the presence of the Senate and the House of Representatives, open all the certificates and the votes shall then be counted." The problem, however, was that no one agreed on what this provision meant. Republicans interpreted the amendment to mean that the president of the Senate had the power to determine which votes would be counted, but this interpretation was no doubt fueled by the political reality that Republican Thomas Ferry was the presiding officer in the Senate. If Ferry decided which votes would count, Hayes would be president. Democrats, in turn, argued that there was simply no fair way of determining which votes should be counted. Therefore, all of the disputed votes should be thrown out. Without either candidate having an electoral majority, this would mean that the election would be decided in the House of Representatives, an outcome that would have favored the Democrats as they controlled that body.

Congress appeared to be at an impasse over how to proceed. However, rising passions in the electorate necessitated a solution, so Congress began entertaining alternative measures. After a great deal of political wrangling, a proposal emerged that appeased everyone. The proposal would create a 15-member independent

As newspapers began declaring Tilden's victory, Republicans were seeking ways to have votes thrown out in Florida.

commission to decide the election, with 10 members being congressmen, divided equally between the two parties, and the other five being justices of the Supreme Court. Of the five justices, four would be split between the two parties and the other four would select the fifth. There was also a widespread assumption that this fifth justice would be David Davis, a man of uncertain political loyalties. Both parties agreed to the arrangement and the commission was created.

Democrats were initially optimistic about the commission. Although Lincoln had appointed Davis, he had ruled against the president in the famous Ex Parte Milligan decision and had briefly been affiliated with the Liberal Republican Party in 1872. This gave Democrats hope that Davis would award at least one electoral vote to Tilden. But then disaster struck for the Democrats. The Illinois state elected Davis U.S. Senator, and he resigned from the commission. His replacement was Justice Joseph P. Bradley, a Republican who had been appointed by Grant. With Bradley casting the tie-breaking vote, Democratic hopes of winning the election were dashed. On every vote, Bradley sided with the Republicans, giving Hayes 185 votes to Tilden's 184.

The Democrats had lost a major battle, but they were not defeated yet. Despite losing the electoral vote decisions of the commission, the Democrats threatened to use various parliamentary tactics in the House to prevent the final count of the electoral votes. With inauguration fast approaching, Republican scrambled to overcome Democratic obstruction. To that end, Republican leaders entered into secret negotiations with Democrats to broker a solution. The result was the now famous (or infamous) Compromise of 1877. The Democrats promised to end their obstruction in the House and allow Hayes to become president. In return, Hayes and the Republicans would formally recognize the Democratic governments in South Carolina and Louisiana, and Hayes would work to remove federal troops from the south as quickly as possible. In short, the Democrats accepted a loss in the election battle to win the war over Reconstruction.

As remarkable as the election of 1876 was, equally amazing was the public reaction, or lack thereof. While the defeat left many rank-and-file Democrats unhappy, the electorate's reaction was largely mute. Party organizations were successful in keeping popular passions in check, which represented the triumph of the new politics of organization over the old politics of ideology. Hayes's inauguration left no doubt that the nation had concluded the final chapter of the history of the Civil War Era; Reconstruction was over. What is less clear, however, is if the victory of organizational politics was also a victory for America. In the end, 15 years of war and turmoil on behalf of the freedmen was silenced by the clamor of party machines.

SEE ALSO: Corruption and Democratic Elections; Election Boards; Electoral College; Florida; Louisiana; Reconstruction; South Carolina; Twelfth Amendment.

BIBLIOGRAPHY. Harry Barnard, *Rutherford B. Hayes and His America* (Bobbs-Merill Co., 1954); Alexander Flick, *Samuel Jones Tilden: A Study in Political Sagacity* (Kennikat Press, 1939); Eric Foner, *Reconstruction: America's Unfinished Revolution, 1863–1877* (Harper Perennial Modern Classics, 2002); P.L. Haworth, *The Tilden-Hayes Disputed Presidential Election of 1876* (Burrows Bros. Co., 1906); Arthur Schlesinger, ed., *History of American Presidential Elections* (Chelsea House Publishers, 1985); C. Vann Woodward, *Reunion and Reaction: The Compromise of 1877 and the End of Reconstruction* (Oxford University Press, 1991).

ERIC C. SANDS
BERRY COLLEGE

Presidential Election of 1880

WITH THE RECONSTRUCTION efforts of the Republicans following the Civil War in the south fully underway with little or no fanfare, small issues arose in the presidential election of 1880, which were mostly resolved with agreement by all parties. However, the presidential election of 1880 is unique in that it is regarded as one of the smallest popular vote victories by a candidate to date and the level of participation by third party candidates demonstrated democracy at its finest.

The presidential election of 1880 began in earnest with the fulfillment of a promise. President Rutherford B. Hayes vowed in 1876 that, if elected, he would serve only one term as president. As the presidential campaign season began, there were five political parties vying for supremacy. They included the Democrats, the Republicans, the Greenback-Labor Party, the Prohibition Party,

and the American Party. The two major parties were the Republican Party and the Democratic Party.

The Republican Party held its national convention in Chicago and was faced with selecting a successor to Hayes. Former President Ulysses S. Grant (in office 1869–77) campaigned for a third term, an idea that did not appeal to many traditionalists within the Republican Party, who adhered to the two-term tradition initiated by President Washington. However, many Republicans supported Grant and were known as Stalwarts. This conservative faction of the Republican Party saw themselves as stalwarts in opposition to the reconstruction of the south. They also backed tariffs and opposed all forms of civil service reform.

At the other end of the spectrum were the liberals, who supported active civil service reform and a tariff that would generate revenue for the states and government as a whole. The other two major candidates vying for the nomination were John Sherman (Ohio) and James Gillespie Blaine (Maine). The "Half-Breeds of the Republican Party" endorsed both Sherman and Blaine. The Half-Breeds supported moderate civil service reform and moderate levels of Reconstruction in the south.

Senator James Garfield (Ohio), a Republican Half-Breed, gave a rousing speech in support of Sherman. The speech was so well-received that Garfield found himself receiving delegate votes and, on the 36th ballot, Garfield garnered 399 delegate votes to Grant's 313 votes, and Blaine's 285 votes, to win the nomination. Despite Garfield's opposition and overwhelming endorsement of Grant, he was selected as the nominee and Grant would return to Ohio to assume Garfield's vacated Senate seat. Chester A. Arthur (New York), a Stalwart, received the endorsement of Garfield as the vice presidential nominee, as Garfield needed the support of the Stalwart faction to be victorious in the general election.

The Democrats decided to meet the Republicans head on, beginning by holding their nominating convention in Cincinnati, Ohio. The convention proved to be a lively event, with dozens of candidates seeking the nomination on the first ballot. However, by the second ballot, retired Civil War General Winfield Scott Hancock received 705 delegate votes to Thomas Bayard (154), Samuel Randall (129), Henry Paine (81), Allen G. Thurman (69), Stephen Field (66), and many others. Hancock had tackled the major issue of Reconstruction in the south and had taken on the Stalwarts

Garfield and Arthur won the popular vote by a mere 9,464 votes, the smallest number in U.S. history in both absolute and percentage terms. Had Hancock carried New York, a shift of a few thousand votes, he would have been elected president.

of the Republican Party by supporting whites and Democrats. William H. English (Indiana) was selected as Hancock's running mate.

Three fairly new political parties surfaced in the election of 1880: the Greenback-National Party, the Prohibition Party, and the American Party. The Greenback-National Party organized from the "greenbacks," a coalition of midwestern and southern farmers whose primary aim was the adoption of a new monetary policy based on the issuance of paper currency. The National Party organized, in 1878, to counter the economic difficulties of the depression of the 1870s. They viewed the depression as caused by a lack of labor oversight and decreased wages due to Chinese immigration. The Chinese immigration issue would surface again later in the election. The Greenback-National Party selected James B. Weaver as its presidential nominee. Benjamin Cham-

bers was selected as the vice presidential nominee. The Prohibition Party, which advocated the prohibition of the use of beverages containing alcohol and played a major role in the temperance movement, also fielded a candidate in the presidential election of 1880, choosing Neal Dow (Maine) and Henry Thompson (Ohio) as their nominees. The American Party, a new political party opposed to the Masonic movement, also fielded a candidate, former Civil War General John Phelps (Vermont), with Samuel C. Pomeroy (Kansas) as the vice presidential nominee.

The campaign was anything but inspiring. Democrats returned to the highly contested 1876 election, while the Republicans focused on the character and the integrity of Garfield. For the Democrats, who felt that the election had been stolen from them in 1876 due to ballot irregularities in Florida, Louisiana, and South Carolina, subsequently settled in the Compromise of 1877, the taste of defeat was hard to fathom. While Republicans addressed tariffs and economic issues, the Democrats went directly after Garfield.

The key controversy facing Garfield focused on "The Morey Letter." On October 20, 1880, a local newspaper in New York published a letter supposedly signed by Garfield and addressed to H.L Morey of Lynn, Massachusetts. Although the letter was only three sentences long and written on Congressional stationary, it proved to have negative effects on Garfield's perception among voters. The letter stated that Garfield supported increasing Chinese immigration, a very polarizing issue among workers. The controversy erupted when Garfield stated he could not remember if he actually wrote the letter or not. Reporters could not find Morley residing in Massachusetts.

Finally, Garfield submitted a sample of his handwriting, albeit six days later, and it was determined that the original letter was a forgery coming directly from the Democratic Party. There was a huge backlash against the Democrats. Garfield spent most of his time working to heal wounds within the Republican Party. A self-identified Half-Breed, Garfield worked with the Stalwarts in secret and agreed to recognize all party factions if elected. During a visit to New York City, Garfield agreed to appoint certain Stalwarts from New York to key positions within his administration. This became known as the Treaty of Fifth Avenue and served as a crucial strategy for Garfield.

The results of the election were as follows: Garfield/Arthur (4,446,158 votes; 48.3 percent of the popular vote; 214 electoral votes); Hancock/English (4,444,260 votes; 48.3 percent of the popular vote; 155 electoral votes); Weaver/Chambers (305,997 votes; 3.3 percent of the popular vote; no electoral votes); Dow/Thompson (10,305 votes; 0.1 percent of the popular vote; no electoral votes) and Phelps and Pomeroy (700 votes; less than 0.1 percent of the popular vote; no electoral votes).

Garfield and Arthur won the popular vote by a mere 9,464 votes, the smallest in U.S. history in both absolute and percentage terms. However, the election results were once again clouded in suspicion as Georgia was scrutinized for its handling of the Electoral College votes. Specifically, the Constitution states that all Electoral College votes shall be cast on the first Wednesday in December. However, Georgia, for whatever reason, did not cast its votes until December 8, 1880, a full week after the deadline. Congress elected to count Georgia's

votes, while many constitutional scholars argued that the votes should be rendered invalid. For many, Hancock should have received 144 votes, not the 155 he was credited with having received. Each candidate carried 19 states. Hancock won the states in the south and most of the border states. Garfield won the northern states and the states in the midwest. He also carried New York by a few thousand votes. Had Hancock carried New York, a shift of a few thousand votes, he would have been elected president of the United States.

SEE ALSO: Electoral College; Presidential Election of 1876; Prohibition Party.

BIBLIOGRAPHY. Atlas of U.S. Presidential Elections, www.uselectionatlas.org (cited August 2007); Ohio History Central, www.ohiohistorycentral.org (cited August 2007).

RONALD ERIC MATTHEWS, JR.
MOUNT UNION COLLEGE

Presidential Election of 1884

IN ONE OF the closest presidential elections in American history, New York Governor Grover Cleveland became the first Democrat to be elected president since before the Civil War when he defeated former U.S. Senator James G. Blaine of Maine, 219 electoral votes to 182. Cleveland's victory was assured by carrying his home state of New York as he won the state's 36 electoral votes by a margin of 1,047 votes out of 1,167,003 votes cast.

THE DEMOCRATS

The Democrats convened in Chicago on July 8, and had four major candidates to choose from. In addition to Cleveland, other Democratic hopefuls included Thomas F. Bayard, a senator from Delaware who had also sought the party's nomination in 1876 and 1880; Thomas A. Hendricks, a former senator (1863–69) and governor (1873–77) from Indiana who had been the Democratic Party's unsuccessful vice presidential candidate in 1876; and Congressman Samuel J. Randall of Pennsylvania, who had served as speaker of the House (1876–81) and had unsuccessfully sought the Democratic nomination in 1880. Ohio's Democrats also put forward Allen G. Thurman, a former U.S. senator from Ohio (1869–81), who had been a "favorite son" candidate for the Democratic nomination in 1876 and 1880.

Cleveland, the front-runner going into the convention, was opposed by Tammany Hall, the Democratic organization in New York City whose dominance he challenged as governor of the Empire State. Tammany supported Hendricks, and tried to rally support for his candidacy, to no avail. Cleveland was a leader of the Bourbon (conservative) faction of the party. Bourbon Democrats supported laissez-faire capitalism, opposed American overseas expansion, and supported the gold standard. The Bourbons also supported civil service reform (which had recently been implemented at the federal level with the passage of the Pendleton Act), and opposed urban political machines, which they believed to be corrupt. Following their selection of Cleveland, the convention selected Hendricks as the vice presidential candidate.

THE REPUBLICANS

The Republican Party also held its convention in Chicago, from June 3 to June 6. The leading candidates were President Chester Alan Arthur, who had succeeded to the office following the assassination of President James Garfield in 1881; James G. Blaine, who had served in the U.S. House of Representatives (1863–76), served as its speaker, and then served five years in the Senate (1876–81) before serving briefly as secretary of state under Garfield and Arthur in 1881; and George F. Edmunds, a U.S. senator from Vermont who was president pro tempore of the body and known as the sponsor of the 1882 Edmunds Act, which designated polygamy a felony and imposed other sanctions on polygamists, who were predominantly members of the Church of Latter Day Saints (Mormons) in Utah Territory. A potential candidate was Civil War hero William Tecumseh Sherman, who had recently retired as commanding general of the U.S. Army. Sherman, who hated politics, and rejected the entreaties of Republicans, stating that, "If drafted, I will not run; if nominated I will not accept; if elected I will not serve."

Blaine, who led throughout the convention, prevailed on the fourth ballot. The convention nominated U.S. Senator John A. Logan of Illinois, who had served in the Mexican War and as a Union General during the Civil War, for vice president. Logan was a member of the radical wing of the Republican Party and his strong following among members of the Grand Army of the Republic (an organization of Union Army Civil War veterans) was a major factor in his selection as Blaine's running mate.

THIRD PARTIES

The U.S. Greenback Party (which had been known as the Greenback-Labor Party) and Anti-Monopoly Parties nominated Benjamin Franklin Butler of Massachusetts for president. Butler, who had been a "political general" during the Civil War, who served in the U.S. House of Representatives (1865–77 and 1877–79) as a Republican, where he was regarded as President Ulysses S. Grant's spokesman. In 1882, he was elected governor of Massachusetts as a Democrat. The Prohibition Party, which wanted to criminalize the sale and consumption of alcoholic beverages, nominated John St. John as its candidate. St. John had served for four years (1879–83) as the Republican governor of Kansas, where he successfully supported the addition of a Prohibition amendment to the state constitution.

THE GENERAL ELECTION

The campaign was noteworthy for personal attacks. The Democrats resurrected the "Mulligan Letters," an old charge that Blaine had accepted bribes. In 1876, a Boston bookkeeper James Mulligan claimed that he had letters of Blaine's that proved that, as speaker of the House, he had engaged in influence peddling. One of these letters indicated that Blaine had received more than $110,000 from the Little Rock and Fort Smith Railroad Company, for which he had secured a federal land grant. These letters had prevented Blaine from receiving his party's presidential nomination in 1876 and 1880. Blaine consistently denied the charges, and his nomination in 1884 was considered a vindication. Nevertheless, Democrats and anti-Blaine Republicans continued the attack with the rallying cry, "Burn, burn, burn this letter," a reference to the alleged ending phrase of Blaine's letters: "burn this letter."

Cleveland also proved to be vulnerable to mudslinging as the Republicans attacked him for having fathered a son out of wedlock. In July 1884, just 10 days after his party's nomination, a Buffalo newspaper reported that Cleveland, a bachelor, had fathered a son out of wedlock 10 years earlier, who had been placed in an orphanage while the mother of the child had been dispatched to an asylum. The Cleveland campaign responded to the charges by acknowledging that the candidate had what they described as an "illicit connection" with Maria

Crofts Halpin, the child's mother. They also contended that, although paternity had not been proven, the boy had been given the Cleveland surname (Oscar Folsom Cleveland) and that by finding the child a home he fulfilled his duty as a father. Further, they claimed that the mother had not been forced into an asylum (although her whereabouts were unknown).

Republicans continued to hammer at Cleveland, often chanting at rallies, "Ma, Ma, where's my Pa?" However, Blaine's morality was not above reproach. Cleveland's supporters claimed that Blaine had married his wife in a "shotgun wedding," and newspaper reports claimed that Blaine had kissed men. Toward the end of the campaign, the Blaine campaign suffered a major setback. A group of Protestant ministers visited Blaine to offer their support. Speaking before the Religious Bureau of the Republican National Committee, the Reverend Samuel Burchard attacked the supporters of the Democrats as backing the party of "rum, Romanism, and rebellion." Blaine's standing among Catholics was already questionable because of his 1875 proposal to amend the Constitution to prohibit the use of public funds for religious schools (which was seen as an attack on the Roman Catholic Church). He was severely wounded by Burchard's anti-Catholic slur as Cleveland's campaign used it to mobilize the large bloc of Roman Catholic voters in New York City, helping deliver a narrow victory in the state (and the election) to Cleveland.

Cleveland, who was known by the nickname, "Grover the Good," for his personal integrity and independence as mayor of Buffalo (1881) and governor of New York (1883–85), attracted the votes of reformers and many liberal Republicans (known as "Mugwumps") who would not support Blaine. While Blaine could not shake his reputation as being politically corrupt (his opponents referred to him as "Slippery Jim"), Cleveland's reputation for attacking the corrupt Tammany Hall and cleaning up the graft in state government, offered a stark contrast to the electorate.

THE OUTCOME

In a very close contest (Cleveland's plurality in the national popular vote was 25,686 out of more than 10 million cast), Cleveland carried the solid south, and battleground states that included Connecticut, Indiana (Hendricks's home state), New Jersey, and New York. Blaine won most of New England, the midwest, and the far West. With the election outcome so close, the

Democratic National Committee dispatched lawyers to New York to insure that Cleveland's victory would survive a recount. While Cleveland won the presidency, the Democrats lost 14 seats in the House of Representatives, reducing their majority to 182. The Republicans won 141 House seats and one member of the U.S. Greenback Party and one Independent were elected to round out the body. The Republicans, who held 42 of the 76 seats in the chamber, would control the Senate.

The Results

	Popular Vote	Percentage	Electoral Votes
James G. Blaine	4,848,936	48.25	182
Grover Cleveland	4,874,621	48.50	219
Benjamin F. Butler	175,096	1.74	0
John P. St. John	147,482	1.47	0
All others	3,619	0.04	0
TOTAL	10,049,754	100.0	401

Source: John W. Wright, ed., *The New York Times Almanac 2007* (Penguin Reference, 2007).

SEE ALSO: Campaigns, Presidential; Candidate Image; Catholic Vote; Greenback-Labor Party; Presidential Elections; Prohibitionist Party; Scandals, Presidential Elections; Tammany Hall.

BIBLIOGRAPHY. Republican National Committee, *The Republican Campaign Text Book for 1884* (Republican National Committee, 1884); F.L. Stetson and W.G. Rice, *Was New York's Vote Stolen?* (North American Review Publishing Co., 1913); M.W. Summers, *Rum, Romanism and Rebellion: The Making of a President 1884* (University of North Carolina Press, 2000).

Jeffrey Kraus
Wagner College

Presidential Election of 1888

THE PRESIDENTIAL ELECTION of 1888 was one of the closest and most controversial presidential elections in the history of the United States. Questionable campaign tactics, coupled with the Constitution rules

Grover Cleveland clearly won the presidency in the popular vote but lost in the Electoral College.

pertaining to the Electoral College, led to the defeat of President Grover Cleveland. The election of 1888 came on the heels of another one of the most controversial presidential elections ever held, the election of 1884. Known for mudslinging and questionable campaign tactics, the atmosphere of the election of 1884 seemed to reemerge in 1888. This presidential election featured four candidates representing different views and political stances.

The Republicans held their national convention in Chicago, Illinois, and initially fielded 14 men for president before deciding on four candidates for the nomination: Russell A. Alger, a former Civil War brigadier general and the governor of Michigan; Walter Q. Gresham from Indiana, a major-general from the Civil War who also served on the U.S. Court of Appeals, Seventh Circuit; John Sherman, a career politician from Ohio who served as secretary of the treasury 1877–81 and was known as the brother of General William Tecumseh Sherman, Union Civil War hero; and Benjamin Harrison from Indiana, who had served as a U.S. Senator 1881–87. After a heated debate and discussion and on the eighth ballot, Harrison was awarded the nomination, receiving 544 delegate votes to Sherman's 249 votes. Alger's 142 votes, and Gresham's 123 votes, followed in third and fourth place, respectively. The delegates also selected Levi Morton from New York (592 votes) as the vice presidential candidate over William Phelps (119 votes) and William Bradley (103 votes).

The Democrat Party unanimously selected President Grover Cleveland, hoping to once again capitalize on the unusual support received from Republicans in the 1884 presidential election. Disgruntled Republicans seeking election reform and integrity had overwhelming supported Cleveland in 1884, and appeared to be prepared to do the same in 1888. Allen Thurman (Ohio), a 75-year-old career politician, was chosen as the vice presidential candidate and selected to lead the campaign, a move that would spell trouble for Cleveland. Thurman received 684 votes at the convention.

The Prohibition Party, which advocated the prohibition of the use of beverages containing alcohol and played a major role in the temperance movement, also fielded a strong candidate in the 1888 presidential election. Clinton Fisk, a senior officer in the Bureau of Refugees, Freedmen, and Abandoned Lands was the party's nominee and vowed to end the sale of alcohol. The Union Labor Party, concerned about labor laws and regulations, placed Alson Streeter on the ballot as their nominee, but received little support.

The campaign of 1888 proved to be laced with controversy and conflict. President Cleveland had alienated many voters leading up to the election and the Republicans, sensing this discord, capitalized on Cleveland's mistakes. Cleveland infuriated his voter base in key pivot states when he decided to return captured Confederate battle flags to southern states. This action incensed Union veterans, who became further outraged when Cleveland vetoed Union veterans' compensation for service in the Civil War. Democratic politicians fanned the flames by opposing civil service reform, and farmers were outraged by Cleveland's adherence to the gold standard, which cut into the farmers' minimal profit margins. But perhaps the most controversial issue during the 1888 presidential election was Cleveland's call for tariff reductions.

Tariffs, viewed by many as very high, protected American goods from competing with lower-priced foreign products, especially those from Great Britain. They also protected thousands of jobs in American industry. Cleveland believed that the tariffs generated excess funds for the Federal Treasury. Cleveland believed that this stifled economic growth and stability, while the Republicans under the leadership of Harrison, countered, arguing that the protection of American jobs was crucial to generate higher pay and more jobs. The tariff issue, however, also carried an ethnic controversy with it.

Great Britain strongly supported the idea of lower tariffs, an idea that frustrated Irish-American immigrants who had arrived in the United States. Any candidate who supported reducing the tariffs was viewed as being pro-Britain and risked the possibility of losing large blocks of Irish-American votes.

In addition to the tariff controversy, two additional issues played a major role in the outcome of the 1888 presidential election. First was the fraud activity known as the "Blocks of Five." Prior to the adoption of the secret ballot in federal elections, political parties printed up their own ballots and distributed them to their voters. The voters would simply fill out the ballot and drop it off at the polling place. In 1888, William Wade Dudley sent a letter to Indiana election officials asking them to locate undecided voters (known as floaters), group them in blocks of five, and put a trusted man with the necessary funds in charge of these blocks. Each "trusted man" was to reward floaters with cash in engage for votes for Harrison. This plan was eventually exposed when a railroad official acknowledged a phony ballot existed. No one knows exactly how many votes were bought. Afterwards, secret ballots were adopted by the states. The second fraud controversy centered on a factious letter written by California Republican George Osgoodby. Under the assumed name of Charles Murchison, Osgoodby asked British Ambassador Sir Lionel Sackville-West who was the best candidate for president. The ambassador responded that he felt that Cleveland was the best man, which infuriated the Irish-Catholics and their voters.

Harrison received 5,443,892 votes, or 47.8 percent of all votes cast, 233 electoral votes. Cleveland received 5,534,488 votes, or 48.6 percent of the popular vote, but only 168 electoral votes. Fisk followed a distant third with 249,819 votes, or 2.2 percent of the popular vote and no Electoral College votes. Streeter brought up the rear garnering 146,602 votes for 1.3 percent of all votes cast and no Electoral College votes. Harrison won the Electoral College by a 233–168 margin, largely by winning Cleveland's home state of New York, with its Irish-Catholic voter base. With each candidate needing just 201 Electoral College votes to win the presidency, Cleveland could have won outright had he carried his home state of New York with 204–197 electoral votes. Cleveland narrowly won (by less than one percent) the popular vote in Connecticut, Virginia, and West Virginia. Cleveland became one of four men to have clearly won the presidency by securing the popular vote, but not winning the Electoral College. Cleveland would be re-elected after a four-year absence in 1892, the only president in the U.S. history to accomplish this feat.

SEE ALSO: Presidential Election of 1884; Prohibition Party.

BIBLIOGRAPHY. Richard Jensen, The Winning of the Midwest: Social and Political Conflict, 1888–1896 (University of Chicago Press, 1971); Wayne Morgan, From Hayes to McKinley: National Party Politics, 1877–1896 (Syracuse University Press, 1969); Joanne Reitano, The Tariff Question of the Gilded Age: The Great Debate of 1888 (Pennsylvania State University Press, 1994); Mark Summers, Party Games: Getting, Keeping and Using Power in Gilded Age Politics (University of North Carolina Press, 2004).

RONALD ERIC MATTHEWS, JR.
MOUNT UNION COLLEGE

Presidential Election of 1892

THE PRESIDENTIAL ELECTION of 1892 featured Benjamin Harrison (1833–1901), and Grover Cleveland (1837–1908). Harrison, the incumbent Republican president, defeated Democrat Cleveland in 1888. Cleveland outpolled Harrison, 48.6 to 47.8 percent in the popular vote. Yet, Harrison convincingly defeated Cleveland in the Electoral College, receiving 233 votes to Cleveland's 168. The 1892 election would see the old adversaries face one another again for the presidency.

The Republican nominating convention in Minneapolis selected Harrison on the first ballot and New York newspaper editor Whitelaw Reid (1837–1912) became his vice presidential nominee. However, William McKinley of Ohio emerged at the convention as a presidential candidate in the making. The Democrats, meeting in Chicago, chose Cleveland on the first ballot, his third consecutive party nomination for the presidency, which was only surpassed by Franklin D. Roosevelt in 1944. Adlai E. Stevenson (1835–1914) of Illinois was chosen as Cleveland's vice presidential running mate.

The 1892 election also saw the rise of a significant third-party challenge to the Democrats and the Republicans from the Populist Party, which emerged on the national scene with agrarian and financial reform messages. The Populists nominated James B. Weaver (1833–1912) of Iowa for the presidency and Virginian, James Gavin Field, as his vice presidential candidate. Other parties, such as the Prohibitionists and the Socialist Labor Party, also fielded candidates, but they would prove to be insignificant factors in the election.

HARRISON AND CLEVELAND

The Republican nominee, Benjamin Harrison, had the advantage as the sitting president. Born in North Bend, Ohio, educated at Miami University, Harrison was the grandson of the 9th President, William Henry Harrison. He built his career as a prominent lawyer and Republican politician in Indianapolis, Indiana. He fought on the Union side in the Civil War, achieving the rank of colonel. In the 1880s, Harrison went to Washington as a senator and was generally seen as a moderate within the party, promoting veterans' issues and the homestead settlement of the West.

As president, however, Harrison is often viewed as less than distinguished. He was not perceived as an effective and dynamic party leader. He supported the Sherman Anti-Trust Act of 1890, and was a protectionist who endorsed the McKinley Tariff of 1890, although with some sugar exemptions. He promoted Pan-American initiatives, allowed silver as a currency, and at the end of his term, submitted a treaty for the annexation of Hawaii. In addition, Harrison pushed to preserve African-American voting rights in the south, which were being eroded by state governments.

Grover Cleveland came to the 1892 election as a former president, serving 1885–89. Although he won the popular vote by approximately 100,000 votes, he lost in 1888 to Harrison in the Electoral College, a situation not repeated until the 2000 presidential election. Cleveland was born in New Jersey, but raised in New York State, and was a lawyer by profession. He came late to politics, becoming mayor of Buffalo in 1881, and New York governor in 1882. He succeeded in the 1884 election by winning over reform-minded Republicans who were dissatisfied with the party candidate, James G. Blaine of Maine. Cleveland went to the White House concerned with the financial abuses of the day, which included corruption in the form of government patronage and fraud. He vetoed numerous Civil War Pension Bills that were subject to fraudulent claims,

and generally tried to stem the tide of bad laws. He endorsed the Interstate Commerce Act of 1887, geared to railroad regulation, and opposed the Republican high tariff protectionist policies. He maintained an aggressive Indian policy, especially in terms of subduing Geronimo and the Apaches, and extended the interpretation of the Monroe Doctrine to broaden America's right to intervene in the hemisphere. In 1886, Cleveland, who had come to the White House a bachelor, became only the second president to marry in office when he married 21-year-old Frances Folsom. Although he was financially prudent and respectful, Cleveland's opponents hounded him with rumors that he fathered an illegitimate child, a claim given credit because of his financial support of the child. Some also questioned his values in the Civil War era, for he had hired a substitute to avoid the Lincoln draft.

The 1892 Populist Party candidate, James B. Weaver, was born in Ohio, but raised in Iowa, where like the other candidates he was admitted to the bar in 1856 and practiced law. He was a devoted abolitionist and fought in the Civil War, rising from the rank of private to general. Initially a Republican, he broke with the party during the Grant administration because of the influence of big business within the party. Weaver opposed the Gold standard, national banks, and the poor state of agriculture that initially drew him to the inflationary policies of the Greenback Party. He represented them as a congressman in the 1870s and 1880s, and through Farmers Alliance activism, moved toward the formation of the Populist Party, where his prominence and experience made him their natural candidate 1892. The 1892 campaign lacked fanfare by either the Republicans or the Democrats, although Weaver actively traveled throughout the country, calling for a "free and fair" election. He boosted his campaign with a Call to Action pamphlet, which detailed the Populist program, hoping that information might win votes.

The fundamental difference between Cleveland and Harrison was Cleveland's opposition to Republican protectionist measures as seen in their high tariff actions. Cleveland backed the gold standard and fiscal control, which attracted business support away from the Republicans and alienated certain free silver Democrats from the south and West. To a lesser extent, Cleveland opposed some of the more expansionist Republican positions. Harrison, on the other hand, although nominated on the first ballot, was not a star performer. His candidacy lacked party enthusiasm and he was not seen as a team player by important elements such as the big city machines, who felt his support for civil service reform undermined their positions. He failed to court key individuals within the party with whom he disagreed, and this denied him the party unity that he needed in a tight race. Many Republicans saw him as a dull and unappealing character and the public seemed to agree.

To make matters worse, Harrison's wife fell desperately ill from tuberculosis during the midst of the campaign, which seriously affected his focus and intensity. In a gentlemanly manner, Cleveland did show deference to this situation and avoided exploiting Harrison's preoccupation. Harrison's wife, Caroline, died on October 25, 1892, just two weeks before the election, and this was a final blow to Harrison's fortunes. It was reported that following his defeat in 1892, Harrison told his family that he felt that he was freed from prison.

In June 1892, the long Homestead, Pennsylvania, Carnegie Steelworks strike began that saw major battles between the union strikers and company agents. This was the most serious union unrest that the nation had seen, and the most violent. It reflected the growing social tensions of the era. Along with deteriorating economic conditions, this became a serious undercurrent that tainted the election, particularly as neither Harrison nor Cleveland identified with the workers' drive toward unionization.

The election November 8, 1892, involved 44 states, with six new western states (North Dakota, South Dakota, Idaho, Washington, Wyoming, and Montana) voting for the first time, after joining the Union 1889–90. Grover Cleveland and Adlai E. Stevenson won 46 percent of the popular vote with 5,553,898 votes, and Benjamin Harrison and Whitelaw Reid took 43 percent of the vote with 5,190,819 ballots cast. James B. Weaver and James Gavin Field for the Populists received 1,026,595 votes or 8.5 percent of the popular vote, drawn primarily from the western states. The Prohibitionist candidates, John Bidwell and James B. Cranfill, took 270,879 votes or 2.2 percent of the vote, and Socialist Labor with Simon Wing and Charles H. Matchett gained 21,173 votes or 0.2 percent of the votes cast. Cleveland's victory was more decisive in the Electoral College, where he received 277 votes to 145 for Harrison and 22 for Weaver. Cleveland's coattails saw the Democrats keep control of the House with 218 seats versus 124 Republi-

cans, and 11 Populists, although the Republicans made major gains over their 1890 performance. The Senate also maintained a Democratic majority in 1892. During the election, the Democrats played on racial fears, particularly about the Republican Federal Elections Bill (Force Bill) that protected African-American voting rights in the south. The Democrats exploited this as an attack on states' rights.

A TURNING POINT

Cleveland's selection made him the first and only president to be elected to two non-consecutive terms. His second term in office would be marred by industrial disputes and consumed by the worst economic depression in American history, the Panic of 1893, during which more than four million of a population of 65 million, were unemployed. He also failed to significantly lower the tariff and reform the patronage system. In addition, Cleveland made use of court injunctions and federal troops to suppress the Pullman strike in 1894, which did not improve his popularity. Cleveland defused Britain's boundary dispute with Venezuela. He maintained an anti-expansionist policy toward Hawaii, and opposed support for the Cuban insurrection.

Cleveland rapidly lost popularity in his second term and the grassroots Democratic Party drifted toward an inflationary free silver monetary policy and adopted other agrarian issues as policy for the 1896 election, which further distanced the Democrats from Cleveland's style and politics. For many, the 1892 election was an important turning point when they first felt the impact of rapid continental expansion and the consequences of freewheeling industrial growth. As a result, increasing labor unrest, economic uncertainty, and drives for overseas expansion led to signal the issues that would dominate early 20th century America politics.

SEE ALSO: Federal Election Bill; Populists and Populist Movements; Presidential Election of 1888.

BIBLIOGRAPHY. H.U. Faulkner, *Politics, Reform and Expansion, 1890–1900* (Harper and Row, 1963); H.P. Jeffers, *An Honest President: The Life and Presidencies of Grover Cleveland* (Harper-Collins, 2000); Matthew Josephson, *The Politicos* (Harvest, 1938); Morton Keller, *Affairs of State: Public Life in Late Nineteenth Century America* (Harvard University Press, 1977); Paul Kleppner, *The Third Election System, 1853–1892: Parties, Voters and Political Culture* (University of North Carolina Press, 1979); G.H. Knoles, *Presidential Campaign and Election of 1892* (Stanford University Press, 1942); Yan Mieczkowski, *The Routledge Historical Atlas of Presidential Elections* (Routledge, 2001); H.W. Morgan, *From Hayes to McKinley: National Party Politics, 1877–1896* (Syracuse University Press, 1969); A.M. Schlesinger, Jr., ed., *History of American Presidential Elections, 1892–1908* (Chelsea House, 1985); H.J. Sievers, *Benjamin Harrison: Hoosier Statesman* (American Political Biographical Press, 1996).

THEODORE W. EVERSOLE, PH.D.
INDEPENDENT SCHOLAR

Presidential Election of 1896

THE AMERICA OF the Gilded Age, with frightening regularity, experienced economic downturns known as panics. The nation did not suffer from want, but from overproduction amid narrow markets. In 1873, 1883, and 1893, the United States experienced financial and economic catastrophes. Farmers believed that the crises they suffered were due to the plutocracy hoarding the wealth of the nation and contraction in the money supply.

In 1890, William Harvey published *Coin's Financial School,* in which a cartoon character, a silver dollar named Coin, explained the need to accept bimetallism. The Democratic incumbent, Grover Cleveland, upon re-entering office in 1893, found the country in the worst panic of the 19th century. Strikes, agrarian unrest, and depletion of the gold supply led to his own party abandoning him in 1896.

THE ISSUE

The chief campaign issue was the free and unlimited coinage of silver at a ratio of 16:1 with gold. The farmers and radicals of the day believed that the use of silver would inflate the currency and increase profits for their crops. It was far too simplistic a notion, but they championed the cause with great fervency. The tariff and other issues that had appeared with regularity since the end of the Civil War also received much debate, but the free and unlimited coinage of silver at a ratio of 16 ounces of silver minted on par in price with one ounce of gold remained the overriding issue of the campaign. The election canvass of 1896 holds the title The Battle of the Standards.

THE CONVENTIONS AND CANDIDATES

The Republicans, long the party of protection and traditional Protestant values, came to their convention in St. Louis anticipating great things. The eventual nominee was William McKinley, former congressman and governor of Ohio. McKinley, who was managed by Marcus Alonso Hanna of Cleveland, Ohio, a gentlemen of perceptive business acumen and, connected with the Standard Oil Corporation, bore the sobriquet of his opponents: Dollar Mark. Hanna was able to obtain the nomination for McKinley without a great deal of opposition.

McKinley ran on a platform of protection and the promise of Republican prosperity. Aging Union veterans supported McKinley overwhelmingly, and as a result the bloody shirt, waved in the Gilded Age breeze. McKinley was moral, upright, honest, conservative, and devoted to his invalid wife. The Republican Platform advocated bimetallism if other nations of the world adopted the same standard, but, in the meantime, endorsed the gold standard.

The Democrats gathered in Chicago and quickly repudiated their own president, the beleaguered Grover Cleveland. The platform committee was swayed by a former congressman from Nebraska and editor of the *Omaha World*, William Jennings Bryan (1860–1925), the powerful orator from Platte River country. Bryan, a dynamic speaker, held the audience spellbound and gave one of the most remembered and powerful speeches in American political history entitled the Cross of Gold. Bryan, with populist rhetoric, class warfare, biblical imagery, historical allusions, and agrarian emphasis, made his case for the free and unlimited coinage of silver on par with gold at a ratio of 16:1. The climax of the speech held the audience in awe: "You shall not press down upon the brow of labor this crown of thorns; you shall crucify mankind upon a cross of gold."

As his speech reached its crescendo, he laid his fingers on his head as if he was donning the crown of thorns, and spread his arms wide in crucifixion pose. After a moment of stunned silence, the hearers erupted. The convention was electrified, and the delegates shouted Bryan's name repeatedly and cried out " No crown of thorns!" "No cross of gold!" Bryan won the nomination on the fifth ballot and the convention gave him Arthur Sewall of Maine as his running mate. The Gold Democrats bolted and nominated their own candidate, John M. Palmer of Illinois, and former

Confederate general Simon B. Butler of Kentucky, on a "gold bug" platform.

The People's Party (the Populists) did not know how to respond. Their convention in St. Louis divided between those who wanted to fuse with the Democrats and those who did not. After all, the Democrats had many of the same concerns and planks in their platform. They hoped that Bryan would take one of their own as a running mate, but he refused; nevertheless, the Populists nominated Georgian Thomas E. Watson for vice president and endorsed Bryan. However, Bryan kept the wealthy plutocrat selected for his running mate by the Democrats.

THE BATTLE OF THE STANDARDS

In the election campaign that followed, the Republicans earned millions of dollars in contributions, while Bryan garnered approximately $300,000–$400,000. McKinley campaigned from his front porch, with delegations coming to see him while he answered prescreened questions. Campaign tracts printed in several languages aided Hanna in getting out the Republican message.

Bryan, on the other hand, traveled 18,000 miles and gave 600 speeches, all by way of whistle-stop campaigns via the train. The election was one of the most exciting in American history, dominated by mass rallies, parades, sharp rhetoric, deep passion, and emotional ecstasy. It also had the highest voter turnout in history, with more than 80 percent of voters casting ballots.

McKinley won a stunning victory with 271 electoral votes, and 7,102,246 popular votes, for 51.1 percent of the total votes cast. There were 45 states in the Union at the time, and his strength was in the populous states of the east and midwest. Bryan won 176 electoral votes, and 6,492,559, or 47.1 percent of the popular votes. Minor party candidates earned approximately 300,000 votes, or 1.2 percent of the ballots cast.

In the end, it was not enough: The well-oiled Hanna machine, the gold strikes in Alaska and abroad easing the pressure on gold, the abating of the panic, and the Republican success in painting Bryan as a radical all served to defeat the Peerless Leader. The Republicans convinced the public that McKinley was the "advance agent of prosperity." However, not all was lost for the

The chief issue of the campaign of 1896 was the free and unlimited coinage of silver at a ratio of 16:1 with gold. The farmers and radicals of the day believed that the use of silver would inflate the currency.

Democracts. Bryan changed the Democratic Party forever by using the liberal ideals of the campaign to reshape liberalism from a limited government point of view to an activist force used on behalf of the underclass. He also became the first candidate to actively campaign among the people, taking his case to them via the rails.

Bryan ran again in 1900 and 1908, but lost each time. Yet, his influence on the Democratic Party was lasting, and after the era of the Great Commoner, the party campaigned on platforms based on class antagonisms. The Democrats remained reactionary for the next generation in their dependence on the solid south and farmers. The election campaign of 1896 was the last presidential election in which farmers would have a major role. By the census of 1920, a majority of citizens no longer lived on farms; therefore, Bryan's themes harkened too much to the past.

REPUBLICAN CONTROL

McKinley began a trend that placed the Republicans in control of the federal government for over a generation. Until the early 1930s, voters identified the Republicans with what McKinley's supporters coined "a full dinner pail." In addition, McKinley began a trend toward much more powerful chief executives. He succeeded in making the United States a power that the Europeans had to respect through his success in winning the Spanish-American War. His acquisitions of territory in the Pacific established the nation as a colonial power for the first time. McKinley's successes would lead to the debate about imperialism and colonization—the chief issue of the second McKinley-Bryan election battle in 1900.

SEE ALSO: Bryan, William Jennings; People's Party; Populism; Presidential Election of 1892; Presidential Election of 1900; Presidential Election of 1908; Realignment.

BIBLIOGRAPHY. W.J. Bryan, *The First Battle: The Story of the Campaign of 1896* (William B. Conkey Co., 1897); R.W. Cherny, *A Righteous Cause: The Life of William Jennings Bryan* (Little Brown, 1985); P.W. Glad, *McKinley, Bryan, and the People* (Lippincott, 1964); E.H. Roseboom, *A History of Presidential Elections* (Macmillan, 1970); D.R.B. Ross, ed. *The Emergence of Modern America: 1865–1900* (Thomas Y. Crowell Co., 1970); A.M. Schlesinger, Jr., ed., *U.S. Political Parties, Volume II: 1860–1910, The Gilded Age of Politics* (Chelsea House, 1973); E.S. West, *The World Almanac of Presidential Campaigns* (World Almanac, 1992).

JAMES S. BAUGESS
COLUMBUS STATE COMMUNITY COLLEGE

Presidential Election of 1900

AS THE NATION calmed after the electrifying election of 1896, known as the Battle of the Standards (over the currency issue), Americans began to enjoy prosperity again, and it seemed that William McKinley and the Republicans delivered on their promise of a "full dinner pail" for all. At first glance, it appeared that Democratic loser William Jennings Bryan's political career had ended at age 37. It only took two years to give Bryan another issue on which to run, and he made the most of it.

The United States suffered from economic downturns known as panics every 10 years. The panics did not occur due to shortages, but to overabundance. The American industrial machine and the nation's farmers produced more than the world had ever seen up to that time.

In 1890, the U.S. Census Bureau declared the frontier closed, which caused a great deal of psychic trauma amid the body politic. Shortly after the revelation of the Census Bureau's report, Frederick Jackson Turner delivered a monumental address at the Columbia Exposition in Chicago in 1893 entitled "The Significance of the Frontier Upon History," in which he declared that the nation experienced economic downturns because the nation needed markets to sell its excess goods. Now that the safety valve of moving west and homesteading was over, the nation needed to look beyond its borders. The Far East, with its teeming millions and precious commodities, seemed an answer to the American economic problem of oversupply.

Turner was not the first individual to see the need for expanding markets. In 1890, Admiral Alfred Thayer Mahan wrote *The Influence of Seapower Upon History*, in which he argued for a large navy to protect an equally large merchant fleet, both of which needed coaling stations en route to the Far East. Mahan also argued for a canal across Central America to decrease travel time by half to the Far East. Senator Henry Cabot Lodge of

Massachusetts and Theodore Roosevelt, assistant secretary of the Navy, agreed with Mahan's thesis that great nations needed powerful vessels that protected merchant fleets. The "large policy" would find its opportunity for implementation at the end of the Spanish-American War.

Cubans had long been in turmoil, struggling to free themselves from the Spanish yoke. Americans, thanks to the "yellow press," sympathized with the Cubans. McKinley, having seen war firsthand as a youth in the Union Army, did not want to go to war to liberate Cuba, but two events resulted in a declaration of war against Spain. First was the discovery of a letter written by Spanish Ambassador Enrique Dupuy De Lôme to a friend in Cuba, claiming that McKinley was:

> ... weak and a bidder for admiration of the crowd, besides being a would-be politician who tries to leave a door open behind himself while keeping on good terms with the jingoes of his party.

The letter appeared in William Randolph Hearst's *New York Journal* on February 9, 1898. The public outcry was deafening. The second event that helped trigger the war occurred on the evening of February 15, when the U.S.S. *Maine* imploded in Havana harbor. Many Americans believed after the insult of the De Lôme letter that the Spaniards destroyed the ship and killed over 200 sailors. By April, the nation was at war with Spain. William Jennings Bryan served with a Nebraska regiment as colonel, but his unit never experienced hostile fire, and he spent the entire conflict in Florida. Bryan resigned his colonelcy immediately after the end of hostilities and returned to Nebraska.

The Spanish-American War, often referred to as "splendid little war," united the north and south for the first time since the antebellum era, and to made the United States a world power. The political fallout came when, in the settlement with Spain, the United States acquired the Philippines and set up occupation forces and bases on the islands. The Filipinos, angered by the occupation, fought a bloody guerrilla war against the United States, and both sides committed atrocities.

Bryan had an issue with which to make another run at the presidency. He argued that the United States had once been a colony and fought a war to free itself from British rule. There was no constitutional basis for becoming an imperial power, and the United States, guilty of as many atrocities as the guerrillas, should leave the Philip-

In 1896, McKinley campaigned by answering questions from his front porch, and in 1900, he sent Roosevelt on the road.

pines to its own devices and get out. An Anti-Imperialist League formed in opposition with many notables in its ranks: Carl Schurz, Andrew Carnegie, Jane Addams, and Mark Twain, all arguing that the nation should not indulge in imperialism. Imperialism for Bryan was the "paramount issue of the campaign."

THE CONVENTIONS

The Republican convention was in Philadelphia, June 19–21. McKinley's nomination was never in doubt. The most issue important issue for the delegates was the nomination of a vice presidential candidate, as Vice President Garrett Hobart died in 1899. McKinley considered a few candidates, and then decided to leave the decision up the convention. The brash and reforming governor of New York, Theodore Roosevelt, a war hero in the most recent conflict with Spain, was the choice of the delegates. Senator Mark Hanna, the national chairman, was aghast at the delegates' decision. "Don't you realize," exclaimed Hanna, "there is only one heartbeat between that madman and the presidency?" Hanna also warned McKinley, "Your duty is to live four years from next March."

Nevertheless, Roosevelt's presence as the vice presidential candidate strengthened the ticket. During the canvass, Roosevelt traveled across the nation, campaigning against Bryan. He went so far as to refer to Bryan as "my opponent" rather than the "Democrat nominee" or "our" opponent. The party platform defended the Republican record of prosperity and success in the war. In addition, the platform declared the party's commitment to the gold standard, protectionism, restriction of cheap labor from foreign lands, raising the age qualification of child workers, renouncing African-American disenfranchisement, and backed the construction of an isthmian canal in Central America.

The Democrats met in Kansas City on July 4 and nominated Bryan on the first ballot. Grover Cleveland's former vice president during his second term, Adlai E. Stevenson, agreed to take a second nomination as the vice presidential nominee. The convention was uneventful, and the only debate was whether to make free silver the paramount issue or imperialism. Imperialism won, but Bryan insisted on a reaffirmation of the silver plank, and the convention agreed to insert it in the platform. The platform condemned imperialism, asked for immediate liberation of Cuba from American influence, opposed private monopoly, demanded strict enforcement of the Chinese exclusion legislation, and demanded the American exit from the Philippines because:

> The Filipinos cannot be citizens without endangering our civilization; they cannot be subjects without imperilling our form of government; and as we are not willing to surrender our civilization nor to convert the Republic into an empire.

THE CAMPAIGN

The campaign was not as exciting as the 1896 canvass. McKinley attempted to look as presidential and dignified as possible traveling between Washington and his hometown of Canton, Ohio. His supporters wore campaign paraphernalia and buttons sporting a print of the full dinner pail. He sent Roosevelt on the road; he surpassed Bryan's performance on the campaign trail. Roosevelt logged 21,000 miles in eight weeks. The

Republican war chest contained approximately $3 million—much more than they needed.

Bryan traveled 16,000 miles in five and one half weeks, but his campaign raised less than $500,000. Bryan's supporters pinned a three-leaf clover to their clothing representing the three main concerns of the Democrat platform: anti-imperialism, anti-trust, and anti-gold. Imperialism did not stir the people and when Bryan tried to resurrect free silver, the public did not respond. The people also ignored the anti-trust emphasis. Momentum and an issue that would stir the voters eluded him.

The lack of intensity did not lessen slogan creation. The Republicans urged "four more years with a full dinner pail," and the Democrats chanted "No Imperialism!" In addition, the Democrats used their usual mantra of class war: "Equal Rights to All—Special Privilege to None!" The voter turnout was lower than in 1896; furthermore, the mass rallies and parades of previous elections faded into memory.

McKinley won the election by a bigger margin than in 1896. Once again, the "Boy Orator of the Platte" suffered defeat. In the end, 45 states participated in the election and McKinley won more votes than in 1896—7,215,525 popular votes, or 52 percent, and 292 electoral votes. Bryan's tally was 6,358,737, or 46 percent of the ballots cast, and 155 electoral votes. The Republicans won 197 seats in the House of Representatives and the Democrats 151. In the Senate, the GOP won 55 seats and the Democrats 31. Voter turnout (70 percent) did not reach the level of the 1900 presidential race. McKinley's victory was short-lived. He died as the result of gunshot wounds at the hands of an anarchist on September 14, 1901. Mark Hanna's worst nightmare then came true: Theodore Roosevelt ascended to the presidency.

SEE ALSO: Bryan, William Jennings; Expansionism; Media, Role in Campaigns; Military Hero; War and Peace.

BIBLIOGRAPHY. O.T. Barck, Jr., and N.M. Blake, *Since 1900: A History of the United States in Our Time* (Macmillan Publishing, 1974); R.L. Beisner, *From the Old Diplomacy to the New, 1865–1900* (Harlan Davidson, 1986); R.W. Cherny, *A Righteous Cause: The Life of William Jennings Bryan* (Little Brown & Co., 1985); F.R. Dulles, *America's Rise to World Power, 1898–1954* (Harper & Row Publishers, 1954); L.L. Gould, *The Presidency of William McKinley* (University Press of Kansas, 1980); L.L. Gould, *The Grand Old Party: A History of the Republicans* (Random House, 2003); B.M. Linn, *The Philippine War: 1899–*

1902 (University Press of Kansas, 2000); E.H. Roseboom, *A History of Presidential Elections from George Washington to Richard M. Nixon: The Definitive Account of Our National Conventions, Campaigns, and Elections* (Macmillan, 1970); A.M. Schlesinger, Jr., *History of U.S. Political Parties: Volume II, The Gilded Age of Politics* (Chelsea House, 1973); Eileen Shields-West, *The World Almanac of Presidential Campaigns* (World Almanac, 1992); T.H. Williams, *The History of American Wars From 1745 to 1918* (Louisiana State University Press, 1981); Jules Witcover, *Party of the People: A History of the Democrats* (Random House, 2003).

JAMES S. BAUGESS
COLUMBUS STATE COMMUNITY COLLEGE

Presidential Election of 1904

THE PRESIDENTIAL ELECTION of 1904, according to the *New York Times*, should have vaulted Democrat Alton B. Parker to the presidency over Republican Theodore (Teddy) Roosevelt concerning the issue of the Panama Canal. The *Times*, however, was wrong and Roosevelt won in a landslide. Despite his long tenure as president, this was the only presidential election that Roosevelt won on his own accord. After the election, he noted, "I am glad to be elected President in my own right." In many ways, Roosevelt was the first modern celebrity president, with great charisma and outstanding oratory skills, and his popularity played a pivotal role in the election of 1904.

Roosevelt, who had become president after William McKinley was assassinated in 1901, won with relative ease over Parker with over 57 percent of the popular vote. He received 336 votes in the Electoral College to Parker's 140 votes. Geographically, the split between Roosevelt and Parker was evident, with Roosevelt sweeping the north and west of the country, while Parker took the south. Of the 45 states in the union at the time, Parker carried all 13 southernmost states, from Maryland down to Florida and over to Texas. This, at least in terms of party, is the reverse of modern politics, whereby the Republican Party usually takes the south and the Democratic Party wins the northeast. Besides Roosevelt and Parker, a third-party candidate, Eugene V. Debs, garnered three percent of the popular vote for the Socialist Party.

At the outset, the election may not have seemed like it would even be close, but Parker had his opportunities with internal Republican quarrels, such as trade issues, and Roosevelt's policies regarding large corporations. Roosevelt had views similar to his predecessor, McKinley, with regards to the Sherman Antitrust Act of 1902, which led to some of his problems with big business. Among other things, the Democratic Party charged that Roosevelt wanted power for many years to come. Instead, he declared on Election Day that he would not seek a third term. Roosevelt would later renege on this commitment as he sought the presidency, in the 1912 election, for the Progressive Party (Bull Moose Party), when he was unable to overtake President Taft for the Republican Party nomination, despite a larger share of the delegates.

ROOSEVELT'S RISE TO POWER

Roosevelt, who had become the youngest president in American history at age 41, used his incumbent status well in the 1904 campaign. His rise to power was imperative to his success in 1904 because, for the first time in history, celebrity mattered. Roosevelt served as police commissioner of New York City in 1895, where he continued to gain experience that would serve him well as president. He also gained popularity, in part, because of his experience as assistant secretary of the Navy under William McKinley in 1897, but left to become lieutenant colonel of the Rough Riders in the Spanish-American War in 1898.

A relative political newcomer, Theodore Roosevelt had served as governor of New York after winning the 1898 gubernatorial election. Garrett Hobart, McKinley's vice president for the 1896 election, died of heart failure midway through the term and was not replaced. Roosevelt then became the Republican vice presidential nominee in the presidential election of 1900 and, with McKinley's victory, became the 25th vice president of the United States.

It was not long into McKinley's presidency that tragedy occurred and brought an unsuspecting Roosevelt into the White House. Roosevelt became the first strong president of the 20th century as his executive powers increased. He referred to the presidency as a "bully pulpit" with which he could influence public opinion to gain support for his programs. It was this advantage that Roosevelt brought into the election of 1904—notoriety as the incumbent president and a great oratory ability that could convince people of his worthiness to remain president.

Teddy Roosevelt's charisma, oratory skills, and popularity made him the first modern celebrity president.

THE NOMINATIONS

Most incumbent presidents are almost automatically nominated as the party choice for the next election. In the case of Theodore Roosevelt, however, there was speculation about challenges given his unpopularity in some Republican circles. The name of Mark Hanna, the chair of the Republican National Committee, was floated as a possible contender to Roosevelt, but this notion was quickly abandoned when Hanna announced that he would not run. Roosevelt was confirmed as the nominee in 1903, and selected Charles W. Fairbanks, a senator from Indiana, as his running mate. Roosevelt had left the vice-presidency vacant between 1901 and the 1904 presidential election.

The presidential election of 1904, on the Democratic side, is best known as the cycle in which William Jennings Bryan did not stand for the nomination. Bryan, who had been the unsuccessful Democratic nominee in

1896 and 1900, did not feel he could adequately challenge Roosevelt. He later returned for the 1908 presidential election, but lost once again. With Bryan out of the race, the only two viable candidates were William Randolph Hearst and Alton B. Parker. Parker went on to win the nomination on a platform of anti-imperialism and adoption of the gold standard. He selected Henry G. Davis of West Virginia as his running mate.

CAMPAIGN ISSUES

Because Roosevelt entered the 1904 presidential election as the incumbent, this election was, in many respects, a referendum on how well he was doing in office. There were plenty of journalists and politicians who thought Roosevelt could be defeated, with the vast majority of metropolitan newspapers with large circulations opposing Roosevelt, most notably those from New York. It was this push in the newspapers that kept the race relatively close because Parker received a great deal of positive press; Roosevelt faced a barrage of negative stories.

The nomination of Parker, however, should have been enough to tip experienced political observers that Roosevelt would win in 1904. The Democrats, after all, passed over William Jennings Bryan in favor of Parker, a judge who was far less charismatic than Roosevelt. On the domestic front, Roosevelt was kept extremely busy with some opposition from political leaders and high-profile men on Wall Street. Roosevelt earned a reputation for his ability to control excessive corporate power, which gained him significant popularity and support. However, this control also gained him powerful enemies who sought to derail his presidency by endorsing Parker during the election.

With regard to foreign policy, Roosevelt saw it as his duty to develop "uncivilized" territories. He implemented his policy in Cuba, the Philippines, and Puerto Rico. This served to expand America's influence in the world, which gained him popularity among voters. His most ambitious plan, however, was to build the Panama Canal Zone, through which ships could pass through the Americas. Panama became an independent country in November 1903, after revolting against Colombia with help from Roosevelt, and the United States benefited from the passage of ships through the isthmus. The issue of Panama again came to the fore in the 1908 election when Joseph Pulitzer made allegations about Wall Street's involvement in the creation of the Panama Canal. It was also an issue in the 1976 Republican primaries when Ronald Reagan held that the United States should retain control of the Canal Zone.

THE FIRST MODERN CELEBRITY PRESIDENT

The election of 1904, the media touted, would be a close race; in the end, it was a landslide. Roosevelt was the first modern president, who used his management of the press to win people over after they backed Parker for the presidency. What is most important about the 1904 election, was that Roosevelt largely stayed off the stump and allowed others to make his case for a full term. The plan worked; Roosevelt was able to deftly sidestep the media, who started off vehemently opposed to him. Roosevelt's popularity was one of the main components of his victory and was the first significant piece of evidence that celebrity appeal matters in modern elections. Even if the election of 1904 was uneventful from a neutral point of view, it did showcase the power of celebrity and the importance of image.

Following his victory in 1904, Roosevelt's inaugural address in March 1905 featured a lavish celebration involving cowboys, Indians, coal miners, soldiers, and students. His celebrity appeal and his ability to showcase his celebrity was pivotal in the election of 1904. It was this match-up with Parker that Roosevelt successfully won, and a significant reason as to why the 1904 presidential election resulted in such a landslide.

SEE ALSO: Debs, Eugene; Issue Coverage by the Media; Media, Role in Campaigns; New York; Presidential Election of 1896; Presidential Election of 1900; Presidential Election of 1908.

BIBLIOGRAPHY. Gilbert Black, ed., *Theodore Roosevelt, 1858–1919* (Oceana Publications Inc., 1969); Paul Boyer et al., eds., *The Enduring Vision* (Houghton Mifflin Co., 1998); R.H. Collin, *Theodore Roosevelt, Culture, Diplomacy and Expansion* (Louisiana State University Press, 1985); O.D. Espino, *How Wall Street Created a Nation: J.P. Morgan, Teddy Roosevelt and the Panama Canal* (Four Walls, Eight Windows, 2001); Lewis Gould, *The Modern American Presidency* (University Press of Kansas, 2003); Theodore Roosevelt, *An Autobiography* (Charles Scribner's Sons, 1920); Frederick Whitridge, *Roosevelt or Parker* (De Vinne Press, 1904).

GLEN M.E. DUERR
KENT STATE UNIVERSITY

Presidential Election of 1908

WITH PRESIDENT THEODORE Roosevelt deciding to not run for a third term, William Howard Taft, Roosevelt's choice for the Republican nomination, handily defeated Democrat William Jennings Bryan, who was making his third run for the office. In 1904, the Democrats turned away from Bryan, nominating Alton Parker, a "gold bug" and conservative, as the party's standard-bearer. Following Parker's devastating defeat by Roosevelt, the Democrats again turned to the progressive wing of their party for a candidate in 1908, and Bryan would once again be a frontrunner for the party's nomination.

Minnesota Governor John Albert Johnson challenged Bryan for the Democratic nomination. Bryan, who had been the Democratic nominee in 1896 and 1900, losing to William McKinley both times, handily defeated Johnson on the first ballot at the Democratic Convention, which took place in Denver, Colorado in July 1908. The party nominated John W. Kern of Indiana for vice president.

When the Republicans met in June 1908 at the Chicago Coliseum, the other candidates seeking the nomination included Joseph Cannon, the speaker of the U.S. House of Representatives; New York Governor Charles Evans Hughes; Wisconsin Senator Robert M. LaFollette; and former Treasury Secretary Leslie M. Shaw, who had resigned from Roosevelt's cabinet in 1907. With Roosevelt's support, Taft secured the Republican nomination on the third ballot. Taft offered the vice presidential nomination to Hughes, who declined and instead ran for re-election in New York. Taft then selected another New Yorker, Congressman James S. Sherman, as his running mate. Sherman was considered a progressive in the party, and Taft chose him over Massachusetts Governor Curtis Guild, Jr., a member of the conservative Stalwart wing of the Republican Party, who had been seeking support for the nomination.

Both parties candidates claimed that they were best qualified to continue Roosevelt's progressive agenda. Bryan, who in his previous two campaigns had run on a platform calling for the United States to lower the gold standard to silver, abandoned that issue in his 1908 campaign. Instead, Bryan offered a progressive agenda similar to Roosevelt's, promoting "trust busting." Bryan said that, if he were elected, he would wage war on the trusts and big banks, and regulate the railroads. He also proposed that the government guarantee deposits held in national banks, a plan that Taft contended would put a premium on reckless banking. Bryan attempted to gain the support of organized labor, but was unsuccessful.

Taft, as Roosevelt's chosen successor, also campaigned on the progressive agenda made popular by Roosevelt. The Republican slogan, "Vote for Taft now, you can vote for Bryan anytime," was a reference to Bryan's many campaigns for the presidency. Taft opposed free trade, contending that the periods of protection in the United States had been the periods of prosperity. This stand insured the support of big business for the Republican ticket. Bryan made a major strategic error when, while campaigning, he called for a takeover by the federal government of the nation's railroads. While the Democrats had called for government regulation of the railroads in their platform, Bryan's stand went beyond that and it backfired, as many voters saw Bryan's plans as socialistic.

Bryan again carried the south, the Democratic Party's electoral bastion during this period. Taft would prevail in most of the rest of the country. Roosevelt's support, as well as Taft's background as a graduate of Yale University, a federal judge, and secretary of war under Roosevelt, swayed enough voters to support the Republican ticket. The only states outside the old Confederacy that were carried by Bryan were Colorado, Delaware, Maryland (Bryan won six of the state's eight electoral votes), Nebraska, and Nevada. Taft carried 28 states to Bryan's 18.

The Results

	Popular Vote	Percentage	Electoral Votes
William Howard Taft	7,662,258	51.38	321
William Jennings Bryan	6,406,801	43.05	162
Eugene V. Debs	420,380	2.82	0
Eugene W. Chaflin	252,821	1.70	0
All others	126,474	0.85	0
TOTAL	14,882,734	100.0	483

Source: J.W. Wright, ed., *The New York Times Almanac 2007* (Penguin Reference, 2007).

SEE ALSO: Bryan, William Jennings; Campaigns, Presidential; Free Trade; Presidential Elections.

BIBLIOGRAPHY. L.W. Koenig, *Bryan, a Political Biography of William Jennings Bryan* (Putnam, 1971); Republican National Committee, *Republican Campaign Text-Book* (Republican National Committee, 1908); W.H. Taft, *Political Issues and Outlooks: Selected Speeches Delivered Between August 1908 and February 1909*, David H. Burton, ed. (Ohio University Press, 2001).

JEFFREY KRAUS
WAGNER COLLEGE

Presidential Election of 1912

THE PRESIDENTIAL ELECTION of 1912 was crucial in American political history. It temporarily reversed the Republican dominance in presidential elections since to 1896. In the 1912 election, Democratic nominee Woodrow Wilson, governor of New Jersey and former college president of Princeton, won the election due to a split in the Republican vote after former President Theodore Roosevelt defected from the Republican Party to form the Progressive Party (Bull Moose Party) after losing the Republican nomination to President William Howard Taft.

The results of the 1912 election had their roots in the results of the 1908 election. In 1908, President Theodore Roosevelt was at the height of his popularity. Four years earlier, he had won the largest landslide in American political history over Democratic opponent Alton B. Parker. However, after winning the 1904 election, Roosevelt announced that he would not run for president again in 1908 because he respected the two-term tradition of George Washington.

In 1908, Roosevelt could have easily received his party's nomination and been elected. However, Roosevelt declined to run and selected his Secretary of War William Howard Taft of Ohio as his successor. In retrospect, Roosevelt overlooked the fundamental differences between his own activist tendencies as president and Taft's very judicial and conservative temperament. Perhaps this was due to Taft's amiable and easygoing nature. Taft's background was primarily judicial; he had served for a number of years as a circuit court judge. He had also served as a solicitor general and governor general of the Philippines. Taft's dream was to serve as chief justice of the Supreme Court. However, Taft's ambitious wife Helen dreamed of being first lady and pushed him in the direction of a political career. Taft received the Republican nomination in 1908 as a result of Roosevelt's influence, and easily defeated perennial Democratic presidential candidate William Jennings Bryan of Nebraska. In November, Taft easily defeated Bryan to become president.

After the 1908 election, Theodore Roosevelt traveled to Africa, content that his successor had been elected president. Unfortunately, while Taft was an honest and amiable man, he lacked Roosevelt's charisma and popularity. As a result, he was unable to hold together the conservative and progressive wings of the Republican Party. During Taft's presidency, a group of insurgent Republicans, including Congressman George Norris of Nebraska, stripped the conservative Republican House Speaker Joseph Cannon from control of the House Rules Committee.

In another instance, Taft, as head of the forest service, fired Roosevelt's primary conservation advisor, Gifford Pinchot. To his critics, Taft appeared to be a fat and lazy man who loved to eat immense amounts of food. Taft was criticized for signing the Payne-Aldrich Tariff bill, which increased duties on imported goods. There were stories of Taft falling asleep at public events. In fairness to Taft, his administration busted more trusts than Roosevelt had, he admitted Arizona and New Mexico into the Union, enacted the eight-hour day for federal employees, and supported making the income tax a constitutional amendment.

Yet for many Republicans, Taft was a step backward from Roosevelt's administration. A break between Roosevelt and Taft was increasingly evident after Roosevelt's return from Africa and Europe in 1910. In the 1910 midterm elections, Roosevelt campaigned for progressive Republican candidates and advocated measures such as inheritance and estate taxes and the recall of judges. These positions clashed with Taft's more conservative positions.

In 1912, Roosevelt decided to wrest the Republican nomination away from Taft. On February 12, 1912, he publicly announced his candidacy. Roosevelt won most of the primaries that he entered (primaries were a new development at the time), including California, Illinois, Maryland, New Jersey, Ohio, Oregon, and South Dakota. In the primary states, Roosevelt received 1,157,397 popular votes and 278 delegates to 761,716 popular votes and 48 delegates for Taft. However, Taft controlled the party machinery and, as a result, won the nomination. Alleging that Taft had rigged the convention, Roosevelt and his supporters responded by storming out of the Republican convention and founding the Progressive (Bull Moose) Party. Roosevelt and the Progressive Party supported a number of reforms, including the direct primary, initiative, referendum, direct election of senators, workmen's compensation, women's suffrage, regulation of trusts, prohibition of child labor, and recall of judges.

Meanwhile, the Democratic Party, realizing that the split in the Republican Party meant that a Democratic victory in 1912 was almost assured, assembled in Baltimore to nominate a candidate. The possibilities included Governor Woodrow Wilson of New Jersey, Governor Judson Harmon of Ohio, Representative Oscar W. Underwood of Alabama, and Speaker of the House James Beauchamp ("Champ") Clark of Missouri. Of the four candidates, Clark was the favorite going into the convention. He won a number of primaries and possessed a seemingly overwhelming lead among the delegates. However, Clark failed to achieve the necessary two-thirds of the delegate required and a deadlock occurred. Eventually, Wilson won on the 46th ballot with 990 votes.

The Socialist Party nominated Eugene Debs (their candidate in 1904 and 1908). In 1912, the Socialist Party was a strong third party. In 1911, 450 Socialist officials had been elected to office. These officials included 56 mayors, 305 city councilmen, and one congressman. One of the most prominent Socialist politicians was Victor Berger, the mayor of Milwaukee, Wisconsin. The Socialist Party platform was to the left of the Democrat and Republican Parties. It advocated public ownership of businesses, property, and the banking system. In other respects, the platform was similar to the platforms of the Democratic and Progressive Parties. For example, the Socialist Party called for the abolition of child labor, shorter working hours, increased safety standards, and female suffrage.

THE GENERAL ELECTION

In the general election, there were four main candidates: Republican William Howard Taft, Progressive Theodore Roosevelt, Democrat Woodrow Wilson, and Socialist Eugene Debs. In reality, the contest was between Wilson and Roosevelt. As a Socialist candidate, Debs had no chance of winning, and Taft was far less popular than either Roosevelt or Wilson. Both

Roosevelt and Wilson seemed to agree on a number of goals, but disagreed about how to accomplish these goals. The best example was the issue of the trusts, the interlocking business combinations, which controlled the American economy and were perceived to be a threat to economic competition. Both candidates were highly critical of trusts. Roosevelt differentiated between "good" and "bad" trusts and believed that they should be regulated, but not abolished. Wilson, on the other hand, considered all trusts to be "bad" and wanted them to be abolished.

Theodore Roosevelt began the general election knowing that he would lose to Wilson, who would undoubtedly benefit from the split in the Republican Party. Nonetheless, he campaigned vigorously throughout the United States on behalf of his candidacy. On one of these campaign swings, in October 1912, Roosevelt was shot on his way to a speech in Milwaukee, Wisconsin, by a deranged bartender named John Schrank. The impact of the bullet was slowed down by Roosevelt's speech manuscript and his eyeglass case. Nonetheless, Roosevelt went to his scheduled speech and spoke for an hour to an astonished audience. Afterwards, he went to the hospital where it was found that the wound was not serious.

The result of the 1912 election was inevitable after the Republican split and Roosevelt's creation of the Progressive Party. Woodrow Wilson won the presidency with 6,293,019 popular votes and 435 electoral votes. Roosevelt received 4,119,507 popular votes and 88 electoral votes. Taft received 3,484,956 popular votes and eight electoral votes. Eugene Debs received 901,873 popular votes, a twofold increase over his showing in the 1908 election.

SEE ALSO: Bull Moose Party; Debs, Eugene; Progressive Party; Socialist Party.

BIBLIOGRAPHY. H.W. Brands, *T.R.: The Last Romantic* (Basic Books, 1997); James Chace, *1912: The Election That Changed the Country* (Simon and Schuster, 2004); J.M. Copper, *The Warrior and the Priest: Woodrow Wilson and Theodore Roosevelt* (Harvard University Press, 1983); Kathleen Dalton, *Theodore Roosevelt: A Strenuous Life* (Random House, 2002); J.A. Gable, *Bull Moose Years: Theodore Roosevelt and the Progressive Party* (Kennikat Press, 1978); William Manners, *T.R. and Will: A Friendship that Split the Republican Party* (Harcourt, Brace & World, 1969); Nathan Miller, *Theodore Roosevelt: A Life* (Morrow, 1992); George Mowry, *Theodore Roosevelt and the Progressive Movement* (Hill and Wang, 1960); Patricia O'Toole, *When Trumpets Call: Theodore Roosevelt after the White House* (Simon and Schuster, 2005).

JASON ROBERTS
GEORGE WASHINGTON UNIVERSITY

Presidential Election of 1916

THE PRESIDENTIAL ELECTION of 1916 occurred during generally uncertain times, and in the midst of a debilitating World War that appeared to have no end. The election was seen as a decision on the direction and intensity of American Progressivism and its continuing place in national politics. Woodrow Wilson was the sitting Democratic American president, elected in 1912 in the face of a divided Republican Party, and he hoped to achieve a second term, to end the trend of one-term Democratic presidents; he became the first Democrat to do so since Andrew Jackson. Wilson and his vice president, Thomas R. Marshall, were re-nominated without opposition at the Democratic convention in June 1916.

Wilson supported neutrality, and he desired the war to end on fair and just terms. This position gave him a degree of popular public support. Further, his stand against Germany's unrestricted submarine warfare seemed to have produced results. However, Germany's brutal occupation of Belgium and French territories boosted the Allied cause in the eyes of the American mainstream. Nevertheless, some Americans, such as the German-Americans and the Irish-Americans, did not have sympathy for an Allied cause as represented by the British Empire.

At the Republican presidential convention held in Chicago in June 1916, Charles Evans Hughes received the presidential nomination on the third ballot, and Charles W. Fairbanks of Indiana became his vice presidential running mate. Although Theodore Roosevelt still had a powerful contingent of Progressive (Bull Moose Republican) supporters, Roosevelt realized that he would only split the party again, as in 1912, and secure victory for the Democrats. With Roosevelt's former vice president Charles Fairbanks on the ticket, it appeared that fences could be mended so that a Republican victory might be achieved.

Charles Evans Hughes was a successful former two-term governor of the influential state of New York, and an associate justice of the Supreme Court. Hughes shared the Progressive agenda and was known as a consensus-builder who could overcome political divides and lead the party to the presidency. He, too, wanted to avoid war if it could be helped, but he was seen to favor the Allied side. During the campaign, Theodore Roosevelt's pro-war convictions seemed to undercut the official Republican position of neutrality based on preparedness and mobilization. It has been claimed that Roosevelt's strident calls for America's involvement in the European conflict allowed Hughes to be painted as a candidate who, if elected, would drag America into the war.

The Democrats exploited the nation's anti-war sentiments, and the slogan "He Kept Us Out of War" persuaded many to support Wilson's election, for he was portrayed as a man of peace and diplomacy. How to handle America's involvement in the war remained the critical issue, and the election unfolded in a climate of concern that was shaped by war propaganda from both the Allied and Central powers. In addition to outside persuasion, American interests were involved (through trade and loans) and both the Germans and the British had violated U.S. maritime rights. A critical case in point was the sinking of the *Lusitania* by a German submarine in May 1915, with the loss of over 1,000 civilian lives, including over 100 Americans. This event had poisoned the German reputation in the eyes of the American public.

Wilson's campaign benefited from the fact that he was the incumbent president and although the platform supported neutrality, it encouraged preparedness in case of war, as well as a post-war association of countries to promote world peace. There were also appeals for Pan American Unity, child labor protection, suffrage for women, and prison reform. Nevertheless, other events in 1916 undermined the administration. Pancho Villa's 1916 raid on Columbus, New Mexico; U.S. military interventions in Haiti and Santo Domingo; and the October 1916 German announcement of a return to search-and-destroy submarine warfare all rattled public confidence.

THE HUGHES CAMPAIGN

In contrast, the Hughes campaign promoted the "America First, America Efficient" agenda. The Dem-

ocrats were attacked over their tariff policies and for their diplomatic failures with Germany and Mexico. The Republicans argued that they could restore the economy and bring efficiency to the federal government by protecting American rights abroad, and promoting the Monroe Doctrine in the Americas. They also called for policy improvements in areas such as conservation, civil service reform, and national transportation. Corporate regulation would continue in ways that were both fair and competitive. Hughes also argued for greater military preparedness in contrast to what was seen as Wilson's more half-hearted efforts.

Initial impressions favored Hughes's election. Voters seemed weary of Wilson's lofty idealism and liberal values. They wanted more concrete results that could be seen, rather than to concepts such as "The New Freedom," which appeared in practice not to differ much from Republican policies.

During the election, Wilson was consumed by other difficulties, including a deteriorating state of affairs with Mexico that could lead to war. Relations with Great Britain were strained, and there was labor unrest and strikes in key industries. This situation gave the Republican Party confidence. Hughes entered the November election clearly assuming that victory would be his. His attacks on Wilson's peace initiatives and foreign policy, particularly toward Mexico, as well as the state of labor relations, were assumed to be crucial vote winners by many pundits.

RESULTS

Although election results were delayed, and for days there was a general uncertainty surrounding the final tally, Wilson confounded predictions when he won 30 states to Hughes's 18. Besides the Democratic south, Hughes lost ground in the west and in certain midwestern states that had sizable German-American populations.

What proved to be of crucial importance was Hughes's loss of California by a margin of less than 4,000 votes. If California had gone with Hughes, he would have become president. California was under the sway of the Progressive Republican governor (and later senator), Hiram Johnson. It has been argued that Hughes failed to make the most of Johnson's popularity and appeared to side with Republican forces in the state that were at odds with Johnson. Nevertheless, Johnson publicly endorsed Hughes for the presidency and argued for his election. This, though, was ultimately insufficient to carry the state.

The election of 1916 saw Wilson's popular vote plurality reduced from 1912, with a winning tally that was only 579,511 votes more than Hughes. He received a total of 9,126,868 votes to Hughes's 8,548,728. This represented 49.2 percent of the popular vote, with Hughes achieving 46.1 percent. This made Wilson the only American president elected without a popular majority in two elections. In addition to the Democratic and Republican candidates, in the 1916 election, Socialist candidate, Allan Louis Benson, received 590,524 votes, 3.2 percent of the popular vote, and Prohibitionist James Franklin Hanly gained 221,302 votes (1.2 percent of the total).

The importance of the California factor was best illustrated when the Electoral College votes were tallied. Here, the result revealed a clearly narrow victory, with Wilson receiving 277 votes to Hughes's 254. A shift in

During Woodrow Wilson's campaign, he was portrayed as a man of peace, but after the election war became inevitable.

California would have made Hughes president. Wilson's Vice President Thomas Riley Marshall's re-election made him the first vice president since John C. Calhoun to achieve two terms in office. Wilson's 1916 victory also carried with it success in the Senate, where the Democrats now held a 53–42 majority. Combined with a thin majority of 216 to 210 in the House, the Democratic Party seemed well-positioned to govern.

The significance of the election of 1916 was not a victory for peace or war. Wilson's second term would see the march toward war become an inevitable prospect for his presidency. Within months, his campaign slogan of keeping the United States out of war seemed hollow. His efforts to achieve a peace without victors and thus, end European bloodshed, became only futile gestures. Events rapidly overtook affairs and put the nature of American domestic Progressivism on the back burner.

In January 1917, Germany resumed unrestricted submarine warfare assuming that they would achieve victory before American forces could make any difference. The revelation of the Zimmerman telegram of February 1917, which proposed a German alliance with Mexico, angered Americans still further at German intervention in American affairs. The Russian Revolution, in March, revealed the instability that the war had brought to Europe. On April 2, 1917, America declared war on Germany and the other Central powers, which made preparedness the crucial issue of the 1916 election, not neutrality. But for Wilson, this was not to be an ordinary war, but an idealistic crusade "to make the world safe for democracy."

SEE ALSO: Presidential Election of 1912; War and Peace.

BIBLIOGRAPHY. J.M. Blum, Woodrow Wilson and the Politics of Morality (Little, Brown, 1956); J.M. Cooper, Jr., Pivotal Decades: The United States, 1900–1930 (Knopf, 1990); L.L. Gould, Reform and Regulation: American Politics, 1900–1916 (Wiley, 1978); August Heckscher, Woodrow Wilson (Scribners, 1991); Richard Hofstader, The Age of Reform: From Bryan to FDR (Knopf, 1955): S.D. Lovell, The Presidential Election of 1916 (Southern Illinois University Press, 1980); A.M. Schlesinger, Jr., ed., History of American Presidential Elections, 1789–1968 (McGraw-Hill,1971).

THEODORE W. EVERSOLE, PH.D.
INDEPENDENT SCHOLAR

Presidential Election of 1920

THE PERIOD FOLLOWING the stirrings and disappointments of World War I was a time for transition, and the presidential election of 1920 symbolized a significant redirection in American politics. The launch of this new tide in politics began with the congressional elections of 1918, which produced a surprise defeat for President Wilson and the Democrats. This was supposedly a time of progress and prosperity, yet the country's mood was against those in power.

Although the armistice of 1918 brought peace to Europe, Woodrow Wilson had also linked America's foreign-policy destiny to the highly ambitious idea of a League of Nations. The League reflected the height of Wilsonian idealism. In theory, such an international body would guarantee that war would no longer plague human society. Wilson took his campaign to ratify the Treaty of Versailles and the League to the nation in 1919, but he encountered a climate of disillusionment that lacked major enthusiasm for this particular project. His vigorous and draining attempt to convert the nation to the cause seemingly contributed to his physical collapse in September 1919, and his remaining months in office were those of a defeated and humiliated invalid.

Theodore Roosevelt had died in 1919, and with Wilson's isolation in the White House, the pre-war Progressive era had lost both support and direction. The nation clearly wanted something different, but it simply was not yet clear what that would be. For a short time, Prohibition, ratified by the 18th Amendment in 1919, seemed to capture the country's mood, and its enforcement mechanism, in the form of the Volstead Act, became law in January 1920.

America faced an uncertain future, where revolutionary upheaval and war could threaten national security. The Bolshevik revolution in Russia, as well as other Communist revolts in Europe, made the threat real. Domestic radical agitation further undercut confidence and brought potential subversion to American shores. In the face of these problems, America was armed only with the moral and religious certainty that a ban on alcohol could in some way make the nation stand victorious and virtuous against all threats foreign and domestic.

By 1920, political troubles were brewing as the economy turned downward in a post-war slump and indus-trial unrest by the unions brought home the fears of social disruption and decline. The Republican nominating convention met in Chicago on June 8, 1920, to decide on a candidate who could best meet the uncertain needs of a new decade. With only modest contenders such as General Leonard Wood, a former Army chief of staff, and Governor Frank O. Lowden of Illinois, the convention was stalemated until the 10th ballot, when a little-known Ohio senator and newspaper publisher, Warren G. Harding, received enough votes to secure the nomination. His political manager, Harry M. Daughtery, engineered his selection from a poor field of candidates and he was supposedly the result of compromises and promises made in "smoke filled rooms." The party selected former Governor of Massachusetts Calvin Coolidge as the vice presidential candidate. Coolidge's suppression of the 1919 Boston Police strike gave him a national reputation for leadership and toughness in the face of controversy.

The Democratic convention met in San Francisco between June 28 and July 6, 1920. Like the Republicans, there were no obvious frontrunners for the nomination. Although ill, President Wilson cast his shadow over the convention, which is said to have prevented his son-in-law and former treasury secretary, and later California senator, William G. McAdoo, from getting the nomination. Likewise, there were moves to nominate A. Mitchell Palmer, the former attorney general who had gained fame leading the Red Scare against radicals, and there was even consideration of the old standard bearer, William Jennings Bryan. Agreement, though, could not be reached and finally on the 44th ballot the convention nominated James M. Cox, also a newspaper publisher from Ohio. The vice presidential nomination went to Franklin Delano Roosevelt of New York, a former assistant secretary of the Navy whose name recognition made him a political asset.

THE CANDIDATES

Warren G. Harding (1865–1923) was a man who spoke in platitudes and supposedly "looked like a president." He was friendly and outgoing and generally obliging to one and all. He was known as an effective party keynote speaker and conciliator who followed the trends in public opinion. After minor offices in local Ohio politics, such as state senator and lieutenant governor, he was elected to the U.S. Senate in 1914, which he found to be a pleasant and not terribly demanding place. Although he married Florence Kling in 1891, Harding's appeal extended to other women as well, and he was known to have an active social life while in the White House. In politics, he was less than fervent, and was generally devoid of strong opinions or policies. William McAdoo said that Harding's speeches represented "an army of pompous phrases moving across the landscape in search of an idea." In office, his outgoing, trusting nature would later prove a weakness as his administration was undone by scandal, including personal scandal involving his much younger lover, Nan Britton, who gave birth to an illegitimate daughter. There were also rumors spread by his opponents that cast doubts about his racial identity.

James M. Cox (1870–1957) shared with Harding a newspaper background and familiarity with Ohio State politics, serving as both a congressman and as a two-term governor. He was a mainstream Democrat on the Progressive side of the party, and shared with Wilson internationalist views that supported membership in the League of Nations. Harding was a jovial backslapper, whereas Cox was by all intents serious and capable. He supported minimum wage and workers compensation programs and would build a successful newspaper-communications business after active politics.

THE CAMPAIGN

Democrats, following the urging of President Wilson, hoped that the election would become a referendum on the League of Nations that had been blocked in the Senate by Republicans. There was particular concern over Article Ten of the League Treaty that could require American participation in any war pursued by the League. This undercut congressional war making powers and unleashed considerable national concern about foreign entanglements.

By taking the nation to war in 1917, Wilson had also alienated many natural Democratic supporters in the Irish-American and German-American communities whose influence could be felt in the growing urban areas of America. In addition, Prohibition hit at the urban populations in a way that alienated many voters particularly from immigrant communities. Cox supported the League in principle, but in the campaign obscured his position with a series of reservations in order to win votes from the disenchanted. Harding argued for a "Return to Normalcy," which was part of his unclear message of "healing not nostrums."

Whereas Cox barnstormed the country with speeches and rallies, Harding ran, like William McKinley in 1896, a "Front Porch" campaign from Marion, Ohio, drawing delegates to him and shaping his views to the interests of the assembled audiences. The Republicans spent money on advertising that far outpaced Cox's campaign expenditures, and they better exploited the new media presence in print, newsreels, and emerging radio. Harding also projected a nationalist spirit with his America First approach. In addition, the handsome Harding photographed well and his image presented better than Cox's. The 1920 election was also the first presidential election in which the newly-franchised women could vote, and perhaps appearance and popular endorsements from entertainment paid Harding dividends with the electorate.

THE RESULTS

When the November 1920 election results came in (1920 was the first election that had radio reports of the returns), the Democrats had suffered a devastating defeat. The Republicans had played on the Democrats as a party unprepared for war or peace and that had left the country in debt. With the exception of Tennessee, the south remained solidly Democratic. Yet, Harding had a landslide victory in the rest of the nation from east to west, winning 16,144,093 votes or 60.3 percent of the total vote with Cox gaining 9,139,661 votes or 34.1 percent. Eugene Debs of Indiana and his Socialist party came in third with nearly a million votes or 3.4 percent of the total. In the Electoral College, the Republicans and Harding had a convincing 404 votes to the Democrat's and Cox's 127.

The rejection of the Democrats and Wilsonism in 1920 extended to Congress, where Harding's coattails brought in major Republican majorities of 302 in the House versus 131 Democrats, and 59 Republican seats in the Senate against 37 Democrats. The 1920 presidential election marked the beginning of a Republican-dominated decade. Harding's death in 1923 during his first term allowed him to escape the scandals, such as Teapot Dome, that would mark his administration and give him a reputation as one of America's worst presidents.

Calvin Coolidge's succession brought a conservative minimalist to the office, but also created a new atmosphere of propriety. The 1920 election did give the Democratic vice presidential nominee, Franklin Delano Roosevelt, national recognition that helped advance his political career, first with election as New

York governor in 1928 and later the presidency in 1932. His popularity was confirmed with re-election to three more terms, serving until his death in April 1945. The presidential election of 1920 introduced the new forces of modernity into American politics. The rise of advertising and the mass media were making appearance and presentation as important as policy. In a rapidly urbanizing nation, party machines could build mass support through exploiting these new methods, based on direct persuasion and appeals to self-interest. Ultimately, such tactics produced voting dividends.

SEE ALSO: Isolationism; Media, Role in Campaigns; Prohibitionist Party.

BIBLIOGRAPHY: W.M. Bagby, *The Road to Normalcy: The Presidential Campaign and Election of 1920* (Johns Hopkins University Press, 1962); J.F. Cebula, *James M. Cox: Journalist and Politician* (Garland Publishing, 1985); R.C. Downes, *The Rise of Warren Harding, 1865–1920* (Ohio State University Press, 1986); Elaine Landau, *Warren G. Harding* (Lerner Publications, 2005); J.A. Morello, *Selling the President 1920: Albert D. Lasker, Advertising and the Election of Warren G. Harding* (Preager Publishing, 2001); C.E. Morris, *The Progressive Democracy of James M. Cox* (Hard Press, 2006); David Pietrusza, *1920: The Year of Six Presidents* (Carroll and Grad, 2006); A.M. Schlesinger, Jr., and F.L. Israel, eds., *The History of American Presidential Elections* (McGraw-Hill, 1971).

THEODORE W. EVERSOLE, PH.D.
INDEPENDENT SCHOLAR

Presidential Election of 1924

THE REPUBLICAN INCUMBENT Calvin Coolidge, the successor to deceased President Warren Harding, won the presidential election of 1924 with 382 electoral votes to his Democratic opponent John W. Davis's 136 electoral votes and Progressive Party candidate Robert LaFollette's 13 electoral votes. Coolidge dominated not only the Electoral College, but also the popular vote, receiving nearly double the popular vote of the Democratic candidate and more votes than all other candidates combined (Coolidge collected almost 16 million votes with Davis and LaFollette receiving over eight million and almost five million, respectively).

REPUBLICAN SELECTION PROCESS

Prior to his election as vice president, Coolidge won national fame as governor of Massachusetts when he quashed the Boston Police strike in 1919. As vice president, Coolidge earned the nickname Silent Cal because of his quiet, reserved nature. Many political analysts believed that the Republicans were vulnerable in the 1924 election due to the late-breaking and far-reaching scandals of the Harding administration. Coolidge did not assuage those fears because he refused to demand the resignations of any of the cabinet members, instead proclaiming he would follow through on the plans of Harding, the man Americans elected. He supported immigration restriction and lowering the income tax.

While a few Republicans wished to be selected as the new Republican standard-bearer, party loyalists decided to remain with the steadfast Coolidge, who had been president since August 1923. Silent Cal won the Republican nomination in Cleveland on the first ballot with all but 44 of the 1,109 votes cast. Frank O. Lowden, governor of Illinois and a front-runner for the presidential nomination in 1920, became the first man in the 20th century to turn down the vice presidential nomination. On the next ballot, Idaho Senator William Borah became the second. On the third ballot, the delegates decided on Illinois banker Charles G. Dawes, the first director of the Bureau of the Budget and the principal architect of the World War I reparations payment plan. Pundits gave Dawes the nickname Hell and Maria based on his outburst during Senate hearings related to his spending as Brigadier General of the Seventeenth Engineers during World War I.

DEMOCRATIC NATIONAL CONVENTION

The Democratic Party's convention in New York City proved the most tumultuous in American history. Californian William G. McAdoo, former secretary of the treasury and the son-in-law of President Woodrow Wilson, was the party favorite for years. In fact, his father-in-law's desire for a third term was likely the greatest obstacle to him securing the party's nomination in 1920. In 1924, McAdoo was the clear favorite, with solid support especially from southern, rural, dry, and Protestant delegates. McAdoo, however, faced equally formidable opponents in the 1924 convention. His relation to Wilson alienated him from many ethnic Americans, especially Irish and Germans who opposed American alignment during World War I. He earned the enmity and opposition of state party bosses by entering into primary campaigns instead of deferring to them. Finally, refusal to distance himself from anti-Catholicism won him the nickname the Klandidate from his ideological opponents in the party.

There were several other hopefuls at the convention, none more important than New York Governor Alfred E. Smith, a product of the Tammany Hall political machine. Dubbed the Happy Warrior by Franklin Roosevelt, this second-generation American found favor with northern party bosses, wets, immigrants, and Catholics. He never secured more than two-fifths of the delegate ballots, but enough to serve as a veto of McAdoo. The unprecedented 103 ballots it took for the Democrats' decision demonstrated the cleavage between the two diametrically opposed and largest factions of the Democratic Party: the southern, rural, dry Protestants versus the northern, urban, wet Catholics. Moreover, the split convention all but assured the nation that Coolidge would ultimately triumph.

The sister contest in the convention dealt not with candidates, but with the official party platform. The party was split on whether to condemn the Ku Klux Klan by name. The Republican convention successfully dodged the issue in committee; it never made it to the floor for debate or embarrassment. For Democrats, the contest proved as contentious as the candidate selection process, and more divisive. Smith controlled the Catholic anti-Klan delegates. Alabama Senator Oscar Underwood, a vocal opponent of the Klan, held the anti-Klan Protestant delegates. This left frontrunner McAdoo with little choice but to remain silent on the Klan issue lest he alienate his southern base and pro-Klan delegates. Several speakers gave passionate speeches supporting their position.

The anti-Klan faction won vocal support from the galleries and seemed it might carry the day until the Prairie Avenger, William Jennings Bryan, gave the final speech urging the plank with the removal of the words "Ku Klux Klan." The two-hour debate that ensued included fist fights, wrestling, and near pandemonium. Only the presence of thousands of police, called in at the culmination of Bryan's speech, prevented a full-scale riot. In the final tally, the anti-Klan plank failed by one vote out of 1,083 votes cast.

The contest in the Democratic convention compelled delegates to select a non-controversial, relatively obscure compromise candidate, John W. Davis. Davis was a highly-respected lawyer, one-term congressman

from West Virginia, and ambassador to the United Kingdom. Davis opposed women's suffrage, African-American political participation, and supported poll taxes. These positions alienated him from considerable constituencies, making his election possibilities all the more remote. His ultra-conservative views no doubt cost him votes and prompted the formation of the Progressive Party as an alternative to the two conservative candidates nominated by the two major parties.

Charles Bryan, younger brother of former Secretary of State and renowned politician William Jennings Bryan, was a compromise selection as the vice presidential candidate. The elder Bryan was too controversial for the general public and unelectable at the convention due to his outspoken position on the Ku Klux Klan plank. The younger Bryan's political career was nearly as uncelebrated as Davis's. He served as Mayor of Lincoln, Nebraska for two years and was elected governor of that state the year prior to the 1924 campaign.

THE PROGRESSIVE PARTY

Successes in defeating conservative Republicans in the midterm elections of 1922 helped to revive the pre-World War I Progressive movement. This groundswell of support prompted Wisconsin's Robert LaFollette to revive the presidential hopes that he carried for at least a dozen years. LaFollette was the acknowledged leader of the liberal wing of the Republican Party. "Fighting Bob" supported far-reaching government reform, labor unions, and non-intervention in World War I.

To solidify the claim that American politics needed bipartisan reform, the Progressive Party selected liberal Democrat Burton K. Wheeler as LaFollette's running mate. Wheeler, a Senator from Montana, was known for supporting labor unions and, while U.S. attorney, refusing to indict anyone under the Sedition Act of 1918. Considered the only liberal ticket in the race, the Progressives won the support of most left-leaning organizations including the American Federation of Labor and the Socialist Party (which had garnered almost one million votes in the last presidential campaign).

THE GENERAL ELECTION

Like Harding four years before, Coolidge did not leave his home to campaign in the general election. Dawes did the campaigning and he spoke out against the Klan, permitting Silent Cal to be true to his moniker and not alienate northern state pro-Republican Klan supporters.

The Republicans adopted the popular campaign slogan "Keep Cool with Coolidge." Republicans ignored Davis and the Democrats in the campaign, instead focusing on the radicalism of LaFollette and his supporters. The strategy was designed to make the American public see the election in terms of choosing between the dependable Coolidge and a radical and dangerous alternative. LaFollette further marginalized the Davis campaign by answering the Republican attacks. Coolidge's young son, Calvin, Jr., died during the campaign, which compelled the grieving Coolidge to conduct a more subdued campaign. The death also garnered the president a great deal of sympathy from the already friendly electorate.

Davis found little Democratic enthusiasm. He received almost no assistance from McAdoo supporters. He fared much better with Smith supporters, but not until late in the campaign. Still, Democrats could expect certain successes. For example, Davis won more than 90 percent of the vote in most South Carolina and Mississippi counties. Democrats won the same states in 1924 that they won in 1920, with the exception of losing Kentucky, but adding Tennessee and Oklahoma. Despite guaranteed Democratic victories in the old south, the Democrats fell apart almost everywhere else. For example, 1924 was the last time a Republican presidential candidate won New York City. In 1928, Smith received almost twice as many popular votes as Davis in 1924.

LaFollette won more than 16 percent of the popular vote, the most for a third-party candidate since Theodore Roosevelt in 1912, and a higher percentage than any other until Ross Perot in 1992. The split in the Democratic convention and the LaFollette candidacy helped Coolidge overcome the scandals of his predecessor and win the presidency in his own right, outdistancing all other candidates combined. Coolidge served four more years as president and did not officially seek re-election in 1928.

SEE ALSO: Bryan, William Jennings; Ku Klux Klan; LaFollette, Robert; Progressive Party; Tammany Hall.

BIBLIOGRAPHY. R.K. Murray, *The 103rd Ballot: Democrats and Disaster in Madison Square Garden* (Harper & Row, 1976); Robert Sobel, *Coolidge: An American Enigma* (Regnery Publishers, 1998); N.C. Unger, *Fighting Bob LaFollette: The Righteous Reformer* (University of North Carolina Press, 2000).

MICHAEL D. JACOBS
UNIVERSITY OF WISCONSIN–BARABOO

Presidential Election of 1928

THE PRESIDENTIAL ELECTION of 1928 took place at the height of 1920s Republican hegemony, and who better to continue the Republican ascendancy than President Coolidge's successful secretary of commerce, Herbert Hoover. In opposition to this continued Republican dominance was the Democratic hopeful, Alfred E. Smith, a popular figure in New York politics.

America was in the midst of a boom with the stock market making ever-higher advances. Worker productivity was also staggeringly efficient. The result of this economic success was that the American standard of living had become the envy of the world. Many thought that the American system had permanently triumphed over poverty and unemployment, making consumer goods and wealth available to the masses in ways that were inconceivable only a few years before. This backdrop of triumph gave the Republicans huge advantages among the population at large, although Democratic appeal could still be guaranteed in the deep south.

The Republican nomination process was open in 1928, because President Calvin Coolidge chose not to seek another term. When the convention met in Kansas City between June 12 and June 15, there were no clear favorites, although old party stalwarts such as Governor Frank O. Lowden of Illinois and Senate Majority Leader Charles Curtis were possibilities. There was also talk of promoting Vice President Charles Dawes to the presidency, but President Coolidge, who disliked Dawes intensely, stifled this. Although not particularly popular within the party or with Coolidge, Secretary of Commerce Herbert Hoover was well known and seemed an able candidate and modernizer who could bridge party divides. Suggestions to have Dawes serve a second term as vice president were also squashed by Coolidge's disdain. Instead, Senator Curtis was nominated to be the running mate. Hoover was overwhelmingly endorsed on the first ballot and the Republican ticket was set.

The Democratic convention occurred between June 26 and June 28 in Houston, Texas. In the midst of Republican-led prosperity, many leading Democrats saw the nomination as a poisoned chalice that would lead to sure defeat. However, Governor Alfred E. Smith of New York was willing to accept the steep challenge and he was nominated on the first ballot with Senator Joseph T. Robinson of Arkansas as his vice presidential running mate. Smith became the first Roman Catholic to be nominated for the presidency, with John F. Kennedy becoming only the second in 1960. Smith had wanted the nomination in 1924, but had failed to get the party's support, and now he saw his chance to bring change to the White House.

In other political parties, the Prohibitionists were divided as to whether they should simply endorse Hoover and the Republicans, but they ultimately fielded William F. Varney and James A. Edgerton as presidential and vice presidential candidates. The Socialist Party nominated Norman Thomas for president (their old standard bearer Eugene Debs had died in 1926) and James H. Maurer as vice presidential candidate. The Communist Party also participated in 1928 with William Z. Foster and Benjamin Gitlow as presidential and vice presidential selections, respectively.

Herbert Hoover was born in 1874 in West Branch, Iowa, of Quaker parents, but following their death, he was raised in Oregon by an uncle. Hoover was to become the first American president born west of the Mississippi. Following various office jobs and a night- school education, Hoover entered Stanford University, and while there met his future wife, Lou Henry, a fellow geology student. He graduated with a degree in geology in 1895 and built himself a successful international career as a mining engineer and consultant. Upon the outbreak of World War I, he became head of the Committee for Relief in Belgium, which brought food relief to the occupied Belgians. Following America's entry into the war, he was appointed by President Wilson to head the nation's Food Administration. After the war, he supervised the American Relief Administration and gained a reputation as a capable and devoted humanitarian.

Although some Democrats saw Hoover as a possible presidential candidate in 1920, he chose to join the Republican administration as secretary of commerce under both Harding and Coolidge. There, he promoted government and business cooperation, and viewed standardization as the key to postwar prosperity and efficiency. He also coordinated relief following the serious 1927 Mississippi floods, which further boosted his positive credentials in the public's eye. Hoover was one of the best known and most respected cabinet officers of the decade, and he maintained a very favorable press image, which helped him enormously during the 1928 campaign.

Alfred E. Smith was born on Manhattan's lower east side to a humble Roman Catholic family. Follow-

The 1928 campaigns were the first to broadly use newsreels, radio addresses, and other new forms of advertising.

ing the death of his father, he left school in order to support his family, eventually working at the Fulton Fish Market. Through hard work and the building of political contacts in New York's Tammany Hall, Smith made a slow advance up the political ladder, gaining election to the New York Assembly in 1903. He became associated with the progressive wing of the party and saw himself as the voice of the Irish Americans, as well as other immigrant groups who were so prominent in New York City. Smith was elected governor in 1918, and after defeat in 1920, was re-elected in 1922, 1924, and 1926. From his New York base he emerged as a significant Democrat leader with national potential, and although overlooked in 1924, he gained the nomination in 1928, as a progressive voice in a divided party split over Prohibition and race.

The 1928 election, even in the face of a crest of Republican strength and confidence, was nevertheless an active campaign with national cross-country speaking engagements. Newspaper advertising, newsreels, and radio addresses became major election features for the first time. The radio took the voices of the candidates into American homes and gave a personal touch to the campaign. Smith was a capable orator, but Hoover's radio style proved more appealing to mainstream America. The Republican platform maintained their support for Prohibition and the Protective Tariff and exploited the nation's well-being to their own ends with slogans such as "Vote for Prosperity" and "Who But Hoover?" One Hoover campaign advertisement that became well known carried the promise: "A chicken in every pot and a car in every garage." Smith and the Democrats did attempt to challenge the Republicans by criticizing Republican farm policies, use of injunctions in labor disputes, and past corruption, as well as the domination of the Philippines. However, it was not by their respective platforms that the 1928 election was decided. The Republicans exploited Smith's Catholicism, his wet position on Prohibition, and Tammany Hall background to discredit him. The slogan "Rum, Romanism and Ruin" suggested the consequences of a Democratic and Smith victory. The still-influential Ku Klux Klan also lambasted Smith's Catholicism and his base of support in the ethnic immigrant community. This further undercut him in the eyes of some voters, making this campaign one marred by base and open prejudice.

The election was held on November 6, 1928, and proved to be a Hoover landslide. Hoover and Curtis received 58.2 percent of the popular vote or 21,427,123 votes as opposed to Smith and Robinson's 15,015,464 or 40.8 percent of the popular vote. Norman Thomas and James H. Maurer's Socialists gained 267,478 votes, which was only 0.7 percent of the votes cast. The Electoral College return was even more devastating for Smith and the Democrats. The Republicans swept the states at large, even making inroads into normally Democratic border and southern states. The Republicans received a decisive 444 electoral votes as opposed to Smith and Robinson's 87 votes. Outside of the deep south, Smith won only in heavily Catholic Massachusetts and Rhode Island. The Republicans also dominated in Congress, picking up several Senate seats to give them a commanding 56-seat advantage. They posted an impressive gain of 32 seats in the House, which consolidated their majority at 270 Republicans to 164 Democrats.

However, Republican victory celebrations would prove to be short-lived. The Wall Street crash of September to October 1929 brought on the Great Depression and sealed Hoover's fate and reputation as president. Although hailed for his skills as an efficient administrator who believed prosperity came only through pro-business policies, the crisis he confronted surpassed even his best abilities. Hoover believed that technology and the Federal Reserve System could moderate the crisis, which it failed to do. In addition, he opposed extensive federal job creation schemes and public assistance programs for the unemployed. Republican thinking was that these issues were better addressed at the state and local level. However, the depth of the Depression left local governments, as well as charities, with a burden they could not manage. Hoover also refused to support repeal of Prohibition, which grew increasingly unpopular as the nation suffered.

Alfred E. Smith's smashing defeat did not destroy the Democratic Party; his campaign helped in the party's realignment, which would produce benefits for Franklin D. Roosevelt in 1932. Smith won majorities in the nation's 12 largest cities, which indicated that the rising urban areas could become instrumental in building a broad-based coalition of interests. Although after 1934 Smith would break with Roosevelt and many of his policies, he did, nevertheless, help reshape the party. In addition, Smith was the embodiment of the American Dream: his career saw him rise above social obstacles and become an individual of power and influence.

SEE ALSO: Catholic Vote; Ku Klux Klan.

BIBLIOGRAPHY. Kristi Anderson, *After Suffrage: Women in Partisan and Elective Politics Before the New Deal* (University of Chicago Press, 1996); G.C. Byrne and Paul Marx, *The Great American Convention: A Political History of Presidential Elections* (Pacific Books, 1976); J.A. Crittenden, *Parties and Elections in the United States* (Prentice-Hall, 1982); C.M. Finan, *Alfred E. Smith: The Happy Warrior* (Hill and Wang, 2002); Herbert Hoover, *The Memoirs of Herbert Hoover: 1920–1933* (Macmillan Press, 1952); A.J. Lichtman, *Prejudice and Old Politics* (Lexington Books, 2000); E.E. Robinson and V.D. Bornet, *Herbert Hoover: President of the United States* (Hoover Institution, 1975); R.A. Slayton, *Empire Statesman: The Rise and Redemption of Al Smith* (Free Press, 2001).

THEODORE W. EVERSOLE, PH.D.
INDEPENDENT SCHOLAR

Presidential Election of 1932

THE 1932 PRESIDENTIAL election is considered one of the more significant elections in American history. It not only signaled a shift from more than a decade of consecutive Republican administrations, it was the first victory for the man who would eventually be the first (and only) American president to be elected to office four times. The collapse of the U.S. economy in 1929, combined with the onslaught of a drought of monumental proportions, led the nation into an unparalleled national depression. The Great Depression caused many Americans to question the leadership abilities of incumbent Herbert Hoover.

The economic depression, which exploded with the 1929 stock market crash, worsened in late 1931 with the collapse of the international economy and the worsening of a severe drought in middle America. Along with the nation's troubles, the crisis of the president, Herbert Hoover, grew more severe. Although easily elected in 1928, Hoover's administration was plagued with problems. He was severely criticized for not doing enough to rectify economic problems, specifically the rapidly-rising unemployment rate. Hoover was an economic conservative who strongly believed in the gold standard doctrine and in adhering to a balanced budget. Many Americans believed Hoover was not taking actions to combat the Depression. In reality, he did make several attempts, beginning with a tax increase, which he believed would cause a "trickle-down" effect that would aid the masses. The Revenue Act of 1932 and the Glass-Steagall Act were further efforts at repairing the tattered economy; they were, however, too little too late.

Hoover believed in people's ability to work and provide for themselves; any charity that might be necessary should come from the private sector, and not the government, according to the president. But as Americans suffered their third winter of the Depression and unemployment reached new highs, this philosophy drew even more fire from critics. The media portrayed Hoover as a rigid man with no emotions, whose inflexible commitment to traditional economic doctrines caused Americans to be cold and hungry. The cardboard box villages that housed the homeless became Hoovervilles, the newspapers used for warmth by vagrants were Hoover blankets, and the state of America was called the Hoover Depression. Despite criticism, Hoover remained dedicated to public service and accepted the nomination of the Republican Party in 1932.

THE NOMINEES

The Democratic nominee, Franklin D. Roosevelt, espoused a very different philosophy of governance than Hoover. Roosevelt voiced his belief that the government should provide relief—this was not an act of charity, but the duty of a democratic society. As governor of New York, Roosevelt endorsed both government-funded old-age pensions and unemployment insurance. He (like Hoover) was concerned about creating a permanent welfare class, but realized that government assistance could be extraordinarily effective, especially if properly organized. Roosevelt began to implement innovative policies in New York, and the rest of the nation started to take notice.

The first hurdle for Roosevelt was to secure the nomination of his party at the 1932 Democratic convention in Chicago. Despite his increasing popularity, Roosevelt's victory was far from assured. He had his critics, amongst them some of the nation's largest newspaper chains, whose editors claimed that Roosevelt would not have the courage to take the necessary actions to combat the Depression. Those involved in big business were also openly against the nomination of Roosevelt. However, the party was facing a dearth of candidates who were well-known on the national level. Roosevelt managed to secure the nomination with his pledge to turn the Democratic Party into a great instrument of social change. Roosevelt broke with tradition by journeying to Chicago to accept before he was even officially notified of his victory. It was during his acceptance speech that he first promised a "new deal" for the American people.

Once the presidential campaign of 1932 began in earnest, it became clear to the electorate and the press that the differences between Hoover and Roosevelt were much greater than their ideas on the economy and government relief. The two men had very different campaign styles. Roosevelt was a career politician who had spent the majority of his lifetime studying how to win votes. He put endless energy into charming voters. Hoover, by contrast, was much more dour and taciturn, particularly when compared to the effusive Democrat. Roosevelt was cognizant that in order to win the election he needed to have a vast number of volunteers and a lot of money—his patrician background and popularity as governor were both important assets in securing these. His wealthy friends donated money and his charisma attracted volunteers by the droves.

THE PLATFORMS

The campaign platform of the Republican Party was unoriginal. After securing the nomination, Hoover advocated an adherence to the status quo—the party had spent so much time espousing traditional Republican actions and policies that to repudiate these ideals was viewed as social suicide. Also, perhaps the fact that the Democrats had not managed to win a presidential contest since 1916 gave the party a false confidence that the electorate would not turn away from the party in the midst of such a crises. The campaign also emphasized the fact that Hoover was a wise leader, one who could be trusted, and who was obviously doing as much as he could to help lead the country during this troubled time. The Republicans criticized the Democrats for endorsing reckless spending.

As for the Democratic platform, it specifically blamed the Republican presidents of the 1920s for the depression, claiming the economy had been disastrously managed since the end of World War I. The platform focused on economic reforms, including the regulation of stocks and banking reforms, and also attacked the Federal Farm Board, pledging agricultural reform as well. Foreign policy was not a focal point in the 1932 election, and was largely ignored by both Hoover and Roosevelt.

Hoover's original intention was to stay in the White House and work during the election period. However, Roosevelt's vigorous stumping (an attempt to show his health would not be a hindrance) and popular advertisements drew Hoover onto the campaign trail. By November, the nation was wholly ready to demonstrate its desire for change. In a sweeping victory, Roosevelt and his running mate, John Nance Garner, defeated Hoover and Charles Curtis by a staggering electoral margin of 472 to 59—a popular vote of 57.4 percent to 39.7 percent.

The presidential election of 1932 is significant for several reasons. It ended over a decade of Republican domination, and led to almost 20 years of Democrats in office. It also demonstrated that Americans were more interested in results than traditional economic and political maneuvers. Additionally, the 1932 election ushered in an era of social change and government relief that had not been seen before in the United States. Franklin Roosevelt's victory also demonstrated that Americans were willing to cross voting lines when voting—he was the victor in many traditionally Republican states such as Kansas and Nebraska. This sweeping victory demonstrated that Americans were ready to embrace a new type of politician as well. Roosevelt is considered by many scholars to be the first modern president, based largely on his enthusiastic interactions with the public and the press.

SEE ALSO: Campaigns, Presidential; Domestic Policy; Democratic Party; Economy; Farm Issues in Campaigns; Government Spending; Great Depression and Realignment; Incumbent.

BIBLIOGRAPHY. M.L. Fausold, *The Presidency of Herbert C. Hoover* (University Press of Kansas, 1985); H.F. Gosnell, *Champion Campaigner: Franklin D. Roosevelt* (Macmillan Co., 1952); D.M. Kennedy, *Freedom From Fear: The American People in Depression and War, 1929–1945* (Oxford University Press, 1999); Steve Neal, *Happy Days are Here Again: The 1932 Democratic Convention, the Emergence of FDR—and How America Was Changed Forever* (William Morrow, 2004); Richard Oulahan, *The Man Who…The Story of the 1932 Democratic National Convention* (Dial Press, 1971); R.N. Smith, *An Uncommon Man: The Triumph of Herbert Hoover* (Simon and Shcuster, 1984).

NICOLE L. ANSLOVER, PH.D.
WALDORF COLLEGE

Presidential Election of 1936

SEVEN YEARS AFTER the onset of the Great Depression, the presidential election of 1936 proved an important turning-point in American electoral politics. President Franklin Delano Roosevelt's New Deal had generated unprecedented growth in the American welfare state. With agencies like the Public Works Administration (PWA), the Works Progress Administration (WPA), and the Social Security Administration (SSA), the New Deal provided unprecedented relief and employment to millions of struggling Americans. During his first term in office, Roosevelt also created the National Labor board, which supported labor unions' rights in collective bargaining. As these policies illustrate, Roosevelt's theory of the role of government could be characterized as one that emphasizes an activist government. Roosevelt's support for big government appealed to some Americans, while repelling others. The election of 1936 determined the future of the American welfare state, serving as an indicator of Americans' preferences for the role of government.

THE PRIMARY ELECTIONS
Incumbent president Franklin Roosevelt and his vice president, John Nance Garner of Texas, once again became the Democratic Party's nominees. Roosevelt

had little noteworthy opposition in the primary election. His most significant challenger was New York's Henry Breckenridge. Breckenridge, a lawyer, was a staunch opponent of the New Deal. He challenged Roosevelt in four primaries, losing each by a substantial margin. At the national Democratic convention in Philadelphia, Pennsylvania, the delegates unanimously re-nominated the president and vice president. Interestingly, Roosevelt's acceptance of the Democratic nomination that year represents the first occasion in American political history that a president personally accepted his party's nomination.

The Republican primary proved more competitive than the Democratic primary. Kansas Governor Alfred "Alf" Landon and Iowa U.S. Senator William E. Borah were the primary contenders for the nomination. In addition to these two candidates, other potential nominees included Illinois newspaperman William Franklin Knox and future Supreme Court Chief Justice Earl Warren, who was then a county district attorney in California. Ultimately, Landon would secure the presidential nomination, and Knox would run as the Republican nominee for vice president.

Third-party candidates in the election of 1936 included the Union Party's William Lemke, Norman Thomas on the Socialist Party ticket, and Earl Browder on the Communist Party ticket. Senator Huey Long, a Democrat from Louisiana, was expected to run for president as a third-party nominee with a "Share Our Wealth" platform; however, Long was assassinated in the fall of 1935.

THE GENERAL ELECTION

The 1936 election represented unprecedented partisan division. As William Leuchtenburg notes,

> the Democratic party, the historic defender of states' rights, had become an instrument of the Welfare State, while the Republican Party, the traditional advocate of a strong national union, now championed a weak central government.

The bulk of the issues dividing the parties pertained to their differing conceptualizations of the appropriate role of the federal government. Roosevelt and the Democratic Party represented firm support for an activist government. From this perspective, big government was the solution to America's problems. Roosevelt effectively painted himself as the opponent of big business and the wealthy, appealing particularly to the urban working-class and to ethnic minorities. His condemnation of a greedy, hostile class of business elites, who he framed as aggressive opponents to the New Deal, comprised a central campaign theme during this election year. On the other side of this debate, Landon and the Republican Party demanded that federal government temper its involvement in American life. Critics of Roosevelt's activist approach to governing advocated a hands-off, free market approach. As such, in 1936, large companies were interested in small government and in an unfettered free market, and directed tremendous financial resources toward the Republican candidates.

During the 1936 election, Roosevelt focused a great deal of attention on cultivating the support of African-American voters. Although efforts to appeal to African-American voters came with the risk of jeopardizing his support in the south, Roosevelt benefited a great deal from their support. Since the Civil War, African Americans had remained faithful to the party of Lincoln: they held fast to the Republican party, while distrusting the Democratic Party's dominance in the segregated south. In the presidential election of 1932, the majority of African-American voters rejected Roosevelt in favor of the Republican nominee, then-incumbent President Herbert Hoover. During Roosevelt's first term in office, however, African Americans became the beneficiaries of some New Deal programs and judged the president favorably for these advancements.

In addition to promoting different positions on central campaign issues, Roosevelt and Landon possessed opposite campaign styles. Roosevelt used his charisma and skill as an orator to create a strong, familiar presence in the lives of American voters. In March 1933, during his first term in office, he delivered his first "Fireside Chat" radio address to the nation. These addresses contributed a great deal to Roosevelt's popularity and strengthened his personal appeal as a candidate. Landon was a foil to the charismatic and articulate Roosevelt. Republican Party leaders accepted the fact that he was a less-than-captivating orator and tried to use this contrast with the president to their advantage. Unfortunately, Landon's ineptitude as a public speaker limited his ability to connect with voters. Unlike Roosevelt, who could use communication skills and engaging personality to attract broad support, Landon was remembered for uttering statements like, "Wherever I have gone in this country, I have found Americans."

In the months leading up to the general election, Americans were uncertain about the outcome. A *Literary Digest* election survey, which included approximately two million responses, predicted that Landon would win the election with 370 electoral votes. Because of *Literary Digest*'s strong record of election forecasting, this prognostication gained a great deal of attention. However, because the majority of the magazine's subscribers were Republican identifiers, the survey sample included a disproportionate number of Republicans and underestimated Roosevelt's performance.

Contrary to the magazine's prediction, the president won a landslide victory with 60.8 percent of the popular vote and 523 electoral votes, while Landon won only eight electoral votes, and 36.5 percent of the popular vote. The day before the election, Democratic Chairman Jim Farley famously predicted that Roosevelt would win a landslide victory, carrying every state with the exception of Maine and Vermont. Roosevelt won 46 of the 48 states, all but Maine and Vermont. Roosevelt's triumphant win included 76 percent of lower income voters, 81 percent of unskilled laborers, and 84 percent of relief recipients. The third party candidates failed to win any electoral votes. Lemke, Thomas, and Brower won two percent, 0.4 percent, and 0.2 percent of the popular vote, respectively.

The election of 1936 represented an important shift in American party politics. In his analysis of this election, historian William Leuchtenburg argues that it exemplifies a capstone of what V.O. Key termed a "critical period." Urban and working-class voters became an important sector of Democratic Party supporters, while farmers provided an important source of Republican Party support. New voters comprised a significant component of the Democratic Party's support during this election. Franklin Delano Roosevelt's landslide victory in this election also solidified the New Deal coalition. The solid support of Catholic, Jewish, African-American, and working-class voters, had a large impact on his re-election. Furthermore, rank-and-file voters, as opposed to political elites, became the central force in American electoral politics.

SEE ALSO: Great Depression and Realignment; Landslides, Election; Presidential Election of 1932.

BIBLIOGRAPHY. Courtney Brown, "Mass Dynamics of U.S. Presidential Competitions, 1928–1936," *American Political Science Review* (v.82/4, 1988); J.P. Fadely, *The Making of a* *Landslide: The Presidential Election of 1936* (Indiana University Press, 1990); V.O. Key and M.C. Cummings, *The Responsible Electorate: Rationality in Presidential Voting, 1936–1960* (Belknap Press, 1966); W.E. Leuchtenburg, *The FDR Years: On Roosevelt and His Legacy* (Columbia University Press, 1971); Louise Overacker, "Campaign Funds in the Presidential Election of 1936," *American Political Science Review* (v.31/3, 1937); A.M. Schlesinger and F.L. Israel, *History of American Presidential Elections 1789–1968* (Chelsea House, 1971); Carter Smith, *Presidents: Every Question Answered* (Hylas Publishing, 2005); M.J. Webber and G.W. Domhoff, "Myth and Reality in Business Support for Democrats and Republicans in the 1936 Presidential Election," *American Political Science Review* (v.90/4, 1996).

DEONDRA ROSE
CORNELL UNIVERSITY

Presidential Election of 1940

THE PRESIDENTIAL ELECTION of 1940 took place as Europe was in the midst of World War II. The Democrats nominated Franklin Delano Roosevelt for a third term, breaking the two-term tradition established by George Washington in 1796. The Republicans nominated a dark-horse candidate, Wendell Willkie, a businessman and lawyer and a Roosevelt delegate at the 1932 convention, who left the Democratic Party in 1939, and became an ardent critic of the New Deal. Roosevelt, who promised there would be no foreign wars, was re-elected.

THE DEMOCRATS

An early frontrunner for the Democratic nomination was Robert H. Jackson, Roosevelt's attorney general. However, Jackson's candidacy suffered a fatal blow when, in January 1938, he appeared on a popular radio program "America's Town Meeting of the Air" to debate New Deal opponent Wendell Willkie. Willkie was perceived to have won the debate, dashing Jackson's hope of being Roosevelt's successor. Speculation then began to center on Willkie, who was still a Democrat at this time. Willkie would not switch to the Republican Party until November 1939.

Roosevelt, while not actively a candidate for re-nomination, made it known that he was willing to be drafted by the Democratic National Convention to run for a third term. For a time, Secretary of State Cordell Hull appeared to be interested in the Democratic nomination, but did not become a serious candidate when it became more obvious that Roosevelt was orchestrating a draft.

Vice President John Nance Garner pursued a presidential candidacy during the primaries. In the latter years of their second term, Garner disagreed with Roosevelt on a number of issues, with Garner supporting a balanced federal budget, opposing Roosevelt's "court packing plan," and believing that the executive branch should not interfere with the internal workings of Congress. He also opposed the notion of any president breaking the two-term tradition. Roosevelt defeated Garner handily in the Democratic primaries and was re-nominated for a third term. With Garner declining to run for another vice presidential term, Roosevelt's running mate was Secretary of Agriculture Henry A. Wallace.

THE REPUBLICANS

The three leading candidates for the Republican nomination were Senator Robert Taft of Ohio, Senator Arthur Vandenburg of Michigan, and Thomas E. Dewey, the Manhattan district attorney who had come to national prominence because of his high profile prosecutions of organized crime figures. All three men were members of the Republican Party's conservative old guard: anti–New Deal isolationists, who opposed American entry into World War II. They were also lackluster candidates who failed to excite the Republican base. As the primaries ended, only 300 of the nearly 1,000 delegates who were going to the Philadelphia convention would be pledged to any candidate, creating the potential for a deadlocked convention.

In contrast, Willkie was the candidate of the party's liberal wing. An anti-isolationist, he argued that Roosevelt had failed to prepare the United States to defend itself, posing a threat to national security as the Nazi regime marched through Europe. Willkie had come to prominence as an opponent of Roosevelt's plan to establish the Tennessee Valley Authority. Willkie, who went to New York in 1929 to serve as general counsel to the Commonwealth and Southern Corporation (C&S), opposed government ownership of utilities (C&S was the largest utility holding company) claiming that it was unconstitutional. He also warned that no business was safe if the government could operate utilities. Willkie would eventually become president (1933) and chief executive officer (1935) of C&S as he

came to national prominence for his opposition to the New Deal. He began to write articles, make speeches, and testify before congressional committees, raising his profile and giving him a national following. By late 1939, he concluded that he could become the Republican nominee in 1940.

As German armies moved into France, support for the isolationist candidates began to decline among Republican voters. A Gallup poll conducted in early May 1940 found Dewey to be the preference of 67 percent of Republican voters. By the time the convention opened on June 24 in the Philadelphia Auditorium, the Gallup poll had Dewey at 47 percent, while Willkie, who had been the favorite of three percent of Republican voters in early May, was second to Dewey at 29 percent.

Willkie, who had never run for public office, was supported by many Republican newspapers, which helped encourage grassroots support for the undeclared candidate. Oren Root, Jr., a young New York lawyer, sent letters to more than 1,000 alumni of Princeton and Yale universities urging them to support a "draft" of Willkie. The news media's coverage of the response to Root's letter led to the creation of Willkie Clubs. These clubs were established throughout the country. They sent telegrams to the convention, circulated petitions that urged the convention to nominate Willkie, and many members came to Philadelphia to support Willkie, chanting, "We want Willkie" from the convention galleries. The convention's keynote speaker, Governor Harold Stassen of Minnesota, came out for Willkie and became his floor manager at the convention. Willkie, who had entered any of the primaries, came to Philadelphia with the fewest delegates of any of the major candidates. On the first ballot, Dewey led with 360 votes; Taft had the support of 189 delegates, and 105 delegates backed Willkie.

Willkie's supporters attempted to convince the delegates and party leaders at the convention that Willkie was the best compromise candidate. However, not all Republicans were responsive to the entreaties of Willkie's supporters. Former President Herbert Hoover, who was to speak at the convention, harbored hopes of emerging from the deadlock for a re-match with Roosevelt (who had defeated him in a landslide in 1932). Forty-five Republican members of Congress sent a message to the convention, urging the delegates to reject any candidate who had not consistently supported Republican principles and policies (a veiled reference to Willkie's recent conversion). His opponents also argued that Willkie was too inexperienced to be elected president. Nevertheless, by the third ballot, Willkie had pulled into the lead and he finally prevailed on the sixth ballot. Reporters called Willkie's victory "The Miracle at Philadelphia."

Willkie selected Charles L. McNary of Oregon, the Republican leader in the U.S. Senate, as his running mate. While McNary differed with Willkie on important issues (he was an isolationist in foreign policy and supported government control of power companies), his selection was intended to make the ticket stronger in the west and to counter one of Willkie's vulnerabilities: his connections to Wall Street financiers.

THE GENERAL ELECTION

Willkie continued his campaign against the New Deal, criticized Roosevelt's decision to seek a third term, and charged the Roosevelt Administration with a lack of military preparedness. Roosevelt's campaign theme was that the war in Europe threatened America, and it was not wise to elect an inexperienced president. The Roosevelt campaign slogan was "Don't change horses in midstream." While polls in the summer of 1940 showed the two candidates to be very competitive, by early October it appeared that Roosevelt was taking the lead.

Willkie had lukewarm support from many Republicans, who regarded him as an outsider who had hijacked their party's nomination. This perception had been given credence by Willkie's brief remarks on the convention's last day when he addressed the delegates as "You Republicans," which only reinforced the belief of many in the party that Willkie was not committed to the party, but had seen it only as a vehicle to seek the presidency. He also had difficulty overcoming the argument that the nation could not afford to replace Roosevelt with an inexperienced leader during perilous times. Toward the end of the campaign, Willkie reversed his strategy by appealing to the isolationists he had spurned earlier. He charged that Roosevelt had made a deal with the allies to bring the United States into the war after the election. Roosevelt, who had not made campaign appeals because he was too busy being president, then made a series of campaign appearances where he denied the Republican candidate's charges.

Roosevelt won an unprecedented third term, defeating Willkie by almost five million popular votes. The Electoral College margin was even wider, as Roosevelt received 449 electoral votes to Willkie's 82. Roosevelt carried 38 states to 10 for Willkie, most of which were in the midwest. Roosevelt's percentage of the popular vote dropped from over 60 percent in 1936 to slightly less than 55 percent in 1936.

The Results

	Popular Vote	Percentage	Electoral Votes
Franklin D. Roosevelt	27,263,448	54.7	449
Wendell Willkie	22,336,260	44.8	82
Norman Thomas	116,827	0.2	0
Roger W. Babson	58,685	0.1	0
All others	65,223	0.2	0
TOTAL	49,840,443	100.0	531

Source: J.W. Wright, ed., *New York Times Almanac 2007* (Penguin Reference, 2007).

SEE ALSO: Campaigns, Presidential; Dark Horse Candidate; Defense; Isolationism; Presidential Elections; Wallace, Henry A.

BIBLIOGRAPHY. Warren Moscow, *Roosevelt and Willkie* (Prentice-Hall, 1968); H.S. Parmet and M.B. Hecht, *Never Again: A President Runs for a Third Term* (Macmillan, 1968); Charles Peters, *Five Days in Philadelphia: The Amazing "We Want Willkie" Convention of 1940 and How it Freed FDR to Save the Western World* (Public Affairs, 2005).

Jeffrey Kraus
Wagner College

Presidential Election of 1944

THE PRESIDENTIAL ELECTION of 1944 took place while the United States was engaged in World War II. As Franklin Roosevelt and Thomas Dewey squared off and battled for the presidency, the American military was making tremendous strides throughout the European and Pacific theatres of war. Roosevelt had led the country since 1933, and re-election seemed certain. The choice for Roosevelt's vice presidential candidate proved to be the most dramatic moment in the campaign, and this decision proved to be the most important. Although Roosevelt did not announce his decision to seek re-election until later in 1944, the State of the Union address in January clearly proclaimed his goals for the following four years. He spoke of changes to the tax system and food distribution, which would speed the continuing war effort. He also spoke of the continued importance of solidarity in America, as the nation faced another year of battles throughout the war.

As the months progressed, Roosevelt realized the need to confront some of his supposed weaknesses and Republican claims. Republicans, and even former administration officials, claimed that Roosevelt was disorganized and too clandestine. There were also rumblings from Republicans that a victory for Roosevelt could lead to a dictatorship or even the beginning of Communism in the United States. Questions of Roosevelt's health also came up in the press regularly; he had a chronic cough and suffered regularly from a variety of illnesses.

REPUBLICAN PRIMARIES

As the Democrats awaited official confirmation from Roosevelt that he would seek re-election, the Republican Party's race began to heat up. Wendell Willkie, the party's presidential nominee in 1940, was the frontrunner throughout the early stages. He campaigned around the country and promoted his book, *One World*, which promoted a strong international organization after the war. Although Willkie displayed strong determination, his isolationist opinions before the war came back to haunt his subsequent campaign. After a very weak showing in the April Wisconsin primary, Willkie dropped out of the Republican race.

New York Governor Thomas Dewey became the clear leader in Republican circles, especially after General Douglas MacArthur decided to remain outside of the political arena. MacArthur disagreed with Roosevelt's New Deal and isolationist policies of earlier years, and many believed his military background would be beneficial to the commander-in-chief post. After consideration, MacArthur resisted the calls for a presidential run. In late June, the Republican convention took place and Dewey won the nomination. Governor of Ohio John W. Bricker was chosen as the vice presidential candidate. The Republicans professed the need to eliminate New Deal strategies and to change the tax system. In his acceptance speech, Dewey proclaimed that 10 million Americans were still unemployed and that conflict

between members of the Democratic Party and Roosevelt were a major detriment to the nation.

DEMOCRATIC CONVENTION

As the Republicans spoke of the need for changes, the Democrats were calling out for Roosevelt. It was understood that Roosevelt would seek a fourth term, but he decided to hold back on the announcement. As the days and months passed, the support for Roosevelt seemed to grow and the call for his nomination increased. Finally, on July 11, one week before the Democratic National Convention, Roosevelt announced his intentions to seek a fourth presidential term.

The only question before the convention revolved around Roosevelt's running mate. Over the previous four years, Vice President Henry Wallace had not garnered a lot of support from the Democrats. Many believed him to be too independent and too liberal for the party. The Democrats realized the need to choose a strong running mate due to Roosevelt's health problems. Many believed that Roosevelt's health was declining quickly. With these concerns circulating throughout Democratic circles, anti-Wallace reports were passed on to Roosevelt. The president, although still supportive of Wallace, realized the disastrous split in the party if he were to choose his current vice president as his running mate once again.

Roosevelt consulted with key Democratic leaders, and Harry Truman's name began to surface as a realistic and safe candidate. The senator from Missouri was the head of the Senate Committee to Investigate the National Defense Program, served in World War I, and was viewed as a conservative in the Democratic Party. Truman was officially recognized as the Democratic vice presidential candidate at the convention.

THE CAMPAIGN

While the running mate drama was unfolding at the Democratic convention, Roosevelt was preparing for a trip to Hawaii. After giving his acceptance speech for the Republican nomination in San Diego, the president examined the city's naval base and departed on a ship bound for Hawaii. While in Hawaii, Roosevelt met with General Douglas MacArthur and discussed the upcoming strategy for the Pacific theater of war. After Hawaii, Roosevelt sailed to the Aleutian Islands to assess the military installations of Alaska. It was obvious that the president would not sacrifice his wartime duties for the

HITLER WANTS US TO BELIEVE THAT:

- Democracy is dying.
- Our armed forces are weak.
- The "New Order" is inevitable.
- Jews cause everybody's troubles, everywhere.
- We are lost in the Pacific.
- Our West Coast is in such grave danger there is no point in fighting on.
- The British are decadent, and "sold us a bill of goods."
- Some sort of "peace" can be made with Nazi Germany.
- The cost of the war will bankrupt the nation.
- Civilian sacrifices will be more than we can bear.
- Our leaders are incompetent; our Government incapable of waging war.
- Stalin is getting too strong, and Bolshevism will sweep over Europe.
- Aid to our allies must stop.
- This is a "white man's war"; our real peril is the Japanese, and we must join Germany to stamp out the "Yellow Peril."
- We must bring all our troops and weapons back to the United States, and defend only our own shores.
- The Chinese, the British, and the Russians will make separate peace with Japan and Germany.
- American democracy will be lost during the war: the two-party system is dead; Congressional elections will never again be held.

THE BRITISH BZ-Z-Z Z-Z-Z-Z-Z   THE AMERICANS BZ-Z-Z Z-Z-Z-Z-Z

AMERICANS WILL NOT BE FOOLED!

A World War II poster. Franklin Roosevelt had led the country since 1933 and re-election seemed certain.

campaign trail. However, Roosevelt's health was beginning to fail. During the trip, photographs of Roosevelt surfaced that portrayed a gaunt and tired man.

After his return to the mainland, he gave a rambling speech at the Bremerton Naval Base adjacent in Seattle, which startled a number of people. Afterward, the polls portrayed that the firm lead Roosevelt once had seemed to be slipping. As September began, Dewey campaigned in Philadelphia and then traveled to the west coast, while Roosevelt met with British Prime Minister Winston Churchill in Quebec to discuss the closing stages of the war. Dewey's campaign focused on the government's labor issues, stating that labor unions were not being treated fairly. He also spoke out for extended Social Security and greater unemployment coverage.

After returning from Quebec, Roosevelt returned to radio airwaves. He spoke of the past 11 years and the positives that he and his administration brought to the

United States. The country under his leadership had survived the Great Depression. He reminded the nation that the Republicans were the ones who believed in isolationism and fought the Democrats in the Lend Lease Act months before the attack on Pearl Harbor. He spoke of the great strides labor leaders had made in the previous few years and the fact that labor supplied the very arms and war machines to the troops overseas.

He closed his radio address with a funny jab at the Republicans, who had days earlier reported false accusations that Roosevelt accidentally left behind his dog, Fala, while he was on the Aleutian Islands. Republicans stated that Roosevelt used American tax dollars to send a ship over to pick up the dog. Roosevelt replied to these bogus accusations with humor: "These Republican leaders have not been content with attacks on me, or on my wife, or on my sons. No, not content with that, they now include my little dog Fala." This speech brought numerous laughs across the country and proved to America that Roosevelt still could bring Americans together. He was still the same leader who brought the country out of the Depression years earlier, and who was holding America together through the war.

Throughout the remaining weeks of the campaign, Dewey and his Republican cronies focused their remarks on the Communist threat. The Congress of Industrial Organization's (CIO) Political Action Committee (PAC) was their main target. The CIO was a federation of labor unions. Many members supported Roosevelt and focused on getting migrants and war workers to vote in the election. Dewey and the Republicans accused the leader of the PAC, Sidney Hillman, of having Communist ties. Republicans also spoke often of the New Deal government that they believed was composed of Communist ideas.

During the final days of the campaign, the military was advancing in Europe as well as in the Pacific. Roosevelt used these advances to his advantage and set forth clear foreign policy plans in a speech given at the Waldorf Astoria in New York City. He addressed the need for the United Nations and the need for the new organization to have the power to display force, if needed. Roosevelt continued his foreign policy addresses with visits to the Philadelphia Naval Yard and Chicago and proceeded to build up fervor for the American war effort.

THE ELECTION

With the war effort going strong and the charismatic Roosevelt in full stride, he was voted in for an unprecedented fourth term. Thomas Dewey and the Republicans could not muster enough anti-Roosevelt feeling. Roosevelt won the election by a margin of 3.6 million votes. This was the closest race in his four presidential election campaigns, but, nevertheless, a very solid showing. The president garnered an incredible amount of support from the northeastern, western, and southern industrial centers. The support from the PAC proved to be beneficial, especially in Michigan, where 170,000 more voters cast ballots.

The concerns for Roosevelt's health rang very true as his body continued to weaken over the upcoming months and into his new term. In April 1945, Roosevelt died, just before the Allies declared victory over Germany in Europe. The decision to choose Truman as his vice president turned out to be the most important decision of his campaign, for Truman took over the reigns of the presidency at the end of World War II.

SEE ALSO: Challengers to Incumbents; Foreign Policy; Labor Vote; Political Action Committee; Wallace, Henry A.

BIBLIOGRAPHY. Conrad Black, *Franklin Delano Roosevelt: Champion of Freedom* (Public Affairs, 2003); R.H. Ferrell, *The Dying President: Franklin D. Roosevelt 1944–1945* (University of Missouri Press, 1998); A.M. Schlesinger, Jr., and F.L. Israel, eds., *History of American Presidential Elections 1789–2001* (Chelsea House Publishers, 2002).

GAVIN WILK
INDEPENDENT SCHOLAR

Presidential Election of 1948

THE 1948 PRESIDENTIAL election was an election in which many voters and pundits believed that the incumbent Democratic President Harry S. Truman was sure to lose to his opponent, Republican nominee and New York Governor Thomas E. Dewey. However, Truman defied predictions and decisively defeated Dewey in an upset election. Doubts about Truman's election prospects were due to concerns about defections from the Democratic Party, mainly from southern Democrats led by J. Strom Thurmond who were angered by Truman's civil rights policies, and Progressives, led by Henry Wallace, who regarded Truman's foreign policy as too militaristic.

Truman was a senator from Missouri, elected in 1934. During World War II, he chaired an investigative committee that dealt with waste in defense. In 1944, Democratic Party bosses made Truman President Franklin D. Roosevelt's running mate. The decision was a significant one because party insiders knew that Roosevelt was an ill man and that his running mate would likely succeed him as president. Further, party bosses did not like Roosevelt's then vice president, Henry Wallace, whom they considered eccentric.

Roosevelt easily won a fourth term against his Republican opponent, Thomas E. Dewey, in 1944. During the time that Truman was vice president, from January 21 to April 12, 1945, he was not kept informed by Roosevelt. On April 12, 1945, Roosevelt died and Truman became president. As president, Truman had to address a number of issues. First was the issue of price controls, which had been instituted during World War II. Second was the issue of business and labor relations. Third was demobilization of American troops. Fourth was the issue of civil rights. Finally, Truman had to handle the issue of what U.S.–Soviet Union relations would be after World War II. There were tensions in the relationship that were set aside due to the focus on the common enemy, Nazi Germany.

Truman lacked Roosevelt's charisma and oratorical abilities, which was an obstacle for him as president. For many Americans, Roosevelt was the only president that they had known, and it was a major adjustment. Many critics viewed Truman as a tool of Tom Pendergast's political machine. Pendergast brought Truman to power in Missouri as a county commissioner and later as a U.S. Senator. Further, Truman spoke with a midwestern nasal twang, which contrasted unfavorably with Roosevelt's warm, confident, aristocratic New York tones. Liberals in Truman's party felt that he was insufficiently liberal and cited his appointment of a number of conservative supporters to the federal government. Many believed that if only Truman possessed Roosevelt's eloquence, he would have more success in pushing his legislative program through Congress.

Truman found that the difficult postwar environment damaged his initial popularity with voters. A major problem was the time the Truman administration took to end wage and price controls. Voters also clamored in 1945 and 1946, for the Truman administration to quickly demobilize the American military at the end of World War II. As a result, by 1946 millions of American soldiers were demobilized. There were also a number of strikes in 1945 and 1946. In 1946, voters, frustrated with the economic situation, elected a Republican Congress.

By 1948, there were splits within the Democratic Party. Southern Democrats, led by Thurmond, walked out of the Democratic convention in Philadelphia because they felt that Truman had gone too far on civil rights (even though the initial civil rights plank had been much weaker and was strengthened by Minneapolis mayor Hubert Humphrey). Among the civil rights policies that Truman supported were a Fair Employment Practices Commission, desegregation of the military, anti-lynching laws, and abolition of the poll tax. Thurmond campaigned on a platform of states' rights and opposition to civil rights.

Henry Wallace (Truman's secretary of commerce until his resignation in 1946), on the other hand, had defected from the Democrats in 1947 to create the Progressive Party, because he considered Truman's foreign policy toward the Soviet Union to be too aggressive and militaristic. The Truman Doctrine, which originated out of the need to aid Greece and Turkey, but called for the United States to aid any country or group that was threatened by the Soviet Union, especially troubled Wallace. There were defections on the right and the left within the Democratic Party because of Truman's domestic and foreign policies.

In contrast, the Republican Party unified behind the candidacy of New York governor Thomas E. Dewey after he defeated Senator Robert Taft of Ohio and Harold Stassen, the former governor of Minnesota. Republicans and many pundits assumed that Dewey would easily win the election. From the beginning, Dewey acted on the assumption that he would win the election. He was frequently cautious in his speeches and wanted to say nothing risky that would upset his presumed victory.

It seemed that Truman was the only one who truly believed that he could be re-elected. Truman gave a defiant speech at the Democratic convention and called the 80th Congress into a special session. Truman forced the Republican Congress to vote on liberal measures that its candidate Dewey professed to support. In the special session, in July 1948, Truman proposed a series of legislative measures including a higher minimum wage, federal aid to education, extension of Social Security benefits, farm subsidies, and civil rights. After two weeks, Congress adjourned, having passed only one or two of Truman's proposals. Truman called the 80th a "do-nothing Congress."

THE GENERAL ELECTION

In the general election, Truman engaged in an energetic "whistle-stop" campaign by train across the nation. Truman sought to appeal to elements of the New Deal coalition formed by Franklin Roosevelt, including farmers, labor, and African Americans. Truman criticized the Taft-Hartley Act and the 80th Congress's agricultural policies. He warned that if another Republican president were elected, there would be another depression similar to the Great Depression, which had started during the presidency of the last Republican President, Herbert Hoover.

Truman also seemed to benefit from his tough foreign policy toward the Soviet Union. One example is the Berlin Airlift, which was the Truman Administration's response to the Soviet Union's economic blockade of West Berlin in the spring of 1948, to drive the United States and its allies out of the city. Likewise, Truman's loyalty and security program was perceived as a strong response to the potential threat of Communists within the federal government. Truman was also made to look tough on Communism by the third-party candidacy of Henry Wallace and the Progressive Party, which was dominated by Communists (though Wallace himself was not a Communist). Wallace criticized Truman's foreign policy, including the Truman Doctrine, Berlin Airlift, and Marshall Plan. During the campaign, Wallace was criticized for blaming Truman's foreign policy for a Soviet coup in 1948, in Czechoslovakia.

In the weeks before the election, pundits predicted a Dewey victory. Some pollsters even stopped polling before the election. For example, pollster Elmo Roper announced in September 1948 that he would cease polling as the outcome was already apparent. Polls before the election showed Dewey leading Truman.

On Election Day, Truman shocked most pundits and much of the electorate by defeating Dewey. Many news outlets were embarrassed, especially the *Chicago Tribune*, which had printed the headline "Dewey Defeats Truman." Truman's victory was either attributed to Dewey's poor campaign and unwillingness to say anything substantive about issues, or Truman's energetic whistle-stop campaigning. Yet, many scholars argue that it was not an upset and was a case of Franklin Roosevelt's New Deal coalition of African Americans, labor, farmers, Jews, city bosses, and white southerners holding together. Some studies of the 1948 election indicate that, absent the third-party candidacies of Thurmond and Wallace, Truman might have won Alabama, Louisiana, Mississippi, New York, and South Carolina. There was also strong evidence that many farmers voted for Truman in protest of the 80th Congress's farm policies, which prohibited farmers from storing their surplus crops. The farm vote helped Truman in traditionally Republican states such as Iowa and Ohio. In addition, the defections of the Dixiecrats, Henry Wallace, and the Progressive Party did not hurt Truman. Most white southerners still voted for Truman and most Democrats did not defect to Wallace. Wallace's association with the Communist Party hurt him and helped Truman.

Truman received 24,105,812 popular votes (49.5 percent) to Dewey's 21,970,065 popular votes (45.1 percent). Truman won 303 electoral votes to 189 electoral votes for Dewey. Both Henry Wallace and Strom Thurmond received slightly over one million votes, with Thurmond receiving 39 electoral votes from Alabama, Louisiana, Mississippi, and South Carolina.

SEE ALSO: Presidential Election of 1944; States' Rights Party (Dixiecrats); Thurmond, J. Strom; Wallace, Henry A.

BIBLIOGRAPHY: G.A. Donaldson, *Truman Defeats Dewey* (University Press of Kentucky, 1999); H.I. Gullan, *The Upset That Wasn't: Harry S. Truman and the Crucial Election of 1948* (Ivan R. Dee, 1998); Alonzo Hamby, *Beyond the New Deal: Harry S. Truman and American Liberalism* (Columbia University Press, 1973); Zachary Karabell, *The Last Campaign: How Harry Truman Won the 1948 Election* (Alfred A. Knopf, 2000); David McCullough, *Truman* (Simon and Schuster, 1992); Irwin Ross, *The Loneliest Campaign: The Truman Victory of 1948* (New American Library, 1968); S.J. Savage, *Truman and the Democratic Party* (University Press of Kentucky, 1997).

JASON ROBERTS
GEORGE WASHINGTON UNIVERSITY

Presidential Election of 1952

IN 1952, INCUMBENT President Harry S. Truman decided not to run. The Democrats nominated Gover-

nor Adlai Stevenson of Illinois. The Republicans nominated General Dwight D. Eisenhower. Eisenhower won the election, ending 20 years of Democratic control of the White House. The fight for the Republican nomination was largely between General Dwight D. Eisenhower and Senator Robert A. Taft of Ohio. The primaries had been split fairly evenly between the two men, and the nomination came down to the wire. When the 1952 Republican National Convention opened in Chicago, most political experts rated Taft and Eisenhower as neck-and-neck in the delegate vote totals.

Ultimately, Eisenhower won the nomination based largely on the perception that he was a sure winner. Eisenhower took the nomination on the first ballot. He chose as his running mate Senator Richard Nixon of California, best known for his pursuit of Alger Hiss, the accused spy. It was felt that Nixon had valuable credentials, as a campaigner and anti-Communist. A March 1952 poll found that Eisenhower was the most admired of all living Americans. Eisenhower would have been a difficult opponent for any challenger. General Eisenhower emerged as a World War II war hero for coordinating the D-Day landing on Normandy. When the war in Europe ended (V-E Day) in 1945, many expected him to enter politics.

The obvious candidate for the Democratic nomination was incumbent President Harry S. Truman. Since the newly passed Twenty-Second Amendment did not apply to whoever was president at the time of its passage, he was eligible to run again. The Twenty-Second Amendment states,

No person shall be elected to the office of the President more than twice, and no person who has held the office of President, or acted as President, for more than two years of a term to which some other person was elected President shall be elected to the office of President more than once.

Truman served three years as president, after Franklin Roosevelt's death, in 1945, and was elected in 1948. The polls showed that Truman entered 1952 with low approval ratings, partly because the Korean War was dragging into its third year. In addition, Wisconsin Republican Senator Joseph McCarthy was involved in a well-publicized search for Communists. "Korea, Communism, and Corruption" were the albatrosses the Republicans were prepared to blame on President Truman in the primaries and general election of 1952, if he ran for a second term of office.

Truman's main opponent was Tennessee Senator Estes Kefauver, who had chaired a nationally-televised investigation of organized crime in 1951, and was known as a crusader against crime and corruption. Senator Estes Kefauver of Tennessee defeated Truman in the New Hampshire primary. A month later, on March 29, 1952, Truman surprised the country by announcing that he would not be a candidate for re-election. Truman liked Illinois Governor Adlai Stevenson as his successor, but Stevenson, who was then running for the Illinois governorship, declared that he was not interested in running for the presidency.

Although Kefauver went on to win most of the other primaries, the majority of states still chose their delegates in state conventions, which meant that the party bosses were able to choose the Democratic nominee. These party bosses (including President Truman) strongly disliked Kefauver because of his investigations of organized crime that had revealed connections between mafia figures and many of the big-city Democratic political organizations. As a result, the party bosses viewed Kefauver as a man who could not be trusted, and they refused to support him for the nomination. Instead, with President Truman taking the lead, they began to search for other, more acceptable, candidates.

Besides Kefauver, the leading contenders for the nomination were Averell Harriman of New York (Truman's pick); Senator Richard Russell of Georgia as the candidate of the southern bloc; and Governor Adlai Stevenson of Illinois, who emerged as the choice of the mainline party leadership. Governor Adlai Stevenson, the grandson of former vice president Adlai E. Stevenson, was known as a gifted speaker, intellectual, and political moderate. In the spring of 1952, President Truman tried to convince Stevenson to take the presidential nomination, but Stevenson refused.

The 1952 Democratic National Convention was held in Chicago. The convention met in the same hall as the Republicans. As the convention was being held in his home state, Governor Stevenson, who still insisted that he was not a presidential candidate, was asked to give the welcoming address to the delegates. He proceeded to give an inspiring speech that led his supporters to begin a renewed round of efforts to nominate him, despite his protests. After meeting with the Illinois delegation, Stevenson finally agreed to enter his name as a candidate for the nomination. The party bosses from other large northern and midwestern states also sup-

ported him. Kefauver led on the first ballot, but had fewer votes than necessary to win. Stevenson gradually gained strength, and was nominated on the third ballot. The convention then chose Senator John Sparkman of Alabama, a conservative, as Stevenson's running mate. Stevenson delivered an eloquent acceptance speech in which he famously pledged to "talk sense to the American people."

THE GENERAL ELECTION

In the general election, Eisenhower campaigned by attacking the conflict in Korea, Communism, and corruption in government. In a major speech, he announced that if he won the election, he would go to Korea to see if he could end the war; however, he never explained what he would do when he got there. This, and his enormous popularity as a World War II commander made him the leader throughout the campaign. During the campaign, the Republicans blamed the Democrats for the military's failures in Korea. Using Senator McCarthy's agenda, they accused the Democrats of having Communist spies within the federal government. Additionally, they accused the Truman administration for having too many officials who had been accused of various crimes.

The Democrats, in turn, criticized Senator McCarthy and other right-wing Republicans as "fear mongers" who were recklessly treading on the civil liberties of government employees. Many Democrats were particularly upset when Eisenhower, on a scheduled campaign swing through Wisconsin, decided not to give a speech he had written criticizing McCarthy's methods, and then allowed himself to be photographed shaking hands with McCarthy as if he supported him. Despite these attacks, Eisenhower retained his enormous personal popularity because of his leading role during World War II.

Both campaigns made use of television ads. A notable ad for Eisenhower was a feel-good animated cartoon with a soundtrack by Irving Berlin called "I Like Ike" (Ike was Eisenhower's nickname). This was the first time that television was used during a presidential campaign. Stevenson also used television, but his ads were not as creative, and he did not have the much-admired composer Irving Berlin on his side. Stevenson concentrated on giving a series of speeches around the nation, and drew large crowds. Although his style thrilled intellectuals and academics, some political experts wondered if he was speaking over the heads of most of his listeners, and they dubbed him an "egghead," based on his baldness and intellectual demeanor. One notable event of the campaign was a scandal that emerged when vice presidential candidate Nixon was accused of receiving various undeclared gifts from wealthy contributors. For a while it appeared that Nixon might be dropped from the campaign, but he gave a tearful televised speech (the "Checkers speech") in which he defended himself and told the public about a dog named Checkers that he had received from a contributor, and how much his children loved it. His speech defused the issue and actually helped the Republicans to win the election.

Eisenhower maintained a comfortable lead in the polls throughout most of the campaign. His military prestige, combined with the public's disillusionment with the conflict in Korea, and the "Checkers speech" gave Eisenhower the final boost he needed to win. On November 4, 1952, Eisenhower won a decisive victory, taking over 55 percent of the popular vote and winning 39 of the 48 states. He took four southern states that the Republicans had won only once since Reconstruction: Florida, Tennessee, Texas, and Virginia, .

SEE ALSO: Advertising, Campaign; Campaigns, Presidential; Campaign Strategies; Challengers to Incumbents; Democratic Party; Incumbent; Military Hero; Nomination Process, Presidential; Scandals, Presidential Elections; Twenty-Second Amendment.

BIBLIOGRAPHY. R.V. Friedenberg, *Communication Consultants in Political Campaigns: Ballot Box Warriors* (Praeger Publishers, 1997); K.H. Jamieson, *Packaging the Presidency: A History and Criticism of Presidential Campaign Advertising* (Oxford University Press, 1996); R.J. Hrebenar, M.J. Burbank, and R.C. Benedict, *Political Parties, Interest Groups, and Political Campaigns* (Westview Press, 1999); M.J. Medhurst, *Dwight D. Eisenhower: Strategic Communicator* (Greenwood Press, 1993); Joanne Morreale, *The Presidential Campaign Film: A Critical History* (Praeger, 1993).

STEPHEN E. SUSSMAN
BARRY UNIVERSITY

Presidential Election of 1956

THE PRESIDENTIAL ELECTION of 1956 was fought between incumbent President Dwight D. Eisenhower for the Republican Party and Illinois governor Adlai Stevenson for the Democratic Party. Eisenhower's running mate was Vice President Richard M. Nixon, and Stevenson's running mate was Senator Estes Kefauver from Tennessee. Eisenhower won with 57 percent of the popular vote and 457 out of 531 electoral votes. Stevenson carried only seven states and won 73 electoral votes, losing one electoral vote to a faithless elector from Alabama who cast his vote for Alabama judge Walter Burgwyn Jones and former Georgia Governor Herman Talmadge.

The 1956 election took place in the middle of a dual foreign policy crisis involving the Soviet invasion of Hungary and the British, French, and Israeli collusion to invade Egypt and retake the nationalized Suez Canal. Stevenson's failure to capitalize on the crises was the last of a series of misjudgments that he had made over the course of the campaign.

THE CANDIDATES

By the middle of 1955, Eisenhower's personal and political popularity, coupled with a general sense of domestic peace and prosperity, made a second term in office seem all the more likely. Even though he had suffered a heart attack in late September 1955 and would need surgery shortly thereafter to treat an intestinal inflammation, Eisenhower had recovered enough by the end of the year to remain a viable candidate in the upcoming campaign season.

Nonetheless, there was a question of whether Vice President Richard Nixon would remain as Eisenhower's choice for a vice presidential candidate. There were a few months of uncertainty where Eisenhower appeared to let Nixon test his own strength within the Republican Party to determine if he had enough support to be viable candidate in his own right. Nixon had built up enough support within the party rank-and-file to help secure his position, and only one Republican politician of note, Harold Stassen, spoke out against his re-selection as running mate. By allowing Nixon to prove his own strength in the party, Eisenhower reaffirmed the strength of their ticket and solidified their joint standing within the Republican Party.

To challenge Eisenhower, the Democratic Party turned, once again, to its favored candidate from the 1952 election, Adlai Stevenson, governor of Illinois. Stevenson had been a reluctant candidate in 1952, but he was prepared to run again. His greatest difficulty was his choice of a candidate for vice president. Stevenson was deeply concerned about the existing method of selecting a vice presidential nominee; it was an unspoken but longstanding tradition, that the presidential candidate would have the decisive voice in selecting the vice presidential nominee. The choice of a vice presidential candidate also had particular implications for the party's future, because the position of vice president appeared to be a method of grooming a selected individual for the job of president. As a result, Stevenson made a novel choice: he declared that he wanted the delegates of the Democratic national convention to choose a vice president without any declared or implied influence, preference, or pressure from him.

This tactic had three effects, all of which Stevenson hoped would operate in his favor. First, an independent selection of a vice presidential candidate would look more democratic. Second, by giving the choice to the national party conference, Stevenson would avoid having to choose among several attractive and qualified potential candidates—including Senator John F. Kennedy of Massachusetts, Senator Hubert Humphrey of Minnesota, and Senator Estes Kefauver of Tennessee. Stevenson hoped to avoid alienating the supporters of the candidates who had not been selected, realizing that their support might shore up his position in states where the vote could go either way.

Finally, Stevenson wanted to remind voters of the important of the vice presidential position: the only thing standing between Richard Nixon and the highest office in the land was President Eisenhower's already weak heart. By emphasizing the relatively undemocratic nature of the vice presidential selection, Stevenson hoped that his more democratic process would make a positive impression on floating or undecided voters. Yet Stevenson's decision, however defensible, was not entirely prudent from a purely political standpoint.

THE CAMPAIGNS

The 1956 presidential campaign was one of the first modern campaigns where state-by-state primaries became a significant factor in the months leading up to the official party conventions and the presidential nominations. In states where the primaries were held at an earlier date, such as New Hampshire, the candidates often faced questions on matters of purely local concern, regardless of whether or not the questions were at all related to larger, more "presidential" domestic or foreign policy issues. Implicit in this more

heavily-weighted focus on local issues was the impression that the average voter was less interested in international affairs than in local affairs—even, in some cases, that the voters did not want to hear about international situations or broader domestic policy issues. Richard Nixon had used his position as vice president to visit states and regions and build support with Republican Party members on the state and local level, bolstering the party's image with the grassroots membership. Stevenson, on the other hand, found this kind of campaigning distasteful; as he saw it, campaigning on local issues to win support in the state primaries made presidential candidates act as if they were running for county sheriff, ignoring the wider issues in favor of pandering to local opinion. Stevenson also disliked two other aspects of the 1956 campaign: the increased spending on the campaigning process (which he believed made candidates too liable to influence by special interest groups) and the dominant role played by television advertisements from both parties (which he thought made the White House look like a "box of cornflakes"). He had attempted to address the democratic deficiencies of the presidential campaigning process within his own party, but he also found much to criticize in the means through which the presidential race was run on the national level.

From the outset, Stevenson's campaign suffered as a result of advice he received from Democratic Party leaders and political pragmatists, who told him that he should focus less on foreign policy issues, which were less likely to have a direct appeal to the electorate. If Stevenson had challenged Eisenhower's foreign policy from the outset, building his case with the eloquence that he had shown during the 1952 presidential campaign, and particularly challenging the aggressive and often belligerent tactics favored by Secretary of State John Foster Dulles, he would have been in an excellent position to gain the full political benefits from the Hungarian and Suez crises at the very height of the 1956 campaign.

Instead, Stevenson avoided foreign policy early in the campaign and focused more on Eisenhower's ill health and on Nixon's likelihood of succeeding to the presidency. This tactic backfired, as it made him seem petty and unable to rise above party politics, reduced to questioning Eisenhower's fitness for duty in a manner that also made him appear somewhat unpatriotic. Meanwhile, the Republicans and Nixon, in particular, played on Stevenson's relative inexperience in foreign affairs and his support for a ban on nuclear testing, further preventing Stevenson from using foreign policy concerns to attack the Eisenhower administration.

The final days of the campaign saw Stevenson still attempting to emphasize Nixon's character and Eisenhower's physical weakness. The fighting continued in Suez even as Americans went to the polls on Election Day, but Stevenson did not fully respond to the opportunity he had been given. He pointed out that the Eisenhower administration had reacted poorly to both Hungary and Suez, but did not offer any concrete answers as to how he would have reacted to put the situation right. If Stevenson had devoted more of the presidential campaign to challenging Eisenhower's foreign policy record, he might have been in a better position to exploit the Suez crisis. Instead, the American public turned to an honored military hero to deal with the crises abroad—a response that caused no small amount of bitterness among Democrats, as their opponents won the election in response to foreign policy fiascoes that Eisenhower's administration had helped to create.

THE RESULTS

The outcome of the election showed a decisive victory for Eisenhower. Stevenson lost by an even greater margin than he had lost in 1952, and also lost in both his own state of Illinois and in Kefauver's state of Tennessee, although he did manage to win his neighbor state, Missouri. The state of Louisiana, to name one notable loss, went Republican for the first time since 1876. Eisenhower, by contrast, won slightly more than 57.7 percent of the popular vote. The only bloc vote that Stevenson was able to swing in the wake of Suez was the Jewish vote, but as Jewish voters had a tendency to vote for Democratic candidates anyway, the increase in votes was marginal.

Adlai Stevenson lost the presidential election of 1956, but he lost to a nationally known, honored, and respected candidate whose military exploits had left him on a par with George Washington. Many of the policy proposals that Stevenson made during the campaign would later be brought into effect during the Democratic administrations of the 1960s, including federal aid to education, broader healthcare coverage for the poorest Americans, and, in particular, the partial nuclear test-ban treaty that would be adopted in 1963. Stevenson had attempted to promote these issues in the campaign, and he took the resounding defeat he received as a bitter personal blow.

As Dwight Eisenhower and Richard Nixon entered a second term of office, Nixon had his sights set four years into the future. In the presidential election of 1960, he intended to prove once and for all that he would win a test of political strength in his own right, free from Eisenhower's long shadow.

SEE ALSO: Presidential Election of 1952; War and Peace.

BIBLIOGRAPHY. Jeff Broadwater, *Adlai Stevenson and American Politics: The Odyssey of a Cold War Liberal* (Twayne, 1994); R.A. Divine, *Foreign Policy and U.S. Presidential Elections 1952–1960* (New Viewpoints, 1974); D.D. Eisenhower, *The White House Years: Waging Peace 1956–1960* (Doubleday, 1965); K.W. Thompson, ed., *Lessons from Defeated Presidential Candidates* (University Press of America, 1994); C.A.H. Thomson and F.M. Shattuck, *The 1956 Presidential Campaign* (Brookings Institution, 1960).

SHANNON GRANVILLE
INDEPENDENT SCHOLAR

Presidential Election of 1960

THE 1960 ELECTION was one of the closest in American political history. It pitted Massachusetts Senator John F. Kennedy, the Democratic nominee, against Vice President Richard Nixon of California, the Republican nominee. The campaign was noted for the youthfulness of the candidates (Kennedy was 43 and Nixon was 46 years old), the first televised presidential debates, and controversy over Kennedy's Catholicism.

On the Democratic side, the candidates were Senate Majority Leader Lyndon B. Johnson of Texas, Massachusetts Senator John F. Kennedy, Missouri Senator Stuart Symington, and Minnesota Senator Hubert Humphrey. Johnson was known for his skill at shepherding legislation through the Senate. On the other hand, many viewed him as deceitful and manipulative and considered him too closely tied to the south—especially his voting record on civil rights, which until 1957 was one of opposition. Kennedy was known for his charm, physical attractiveness, attractive wife Jacqueline Bouvier Kennedy, his distinguished service as a Patrol Torpedo boat captain in World War II, and the Pulitzer Prize he had won for his book *Profiles in Courage* in 1957. On the other hand, many considered his religion and his youthfulness (Kennedy was 42 years old when he announced his candidacy in January 1960) to be liabilities. Symington was an expert on defense issues, having served as President Harry Truman's first secretary of the Air Force. Humphrey, who had once been the mayor of Minneapolis, was a long-standing advocate of civil rights.

THE KENNEDY CAMPAIGN

From the beginning, John F. Kennedy's strategy was clear. It was to court the press and to win enough primaries to persuade skeptical party leaders who had reservations about Kennedy's youth, religion, and experience. Kennedy argued that he was the same age as George Washington when he commanded the Continental Army and Christopher Columbus when he discovered the New World. He ran in the Wisconsin and West Virginia primaries; his direct competition was Hubert Humphrey. In Wisconsin, which neighbored Humphrey's state of Minnesota, Kennedy won, receiving 56 percent of the vote. However, many pundits did not consider Kennedy's victory decisive because Humphrey had performed well in Protestant areas while Kennedy performed best in Catholic areas of the state.

Kennedy then moved his campaign to West Virginia. Initially, Kennedy led in the polls in West Virginia. However, that was before the residents of the predominantly Protestant state learned that Kennedy was a Catholic. Kennedy sought to allay concerns about his religion by assuring voters that he would follow the Constitution and not the Pope. He insisted that he believed strongly in the separation of church and state. Kennedy frequently told audiences that no one asked his brother his religion when he volunteered for his last bomber mission in World War II, and that no one asked Kennedy his religion when he commanded PT-109 in World War II. Franklin Roosevelt, Jr., the son of President Franklin Roosevelt, aided him in his campaign. President Roosevelt was revered in the state of West Virginia and the support of one of his sons clearly helped Kennedy. Kennedy won the West Virginia primary, receiving 61 percent of the vote. The victory gave him momentum going into the Democratic convention in Los Angeles.

At the convention, Lyndon Johnson sought to derail the Kennedy candidacy. He accused Kennedy's father, former ambassador to Great Britain, Joseph P. Kennedy, of appeasing Adolph Hitler. Likewise, he raised question about the state of Kennedy's health. However, the Kennedy campaign was too efficient and strong and Kennedy was easily nominated on the first ballot. In an initially controversial decision, Kennedy chose Lyndon Johnson as his running mate. Many at the convention (including Kennedy's brother Robert) were initially hostile to the decision because they did not see Johnson as a reformer and were stung by his attacks on the Kennedy campaign. However, the decision turned out to be wise as it strengthened Kennedy's chances in the south and lent geographical balance to the ticket.

THE NIXON CAMPAIGN

On the Republican side, the main candidates were Vice President Richard Nixon and Governor Nelson Rockefeller. Nixon had made a name as a congressman from California on the House Un-American Activities Committee investigating whether or not former State Department official Alger Hiss was a Communist. Ultimately, Hiss was indicted for perjury for a grand jury and convicted by a jury. As a result, Nixon quickly ascended the political ladder. He was elected to the U.S. Senate from California in 1950. In 1952, the Republican nominee and the former Allied Supreme Commander in Europe during World War II, Dwight D. Eisenhower, chose him as his vice president. After allegations of a secret slush fund, Nixon saved his spot on the ticket with an impassioned speech.

Nixon's main strength was that he had eight years of foreign policy experience as Eisenhower's vice president. This included trips to Latin America and the Soviet Union. On the other hand, Eisenhower seemed ambivalent about his vice president and was to show this frequently during the campaign. Nixon also had a tendency to aggravate his political opponents with accusatory rhetoric. For example, he accused President Harry Truman and his Secretary of State Dean Acheson of being soft on Communism.

Rockefeller dropped out of the race (he had refused to run in the primaries) only after forcing a meeting with Nixon in which they sat down and drafted the party's platform. Rockefeller included increased defense spending, which was something that Eisenhower, had sought to restrain during his presidency, and vehemently opposed.

THE ISSUES

A number of issues were at the forefront in the 1960 campaign. Among them were the state of the economy, civil rights, and national security. In 1960, the economy

The campaign of 1960 was notable for the youth of John Kennedy, as well as the first televised presidential debates.

into outer space in 1957. Kennedy alleged that there was a "missile gap" in favor of the Soviet Union; furthermore, Kennedy alleged that American prestige around the world had declined during the Eisenhower administration. In addition, he attacked the Eisenhower administration for its failure to overthrow Cuban leader Fidel Castro. Kennedy's charges put Nixon in an awkward position because he agreed with Kennedy, but was forced to defend the policies of the Eisenhower administration.

Kennedy's religion also continued to be a significant issue in the general election campaign. Even though Nixon did not address the issue, many Protestant ministers openly expressed doubt that a Catholic president could run the United States without taking orders from the Pope. For example, the well-known Protestant minister, Norman Vincent Peale, opposed Kennedy's candidacy based on his religion. Kennedy responded to questions about his religion before a gathering of Protestant ministers in September 1960. Kennedy argued that the Constitution prohibited religious tests for elective offices and emphasized his belief in the separation of church and state. Many observers then and later believed that this speech effectively answered questions about his religion.

THE GENERAL ELECTION

Of the two candidates, Kennedy ran a near-perfect campaign, while Nixon made a number of mistakes. Kennedy chose a running mate, Lyndon Johnson, who lent geographic balance to the ticket and was an effective campaigner. Nixon, on the other hand, chose Henry Cabot Lodge, former U.S. senator from Massachusetts, whom John F. Kennedy had unseated. Lodge turned out to be an ineffective campaigner and did not contribute much to the ticket. Kennedy selectively campaigned, picking crucial states that could be the key to victory. Nixon, on the other hand, unwisely campaigned in all 50 states, which physically exhausted him. Nixon's failure to help Martin Luther King, Jr., lost him support from African-American voters. In addition, Nixon waited until late in the campaign to ask Eisenhower to campaign for him.

Perhaps Nixon's most significant mistake was agreeing to debate Kennedy. In high school and in college, Nixon had been a champion debater. He had prided himself on outdebating his political opponents in both his House and Senate races. He had even appeared in the "kitchen debates" with Soviet Premier Nikita Khrushchev during a trip to the Soviet Union in 1959. The 1960 debates were

was in recession. Kennedy promised to get the country moving again and to get it out of the Eisenhower recession. Civil rights became a key issue in the campaign because of the way that both candidates responded to the arrest of civil rights leader Martin Luther King, Jr. in Georgia. The King family, in 1960, supported Nixon, who had supported civil rights legislation during his time as vice president. However, it was John F. Kennedy who called King's wife Coretta, expressing his sympathies, and asking what he could do to help. It was Robert Kennedy, Kennedy's brother and campaign manager, who persuaded the local judge in Georgia to release King from jail. As a result, the King family shifted their support from Richard Nixon to John F. Kennedy. The incident received attention in the African-American community and energized African-American voters in support of the Kennedy campaign.

Likewise, national security was front and center in the campaign. John F. Kennedy charged that the United States had fallen behind the Soviet Union during the Eisenhower administration. He pointed to events such as the Soviet Union sending the first satellite, Sputnik, the first televised presidential debates. While Nixon may have done well in terms of substance (those who listened on the radio thought he had won the first debate), he did not look presidential to the television viewers. Sweat poured from his face, which appeared dark and unshaven. By contrast, Kennedy appeared tanned, cool, calm, and confident besides Nixon. In effect, Kennedy appeared presidential to over 70 million viewers. Viewership was high, but decreased for the final three debates. The debates gave Kennedy momentum going into the final weeks of the campaign.

Despite Nixon's mistakes and the efficiency of Kennedy's campaign, the election was close. Kennedy won by 118,000 popular votes and received 303 electoral votes to 219 for Nixon. Kennedy received 34,221,463 popular votes (49.7 percent) to 34,108,582 popular votes (49.6 percent). Kennedy won the popular vote by one-tenth of one percent. A shift of a couple of thousand votes in swing states such as Illinois, Michigan, Missouri, and Texas could have given the election to Nixon. Many pundits believed then and now that Kennedy's religion both helped and hurt him. It hurt him in that there were many Protestant Democrats who voted for Nixon. On the other hand, many Catholics who had voted for Eisenhower in 1952 and 1956, voted for Kennedy in 1960.

SEE ALSO: Civil Rights; Religion and Voting Behavior; Religious Issues in Campaigns.

BIBLIOGRAPHY. S.E. Ambrose, *Nixon: The Education of a Politician* (Simon and Schuster, 2003); Christopher Matthews, *Kennedy and Nixon: The Rivalry that Shaped Postwar America* (Simon and Schuster, 1996); A.M. Schlesinger, Jr., *A Thousand Days: John F. Kennedy in the White House* (Houghton and Mifflin, 1965); Theodore Sorenson, *Kennedy* (Bantam Books, 1965); Theodore White, *Making of the President 1960* (Atheneum Publishers, 1961).

JASON ROBERTS
GEORGE WASHINGTON UNIVERSITY

Presidential Election of 1964

THE 1964 PRESIDENTIAL election was won by one of the largest margins in American history, the result of a number of factors that highlighted the unique political climate of the time. Though incumbent Democrat Lyndon Johnson faced little difficulty, his opposition was and remains significant to the course of American politics; though liberalism prevailed, the election was a watershed for American conservatism. President John F. Kennedy was assassinated less than a year before the election, during what was essentially campaign season, only a few months before the party primaries.

He would not have been expected to face any real competition in earning the Democratic Party's nomination, but the Republicans would have been another matter. When Kennedy was killed, though, the Republicans took a step back, not only halting their campaigns for the upcoming primaries, but also putting a damper on criticism of the administration. It was an awkward position, and it made for an unwinnable election, unless Johnson should prove wildly unpopular.

THE CANDIDATES

Johnson inherited the presidency, preserving Kennedy's legacy and the majority of his staff. The late president's brother, Bobby, remained as attorney general until resigning to challenge Kenneth Keating for his seat in the Senate. Though Bobby Kennedy and Lyndon Johnson had disagreed on many issues, each supported the other in their respective races, further shoring up their chances, their popularity, and the appearance of a unified front to carry on Jack Kennedy's political mission. The appearance was only that, though. Bobby wanted Johnson to make him his running mate, which Johnson adamantly refused to do (Bobby had tried to persuade him against running on Jack's ticket in 1960), and in order to make this refusal public without singling Kennedy out, he announced that none of his cabinet members were under consideration as running mate. Johnson further rescheduled Kennedy's planned speech at the Democratic National Convention, but it had no effect on the future senator's popularity: the speech and short tribute film to JFK are famous now for the 22 minutes of applause that followed.

Although Johnson faced no real competition for the Democratic nomination, Alabama Governor George Wallace, who loathed the president's position on civil rights as much as he had Kennedy's, opposed him. Wallace was unable to be an effective spoiler, though, as usual he performed better than most expected. Race and civil rights were a bigger issue in the matter of the

Mississippi delegation than in the primary campaign: Mississippi's Democratic primary had excluded African Americans, and as the southern Democrats saw the national party moving further and further away from them, many refused to support Johnson and his platform, including the Mississippi delegates.

Meanwhile, the Mississippi Freedom Democratic Party had held an integrated primary open to registered voters of all races, and claimed the right to replace the delegates from the main body of the party, arguing that the whites-only primary should be rendered invalid. The convention was torn on how to handle the situation; it was largely left to the states to determine how to handle their primaries and delegates, especially in the days before the 1968 reorganization. Johnson was already worried about his chances of carrying the south in the November election, though it was not until 1968 that Richard Nixon's "Southern strategy" would specifically aimed at swaying southern Democrats to the Republican Party. The change in the air was unmistakable, and Johnson suspected many of those Democrats would vote Republican when the time came. Refusing the Mississippi delegation would not help his chances.

A coalition of convention attendees including Martin Luther King, Jr., and Hubert Humphrey (Johnson's eventual running mate, and one of the speakers in favor of civil rights at the 1948 convention, which prompted the walk-out of the Dixiecrats) proposed a compromise. The integrated delegation would be granted two seats; the segregated delegation would take the rest, on the understanding that they would be required to support the party's choice and that no "Jim Crow primaries" would be accepted in the future. The compromise managed to offend all sides and several delegates walked out. In the end, Johnson carried the south, but not Mississippi, and it was the last election in which the Democrats won the white southern vote.

Meanwhile, the Republican Party suffered a greater identity crisis than that of the Democrats. Their 1960 candidate, Richard Nixon, bided his time and decided not to run, depriving the party of a clear frontrunner; at the same time, many who might have challenged Kennedy saw no hope in fighting a dead man's legacy. Many considered Governor Nelson Rockefeller of New York, a prominent Republican of the moderate faction, the obvious choice. He was well-connected and charismatic, with strong financial backers. But the party was home to a new breed of conservatism, informed by the Cold War

and reacting to the new liberalism in the Democratic Party and on college campuses. Barry Goldwater was the candidate of this conservatism. Senator Goldwater was a throwback, in some ways, to the opponents of the New Deal, and even to the anti-federalists. His dislike of big federal government and a "welfare state" meshed well with the states' rights supporters in the south, which was a large part of why Johnson feared the southern Democrats would support him. Though vocally anti-Soviet through the 1950s, he had rejected the extremes of men like Senator McCarthy, instead attacking the Communist threat through his writing. His 1960 *Conscience of a Conservative* remained a critical text among the new American conservatives for a generation to come. He supported many civil rights initiatives, but challenged the federal government's right to "legislate morality" and to interfere with state or popular sovereignty.

In the primary campaign, Goldwater painted Rockefeller and other moderate candidates as little more than Democrats of another stripe, political insiders who sought to build up government just as much as Johnson did. There was more difference between Goldwater and Johnson, or Goldwater and Rockefeller, for that matter, than between Rockefeller and Johnson, which strengthened his claims. The opposition to Goldwater was bitter enough, though, that as Rockefeller lost votes (due, in part, to the widespread speculation that he and his wife had been carrying on an adulterous affair when both were still married to others), they went to Governor William Scranton of Pennsylvania, another East Coast moderate.

THE CAMPAIGNS

Goldwater won the nomination by a considerable margin, with Scranton, Rockefeller, and a number of minor candidates splitting barely a third of the votes. His acceptance speech included the statement for which he has become famous, and which must have seemed foreboding to the moderates: "Extremism in defense of liberty is no vice." Cut off from much of the Republican Party infrastructure, Goldwater's campaign is sometimes described as a grassroots campaign, and many future politicians got their start working for him in 1964. His platform called for an escalation of the war in Vietnam, tax cuts, and cuts to government programs, limited federal interference in the business of states and the state of business, and vicious condemnation of the Kennedy-Johnson foreign policy, which Goldwater saw as soft on Communism. His choice of words was often unfortunate, and an insider like Rockefeller would have been more politic in his comments. Although Eisenhower endorsed Goldwater, Goldwater made dismissive remarks about his presidency, comparing it unfavorably to the liberalism of the New Deal era. Unlike other conservatives, Goldwater was not reluctant to discuss the possibility, or even the likelihood and desirability, of using nuclear weapons in the war against Communism; this would ultimately be his undoing.

The Goldwater campaign was based on an emotional appeal, invoking Cold War fears. "In your heart," the slogan said, "you know he's right." "In your guts," the Johnson campaign countered, "you know he's nuts." The Johnson campaign wasted no time in painting Goldwater as a dangerous extremist, and premiered the "Daisy girl ad" two months before the election. In the ad (premiering during the NBC broadcast of *David and Bathsheba*), an endearing young girl plays in a meadow, counting off the petals of a daisy, and her counting segues into the countdown of a missile launch. As the little girl looks into the sky, the camera zooms in on her eyes and fades to black, before cutting to a bright flash and the mushroom cloud of a nuclear explosion.

Three weeks later, the Warren Commission report on Kennedy's assassination was released, and although its conclusions were hardly heartwarming or enlightening, the publicity surrounding it may have helped to reinforce in the public's mind the idea of Johnson as Kennedy's chosen successor. He won 61 percent of the popular vote, and all but six of the states. Goldwater took only his home state of Arizona and five southern states alienated by Johnson's civil rights initiatives. Despite this loss, though, he won something significant: it was the first time the deep south had been won by a Republican since Reconstruction, and it laid the groundwork for Nixon's southern strategy and the Reagan Democrats who would help to further a muted form of Goldwater's conservatism.

SEE ALSO: Civil Rights; Conservatism; Presidential Election of 1960; Presidential Election of 1968; Southern Democrats; States' Rights Party (Dixiecrats).

BIBLIOGRAPHY. M.C. Brennan, *Turning Right in the Sixties: The Conservative Capture of the GOP* (University of North Carolina Press, 1995); Gary Donaldson, *Liberalism's Last Hurrah: The Presidential Campaign of 1964* (M.E. Sharpe, 2003); Kari Frederickson, *The Dixiecrat Revolt and the End of the Solid South, 1932–1968* (University of North Carolina Press, 2000); Sean Wilentz, *The Rise of American Democracy* (W.W. Norton, 2005); Godfrey Hodgson, *The World Turned Right Side Up: A History of the Conservative Ascendancy in America* (Houghton Mifflin, 1996); N.C. Rae, *Southern Democrats* (Oxford University Press, 1994).

BILL KTE'PI
INDEPENDENT SCHOLAR

Presidential Election of 1968

THE 1968 PRESIDENTIAL election was an important turning point for both the Democratic and Republican parties. In the general election, former Vice President Richard M. Nixon won the first of his two terms, defeating Vice President Hubert H. Humphrey, with Alabama Governor George C. Wallace as a significant third-party candidate.

At the start of the year, the race appeared to belong to President Lyndon Baines Johnson. A Democrat from Texas, Johnson had won with one of the largest landslides in American history in 1964. The United States was successfully engaged in a large-scale effort against poverty and in favor of civil rights for African Americans and others. The country was also fighting a war in Vietnam. It is generally believed that war is good for an incumbent president, because many people who would ordinarily vote for a challenger will vote for the incumbent out of patriotism. This suggests that Johnson could have counted on many Republican votes. However, before Johnson could appeal to Republicans or anyone else in the general election, he had to win the Democratic presidential nomination. Winning the party nomination is ordinarily no contest for an incumbent president, however, opposition to the war had been building among Democratic activists since mid-1967, a time of urban unrest and growing agitation among young people who were subject to the military draft.

Democratic Senator Eugene J. McCarthy of Minnesota challenged Johnson's position on the war, and he did very well in the critical first primary election, in New Hampshire. Johnson won the primary handily, taking 49 percent as a write-in candidate, but as an incumbent president, he expected nothing more than token opposition. He found McCarthy's 42 percent of the vote to be humiliating, and he expected there would be worse to come for him in subsequent primaries. The Vietnam War was not going well, with a major offensive by the enemy leading to record American casualties in the first quarter of 1968. On March 31, 1968, Johnson announced in a televised address to the nation that he would not seek another term. The officially stated reason was that he wanted to devote all of his remaining energies to winning the war.

THE CANDIDATES

Johnson's withdrawal sent the Democrats into a frenzy. Vice President Hubert H. Humphrey (also of Minnesota) stepped into Johnson's campaign. Less than a week after Johnson's withdrawal, civil rights leader Martin Luther King, Jr., was assassinated in Memphis, adding another note of strife to what was already a turbulent year. Humphrey and Johnson (he had withdrawn too late for his name to come off the ballot) were swamped by McCarthy in the Wisconsin primary. Senator Robert F. Kennedy of New York, brother of President John F. Kennedy, whose assassination in 1963 had made Johnson president, also ran.

Humphrey was doing well among the Democratic elite in caucuses and conventions, in states where Democratic convention delegates were chosen behind the scenes, while Kennedy was doing better in states where ordinary voters participated in primary elections that were conducted in the open. Some of the primaries in both the Democratic and Republican parties had no impact on the selection of delegates; they were advisory votes only, known derisively as "beauty contests."

The primary election season climaxed on June 5 with the California primary. Kennedy won, defeating McCarthy 46 to 42 percent (Humphrey did not enter) and this put his share of convention delegates close enough to Humphrey's count that it looked like the convention might go to more than one ballot. The last American major-party convention to take more than one ballot to choose a presidential nominee had been in 1952. This suspense was ended that same night, when Kennedy was assassinated at his victory party at the Ambassador Hotel in Los Angeles, by Sirhan Sirhan, a Palestinian.

Meanwhile, Nixon coasted through a series of primary and caucus victories. His only primary loss came in Massachusetts where he was a write-in candidate and lagged behind both New York Governor Nelson A. Rock-

efeller (who would eventually become vice president as a result of Nixon resigning the presidency) and favorite son Congressman Joe Volpe. Michigan Governor George Romney (father of 2008 candidate Mitt Romney), California Governor Ronald Reagan, and Rockefeller never got their campaigns competitive with Nixon's.

THE REPUBLICAN NATIONAL CONVENTION

Nixon was nominated on the first ballot at the Republican National Convention in Miami Beach, Florida with 692 votes to 277 for Rockefeller, 182 for Reagan (including all 86 as California's favorite son, although Nixon got every vote in the primary there), 55 for Senator John Rhodes of Arizona, 50 for Romney, and 77 for a scattering of others.

The surprise of the convention was Nixon's choice of Maryland Governor Spiro T. Agnew as his running mate. Polling done by the Nixon campaign showed that none of the runners-up from the nomination race added anything to Nixon's electoral chances; it actually seemed better if Nixon ran alone. As a practical matter, a candidate could not do this, or he or she would risk sending the election of the vice president to the Senate, which at the time was overwhelmingly in Democratic hands. Nixon decided the best alternative was to pick a running mate who was a complete cipher in the public mind. The choice of Agnew was the source of much derision among Democrats and a major theme of attack at their convention and in their media campaign, although, as Nixon intended, it did not make much difference in the election.

THE DEMOCRATIC NATIONAL CONVENTION

With Bobby Kennedy's death, Humphrey's accession to the presidential nomination became a mere formality. Humphrey was nominated on the first ballot, taking 1,760.25 votes to 601 for McCarthy, 146.5 for anti-war candidate George McGovern (who would win the party's nomination four years later), and 98.25 for a scattering of others. However, the convention in Chicago served as a flashpoint between the young anti-war activists and traditional authority.

Protestors clashed with police at several locations in Chicago, and this violence received as much television coverage as the proceedings inside the convention hall. Chicago Mayor Richard J. Daley, long a symbol of Democratic Party power, became as much an object of scorn on the left as he had previously been on the right, because of his support of the police's heavy-handed actions against the protestors. The convention, which was supposed to be a weeklong public relations campaign for the party, instead turned out to be a disaster for Humphrey. Within weeks, Nixon was running television ads juxtaposing images of Humphrey and the Democratic convention with the riots in the streets of Chicago, set to a jarringly dissonant musical score.

THE CAMPAIGNS

The events in Chicago neatly fit into the strategy that Nixon had been developing all along. Nixon was running a "law and order" campaign, in which he articulated traditional American values, especially respect for the law and maintaining an orderly society. He often denounced what he and most Republicans saw as chaos reigning in the land, especially the youth and countercultural movements and the sexual revolution agitating unchecked.

The Supreme Court had issued a series of decisions increasing the rights of criminal defendants, pornographers, and other types not typically favored by Republicans. Nixon ran almost as strenuously against the Supreme Court and its liberal Republican Chief Justice, Earl Warren, an old foe of his from California, as he did against the Democrats. Warren was appalled at the prospect of Nixon being elected and appointing a new Chief Justice, so he resigned in order to give Johnson the opportunity. Johnson overplayed his hand, appointing one of his best Washington friends, Associate Justice Abe Fortas to the post, and one of his best Texas friends, Judge Homer Thornberry, to Fortas's seat. Presidents typically have low political capital for making such appointments in the fourth years of their terms, and the Senate was unable to overcome a filibuster on the Fortas nomination. Thus, Nixon arrived in office with the resignation of the Chief Justice waiting for him.

Humphrey was undercut by the left wing in his party, which was very sympathetic to the anti-war protestors. The Democratic convention had backed Humphrey's moderate stance on the war, rejecting an anti-war minority report 60 to 40 percent. The left-wing movement felt that Humphrey would not do enough to end the war, and that they were better off either supporting a fringe party anti-war candidate like Eldridge Cleaver, or not voting at all. Humphrey, in fact, wanted to end the war, but believed that vigorously stating this view would be a disservice to Johnson. Johnson's selection of Humphrey as vice president in 1964 he credited with making his rise to presidential nominee possible. It was not until too late

in the campaign, in mid-October, in a speech at Ohio State University in Columbus, that Humphrey vociferously outlined his true position on the Vietnam War.

THE RESULTS

The popular vote was quite close; Nixon beat Humphrey by only 0.7 percent. However, Nixon won handily in the electoral college, taking 301 votes to Humphrey's 191, and 46 for Wallace, the last third-party candidate to win electoral votes. Wallace carried Alabama, Arkansas, Georgia, Louisiana, and Mississippi and was popular enough in the other southern states that Nixon was able to beat Humphrey in what had previously been solid Democratic states. Humphrey carried the northeast, except for New Hampshire, Vermont, New Jersey, and Delaware; and also Hawaii, Michigan, Minnesota, and Washington.

Had Wallace been able to carry three other states, the Carolinas and Tennessee, perhaps, Nixon would have been denied a majority and the election would have been decided by the House of Representatives. In that instance, Wallace was planning to instruct his electors to vote for whomever, Humphrey or Nixon, offered him the best deal, possibly to include the chief justiceship. This concept of a brokered deal has been used as an argument for the abolition of the Electoral College ever since.

According to some views, Nixon's victory was the beginning of a Republican ascendancy. To others, it was a blip in Democratic dominance that did not end until the election of Ronald Reagan. In either case, the election turned the Republican Party away from the doctrinaire conservatism that had led them to nominate Barry Goldwater in 1964, and instead, to focus on electability.

The election led the Democrats to institute a series of party reforms intended to increase the value of participation of ordinary party members, since elites so visibly dominated the nominating process in 1968. In the Democratic Party, beauty contest primaries and favorite sons were eliminated, and proportional representation was instituted at every level. The imbroglio in Chicago led to a revision of the time-honored wisdom that hosting a convention increases a party's chances in the host state. In 1972, some venues that had vied for conventions in the past, shied away from hosting, and Chicago, which had been the most frequented convention location in the 20th century, did not host a national political convention again until 1996. The biggest loser was probably McCarthy, who declined to seek re-election to his senate seat in 1970, in anticipation of his ouster by pro-Humphrey forces; Humphrey was, in fact, elected to the seat that year. McCarthy became a fringe figure and remained so for the rest of his life.

SEE ALSO: Vietnam; Wallace, George C.

BIBLIOGRAPHY. Albert Eisele, *Almost to the Presidency: A Biography of Two American Politicians* (Piper, 1972); L.L. Gould, *1968: The Election That Changed America* (Ivan R. Dee, 1993); David Lebedoff, *Ward Number Six* (Scribner, 1972); Kevin Phillips, *The Emerging Republican Majority* (Arlington House, 1969); Dennis Wainstock, *The Turning Point: The 1968 United States Presidential Campaign* (McFarland, 1988).

TONY L. HILL
MASSACHUSETTS INSTITUTE OF TECHNOLOGY

Presidential Election of 1972

PEOPLE REMEMBER THE presidential election of 1972 most often for its connection to Watergate, but its importance went beyond dirty tricks or the break-in at the Democratic National Committee headquarters by Nixon operatives. The election was significant because it marked the beginning of the rise of conservatism as a major political force, as well as the decline of liberalism.

The nominations of Richard Nixon and George McGovern to the head the Republican and Democratic tickets, respectively, indicated party responses to the social, economic, and political situations arising from the tumultuous 1960s. By 1972, the social turmoil created by the Civil Rights Movement and the Vietnam War started to recede, while the country's economic situation continued to deteriorate. Moreover, Americans' faith in government-sponsored solutions began to decline by the early 1970s, pushing the electorate to the right of center.

THE CANDIDATES

As the incumbent, Richard Nixon seemed the likely nominee for the Republican Party in 1972. During his first term, Nixon looked for policies that would appeal across a broad political spectrum to the silent majority. His foreign policy initiatives—namely, détente with the Soviet Union and China—helped define his image as a

man of peace and grand vision. Moreover, the New Economic Policy outlined in August 1971, including wage and price controls, gave the impression that Nixon had taken steps to curb inflation and unemployment. However, Nixon faced challenges for the Republican nomination. On the left, Pete McCloskey, a congressman from California, ran on an anti-Vietnam War platform. On the right, John Ashbrook, a congressman from Ohio, objected more generally to the liberalism of Nixon's foreign and domestic policies. Nixon won all of the primaries he entered. McCloskey and Ashbrook never made a dent in his drive for re-election.

On the Democratic side, several candidates fought for the party's nomination. Edmund Muskie, a Senator from Maine, emerged as an early frontrunner. However, his campaign lost steam after the New Hampshire primary. George McGovern, a senator from South Dakota with a doctorate in history, made a strong showing in the Florida and Wisconsin primaries where he focused on the Vietnam War, inflation, and taxes. George Wallace, Alabama's governor, ran on a socially conservative platform that stressed limited government. Wallace remained a strong contender for the nomination until an assassination attempt on May 15, 1972, caused him to pull out of the race. Hubert Humphrey, the former vice president and presidential nominee in 1968, entered the race before the California primary in June. He represented the interests of Democrats who saw the party moving too far to the left. While McGovern won in California, Humphrey's challenge foreshadowed the problems arising at the convention in July.

THE CONVENTIONS

Although the Democrats made a major effort to reform the selection process for delegates and make the state delegations more representative of the population before 1972, divisions within the party still plagued them at their convention in Miami, from July 10 to July 13. George McGovern easily won the nomination. Selecting Thomas Eagleton as the vice presidential nominee was challenging because of the number of candidates in the running. However, platform deliberations proved even more troublesome, particularly with respect to Vietnam and civil rights. Party regulars felt increasingly distant from the proceedings and the resulting platform, as the convention had more women (38 percent), African Americans (15 percent), and youth (23 percent) representatives than ever before.

The Democrats, while not going as far as McGovern did in his primary campaign, called for a lower defense budget and income supplements for the poor in their platform. They pledged to find jobs for the unemployed, bring down inflation through better government management, to end unjust tax practices, distribute the cost of government more equitably among all income classes, secure an immediate withdrawal from Vietnam, oppose the draft, support gun control, and fight capital punishment.

When the Republicans met in Miami Beach from August 21 to 23, Richard Nixon and his running mate, Spiro Agnew, easily won renomination. The Committee to Re-elect the President carefully managed the entire convention to show the president in the best possible light—especially for the television cameras. The White House also wrote most of the Republican platform, which responded to the Democrats' platform, and celebrated the administration's ability to restore order, reason, and hope.

Specifically, the Republican platform pledged to uphold Nixon's strategy of peace, which would contribute to increased national strength. It also renewed Nixon's promise to end the war in Vietnam honorably. Domestically, the Republicans pledged to be the party of prosperity through monetary policies to cut inflation, responsible budgets to expand the economy, and reforms in the tax code to spread the burden more equitably. Finally, they pledged to improve the quality of life in America by making government more responsive to individual needs.

THE CAMPAIGNS

Richard Nixon campaigned with the slogan "Nixon: Now More than Ever." He successfully emphasized issues that appealed to average Americans, including limited government intrusion, family values, and self-reliance. Nixon employed a Rose Garden strategy, one that capitalized on his incumbency, making only five public appearances in support of his re-election after the convention. The approach allowed him to highlight his leadership and it allowed him to avoid a campaign that would alienate voters disgruntled with the Democratic Party.

Nixon also looked to illegal political avenues to help determine the course of the election. The results of the 1970 congressional races pushed Nixon to a more aggressive effort against potential opponents in both parties. His re-election team started using dirty tricks—including forging documents, leaking false statements, and canceling appearances by Democratic candidates—

to discredit opponents on a scale beyond anything seen in previous elections in the 20th century. The operations, some more sinister than others, eventually led to the break-in at the Democratic National Committee headquarters at the Watergate, for purposes of political espionage. Nixon knew the basic outline of the dirty tricks program, but was unaware of its specific details until after the Watergate burglary became public knowledge. Revelations about the break-in had little effect on the election in November.

George McGovern's campaign received little in the way of a post-convention boost because of the divisions in Miami. Then, the Eagleton Affair hampered his bid for the presidency even more; the media reported that the vice presidential nominee had been treated for depression and mental fatigue. McGovern stood behind his running mate at first, but eventually conceded that he would have to withdraw from the race. Party leaders forced Eagleton from the ticket, claiming he weakened the entire party, and replaced him with R. Sargent Shriver (a Kennedy family in-law). The party's decision hurt McGovern's image as a principled man because he had supported Eagleton "1,000 percent."

Moreover, McGovern's campaign strategy proved ineffective in attacking the Nixon machine. His campaign slogan "Come Home America" had appeal, but McGovern failed to convince many voters that he was not as radical as his opponents painted him, or that Nixon's solutions had failed to resolve the country's problems. He also found it difficult to balance his supporters and his opponents in the Democratic Party. Many Democratic politicians refused to endorse McGovern's campaign because the platform focused too much on cultural, and not enough on economic, issues.

THE RESULTS

On Election Day, November 7, 1972, only about 55 percent of those eligible voted. Richard Nixon easily outpolled the George McGovern, as well as a host of Independent candidates, including John Hospers (Libertarian), John Schmitz (American), Benjamin Spock (People's Party), and Linda Jenness (Socialist Workers). Nixon took close to 61 percent of the popular vote to McGovern's 38 percent, while the rest of the candidates polled less than two percent of the ballots cast.

McGovern did not even win his home state of South Dakota, taking only Massachusetts and the District of Columbia. Nixon received 520 electoral votes to McGovern's 17 (one elector, pledged to Nixon, cast his vote for Hospers instead). The presidential election of 1972 ultimately showed that the United States had begun the process of moving away from the tumultuous 1960s, toward the seemingly more traditional American values that became politicized by the 1980 election.

SEE ALSO: Civil Rights; Presidential Election of 1968; Presidential Election of 1980; Vietnam; Watergate.

BIBLIOGRAPHY. W.C. Berman, *America's Right Turn* (Johns Hopkins University Press, 1998); P.F. Boller, *Presidential Campaigns* (Oxford University Press, 1984); Peter Carroll, *It Seemed Like Nothing Happened* (Rutgers University Press, 1982); George McGovern, *Grassroots: The Autobiography of George McGovern* (Random House, 1977); Richard Nixon, *RN: The Memoirs of Richard Nixon* (Simon & Schuster, 1990); Melvin Small, *The Presidency of Richard Nixon* (University of Kansas Press, 1999); R.P. Watson, ed., *George McGovern: A Political Life, A Political Legacy* (South Dakota State Historical Press, 2004).

SARAH KATHERINE MERGEL
GEORGE WASHINGTON UNIVERSITY

Presidential Election of 1976

THE PRESIDENTIAL ELECTION of 1976, pitting Republican Gerald Ford against Democrat Jimmy Carter, focused primarily on the perception of the candidates, not policy issues. Richard Nixon's forced resignation after Watergate created a political and social crisis in the United States. Americans lost faith in their government and questioned the social and cultural changes since the 1960s. Moreover, stagflation—high inflation and high unemployment—took hold because of the oil embargo in 1973, and worldwide food shortages. While Americans cared about the deteriorating economic solution, they really wanted a leader to restore their faith in themselves and in their country. Both Carter and Ford tailored their campaigns to that desire.

Gerald Ford, who succeeded Richard Nixon when Nixon resigned, seemed the likely candidate for the Republican nomination. However, Ronald Reagan entered the primaries to challenge Ford from the right. Ford, a moderate from Michigan, benefited from his incumbency and the resources it provided, but he struggled to stop Reagan's early momentum. Voters remained concerned about Ford's leadership qualities, especially because he pardoned Nixon. Conservative Republicans had supported Reagan in 1968, and he emerged as their candidate of choice, again, in 1976. Reagan, since his first run for governor of California in 1966, successfully sold conservatism to a wider audience—especially the merits of limited government.

Ford narrowly defeated Reagan in the New Hampshire primary, but Reagan continued his fight, attacking Ford on détente and negotiations on the future of the Panama Canal. Ford and Reagan split the remaining primaries; Ford took the northeast and midwest, while Reagan prevailed in the Sunbelt. As the convention approached, Ford and Reagan looked to secure uncommitted delegates. Ford dropped Vice President Nelson Rockefeller as a possible running mate because conservatives considered him too liberal. Reagan, in an unusual step, announced he preferred Richard Schweiker, a liberal from Pennsylvania, for the second spot.

Divisions in the Democratic Party made for a crowded field, including Morris Udall, Henry Jackson, George Wallace, Jimmy Carter, Pat Brown, and Frank Church. Each candidate appealed to a different wing of the party—Udall for liberal intellectuals, Jackson for cold warriors, Wallace for social conservatives, and Church for party regulars. Jimmy Carter attracted supporters in several of these groups and became an early frontrunner, with wins in the Iowa Caucus and the New Hampshire Primary.

Carter used the expanding number of primaries to his advantage. He took the campaign to the people, drawing on populist themes and his outsider status. Carter appealed to his image as a common man with a missionary message. He knocked out Wallace in Florida, Jackson in Pennsylvania, and Udall after Michigan and Wisconsin. While Church and Brown challenged Carter in California, these latecomers simply did not have enough time to build up support before the convention. Carter's victory in Ohio, and his support from Richard Daley's Democratic Party machine in Chicago, meant he possessed a solid lead before the convention.

When the Democrats met in New York City from July 12 to July 15, the delegates nominated Jimmy Carter on the first ballot. In Carter, they found a candidate able to lessen the party's image as ideologically extreme after McGovern's defeat in 1972. Carter selected Walter Mondale, a liberal senator from Minnesota, as his choice for

Gerald Ford (center, right) struggled to stop Ronald Reagan's early momentum; conservative Republicans had supported Reagan (center, left) in 1968, and the vote was very close at the convention of 1976.

vice president. Carter opened his acceptance speech simply by saying: "My name is Jimmy Carter, and I'm running for President." Then he emphasized that it was not only a year for hope and inspiration, but also a year to give the government back to the people and get the country moving again.

The Republicans chose Gerald Ford at their convention in Kansas City, August 16 to August 19. Ford, with 1,187 votes, narrowly edged out Reagan, with 1,070 votes, on the first ballot. Ford chose Robert Dole, a conservative senator from Kansas, as his running mate, although some delegates wanted him to choose Reagan. In his acceptance speech, Ford mended fences with conservatives in the party, and showed his capacity for vigor. Ford highlighted his administration's efforts to combat inflation and placed blame for continued increases in the hands of the Democratic Congress. He looked toward building an America "where people feel proud about themselves and about their country." Finally, Ford

proclaimed to like what he saw about America and reaffirmed his commitment to do right by the country.

Both parties hoped to see their platforms unify their members. The Democratic platform seemed more liberal than some observers expected given that Carter portrayed himself as a conservative populist. Specifically, it highlighted Republican misuse and mismanagement of the national government, which only caused hardship for Americans. The Republican platform suggested that the Democrats planned to further burden taxpayers with more government programs, whereas they proposed using the private sector to meet the needs of the people. The Republicans took a conservative position on foreign policy, essentially denouncing Ford's previous stances. However, Ford went along in the name of party unity. The platforms differed on several issues. The Republicans wanted to end deficit spending to solve unemployment, whereas the Democrats sought to increase spending to help put people to work. The Republicans supported an amendment to protect the unborn, while the Democrats opposed any restrictions on abortion. The Democrats hoped to enact a federally financed health insurance program; the Republicans extolled the virtues of private insurance. The Republicans called for more spending on advanced weapons systems and an increase in the size of the armed forces; the Democrats sought overall reductions in the defense budget.

Jimmy Carter had a significant lead in the polls after the summer conventions. As the election drew closer, Gerald Ford closed the gap. For the first time since 1960, the candidates engaged in public debates sponsored by the League of Women Voters. However, these debates gave little indication of what the candidates would do if elected. Ford's campaign strategy centered on his incumbency and stressed his integrity, fiscal conservatism, and patriotism. He sought to assure voters that he was the safe choice and that he was an effective leader. The Ford team focused their efforts in the northeast, midwest, and West. Ford also avoided partisan attacks on his opponent in hopes of drawing voters from across party lines. Carter based his campaign on his outsider status, his religious values, and his southern roots. He proposed to be "a leader for change." Carter used the economic situation to his advantage and hit Ford hard on the misery index—a phrase used to describe inflation and unemployment rates. Confident that he had the south, Carter focused on attracting voters in the west.

THE RESULTS
When Election Day arrived, the candidates remained locked in a dead heat. The final tally showed that Carter won 50 percent of the popular voter to Ford's 48 percent. Third-party candidates—including Eugene McCarthy (no affiliation), Roger MacBride (Libertarian), Lester Maddox (American Independent), Thomas Anderson (American), and Peter Camejo (Socialist Workers)— accounted for less than two percent of cast ballots. With victories in 23 states, Carter won the electoral vote 297 to 240. He took the south, except Virginia, and portions of the northeast and midwest. Although Ford had a solid hold on the west, Carter managed to pull in voters lost to Nixon in 1972, because of his social conservatism.

The presidential election of 1976 reasserted, albeit briefly, the importance of party affiliation in presidential politics. By not focusing on the issues, Ford and Carter allowed the voters the opportunity to make their decisions based on presence and style. In the end, voters concluded, if only by a slight margin, that Jimmy Carter would better help the country move out of its economic slump and its post-Watergate mindset.

SEE ALSO: Delegates, Convention; Economy; Populists and Populist Movements; Presidential Election of 1972; Watergate.

BIBLIOGRAPHY. Patrick Anderson, *Electing Jimmy Carter* (Louisiana State Press, 1994); W.C. Berman, *America's Right Turn: From Nixon to Clinton* (Johns Hopkins University Press, 1998); P.F. Boller, *Presidential Campaigns* (Oxford University Press, 1984); Peter Carroll, *It Seemed Like Nothing Happened* (Rutgers University Press, 1982); Jimmy Carter, *Why Not the Best* (Broadman, 1975); J.R. Coyne, Jr., "Eating Crow in California," *National Review* (v.28, 1976); Gerald Ford, *A Time to Heal* (Harper & Row, 1979); J.D. Gopoian, "Issue Preference and Candidate Choice," *American Journal of Political Science* (v.26, 1982); Jules Witcover, *Marathon* (New American Library, 1978).

SARAH KATHERINE MERGEL
THE GEORGE WASHINGTON UNIVERSITY

Presidential Election of 1980

THE 1980 PRESIDENTIAL election arrived on the heels of a tumultuous first term for President Jimmy Carter. During the previous four years, Carter had struggled with a major economic downturn, an energy crisis, increased foreign threats (particularly from Iran and the Soviet Union), and an overall decline in patriotism and morale among the American citizenry. In a speech delivered on July 15, 1979, Carter lamented these troubles and declared that Americans were experiencing a crisis of confidence.

Taking advantage of Carter's troubles, Ronald Reagan entered the 1980 election with a promise to restore America's prosperity, strength, and patriotism. Throughout his campaign for the presidency, Reagan focused on Carter's failure to solve the country's foreign and domestic woes. In the end, discontent among the electorate paved the way for Reagan's ascension to the presidency.

THE 1980 PRESIDENTIAL PRIMARY CAMPAIGN
In early 1979, Carter found himself at risk of having his re-election chances foiled by a primary challenger. The strongest challenge came from Massachusetts Senator

Edward "Ted" Kennedy, although others such as William Proxmire and Jerry Brown, also posed a threat. Kennedy hoped that Carter's negative image and poor first-term performance would allow him to surpass the incumbent as the Democratic Party's choice for presidential candidate. In fact, early public survey polls indicated that Democrats favored Kennedy over Carter by nearly a two-thirds margin. Fortunately for Carter, however, Ted Kennedy was unable to make a strong case for his candidacy. During a number of key interviews with the media at the outset of his campaign, Kennedy struggled to provide a clear explanation of his policy views and his motivations for entering the campaign.

Not long afterward, a sudden crisis emerged when Iran took 63 Americans hostage in Tehran. In response, the American public immediately rallied behind Carter to display their patriotism and to show support for the hostages. However, Carter's support would later diminish after a botched rescue attempt, Operation Eagle Claw, on April 24, 1980, left eight servicemen dead and forced Carter to abort the mission.

After Kennedy's missteps and the rally effect in the wake of the hostage crisis, Carter regained support in the polls and eventually beat Kennedy in the key primary battles in Iowa and New Hampshire. Carter then followed with victories in nearly all the remaining primary elections, save for Kennedy's expected victory in the Massachusetts primary and a couple of surprise victories in New York and Connecticut. Thereafter, at the 1980 Democratic convention, delegates once again nominated Carter as the party's candidate for president.

The primary battle for the Republican Party nomination produced a much wider array of aspiring candidates, including Ronald Reagan, George H.W. Bush, John Anderson, Howard Baker, John Connally, Phil Crane, and Bob Dole. Having nearly defeated Gerald Ford in the 1976 Republican primary, Ronald Reagan began as a hands-down favorite for the candidacy, until George H.W. Bush pulled a surprising victory over Reagan in the opening Iowa primary election. Reagan responded with a strong showing at a debate sponsored by the *Nashua Telegraph*. Reagan went on to receive the nomination of the Republican Party by an overwhelming margin.

Soon afterward, Reagan began to court Gerald Ford to be his running mate, but Ford declined. Thus, despite Reagan and Bush's hostility toward each other during the primary campaign, Reagan eventually chose Bush as his running mate and soon developed a close friendship and working relationship with the former Central Intelligence Agency director and future 41st president.

THE GENERAL ELECTION

As with previous presidential elections, Carter and Reagan both began their general election campaigns on Labor Day. Carter chose the city of Tuscumbia in Alabama as the site of his official re-election campaign kick-off. In a bid to warm up to southerners, Carter encircled himself with an arsenal of top southern politicians and labor leaders. In the meantime, Reagan gave his speech on the Hudson River waterfront in New Jersey in front of the Statue of Liberty. His campaign team framed the event as an "ethnic picnic" and Reagan drew the attendance and support of, among others, Stanislaw Walesa, the father of the leader of the Polish Workers' movement against Communism and the Soviet Union.

During the general election, Reagan focused on Carter's record, often referring to Carter's performance as a failure. In contrast, Carter focused more on Reagan's character, referring to Reagan as someone who preferred war to peace, who did not care about the working class, and who supported policies that would worsen class and racial cleavages across the country. Although he denied calling Reagan a racist, Carter often suggested indirectly that Reagan had racist leanings. He pointed to Reagan's use of the term "states' rights" as an indication that Reagan was using "code words" to pander to those who opposed the Civil Rights Movement.

Reagan reacted to Carter's attacks mildly, by downplaying their importance and using terms such as "saddened" and "surprised" in reaction to the claims. This tactic, coupled with Reagan's continued focus on attacking Carter's performance record without attacking his character led much of the media to interpret Carter's attacks as a sign of weakness and as a reflection of Carter's inability to draw attention away from the economic downturn or the worsening Iran hostage crisis.

THE PRESIDENTIAL DEBATES

For some observers of the 1980 election, the presidential debates played a key role in propelling Reagan ahead of Carter in the polls. The first presidential debate took place in Baltimore, Maryland, on September 21. Although, as with most presidential debates, very few people watched or recalled the key exchanges between the candidates, one fact did appear to make a significant impact on the campaign: President Carter's absence from the debate. Carter refused to participate when he learned that the Independent candidate, John Anderson, would attend. Consequently, the media widely criticized his absence. By October, polls taken at the state level indicated a strong and growing lead for Reagan, although the national polls continued to suggest a close race. That same month, observers witnessed a shift in the polls toward Carter, stemming mainly from increased negative media coverage concerning Reagan's shift from the right to the center of the voting spectrum since the primary campaign.

A week before the election, however, Reagan and Carter clashed in a key final debate in Cleveland, Ohio. Because the debate occurred so close to the day of the election, it received an unusually large amount of attention in the media. Moreover, post-debate surveys revealed that a surprising percentage of viewers who identified themselves as Democrats and an even greater percentage of Independents indicated that Reagan's performance impressed them more than Carter's, and that the debate would have a notable influence their vote choice. Although subsequent media coverage scored the final debate as "fairly even," most coverage also took note of the public's positive reaction to Reagan and highlighted Reagan's rhetorical skills during the event. News outlets also took special note of Reagan's memorable closing statement, in which he directed voters to ask themselves whether they were better off in the present-day than they were four years before.

ELEVENTH-HOUR DRAMA

In the final days leading to the election, the likelihood of Reagan's victory continued to increase. However, both campaign teams experienced a brief jolt when news suddenly emerged that the Iranian government might allow the American hostages to return home under certain conditions. Immediately, the Carter camp rushed the president back to Washington, D.C., in dramatic fashion to readdress the crisis.

After mulling over the demands of Iran, Carter decided to reject what he viewed as unacceptable terms of release the Sunday before the election. In the end, the Iranian government would not release the captives until after the election was over. On the eve of the election, the final polling numbers indicated that Reagan was ahead, but not by much. In fact, most pollsters claimed that the election was too close to call, with only the Harris

poll displaying enough confidence to predict Reagan's impending victory.

REAGAN'S VICTORY

Reagan's 1980 election victory was an overwhelming success. In total, Reagan received nearly 44 million votes, compared to Carter's 35.5 million. Reagan also clinched 44 out of the 50 states, which gave him 489 out of a possible 538 electoral votes. In comparison, Carter carried only his home state of Georgia, Maryland, Minnesota, Rhode Island, West Virginia, Hawaii, and the District of Columbia. Reagan also received a majority of the vote, with 50.7 percent, compared to Carter's 41 percent, and Independent John Anderson's 6.6 percent. Overall, Reagan achieved a narrow popular vote majority and a historically large Electoral College majority. Across states, Reagan was most successful in the prairie and mountain states in the west, claiming a 20-plus-percent margin of victory in seven of those states. Reagan also dominated in the south, even though he achieved most of his southern victories by five percent or less. Although Reagan's national support waned among minority, low-income, and working-class voters, Reagan nevertheless received an overall wide degree of support across most of the national electorate.

Reagan also witnessed a changing of the guards in the Senate, where Republicans gained 12 seats to take control of the upper chamber. Republicans also added 33 seats in the House, although Democrats retained their majority control. In retrospect, the American public voted for change in 1980, because of a national sense of discontent with Carter's first-term performance. Americans elected Ronald W. Reagan, remembered as the Great Communicator, as the 40th president of the United States.

SEE ALSO: Campaigns, Presidential; Nomination Process, Presidential; Presidential Debates; Presidential Elections; Presidential Primaries.

BIBLIOGRAPHY. P.R. Abramson, J.H. Aldrich, and D.W. Rhode, *Change and Continuity in the 1980 Elections* (CQ Press, 1980); A.E. Busch, *Reagan's Victory: The Presidential Election of 1980 and the Rise of the Right* (University Press of Kansas, 2005); Elizabeth Drew, *Portrait of an Election: The 1980 Presidential Campaign* (Simon and Schuster, 1981); J.W. Germond and Jules Witcover, *Blue Smoke and Mirrors: How Reagan Won and Why Carter Lost the Election of 1980* (Viking

Press, 1980); Richard Harwood, ed., *The Pursuit of the Presidency 1980* (Berkley Books, 1980); Jonathan Moore, *The Campaign for President: 1980 in Retrospect* (Ballinger, 1981); G.M. Pomper, ed., *The Election of 1980: Reports and Interpretations* (Chatham House Publisher's Inc., 1980); Austin Ranny, ed., *The American Elections of 1980* (American Enterprise Institute, 1981); K.W. Ritter, ed., "The 1980 Presidential Debates," *Speaker and Gavel* (v.18/2, 1981); Ellis Sandoz and C.V. Crabb, Jr., eds., *A Tide of Discontent: The 1980 Elections and Their Meaning* (CQ Press, 1981).

José D. Villalobos
Texas A&M University

Presidential Election of 1984

THE PRESIDENTIAL ELECTION of 1984 was fought between incumbent President Ronald Reagan for the Republican Party, and former Vice President Walter Mondale for the Democratic Party. Reagan's running mate was Vice President George H.W. Bush, and Mondale's running mate was Representative Geraldine Ferraro of New York. Reagan won with nearly 60 percent of the popular vote and an overwhelming 525 out of 538 electoral votes, while Mondale carried only his home state of Minnesota (which he won by barely 4,000 votes) and the District of Columbia. Reagan's landslide victory was the worst defeat for any Democratic presidential candidate in U.S. history.

Reagan was elected in 1980 on a platform of tax cuts and deregulation, but during his first term in office, his popularity ratings were among the lowest ratings received by first-term presidents elected since 1945. In late October 1983, near the start of the 1984 presidential campaign season, Reagan's foreign policy experienced both severe crisis and notable success in the course of approximately 72 hours.

On October 23, 1983, two truck bombs struck the barracks that housed members of the U.S. and French military forces in Beirut, Lebanon, killing 241 U.S. Marines and 58 French soldiers. The U.S. military had been sent as part of a peacekeeping force in the Lebanese civil war, and the devastating bombing renewed calls by Reagan's political opponents to remove U.S. troops from Lebanon. This particular low point of Reagan's foreign policy was followed two days later by the successful invasion of the Caribbean island of Grenada, where the U.S. military was able to overthrow a hard-line Marxist government that had been established by a coup on October 19. The invasion was condemned by a number of American allies—not least of who was British Prime Minister Margaret Thatcher—and Democratic presidential candidates criticized Reagan's decision to invade as "trigger-happy" gunboat diplomacy. Yet in contrast to the bombings in Lebanon, the invasion of Grenada was fast and successful with very minor casualties, and the resulting publicity was a public-relations coup for Reagan's foreign policy. Both Reagan and Bush were renominated at the Republican National Convention in Dallas, Texas, in the summer of 1984.

In contrast, the race for the Democratic nomination featured many candidates, all of whom hoped to capitalize on Reagan's unpopular domestic and foreign policies, and appeal to voters. The initial primaries reduced the candidates to two; Senator Gary Hart from Colorado and former Vice President Walter Mondale. Hart and Mondale ran a close race in the primaries, with Hart winning the important New Hampshire, Ohio, and California primaries, and showing stronger support in the western states.

A third candidate, the Reverend Jesse L. Jackson of Illinois, came in third behind Mondale and Hart. Jackson was the second African American to run for the presidency, and he had managed to gain backing from minority voters. But at the Democratic National Convention, in San Francisco, California, Jackson received less than 500 votes to Hart's 1,200, and both of them trailed the nearly 2,200 votes that Mondale received. As the presidential nominee, Mondale chose the New York City-based Representative Geraldine Ferraro as his running mate.

Mondale's choice of Ferraro as a running mate added a new dimension to the 1984 election campaign. Rather than selecting the runner-up Gary Hart, Mondale made history by nominating the first woman candidate for vice president—a tactic that was highly praised at the convention, but did little to bring Hart's supporters in the west to Mondale's side. Some of Hart's supporters criticized Mondale's choice as an attempt to pander to special interest groups, a charge that Mondale was frequently accused of over the course of the campaign.

Reagan, in his own defense, was forced to point out his track record of appointing women to high positions, such as Supreme Court Justice Sandra Day

O'Connor, United Nations Ambassador Jeane Kirkpatrick, and cabinet members Margaret Heckler and Elizabeth Dole.

However, the high-profile nature of Ferraro's nomination added to the crisis that hit the Mondale-Ferraro campaign in the summer of 1984. There was confusion over whether Ferraro would release both her tax returns and financial statements and those of her husband, real estate agent John Zaccaro. When Ferraro first agreed to do so, then stated that she would release only her own, then refused to release her husband's financial statements even when pressed, press speculation circulated that Zaccaro had connections to shady business dealing and real estate transactions.

Ferraro managed to save her campaign in a well-spoken press conference on August 21, but Mondale had been conspicuously absent during the whole ordeal. He had made a statement of support for her, but the weak statement and his lack of visible support for her damaged public perceptions of both of them. The increased scrutiny of Ferraro as a running mate proved problematic for Mondale, and he found himself badly prepared to handle a potential financial scandal.

THE CAMPAIGNS

The presidential campaign between Mondale-Ferraro and Reagan-Bush focused heavily on Reagan's administration of the economy and his defense policies. In his acceptance speech at the Democratic Convention, Mondale said that while both he and Reagan intended to raise taxes, he would admit to it while Reagan would not. The attempt to depict Reagan as a hypocrite made it seem as if Mondale had just made raising taxes a part of his campaign platform, and this was the statement that was most remembered by voters.

The Reagan campaign also used television advertisements very effectively to promote Reagan's strength on economic issues—the campaign commercial widely known as "Morning in America" stated that economic improvements were the result of Reagan's wise economic policy choices, in contrast with the economic fiascoes of the Carter years. Another memorable Reagan commercial highlighted the administration's careful defense policy, hinting that there was a "bear in the woods" that might or might not be harmless—a transparent reference to the perceived threat of the Soviet Union's military strength. These commercials highlighted the degree to which the Republican's simple messages of economic growth and national security appealed to voters during the 1984 campaign.

THE OUTCOME

The outcome of the election was a landslide victory for Reagan. Mondale just barely won the 10 electoral votes of his home state of Minnesota, and the three electoral votes of the District of Columbia. The congressional elections were more reassuring for the Democratic Party, as the presidential victory did not translate to a Republican majority in Congress. Though the Republicans gained seats in the House, the Democrats gained seats in the Senate and kept the overall majority in both houses.

There are two main reasons that Reagan won and Mondale lost the 1984 election. The first is the straightforward fact that it is difficult for a presidential challenger to defeat the incumbent in a time of peace and prosperity, especially when the incumbent has managed to avoid aggravating the public to the point of losing votes. The second reason concerned the 1980 presidential election, when Mondale ran as Carter's vice president. In 1984, Mondale was the ideal candidate for a Republican opponent. A vote for Mondale, Carter's vice president, would suggest that the presidential election of 1980 had been a mistake and that the nation would be better off returning to the status quo before Reagan had entered office: higher taxes, high inflation, high unemployment, and a sense that the United States had been weakened on national and international levels.

Reagan was re-elected because voters believed that he had succeed where Carter had failed, and the campaign of 1984 was almost more of a vote against Carter than it was a vote for Reagan. Reagan had been able to convince the voters in 1980 that he was a viable alternative to Carter. As such, it is doubtful that any Democratic ticket, regardless of the combination of presidential and vice presidential candidates, could have unseated the incumbent Reagan in 1984. When the Democrats nominated Carter's vice president in 1984, it was an open invitation for the voters to repeat the last few years of the 1970s, and the voters clearly indicated that they had no intention of doing so.

A political phenomenon that came to particular attention in the 1984 election was a group of voters referred to as "Reagan Democrats"—people who normally considered themselves Democrats, but who voted for Reagan.

An examination of the group showed that the average Reagan Democrat was a southern white or northern working-class (blue-collar) voter, who supported Reagan because he or she regarded Reagan as strong on national security and strict on economic reforms. Reagan Democrats regarded the actual Democratic Party as being too concerned with supporting the poor and the unemployed at the expense of the hard-working middle class taxpayers, as being too attached to special interest groups such as minorities and women's rights organizations, and as insufficiently strict on moral issues such as pornography, birth control, and abortion. The existence of Reagan Democrats indicated the degree to which the Democratic Party had lost touch with the working-class voters who had once provided its core of support.

The 1984 election also pointed to the impact that party unity, or the perception of party unity, can have on a presidential candidate's chances of success. Beginning with Lyndon Johnson's election in 1964, the winner of each presidential election was the candidate with the most united party. Even as party unity became more difficult to achieve with the passage of time, it acquired greater importance to both candidates and voters.

In 1984, Mondale and Ferraro were running on the ticket of a divided and demoralized party. The Democratic Party was caught up in a generational and class-based clash that pitted the older and more socially conservative working-class whites against a wealthier, better educated, and more liberal younger generation. Walter Mondale was one of the last of the New Deal liberals, and had been involved in Democratic politics since the days of the Truman administration, but he was ill equipped to cope with the sea change in the demographics of his party. He failed to appreciate the power of television in campaigning, particularly when it came to the campaign advertisements that had made Reagan's campaign so memorable. Even Mondale's fellow Democrats accused him of pandering to special interest groups (in his nomination of Ferraro), making him seem out of touch. His loss indicated the degree to which the Democratic Party would have to reform and redefine itself and its electoral base before it would be able to win a national election once more.

The presidential election of 1984 was more the result of personal triumphs rather than the specific success of the Republican Party as a political unit. Reagan had polarized the electorate to a much greater degree than any candidate had since the end of World War II, but in the end the electorate voted for Reagan's specific accomplishments: tax cuts, deregulation, and a general improvement of the U.S. economy. He was a safe choice, and the election itself changed very little about the political landscape. The "Morning in America" commercial had ended with the tagline "Ronald Reagan—Leadership That's Working." As a result, the prospect of a return to the high inflation and unemployment of the Carter years seemed to have prompted voters to vote for the leadership that they felt was working—even though they may not have always agreed with the specific policy decisions that the current leader chose to make.

SEE ALSO: Advertising, Campaign; Presidential Election of 1980.

BIBLIOGRAPHY. John Forest, *Warriors of the Political Arena: The Presidential Election of 1984* (Vantage Press, 1986); T.R. Marmor, "The Lessons of Mondale's Defeat," *Political Quarterly* (v.56, 1985); N.W. Polsby, "Party Realignment in the 1980 Election," *Yale Review* (v.72, 1982); Austin Ranney, ed., *The American Elections of 1984* (Duke University Press, 1985); William Schneider, "The Jewish Vote in 1984: Elements in a Controversy," *Public Opinion* (December–January, 1985); K.W. Thompson, ed., *Lessons from Defeated Presidential Candidates* (University Press of America, 1994); M.P. Wattenberg, *The Rise of Candidate-Centered Politics: Presidential Elections of the 1980s* (Harvard University Press, 1991).

SHANNON GRANVILLE
INDEPENDENT SCHOLAR

Presidential Election of 1988

THE 1988 PRESIDENTIAL election was the first election in 20 years that did not feature a president seeking re-election. Ronald Reagan, elected in 1980 and re-elected in 1984, was barred by the Twenty-Second Amendment from seeking a third term. Vice President George H.W. Bush won the Republican Party's nomination, while the Democrats nominated Michael S. Dukakis, the governor of Massachusetts. Bush, relying on Reagan's popularity, handily defeated Dukakis.

The Democrats were optimistic going into 1988. The party re-captured control of the U.S. Senate in the 1986 midterm elections, ending six years of Republican control. The departure of President Reagan, a former Democrat, from the political scene heartened the Democrats, and encouraged a number of candidates to enter the contest for the party's presidential nomination.

THE DEMOCRATS

The Democratic field included Bruce E. Babbitt, who had served as governor of Arizona 1978–87; three United States Senators: Joseph R. Biden, Jr., (Delaware), Albert A. Gore, Jr. (Tennessee), and Paul M. Simon (Illinois); Governor Dukakis; two members of the House of Representatives: Richard A. Gephardt (Missouri) and Patricia Schroeder (Colorado); and two candidates who had sought the nomination in 1984: former U.S. Senator Gary Hart and the Reverend Jesse L. Jackson. New York Governor Mario Cuomo, who emerged as a national figure after his keynote address at the 1984 Democratic Convention, was urged to run by many Democratic leaders, but ultimately remained on the sidelines.

Hart, who had run a very strong race for the nomination against former Vice President Walter Mondale in 1984, was considered to be the early frontrunner in the campaign. Hart was leading in the polls when, on May 2, 1987, the *Miami Herald* reported that the former senator was involved in an extramarital affair with Donna Rice, a 29-year old model and actress. The *Herald* reported that two of their reporters had observed Hart and Rice entering his Washington home on two consecutive evenings and the paper published a picture of Rice sitting in Hart's lap on board his boat. While initially denying that he was having an affair, Hart withdrew from the race a week after the story was published. Hart would re-enter the race in December 1987. However, the scandal had already damaged his prospects.

Senator Biden would also see his campaign collapse under the weight of a scandal. A videotape was released in which Biden gave a speech in Iowa that was found to have been, nearly word for word, a speech given by Neil Kinnock, the leader of the British Labor Party. There were also allegations that Biden had committed plagiarism while a student at the Syracuse University College of Law. Biden withdrew from the race in late September 1987. After first denying that his campaign had anything to do with exposing Biden, Governor Dukakis revealed that his campaign had supplied the tape to the news media, and he fired campaign manager John Sasso.

Congresswoman Schroeder also withdrew in September 1987. Schroeder, who had traveled the country

Dukakis hoped that the "election would not be about ideology, but competence," but failed to counter Republican attacks.

to determine if she should get into the race, said she was not running because she believed she would be unable to maintain personal contact with the voters. During the press conference where she made her announcement, Schroeder burst into tears and was comforted by her husband. As the caucuses and primaries began in early 1988, no frontrunner emerged. Gephardt, who ran television advertisements criticizing the protectionist trade policies of South Korea and Japan, won the Iowa caucuses and an early primary in South Dakota. However, Gephardt was targeted in negative advertisements by the Dukakis campaign, which criticized him for flip-flopping votes in Congress. Gephardt's campaign was staggered by the decision of the United Auto Workers to rescind their endorsement of his candidacy, and he dropped out after doing poorly in the Super Tuesday round of primaries.

Dukakis won New Hampshire's first in the nation primary, as Babbitt, who had advocated a national sales tax, dropped out. Super Tuesday demonstrated how fragmented the Democratic field remained, as Dukakis won six primaries, Gore and Jackson each won five, and Gephardt won one. Native Son Paul Simon won the Illinois primary, and the nomination was not really decided until Dukakis defeated Gore and Jackson in the New York primary. At the Democratic convention held in Atlanta, the Democrats nominated Dukakis and Texas Senator Lloyd Bentsen as his running mate. Bentsen was selected to help the Democrats carry Texas.

THE REPUBLICANS

Vice President Bush was the frontrunner in his second campaign for the presidency. In 1980, Bush had campaigned against Reagan as a moderate, at one point describing the former Californian's economic plan as "voodoo economics." Following his selection as Reagan's running mate, Bush took conservative positions that were similar to those held by the president. In the campaign, Bush made what would become famous as his "read my lips, no new taxes" pledge. This endeared him to Reagan's supporters, but would come back to haunt him four years later. He promised to continue Reagan's economic policies and, like the popular president, he would only negotiate with the Soviet Union from a position of strength. He did indicate that he would be more responsive to environmental concerns.

Notwithstanding Bush's status as Reagan's "heir apparent," six candidates challenged Bush for the nomination: Bob Dole, the Senate Minority Leader; Pete DuPont, who had been Governor of Delaware (1977–85); Alexander Haig, a former military officer who had served as White House chief of staff under Nixon and Ford (1973–74) and as Reagan's first secretary of state (1981–82); New York Congressman Jack Kemp; Pat Robertson, the Evangelical minister, founder of the Christian Broadcasting Network (CBN), and host of the *700 Club*; and Donald Rumsfeld, White House chief of staff (1974–75) and secretary of defense (1975–77) in the Ford administration.

The campaign began with Bush coming in third in Iowa, behind Dole and Robertson. In New Hampshire, where Dole was ahead in early public opinion polls, the Bush campaign started running television commercials depicting Dole as someone who had raised taxes. The state's popular governor, John Sununu, who campaigned for Bush, also bolstered the campaign. Bush won the primary, and then went on to dominate the primaries held on Super Tuesday, insuring that he would win the Republican nomination. The Republican convention, held in New Orleans, unanimously nominated Bush. He selected Senator Dan Quayle of Indiana as his running mate.

THE GENERAL ELECTION

In his acceptance speech, Governor Dukakis said that the "election would not be about ideology, but competence." Nonetheless, the Republican campaign defined Dukakis as a "Massachusetts liberal," who opposed the reciting of the Pledge of Allegiance in schools; was soft on crime, and was not knowledgeable about military matters. Dukakis's efforts to counter the Republican message were not effective. In response to the charge that he would not be an effective commander-in-chief, Dukakis agreed to a photo opportunity where he drove a tank. The footage was so embarrassing that it ended up in Bush campaign advertisements as proof that he could not be trusted to lead America's military. Another advertisement, "Boston Harbor," attacked Dukakis's environmental record.

Dukakis was also attacked for his support of Massachusetts's prison furlough program. The "Willie Horton" advertisement, paid for by the National Security Political Action Committee, and the Bush campaign's "Revolving Door" commercial, attacked Dukakis for being soft on crime. This image was reinforced by Dukakis's response to a question from Cable News Network (CNN) anchor Bernard Shaw, who asked Dukakis (a death penalty opponent) whether he would support the death penalty if his wife were raped and murdered. Dukakis replied by citing the ineffectiveness of the death penalty as a deterrent.

The Dukakis campaign attempted to link Bush to the scandals of the Reagan administration. It also attacked the credentials of Dan Quayle as "a heartbeat away from the Presidency" because of his inexperience. One of the few bright spots for the Democrats was the vice presidential debate between Quayle and Bentsen. Quayle compared himself to John F. Kennedy, when he said; "I have as much experience in the Congress as Jack Kennedy did when he sought the presidency." Bentsen went on the offensive, stating, "Senator, I served with Jack Kennedy. I knew Jack Kennedy. Jack Kennedy was a friend of mine. Senator, you're no Jack Kennedy." The attacks on Quayle did not have a significant effect on the Bush campaign.

THE OUTCOME

Bush won 53 percent of the popular vote and won 40 states (426 electoral votes), while Dukakis polled 45 percent of the popular vote and carried 11 states and the District of Columbia (112 electoral votes). Bush's victory was based on Reagan's popularity and the electorate's satisfaction with the direction of the country. Unable to vote for Reagan because of the Twenty-Second Amendment, the electorate chose to continue his policies by voting for his vice president, making Bush the first sitting vice president since Martin Van Buren in 1836 to be elected president.

The Results			
	Popular Vote	Percentage	Electoral Votes
George H.W. Bush	48,881,011	53.4	426
Michael S. Dukakis	41,828,350	45.6	112
Ronald E. Paul (Libertarian)	431,499	0.5	0
Lenora Fulani (New Alliance)	218,159	0.2	0
All others	226,852	0.3	0
TOTAL	91,594,686	100.0	538

Source: J.W. Wright, ed., *The New York Times Almanac 2007* (Penguin Reference, 2007).

SEE ALSO: Advertising, Campaign; Campaigns, Presidential; Law and Order; Negative Campaigning.

BIBLIOGRAPHY. C.M. Black and Thomas Oliphant, *All By Myself: The Un-making of a Presidential Campaign* (Globe Pequot Press, 1989); Sidney Blumenthal, *Pledging Allegiance: the Last Campaign of the Cold War* (Harper and Row, 1990); Bruce Buchanan, *Electing a President: the Markle Commission Research on Campaign 1988* (University of Texas Press, 1991); Jack Germond and Jules Witcover, *Whose Broad Stripes and Bright Stars? The Trivial Pursuit of the Presidency 1988* (Warner Books, 1989); Penn Kimball, *Keep Hope Alive! Super Tuesday and Jesse Jackson's 1988 Campaign for the Presidency* (Joint Center for Political and Economic Studies, 1992).

JEFFREY KRAUS
WAGNER COLLEGE

Presidential Election of 1992

IN LATE FEBRUARY of 1991, President George H.W. Bush commanded an 89 percent job approval rating in a Gallup poll of 1,012 registered voters. Coming as it did just weeks after the liberation of Kuwait and the successful conclusion of the first Gulf War with Iraq, Bush's approval ratings were remarkably high, and portended a relatively easy path for the incumbent Republican to re-election in 1992. By late July 1992, however, just 17 months later, this same president's approval ratings had dipped to 29 percent, a loss of 60 percent. What seemed like an easy path to re-election only a year-and-a-half before turned into a treacherous road to electoral defeat in the presidential election of 1992.

The swift and certain conclusion to the Persian Gulf War in early 1991, coupled with the coincident collapse of the Soviet Union, worked to drive foreign policy from the nation's attention. For many Americans in late 1991 and early 1992, foreign policy questions and concerns seemed distant and relatively stable. Much more immediately relevant was the economic downturn facing the United States in 1991–92. By the early summer of 1992, the unemployment rate in the United States was 7.8 percent and overall productivity declined from 6.8 percent in the first quarter to 3.3 percent in the fourth quarter after posting an annual rate of 1.6 percent for 1991. Average hourly earnings were largely stagnant during this period, while the overall level of economic growth was lackluster.

Americans were concerned about significant social upheaval and occurrences separate from foreign policy as well as the U.S. economy as they prepared to select a president in 1992. In March of 1991, an African-American motorist named Rodney King was arrested in Los Angeles and was severely beaten by the arresting officers—an event captured surreptitiously on videotape and played endlessly on American televisions. When the four officers charged in the incident were acquitted in April of 1992, violence erupted throughout Los Angeles, resulting in a number of deaths and significant looting.

In the summer of 1991, President Bush nominated for the Supreme Court an African-American judge named Clarence Thomas to replace the retiring Thurgood Marshall. One of the signature political events of the early 1990s, the Clarence Thomas confirmation hearings were transformed from a staid discussion of constitutional jurisprudence into a provocative display of race, sex, and power when University of Oklahoma law professor Anita Hill came forward to accuse the nominee of sexual harassment. Though Thomas was confirmed for the high court, his hearings brought new attention to issues of sexual harassment and the role and place of women in the workplace and in society.

On October 3, 1991, a relatively unknown governor of the small southern state of Arkansas announced on the steps of the governor's mansion in Little Rock that he would seek the Democratic nomination for president. Bill Clinton went where few Democrats dared to go in the fall of 1991. Many of the party's most prominent leaders—like New York Governor Mario Cuomo, Tennessee Senator Al Gore, and Missouri Congressman Richard Gephardt—opted not to seek the Democratic nomination, believing that George H.W. Bush would be re-elected with relative ease. After all, the week that Clinton declared his candidacy, the president's approval rating was a strong 65 percent.

Clinton joined several other Democrats in seeking his party's nomination in 1992. Some were less well-known, such as the mayor of Irvine, California, Larry Agran or the actor and director Tom Laughlin, best known for his portrayal of Billy Jack in the 1971 film of the same name. Others were more familiar: former Massachusetts Senator Paul Tsongas, Nebraska Senator Bob Kerrey, Iowa Senator Tom Harkin, former California Governor Jerry Brown, and Virginia Governor Douglas Wilder.

Traditionally first on the presidential nominating calendar, the Iowa caucuses were less relevant in 1992 because of the presence of favorite son Harkin in the Democratic field. New Hampshire would instead play the critical first role in the nomination process for the Democrats. Dogged by scandal in late 1991 and early 1992, the Clinton campaign was reeling as they headed to New Hampshire. Clinton confronted allegations of draft dodging and womanizing as the New Hampshire primary neared; the governor made a dramatic post–Super Bowl appearance on the CBS newsmagazine *60 Minutes* with his wife, Hillary Rodham Clinton, to admit to mistakes in his marriage and to attempt to salvage his campaign.

Clinton's second-place finish in New Hampshire, behind Paul Tsongas from neighboring Massachusetts, allowed the Arkansas governor to claim victory and reenergize his campaign, calling himself the Comeback Kid on election night. After sweeping most of the Super Tuesday primaries on March 10, Clinton faced only a relatively weak challenge from former California governor Jerry Brown on his way to the nomination. He selected Tennessee senator Al Gore as his vice presidential nominee that summer.

President Bush faced a surprisingly strong challenge for the Republican nomination from television columnist and former Nixon speechwriter Patrick Buchanan. Though he did not have a realistic chance of securing the GOP nomination, Buchanan still managed to pull many votes in early primary contests from Bush, highlighting the president's vulnerability, especially from the Republican right wing. Angry that Bush abandoned his famous "Read my lips, no new taxes" pledge from the 1988 campaign, these base voters used the Buchanan challenge as an opportunity to express their displeasure with the president. David Duke, a former member of the Ku Klux Klan, also sought the Republican nomination. Bush was renominated and kept on the ticket the sitting vice president, J. Danforth Quayle, despite some calls to replace him. Quayle was perhaps best known for his attacks against the "family values" of a primetime television character, Murphy Brown, and for misspelling "potato" at a New Jersey school in June of 1992.

THE CONVENTIONS

The 1992 Democratic convention, held in July in New York City, was hailed as a successful introduction of Bill Clinton to the American public. Clinton received a significant increase in the polls following the convention, in large measure because of the surprise withdrawal from the campaign of H. Ross Perot on the last day of the convention. In February of 1992, on CNN's *Larry King Show*, the Texas billionaire and businessman announced that he would be a candidate for president if his supporters were able to secure his place on the election ballots in all 50 states. Perot's insurgent bid captured considerable media attention in the spring and early summer of 1992. By July, facing increased scrutiny of his personal and professional life, Perot announced he was withdrawing from the campaign, in part because of what he saw as a reenergized Democratic Party. At the time, his named was secured on only 24 state ballots.

The Republicans met for their convention in Houston, Texas, in August. With the renomination of the Bush-Quayle ticket secure, the convention lacked excitement or suspense. That changed, however, when defeated candidate Patrick Buchanan declared from the podium the beginnings of a "culture war" and a "religious war" for the "soul of America." His speech attacked both Bill and Hillary Clinton and was followed by an address later at the convention from Marilyn Quayle who asserted that the cultural memory of the 1960s was flawed and that

"Not everyone demonstrated, dropped out, took drugs, joined in the sexual revolution or dodged the draft"—a clear and unmistakable character attack on the Democratic nominee.

THE CAMPAIGNS

George H.W. Bush based his campaign for re-election on the premise that an uncertain world demanded a president with character and experience. The president repeatedly emphasized his considerable résumé and his campaign commercials claimed that "The World is in Transition" and that only Bush possessed the experience to handle such changes. His spots also attacked Clinton's proposals to increase government spending, claiming that the Democrat would increase taxes on all Americans, and invited voters to find out more by calling "1-800-MEGA-TAX." Only late in the campaign did the president highlight Clinton's perceived character flaws, attacking him on CNN for visiting Moscow during the Cold War and for organizing protests against the Vietnam War on foreign soil while the Democrat was a student at Oxford University.

For his part, Clinton argued in the general election campaign that change was necessary, especially as it concerned economic policy, reflecting his campaign's internal mantra—"it's the economy, stupid." He endorsed tax increases for wealthy Americans, greater public investment, and reform of both healthcare and welfare policy. Charging in television ads that Bush had "the worst economic record of any president in 50 years," the Clinton campaign sought to motivate voters with the claim that it was "putting people first." The campaign also tried to communicate its message of youth and vigor with bus tours around the country and with appearances on unconventional, non-news, and media outlets.

Both campaigns also confronted the reentry into the campaign of H. Ross Perot. On October 1, Perot declared that he would again be a candidate for president. His place on ballots nationwide was secure and he selected as his running mate James Stockdale, a former Navy admiral and Vietnam War veteran. Perot's campaign was largely premised on economic fears about increased free trade and ballooning budget deficits, and the candidate took the innovative step of purchasing national television time for 30-minute infomercial-style campaign programs where he used flip charts and graphs to detail his take on the economy for the voters.

While other presidential contests have featured a particularly notable television spot ad, or a specific candidate gaffe as a critical event in the campaign, in 1992 such an event came in the second presidential debate in Richmond, Virginia, on October 15. This debate was unique in presidential campaign history as the first to employ a "town hall" format, with questions coming not from journalists and politicians, but from citizens. One of these citizens, a young African-American woman, asked the candidates to reflect upon how the national debt affected them personally. Unable to comprehend the question, President Bush was forced to admit, after seeking clarification from the moderator, that he loved his grandchildren and that he was concerned about rising levels of teenage pregnancy in African-American communities. Governor Clinton, conversely, was able to both personalize the issue while also using it to pivot to his call for more government investment to spur economic growth. The debate also featured several shots of the president looking at his watch, as if bored and uninvolved. Bush later revealed to Jim Lehrer that he took a "huge hit" from the Richmond debate and that when he was looking at his watch, he was thinking, "only 10 more minutes of this crap."

Bill Clinton was elected president on November 3, achieving a decisive victory in the Electoral College—370 to 168. This victory is somewhat deceptive, as Clinton only achieved 42.9 percent of the popular vote to President Bush's 37.1 percent. Surprisingly strong, Ross Perot took 18.8 percent of the popular vote, even if he was unable to secure any votes in the Electoral College. Clinton's electoral victory was broad-based, as he won states from the old south to the Pacific Northwest, from New England to the industrial heartland. On January 20, 1993, Clinton was inaugurated as the 42nd president of the United States.

SEE ALSO: Economy; Perot, Ross; Presidential Debates; Racial Justice.

BIBLIOGRAPHY. P.R. Abramson, J.H. Aldrich, and D.W. Rohde, eds., *Change and Continuity in the 1992 Elections* (CQ Press, 1995); R.M. Barrus and J.H. Eastby, eds., *America Through the Looking Glass: A Constitutionalist Critique of the 1992 Election* (Rowman & Littlefield, 1994); James Ceaser and Andrew Busch, *Upside Down and Inside Out: The 1992 Elections and American Politics* (Rowman & Littlefield, 1993); J.W. Germond and Jules Witcover, *Mad as*

Hell: Revolt at the Ballot Box, 1992 (Warner Books, 1993); Peter Goldman et al., *Quest for the Presidency 1992* (Texas A&M University Press, 1994); Matthew Kerbel, *Edited for Television: CNN, ABC, and American Presidential Elections* (Westview Press, 1998); Clarence Lusane, *African Americans at the Crossroads: The Restructuring of Black Leadership and the 1992 Elections* (South End Press, 1994); Michael Nelson, ed., *The Elections of 1992* (CQ Press, 1993); S.J. Parry-Giles and Trevor Parry-Giles, *Constructing Clinton: Hyperreality and Presidential Image-Making in Postmodern Politics* (Peter Lang, 2002).

SHAWN J. PARRY-GILES
UNIVERSITY OF MARYLAND
TREVOR PARRY-GILES
UNIVERSITY OF MARYLAND

Presidential Election of 1996

PRESIDENT BILL CLINTON'S first term can be divided into two halves. During the first half, Clinton was bedeviled by minor scandals about expensive haircuts and the White House Travel Office, while also confronting the more significant controversy over the service of gay men and lesbians in the U.S. military. His Justice Department, FBI, and Bureau of Alcohol, Tobacco, and Firearms were heavily criticized for their handling of a siege at a religious compound near Waco, Texas, in 1993 that ended with the deaths of almost 80 people. At the same time, the president secured passage of the North American Free Trade Agreement, saw his Omnibus Budget Reconciliation Act pass by one vote in the House of Representatives in 1993, and signed the popular Family and Medical Leave Act.

Nevertheless, he also witnessed the collapse of his healthcare reform plan and watched as the opposition Republicans took control of both houses of Congress for the first time in 40 years in the 1994 off-year elections. By any measure, at this stage in his presidency, Bill Clinton's re-election looked doomed. Just two years later, in 1996, Clinton became only the third Democrat in the 20th century to achieve re-election. Facing approval ratings consistently in the low to mid 40 percent range, and a new opposition Congress, Clinton was forced rather pathetically to assert his continued relevance as president in an April 1995 press conference, saying, "The

Constitution gives me relevance. The power of our ideas gives me relevance…The President is relevant here."

The next day, a bomb exploded at the Alfred P. Murrah Federal Building in Oklahoma City, killing 169 people. Providing Clinton the opportunity to act "presidential," the Oklahoma City bombing ushered in the second half of the Clinton first term, dominated by conflicts with Congress over budget matters. Twice in late 1995 and early 1996, the federal government shut down because of disagreements between Congress and the White House over spending priorities and tax policies. Out of this conflict, Clinton emerged as a leader fighting for principles and preserving important social programs while his Republican opponents in Congress—House Speaker Newt Gingrich and Senate Majority Leader Bob Dole—were depicted as seeking deep and harmful cuts in federal spending. During this period, the president's approval ratings in most polls were in the mid to high 50 percent range. The second half of Clinton's first term also featured passage of a welfare reform bill that angered many progressives and Democrats, but that allowed the president to "triangulate" between the Republican and Democratic positions while also achieving a significant campaign pledge from the 1992 election.

Heading into the beginning of the 1996 campaign, then, Republicans faced an incumbent president with a mixed domestic record during his first term. The economy was relatively stable, though conflicts persisted with Congress over budgets and fiscal policy. The president had secured some legislative successes, while the signature achievement of his first term, healthcare reform, had failed. President Clinton's first term was dominated by concerns over Iraq's Saddam Hussein, ethnic strife in former Yugoslavia, and tensions in the Middle East between Israelis and Palestinians. Scandals also lingered around Bill Clinton: Paula Jones filed her sexual harassment lawsuit against the president in May of 1994; the secretary of Housing and Urban Development, Henry Cisneros, was facing an independent counsel's investigation that began in 1995; and the secretary of Agriculture, Mike Espy, resigned in 1994 under suspicion of accepting bribes. There was the Travel Office scandal and the beginnings of what would become the Whitewater episode.

In this turbulent political context, 11 Republicans sought their party's nomination to face Bill Clinton in the 1996 presidential election. Some were obscure candidates with little or no national political profile, including Ohio business executive Morry Taylor and Maryland radio talk-show host Alan Keyes. Former Tennessee governor Lamar Alexander and the current governor of California, Pete Wilson, were in the field, as were four sitting U.S. senators: Bob Dole (Kansas), Phil Gramm (Texas), Richard Lugar (Indiana), and Arlen Specter (Pennsylvania). Also vying for the nomination were California congressman Robert Dornan, magazine publisher Steve Forbes, and television commentator and former Nixon speechwriter, Patrick Buchanan.

Though Buchanan and Forbes prevailed in some early primaries and caucuses, Dole's path to the nomination was assured with his victories in the North Dakota and South Dakota primaries. Realizing that the pursuit of the presidency required his full-time attention, Dole tearfully resigned from the U.S. Senate in the summer and prepared for the upcoming general election campaign. He selected Jack Kemp, former congressman and former secretary of Housing and Urban Development, as his running mate.

THE CAMPAIGNS

There was no serious opposition within the Democratic Party to Bill Clinton's renomination, allowing the president to raise substantial funds for the general election—a fundraising effort that would later raise significant questions and legal challenges. With his hefty bankroll, the Clinton campaign was able to run a series of early campaign ads in the spring and summer months that touted the president's achievements and attacked Republican obstructionism on issues ranging from Medicare to the environment. Because Dole was unable to respond, largely for financial reasons, the Clinton campaign effort crafted a lead in most public opinion polls that would be sustained for the entirety of the campaign.

In part, the Clinton effort succeeded because his campaign capitalized on the perception of Dole as old and out of touch. This perception was, at least to some degree, of Dole's own making. The candidate was 73 years old in 1996 and would have been, if elected, the oldest president ever inaugurated. Seeking to turn his age to his advantage, Dole implored his audience in his acceptance speech to the August GOP convention meeting in San Diego that:

Age has its advantages. Let me be the bridge to an America that only the unknowing call myth. Let me be the bridge to a time of tranquility, faith and confidence in action. And to those who say it was never

so, that America's not been better, I say you're wrong. And I know because I was there. And I have seen it. And I remember.

Add to this a series of incidents over the course of the campaign—Dole falling from a platform in Chico, California, or referencing a no-hitter thrown by a pitcher for the "Brooklyn Dodgers"—and the perception stuck.

Clinton, conversely, ran a campaign that emphasized future themes and sought diligently to blunt expected character attacks and negative campaigning about scandals. In his acceptance speech to the Democratic convention meeting in Chicago, Clinton praised Dole and Kemp for their service to the nation, and added "But with all respect, we do not need to build a bridge to the past. We need to build a bridge to the future. And that is what I commit to you to do. So tonight, let us resolve to build that bridge to the 21st century, to meet our challenges and protect our values." The "bridge to the 21st century" theme was ubiquitous in the Clinton campaign and worked to reinforce the perceptions of the younger Clinton vying against an older, and disconnected, Dole. Never able to break that perception, unwilling to engage in attacks on the president's character, Dole was ultimately defeated by the president.

The two debates between Clinton and Dole did little to alter the dynamics of the contest. Both were relatively civil affairs, devoid largely of personal attack or signature moments. Perhaps most notable about the 1996 presidential debates was the absence of Ross Perot, a participant in all three debates in 1992. Perot once again ran for president as the candidate of the U.S. Reform Party, but was excluded from the debates along with candidates from such organizations as the Natural Law Party, the Libertarian Party, and the Socialist Party.

Even with his exclusion from the debates, Perot still captured 8.4 percent of the popular vote when Americans cast their ballots on November 5. The president secured 379 electoral votes to Dole's 159, winning many of the states that he won in 1992, surrendering Georgia, Colorado, and Montana to the Republicans, but adding Florida and Arizona, for a net electoral vote gain of nine votes. Despite his considerable victory in the Electoral College, Clinton was unable to attract a majority of the popular vote, prevailing with 49.2 percent of voters to Dole's 40.7 percent. Clinton would remark some years later in his memoirs that because his popular vote total was lower than his job approval rating as president, the election results were a "sober reminder of the power of cultural issues like guns, gays, and abortion" on certain key segments of the American electorate.

SEE ALSO: Perot, Ross; Presidential Debates; Scandals, Presidential Elections.

BIBLIOGRAPHY. P.R. Abramson, J.H. Aldrich, and D.W. Rohde, *Change and Continuity in the 1996 Elections* (CQ Press, 1998); J.W. Ceaser and A.E. Busch, *Losing to Win: The 1996 Elections and American Politics* (Rowman & Littlefield, 1997); L.L. Kaid and D.G. Bystrom, *The Electronic Election: Perspectives on the 1996 Campaign Communication* (Lawrence Erlbaum, 1999); L.L. Kaid, Mitchell McKinney, and J.C. Tedesco, *Civic Dialogue in the 1996 Presidential Campaign: Candidate, Media, and Public Voices* (Hampton Press, 2000); Michael Nelson, ed., *The Elections of 1996* (CQ Press, 1997); S.J. Parry-Giles and Trevor Parry-Giles, *Constructing Clinton: Hyperreality and Presidential Image-Making in Postmodern Politics* (Peter Lang, 2002); G.M. Pomper et al., *The Election of 1996: Reports and Interpretations* (Chatham House, 1997); Evan Thomas et al., *Back from the Dead: How Clinton Survived the Republican Revolution* (Atlantic Monthly Press, 1997); H.F. Weisberg and J.M. Box-Steffensmeier, eds., *Reelection 1996: How Americans Voted* (Chatham House, 1999); Bob Woodward, *The Choice* (Simon & Schuster, 1996).

TREVOR PARRY-GILES
UNIVERSITY OF MARYLAND
SHAWN J. PARRY-GILES
UNIVERSITY OF MARYLAND

Presidential Election of 2000

ON NOVEMBER 7, 2000, Americans went to the polls to cast their vote for the presidential candidate they wanted to succeed William "Bill" Clinton. As the votes were cast, Americans across the country witnessed one of the closest presidential elections in history. The American public was able to take part in a contest that would ultimately be decided not by the votes cast by the electorate, but by the final ruling of the Supreme Court.

Governor George W. Bush, the son of the 41st President George H.W. Bush, was elected as the Republican governor of Texas in 1994 and served for two consecutive terms until his bid for the White House in 2000. Governor Bush received his bachelor's degree in history

from Yale University in 1968 and a Masters in Business Administration from Harvard University in 1975. Prior to entering the world of politics, Governor Bush participated in several business ventures that included the development of an independent oil company called Arbusto, in the mid-1970s, and the eventual purchase of a Major League Baseball team, the Texas Rangers, in 1988. His political career prior to entering the Texas governorship included a failed bid for the House of Representatives in 1978, and working as a campaign manager on Vice President George H.W. Bush's bid for the White House in 1988.

Vice President Albert A. Gore, Jr., a graduate of Harvard University, sought the White House for the Democratic Party in 2000 following his two successive terms as vice president during the Clinton Administration. The son of a former representative and senator from the state of Tennessee, Vice President Gore followed in his father's footsteps by serving as a representative 1977–85 and then as a senator 1985–93, prior to assuming the office of vice president in 1993. During his tenure as vice president, Al Gore urged the Clinton administration to improve governmental bureaucracy and was a steady advocate for environmental concerns.

During the Republican primary season, Senator John McCain (R-Arizona), who had an extensive résumé that highlighted his service in the Senate and his decorated history as a Vietnam War hero, principally opposed Governor Bush. After earning the reputation of being a "maverick" and boarding his tour bus, "The Straight Talk Express," McCain was a formidable opponent, but was eventually eliminated following a poor showing on March 9, or Super Tuesday. Following the defeat of his opponent, Governor Bush was faced with the challenge of selecting a vice presidential candidate who would complement the ticket and appease those in the Republican Party who had concerns regarding Bush's apparent lack of experience.

In response, Governor Bush tapped former U.S. Representative Richard "Dick" Cheney to run as vice president. Cheney had the experience in national politics as well as foreign affairs, serving as a representative from the state of Wyoming and as a member of several presidential administrations, which George W. Bush's résumé lacked.

Vice President Gore also faced a fair challenger in the form of Bill Bradley, former National Basketball Association star and U.S. senator from New Jersey. While

Bradley seemed to be able to raise funds at a rate comparable to that of Gore, he was never able to mount a serious challenge and was swept in every primary, eventually conceding his bid for the nomination following a crushing defeat on Super Tuesday. To combat his apparent leftist leanings and the "heavy Clinton baggage he carried," Vice President Gore selected Joseph Lieberman, a longtime senator from the state of Connecticut, an avid critic of the Clinton administration during the scandals of the late 1990s, and a Jewish senator who could reach out to those in the Democratic Party that Gore could not easily obtain on his own.

In a campaign that was portrayed by many political pundits as a choice between two very similar candidates, a closer inspection of the platforms for both parties demonstrates very distinct differences between the candidates for the presidency. The Republican Party and Governor Bush supported increasing tax cuts for low-income families, supported a constitutional amendment to ban abortion procedures, advocated the development of personal savings accounts for Social Security, and the use of federal tax dollars for voucher programs to remove students from failing schools and place them in private schools.

In contrast, the Democratic Party and Vice President Gore advocated the promulgation of a staunchly different program that included a tax program that targeted the middle-class population, general government support for a woman to decide whether or not to seek an abortion, a call to avoid establishing private accounts and to preserve the Social Security program as is, and increasing funding for public schools and establishing standards that would hold teachers more accountable for their actions within the classroom.

THE GENERAL ELECTION

Leading up to Election Day on November 7, a clear winner had not yet been established. Early election results indicated that Al Gore was collecting the majority of Democratic strongholds, including New York, Michigan, California, and Washington. George H.W. Bush was collecting states that he was polling quite strongly in, including much of the midwest and southern states, which appealed to his stronger characteristics.

Ultimately, the contest would rely on the election results from the state of Florida. Looking to legislative elections proved to be little help in determining who would capture victory in the presidential election. Only

48.5 percent of registered voters cast a ballot for their member of Congress, and the final results ended in a tie in the Senate, with 50 seats each for both the Republicans and the Democrats, and a slight majority for the Republicans in the House with a total of 221 seats for the Republicans and 212 for the Democrats.

When it was evident that there were considerable problems with the ballots cast in multiple districts in Florida, legal advisors for both candidates started to file petitions in court. The Gore campaign claimed that there were problems with the ballots in several counties and that, if they were to be counted by hand, enough votes would be discovered to grant Gore the victory. The Bush campaign, on the other hand, sought to have all recounts halted because of the discrepancy that would inevitably occur when hand counting began.

THE CONTROVERSY

On December 11, 2000, the Supreme Court in the case of *Bush v. Gore*, in a 5–4 vote, opted to halt the manual recount that was established by the Florida Supreme Court. Chief Justice Rehnquist, writing for the majority, argued that only the state legislature had the ability to craft election law, not the courts. Furthermore, the majority opinion argued that the recount procedure was unfair and that there was insufficient time to develop a fair election law before the Florida State Legislature was set to certify the election results. There were four independent dissenting opinions from Justices Breyer, Ginsburg, Souter, and Stevens. The dissenting arguments suggested that there were constitutional safeguards against artificial timetables when fundamental rights were being infringed upon, and that the nature of federal government required that each state individually establish election rules for counting and verifying ballots.

Ultimately, Governor Bush was awarded the electoral votes from the state of Florida and captured the majority of votes needed to win the presidency, with 271 votes in the Electoral College, while securing fewer popular votes than his Democratic challenger, Al Gore. This election, which had a turnout of 67.4 percent of registered voters, generated considerable debate among the public, scholars, and political pundits about the role of the courts in the election process, the fairness of the presidential election system, and the necessity for every vote to be counted before the mass media announces a victor.

SEE ALSO: Ballot Controversies; Ballot Issues; Exit Poll; Florida; Jewish Vote; Nader, Ralph; Polling; Protest Voting; Third Parties; Vote by Mail; Voting Methods.

BIBLIOGRAPHY. Biography.com, www.biography.com (cited August 2007); Kenneth Janda, J.M. Berry, and Jerry Goldman, *The Challenge of Democracy: Government in Action* (Houghton Mifflin, 2006); L.J. Sabato, *Overtime: the Election 2000 Thriller* (Longman Publishers, 2002); The White House, www.whitehouse.gov (cited August 2007).

Ian Farrell
Independent Scholar

Presidential Election of 2004

THE PRESIDENTIAL ELECTIONS of 2004 placed incumbent President George W. Bush against fourth-term Massachusetts Senator John F. Kerry. The Republican nomination went uncontested, with Bush again choosing Richard ("Dick") Cheney as his vice presidential running mate. Democratic electioneering commenced early and, by the end of 2003, the media declared flamboyant Vermont Governor Howard Dean the party's frontrunner. However, the primaries brought a different reality. One hand-written sign summarized it best: Democrats may have "dated Dean, but married Kerry." Kerry handily won 27 of the 30 primaries. First-term South Carolina Senator John Edwards, well spoken with a slight populist accent, ran a positive campaign and garnered a strong second-place showing. After launching a few trial balloons (including thoughts of a bipartisan ticket including Arizona Republican John McCain), Kerry offered Edwards the vice presidential spot.

Underlying the contest were questions from the presidential election of 2000. Democrat Al Gore had won the popular vote, but after irregularities occurred, particularly in Florida, the Republican-dominated Supreme Court determined the electoral vote. Congress responded two years later with the Bipartisan Campaign Reform Act (BCRA) and Help America Vote Act (HAVA). Both emerged ready for implementation during the 2004 campaign. This contest would be remembered as the moment when 50-year assumptions about voting behavior were reduced to a race of blue states versus red states.

THE CANDIDATES

The Democratic field initially spanned diverse backgrounds and interests, from the anticipated congressional contingent to retired Allied Supreme Commander Wesley Clark, to grassroots-based African-American leader Reverend Al Sharpton. Vermont Governor Howard Dean, a physician by profession and first-time national office seeker, claimed distinction as the first to forcefully question U.S. involvement in Iraq. His pioneering nature served him well on another front: according to one estimate, internet use of political news and information increased 83 percent 2000–04. Dean visibly tapped this source, attracting young voters and legions of small donors online. With assistance from Meetup.com, his campaign began sponsoring its own "Meetups," mainly metropolitan soirees that offered social mingling and political bonding. During the first nine months of 2003, Dean raised $25 million, the most ever recorded up to that time by a non-incumbent. The 2000 Democratic candidate, former Vice President Al Gore, threw his support to Dean in early December

George W. Bush in 2004. Seventeen million more Americans voted in 2004 than in 2000.

2003 and veteran newscaster Ted Koppel subsequently opened a televised New Hampshire debate by asking all the Democratic candidates if they felt Dean could defeat George W. Bush. Energy did not translate into effectiveness, however. Dean diffused his youthful supporters en masse to small towns, where they failed to make an impact on older, more reserved voters. In addition to several tactical blunders, the infamous Dean "scream" of confidence (or perhaps nervousness) after the Iowa Caucus portrayed his more brash, uncontrollable side, effectively ending his presidential aspirations.

John Kerry appeared calmly presidential. Liberal in politics and conservative in manner, he confronted Dean's momentum by shuffling his staff and securing a $6.4 million second mortgage on his Boston home. Besides affirming his serious commitment to the race, this infusion temporarily freed him from the restrictions of federal hard money under the BCRA (or, McCain-Feingold, after its authors). Consequently, Kerry could allocate his primary funds more strategically.

MCCAIN-FEINGOLD CAMPAIGN FINANCE REFORM

In fact, McCain-Feingold influenced the 2004 elections in many ways, confounding business as usual and inspiring some creative tactical thinking. BCRA doubled contribution ceilings to candidates (from $1,000 to $2,000) and to state, district, or local parties (from $5,000 to 10,000). It capped donations to national parties at $25,000 rather than $20,000. Within a campaign finance framework, the new law distinguished among federally-circumscribed hard money and soft money; specified the interactions between campaigns, national committees, and more localized operations; and defined electioneering communications. Finally, whereas political action committees (PACs) representing various issues and special interests had been the watchword of the 1980s, McCain-Feingold catapulted 527s in the political limelight. These organizations (identified under section 527 of the tax code) were political parties, committees, or associations formed for the purpose of influencing the selection, nomination, or appointment of any individual to public office.

President Bush enjoyed the benefits of incumbency. He did not need to squander his funds on primaries, and both he and the Republican National Committee (RNC) could slowly, methodically develop a strategic infrastructure. When Bush's campaign formally revved

up in June 2003, they petitioned steadfast supporters—realizing that BCRA made considerably larger donations possible. The Republicans entered the presidential campaign season with well over $200 million. Bush presented himself as a strong national leader. Mindful of the electoral tendency to rally around the president during crisis, his media messages included visuals of 9/11 and emphasized a quick, reassuring response. But the image became grainy. The national economy appeared to stagnate, producing few new jobs, and the weapons of mass destruction that precipitated U.S. involvement in Iraq had yet to be found. A Vietnam veteran decorated with a Bronze Star and two Purple Hearts, John Kerry initially added voice and credibility to the antiwar rumblings that began with Howard Dean and the Democratic 527 group MoveOn.org. Bush's approval ratings in May 2004 tumbled to 41 percent (according to a CBS News poll), the lowest of his term. Except for Harry Truman, no sitting president with a rating below 50 percent had ever won re-election.

THE 527 GROUPS

Both parties held their national conventions in midsummer. Less than a week after the Democratic convention, however, a 527 group called Swift Boat Veterans for Truth plunked down the relatively small sum of $550,000 to release a 60-second advertisement in several media markets. It falsely impugned Kerry's war record and reopened the painfully deep gashes remaining from the Vietnam War. Replayed and discussed countless times across the country—which amounted to free distribution—the controversial ad reached far beyond its original markets. Kerry could make life or death decisions on the Mekong delta, but when it came to campaign tactics, he sought ample consultation and deliberated, endlessly. It took him two weeks to refute the Swift Boat charges, raising doubts about his service record. The "Veterans" immediately followed up with a new, more expansive ad, "Sellout"; ultimately, the bill for these smear tactics escalated from the original $500,000 to $20 million.

The Swift Boat incident also gave insight, more positively, into the Bush campaign's primary method for reaching otherwise elusive supporters—micro-targeting. Essentially, the campaign staff obtained and cross-referenced both political and commercial databases. Applying modeling methods, they developed profiles of consumer groups that agreed with the president's positions, but were not regular voters or supporters.

The campaign fine-tuned 32 media messages, simultaneously working at the grassroots level to separate the individuals from the typologies, link them with committed Republic peers, and activate them through Bush rallies and partisan events.

THE GENERAL ELECTION

The presidential election of 2004 was a polarizing contest. However, exit polls did not match results in some important states. Part of the reason may have been unanticipated participation. Seventeen million more Americans voted in 2004 than in 2000, accounting for 59.4 percent of the electorate. Not since the 1960s had turnout approached that level, 55.3 percent in the presidential election. Fundamental processes also were in flux. Among other provisions, HAVA sought to move the nation uniformly from ballots and levers to electronic machines, and implement statewide registration lists that would facilitate voting, even if a person had moved. The problem was that 2004 was a transitional year. Election districts varied, as did the documentation required to cast a ballot. And new systems did not always function smoothly, long lines formed, and issues were raised. Residual suspicions from 2000 also mobilized 25,000 volunteers to monitor field operations in 17 states.

The final count showed President Bush with 50.7 percent of the vote to Kerry's 48.3 percent, and one percent for third-party candidates, primarily Ralph Nader. Bush's popular margin, 2.4 percent, was the slimmest ever for an incumbent president. On the other hand, during the previous 30 years, three sitting chief executives (Gerald Ford, Jimmy Carter, and Bush's own father, George H.W. Bush) were not returned to office. The younger Bush in 2004 won 31 states and 286 electoral votes, on 16 more than the number required to win, and 15 more than he received after the contested Florida count was validated in 2000.

Long-held notions of voting behavior also receded. Bush secured the Catholic vote, 52 to 47 percent, though Kerry was a coreligionist. The Democratic primary season offered other examples of change. According to a member of his campaign committee, former vice presidential nominee Joe Lieberman's effort foundered, in part, because anticipated Jewish contributions did not materialize. Similarly, Reverend Al Sharpton failed to win states where African Americans constituted a large percentage of the Democratic voters, and where Jesse Jackson had triumphed only 16 years earlier. Although Republican micro-targeting ultimately did a better job of getting out the votes, the internet-savvy Democratic National Committee (DNC) for the first time in recent memory raised more money than the RNC, $391 to $384 million. Democratic-leaning 527s gathered $266 million in contributions, in contrast to their opponents' $144 million.

The lingering snapshot of 2004 was a red-blue state divide, little changed from 2000, but radically different than the mid-20th century. Bush claimed Iowa and New Mexico, and Kerry won over New Hampshire, further asserting regional voting identities. Yet, the election paired fast-changing technology with old-fashioned grassroots politicking. The incoming DNC chair, Howard Dean, dumped the obvious (and losing) red-blue strategy for a "50 State" plan—that turned both the Senate and the House Democratic in 2006.

SEE ALSO: Blue States; Campaign Finance, Federal Elections; Campaign Finance, Politics of; Campaign Reforms; Campaign Spending; Help America Vote Act; Internet Use in Political Campaigns; McCain-Feingold Campaign Finance Reform; Political Action Committee; Presidential Election of 2000; Presidential Election of 2008; Race and Voting Behavior; Red States; Religion and Voting Behavior; War and Peace.

BIBLIOGRAPHY. Dana Dunnan, *Burning at the Grassroots: Inside the Dean Machine* (PageFree Publishing, Inc., 2004); Electiononline.org, "Briefing: The 2004 Elections," www.electionline.org (cited August 2007); Heather Havenstein, "Dems Deploy Data Tools; GOP Expands Microtargeting," *Computerworld* (November 6, 2006); L.J. Sabato, *Divided States of America: The Slash and Burn Politics of the 2004 Presidential Election* (Pearson Longman, 2006); William Saletan and the Staff of Slate.com, *Slate's Field Guide to the Candidates 2004* (Plume/Penguin Group, 2003).

Lynn C. Kronzek
Independent Scholar

Presidential Election of 2008

THE 2008 PRESIDENTIAL election will most likely be a landmark election as the frontrunners in each of the two major parties offer a rare or unique characteristic to the White House. As of February 2008, The front-runners for the Democratic Party included New York Senator Hillary Clinton and Illinois Senator Barack Obama. The frontrunner for the Republican Party was Arizona Senator John McCain. If the United States is still engaged in the war in Iraq at the time of the presidential election on November 4, 2008, the United States will have been in the war for five years and eight months. The next president will then decide the fate of the United States in the war in Iraq and will help shape the future of American domestic and foreign policy.

THE ISSUES AT STAKE

There are several issues that will be of great importance when voters decide who to cast their vote for in the presidential election of 2008. An issue of high importance will be the war in Iraq. All of the candidates will need to form positions on an Iraq exit strategy. Voters will need to decide which of these exit strategies they prefer when making the decision for whom to cast their ballot. Clinton and McCain both voted for war authorization and their positions will need to revolve around their decision to authorize war in Iraq in 2003. Obama was not yet in the Senate when the decision to authorize war was made.

Other issues of great importance are the U.S. economy, oil prices, immigration, abortion, healthcare, and Medicare. First, the U.S. economy is struggling to compete for growth in the world and needs to continue to grow or it will be eclipsed by other, faster-growing economies. Second, oil prices are increasing and this could wreak havoc on the American economy and U.S. consumers.

The American economy will struggle if oil prices continue to increase because businesses will suffer with additional costs; for example airlines will struggle to offer affordable plane tickets. The American consumer will suffer from increased heating and gasoline prices. If consumers and businesses both suffer from the increasing oil prices, then this will further hinder U.S. economic growth.

Third, immigration is becoming more salient in the minds of voters. With approximately 12 million illegal immigrants, the controversy surrounding the benefits and costs of illegal immigration is creating a sense of urgency in the American public. Fourth, abortion has been an extremely important issue since

Roe v. Wade, but with the recent Supreme Court decisions upholding the partial birth abortion ban (*Gonzales v. Carhart* and *Gonzales v. Planned Parenthood*) and the appointment to the Supreme Court of more conservative justices, abortion is becoming a polarizing issue in the American public. Finally, healthcare and Medicare have become important voting issues, as close to 50 million Americans have no healthcare insurance and Medicare's financial future remains uncertain.

THE DEMOCRATIC HOPEFULS

Hillary Clinton, if elected president, would be the first woman president in U.S. history. In 1992, when Bill Clinton was elected president, Hillary Clinton took on the role of first lady. She served in this role for the eight years her husband was in office. In 2000, Hillary Clinton became a New York senator, the first woman to be elected to a statewide office in New York. She has served on the Education, Health, Labor and Pensions Committee, Environment and Public Works Committee, the Special Committee on Aging, and is the first New York senator to serve on the Senate Armed Services Committee.

Barack Obama, if elected president, would become the first African-American president in U.S. history. In 2004, Obama was elected senator from Illinois. Obama has served on the Health, Education, Labor and Pensions Committee, Foreign Relations Committee, Veterans' Affairs Committee, and the Environment and Public Works Committee. Before serving in the senate, Barack Obama served eight years as an Illinois state senator.

THE REPUBLICAN HOPEFULS

This was the first time since 1928 that the vice president of the United States has not run in the presidential election after an incumbent president could not run for re-election. This election will mark 80 years since neither an incumbent president or vice president is running for president, which is significant because it means that all candidates will have no direct ties to the White House from the previous year.

As of February 2008, John McCain was the frontrunner in the race for the Republican presidential nomination. McCain was elected to the U.S. Senate from Arizona in 1986 to replace Barry Goldwater. McCain is known for his military experience and serving as a prisoner of war for five years. If McCain is elected to the presidency, he will be the first active senator to become president since John F. Kennedy in 1960.

IMPORTANCE

The presidential election of 2008 will probably be the most expensive election campaign in history. It is argued that a presidential hopeful will need to raise at least $100 million by the end of 2007 in order to be considered viable as a presidential candidate. With many contenders for each party's nomination, there will be an enormous sum of money spent.

For the past 60 years, presidential elections have followed a fairly regular pattern. Harry Truman (D) served eight years, Dwight Eisenhower (R) served eight years, John F. Kennedy/Lyndon Johnson (D) combined served eight years, and Richard Nixon/Gerald Ford (R) combined served eight years. Jimmy Carter (D) then served four years and Ronald Reagan/George H.W. Bush (R) served 12 years. Bill Clinton (D) served eight years and George W. Bush (R) served eight years. Approximately every eight years, the party in the White House changes. If this trend continues, a Democrat is destined to take office in 2008. The future president will have to provide strong leadership and most likely work with a Democratic Congress.

SEE ALSO: Abortion; Economy; Healthcare; Immigration; New York.

BIBLIOGRAPHY. Carl Bernstein, *A Woman in Charge: The Life of Hillary Rodham Clinton* (Vintage, 2008); Hillary Clinton, clinton.senate.gov (cited August 2007); John McCain, mccain.senate.gov (cited August 2007); New York City, www.nyc.gov (cited August 2007); Barack Obama, obama.senate.gov (cited August 2007); Barack Obama, *The Audacity of Hope: Thoughts on Reclaiming the American Dream* (Three Rivers Press, 2007); Source Watch, "Issues for 2008," www.sourcewatch.org (cited August 2007); The White House, www.whitehouse.gov (cited August 2007).

JONATHAN DAY
UNIVERSITY OF IOWA

Presidential Elections

AMERICAN PRESIDENTIAL ELECTIONS determine who is elected president and vice president of the United States. Local election boards throughout the 50 states and the District of Columbia administer presidential elections, and Article II, Section 1 of the U.S. Constitution, as amended by the Twelfth, Twenty-Second, and Twenty-Third amendments, prescribe the general requirements for how the president and vice president are to be elected. Presidential elections are held every four years on the first Tuesday after the first Monday in November (established by Congress in 1854).

Although Americans go to the polls on Election Day to select the presidential and vice presidential candidates of their choice, they actually do not vote for these candidates directly. Rather, they vote for a list of party electors who have pledged to vote for their party's candidates in a separate election. The winning electors from each state make up the Electoral College. Thus, in the American presidential election system, the general electorate indirectly chooses the winning ticket by voting for electors who directly elect the president and the vice president. On Election Day, Americans also elect the entire U.S. House of Representatives and one-third of the U.S. Senate, as well as many state and local officials.

The selected electors then meet in their respective state capitals on the first Monday after the second Wednesday in December to cast their votes for president and vice president. These votes are sent to the nation's capital to be officially counted and certified by the president of the Senate (who is also the vice president of the United States) in front of a joint session of Congress the following sixth of January. The presidential and vice presidential candidates who receive a majority of the Electoral College vote are declared the winners, and assume their duties at noon on January 20th.

If no candidate wins a majority of the electoral vote, then the presidential election is decided by the U.S. House of Representatives (from among the three candidates receiving the largest number of electoral votes), with each state having one vote. The vice presidential election is decided by the U.S. Senate (from the two candidates receiving the largest number of electoral votes), with each senator having one vote. The presidential elections of 1800 and 1824, and the vice presidential election of 1836, are the only elections that have been decided in this manner. In 1800, running mates Thomas Jefferson and Aaron Burr each received the same number of votes (as votes for the presidency were not differentiated from votes for the vice presidency until passage of the 12th Amendment in 1804). The House of Representatives elected Jefferson as president, and Burr became vice president. In 1824, when no candidate received a majority of the Electoral College vote, the House of Representatives chose John Quincy Adams as president; despite the fact that Andrew Jackson had won a plurality, but not a majority, of both the electoral and the popular vote. In 1836, no vice presidential candidate received a majority of the Electoral College vote, and the Senate decided the election.

The Constitution allows each state to appoint "in such manner as the Legislature thereof may direct, a number of Electors, equal to the whole number of Senators and Representatives to which the state may be entitled in the Congress." Currently, this number is set at 538 (with the District of Columbia receiving three electors). Although most electors were originally selected by the state legislatures, by the mid-19th century, all states chose their electors by popular vote, with state parties designating a slate of electors in each state, and voters choosing the winning slate.

Every state, with the exception of Maine and Nebraska, awards all of its electoral votes to the winner of the popular vote in that state (winner-take-all system). Although it happens rarely, this formula can result in a scenario where the candidate receiving the largest number of popular votes does not win the electoral vote, as was the case in 1824, 1876, 1888, and 2000. The system also leads presidential campaigns to target aggressively those states with many electoral votes, as well as those considered to be swing or battleground states where the election is expected to be so close that it could easily go for one candidate or the other.

Running for the U.S. presidency is a long and protracted process. For much of American history, however, this was not the case. Until the end of the 19th century, most presidential candidates did not actively campaign, because such activity was considered demeaning to the office. Now, candidates actively campaign across the country and aggressively seek election. Most major-party candidates (Democratic and Republican) who decide to run for the presidency begin campaigning, usually with the formation of a campaign exploratory committee, at least two years before Election Day. The primary season now starts in January of the presidential election year, with the Iowa caucus and New Hampshire primary. During this time, candidates raise large sums of money to support field organizations and campaign staffs and to familiarize voters with their views through advertising. After the primary season is over, each of the two major parties holds a national nominating convention where it officially nominates its presidential candidate (the individual with the most delegates obtained through the primary system) and his/her running mate (chosen by the presidential candidate). The general election campaign season is then set to begin.

Presidential campaigns are characterized by numerous candidate appearances, partisan appeals, fundraising events, political advertisements, and televised presidential and vice presidential debates (the first presidential debate took place in 1960, and they have been the norm in every election since 1976). Today, running for the presidency involves highly sophisticated, increasingly professionalized, and ever more expensive campaigns that seek to maximize a candidate's chances of winning the election.

SEE ALSO: Campaigns, Presidential; Conventions, National Nominating Party; Elections Laws, Federal Elections; Electoral College; Nomination Process, Presidential; Presidential Debates; Presidential Primaries; Winner-Take-All System.

BIBLIOGRAPHY. P.R. Abramson, John Aldrich, and D.W. Rhode, *Change and Continuity in the 2004 Elections* (CQ Press, 2006); J.E. Campbell, *The American Campaign: U.S. Presidential Campaigns and the National Vote* (Texas A&M, 2000); W.G. Mayer, ed., *The Making of the Presidential Candidate 2004* (Rowman and Littlefield, 2004); Michael Nelson, ed., *The Elections of 2004* (CQ Press, 2005); Thomas Patterson, *The Vanishing Voter* (Knopf, 2002); S.J. Wayne, *The Road to the White House, 2004* (Thomson/Wadsworth, 2004).

CARLOS E. DÍAZ-ROSILLO
HARVARD UNIVERSITY

Presidential Primaries

PRESIDENTIAL PRIMARIES HAVE been the dominant method for choosing delegates to the national conventions since the 1972 presidential elections. The proliferation of presidential primaries has transformed the presidential nomination process by transferring political power from the party organizations and party leaders, to the candidate organizations and rank-and-file voters. Presidential primaries also have affected the quality of nominees. Some argue that candidates are now less in debt to party bosses and are more representative of the voting population. Others argue that nominees have to be narrowly focused on drawing support from a minority of voters within each major party. Therefore, nominees are not more representative of the public, but of a certain factional balance within each major party.

TYPES OF PRIMARIES

Presidential primaries can be classified into two types: binding primaries and presidential preference contests, or "beauty contests." In states with primaries, nearly all have adopted binding primaries, where voters elect delegates who are legally bound to vote for a candidate they declared prior to the primary date. In some states, election results bind all delegates, whereas in other states, party organizations select some of the delegates who are not bound by the results of the primary.

In presidential preference contests, voters choose the candidate they prefer. This preference vote does not result in the directc selection of any delegates. In some states, voters choose delegates and candidates. Both parties have rules to designate superdelegates who are not legally bound by the results of the primary results. Of the 4,353 delegates to the 2004 Democratic National Convention, 830 (19 percent) were superdelegates. Designating superdelegates is the party organizations' attempt to retain some influence in the nominating process.

In the early 20th century, progressive leaders thought that direct primaries could be used in presidential nominations. Because direct primaries have been instrumental in removing power from the vested interests that controlled state and local nominations, progressives sought similar results in adopting direct primaries for presidential nominations. They believed that, in time, the national party convention's sole function would be to ratify the choice of the voters in state primaries. Even though the first presidential primaries emerged in the early 20th century, it was not until 1972 that presidential primaries became the dominant method. By 1916, 25 states had passed presidential primary laws. However, the time between the World Wars saw an ebb when eight states repealed primary laws and candidates largely ignored primary campaigning. It was only after 1968 that the number of primary states jumped from 15 to 33, in just three presidential elections. The percentage of delegates selected in the presidential primary states jumped from 37 percent in 1968 to 72 percent in 1976. By 2000, 41 states held presidential primaries.

Until the proliferation of primaries in the late 1960s, a presidential candidate ignoring presidential primaries could hope that the national convention would still choose him or her as the party's candidate, perhaps as a compromise candidate if the convention was deadlocked. However, since 1972, it has become virtually impossible for a candidate to win the nomination without campaigning and winning in the primaries. In fact, since Hubert Humphrey secured the nomination despite several primary victories for Eugene McCarthy, the candidate who was the most successful in primaries has been nominated at the national convention. Thus, from the 1960s to 1980, the presidential nomination process was gradually transformed from a closed system dominated by party leaders to a popular, open system that gave more power to candidate organizations and rank-and-file voters.

Presidential primaries span a period of about six months, with preparations beginning about a year before the first primaries. During this period, presidential primaries create unique electoral dynamics. Candidates who can start with a few impressive primary results usually ride this momentum to win nominations. Because of the importance now given to momentum-building, early primaries have gained added attention.

IMPACT

The New Hampshire Primary and the Iowa Caucus get much media attention and candidates usually spend a lot of campaign resources on winning these early contests. However, this increased attention also creates some controversy. Some argue that the publicity Iowa and New Hampshire get distorts the representativeness of the primary system. Candidates who carry New Hampshire also lure voters in the following primaries. Critics say that this momentum is harmful for representativeness because by the time the last primaries are due, the nomination is practically over, and late primary states have no say in the process.

Presidential primaries have transformed the nomination process. Party organizations and leaders have lost their dominant influence on presidential nominations. Together with primary elections for all other offices, presidential primaries give the power of political leader selection to the rank-and-file voters. In addition to the voters, candidate organizations and mass media also have benefited from the presidential primaries. The media have not only gained a longer-running story from primaries, but also more influence over the nomination process.

SEE ALSO: Iowa Caucus; New Hampshire Primary; Presidential Election of 1972; Presidential Primaries.

BIBLIOGRAPHY. L.M. Bartels, *Presidential Primaries and the Dynamics of Public Choice* (Princeton University Press, 1986); J.W. Davis, *Presidential Primaries: Road to the Whitehouse* (Greenwood Press, 1980); J.W. Davis, *U.S Presidential Primaries and the Caucus-Convention System: A Sourcebook* (Greenwood Press, 1997); E.R. Gerber and R.B. Morton, "Primary Election Systems and Representation," *Journal of Law, Economics and Representation* (v.14/2, 1998).

Eser Sekercioglu
Stony Brook University (State University of New York)

Primaries, State and Local Elections

PRIMARIES ARE THE method by which voters nominate party candidates. In the United States, primaries are used at federal, state, and local levels. Before the advent of the direct primary, the standard method of nomination in the United States was through party conventions. In many states, each township or district elected delegates to the county convention, where delegates for congressional and state conventions were then selected. At each of these stages, delegates negotiated, bargained, and voted to make nominations. Often, the first level of this layered process, the township or district meetings, were called primary elections, or primaries. For this reason, when the nomination of candidates by popular vote was introduced, the method was referred to as a direct primary to distinguish it from the local meetings held under the convention method.

The statewide application of primaries for most elected offices, except the U.S. presidency, was imposed on political parties by legislatures in many states during the Progressive era. This was done to nullify the political clout corrupt party machines exerted under the convention method. Revisionists, however, argue that urban middle-class reformers intended to take back political power from lower-class immigrants who were mobilized by party bosses. Recent studies suggest that the emergence of increasingly aggressive candidates and the necessity of institutionalization in response to societal urbanization may have induced the political parties to initiate this reform. One important historical fact those making these arguments neglect, is that nominating by the direct primary system was initially adopted by county party organizations. The oldest known case was the Democratic party of Crawford County, Pennsylvania, in 1842. The method was eventually referred to as the Crawford County system, and was adopted at the county level in more than 25 states by the early 20th century.

Primaries, regulated by state laws in most cases, and are diverse, but can typically be categorized into four types: open, closed, non-partisan, and blanket. Eleven states have an open primary system in which voters can choose their party after they enter the voting booth (thus called a pick-a-party primary). No party registration is needed, but voters may only vote for candidates from the same party for all offices. Eleven mostly southern states utilize a variation of the open primary, called a semi-open primary, in which voters do not have to register with a party in advance, but have to declare openly at the polls in which party's primary they wish to vote.

Fourteen states use a closed primary, in which voters must be registered with a party in advance to vote in its primary. Also, 14 states employ a semi-closed primary, in which voters are permitted to register or change party affiliation on Election Day, or unaffiliated Independent voters are allowed to participate in partisan primaries. Florida has a closed primary system, allowing all qualified voters, regardless of party affiliation to participate in a partisan primary if no candidate from another party is running for the office (called a universal primary). Louisiana has a unique non-partisan primary, in which all candidates for an office are listed on the same ballot with their party affiliation appearing after their names. If a candidate receives a majority of votes cast in the primary, he or she is elected to the office with no general election to follow. Otherwise, the top two finishers of the primary, even if they are from the same party, proceed to the general election.

The blanket primary is no longer in use. At one time utilized by Washington, Alaska, and California, the blanket primary allowed voters to switch between parties to participate in nomination from office to office. This method was ruled unconstitutional by the U.S. Supreme Court in 2000, on the grounds that it violated the parties' First Amendment rights of free political association.

Primaries are usually run by plurality rule, in which the candidate who receives the most votes wins. However, 12 mostly southern and border states use the run-off primary system where the top two contenders proceed to a second round, known as a runoff primary, if no candidate receives a majority of the votes in the first round. Political parties prefer a closed primary to an open primary because they can focus on appealing to registered, partisan voters. Parties also fear strategic crossover voting under the open primary system, characterized by supporters of one party participating in the other party's primary in an attempt to nominate the weaker candidate. However, researchers have found that voters resist this temptation, and that crossover voting tends to be less strategic than sincere.

Still, the shift from party conventions to primaries of any type is said to have weakened political parties. Party leaders lost the power to nominate the candidates who are most likely to win the general election. Candidates are now nominated in primaries that are often plagued with low competition, low turnout, and unrepresentative participants who are typically older, whiter, wealthier, and with more extreme policy preferences than general election voters. In an attempt to exert some influence under the primary system, parties struggled to retain the elements of the convention system. As a result, in many states, parties are required to hold conventions, or allowed to choose between party convention and primary. Seven states by law provide for preprimary endorsements by party conventions. Although the likelihood of party-endorsed candidates winning primaries is on the decline, party endorsement still functions as a vehicle for party organization amidst the candidate-centered style of politics that the adoption of primaries has enhanced.

Primaries are used for most partisan offices, including statewide elected offices, state legislatures, and party county central committees. In many states, judicial, municipal, and school board elections are nonpartisan; for these offices, nonpartisan primaries are used to reduce the set of candidates that go on to the general election, usually to the top two candidates in a primary. In nonpartisan primaries, candidates are not allowed to list a party affiliation. County offices are partisan in some states, while nonpartisan in others. In California, county offices are nonpartisan, and appear only on the primary ballot. In the case where no candidate receives a majority of the vote, the race between the top two candidates receiving the highest number of votes will appear on the general election ballot. By contrast, in Tennessee, county offices are partisan, but primaries are not mandatory. Each of the two major political parties in a county has the right to call a county primary election for any or all of the county offices in election years.

SEE ALSO: Election Laws, State and Local; Nonpartisan Election; Presidential Primaries; Primary Elections.

BIBLIOGRAPHY. Virginia Gray and R.L. Hanson, *Politics in the American States: A Comparative Analysis* (CQ Press, 2004); J.C. Kuzenski, "The Four. Yes, Four. Types of State Primaries," *PS: Political Science and Politics* (v.30/2, 1997); J.F. Reynolds, *The Demise of the American Convention System, 1880–1911* (Cambridge University Press, 2006); Alan Ware, *The American Direct Primary: Party Institutionalization and Transformation in the North* (Cambridge University Press, 2002).

KAORI SHOJI
COLUMBIA UNIVERSITY

Primary Elections

IN EXISTENCE SINCE the early 20th century, primary elections are a defining characteristic of politics in the United States. No other democracy, with the exception of Canada, allows so much popular influence in the selection of political leadership. American voters elect the candidates who run in presidential, congressional, and gubernatorial elections, as well as elections for other state offices. Primary elections are usually traced to the U.S. progressive movement. Until about 1910, the convention system, which had replaced the legislative caucus in mid-19th century, had remained the dominant method of party candidate nomination. However, conventions were increasingly seen as instruments of machine politics and state party leaders. Backed up by the rising middle class, consisting of small businesspersons, professionals, and independent farmers, progressive reformers at the turn of the 20th century championed the adoption of direct primary elections to undercut the power of machine politics at both local and state levels. In the south, while progressives also favored adoption of direct primaries, primary elections were part of the electoral institutions designed to disenfranchise African Americans and further strengthen Democratic Party dominance. Thus, primary elections emerged out of two different historical and political conditions.

Extension of the primary elections to nominating presidential candidates took a little longer, but by 1916, 25 states had passed presidential primary laws. However, the state conventions and caucuses retained the lion's share in the nomination process until the 1970s when the number of states with presidential primaries grew from 25 to 33. After 1972, the number of states that held presidential primaries continued to increase, fluctuating from election to election. For example, in 2000 a total of 41 states held presidential primaries compared to 36 in 2004. Unlike other federal and state elections, presidential primaries attract much attention from the mass media. Presidential primaries not only give people a say in selecting their leaders, but also provide the media with a long-running and exciting story line. In presidential primaries, turnout has increased from less than 10 percent of the voting age population, to about 25–30 percent in the early 21st century.

There are several types of primary elections: in closed primaries, only registered voters of the party can participate; in semi-closed primaries, both registered voters of the party and unaffiliated voters can participate; in a blanket primary, voters are given a list of candidates and they can choose candidates without regard to party lines. Blanket and non-partisan primaries are considered variants of open primaries, because voters are either not required to declare party affiliation, or may declare affiliation on the election day. In a blanket primary, voters are given a list of candidates and they can choose candidates without regard to party lines.

Blanket primaries are now used by very few states, though several states would like to adopt blanket prima-

ries. Louisiana, for example, uses a nonpartisan variant of a blanket primary, which many states see as a model to adopt after the U.S. Supreme Court ruled in 2000 that a state cannot mandate that political parties use a blanket primary (*California Democratic Party v. Jones*). Ultimately, Washington, California, and Alaska had to change their blanket primary systems. Several states see blanket primaries as a solution to decreasing political participation. Because blanket primaries do not force voters to chose a party and allow unaffiliated voters to participate, adoption of blanket primaries can reinvigorate interest in the nomination process. Proponents of the blanket primary also argue that blanket primaries would lead to more moderate candidates and give voters more varied choices.

Political parties, in contrast, prefer closed primaries to open primaries because of the fear of strategic voting. Low turnouts make it relatively easy to influence primary election results. In open primaries, because voters are not required to declare party affiliation, supporters of one major party could vote for a weak candidate in the primary elections of the other major party, thus increasing their own party candidate's winning chances in the general elections. Though such strategic voting or raiding has not been documented, it is deemed possible, especially in low turnout elections.

The type of primary elections used in a state affects the characteristics of candidates nominated for general elections. Open and semi-closed primaries result in more moderate candidates than closed primaries. Because only registered voters who declared affiliation with the party can participate, electorates in closed primaries tend to have stronger party ties and more extremist policy preferences. Therefore, winning candidates in closed primaries appeal to this subset of partisan electorate. In open and semi-closed primaries, on the other hand, moderate voters who are not affiliated with either party can cast votes. Thus, the winning candidate has to be appealing to an electorate, which is, on average, more moderate than the electorates in closed primaries.

SEE ALSO: Presidential Primaries; Primaries, State and Local Elections.

BIBLIOGRAPHY. J.W. Davis, *Presidential Primaries: Road to the Whitehouse* (Greenwood Press, 1980); L.M. Bartels, *Presidential Primaries and the Dynamics of Public Choice* (Princeton University Press, 1986); E.R. Gerber and R.B. Morton, "Primary Election Systems and Representation," *Journal of Law, Economics and Representation* (v.14/2, 1998); Robert Hogan, "Sources of Competition in State Legislative Primary Elections," *Legislative Studies Quarterly* (v.28/1, 2003).

ESER SEKERCIOGLU
STONY BROOK UNIVERSITY (STATE UNIVERSITY OF NEW YORK)

Progressive Party

THE PROGRESSIVE PARTY has been the name of three different national third parties during the first half of the 20th century. The three parties were Theodore Roosevelt's Bull Moose Party (1912), the Progressive Party of "Fighting Bob" LaFollette, and the 1948 campaign of Henry Wallace.

THE BULL MOOSE PARTY

The Progressive Party (1912) came about as a result of a split in the Republican Party. Theodore Roosevelt, who left the presidency in 1909, was disappointed by the policies of his handpicked successor, William Howard Taft. After failing to win the Republican nomination, despite winning nine of the 12 presidential primaries held that year, Roosevelt called his own convention in Chicago, which nominated him for president and California's Republican governor, Hiram Johnson, for vice president. The Progressive Party platform called for the federal government "to dissolve the unholy alliance between corrupt business and corrupt politics." In his acceptance speech, Roosevelt told the delegates that, "we stand at Armageddon. And we battle for the Lord."

Most Republican leaders refused to bolt the party to support Roosevelt (including his son-in-law Nicholas Longworth), believing that joining the new party was too risky a step. The Progressive Party's leading financial supporters were newspaper and magazine publisher Frank A. Munsey and George W. Perkins, a financier who was a partner in the House of Morgan. Roosevelt's supporters included the social worker Jane Addams, former U.S. Senator Albert J. Beveridge of Indiana (who would be the party's unsuccessful candidate for governor in 1912, and the U.S. Senate in 1914), and U.S. Senator Joseph M. Dixon of Montana (who served as Roosevelt's campaign manager).

While campaigning in Milwaukee, John Schrank shot Roosevelt, who survived, stating, "it takes more than a bullet to stop a bull moose" (giving the party its nickname). Roosevelt came in second in the election, polling 27 percent of the popular vote and winning 88 electoral votes, more than Taft, but allowing Woodrow Wilson to win the presidency. The Progressives would run a number of candidates for the House of Representatives, winning nine seats. However, the real impact of the Progressives on the House was that, in a number of races, the Progressives split the Republican vote, allowing the Democrats to pick up 61 seats, expanding their majority to 290 in the 435 seat chamber.

The party continued after the 1912 elections. Perkins, the party's executive secretary, caused a split in the party in 1913 when he came out against anti-trust laws. Many Progressives had joined the party because of Roosevelt's reputation as a "trust buster." In 1914, the Progressives would win only six seats in the House of Representatives (a loss of three). In 1916, Roosevelt rejected the Progressive Party nomination after the Republicans nominated Supreme Court Justice Charles Evans Hughes for president. Not wishing a repeat of the 1912 contest, Roosevelt campaigned for Hughes, who was narrowly defeated by President Wilson. In the congressional elections, the Progressives would win three seats, but by joining with the Democrats, they allowed the Democrats to remain in control of the House (the last time that the House would be controlled by a coalition of parties, rather than a single party).

The party disbanded as a national party after the 1916 elections, with many of its members returning to the Republican Party. During its short existence, the party elected 13 different men to the U.S. House of Representatives, the governor (Hiram Johnson) and lieutenant governor (John Morton Eshleman) of California; one senator elected as a Republican, Miles Poindexter of Washington, would formally switch to the party for the 63rd Congress (1913–15).

THE LAFOLLETTE PROGRESSIVES

In 1924, Robert Marion "Fighting Bob" LaFollette, Sr., a Republican senator from Wisconsin, established the United States Progressive Party to run for president in 1924. LaFollete's running mate was Democratic Senator Burton K. Wheeler of Montana. The American Federation of Labor, the Socialist Party of America, the Non-Partisan League and many former "Bull Moose" Progressives supported LaFollette. Unlike the Bull Moose Progressives, the LaFollette party did not seek other offices. LaFollette's platform called for government ownership of railroads and electric utilities, more access to credit for farmers, the abolition of child labor, laws protecting labor unions, more protection of civil liberties, an end to American imperialism in Latin America, and support for a constitutional amendment that would require a referendum before a declaration of war. LaFollette carried Wisconsin and its 13 electoral votes, and won 17 percent of the national popular vote. The party disbanded after the election and LaFollette died in June 1925 from cardiovascular disease.

In 1934, Robert M. LaFollette, Jr., who had succeeded his father in the Senate as a Republican, left that party and established the Progressive Party of Wisconsin. That year, the party dominated the state's elections, with Philip LaFollette (brother of the Senator) elected governor and seven of the party's candidates winning election to the U.S. House of Representatives. In 1936, the Progressive Party of Wisconsin endorsed President Franklin D. Roosevelt for re-election. Philip LaFollette established a National Progressive Party in 1938, but LaFollette was defeated for re-election in 1938, and the national party failed to gain support. In 1942, Orland Steen Loomis was elected governor of Wisconsin as a Progressive, but died before he could take office. The last Wisconsin Progressive to hold public office was Merlin Hull, a congressman, who served as a Progressive 1935–47 (he was re-elected four more times as a Republican).

HENRY WALLACE'S CHALLENGE TO TRUMAN
In 1946, the Progressive Citizens of America (PCA) was formed as a left-of-center advocacy group to support the continuation of Franklin Roosevelt's policies. The group's members had become disillusioned with Harry Truman, especially his policies toward the Soviet Union. Its more prominent members included former Interior Secretary Harold Ickes (who had been a leader in the Bull Moose Party). By 1948, the group had decided to move toward becoming a new political party (initially, the party was referred to as the New Party). The purpose of the party was to elect Henry Agard Wallace, who had served as secretary of agriculture (1933–40), vice president (1941–45), and secretary of commerce (1945–46). President Harry S. Truman fired Wallace from his post as commerce secretary for

Theodore Roosevelt's Bull Moose Party managed to elect 13 men to the U.S. House of Representatives.

criticizing Truman's policy toward the Soviet Union. He then became editor of *The New Republic*, where he continued to criticize Truman.

The Progressive Party, meeting at its organizing convention in Philadelphia, nominated Wallace for president and U.S. Senator Glen H. Taylor of Idaho for vice president. The party called for an end to segregation, full voting rights for African Americans, and the introduction of universal health insurance. The party also opposed Truman's foreign policy (including the Marshall Plan and the Truman Doctrine), was against the continuation of the military draft during peacetime, and called for the abolition of the House of Representatives Committee on Un-American Activities. The Progressive ticket was endorsed by New York's American Labor Party (ALP), giving Wallace a ballot line in New York (Wallace's name would appear on the ballot in every state), and by the Communist Party USA.

The Progressive Party attracted the support of left-wing Democrats who, like Wallace and Taylor, were alienated by what they perceived as Truman's rightward-shift, and Communists, whose presence in the Progressive campaign was criticized by the Democratic and Republican campaigns. Some of the more prominent figures in the party were former U.S. Senator Elmer Benson of Minnesota (who was Wallace's campaign manager), and actor Paul Robeson, The presence of Communists in the campaign, and Wallace's unwillingness to repudiate that party's endorsement, cost the ticket support. In the election, the Wallace-Taylor ticket polled over 1.1 million votes, with more than 40 percent of his votes coming from New York.

After the election, many of the party's moderate supporters, including Wallace, would leave the party. By 1952, the party's base came from the far left of the political spectrum. In 1952, the party would nominate Vincent Hallinan, a lawyer from California, for president. His running mate was Charlotta Bass of New York, the first African-American woman to run for national office. The Hallinan-Bass ticket received 140,000 popular votes. The party disbanded in 1955. The party had been built around Henry Wallace, who left the party, and most of its more committed members had come from the Communist Party, and opposed any criticism of the Soviet Union. Given its opposition to U.S. foreign policy during this era, it would be difficult for any party that was not perceived as anti-Communist to survive.

Since Wallace's time, a number of third parties known as Progressive parties have developed at the state level. In 1981, the Vermont Progressive Party was established with the election of Bernie Sanders as Mayor of Burlington (1981–89). Sanders was elected to the first of his eight terms in the U.S. House of Representatives in 1990, and was elected to the U.S. Senate in 2006. In 2003, a Washington State Progressive Party was established.

SEE ALSO: Anti-Communism; Bull Moose Party; LaFollette, Robert M.; Presidential Election of 1912; Presidential Election of 1924; Presidential Election of 1948; Third Parties; Wallace, Henry A.

BIBLIOGRAPHY. Brett Flehinger, *The 1912 Election and the Power of Progressivism: a Brief History with Documents* (Bedford/St. Martins, 2003); J.A. Gable, *The Bull Moose Years: Theodore Roosevelt and the Progressive Party* (Kennikat Press, 1978); C.D. MacDougall, *Gideon's Army* (Marzani and Munsell, 1965); K.C. MacKay, *The Progressive Movement of 1924* (Columbia University Press, 1947); R.B. Nye, *Midwestern Progressive Politics: A Historical Study of Its Origins and Development, 1870–1958* (Michigan State University Press, 1959); Amos Pinchot, *History of the Progressive Party, 1912–1916* (New York University Press, 1958); K.M. Schmidt, *Henry A.*

Wallace, Quixotic Crusade 1948 (Syracuse University Press, 1960); N.C. Unger, *Fighting Bob LaFollette: The Righteous Reformer* (University of North Carolina Press, 2000).

JEFFREY KRAUS
WAGNER COLLEGE

Prohibitionist Party

BEHIND ONLY THE Democratic and Republican parties, the Prohibitionist Party is the oldest political party still in existence in the United States. Since 1872, the party has fielded a presidential ticket in every election. Though, like other minor parties, it never had great electoral success, the party did contribute to the passage of various notable reforms, including the prohibition of alcohol, women's suffrage, and the direct election of U.S. senators.

Many of the party founders were originally enthusiastic supporters of the Republican Party. They were fervent abolitionists, and saw the Civil War as a great Christian crusade against the south's peculiar institution. After the war, they hoped the Republicans would take up the next great social evil—alcohol. When this did not happen, their disillusionment grew, and they were frustrated that the party was more interested in the economic than the moral transformation of the country. To have "a land redeemed from drink," it was decided, in 1869, that the best course of action was to abandon two-party politics and form their own party to advance Christian values, with the prohibition of alcohol chief among them. Not surprisingly, given its faith in being dry, the camel, over time, became the party's symbol.

At the presidential level, the party's best years were 1884–1924, when it typically received one to two percent of the popular vote. During this time, its nominees were quite experienced by minor party standards. Among its nominees were three Union Army generals, two former state governors, and a former congressman. Its 1924 ticket made history, with Marie Brehm as its vice presidential nominee, the first woman to be legally chosen by an American party to be a presidential running mate. Two prohibitionists were also elected to the U.S. House, and, in 1916, Sidney Catts was elected governor of Florida. In 1932, in the shadow of Prohibition's repeal, Reverend Robert Shuler ran for the U.S. Senate in California and earned the largest vote total (more than

The Prohibition Party backed women's suffrage. Above, Elsie Hill, representing the Congressional Union for Woman Suffrage Woman's Party, addresses a crowd in St. Paul, Minnesota during a July 1916 party convention.

500,000 votes) ever for any Prohibitionist candidate. After the ratification of the Nineteenth Amendment, the party was among the first to run women for the U.S. Senate. In 1920 and 1922, in multiparty contests, Prohibitionist women (Ella Boole, Leah Cobb Marion, and Rachel Robinson) won over five percent of the statewide vote in New York and Pennsylvania.

After the 1920s, the party rapidly declined. In recent years, the Prohibition Party has been more a one-person hobby than a viable party. Since 1976, Earl Dodge of Colorado, a political button vendor, has been on the party's national ticket eight consecutive times, twice as the vicepresidential nominee (1976–80) and six times as the presidential nominee (1984–2004). In 2000 and 2004, Dodge received a mere 208 and 140 votes, respectively.

SEE ALSO: Nineteenth Amendment; Religious Issues in Campaigns; Republican Party; Third Parties.

BIBLIOGRAPHY. John Kobler, *Ardent Spirits: The Rise and Fall of Prohibition* (G.P. Putnam's Sons, 1973); R.C. Storms, *Partisan Prophets: A History of the Prohibition Party* (National Prohibition Foundation, 1972).

D. JASON BERGGREN
FLORIDA INTERNATIONAL UNIVERSITY

Proportional Representation

IN A PROPORTIONAL representation system, the goal is to translate as closely as possible each party's share of votes into a share of seats in the legislature. Proportional representation facilitates the existence of multiparty systems and coalition governments. While proponents point out that this ensures a better representation of minorities and greater consideration of a wider range of policies in the government, critics claim that it encourages fragmentation, indecision, instability, and possibly opens the door to extremist parties. Proportional representation emerged in continental Western Europe at the end of 19th century. It was first used in some Swiss cantons in the 1890s, and Belgium was the first country to use it for national elections in 1900. Currently, all countries in the European Union, with the exception of France and Britain, use some form of proportional representation. The system is also widely used in Latin America. In the United States, proportional representation has been used in many cities (for example, on city councils and school boards). It is also used for apportioning seats to states in the House of Representatives.

THE SYSTEM

The party list vote is the most widely used form of proportional representation, and the most frequently used electoral system in the world, currently employed in about 70 countries. Each party presents a list of candidates, and the voter chooses from among these lists. The total vote for each party determines the number of its candidates who get elected. For example, in a 100-member legislature, a party receiving 10 percent of the vote will be entitled to 10 seats. In a closed party list system, these individuals will be the top 10 candidates on the list (the order on the list is decided by the party leaders). In an open party list system, voters can express their preference for a specific candidate, but these votes will first be added up to give a total party vote. This total will determine how many seats a party will get; for example, the 10 individuals who are elected are the top 10 vote getters.

By definition, proportional representation requires multi-member electoral districts, and the number of representatives elected in a district is referred to as district magnitude. This number ranges from Chile's two-member districts to Ukraine's nationwide, 450-member district. In the latter case, the whole country is treated as a unique district for the purpose of electing the members of its legislature. Most countries want to retain some degree of local representation, thus the country is divided into a set of multi-member districts, and seats are allocated within each district. There is a tradeoff between proportionality, on the one hand, and the closeness of the relationship between representa-

tives and constituents on the other. In a case such as Chile, with only two members elected within each district, the relationship is much closer than in Ukraine, and resembles the constituents-representative link in a single-member district system as in the United States. However, this comes at a heavy price for proportionality: a party must win at least one-third of the total vote to be guaranteed a seat. Thus, smaller parties are essentially excluded from competition in such a system.

District magnitude is essential for the proportionality of the system. The lower the magnitude, the more disproportional the system. Another way to limit the proportionality and, consequently, to ensure that the legislature does not become too fragmented is to raise the legal threshold, the minimum percentage of votes required by law to gain representation. In practice, this legal threshold varies from the Netherlands' 0.67 percent to Turkey's 10 percent.

The Netherlands combines this low threshold with a single, nationwide district (the district magnitude equals the size of the legislature, 150 members), and creating an almost perfect match between votes and seats, or real proportional representation. This leads to the representation of a wide array of parties and an extremely fragmented legislative body. For instance, after the Netherlands' 1994 parliamentary elections, 12 parties gained representation, including two parties representing pensioners. The result is that no party ever gains a majority, and the government is always a broad coalition of parties. Such governments tend to be short-lived: The Netherlands has had 28 changes of government since 1945. Other democratic regimes using proportional representation provide even more extreme examples of governmental instability. One such example is the French Fourth Republic, which had 21 prime ministers in less than 12 years (1947–58).

Even a moderate threshold can lead to a significant decrease in the number of parties. Between 1961 and 1980, Germany's five percent threshold kept down the number of parties represented in the federal parliament to just three. An even higher threshold, such as Turkey's 10 percent, can lead to a substantial number of wasted votes (that is, votes cast for parties that do not cross the threshold). In Turkey's 2002 parliamentary election, only two parties gained representation, and 46 percent of the votes were wasted. This illustrates the inherent tension that exists in proportional representation systems. If the system is too proportional, it can lead to fragmentation and instability. If the system is made less proportional, either through low district magnitude or through a high threshold, it starts resembling a winner-take-all system, and by doing so defeats the very purpose of proportional representation.

SEE ALSO: Multiparty System; Plurality Vote; Winner-Take-All System.

BIBLIOGRAPHY. D.J. Amy, *Real Choices/New Voices: The Case for Proportional Representation Elections in the United States* (Columbia University Press, 2001); Vernon Bogdanor, *What Is Proportional Representation?* (Blackwell, 1984).

FLORIN FESNIC
UNIVERSITY OF BUCHARES

Protectionism

PROTECTIONISM FORMS PART of an American political legacy inherited from the colonial era as part of Great Britain's mercantilist traditions. Independence did not change the need to protect America's infant industries. Hence, protectionism formed a critical part of Secretary of the Treasury Alexander Hamilton's approach to the economy as reflected in his *Report on Manufacturers* (1791). The method employed to deliver this protection from foreign competition was a system of import charges or duties.

Protectionism also offered the federal government a way to raise revenue, which was the clear purpose behind the first tariff in 1789. The tariff would remain the principal source of government revenue until World War I and the onset of income tax. Other early tariffs, such as the 1816 Tariff, were clearly protectionist. This tariff charged a 25 percent rate on imported textiles, and even more on certain manufactured goods. The 1824 Tariff expanded these rates to include a wider range of imported goods such as wool, iron, lead, and glass.

The height of this early protectionist drive came in the Tariff of 1828, also known by its opponents as the Tariff of Abominations, which increased rates to almost 50 percent. Although beneficial to the emerging economic interests of New England manufacturers, it was seen in other areas as a penalty on their economies. This was

particularly the case in South Carolina. Enforcement hurt cotton exports and made the cost of manufactured imports astronomical. Southern criticism of the tariff became a campaign issue that benefited Andrew Jackson's faction in what would soon become a separate Democratic Party.

Jackson exploited this unpopularity in his 1828 campaign against President John Quincy Adams, who had signed the tariff bill. Although Jackson benefited from this opposition, and by 1832 had overseen tariff reductions, the tariff still created bitter feelings in the south, a situation that was exploited by South Carolina's Senator John C. Calhoun. Calhoun elevated the disagreement to the point that it is remembered as the Nullification Crisis. South Carolina threatened secession from the union if tariff reduction did not occur. The tariff had emerged by mid-century as a key political divide. The Whigs were committed to protective tariffs, while the Democratic Party opposed high tariff legislation.

Whig control of Congress allowed the tariff to be increased in 1842. With the Democrats in a majority and James K. Polk in the presidency, the tariff was lowered in 1846. Duties were further lowered in 1857, under Democratic President James Buchanan to a 20 percent average. The Civil War transformed America and saw the rise of Republican dominance of both the presidency and Congress with the withdrawal of southern Democratic opposition. Republican support of high tariff policies that favored domestic manufacturing over agriculture became a political mainstay of the party.

The period after the Civil War became an era of protectionist Republican tariffs. This shaped national debate on the issue, and Republican practice until 1913. Rates generally remained high, but a number of exemptions were included in the legislation. American industrial strength had expanded during these years and did not seem in need of so much protection, nevertheless, high tariff policy was embraced in exchange for native business support.

In the latter decades of the 19th century, such increased protectionism was opposed in the campaigns of Grover Cleveland, who fell on the free trade side of the Democratic Party. However, Cleveland was defeated by Benjamin Harrison and the Republicans, who built protectionism into the McKinley Tariff of 1890. Republican platforms maintained support for the protective tariff into the 20th century, as seen in the

Dingley Tariff of 1897, and the Payne-Aldrich Tariff of 1909 during President William Howard Taft's administration. A general policy of tariff reduction formed part of Woodrow Wilson's successful 1912 campaign, and during his first administration, the 1913 Underwood Tariff was passed, which represented a reduction.

However, the Republican ascendancy following World War I saw the return to protection in the form of the Fordney-McCumber Tariff of 1922, which increased rates generally by as much as 50 percent, to be determined by the president. Even with the collapse of trade following the Great Depression, the Republicans maintained the high tariff mind set and produced the 1930 Smoot-Hawley Tariff, which increased rates enormously above those of the Underwood Tariff. As the worldwide economic crisis increased, such protectionism made matters worse internationally and deepened the collapse of world trade.

FREE TRADE AGREEMENTS

The lessons learned following Smoot-Hawley and World War II saw both the Republican and Democratic parties adopting free trade principles, which were geared to the reduction of international trade barriers. In 1947, during Democratic President Harry Truman's administration, the United States led the way in establishing the General Agreement on Tariffs and Trade (GATT), which reduced restrictions on world trade. In the next decades, there would be a series of rounds such as the Kennedy Round, Tokyo Round, and the Uruguay Round that further liberalized trade. Although tariff removal or reduction symbolizes the modern political position over protectionism, a variety of other protectionist practices have an impact on government policy. The use of product quotas, direct subsidies such as those on manufacturing or agricultural goods and crops, and other governmental interventionist trade restrictions, as well as the devaluing of exchange rates, often produce protectionist outcomes.

The general trend for both Republican and Democratic parties is to support free trade agreements as seen in President Clinton's support for NAFTA (North American Free Trade Agreement) in 1993, and President George W. Bush's support for the CAFTA (Central American Free Trade Agreement) in 2004. Both measures were anti-protectionist and furthered a globalized approach to economic welfare through expanded markets and investments without national-

ist barriers. However, there are protectionist voices in both parties and remain potent influences on political campaigns, particularly in some local areas and states, which can affect certain congressional districts. Many special interests, such as unions or specific industries, still desire protection for their members, employees, and stockholders.

These protectionists can be found among conservative factions within the Republican Party, as well as among union, manufacturing, agricultural, and other special interests within the Democratic Party. Nevertheless, the generally-held political view is that protectionism hurts economic development in both developed and undeveloped countries. Trade liberalization increases investment and exports, while reducing poverty. Yet, certain national interests, regional trading blocks, and left-wing anti-globalization forces still favor protectionist practices, making protectionism a continuing issue for both American political parties.

SEE ALSO: Economy; Free Trade; Isolationism.

BIBLIOGRAPHY. I. M. Destler, *American Trade Politics* (Institute for International Economics, 2005); A.E. Eckes, *Opening America's Markets: United States Foreign Trade Policy Since 1776* (University of North Carolina Press, 1999); J.S. Gordon, *An Empire of Wealth: The Epic History of American Economic Power* (Harper-Collins, 2004); Sidney Ratner, *The Tariff in American History* (Van Nostrand, 1972); R.W. Thompson, *The History of Protective Tariff Laws* (Garland Publishing, 1974); Morgan Witzel, ed., *Free Trade, Reciprocity and Protectionism: The American Debate, 1890–1914* (Thoemmes Continuum, 2003).

THEODORE W. EVERSOLE, PH.D.
INDEPENDENT SCHOLAR

Protestant Vote

AMONG OTHER DEVELOPED countries, the United States stands out as remaining a highly religious country. Not only is it religious, it is mostly Christian and Protestant. By virtue of this demographic, the Protestant vote is amongst the most important blocs in American politics. In fact, it is nearly impossible to win the White House without seriously appealing to Protestant voters. Protestantism, whether practiced or nominal, is self-identified by approximately 60 percent of the population. In the political arena, the Protestant vote is often associated with the Republican Party. However, Protestantism, especially in the United States, is largely decentralized, which has led to a highly independent and libertarian group of people.

Regionalism also plays a role, since there are a greater number of self-identifying Protestants in the south relative to the rest of the country. Yet, there are still significant numbers of Protestants in the other regions of the country and the Protestant vote goes to both major parties. Within the Protestant vote, the issue of race plays an important role. The racial difference is that upwards of 90 percent of African Americans have voted for the Democratic Party in recent elections. This stands in stark contrast to white Protestant voters, especially white Evangelical voters. Overwhelmingly, African-American Protestants will vote for Democrats based on issues such as poverty and affirmative action.

Protestantism has hundreds of different categories and denominations. There is a significant difference between what is considered a mainline Protestant (for example Lutheran, Episcopalian, or Presbyterian), an Evangelical, and a fundamentalist. Although both fundamentalists and Evangelicals are born again, Evangelicals tend to emphasize a personal relationship with Jesus Christ as the key to salvation. The simplest distinction between the two groups is that a fundamentalist tends to take a very literal translation of the Bible, whereas an Evangelical will look at the meaning behind the text. Upwards of one-third of Americans are Evangelical Christians, and this bloc, in particular, has been influential in electing Republican presidents in recent years. Evangelicals and fundamentalists vote for the Republican Party, whereas mainline Protestants are much more split.

PROTESTANT VOTING IN RECENT ELECTIONS
The Evangelical vote is overwhelmingly cast in favor of the Republican Party. It was the driving force that gave the White House to George W. Bush in 2000 and 2004. Likewise, the Evangelical vote was significant in the election of Ronald Reagan in 1980 and 1984. This is not to say that Evangelicals, across the board, vote for Republicans, but to say that the ratio is approximately 4:1 favoring Republicans over Democrats. Despite this, the Evangelical vote did help Jimmy Carter, who identified himself as a born-again Christian, win the presidency in 1976.

When preachers in the Evangelical and fundamentalist churches wade into the political arena in an organized manner, the distinctions between religion and culture become blurry. For example, the most notable organization hoping to mobilize Christians politically, the Christian Coalition, was founded in the late 1970s to affect issues such as abortion and prayer in school (this was later extended to the issue of same-sex marriage). One of its leaders, Marion (Pat) Robertson, attempted to win the Republican nomination for the 1988 election. Robertson had some initial success in a Michigan straw poll and came in second in Iowa (ahead of the eventual nominee, George H.W. Bush). However, after a number of problematic incidents, Robertson conceded after significant losses on Super Tuesday, including some largely Christian states such as Texas.

DOMESTIC ISSUES
There are a number of issues that help to explain why many Protestant voters elect Republican candidates. Abortion is probably the most central issue for many Protestant voters, but prayer in school and same-sex marriage are also important issues. The *Roe v. Wade* decision of 1973, which legalized abortion, shaped the voting patterns of many Protestants throughout the country. Evangelicals and fundamentalists are, in most cases, vehemently opposed to abortion. The issue of same-sex marriage, after the Massachusetts state court legalized same-sex unions in 2004, has also become a significant factor for the national electorate.

Therefore, the 2004 election, in many ways, revolved around moral values, and including appeals on the part of President Bush to press Congress to support a constitutional amendment banning same-sex marriage. These issues, therefore, became wedge issues that helped cement Protestant support for the Republican Party (especially among Evangelicals and fundamentalists). This is not to say, however, that the Protestant vote is always cast in one direction. In recent years, many traditionally conservative Evangelicals have taken on some more liberal issues such as lobbying for environmental protection. Viewed as protecting "God's creation," this has become an important niche sector of the Evangelical vote.

FOREIGN POLICY AND PROTESTANT VOTING
Often cast by the mainstream media as simplistic, the Evangelical vote has become increasingly sophisticated,

lobbying for the rights of the persecuted church abroad. This has led many Evangelicals to become well-informed about countries throughout the world that are known for religious persecution. Many Evangelicals, given their desire for world missions, have traveled abroad and have gained increased perspective from this. Subsequently, their votes have increasingly gone to candidates who are well-versed in foreign policy. In contrast, mainline Protestant groups have decreased their involvement in world missions. This has led to a greater influence from more liberal sources such as academia and, to some extent, the media.

With regards to foreign policy, many fundamentalists and Evangelicals have been influenced by the highly popular book series *Left Behind*, written by Tim LaHaye and Jerry Jenkins. The *Left Behind* series is a fictional future account of the rapture (when Jesus returns, Christians believe that they will ascend into heaven) which, some Christians believe, will mark the tribulation when the earth will undergo seven years of intense hardship before Jesus will return to defeat Satan. The eschatology (study of End Times) of fundamentalist Christians has led many to support the War on Terrorism because of the inherent view of good versus evil in the world.

Because of their belief in certain prophetic occurrences ushering in the return of Jesus, many fundamentalists support Israel in any crisis in the Middle East, as do some Evangelicals. Mainline Protestants vary between support for Israel and support for the Palestinians. Evangelical and fundamentalist interests in foreign policy are not, however, limited to Israel. Many have serious interests in the War on Terror, especially with U.S. troops in Afghanistan and Iraq.

The issue of religious freedom in China has become popular with Protestants, as has support for Christian martyrs around the globe. The genocide in the Darfur region of Sudan, too, has become a rallying point in Christian circles. This was, in some sense, a continuation of Christian lobbying on the part of fellow Christians in another Sudanese civil war involving the Arab Muslim government in Khartoum against the black animist and Christian population in the south of the country.

SEE ALSO: Abortion; Gay Rights; Presidential Election of 2004; Religion and Voting Behavior; Religious Issues in Campaigns; War on Terrorism.

BIBLIOGRAPHY. Hugh Heclo, "Is America a Christian Nation?" *Political Science Quarterly* (Spring 2007); Allen Hertzke, *Freeing God's Children: The Unlikely Alliance for Global Human Rights* (Rowman & Littlefield Publishers, 2004); W.R. Mead, "God's Country?" *Foreign Affairs* (September/October 2006); Clyde Wilcox and Ted Jelen, eds., *Religion and Politics in Comparative Perspective: The One, The Few, and the Many* (Cambridge University Press, 2002).

Glen M.E. Duerr
Kent State University

Protest Voting

PROTEST VOTING IS voting for an outsider candidate, perceived as having no chance to win, as an expression of dissatisfaction with traditional parties. What distinguishes it from regular voting is its negative connotation: it is a vote of rejection, rather than a vote of support for the recipient. Its goal is to send a signal to one's own party or the political elite, in general, rather than to promote a particular candidate, party, or policy. Protest voting is different from split-ticket voting, when a voter simultaneously casts votes for candidates of different parties, and from strategic voting, when a voter votes with the better-positioned candidate rather than with the one that represents him or her better.

Protest voting is a form of expression of political discontent akin to returning a blank vote, spoiling the vote, and nonvoting (when not due to political indifference). Unlike these other forms of voting that ultimately amount to abstention, a voter engaged in protest voting actually casts a vote for a party or candidate. While the intent of the protest vote is to scare political leaders, in some instances the protest vote is credited as having changed the outcome in close elections.

PRESIDENTIAL ELECTIONS

The most often-quoted instances of protest voting take place in presidential elections. In the 1992 U.S. presidential election, the popular vote was divided between Bill Clinton (42.9 percent), George H.W. Bush (37.1 percent), and Independent Ross Perot (18.8 percent). Many of the votes received by Ross Perot were seen as protest votes. Public opinion research have shown that Perot supporters were more likely than the voters choosing the others two candidates to mistrust the government and to fear public officials' corruption. Although Perot succeeded in attracting new voters to the political process, he also took away votes from the two major parties. Some claimed that he disproportionately hurt Bush, therefore allowing Clinton to win the election, however his overall impact on the outcome is difficult to assess. In the extremely close 2000 election between George W. Bush and Al Gore, Ralph Nader, a candidate for the Green Party, received many thousands of votes that otherwise likely would have been cast for Gore. In Florida alone, Nader received 97,421 votes. Bush won Florida by a mere 537 votes, giving him the electoral votes needed to win the presidency. Most political analysts believe that these protest votes for Nader cost Gore the presidency, because the vast majority of these votes would have gone to Gore, the more liberal feasible alternative, had Nader not been on the ballot.

Protest voting is not limited to the United States. Presidential runoff elections, common to many democracies around the world, highlight another remarkable feature of this form of protest. Sometimes, dissatisfied electors vote in the first round for a marginal candidate, who every so often makes a surprising appearance into the second round, only to have voters turn against him or her in the run-off. There might be a political cultural dimension associated with this behavior, as voters in some countries, such as France, resort to it frequently as a protest mechanism, while voters in other democracies might choose a different form of protest.

A notorious instance of protest voting was the French 2002 presidential election, when the far right nationalist Jean-Marie Le Pen of the National Front came in second, defeating the left candidate Lionel Jospin. In the runoff, however, incumbent president Jacques Chirac of the right defeated Le Pen by a large margin: 82.2 percent to 17.8 percent. This result showed that Le Pen attracted a large number of unhappy voters, without being seen by the French public as a viable alternative.

The consequences of protest voting in parliamentary elections depend on the electoral system. Plurality elections, such as those in the United States and United Kingdom, may encourage protest voting. Under these rules, there have been many failed attempts by third parties to enter the political arena, but the electoral system systematically discriminates against them. Casting a protest vote for a third party, such as the Liberal Democrats in the United Kingdom, and the Reform and Libertarian parties in the United States, adds to the core supporters of such a party, but is unlikely to bring them into power.

Occasionally, third parties fuelled by protest votes manage to produce surprises, such as the 2007 victory of the separatist Scottish National Party. In proportional representation electoral systems, the protest vote can be very consequential. In the absence of a high electoral threshold, it may promote political fragmentation and makes coalition formation difficult. In the Dutch 2006 parliamentary election, several small parties, such as the Party for Animals, captured protest votes from the main political players, weakening the major player's bargaining power during coalition formation. It is not uncommon for the beneficiaries of the protest vote to have a vaguely defined ideological platform and even self-mocking names, such as the Blah! Party (United Kingdom), or The Free to Change Party (Romania).

THE PROTEST VOTE AND EXTREMISM

A much-debated topic concerns the relationship of the protest vote to the far left and far right. In Western Europe, increased support for nationalist anti-immigrant parties is often interpreted as protest voting. Others argue that, at least in some countries, anti-immigrant parties have their own electoral support and those votes should not be interpreted as protest votes. The debate stems from problems with the concept and its measurement. Identifying a protest vote entails access to the motivation of a rational, but teasing voter. Transitory spikes in popularity for marginal parties or candidates, in conjunction with public opinion data, suggest dissatisfaction with mainstream political parties, and lack of identification with the recipient of the vote, provides support for protest voting.

The new post-Communist democracies abound with such instances. In the 2000 Romanian parliamentary election, the far right Greater Romania Party with 23 percent of the popular vote, was the second-largest party in the legislature. Considered to be the result of a protest vote, the party declined only slightly after the 2004 election, and maintained third place in the Romanian legislature. In 2007, the Great Romanian Party was able to place five of its members in the European Parliament, and together with a similar party from Bulgaria, played a decisive role in the formal recognition of the far-right political group Identity, Tradition, Sovereignty in the European Parliament.

SEE ALSO: Nader, Ralph; Nonvoters; Perot, Ross; Plurality Vote; Presidential Election of 2000; Proportional Representation; Split Ticket Voting; Third Parties.

BIBLIOGRAPHY. Hans-Georg Betz and S. Immerfall, eds., *The New Politics of the Right; Neo-Populist Parties and Movements in Established Democracies* (Macmillan, 1998); "Leader: France's Loss of Legitimacy," *Financial Times* (April 22, 2002); Won-Taek Kang, "Protest Voting and Abstention under Plurality Rule Elections. An Alternative Public Choice Approach," *Journal of Theoretical Politics* (v.16/1, 2004); Jeffrey Koch, "The Perot Candidacy and Attitudes toward Government and Politics," *Political Research Quarterly* (v. 51/1, 1998); Marion Kraske and Hans-Jürgen Schlamp, "Far-right MPS Join Forces in EU Parliament. A Small Thorn in The EU's Side," *Spiegel Magazine* (January 23, 2007); Lorna Martin, "Labour Launches Fight to Stop Protest Vote," *Observer* (April 8, 2007); Wouter Van Der Brug and Meindert Fennema, "Protest or Mainstream? How the European Anti-immigrant Parties Developed into Two Separate Groups by 1999," *European Journal of Political Research* (v.42, 2003).

OANA I. ARMEANU
UNIVERSITY OF SOUTHERN INDIANA, EVANSVILLE

Provisional Ballots

PROVISIONAL BALLOTS FORM part of the electoral reform process that emerged following the voting difficulties encountered in the 2000 U.S. presidential election. Provisional ballots fall under the guidelines of the Help Americans Vote Act, Public Law 107-252, of 2002. The provisional ballot forms part of a general process to guarantee voting rights to all, and to ensure transparency so that those eligible to vote are not denied because of local procedural or mechanical irregularities. By creating such a system, eligible voters can deliver their vote as a provisional ballot if they satisfy individual state and precinct rules. These new federal guidelines are outlined in the legislation. Each state has therefore introduced new procedures to meet these contingencies.

In practice, provisional ballots offer a method to reduce the number of people who wanted to vote, but were denied the opportunity due to certain voting rules and procedures. Under the provisional system, a voter can vote if they claim to be registered, but do not appear on a particular voting list. They might also be given a provisional ballot as a first-time voter who lacks proper identification at the time of voting.

Those who have applied to vote by mail, but have not been issued a postal ballot or have not returned one, can use provisional ballots. The provisional ballot might also be used by those attempting to vote in a precinct other than the one they had originally registered in, or by a potential voter who is on a polling list, but whose address falls outside of a specific voting precinct. In addition, voters trying to vote in precincts with extended polling hours might use the provisional ballot.

The principle behind the provisional ballot is to close those gaps that have excluded certain individuals from the voting process, and to increase voter participation. This type of ballot potentially eliminates voter rejection because of registration issues, particularly, omission from polling lists or improper identification requirements for specific districts. Those whose previous political party registration makes them ineligibile for a primary election might use the provisional ballot. There could also be specific court action at either the federal or state levels that allows a provisional ballot to be issued.

The provisional ballot contains the same information on candidates as the normal ballot, but will be distinguished by a different color and labeling to show it is a provisional ballot; this might include a separate provisional ballot envelope. The local board of elections will then have a short period of time (normally 10 days for a primary election and 14 days for a general election) to determine if the provisional ballot is legitimate and, therefore, should be included in the total election count. The provisional ballot can be denied or challenged if it does not conform to other registration requirements, such as the voter not appearing on any acceptable registration list, wrong precinct or address information, and inaccurate or fraudulent documentation of identity, residence, or eligibility.

As the law states, the provisional ballot was established:

… to ensure that every eligible voter who is registered or who believes they are registered can cast a ballot in federal elections with the knowledge that a fair process will be followed to determine if this provisional ballot is eligible to be counted.

States have been given the task of creating voting procedures that meet these federal guarantees. For critics, provisional voting is not a solution to voter discrimination and denial. Instead, provisional voting might allow felons, foreigners, and others to vote illegally unless local precincts can properly supervise the voting process within the time and financial constraints placed upon the recording agents.

SEE ALSO: Election Boards; Help America Vote Act; Voting, Obstacles to; Voting Methods.

BIBLIOGRAPHY. Tracy Campbell, *Deliver the Vote: A History of Election Fraud, an American Political Tradition* (Carroll and Graf Publishers, 2005); Committee on Government Reform, U.S. House of Representatives, *Election 2000: An Investigation of Voting Irregularities* (Cosimo, 2005); Bev Harris, *Black Box Voting: Ballot Tampering in the 21st Century* (Talion Press, 2004); S.E. Schier, *You Call This an Election?: America's Peculiar Democracy* (Georgetown University Press, 2003); Craig Varoga, "Collecting Provisional Ballots: Using Stock Photos on Campaign Websites," *Campaigns and Elections* (v.26/7, 2005).

THEODORE W. EVERSOLE, PH.D.
INDEPENDENT SCHOLAR

Psychological Reasons for Voting and Nonvoting

VOTER TURNOUT IN any given election is minimal when juxtaposed with eligible voters. The proportion of those who vote compared to those who are eligible to vote in the United States is also smaller compared to many other countries, some of which (such as Australia) have compulsory voting laws. Thus, voting behavior is an important topic for political researchers, who examine demographic, sociological, and psychological factors that may influence the choice to vote.

Some researchers suggest morality comes into play when individuals compare themselves to those who live under dictatorships or other non-democratic rulers who prevent individuals from exercising electoral rights. Citizens of democratic countries may define morality as doing what a "good citizen" does. If one perceives him or herself to be a good citizen, and the perception of a good citizen includes voting, then according to cognitive dissonance theory, there will be an uncomfortable tension experienced if he or she

does not vote. The congruity between self-perception and action is maintained by acting as an ideal citizen and voting. Similarly, some citizens vote for symbolic reasons. The very act of voting reaffirms the democratic right to do so.

Although some longitudinal researchers find that those who participate in one election may not participate in the next, other researchers report longstanding psychological drives to vote. One such drive is a deep-seated feeling of civic obligation. This differs from other reasons because it implies more of a duty and less of a choice. Another drive to vote is interest in political affairs. The more interest in the governmental process a person has, the greater the impetus to vote.

The perceived need for control in one's life can also be a predictor of if one casts a vote. Under some conditions, researchers report that those who experience low levels of personal control demonstrated increased participation in voting. Other researchers have examined aggregate increases in voting behavior over time. Interestingly, the most influential factor has been an increase in civic consciousness. Voting behavior positively correlates with awareness of governmental processes and those involved in governing.

Perhaps the most frequent psychological factor reviewed that seems to encourage or discourage voting is efficacy. Specifically, efficacy breaks down into two subtypes: internal and external. Internal political efficacy is the belief that a person has the necessary resources or skills to influence the government. External political efficacy focuses on personal beliefs, whether or not they believe the government is responsive to their influence. Thus, the greater the perceptions of each internal and external political efficacy, the greater the likelihood exists that the individual will vote. Some researchrs show that for those with high efficaciousness, a feeling of anxiety about a candidate increases the probability they will vote.

Reinforcement theory offers a different perspective on why people choose to vote or abstain, based on their participation in the last election and the election results. This application of reinforcement theory relates to citizens' internal political efficacy, with election outcomes either augmenting efficacy beliefs or diminishing them. For example, if an individual voted and the desired candidate won, then that individual is likely to vote again. If the individual did not vote, but his or her preferred candidate won anyway, then the individual's nonvoting was reinforced, and not voting in the next election is predicted. However, if an individual did not vote and his or her favored candidate lost, then this encourages him or her to alter behavior and vote in an upcoming election.

Whereas civic duty serves as a motivational impetus for some to vote, for others the argument that Americans should be good citizens holds far less weight than it does for citizens of other democratic countries. U.S. citizens are far more individualistic than other citizenry, and focus more on self than on the collective body of the country's well being. Voting becomes of lesser importance than other activities that are more directly self-serving. Carried one step further, self-interested Americans may choose not to vote as a means of deviancy.

Other researchers suggest that would-be voters are ignorant of the process, candidates, and issues. Some researchers hypothesize that non-voters are filled with cynicism, apathy, or perhaps feel alienated. The number of Americans who report themselves as engaged in public or political life has declined. While some pin nonvoting on purely internal characteristics, others point to external factors, blaming nonvoting on the declining ability of major parties to stimulate political activity. Along these lines, criticism is directed to a lack of new campaign marketing techniques, or even voter weariness when new marketing ventures are attempted. And, although voting impediments such as assessments have been removed or lessened over time, there is still a psychological perception that there are legal and procedural roadblocks to voting.

Examining nonvoting from the perspective of rational choice theory, choosing not to vote is logical. Technically, it is rarely in an individual's self-interest to vote, given that the act of voting is psychologically classified as low-cost, but more importantly, low-benefit. Voting research commonly consists of asking individuals to self-report voting behavior. Some researchers have demonstrated a gap between those who claim to have cast ballots and those who actually did. This research also examined some psychological factors of voters, nonvoters, and those who misrepresented themselves as voters. Psychologically, misrepresenters fall in between voters and non-voters, but more closely resemble the former. Most researchers define a voter as someone who voted in a given election. This holds an implied assumption that a voter typically votes and a non-voter usually

does not. However, there is some longitudinal research that has tracked validated electoral data over time and found voter turnout and those who voted varied noticeably over time. Many vote only sometimes.

SEE ALSO: Social Groups and Electoral Behavior; Voter Alienation; Voter Apathy; Voter Disenfranchisement; Voter Knowledge/Ignorance; Voter Registration; Voter Self-Interest; Voting; Voting, Incentives for; Voting, Obstacles to.

BIBLIOGRAPHY. J.H. Aldrich, "Rational Choice and Turnout," *American Journal of Political Science* (v.37/1, 1993); D.P. Bannon, "Voting, Non-Voting and Consumer Buying Behaviour: Non-Voter Segmentation (NVS) and the Underlining Causes of Electoral Inactivity," *Journal of Public Affairs* (v.3/2, 2003); J. Fraser, "The Mistrustful-Efficacious Hypothesis and Political Participation," *Journal of Politics* (v.32/2, 1970); A.S. Gerber, D.P. Green, and R. Shachar, "Voting May Be Habit Forming: Evidence from a Randomized Field Experience," *American Journal of Political Science* (v.47/3, 2003); S. Kanazawa, "A Possible Solution to the Paradox of Voter Turnout," *Journal of Politics* (v.60/4, 1998); F.F. Piven and R.A. Cloward, *Why Americans Don't Vote* (Pantheon, 1989); S.A. Renshon, "Psychological Needs, Personal Control, and Political Participation," *Canadian Journal of Political Science* (v.8/1, 1975); T.J. Rudolph, A. Gangl, and D. Stevens, "The Effect of Efficacy and Emotions on Campaign Involvement," *Journal of Politics* (v.62/4, 2000); L. Sigelman, "The Nonvoting Voter in Voting Research," *American Journal of Political Science* (v.26/1, 1982); L. Sigelman et al., "Voting and Nonvoting: A Multi-Election Perspective," *American Journal of Political Science* (v.29/4, 1985); R.M. Stein, J.E. Leighley, and C. Owens, "Who Votes, Who Doesn't, Why and What can be Done?" (Federal Commission on Electoral Reform, 2005).

JALANE M. MELOUN
BARRY UNIVERSITY, MIAMI SHORES, FLORIDA

Public Funding of Campaigns

PUBLIC FINANCING IS the appropriation of money from a public treasury to candidates or parties for the express purpose of aiding them in funding electoral campaigns. Public financing schemes are generally designed to combat perceptions of widespread inequity or financial malfeasance in elections at the federal, state, and local levels of American government. There is a substantial diversity in the construction of public financing systems. However, they generally possess three key commonalities: they provide viable candidates with subsidies sufficient to pay for all or part of a campaign, candidates usually agree to limit their spending to a predetermined amount, and candidate participation in public funding programs is optional because mandatory spending restrictions have been deemed unconstitutional by the Supreme Court.

There are at least four broad issues that public subsidies seek to confront. The first is the elimination of special interest influence-peddling. Because many public funding systems proscribe the solicitation of special interest contributions, or severely restrict them, public funding is intended to mitigate the influence of resource-laden pressure groups. Second, public funding is intended to curb the growth of campaign spending, in general, allowing a greater degree of access for potential challengers. The Supreme Court ruled in *Buckley v. Valeo* (1976) that political spending equates to speech, thus striking down mandatory campaign spending caps. Public funding provides an incentive to participate in an optional program that incorporates spending limits, thus reigning in spending without mandatory limits.

Third, public subsidies work to combat the notion of the unbeatable incumbent. With name recognition, professional staff, and more highly-developed resource networks at their disposal, incumbents are difficult for a challenger to defeat. Because private donations are generally not allowed if public funding is accepted, optional election subsidies reduce disparities in funding between challengers and incumbents, allowing the former the resources to mount more effective campaigns against entrenched officeholders. Fourth, by providing them with funds directly, public financing seeks to alter the routines of candidates, freeing them from the onerous burden of fundraising with the supposition that they will reinvest that time into engaging voters directly. The assumption is that absent spending caps, candidates must devote so much time to raising money that their ability to interact with voters (and, in the case of incumbents, to represent their constituencies) is substantially undermined.

At the federal level, the presidency is the only office for which public election subsidies are available. The Federal Election Campaign Act of 1974 created a system of partial public funding in presidential primaries and full funding for the general election. In both instances, candidates accept spending limits as a condition of participation. In the 2008 primaries, candidates must first qualify by raising $5,000 in 20 separate states, and agree to spending limits of slightly more than $40 million overall, and no more than $200,000 in any one state. The federal government then matches the first $250 of every individual contribution. Major party candidates who win their party's nomination for president receive a subsidy of $81.8 million. While the program enjoyed unanimous participation from its inception through 1996, participation has recently lessened. In 2000, George W. Bush refused public funds in the primary, and neither Bush nor his 2004 opponent, John Kerry, accepted general election funds and spending limits that year. The evidence indicates that this trend will continue.

In addition to the presidential program, some mechanism of public funding exists in over half of American states and at least four municipalities. The nature and scope of the state programs vary substantially; in some states, all offices are eligible for public funding, while in others, only candidates for governor or the judiciary can take public money. In many instances, subsidies are not granted for the full amount of the spending limit, forcing candidates to raise the remainder from private sources. Recently, advocates of legislation called Clean Money, Clean Elections have had some success, passing full public financing in seven states. Through the 2006 election, only Maine and Arizona had funded their programs at levels sufficient to grant full public subsidies to all candidates for state office since 2000. North Carolina enacted full public funding, but only for candidates for the judiciary. Given the widespread perception that money is the root of evil in American politics, public funding programs may become increasingly common.

SEE ALSO: Campaign Finance, Federal Elections; Campaign Finance, Politics of; Campaign Finance, State Elections; McCain-Feingold Campaign Finance Reform.

BIBLIOGRAPHY. P.L. Francia and P.S. Herrnson, "The Impact of Public Finance Laws on Fundraising In State Legislative Elections," *American Politics Research* (v.31/5, 2003); C.M. Mathias, Jr., "Should There Be Public Financing of Congressional Campaigns?" *Annals*, AAPSS (v.486, July 1986); K.R. Mayer and J.M. Wood, "The Impact of Public Financing on Electoral Competitiveness: Evidence from Wisconsin, 1964–

1990," *Legislative Studies Quarterly* (v.20/1, 1995); F.J. Sorauf, *Inside Campaign Finance: Myths and Realities* (Yale University Press, 1992); Fred Wertheimer and S.W. Manes, "Campaign Finanace Reform: A Key to Restoring the Health of Our Democracy," *Columbia Law Review* (v.94/4, 1994).

MICHAEL G. MILLER
CORNELL UNIVERSITY

Push Polls

PUBLICLY CONDEMNED BY professional polling agencies and associations, a push poll is not a poll at all, but a campaign technique designed to deride the opponent. Though it follows the format of a poll, those conducting a push poll do not care about the respondent's answer. Like a rhetorical question, it only asks in order to pass on information and ideas. For instance, a multi-question poll may open with a block of information and a leading question to which, as phrased, there is only one reasonable answer; a follow-up question will then indict the target of the poll, the first question having warmed up and conditioned the respondents to get them thinking about the issue.

In the guise of seeking a voter's opinion, a push poll seeks to influence and even deceive a voter. Often, a large block of information will be presented, with only one question asked, "Will this affect the likelihood of your voting for Candidate Smith?" The question reinforces the idea that the respondent's opinion is important; respondents may extemporize beyond the simple *yes* or *no*, but what matters to the pollster is that they listened to that block of information. Consequently, often many more voters are contacted in push polls, since one common objective of a push poll is to smear the opposition candidate. It may have concerned candidate Smith's voting record, for example, perhaps honestly (as a way to notify voters of candidates who have supported positions unpopular in the voter's neighborhood) and perhaps deceptively (a senator voting in support of civil unions may be described as voting against traditional heterosexual marriage).

But the information passed on by a poll need not even be true. During the 2000 South Carolina presidential primary, a polling agency assumed to be affiliated with the Bush campaign called voters and asked them if their vote would be affected by the revelation that John McCain had fathered an illegitimate child with a black woman. He had not done so, nor did the poll actually state that he had, but if treated as a fair and honest poll, it sounds as though it is making that claim. Given the human tendency to remember information better than its source, the poll must have been very effective at spreading and creating this rumor, and McCain lost the primary and the election.

SEE ALSO: Canvassing Voters in Campaigns; Election Outcome Forecasting Models; Negative Campaigning; Polling; Polls, Pre-Election.

BIBLIOGRAPHY. E.J. Dionne, *Why Americans Hate Politics* (Simon and Schuster, 2004); J.B. Judis, *The Paradox of American Democracy: Elites, Special Interests, and the Betrayal of the Public Trust* (Routledge, 2001); Hal Malchow, *The New Political Targeting* (Campaigns and Elections, 2003); D.R. Shaw, *The Race to 270: The Electoral College and Campaign Strategies of 2000 and 2004* (University of Chicago Press, 2006); J.M. Stonecash, *Political Polling: Strategic Information in Campaigns* (Rowman and Littlefield, 2003).

BILL KTE'PI
INDEPENDENT SCHOLAR

Race and Voting Behavior

THE STUDY OF the differences in demographics, such as education level, socioeconomic status, gender, age, and race, among voters can help determine how and why different people vote. It also provides political parties with the information they need to attract voters. These parties must know who is most likely to cast a vote in their favor. If they are unlikely to actually go to the polls, it is important to determine why they do not vote, and how to encourage them to do so. It is essential for campaigns to direct advertising and get-out-the-vote drives to those individuals who are most likely to vote for their particular party.

It is likely that people of certain races, education levels, socioeconomic status, and other characteristics will be attached to one party over another. Overall, the race of an individual has a greater impact on voting behavior than other characteristics, including socioeconomic status. In order to understand the voting behavior of different races, their journey to the polls must be traced with particular emphasis on the obstacles they faced in obtaining the goal of full membership in the U.S. system of participatory democracy.

The U.S. Census Bureau has projected that by 2050, the country's Caucasian population decline to 52.5 percent of the population, the Hispanic population will increase to 22.5 percent, the African-American population to 15.7 percent, the Asian and Pacific Islander population to 10.3 percent, and the Native American, Eskimo, and Aleut populations will be approximately 1.1 percent. This rise in the minority population of the United States will make it increasingly important for political parties to understand the voting behavior of these groups to ensure that they are able to properly cater to the voters on which they must rely to get elected—their new support bases.

BARRIERS TO VOTING

Poll taxes, grandfather clauses, registration requirements, literacy tests, residency requirements, the institution of white-only primaries, as well as a host of intimidation tactics have kept minorities from the polls and effectively disenfranchised them. Such devices prevailed despite the passage of the Fifteenth Amendment in 1870, which guaranteed all races the right to vote in all elections. It was not until Congress passed the Voting Rights Act of 1965 that the promise of the right to vote began to be fulfilled. The Voting Rights Act of 1965, most recently renewed in 2006 by President George W. Bush, along with its various amendments, slowly removed the barriers that had been created in the southern states to keep minorities from exercising their constitutional vote. The removal of these barriers to the voting booth

689

increased voter registration for African Americans from 12 percent to 62 percent in southern states over approximately 20-years.

However, the barriers to voting for minorities were not completely removed by this act. The basic requirements inherent in the voting system still keep many individuals from voting in federal and state elections. For example, the requirement of registration prior to being able to vote often limits participation because of the fact that individuals have a deadline by which to be registered in order to be able to vote in a particular election. Often people do not become interested in an election until it is very close to the actual vote. Interest drives the willingness to participate, but a lack of interest in the months prior to the election means registration to vote may not have occurred by the deadline date and therefore people are prevented from going to the polls.

There are various other barriers related to the structure of the political system that affect participation, but it is now believed that individual voting behavior relates more to individual characteristics than to external factors. These characteristics include: Race, education, socioeconomic status, trust in government, interest in politics, belief that one's vote makes a difference, and the attachment (or lack thereof) to a political party.

AFRICAN-AMERICAN VOTING BEHAVIOR
African Americans are more likely to vote in a given election when compared with whites of an equivalent status once socioeconomic levels are controlled for, despite the variety of barriers that African Americans have had to overcome. African Americans tend to be highly politically motivated because of their involvement in groups and organizations that have concentrated their efforts and resources and provided members with incentives and education. By encouraging political activity, these groups ensure large numbers of African Americans are involved in politics, even if that involvement is limited voting. As race-conscious individuals, they work hard in the political arena to ensure that African Americans are elected to political office to improve the lot of the entire race. This race-consciousness has led to a large degree of distrust in the political system and those who work within it. This distrust drives them to participate and to work toward political change, as long as political efficacy already exists within the group.

Since 1964 the Democratic Party has been the recipient of the largest share of the African-American voting bloc. African Americans are now approximately one quarter of the core base of the Democratic Party. However, this does not mean that the Democratic Party can rely on the fact that the receipt of this vote will be a foregone conclusion in every election. The party needs to continue to cater to this voting block, as it could be lost to a strong, pro–African-American, third party candidate. Nevertheless, African Americans are a part of the Democratic Party today because of the support the African-American community has received and because of shared ideological beliefs.

LATINOS, ASIANS, AND OTHER GROUPS
Many Latinos and Asians in the United States are unable to register to vote because many inhabitants of these communities are not native or naturalized U.S. citizens. They face even more problems as a result of the lengthy and complicated process involved in becoming naturalized citizens, lack of time and money to go through the process to become naturalized citizens, a lack of knowledge of the information on which they are tested in the naturalization examination, and language barriers. Asians are 23 percent less likely to vote than whites of equivalent demographic characteristics, while Latinos and Native Americans vote in similar levels to whites.

Asians and Latinos each include a variety of ethnicities. For example, Cubans are more likely to vote than whites, and Puerto Ricans are the most likely Latinos to vote overall. Also, the Filipino and Vietnamese ethnic groups are the most likely Asians to vote. Therefore, blanket statements about Latinos or Asians cannot possibly cover the numerous differences that exist among the variety of ethnicities one finds in these two groups.

The power of the Latino voting bloc is especially felt in Florida and California, where they make up a large percent of the voting public. Especially in these areas, Latino political representation has greatly increased, enabled by the use of Spanish language television, advertising in Spanish, and a Spanish version of the voting ballot.

SEE ALSO: African-American Suffrage; African-American Vote; Asian-American Vote; Democratic Party; Educational Level and Voting Behavior; Fifteenth Amendment; Hispanic

Vote; Income and Voting Behavior; Trust in Government; Voting Rights Act of 1965.

BIBLIOGRAPHY. Y.M. Alex-Assensoh and L.J. Hanks, *Black and Multiracial Politics in America* (New York University Press, 2000); L.J. Barker, M.H. Jones, and Katherine Tate, *African Americans and the American Political System* (Prentice-Hall, Inc., 1999); S.L. Croucher, *Imagining Miami: Ethnic Politics in a Postmodern World* (University Press of Virginia, 1997); J.C. Day, "National Population Projections," U.S. Census Bureau, www.census.gov (January 18, 2001); D.C. Nelson, "Ethnicity and Socioeconomic Status as Sources of Participation: The Case for Ethnic Political Culture," *American Political Science Review* (v.73/4, 1979); R.G. Niemi and H.F. Weisberg, eds., *Controversies in Voting Behavior* (CQ Press, 1993); R.D. Shingles, "Black Consciousness and Political Participation: The Missing Link," *American Political Science Review* (v.75/1, 1981); Katherine Tate, *From Protest to Politics: The New Black Voters in American Elections* (Russell Sage Foundation, 1994); V.M. Valle and R.D. Torres, *Latino Metropolis* (University of Minnesota Press, 2000).

RACHEL YFF
UNIVERSITY OF FLORIDA

Racial Justice

THOUGH RACIAL JUSTICE overlaps with civil rights, the overlap is not complete. Civil rights encompass non-racial issues, and though the Civil Rights Movement responded principally to race-based problems, in American politics the fight for civil rights has included the rights of women, homosexuals, and non-ethnic minorities, as well as rights denied and owed to all citizens. Racial justice, meanwhile, is more than a simple guarantee and protection of rights: under the umbrella of racial justice, organizations such as the American Civil Liberties Union (ACLU) include the condemnation of racial profiling and the race disparity in prisons, and advocacy of affirmative action programs. The pursuit of racial justice has generally focused on African Americans and Native Americans, the two ethnic groups most frequently targeted by unfair or unjust legislation.

The two earliest issues of racial injustice in the United States were the enslavement of Africans and the treatment of, and breaking of treaties with, Native Americans. However, not until the expansion of the 19th century did these issues really become politicized. As the country acquired more and more territory and slavery became unprofitable or illegal in most of the rest of the world, Americans debated whether they were a slave-holding or free nation. As northerners and southerners argued whether new territories should outlaw or legalize slavery, they were really arguing over which position was the "default American stance" and which was the exception.

SLAVERY

Most northerners were perfectly willing to let southerners own slaves, so long as it was clear that an allowance was being made for the slave states. Abolitionists obviously went further than that, calling for an end to slavery in all states, territories, and other holdings, but the argument had raged for decades before the abolitionists' voices became as loud as the others. The importation of new slaves was banned as early as 1808, but as long as the children of slaves remained slaves, all that did was limit the slave trade, not slave ownership. Free African Americans continued to be kidnapped and forced into slavery.

Throughout the 19th century, slavery and the treatment and position of former slaves were the most prominent issues in American politics, alongside currency. Free African Americans were continually treated as lesser citizens than whites, especially because for most of the antebellum period, more than half of free African Americans lived in the southern states or territories. The later codified practice of segregation originated (in a sense) with the creation of free African-American institutions by free African Americans, who established their own businesses and schools because of their exclusion (whether official or not) from white institutions. This also established an African-American power base, which, while limited, in many parts of the country (for example, New Orleans) became significant. The African-American middle class, though all but invisible to most whites, originated in the 19th century among the growing numbers of free African Americans. This development likely felt as much like a threat to pro-slavery southerners as northern abolitionists.

By the middle of the 19th century, the treatment of African Americans was the preeminent issue in federal politics. After the Bleeding Kansas dispute over the issue of slavery in the new state of Kansas, with fears that slaves in Missouri would escape to a free Kansas boiling over into riots and arson, and after the assault on Massachusetts Senator Charles Sumner by South Carolina Congressman Preston Brooks, and the kidnapping and murder of five pro-slavery Kansans by radical abolitionist John Brown, the Supreme Court decided in the 1857 Dred Scott Decision that no one of African descent, regardless of whether they had ever been a slave, could be a citizen of the United States. It was in some sense a worse blow to racial justice than slavery itself, the American practice of which at least provided for the ability of slaves to be freed and, theoretically, enjoy the same rights as other Americans.

The Civil War broke out less than four years later, with the election of Abraham Lincoln. Slaves were theoretically freed during the war, though the Emancipation Proclamation only freed slaves in areas the Union did not actually control; nevertheless, at war's end the Thirteenth Amendment to the Constitution ended slavery, the Fourteenth Amendment overturned Dred Scott and granted citizenship to African Americans, and the Fifteenth Amendment granted African-American males the right to vote.

RECONSTRUCTION

From 1865 to 1877, Union troops occupied the former Confederate states, overseeing and enforcing the reforms of Reconstruction. Southern African Americans not only voted, but were elected or appointed to public office at the local, state, and federal levels, and, for the first time, a significant number of African Americans moved to the south from the north, to take advantage of the growing African-American community there. Reconstruction was not a smooth process for African Americans or whites, too often suffering from the mismanaged attempts at compromise between President Andrew Johnson, who seemed to want to fulfill Lincoln's wish for a non-punitive Reconstruction, and the conservatives in Congress who wanted to punish the former Confederates for their rebellion.

The poor treatment of southerners by northerners and federal authorities only increased their resentment, and while the first Ku Klux Klan did not last for long, white southerners resumed their mistreatment of African Americans, taking out their frustrations on them as soon as they regained power. Northerners, meanwhile, saw a greater number of African Americans moving to the industrial cities. Lynchings soared, the practice of sharecropping put many free African Americans in the same economic position in which slavery had kept them, and Jim Crow laws disenfranchised African Americans, discouraged their education and political participation

in cases where it was not possible to forbid either, and clearly established separate African-American and white Americas, at least in the south.

The period from Reconstruction to the early 20th century, though coinciding with the Progressive Era that sought reforms for the benefit of so many, is sometimes called "the nadir of American race relations." Racism was blatant, and tolerated, and the same scientific advances that inspired so many Progressive reforms were used to justify scientific glosses on racism. These included claims of biological evidence of white supremacy, eugenics, and support for treatment of African Americans as a separate species.

South Carolina Senator Ben Tillman, in a statement often quoted as emblematic of the era, but not nearly so shocking at the time, bragged in 1900 about the efforts made by whites in his state to prevent African Americans from voting. And though Jim Crow laws are primarily remembered for enforcing the practice of segregation, their more serious effect at the turn of the century was to skew the judicial system against African Americans. Because African Americans were forbidden to serve on juries, on the rare occasion that a white person was prosecuted for a crime against an African American, the jury was likely to find them innocent, and there was virtually no point in an African American suing a white person in civil court.

RACIAL JUSTICE ISSUES

Throughout the 20th century, the Civil Rights Movement fought for the end of the mistreatment of African Americans, and, in time, came to focus on ending segregation and protecting the right to vote. The 1896 Plessy v. Ferguson decision by the Supreme Court had upheld segregation by introducing the "separate but equal" doctrine, which was not reversed until the 1954 *Brown v. Board of Education* decision, in which the court unanimously declared, "Separate educational facilities are inherently unequal." With the growing importance of public education in the aftermath of World War II, the desegregation of schools, which were providing more and more facilities and opportunities for white children, while denying them to African Americans, became more critical. Education represented a clear and practical gain compared to the more symbolic victories of desegregating transportation and other facilities. Over time, the desegregation of the Armed Forces and the federal government paved the way for

Martin Luther King, Jr. at the March on Washington in 1963. The Voting Rights Act of 1965 helped increase voting registration for African Americans from 12 percent to 62 percent in southern states.

desegregating the schools and, at least in theory, every public institution in the country allowed for full participation of African Americans in American government and society, a little more than a century after the end of slavery.

Desegregating schools didn't prevent the existence of all or mostly white and African-American schools as a result of local demographics. The correlation between race and economics meant a disparity in funding African-American schools and white schools. School busing—transporting students from one district to the schools of another—was used to combat this in some districts, and remains the target of controversy. The practice of affirmative action also developed in an attempt to deal with imbalances left as a result of historical mistreatment. Because centuries of racial injustice created tenacious inequalities, affirmative action policies in hiring practices or university admissions

attempted to redress that to restore a balance. The specifics vary, and both African Americans and whites have disagreed with the system or the implementation of it. Affirmative action has been a hotly contested campaign issue since the 1960s, and the term is sometimes used as shorthand by conservative factions to conjure up ideas of whites, and especially poor or middle-class white males, being disenfranchised for the benefit of less-qualified African Americans and other minorities.

The ACLU and a score of other organizations quickly point out that great race-based disparities still persist. Some are a matter of historical circumstance, with no apparent solution: the old money that shores up so many institutions is almost purely white; there are no African-American Rockefellers, no African-American Cabots or Lodges. At the same time, the ratio of African Americans to whites in prison and especially on death row is wildly disproportionate; even if economic disparity accounts for a higher percentage of African Americans committing crimes, whites are statistically more likely to be found innocent, especially as a result of some point of law that only an expensive attorney can bring to light.

Many opponents of the death penalty oppose it not only because they oppose the concept of execution in principle, but because in practice it results in far more deaths of African Americans than whites, even relative to the ratio of African Americans to whites in murder convictions. Whatever the reason or explanation, African Americans are more likely to be sentenced to death, and once so sentenced, are more likely to have that sentence carried out rather than succeeding in an appeal. A University of North Carolina study has also found that murders involving non-white victims are less likely to result in the death sentence, which is a different sort of discrimination.

Though the practice of slavery has meant that many of the racial justice issues facing the American electorate have concerned African Americans, the 20th century saw the political mobilization of the disenfranchised Native American as well. There has never been the sort of wide-scale course-correction to counter the mistreatment of Native Americans, both in Colonial times and in the first half of this country's history that there has been for African Americans—no Native-American Reconstruction.

Reservations are simultaneously emblematic of the federal government's corralling of tribes into assigned locations, and those tribes' source of sovereignty. The redistribution of land in order to redress the seizures of tribal land by past generations would be very unpopular. The American Indian Movement and other Native American political groups were very active during the 1960s and 1970s, but never drew the same degree of support as the mainstream Civil Rights Movement, nor did they have as clear an issue as school segregation around which to rally.

SEE ALSO: Civil Rights; Civil War and Realignment; Northern Democrats; Presidential Election of 1860; Presidential Election of 1948; School Integration.

BIBLIOGRAPHY. Stuart Banner, *The Death Penalty: An American History* (Harvard University Press, 2002); B.T. Bates, *Pullman Porters and the Rise of Protest Politics in Black America, 1929–1945* (University of North Carolina Press, 2001); John Egerton, *Speak Now Against the Day: The Generation Before the Civil Rights Movement in the South* (Alfred A. Knopf, 1994); Harvey Fireside, *Separate and Unequal: Homer Plessy and the Supreme Court Decision That Legalized Racism* (Carroll and Graf, 2004); Richard Kluger, *Simple Justice: The History of Brown v. Board of Education and Black America's Struggle for Equality* (Vintage Books, 1976); Manning Marable, *Race, Reform, and Rebellion: The Second Reconstruction in Black America, 1945–1982* (University Press of Mississippi, 1984).

BILL KTE'PI
INDEPENDENT SCHOLAR

Rational Voter Model

THE RATIONAL VOTER model is one of the major alternative explanations of voting behavior to arise in the wake of the now-classic American Voter study by Angus Campbell, Phillip Converse, Warren Miller, and Donald Stokes, released in 1960. While it was not the first in-depth examination of voter behavior, it is certainly the most influential and controversial. It is not an overstatement to say that this study has dominated work on, as well as our collective understanding of, electoral behavior in the United States for the last half-century.

One proponent of this model was the legendary political scientist V.O. Key. Published posthumously in 1966, with the assistance of Milton Cummings, "The Responsible Electorate" was not only Key's response to the American Voter study, but his defense of the American electorate. Key's primary argument can be summarized by a statement early in the text in which he claims, "Voters are not fools." While largely criticized and discredited in the American Voter Study, Key finds that the electorate is, for the most part, responsible, reasonable, and rational.

It is always dangerous to attempt to summarize a study as involved as Key's, but in order to understand his conclusion it is important to look at how he approached his work. Key categorized voters as either "standpatters" (if they voted for candidates from the same party in two consecutive elections), "switchers" (if they voted for candidates from different parties in two consecutive elections), or "new voters" (if they voted in one election, but not the previous one). He then examined the behavior of voters within each of these three categories to determine if they had acted rationally. Key found that the switchers were not only the smallest of the three groups, but also the most rational. Unlike the other two, the switchers based their vote on how they were treated between elections. Moreover, they behaved this way regardless of how they voted in the past. Key also determined that standpatters, the largest group, were rational. He was less upbeat when it came to new voters.

Consequently, while the influential American Voter model suggested that voters were not well informed or concerned and thus often cast their votes irrationally, Key claimed this was not necessarily the case. Key's study presented a picture of the American voter as careful to consider what happened since the last election and to cast their vote retrospectively, on the basis of a reasonable assessment of past performance; to this extent Key argued they were responsible and behaving rationally. Key's defense of the American voter not only served as an important counterpoint to the American Voter model, it has influenced subsequent work in this area as well.

Out of Key's notion of a more reasonable, rational electorate has grown an entire body of literature on electoral behavior from scholars such as Morris Fiorina, Charles Franklin, John Jackson, and many others. Like Key, for example, Fiorina argued that voters behave rationally. Fiorna's work has been influenced not only by Key, but other scholars such as rational choice theorists like Anthony Downs.

The model of rational voting that has developed in subsequent years has been used to help address important questions regarding electoral behavior, such as: Why do people vote? (For instrumental rather than altruistic reasons, in short they expect to benefit in some way). Who votes? (The rational, reasonable, self-interested). While it is appealing in many ways, as is rational choice theory itself, the rational voter model is not without its critics and detractors. One major criticism is that despite its popularity, in the last several decades there is still not enough empirical evidence to support its major assumptions and claims.

SEE ALSO: Voter Knowledge/Ignorance; Voter Self-Interest.

BIBLIOGRAPHY. Angus Campbell, Philip E. Converse, Warren E. Miller, and Donald E. Stokes, *The American Voter* (University of Chicago Press, 1980).

JEANNE ZAINO
IONA COLLEGE

Realignment

REALIGNMENT THEORY EMERGED as the result of a straightforward observation: American political life has been dominated by only two parties since the Civil War, but their ideologies, their electoral base, and the balance of power between them have changed radically more than once. Realignment theory is the attempt to explain when, why, and how these changes occur. Realignments account for changes in the patterns of two-party competition in the United States as the joint effect of two processes. First, adjustments of the policy positions endorsed by the two parties cause realignments. Second, shifts in partisan support from various constituencies as a response to these adjustments create realignments. To qualify as realignments, these changes must be durable. Typically, realignments start with a national election where the balance of power between the two parties is altered significantly.

There are several ways in which realignments can be analyzed and assessed. One approach is to look at survey data, and see if any changes in the patterns of partisan support are discernible at the individual level. Unfortunately, survey data are not available for most of the last two centuries. However, scholars have analyzed aggregate electoral returns available at state, county, town, or precinct levels, to detect differences or changes in voting patterns across various regions or between urban and rural locations.

Comparing the regional bases of support for each party in presidential elections with those of legislative elections offers useful information about the process of realignment. For instance, the results for the Democratic Party in the south have traditionally been better in the elections for Congress than they were in presidential elections. The same can be said about the results of the Republican Party in New England. The explanation is simple: there were liberal and conservative wings in both parties, and in each case, the presidential candidate represented the dominant faction, liberal in the Democratic case, conservative in the Republican case. The Democratic incumbents in the conservative south represented that party's conservative minority, and the Republican incumbents in the liberal northeast represented that party's liberal minority. These gaps were only closed when conservative Republican legislators replaced conservative Democrats in the south, and when liberal Democrats replaced liberal Republicans in

New England. In both cases, the result was that parties became more homogeneous ideologically, with many voters changing their party allegiance in the process.

Another approach is to compare shifts in the voting patterns of rural versus urban locations. V.O. Key, one of the intellectual fathers of the theory of realignments, used this approach to compare electoral returns in two localities in Massachusetts. He compared Somerville, a city with a large percentage of foreign-born inhabitants, and an equally large number of Catholics, with Ashfield, a small, overwhelmingly native-born and Protestant community. In the early 1900s, the Democratic candidates' share of the vote in presidential elections in the two communities was virtually the same. By the 1920s, the Democratic vote in Somerville started to rise, whereas in Ashfield it started to fall, so that by 1932 the gap between the two localities in Democratic support was 50 percent.

To show changes in partisan support among various ethnic groups, Key compared Republican registration in three Boston wards, ward 5 (predominantly "Yankee"), ward 14 (Jewish), and ward 15 (Irish), between 1928 and 1952. In both ward 5 and ward 15, Republican registration remained about the same throughout the period (above 60 percent in the first case, less than 15 percent in the second). In the Jewish ward, though, the change was dramatic. There was a fourfold decrease in Republican registration, from an almost 80 percent high in 1928 to less than 20 percent in 1952.

These examples show creative ways in which scholars have circumvented the absence of survey data. Equally important, they highlight the type of changes in the electoral base of the two parties that constitute a central element of realignments. To explain realignments, it is useful to consider the liberal-conservative dimension typically used to describe political competition. Such a one-dimensional view is of limited use here, and cannot readily explain the changes in party positions and voter support that are associated with realignments. Instead, competition involves at least two dimensions: an economic dimension and a social dimension. While the Republican Party represents conservative policy positions on both dimensions, and the Democratic Party represents the liberal positions, it was not always like this.

In the early 20th century, the Republican Party was at least as liberal as the Democratic Party on social issues. As civil rights issues moved into the forefront of political debate during the 1950s and 1960s, the Republican Party was gradually taken over by its conservative wing, and moved toward a more conservative position on social issues, whereas the Democratic Party moved in the opposite direction. A process of voter adjustment followed this process of changing the policy positions endorsed by each party. For example, libertarian voters, who are economically conservative, but socially liberal, did not feel represented by either party. Some tried to find a different vehicle for representation, such as the Libertarian Party. Others tried to take over one party or the other, moving it into a libertarian position. If they succeeded, the outcome would be another realignment.

While there is disagreement about how many realignments have occurred so far, and their exact timing, the most serious contenders for the title of realigning elections are 1828, 1860, 1896, and 1932. Whether there has been an additional realigning election since the 1960s is debatable, but the current positions of the two parties and their electoral base are very different from what they were at the time of the New Deal. Thus, if there has not been a realigning election since, perhaps there has been a secular (or creeping) realignment, whose end result is similar to that of a realigning election. Although the concept of realignment was developed in the context of American politics, it can be useful to explain political developments elsewhere, for instance, to account for the rise in middle-class support for moderate left-wing (especially Green) parties in other advanced industrial democracies.

SEE ALSO: Conservatism; Election Types; Liberalism.

BIBLIOGRAPHY. V.O. Key, "A Theory of Critical Elections," *Journal of Politics* (v.17/1, 1955); Norman Schofield, Gary Miller, and Andrew Martin, "Critical Elections and Political Realignments in the USA: 1860–2000," *Political Studies* (v.51/2, 2003); J. M. Stonecash, M.D. Brewer, and M.D. Mariani, *Diverging Parties: Social Change, Realignment, and Party Polarization* (Westview, 2003).

FLORIN FESNIC
UNIVERSITY OF BUCHAREST

Recall

THE RECALL IS an election to remove a public official from office before the end of his or her term. It is a form of direct democracy similar to referendum and initiative, in which the election is set in motion by the public because of dissatisfaction with the performance of an elected official, usually by a petition that requires a given number of signatures. If a majority votes in favor, a new election is scheduled to fill the vacancy.

The origin of the recall can be traced to ancient Rome, where the Plebeian Assembly is known to have removed officials from office. The recall has gained influence in the United States due to the efforts of the Progressive Party, which around the turn of the 20th century advocated for a Swiss type of direct democracy, to limit the influence of political parties. That was a period when rapid economic development led to massive social disruption and pressure for political participation by the newly emerging groups. The recall was used for the first time in the United States in Los Angeles in 1903, against a councilman who was successfully removed. Another successful recall of the Progressive era was that of North Dakota Governor Lynn J. Frazier in 1921. Despite a long history, the recall has encountered strong opposition on the part of legislators, and currently only 18 states allow it, although a majority of state constitutions provide for some type of direct democracy.

The last 30 years in the United States have seen an increase in various forms of direct democracy, mostly initiative, through which voters place legislation on the ballot, and to a lesser extent, recall. The latter has been particularly dominant at the local level and has served to remove many local officials. Recall attempts at the top levels generally have failed, with few exceptions. The California recall of 2003 was widely publicized; it removed the newly re-elected Democratic governor Gray Davis, replacing him with the Republican Arnold Schwarzeneger. The 2003 recall followed 31 failed attempts to recall a California governor, in a state requiring only 12 percent of signatures to fill the petition.

Worldwide, one of the most controversial recalls was the 2004 recall of Venezuelan president Hugo Chavez. Despite repeated attempts by the Chavez administration to reject the petition on technical grounds and to punish the signatories by firing them from public jobs, the opposition to the president collected a second set of the 20 percent of signatures required. The recall failed to remove the president amid accusations of fraud.

The debate about recall is rooted in philosophical arguments about representative democracy and public control. The recall is based on the agency view of democracy, which sees elected representatives as agents of the public, under the direct control of the people. The recall has powerful symbolic significance as a form of direct participation and is intended to provide feedback within the political system. It is expected to increase government responsiveness and accountability by removing, or threatening to remove, elected representatives who are corrupt, inefficient, unresponsive, or unpopular, and hence to have the overall effect of strengthening democracy.

In opposition stands the delegation theory of democracy, arguing that public officials should act based on their best judgment, without being bound by the will of their constituents. The belief is that they would behave more responsibly if they were isolated from populist pressures. Experience has shown that recall is a costly and ineffective form of democracy. The rare cases of success may occur for the wrong reasons, such as a millionaire backing the recall, and hence the results are by no means an accurate thermometer of public dissatisfaction. Critics of recall fear that political parties and special interests that want to score political points might abuse the procedure, because money may play a larger role in recall than in regular elections.

The recall also raises some important technical issues, such as the appropriate percentage of petitioners needed to trigger a recall, the timing of the new election to fill the vacancy, and the election of a new official with fewer votes than those in favor of the incumbent. This is a troubling possibility raised by the California recall rules, in which a combination of a high number of candidates, the concomitant scheduling of the recall and the election for the replacement, and the plurality electoral system, may create the opportunity to substitute a sitting official with one who musters even less public support than the previous officeholder.

SEE ALSO: Direct Democracy; Progressive Party.

BIBLIOGRAPHY. T.E. Cronin, *The Politics of Initiative, Referendum, and Recall* (Harvard University Press, 1999); M.L. Ford, *When Voters Change Their Minds: Recall Elections* (Council of State Governments, 1984); Lawrence Sych, "State Recall Elections: What Explains Their Outcomes?," *Comparative State Politics* (v.17, October 1996); J.F. Zimmerman, *The Recall: Tribunal Of the People* (Westport: Praeger, 1997).

OANA I. ARMEANU
UNIVERSITY OF SOUTHERN INDIANA, EVANSVILLE

Reconstruction

THE END OF the south's failed quest for independence, the destruction of its peculiar institution of slavery, and the death knell of secession as a viable political theory, resulted in the need to remake southern institutions and society. From the issuance of the Emancipation Proclamation in 1863 and Abraham Lincoln's generous Ten Per Cent Plan in 1864 culminating in the outcome of the controversial election of 1876, the Republican Party struggled to build a two-party system, provide justice for the freedman, and unity to the nation. Despite their valiant efforts and modest successes, most historians view the Reconstruction as a failure. The issue of Reconstruction policy dominated the presidential campaigns of 1868 and 1872, and the presidential election of 1876 resulted in ending Reconstruction.

The assassination of Abraham Lincoln in April 1865 dashed the hopes of many newly-freed slaves, and the ascension of Vice President Andrew Johnson, a southerner, and a man of extremely negative views toward African Americans, served to hinder their progress toward equality of opportunity. Johnson would prove to be an implacable enemy of the newly-emancipated people. Johnson, working under Lincoln's policy of generosity and leniency toward the former Confederates, outraged Radical Republicans in Congress by vetoing the renewal of the Freedman's Bureau and the Civil Rights Act of 1866; however, Johnson's tactless and public name calling of his opponents resulted in the overriding of his vetoes. To prevent the negation of basic civil rights for the freedman, Congress passed the Fourteenth Amendment in 1868, defining citizenship for all persons born in the United States, regardless of past servitude.

Johnson, fearing the loss of control by the Union Party (the new name of the wartime Republicans), decided to take his case to the people in the infamous "swing around the circle," in which he traveled from Philadelphia to various cities as far as St. Louis, ending in Pittsburgh. In many cities, he faced well-placed hecklers, who taunted him and provoked him unmercifully, and the president, in turn, resorted to intemperate name-calling and return jibes. Johnson lost much support in the country and with Congress, and was impeached. He did was not nominationed to run again in 1868.

When the Republican Party met in convention in the summer of 1868, they nominated General Ulysses S. Grant of Illinois for president and Schyler Colfax of

As a popular war hero, Ulysses S. Grant had first been seen as the key to reuniting the nation after the chaos of the Civil War.

Indiana for vice president on a ticket based on a phrase within a letter written by Grant in which he pleaded to "let us have peace." The convention, in the platform adopted, opened with congratulations to Congress for conducting Reconstruction policy, and promised to prevent the states formerly in rebellion from reverting to "anarchy and military rule." The platform did not mention African Americans directly; however, the National Union Republicans promised that Congress would guarantee the equal suffrage of all loyal men of the south, but negated the hope of federal intervention by declaring "the question of equal suffrage in all the loyal States properly belongs to the people of those states." Finally, convention delegates declared readiness to forgive the participants of the rebellion who were now serving as loyal citizens.

When the Democrats, Johnson's prewar party, met in the summer of 1868, Reconstruction, and the restoration of the former Confederate states served as the key issue, both at the convention and in the canvass. The party called for the "immediate restoration" of the former Confederate states, amnesty for the former rebels, and the right to vote for all the citizens of the states, and concluded with the accusation that the Radicals in Congress had negated and circumvented the constitution. In addition, they accused the Republicans of not restoring the Union, but of dissolution of the nation, and worse, "subjected ten states in a time of profound peace to military despotism, and negro supremacy." The Democrats nominated Horatio Seymour of New York for president and Francis Blair of Maryland as his running mate. The Democrats made it clear they wanted Reconstruction ended and the solid south in the national party.

In the end, Grant crushed Seymour in both the Electoral College and popular vote. Grant and Colfax won 214 electoral votes and 3,012,833 popular votes. The Seymour-Blair ticket garnered 80 votes in the Electoral College and a popular vote of 2,703,249. The Radical Republicans would now most certainly control Reconstruction, but the triumph was short-lived.

The corruption of the Grant administration caused a revolt in the Republican ranks, enough of an uprising so that the intra-party squabble led the formation of a new Liberal Republican Party led by *New York Tribune* editor Horace Greeley. The Democrats chose to back Greeley against Grant rather than nominate their own candidate. Liberal Republicans pledged "to maintain the union of these States, emancipation and enfranchisement; and to oppose any reopening of the questions settled by the thirteenth, fourteenth and fifteenth amendments of the Constitution."

In addition, Greeley and the delegates demanded "the immediate and absolute removal of all disabilities imposed on account of the rebellion," and that universal amnesty would "result in complete pacification in all sections of the country." Local self-government, with impartial suffrage, would guard the rights of all citizens more securely than any centralized power. Furthermore, the delegates demanded "the largest liberty consistent with public order; for the State, self-government, and for the Nation a return to the methods of peace and the constitutional limitations of power." Greeley lost by a wide margin, and despite the corruption, Grant stayed in office. A month after his humiliating defeat, Greeley died.

Grant's second term was even less successful than the first, and that fact served to make the election of 1876 close. One again, Reconstruction was a political issue. In the National Union Republican Convention in Cincinnati, June 14–16, the Republicans produced a platform that began with a preamble of waving the bloody shirt. The third plank of the document promised the "permanent pacification of the southern section of the Union, and the complete protection of all its citizens in the free enjoyment of their rights, are duties to which the Republican Party is sacredly pledged." They also repudiated sectionalism, and accused the Democrats of trying to hinge their hopes on the votes of those formerly arrayed against the Union. Worse, the platform stated that the Democratic Party was the same in character at present as it was when it "sympathized with treason."

The Democrats, meeting in St. Louis in late June, responded with a pledge to accept the outcome of the war, the newly-added constitutional amendments, and that they were not traitors and resented the assertion; further, they believed that such planks on the party of their opponents would stir up more sectional animosity and strife. Samuel J. Tilden of New York received the presidential nomination, with Thomas J. Hendricks of Indiana as his running mate. On the night of the election, it appeared that in the final states still occupied by federal troops (Louisiana, Florida, and South Carolina), voting irregularities occurred. It was obvious that both sides tampered with the vote, and, as usual, white supremacists tried to scare African Americans away from the polls.

After a compromise between the parties, an election commission of eight Republicans and seven Democrats awarded the election to Hayes, and in exchange, the Republican administration removed the final federal troops from the three states. Reconstruction ended with the inauguration of Hayes in 1877. The Reconstruction period, despite its successes, failed because of the north's weariness with the process, racial prejudice entrenched in both sections, and the victor's desire to get the issues of the war behind them.

SEE ALSO: Fifteenth Amendment; Fourteenth Amendment; Greenback-Labor Party; Jim Crow Laws; Ku Klux Klan; Liberal Republican Party; Racial Justice as a Political Issue.

BIBLIOGRAPHY. David and Jeanne Heidler, *Encyclopedia of the American Civil War* (ABC-Clio, 2000); Michael Perman, *Emancipation and Reconstruction* (Harland Davidson, 2003); E.H. Roseboom, *A History of Presidential Elections From George Washington to Richard M. Nixon: The Definitive Account of Our National Conventions, Campaigns, and Elections* (Macmillan, 1970); A.M. Schlesinger, Jr., ed., *History of U.S. Political Parties,*

Volume II, 1860–1910: The Gilded Age of Politics (Chelsea House, 1973); B.D. Simpson, *The Reconstruction Presidents* (University Press of Kansas, 1998); A.W. Trelease, *Reconstruction: The Great Experiment* (Harper & Row, 1971).

JAMES S. BAUGESS
COLUMBUS STATE COMMUNITY COLLEGE

Red States

THE TERM *red states* denotes states that disproportionately support the Republican Party, especially for president. Republicans dominate the red states of the south, much of the farm belt, and the mountain west. States in which the Democratic Party is dominant, on the other hand, are deemed *blue states*. Though the red state/blue state terminology is relatively new, regional differences have long marked the American political landscape. The perception of a divide between red states and blue states largely rests on the belief that the political divisions within the states are relatively stable and that red states and blue states are becoming more polarized politically.

At the presidential level, this has become the case; due to the winner-take-all nature of the Electoral College, relatively few states (about one-third of all states in the 2004 presidential election) are considered swing states that could potentially go red or blue. This is a noticeable shift from a generation ago. In 1976, for example, 20 states with 299 electoral votes were decided by a margin of less than five percents. In 2004, only 10 states with 106 electoral votes were decided by a margin of less than five percents.

The red state/blue state dichotomy rests, to a large degree, on the premise that red states are culturally different from blue states, and that this explains much of the political differences between red and blue states. Cultural divisions unquestionably impact the differences in political attitudes in the United States. Researchers find a widening and deepening of a cultural values-based realignment of the American electorate. In red states, moral traditionalism has exerted a stronger influence on vote choice through party identification. The result is a process of realignment in the electorate along a moral traditionalism divide, as states with more morally traditional citizens become more Republican. The growing importance of values and the cultural divide has served

to nationalize citizens' vote choices, with voters more willing to cast their ballots on the basis of national issues that usually are only thought to affect presidential vote choice. As a result, the red states have become "redder"— that is, more Republican. Since the 1960s, cultural issues have increasingly become the focal point differentiating the parties, with a culturally traditional Republican Party dominant in red states and a culturally progressive Democratic Party dominant in blue states.

The defining characteristic differentiating red states from blue states may be religion. The religious polarization among red states and blue states is associated with a growing schism on cultural issues such as abortion, women's rights, and gay rights. The more religious an individual, the more likely he or she is to vote for, and identify as, a Republican. This has not always been the case; in 1960, for example, regular churchgoers were actually more Democratic in their vote for president. Committed Evangelicals, who have distinct political attitudes and who live disproportionately in the red states of the south, have steadily ascended within the Republican Party since the 1970s. Today, more than 70 percent of white evangelicals align themselves with the Republican Party. As the religious right has increasingly influenced the Republican Party, the base of the party—the red states—has moved to the south. This, in turn, has influenced how the American polity is viewed. A popular post-2004 election map that circulated on the internet had the United States divided in two: "The United States of Canada" (blue states joined to Canada) and "Jesusland," representing red states.

To critics, however, the red state/blue state cultural divide is overstated, exaggerating the geography of electoral polarization and creating a cultural war myth. It is certainly an oversimplification to argue that all red states vote Republican simply on the basis of religion or cultural issues. The political values of red states in the west and the plains, for example, are not necessarily in tandem with the political values of the south. Southern states are 50–60 percent Evangelical Christian, which is nearly double the figure for some western red states, such as Montana. Western red states are far more libertarian and secular than southern states, indicating that red states are not automatically more religious and socially conservative than blue states. Yet, at the same time, economic issues appear to be less important than they used to be. There is a correlation between income and support for the Republican Party at the individual level, but at the aggregate level it is the Democrats who do better in wealthier states. Economically, therefore, red states tend to be poorer than blue states. Some of the lowest-income states in the United States cast overwhelmingly Republican votes.

The fact that some of the poorest areas in the country are also the most Republican is a consequence of the Republican Party's dominance in the south, the country's poorest region. Though African Americans in the south vote overwhelmingly Democratic, among conservative southern whites there has been a steady movement toward the Republican Party since the 1970s, making southern states safely red states. In turn, voters in both the south and non-south are responding to the increasing southern influence on the Republican Party and the decreasing southern influence on the Democratic Party, making red states redder and blue states bluer. Though some find the increasing red-blue political divide in American politics problematic, it simply may be a natural product of American federalism. At the national level, the parties are extremely competitive, as the results of the 2000 and 2004 presidential elections show. But at the state level, the red states and blue states are becoming more polarized. The growing intensity of partisanship within red and blue states is creating parties with increasingly distinct identities.

The emergence of a more partisan electorate is a product of long-term realignment and social change. Public opinion is of major importance for the determination of state policy. In terms of ideological direction, state policies tend to reflect the ideological sentiment of the state electorates. The strongest red states enact the most conservative policies and the strongest blue states enact the most liberal policies. The result of this realignment is a "responsible" party system, with the Republican-dominated red states advocating very different ideological agendas than Democratic-dominated blue states.

SEE ALSO: Blue States; Income and Voting Behavior; Partisanship; Political Culture; Political Socialization; Religion and Voting Behavior; Two-Party System.

BIBLIOGRAPHY. M.D. Brewer and Jeffrey Stonecash, *Split: Class and Cultural Divisions in American Politics* (CQ Press, 2007); Morris Fiorina, *Culture War?: The Myth of a Polarized America* (Pearson Longman, 2005); Jonathan Knuckey, "A New Front in the Culture War?," *American Politics Research* (v.33, 2005); G.C. Layman, "'Culture Wars' in the American Party System," *American Politics Quarterly* (v.27, 1999); Kara Lindaman and D.P. Haider-Markel, "Issue Evolution, Political Parties, and the Cultural Wars," *Political Research Quarterly* (v.55, 2002); J.M. Stonecash, M.D. Brewer, and M.D. Mariani, *Diverging Parties: Social Change, Realignment, and Party Polarization* (Westview Press, 2003); J.K. White, *The Values Divide: American Politics and Culture in Transition* (Chatham House, 2002).

PATRICK FISHER
SETON HALL UNIVERSITY

Reform Party

THE REFORM PARTY is a third party in American politics that emerged from Ross Perot's 1992 Independent presidential campaign. The goal of the Reform Party is to reform the current political system by electing candidates who will make government fiscally responsible and more responsive to citizens. The key issues for Reform Party members have been campaign finance reform, term limits, a balanced federal budget, foreign trade, and Social Security and Medicare reform. The forerunner of the Reform Party was United We Stand America (UWSA), which was established in early 1992 for the purpose of gathering enough signatures in each state for Perot, a businessman, to appear on the ballot. The grassroots organization, based in Dallas, Texas, was organized into state chapters, which facilitated the collection of signatures under state ballot access laws.

Following his 1992 campaign, Perot decided to keep UWSA going as a non-partisan "educational group," appointing Russell Verney, who had worked on his campaign, as executive director. The organization's principal purpose was to channel Perot's opposition to the North America Free Trade Agreement (NAFTA), although the organization also supported campaign finance reform and balancing the federal budget. In 1995, Perot founded the Reform Party. The Federal Elections Commission (FEC) ruled that the party would be eligible for $30 million in federal funds in the 1996 presidential election campaign as a result of Perot having received 19 percent of the popular vote in 1992, provided that Perot was its candidate. Perot planned to incorporate UWSA into the new party, appointing Verney its national chair. However, there was opposition to Perot: some opposed turning UWSA into a partisan political organization, while others opposed the plan because they hoped to support former Colorado Governor Richard Lamm's candidacy for the new party's presidential nomination, and believed that Perot's supporters, who controlled the new party organization, would insure his selection as the party's candidate for 1996. This resulted in the creation of competing organizations: the Reform Party and United We Stand America.

Perot did win the nomination (his running mate was Pat Choate, a radio talk show host, college professor, and like Perot, an opponent of free trade), however, the split between Perot and Lamm supporters handicapped the party in the general election, as Perot's percentage of the popular vote dropped to eight percent. Following the election, the party's leadership attempted to distance itself from Perot to attract more support. Some of Lamm's supporters left the party in 1997, to form the American Reform Party.

In 1998, Jesse Ventura was elected governor of Minnesota as the Reform Party candidate. Ventura, a former professional wrestler, movie actor, radio talk show host, and mayor of Brooklyn Park, Minnesota (1991–95) won the election despite not receiving support from Perot or the national party. During the next two years, there was skirmishing between supporters of Perot and Ventura for control of the party. In 1999, Ventura's supporters took control of the party, electing Jack Gargan as the party's national chair. Ventura (who did not seek re-election in 2002) left the party, contending that it lacked leadership and could not escape from Perot's shadow.

In the 2000 election cycle, Republican Pat Buchanan (who had sought the 1992 Republican presidential nomination) secured the Reform Party nomination, as his "Buchanan Brigades" were able to take control of the party by re-registering as Reform Party members. Choate, the 1996 vice presidential candidate (and Buchanan supporter), became the national chair of the party. Another Buchanan supporter, Gerald Moan, would succeed him as party chair. When challenges to Buchanan's nomination arose, his supporters on the national committee successfully blocked the effort. John Hagelin challenged Buchanan and won the Reform Party primary. Buchanan and his supporters challenged Hagelin's candidacy at the FEC, which ruled in favor of Buchanan, awarding him the $12.5 million in federal funds earmarked for the Reform Party. A number of state reform party organizations, led by the Minnesota Party, left the

Reform Party. Buchanan received less than one percent of the popular vote. Buchanan, who had promised that he would give the party a five-year commitment, left the party shortly after the election. By 2002, his followers would be removed from the party's leadership. However, by that time, the party was in organizational disarray and financially insolvent.

In 2004, the party supported consumer advocate (and 2000 Green Party presidential candidate) Independent Ralph Nader as its presidential candidate. Nader, who appeared on the ballot in a number of states under a number of party labels, received less than one percent of the popular vote. The party continues to be divided into competing factions, each claiming to be the Reform Party. One faction, headed by Charles Foster, is headquartered in Abilene, Texas. A second faction, chaired by Rodney Martin, operates out of El Cerrito, California. In July 2006, they filed a Racketeer Influenced and Corrupt Organizations (RICO) statute lawsuit against the Foster group, alleging that they were misrepresenting themselves as the Reform Party.

Where the party once had active organizations in all 50 states, as of May 2007 there were functioning Reform Party organizations in 15 states. The party (as of May 2007) had ballot access for the 2008 election in four states: Florida, Kansas, Louisiana, and Mississippi. Since Perot's withdrawal from active participation in the party, it has not been able to attract the same media attention or voter interest.

SEE ALSO: Campaign Finance, Politics of; Free Trade; Nader, Ralph; National Debt; Perot, Ross; Presidential Election of 1992; Presidential Election of 1996; Third Parties.

BIBLIOGRAPHY. Tricia Andryszewski, *The Reform Party: Ross Perot and Pat Buchanan* (Millbrook Press, 2001); T.G. Jelen, ed., *Ross for Boss: The Perot Phenomenon and Beyond* (State University of New York Press, 2001); A.J. Menendez, *The Perot Voters and the Future of American Politics* (Prometheus Books, 1996); Gerald Posner, *Citizen Perot: His Life and Times* (Random House, 1996); R.B. Rapoport and W.J. Stone, *Three's a Crowd: the Dynamic of Third Parties, Ross Perot and Republican Resurgence* (University of Michigan Press, 2005); Micah Sifry, *Spoiling for a Fight: Third Party Politics in America* (Routledge, 2002).

JEFFREY KRAUS
WAGNER COLLEGE

Religion and Voting Behavior

RELIGION IS ONE factor that can potentially influence voting patterns and the choices made on Election Day. However, religion is but one part of the complex social mix found within the American electorate. Other forces such as gender, social status, income, and ethnic identities also shape voting. In the distant past there have been other special interests such as regional identity, state rights, western and foreign expansion, attitudes to immigration, and common economic aspirations that have influenced voting decisions. Religion as a political device faces difficulties within the existing American constitutional framework. The U.S. Constitution, through the Establishment Clause found within the First Amendment, demands a clear separation of church and state, a position that has steadily evolved since the 1790s. This has meant that at all levels there is a secular approach to governing and government. It has also been the desire of repeated administrations to keep religion outside of the state in order to promote national harmony, given the wide variety of competing religions.

Although the nation manifested a primarily Protestant religious identity in its early creation, the arrival of large numbers of Irish Catholics in the 1840s, who were soon joined by German and other European Catholics as the century unfolded, challenged the status quo. The Democratic Party welcomed these new Catholic voters, at least in the northern, midwestern, and western branches of the party. More recently, the rise of a more fundamentalist Christianity, particularly since the 1980s, has found an outlet, and has exerted political influence on the conservative section of the Republican Party. Their emphasis on religious values has seemingly produced recent dividends in Republican voter turnout, and, perhaps, election victories.

Even with a strong religious base, voter participation is not guaranteed nor do the issues remain constant. Demands change with the times as circumstances shift. For a time, 9/11 brought a unified patriotic response to an external threat that increased citizen consciousness above narrow concerns, religious and otherwise. Meeting such threats was more important initially than party policies or political personalities, but religion can enter the discussion when a search for understanding is undertaken. This can lead to a common religious orientation becoming entwined with the nation's perceived destiny. This situation can be manipulated into an electoral advantage, especially when parties differ over concepts of national security.

Religious voter orientation, though, can be hotly debated. While religion is a driving force, and Americans for the most part consider themselves God-fearing and church-going, American voter participation has declined to the point where only approximately 50 percent of the electorate actually votes. This indicates that voting is becoming a minority event where only a small number of those eligible to vote find the motivation to vote. As a consequence, those with a particular agenda, who are sufficiently motivated, perhaps by religiously-shaped loyalties, can exert a disproportionate effect on an individual election. But simply being a believer in God doesn't make one vote or vote in a particular way. Given a small voter turnout, religion might influence American election outcomes, especially in a state or local context. This becomes more significant when certain religious denominations

Since 2002, exit polls have shown a very high correlation between church attendance and voting.

assert their goals within the body of a political party and help define platforms. Traditionally, Protestants identify with the Republicans. Religious devotion and commitment, if it leads to activism, can raise political expectations. This can increase the willingness to vote in a particular direction, along with other factors such as established personal histories and loyalties.

In recent decades, there has been a mixing of religion and politics in the conservative wing of the Republican Party that has received much attention and comment. It has been argued that there is a gender factor in this development, with fundamentalist women leading the way in spreading a more conservative message to candidates. Results are not overwhelmingly conclusive. Women fundamentalists did prefer Ronald Reagan in the 1980s, as did some more traditional Catholic women; however, this did not lead to a serious religious gender-voting gap. Neither did it mean in a generalized sense that religious women as a group are more conservatively-orientated in their voting.

American Catholics are not associated in the modern era with a particular political party, although certain controversial issues can absorb the Church and its teachings. This does not necessarily translate into voting behavior that follows the Church's exhortations, practices, or condemnations. For instance, powerful issues involving women's rights in areas such as contraception and abortion have not led to a guaranteed Catholic voting bloc opposed to these issues. Politicians who have held contrary views have not lost the Catholic vote.

President Reagan's brand of social conservatism did attract conservative Catholics. Yet in the 1992 election, the Catholic vote was clearly divided, with 44 percent choosing Bill Clinton over George H.W. Bush or Ross Perot. The Protestant Clinton increased his Catholic appeal in 1996, gaining 53 percent of the vote. In the 2000 election, the Catholic vote was even more evenly split between Al Gore, with 49 percent, and George W. Bush with 47 percent. Evidence suggests it was not religious identities that influenced voting behavior in a particular direction, but individual preferences in reaction to the pressing issues of the time.

While the Catholic vote has become more neutral, Jewish-American voting behavior seems permanently attached to the Democratic Party. Approximately 80 percent of the Jewish vote supports Democratic goals and candidates regardless of the candidate or era. However, there does not seem to be a religious basis for this

pattern. Instead, the vote seems to be determined by a more liberal cultural bias and family voting traditions.

RISE OF THE RELIGIOUS RIGHT

The rise of the religious right since the 1980s has created a sense that religious affiliation has become a more telling force in politics, and one that is just as important as ethnic, gender, and racial preferences. Some scholars suggest that regular church attendance can indicate a tendency to vote Republican as opposed to Democrat, but much depends on the issues at a given time and election. Some argue that the current situation reflects a religious gap between the parties, but this is far from absolute or, for that matter, necessarily permanent. Moral distress can influence the vote, but value-based issues can change from one election to another with more complex and pressing concerns overriding purely religious issues or even gender.

In recent presidential elections there is evidence that George W. Bush gained support from those that frequently attended church, and of this group the fundamentalist religious right overwhelmingly supported him. But other Christian churches including the Mormons, Pentecostals, Christian Scientists, Eastern Orthodox, and many others with records of strong religious devotion also joined the Republican vote. Yet, in contrast, Evangelical African-American Protestants, Jews, and Latino Catholics gave substantial voting majorities to Al Gore and the Democrats in 2000.

At the congressional level, the strict voting preferences based on religious identifications can become less direct. This includes Jewish and secular voting as well as Catholic and other non-Protestant groupings. Republicans can attract crossover voting if other local or national issues such as war or tax policy appeal to the voters' own views of their interests. This would suggest that the religious gap is one that is less distinct than is generally believed, with a number of offsetting features that can undermine assumptions of the religious right's domination of contemporary politics.

VOTING PREFERENCES

The issues that can affect voting behavior are subject to periodic analysis. Typically, Jewish groups and mainstream denominations have taken a pro-choice stance regarding abortion, whereas Catholics, Mormons, and more evangelical Protestants have maintained a pro-life position. This would indicate that religion could influence abortion-based voting and therefore exert pressure on legislative programs and candidates' platforms. However, ultimate influence on the courts is far more muted.

Although there are a multitude of factors that can shape a vote such as age, gender, class, and race, religion can forge another connective link in the voting process, particularly if there are dominant moral issues involved. This can be as important as party, or other demographic affiliations. Evangelical fundamentalists remain overwhelmingly committed to the Republican Party, whereas non-Evangelicals have greater Democratic Party leanings. Disenchantment can change these allegiances. Religion can also be more important than historic regional differences. This can partially explain Republican gains in the former Democratic south. Single issues such as abortion can attract religious campaigning. Religion could be influential if are clear divisions between candidates, but whether it is enough to change an election outcome remains unclear.

There is some consensus concerning religious identification and voting preferences. Since the New Deal the Democrats have usually attracted the Jewish and, to a lesser extent, the Catholic vote, whereas the Republicans have drawn support from mainstream Protestants, as well as the growing Evangelical-fundamentalist movement. Some variations see the Catholic vote as neutral, except in certain ethnic areas. The electoral problem is made more complex because the issues are not necessarily ideologically consistent or unchanging. As voters mature, other, more pressing issues such as employment, crime, immigration, and foreign affairs, can override religious bias. Secular and religious concerns can mingle and be equally influential in final voting decisions. The assumption is that religious commitment has benefited Republicans.

The rise of the religious right has had an impact upon the Republican Party and on its programs and policies. However, this voice within the party does not dictate the party's agenda, except in the eyes of its critics. The reality is far more complex. The supposed connection between Evangelicals and Republican conservatism is truer for the fundamentalist minority than for the broad spectrum of evangelicals. There also seems to be a concern about religious influence on only one side of the political divide. The atheist, agnostic, or not religiously affiliated identity within the Democratic Party does not raise the same time level of interest or analysis with regard to its domination of policy or influence on individual voting.

In the 2000 presidential election, over 10 million evangelicals voted for Al Gore, which suggests that one's religious enthusiasm does not necessarily produce a conservative voting preference. The idea that the religious right dominates voter turnout is also not as as is sometimes portrayed. The 56 percent religious turnout in 2000 for George W. Bush was not beyond challenge from other equally committed special interests. In addition, there is evidence that on the congressional or local level, religion as a factor in voting is becoming less significant.

When there are glaring issues that threaten individual religious beliefs or moral values such as homosexuality, gay and lesbian marriage, or even environmental concerns, a candidate's position on these issues can affect how one votes. However, this does not mean that the voter will decide these issues alone. Candidate consistency might be more important than a specific issue. Abortion, stem cell research, and the teaching of evolutionary science in public schools can produce an outpouring of religious positions that vary according to denomination and an individual's own interpretation of moral practice. This does not produce an religious voting base or guarantee a homogenous voting block. Religion remains a factor in voting preference, but its dominance is open to question.

SEE ALSO: Abortion; Catholic Vote; Gay Rights; Jewish Vote; Protestant Vote; Religious Issues in Campaigns.

BIBLIOGRAPHY. Clem Brooks and Jeff Manza, "The Religious Factor in U.S. Presidential Elections: 1960–1992," *American Journal of Sociology* (July 1997); E.L. Cleary and A.D. Hertzke, eds., *Representing God at the Statehouse: Religion and Politics in the American States* (Rowan and Littlefield, 2005); Chris Fastnow et al., "Holy Roll Calls: Religious Tradition and Voting Behavior in the U.S. House," *Social Science Quarterly* (December 1999); R.B. Fowler et al., *Religion and Politics: Faith, Culture and Strategic Choices* (Westview Press, 2004); J.L. Guth et al., *The Bully Pulpit: The Politics of the Protestant Clergy* (University of Kansas Press, 1997); J.L. Hammond, *The Politics of Benevolence: Revival Religion and American Voting Behavior* (Ablex Publishing, 1979); Andrew Kohut et al., *The Diminishing Divide: Religion's Changing Role in American Politics* (Brookings Institute, 2000); M.J. Rozell et al., *Interest Groups in American Campaigns: The*

New Face of Electioneering (CQ Press, 2006); H.S. Stout, *New Directions in American Religious History* (Oxford University Press, 1997).

THEODORE W. EVERSOLE, PH.D.
INDEPENDENT SCHOLAR

Religious Issues in Campaigns

AMERICAN POLITICAL LIFE has always been affected by religious convictions and beliefs. Religion continues to be at the forefront of American politics and government. Elections are no exception. From the first colonists arriving in the new world with the hope of religious freedom, to President George Bush rallying his armies of compassion, religion and faith have served as a cornerstones in American elections and campaigns and religion has served as a major force in the political lives of its citizenry.

Researchers note that individuals and groups use religion as a filter in the decision-making process in politics and public policy in two primary ways. First, religion can be viewed as a set of internal beliefs that one acquires primarily within the cognitive sphere. Viewing religion from a cognitive or theological perspective, individuals utilize their own beliefs to develop a certain political or social view about politics, a campaign, an issue, or a political candidate.

Second, religion can be viewed as a participatory activity of civic engagement, or "belonging," which emphasizes group dynamics as a form of expression and involvement. In this case, a certain view about a campaign issue or public policy program would be funneled through the beliefs of a specific religious tradition or faith. When combined, believing and belonging have a tremendous effect on political campaigns and elections. They affect who gets elected and who does not, the platforms of candidates, and in many cases, religious issues affect campaigns and elections by serving as referendums.

Religion and religious issues, affect who gets elected and who does not. In 1928, Alfred Smith (New York), the Democratic nominee for president and self-identified Roman Catholic, ran against Republican Herbert Hoover. Hoover, besides using the famous slogan "a chicken in every pot and a car in every garage," attacked Smith by using religious rhetoric and religious bigotry. With the two major themes in the campaign focusing on religion and prohibition, Hoover and others convinced the electorate that, if elected, Smith would make Catholicism the national religion and suggested that Smith would adhere to the words of the Pope in lieu of the Constitution. In the end, Hoover beat Smith by more than 18 percent of the popular vote.

John F. Kennedy (D-Massachusetts), another Roman Catholic, would take a page from the Hoover campaign and use it to his advantage in 1960, by suggesting that anyone who would not vote for him because he was Catholic could be labeled a religious bigot, noting that he was not the Catholic candidate for president, he was the Democratic Party's candidate for president, who happened to be a Catholic. Kennedy's ability to separate his religion from his candidacy served as the cornerstone for future debates on religion and politics and led to his victory against Richard Nixon (R-California) in 1960.

George W. Bush (R-Texas), a self-proclaimed Evangelical, used religion to court the conservative Republican, religious right vote in both the 2000 and 2004 presidential elections. During his campaigns, Bush often quoted Bible verses, referenced his daily prayer activities, and discussed issues he viewed as biblically immoral: homosexuality, same-sex marriages, and abortion. Despite being involved in a highly controversial war in Iraq, Bush was re-elected in 2004, in part due to the conservative Christian voter turnout in key states.

Pat Robertson, founder of the Christian Coalition, used the perceived moral decline of society as evidenced by the breakdown of the family to launch an unsuccessful bid for president in 1988. Likewise, the Reverend Jesse Jackson campaigned on the importance of a moral community and social justice while running for president, in 1984 and in 1988. Religious issues also play an important role in the election process without being on a candidate's election platform. Religious issues can stand alone as referendums, or ballot initiatives, and affect voter participation and voter turnout. A classic example of this is the 2004 "same-sex marriage amendments" that were placed on the ballot in 11 key states. Other key issues on the ballot in state elections have focused on abortion rights, prayer in schools, embryonic stem cell research, and sodomy laws.

Just as beliefs have played an important role in elections and campaigns, so too, has belonging to religious groups. Robertson and Jackson each mobilized specific religious groups to advance their beliefs through campaigns and such groups have played an important role in subsequent presidential and congressional elections. Robertson and Jackson demonstrated that populist candidates could use churches as conduits for organizing people at the local level, and that churches could serve as key strategic locations for fundraising and social activism.

Religious groups function as sociological and political communities, and each community has differences in opinions, levels of activism, and beliefs. Jehovah's Witnesses, for example, eschew forms of political activism, including voting, while the Christian Coalition encourages members to become very involved in the political process, including elections and campaigns. Mennonites and certain Church of God denominations oppose church and state involvement, and strongly denounce war.

Two of the easiest ways to measure the effect religious belonging has on the election process and campaigning, in general, is to look at voting behavior and campaign involvement. Researchers find that since the 1964 election, Jews exceed all other religious groups in voting. Roman Catholics and mainline Protestants follow, and are very similar in their voting behavior. African-American Protestants have the lowest voter turnout, and white Evangelical Protestants, especially those associated with the Christian Coalition and the Religious Right, have higher levels of voter participation.

Using a campaign behavior index to measure religious constituents attendance at meetings, work on a specific campaign, attempts to influence another's vote, displays of campaign materials, and work for a political party, can document religious influence. Since 1960, Jews have overwhelmingly played a more active role in campaigning, followed by mainline Protestants, Roman Catholics, white Evangelical Protestants, and, finally, African-American Protestants. Also, since 2002, exit polls have shown a very high correlation between church attendance and voting. The more frequently people go to church, the more likely they are to vote Republican.

Religion can operate in many ways to influence elections and political campaigns. Through the development of a systemic belief structure, religion can influence one's actions and behavior in areas related to voting and political involvement. The religious beliefs and religious affiliation of political candidates have a tremendous bearing on the tone and outcome of an election. George W. Bush's acknowledgement that he looked to Jesus Christ for answers, coupled with Sena-

tor John Kerry's decision to have Joseph Lieberman, an orthodox Jew, serve as his running mate, had major repercussions for the 2004 presidential election. Candidates can use key moral issues to affect voter turnout and grassroots involvement by religious organizations such as the Religious Right can help determine the outcome of elections.

SEE ALSO: Issue Framing; Populists and Populist Movements; Presidential Election of 1928; Presidential Election of 1960; Presidential Election of 1984; Presidential Election of 1988; Presidential Election of 2004; Religion and Voting Behavior.

BIBLIOGRAPHY. James Guth, *The Bully Pulpit* (University of Kansas, 1997); Corwin Smidt, *In God We Trust: Religion and American Political Life* (Baker Press 2001); Kenneth Wald and Corwin Smidt, *Rediscovering the Religious Factor in American Politics* (M.E. Sharpe, 1993); Peter Wielhouwer, "Releasing the Fetters: Parties and Mobilization of the African-American Electorate," *Journal of Politics* (v.62, 2000).

RONALD ERIC MATTHEWS, JR.
MOUNT UNION COLLEGE

Representative Democracy

TO ADOPT LINCOLN'S Gettysburg declaration that democracy is government of the people, by the people, and for the people, is to endorse a formula that only begins to explain the diversity of regimes that have labeled themselves democratic. A great deal depends on how government might be said to belong to the people and how governments actually operate. A key variable in such considerations is the nature of political representation.

Governments that claim to be "of the people" will vary in the extent to which they represent the range and diversity of voices that constitute the polities that elect them. Apart from those who have been elected, government of the people also depends on who is represented between elections. If government is by the people, it matters which people come to be the people's representatives in government. Only in very small polities can there be any meaningful form of direct democracy. In modern democratic states with mass franchises, some form of representation is necessary. Given the necessary selectivity of this process, it is important to know who runs and who does not run for office, and what chance they have of election. The electoral system itself influences who runs for office and who is elected. Government that is for the people presumably acts in their interests. Mechanisms are needed to assess such interests and how to represent them. Governments vary in how far they are prepared to go on behalf of their people, and may represent forces other than the interests of the people. A major challenge is to come up with people and practices to faithfully represent the public.

Democratic representation is associated with the rise of complex modern societies, notably those that have evolved over the past 200 years. Contemporary democracies have given rise to the growth of political institutions, such as legislatures, and political organizations such as political parties and interest groups. Representative democracy is complex and an adequate understanding of it is grounded in an appreciation of how institutional structures, political organizations, and political movements interact. Despite this, the basic model of representation is quite simple, it is inherent in all forms of political life, even those that existed in egalitarian pre-modern societies. From the beginning, human groups have found it useful to establish roles and select persons who are able to express the ideas, the purposes, or the visions of a number of others.

Representation has at least four distinct meanings in contemporary representative democracies, and particular political systems and eras can be characterized on the basis of particular mixes of these. Mandate representation consists of attempting to transmit, as faithfully as possible, precisely what the people have instructed them to do. In sociodemographic representation, individuals represent others to the extent that they approximate them in their background and personal characteristics such as age, sex, race, region, and religion.

Contemporary polities have been built around political parties. These are organizations that aggregate the generalized political will of large numbers of people. Members of political parties are bound by adherence to the party line; to the extent that they follow it, they manifest partisan representation. People held in high esteem, those who are knowledgeable, intelligent, and of good character, can be said to represent others based upon intrinsic qualities that set them apart from others and fit them for leadership. Philosopher Edmund Burke referred to such qualities as virtual representation.

A representative democracy is in practice limited in certain respects. Populist versions of representative democracy envision that a majoritarian will can be translated into blunt forms of mandate representation. However, in practice, the majority does not always rule in an unrestricted manner. Forms of constitutional democracy or parliamentary democracy exist to ensure that fundamental rights and freedoms set limits on what the people's representatives can do. The Rule of Law, guaranteed rights of certain minorities, the independence of the judiciary, and the supremacy of the Constitution, act further to restrict elected officials. The complexity of contemporary governance, the challenges of public stewardship, and the diversity of voices to be taken into account suggest the need for sociodemographic considerations and for virtual representation. Partisan representation reflects the ongoing challenges of piecing together winning coalitions of support that most broadly represent the political will of a plurality, while taking into account the needs and aspirations of minorities.

Existing structures of representative democracy have been criticized for a range of inadequacies including: excessive political centralization in the hands of executive branches, the irrelevance of legislators, the impotence of judiciaries, and the control of political agendas by those who control the economy. There are various suggestions for enhancing representative democracy: a reformed electoral system, a reassertion of the power of the legislature as people's representatives, controls over election financing and political financing between elections, a system of guaranteed and routine public consultations, and the active sustaining of channels of communication between the state and civil society.

SEE ALSO: Majority Rule; Participatory Democracy; Political Elites; Political Legitimacy and Democracy.

BIBLIOGRAPHY. Paul Hirst, *Representative Democracy and Its Limits* (Polity Press, 1990); Nadia Urbinati, *Representative Democracy: Principles and Genealogy* (University of Chicago Press, 2006).

Paul Wingfield Nesbitt-Larking, Ph.D.
Huron University College, Canada

Representative Role Types

IN CONTRAST TO direct democracy, in which citizens directly vote on public policy, representative democracies require an intermediary who represents the interests of those who elect them. How this representational duty is accomplished can be more complicated that it might first appear. Legislators may perceive their roles in different ways. There are three main representative role types (also called "role orientations" or "models of representation"), used for classification by political scientists. They are the "delegate," the "trustee," and the "politico."

The delegate role type is also sometimes referred to as the "instructed delegate." Elected officials who view their role as that of a delegate will strive to directly reflect the will of the people they represent as accurately as possible. They see themselves as reflecting the way the entire group would vote were such a thing possible. Strict delegates would put the views of their constituents first, even if these conflict with their own judgment. For this reason, representatives with a delegate orientation will expend a great deal of energy watching polls and otherwise gathering information about the wishes and needs of those they represent.

The trustee role type is also sometimes called Burkean after the 18th century political philosopher and member of the British House of Commons, Edmund Burke, who advocated for a trustee role orientation. Representatives who sees themselves as trustees will be concerned with the broad dispositions of their district, but will feel free to exercise their own best judgment when making decisions. Trustees tend think voters expect judgment, wisdom, and expertise from their representatives, more than direct mirroring of public opinion on specific issues.

Clearly, there are disadvantages to either of these role types. In reality, it is impossible to be a pure delegate for several reasons. For one, constituencies are not uniform, and will invariably have divergent needs and opinions. Even attempts to represent the majority within an electorate can be impossible when there is no reliable means of discerning what that opinion might be. Also, even when public opinion data are available, citizens often express desires for conflicting goals such as wanting more government services as well as lower taxes. Even a committed delegate will have to make some tough decisions. Delegates focus on the needs of their particular electorate, and, as a result, may not be as concerned about the good of the whole state or country, especially if it conflicts with the interests of their constituents.

The trustee orientation comes with its own difficulties. Though ideally, trustees would be concerned with accurately representing the general will of their constituents, if they do not actively assess that opinion, they may be misguided. The main concern is that trustees may rely on their own judgment, and that judgment could differ from that of their constituents. In the most extreme case, trustees could act counter to the will of the majority of those they represent, and could arguably be behaving in an undemocratic way.

In practice, most representatives do not see themselves as pure trustees or pure delegates, but somewhere in between. Political scientists sometimes refer to those who vacillate between the two roles as politicos. A politico typically acts as a trustee on matters for which there is no explicit public guidance, but feels compelled to act as a delegate when constituents express a strong and consistent opinion on an issue. Studies by political scientists have shown that legislators are more likely to begin their careers on the delegate end of the spectrum, but end up closer to the trustee end over time. However, elected officials are also highly motivated by the desire for re-election. If representatives acts in ways that defy the explicit desires of those who elected them, there can be a political or electoral price to pay. This reality keeps a check on the excesses of those who fit the trustee model.

Political discourse often makes reference to these styles, if not by name, then by substance. For example, delegates are sometimes accused of "holding a finger up in the wind" to see which way the winds of opinion are blowing before making a decision. They are also sometimes criticized for "following the polls," which is only really a criticism if one favors the trustee model. Trustee-type leaders are sometimes accused of behaving in an imperial, autocratic, or undemocratic way.

SEE ALSO: Majority Rule; Representative Democracy.

BIBLIOGRAPHY. Heinz Eulau et al., "The Role of the Representative: Some Empirical Observations on the Theory of Edmund Burke," *American Political Science Review* (v.53/3, 1959); D.J. McCrone, et al.., "The Delegate Theory of Representation," *American Journal of Political Science* (v.23/2, 1979).

KIMBERLY L. NALDER
CALIFORNIA STATE UNIVERSITY, SACRAMENTO

Republican National Committee

THE REPUBLICAN NATIONAL Committee (RNC) is the official organization representing the Republican Party in the United States. According to the party rules, the Republican National Committee "shall have the general management of the Republican Party, subject to direction from the national convention." Under party rules, the committee is required to meet at least twice a year. The primary responsibilities of the Republican National Committee are to develop and promote the Republican Party's political agenda, coordinate fundraising and election strategy, support Republican Party office holders and candidates, and organize and run the quadrennial Republican National Convention. Also, under party rules, a vacancy on the national ticket would be filled by a vote of the national committee.

The committee was established in 1856 to organize the first Republican National Nominating Convention. The first chair of the Republican National Committee was Edwin D. Morgan, a former Whig. Initially, one national committee member, who would be elected by the state party organization for a four-year term, represented each state and U.S. territory. In 1924, following the ratification of the Nineteenth Amendment that extended the franchise to women, the membership of the Republican National Committee was expanded to include a national committeeman and national committeewoman from each state, U.S. territory, and the District of Columbia.

In 1952, the composition of the Republican National Committee was again modified, for the purpose of providing bonuses to state parties that did well on behalf of the party. A state that had voted Republican in the previous presidential election, had a Republican majority in its congressional delegation, or had a Republican governor, would be given an extra seat on the RNC to be occupied by its state party chair. In 1968, the composition of the Republican National Committee was established: state party chairs, national committeeman, and national committeewoman representing each state, territory, and the District of Columbia. The terms of the national committee members are four years, while the state party chair remains a member of the RNC as long as they are chair of their state party organization. The national committee has 165 members.

The leadership of the Republican National Committee consists of the chair and co-chair, elected by the members of the RNC. Under party rules, the chair and co-chair must be of the opposite sex. They are also full-time employees of the party. In addition, the RNC elects eight vice chairs: a male and female from each of the four regions (the Western States Association, the Midwestern States Association, the Northeastern States Association, and the Southern States Association), a secretary, and a treasurer. All officers are elected for two-year terms.

The Republican National Committee has a number of standing committees. The Executive Committee consists of 28 members, including all RNC officers, and is responsible for acting on behalf of the committee between its meetings. The Rules Committee, consisting of one delegate from every state, makes recommendations regarding the party rules to the national committee and the national convention. The Budget Committee develops the budget and reviews the income and expenditures of the RNC. The RNC Chair appoints three of the seven members, and the other four are selected from the regional caucuses. The Committee of Resolutions, informally known as the Platform Committee, is responsible for preparing the party platform presented to delegates for their consideration at the national nominating convention every four years. The committee consists of eight members (two from each of the four regions) and a chair appointed by the RNC Chair.

The Committee on Arrangements is responsible for the planning and management of the convention, including selecting the officers of the convention. The chair and co-chair of the RNC serve on this committee, and the RNC chair appoints at least one member from each state to the committee. The Committee on Contests hears any disputes on matters relating to the convention. There are eight members (two from each of the four regions) and a chair appointed by the RNC Chair.

The Site Selection Committee reviews the bids by cities to host the nominating convention, and then makes a recommendation for a convention site to the RNC, which make the final decision. The nine-member committee is made up of two members from each region and is chaired by the RNC Co-chair. The Committee on the Call is made up of a chair and seven members. They assist the RNC with the issuance of the party call for the next national convention, including writing the rules and procedures for the convention. The RNC staff organization includes a number of different departments, which include political, communications, research, membership services, outreach, chairman and co-chair's office and finance.

The RNC's headquarters is located at 310 First Street, Southeast, Washington, D.C., in a building they share with the National Republican Congressional Committee and the Republican Governors' Association. The RNC chair is Robert M. "Mike" Duncan (who became the 60th Chairman of the RNC in January 2007), and Jo Ann Davidson is the co-chair (having taken office in January 2005).

SEE ALSO: Democratic Party; Political Parties in American Elections; Republican National Party Finance Committees; Republican Party; Republican State Party Organizations.

BIBLIOGRAPHY. C.P. Cotter and B.C. Hennessy, *Politics Without Power: The National Party Committees* (Atherton Press, 1964); P.A. Klinkner, *The Losing Parties: Out-party National Committees, 1956–1993* (Yale University Press, 1994).

JEFFREY KRAUS
WAGNER COLLEGE

Republican National Party Finance Committees

THE AMERICAN POLITICAL system is a two-party system, with most contests between two candidates, one from the Republican Party and one from the Democratic Party. Each major political party has several national committees formulated to carry out the specific needs of their respective party and to insure victory for their respective candidates. The Republican Party has the Republican National Committee, the National Republican Congressional Committee, and the National Republican Senatorial Committee. The financial activities of these committees are regulated by federal law and play an important role during an election cycle.

Like federal candidates, the Republican National Party Finance Committees can raise only hard money. The Republican National Party Finance Committees are permitted to receive contributions of up to $26,700 per year (for the years 2005 and 2006) from any individual, and up to $15,000 per year from a multi-candidate Political Action Committee (PAC). The Republican National

Party Finance Committees cannot raise any funds from corporations, labor unions, or other restricted sources, although individuals affiliated with these entities can donate through the entities' connected PACs.

As a result of the Bipartisan Campaign Reform Act of 2002 (McCain-Feingold Bill), there are very specific rules regarding contributions. The Republican National Party Finance Committees can make contributions directly to federal candidates of up to $5,000 per election, with the exception of Senate candidates, to whom they may contribute a total of $37,300 per candidate per election cycle (for the 2005–06 cycle).

In addition, the Republican National Party Finance Committees can make coordinated expenditures on behalf of their candidates. In House races, these coordinated expenditures can reach a total of $38,300 per candidate for 2005. In Senate races, the amount depends on the population of the state, but ranges from a total of about $60,000 in the smallest states to well over $1 million in the largest states. In the presidential general election race, the Republican National Party Finance Committees can each spend about $16 million in coordination with their respective presidential nominee.

The Republican National Party Finance Committees are successful at what they do. They out-raised the large amounts of money that the Democratic National Finance Committees raised, in many cases doubling the funds raised by the Democrats. Consider the following:

- The Republican National Party raised more than $514,015,523 1990–2002.
- Individuals were responsible for more than $487,938,939 during this same period.
- Disbursements from the National Republican Party totaled more than $455,756,468 during this 12-year cycle.
- The Republican Senatorial Campaign Committee, aimed at raising money for those seeking office in the Senate, raised more than $297,911,284 in that 12-year period.
- The Republican Senatorial Campaign Committee spent more than $240,262,379 during this time period to campaign for their candidates.
- The Republican Congressional Committee increased their fundraising efforts from just over $23 million in 1990, to more than $65 million in 2002. The total amount of monies raised during this time period was $275,497,285.

- The Republican Congressional Committee spent more than $238,403,575 on behalf of those seeking congressional offices during this cycle.
- At the state and local level, the Republican Party Finance Committees raised more than $364,555,944 and spent more than $289,390,496.
- All of the National Finance Committees of the Republican Party raised a combined total of $1,404,965,430 and spent $1,176,798,312 during this period.

The Republican National Party Finance Committees have done a remarkable job, having out-raised the Democratic National Party Finance Committees by more than $600 million. It is important to remember as one looks at these numbers that the connection between money and election campaigns are costly. Researchers suggest that in the 1999–2000 election cycle more than $3 billion was spent at all levels of campaigns with more than $800 million spent on the George W. Bush-Al Gore presidential election battle.

SEE ALSO: Campaign Finance, Federal Elections; Campaign Finance, Politics of; Democratic National Party Finance Committees; Republican Party.

BIBLIOGRAPHY. Federal Election Commission, www.fec.gov (cited August 2007); Republican Party, www.gop.com (cited August 2007).

RONALD ERIC MATTHEWS, JR.
MOUNT UNION COLLEGE

Republican Party

THE REPUBLICAN PARTY is one of the two parties that constitute the two-party system in the United States. The party was one of a number of third parties that appeared during the 1840s and 1850s, and emerged as a major party following the election of Abraham Lincoln in 1860. Since that time, the Republicans and Democrats have dominated the American political system. The party has long been known as the GOP, an acronym for the Grand Old Party. However, when originally introduced in 1875, it was understood to stand for the Gallant Old Party. The contemporary Republican Par-

ty's core principles are that individuals, not government, make the best decisions; that all people are entitled to equal rights; and that decisions are best made close to home. The party, due to the influence of social conservatives, has become the defender of traditional values in American society.

THE FOUNDING OF THE PARTY

As the slavery controversy intensified during the 1840s and 1850s, a number of antislavery political parties appeared, in large part because of the failure of the two major parties of the day, the Democrats and the Whigs, to respond to the developing crisis. Among the parties that appeared during this time were the Liberty Party (1840–48), the Free Soil Party (1848–55), the Anti-Nebraska Party (1854), the Opposition Party (1854–58), and the Constitutional Union Party (1860). Opponents of slavery and supporters of the notion that the federal government should offer free land in the west to settlers formed the Republican Party in the early 1850s.

The first county convention of the Republican Party was held in Ripon, Wisconsin, on March 20, 1854 (the moderate Republican group, the Ripon Society, takes its name from the site of the first party meeting). The first statewide Republican convention took place on July 6, 1854, in Jackson, Michigan. The convention adopted a platform that opposed the expansion of slavery into the west and nominated a slate of statewide candidates, including Kinsley S. Bingham, who would be elected governor that year. Alvan E. Bovay, who organized the Wisconsin meeting, chose the name Republican because it was reminiscent of Thomas Jefferson's "Republican" party of the early republic.

The new party drew supporters from antislavery elements of the Whig (who were known as the Conscience Whigs) and Democratic Parties, and would eventually attract many former Free Soilers, Anti-Nebraska Party members, and members of the Opposition Party. It attracted both abolitionists, who wished to eliminate slavery (who became known as the radical wing of the party); and anti-expansionists (known as the conservative wing), who opposed the expansion of slavery into the territories (made possible by the Kansas-Nebraska Act), but were unwilling to outlaw slavery in the states where it was already in place.

By 1856, the Republicans had become a national party, with its base primarily in the northeast and midwest. The party also had organizations in Delaware, Kentucky, North Carolina, and Virginia. Their first national convention was held in Pittsburgh in February 1856. The party's first nominating convention was held at Philadelphia's Musical Hall Fund in June, 1856, where the new party nominated John C. Fremont, the "pathfinder" and former Democrat who had conquered California during the Mexican War, for president. William Lewis Dayton of New Jersey, a former Whig, was selected as his running mate. The party slogan was "Free soil, free labor, free speech, free men, Fremont." The party platform opposed the extension of slavery into the western territories. Fremont received 33 percent of the popular vote, and carried New England, New York, Iowa, Michigan, Ohio and Wisconsin. However, Fremont had no support in the south, and Democrat James Buchanan won the election.

THE THIRD PARTY SYSTEM 1860–96

By 1860, the Republicans were now the principal alternative to the Democratic Party in national politics. Meeting at the "Wigwam" in Chicago, the Republicans selected on the third ballot a dark horse candidate, Abraham Lincoln, as the party's standard-bearer in the general election against a Democratic Party fractured by the slavery issue. Lincoln, who opposed the expansion of slavery into the western territories, but believed that the federal government did not have the authority to ban slavery, was elected. The southern states, seeing the new Republican administration as a threat to slavery, seceded from the Union, leading to the Civil War.

While Lincoln is most remembered for leading the Union during the Civil War, his administration also established the Department of Agriculture (1862), the Bureau of Internal Revenue (1862), and the Comptroller of the Currency (1864). Two important bills enacted during Lincoln's presidency were the Homestead Act (1862), which gave 160 acres to settlers, and the Morrill Land Grant College Act, which gave federal land to states for the purpose of establishing agricultural and engineering colleges. In 1863, Lincoln issued the Emancipation Proclamation, ending slavery in the rebellious states.

Following the Civil War, the radical Republicans who dominated Congress (over the opposition of Andrew Johnson, who became president after Lincoln's death), oversaw the reconstruction of the Union, which included the enactment of legislation to improve the plight of the newly-freed slaves, the "reconstruction amendments" (Thirteenth, Fourteenth, and Fifteenth Amendments) to the Constitution, and the occupation of the south by federal military forces. The radicals also imposed Republican rule on the former Confederate states, through a coalition of freed slaves, Scalawags (southern whites who joined the Republican Party and called for acceptance of the radicals' reconstruction policies) and Carpetbaggers (northern whites who moved into the former Confederate states during reconstruction).

The party would become dominant in presidential elections, winning six of the eight presidential elections 1864–92. The only Democrat elected during this period was Grover Cleveland, who was elected in 1884 and 1892. In 1876 (Tilden) and 1888 (Cleveland), the Democratic candidate won the popular vote, but lost the electoral vote. Following the contested presidential election of 1876, President Rutherford B. Hayes removed federal troops from Florida, Louisiana, and South Carolina, the last three states under military occupation. With the end of Reconstruction, the Republican Party would virtually disappear from the south until the middle of the 20th century, as the south went Democratic. It was during this era that the party's traditional symbol, the elephant, came into use. A political cartoon drawn by Thomas Nast was published in the November 7, 1874, edition of *Harper's Weekly* and depicted a Republican elephant and a Democratic donkey; both symbols endure.

THE FOURTH PARTY SYSTEM 1896–1932

By 1896, a new era was emerging in American politics. The Civil War and Reconstruction were no longer salient issues in American politics. The Industrial Revolution had transformed America, and it would transform the competition between the two major political parties. By 1896, the Republicans supported big business, the gold standard, protective tariffs, and pensions for Union military veterans. The 1896 Republican platform was also the first to call for women's suffrage. The Republican presidential candidate in 1896, William McKinley of Ohio, won an overwhelming victory over the Democratic candidate, William Jennings Bryan, the "free silver" advocate who had captivated the Democrats at their convention with his "Cross of Gold" speech. In doing so, McKinley (and his campaign manager, industrialist and politician Marcus Hanna) made the Republican Party the "pro-business" party that also had the support of America's emerging middle class.

Once again, the Republicans would dominate the presidency. Between 1896 and 1928, only one Democrat, Woodrow Wilson, captured the presidency. The Republicans would also control both houses of Congress during 30 of the 36 years between 1896 and 1932. Wilson's first victory, in 1912, was due to a split in the Republican ranks. Theodore Roosevelt, who had become president following the assassination of William McKinley in 1901, and was elected in 1904, returned after four years to seek the Republican nomination.

Roosevelt, who was a Progressive, was disappointed with his hand-picked successor, William Howard Taft, whom Roosevelt believed had betrayed the Progressive cause by supporting conservative Republican measures such as the protectionist Payne-Aldrich Tariff Act of 1909. Denied the Republican nomination despite winning most of the primaries, "TR" became the nominee of the Progressive Party. In the 1912 election, Roosevelt actually came in ahead of Taft; but the split between the two candidates allowed Wilson to win. It also allowed the Democrats to begin their brief period of control of both houses of Congress during this era.

While Roosevelt's presidency made the party a progressive force in the early 20th century, by the 1920s the Republican Party's economic ideology had become promotion of business interests, as exemplified by the party's support of protectionist tariffs. The party also opposed American entry into the League of Nations. The stock market crash of October 1929 would set the stage for the end of the fourth party system and the end of the era of Republican domination. President Herbert Hoover, elected in a landslide in 1928, opposed the establishment of direct relief programs to ease the suffering caused by the economic crisis. In the 1930 election, the Democrats would narrow the Republican majorities to one seat in the United States Senate and two seats in the U.S. House of Representatives.

THE FIFTH PARTY SYSTEM 1932–68
In defeating Hoover in 1932, Roosevelt would bring together a New Deal Coalition of white ethnic voters in big cities, southern whites, and African-Americans, that would make the Democrats the dominant party in American politics for nearly 40 years. The New Deal policies made Roosevelt and the Democrats incredibly popular with the electorate, and the 1936 election saw Roosevelt carry 46 of the 48 states in the Union, and reduced the Republican Party's numbers in Congress to

17 (out of 96) in the U.S. Senate, and 89 (of 435) in the U.S. House of Representatives.

In 1938, the Republicans, capitalizing on the unpopularity of Roosevelt's court packing plan, would gain six seats in the Senate and 80 in the House of Representatives. In 1946 capitalizing on President Harry S. Truman's unpopularity (Truman became president following Roosevelt's death in 1945), the Republicans re-captured both Houses of Congress for the first time since 1932. However, Republican control was short-lived as the Democrats would re-take control in 1948 when Truman upset New York Governor Thomas E. Dewey for the presidency. In 1952, Dwight D. Eisenhower, the supreme commander of Allied Forces in Europe during World War II, was elected president. He also had coattails that helped the Republicans take control of both houses of Congress during the 83rd Congress (1953–55), only to lose control to the Democrats in the 1954 elections. It would be another 40 years until the Republicans would control both houses of Congress again.

During this period, there were two wings in the Republican Party. The party's liberal wing supported most of the New Deal, but believed that these programs, as well as other social programs proposed by the Democrats, could be run more efficiently. They also tended to be internationalists. This wing of the party was geographically centered in the northeast, and numbered among its leaders Governor Dewey, his Republican successor Nelson A. Rockefeller, New York Senator Jacob Javits, Eisenhower, and Richard Nixon.

The conservative wing of the party opposed the New Deal and, after 1938, joined with conservative Democrats in Congress to block most liberal initiatives until Lyndon Johnson and the Great Society of the 1960s. Senator Robert Taft of Ohio was the longtime leader of this wing, whose base was in the midwest. During the 1950s, Arizona Senator Barry Goldwater and other conservative Republicans considered leaving the party to start a new conservative party with conservative Democrats. Goldwater rejected that option, and instead sought the Republican presidential nomination in 1964. While Goldwater lost to Johnson in a landslide, he set the stage for the rightward shift of the Republican Party, a shift that would culminate in the election of Ronald Reagan in 1980.

THE ERA OF DEALIGNMENT 1968–2008
The Democrat's New Deal Coalition began to collapse in the late 1960s, as white ethnic and southern

white voters began to drift away from the party. The 1966 midterm election, where the Republicans picked up four seats in the senate and 47 in the House, was characterized as a "white backlash" against Johnson's "Great Society" social welfare policies, the Democratic Party's support of the Civil Rights Movement and the urban riots. The south, which had been a Democratic stronghold since the end of reconstruction, shifted to the Republican column, prompted by President Nixon's southern strategy.

Under Ronald Reagan's leadership, the party moved sharply to the right. Reagan, an actor and former Democrat who switched parties in 1962, became a national political figure as a result of his "A Time for Choosing" speech made on behalf of Goldwater at the 1964 Republican convention. Reagan was elected governor of California in 1966; in 1968 he briefly ran for president as part of an unsuccessful "Stop Nixon" movement, receiving 182 votes at the convention. In 1976, he made a more serious run, nearly taking the nomination from Gerald Ford, who had become president following Nixon's resignation on August 9, 1974.

Reagan won a landslide victory over President Jimmy Carter, attracting the votes of Reagan Democrats, who were white, Roman Catholic, and blue-collar voters who supported Reagan because of his social conservatism (opposition to abortion and gay rights) and his anti-Soviet rhetoric. The 1980 Republican platform, at Reagan's behest, dropped support for the Equal Rights Amendment (the Republicans had, in 1940, included a platform plank calling for the ratification of an Equal Rights Amendment, four years before the Democrats would add a similar plank), based on the premise that such an amendment was an intrusion by Congress and the federal courts into what was a state matter. Reagan was re-elected in 1984, winning 49 of the 50 states and his vice president, George H.W. Bush, was elected president in 1988.

After Democrat Bill Clinton defeated George H.W. Bush in 1992, the Republicans won majorities in both houses of Congress in the 1994 midterm elections. Led by House Republican whip Newt Gingrich (who would become speaker), the Republicans ran on the Contract With America, which called for a number of reforms, including a balanced budget, welfare reform, and term limits. For the first time in more than 40 years, the Republicans would control both houses of Congress (they had controlled the Senate 1981–87). For the next

12 years, the Republicans controlled both chambers (except for the period from June 6, 2001, to January 3, 2003, when the Democrats controlled the Senate after Senator James Jeffords of Vermont left the Republican Party to sit as an Independent).

In 2000, George W. Bush was elected president, despite trailing Vice President Al Gore in the popular vote by 543,816 votes. It was the first time since 1888 that a candidate who did not receive at least a plurality of the popular vote was elected president. It was also the first time since 1952 that the Republicans would control the presidency and both houses of Congress simultaneously (this domination was short-lived as a result Jeffords decision to leave the party in June 2001 to sit as an Independent).

Following 9/11, President Bush gained widespread support as he prosecuted the War on Terrorism. The invasion of Afghanistan, the enactment by Congress of the USA PATRIOT (the Uniting and Strengthening America By Providing Appropriate Tools Required to Intercept and Obstruct Terrorism) Act of 2001, and the president's popularity, helped the Republicans in the 2002 midterm election, allowing them to re-take control of the Senate and maintain their majority in the House of Representatives.

In 2004, President Bush was re-elected, with 51 percent of the popular vote and 286 electoral votes to Senator John Kerry's 251. Days after the election, the president told supporters that he had "earned capital in the campaign, political capital, and now I intend to spend it." In the first months of his second term, Bush's proposal to modify the existing Social Security system by adding personal savings accounts failed to gain public support.

The administration's response to Hurricane Katrina was seen as, at best, inadequate. The Director of the Federal Emergency Management Agency (FEMA), whom the president had said was "doin' a heck of a job," resigned. The war in Iraq, as the situation continued to deteriorate, grew unpopular. An October 2007 CBS News/*New York Times* poll found the president's approval rating at 34 percent.

The Republican Party suffered a serious setback as President Bush's declining popularity, rising opposition to the American military presence in Iraq, and voter disgust with what the Democrats called the "culture of corruption" that was reflected by number of scandals involving Republican members of Congress resulted in a sweeping Democratic victory in the 2006 midterm elections. Democrats returned to power in the House of Representatives and the Senate, and took control of a majority of state governments.

CURRENT PARTY STRUCTURE

The principal national party organization is the Republican National Committee (RNC). The committee is responsible for promoting the party and its activities, organizing the quadrennial convention, and coordinating fundraising and political strategy. The members of the national committee elect the chair of the Republican National Committee. Generally, when a Republican is president, the president chooses the chair of the national committee. When the party is out of power, the selection process is open. The current chair of the Republican National Committee is Mike Duncan, who was elected January 19, 2007. The committee is made up of 165 members, representing each state, the District of Columbia, and U.S. territories. The delegation from each state consists of the state party chair, a national committeeman, and national committeewoman. They are elected for four-year terms.

In addition to the national committee, there are campaign committees in each chamber of Congress. The National Republican Congressional Committee (NRCC), which was established in 1866, and the National Republican Senatorial Committee (NRSC), founded in 1916, recruit candidates, raise money, and provide campaign support in targeted races in each election cycle. The Republican Governors Association (RGA), founded in 1963, has historically been a discussion group for Republican governors. Recently, the RGA has begun to play a role in gubernatorial elections similar to that of the "Capitol Hill" campaign committees.

Party grassroots organizations include the College Republican National Committee (CRNC), the Young Republican National Federation (YRs), and the National Federation of Republican Women (NFRW). The CRNC was established in 1892, and presently has more than 250,000 members at over 1,800 college campuses in the United States. The purpose of the organization is to help elect Republicans and recruit and develop new party activists and leaders.

The Young Republicans are a grassroots organization open to members of the party who are between 18 and 40 years of age. The NFRW, founded in 1936, has over 100,000 members in more than 1,800 clubs throughout the United States. There are state Republican Party organizations in each state, and within each state there are local party organizations. State party organizations' state election laws determine structure and state party rules. As of July 2007, the party's general chairman is Mel Martinez, who is also a U.S. Senator from Florida. The party headquarters is located at 310 First Street, Southeast, in Washington, D.C.

SEE ALSO: Abortion; Affirmative Action; Civil War and Realignment; Homeland Security; Liberal Republican Party; Political Parties in American Elections; Republican National Committee; Republican National Party Finance Committees; Republican State Party Organizations; Seventy-Two-Hour Program; Slavery; State Campaign Committees; Two-Party System.

BIBLIOGRAPHY. J.A. Aistrup, *The Southern Strategy Revisited: Republican Top-Down Advancement in the South* (University Press of Kentucky, 1996); Earl Black and Merle Black, *The Rise of Southern Republicans* (Harvard University Press, 2002); M.C. Brennan, *Turning Right in the Sixties: The Conservative Capture of the GOP* (University of North Carolina Press, 1995); M.K. Fauntroy, *Republicans and the Black Vote* (Lynne Rienner Publishers, 2007); Jim Geraghty, *Voting to Kill: How 9/11 Launched the Era of Republican Leadership* (Simon and Schuster, 2006); Newt Gingrich and R.K. Armey, *Contract With America: the Bold Plan By Representative Newt Gingrich, Representative Dick Armey and the House Republicans to Change the Nation*, ed. by Ed Gillespie and Bob Schellhas (Times Books, 1994); Lewis Gould, *Grand Old Party: A History of the Republicans* (Random House, 2003); Tom Hamburger and Peter Wallsten, *One Party Country: the Republican Plan for Dominance in the 21st Century* (John Wiley and Sons, Inc., 2006); Patrick Hynes, *In the Defense of the Religious Right: Why Conservative Christians are the Lifeblood of the The Republican Party and Why that Terrifies the Democrats* (Nelson Current, 2006); Steve Jarding, *Foxes in the Hen House: How the Republicans Stole the South and the Heartland and What the Democrats Must Do to Run 'em Out* (Simon And Schuster, 2006); R.A. Rutland, *The Republicans: From Lincoln to Bush* (University of Missouri Press, 1996); M.D. Tanner, *Leviathan on the Right: How Big Government Conservatism Brought Down the Republican Revolution* (Cato Institute, 2007).

JEFFREY KRAUS
WAGNER COLLEGE

Republican State Party Organizations

ALL STATE PARTY organizations played a critical role in the development of the political system in the United States, though the Grand Old Party (GOP) differs somewhat from the Democratic organizations. The Republican Party officially began in the early 1850s and was committed to the abolishment of slavery and free westward expansion. The first Republicans a were combination of members from the Whig, Democrat, and Free Soil Parties. They collaborated on ideas based on their anger over the Kansas-Nebraska Act, which gave new territories the choice of accepting slavery. The history of the Republican Party as a party of reform meant that the structure of the local organizations—mostly at the state level—would have a somewhat different structure and greater power than their Democratic counterparts.

The party first became nationally known when one of its members, John C. Fremont, was nominated for President. The Republican platform was publicized with Fremont's slogan "free soil, free labor, free speech, free men, and Fremont." The attempt to win the presidency was genuine, but with the Republican Party still a third party, it was unlikely one of its candidates would win. It was not until four years later that a Republican made it into the White House. The first Republican president was Abraham Lincoln. Success at the presidential level opened a completely new set of doors for the Republican Party; it finally had its chance to fulfill its original platform. Lincoln took the first step for the party's platform by signing the Emancipation Proclamation; later the party was able to pass the Thirteenth, Fourteenth, and Fifteenth Amendments, all supporting African-American rights. Some say that it was Lincoln's leadership during the Civil War and his time in office that led the Republicans into a "period of dominance" that lasted over 50 years.

State party organizations for the GOP took on the critical task of developing a voting base from disenchanted Whigs and Northern Democrats, asserting an electoral role for the party organizations at a very early stage. The state organizations still exert a great deal of leverage over national party decision-making. The mission of state organizations really falls into three distinct, though intertwined, roles: liaison between the local organizations and the national party, electoral mechanism, and power within the state political apparatus.

In the first role, that of liaison between the local organizations, individuals, and Republican-oriented groups within the state, the state party functions as an "interest aggregator," representing, through its delegates to the Republican National Committee, the interests of Republicans and their supporters in the state. It is in this role that the state organization will nominate persons to the National Platform Committee, advise the national party on issues of policy, and work with the national party to raise awareness of national initiatives by the party as manifested in that state.

The second role, that of an electioneering organization, is the function with which most people are familiar. Here, the state party organizes, sets many of the rules for, and takes responsibility for the state's party primary, convention, or caucus (depending on the state). The state party also raises and disperses party money for local candidates, launches advertising campaigns for electoral purposes, recruits candidates for office, and acts as a conduit between the national party's efforts and local candidates and their organizations, coordinating efforts to gain office. Finally, the state party is the local representative of, and to, the national party in policy efforts. It is in these roles that state GOP organizations disseminate the party's position on various issues and pass them down to the rank and file.

The responsibility and roles that each state organization take vary greatly from organization to organization. In order to explore the variability it is helpful to simply compare a few states. When comparing the activities of New York's Republican Party and the Vermont Republican Party, it is easy to see the differences. New York's Republican organization has over 20 events listed on their website, and each of which is a fundraising opportunity for the state to raise money for their party. It is possible for those interested to become involved in the fundraising process. In Vermont, there are five listed events; a majority of which are meetings at the state level—Vermont is not holding as many parties and events in which it is raising money for the Republican Party.

The availability of news relating to the Republican Party also varies with each state. The New York organization offers a long list of recent news as well as the opportunity to look up past articles and information. The list that Vermont offers is slightly shorter. It is very important for a state to make as much information available to the people as possible, but possibly the most important aspect of the state organization is the ease of getting involved or volunteering. Unlike Vermont, New York offers a detailed map of each county; once a county is selected, it is easy to find information about the events taking place in an area close to one's home.

State organizations can be expected to vary according to the level of influence the party has, the wealth of the state, the number of delegates the states sends to the national convention, and the competitiveness of the GOP for office in that state. Thus, small and less significant organizations are found in states that are predominantly Democratic; while state organizations serving states with large numbers of Republican officeholders will tend to be far more active.

Democratic and Republican state parties are similar in scope and institutional purpose, but the difference with the GOP lies in the level of autonomy Republican state parties may have from the national organization. Perhaps because of their reforming efforts early on (and the representation of GOP organizations as progressive alternatives to Democratic "machine" politics in the early part of the 20th century), Republican state organizations tend to depart from the "party line" of the national party perhaps more often than their Democratic counterparts do.

SEE ALSO: Republican National Committee; Republican National Party Finance Committees; Republican Party.

BIBLIOGRAPHY. New York State Republican Committee, www.nygop.org (cited August 2007); Republican Party, www.gop.com (cited August 2007); Vermont Republican Party, www.vtgop.org (cited August 2007).

R. Bruce Anderson
Baker University

Retrospective Voting

RETROSPECTIVE VOTING IS voting that takes place as voters look backward in time. It is contrasted with prospective voting, which takes place as voters look forward in time. Retrospective voting is encouraged by incumbents who want to highlight their accomplishments, and also by challengers who want to focus on the incumbents' missteps. One of the leading exponents of retrospective voting was Ronald Reagan. When he ran for president as a Republican in 1980, challenging Democratic incumbent Jimmy Carter, he asked the question in the only presidential debate with Carter, "Are you better off now than you were four years ago?" In this mode, he was both asking voters to vote their pocketbooks, and encouraging them to practice retrospective voting. Carter, meanwhile, wanted voters to overlook the economic recession that had fallen on the country in the past year and, instead, encouraged them to vote prospectively by reminding them of the possibility of a right-wing revival under Reagan, and by painting Reagan as a warmonger.

Four years later, Reagan remained in retrospective mode. In a debate with Democrat Walter F. Mondale (who had been Carter's vice president), Reagan once again asked the question, "Are you better off now than you were four years ago?" He was asking voters to focus once more on their pocketbooks and to contrast the very low inflation of 1982–84 with the double-digit inflation of 1979–80. Mondale urged both prospective voting (as he subtly called attention to the 73-year-old president's declining agility) and retrospective voting (as he campaigned against the huge deficit spending Reagan supported).

Regardless of how politicians campaign, political scientists use public opinion research to find out what voters are looking at in determining their vote choice. Many political scientists believe that economic performance is key and that elections can be predicted on the basis of economic performance in the period leading up to the election. Implicit in this is the idea that voters are paying attention retrospectively. This has led to the development of economic-based voting models that look only at key economic indicators and do not consider such usually central ideas to voters, such as party identification, public opinion, and war. Despite their mechanical nature, these models have correctly projected 12 of the last 15 presidential elections through 2004.

One key challenge to the supremacy of retrospective voting was the 2000 presidential campaign of Al Gore. Many believed that Gore should have focused his campaign on the peace and prosperity of the eight years he had served as vice president under President Bill Clinton. Under the framework of retrospective voting, the economic voting models predicted a comfortable landslide win by Gore. However, Gore seemed to ignore the prosperity of the previous eight years and instead focused his campaign on the future, an obvious appeal to prospective voters. Some believe that Gore refused to campaign on the Clinton record because of the acrimonious tarring of Clinton that had occurred during his administration as a result of a series of personal scandals, which had not touched Gore.

Thus, while lambasting Clinton did not drive him from office, Republicans can claim victory because their agitation kept Gore from campaigning (and according to conventional political science, being elected) on the Clinton-Gore record. The challenge to the operation of the retrospective voting models comes not only from Gore's failure to campaign according to their script, but voters' seeming inability to pick up the economic cues anyway (although Gore won the popular vote very narrowly.)

SEE ALSO: Determinants of Vote Choice; Rational Choice Model.

BIBLIOGRAPHY. Morris Fiorina, *Retrospective Voting in American National Elections* (Yale University Press, 1981); V.O. Key, Jr., *The Responsible Electorate: Rationality in Presidential Voting* (Vintage, 1966); John Zaller, *The Nature and Origins of Mass Opinion* (Cambridge University Press, 1992).

TONY HILL
MASSACHUSETTS INSTITUTE OF TECHNOLOGY

Rhode Island

EUROPEANS FIRST VISITED the State of Rhode Island and Providence Plantations (its full name), in 1524 when Italian navigator Giovanni de Verrazzano sailed there. He described it as being about the same size as the island of Rhodes, with the subsequent Dutch explorer calling it Roodt Eylandt. Under the British, it came to be known as Rhode Island. It was occupied by Roger Williams and others beginning in 1636, after Williams had been banished from the Massachusetts Bay Colony for his religious views. In 1772, people in Rhode Island attacked the British soldiers in the area, and took a leading role in the American War of Independence. At that time the slave population of the colony was 6.3 percent, far higher than any other colonies in New England. Merchants from Rhode Island controlled up to three-quarters of the slave trade from Africa to the American states.

Nicholas Cooke was the first governor of Rhode Island's after its independence, serving from 1775 to 1778

Rhode Island was the first of the 13 colonies to declare its independence from England on May 4, 1776, and was the last to ratify the U.S. Constitution, only doing so because it was feared that its trade might suffer if it was regarded as a foreign country. The first governor after independence was Nicholas Cooke, who was succeeded by William Greene. During this period, the industrialization of Rhode Island started. Industries involved with building materials, then builders, and services for the new population with other industries enlarging the local economy.

Many laborers came to Rhode Island for work who did not own land and were not allowed to vote in state elections. By 1829 some 60 percent of free white males did not have the franchise. The problem became so important that Thomas Dorr, who staged two insurrections in the state, in 1841 and again in 1842, managed to change the electoral system. In 1842, a referendum eventually led to a new liberal constitution, although two rival state governments were briefly elected. Dorr had to flee the state, returning in 1844, he was convicted of high treason, and sentenced to life imprisonment with hard labor, although he was released in the following year and pardoned nine years later. By this new constitution, any white male who either held land or could pay a poll tax of one dollar was able to vote.

In 1854, William W. Hoppin, a former Whig, was elected as governor for the Know-Nothing Party. He became a major force in the Republican Party in the state, and his successor, Elisha Dyer, elected in 1857, was the first Republican governor of the state. In 1859, Thomas G. Turner, another Republican, won the gubernatorial elections, and in the following year William Sprague IV was elected, also for the Republican Party. Aged 29, he was the youngest governor of the state at the time; his uncle, William Sprague III, a member of the Democratic Party had served as governor 1838–39.

In the 1860 gubernatorial elections, many conservatives were unwilling to support the radical Republicans, and managed to reject Seth Padelford, who had hoped to be chosen as the Republican Party candidate. This helped prevent the Republican Party at the federal level from picking William H. Seward as their candidate, believing he might alienate states such as Pennsylvania. This helped Abraham Lincoln's nomination at the Republican Party convention in Chicago. In the 1860 U.S. presidential election, Rhode Island voted convincingly for Abraham Lincoln, who won with 12,244 votes (61.4 percent) to Stephen Douglas who received 7,707 votes (38.6 percent), even though he was standing on a fusion ticket with John Breckinridge and John Bell.Most members of the Democratic Party remaining loyal to their party. William Sprague, who was re-elected in 1860, fought in the First Battle of Bull Run.

Although Democrat William C. Cozens served as governor in 1863, Republican James Y. Smith won the gubernatorial elections in 1863. The next governor, also from the Republican Party, was Ambrose Everett Burnside, a railroad executive, and later a Union general popularly regarded as one of the worst Civil War generals. His proliferation of facial hair gave rise, subsequently, to the term sideburns.

Republicans won the gubernatorial elections until 1887, when Democrat John W. Davis was elected. He served for one term, with Royal C. Taft of the Republican Party winning the subsequent gubernatorial election. Taft was succeeded by Herbert W. Ladd, also Republican. In 1890, John W. Davis returned to the

governorship. After he left office, the next 10 years saw Republican governors until 1902, when Lucius F.C. Garvin was elected.

THE 20TH CENTURY

Garvin served one term, and then Republican George H. Utter won the next gubernatorial election. Since then, neither party has held the governorship for long. Rhode Island became a swing state, although the Democrats failed to win control of the state legislature in 1934, ending an opportunity to change the state constitution.

In 1938, William H. Vanderbilt III, of the famous Vanderbilt family of New York, was elected governor of Rhode Island. When Vanderbilt became governor, he refused to appoint fellow Republicans to state positions, preferring to appoint on merit, and quickly lost the support of his party base. His successor, Democrat James Howard McGrath, was a district attorney before he became governor, and served 1941–45. The next governor, John Orlando Pastore, a Roman Catholic, was the first Italian-American governor of Rhode Island, elected in 1946 and again in 1948. He delivered the keynote address at the Democratic National Convention at Atlantic City, New Jersey, where Lyndon B. Johnson was nominated for the presidency. By that time Pastore was serving his third of five terms in the U.S. Senate.

In 1958, Republican Christopher Del Sesto was elected governor, and two years later, Democrat John A. Notte, Jr., won the gubernatorial election. In the 1960 U.S. presidential election, Rhode Island voted for the Democrats, giving John F. Kennedy 258,032 votes (63.6 percent) to Richard M. Nixon's 147,502 votes (36.4 percent). In 1962, John H. Chafee was elected governor of the state, and remained governor until 1969.

In the U.S. presidential election in 1964, Rhode Island again voted Democratic, giving Lyndon Johnson 315,463 votes (80.9 percent) to Barry Goldwater's 74,615 votes (19.1 percent), the largest margin by which Johnson won any state (although the District of Columbia did record a higher percentage for him, 85.5 percent); and in 1968 voted Democratic again, supporting Hubert Humphrey who received 246,518 votes (64 percent) to 122,359 votes (31.8 percent) for Richard M. Nixon, and 15,678 votes (4.1 percent) for George Wallace. In the 1968 gubernatorial election, Chafee lost to Democrat Frank Licht, the first Jewish person to be elected governor in Rhode Island. In January 1969, Richard M. Nixon appointed Chafee secretary of the Navy.

Licht, as governor, went back on campaign pledges not to introduce state income tax, and this led to a voter backlash against him, but not against the Democratic Party. Democrat Philip William Noel, the mayor of Warwick, was elected governor in 1972, and remaining in office until 1977 when J. Joseph Garrahy became the governor.

Garrahy held office 1977–85, becoming one of the few governors to serve eight years in that position. His successor, Edward D. DiPrete, a Republican, won the 1984 gubernatorial elections, and remained in office until 1991, losing the 1990 gubernatorial election to the former federal prosecutor Bruce Sundlun in a landslide. Sundlun, the second Jewish governor of the state, was a decorated World War II hero, and had been defeated by DiPrete in 1986 and 1988, and expected to lose again in 1990. Instead, he won the election by 74 percent to 26 percent.

However, in the 1994 gubernatorial election, Sundlun lost the Democratic Party primary to Myrth York, who went on to lose the election to Lincoln C. Almond, a Republican. York lost by only three percent, defeated by Almond again in 1998 by nine percent. In 2002, she stood for the third time, but lost to Donald Carcieri, by 10 percent, Carcieri getting 55 percent to York's 45 percent. Carcieri was re-elected in 2006, and tried to reform the electoral system in the state. Rhode Island is one of 19 states that elects its governor and lieutenant governor in separate elections, with the result that they are often from different political parties.

SEE ALSO: Catholic Vote; Know-Nothing Party; Poll Tax; Republican Party; Suffrage; Whig Party.

BIBLIOGRAPHY. M.R. Di Nunzio and J.T. Galkowski, "Political Loyalty in Rhode Island—a Computer Study of the 1850s," *Rhode Island History* (v.36/3, 1977); P.A. Grant, "Party Chaos Embroils Rhode Island," *Rhode Island History* (v.27/1, 1968); C.G. Hoffman and Tass Hoffman, *Brotherly Love: Murder and the Politics of Prejudice in Nineteenth-Century Rhode Island* (University of Massachusetts Press, 1998); J.L. Huston, "The Threat of Radicalism: Seward's Candidacy and the Rhode Island Gubernatorial Election of 1860," *Rhode Island History* (v.41/3, 1982); Dan King, *The Life and Thomas of Thomas Wilson Dorr* (privately published, 1859); D.S. Lovejoy, *Rhode Island Politics and the American Revolution 1760–1776* (Brown University Press, 1969); Maureen Moakley and E.E. Cornwell, *Rhode Island Politics and Government* (University of Nebraska Press, 2001); M.J. Smith, "The Real McCoy in the Bloodless Revolution of 1935," *Rhode Island History* (v.32/3, 1973).

JUSTIN CORFIELD
GEELONG GRAMMAR SCHOOL, AUSTRALIA

Right-Wing Candidates

IN THE POLITICAL arena, the term *right-wing* usually refers to sections or categories within the political continuum that are conservative in nature. In the simplest of terms, Right-wing conservative politics stand in direct opposition to left-wing liberal politics. Right-wing politics have also been referred to as neo-liberalism, traditionalism, the Religious Right, American conservatism, and some forms of populism.

Right-wing ideology is most commonly associated with traditional values, especially in social issues and social policy. These issues, often viewed through the lens of religious values, morals, and norms, commonly involve constraining government power while promoting individual rights. Right-wing political advocates encourage and support the idea of obedience through authority rather than liberty and, as such, are willing to give up some basic rights for the well-being of others, especially those of the privileged class. As a result of this stand, right-wing politics has over time become associated with traditionalism coupled with privilege.

As there are varying degrees of political ideology on the overall spectrum of political thought, there are also varying degrees of political conservatism within right-wing ideology. Not all right-wing political advocates are staunch conservatives; many are conservative in only limited aspects and for the most part they focus on changes that are not sociopolitical in nature unless they deal with reactionary politics. Many researchers hold the term *reactionary politics* and conservatism in the same light; reactionary political figures react against change and development, especially those that have an immediate impact on them. This provides the connection with conservatism.

Right-wing politics is a strong force in the United States, with more than 60 national organizations in the country. These include, but are not limited to, the

American Civil Rights Institution, American Family Association, Focus on the Family, Christian Legal Society, and the New Coalition for Economic and Social Change. Each of the more than 60 organizations has specific issues that they advocate, but all have both conservative and religious/moral overtones.

They deal with such issues as the opposition to gay and lesbian civil rights, the prohibiting of the teaching of evolution in public schools, requiring all sex-education courses in public schools to teach abstinence, and the promotion of prayer in public schools. Furthermore, they have worked on supporting specific right-wing judicial nominees, carried out voter registration drives, supporting political candidates via religious institutions, and raised millions of dollars to mobilize voters and endorse anti-left congressional candidates. Right-wing political organizations have always nominated members to run for congressional and political offices in the United States. Three notable organizations are: the Traditional Values Coalition, the Religious Right, and the Christian Coalition of America. While their names imply a religious connotation, it is their practices and their common stances on key issues that truly demonstrate their right-wing political leanings.

THE TRADITIONAL VALUES COALITION

The Traditional Values Coalition (TVC) is a 501C-4 organization with more than $6 million in contributions yearly. TVC describes itself as the largest church lobby in the United States, whose aim is to restore America's cultural heritage by opposing gay and lesbian civil rights, reproductive freedom, the teaching of evolution in public schools, and sex education curricula that do not stress abstinence. TVC seeks to accomplish these goals through lobbying Congress and, as a grassroots organization, they give "marching orders" to churches to oppose local, state, and federal legislation. TVC claims to have more than 43,000 churches involved in their organization representing 12 denominations. They send out monthly newsletters highlighting key issues, along with action alerts and special letters from their founder.

They have formed a sister organization known as the Traditional Values Education and Legal Institute, and at one time ran a third organization, the Task Force for the Preservation of the Heterosexual Ethic in America, which is now defunct. TVC worked to support the nomination of John Roberts to the Supreme Court, creating a Supreme Court Action Center, and has openly supported hundreds of candidates at the local and state level, as well as being involved in numerous state ballot initiatives. TVC's founder, Reverend Louis P. Sheldon, has recently been linked to Jack Abramoff and the lobbying scandal of 2006.

FOCUS ON THE FAMILY

Focus on the Family supports right-wing politics and political views from a conservative standpoint. This group, with its founder Dr. James Dobson, uses its media outlets (radio and magazine) to discuss public policy issues and political events from a conservative pro-family, pro-life perspective. In addition to Focus on the Family, Dobson has formed Focus on the Family Action (also known as Focus Action), which addresses conservative social issues within a political framework.

With traditional family values serving as its foundational cornerstone, Focus on the Family and Focus Action promotes political activism that is rooted in conservative religious Christian values. They actively support the state of Israel and oppose abortion, pornography, premarital sex, and extramarital sex. One of the strongest issues that they support is the union of church and state along with school prayer and corporal punishment. While Focus on the Family may serve as a 501C-3 organization and, as such, cannot endorse candidates, Focus Action has played key roles in supporting President Bush and has openly campaigned for conservative Supreme Court Justices Samuel Alito and John Roberts.

THE CHRISTIAN COALITION

The third right-wing organization that has played a major role in the election process through the advancement of a conservative right-wing apolitical agenda is the Christian Coalition of America, founded by Reverend Pat Robertson, following his defeat for president in 1988. From 1989 to 1997, the Christian Coalition was a leading force in both political parties primarily due to the creation of voter's guides. To be listed in the voter guides as anti-Christian was viewed by many as a huge blow to a political campaign and, as such, many politicians played close attention to the Christian Coalitions views on social and political issues.

In 1996, the Christian Coalition believed it had enough support to elect a conservative Christian to the presidency but the support quickly faded. Caught up in a legal battle with the Internal Revenue Service over tax-exempt status, the Christian Coalition began to lose influence within the Republican Party and, by 2005, they were more than $2 million in debt. However, the idea of voter guides remained a focal point of elections. In 2000, the Christian Coalition claims that it distributed over 70 million voter guides to churches across the country. More than five million were translated into Spanish and distributed in states with high concentrations of Mexican-Americans. (Florida received more than two million guides.) In 2004, the Christian Coalition indicates that it distributed more than 30 million voter guides to specific areas of the country: areas with highly competitive races, or with large concentrations of Christians. In 2006, the Christian Coalition pledged its alliance to Network Neutrality.

PAST AND PRESENT CANDIDATES

Clinton Fisk may be regarded as one of the earliest and most successful right-wing candidates. Fisk joined the Union Army in 1862 and served throughout the campaign. Following the south's surrender, Fisk became a senior officer in the Bureau of Refugees, Freemen and Abandoned Lands. Fisk also became a leading supporter of the temperance movement and joined the Prohibition Party.

The Prohibition Party advocated the abolishment or prohibition of the use of beverages containing alcohol. Viewed by many to be right-wing and very conservative at the time, the Prohibition Party would eventually lobby for the successful passage of the Eighteenth Amendment to the Constitution, which outlawed the production, transportation, import and export of alcohol. Fisk ran for president of the United States representing the Prohibition Party, finishing third (249,506 votes) behind Benjamin Harrison and Grover Cleveland. Both Cleveland and Harrison would serve as presidents and the Prohibition Party would continue as a right-wing political party, having run a candidate for president in every election since 1872.

Pat Buchanan, a well-known conservative politician and journalist, ran for president in 1992 and 1996. Buchanan had years of political experience in both the Nixon and Reagan administrations, and was seasoned by the Watergate Scandal and the Contra Affair. Following the election of Vice President George H.W. Bush to the presidency in 1988, Buchanan began to gather his forces for a run in 1992. Buchanan attacked incumbent Bush for being both liberal and a backroom dealer and began

publishing a newsletter entitled "Patrick J. Buchanan: From the Right," which highlighted his right-wing stance within the Republican Party. His 1992 presidential campaign platform focused on economic nationalism, curbing immigration through swift reforms, and opposing gay rights, abortion, and multiculturalism.

Right-wing politics caught fire initially as Buchanan garnered 38 percent of the primary vote in New Hampshire, seriously challenging Bush, who was dealing with his "read my lips, no new taxes," blunder. Buchanan's campaign lost momentum throughout the primary season and Bush won the nomination. Buchanan, who received more than three million votes in the primaries, was relegated to delivering a keynote address at the Republican National Convention. Buchanan strongly attacked the Democrat nominee, William Jefferson Clinton, (D-Arkansas) and alienated many within the Republican Party as he called for returning to traditional values and not tolerating homosexuals, abortion, or women in combat.

Following his defeat in 1992, Buchanan returned to journalism anchoring the CNN show *Crossfire*. He also founded a neo-conservative foundation, The American Cause, aimed at returning America to conservative values and federalism. On March 20, 1995, Buchanan announced his candidacy for president in 1996. Buchanan entered the campaign denouncing the North American Free Trade Agreement (NAFTA). In the New Hampshire Primary, Buchanan shocked the Republican Party by besting Senator Bob Dole (R-Kansas) by more than 3,000 votes.

Leading up to Super Tuesday, Buchanan was poised to pull another major upset, but all plans were derailed when the Center for Public Integrity linked Buchanan's campaign director, Larry Pratt, with white supremacists. Buchanan and Pratt denied the accusation, but the damage had already been done; Dole defeated Buchanan by large margins on Super Tuesday and on March 21 Buchanan dropped out of the race, having collected 21 percent of the total votes in all the state primaries. Buchanan returned to *Crossfire*, contemplating another run at the presidency.

Buchanan returned to campaign for the presidency in 2000, but not as a representative of the Republican Party. Having lost in the Iowa primary, Buchanan switched to the Reform Party, once headed by political maverick Ross Perot. After a split in the Reform Party between Buchanan and John Hagelin,

Buchanan received the Reform Party nomination and the $12.6 million in campaign funds secured by Perot's electoral support in 1996. In his acceptance speech, Buchanan proposed expelling the United Nations from New York, abolishing four Executive Offices (Departments of Housing and Urban Development, Department of Education, Department of Energy and the Internal Revenue Service) and withdrawing from the United Nations.

In the end, Buchanan finished fourth in the general election for president, garnering 449,895 votes (0.4 percent of the popular vote). Yet, he will be remembered for receiving 3,407 votes from what was perceived as very liberal Palm Beach County, Florida—enough votes that many skeptics believe smells of conspiracy, and many Republicans viewed as legitimate. In the end, George W. Bush beat Al Gore and won Florida by a few hundred votes. Following his performance in 2000, Buchanan indicated that he would never seek the presidential nomination again, and returned to television and politics as a self-proclaimed neo-conservative.

Another major right-wing candidate was Pat Robertson. Robertson, an ordained minister of the Southern Baptist Convention, is most famous for starting the Christian Broadcasting Network (CBN) in 1960. Today, CBN is seen in 180 countries and broadcast in 71 languages. He also founded Regent University (formerly CBN University) in 1977 and the American Center for Law and Justice, which advocates First Amendment Rights: pro-family, pro-liberty and pro-life. Robertson saw this political activism as an opportunity to run for president, and in September of 1986, Robertson announced his candidacy for the 1988 nomination. However, there would be one catch: Robertson would only seek the nomination if three million people would sign up to volunteer for his campaign, within one year. Surprisingly, more than three million people pledged to volunteer, Robertson raised millions of dollars in campaign contributions, and officially entered the race in September 1987.

The Robertson campaign platform was simple: ban pornography, reform the education system, require a constitutional amendment to balance the budget, and eliminate the Departments of Education and Energy. Despite being viewed as a political long shot, Robertson was prepared to do battle with George W. Bush by portraying himself as the conservative political candidate. Robertson's campaign got off to a strong start with a second place finish in Iowa, but he did poorly in New Hampshire. Many believe that this spiral downward was the result of Robertson presenting false information about his military record, claiming he had served as a combat Marine in Korea when he never saw combat in the field. Robertson never recovered from the debacle and his campaign lost steam, especially as the multiple-state primaries began. After winning Washington, Robertson bowed out of the primaries and at the Republican Convention in New Orleans he threw his support behind the eventual nominee, George Bush.

Robertson returned to CBN but did not disappear from the political arena. Following his early exit from the campaign, Robertson formed the Christian Coalition. Now the Christian Coalition of America, it promotes Christian values, highlighting family issues and conservatism in government. With more than 1.7 million members, the Christian Coalition promotes conservative candidates and judicial appointees. Robertson is extremely popular with Protestant Evangelical and other Christian organizations, and he has also received the State of Israel Friendship Award and other awards for his support of Israel.

SEE ALSO: Conservatism; Candidate Image; Third Parties.

BIBLIOGRAPHY. Pat Buchanan, *Right from the Beginning* (Regnery Gateway, 1990); Christian Coalition of America www.cc.org (cited August 2007); D.J. Marley, *Pat Robertson: An American Life* (Rowman-Littlefield Publishers, 2007); People for the American Way, www.pfaw.org (cited August 2007); Traditional Values Coalition, www.traditionalvalues.org (cited August 2007).

RONALD ERIC MATTHEWS, JR.
MOUNT UNION COLLEGE

Roper, Elmo (1900–71)

ELMO ROPER WAS a pioneer and leader in the field of modern survey research. In the 1930s, he was one of three major pollsters who helped usher in a new era of scientific survey research. Roper was born in Hebron, Nebraska. As a young man, he operated a jewelry store with his brother in Creston, Iowa (1922–28) and worked for manufacturing companies (1928–33). He got his first taste of customer research while employed by the Traub Company. Shortly thereafter, he joined with Paul T. Cherington and Richard Wood to found one of the first market research firms, Cherington, Roper, and Wood (1933–38).

In 1935, publisher Henry Luce asked Roper to serve as director of the *Fortune* survey. Roper and two other young pollsters, George H. Gallup and Archibald Crossley, predicted accurately (but not with statistical precision) President Franklin Roosevelt's victory over Republican challenger Alfred (Alf) Landon in the 1936 presidential election. This election proved to be a turning point. *Literary Digest* magazine ran the major survey at the time. Until that election, *Literary Digest* had accurately predicted election outcomes, but in 1936 a series of methodological mishaps resulted in failure. Roper headed one of three organizations that employed "scientific methods" to poll a fraction of the *Literary Digest*'s two million respondents and accurately project the outcome of the race.

In the late 1930s, Roper left Cherington to establish and head his own firm, Roper Research Associates. He also successfully predicted Roosevelt's two subsequent electoral victories. The viability of scientific polling was cemented in 1940 when President Roosevelt asked Roper and Gallup to measure public support for the Lend-Lease Deal. Roper continued to poll extensively during World War II.

Among other things, he served as deputy director of the Office of Strategic Services and helped convince the military establishment to use public opinion polling. If 1936 established the viability of scientific survey research, 1948 showed that it was not infallible. During that election, all three of the nation's top pollsters, Roper, Crossley, and Gallup, inaccurately projected Thomas E. Dewey would defeat Harry Truman by five to 15 percent.

Truman not only won by 4.5 percent, but the image of him holding a copy of the *Chicago Tribune* bearing the headline "Dewey Defeats Truman" has become one of the most famous photos of the mid-20th century. Roper responded to the debacle by saying that his face was "just as red as President Truman said it would be." He and the other major pollsters not only took responsibility for the errors, but also took steps to correct them. Among other things, they explored new sampling techniques. In 1948, most pollsters used quota sampling, in subsequent elections this was abandoned in favor of probability sampling, a technique that is still used today.

In addition to polling, Roper was an editor for the *Saturday Review*, a newspaper columnist, radio commentator, television analyst, and a popular speaker on the lecture circuit. He also served on the boards of several well-known organizations and businesses, was a member of the Urban League, the Connecticut Civil Rights Commission, and the U.S. Citizen's Commission on the North Atlantic Treaty Organization (NATO). While Roper never completed his undergraduate studies, he was the recipient of honorary degrees from the University of Minnesota, Williams College, and the University of Louisville.

Among his most enduring legacies was his decision, in 1946, to establish the first archive of public opinion data, the Roper Center for Public Opinion Research at Williams College. Roper convinced fellow pollsters Gallup and Crossley to house their data at the center as well. A firm believer in the important role of opinion in democracy, Roper hoped the repository would encourage scholars and policymakers to study opinion carefully and use it responsibly. The archive was later moved to the University of Connecticut, Storrs, where it remains today and has become the world's largest library of opinion data, with collections from around the world and data that goes back to the 1930s.

SEE ALSO: Crossley, Archibald; Gallup, George; Mitofsky, Warren; Polling and Election Studies Organizations; Polls, Pre-Election; Zogby, John.

BIBLIOGRAPHY. Irving Crespi, *Public Opinion, Polls, and Democracy* (Westview Press, 1989); G.H. Gallup and Saul Forbes Rae, *The Pulse of Democracy: The Public Opinion Poll and How It Works* (Simon and Schuster, 1940); P.J. Lavrakas, *Election Polls, the News Media, and Democracy* (Chatham House Publishers, 2000); D.W. Moore, *The Superpollsters: How They Measure and Manipulate Public Opinion In America* (Four Walls, Eight Windows, 1995); Frederick Mosteller, *The Pre-election Polls of 1948* (Social Science Research Council, 1949).

JEANNE S. ZAINO
IONA COLLEGE

Rose Garden Strategy

THE TERM *Rose Garden strategy* refers to the re-election strategy of incumbent American presidents who focus on events in the White House, taking advantage of the grandeur and aura of their office to look presidential. By following this strategy, presidents hope to underscore their competence in office. While challengers must work hard to look presidential, incumbent presidents appear presidential by staying focused on the business of governing, often remaining above the political fray.

A classic Rose Garden strategy is filled with photo opportunities and presidential imagery. The term makes reference to the Rose Garden because this setting reflects the majesty and grandeur of the presidency. It is a lush, impeccably landscaped garden, covering an area approximately 125 by 60 feet, that borders the Oval Office just outside the West Wing of the White House. Known as the Rose Garden since 1913, it is used as a venue for informal and official White House events, including formal announcements, bill-signing ceremonies, press conferences, and photo opportunities with foreign dignitaries and notable Americans. As incumbents take part in these highly-staged, but relatively low-cost events, they hope the media coverage will cast a positive light on their stewardship.

For a Rose Garden strategy to be effective, the president has to emphasize the presidential, highlighting the image of a competent leader, and de-emphasize the political, downplaying the image of a partisan candidate. The strategy, however, does not dictate that the president has to remain exclusively in the White House. The exigencies of modern presidential campaigns require that candidates, including incumbent presidents, travel extensively throughout the country. The strategy does involve making choices about when to go on the campaign trail and when to stay in the Rose Garden. These choices determine whether the president can, at any one time, improve the odds of re-election by campaigning on the road or by staying in the White House.

President Gerald Ford, campaigning for the presidency in 1976, made extensive use of the Rose Garden strategy. For much of the early campaign season, he stayed in the White House, seeking to covey the message that he enjoyed his job and that he was good at it. As his opponent, Jimmy Carter, struggled to get media attention, Ford enjoyed the free publicity that came with his Rose Garden strategy. Although it proved successful in gaining positive attention for him, the president wanted to campaign more actively and, thus, abandoned this strategy late in the summer.

Interestingly, President Jimmy Carter, who had criticized Ford's use of the Rose Garden strategy when he was running against him, used the same strategy four years later when running for re-election against Ronald Reagan. Preoccupied with the Iran hostage crisis, Carter rarely left the White House during the early months of the campaign. As the crisis worsened and the media portrayed him as an isolated, ineffective president, he abandoned his Rose Garden strategy in favor of a more aggressive campaign.

The Rose Garden strategy has been used at various points and to different degrees by all successive presidents. Possibly President Richard Nixon used the Rose Garden strategy best in his 1972 re-election campaign against Democratic rival George McGovern, even refusing to debate him. McGovern, a severe critic of Nixon's Vietnam policies, became a frustrated campaigner because Nixon, way ahead in the polls, largely ignored him. Nixon's strategy was to simply to act presidential, frequently presenting his issue stands from the calm of the Rose Garden.

However, since 1972, all incumbent presidents have had to avoid an extreme Rose Garden strategy, not only because modern campaigns have become more intense and competitive, but also because they have been compelled to debate their challengers in almost obligatory live television debates. With the rise of what has been termed the "permanent campaign," many observers argue that those in the White House have increased their focus on politics, displacing the traditional Rose Garden strategy. Some see the strategy in a pejorative way, claiming that it is too passive, potentially conveying the image of a president out-of-touch, concerned more about style than substance. Whatever its effectiveness, however, the rationale behind the Rose Garden strategy is clear: the best strategy for an incumbent president is to go about the business of governing and look presidential.

Although the original term refers to an American presidential strategy, it also used to describe the strategy of other political chief executives, including governors, mayors, and even foreign executives, who want to bring attention to their incumbency, even in the absence of a Rose Garden per se. Thus, like the presidential analogue, the phrase may be employed to describe the strategy of a governor inviting the media to the governor's mansion for a bill-signing ceremony. Similarly, it could be extended outside the electoral domain, to an executive interested in bolstering public support.

SEE ALSO: Campaigns, Presidential; Campaign Strategies; Challengers to Incumbents; Presidential Election of 1976; Presidential Election of 1980.

BIBLIOGRAPHY. S.L. Popkin, *The Reasoning Voter: Communication and Persuasion in Presidential Campaigns* (University of Chicago Press, 1994); K.D. Tenpas, *Presidents As Candidates: Inside the White House for the Presidential Campaign* (Routledge, 2003).

CARLOS E. DÍAZ-ROSILLO
HARVARD UNIVERSITY

Rural Vote

FOLLOWING THE MIGRATION by rural America to the big cities of the north, the rural vote seemed to be overlooked. While rural voters served as the cornerstone for Franklin Delano Roosevelt's New Deal Programs that led to his re-election for an unprecedented fourth term, rural voters seem to be more conservative in recent presidential elections. The Center for Rural Strategies reports that George W. Bush won the rural vote by 22 points and in crucial battleground states he won the rural vote by more than 16 points in 2000.

Bush duplicated this feat in 2004 by winning the national rural vote by 19 points and the rural vote in battleground states by 29 percent. If either Al Gore (D-Tennessee) in 2000, or John Kerry (D-Massachusetts) in 2004 had tapped into this large base of rural voters, he would have easily won the election. It appears that since the Clinton sex scandal, rural voters have shifted toward a more moral agenda with emphasis on Christian values in areas related to abortion, same-sex marriages, and the right to bear arms. Conservative talk radio flourishes in rural America as talk show hosts such as Reverend James Dobson and Rush Limbaugh intertwine Christian values with conservative politics—ideas and norms that resonate in rural communities.

Two exceptions to this principle warrant mentioning. First, Jimmy Carter (D-Georgia) captured the rural vote in grand fashion following the presidential pardon of Richard Nixon by Gerald Ford. Carter was extremely popular with rural America, both as a peanut farmer and as a self-proclaimed born-again Christian. William Jefferson Clinton also won the rural vote. Having served as the Governor of Arkansas, a poor rural state, Clinton campaigned as a "new Democrat," promising to move people off the welfare rolls and into the work force. This idea was extremely popular in rural America, where the work ethic is highly-valued.

Coming on the heels of the Clinton-Lewinsky scandal, Governor George W. Bush (R-Texas) campaigned on the idea of bringing integrity and honesty back to the White House. Al Gore (D-Tennessee) ran in the shadow of the scandal and lost to Bush by the narrowest of margins. To show how important the rural vote was to Gore, consider the following: Gore won the urban vote in Ohio by 48,000 votes, but lost the rural vote by 117,000 votes (22 points). In the end, this deficit was too large to overcome and Gore lost the state of Ohio by a only 69,000 votes.

This trend would continue in 2004 as Kerry (D-Massachusetts) would lose to Bush because of his poor showing in the rural counties of Ohio. An important factor associated with religious values brought out the rural vote in large numbers. State ballot initiatives surfaced in 11 states such as Ohio and Missouri, and rural Americans came out in droves to place state constitutional bans on same-sex marriages. Fueled by conservative talk radio hosts like Limbaugh and Dobson, the Republican Party capitalized on rural votes using conservative evangelical values and rhetoric. The Center for Rural Strategies notes that more than 2,100 radio stations carry Dobson's "Focus on the Family Program" and that 70 percent of those stations are found in rural counties. There is no doubt that Dobson and Limbaugh played a key role in getting rural voters to the polling stations in the 2004 presidential election.

To see the vital role the rural vote plays in elections, consider the 2006 Congressional elections. Following the sweeping results of the 2004 presidential election in which the GOP saw huge victories in the Red States, the Republican Party was relishing its success and perceived control. Two other factors had helped to bolster their support: the country was more focused on a moral agenda, and on economic factors, thanks in part to the Christian right and the patriotic support for the war on terrorism fueled by the threat of an additional attack. However, the Republican Party and President Bush took the rural vote for granted, choosing to nationalize the 2006 election and attempt to capitalize on the popularity of the president to focus on national security. While these issues became key factors in the outcome of the 2006 congressional midterm elections, the outcome was not what the Republican Party and the president had hoped for.

The Center for Rural Strategies notes that the war in Iraq and national security were the two major issues on the minds of the electorate. Using national poll tracking survey data for rural voters, statistics showed that 55 percent of those surveyed wanted the United States to withdraw from Iraq, and 59 percent said the war was not winnable. Also, 75 percent of those surveyed knew someone from a rural area who had served in the war in Iraq or Afghanistan.

By October 2006, just weeks before the election, rural voters listed the war in Iraq (38 percent), jobs and the economy (25 percent), Social Security (21 percent) and healthcare (20 percent) as their top issues to be addressed in the election. The Republicans and President Bush, while working to nationalize the election, had succeeded in doing so, but focused on the wrong issues. The fact that the war in Iraq was seen as a losing battle, with more lives lost and increased requests for taxpayer monies to fund military activities, did not bode well for Republicans seeking office in 2006. In hindsight, there was also nothing new on the agenda that was perceived as an attack on moral values as there had been in 2004, a clear indication that rural voters may not come out in force to the polls. Two issues that many strategists expected to bring out the rural voters never materialized as national issues: immigration and an increase in the minimum wage. Rural voters were divided on both the immigration issue and the minimum wage increase.

The 2006 congressional midterm election was a major political event. Democrats picked up six seats in the Senate and 30 seats in the House of Representatives. Not only did this landslide victory of the Democrats, which enabled them to gain control of both Houses of Congress, affect the political culture of the United States, but it also showed that elections are won by altering or modifying the national debate. Furthermore, the Center for Rural Strategies reported that the sweeping changes in the 2006 congressional midterm elections were the result of dozens of very close elections. These elections were close for three important reasons: the shift among rural voters in the Democratic Party, who collectively disapprove of the war in Iraq, the lack of a moral issue among rural voters, thereby limiting their participation in the election, and the reprioritizing of issues in rural America. The importance of the rural vote cannot be overlooked when approximately 55 million Americans live and work in rural America.

SEE ALSO: Presidential Election of 2000; Presidential Election of 2004; Presidential Election of 2006; Voter Turnout; Voting by Regions.

BIBLIOGRAPHY. Center for Rural Strategies www.RuralStrategies.org (cited August 2007); Niel Ritchie, "Harvesting the Rural Vote: The Key to Building Party Majority," *Campaigns and Elections* (2005).

RONALD ERIC MATTHEWS, JR.
MOUNT UNION COLLEGE

Safe Seats

THE AMERICAN ELECTORAL process is designed to promote the power of the Democratic and Republican parties and discourage independent candidates and minority parties from seeking office. Safe seats are those in which members of Congress are re-elected year after year with little or no opposition. Every two years, Americans go to the polls to choose 435 members of the United States House of Representatives and one-third of the 100 Senate seats. When writing Article I of the United States Constitution, the Framers said little about congressional elections, requiring only that each state legislature determine "times, places and manner of holding elections," and specifying that House members serve two-year terms, and Senators six. Because many Americans vote by party label, or for those candidates with the highest name recognition and level of experience, incumbents are regularly returned to office.

Many political watchers insist that politicians who inhabit safe seats are not held accountable for their actions. While this may be true of political actions, it may not always follow when moral issues come into play. When it was discovered in 2006 that Florida Republican Mark Foley had been sending sexually explicit online messages to former congressional pages, his safe seat became highly vulnerable. Democrats took the high moral ground, accusing Republican House leaders of failing to act even when they were aware of Foley's behavior. The scandal helped to propel a number of Democrats into office in 2006, giving the party control of both houses of Congress, and a majority of gubernatorial and state legislative seats. It is assumed in political science that although Congress as a body is generally unpopular, this disapproval does not affect support for its individual members. In 2006, in the wake of several congressional scandals, a *Washington Post*-ABC News Poll revealed that congressional approval had declined by 32 percent. Nevertheless, 60 percent of respondents expressed support for their own members of Congress. A 2006 *Congressional Quarterly* survey found that 81 percent of incumbents were considered "safe."

Between 1980 and 1990, 95 percent of incumbents were re-elected to office. In 1986, a record 98 percent of House incumbents won re-election. In 85 percent of those races, candidates won with at least 60 percent of the vote. Eight years later, voters, who were disgusted by the stalemate between President Bill Clinton and the Democratic Congress, helped to launch the so-called "Republican Revolution" in which the opposition party gained 54 House and eight Senate seats. In 1996, voters returned Clinton to the White House, but

76.7 percent of congressional races were virtually a foregone conclusion, with less than 40 races considered up for grabs. In the off-year elections held two years later, serious competition was absent in 79.6 of all congressional elections, resulting in a re-election rate of 97 percent.

Once in office, incumbents have distinct advantages in addition to name recognition and party labels. Those who have been in Congress for many years have often risen to positions of leadership, and may chair important committees, promoting the interests of their states and districts. However, in recent years, even those members who are considered "safe" may be under pressure to raise increasingly large sums for re-election campaigns. This is particularly true of vulnerable members who are facing well-financed opposition. Because of their access to millions of dollars, political parties play a major role in re-electing incumbents.

In the 1960s in a series of cases, the United States Supreme Court held that states must draw district lines so as to reflect the concept of "one-person, one vote" as nearly as possible. These decisions require states to redraw district lines for the United States House of Representatives and local legislatures after every national census, to reflect changes in population. In eight states, redistricting is carried out by special commissions, and joint legislative/commissions plan for redistricting in Connecticut, Indiana, and Iowa. Results have been varied. In Iowa and Washington, for instance, elections have become competitive. In New Jersey, on the other hand, only one of 13 congressional races held in 2006 was considered competitive. In the remaining states, responsibility for redistricting lies with state legislatures.

Critics of frequent redistricting argue that it encourages gerrymandering, the practice of designing congressional districts to promote specific political goals. In cases where a political party controls the governorship and holds a majority in the state legislature, the party may be able to manipulate redistricting to its own advantage, with the overall goal of creating safe seats to help the party retain control of the political process. In 2003, the redistricting process in Texas became increasingly acrimonious. With the help of the George W. Bush White House, Republicans designed a redistricting plan to give the party an advantage in 22 of 32 House seats. Fifty Democratic legislative members left the state, well aware that without a quorum, the Republican plan could not come to a vote.

SEE ALSO: Agenda Setting; Campaigns, U.S. Representatives; Campaigns, U.S. Senate; Challengers to Incumbents; Incumbents.

BIBLIOGRAPHY: Richard Cohen, "When Campaigns Are Cakewalks. National Journal (March 16, 2002); Joanne Dann, "Safe But Sorry: The Way We Redistrict Destroys the Middle Ground." Washington Post (December 2, 2001); Peter F. Galderisi, et al, editors, Congressional Primaries and the Politics of Representation (Rowman and Littlefield, 2001); K. Jost, "Redistricting Disputes." CQ Researcher, v14 (cited January 22, 2008); Liz Marlantes, "Redistricting Shifts Clout, but Plays It Safe." Christian Science Monitor (June 10, 2002); Alison Mitchell, "Redistricting 2002 Produces No Great Shake-Ups." New York Times (March 13, 2002); "Politics as Warfare." The Economist (January 22, 2008).

ELIZABETH PURDY, PH.D.
INDEPENDENT SCHOLAR

Scandals, Presidential Elections

PRESIDENTIAL SCANDAL IS now a permanent part of the American political landscape. Among the modern presidents, four—Richard Nixon, Ronald Reagan, Bill Clinton, and George W. Bush—have been or had members of their administrations implicated in high-profile scandals. In each of the scandals, illicit activity, concealment of those activities, and press revelations about those activities were the engines that propelled the president's activities into the public spotlight. Modern presidential scandals all have received substantial media attention, some have prompted impeachment votes, others have permanently damaged the president's approval rating and, in Nixon's case, a sitting president was driven from office. Moreover, presidential misdeeds appear to more often fall on the president's party in subsequent congressional and presidential elections.

HARDING THROUGH CLINTON

The most immediate precursor of the modern presidential scandal was the investigation of "Teapot Dome." President Warren G. Harding's Secretary of the Interior Albert B. Fall secretly leased three U.S. Navy strategic petroleum reserve sites to oil companies and received

$409,000 in kickbacks for doing so. The *Wall Street Journal* exposed Fall's activities and the subsequent congressional investigation saw him become the first presidential administration official to receive a prison term. President Harding avoided any adverse electoral effects from this scandal: he died in office in 1923. Perhaps most importantly, Teapot Dome prompted the 1927 Supreme Court decision, *McGrain v. Daugherty*, which restrained the executive's power to conduct secret activities by providing the House and Senate the power to compel the president's staff and aides to testify before their committees.

The modern presidency recognizes Watergate as a watershed moment for presidential scandal. Watergate had its antecedents in a series of illegal wiretaps and break-ins authorized by President Nixon between 1969 and 1972 to uncover leakers of the Pentagon Papers and information about U.S. bombing in Cambodia. Nixon's Committee for the Re-Election of the President (CREEP), in 1972, broke into the Democratic National Committee's (DNC's) headquarters in the Watergate Apartment Complex to monitor DNC communications. CREEP operatives were caught in the early morning hours of June 17, 1972 attempting to adjust previously installed recording equipment.

The subsequent cover-up and directions by Nixon to squelch investigators' efforts were exposed by the *Washington Post*'s Bob Woodward and Carl Bernstein and later documented in their book *All the President's Men*. The scandal resulted in the 1974 obstruction of justice convictions and sentencing for Nixon's Attorney General, Chief of Staff, former chief domestic adviser, and former special counsel. Nixon was impeached by the House of Representatives in July 1974, and, before standing trial in the Senate, resigned from office effective August 9, 1974. He eventually was pardoned by President Gerald Ford in 1975, and faced no prison time for his role in the cover-up. Watergate prompted Congress in 1978 to conclude that the president cannot impartially initiate investigations against himself or members of his administration. The resulting Independent Counsel Act still guides investigation executive misconduct.

The Iran-Contra scandal had its origins in the Reagan administration's support for the Contras, a right-wing rebel group in Nicaragua fighting against the leftist Sandinistas. Although Congress—supported by Reagan—in 1982 banned financial support for the Contras, Reagan's National Security Council contravened this order. It did so not by requesting congressional appropriations, but by selling arms to Iran, a country banned by the Arms Export Control Act from receiving such shipments. The administration calculated that arms sales to Iran would bolster its diplomatic relationship and would provide an incentive for Iran to negotiate with Hizballah for the release of U.S. hostages held by the group. President Reagan approved the shipment of defensive arms and parts to Iran in 1985, the operation was revealed on November 3, 1986 by the Lebanese magazine *Ash-Shiraa*, and

Oliver North, a key figure in the Iran-Contra scandal, pictured later in 2004 as a correspondent for Fox News in Iraq.

President Reagan confirmed the affair on November 13 during a televised speech.

As with Watergate, the cover-up—which involved the shredding of documents pertinent to the case—caused the administration its most significant problems and resulted in indictments on multiple charges against National Security Council aide Oliver North and National Security Adviser John Poindexter. President Reagan acknowledged on March 4, 1987 that his administration had, in fact, attempted to trade arms for hostages and that his Vice President, George H.W. Bush—despite previous denials—was aware of the plan's details.

Bill Clinton's "Monica-gate" and Whitewater scandals were different because both involved the personal life and choices of a president. Clinton, the former Arkansas governor, was dogged during his 1992 presidential campaign by claims of sexual misconduct, including a 12-year affair with Genifer Flowers, an Arkansas state employee, and for sexually harassing Paula Jones, another Arkansas state employee. The Jones case required the president to disclose improper relationships he had with other women, one of whom was Monica Lewinsky, a former White House intern.

According to the special prosecutor's report, Clinton attempted to deter Ms. Lewinsky from testifying about the relationship the two had, and tried to influence her testimony. Further, Clinton mislead prosecutors and the grand jury in the Jones case by claiming to have never had a sexual relationship with Ms. Lewinsky, despite having carried one on between 1995 and 1997. The president was found to have committed perjury in the Jones case and subsequent investigations ordered by the Republican Congress through the Independent Counsel Act supported this finding.

In December 1998, the House of Representatives considered four articles of impeachment against President Clinton, approving Article I (giving false, perjurious, and misleading testimony) and Article III (obstruction of justice). In January 2001, former President Clinton signed a consent agreement in which he accepted a five-year suspension of his law license, paid a $25,000 fine, and acknowledged violating the Arkansas rules of professional legal conduct.

The George W. Bush administration presents a series of potential scandals, although none have carried that label yet. The Iraq-Weapons of Mass Destruction, Federal prosecutor firings, secret Central Intelligence Agency prisons, and the Valerie Plame leak all may aspire to the scandal designation, however. Each may have involved illegal, or accusations of, illegal activity by the president and his staff; an attempted cover-up of those illegal activities by the president or his advisers; and media revelations about, and subsequent congressional inquiries into, the president's misdeeds.

PRESIDENTIAL SCANDAL CAUSES ...

Scandal in the White House has its grounding in five principal concerns: the psychology and resulting behaviors of the president and his staff; a failure by the president to execute strong, ethical leadership; the institutional or structural arrangements of particular presidential staffs; a social acceptance of the polarization of U.S. politics; and the print, press, and internet media's cultivation of a market for nonsubstantive political news. These explanations individually and in combination provide a structure for interpreting the causes of presidential scandals such as Watergate, Iran-Contra, the Monica Lewinsky affair, and Iraq/Weapons of Mass Destruction, and Valerie Plame leak incidents, during the George W. Bush administration.

Scholars such as James David Barber, Fred Greenstein, and Richard Neustadt suggest that the president's psychological predispositions and leadership style provide an explanation for the emergence of events such as White House scandals. Under his active-passive/positive-negative model for presidential character, James David Barber suggests that Nixon's authorization of the Watergate break-in, for example, owed to his paranoid personality, obsession with success and failure, and a desire to maintain control of both his political adversaries and allies. Extrapolating, Bill Clinton's marital misdeeds could be attributed to a need for approval and more fundamental psychological concerns related to his relationship with his single-parent mother.

Presidential scandal may instead owe to a president's management style or the structure of his staff. Nicole Woolsey Biggart notes that deviant staff behaviors and a lack of presidential oversight, or organizational management, drive the emergence of scandal and its eventual cover-up by presidential staff members. In examining the Iran-Contra affair, President Reagan's commitment to the Contras and a lack of specific guidance to the members of his National Security Council may have fostered an environment that encouraged his staff's illegal activities.

The same might be said for the George W. Bush administration, where the president's subordinates, the office of the vice president, in particular, were given autonomy that resulted in the activities that one might regard as scandals. The American public's interest in scandal and the media's willingness to cover it also drive the increasing press time devoted to presidential misdeeds. Nicole Woolsey Biggart suggests that the moral decay or acceptance of corruption in the U.S. political system by the electorate creates a permissive environment for presidential scandal to occur and, also establishes media markets for the coverage of such scandals.

... AND CONSEQUENCES

While presidential scandals lead to some obvious consequences—impeachment among them—identifying the systematic electoral, public approval-related, or legislative impacts of presidential scandal is more challenging. The most obvious harm presidential scandal causes should be to the president's party in Congress or to those associated with the president and his scandal. For example, in the 1974 midterm election, Republicans lost five seats in the Senate and 48 seats in the house. Because Watergate occurred during Nixon's second term, one only can interpret the scandal's broader electoral importance by examining Gerald Ford's fortunes in the 1976 election. Ford's role as Nixon's former vice president and his pardon of Nixon contributed to his two percent loss to Jimmy Carter.

Reagan's situation clearly was different than Nixon's. He faced no midterm election during the Iran-Contra period, nor was he eligible for re-election, so one must instead look to those associated with his administration to understand the electoral impact of the Iran-Contra affair. As with Gerald Ford, one might imagine that Reagan's former vice president and successor, George H.W. Bush, would suffer for his awareness of the arms-for-hostages scandal. This was not the case. Instead, Bush defeated his opponent, Michael Dukakis, by more than eight percent and continued Reagan's White House legacy for another four years.

The electoral legacies of Bill Clinton's scandals are similarly mixed. The Democratic Party gained five seats in the House and had neither a gain nor a loss in the Senate during the 1998 midterms. Clinton was ineligible for another term, so it is necessary to look at others' fortunes to understand the electoral impact of his administration's scandals. As with Gerald Ford in 1976, it appears that those associated with the Clinton administration, including his former vice president and 2000

presidential candidate Al Gore, may have suffered for that relationship.

In a Pew Research Center poll conducted in March 2000 and reported by Julie Yioutas and Ivana Segvic, it was noted that 41 percent of those surveyed would be less likely to vote for Gore because of his association with the scandal-ridden Clinton administration. During the 2000 election, Gore attempted to limit his relationship with Clinton by criticizing Clinton for his misdeeds and excluding Clinton from the campaign trail. Clinton's scandals may have had direct and indirect effects: the public's perceptions of Al Gore were shaped by his association with the Clinton administration and, in distancing himself from Clinton, Gore was unable to seize on the potential benefits from associating himself on the campaign trail with the popular former president.

The relationship between presidential scandal and approval are also unclear. Paul Gronke and John Brehm found weak (statistically insignificant) results suggesting a negative relationship between presidential scandal and public approval of the president. Their models are saturated, however, and control for a variety of exogenous events such as war, the economy, and the president's policy accomplishments. Removed from these well-controlled models, presidential approval appears to have a strong negative correlation with the emergence and persistence of presidential scandals. During the period immediately prior to the Watergate scandal, Nixon enjoyed a 62 percent approval rating; when he left office, that approval rating had dropped to 24 percent. Ronald Reagan's public approval also dropped during the Iran-Contra affair. One month prior to the scandal breaking in November 1986, Reagan's approval was at 63 percent. At the height of the investigation into the Iran-Contra cover-up, in April 1987, Reagan's approval rating had dipped to 45 percent.

Bill Clinton, however, proved to be the exception to this rule. At the height of the Monica Lewinsky/Whitewater scandal and during his impeachment trial, Clinton's approval rating was at a stunning 66 percent. Brian Newman offers an explanation for these divergent findings among modern presidential scandals, noting that the public emphasizes political, social, economic, and personal judgments about presidents' character differently at different times. Indeed, Julie Yioutas and Ivana Segvic report that citizens polled during the height of the Monica Lewinsky scandal were more concerned with the economy (52 percent) than they were with the president's moral problems (42 percent).

While the electoral and public opinion effects of scandal lack some transparency, it is clearer that presidential misdeeds harm the president's ability to legislate effectively in Congress. Scott Meinke and William Anderson find that the Watergate, Iran-Contra, and Monica Lewinsky scandals prompted lower levels of support from members of the House of Representatives on key votes before Congress than they would have absent the scandal. So while scandal has variable effects on an ambivalent public, the increasingly polarized partisans in Congress appear to have taken more notice of the presidents' troubles and punish them.

CONCLUSION

Presidential scandal is part of the modern political landscape. A president's psychological predispositions, their ability to manage down and across their staff, and the media's and public's interest in scandal all appear to drive both the emergence and persistence of presidential scandal in today's politics.

The consequences of presidential scandal are opaque, however. In the modern era, the president's party and those associated with the administration—rather than the president alone—have experienced the electoral consequences of presidential misdeeds. The more concrete harm suffered by the president appears to happen in the legislative branch, where presidents and their agendas can be checked, and his behavior punished or rewarded—by an increasingly polarized Congress.

SEE ALSO: Campaigns, Presidential; Campaigns, U.S. Representatives; Campaigns, U.S. Senators; Congressional Elections; General Elections; Political Parties in American Elections; Presidential Approval Ratings; Presidential Election of 1924; Presidential Election of 1976; Presidential Election of 1988; Presidential Election of 2000; Presidential Elections.

BIBLIOGRAPHY. J.D. Barber, *Presidential Character: Predicting Performance in the White House* (Prentice Hall, 1992); N.W. Biggart, "Scandals in the White House: An Organizational Explanation," *Sociological Inquiry* (v.55/2, 1985); Fred Greenstein, *The Presidential Difference: Leadership Style from FDR to George W. Bush* (Princeton University Press, 2004); Paul Gronke and John Brehm, "History, Heterogeneity, and Presidential Approval: A Modified ARCH Approach," *Electoral Studies* (v.21/3, 2002); S.R. Meinke and W.D. Anderson, "Influencing from Impaired Administrations: Presidents, White House Scandals, and Legislative Leadership," *Legislative Studies Quarterly* (v.26/4, 2001); Richard Neustadt, *Presidential Power and the Modern Presidents: The Politics of Leadership from Roosevelt to Reagan* (Free Press, 1991); Brian Newman, "Integrity and Presidential Approval: 1980-2000," *Public Opinion Quarterly* (v.67, 2003); Julie Yioutas and Ivana Segvic, "Revisiting the Clinton/Lewinsky Scandal: The Convergence of Agenda Setting and Framing," *Journal and Mass Communication Quarterly* (v.80/3, 2003).

WILLIAM D. ANDERSON
UNIVERSITY OF SOUTH DAKOTA

Scandals, State and Local Elections

GIVEN THAT THE high stakes in most elections create incentives to do wrong, the history of state and local election scandals is in large part a history of the law's ineffective or belated attempts to catch up with the ingenuity of humans bent on ensuring victory in elections for the "right" side or issue.

Although election scandals are traditionally downplayed in order to sustain public confidence in the process of elections, the long and detailed history of election scandals tells a story of systemic and regular corruptions of the procedural justice of elections.

The vast majority of elections in the United States are state and local races (and not federal races). Surveying the scene of election scandals in the late 1800s, President Benjamin Harrison provided a candid overview of the status of elections in the United States at that time, certain attributes of which he termed both "depressing and undeniable:"

If any intelligent and loyal company of American citizens were required to catalogue the essential human conditions of national life, I do not doubt that with absolute unanimity they would begin with free and honest elections. And it is gratifying to know that generally there is a growing and nonpartisan demand for better election laws; but against this sign of hope and progress must be set the depressing and undeniable fact that election laws and methods are sometimes cunningly contrived to secure minority control, while violence completes the shortcomings of fraud.

Many maintain that President Harrison himself, as well as President "Rutherfraud" B. Hayes, were helped to election by virtue of the fraud of sympathetic supporters. Notably, neither President was required to issue instructions to supporters as to what to do, and when to do it, and why, because all of these factors were already known to anyone familiar with the news of the day.

It should to be noted that incumbents create election laws, even though these laws govern the circumstances of their own elections—a classic conflict of interest since procedural integrity is the goal of those elections.

While statements such as Harrison's rarely make it into textbooks, scholarly reviews such as Tracy Campbell's "Deliver the Vote: A History of Election Fraud, An American Political Tradition, 1742-2004" provide support for the long history of pressure on elections oftentimes spilling over into fraud, violence, death and scandal. General George Washington himself held liquor "treating" parties where alchohol was provided on Election Day to those willing to ride into town to vote for Washington. Treating parties were subsequently outlawed by the Virginia House of Burgesses.

The history of election scandal goes back even further, for example, in 1675, authorities in a Boston Town-Hall meeting noticed during an election that a man submitted about a dozen ballots with the word "Yea" on them, and he was fined ten pounds for this ballot box stuffing. During the earlier days of *viva voce* (by voice) voting in the United States, politicians, such as one in Pennsylvania, in 1765, sent out a message that his supporters should put on a "bold face" and that each would be provided "with a good *shillelagh* [a club or mace]" for election day.

Although political representatives were originally selected by towns or townships, the principle of "one person, one vote" came to be increasingly honored, and the practice of making approximately equal political districts began. However, around 1812, Massachusetts Governor Gerry became immortalized for the "gerrymander" adjusting of political districts that favor certain politicians or interests above others, allowing minorities to be majorities in the Legislature.

Among the greatest election-related scandals in U.S. history involved the "Tweed Ring" of Boss Tweed. After becoming active in politics in 1852, Tweed was reputed to have run New York City from 1863–72, capturing Tammany Hall in 1863, and giving jobs to dozens of his friends. After a series of corrupt acts that included millions in overpayments for a courthouse construc-tion project, rigged vote counting, the government was reduced to a victor spoils system, Tweed's ring was eventually ousted and Tweed was sentenced to the state penitentiary. Memorable quotes attributed to Tweed include "You have the liberty of voting for any one you please; but we have the liberty of counting in any one we please."

The corruption of state and local political parties also had considerable effect on American politics. Because both the law and the public look upon political parties as private organizations, political parties are less observed, less accountable, and less regulated than the government itself. Political parties are not only seen as a group to be supported, but also extract conditions on their continuing support of candidates. For example, as a condition of re-nomination or support, there were longstanding practices of making "assessments," whereby an office-holder or government employee would pay a percentage of their salary (such as 2 percent, even for an un-elected civil service position) for the privilege of keeping their job and/or enjoying political party support.

Another class of corrupt practice that was nearly universally outlawed by the turn of the 20th century was corporate campaign contributions. Legislation originally passed against this in 1907 was recodified in 1925, as the federal Corrupt Practices Act.

In 1922, an unusually honest registrar of elections in San Francisco, named J.H. Zemansky, stated that "a free ballot, a secret ballot, a fair count, or an honest election can be secured only on rare occasions, when conditions are favorable and large sums of money paid to persons to watch the count."

Although political parties are commonly quite adverse to each other, they often find common ground on some issues, such as in mutual animosity for any competition from third parties. In the late 19th and early 20th centuries, arrangements developed where the parties overlooked the other party's cheating practices. These arrangements were found to be "very common" by the 1918 Report of the Honest Ballot Association. State-based referenda on women's suffrage were often defeated by ballot box stuffing and other fraudulent devices, as reported by Catt and Shuler in "Woman Suffrage in Politics."

Throughout American history, a primary deterrent to scandal has been the power of the press. Thus, hearing about a scandal means that the system, though perhaps too late, has caught and exposed a particular wrongdoing. In many ways, because election laws react to perceived abuses, a detailed history in a given state of the evolution of the election laws will give a good picture of the history of scandals and corrupt practices by the residents and businesses in a given state. Thus, laws against violence at the polls, bribery, skippers or multiple voters, public review of vote counts, voter registration, the Australian or secret ballot system, and many other reforms over the years are in large part responses to specific problems or scandals. Other reforms include laws against false registration, soliciting media support, failure to furnish required disclosures or information, removal, mutilation or destruction of election booths, supplies, poll-lists or cards of instruction, refusal to permit employees to attend election, misconduct in relation to certificate of nomination and official ballot, misconduct in relation to petitions, violations of election law by public officers or employees, illegal voting, double voting, repeat voting via "floaters" or "rovers," unlawful use of stickers on ballots, executing false or fraudulent election returns, giving money or entertainment to induce attendance at polls, giving or receiving consideration for a vote, duress and intimidation of voters, conspiracy to prevent elections, corrupt use of position or authority to manipulate elections, procuring fraudulent documents in order to vote, and destroying or delaying election returns.

More recently, convictions have been obtained for fraudulently requesting absentee ballots on behalf of persons not intending to vote, rigging the recounts in Cuyahoga County in the presidential election of 2004, and selling ballots for prices as high as $200 in Kentucky, in 1987. Adding incompetence to injury, the Election Assistance Commission in 2006 announced the claim that no systematic study of election crimes has yet been done, despite the strong need for defending the integrity of elections.

There is no doubt that a free and fair election has not always been acheived in American history. Nor, as the disputed election of 2000 shows, does this problem seem to be going away. Frustration with the corrupted system of elections played a part in the Chicago Haymarket Riot of May, 1886. Six years before the Haymarket Riot, Socialist candidate Frank Stauber sued, after having lost a race for alderman. The court found excessive fraud, and restored Stauber's seat, but the jury refused to convict the "good faith" poll workers. This episode, among many like it, destroyed the surging Socialists' faith in the ballot. Later, when anarchists on strike for an eight-hour work day clashed with police, a bomb was thrown, and

seven police died. Four accused anarchists were hanged for this, but the bomber was never identified.

There is a long and sordid history of Jim Crow suppression of the votes of African Americans, resulting in the application of the Voting Rights Act of 1964, to state elections as well as federal elections. This might not have been constitutionally permissible if it were not for a history of scandalous discrimination against the voting rights of African Americans through literacy tests, poll taxes, and differential application of laws, together with outright intimidation toward minority voters.

Despite all the changes in the mechanics of voting, and the apparent safeguards, fraud (both flagrant and subtle), has persisted. There is a movement to shift to the secret electronic counts, obtained from voting on a computer. Voting machines form bottlenecks, forcing voters to stand in lines, and the numbers of machines allocated to each polling place is another manipulation technique, as long lines may deter voters.

Most problematically, election fraud is a crime that typically has a pay-off, in part because a successful election fraud results in that person being put into office, putting the wrong-doer in a position to perpetuate even more fraud as a newly-elected insider.

It should be noted that partisans of the various sides hotly disputed the veracity of these reported election fraud incidents. However, the truth tends to be known over the course of history, once the political impact of the story is not as acute. Likewise, as to modern controversies about computerized secret vote counts and allegations of stolen elections via computerized voting machines, the allegations will continue to be disputed until time and history are able to have their clarifying effects. Indisputably, however, there continues to be strong pressures for elections to come out the "right" way, on behalf of those who care deeply about politics.

SEE ALSO: Ballot Controversies; Corruption and Democratic Elections; Jim Crow Laws; Tammany Hall.

BIBLIOGRAPHY. Tracy Campbell, *Deliver the Vote: A History of Election Fraud, an American Political Tradition—1742-2004* (Carroll & Graf, 2005); Election Assistance Commission, Election Crimes: An Initial Review and Recommendations for Future Study, http://www.eac.gov/clearinghouse/docs/reports-and-surveys-2006electioncrimes.pdf (cited October

2007); Andrew Gumbel, *Steal This Vote: Dirty Elections and the Rotten History of Democracy in America*, (Nation Books, 2005); Albert Bushnell Hart, *National Ideals Historically Traced* (Harper & Brothers, 1907).

PAUL R. LEHTO
INDEPENDENT SCHOLAR

School Integration

SCHOOL INTEGRATION OR desegregation is an issue that has always divided America. In *Roberts v. City of Boston* (1849), the U.S. Supreme Court found that assigning African-American children to separate schools was reasonable. Plaintiffs in the Roberts case argued that segregated schools created "a feeling of degradation in the blacks and of prejudice and uncharitableness in the whites," a similar argument that would be heard over 100 years later. Following Reconstruction in the south, the rise of segregation was facilitated by a new wave of discriminatory laws known as Jim Crow. Discrimination was further sanctioned in the case of *Plessy v. Ferguson* (1896), when the Supreme Court announced its "separate but equal" doctrine. Southern states began to pass and enforce more Jim Crow laws.

Eventually, it became clear that "separate was not equal." The National Association for the Advancement of Colored People (NAACP) played a pivotal role toward outlawing "separate but equal." The NAACP first attacked higher education, followed by an attack on segregation in elementary and secondary schools. Although none of the higher education cases overturned the "separate but equal" doctrine, they were the pre-cursor to its reversal.

As lead counsel of the Legal Defense and Education Fund, Thurgood Marshall challenged segregation in Kansas, Delaware, Virginia, South Carolina, and the District of Columbia in the consolidated case, *Brown v. Board of Education* (1954). The newly appointed Chief Justice Earl Warren announced the court's unanimous decision on May 17, 1954, which declared separate education facilities were inherently unequal, thus in effect, overturning the *Plessy* decision. In implementing *Brown*, the court primarily deferred to the local school districts and left it up to the federal district courts to determine if the state and/or local school districts were in compliance. The public was not in favor of the court's

ruling, and massive resistance developed. In 1956, over 100 members of Congress signed a Southern Manifesto, vowing to use all means necessary to reverse Brown. Most school districts made little or no effort to desegregate. In those districts that attempted to integrate, African-American students were met with violence and intimidation. In 1957, when nine black students attempted to integrate Little Rock High School, Governor Orval Faubus used the Arkansas National Guard to block their entrance. The students faced an angry mob that harassed and spit upon them. To ease the situation, President Dwight D. Eisenhower had to federalize the Arkansas National Guard and send in paratroopers.

The New Orleans school crisis played a significant role in the contest for the state's governorship in late 1959 and early 1960, when three hard-core segregationists faced each other in a bitter fight for the Democratic nomination. Jimmy Davis won the governorship and in his inaugural address, he promised to "maintain separate but equal facilities." Following his inauguration, the Orleans Parish School Board, the governor, federal and state authorities, parents, and various citizen groups became embroiled in a bitter battle over the issue of school desegregation. Ten years after Brown, most of the schools throughout the country remained segregated. Over 300 school desegregation cases had been filed throughout the south. Finally, the court announced that time had run out for compliance. In fear of losing billions of dollars in federal funding, local school districts began to integrate. As a result, the enrollment of African-American students attending integrated schools rose from 1.17 percent in 1964 to 6.01 percent the following year.

The desegregation schemes that judges approved were either criticized by school districts as going too far, and by the civil rights advocates, as not going far enough. In the 1971 case of *Swann v. Charlotte-Mecklenburg Board*, the Supreme Court upheld for the first time the idea of intra-city busing to achieve desegregation. The Swan decision was divisive and polarized opinion against school desegregation.

Two days after the 1972 presidential election, Nixon proposed a moratorium on busing. In *Keyes v. School District #1, Denver Colorado* (1973), the Supreme Court upheld busing in Denver for the first time outside of the south. However, in *Miliken v. Bradley* (1994), the Supreme Court reversed a lower court's decision to bus students on a metropolitan basis in the Detroit area.

Clinton, Tennessee, 1956: A news photo captures the moment when an African-American boy walks through a crowd of white boys during a period of violence related to school integration.

The busing issue played out in elections throughout the country, from school boards to presidential elections.

George Wallace made busing the foundation of his campaign in the Florida primary, when vying for the 1968 presidential nomination. He lashed out at the administration and his opponents for supporting court-ordered busing. With mandated busing, many white families fled to the suburbs or created private schools, leaving the inner cities with predominantly segregated schools made up of African Americans and Latinos. By the mid-1990s, civil rights advocates complained about the resegregation of African Americans and Latinos. According to Kenneth Jost, "by 2001, at least two-thirds of black students and at least half of Latino students nationwide were enrolled in predominately minority schools."

As the federal courts eased up on mandated busing, other techniques were implemented to achieve racial balance, such as magnet school, voucher programs, and race-based assignment of students. White parents began to challenge the policy of assigning students to schools based on race and/or ethnicity guidelines. In 1991, the First Circuit Court of Appeals ruled against the policy the Boston School Committee used in assigning pupils to the elite Boston Latin School. On June 27, 2007, the Supreme Court announced its decision in the diversity cases of Louisville, Kentucky and Seattle, Washington. The court ruled 5–4 that assigning students to schools on the basis of race was a violation of the equal protection clause of the Fourteenth Amendment. However, Justice Kennedy wrote a concurring opinion, stating that race may be a factor in school diversity plans.

SEE ALSO: Civil Rights; Jim Crow Laws; Racial Justice; Urban Vote; Wallace, George C.

BIBLIOGRAPHY. H.J. Abraham and B.A. Perry, *Civil Rights and Liberties in the United States* (Oxford University Press, 1994); K.T. Andrews, "Movement-Countermovement Dynamics and the Emergence of New Institutions: The Case of "White

Flight" Schools in Mississippi," *Social Forces* (March, 2002); T.R. Ascik, "The Anti-Busing Constitutional Amendment," *Heritage Foundation Issue Bulletin* (v.47, 1979); Harry Ashmore, *Civil Rights and Wrongs: A Memoir of Race and Politics 1944–1996* (University of South Carolina Press, 1997); Derrick Bell, *Silent Covenants: Brown v. Board of Education And the Unfilled Hopes for Racial Reform* (Oxford University Press, 2004); Lee Epstein and T.G. Walker, *Constitutional Law for a Changing America: A Short Course* (CQ Press, 2005); Mark Sherman, "Supreme Court Rejects School Race Plans," *Washington Post* (June 28, 2007).

Naomi Robertson
Macon State College, Georgia

Senior Citizen Issues

UNDERSTANDING demographic conditions in the United States is a key element to understanding the issues facing senior citizens. An aging population has implications for the financial well-being and quality of health and social service programs, and public policymaking. A Reuters 2007 article reports that recent statistics show hospital and doctor visits in the United States have surged by 20 percent in the past five years. The baby boom generation, born between 1946 and 1964, are now key users of the medical system. According to U.S. Census Bureau projections, an increase in the number of senior citizens will occur when the Baby Boom generation begins to turn 65 in 2011. Those 65 and older are projected to double from 36 million in 2003 to 72 million in 2030, and to increase from 12 percent to 20 percent of the population. By 2050, this older population is expected to reach 86.7 million. Those aged 85 and older are projected to double from 4.7 million in 2003 to 9.6 million in 2030, and to double again to 20.9 million in 2050.

Social Security and Medicare are two of the largest social welfare entitlement programs in the United States. As a result, senior citizens are considered a powerful voting bloc, and exercise enormous political power. Additionally, although young people are more likely to take part in political protesting, they are less likely to participate in conventional politics, such as voting. According to Sidney Verba and N.H. Nie in *Participation in America*, voting rates tend to increase as people grow older. However, as physical problems begin to set in, voter participation declines. Thomas Dye, in *Politics in America*, explains that senior citizens are the most politically powerful age group in the population. They make up 28 percent of the voting population. Citizens over 65 years old average a 68 percent turnout rate in presidential elections and a 61 percent rate in congressional elections. By comparison, those aged 18 to 21 have a 36 percent turnout rate in presidential elections and 19 percent in congressional elections. Senior citizens are a powerful political force and are well represented in the political environment. So much so, that the American Association of Retired Persons (AARP) is the largest organized national interest group. Because of the financial influence of the AARP and the large senior citizen voting bloc, politicians cannot afford to distance themselves from this group.

Medicare is an important issue to senior citizens. Medicare was signed into law by President Lyndon Johnson in 1965 and is the U.S. version of national healthcare for the aged. It has an age requirement, but not a means-test. It is the primary source of publicly funded healthcare for the elderly.

Medicare is a federal health insurance program that provides healthcare coverage for individuals aged 65 and older. The program also covers certain persons under age 65 with disabilities. The program was authorized under Title XVIII of the Social Security Act. Medicare eligibility is available to individuals who fall into categories defined by either age or disability. At age 65, individuals qualify for Medicare if they or their spouses paid Social Security taxes for at least 40 calendar quarters (10 years). The Social Security Act was first passed in 1935. It is also sometimes referred to as the "third rail" of politics; touching it can cause political suicide. According to AARP (2007) figures, more than 47.5 million people receive monthly Old Age, Survivors and Disability Insurance benefits (OASDI). Based on an AARP report, the poverty rate for those 65 and older is 10.2 percent. Without Social Security, that rate would rise to almost 50 percent. Close to 80 percent of African Americans and 76 percent of Hispanics age 65 and older depend on Social Security for more than 50 percent of their income. Almost 75 percent of unmarried women rely on Social Security for half or more of their income.

Social Security is at the heart of a controversy. As baby boomers age and fewer working people replace them, it

Medicare and other healthcare concerns are paramount among senior citizen issues in most elections.

of 65. However, the life expectancy of a child born in 1990 is 74 years. When the Social Security system was created, the dependency ratio was 10–1; by 2010, the dependency ration will be 2–1, or two workers for each Social Security recipient.

Issues important to senior citizens include, strengthening Social Security; making healthcare affordable; making prescription drugs more affordable; providing affordable housing; and expanding job opportunities so people can keep working and contributing to society as they get older. The source of most legislation and benefits for senior citizens is the federal government. Legislative polices for senior citizens can be divided into various policy areas, focused on specific issues. Income policies are intended to provide supplemental income in retirement or to compensate or replace money lost due to early retirement or disability, or to provide a minimal income for the very poor. These include the Old-Age Survivors Insurance (private or public), Disability Insurance, and Supplemental Security Income. Additionally, seniors are concerned with COLAs, cost-of-living-adjustments mandated by law. Because of the efforts of senior citizen interest groups, such as the AARP, COLAs have given retirees some protection against inflation. Health policies such as Medicare are intended to cover costs associated with hospital care and certain medical services for the elderly. Medicaid is designated a healthcare coverage program for the very poor.

Publicly-subsidized housing and rent for senior citizens, and tax credits to mortgage firms and developers are the key aspects of housing policy. Primary programs include public housing, with specific units designed for the elderly. The Older Americans Act, originally signed into law in 1965, covers services such as transportation, employment and training, and case-management programs. Additionally, civil rights policies benefit the elderly. These include antidiscrimination laws and enforcement agencies. Efforts to combat age discrimination resulted in establishment of the Age Discrimination in Employment Act of 1967 (ADEA). Political participation is usually tied to socioeconomic status; the higher the income, the more likelihood of conventional political participation. A.L. Campbell (2003) argues that Social Security recipients are an exception to the usual relationship between higher socioeconomic status and higher rates of participation. Campbell finds that low-income seniors display a higher level of interest in Social Security than the more affluent seniors because

may become more difficult to finance Social Security in the current manner. However, the thought of tampering with it creates considerable anxiety among many who rely on it. A 2007 AARP policy report states that the graying of America has caused concern among many experts that the future cost of federal health and retirement programs will create huge federal deficits, and jeopardize long-term economic growth. The dependency ratio, according to Thomas Dye, is the number of recipients as a percentage of the number of contributing workers. A person born in 1935 would expect to live only to age 61, four years before the retirement age the benefits that they receive constitute a larger proportion of their incomes.

SEE ALSO: Age and Voting Behavior; Voter Turnout; Voting; Voting Rights Act of 1965; Voter Self-Interest.

BIBLIOGRAPHY. A.L. Campbell, *How Policies Make Citizens: Senior Political Activism and the American Welfare State* (Princeton University Press, 2003); J.W. Ceaser and A.E. Busch, *Losing to Win: The 1996 Elections and American Politics* (Rowman & Littlefield, 1997); Thomas Dye, *Politics in America* (Prentice Hall, 2005); R.P. Hart, *Campaign Talk: Why Elections Are Good for Us* (Princeton Univrsity Press, 2000); F.M. Torres-Gil, *The New Aging: Politics and Change in America* (Auburn House Paperback, 1992); Sidney Verba and N.H. Nie, *Participation in America: Political Democracy and Social Equality* (University of Chicago Press, 1987).

STEPHEN E. SUSSMAN
BARRY UNIVERSITY

Seventy-Two-Hour Program

THE SEVENTY-TWO-HOUR PROGRAM is the name for the Republican Party's plans for their get-out-the-vote drives (GOTV) that have been operational since the 2002 midterm elections. The purpose of these efforts has been to increase turnout among likely Republican voters. Karl Rove, the chief strategist for George W. Bush's 2000 presidential campaign, assembled a task force after that election to study how Democrats mobilized voters in the 72 hours prior to an election. The purpose of this study was to come up with a program where the Republicans could compete with the Democrats in mobilizing voters, an area where the Democrats, because of organized labor and party organizations in urban areas, had historically enjoyed an advantage. GOTV drives are critical in close contests, where effectively mobilizing voters can be the key to victory. GOTV drives typically include targeting likely voters, reminding targeted voters to vote, helping them get to the polls, and making them feel that they are performing an important civic duty.

Prior to the 2002 midterm elections, Rove implemented a program where the Republicans would counter organized labor and Democratic Party activists by building local organizations and targeting key Repub-

lican constituencies, notably voters in rural and exurban areas. It also included identifying voters who were, for example, opposed to abortion, gay marriage, and gun control; all issues where there are clear distinctions between Republican and Democratic identifiers. It also included an effort to mobilize voters who regularly attend religious services, as one of the components of the program was to gather membership directories from churches around the country. Their 2002 program also called for registering new voters in Republican constituencies, recruiting more than 2,000 GOTV coordinators, and more than 100,000 volunteers in key congressional races around the country. In undertaking these efforts, the Republicans were attempting to match the Democrats labor-based and party-activist centered field organization. A Volunteer Deployment Program, which sent Republican volunteers from Washington, D.C., into local areas to knock on doors, would supplement this grass-roots organization and staff phone banks. The program also incorporates pro-Republican groups. Conservative Christian radio host James C. Dobson's organization, Focus on the Family, mobilized Evangelical voters in battleground states.

In Missouri, Republican GOTV efforts, which included the state Republican Party paying individuals to help with the Election Day operation, was considered critical to former Congressman Jim Talent's victory over Senator Jean Carnahan by 21,254 votes out of more than 1.8 million cast. By increasing turnout in Republican areas of the state, the GOTV effort provided Talent with the margin of victory. In 2004, the Republicans refined their targeting with polling, census, and commercial data to "micro-target" small groups of voters. By the end of the campaign, the Republicans had developed a 165 million-name database, known as Voter Vault. These tactics are credited for President Bush's victory, as well as the increase of four seats in the House of Representatives. In that election, although the Democrats surpassed all previous turnout records, the Republicans, through their efforts, turned out even more voters.

The Democrats, recognizing that the Republicans had gained an advantage in GOTV, commissioned their own study after the 2004 election to determine a new course of action. In response, the Democrats began to develop their own micro-targeting techniques for the 2006 midterm elections. The Democratic National Committee (DNC), as part of DNC Chairman Howard Dean's "50-state strategy," hired organizers to work with the state parties to build GOTV efforts. This strategy caused some tension with the party's congressional campaign committees, which favored targeting the effort on key races. The Democrats took control of both Houses of Congress in 2006. Whether these victories can be attributed to their new GOTV efforts, or to President Bush's unpopularity, or to other factors, is unclear. In one study conducted after the election, Harvard political scientist Elaine Kamarck found that the Democratic vote increased by 4.7 percent nationally, but increased by 9.8 percent in the 35 districts where a DNC field worker was placed.

SEE ALSO: Campaign Strategies; Canvassing Voters in Campaigns; Get-Out-the-Vote (GOTV) Drives; Republican Party; Republican State Party Organizations; Targeting Strategies; Voter Turnout.

BIBLIOGRAPHY. Ari Berman, "Ground Game '06," *Nation* (November 13, 2006); Tom Hamburger and Peter Wallsten, *One Party Country: the Republican Plan for Dominance in the 21st Century* (John Wiley and Sons, 2006); Elaine Kamarck, "Assessing Howard Dean's 50-State Strategy and the 2006 Midterm Elections," *Forum* (v.4/3, 2006); James Moore and Wayne Slater, *The Architect: Karl Rove and the Master Plan for Absolute Power* (Crown Publishers, 2006).

JEFFREY KRAUS
WAGNER COLLEGE

Single-Issue Voting

SINGLE-ISSUE VOTING REFERS to individual or group voting behavior based on a candidate or party's stand on a single issue. It is a specific case of the more general concept of issue voting, which occurs when voters make decisions based on policy issues rather than on other considerations, such as party identification, political ideology, or candidate traits.

Although single-issue voters may be interested in a variety of policy areas, they are different from other voters in that they care so deeply about a particular issue that their vote choice is based on that issue. Thus, they behave as if there were only one issue in the policy space. Single-issue voting is not a new phenomenon. Americans have gone to the polls for over two centuries in support of candidates based on their stands on single issues. Although some of these issues can fade away rather quickly, others (such as slavery and civil rights) can influence voter behavior for generations and remain on the political scene until they capture the interest of a majority of the electorate, or become redefined by a change in the policy landscape. The phenomenon is also not unique to American politics.

Some of the most prominent issues for single-issue voters in the United States are abortion, affirmative action, crime, the economy, education, the environment, gay rights, gun control, and war. To induce single-issue voting and mobilize support for a candidate, a political campaign may focus on a singular issue rather than on a broad range of issues. In some cases, this may be done to mobilize core voters to support a candidate based primarily on his or her stand on that issue. In other cases, campaigns may use single issues as wedge issues, which target voters who might generally prefer another candidate or party, but who strongly disagree with that candidate or party on a particular issue. In this case, the single issue creates cross-pressures on voters that go contrary to their general political disposition. New technologies that permit campaigns to micro-target messages to individual voters have increased the viability of the use of single issues in political campaigns.

Such a strategy, however, comes at the risk of potentially alienating those voters who disagree with a candidate's emphasis or stance on the issue. Single-issue voting is more prominent among those who feel strongly about an issue than among the general population. That is, it is more prevalent among those voters with extreme attitudes (either positive or negative) about the particular issue than among those who hold more moderate views or feel indifferent about it.

Single-issue voting can lead to the formation of single-issue interest groups and, especially in electoral systems based on proportional representation, to single-issue parties. Although the general electorate in the United States tends to be broad-based, sometimes a single issue may come to dominate an election to the extent that it becomes the main issue in a campaign. In a close race, an election could be decided by single-issue voting. Furthermore, even when single-issue voting is not the determining factor in an election, it can influence the policy agenda after the campaign is over. To some observers, single-issue voting raises normative concerns about its impact on the polity. Some argue that it can lead to decreased voter satisfaction with the political system because single-issue voters hold very strong views on particular issues even in cases where the majority of the electorate is not interested in those issues. Critics also question if elected officials should pay special attention to an opinionated minority on issues about which the majority may be disinterested. On the other hand, single-issue voting is a vehicle that can give particular weight to voters who care deeply about an issue, allowing them to express not only a simple preference, but also the intensity of their interests. Single-issue voting remains a prevalent phenomenon in contemporary campaigns and elections and an increasingly important factor in the study of electoral behavior.

SEE ALSO: Campaign Strategies; Cross-Pressures, Sociopolitical; Determinants of Vote Choice; Issue Evasion; Issue Framing; Issue Salience and Voting Behavior; Special Interests.

BIBLIOGRAPHY. T.M. Carsey and G.C. Layman, "Changing Sides or Changing Minds? Party Identification and Policy Preferences in the American Electorate," *American Journal of Political Science* (v.50/2, 2006); Pamela Conover, Virginia Gray, and Steven Coombs, "Single-Issue Voting: Elite-Mass Linkages Political Behavior," *Political Behavior* (v.4/4, 1982); D.S. Hillygus and T. Shields, *The Persuadable Voter: Strategic Candidates and Wedge Issues in Presidential Campaigns* (Princeton University Press, 2008); W.E. Miller and J.M. Shanks, *The New American Voter* (Harvard University Press, 1996); R.G. Niemi and H.F. Weisberg, *Controversies in Voting Behavior* (CQ Press, 2001).

CARLOS E. DÍAZ-ROSILLO
HARVARD UNIVERSITY

Slavery

THE 1860 PRESIDENTIAL election had many issues to address, but none more important than the future course of the country and the south's "peculiar institution of slavery. With the invention of Eli Whitney's cotton gin in 1793, the plantation system in the south received an economic boost and as the cotton economy blossomed, the internal slave trade increased. The south became committed to slavery as it became vital to their existence. With the threats of slave insurrections and the North's denunciation of the south's institution, the south became defensive about their rights. Although the majority of whites did not own slaves, their racial ideology was questioned and many felt that emancipation for blacks meant the end of white rights (supremacy). With increasing agitation by abolitionists on the slavery issue, sectional hostilities were increased Many Americans had opposed slavery since colonial times. In 1877, Vermont was the first United States territory to ban slavery and the state of Pennsylvania followed suit in 1790.

By 1804, Northern states had voted to abolish slavery within their borders. In the half century leading up to the Civil War, white and black activists, women and men, worked together under the abolitionist umbrella though not always in harmony. Abolitionists put forward a wide range of approaches to end slavery from moral pervasion to boycotts, to the endorsements of violent rebellions. William Lloyd Garrison believed that slavery was a moral issue. He sought the immediate release of all slaves, as the only justifiable solution. As he became more radical, Garrison called for the Northern secession from the slaveholding south. James Gillespie Birney believed that political action and the power of religion were the key to ending slavery. Born in Kentucky to a slaveholding family, he freed his slaves and became one of the nation's most prominent abolitionists. Frederick Douglass believed that both moral arguments and political action should be used in the fight to achieve abolition. Born into slavery, Douglass escaped bondage in 1838 and became one of the eloquent voices of the abolition movement.

Lincoln and William Seward, who fought for the Republican nomination of 1860, acknowledged the existing problems. Lincoln had recently lost the 1858 Senate race to Stephen Douglas and was not in office at the time of the presidential campaign. Seward was a sitting Senator, but lost favor with Republicans because of his "political insider" status and for his radical abolitionist opinions, as previewed in his speeches. Republicans feared that Seward could not carry states sympatric to slavery. "Slavery is not, and never can be, perpetual," said Seward. "It will be overthrown either peacefully or lawfully under the Constitution or it will work to the subversion of the Constitution, together with it own overthrow, then the slaveholders would perish in

Exeter Hall, filled with a large crowd for the Anti-Slavery Society meeting, London, England, 1841. America's territorial disputes about slavery were influenced by European views on America's "peculiar institution."

the struggle." Lincoln advocated a more modern party plank designed to preserve the Union. Although we remember Lincoln as the president who ended slavery in the states where it was already present, he also promised to prohibit expansion in the Western territories. Lincoln also disavowed John Brown and his anti-slavery activities. This more moderate position earned Lincoln the Republican nomination, but it was questioned if it would be enough to win the White House.

President James Polk's (1841–45) administration had been credited with great expansion and investment with the annexation of Texas, the treaty with Great Britain for the Oregon Territory, as well as the addition of California and New Mexico. This was a source of great national pride and many thought expansion was the fulfillment of both God's will and America's mission to

spread its republican institutions, but there was great concern about slavery.

The slavery issue became inextricably linked to several territorial conflicts, such as the Mexican Cession, the Kansas-Nebraska Act, the Louisiana Purchase, the Missouri Compromise, as well as the nationalistic Manifest Destiny. There were a host of specific incidents: the Fugitive Slave Law (1850), the publication of *Uncle Tom's Cabin* (1852), the *Dred Scott Decision* (1857), and the hanging of John Brown (1859) that polarized the north and the south. Slavery was the common-binding these incidents. The north had a sense of moral revulsion toward the south. During the 1850s, different views about slavery's expansion and its place in America fueled suspicion and bitterness between northerners and southerners.

This issue shattered the nation's two-party system, which had served for a generation to pull sections and interests into two powerful national institutions. Of the two major parties, the Whig organization succumbed in the mid-1850s. Lincoln's careful stand on a variety of these issues guided him into a meager victory in a year when the country and its political parties were ravaged by a maelstrom of complicated and volatile issues. Like the Whigs, the Democratic Party also cracked beneath the weight of the issues at hand. States that favored slavery in the territories walked out of the Democratic Convention at Charleston, South Carolina, preventing Stephen Douglas from winning the party's endorsement.

A reconvened convention eventually nominated Douglas, but kept slavery out of the platform. As a result of the disagreement over the issue of slavery, splintered parties were formed. The Southern Democratic Party was formed by traditional Democrats to nominate John Breckenridge, an advocate for slavery in the West. Republicans breakaways formed the Constitution Union Party. They nominated John Bell who would not address the issue of slavery at all, but rather spoke of upholding the Constitution. With four candidates in the race, Lincoln won the 1860 election. But by the time he took office in March of 1861, seven southern states had already seceded from the Union.

With the first shot that rang out at Fort Sumter, just one month after Lincoln took office, the Civil War began. Lincoln's hopes for peacefully preserving the Union were gone. In 1863, Lincoln issued the Emancipation Proclamation. He also promoted a Constitutional amendment to permanently abolish slavery. This marked a shift from Lincoln's more moderate campaign position on slavery issues, and also changed the focus of the war from preserving the Union to freeing slaves. Although, there were thoughts of suspending the Civil War, during the election of 1864, Union soldiers were given absentee ballots or furloughed to permit them to vote. With mounting Union victories, the votes of soldiers and the campaign slogan "Don't switch horses in mid-stream," Lincoln won the election. Unfortunately, he did not live to see passage of the Thirteenth Amendment that abolished slavery forever. He was assassinated just five day after Ulysses S. Grant celebrated his victory over Robert E. Lee at Appomattox.

SEE ALSO: Civil War and Realignment; Presidential Election of 1860.

BIBLIOGRAPHY. Herman Belz, *Lincoln and Freedom: Slavery, Emmancipation and the Thirteenth Amendment* (Southern Illinois University Press, 2007); John Mack Faragher, et al, *Out of Many: History of the American People* (Prentice-Hall, New Jersey, 1997. James McPherson, *Battle Cry for Freedom: The Civil War Era* (Oxford University Press, 1984).

FRED LINDSEY
INDEPENDENT SCHOLAR

Social Concerns

THERE ARE SIGNIFICANT differences between the two major political parties over social concerns. Within the Republican Party there are factions concerned with economic issues, while in the Democratic Party many social issues split the group. Often these issues mirror the concerns of the general electorate and, as such, issues can serve as major campaign issues, especially during presidential campaigns. Fortunately, researchers such as the Pew Center for the People and the Press conduct surveys pertaining to social issues and concerns and provide statistics related to voting behaviors.

As has been the pattern since 2001, Americans feel that protecting the country against another terrorist attack ranks as the most important social concern issue. Over 80 percent of those surveyed indicated that they felt a terrorist attack was imminent. Yet, in the wake of Hurricane Katrina, more than 57 percent said it was more important for President Bush and Congress to focus on domestic issues than foreign policy issues such as terrorism and the war in Iraq.

Approaching the 2008 election campaign, specific domestic priorities seem to be more important than others: dealing with the nation's energy crisis (up 11 percent from 2005), reducing crime (up nine percent); protecting the environment (up eight percent) followed by regulating health maintenance organizations (up six percent) and dealing with morality issues (up six percent). When asked, most Americans feel very optimistic about the economy, noting that they feel the economy will not get better or worse, and for that they are cautiously optimistic. When asked to specifically identify key social concerns as they pertain to the economy, the following very big/big problems:

gasoline prices (82 percent), home heating prices (87 percent), healthcare affordability (90 percent), federal budget deficit (77 percent), retirement affordability (75 percent), job situation (70 percent), housing prices (65 percent), inflation (61 percent), and interest rates (48 percent). Economic issues at the personal level are also intriguing: eight percent of Americans surveyed indicated that they owed a lot more than they could handle, and 15 percent a little more than they can handle on credit cards and other loans. Most note that the debt they carry is manageable, while surprisingly, 21 percent say they have no debt at all. Democrats list these issues as very big problems, more frequently than Republicans or moderates.

THE NEEDY AND THE ENVIRONMENT

Two of the most divided and controversial social issues facing the American electorate pertain to expanding government assistance for the needy and the role of government in protecting the environment. More than 69 percent of Democrats surveyed feel that dealing with the problems of the poor should be a top governmental priority. Republicans were less interested in the needs of the poor; only 39 percent listed poverty as a need requiring governmental attention. Democrats, compared to Republicans, felt that one way to help the needy was through the providing of health insurance (Democrats 71 percent; Republicans 41 percent) and that increasing the minimum wage was another key strategy (Democrats 55 percent; Republicans 33 percent).

Immigration is a major social issue in the 2008 election. Over 51 percent of those surveyed list placing restrictions on illegal immigration as a top priority, while only 17 percent feel the same about a proposal for a guest-worker program. When specifically asked about a guest-worker program, 47 percent support it and 46 percent oppose it. There is a sharp divide based on political ideology among conservatives and liberals concerning illegal immigration: over 63 percent of conservatives view this as a top priority, while only 39 percent of all liberals listed it as a social concern or issue.

One issue that has shown a degree of bipartisanship centers on the guest worker program: 56 percent of liberal democrats and 55 percent of conservative Republicans support the idea, with those in the middle denouncing the program. Many social concerns find their way onto the public policy agenda and, as a result,

are debated more frequently among political candidates, especially those seeking the office of the presidency. These include: abortion, stem cell research, creationism, and the Supreme Court. Each of these issues clearly has religious overtones and as such, they become very divisive, very quickly.

Since the Supreme Court decision to legalize abortion in 1973 (*Roe v. Wade*), the issue of abortion has been a hot topic among the electorate and those seeking political office. The abortion issue seems to be divisive on four main concerns: church involvement in public policy issues, the moral question surrounding when life begins (at conception or birth); the right to terminate life regardless of when it began, and the right of a woman to decide what she can do with her body.

Since the mid 1940s, interest groups and religious institutions have sought to keep reproductive rights (birth control, abortion, and sterilization techniques) out of the public view and even to make it a crime to discuss them. Prior to the Civil War, most states allowed for some form of abortion. However, with the influx of Catholic immigrants and the increase in Evangelical movements around the turn of the 20th century, public opinion about abortions changed.

By 1910, every state but Kentucky had made it illegal to receive an abortion. However, the pendulum began to swing back, and in landmark decisions in 1965 (*Griswold v. Connecticut*) and 1972 (*Eisenstadt v. Baird*), the Supreme Court ruled that reproductive rights were not the concern of the government. This opened a floodgate of lawsuits against the practice of banning abortions.

LANDMARK CASE

Roe v. Wade is viewed as a landmark case because of its stance on matters of personal privacy. In essence, the court ruled that a woman's body belonged to her and, as such, her right to privacy included her right to have an abortion. While the court upheld the notion that states have the constitutional right to protect human life, it was vague in determining how involved the state could become in the private life of the mother. During the first three months, there would be no involvement by the state; during the second three months, only if there was "reasonable" cause; and in the final three months there would be no abortions except if the mother's life were in jeopardy.

This ruling set off a firestorm of controversy as elected officials and those campaigning began to use the abortion issue as a campaign issue. States interpreted the ruling in different ways. Some states imposed waiting periods, others required parent notification, some required that the father of the child be notified, and some attempted to limit access to abortion clinics. Each one of these issues would become political fodder for those seeking office and those seeking re-election at the state level. At the federal level, it became an issue as well. Members of Congress ran on campaign promises to pass a constitutional amendment banning abortion, which ultimately failed. Others promised their constituents they would place tighter restrictions of abortion.

Over 30 laws, ranging from Medicaid funding for abortions (upheld by the Supreme Court in 1980), to parent notification were passed. Abortion continues to be a major campaign issue, especially as it pertains to so-called partial-birth abortion (supported by Democrats; opposed by Republicans). Statistics show that 55 percent of Americans oppose making it more difficult for a woman to obtain an abortion, while 36 percent favor greater restrictions. Republicans tend to favor greater restrictions and Democrats tend to oppose them.

There has been a steady up-tick in the overall salience of stem-cell research since 2002, and today, most Americans have at least heard something about the issue. In March 2002, 27 percent of respondents reporting hearing a lot about stem cell research. By August 2004, this was up to 42 percent, and, since then, has hovered at just slightly under 50 percent. In March 2002, some 43 percent of respondents favored conducting research, while 38 percent favored protecting human embryos over conducting stem-cell research (19 percent did not know). Over time, opinions shifted toward favoring the research (52 percent by August 2004) but, since December 2004, patterns have held relatively stable with about 55 percent favoring stem-cell research and some 30 percent speaking out against it, at least in part, because they do not wish to destroy human embryos.

Thus the divide on stem-cell research is not quite as stark as in 2002, but polling suggests that it persists and is often understood as a debate between conducting potentially lifesaving research for the common good and protecting the sanctity of life. What is unique among the electorate is the apparent political split in support for stem-cell research. Democrats distinctly support stem-cell research (over 80 percent), while Republicans are evenly split (38 percent to 40 percent).

Religious issues will continue to be campaign issues in the 2008 election. Specifically, two social issues are viewed by political observers as key issues in local and state elections: the teaching of creationism in public schools and the displaying of the Ten Commandments in government buildings. Majorities of Americans support both of these ideas, with 74 percent supporting the Ten Commandments issue and 57 percent in favor of teaching Bible-based creationism, provided evolution is taught at the same time. Only one-third of those surveyed support only teaching creationism instead of evolution. Most Democrats line up with Republicans on these issues.

Finally, a social concern that will be an issue in the 2008 election involves the selection of Supreme Court justices. On this issue the country appears to be split: over half want the next president to select a justice that will make the court more conservative, and half want the president to select a justice that will lean the court toward a more liberal stance. In the end, it is the social issues that drive a campaign and involve the electorate.

SEE ALSO: Abortion; Democratic Party; Economy; Republican Party; Social Groups and Electoral Behavior; Special Interests.

BIBLIOGRAPHY. Robert Baird and Stuart Rosenbaum, *Ethics about Abortions* (Prometheus Books, 2001); Kurt Finsherbusch, *Taking Sides-Clashing Views on Social Issues* (McGrawHill Publishers, 2006); Pew Center for the People and the Press, www.people-press.org (cited August 2007); Michael Ruse and Chris Pynes, *The Stem Cell Controversy* (Prometheus Books, 2006).

RONALD ERIC MATTHEWS, JR.
MOUNT UNION COLLEGE

Social Groups and Electoral Behavior

VOTERS RECEIVE INFORMATION about candidates from many sources, including the people around them and groups they associate with. These social factors can be analyzed according to the level of direct contact the individual or groups have with the person. Those with the most immediate contact with voters are family and friends. At the next level are coworkers, and then other groups and organizations with which the person is involved. Last is the person's perceived social status (or class). All of these social contacts exert some amount of pressure on voter choice.

Within the group of family and friends, most people tend to associate with people of similar political views. While not a foolproof indicator, most people's spouses tend to be of the same political party as the voter. Friends of the voter also tend to be heavily weighted toward members sharing the same political party. This is in part due to the closeness of their relationships. These people are the ones who can bring the most pressure to bear on the voter. The voter, in turn, will tend to associate with people who have similar views, and the voter has the most control over who is in this group.

With respect to coworkers, the voter normally has little choice of whom they work with, and therefore cannot choose people with whom they share a common political view. There are several mitigating factors, however. One is that the voter has the option of not discussing politics with coworkers. The other is that some jobs tend to attract people of similar political alignment, for example a job where the person is required to be a member of a union or a professional organization. People in these types of membership organizations often have similar political views.

In addition, the voter is more likely to gravitate towards coworkers with similar views and will have only limited interaction with those of differing views. With these groups, there are several things to keep in mind. Politics are unlikely to play a large role in their daily lives. Although people tend to gravitate toward people of similar political views, this may be a product of similar social and economic factors. In addition, within most of these social groups, individuals are not interested in dealing with high levels of political pressure from members of the group. People tend to gravitate towards others who have similar backgrounds and status in society, which includes not just economic and social factors, but also people of similar racial and ethnical backgrounds.

Groups that have less direct contact with the voter include those where members tend to have similar interests. These groups include associations, unions and professional organizations, and religious organizations. Because these groups are made up of similar people, they will tend to have similar political views. In part, this comes from the fact that the group members have had similar life experiences. These groups become important when the voter uses them as a guide in forming opinions. These references can be positive or negative. Positive reference comes about when the voter is in agreement with the positions of the group, while negative reference comes from the voter's disagreement or dislike of the group. This reference becomes more powerful the more the voter identifies with the group. Also important is the perceived level of power or importance of the group. The more powerful the group, the more voters associated with that group will be influenced. As a group's power declines, the voter is less likely to use that group as a guide to forming opinions. It is also possible for these groups to become important temporarily, for example, for one election cycle.

The final social influence is how people perceive themselves. For most people, this centers on whether they are middle-class or working-class. In European politics, this tends to be more important than in America. The ability to determine a person's political inclination based on their perceived social class has been on the decline in America since the 1950s. In part, this is because American politicians have tended to avoid social class as an issue when campaigning.

SEE ALSO: Martial Status and Voting Behavior; Occupation and Voting Behavior; Race and Voting Behavior; Religion and Voting Behavior.

BIBLIOGRAPHY. W.H. Flanigan and N.H. Zingale, *Political Behavior of the American Electorate* (CQ Press, 1998); L.S. Maisel and K.Z. Buckley, *Parties and Elections in America: The Electoral Process* (Rowman & Littlefield Publishers, 2005).

DALLACE W. UNGER, JR.
INDEPENDENT SCHOLAR

Socialist Party

THE SOCIALIST PARTY of America was formed in 1901 by dissident members of the Socialist Labor Party known as the constitutional or Kangaroo wing socialists (founded in 1876) led by Job Harriman, Max Hayes, and Morris Hillquit; the Social Democratic Party (founded in 1898), led by American Railway Union leader and pacifist Eugene V. Debs; and a number of independent socialist parties. The first National Secretary of the party was Leon Greenbaum. In its early years, it received support from a number of new immigrants in urban areas. In 1910, a youth organization, the Young People's Socialist League, was established. The party was a democratic socialist party, advocating change through elections rather than through revolution. In the early years of the 20th century, under Debs' leadership, the party was an important third party. Debs was a socialist presidential candidate five times between 1900 and 1920 (the last time while in prison for violating the World War I-era Espionage Act), receiving over 919,000 votes in 1920. Membership peaked in 1912, at slightly over 118,000.

The Socialist Party elected a number of congressman, mayors, and other public officials 1910–50. The first socialist elected to the U.S. House of Representatives was Victor L. Berger, who was elected to represent Wisconsin's fifth congressional district in 1910. Meyer London was elected to the House from New York's 12th congressional district, which included the Lower East Side, in 1914. Daniel Hoan became Mayor of Milwaukee in 1916, and would serve until 1940. More than 70 cities would elect socialist mayors in the years before World War I, as the party attracted support from Jewish and German immigrants in urban areas, some Marxists, Christian socialists, and from coal miners and some farmers in rural areas.

INTERNAL DIVISION

However, the party was internally divided over American involvement in World War I. The Debs faction of the party opposed American involvement in the war, claiming that the war had been caused by imperialism and that the United States should remain neutral. After the United States entered the war, Debs made an anti-war speech, urging men to refuse to sign up for the draft. Debs would be convicted of violating the Espionage Act, a law that made it a crime to make speeches that undermined the war effort, in 1919, and was sentenced to 10 years in prison (he was released by President Warren G. Harding in 1921, who commuted his sentence to time served). Another faction of the party supported America's entry into the war.

Following the war, the party became fractionalized over the issue of the relationship with the new Bolshevik government in Russia. The party voted to expel its pro-Bolshevik faction in early 1919. This faction of the party formed, in September 1919, the Communist Party of America (which was made up mainly of the foreign language federations in the Socialist Party) and the Communist Labor Party, which was led by the journalist John Reed, further fracturing the left in American politics (under pressure from Moscow, the two parties would merge into the Communist Party USA in 1921). In 1920, the party convention voted to make American citizenship a requirement to serve as a party officer or delegate to the party convention. The following year, a faction of the party that wanted to join the Third International in Moscow broke away and formed the Workers Party of America. In 1924, the party convention endorsed the presidential candidacy of Progressive Party candidate Robert M. LaFollette. The party's goal, in joining with the Progressives, the American Federation of Labor, and a number of other unions in supporting LaFollette was to create a permanent farmer-labor party. This effort would, ultimately, be unsuccessful.

PARTY MEMBERSHIP

Following Debs's death in 1926, Norman Thomas, a Protestant minister and journalist, became the leader of the party. He was the party's presidential nominee in 1928, 1932, 1936, 1940, 1944, and 1948. In 1932, during the Great Depression, Thomas polled 883,000 votes (2.2 percent). In 1936, a number of party leaders, notably David Dubinsky, supported Franklin Roosevelt, and Thomas's vote total dropped to 185,000. During the years after World War II, the party's membership fell to less than 2,000. A number of party members, including Walter Reuther, A. Philip Randolph, and Bayard Rustin left the party, believing that they could do more to achieve progressive reforms by becoming active in the Democratic Party. Also, McCarthyism, while targeting Communists, had a negative impact on all left-wing parties. In 1958, the Independent Socialist League dissolved, with most of its members joining the Socialist Party. Their leader, Max Shachtman, urged the Socialists to realign with the Democratic Party, while explicitly rejecting Soviet-style Communism.

During the 1960s, the party continued moving rightward under Schactman's influence. In 1968, the Socialist Party's national convention rejected a resolution urging American withdrawal from Vietnam. The party also voted to endorse Hubert Humphrey, despite the opposition of Norman Thomas. In the early 1970s, the Socialist Party of America split into three different organizations. The split developed in 1972 after Shachtman's Unity Caucus had taken control of the party and blocked a resolution opposing the Vietnam War. In that year's presidential election, the Unity Caucus first supported Democratic Senator Henry (Scoop) Jackson of Washington. After Jackson dropped out of the Democratic contest, Shachtman and his followers refused to oppose President Richard Nixon's re-election. Michael Harrington then formed the Democratic Socialist Organizing Committee (which became the Democratic Socialists of America), supporting Democratic nominee George S. McGovern. This group believed it was important to work within the Democratic Party and try to pressure the party to the left.

The Party's Debs Caucus, led by David McReynolds, formed the Union for Democratic Socialism and supported the anti-war candidacy of People's Party presidential candidate, Benjamin Spock. In 1973, this group became the Socialist Party USA, while the Shachtman group re-named itself Social Democrats USA. The Debs Caucus believed it was important to maintain an independent Socialist Party.

This group became the Socialist Party USA, a new third party. In 1976, the new party ran its first presidential candidate. Frank Zeidler, who had been the Socialist Mayor of Milwaukee 1948–60, received 6,000 votes and was on the ballot in 10 states. The Socialist Party USA's candidates since that time have included David McReynolds (1980 and 2000), Willa Kenoyer (1988), Quinn Brisben (1992), Mary Cal Hollis (1996), and Walter F. Brown (2004).

Today, the Democratic Socialists of America (DSA) is the official U.S. member of the Socialist International, which includes Great Britain's Labour Party; the French Parti Socialiste and 140 other political parties around the world. The DSA does not run candidates for office. Instead, they engage in political education and grassroots organizing in order to establish "an openly socialist presence in American communities and politics." The Social Democrats USA are an ideologically centrist group that is aligned with the Democratic Party. The Socialist Party USA continues as a separate party, with about 1,600 members nationally. The party's headquarters is located in New York City.

SEE ALSO: Debs, Eugene; Left-Wing Candidates; Third Parties.

BIBLIOGRAPHY. Ira Kipnis, *The American Socialist Movement, 1897–1912* (Columbia University Press, 1952); S.M. Miller, *Victor Berger and the Promise of Constructive Socialism, 1910–1920* (Greenwood Press, 1973); H.W. Morgan, *Eugene V. Debs: Socialist for President* (Greenwood Press, 1973); M.B. Selder, *Norman Thomas: Respectable Rebel* (Syracuse University Press, 1967); F.A. Warren, *An Alternative Vision: the Socialist Party in the 1930s* (Indiana University Press, 1974).

Jeffrey Kraus
Wagner College

Social-Labor Party

THE SOCIAL-LABOR PARTY is a political party that advocates Marxism. The party was founded in Newark, New Jersey in 1876 as the Workingmen's Party of America. It took on its current name the following year. It was a network of local socialist political parties and American supporters of Marx's First International and was strong in New York City, having its base in the city's large German population (who referred to the party as the Sozialistische Arbeiter Partei). In 1881, the party suffered the first of many break-offs as an anarchist faction of the Socialist Labor Party left to form the Revolutionary Socialist Labor Party (two years later, this group would merge with a number of other groups to form the International Workingman's Association).

During this time, the party's positions were influenced by the views of Ferdinand Lassalle, Lassalle, a rival of Marx, believed that workers should form political parties to win control of the state. In 1886, the party joined the movement for an eight-hour day. On May 4, 1886, at a meeting to protest the riot at the McCormick plant in Chicago, the Haymarket Square bombing occurred and eight police officers were killed. While the bomber was never identified, a number of party members, including August Spies, Albert Parson, Adolph Fisher, and George Engel, were convicted of conspiracy to murder and executed.

In 1890, Daniel DeLeon, a Columbia University Law School lecturer, became the leader of the party, introducing changes in the party that have become known as

DeLeonism. He introduced English as the party's official language, replacing German, and moved the party towards Marxism. DeLeon also started the publication of a party newspaper in 1891, *The People* (which is still published). In 1892, the Socialist Labor Party nominated its first presidential candidate, Simon Wing, who (along with running-mate Charles H. Matchett) received 21,163 votes. Hatchett would be the party's standard-bearer in 1896, receiving over 36,000 votes. Another split in the party took place in 1901, when anti-DeLeon members of the Socialist Labor Party left and joined with Eugene V. Debs's Social Democratic Party to form the Socialist Party of America.

During the 1890s, the Social-Labor Party attempted to establish militant trade unions. Marx believed that unions could be a training ground where workers would develop a class-consciousness that would eventually lead to worker control of the state. Their efforts to convert the Knights of Labor into a revolutionary movement by what was called "boring from within" failed, and in December 1895, members of the Knights sympathetic to the Socialist Labor Party met in New York City to establish the Socialist Trade and Labor Alliance (STLA), an effort to establish a revolutionary trade movement in the United States that would compete, in each industry, with the more conservative unions of the American Federation of Labor.

At its 1896 convention, the party endorsed the STLA. In 1905, the Social-Labor Party helped found the Industrial Workers of the World (IWW), an international union. The STLA, at the party's behest, merged with the IWW. However, there was a falling out between DeLeon and the IWW, and DeLeon would form a rival organization, the Workers International Industrial Union, in 1908 (it would disband in 1924).

Following DeLeon's death in 1914, other left-leaning third parties eclipsed the party. In 1944, Edward A. Teichert, the party's presidential candidate, received 45,226 votes (appearing on the ballot in 15 states). In 1964, Eric Hass (who was also the party's presidential candidate in 1952, 1956, and 1960) polled 45,187 votes (on the ballot in 16 states), more than any other third party candidate. In 1972, the ticket of Louis Fisher and Genevieve Gunderson polled 53,851 votes (appearing on the ballot in 12 states), the most in the party's history. However, four years later, the party's ticket of Jules Levin and Constance Blomen received 9,265 votes in 10 states. Since that time, the party has not run a presidential candidate, claiming that restrictive state ballot access laws and the expense of national campaigns forced the party to focus its efforts on campaigns for offices at the state and local level.

In 1980, the party's Minnesota affiliates, claiming that a small authoritarian group dominated the party, left to form the New Union Party. The Social-Labor Party's goal is what it calls:

> … a classless society that is based on collective ownership and control of the industries and social services, these to be administered in the interests of all society through a Socialist Industrial Union government composed of democratically elected representatives from all the industries and services of the land.

The party platform calls for the abolition of capitalism. The party holds a national convention every two years. The convention elects national officers and a seven-member national executive committee. The National Secretary is Robert Bills, who has held the office since 1980. The party is headquartered in Mountain View, California.

SEE ALSO: Eight-Hour Day; Socialist Party; Third Parties.

BIBLIOGRAPHY. Frank Girard and Ben Perry, *Socialist Labor Party, 1876–1991: A Short History* (Livra Books, 1991); Eric Hass, *The Socialist Labor Party and the Internationals* (New York Labor News Co., 1949); Henry Kuhn, *The Socialist Labor Party During Four Decades: 1890–1930* (New York Labor News Company, 1931); L.G. Seratan, *Daniel Deleon: The Odyssey of an American Marxist* (Harvard University Press, 1979).

JEFFREY KRAUS
WAGNER COLLEGE

Social Security

SOCIAL SECURITY HAS often been a political campaign issue in presidential and congressional elections. Social Security has been referred to as the Third Rail of American politics, meaning that if political candidates attempt to advocate benefit changes or reductions, they will suffer defeat at the polls. The election of President Franklin D. Roosevelt in 1932 provided a focus on the issue of social insurance that eventually resulted in the enactment of the Social Security Act of 1935. In each of the successive presidential election cycles, Social Security has been a campaign issue in American politics, which has often resulted into expansions and modifications of the current system.

ADVOCACY GROUPS

Prior to the enactment of Social Security in 1935, the issue attracted the attention of a variety of political leaders and spawned a diverse group of state and national advocacy groups. President Roosevelt made a political calculation that enactment of a national social insurance program would benefit his Democratic Party at the polls in successive elections. In the midst of the Great Depression, Roosevelt's party enacted a host of legislation aimed at helping Americans that were devastated by the economic collapse of the 1930s. Social Security became a central campaign issue for Roosevelt, which allowed his party to control the White House and Congress for more than two decades.

In successive election cycles, both major political parties advocated continuing Social Security, and even expanding provisions of the program. The electoral pressures to expand benefits began to grow, and in 1950, the Congress and President Harry S. Truman enacted a Cost of Living Adjustment or COLA that increased monthly benefit payments. The 1964 election cycle brought about a landslide electoral victory for President Lyndon B. Johnson. This allowed an overwhelmingly Democratic-controlled Congress to enact the Medicare program in 1965, guaranteeing health care coverage to Social Security recipients. This was a major expansion of the entitlement provisions of the Social Security Act that many scholars concluded was motivated by the electoral calculations of Congress and the president. Benefit and program cost increases continued during the administration of President Richard M. Nixon when the cost of living and the effects of inflation became a campaign issue in the 1972 and 1974 election cycles. Congress enacted a formal procedure that made automatic COLA adjustments to the program beginning in 1975. As a result, the current 46 million recipients receive an automatic annual increase in monthly checks based upon cost of living and inflation calculations from the U.S Bureau of Labor Statistics.

However, academics, government economists, and actuaries from the Social Security Administration began to signal potential shortfalls in the program in the 1980s that eventually led to the creation of a formal commission to study the potential liabilities of the program. The 1983 Commission, chaired by Alan Greenspan, concluded that the solvency of the program was at stake and urged the Congress to make changes to protect future beneficiaries. Many of the 1983 Commission recommendations were enacted into law, which would eventually raise the eligibility age above 65. During this period of time, advocacy groups, such as the American Association of Retired Persons (AARP), fiercely defended the entitlement provisions of the Social Security Act and used their constituency to either help or punish candidates who attempted to change the major provisions of Social Security. AARP and similar senior citizen groups continue to be a major political force in federal elections.

POLITICAL RAMIFICATIONS

The political ramifications of Social Security and the Medicare program are evidenced by the continued program support of both major political parties. Public opinion data confirm the popularity of the program among the current 46 million beneficiaries and the voting public at large. The elections of 2000 and 2004 demonstrated the political importance of the program; Congress expanded the Medicare program to include a new entitlement for prescription drugs. President George W. Bush advocated this expansion of Medicare along with Republican candidates for Congress, which enacted the new prescription drug entitlement in 2003.

The trustees of the Social Security Trust Fund have issued reports that expect the program to begin paying more out in benefits than they are taking in through taxes in the coming decades. Most academic and professional economists who have studied Social Security and Medicare financing indicate there will be significant fiscal pressures by 2040, when there will be only three taxpayers supporting each beneficiary. By most estimates, including that of the Congressional Budget Office, at current program entitlement levels, the Social Security and Medicare program could comprise almost 50 percent of all federal spending by 2050. Given the past political pressures associated with increasing and enhancing existing benefits, the political realities and electoral pressures on the president and Congress will be tested. Academicians, business interests, and groups that advocate for senior citizens and current Social Security beneficiaries have advanced a wide variety of reform efforts. It is anticipated that reform initiatives will continue to proliferate in political campaigns as the solvency of Social Security is questioned.

SEE ALSO: Age and Voting Behavior; Domestic Policy; Great Depression and Realignment; Healthcare; Senior Citizens Issues; Social Security Reform.

BIBLIOGRAPHY. J. Baggette, R.Y. Shapiro, and L.R. Jacobs, "Poll trends: Social Security, An Update," *Public Opinion Quarterly* (v.59, 1995); E.D. Berkowitz, *America's Welfare State: From Roosevelt to Reagan* (Johns Hopkins University Press, 1991); Congressional Budget Office, *Social Security: A Primer* (U.S. Government Printing Office, 2001); Larry DeWitt, *A Historical Background and Development of Social Security* (Social Security Administration, Office of the Historian, 2003).

DAVID RANDALL
KENT STATE UNIVERSITY

Social Security Reform

SOCIAL SECURITY REFORM is an issue that political leaders in Washington, D.C., do not like to deal with because there are 46 million current program beneficiaries and, thus, the potential for adverse political consequences of reform is great. However, there have been a variety of reform proposals in recent years concerning Social Security. Since the inception of the program in 1935, successive congresses and presidents have campaigned on, and eventually enacted, reforms based largely on the demands of their constituents.

In recent years, more political attention has been focused on the solvency of the Social Security system as a large number of potential beneficiaries will retire in the coming decades. The future of Social Security has become a campaign issue as a result of those demographic and fiscal pressures.

Reforming Social Security is often a campaign issue in federal elections. In the 1960s and 1970s, the issue became prevalent as President Lyndon Johnson advocated a healthcare program for those over the age of 65 that became the Medicare program in 1965. Cost of Living Adjustments (COLAs) also became a campaign issue that Congress addressed in 1973, by enacting automatic increases in monthly benefit payments tied to data supplied by the U.S. Bureau of Labor Statistics. Both of these issues become relevant as new reforms to the entitlement nature and fiscal solvency of Social Security and Medicare have both become campaign and political issues.

MEDICARE MODERNIZATION
During the 2000 election cycle, candidate George W. Bush advocated an expansion of Medicare by adding a prescription drug entitlement program. After Bush won the election, Congress enacted the Medicare Modernization Act of 2003, marking the largest expansion of Social Security benefits since the 1965 enactment of Medicare.

During this period, the Bush administration convened a commission to study the future solvency and program viability of Social Security. By most estimates from economists and academics, the Social Security system will experience fiscal stress by at least 2040, based upon projected beneficiaries and monthly entitlement payments. As a result of these studies, President George W. Bush proposed a partial privatization of Social Security to allow individuals to manage and own their accounts. Advocacy groups, including the American Association of Retired Persons (AARP), objected and the Congress did not enact any of the provisions advocated by President Bush.

The political strength of advocacy groups and the political activity of Social Security and Medicare beneficiaries give pause to members of Congress and even presidential candidates in proposing reforms that could potentially cost them political support and, ultimately, electoral success.

Beyond the proposal by President George W. Bush to partially privatize Social Security accounts, there are numerous proposals that have been discussed by candidates for federal office. The issues discussed in political campaigns include: raising the retirement age for Social Security eligibility from age 65; establishing a means or income test for Medicare benefits; adjusting the automatic nature of COLAs yearly increases; and allowing for a partial privatization of Social Security funds held by the government or by individuals as the Bush administration has advocated.

Public opinion, as a major influence on electoral outcomes, does not support any major reform of the current system of benefits that includes benefit reduction or a form of account privatization. Unless public sentiment were to support one or more of the reform initiatives, it is unlikely that Congress or any future president will risk political defeat to change the current system in any manner that would potentially harm current beneficiaries or anger senior citizen advocates. However, many public opinion surveys indicate that future beneficiaries do not believe that Social Security will be able to pay monthly benefits to them when they become eligible. In short, the ramification of electoral politics has a direct relationship to policy outcomes based on the nature, influence, and scope of the interests associated with reforming Social Security.

In the 2008 election cycle, the issue of Social Security reform has not emerged as a major issue of importance with candidates for president from either the Democratic or Republican parties. As in past election cycles, candidates for Congress will emphasize their support for the program, maintenance of the status quo benefit structure, and even marginal expansion of the program.

While the near-term prospects for reforming Social Security may not be prevalent, the various reports issued by government commissions, interest groups, and academics will continue to bring political attention to the fiscal stability of Social Security and related benefit programs.

SEE ALSO: Age and Voting Behavior; Domestic Policy; Great Depression and Realignment; Healthcare; Senior Citizens Issues; Social Security Reform.

BIBLIOGRAPHY: R.D. Arnold, "The Politics of Reforming Social Security," *Political Science Quarterly* (v.113, 1998); J. Baggette, R.Y. Shapiro, and L.R. Jacobs, "Poll Trends: Social Security—An Update," *Public Opinion Quarterly* (v.59, 1995); E.D. Berkowitz, *America's Welfare State: From Roosevelt to Reagan* (Johns Hopkins University Press, 1991); J. Cogan and O.S. Mitchell, "Perspectives from the President's Commission on Social Security Reform," *Journal of Economic Perspectives* (v.17, 2003); Congressional Budget Office, *Social Security: A Primer* (U.S Government Printing Office, 2001); Larry DeWitt, *A Historical Background and Development of Social Security* (Social Security Administration, Office of the Historian, 2003).

DAVID RANDALL
KENT STATE UNIVERSITY

South Carolina

THE FIRST EUROPEAN settlers in South Carolina came from Barbados and other islands in the 1670s, followed by the arrival of French Huguenots. Pioneers from Pennsylvania and Virginia opened up inland South Carolina, and South Carolina was proclaimed a royal colony in 1729. It took a leading role in the American War of Independence, and was the first state to ratify the first U.S. Constitution, the Articles of Confederation, and became the 8th state of the Union on May 23, 1788. Initially elections in South Carolina, as stipulated in the state's 1776 constitution, were conducted to elect the General Assembly of the state, which, in turn, elected the president (the office was renamed governor in 1778). This meant that the General Assembly, which consisted of a senate and a house of representatives, remained all-powerful. Prior to the 1964 Supreme Court ruling in *Reynolds v. Sims*, a senator represented each county in the state, and each county elected at least one member of the House of Representatives based on the population of the county.

The presidents elected under the Constitution of 1776 were John Rutledge and Rawlins Lowndes, the former a brother to a signatory to the U.S. Declaration of Independence and himself a signatory to the U.S. Constitution, and the latter, born in the West Indian island of St. Kitts, was a lawyer who was a prisoner of the British during the part of the American War of Independence. Under the Constitution of 1778, John Rutledge was elected for a second term, followed by two lawyers, two soldiers, and Charles Pinckney, a soldier who was the son of a lawyer, and also another signatory to the U.S. Constitution. Although the Constitution was revised in 1790, the election of the governor was still through the General Assembly, which also decided on the allocation of the electors for the Electoral College in U.S. presidential elections. That the state representatives and the senators could not only chose the executive officials of the state, but also decided on whom the state would support in presidential elections, made South Carolina unique.

Although African Americans were not able to vote in South Carolina until after the U.S. Civil War (prior to the war the vast majority of them were slaves) South Carolina was the first state to adopt the system of allowing white male suffrage in elections. It was a move introduced early in the career of John Caldwell Calhoun, the politician most identified with the state from the 1820s until the 1840s. He believed passionately in states rights, and also in the rights of minorities, such as slave-owners. Calhoun was the U.S. secretary of war 1817–25, and 1825–32 he was the seventh vice president of the United States, serving under John Quincy Adams and Andrew Jackson. Calhoun first entered politics as a member of the South Carolina General Assembly, before moving to Washington, D.C., as a member of the House of Representatives 1811–17, and then in the cabinet and as vice president for the next 15 years, the U.S. Senate for the next 18 years, excepting just under a year when he was U.S. secretary of state. Calhoun's major contribution to U.S. politics was his concept of Nullification, by which any state legislature could nullify any laws that it did not like.

Although this was initially tested over federal tariffs in 1832, the real test obviously would be to block any attempt to abolish slavery. Calhoun was a figure of controversy throughout the United States, hated by northerners and beloved by southerners, elected and re-elected on many occasions. Calhoun's articulate defense of minority rights (in this case, slave-owners), was later used by the Civil Rights Movement in the United States, campaigning for equal rights for the African-American minority.

VOTING PATTERNS

The General Assembly of South Carolina, after the introduction of its Constitution of 1790, elected two Federalists, and then 1796–1826 elected Democratic-Republicans, and then from 1828 until the American Civil War elected Democratic governors. Although the original 1776 Constitution did allow for governors to be elected for two consecutive terms, this was amended, and during this period not only were governors not allowed to serve a consecutive term, but they also could not return to office until four years after their previous term had ended.

Only two governors during this period were to hold office twice. In presidential elections, South Carolina remained the only state where the people did not vote. The General Assembly put the state's votes, in 1860, clearly behind John Breckinridge of the southern Democrats. When news of Abraham Lincoln's victory reached South Carolina, the General Assembly immediately issued a call for elections for a secession convention. However, initially secession was not certain as soon

after the presidential election, the General Assembly voted to rejecct the secessionist and fire-eater Robert Rhett as governor. Instead they chose Francis W. Pickens, a moderate, for the governorship. However, in spite of the choice of Pickens, when the secession convention gathered at Charleston on December 20, the 169 delegates voted for South Carolina to secede, which took place later that day.

CONFEDERATE STATE

During the American Civil War, South Carolina was one of the most robust members of the Confederate States. After being invaded and occupied by Union soldiers, in 1865 a new constitution was promulgated that called for the direct election of the governor, although the franchise continued to be restricted to white males. In the election on October 18, 1865, James Lawrence Orr was the first governor of South Carolina to be elected by the people. Orr represented no party, and in office for slightly less than three years. When South Carolina refused to adopt the Fourteenth Amendment to the U.S. Constitution, ensuring equal rights for all people regardless of race, a temporary military government was established in the state, and the 1868 constitution was drawn up. This continued the practice of the governor's election by all male citizens above the age of 18, with no reference to race; a governor was now allowed a maximum of two consecutive terms.

Only three months after the surrender of Robert E. Lee at Appomattox, African Americans met in a convention in South Carolina and provided the impetus for the establishment of the South Carolina Republican Party in 1867. African Americans and whites worked together in the party, electing Robert Kingston Scott as the first Republican governor of South Carolina; he took office in July 1868. Scott was re-elected in 1870, and was the first governor of the state to serve two consecutive terms. In the 1870 election, the turnout was 136,608, and Scott had a comfortable majority of 33,534 votes over his Democrat opponent. He survived an impeachment attempt in 1871, and in the 1872 election, Franklin J. Moses Jr. was elected as the second Republican governor, holding office for one term, and succeeded by Daniel Henry Chamberlain, another Republican, who also held office for one term.

The return of the Democrats to the governorship only happened in 1876 when Wade Hampton III, a

Confederate cavalry officer, was elected as the first successful southern gubernatorial candidate to have run on a platform of total opposition to Reconstruction. The 1876 elections were particularly violent, with supporters of the incumbent governor, Chamberlain, who was running against Hampton, regularly being involved in street battles with Hampton supporters. The results were so close that both parties claimed victory. There were also two rival legislatures in the state, which led to even more trouble, until that was finally resolved in April 1877. Most historians now recognize that Hampton's victory relied on the mass intimidation of African-American voters, with Governor Chamberlain unable to protect his own supporters.

DEMOCRATIC GOVERNORS

The Democrats also benefited from the withdrawal of Union soldiers, many of whom would have voted Republican, in spite of the Board of Canvassers invalidating ballots which came from counties where voting fraud was believed to have taken place. Even when President Ulysses S. Grant did finally send in soldiers, they were unwilling to become too involved. During Hampton's first term, he helped introduce tactics that made it harder for African Americans to vote. He was re-elected in 1878, but resigned from the governorship in the following year to serve two terms in the U.S. Senate. From Hampton's victory in 1876 until the gubernatorial election of 1974, the Democrats won the governorship at each election. Many governors served one or two terms, with a few, such as Hugh Smith Thompson, moving to Washington, D.C., in his case as assistant secretary of the Treasury. A level of unity in the state marked Thompson's governorship, with his nomination by the Democratic Party unchallenged.

Although the Democrats won the gubernatorial elections, their control of the state legislature was not entirely taken for granted. In 1881, when the Republicans and Independents combined to win the state elections in Virginia, the Republicans in South Carolina tried to win over the Progressives, but lost the 1882 state legislature elections. The 1890 gubernatorial election was particularly notable, with Benjamin Tillman taking over the South Carolina Farmers Alliance and using it as a platform for his political career. The election was not fought on the issue of race, but between agrarian interests and the Bourbon Democrats. Part of this was because the Republican Party posed little threat; the real

contest was the Democratic Party's state primary. In this campaign, Tillman managed to get the support of poor whites who were worried about agrarian reform, and these votes enabled him to defeat his Democratic Party rival, Alexander Haskell.

In the 1920s, Cole L. Blease emerged as a powerful political force in the South Carolina senate, winning the elections in 1924, and urging maintenance of the policy of state isolation. However, it was his final victory; the Democrat Party, nationwide, changed dramatically during the presidency of Franklin D. Roosevelt. This manifested itself in South Carolina as a shift from the control of the state Democrat Party by farmers from the western counties. In 1938, the victory of Burnett Rhett Maybank, an aristocrat from Charleston who supported Roosevelt, in the primary for the gubernatorial elections, over Wyndham Meredith Manning, a farmer from the west, confirmed this.

In the 1960 U.S. presidential election, the Democratic Party saw South Carolina as a "barometer" state. The cities voted overwhelmingly Republican, but the countryside continued to be Democratic Party heartland, with the state going to John F. Kennedy by 198,129 votes (51.2 percent) to 188,558 for Richard M. Nixon. However, by 1964, voting patterns changed considerably. With Lyndon B. Johnson urging for greater rights for African Americans, and race the dominant issue, the state voted for Barry Goldwater of the Republican Party, giving him 309,048 votes (58.9 percent) to Johnson's 215,700. It was the first time since the Reconstruction period that the Republicans had won such a victory in the state. Despite being courted heavily by George Wallace in the 1968 U.S. presidential election, South Carolina voted for Richard M. Nixon by 254,062 votes (38.1 percent) to Wallace's 215,430 votes (32.3 percent), and Hubert H. Humphrey picking up 197,486 votes (29.6 percent). With South Carolina voting Republican again in 1972 (as did all but one state of the Union), it was only a matter of time before a Republican governor was elected.

In the 1974 gubernatorial elections, James Burrows Edwards was elected as South Carolina's first Republican governor since 1876, and he remained governor until 1979. Richard W. Riley of the Democrats won the 1978 gubernatorial elections, and also served for eight years, with the Republicans in office since 1987, with the exception of the period from January 1999 until January 2003, when James H. "Jim" Hodges of the Democrats was governor. Mark Sanford was elected governor in 2002, defeating Lieutenant Governor Bob Peeler in the Republican Primary, and Jim Hodges in the election, by 53 percent to 47 percent.

SEE ALSO: African-American Suffrage; African-American Vote; Democratic-Republican Party; Slavery; Suffrage.

BIBLIOGRAPHY. Martin Abbott, "Freedom's Cry: Negroes and Their Meetings in South Carolina, 1865–1869," *Phylon* (v.20/3, 1959); B.M. Barnes, "Southern Independents: South Carolina, 1882," *South Carolina Historical Magazine* (v.96/3, 1995); M.L. Cann, "The End of a Political Myth: The South Carolina Gubernatorial Campaign of 1938," *South Carolina Historical Magazine* (v.72/3, 1971); W.J. Cooper, Jr., "Economics or Race: an analysis of the Gubernatorial Election of 1890 in South Carolina," *South Carolina Historical Magazine* (v.73/4, 1972); *William Cooper, The Conservative Regime: South Carolina, 1877–1890* (University of South Carolina Press, 2005); D.W. Hollis, "Cole L. Blease and the Senatorial Campaign of 1924," *Proceedings of the South Carolina Historical Association* (1978); *B.H. Kalk, The Origins of the Southern Strategy: Two-Party Competition in South Carolina, 1950–1972* (Lexington Books, 2001); R.F. King, "Counting the Votes: South Carolina's Stolen Election of 1876," *Journal of Interdisciplinary History* (v.32/2, 2001); P.M. Mercer, "Tapping the Slave Narrative Collection for the Responses of Black South Carolinians to Emancipation and Reconstruction," *Australian Journal of Politics and History* (v.25/3, 1979); Diane Neal, "Agrarian Reform Versus Bourbon Democracy: The South Carolina Gubernatorial Campaign of 1890," *Proceedings of the South Carolina Historical Association* (1983); J.B. Scroggs, "Carpetbagger Constitutional Reform in the South Atlantic States, 1867–1868," *Journal of Southern History* (v.27/4, 1961).

JUSTIN CORFIELD
GEELONG GRAMMAR SCHOOL, AUSTRALIA

South Dakota

THE STATE OF South Dakota has been inhabited by Native Americans for several thousand years; the first European explorers, mainly French, visited the territory in the 18th century. In 1803, South Dakota, still largely unexplored by Europeans, was part of the Louisiana Purchase and became a part of the United States. It was visited during the Lewis and Clark Expedition, with the U.S. army setting up outposts in the 1850s. In 1856, Sioux Falls was established, with Yankton three years later. In the meantime, in 1858, the Yankton Sioux had been forced to sign a treaty ceding most of their lands. The Dakota Territory, as it was known at the time, had few European settlers until the discovery of gold in the Black Hills in 1874 during an expedition by Colonel George A. Custer. When the Sioux refused to grant mining rights or land in the Black Hills, skirmishes began between prospectors and Native Americans, leading to major fighting, with Custer being killed at the Battle of the Little Bighorn in June 1876, but the Native Americans eventually losing. Railroads were built across the Dakotas, and on December 29, 1890, the Massacre at Wounded Knee saw the killing of 300 Sioux, many of whom were women and children.

On November 2, 1889, South Dakota and North Dakota were admitted as states to the Union with Arthur C. Mellette, a Republican, elected as the first governor. From 1889 until 1974 the governor served a two-year term, with the number of consecutive terms limited to two in the 1940s, although in 1974 the governor's term was extended to four years, they were still allowed to serve only two consecutive terms. Arthur Mellette was from Indiana and had moved west when his wife fell ill, and hoped to find a more conducive climate for her. In November 1885, he ran unopposed for the office of governor of the Dakota Territory and in 1889 when voters approved the new constitution for South Dakota, just prior to statehood, they also elected him as governor.

In 1892, at the state Republican Convention, Charles H. Sheldon was nominated for governor. He had also moved to the Dakota Territory to seek a better climate, in his case, for his son. In the subsequent gubernatorial elections, the first after the granting of statehood, Sheldon defeated A.L. Van Osdel, an Independent, and Peter Couchman of the Democrat Party. In 1896, the Norwegian-born Andrew E. Lee was elected governor of South Dakota for the Populist Party. Lee then won re-election two years later. In that election, the 1898 gubernatorial elections ex-governor Charles Sheldon was asked to go on a speaking tour, but caught a cold during it and died of pneumonia five days after his last speech at Deadwood on October 15, 1898. Although the Populists at their convention in Sioux

Falls nominated Lee for Congress, he lost in a Republican landslide that ended the short political influence of the Populist Party in South Dakota, with many of its adherents later joining the Democratic Party. The 1898 elections were also important, as they were the first time that any state in the Union allowed citizens to vote on policy propositions.

From 1900 until 1926, the Republicans won every gubernatorial election. The careers of some of the governors explain the nature of politics at the time. Frank M. Byrne, who was governor 1913–17, was from a family of poor Irish migrants. He entered politics when a in dispute over the county seat of Potter County, he took part in a raiding to take the county records from Forest City to Gettysburg. Two other Republican governors, Peter Norbeck and Carl Gunderson, were both born in Vermillion in what was then the Dakota Territory (now South Dakota), to Norwegian migrants. Subsequently, there were six more governors of Norwegian ancestry, all of them Republicans. Sigurd Anderson (governor 1951–55) was born in Norway, while George T. Mickelson (governor 1947–51; whose son George S. Mickelson was governor 1987–93), Joe Foss (governor 1955–59), and Archie M. Gubbrud (governor 1961–65) all had Norwegian fathers. Leslie Jensen's (governor 1937–39) family was Danish.

FIRST DEMOCRATIC GOVERNOR

In the gubernatorial elections in 1926, William J. Bulow was elected as the first Democratic governor of South Dakota, and received the highest vote achieved by any Democratic Party candidate up to that time. After his period as governor, he served two terms in the U.S. Senate. Warren Green, the next governor, faced an enormous state debt and had to introduce tax reforms, budget cuts, and reduce government salaries by 10–20 percent. He lost the 1932 gubernatorial election to Thomas Matthew "Tom" Berry, who was re-elected as governor in 1934. In 1936, Berry lost while attempting to get an unprecedented third term, defeated by Republican Leslie Jensen. In the 1938 gubernatorial elections, he managed to defeat U.S. Senator Herbert Hitchcock in the primary for the Democratic Party, but lost the election itself to Chan Gurney. In 1942, he again won a closely-fought Democratic Party primary, defeating the incumbent senator, William J. Bulow, and then lost the subsequent gubernatorial battle against Harlan J. Bushfield.

In the 1960 U.S. presidential election, South Dakota voted strongly for Richard M. Nixon with 178,017 votes (58.21 percent) going to the Republicans, and Kennedy getting 128,070 votes (41.79 percent). In that year, at the gubernatorial elections, Archie M. Grubbrud won for the Republican Party. Four years later, Lyndon B. Johnson easily carried South Dakota in the presidential elections with 163,010 votes (55.61 percent) against Goldwater's 130,108 votes (44.39 percent). That a Republican won the gubernatorial contest at the same time showed the Republican Party machine the unpopularity of Goldwater. In the 1968 presidential election, Richard M. Nixon won the state with 149,841 votes (53.3 percent), with Hubert Humphrey, who had been born in the state, getting 118,023 votes (42 percent), and George Wallace getting the remaining 4.7 percent.

REPUBLICAN RECORD

Since 1968, South Dakota has always voted Republican in presidential elections. However, during the 1968 elections George Wallace gained 13,400 votes (4.7 percent); in 1980, Independent John Anderson gained 21,431 votes (6.5 percent), in 1992, Ross Perot gained 73,295 votes (21.8 percent), and in 1996, the Reform Party managed to gain 31,250 votes (9.65 percent). In spite of the Republicans winning the state in the presidential elections, there have been two Democratic governors. Richard F. Kneip was a governor from the Democratic Party 1971–78. When he resigned to become ambassador to Singapore, Harvey L. Wollman completed his unexpired term. Kniep, on his first election, was the youngest person ever to be governor in South Dakota, and his success at winning re-election in 1972 and again in 1974 owed much to his election campaign style, which was well-organized and resulted from an overhaul of the state party machine. In 1978, William J. Janklow was elected as governor and won a second term in 1982, and 1995–2003 served two more consecutive terms, making him the longest-serving governor in South Dakota politics, and the only one to win four gubernatorial elections.

SEE ALSO: North Dakoka; Populist Party and Populist Movements.

BIBLIOGRAPHY. R.F. Durden, *Reconstruction Bonds & Twentieth Century Politics: South Dakota vs North Carolina* (Duke

University Press, 1962); A.L. Clem, *Prairie State Politics: Popular Democracy in South Dakota* (Public Affairs Press, 1967); A.L. Clem, *Government by the People?: South Dakota in the Last Third of the Twentieth Century* (Chiesman Foundation for Democracy, 2002); J.G. Matsusaka, "Direct Democracy Works," *Journal of Economic Perspectives* (v.19/2, 2005).

JUSTIN CORFIELD
GEELONG GRAMMAR SCHOOL, AUSTRALIA

Southern Democratic Party

THE DEMOCRATIC PARTY in the south has had a complex, oftentimes problematic past. It had its modern start in the pursuit and maintenance of white supremacy, was transformed, sometimes painfully, into the party of reform and equal rights, and continues with faction-ridden, locally charged, and fractious politics. From the end of Reconstruction in the 1870s, through the early 1960s, the south, as defined as the states that succeeded from the Union prior to the Civil War, was almost entirely dominated by the Democratic Party. The Democrats held the solid south through a sharply narrow states' rights agenda wholly consumed with the preservation of the white elites at the expense of African-American opportunity. The national party winked at this central agenda in return for solid support for the national Democratic Party, particularly in presidential elections, but also in the Congress in terms of loyalty to the party policy agenda.

This coalition between southern white supremacists and an increasingly liberal national party held, almost seamlessly, until the end of World War II. When Democratic President Harry Truman commissioned an inquiry into the state of civil rights in the south in the late 1940s, the first cracks began to appear between the national and southern state Democrats. Truman's re-election effort in 1948 saw the defection of four southern states (South Carolina, Alabama, Mississippi, and Louisiana) under the banner of South Carolina's Senator J. Strom Thurmond's Dixiecrats (States' Rights Party): in Louisiana, Truman did not even appear on the ballot.

Further fissures appeared after the 1954 *Brown v. Topeka Board of Education* (often shortened to *Brown v. Board*) Supreme Court ruling, signaling the beginning of the end of segregation in southern schools. As the decade of the 1950s ended, the first signs of a two-party system began to surface. Though Republicans had held small outposts since the Civil War era (mountain Republicans in Tennessee and North Carolina, for example, who had opposed secession), no Republican had won statewide office in the deep south until John Tower was elected senator from Texas in 1961. The election of John F. Kennedy and Lyndon Johnson (a southerner himself) saw some defections, but it was the public support of the voting rights movement in the south by the national party that fired up open political warfare between southerners and their northern and western counterparts.

The passage of the Civil Rights Act (1964) and the Voting Rights Act (1965) during the Johnson administration signaled the end of the total dominance of white elites over the electoral process in the south. For decades, the state Democratic parties, as private associations, had had total control over the party and, by fiat, over the party's primary elections: in a solidly Democratic south. These "white primaries" sometimes explicitly excluded African Americans from the voting process; while the strategies were more covert (for example, through the use of rigged literacy tests and dizzyingly complex registration processes) they were nonetheless very effective at disfranchising the African-American population. The Voting Rights Act effectively ended the period of legal restrictions on African-American political activity, though many would argue that years would pass before there was effective enfranchisement of African Americans.

The Democratic Party, which emerged from the turmoil of the 1960s, was a very different party than the organization that had preceded it. As the GOP gained ground in the south, southern Democrats moved to appeal to African Americans, both as voters and as candidates. Many African Americans, wary of the conservatism of the Republican Party at the national level, moved quickly to consolidate their position in the resultant coalition between New Democrats and the national party of the 1970s and 1980s. Though many conservative Democrats remained in the party during the 1980s, this was also a period of party switching in which some more traditionally-minded whites left the party and joined the more ideologically heterogeneous Republicans. For some, this signaled the end of their careers (Governor "Buddy" Roemer III of Louisiana, a popular legislator and Democratic officeholder, was unceremoniously pitched from the governor's chair after his conversion), but many (House member, then Senator, Phil Graham of Texas, for example) went on to great success without taking a political breath. The Democratic Party of the 1990s and 2000s has been a very successful and competitive blend of liberal urbanites and more populist conservative voters and candidates from the rural areas.

SEE ALSO: Democratic Party; States' Rights Party (Dixiecrats); Thurmond, J. Strom.

BIBLIOGRAPHY. E. Black and M. Black, *Politics and Society in the South* (Harvard University Press, 1987); V.O. Key, Jr., *Southern Politics: In State and Nation* (Alfred A. Knopf, 1949); A.P. Lamis, *The Two-Party South* (Oxford University Press, 1984); W. Parent, *Inside the Carnival: Unmasking Louisiana Politics* (Louisiana State University Press, 2004).

R. Bruce Anderson, Ph.D.
Baker University

Special Election

A SPECIAL ELECTION, sometimes called a by-election, is an election held to fill a political office that has become vacant between regularly scheduled elections. Such a vacancy can occur as the result of the death or resignation of the incumbent, or because the incumbent has become ineligible for office due to a recall, felony conviction, or another disqualifying event. The rules governing whether a special election must be held following a vacancy, and the conduct of a special election, vary considerably across jurisdictions. The most common special elections are those held to fill vacancies in legislative bodies, including the U.S. Congress and state legislatures.

The most visible special elections in the United States are those to fill vacancies in the U.S. Congress. The Constitution requires a special election to fill all vacancies in the House of Representatives, although it allows each state to determine its own election procedures. The filling of vacancies in the Senate is governed by the Seventeenth Amendment, which requires a special election, unless a state's legislature has empowered a governor to make a temporary appointment to fill the Senate vacancy until it is filled by an election as directed by the legislature.

The results of special legislative elections are often viewed as a bellwether for the outcome of the next midterm or general election, especially as a referendum on the performance of the president. However, the dynamics of special legislative elections generally resemble open-seat elections where local candidate and constituent preferences often shape the outcome more than national factors. The level of partisan change in special elections is the same as in open seat elections.

Special elections are an important source of turnover in Congress, where incumbents enjoy a very high rate of re-election. Because special elections occur outside the normal election cycle, they offer a useful way to study the effects of sudden, unexpected changes in representation. Traditionally underrepresented groups have successfully utilized special elections to increase their ratio of membership in the U.S. House. This is especially true for women. Nearly a third of women entering the House in the 1980s and 1990s won their seats in special elections.

SEE ALSO: Election Laws, Federal Elections; Election Laws, State and Local Elections.

BIBLIOGRAPHY. F.B. Feigert and Pippa Norris, "Do By-Elections Constitute Referenda," *Legislative Studies Quarterly* (May, 1990); R.K. Gaddie and C.S. Bullock III, "Structural and Elites Features in Open Sat and Special U.S. House Elections: Is there a Sexual Bias?," *Political Research Quarterly* (June, 1997); R.K. Gaddie, C.S. Bullock III, and S.E. Buchanan, "What is So Special About Special Elections," *Legislative Studies Quarterly* (February, 1999); D.L. Nixon and R. Darcy, "Special Elections and the Growth of Women's Representation in the U.S. House of Representatives," *Women and Politics* (October, 1996).

Eric H. Hines
University of Montana

Special Interests

INTEREST GROUPS HAVE a long history of involvement in American campaigns and elections, but the nature of that involvement has changed considerably over the years. In addition, campaign reforms since the early 1970s have made more information available concerning some facets of group involvement. Some aspects of group involvement are visible, but other aspects are less likely to be noticed by the average citizen. Much of the typical group's focus is on the campaigns of candidates, but in recent years have witnessed increasing interest group involvement in initiative, referendum, and recall campaigns.

CAMAIGN RESOURCES

Some of the most visible and widely discussed interest group actions in campaigns involve providing campaign resources to candidates or parties. The most controversial of those resources is money. Since World War II, interest-group funding of campaigns has risen dramatically, although some of the apparent increase is due to improved reporting requirements. However, much of the conventional reporting of interest group funding emphasizes contributions from political action committees (PACs), the vast majority of which are affiliated with interest groups. Unfortunately, those numbers understate the amount of interest-group money in campaigns.

First, a group may encourage its members to contribute as individuals. If the members include a letter with their donation or identify their professions and employers on the contribution forms, the recipients will know that some donors are autoworkers, realtors, chiropractors, or bankers.

Second, a group may sponsor a fundraising reception or dinner in order to help a candidate raise money. A smaller group may sponsor one or more tables at a large reception. Much of the money raised in that fashion will be officially classified as being from individuals, but the candidate or party receiving the money will know of the group's involvement. Third, one or more group members may collect contributions from colleagues in the group and then pass the contributions along to the preferred candidate or party.

Groups desiring more direct policy impact may provide funding for initiative, referendum, and recall campaigns. A group may help to finance signature gathering for initiative or recall campaigns (where state laws permit the use of paid signature-gatherers).

If the proposal qualifies for a public vote, interest-group contributions may help to finance advertisements and other expenses of the referendum or recall campaigns. In some cases, the group may set up an organization with a somewhat misleading name ("Citizens for Insurance Reform" when the group is actually from the insurance industry) if that name may be politically beneficial.

Groups with large numbers of members, especially highly-motivated ones, may provide volunteer workers to assist with a campaign. Many campaigns suffer from a severe shortage of volunteers, who can perform all sorts of tasks, including campaigning door-to-door, staffing telephone banks, and prepare literature for mailing. Organized labor has traditionally been a significant source of campaign volunteers, but many other groups also provide some campaign helpers.

Some groups also provide in-kind resources for campaigns, although that practice appears to be less common than giving money. A group may provide polling data to help a candidate develop a clearer picture of public sentiments, including the public's views of other candidates and preferences on major issues. A group may provide transportation to assist a candidate's travels around the state or country. Some groups also provide research support: an analysis of one or more policy proposals or the public record of a political rival may be a great help to a candidate.

If a group has reached the maximum amount that it can give to a given candidate or party, both as a group and by its individual members, there are still ways to provide financial assistance. One option is to contribute money to another organization that will then distribute the money. Many state legislative and congressional leaders have formed leadership PACs that raise money, a good bit of it from interest groups, and then pass much of it on to other legislative candidates.

DONATION LIMIT

An interest group that has reached the donation limits may also provide additional help for a campaign by using so-called independent spending. For example, groups that prepare and run a commercial attacking or praising a candidate, party, or referendum proposal. By 2004, independent spending reached nearly $100 million. In addition to enabling groups to bypass donation limits, independent spending can be used to finance attack ads that may damage one candidate's image without making the favored candidate appear to be mudslinging. That insulation may be especially important if the attack ads are false or misleading, as they sometimes are.

In a variety of ways besides giving money, a group may help to publicize a candidate, party, or viewpoint.

Some of those efforts are relatively visible to the general public, but others have a much lower profile. One relatively visible method is to sponsor a forum for a group of candidates. The forum may be particularly helpful if it attracts coverage from the mass media.

Groups may also help individual candidates gain exposure by inviting them to speak at group meetings or conferences. Those appearances are often ignored by the mass media, but the group may help to publicize the event through its own publications: newsletters, magazines, or electronic communications. Even without a candidate's personal visit, a group may give him or her some publicity through the group's own communication apparatus. Those specialized communications networks connecting people with a common interest are of great value to candidates who want to tailor their messages to topics people care about. Those internal communications systems can also be used for initiative, referendum, and recall campaigns.

GAINING EXPOSURE

Other common devices for helping candidates to gain exposure are interest group endorsements, scorecards or ratings, and hit lists. A group may issue a press release or place an advertisement indicating support for a candidate, rating a candidate on votes or decisions important to the group, or attacking a candidate's record. Those ratings and other evaluations can also be circulated through the group's own internal communications systems, through the mass media, or both. The same devices may be used to spread the group's support or opposition to an initiative, referendum, or recall campaign.

Some of the least visible ways in which interest groups become involved in the electoral process include efforts to encourage people to run for office, begin an initiative campaign, train candidates, and advise candidates and other participants in campaigns. Candidate recruitment may be most critical at the local level, where candidates are sometimes in short supply, especially in smaller communities. Recruitment activities also appear to be somewhat more important for female candidates. They are somewhat less likely than men to be self-starters in running for office.

Groups sometimes try to encourage their own members to run for office in the belief that they are likely to be more supportive of the group's values than are outsiders. The literature on state legislatures mentions the phenomenon of the "legislator-lobbyist": a member of the legislature who is also a member of an interest group. The large number of part-time elected officials in state and, especially, local governments makes recruiting group members as candidates especially attractive. Moreover, many local governments have only a single responsibility, as do school districts; groups can target their member-candidates to the governments specializing in the group's areas of interest. Many school boards have a number of members with ties to the education profession. Many local boards dealing with planning, zoning, and other land use controls have members who are realtors, building developers, and representatives of the financial industry.

In a related vein, a group may help develop a ballot proposal for an initiative campaign or recall effort. The average citizen does not have the skills or the time to develop a ballot proposal. Groups can help to broaden the range of options presented to the public, although groups are likely to place a premium on protecting or advancing their own interests. In addition, groups sometimes create intermediary organizations with names that conceal the groups' involvement.

Some groups also provide training for candidates and political activists. That training is particularly important for candidates who are relative beginners in the political process, and those beginners are especially common at the local level, where many political careers begin. Newcomers are often unfamiliar with many aspects of campaigning, from the costs of running for office to the time commitments, dealing with the media, and coping with hostile questions from individual citizens. A good training program can reduce the risk of mistakes in a campaign and improve its effectiveness.

CAMPAIGN ADVICE

In a related vein, members of a group can give a candidate advice as a campaign proceeds. Even if a candidate begins with a sound campaign plan, unexpected issues or problems may erupt and demand a response. Group members can provide guidance regarding their members' likely reaction to various options, suggestions regarding substantive aspects of the problem, and/or help in dealing with the news media.

The impact of group efforts to influence elections has been studied from a number of perspectives and vantage points. There are noticeable differences of opinion in the literature, but researchers have identified general patterns. Some groups pursue an electoral strategy, in which they try to influence the outcomes of elections. The largest body of research on this aspect of group efforts has focused on campaign contributions and election outcomes. The findings are quite clear: there is a strong relationship between the distribution of campaign funds and the outcomes of elections, particularly for candidates who are not well-known at the beginning of the campaign. Money does not guarantee success; it is only one factor in election outcomes, and not always the most influential. However, poorly-funded campaigns are very likely to end in defeat unless there is no opposition or people are furious at the other candidate.

Efforts to assess the impact of money on election results are complicated by groups that follow an access strategy. These groups are primarily interested in building or maintaining a positive relationship with elected officials. As a result, they tend to funnel money to candidates that are likely to win. Consequently, the causal link between political money and election outcomes may be partially reversed: people who look like they will win find that fundraising is much easier than it is for candidates trailing in the polls. The availability of polling data, coupled with the fact that many elected offices have high re-election rates, make predicting the outcome of many races relatively easy. When a candidate wins unexpectedly, groups pursuing an access strategy will immediately send a contribution, backdating the letter and check to make it appear that it was sent before Election Day.

Research on the impact of the access strategy yields mixed results. Busy elected officials do appear to spend more time with donors than with non-donors, and campaign contributions do appear to give groups more influence over which issues receive attention and which do not. However, the policy impact of giving money and other group support or pressure is sometimes substantial and sometimes weak. There have been instances of multi-pronged group campaigns that helped to reverse or derail a policy or proposal.

However, campaign contributions do not appear to be very successful in changing officials' minds on matters about which they have long-held opinions, unless there is accompanying pressure from the public. However, if a group is successful in electing friendly officials, the group can indirectly exert significant impact on public policies. The beliefs of officials often affect their policy decisions. Putting sympathetic people in office makes influencing their actions much easier.

SEE ALSO: Campaign Finance, Politics of; McCain-Feingold Campaign Finance Reform.

BIBLIOGRAPHY. Robert Alexander, *The Classics of Interest Group Behavior* (Thomson Wadsworth, 2006); R.K. Godwin, *One Billion Dollars of Influence* (Chatham House, 1988); Paul Herrnson, Ronald Shaiko, and Clyde Wilcox, *The Interest Group Connection* (Chatham House, 1998); Mark Rozell, Clyde Wilcox, and David Madland, *Interest Groups in American Campaigns* (Congressional Quarterly, 2006); Darrell West and Burdett Loomis, *The Sound of Money* (Norton, 1998).

DAVID NICE
WASHINGTON STATE UNIVERSITY

Split Ticket Voting

SPLIT TICKET VOTING is the decision by a voter to choose candidates from two or more parties on the same ballot. Split ticket voting contrasts with straight ticket voting, when a voter chooses candidates from the same party. Prior to the 1880s, in the United States, ballots were printed and distributed by parties. While voters could choose to literally rip their ballots and cast votes for candidates from different parties, this practice was discouraged and, consequently, limited in use. By 1892, however, all states adopted provisions for election by a secret ballot, also called the Australian ballot, which lists all the candidates for office, regardless of party. As a result, voters could choose any candidates they liked, regardless of party affiliation. The institution of secret voting provided voters with the opportunity to cast split tickets for multiple parties' candidates.

A voter may decide to split his or her ticket for any number of reasons. One commonly held view is that voters choose presidents to represent their national interests, while they choose House representatives to represent their local interests. This view posits that the Republican Party coordinates national policies, while the Democratic Party coordinates local issues. These divergent emphases allow voters to choose two different parties to represent their interests, resulting in split ticket voting.

Another theory is that voters choose to split their tickets strategically between the two major parties to create moderate policies. This perspective holds that voters wish to divide the government between the two parties to diffuse power, rather than to concentrate power in one party. The consequence of split ticket voting, then, is divided government. Divided government results in each party controlling one branch of the federal government. The Democratic and Republican parties must compromise in order to coordinate policy action between the different branches of the government. As a result, it may be argued that voters directly influence the laws that govern them by splitting their votes.

SEE ALSO: Australian Ballot; Balanced Ticket; Divided Government and Electoral Behavior; Proportional Representation; Straight Ticket Voting.

BIBLIOGRAPHY. Gary Cox, *Making Votes Count: Strategic Coordination in the World's Electoral Systems* (Cambridge University Press, 1997); Morris Fiorina, *Divided Government* (Macmillan Publishing, 1992); Bernard Grofman, et al., "A New Look at Split-Ticket Outcomes for House and President: The Comparative Midpoints Model," *Journal of Politics* (Winter, 2000); Michael Lewis-Beck and Richard Nadeau, "Split-Ticket Voting: The Effects of Cognitive Madisonianism," *Journal of Politics* (Winter, 2004); David Mayhew, *Divided We Govern* (Yale University Press, 1991); Charles Smith, Jr., et al., "Party Balancing and Voting for Congress in the 1996 National Election," *American Journal of Political Science* (Fall 1999).

JESSICA DAY
UNIVERSITY OF IOWA

Stalking Horse

GENERICALLY, A STALKING horse is employed to cover one's real purpose; in other words, a stalking horse is a decoy. Stalking horse is archaic terminology. In America, the term became popular in the Great Plains of the old west, when hunters used their horses as decoys to sneak up on wild birds, buffalo, and other game so they could shoot them from a short distance, although the origin of the concept dates back to 16th century Europe. In political campaigns, there are different types of stalking horses. One type of stalking horse runs, not as a serious candidate with any intention of winning, but just to test the strength of a particular political cause or candidate. For instance, it was charged by some political pundits that in the U.S. presidential campaign of 1964, Republican Barry Goldwater ran as a stalking horse, put up by the Republican National Committee, to test the strength of the right wing of the Republican Party before the voters. It was well known that Goldwater stood no chance of defeating the popular incumbent, President Lyndon Johnson.

Another type of stalking horse enters a campaign, especially in party primaries, as a front or decoy for a legitimate, but unannounced, candidate. The true purpose of the stalking horse candidate is to pave the way for the more viable candidate. When the time is right, the stalking horse candidate withdraws and the real candidate enters the race, benefiting politically from the stalking horse's withdrawal. In the California recall election of Governor Gray Davis, in 2003, it is thought that Republican Representative Darrell Issa acted as a stalking horse candidate for actor Arnold Schwarzenegger. Issa pushed hard for the recall of Davis, blasting Davis for his incompetence as governor and entering the recall contest. Yet, with no chance of winning, Issa backed out, leaving Schwarzenegger in a solid political position to win.

Probably the most common kind of stalking horse is a candidate who runs as a spoiler. Such a stalking-horse candidate runs to spoil the chances of another candidate winning by eroding or splitting the vote, usually between the two main candidates. For example, in inner city primary elections, African-American candidates, if in the minority, have been able to win by getting a white stalking horse candidate in the race to split the vote among white voters. Although using stalking horses to split the vote is common in politics, it sometimes can be illegal. For example, in the 1993 primary race for comptroller in St. Louis, Missouri, federal charges of mail fraud in an attempt to defraud Missouri voters were brought against Virvus Jones, candidate for comptroller, not just because he placed a stalking horse candidate in the race to draw votes away from his main opponent, James Shrewsbury, but because there was evidence that he even helped fund the stalking horse's campaign.

Historically, stalking horses have played a pervasive and significant role in American elections, as well as in election contests in other countries. Most stalking horse candidates have no realistic chance of winning, as, inevitably, only the strongest candidate can win. They do, however, influence election results. Some candidates run to test their popularity for future elections, to advance a cause, or to send some message.

In democratic elections, all candidates, weak or strong, increase or decrease another candidate's chances of winning. Ross Perot's candidacy weakened President George H.W. Bush's chances of re-election in the 1992 presidential election, while Ralph Nader's presidential run likely cost Al Gore the presidency in the 2000 presidential race.

SEE ALSO: Nader, Ralph; Presidential Election of 1964; Presidential Election of 1992; Presidential Election of 2000.

BIBLIOGRAPHY. Ed Finn, "What Exactly Is a Stalking Horse?," *Slate Magazine*, www.Slate.com (September 23, 2003); K.F. Warren, "A Long History of Stalking Horses," *St. Louis Post-Dispatch* (December 18, 1995).

KENNETH F. WARREN, PH.D.
SAINT LOUIS UNIVERSITY

State Campaign Committees

LEGISLATIVE LEADERS USE state Legislative Campaign Committees to raise campaign contributions that are then distributed to candidates. These committees are similar to the Capitol Hill committees established by the Republican and Democratic Party conferences in each house of Congress. State legislative committees developed in response to the state party organizations' loss of traditional bases of power, their ability to control nominations, and attract volunteers.

The decline of the state party organizations meant that they could no longer effectively assist candidates for the state legislature. Even in the states where party organizations resisted the trend, they tended to direct their resources on statewide and congressional contests, leaving state legislators and their challengers to fend for themselves.

Generally, each state's polity will contain four state legislative campaign committees: one for each party in both chambers of the state legislature. Although the

first state legislative campaign committees were established in the early 1970s, they existed in most states by the mid-1990s. State legislative campaign committees are usually run by the party's legislative caucus or leadership, and raise money that is then distributed strategically to legislative candidates. In many states, the staff of the legislative caucuses (paid with taxpayer funds) play a major role in managing the day-to-day operations of the state legislative campaign committees. Depending upon state election laws, campaign contributions are usually solicited from individuals, political action committees (PACs), corporations, trade associations, and unions.

Although initially established for fundraising purposes, state legislative campaign committees have broadened their role as they now support and manage legislative campaigns. Originally, state legislative campaign committees were designed to protect and expand the party's representation in a legislative chamber by providing financial support to vulnerable incumbents and to non-incumbents running in targeted districts. However, it soon became clear to state legislative leaders that they needed to play some role in helping candidates spend the monies they were given or they might be wasted. Today, state legislative campaign committees vary from state to state, but their activities often include recruiting candidates, providing candidates with campaign media assistance, polling, issue/opposition research, direct mail, formulating campaign strategy, and even management of the campaign.

Nevertheless, financial support of legislative candidates is still the principal responsibility of most state legislative campaign committees. State legislative campaign committees can provide three forms of financial support to candidates: direct cash contributions to the candidate's campaign committee, expenditures that are made by the state legislative committee on behalf of the candidate (for example, a mailer that includes a disclaimer that it was paid for by the legislative campaign committee), and independent expenditures that can have no connection to the candidate. State legislative committees tend to make expenditures on behalf of candidates for two reasons.

First, it allows the state legislative campaign committee to retain control over how the funds are spent. Also, expenditures on behalf of candidates by state legislative campaign committees are often not limited, while direct cash state campaign-finance laws often limit contributions to candidate committees. Party leaders who control state legislative campaign committees tend to distribute campaign resources to help candidates in close races, as their goal is to maximize their party's representation in the legislative body. They often direct candidates as to which consultants to hire or which vendors to use for an array of goods and services that campaigns will buy.

Critics of state legislative campaign committees have called them "legal money laundering operations" that raise large sums of money from special interests that benefit legislative candidates, but allow those candidates to appear to be free of influence from such groups since they do not have to report such contributions in their campaign finance disclosure statements. "Good government" groups are often the most critical of state legislative campaign committees, arguing that the committees enhance the influence of special interest groups, diminish the role of political party organizations, make individual legislators more beholden to their leaders and less responsive to their constituents, and often reduce the competitiveness of races by increasing the number of uncontested races.

Some states have imposed limits on state legislative campaigns. For example, in Minnesota, legislative caucus fundraising events are prohibited during the period when the state legislature is in session. In Tennessee, lobbyists are prohibited from contributing to state legislative caucus committees. In late 2001, as a result of investigations into caucus employees working on campaigns on state time, the legislative caucus committee staffs in Wisconsin were dismantled.

SEE ALSO: Campaign Finance, State and Local Elections; Campaigns, State; Democratic State Party Organizations; Fundraising, State Campaigns; Republican State Party Organizations; Special Interests.

BIBLIOGRAPHY. Anthony Gierzynski, *Legislative Party Campaign Committees in the American States* (University Press of Kentucky, 1992); D.M. Shea, *Transforming Democracy: Legislative Campaign Committees and Political Parties* (State University of New York Press, 1996); Wisconsin Democracy Campaign and Common Cause of Wisconsin, *Legal Laundering: A Report Examining the Link Between Special Interests and Legislative Leadership* (Wisconsin Democracy, 1999).

JEFFREY KRAUS
WAGNER COLLEGE

States' Rights Party (Dixiecrats)

THE STATES' RIGHTS Democratic Party, or Dixiecrat Party, was founded in 1948 in response to the Democratic Party's growing support of civil rights and opposition to segregation. The solid south had been staunchly and reliably Democratic since the Civil War, but President Truman's integration of the army and the party's adoption of a civil rights platform in its presidential campaign ended that relationship. At the urging of South Carolina Governor J. Strom Thurmond, 35 delegates walked out of the Democratic National Convention, and reconvened in Alabama, where they nominated Thurmond as their presidential candidate, with Mississippi Governor Fielding Wright as his running mate. In four states, Thurmond's South Carolina, Wright's Mississippi, and the deep south states of Louisiana and Alabama, the Dixiecrats took the Democrats' spot on the ballot, and carried the electoral votes in just those states. With the addition of a single electoral vote from Tennessee, the Dixiecrats had a total of 39, well below what was needed, but a significant number for a third party.

Meanwhile, further demonstrating the identity crisis among the Democrats, liberal Democrats formed the Progressive Party (unrelated to previous parties by that name) on an anti-war platform; it earned no electoral votes, but Progressive candidate Henry Wallace won nearly as many popular votes as Thurmond. The three-way split among the Democrats was expected to hand the election to Republican Thomas Dewey (though Truman won, in the end).

Though the States' Rights Democratic Party disbanded after the election, the Dixiecrats remained a power in politics. The Democratic hold over the white south's electoral votes crumbled between 1948 and the 1960s. After the *Brown v. Board of Education* ruling by the U.S. Supreme Court, the Southern Manifesto was signed in 1956 by 19 senators and 77 congressional representatives: all but two of the 96 signatories were southern Democrats.

The Manifesto declared that the ruling had been an abuse of judicial power, and accused integrationists of worsening southern race relations by interfering with the balance that had been "created through 90 years of patient effort." The author of the Manifesto was Virginia

Senator Harry Byrd, who received 134,000 votes in the 1956 presidential election (even though he was not a candidate). In 1960, when the Democrats nominated John F. Kennedy, Byrd (still not a candidate) received 15 electoral votes, all from southern states, and he actually carried Mississippi. Outspoken Alabama Governor George Wallace, a charismatic and popular segregationist, ran for president in every election 1964–76 (as the candidate for the American Independent Party in 1968), consistently garnering more votes than anyone expected, though not nearly enough to be a serious contender.

All of these events were a signal to the supposed party of the opposition, that Democrats in the south could be lured away; if nothing else, the two parties were on closer to equal ground, each of them representing a different period of federal imposition on the sovereignty of southern states. Republican Richard Nixon's southern strategy worked by targeting southern Democrats and highlighting the differences between their values and those of the Democratic National Party. A number of prominent Democrats changed their party affiliation, tossing their hats in with the Republicans (including Thurmond, who endorsed Barry Goldwater in 1964 and was an important unofficial advisor to Nixon). Beginning with presidential elections, the south gradually shifted allegiance to the Republican Party, with the Grand Old Party (GOP) winning more and more statewide elections as the 20th century waxed on.

The Democratic Party, particularly in the pre-Bill Clinton era, continued to be popular in the south for state offices, where the national party platform was less relevant. Southern Democrats, especially the more conservative ones, have often been called Dixiecrats, invoking Thurmond and his party.

Many of the Reagan Democrats, who, as a group, have been described as Kennedy supporters in the 1960s and Reagan supporters in the 1980s, were Dixiecrats. They saw the national party as a party of special interests rather than of the workingman, the middle class, and the American family. National security and federal taxes were also divisive issues, with southern Democrats generally siding with Reagan. This may have laid some of the groundwork for the growing popularity of the Republican Party in the south in the 1990s. Dixiecrats tend to be social conservatives compared to northern Democrats, pro-life, friendly with Evangelical groups, more likely to support school prayer, and especially concerned with maintaining a division between the power of the federal government and the sovereignty of state governments.

SEE ALSO: Civil Rights; Conservatism; Populists and Populist Movements; Presidential Election of 1948; Sectionalism; Thurmond, J. Strom.

BIBLIOGRAPHY. Jack Bass and M.W. Thompson, *Strom: The Complicated Personal and Political Life of Strom Thurmond* (Public Affairs, 2005); Nadine Cohodas, *Strom Thurmond and the Politics of Southern Change* (Mercer University Press, 1994); Kari Frederickson, *The Dixiecrat Revolt and the End of the Solid South* (University of North Carolina Press, 2001); Dewey Grantham, *The Life and Death of the Solid South* (University Press of Kentucky, 1992); Forrest McDonald, *States' Rights and the Union* (University Press of Kansas, 2000).

BILL KTE'PI
INDEPENDENT SCHOLAR

Straight Ticket Voting

STRAIGHT TICKET VOTING can refer to both individuals' behavior, and an institutional feature of elections designed to simplify the process of voting. As a behavior, straight ticket voting refers to the propensity of an individual to cast all votes on a ballot for candidates from the same party. As an institutional feature, several states have, and continue to offer voters, the option to cast just one party vote that would apply to all races in the election. As of 2007, the following 13 states present voters with the straight ticket option in all elections: Alabama, Indiana, Iowa, Kentucky, Michigan, New Hampshire, New Mexico, Oklahoma, Pennsylvania, South Carolina, Texas, Utah, and West Virginia. New Jersey restricts straight ticket voting to primary elections. Rhode Island is the opposite, allowing straight ticket voting only in general elections. Finally, North Carolina and Wisconsin allow straight ticket voting in all elections except those for president.

Straight ticket voting, despite its accessibility as a ballot feature in the states listed, is far more significant as a behavior. Even if all states were to do away with the straight ticket voting option, many voters who make use of it now would simply cast individual ballots for members of the same party. For both the behavior or

As an electoral behavior, straight ticket voting refers to the propensity of an individual to cast all votes on an election ballot for candidates from the same political party.

the institution, it is important to know what drives individuals to select all members from the same party even if listed in other ways, or select the straight ticket option where available. There are two important individual characteristics that influence straight ticket voting: partisanship and sophistication. Partisanship can be simply defined as a psychological attachment to a political party. As typically measured, partisanship has two distinguishing characteristics. Direction refers to whether the individual considers him or herself a Democrat or Republican, whereas Independent is considered the absence of direction. Intensity categorizes the strength of attachment to the party label. As partisan intensity increases, there is more likelihood of straight ticket voting behavior. Simply, as one's attachment to a political party increases, one is more willing to vote for every candidate representing that party. Sophistication has the opposite effect

from partisanship. As sophistication increases, a voter is expected to be more knowledgeable about politics and the candidates, and less reliant on party labels as cues to perceived proper behavior.

Institutionally, there has been increasing resistance to straight ticket voting. Since 1994, four states have successfully abolished the institutional practice of straight ticket voting: Georgia, Illinois, Missouri, and South Dakota. Michigan attempted to abolish the practice by law in 2001, but the law was repealed in 2002 by statewide balloting. Proponents of the option believe that it increases turnout by providing individuals with an easier means of participating in elections and by making lines at precincts move more quickly. Those who oppose straight ticket voting argue that it promotes decreased responsibility among voters for becoming knowledgeable about issues and candidates. Additionally, it may limit electoral choice by disadvantaging Independent and third-party candidates. If the situation in Michigan is a bellwether to public opinion regarding straight ticket voting options, voters appear to prefer having the alternative available on the ballot, despite objections from elected state officials.

SEE ALSO: Partisanship; Split Ticket Voting; Voter Knowledge/Ignorance; Voting Methods.

BIBLIOGRAPHY. Richard Born, "Split-Ticket Voters, Divided Government, and Fiorina's Policy Balancing Model," *Legislative Studies Quarterly* (v.19/1, 1994); Richard Born, "Congressional Incumbency and the Rise of Split-Ticket Voting," *Legislative Studies Quarterly* (v.25/3, 2000); Angus Campbell, et al., *The American Voter* (University of Chicago Press, 1960); D.M. Ogden, Jr., "A Voting Behavior Approach to Split-Ticket Voting in 1952," *Western Political Quarterly* (v.11/3, 1958); J.G. Rusk, "The Effect of the Australian Ballot Reform on Split Ticket Voting: 1876–1908," *American Political Science Review* (v.64/4, 1970).

ANDREW H. SIDMAN
JOHN JAY COLLEGE, CITY UNIVERSITY OF NEW YORK

Suburban Vote

AS SUBURBANIZATION CAME about after World War II, suburban voters initially supported Republican candidates. This was believed to be, in part, because they were upwardly mobile, not very diverse, and financially well-off. These characteristics are the same as those of Republican voters, so it was not unusual that those from the suburbs supported Republican candidates. Researchers have shown that, on average, there were more Republicans than Democrats in the suburbs initially, but this trend was not static and would swing in favor of the Democrats at times. Another seemingly important factor was the location of the suburb, as well as who was moving into the area. However, a voter's behavior is not solely controlled by where he or she lives, but also by experiences, family, friends, co-workers and groups the voter associates with.

Following the New Deal and World War II, the political system moved away from the Democratic-controlled electorate into a more balanced split in the electorate. The increase in prosperity and the corresponding increase in economic security that occurred at this time characterize the Republican Party. The urban electorate tends to be Democratic because it tends to be made up primarily of blue-collar workers. On the other hand, the rural electorate (made up of primarily southern, white, religious people) tends to support the Republican Party. Initially all the reasons for moving to the suburbs; more room, less traffic, lower crime, and a slower pace to life, lead to the assumption that this would lead suburban voters to vote for Republican candidates.

Indeed, when viewed as a whole, initially the suburban electorate favored Republican candidates. Not every suburb was predominantly Republican, some were Democratic, while others have changed from Republican to Democratic when blue-collar workers moved in and displaced the white-collar voters who lived there. With exposure to a different political climate, it is possible that person's political alignment may shift towards that of his neighbors. Thus, as more people moved to the suburbs, it is likely that these new members would tend to adapt new political views. Also during this time, there was an ongoing increase in the percentage of the electorate from the suburbs. This increase came from more people moving to the suburbs. The inclination of the electorate in the suburbs to support Republican candidates shifted in the 1990s towards the Democratic Party.

Part of this change started in the mid-1970s as the population in the suburbs increased. The height of the Republican strength was during the Reagan administration, with support for the Republican Party being strongest in southern Suburbs. This changed in the elections of the 1990s when the Democrats gained a majority of the suburban votes. However, the margin was never very large. The question is where, and why has this change taken place. Some believe that, in part, it was driven by the perception that the Republican Party has moved to the right, while the Democratic Party has moved towards the center.

While examining voting behavior regionally, it was found that southern suburban areas were more likely, prior to the 1990s, to vote Republican. However, both northern and southern suburbs had Republican leanings through the Reagan presidency. In the 1990s, both regions then switched to supporting the

Democratic Party. This trend changed in 2000 when the southern suburbs moved back to support for the Republican Party. While it is not clear at this time, it is possible that the support for the Democratic Party by suburban southern voters was actually support just for President Bill Clinton because he was from the south. The switch by southern suburban voters back to the Republican Party in the 2000 election would support this thought also.

Compared to urban areas, the suburbs have always been supportive of the Republican Party. In the south, this tendency has been even more pronounced. This difference between to urban and suburb voters diminished starting in the 1990s, so that now a voter in the suburbs is as likely to support the Democratic Party as is an urban voter.

Part of the reason for this homogeneity between the two areas was thought to have to do with migration of people from one area to another. The idea was that there was a diversification of the suburbs causing the change in voting habits. Instead, Census data showed that while there was some diversification, it was not sufficient to cause the change in the voting habits of the suburbs. Another explanation was a change in the wealth level of the voters living in the suburbs. Researchers found that an increase in homeownership would suggest that the voters should be more likely to vote Republican, rather than less likely.

Another possible explanation was that white liberal residents from the cities had moved to the suburbs, but there are no data to support that explanation. Having ruled out the possibility of an influx of voters to the

Research has shown that on average there were more Republicans than Democrats initially in the suburbs, this trend was not static and would swing in favor of the Democrats at times.

suburbs as the reason for the change away from the Republican Party, the likely answer lies with a change in the voting habits of the voters themselves.

This change in suburban voting habits from strongly Republican to a more balanced vote has made the suburbs more contested. In addition, with the increase in the number of voters living in the suburbs, the suburban vote has become more critical to the outcome of an election.

SEE ALSO: Age and Voting Behavior; Cross-Pressures, Sociopolitical; Education Level and Voting Behavior; Electoral Behavior; High and Low Stimulus Elections; Income and Voting Behavior; Independent Voters; Occupation and Voting Behavior; Race and Voting Behavior; Rural Vote; Social Groups and Electoral Behavior; Urban Vote; Voter Self-Interest.

BIBLIOGRAPHY. Angus Campbell, Philip E. Converse, Warren E. Miller, and Donald Stokes, *The American Voter* (University of Chicago Press, 1960); Angus Campbell, Philip E. Converse, Warren E. Miller, Donald E. Stokes, *Elections and the Political Order* (John Wiley and Sons, 1966); Matthew D. Lassiter, *The Silent Majority: Suburban Politics in the Sunbelt South (Politics and Society in Twentieth Century America)* (Princeton University Press, 2005); Norman H. Nie, Sidney Verba, and John R. Petrocik, *The Changing American Voter* (Harvard University Press, 1979); Eric J. Oliver, *Democracy in Suburbia* (Princeton University Press, 2001); "Suburban Voting and National Trends: A Research Note," *The Western Political* Quarterly (September 1968); "Suburban Voting in Presidential Elections," *Presidential Studies Quarterly* (March 2003).

DALLACE W. UNGER, JR.
INDEPENDENT SCHOLAR

Suffrage

SUFFRAGE REFERS TO the civil right to vote. The inclusion or exclusion of a given group can have serious repercussions. Who votes and whose vote counts is the essence of representation. If congresspersons did not have to respond to the entire population within their district or state get elected, there would be no mechanism to induce them to be responsive to the issues pertinent to the population. Thus, expanding or including individuals who were once excluded can have serious repercussions, not only for their representatives, but also for the issues that will be raised in Congress, state legislatures, and local governments.

As such, the concept of suffrage and its history within a polity can serve as a starting point for any discourse regarding representation or government that is based on the will of the people. The expansion of voting rights has occurred four times via constitutional amendment. The Fifteenth, Nineteenth, Twenty-Fourth, and Twenty-Sixth amendments secured suffrage for racial or ethnic minorities, women, the poor, and 18-year-olds, respectively. Although these were all formal declarations by the federal government ratified by at least two-thirds of the states, and most have been readily accepted, but in case of racial minorities, compliance has varied.

RACIAL MINORITIES
The Fifteenth Amendment, passed by Congress as part of the Civil War Amendments and ratified by the several states on February 3, 1870, established that the right to vote of a citizen would not be "denied or abridged … on account of race, color, or previous condition of servitude." While this offered a formal protection in the Constitution, full suffrage for racial minorities remained elusive.

After ratification, state and local legislation, especially in the south, still erected barriers, which were more inventive than bans on voting rights. Often referred to as "Jim Crow" laws, these barriers, despite appearing to be race neutral, had the purpose and effect of denying the right to vote to racial minorities, particularly African Americans. The states have the power to restrict voting rights in Article I, Section 2 of the Constitution, which allows the states to determine the qualifications of electors. Therefore, states, in theory, had the power to determine the requirements a citizen needs in order to vote.

All that the Constitution required is that the laws not abridge the right to vote based on race, color or previous condition of servitude. As a result, Jim Crow laws arose in the south. Several of the methods included white-only voting in Democratic Party primary elections, hefty registration requirements, literacy and understanding requirements, ownership or rental of real property as a requirement for voting on property tax issues, and poll taxes. These laws had the intended effect; African-American participation in voting in the south was rare.

It was not until the federal government, working from the Enforcement Clause (Section 2) of the Fifteenth Amendment in the 1960s, that removal of these barriers began. Bringing suit against the discriminatory laws, the federal government sought to rectify the denial of full suffrage to racial minorities. The Supreme Court, in several pivotal cases concerning voting rights ruled that state laws that discriminated and denied access to the ballot box would not be tolerated. In *Louisiana v. United States* (1965), the court struck down the use of literacy and understanding tests as a qualification for voting. In *Kramer v. Union Free School District* (1969), the court struck down the ownership or rental of real property requirement. In *Dunn v. Blumstein* (1972), the residency requirement of a year as a qualification for voting was deemed unconstitutional.

Moreover, the ratification of the Twenty-Fourth Amendment on January 23, 1964, removed the poll tax in federal elections; the court's decision in *Harper v. Virginia State Board of Elections* (1966) effectively eliminated the use of poll taxes in state elections. While many would consider the Twenty-Fourth Amendment as a removal of a barrier to voting for the poor, the intent of the amendment, as Congress suggested, was to correct states' circumvention of the Fifteenth Amendment's purpose and intent. Levying a tax on the right to vote was designed to keep African Americans away from the polls and the ratification of the Twenty-Fourth Amendment sought to end such discriminatory practices.

Despite these legal victories, registration of African Americans in the south remained low. Given the ability of the states to determine the qualifications of electors, formal protections would not be enough to secure the right to vote for racial minorities. Thus, Congress passed the Voting Rights Act of 1965. With this legislation, Congress established a coverage formula to target states or counties for possible discrimination or denial of voting rights.

The two criteria were: the presence of a discriminatory mechanism or test in November 1964, and less than 40 percent of the voting population registered to vote or voted in the 1964 general election. If a state "triggered" this formulation by meeting the criteria, they were subject to federal government oversight. Federal examiners, appointed by the U.S. attorney general,

would supervise registration and voting procedures if the Justice Department determined that lower African-American participation was due to state- or county-sponsored discriminatory practices. The state covered under this triggering formula were Alabama, Alaska, Georgia, Louisiana, Mississippi, South Carolina, Virginia; also included were portions of Arizona, Hawaii, Idaho, and North Carolina. Any changes to election law in these states were subject to review and needed approval from the attorney general (or a U.S. District Court for the District of Columbia).

In *South Carolina v. Katzenbach* (1966), the court affirmed the federal government's ability to regulate and rectify voting discrimination on the basis of race. The Voting Rights Act of 1965, as well as extensive voter registration efforts by civil rights groups would eventually raise southern African-American voting participation to levels slightly lower than southern whites.

WOMEN

The Nineteenth Amendment, ratified by the several states on August 18, 1920, established in the Constitution that the right of a citizen "to vote shall not be denied or abridged by the United States or by any State on account of sex." While the post-Amendment era for the Nineteenth Amendment did not present as many state-sponsored roadblocks as the Fifteenth Amendment, the struggle for suffrage still had barriers to overcome. The suffrage movement lost much steam and encountered some fractionalization after the passage of the Civil War Amendments. First, resentment formed among some women because racial minority citizens received the right to vote (Fifteenth Amendment) and racial minorities received equal protection (Fourteenth Amendment) prior to women. Second, in *Minor v. Happersett* (1875), the court ruled that women may indeed be citizens, but not all citizens, especially women, are voters.

The movement gained ground again with the Progressive Movement in the late 19th and early 20th centuries. Several reasons explain this. First, the Progressive Movement was a grassroots effort to reform local and state governments. Second, without sufficient support in of states, many leaders in the suffrage movement believed that it could not achieve success at the national level. Third, many of the issues that were vital to Progressive reforms—ending child labor, pure food and drug regulation—required the support of women in order to achieve success. Steadily, territories began

Suffragettes at the U.S. Capitol in 1913. Many of the issues that were vital to Progressive reforms—ending child labor, pure food and drug regulation—required the support of women in order to achieve success and realization.

enfranchising women. Wyoming, in 1869, became the first territory to offer women the right to vote. Utah, (1870), Colorado (1893), and Idaho (1896), followed suit. After the turn of the century, Washington (1910), California (1911) as well as Oregon, Kansas and Arizona (1912) enfranchised women voters. This push for suffrage gained even more momentum with the re-ascension of Carrie Chapman Catt to the leadership of the National American Woman Suffrage Association in 1915, and her pursuit of the "winning plan," which argued for partial rather than full suffrage. With the conversion of Woodrow Wilson to the suffrage movement, as well as other states enfranchising women,

Congress passed the Ninteenth Amendment and submitted to the states for ratification.

Despite the fact that the Nineteenth Amendment's passage was not met with as much antagonism as the Fifteenth Amendment, there are several issues to note regarding woman's suffrage and its effects on the polity. First, the achievement of the Nineteenth Amendment was a victory for the woman suffrage movement that saw a strong coalition form, but with this win, some scholars have suggested, the women's movement actually lost. The one issue—suffrage—that held fractionalized and polarized groups together soon fell apart. Women failed to vote as a "bloc" as racial and ethnic minorities did, and do still. Second, even with suffrage, there still remains a gender gap between men and women. Political participation for women in the form of voting remains distinctly and consistently lower than for men. This gender gap, as some researchers in political science and history opine, remains pervasive not only in political participation, but also across other factors that seem to be strong predictors of political involvement: political knowledge, awareness or sophistication, as well as partisan strength and attachment.

EIGHTEEN-YEAR-OLDS

The Twenty-Sixth Amendment, ratified on July 1, 1971, established that the right to vote for any citizen who is 18 years of age or older "shall not be denied or abridged by the United States or by any state on account of age." Most states, prior to 1971, determined the minimum voting age, ranging from 18- to 21-years-old. The Constitutional amendment was proposed in reaction to the Supreme Court's decision in *Oregon v. Mitchell* (1970). There, the court decided that Congress had the right to impose a minimum age for voting in federal elections, but could not do so in state and local elections. Rather than induce possible confusion by having different minimum age standards for federal and state elections, Congress proposed the Twenty-Sixth Amendment.

As was the case with the Nineteenth Amendment, the Twenty-Sixth Amendment had several notable effects. First, the amendment's ratification can be seen as a culmination of the highly-publicized student free speech movement at colleges and universities nationwide. The movement highlighted political involvement and awareness of students even though they could not all participate by voting at the polls due to being too young. The Twenty-Sixth Amendment rectified that. Second, and very similar to women, young voters did not vote as a bloc and, as such, did not capture much attention from legislators and congressmen. Even if younger voters did participate in the system, their level of participation—as documented in subsequent elections since ratification—is nowhere near the level of voters in their 30s or older.

While most may see suffrage as an issue long-settled, it continues to be pertinent. For example, the California State Legislature, in 2004, considered a bill that would have expanded the right to vote to teenagers; 14-year-olds would count as a quarter of an adult vote and 16-year-olds would count as a half vote. Although in most discussions of suffrage, the focus has been on the expansion of voting rights to a given group based on race, sex or age, other actions can also expand suffrage. For example, the introduction of an open primary, where all eligible voters may participate in partisan primaries, can be seen as an expansion of voter rights. Regardless of partisan affiliation, these blanket or open primaries allow individuals to choose the candidates who will represent the major parties in the general elections.

There are many proponents and opponents for the use of open primaries as a modern day application of suffrage. Rather than being based on gender, age or race, this use of open primaries must determine whether partisanship, or at least a formal declaration of partisan affiliation, serves as an appropriate means to include or exclude individuals from their civil right to vote.

SEE ALSO: Representative Democracy; Voting, Obstacles to; Voting Disenfranchisement.

BIBLIOGRAPHY. C.K. Chaney, Michael Alvarez, and Jonathan Nagler, "Explaining the Gender Gap in U.S. Presidential Elections, 1980–1992," *Political Research Quarterly* (1998); Chandler Davidson and Bernard Groffman, eds., *Quiet Revolution in the South: The Impact of the Voting Rights Act, 1965–1990* (Princeton University Press 1994); Lee Epstein and T.G. Walker, *Constitutional Law for a Changing America: Rights, Liberties, and Justice* (CQ Press, 2007); Bernard Grofman and Chandler Davidson, eds., *Controversies in Minority Voting: The Voting Rights Act in Perspective* (Brookings Institution, 1992); K.L. Hall, ed., *The Oxford Companion to the Supreme Court of the United States* (Oxford University Press, 1992); Karen Kaufman, "Culture Wars, Secular Realignment, and the Gender Gap in Party Identification," *Political Behavior* (2002); Karen Kaufmann and John Petrocik, "The Changing Politics of American Men: The Sources of the Gender Gap," *American Journal of Political Science* (1999); A.M. Thernstrom, *Whose Votes Count? Affirmative Action and Minority Voting Rights* (Harvard University Press, 1987).

Maxwell H.H. Mak
Stony Brook University (State University of New York)
Andrew H. Sidman
John Jay College, City University of New York

Tammany Hall

TAMMANY HALL was a Democratic political machine whose control of New York City politics persisted in varying degrees from the 1790s until the 1960s. Tammany Hall was the epitome of a political machine, in that political principles were secondary to the economic and political empowerment of members and leaders (also known as bosses). The loyalty of members and their families to the political machine was guaranteed through a system of political rewards. It was often through corrupt means that Tammany Hall met its members' needs and ensured its politicians were elected to public office. Tammany Hall, like other political machines, took advantage of communities that were weak and vulnerable as a result of poverty, political chaos, and social disorganization.

The presence of such vulnerabilities often fell disproportionately on certain ethnic and immigrant groups that Tammany Hall catered to in order to induct them as loyal followers. Provision of services to its constituents ensured its political relevancy and, therefore, it worked diligently to ensure that other entities did not fulfill its constituents' needs. Without the reliance of its constituents for the fulfillment of needs, political machines lose power and eventually die out. This was eventually the fate for Tammany Hall.

The Society of Tammany was created on May 12, 1789, based on the principles by which Indian Chief Tamanend lived his life. Tamanend was legendary throughout the colonies for his compassionate nature and his acumen. Members established this organization intending it to be a guiding light for both governmental actions and the public's patriotism. Over time, this society became less of a social club and more of a political institution. The Society of Tammany and Tammany Hall have their differences. Matthew Davis is credited with the foundation of Tammany Hall, which reigned in New York City until the 1960s, as he brought together the Society (an organization based on patriotism), and the general committee of Tammany Hall (an organization based on politics).

In 1809, after the initial melding, Tammany Hall began to weed out its enemies with methods of intimidation that would come to epitomize the organization. Aaron Burr is credited with being the first leader of Tammany Hall to use these tactics to change the society into a political institution. By 1816, it had taken root in New York City and, by the 1830s, its power was tremendous. Using its influence and connections with businesspeople (especially bankers), Tammany Hall worked to get its supporters elected. It bought votes from the mass public with promises of support. By 1854, Tammany was in control, not only of politics, but also of businesses,

Tammany Hall on 14th Street in New York City, c.1913. The Democratic political machine controlled New York City politics and persisted in varying degrees from the 1790s until the 1960s.

and its bosses were able to use corrupt means to enrich themselves. The most infamous of these was William Tweed or Boss Tweed, who was the first "boss" of Tammany Hall. Tweed used Tammany Hall to consolidate his power over New York City; and he was also at the center of corruption in the city. By the 1880s, Tammany and the Democratic Party within New York City had practically become the same organization.

Tammany Hall was dominated by the Irish and supported by the Jews. They worked together to ensure each of their political goals was met. The Irish wanted patronage and power, while the Jews wanted to end discrimination and help the poor. In order to gain power, the organization needed to obtain mass support from loyal voters. Therefore, Tammany preyed on the disad-

vantaged by providing them necessities (such as food, clothing, and jobs) in return for their support of Tammany Hall politicians.

In the 1930s, Franklin Roosevelt took federal patronage away from Tammany by enlarging the federal government's role in social programs. By the 1940s, with the advent of federal government relief programs, Tammany had nothing left to entice further loyalty from its members. Furthermore, the Irish and Jews had less need for this organization and it was considered to be at its weakest point. In the 1950s, the last head of Tammany Hall, Carmine De Sapio, attempted to reinvigorate this dying institution and, for a while, he was successful. However, he ultimately failed in this attempt and his leadership ended in 1961, taking with it the last vestiges of Tammany Hall. Overall, Tammany Hall's success for such a long period of time was because of its ability to meet the needs of a diverse group of people that were not being met. For politicians and businesspeople, it provided economic and political power, and for the poor, it provided a support system. In return these individuals were loyal and voted the way they were told, making Tammany Hall a powerful political force.

SEE ALSO: Machine Politics and Political Bosses; New York; Patronage System; Tweed, William.

BIBLIOGRAPHY. Peter Baida, "The Corrupting of New York City," *American Heritage Magazine* (December 1986); Charles LaCerra, *Franklin Delano Roosevelt and Tammany Hall of New York* (University Press of America, Inc., 1997); Chris McNickle, *To be Mayor of New York: Ethnic Politics in the City* (Columbia University Press, 1993); Warren Moscow, *The Last of the Big-Time Bosses: The Life and Times of Carmine DeSapio and the Rise and Fall of Tammany Hall* (Stein and Day Publishers, 1971); Jerome Mushkat, *Tammany: The Evolution of a Political Machine 1789–1865* (Syracuse University Press, 1971); Gustavus Myers, *The History of Tammany Hall* (Dover Publications, Inc., 1971).

RACHEL YFF
UNIVERSITY OF FLORIDA

Targeting Strategies

THE ABILITY OF political parties, candidates, and political movements to target their messages to a particular audience is a crucial component of contemporary political campaigns in the United States. Campaigns target different aspects of their messages at different groups of voters, whom the campaigns segment according to a variety of characteristics, including, but not limited to, political party, age, gender, ethnic background, socioeconomic status, profession, religion, and geographic location. Targeting strategists use polling data, focus groups, and even door-to-door canvassing to identify, which messages will resonate best with each segment of a voting public that may potentially support a candidate or initiative at the polls. Over the course of history in the United States, each party's targeting strategy has changed along ethnic and geographic lines, among other

segments. However, despite shifting allegiances among some populations, each party has always counted on the support of certain segments of the voting public.

Use of targeting strategies in early political campaigns in the United States was primitive, if present at all. Early political campaigns of the late 18th, and early 19th, centuries depended on campaign tools such as rallies, pamphlets, and the partisan press. These early campaign strategies were not targeted at any one segment of the voting population. Rallies sought to attract as many people as possible, regardless of political affiliation or other identifying characteristics. Gradually, political campaigns began to target their messages at different audiences. The election of 1840 saw Whig candidate William Henry Harrison triumph over incumbent Democrat Martin Van Buren, by focusing on Populist politics. Harrison's campaign targeted the frontier commoners, in contrast to the aristocratic supporters of Van Buren, marking perhaps one of the earliest forms of targeting strategy.

While Harrison and his presidential successors keyed on these strategies of trying to give the people what they wanted, these strategies were still a far cry from the sophisticated political targeting strategies we see in contemporary political campaigns. Most notably, these early campaigns were not engaged in polling or other means of research to find out what was actually important to voters. This practice would not become prevalent until the late 19th century, when the reform movements of that period employed polling data to focus on issues that concerned voters the most.

In 1896, William McKinley triumphed over William Jennings Bryan by branding himself in a way that better appealed to the preferences of the people and, more importantly, by employing one of the period's new media developments: direct mail. McKinley used the U.S. Postal Service's new rural home delivery to distribute over 250 million pieces of campaign literature to voters.

By capitalizing on the use of new communication with a important segment of the electorate, rural voters, McKinley was able to target a group of voters who had previously been difficult to reach due to their somewhat isolated status compared to urban voters. McKinley's focus on the rural voters of that period through specifically tailored messages and new media technology (direct mail) represented an important step toward modern political targeting strategy.

In modern models of political campaign communication, targeting strategy is often referred to as voter segmentation and, along with positioning, and strategy planning and implementation are three elements of the broader practice of political marketing. The concept of political marketing emerged from political strategists' adoption of product marketing principles. The traditional four P's of marketing are product, promotion, price, and place of distribution. Bruce Newman identifies four P's in his widely used model of political marketing. These are product, equivalent to the campaign platform; push marketing, which includes grass-roots strategy; pull marketing, which recognizes the role of the mass media in the campaign; and polling, which gauges public opinion and provides the campaign with a measure of feedback from voters.

VOTER NEEDS

In order to assess voter needs and provide accurate voter profiles, campaign practitioners must first attempt to understand what factors motivate voter behavior. Among these factors are political issues, stereotypes of candidates or political parties, the character traits of the candidate, political conditions or current events, and the desire for change (or lack of change) in leadership.

Each of these factors strongly influences how a candidate will be viewed among a certain segment of the voting population. Thus, the candidate and his or her campaign staff must carefully consider each of these factors when planning a targeting strategy for the campaign. With respect to political issues, different segments of the electorate will not only hold different opinions on various issues, but different segments will also have varying levels of interest in different issues. For example, retired voters will typically have more interest in Social Security issues, while working-age adults will have more interest in job issues.

Another factor is party or candidate stereotypes. Voters hold preconceived notions about how different candidates and the two major political parties will govern the country. John Petrocik's theory of issue ownership suggests that there are certain issues that voters believe are better handled by one party than the other. For example, Democrats are typically believed to better handle issues of healthcare and education, while Republicans are considered to better handle issues of national defense and limiting or cutting taxes. Certainly there are

exceptions to this rule depending on situational factors such as the economy. However, the theory of issue ownership suggests that Democratic and Republican candidates who focus their campaigns on issues owned by their respective parties will be more successful in their election quests.

Campaigns are also likely to target certain voter segments related to the characteristics of the candidate. Typically, applying this strategy, voters will be targeted based on characteristics that they share with the candidate. For example, older candidates Bob Dole and Ronald Reagan targeted their campaigns at elderly voters. Similarly, relatively younger candidates John F. Kennedy and Bill Clinton successfully targeted more youthful voters by contrasting themselves with their elder opponents. Similarly, female candidates are likely to more heavily target the woman vote, and minority candidates typically will attempt to target minority voters.

The remaining targeting strategies based on current events, and a desire for change, are often consolidated with the other strategies. Both parties always target independent voters. However, such voters are pursued even more aggressively when political conditions exist that have angered Independent voters and less loyal partisans who are likely to change parties. For example, during periods of economic hardship, out of work voters are likely to be a heavily-targeted segment of voters.

HISTORICALLY RELIABLE

Just as issue ownership theorists identify issues that candidates are likely to target in the campaign, there are certain segments of the electorate that are historically reliably Republican or Democrat. For example, Republicans, for the duration of the last half of the 20th century, have reliably targeted the military, wealthy voters, business owners, and socially conservative voters. During the same time, Democrats successfully targeted women, organized labor, and socially liberal voters. However, the last half of the 20th century has also seen a shift in other historically partisan groups.

Historically, African-American voters had been faithful to the Republican Party, dating back to the post-Civil War period of Reconstruction when they first earned the right to vote. Similarly, European-American voters in southern states were unquestionably loyal to the Democratic Party. These two groups have dramatically shifted their allegiances since the civil rights reforms of the 1950s and 1960s. By the start of the 21st century, the Republican Party had all but abandoned the strategy of targeting minorities. Similarly, beginning with the 2004 election, Democrats noticeably shifted the focus of their targeting strategy away from the southeast United States and toward the growing population of Hispanic-American voters in the west and southwest. Ultimately, ever-changing policy priorities, demographics, technological advances, and social trends are likely to gradually change the targeting strategies applied by both parties in U.S. political campaigns.

SEE ALSO: Advertising, Campaign; Age and Voting Behavior; Campaign Strategies; Campaigns, Presidential; Electoral Behavior; Gender and Voting Behavior; Income and Voting Behavior; Issue Ownership Theory; Occupation and Voting Behavior; Presidential Election of 1840; Presidential Election of 1896; Presidential Election of 2004; Race and Voting Behavior; Reconstruction.

BIBLIOGRAPHY. R.V. Friedenberg, *Communication Consultants in Political Campaigns* (Praeger, 1997); L.L. Kaid, ed., *Handbook of Political Communication Research* (Lawrence Erlbaum Associates, 2004); B.I. Newman, ed., *Handbook of Political Marketing* (Sage, 1999); B.I. Newman, *The Marketing of the President: Political Marketing as Campaign Strategy* (Sage, 1994); R.M. Perloff, *Political Communication: Politics, Press, and Public in America* (Lawrence Erlbaum Associates, 1998); J.R. Petrocik, "Issue Ownership in Presidential Elections, with a 1980 Case Study," *American Journal of Political Science* (v. 40/3, 1996); S.J. Rosenstone and J.M. Hansen, *Mobilization, Participation, and Democracy in America* (Longman, 2003).

COREY B. DAVIS
UNIVERSITY OF MISSOURI-COLUMBIA

Taxes

THE FEDERAL, STATE, and local tax systems in the United States have changed significantly over the years. During the colonial days, taxes varied from colony to colony, but were largely limited to taxes on imports and exports, poll taxes, and excise taxes. The same types of taxes continued after the American Revolution, which was, in part, inspired by the English Parliament's imposition of Stamp and tea taxes on the colonies.

During the Civil War, Congress passed new excise taxes on items such as playing cards, gunpowder, feathers, telegrams, iron, leather, pianos, yachts, billiard tables, drugs, patent medicines, and whiskey. Many legal documents were also taxed, and license fees were collected for almost all professions and trades. Congress also passed the first federal income tax, which was levied at 3 percent on all incomes over $800 per year.

The Federal government's demand for revenue declined sharply after the Civil War and many taxes were repealed. By 1868, the main source of Federal revenue was derived from liquor and tobacco taxes. The income tax was abolished in 1872, and from 1868 to 1913 almost 90 percent of all revenue was collected from the remaining excises.

THE INCOME TAX

Under the Constitution, Congress could impose direct taxes only if they were levied in proportion to each state's population. Thus, when a flat rate federal income tax was enacted in 1894, it was quickly challenged and in 1895, the U.S. Supreme Court ruled it unconstitutional because it was a direct tax not apportioned according to the population of each state.

By 1913, 36 States had ratified the Sixteenth Amendment to the Constitution. In October, Congress passed a new income tax law with rates beginning at one percent and rising to 7 percent for taxpayers with income in excess of $500,000. Less than one percent of the population paid income taxes at this time. Form 1040 was introduced as the standard tax reporting form and, though it has changed and grown much more complicated over the years, it remains in use today.

Prior to the enactment of the income tax, most citizens were able to pursue their private economic affairs without the direct knowledge of the government. Individuals earned their wages, businesses earned their profits, and wealth was accumulated and spent with little or no interaction with the government. The income tax fundamentally changed this relationship, giving the government the ability to know all about an individual and business' economic life. Presidents Franklin Delano Roosevelt and Richard Nixon, among others, have used the Internal Revenue Service to harass their political enemies.

TAX PROTESTORS

Many people in the United States are known as tax protestors, refuse to pay taxes under the belief that income taxes are unconstitutional or were passed illegally. Tax Protestors argue that forcing people to engage in "voluntary compliance" is unconstitutional under the Fifth Amendment prohibition against forcing citizens to testify against themselves. Tax Protestors have limited success in the U.S. court system.

WORLD WAR I AND THE 1920s

The entry of the United States into World War I greatly increased the government's demand for revenue and Congress responded by passing the 1916 Revenue Act. The 1916 Act raised the lowest tax rate from one percent to 2 percent and raised the top rate to 15 percent on taxpayers with incomes in excess of $1.5 million. Through out the war, taxes continued to increase. By 1918, the bottom rate was 6 percent and the top rate was 77 percent. Even in 1918, however, only 5 percent of the population paid income taxes.

During the 1920s taxes were cut somewhat, but this trend reversed after Franklin Delano Roosevelt entered office. By 1936, the lowest tax rate was four percent and the top rate was 79 percent. In 1939, Congress systematically codified the tax laws so that all subsequent tax legislation, until 1954, amended this basic code. The combination of a shrunken economy and the repeated tax increases raised the Federal government's tax burden to 6.8 percent of Gross Domestic Product (GDP) by 1940.

SOCIAL SECURITY AND MEDICARE TAXES

In 1935, the Social Security Act was passed. This law provided payments to workers who lost their jobs and gave public aid to the aged, the needy, the handicapped, and to certain minors. These programs were initially financed by a two percent tax, one half of which was subtracted directly from an employee's paycheck and one half collected from employers on the employee's behalf. The tax was levied on the first $3,000 of the employee's salary or wage. In 1965, Congress enacted the Medicare program, providing for the medical needs of persons aged 65 or older, regardless of income. The 1965 Social Security Amendments also created the Medicaid programs, which provides medical assistance for persons with low incomes and resources.

Of course, the expansion of Social Security and the creation of Medicare and Medicaid required additional tax revenues, and thus the basic payroll tax was repeat-

edly increased over the years. Between 1949 and 1962 the payroll tax rate climbed steadily from its initial rate of two percent to six percent. The expansions in 1965 led to further rate increases, with the combined payroll tax rate climbing to 12.3 percent in 1980. In 1983, Congress passed legislation to increase the payroll tax rate to 15.3 on an increasing maximum salary, which is now around $100,000.

These payroll tax increases were recommended by a commission appointed by President Ronald Reagan and chaired by Alan Greenspan. Senators Robert Dole and Daniel Patrick Moynihan were also members. Even with all these tax increases the federal government's entitlement programs have unfunded liabilities well in excess of $10 trillion.

WORLD WAR II

During World War II the federal government continued to increase taxes. Reductions in exemption levels meant that taxpayers with taxable incomes of only $500 faced a bottom tax rate of 23 percent, while taxpayers with incomes over $1 million faced a top rate of 94 percent. Federal taxes as a share of GDP grew from 7.6 percent in 1941 to 20.4 percent in 1945. Beyond the rates and revenues, however, another aspect of the income tax that changed was the increase in the number of income taxpayers from $4 million in 1939 to $43 million in 1945. Another important change was the return to income tax withholding as done during the Civil War. This greatly eased the collection of the tax for the Bureau of Internal Revenue. It also greatly reduced the taxpayer's awareness of the amount of tax being collected, that is, it reduced the transparency of the tax, which made it easier to raise taxes in the future. Withholding was supposed to be a temporary measure during the war years, but was never repealed.

Tax cuts following the war reduced the federal tax burden as a share of GDP from its wartime high of 20.9 percent in 1944 to 14.4 percent in 1950. However, to pay for the Korean War and the extension of Social Security coverage to self-employed persons, the government demanded more money. By 1952 the tax burden had returned to 19.0 percent of GDP.

John F. Kennedy pushed for tax cuts during his administration, which were passed after his death. Among other changes, the top marginal tax rate was cut from 91 to 70 percent. During the 1980s a series of tax cuts were passed by Congress and signed by President

Ronald Reagan. Tax reforms passed during this era lowered the top personal marginal income tax rate from 70 percent down to 28 percent, reduced the number of tax brackets from 16 to 2, and indexed individual tax brackets to inflation. Innovations such as the Individual Retirement Account (IRA) were also developed. The top marginal corporate tax rate was reduced from 50 percent to 35 percent, and the Accelerated Cost Recovery System, which greatly reduced the disincentive facing business investment, was created.

One of the primary arguments used to justify these tax cuts was the Laffer Curve. If people are taxed at very high rates, they do not bother to work, and therefore produce no taxes. Therefore, in many circumstances, cutting marginal tax rates will increase government revenues.

Between 1986 and 1990 the federal tax burden rose as a share of GDP from 17.5 to 18 percent. Despite this increase in the overall tax burden, persistent budget deficits existed due to even higher levels of government spending. In 1990, the Congress enacted a significant tax increase raising the top tax rate from 28 to 31 percent. This act was signed by President George Bush breaking his famous "Read My Lips, No New Taxes" pledge. Bush did not believe in the economics behind the Laffer Curve having referred to it as Voodoo Economics. The Recession of 1990-91 soon followed.

Shortly after his election, President Clinton insisted on and the Congress enacted, a second major tax increase in 1993, in which the top tax rate was raised to 36 percent and a 10 percent surcharge was added, leaving the effective top tax rate at 39.6 percent. Despite the higher tax rates, other economic fundamentals such as low inflation and low interest rates, an improved international picture with the collapse of the Soviet Union, and the advent of qualitatively and quantitatively new information technologies led to a strong economic performance throughout the 1990s.

THE BUSH TAX CUT

In 2001, the Economic Growth and Tax Relief and Reconciliation Act was passed. This act lowers the top marginal federal income tax rate from 39.6 percent to 33 percent, expands a variety of savings incentives, and puts the estate, gift, and generation-skipping taxes on course for eventual temporary repeal. Unlike previous tax cuts, many provisions of the tax cut are temporary. For example, while the inheritance tax is repealed by 2010, it automatically returns at a very high tax rate

in 2011. Currently popular alternatives to the federal income tax system include the flat tax and the fair tax. The flat tax would be a drastic simplification of the federal income tax, whereas the fair tax would be a national sales tax as an alternative to the federal income tax.

SEE ALSO: Conservatism; Economy; Government Spending; Libertarian Party; Liberal Republican Party; Limited Government; National Debt; Socialist Party; Social Security.

BIBLIOGRAPHY. Neal Boortz and John Linder, *The FairTax Book: Saying Goodbye to the Income Tax and the IRS* (William Morrow, 2005); Burton Folsom, "The Progressive Income Tax in U.S. History", *The Freeman* (2003); Steve Forbes, *Flat Tax Revolution: Using a Postcard to Abolish the IRS* (Regnery Publishing, 2005); Greenspan Commission, *Social Security Online* (1983); "History of the U.S. Tax System", *Fact Sheets: Taxes* (2007); "Individual Income Tax Brackets, 1945-2007", *Tax Policy Center* (2007); Arthur B. Laffer, *Laffer Curve: Past, Present, and Future* (2004); "Nixon's Enemies List", *Wikipedia* (2007); Irwin Schiff, *How Anyone Can Stop Paying Income Taxes* (Freedom Books, 1982); "Social Security Insolvency Accelerating", *Budget and Tax News* (2005).

KIRBY R. CUNDIFF, PH.D.
NORTHEASTERN STATE UNIVERSITY

Technology

TECHNOLOGY HAS HAD more of an impact on recent political campaigns and American elections than ever before. The elections of 1996 and 2000 occurred in conjunction with the rise of the internet, while the 2004 election signaled extensive use of online discussion sites. The 2008 election may likely become known as the "YouTube election" for its use of video technology to communicate a candidate's position. Voters and politicians alike have found new ways to interact by transporting them to any place on the World Wide Web they chose.

Web surfers with a political bent can peruse the positions taken and speeches captured of their favorite candidates and, similarly, understand the rationale of competing viewpoints. Instant feedback and campaign contributions can be provided just as easily. The national election of 2004 and the 2006 midterm elections saw an increase in volunteers registering online, the number of polling booths replacing paper ballots with electronic ballots, and the use of email and electronic surveys used to aid candidates in understanding the "top-of-mind" issues in their district. Technology is now an integral part of every political campaign and election.

Politicians use technology today to reach a new voting bloc never before tapped. This group is typically younger, mobile, and impatient to get to the point. Consequently, the use of text message updates, interactive website surveys, and podcasts have opened up new avenues for getting the message out and compelling new voters to enter the world of active politicking. The net effect has been to increase the number of registered voters across the country and set the stage for even greater voter turn out in subsequent elections. Technology assists here, too. Absentee balloting has increased in many counties that offer this voting tool. Sonoma County, California found that more than half of the registered votes cast in the 2004 general election were absentee ballots: about 113,000 absentee ballots versus 110,000 precinct ballots. Technology enhances direct democracy. With the internet, candidates or elected officials communicate directly with the majority of their constituents. Intermediaries such as party officials have become mostly irrelevant. Elected officials take their direction from voters and local referenda. Only the funding provided by lobbyists continues to hold sway over politicians today.

LEVERAGING TECHNOLOGY

New technology, when properly leveraged by a candidate, can lead to electoral success. John F. Kennedy made television politics his own and took his party to national victory in the 1960s, while Jesse Ventura owned internet campaigning in his successful bid to become the governor of Minnesota 30 years later. Television and digital politics have arrived, but with an escalating cost. One reason for this expense is how candidates use technology to get their message out. In the past, party activists volunteered to visit voters to get the word out. Today, radio and television time must be secured to deliver the message. Money for Website development and direct mail campaigns must also be raised to reinforce the candidate's message. By the 1990s, nine of 10 senate campaigns and 70 percent of House candidates spent money for television

advertising. In addition to message-placement "buys," politicians feel compelled to hire professionals to run their campaigns. These advisers mold the candidate, shape their message, and define the winning strategy. Associated with this program are a new collection of consultants to lead the way including pollsters, media experts, fundraisers, strategists, direct-mail specialists, and more. Technology integration, the process of image shaping, and the cost of specialists makes political campaigning an expensive proposition.

Ronald Reagan's ascendancy was, in part, due to the extensive use of technology relative to his rivals. Republican party leaders, in 1979, recognized the power of enabling state and local party organizations to leverage national party-owned equipment for next to nothing. The success of the Reagan campaign signaled that modern-day election campaigns required the latest in computer technology, targeted survey research, television advertising, and direct-mail techniques to carry the candidate to victory.

Joe Andrew, before becoming Democratic National Convention chair, applied database technology to Indiana's voter rolls to better target the voting public. In 1996 and 1998, Andrew augmented the voting list with metrics such as age, income, religion, ethnicity, and even magazine subscriptions to profile prospective voters. He then messaged the data and provided it on CD-ROM disks to Indiana's local organizers. The valuable data allowed the local Democratic party to better target who to personally call, send direct mail, transmit e-mails, and canvass in person. Voter turnout was boosted and the Democrats elected more candidates during these two elections alone since the race of 1932. Use of technology and database management provided an effective plan for tactical engagement of the electorate. At the national level, as early as 1996, the major presidential candidates, including Bill Clinton, Bob Dole, and Ross Perot, established a presence on the web. Furthermore, in key swing states, extensive television advertising ran at least two times a week for 18 months.

Prior to 1990, there were only a handful of computers linked to the internet. By the mid-1990s this number shot up to one million computers connected to some 50,000 global networks. Businesses began to invest in e-commerce, which opened up opportunities for new companies like Amazon and enhanced existing retail outlets such as Barnes & Nobles with online shopping outlets. By 2003, more than 60 percent of U.S. house-

The rise of the web has made it easier to establish, maintain, and then broaden the reach of a third party. Many political commentators and media analysts believe the internet is the enabler for the rise of a multiparty system in American politics.

holds had computers and almost 55 percent of them were connected to the internet. The internet, like the computer, became an accepted tool for both business and personal use. It also ensured easy access to local, state, and national political leaders. Today, no viable candidate ignores this indispensable tool, especially as more than 70 percent of voting-age Americans are registered and most of them are online.

Technology plays a major role while voters cast their ballots on Election Day. The science of random sampling and computers permits television networks to conduct exit polls and accurately predict winners, even before the polls close. This scientific analysis takes away much of the drama of election night, but feeds the desire of many people to quickly learn about an outcome.

Sophisticated database management using desktop computers was a boon to all politicians. They can easily compile fundraising lists and recruit volunteers easily. The widespread acceptance of computers and internet connectivity has provided new ways to generate excitement and raise campaign funds. Momentum is a powerful incentive for many voters to contribute to a campaign, especially during the presidential season. An example of how the internet keeps the momentum of a campaign rolling was the April 2007 surprise that newcomer Senator Barack Obama raised more money than the seasoned Senator Hillary Clinton. During the first quarter on the road to the 2007 presidential primary season, Obama raised $6.9 million from 100,000 internet donors compared with Clinton's $4.2 million from 50,000 donors. Obama's support was more broad-based with donors averaging $100 each, versus Clinton's donors contributing the maximum amount of $2,300 each. The impulse to contribute to a candidate enables them to receive quick cash from the electorate to keep the campaign rolling. Besides cash, Obama had more "friends" in cyberspace as defined by the popular social networking site MySpace. He outdistanced Clinton by a factor of two-to-one.

Internet technology use also enables third parties to more actively participate in politics. Activists in minority parties are more able to communicate with voters. The rise of the web has made it easier to establish, maintain, and then broaden the reach of a third party.

Many political commentators and media analysts believe the internet is the enabler for the rise of a multiparty system in American politics. It was outsiders who brought internet technology and an associated web presence to the political arena. Ross Perot did so on a national scale in his bids for the White House, while Jesse Ventura leveraged his virtual presence in his successful bid to become governor of Minnesota. Both Perot and Ventura employed the internet as a powerful campaign tool in the 1990s.

Technology can be a double-edged sword when it is not properly integrated into a process involving many people with diverse backgrounds. The infamous 2000 presidential election and how it unfolded in Florida is a subject of much debate. It led to federal bills for election reform because Florida voter technology failed. Poor state administration squeezed county election supervisors in terms of money and training. Voters appeared at the polls in record numbers, but were untrained in the use of optical scan systems in some counties and suffered through the use of unreliable punchcard ballots in other counties. In spite of the Florida voting debacle, it highlighted the need for a major overhaul of the technology used at the time of elections. In spite of this incident it appears the use of technology as applied to campaigns and elections is here to stay.

SEE ALSO: Ballot Issues; Campaign Advertising; Direct Democracy; Internet Use in Political Campaigns; Polling Place.

BIBLIOGRAPHY. ABC, "Obama Bests Clinton in Primary Fundraising," www.abc.com (cited April 2007); Joe Garofoli, "Candidates and Voters Relying More on Internet," *San Fran-cisco Chronicle* (January 18, 2007); Martin Merzer, *The Miami Herald Report: Democracy Held Hostage* (St. Martin's Press, 2001); J.K. White and D.M. Shea, *New Party Politics: From Jefferson and Hamilton to the Information Age* (Bedford/St. Martin's Press, 2000).

ROBERT KARL KOSLOWSKY
INDEPENDENT SCHOLAR

Tennessee

NATIVE AMERICANS HAD settled Tennessee from about 9,000 B.C.E., with Hernando de Soto becoming the first European in the area in 1539–43. During the 17th century, European settlement opened up Tennessee, with some tribes from the east coast such as the Chickasaw and the Choctaw being resettled there. There was some fighting in Tennessee during the American War of Independence, but it was not until 1796 that Tennessee was granted statehood and formally became the 16th state of the Union. The first elected governor was John Sevier from the Democratic-Republican Party, of French Huguenot extraction, who served 1796–1801, completing three successive terms, the maximum allowed in the state Constitution. He was succeeded by Archibald Roane, also from the Democratic-Republicans, and, as with Sevier, a hero from the American War of Independence, but a bitter enemy of Sevier. Sevier returned to the governorship 1803–09, completing another three consecutive terms, making him the second longest serving governor in the history of the state, William Carroll serving only slightly longer.

Willie Blount, the fourth elected governor (Sevier is counted as both the first and third governor) was the younger half-brother of North Carolina politician William Blount. A lawyer, he was elected governor in 1809, served three terms, and was a strong supporter of the War of 1812. The fifth governor, Joseph McMinn was also "term limited," served three consecutive terms, with the interesting fact it was that McMinn who had helped introduce the constitutional requirement barring any governor from more than three consecutive terms when the 1796 constitution of the state was drafted. The next governor, William Carroll, was from Pennsylvania, as were Archibald Roane and Joseph McMinn. He also served three consecutive terms. With little opposition, there were two Democratic-Republican candidates in the 1827 gubernatorial elections Sam Houston was elected as governor, defeating former governor William Blount. Houston went on to serve as the seventh governor of Texas, becoming one of the few U.S. politicians to be governor of two different states. After Houston, William Hall was briefly governor, and then William Carroll returned to office to complete three more consecutive terms, making him the longest serving governor in the history of the state.

The demise of the Federalists led to state election contests between the Democrats and the Whigs. In 1838–39, many Native Americans from Tennessee were forcibly uprooted and moved to the Indian Territory (now Oklahoma), an action that killed of 4,000 of the 17,000. This changed the nature of the state, with more settlers from the east coast arriving as more land, previously occupied by the Native Americans, became available. In 1839, James K. Polk was elected governor of the state, serving only one term; in 1844, he was elected the 11th president of the United States. The 1841 senatorial election in Tennessee showed the power of the Whigs, but 13 Democratic Senators, who were nicknamed the "immortal thirteen" maneuvered to prevent two Whigs from taking their places in the U.S. Senate, and the state was unrepresented until 1843.

BORDER STATE

By the 1850s, the issue of slavery divided Tennessee, which was one of the border states. It was a period when men such as Thomas A.R. Nelson, Andrew Johnson, and William G. "Parson" Brownlow dominated state elections, including the governorship and the state legislature. Supporters of Nelson and Brownlow, both Whigs, fought those of Johnson, a Jacksonian Democrat, but in the gubernatorial election of 1853, Johnson, one of the "immortal thirteen," later U.S. vice president and then president, was elected and served until 1857. He was opposed to slavery, but many people in Tennessee hoped that war could be avoided. In the 1860 U.S. presidential election, Tennessee became one of the only three states to vote for John Bell of the Constitutional Union Party. He received 69,728 votes (47.7 percent) against John Breckinridge who received 65,097 votes (44.6 percent), and Stephen Douglas who managed only 11,281 votes (7.7 percent). The election of Abraham Lincoln,

who had not appeared on the ballot in the state, split Tennessee, breaking down traditional party lines. The initial moves to secede, initiated by Governor Isham Green Harris received qualified support from the state legislature, which finally resolved that the matter be decided by a state referendum. On June 8, 1861, a referendum was held with 104,913 voting to leave the Union, and only 47,238 voting to stay. In the west of the state, 83 percent voted for secession, in mid-Tennessee 88 percent voted for secession, but in Tennessee, support for secession was only 31 percent. A Unionist convention convened on June 17–20 in Greeneville, urging for eastern Tennessee to be given statehood, which did not take place, and on July 22, Tennessee joined the Confederate States of America.

CONFEDERATE STATE

The military governor of the state (appointed by the Union) 1862–65 was Andrew Johnson, the pre-war governor. During the Civil War, Johnson, Brownlow and Nelson all supported the Union, with the Emancipation proclamation bringing Johnson and Brownlow into a political alliance against Nelson. A War Democrat, so-named for his support for the Union during the Civil War, Johnson became a member of the newly-founded National Union Party, and was chosen to run as the vice presidential candidate in Abraham Lincoln's re-election bid. Johnson became vice president, and at the assassination of Lincoln became the 17th president of the United States. In a curious twist it was Nelson, Johnson's enemy in Tennessee state politics, who was to defend the president during Johnson's impeachment proceedings.

Johnson's harsh pronouncements on the Confederates won him support from the Radical Republicans, but Tennessee, which saw heavy fighting during the war, voted in William G. Brownlow, a Whig, as governor 1865–69, a move that was helped by Johnson no longer being involved in state politics. The gubernatorial election of 1867 saw a significant heightening of political tensions, with Brownlow supported by the Radical Republicans against Henry Emerson Etheridge, who was supported by the Conservative Unionists. Brownlow's supporters prevented many Confederate supporters from voting, and allowed many African Americans to vote. In 1869, DeWitt Clinton Senter was elected as governor in a backlash against Brownlow, ending the political power of the Radical

Republicans. The Democrats held successive gover-norships until Alvin Hawkins was sworn in as the first Republican governor of the state in 1881, having only won the gubernatorial election of the previous year due to a bitter split in the Democratic Party over the issue of state debt.

Hawkins served only one term, and the state returned to the Democratic fold. In the 1886 gubernatorial election, Alfred Alexander Taylor (1848–1931) lost to his younger brother, Robert Love Taylor (1850–1912). Alfred was later elected governor, and served 1921–23. The only break in 28 years of Democrat governors was the election in 1890 of John Price Buchanan. He was from the Farm-Labor Party and served as governor from 1891–93. Buchanan controversially introduced a pension for Confederate soldiers and civil servants, and also enlarged government secondary education. His governorship was rocked with violence in Nashville and other cities, and the state voted for Democrats continu-ously until the election in 1910.

PROGRESSIVES AND DEMOCRATS

Although the Democrats managed to win most of the gubernatorial elections in Tennessee in the 20th cen-tury, the 1900s saw a rise of the Progressives with both the Democrat candidate Malcolm Rice Patterson, and the Republican, H. Clay Evans, supporting economic and social reforms in their 1906 gubernatorial election campaigns. During 1908–12 the Democratic Party in Tennessee split over the issue of Prohibition, and this allowed the Republicans to briefly take back the gover-norship with Ben W. Hooper serving four years as gov-ernor, 1911–15. The dominance of the Democrats led to the emergence of many factions within their party, and many bi-factional election contests in the state for much of the rest of the 20th century.

The only occasion that the Republicans were able to win the governorship of the state was when Alfred A. Taylor won the 1920 gubernatorial election, defeating incumbent Albert H. Roberts. Much of this can be attrib-uted to the swing at a federal level toward the Republi-cans with the election as President of Warren Harding, as well as Roberts trying to introduce unpopular mea-sures, such as tax reform. Roberts had to survive a bitter Democratic primary campaign, trying to enfranchise women. Since then, the state voted Democratic in all gubernatorial elections until 1970 when a Republican, Winfield Dunn, was elected governor.

The concept of merchandising a candidate first emerged in Tennessee after World War I, with Clarence Saunders, who had founded the Piggly Wiggly grocery chain in Memphis, using advertising to successfully mer-chandise Austin Peay in the 1922 gubernatorial election, although he tried to undermine him soon afterwards. This was the period of the emergence of Democrat Party "boss," Edward Crump, who won a three-way primary campaign in 1932, that resulted in Harry Hill McAlister winning a narrow victory over Lewis Pope in an elec-tion campaign that revolved heavily around racism. In the 1936 gubernatorial elections, Gordon Browning campaigned hard and won a landslide victory in the Democratic primary, with the support of Crump and the Democratic Party machine from Memphis.

In the 1952 gubernatorial election, during the Dem-ocratic Party primary, incumbent governor Gordon Weaver Browning lost to Frank Goad Clement, who used evocative religious oratory to rally supporters, won the election, and remained governor until 1959. In the 1960 U.S. presidential election, Richard Nixon carried the state with 556,577 votes (52.9 percent) to John F. Kennedy's 481,453 votes (45.8 percent); and two years later Clement was re-elected as governor. In the 1964 U.S. presidential election, Lyndon B. Johnson carried the state with 635,047 votes (55.5 percent) to Barry Goldwater's 508,965 votes (44.5 percent). In 1968, Richard M. Nixon carried the state with 472,592 votes (37.8 percent), to George Wallace's 424,792 votes (34.1 percent), with Hubert Humphrey coming third with 351,233 votes (28.1 percent).

THE GORES

In the 1970 gubernatorial elections, Winfield Dunn was elected the first Republican governor since 1923. A prominent dentist, he served for four years, succeeded by Democrat Ray Blanton, who in turn was succeeded by Lamar Alexander, who was later U.S. Secretary of Edu-cation 1991–93, and who made unsuccessful runs for the U.S. presidency in 1996 and 2000. In both primary campaigns Alexander was forced out of the race before the Super Tuesday primaries when he was expected to pick up support from his home state and other southern states, but did not.

Al Gore, Jr., was prominent in Tennessee politics as a member of the U.S. House of Representatives 1977–85, the U.S. Senate 1985–93, and vice president of the United States 1993–2001. His father, Albert Gore, Sr., was U.S. Senator for Tennessee 1953–71. In 1994, Donald Sundquist was elected the 47th governor of Tennessee, the first governor of the state of Swedish descent. A Republican, he served two terms as governor, and in 2002, Phil Bredsen, a Democrat, won the gubernatorial elections. Although Tennessee supported Al Gore, Jr., in the 1992 and 1996 U.S. presidential elections, voting Democratic on both occasions, in the 2000 and 2004 U.S. presidential election, Tennessee supported Republican George W. Bush.

SEE ALSO: Constitutional Union Party; Democratic-Republican Party; Federalist Party; Machine Politics and Political Bosses; Slavery.

BIBLIOGRAPHY. J.M. Atkins, "Party Politics and Debate over the Tennessee Free Negro Bill," *Journal of Southern History* (v.71/2, 2005); H.J. Bingham, *Municipal Politics and Power: Tennessee Municipal League in Action* (Municipal Press, 1986); Earl Black, "A Theory of Southern Factionalism," *Journal of Politics* (v.45/3, 1983); L.S. Greene, *Lead Me On: Frank Goad Clement and Tennessee Politics* (University of Tennessee Press, 1982); William Lyons, J.M. Scheb and Billy Stair, *Government and Politics in Tennessee* (University of Tennessee Press, 2001); A.S. Macaulay, Jr., "Growing Pains: The Immortal Thirteen, the Destructive Twelve, and the Emergence of Two-Party Politics in Antebellum Tennessee," *Journal of East Tennessee History* (v.70, 1998); W.R. Majors, *Change and Continuity: Tennessee Politics since the Civil War* (Mercer University Press, 1986); L.E. Maness, "Henry Emerson Etheridge and the Gubernatorial Election of 1867: A Study in Futility," *West Tennessee Historical Society Papers* (v.47, 1993); J.R. Vile and Mark Byrnes, *Tennessee Government and Politics: Democracy in the Volunteer State* (Vanderbilt University Press, 1998).

JUSTIN CORFIELD
GEELONG GRAMMAR SCHOOL, AUSTRALIA

Texas

ORIGINALLY SETTLED BY the Spanish and the French, the United States, after the Louisiana Purchase of 1803, claimed some of the area which was to become Texas with the Spanish, and later the Mexicans, also making a claim. In 1821, Texas became a part of the Republic of Mexico and, two years later, Stephen F. Austin established a colony of 300 Anglo-Americans along the Brazos River, with the permission of the new Mexican authorities. In 1835, when Antonio López de Santa Anna became president of Mexico, he wanted to change the system of a federal government to establish greater central authority. Many Texan settlers opposed this, and, in 1836, they held a convention that signed a Declaration of Independence, defeating the Mexicans at the Battle of San Jacinto later that year.

The first president of the Republic of Texas was David G. Burnet, but in elections held on September 5, 1836, Sam Houston was elected president. He had been governor of Tennessee 1827–29, with many people believing that he had the administrative experience to lead Texas. Although Houston's term was not meant to begin until December, Burnet resigned from office on October 22, with Houston immediately assuming the office. Soon after Houston's election, debate started in Texas about whether the judiciary should be elected or appointed. The crises that faced early Texas meant that initially both houses of the state legislature elected the judiciary, a situation that continued until 1849, when the Texas constitution was altered to allow for popular election of all judges. In 1838, in the second presidential election, Mirabeau B. Lamar was elected president, with Burnet as his vice president.

When Lamar's term in office ended, the 1841 election was fought, with Houston getting 75 percent of the votes, easily defeating Burnet. In September 1844, Anson Jones, ran a quiet campaign, in contrast to the bitterness of 1841, when Burnet challenged Houston to a duel. Jones was elected, and urged for Texas to become a part of the United States. Texas was admitted to the Union on December 29, 1845.

James Pinckney Henderson, elected the first governor of Texas in November 1845, started a tradition of Democrat governors, with only four non-Democrats elected until 1979, two of which were Republicans elected immediately after the Civil War. In 1847, Mexican War hero George T. Wood was elected governor, and in the following year, Sam Houston was elected to the U.S. Senate by the Texas legislature. In 1848, there was a resurgence of the Whig Party in Texas in the presidential election, with the Whigs opposing the annexation of Texas. With much support throughout Texas, the Whigs in 1848, and 1852, attracted professional men as well as business interests who felt they would gain from federal projects. Governor Wood lost the 1849 election, and in the following year an election was held to determine a permanent site of the state capital, with Austin, the temporary capital, easily being the popular choice, especially for people in central and western Texas. The municipality that came in second was Tawakanah, which had the advantage of being centrally-located, and Palestine was the choice of most voters in eastern Texas.

The first non-Democrat governor was Elisha Marshall Pease, a former Democrat from Brazoria County, West Texas, who had lost the 1851 election, but won in 1853 as a Unionist candidate, where sectional rivalry between the west and the east of Texas was obvious. Pease was re-elected in 1855, with the American Party, popularly called the Know-Nothings, winning the state elections. In 1859, Sam Houston was elected governor, the first (and to date the only) person to be elected governor of two different states. Houston opposed the secession of Texas in 1861, but an election was held for delegates to a convention which authorized Texas to secede, which took place on February 1, 1861. This was approved by a referendum held exactly a month later. Houston, who refused to take an oath of loyalty to the Confederacy, was deposed and replaced by Edward Clark. He was then replaced by Francis R. Lubbock, who had been elected lieutenant governor in 1857, lost the position in the 1859 election, and in 1861 was chosen as governor.

CONFEDERATE ROLE

During the American Civil War, Texas provided many troops and supplies for the Confederate States. However, by the end of the war, the state was in chaos. Elisha Pease returned to mainstream politics in 1867, and was elected as the first Republican governor of the state, less than 10 years since he had previously held that office. Following him, Edmund J. Davis, a radical Republican, defeated moderate Republican Andrew J. Hamilton, who had gained support from some Democrats. This election was one of the closest in U.S. history up to that time, with nearly 80,000 votes cast, and Davis winning by only 783 votes. There were many allegations of intimidation of African-American voters by both sides. However, the following Texas gubernatorial election, in 1873, was even more controversial. It resulted in Richard Coke winning back power for the Democrats, the party winning every

subsequent Texas gubernatorial election until 1979. The 1873 election was heavily disputed, with the Texas Supreme Court eventually ruling that the event was unconstitutional, attempting to prevent Coke from taking office. In 1888, Texas started using the Australian (secret) ballot system, whereby ballots are printed at the public expense only at polling stations, contain the names of all candidates, and are marked in secret by the voter. A major modification was made in which the Texan ballot was to include the party candidates' affiliation on the ballot, which was not done in Australia at that time.

SOLIDLY DEMOCRATIC

For the rest of the 19th century, Texas remained solidly Democratic, although there were attempts to promote the Republicans in the 1890 gubernatorial election when the American financier Jay Gould visited Texas, urging the creation of a regulatory agency for railroads. In the early 20th century, James Edward "Pa" Ferguson emerged as a major political force, was elected governor in 1914, and sworn in on January 19, 1915. Re-elected in 1916, he tried to get the University of Texas to remove members of their faculty who he did not like. When the university refused, Ferguson vetoed the appropriations for the university, a move that was to lead for calls for his impeachment. Indicted in July 1917, he was convicted of 10 of the 21 charges brought against him, with the Texas Senate removing him as governor and declaring him ineligible to hold office again in the state. In spite of this, he did contest the 1918 election, losing to the incumbent, William Petty Hobby, Sr. This spurred him to run in the 1920 presidential election for the American Party, only appearing on the ballot in Texas, where he managed to get 47,968 votes (9.86 percent of Texan votes). He also failed to get a seat in the U.S. Senate in 1922. However, he remained popular, and his wife, Miriam A. Ferguson (known as "Ma Ferguson") was elected governor for two terms (1925–27 and 1933–35).

Miriam Ferguson openly proclaimed that if she were elected, the people of Texas would get "two governors for the price of one." She was the first female governor of any state in the Union. However, her time in office was extremely controversial. She refused to allow foreign languages to be taught in public schools in Texas saying, "if English was good enough for Jesus Christ, it ought to be good enough for the children of Texas."

She also granted many prisoners pardons, averaging 100 per month, with many allegations (although none were ever proven) that the pardons were in return for bribes. In 1926 and 1930, she tried to run as a Democrat in the gubernatorial election, but was defeated in the primaries. Narrowly winning the Democratic Party primary in 1932, defeating the incumbent Ross S. Sterling, she defeated Republican Orville Bullington who, nevertheless, did far better than most other Republicans had done in Texas state politics. In the 1932 gubernatorial election, George Washington Armstrong launched his Jacksonian Democratic Party bid, which was based on conspiracy theories of international Zionist threats. He only received about 1,000 votes. Miriam Ferguson retired in 1935, but did try to run again in 1940.

Throughout the remainder of the 1930s and through the 1960s, Texas remained staunchly Democratic. In the 1948 Texas Senate election, there was a battle between the Texas Loyalists, who supported Harry S. Truman, and white supremacists known as the Texas Regulars. Austin Congressman Lyndon B. Johnson defeated the former governor Coke R. Stevenson by only 87 votes. It was the closest senatorial vote in U.S. history, and there were doubts over what became known as "Ballot Box 13," which contained returns from the 13th Precinct town of Alice, Jim Wells County, which were believed to be fraudulent. The victory by Johnson led to a number of conspiracy theories, one, advanced by Ray Brown and Don Lasseter in their book *Broken Silence,* was that knowledge of this might have given Johnson a plausible reason to become involved in the assassination of John F. Kennedy.

On July 11, 1949, Governor Beauford H. Jester died, the only Texas governor to die in office. He was succeeded by Allan Shivers, the leader of the conservative wing of the Texas Democratic Party, who was to be governor for the next seven and a half years, the longest continuous tenure for a governor of Texas. One reason for Shivers's success was because his campaign assistant, Jake Pickle, established political organizations in 15 counties in east Texas in 1949, getting many of the urban middleclass to support the Democrats, who had previously relied heavily on rural voters. Gradually, Shivers became more Republican in his outlook, supporting Dwight Eisenhower's election bid in 1952, delivering Texas to the Republicans for only the second time since Reconstruction.

Senator (later president) Lyndon B. Johnson when he was the powerful Senate Majority Leader in 1955.

Shivers defected to the Republicans for the 1954 gubernatorial race, and defeated Ralph Yarborough, who gained most of his support from the workers and liberals. Shivers raised the worry of Communism (during the height of McCarthyism) and used racism to influence people in the election. Shivers was re-elected and retired from politics when his term in office finished in 1957. Six years later, John F. Connally, Jr. became arguably the most famous governor of Texas, because he was with President John F. Kennedy in Dallas on November 22, 1963, when Kennedy was assassinated.

In 1971–72, the Sharpstown Bank scandal occurred, involving Houston banker and insurance company manager, Frank Sharp, who granted bank loans of $600,000 for state officials who bought shares in National Bankers Life, the price of which Sharp artificially inflated. Allegations of bribery were made against Texas House Speaker Gus Mutcher, Jr., State Representative Tommy Shannon, and Elmer Baum, Chairman of the Texas Democratic Party, as well as against Lieutenant Governor Ben Barnes and Governor Preston Smith. In the state election held in 1972, which coincided with the presidential election, and thus resulted in an abnormally high turnout, Texas voters rejected everyone tainted by the scandal, with moderate Democrats, Republicans, and reformist candidates elected.

The scandal also had the longer-term effect of voters gradually beginning to decide their allegiance, not for party or historical reasons, or even on the main issues, but on the perceived personality of the candidates. Campaign advertising considerably increased the cost of elections. John Hill won the 1978 Democratic Party primaries, defeating incumbent governor Dolph Briscoe; and William P. "Bill" Clements won the election, becoming the first Republican governor of Texas since Reconstruction. It was the same trend that also saw Mark White defeat Price Daniel, Jr., in the Democratic primary for attorney general, and managed to defeat Republican Jim Baker in the election.

Bill Clements had won the Republican primary in 1978 with a landslide, getting 115,345 votes to 38,268 for Ray Hutchison, a prominent attorney from Dallas. The final election was very close with Clements getting 1,183,828 votes (49.96 percent) to former Supreme Court Chief Justice John L. Hill's 1,166,919 votes (49.24 percent), with the remaining three candidates getting 18,942 votes. The turnout was low and the Democrats won the 1982 gubernatorial election when a higher turnout favored them. In that election Clements received 1,465,537 votes (45.9 percent) with the winner, Democratic Attorney General Mark White securing 1,697,870 votes (53.2 percent). Clements returned as governor in 1987, after winning the 1986 elections, but decided not to run for a third term, with the Democratic State Treasurer Ann Richards winning the next election.

By this time, there was a clear two-party system in Texas, with the Republicans beginning to win more often than the Democrats. In the 1994 elections, Richards outspent her Republican rival, George W. Bush, by $2.6 million. Richards hoped that Bush would show his inexperience, but she lost popularity after calling Bush "some jerk." Bush won comfortably with 53 percent of the vote to 46 percent for Richards, and he served until December 21, 2000 when he stepped down to prepare for his inauguration as president. Lieutenant Governor Rick Perry succeeded him, and was elected in his own right in 2002, and again in 2006.

SEE ALSO: American Party; Australian Ballot; Know-Nothing Party; Whig Party.

BIBLIOGRAPHY. Dale Baum, "Chicanery and Intimidation in the 1869 Texas Gubernatorial Race," *Southwestern Historical Quarterly* (v.97/1, 1993); Dale Baum and J.L. Hailey, "Lyndon B. Johnson's Victory in the 1948 Texas Senate Race: A Reappraisal," *Political Science Quarterly* (v.109/4, 1994); T.M. Carsey, "Gubernatorial Electoral Coalitions in the Great Plains," *Great Plains Research* (v.1, 1997); F.A. Day and A.L. Jones, "A Portrait of Modern Texas Politics: The Regional Geography of the 1990 Governor's Race," *Social Science Journal* (v.31/2, 1994); R.F. Dobbs, "Lions, Lawyers and 'Lead Men': Allan Shivers' East Texas Political Network, 1950," *East Texas Historical Journal* (v.43/1, 2005); K.E. Hendrickson, Jr., "The Last Populist: George Washington Armstrong and the Texas Gubernatorial Election of 1932, and the "Zionist" Threat to Liberty and Constitutional Government," *East Texas Historical Journal* (v.40/1, 2002); K.E. Hendrickson, Jr., "The Last Populist: George Washington Armstrong and the Texas Gubernatorial Election of 1932," *Journal of the West* (v.41/4, 2002); Chris Klemme, "Jacksonian Justice: The Evolution of the Elective Judiciary in Texas, 1836–1850," *Southwestern Historical Quarterly* (v.105/3, 2002).

JUSTIN CORFIELD
GEELONG GRAMMAR SCHOOL, AUSTRALIA

Third Parties

THIRD PARTIES IN the United States describes both established parties other than the Republican and Democratic parties, and candidate-centered episodic organizations. Although a third party candidate has never won a major election, their performance varies wildly from election to election. In many presidential elections, the vote totals for third parties do not exceed one percent, while in some elections third-party candidates receive as much as 20 percent of the popular vote. Despite sustained electoral success, third parties serve an important function in American political life: they provide major parties with important cues and provide a channel for the voters to express their discontent. Third-party involvement in the American political process has transformed from the well-organized party involvement in the 19th century to candidate-centered, episodic, short-lived outbursts in the 20th century.

THIRD PARTIES IN THE 19TH CENTURY

Third parties in the 19th century were relatively successful in House, Senate and gubernatorial elections. In the last decade of the 19th century, and in early 20th century, third parties frequently won more than 10 percent of the popular vote in congressional and gubernatorial elections in many states. Third parties during the 19th century were, for the most part, established political organizations. Many third parties in this period were long-standing organizations that endured more than two presidential elections. Several third parties in this period were quite influential in American politics. The Free Soil Party was a substantive organization for three presidential elections before it became part of the Republican Party.

The Prohibition Party, even though it has never won more than three percent of the popular vote in presidential elections, has entered all presidential elections since 1872. The Greenback Party and People's Party (Populists) were anti-industrial pro-farmer/labor parties, that operated in the 1870s and 1890s, respectively. The Know-Nothing (American) Party was a nativist party supported by those who felt threatened by the record numbers of incoming immigrants in the 1840s and 1850s. Until the party was torn apart by the slavery issue during the 1856 convention Know-Nothing Party candidates won several elections, and controlled state legislatures in several states following the 1854 elections.

Third parties of the 19th century were not dependent on a single charismatic leader. They ran in federal, state, and local races and were able to attract experienced candidates. Even though a third-party candidate never won the presidency, third-party candidates have won several House and Senate seats, as well as governorships. However, third-party performance in congressional and gubernatorial elections declined sharply in 1930s. Some scholars attribute this decline to the introduction of the direct primaries and the Australian ballot. With its introduction in the 1890s, parties could no longer provide ballots to the voters. Providing ballots directly to the voters had allowed minor parties access to polling places and voters. Direct primaries also affected the third-party performance by opening the major parties to candidates who would otherwise seek the third-party route, discouraging campaign contributors and special interests to from supporting third parties.

Other scholars argue that electoral laws have not played that much of a role in the decline of third-party voting. They argue that it was the Democratic Party's cooptation of the left-wing policies during the New Deal era that led to the decline. According to this argument, the Democratic Party adopted policies that were previously the impetus for most left-wing third parties.

THIRD PARTIES IN THE 20TH CENTURY

Throughout the 20th century, several third-party candidates had strong showings in the presidential elections. Theodore Roosevelt's 1912 Bull Moose campaign under the Progressive Party ticket brought him 27 percent of the popular vote, but not the presidency. After Howard Taft succeeded Roosevelt as president in 1909, and failed to follow his progressive reforms, the Republican Party started to unravel. Roosevelt and Taft tried to reunite the party, but neither succeeded. Roosevelt decided to form a new party (Bull Moose) and run for the presidency. Roosevelt's decision to run for the presidency was markedly different from the third-party campaigns of the previous century. Before Roosevelt, every third-party run had beuan with an established party, which nominated its candidate. In Roosevlet's case, it was the candidate who founded the party.

Under similar conditions and following policy positions similar to Roosevelt's, LaFollette ran a Progressive campaign in 1924. Drawing support from farmers and labor he won almost 17 percent of the popular vote and Wisconsin's 13 electoral votes. Yet, his campaign experienced many difficulties. His reluctance to create a formal party organization disaffected both socialists who were trying to organize for future and Progressives alike. He could not raise nearly enough money to launch an effective campaign (he was outspent 20 to one by the Republicans). George Wallace's bid for the presidency grew in the south, where Wallace found support for his segregationist position. He won more than 13 percent of the popular vote and carried five southern states, with 46 electoral vote, which forced Nixon to adopt a more conservative position.

John Anderson's 1980, and Ross Perot's 1992, campaigns are the other strongest third-party performances in presidential elections. Ross Perot in 1992 even led in the opinion polls as late as five months prior to the elections. Perot's campaign was centered on two issues: balancing the budget and major party failure. He blamed both major parties for the huge public debt and promised to take steps to balance the budget. His message got to the people. His self-financed campaign brought him almost 19 percent of the popular vote, but no electoral votes because he could not beat both major parties in any state. After 1992, he founded the Reform Party and ran for president under Reform Party ticket in 1996, winning about eight percent of the vote. The common characteristic of 20th-century third parties was their dependence on individual candidates. Unlike their 19th century counterparts, third parties in the 20th century lacked longevity; they were not well-established organizations. In fact, most third-party campaigns during this period were little more than the individual efforts of candidates and their candidate organizations.

CONSTRAINTS

In addition to the third-party decline in non-presidential elections in the 20th century, life has never been easy for third parties in the United States. Third parties face a host of constraints in their bid for electoral success. There are three major constraints: barriers, which are legal institutional arrangements that make it harder for third parties to run; handicaps, which are systematic practical difficulties third parties face; and major party strategies.

Barriers are of several types; it is generally accepted that single-member districts and plurality voting facilitate a two-party system. Third parties fall victim to strategic voting (for example, voting for a candidate other than one's favorite in order not to waste the vote for a candidate who has no chance of winning). Also, ballot access restrictions, especially in presidential elections, hurt third parties' chance of running and launching effective campaigns. Even when third parties could secure ballot access in as many states as needed, this access usually has a very high price. Candidates have to

spend a lot of time and money to gain access. In 1980, John Anderson had no money left to advertise on television after securing ballot access in all states. Campaign-finance laws also hamper the third-party prospects. Major parties receive guaranteed federal support, while third parties must have ballot access in at least 10 states and receive at least five percent of the popular vote. Only 12 of over 150 third-party presidential candidates since 1840 would have secured this support had the law existed then. In 2000, Ralph Nader and the Green Party campaigned hard to pass this five percent threshold, but failed.

Apart from the legal obstacles, third parties also face practical inconveniences that make it hard for them to succeed at the polls. These handicaps have several sources. First, third parties usually do not have the necessary resources to run effective campaigns. In most presidential elections third parties do not have even 10 percent of the campaign resources of either major party. When third-party candidates can spend as much as the major party candidates, they also fare better at the polls. Theodore Roosevelt spent 60 percent of the average major party candidate and won 27 percent of the vote. Similarly, Ross Perot spent 119 percent of the average major party candidate and won 18 percent of the popular vote.

The resources available to third-party candidates are almost always a fraction of the major party opponents and even when third-party candidates raise money they have to spend it for securing ballot access, building a campaign organization, and so on, instead of advertising on the television and campaigning around the country. In addition to lack of campaign resources, third parties also lag behind the major parties in terms of the media coverage they receive. Third-party candidates are not invited to television debates anymore because they must show at least 15 percent support in national public opinion polls, an unrealistic threshold set by the Commission on Presidential Debates. Candidates are not invited to television debates and most commentary time is devoted to major party candidates. Without enough publicity via television and other forms of communication, third parties find it hard to make their candidates known.

Major parties also strategically act to cut third-party support. By adopting third-party positions as their own major parties try to capture as many votes from third parties as they can, as well from each other. Growing third-party support in the opinion polls signals major parties that there are disaffected voters and they hope to win their vote by adopting the position of the third party these voters support. Three types of constraints, then, restrict third parties and make it very difficult for them to successfully challenge the major parties in elections.

Third parties have not won elections in recent years, but they remain important, and do influence election outcomes. In the 2000 presidential elections, Ralph Nader won over 97,000 votes in Florida. The winner in Florida (George W. Bush) was decided by only a few thousand votes and many scholars, assuming most Nader voters are liberals, think that Ralph Nader cost Vice President Al Gore the election. In most presidential elections, the difference between the two major parties' votes is less than the third-party votes. Third parties also provide a channel for voters to express their discontent with the major parties and signal their desire for change. Major parties take this dissatisfaction seriously, occasionally by co-opting third parties.

SEE ALSO: Know-Nothing Party; Nader, Ralph; Presidential Election of 1912; Presidential Election of 1992; Prohibition Party.

BIBLIOGRAPHY. P.R. Abramson, et al., "Challenges to the American Two-Party System: Evidence from the 1968, 1980, 1992 and 1996 Presidential Elections," *Political Research Quarterly* (v.53, 2000); P.R. Abramson, et al., "Third Party and Independent Candidates: Wallace, Anderson, Perot," *Political Science Quarterly* (v.110, 1995); J.F. Bibby and L.S. Maisel, *Two Parties—or More? The American Party System* (Westview Press, 2003); Shigeo Hirano and J.M. Snyder, Jr., "The Decline of Third Party Voting in the United States," *Journal of Politics* (v.69/1, 2007); D.A. Mazmanian, *Third Parties in Presidential Elections* (Brookings Institution, 1974).

ESER SEKERCIOGLU
STONY BROOK UNIVERSITY (STATE UNIVERSITY OF NEW YORK)

Thurmond, J. Strom (1902–2003)

PERHAPS THE MOST significant third-party presidential candidate of the 20th century, J. Strom Thurmond was also the oldest serving senator, and at the time he left office, had served the longest senatorial career. A South Carolinian lawyer, Thurmond served in the state Senate and as a judge in the Eleventh Circuit Court before joining the army during World War II. He returned heavily decorated, and was elected governor in 1946. As a young man, he fathered an illegitimate child with an African-American woman, Carrie Butler, a fact that was only revealed after his death, though throughout his daughter's life, he offered her financial and emotional support.

During his term as governor, the national debate over segregation intensified. At the 1948 Democratic National Convention, a number of the conservative Southern Democrats, Thurmond included, expressed their outrage over Truman's growing support of integration, and his integration of the U.S. Army. When the party adopted an antisegregation platform over southern protests, 35 delegates walked out. These delegates formed the States' Rights Democratic Party (also known as the Dixiecrats), which upheld segregation as a matter to be determined by individual states according to rights guaranteed them by the Constitution. It was a drastic split with tradition: since the Civil War, the solid south had been staunchly Democratic.

Thurmond had organized the walkout, and was nominated the Dixiecrat candidate, with Mississippi governor Fielding Wright as his running mate. In several southern states, including Thurmond's South Carolina, the Dixiecrat candidates were listed as the official Democratic ticket, which accounted for Thurmond's success in garnering 39 electoral votes (of 531). Though Thurmond had only 2.4 percent of the popular vote, compared to third-party candidate Ross Perot's 18.9 percent in 1992, Perot won no electoral votes. That Thurmond's share of the electoral vote was quadruple that of his popular support demonstrates the strong regional nature of his appeal.

After losing a senatorial campaign in 1950, Thurmond was forced to run as a write-in candidate in 1954, when the South Carolina Democratic Party refused to nominate him because he had supported Republican candidate Dwight Eisenhower in the 1952 presidential election. He became the only senator elected as a write-in candidate, and pursued his anti-integration platform aggressively in the Senate. When the majority of southern Democrats agreed not to filibuster the Civil Rights Act of 1957, Thurmond ignored them. His filibuster set a still-unbroken record of 24 hours and 18 minutes, though the bill passed. In 1964, discontent with the civil rights platform of the Democratic Party, he switched affiliation to the Republican Party, and drummed up support in South Carolina for presidential candidate Barry Goldwater.

In the 1968 presidential election, Thurmond's support of Richard Nixon was one of the factors that informed Nixon's "Southern strategy," by which electoral votes were courted in the south, long-ignored by the GOP as a Democratic stronghold. Thurmond, as a sort of unofficial southern ambassador to the party, was instrumental in Nixon's choice of Maryland governor Spiro Agnew as his running mate, and became a significant force in 1970s Washington, after spending the previous decade and a half concerned with little beyond his opposition to civil rights. This power waned in the Reagan years, though, because of Thurmond's broken promise to support Reagan's candidacy (he endorsed dark horse John Connally, who like Reagan and Thurmond was a Democrat turned Republican). His views on race mellowed as the times changed, and his blanket opposition to the nomination of African Americans to various positions ended; he was one of the senators who voted to make Martin Luther King Jr.'s birthday a national holiday.

Thurmond served as president pro tempore of the Senate 1981–99. Although by this time he took a more moderate position than many southern conservatives, American liberals often referenced him as a symbol of dated southern conservatism, recalling his Dixiecrat candidacy, his filibuster, and his many speeches in support of segregation. He never denounced or distanced himself from those views; he simply stopped expressing them. He retired from the Senate after 2002, and died in June of the following year at the age of 100.

SEE ALSO: Jim Crow Laws; Populists and Populist Movements; Presidential Election of 1948; Sectionalism.

BIBLIOGRAPHY. Jack Bass and M.W. Thompson, *Strom: The Complicated Personal and Political Life of Strom Thurmond* (Public Affairs, 2005); Nadine Cohodas, *Strom Thurmond and the Politics of Southern Change* (Mercer University Press, 1994); Kari Frederickson, *The Dixiecrat Revolt and the End of the Solid South* (University of North Carolina Press, 2001); E.M. Washington-Williams, *Dear Senator* (Regan Books, 2005).

BILL KTE'PI
INDEPENDENT SCHOLAR

President Ronald Reagan (left) greeting Senator J. Strom Thurmond at the White House.

Travel

THE GOAL OF any political campaign is to promote a candidate through a series of effective messages that connect with and encourage an optimal number of voters. Over time, campaigns have accordingly developed innovative ways to give candidates a visible presence. But there are many time-honored ways to further define and establish the mission of the candidacy, communicate it to followers, and otherwise familiarize voters with a candidate. Among such strategies and tactics is the campaign stop, a personal appearance made by a candidate that requires the candidate travel from one place to another. As new modes of transportation have been invented, travel plans and patterns have changed dramatically, yet have remained a basic element of the political campaign.

While politicians have increasingly traveled beyond their home bases in efforts to shape public opinion, campaign-related travel has long depended heavily on

Air Force One *can make a powerful impression during a presidential campaign. Above, President Gerald Ford (left) on a campaign trip aboard* Air Force One *through the deep south in 1976.*

status. How far a distance and where a candidate or political personality travels depends on a number of factors, including notoriety, popularity, and electability. It also is contingent on the individual's position on key issues, as well as which type of office the candidate or personality is running for or holds at the time. For example, many sources indicate that incumbent members of Congress are often re-elected, in part, because taxpayers support an unlimited number of House members' trips between Washington, D.C., and their districts. From a similar perspective, sitting presidents have the unmatched opportunity to use the symbols and importance of their office to simultaneously govern and campaign.

Presidential travels became a part of American conscience when, in his first three years as chief executive, George Washington officially visited each of the states in

the newly-formed union. Records from 1789 and 1790 recall tours he took to the parts of New England that had ratified the constitution; in 1791, he devoted four months to traveling throughout the southern states. Of his travels was born a custom of exchange whenever he came to a community: Washington would be greeted and honored by a welcoming committee, and would reply to the public reception with patriotic messages and commendations of the community. He also designated these visits as opportunities to better connect the American people with their government, rather than events at which to promote any administration policy.

These tours are also noteworthy because Washington rode on horseback or via horse-and-carriage over poor roads that made travel unpleasant. Due to the relative hardship of travel, and despite the invention of the steamboat, Washington's successors chose to remain close to the nation's capital. Such was the case until the advent of the railroad in 1829. In 1833, Andrew Jackson became the first president to ride on a train, and Lincoln rode one to Gettysburg, Pennsylvania, 30 years later. As the system expanded, Lincoln's travels by railroad increased in frequency, especially following Civil War battles, further encouraging a consistent trend of travel and exposure.

By the 1950s, airplanes emerged as a means for candidates to more readily participate in direct campaigns throughout the states and across the country. Although Franklin D. Roosevelt had, in 1943, become the first sitting president to be flown in an aircraft and Dwight D. Eisenhower initiated use of the jet-powered passenger airliner in 1959, it was during John F. Kennedy's administration that the use of an aircraft is considered to have first became a political symbol. Since Kennedy, every president has flown aboard— and used as a backdrop—the various incarnations of the unmistakable, specialized aircraft known as *Air Force One*.

IMPORTANT SYMBOLS

The power of the presidency has often provided access to innovative modes of transportation. It has also served as a standard-bearer for new adventures in travel, especially with the sense that the president is engaged in a "permanent campaign" of governing while nourishing popularity. The mode of transportation a candidate uses during a campaign is not only an important symbol, but also a means through which a candidate can be identified. One example of the use of travel to add spectacle to a campaign occurred during in the nomination Franklin D. Roosevelt for president in 1932. The then-governor of New York and his entourage flew from Albany, New York to Chicago, where, upon landing, they were met by a motorcade that escorted Roosevelt to his official acceptance as the Democratic Party nominee.

The precedent for modern campaign travel emerged from the 1948 presidential campaign in which the Democratic incumbent Harry S. Truman was challenged by the Republican nominee Thomas Dewey. Truman sought re-election, but consistently received low approval ratings in public opinion polls and lagging support from members of his own party. This, combined with media coverage, helped Dewey build a significant lead in the run-up to the election. In response, Truman embarked on a "Whistle Stop" tour of the United States.

The "Whistle Stop" campaign was designed to allow Truman to deliver short messages from the back of a train that made brief stops in front of people in small communities, large towns, and big cities. It essentially brought localized activity to what was a national campaign. That is, the strategy was based on the simple logic that a personal appearance would provide an opportunity for a candidate to communicate directly with people. And because such events would be held without the interfering presence of other candidates, the individual candidate could likely generate more localized media coverage and exposure through which to convey a message.

Despite prevailing belief, candidate visits and direct campaigning do not necessarily translate into shows of support by voters. But Truman eventually won both the popular and electoral votes—a come-from-behind victory that was largely attributed to his "Whistle Stop" campaign. His success has since compelled candidates to attempt to discover similar ways to reach voters.

Personal appearances provide messages that, reinforce the decisions of individuals who believe in, and want to associate themselves with, a candidate they feel will be successful. Today, many political actors—whether they are candidates, potential candidates, or individuals campaigning on behalf of candidates—travel virtually any distance to carefully-orchestrated events to maximize media coverage and exposure. These events can include an address to reinforce policy to a political base, to persuade legislators and their constituents in a swing state, or merely to keep one's name in the news media. At other times, the same individuals may choose more private travel plans and events designed to avoid the media altogether.

FUNDING TRAVEL

Toward the end of the 20th century and in the first years of the 21st century, there has been increased attention paid to campaign finance reform, especially whether "soft-money" or "hard-money" is used to fund such arrangements. Nevertheless, innovations and changes in transportation, logistics, communication, polling data, number of delegates, and number of electoral votes have combined to create a matrix of available options for campaign itineraries. Candidates can choose to travel by airplane, private bus, or some other mode of transportation. Attitudes and ideas about campaigning have changed over time, both as a cause of, and as a response to, attitudes and ideas about travel.

SEE ALSO: Battleground States; Campaign Spending; Candidate Image; Local Media Coverage of Campaigns; Media, Role in Campaigns; Presidential Election of 1948.

BIBLIOGRAPHY. Sidney Blumenthal, *The Permanent Campaign: Inside the World of Elite Political Operatives* (Beacon Press, 1980); R.B. Cialdini, *Influence: The Psychology of Persuasion* (Collins, 2006); Von Hardesty, *Air Force One: The Aircraft that Shaped the Modern Presidency* (Creative Publishing International, 2003).

LEE H. IGEL
NEW YORK UNIVERSITY

Trust in Government

THE STRUCTURE, PROCEDURES, and legitimacy of American democracy rely on a system in which a body of citizens freely elects its government representatives. For this form of government to function effectively, it must be accountable to the people and the people must have trust in it. The extent to which people have trust in government is of great importance because it affects how and why they vote, which can have an enormous influence on the composition and function of government. Trust is a psychological dimension. It comes in many forms and from many sources, so people evaluate or perceive it differently. There is, however, general consensus on how citizens determine their degree of trust in government. People tend to have more trust in government when they feel satisfied with the performance of their leaders and institutions. However, government is susceptible to lower degrees of trust among the public during times of deception, controversy, or inattentiveness to the needs and interests of the population.

Because citizens have the right to vote for their government representatives, trust is an important feature of the process and outcome of voter decisions. Varying degrees of trust in government affect how voters feel about particular candidates, policy propos-

als, issues, institutions, and the overall legitimacy of government. Whether the people of a democracy trust their government can alter the result of an election. A relationship predicated on trust between people and government is concept expressed in the Constitution and other documents and works authored by founding fathers such as Thomas Paine, Thomas Jefferson, James Madison, and Alexander Hamilton. Implicit in their thoughts was the knowledge that the citizenry would not always be in favor of government policy and action; they consequently instituted representative government as a means by which to protect against any public inclination toward a system of direct control. However, at the core of their doctrine was the notion that the primary source of political power in a democracy lies with the people.

Although there are many ways to measure trust, scholars, pollsters, and observers agree that people's trust in government has been in decline since the 1960s. As the United States developed through the 19th century and into the 20th century, people increasingly believed U.S. government was capable enough and could be relied on to do almost anything. This view was fostered by government's effective organization and mobilization during World War I and World War II, and exemplified by people's dependence on government to relieve the Great Depression. But by the 1960s, government had become increasingly bureaucratic. Government bureaucracy, together with changing social norms, expanding media scrutiny, controversy over the war in Vietnam, and the Watergate scandal in the early 1970s, left the public increasingly disenchanted with, and distrustful of government. Through the remainder of the 20th century and into the early 21st century, remnants of these affairs combined with various other economic, social, and political events to continue—with a few exceptions, such as the months following the attacks of 9/11—this downward trend.

Although the economic, social, and political issues that dominate the headlines often shape people's perceptions of government, less visible and less direct factors also contribute to their trust in government. These underlying variables include people's identification with a political party, whether government policy reflects (or otherwise aligns with) public preferences, and perceptions about the fairness, openness, and responsiveness of government and political figures.

Identification with a political party provides a short-cut through which people acquire context and clarity about the vast amount of information contained in the political world. It also increases the likelihood that people will vote, and is an indicator of which candidates and policies they will support. Further, people who identify with a particular party usually have a lot of confidence in it.

When their party is in control of government institutions, and especially when that group or individuals within it are politically successful, people tend to be more approving and trusting of government; when they identify with a losing party, people tend to be less supportive and trusting of government, its institutions, and it agents and officials.

At the same time, if a political party and its leadership hope to receive the trust of their followers, as they must satisfy those followers with policy generation. That is, followers, or partisans, typically remain trusting of the party with which they identify so long as it pursues policies similar to their own, even in instances in which the policy outcome is not in accordance with policy preferences. In addition, because democratic institutions are highly dependent on integrity, citizens check for indications of whether political representatives are upholding the public trust. When citizens perceive or discover politicians to be dishonest, reckless, dominated by special interests, or in other ways inefficient, they generally treat government and its operations with a degree of mistrust. The rise in public distrust has increasingly been attributed to a preponderance of critical and negative portrayals of political figures and institutions by mass media.

How much of a direct effect such actions have on trust is difficult to measure. Nationally or locally, how people evaluate government is due in large part to the combination of features inherent in democracy, including partisanship, which party is in control of the executive branch, and which party is in control of the bicameral legislative branch.

Thus, a complex array of possible causes of satisfaction or dissatisfaction with politicians and institutions must be considered to fully understand people's trust in government. Whether people trust government or not is of profound importance in a democracy because it influences their willingness to participate in a government that is fundamentally of, for, and by the people.

SEE ALSO: Corruption and Democratic Elections; Direct Democracy; Participatory Democracy; Political Legitimacy and Democracy; Presidential Approval Ratings; Psychological Reasons for Voting and Nonvoting; Representative Democracy.

BIBLIOGRAPHY. P.F. Drucker, *The Age of Discontinuity* (Harper and Row, 1969); Sissela Bok, *Lying: Moral Choice in Public and Private Life* (Vintage Books, 1978); R.B. Cialdini, *Influence: Science and Practice* (Allyn & Bacon, 2000); J.S. Nye, Jr., P.D. Zelikow, and D.C. King, eds., *Why People Don't Trust Government* (Harvard University Press, 1997).

LEE H. IGEL
NEW YORK UNIVERSITY

Tweed, William (1823–78)

ONE OF THE most powerful politicians in New York City in the years following the Civil War, William Marcy "Boss" Tweed for a time led the formidable Tammany Hall political ring, but ultimately died behind bars a broken man. While in power, Tweed personified the political and financial corruption that often plagued American cities during the Gilded Age.

Tweed was born in New York City and, in early life, held a variety jobs including bookkeeper, chair maker, and volunteer fireman. It was through his work with the fire department that Tweed first became involved in ward politics. He parlayed his local influence into a seat as an alderman in 1852, and soon afterwards he won election as a Democrat to the U.S. House of Representatives. By 1856, Tweed was back in New York City, where he won election to the New York Board of Advisors. Tweed became a true political force after his 1863 election as "Grand Sachem" of the Society of Tammany. The group was originally a fraternal organization, but by the Civil War it had become heavily involved in New York City politics.

From his position as leader of "Tammany Hall," Tweed held power through his ability to control patronage in the city. He made certain that corrupt friends were appointed to important offices, and held several positions himself. Following the Civil War, "Boss" Tweed and his Tammany Hall friends had a fierce grip on politics in the city, controlling not only patronage, but New York

A political cartoon of Tammany Hall Boss Tweed by illustrator Thomas Nast, 1876.

to expose the Tammany ring. In his popular caricatures, Nast usually portrayed Tweed as a bloated, well-dressed swindler with no conscience, and at least some New Yorkers began to take notice. Tweed and his friends unsuccessfully pressured the magazine to fire Nast, and reportedly offered the cartoonist a bribe of several hundred thousand dollars to cease his activities. Eventually, Tweed's conduct drew significant public attention, and New York governor Samuel Tilden established a commission to investigate fraud and corruption in New York City. Hoping to topple the boss from power, Tweed's rivals within the Democratic Party began cooperating with the investigation, offering evidence of Tweed's crimes. In 1873, Tweed was convicted of corruption and sentenced to 12 years in prison. While the initial sentence was reduced, the state of New York sued the disgraced politician for millions of dollars and filed additional charges. In 1875, Tweed escaped from prison, fled to Cuba, and eventually made his way to Spain, where he was arrested by Spanish authorities who identified him using one of Nast's cartoons. Tweed was extradited to the United States and died in prison on April 12, 1878.

SEE ALSO: Machine Politics and Political Bosses; New York; Scandals, State and Local Elections; Tammany Hall.

BIBLIOGRAPHY. K.D. Ackerman, *Boss Tweed: The Rise and Fall of the Corrupt Pol Who Conceived the Soul of Modern New York* (Carrol & Graf, 2005); S.J. Mandalbaum, *Boss Tweed's New York* (Blue Ribbon Books, 1931).

BEN WYNNE
GAINESVILLE STATE COLLEGE

City's cash flow as well. Corruption was widespread as the group siphoned away millions of public dollars for their own use. Estimates vary widely, but the Tammany ring may have stolen as much as $100 million 1868–70.

Like other political bosses of the period, Tweed led a ring that was efficient in providing city services, regardless of his personal misdeeds. His organization secured various types of relief for the poor, funding for increased construction and renovation of hospitals, public buildings, and city streets, and land for museums and parks. This made Tweed very popular with many New York voters, especially the working class, who came to view him as a larger-than-life Robin Hood figure and did not question his methods.

As Tweed lined his pockets, Thomas Nast, an influential cartoonist for *Harper's Weekly*, began a campaign

Twelfth Amendment

THE TWELFTH AMENDMENT, adopted in 1804, ensures that members of the Electoral College cast separate, specific votes for president and vice president, effectively guaranteeing party tickets. It also specifies that the House of Representatives elects the president when no candidate receives a majority of electoral votes. In that instance, the House is to choose from among the three candidates who received the most electoral votes, by state delegation (each state has an equal vote, regardless of how many representatives are in each delegation).

The presidential election of 1800 was hotly contested. Democratic-Republicans Vice President Thomas Jefferson and Aaron Burr challenged incumbent Federalist President John Adams and Charles Pinckney. Jefferson and Burr received more popular votes than their opponents, but each party received the same number of electoral votes.

Under the applicable constitutional provision (Article II, section 1) electors were directed simply to cast two votes for president, with whoever received the most electoral votes becoming president and whoever received the second-most becoming vice president. It was unclear who would assume which office, although Jefferson was the intended presidential candidate, and Burr was the intended vice presidential candidate, Burr would not stand down. The fact that Federalists controlled the outgoing Congress further complicated matters. Many Federalists supported Burr, simply to oppose Jefferson, knowing that neither of the Federalist candidates could assume the presidency. They could at least frustrate the opposition by switching the two officeholders. Federalist Alexander Hamilton lobbied members of his party to support Jefferson, even though Hamilton disagreed with Jefferson politically, and personally liked Burr better. After tense negotiations, including alleged offers and acceptances of deals by both Jefferson and Burr, Jefferson prevailed on the 36th ballot a mere two weeks prior to inauguration.

In the 1824 presidential election, no candidate received an electoral vote majority. Four candidates, all of the Democratic-Republican Party, received electoral votes: Andrew Jackson, military hero and senator from Tennessee (99 votes), John Quincy Adams, secretary of state (84), William Crawford, secretary of the treasury (41), and Henry Clay, speaker of the house (37). Under the terms of the amendment, the House of Representatives was to choose from among Jackson, Adams, and Crawford.

Even though as the fourth candidate he was ineligible for election, Clay's position as speaker assured that he would play on important role in the House proceedings. Clay believed that Adams was the best of the available options, though he disagreed with him on several issues. Clay mistrusted Jackson based on his military service and his fear of the military threat to democratic rule, and was concerned about Crawford's failing health (he had suffered a paralytic stroke in late 1823). In large part due to Clay's sup-

port, Adams was able to win the presidency on the first ballot in the House.

In the 1876 election, an ambiguity in the amendment came to light. Although it calls for electoral votes to be counted in the presence of the House and Senate, neither the amendment nor the language it replaced specified who was to count; nor did it state what to do in the case of multiple returns. Several states submitted multiple sets of electoral ballots, and both the Democratic House and Republican Senate favored different interpretations of who had the power to count and rule on the validity of the ballots. In the end, an extra-constitutional Electoral Commission was used to award the White House to Republican Rutherford B. Hayes. A federal law adopted in 1887 further specifies the powers pertaining to counting and ruling on the validity of electoral votes.

SEE ALSO: Democratic-Republican Party; Electoral College; Federalist Party; Presidential Election of 1800; Presidential Election of 1824; Presidential Election of 1876.

BIBLIOGRAPHY. Jonathan Daniels, *Ordeal of Ambition: Jefferson, Hamilton, Burr* (Doubleday, 1970); Mary Hargreaves, *The Presidency of John Quincy Adams* (University Press of Kansas, 1985); Roy Morris, Jr., *Fraud of the Century: Rutherford B. Hayes, Samuel Tilden, and the Stolen Election of 1876* (Simon & Schuster, 2003).

Scott Markowitz
University of Florida

Twenty-Fourth Amendment

ONLY FIVE STATES still imposed a poll tax on their voters in August of 1962 when the Twenty-Fourth Amendment was proposed. This amendment, also known as the anti-poll-tax amendment, made it illegal for the states to require voters to pay a poll tax to be eligible to vote in presidential and congressional elections. Once submitted to the states for ratification, it took less than two years for the amendment to become part of the Constitution. Then, the Voting Rights Act of 1965 gave the attorney general, under the Fourteenth and Fifteenth Amendments, the power to prosecute any state that made the payment of a poll tax a prerequisite to the voting process. The act also allowed private individuals to sue such entities for imposing such a tax. Finally, in 1966, the Supreme Court determined that the poll tax violated the Equal Protection Clause of the 14th Amendment, and therefore it was formally declared unconstitutional, not only for presidential and congressional elections, but also for state and local elections.

From the mid-19th century to the mid-20th century, a poll tax (a fixed amount of money required to be paid prior to being allowed to register to vote in presidential, congressional, state, and local elections) was used by a number of southern states for the stated purpose of ensuring that each person only voted once per election cycle.

However, the true reason for this tax was to ensure that the only eligible voters in these elections were wealthy and white. Even after the passage of the Fifteenth Amendment, which extended the right to vote to all races, many southern states found a way to continue their discriminatory practices. This was achieved by including a grandfather clause within the poll tax allowing men who had either a father or grandfather eligible to vote prior to the abolition of slavery to vote without paying the tax. This ensured that Native Americans, a large portion of poor whites (for the most part immigrants), and African Americans were effectively disenfranchised.

While there were proposals over the years to abolish this tax, it was not until 1962 that an amendment was passed declaring such taxes illegal in presidential and congressional elections. Congress may not have been able to pass such an amendment until the 1960s, but all but five of the states had, by this time, voluntarily rescinded their poll taxes. On January 23, 1964, poll taxes were no longer allowed in federal elections.

The Supreme Court first interpreted this amendment in 1965 in *Harman v. Forssenius*. It determined that Virginia's prerequisites, the requirement of filing a residency certificate before each election or, alternatively, paying the poll tax, prior to citizens being allowed to vote was in violation of the Twenty-Fourth Amendment. As such, the Court struck down this requirement.

Then in 1966, in *Harper v. Virginia State Board of Elections*, the court declared the use of a poll tax in any election within the United States to be unconstitutional and in violation of the Equal Protection Clause of the Fourteenth Amendment.

Finally, Congress sealed the death of the poll tax by including in Section 10 of the Voting Rights Act of 1965, a direct order to the attorney general to seek out and obtain injunctive relief from states that used the poll tax as a prerequisite to the ability to vote in federal, state, or local elections. This section also provided the ordinary citizen with the right to litigate against the enforcement of this tax.

SEE ALSO: Court Cases, Federal Elections; Court Cases, State and Local Elections; Fifteenth Amendment; Poll Tax; Voting Rights Act of 1965.

BIBLIOGRAPHY. Joan Biskupic and Elder Witt, *The Supreme Court & Individual Rights* (CQ Press, 1997); Johnny Kilman and Kenneth Thomas, eds., *The Constitution of the United States of America: Analysis and Interpretation* (U.S. Government Printing Office, 2006); J.W. Peltason, *Understanding the Constitution* (Harcourt Brace College Publishers, 1997); S.J. Rosenstone and R.E. Wolfinger, "The Effect of Registration Laws on Voter Turnout," *American Political Science Review* (v.72/1, 1978).

RACHEL YFF
UNIVERSITY OF FLORIDA

Twenty-Second Amendment

ALTHOUGH A PRECEDENT had been set in the 19th century that presidents of the United States should only serve two terms in office, Franklin D. Roosevelt ignored this tradition in 1940. As a result, many in Congress felt that the time had come to make the long-standing precedent a firm constitutional requirement. Therefore, on March 24, 1947, the Twenty-Second Amendment to the U.S. Constitution was proposed, limiting the president to two terms in office. It also set a limit for any president who serves more than two years of another's presidency to one term in office.

Within four years of its proposal, on February 27, 1951, the amendment had been ratified by more than the required three-fourths of the states. While the creation of the tradition of two terms in office has often been attributed to George Washington, in his 1796 Farewell Address, it was actually Thomas Jefferson, in 1788, who first expressed concern over the ease with which the presidency could become a lifetime position. Franklin D. Roosevelt broke this tradition when he decided to run not only for a third term in 1940, but for a fourth term in 1944.

The amendment was a direct result of Roosevelt's four terms in office. The Republican-led Congress proposed a constitutional amendment limiting the president to two terms in office. The rationale for the amendment was based on the belief that without term limits the presidency could turn into a dictatorship. Democrats, however, felt that it was an attempt to reach beyond the grave to admonish Roosevelt. The extreme partisan nature of this issue was barely hidden behind the veil of constitutional debate, which never focused on the fact that the delegates at the Constitutional Convention did not include any eligibility limitations on the presidency in the U.S. Constitution.

Nevertheless, the House passed the presidential term limit amendment by a vote of 285 to 121 on February 6, 1947. The Senate passed the amendment on March 12, 1947 by a vote of 59 to 23. In both the House and the Senate, Republicans passed the amendment unanimously, while the yea votes from the Democrats consisted mainly of southerners.

The amendment was then sent for ratification by three-fourths of the states. It took 41 states approximately four years to ratify this amendment. By the end of 1947, the 18 states that had ratified the amendment were mostly Republican strongholds. From this time until February 27, 1951, the remaining 18 states needed to reach the three-fourths requirement were obtained, mostly from conservative Democratic southern states.

The issue of presidential term limits was visited again during Ronald Reagan and William J. Clinton's terms in office. During Reagan's presidency, many Republicans considered repealing the amendment to allow him to serve a third term. However, this idea was quickly dropped when it became clear that Reagan would not be a viable presidential candidate in another election. At the end of Clinton's second term in office, there was also discussion about the possibility of repealing the amendment. However, Clinton supported modifying the amendment in order to allow individuals to serve more than two terms in office as long as they were non-consecutive. However, this has also not been seriously considered by the U.S. Congress.

SEE ALSO: Elections Laws, Federal Elections; Presidential Election of 1940.

BIBLIOGRAPHY. Karen O'Connor and L.J. Sabato, *American Government: Continuity and Change* (Pearson Education Inc., 2004); Sidney M. Milkis and Michael Nelson, *American Presidency: Origins and Development, 1776–1998* (CQ Press, 1999.); B.G. Peabody and S.E. Gant, "The Twice and Future President: Constitutional Interstices and the Twenty-Second Amendment," *Minnesota Law Review* (v.83/3, 1997); J.W. Peltason, *Understanding the Constitution* (Harcourt Brace College Publishers, 1997).

RACHEL YFF
UNIVERSITY OF FLORIDA

Twenty-Sixth Amendment

THE ADOPTION OF the Twenty-Sixth Amendment to the Constitution on March 10, 1971 marked a reduction of the minimum voting age from 21 to 18 years of age. Its passage also signaled a conclusion to a debate dating back to the Civil War, regarding a controversy over the military draft and the minimum voting age. It seemed ironic and unfair to some Americans that the government could draft soldiers between the ages of 18 and 21 to fight in a war and risk their lives on the battlefield, but not allow those soldiers to vote. Consequently, a voice of dissention arose (which reached its height during the Vietnam War) contending that all soldiers should be able to vote for or against those government officials who have the authority of deciding whether or not to send them to war. Soon after the United States' entry into World War II, a resurgence of the debate led members of Congress to act on the issue. Beginning in 1942, Senator Arthur Vandenberg (R) and Representative Jennings Randolph (D) introduced legislative initiatives to lower the voting age, and many others followed. Others, such as Representative Emanuel Celler (D), pushed for a permanent freeze of the voting age at 21. By 1971, Congress had introduced over 150 proposals in support and dissent on the subject.

Members of Congress were not alone in their determination to address the issue. Presidents Dwight D. Eisenhower, Lyndon B. Johnson, and Richard M. Nixon also joined the debate. President Eisenhower called for a reduction of the voting age in his 1954 State of the Union Address. In the summer of 1968, President Johnson began calling on Congress to propose and adopt an amendment to the Constitution. As a presidential candidate that year, Richard Nixon also voiced his support for allowing 18-year-olds to vote, but was skeptical regarding the constitutionality of having the reform passed as a legislative statute. Between 1968 and 1970, Congress also held a number of key hearings on the matter. In addition to the issue of military service, proponents for reducing the voting age pointed to the ability of the age group to hold jobs, pay taxes, attend college, be tried in court as adults, drive an automobile, and, at the time, drink alcohol. In the end, public pressure during the Vietnam War and a key decision by the Supreme Court paved the way for the Twenty-Sixth Amendment.

When the Voting Rights Act of 1965 expired in 1970, Congress renewed it with a provision for lowering the voting age. President Nixon signed the legislation into law, but openly reiterated his reservations regarding its constitutionality as a legislative statute. Shortly thereafter, the Supreme Court addressed the constitutionality of the provision in *Oregon v. Mitchell* (1970). In its ruling, the Supreme Court held that, although Congress had the power to lower the voting age at the federal level, such power did not extend to state or local elections. In light of this decision, some states would need to create a dual voting system or amend their respective constitutions in order for 18 to 21-year-olds to be able to vote.

With the elections of November 1972 looming ahead, a number of state legislatures realized that they would be unable to overcome such legal requirements before Election Day. Subsequently, Senator Jennings Randolph (D) of West Virginia reintroduced the provision in 1971 as a proposed amendment to the Constitution. This time, the amendment passed by lopsided votes of 401–19 in the House of Representatives and 94–7 in the Senate.

Ratified in just 107 days by 42 states, it was the fastest ratification of an amendment in U.S. history and enfranchised an estimated 11 new million voters. With the general decline in U.S. voter participation, however, voting and other forms of political participation among those 18 to 21 years of age have decreased considerably since the 1972 elections.

SEE ALSO: Military Vote; Suffrage; Voter Disenfranchisement; Voting Rights Act of 1965.

BIBLIOGRAPHY. George Anastaplo, *The Amendments to the Constitution: A Commentary* (Johns Hopkins University Press, 1995); A.P. Grimes, *Democracy and the Amendments to the Constitution* (Lexington Books, 1978); W.L. Katz and Bernard Gaughran, *The Constitutional Amendments* (Franklin Watts, Inc., 1974); J.R. Vile, *Encyclopedia of Constitutional Amendments, Proposed Amendments, and Amending Issues, 1789–1995* (ABC-CLIO, 1996).

JOSÉ D. VILLALOBOS
TEXAS A&M UNIVERSITY

Twenty-Third Amendment

PROPOSED ON JUNE 16, 1960 and ratified on March 29, 1961, the Twenty-Third Amendment gave the District of Columbia the right to appoint electors of the president and vice president to the Electoral College. The number of electors was limited to the same number of electors as the least populous state.

This provided the District of Columbia with three electoral votes, the same as the state of Wyoming. Until 1961, the residents of the District of Columbia had no say in who became president and vice president of the United States. Although the seat of the federal government, with a population greater than 13 of the 50 states at that time, the residents of the District of Columbia had neither the right to go to the polls to vote in presidential elections, nor the ability to designate electors to the Electoral College. Nevertheless, they were required to fulfill all expectations of citizens of the United States, such as payment of taxes.

The amendment provided that the District of Columbia would be allowed to choose the same number of electors as a state with its population would be allowed to elect. The number of electors a state is allotted equals the number of Senators, plus the number of House Representatives who represent a state in Congress. However, the amendment also limited the number of electors the District of Columbia was allowed to obtain to an amount equaling the number of electors in the least populous state. This state, Wyoming, has three electors; therefore, the District of Columbia was given three presidential electoral votes. Three electoral votes is the least number of electors any state, regardless of its population, may be allotted because every state has at least one member of the House of Representatives and two Senators. Congress submitted the amendment to the states and it took only nine months for the required three-fourths of the states to ratify the amendment, which took place on March 29, 1961. Of the states that considered the amendment, a total of 40 ratified it, with only one state refusing to do so.

Based on Census data 1964–2000, this amendment prevented the District of Columbia from obtaining its true number of electoral votes based on its population. Based on its population during this time, the District of Columbia should have had four electors in presidential elections. However, 1980–2004, the District of Columbia has been designated the correct number of electoral votes for its population.

Every amendment prior to the Twenty-Third Amendment included a requirement that ratification by three-fourths of the states was required within seven years of submission of the amendment. Beginning with the Twenty-Third Amendment, instead of placing this requirement within the body of the amendment, Congress put it in the submissions of the amendments to the states for ratification. While a strict time limit is still placed on the states, it is no longer part of the amendment.

In 1978, an amendment was proposed which, if ratified, would have repealed the Twenty-Second Amendment. The District of Columbia would have been provided the same number of members of Congress, as well as the same number of electoral votes as if it were a state. It would also have been given the power to participate in the ratification of constitutional amendments. However, the amendment was not ratified. Also, the movement to designate the District of Columbia a state has not been well received, despite numerous attempts over the years to ratify such an amendment.

SEE ALSO: District of Columbia; Electoral College; Electors.

BIBLIOGRAPHY. Johnny Kilman and Kenneth Thomas, eds., *The Constitution of the United States of America: Analysis and Interpretation* (U.S. Government Printing Office, 2006); L. Sandy Maisel and Kara Z. Buckley, *Parties and Elections in America: The Electoral Process* (Rowman & Littlefield Publishers, 2005); J.W. Peltason, *Understanding the Constitution* (Harcourt Brace College Publishers, 1997).

Rachel Yff
University of Florida

Two-Party System

A TWO-PARTY SYSTEM is found in democracies such as Great Britain and the United States, where only two parties gain the vast majority of votes and offices at all levels of government. Two-party systems are rare outside Great Britain and former British colonies; they are typically associated with a relatively simple cleavage structure and single-member district plurality elections.

Proponents praise the simplicity of such a system, arguing that it ensures governmental stability, it indicates clearly where responsibility lies, and has a moderating influence over the main political actors. In a parliamentary system, in addition to making the choice easier for voters, the two-party system is considered more democratic because it gives voters an opportunity to choose the government, unlike multiparty systems where government is the result of post-election negotiations among party leaders. Critics say that a two-party system limits representation and the range of policies considered for enactment.

There is more than one kind of two-party system; British two-partyism is very different from the American two-partyism. The institutional context is crucial for how a two-party system actually works and for its effects on policymaking. The key distinction here is between America's presidential system and Britain's parliamentary system. Although the logic of a two-party system is inherently majoritarian, the existence of separation of powers opens the door for divided government. This can mitigate the winner-takes-all effect of the two-party system when, as it is often the case in the United States, one party is in control of Congress and the other party controls the White House. The British parliamentary system, with its fusion of legislative and executive powers, prevents such an occurrence. In a parliamentary regime, a two-party system means that the party that has a majority in the legislature is also forming the government. Such single-party governments have a higher life expectancy than multiparty governments.

Party discipline is another important difference between the British and the American two-party system, and is largely a result of the different institutional incentives provided by presidentialism and parliamentarism. In Britain, the prime minister is also the leader of the legislative majority, and therefore has the means to ensure the compliance of the rank-and-file members of parliament representing the majority party. Parties select the candidates for office, as in other European nations. British parties are centralized and disciplined, and representatives from the same party tend to vote as a bloc. Those who follow the party line enhance their chances for being rewarded in the future with a better position in the government, and party dissidence is rare.

American parties are decentralized and undisciplined; party dissent is more common than in Britain. Thus, unlike the impact of parliamentarism in Britain, which maintains the cohesiveness of the two major parties, American-style presidentialism has somewhat contradictory effects on the party system. It reinforces the existing two-party system, as only the two major parties have a chance to capture the most important office, but it weakens the two parties, because it lacks the additional incentive (the fusion between legislative and executive power) that makes their British counterparts so disciplined and cohesive. Finally, having the candidates for office selected through primary elections, rather than party organizations, as in Britain, further enhances the independence of office holders.

Equally important in accounting for the differences between American and British two-partyism are the differences between the two societies. America is much larger than Britain, in geography and population, and significantly more diverse. The consequence of this is that American legislators from the same party represent constituencies that are more diverse than British members of parliament from the same party and this, in turn, makes American parties more divided internally than their British counterparts.

Two arguments in favor of two-partyism are the argument that a two-party system has a moderating influence, and that the existence of only two parties offers voters a clear choice. Because the truth of either claim makes the other less plausible, proponents tend to focus on only one or the other. Typically, the first argument was advanced in the American context, and the second claim in the British context.

During the 1970s and 1980s, there were dramatic shifts in policies whenever there was a transition from a Labour government to a Conservative government and vice versa, with Labour nationalizing major industries which were then returned to private owners by Conservatives. During the same time, the ideological distance between America's major parties appeared comparatively narrow. Thus, depending on the country, either claim could be confirmed empirically.

In recent years, though, things appear to have changed in both countries. In Britain, Labour's success in is largely due to the party's adoption of moderate policy positions. Currently, British politics is less polarized than in the 1980s. At the same time, there is a widening policy gap between the positions endorsed by the Republicans and the Democrats in the United States. America's diversity as a society is not mirrored at the constituency level; an increasing number of representatives are elected either from rural (or suburban), predominantly white, conservative districts, or from urban, minority-dominated, liberal districts. There is an increasing heterogeneity across districts, but an increasing homogeneity within districts. The result is that the ideological distance separating the two parties is currently greater than it was at any point in the last 50 years.

Although two-party systems tend to be associated with single-member district plurality elections, plurality is neither necessary, nor sufficient for the existence of a two-party system. There are examples of countries such as Malta and, until the 1980s, Austria that maintained a two-party system for a long time, in spite of using proportional representation. There are also examples of countries such as Canada or India that have multiparty systems, even though they use plurality elections.

SEE ALSO: Multiparty System; Plurality Vote; Realignment.

BIBLIOGRAPHY. Jean Blondel, "Party Systems and Patterns of Government in Western Democracies," *Canadian Journal of Political Science* (v.1/2, 1968); Maurice Duverger, "Party Systems," in *Party Politics and Pressure Groups* (Thomas Y. Crowell, 1972); T.J. Lowi and Joseph Romance, *A Republic of Parties? Debating the Two-Party System* (Rowman & Littlefield, 1998).

FLORIN FESNIC
UNIVERSITY OF BUCHAREST

Undecided Voters

IN PRE-ELECTION POLLS, many respondents declare themselves as undecided. These voters, also called swing voters, are usually a sizeable minority, ranging between 10–20 percent. Undecided voters undermine polls' precision, but more importantly, they can change the fate of an election. Polls normally have a two percent margin of error, while the percentage of the undecided vote is usually in the double digits. Some pollsters ignore undecided respondents, as if they remain undecided and will not show up to vote. This assumption is obviously wrong for the countries where voting is mandatory, and has proven largely inaccurate even for countries where voting is not mandatory.

Other investigators prefer to split them based on the other responses in the sample. There are, however, several examples when undecided voters made the difference in contests. In a 1978 gubernatorial campaign, for instance, the polls indicated a landslide victory of 66 percent for one candidate, and only six percent for his opponent. The election results, however, suggested that most of the 28 percent of undecided voters voted for the underdog, since the final tallies showed that only 67 percent of the votes went to the favorite. Given that the winner was an incumbent governor, many experts believe that the undecided voters did not want to dis-

close their choices. The same phenomenon was noticed in some mayoral races that pitted African-American and white candidates against each other. In these polls, most of the undecided white voters ultimately voted for the white candidate. Different techniques are used to encourage people to express their preference during polls. One, used by Gallup, replaces the face-to-face interview with dropping a ballot in a box. Another is to ask for the softer preference, for example, which candidate the interviewee leans toward.

Although undecided voters are common in all democracies, they exert the largest influence in plurality systems, such as those of the United Kingdom and the United States. In presidential elections in the United States, for example, most of the states will predictably vote for Republican or Democratic candidates. Candidates can win only few additional states, the battleground or swing states. Candidates will spend a considerable amount of time and money to attract undecided voters in battleground states, neglecting their constituents in other states.

Candidates and their political advisors try to identify undecided voters and battleground states. Although battleground states change over time (from example, Illinois and Texas, which were once battleground states, but are now a blue and red respectively), battleground states are relatively stable and easy to identify based on previous elections. It is much more difficult to identify undecided voters. In general, they tend to be white, less engaged in politics, with a low- to middle-class income. In the past, the undecided voter was located in the center of the political spectrum, and political discourse tended to cater to centrists. Now, swing voters have no one dominant issue that they care about, but, rather, they are loosely interested in multiple areas, which might include the Iraq War, abortion, stem cell research, same-sex marriage, and gun control. With no candidate clearly overlapping with their positions, they have a hard time deciding upon a candidate. The soccer mom and the NASCAR-fan dad have been depicted as decisive swing voters for George Bush's electoral victory in the 2000 presidential election. Attracting swing voters also served Bill Clinton well in the 1992 and 1996 campaigns. However, in the 2004 presidential election, the George W. Bush campaign focused less on capturing the undecided voters, and more on driving up the turnout rate of its own natural voting base.

Because undecided voters are less engaged politically, and have lower levels of information compared to loyal party supporters, many observers believe that for them emotions may play as big a role as reason in forming opinions about candidates. Televised presidential debates appeal directly to undecided voters, changing the battlefield substantially. The way that candidates present themselves becomes more important than their messages. Presidents such as John F. Kennedy, Ronald Reagan, and Bill Clinton attracted many swing voters by being much more telegenic than their opponents. Some scholars warn about the potential danger to democracy that is associated with the increasing role of emotional appeal to the detriment of policy analysis.

SEE ALSO: Battleground State; Pre-Election Polls; Presidential Debates; Voter Knowledge/Ignorance.

BIBLIOGRAPHY. J.B. Ozols, "An Expert on the Mind of the Undecided Voter. How Do Swing Voters Make Up Their Minds? A Harvard Psychologist Has Some Insights," *Newsweek*, www.msnbc.msn.com (cited October 15, 2004); Ruy Teixeira and Joel Rogers, *Why the White Working Class Still Matters. America's Forgotten Majority* (Basic Books, 2000); Penny Visser, et al., "Improving Election Forecasting: Allocation of Undecided Respondents, Identification of Likely Voters, and Response Order Effects," in P.J. Lavrakas, et al., eds., *Election Polls, the News Media, and Democracy* (Chatham House Publishers, 2000); John Zaller, "Floating Voters in U.S. Presidential Elections, 1948–2000," in W.E. Saris and P.M. Sniderman, eds., *Studies in Public Opinion: Attitudes, Measurement Error, and Change* (Princeton University Press, 2004).

Oana I. Armeanu
University of Southern Indiana, Evansville

United Nations

THE VIEW OF the United Nations (UN) by the U.S. government and its citizens reflects to some extent the ongoing national debate about whether the United States should act unilaterally, or seek consensus within the parameters of the United Nations. While the United States was one of the founding members of the United Nations and maintains a permanent seat on the Security Council, political leaders in the United States have increasingly challenged UN operations on a number of fronts, particularly regarding its peacekeeping missions. Questions regarding the UN have raged in the political arena of the United States periodically since 1952, when Republican Senator Joseph McCarthy held hearings regarding the loyalty of U.S. citizens employed by the UN. The investigation provoked such a furor that a federal grand jury was called in New York on the very subject. The collapse of the Soviet Union led officials in both President George Bush and Bill Clinton's administrations to hope that the United Nations would assume a major role in world peace that was envisioned upon its establishment. Many saw UN actions in the 1991 Persian Gulf War against Iraq as an example of the role the UN could and should assume regarding world peace.

However, the failure of the 1993 UN mission in Somalia and the failure to prevent or respond to ethnic cleansing in Bosnia and the genocide in Rwanda led to a political backlash in Congress. In 1994, Congress held back U.S. payments for UN missions in Somalia and Bosnia and passed legislation that limited U.S. contributions to one-fourth of the UN peacekeeping budget. The 1994 Republican Contract with America called for legislation that would prohibit U.S. forces from being placed under the command of non-U.S. commanders while participating in UN peacekeeping missions. While this proposal passed in the House, it never became law. Republican reluctance to support further UN peacekeeping missions forced the Clinton administration to scale down their support of such missions. In 2000, the Clinton administration failed in its attempts to pass a supplemental appropriations bill to support new UN peacekeeping missions in Kosovo and East Timor. Republican Senator John Warner of Virginia complained over the failure by European countries to fulfill their peacekeeping pledges and of the need for the UN to address existing peacekeeping missions. Other Republican congressional leaders, such as Congressman Benjamin Gilman, expressed concern over the poor organization and definition of U.S. missions. Congressional support for U.S. missions was further weakened in May 2000 when 500 UN peacekeepers were captured and held hostage by rebel forces within Sierra Leone.

U.S. lawmakers have traditionally had a more limited view of the role of UN peacekeeping: support for peacekeeping versus efforts at peacemaking. Congressional, and some military leaders such as the former commander of North Atlantic Treaty Organization (NATO) forces in Kosovo, General Wesley Clark, argue in favor of regional organizations and forces to address regional peacekeeping issues. The 2000 Republican ticket of George Bush and Dick Cheney criticized the Clinton administration for its willingness to commit U.S. forces to UN missions. The political debate caused by UN peacekeeping issues and Iraq was heightened when Libya assumed the chair of the UN Commission on Human Rights. Republican Representative Ron Paul of Texas called for the United States to leave the UN due to UN hostility to American interests, arguing that membership compromises U.S. sovereignty.

Another UN issue that stirs hot political debate within the United States is the establishment of the International Criminal Court (ICC). The Clinton administration opposed the ICC Treaty, but the Bush administration adopted an even more hostile attitude toward the court over the refusal to grant American, and other peacekeepers, immunity from prosecution. In his book *Diplomacy*, former U.S. National Security Advisor and Secretary of State Henry Kissinger describes the United Nations as ineffective in dealing with the problems of the world. Growing calls for reform of the United Nations, and anger over failed UN peacekeeping missions led the United States to begin to withhold

Soviet Union leader Nikita Khrushchev at the UN in 1960. The UN has always been problematic for the United States.

its UN dues during the Clinton administration, a policy continued early in the George W. Bush administration. The United Nations responded, in 2001, by voting the United States off of several UN subcommittees. The decision by the UN Security Council not to authorize the use of force in Iraq even thought earlier UN sanctions were routinely ignored by Iraq was ignored by the George W. Bush administration and viewed as further proof of the weakening of UN influence.

Reports of financial improprieties and nepotism regarding vast aid to Iraq during the tenure of Secretary-General Kofi Annan damaged the reputation of the UN within both U.S. political parties and increased the call for a major reform of the UN organizational structure.

SEE ALSO: Foreign Policy; Presidential Election of 1996; War and Peace.

BIBLIOGRAPHY. Cullen Thomas, ed., *U.S. National Debate Topic 2004–2005, The United Nations* (H.W. Wilson Co., 2004); Paul Johnson, *A History of the American People* (Weidenfeld & Nicolson, 1997); E.C. Luck, *Mixed Messages: American Politics and International Organization, 1919–1999* (Brookings Institution Press, 1999); S.C. Schlesinger, *Act of Creation: The Founding of the United Nations* (Westview Press, 2003).

ABBE ALLEN DEBOLT
COLUMBUS STATE COMMUNITY COLLEGE

Urban Vote

SINCE THE NEW Deal era, the urban electorate has played a role in the outcome of presidential elections. The size and political importance of this electorate grew as a result of the mass migration of people from the countryside into the city; this made cities across the country the most concentrated areas of political support available to political parties.

The true importance of this concentrated population of voters was seen in those presidential elections that took place between the early 1930s and the early 1960s. During this time, the Democratic Party was the main benefactor of the urban vote, allowing it to create and implement its New Deal policies. However, since the 1960s, the ability of the urban vote to play an influential role in presidential elections has declined because of the exodus of voters from the cities to the suburbs. This suburban vote has mainly benefited the Republican Party.

Electoral realignment is inextricably linked with the urban vote and its influence on presidential elections. Electoral realignment occurs when the party in power is voted out approximately once every generation, normally after a triggering crisis, because of its inability to meet the changing needs of the electorate. Soon after a crisis, a critical election takes place. This is an election from which a realignment, which is both sudden and durable, occurs. Into this void a new party comes to power with the ability to meet the electorate's growing needs and to deal with the crisis in a manner approved of by a majority of the public. For such an election to be considered the beginning of a durable realignment, this new party must be in power for a great deal of time after its initial rise to governmental control.

In 1932, one of the major critical elections of the 20th century took place. Unlike other realignments, where a new party is created, or there is the destruction or absorption of an old party, in this realignment the parties remained the same. There was simply a change in the policies and support bases of the parties as new issues took center stage. It was in this election that President Franklin Roosevelt was able to capitalize on the growing urban electorate and bring it into the fold of the Democratic Party where it would remain for a number of years. This urban electorate was made up of the working class, as those who migrated to the city were mostly poor, seeking a living after the Great Depression hit them. Through this large block of support, President Roosevelt was able to ensure the passage and implementation of his New Deal policies. In order to keep this bloc of support loyal to Democratic presidential and congressional candidates, New Deal policies centered on the improvement of urban areas across the country and direct financial relief for urban workers.

However, once urbanites began fleeing to the suburbs, the Democratic Party lost this core of support to the Republican Party. This flight was the result of improving education, a move from menial to more professional occupations, and an increase in income, all of which allowed individuals to move out of the cities to the suburbs. Once in the suburbs, these individuals turned to the Republican Party to meet their new needs. Those fleeing to the suburbs were middle class whites, leaving the urban population mostly composed of minorities. In order to keep the urban vote alive, Democrats had to cater to the needs of minorities, which cost them votes from other blocs of support, especially southern Democrats. However, because of the necessity of keeping the urban vote in the Democratic camp and the growing opposition to segregation outside the south, the Democratic Party created a strong civil rights platform as early as the late 1940s to the early 1950s.

SEE ALSO: Democratic Party; Presidential Election of 1932; Realignment; Republican Party; Suburban Vote.

BIBLIOGRAPHY. Kristi Anderson, *The Creation of a Democratic Majority 1928–1936* (University of Chicago Press,

1979); C.N. Degler, "American Political Parties and the Rise of the City: An Interpretation," *Journal of American History* (v.51/1, 1964); T.B. Edsall and M.D. Edsall, *Chain Reaction: The Impact of Race, Rights, and Taxes on American Politics* (W.W. Norton & Company, 1991); Samuel Lubell, *The Future of American Politics* (Harper & Brothers, 1952); J.H. Mollenkopf, *The Contested City* (Princeton University Press, 1983); Richard Sauerzopf and Todd Swanstrom, "The Urban Electorate in Presidential Elections, 1920–1996," *Urban Affairs Review* (v. 35/1, 1999); J.L. Sundquist, *Dynamics of the Party System: Alignment and Realignment of Political Parties in the United States* (Brookings Institution, 1983).

RACHEL YFF
UNIVERSITY OF FLORIDA

Utah

THERE IS ARCHAEOLOGICAL evidence that Native Americans lived in Utah as long ago as 10,000 B.C.E., with Francisco Vásquez de Coronado, a Spanish explorer, visiting the region in 1540. The major settlement of Utah did not take place until 1847 when some 11,000 Mormons (members of the Church of Jesus Christ of Latter-day Saints) arrived at Salt Lake City after having fled from Illinois following the death of their leader Joseph Smith. At that time, Utah was a part of Mexico. After the Mexican-American War, the Treaty of Guadalupe Hidalgo on February 2, 1848 saw Utah become a part of the United States. Brigham Young, the leader of the Mormons after the death of Joseph Smith, became the first state governor.

On January 4, 1896, Utah was admitted to the Union becoming the 45th state, with Heber Manning Wells elected as its first governor. Wells, a Republican, a prominent Mormon born in Salt Lake City, had lost the election for mayor of Salt Lake City in 1892. During his first term as governor, Wells introduced legislation, including a law for the use of the secret ballot. At the end of his first four-year term, in 1900, Wells was elected, defeating James H. Moyle of the Democratic Party. Although he initially wanted to run for the U.S. Senate, he was persuaded to run again for governor in 1904, he lost to John C. Cutler.

There had already been controversy over Senate elections in Utah with the state legislature choosing the senators, a practice that was to be terminated by the Seventeenth Amendment in 1913.

In 1899, when the Republican Frank J. Cannon's term expired, the Democrat-controlled Utah legislature failed to elect a senator, and in the following year the Republicans had been able to use the legislature to split the state Democratic Party.

Cutler had been born in Sheffield, England, and was 18-years-old when he and his parents left for Utah after having become a Mormon. In the 1908 gubernatorial elections, Republican William Spry, managed to defeat Democratic Party candidate J. William Knight, in spite of James A. Street of the American Party making a strong showing. As with his predecessor, Spry was born in England, his family becoming Mormons before moving to Salt Lake City. In the election campaign, Spry had promised to introduce governmental reforms, but these were rejected by the state legislature. He did, however, get authorization to build the state capitol, and, in 1912, was re-elected, defeating John F. Tolton from the Democratic Party, and Nephi L. Morris of the Progressive Party.

In the gubernatorial elections in 1916, Democrat Simon Bamberger won the elections. He was born in Germany, migrated to the United States at the age of 14, and later moving to Salt Lake City. Although he was not a Mormon (Bamberger was the second Jewish person to be elected as a governor in the United States), during the 1916 election campaign, Bamberger gained the support of Brigham H. Roberts, a member of the Council of Seventy of the Church of Jesus Christ of Latter-day Saints. Roberts wanted to stop supporting people solely on the basis of church affiliation, and this helped Bamberger defeat a Mormon, Alfred W. McCune, a wealthy mine owner, in the Republican primary.

Bamberger promised that, if elected, he would support Prohibition. His Republican rival, Nephi L. Morris, formerly of the Progressives, made opposition to Prohibition his major campaign issue. In his one term as governor, Bamberger introduced financial restraints, with a new audit of government expenditure that resulted in the recovering of about $1 million in misallocated funds. He had the support of a Democrat-controlled state legislature, and urged that the franchise be extended to women, as well as supporting other policies which had been proposed by the Progressive Party.

The Mormon Temple in Salt Lake City, Utah. Church and state have mingled on the ballot and in the politics of Utah.

In the 1920 gubernatorial elections, Charles Rendell Mabey, a Republican, was elected, defeating the Democratic Party candidate T.N. Taylor by a large margin. Mabey had campaigned for further economic restraint and he totally reorganized the state administration, saving large sums of public money. In 1924, George Henry Dern, born in Nebraska, and a powerful Utah industrialist, won the gubernatorial election; he was re-elected in 1928. A Democrat, and not a Mormon, he was in the 1932 U.S. presidential election he was a strong supporter of Franklin D. Roosevelt, who appointed him as U.S. secretary of war.

In 1932, Democrat and Mormon businessman, Henry Hooper Blood was elected governor, defeating the Republican former legislator William W. Seegmiller. Blood inherited a state as many as a third of

the population unemployed. The percentage of the population on welfare relief was the highest in the United States, with the 1934 drought making the situation even worse. Franklin D. Roosevelt endorsed Blood, who was able to win the Democratic renomination in 1936, in spite of a strong challenge by Herbert Brown Maw, the leader of the liberal wing of the state Democrats. In the succeeding gubernatorial election, Blood defeated Republican Ray E. Dillman, a former state senate president from, and Harman W. Peery, an Independent-Progressive who was Mayor of Ogden, in northern Utah. Blood did not run for re-election in 1940, and died two years later.

The liberal Democrats had rallied around Herbert Brown Maw, and, in 1940, Maw won the state's first direct Democratic Party primary, defeating Henry D. Moyle and won the gubernatorial election, defeating Don B. Colton, a former Republican congressman. The 1944 gubernatorial election was particularly controversial; Maw supporters produced the pamphlet *Morals and the Mayor,* which suggested that Joseph Bracken Lee, mayor of Price, and the Republican gubernatorial candidate, had been lax in collecting local taxes. Lee had been elected as mayor of Price in 1931, winning his first election by two votes, but later winning another five terms. Maw managed to win the governorship, but only by a majority of 1,056, which Lee unsuccessfully contested. In 1948, Maw sought a third consecutive term as governor, but lost when conservative Democrats deserted him, and a campaign letter by Maw to fellow Mormons backfired. J. Bracken Lee was elected and served two terms, losing the Republican Primary in 1956 and failing to win after running as an Independent. George Dewey Clyde won the Republican nomination, gaining crossover votes from Democrats. A supporter of Dwight D. Eisenhower, Clyde was elected in 1956, defeating both Lee and L.C. Romney, the Democrat candidate.

In the U.S. presidential election of 1960, Richard M. Nixon won the state with 205,733 votes (54.8 percent) to John F. Kennedy's 169,248 votes (45.2 percent). In the Utah gubernatorial election, Clyde won re-nomination for the Republicans, defeating Lamont B. Gunderson, chair of the Salt Lake County Commission, and defeated the mayor of St. George, William A. Barlocker. Clyde had been frustrated in 1959, when Democrats won control of the state legislature, and fought them on many issues. In the 1964 elections, Democrats won throughout the state, voting by a margin of 54.6 percent (219,628 votes) for Lyndon B. Johnson to 45.1 percent (180,682 votes) for Barry Goldwater. The Democrats also retained their seat in the U.S. Senate, regained a House seat, all with 57 percent of the vote; they won all five state elective offices with Democrat Calvin L. Rampton elected as governor, as well as control of both houses of the Utah legislature. Much of this seems to have been a reaction against the far right policies of Barry Goldwater and the Republican Senate nominee Ernest Wilkinson, as well as the support for Lyndon B. Johnson by David O. McKay, the president of the Mormon Church. Wilkinson, who had been president of Brigham Young University, had defeated Sherman P. Lloyd in the primary and felt that with the support of McKay, he could win, but McKay supported the Democrats, and Wilkinson lost to Frank E. Moss.

In the 1968 U.S. presidential election, Utah voted Republican. Nixon won a large majority in the state, with 238,728 votes (56.5 percent), to 156,665 votes (37.1 percent) for Hubert H. Humphrey, and 26,906 votes (6.4 percent) for George Wallace. In the gubernatorial elections, Rampton was re-elected, and again in 1972, making him the first governor to win three terms. Rampton decided not to stand for a fourth term, and Scott Milne Matheson, who succeeded him, won two terms. Matheson decided to retire rather than seek a third term that he likely would have won. Although Matheson had been an active Democrat, the governorship was his first elected office. A strong administrator, Matheson restructured the local government and became famous for his opposition to the positioning of MX missiles in Utah.

In the gubernatorial election of 1984, Borman Howard Barngeter was the first Republican to be elected governor of Utah in 19 years. A prominent Mormon, and the founder of a successful construction company, he served two terms and then retired to run to his company. By then, Utah was a strong Republican state with

Michael Okerlund Leavitt, a Republican, elected as the 14th governor with 42 percent of the vote, to Independent Merrill Cook's 34 percent, and Democrat Stewart Hanson's 23 percent. In 1996, Leavitt won an unprecedented 75 percent of the vote, with Democrat Jim Bradley getting 23 percent. Four years later, Leavitt was elected for a third time, taking 56 percent of the vote to Democrat Bill Orton's 42 percent.

In 2003, Leavitt left the position of governor after being nominated by George W. Bush as the secretary of Health and Human Services. Olene Smith Walker became governor, completing Leavitt's unexpired term, and was the first female governor of the state. Christine Durham, the female chief justice of the Utah Supreme Court, swore her in. In 2004, Utah voted for George W. Bush in the U.S. presidential election, and elected Jon Meade Huntsman Jr., the former U.S. ambassador to Singapore, as governor.

SEE ALSO: American Party; Progressive Party; Prohibitionist Party; Wallace, George C.

BIBLIOGRAPHY. G.J. Bergera, "'A Sad and Expensive Experience': Ernest L. Wilkinson's 1964 Bid for the U.S. Senate," *Utah Historical Quarterly* (v.61/4, 1993); S.L. Grow, "Utah's Senatorial Election of 1899: The Election That Failed," *Utah Historical Quarterly* (v.39/1, 1971); F.H. Jonas, "The 1964 Election in Utah," *Western Political Quarterly* (v.18/2, 1965); F.H. Jonas and D.E. Jones, "The 1970 Election in Utah," *Western Political Quarterly* (v.24/2, 1971); D.L. May, *Utah: A People's History* (Bonneville Books, 1987); S.M. Olson and Christina Batjer, "Competing Narratives in a Judicial Retention Election: Feminism Versus Judicial Independence," *Law & Society Review* (v.33/1, 1999); W.L. Roper and L.J. Arrington, *William Spry: Man of Firmness, Governor of Utah* (University of Utah Press, 1971).

JUSTIN CORFIELD
GEELONG GRAMMAR SCHOOL, AUSTRALIA

Vermont

THE STATE OF Vermont in New England was the 14th state to be admitted to the Union, which took place on March 4, 1791, ending the short-lived Vermont Republic, and making the state the first to join after the original 13 colonies. As a counterweight to Vermont as a free state, Kentucky, a slave state, joined soon afterwards. Until 1836, Vermont had a unicameral legislature.

Before Vermont joined the Union, it had its own general assembly, elected by freemen, and a democratic tradition. When the issue of joining the United States arose, the assembly called a convention that met at Bennington on January 6, 1791. They eventually voted to join the Union by 105 votes to three, with Nathaniel Chipman and Lewis R. Morris delegated to carry out the negotiations. The U.S. Congress agreed to the final admission unanimously. The *Vermont Chronicle* of October 18, 1791 detailed the first "election day" in the state of Vermont. The day began with Thomas Chittenden, the governor-elect, and Lieutenant Governor Peter Olcott, along with members of the council, meeting some distance from the state capital and then riding into Windsor in their best uniforms. They waited for the official results to be proclaimed, followed by a 15-gun salute. In the late 18th and early 19th century,

election day in Vermont was on the first Tuesday in September, with annual elections for legislators, judges, and state officials. The various candidates often established booths offering food and drink to voters as they were heading to the polls. It was also common that as soon as the results were declared, the winning candidate would buy large quantities of food and drink to dispense to the voters.

That Vermont had briefly been an independent Republic (1777–91) led to a certain degree of political free thought in the state, and after Thomas Chittenden, Paul Brigham was elected as their second governor. As Vermont was split geographically by the Green Mountains, there was an informal arrangement by which the governor and the lieutenant governor would come from different sides of the mountains. This held with the choice of U.S. senators and representatives until 1932, when Vermont was reduced to one member in the House of Representatives; it held for governors until 1974.

From 1797 until 1820, Vermont voters supported Federalist and Democratic-Republican governors alternately, with the Democratic-Republicans holding office 1815–26, when Ezra Butler of the National Republicans took office. During the 1826 gubernatorial election campaign, the issue of Freemasonry was actively debated, benefiting Butler as a Baptist elder from Waterbury. He was from east of the Green Mountains, while the early governors were from the west. The nomination of Butler by private citizens circumvented the system of a caucus, and raised concerns about the election of clergymen to state office. With the agrarian population worried that this might lead to domination of the state by the largely town-based merchants, many who were Freemasons, the farmers took up the issue of anti-Masonry. By 1827, many voters of Vermont started supporting the Anti-Masonic Party, leading to William A. Palmer's election as governor; he held that office until 1835, managing to win the election, despite campaigning on a single issue. In 1835, Silas H. Jennison of the Whig Party was elected, and the next seven governors were all Whigs. However, in October 1853, John S. Robinson became the first Democratic governor, and the only one until the election of Philip H. Hoff in 1962.

Vermont was opposed to slavery, and the first article of the state constitution proudly declared the rights of all men. An abolitionist movement emerged in the state and during the early 1850s, public opinion shifted from a belief in containing slavery, to the abolition of it, with many people beginning to support the Pennsylvanian abolitionist and radical Republican Thaddeus Stevens. With the gradual disintegration of the Whig Party, and the formation of the Republican Party, Vermont voters started supporting Republicans for state office, and, in 1859, turned on John Godfrey Saxe, a poet who ran in the gubernatorial elections as a Douglas Democrat after he (Saxe) equivocated on the issue of the abolition of slavery.

In 1860, the state gave Abraham Lincoln the largest margin of victory of any state in the Union. Later, Lincoln's only son to survive childhood, Robert Todd Lincoln, relocated to Vermont and built a house at Hildene. Since the Civil War, Vermont voters have voted Republican, only electing two Vermont senators since then who were not Republicans: Patrick Leahy, Democrat, elected in 1975, and Bernard Sanders, an Independent elected in 2007.

Vermont's strong support for the abolition of slavery was matched by a championing of women's rights in the 1870s. On December 18, 1880, women were allowed to vote for the first time in town elections, with the franchise later extended to cover state legislative races. Traditionally, Maine had been the barometer of public opinion in U.S. presidential elections, with the saying "As Maine goes, so goes the nation." However, in the 1936 elections, Maine voted for Republican Alf Landon

over Franklin Delano Roosevelt, and because Vermont was the only other state to vote for Landon, Democratic strategist James Farley commented, "As Maine goes, so goes Vermont."

Up until the 1960s, rural interests dominated the state legislature, which resulted in some urban decay, especially in parts of Burlington and Winooski, with many residents from those areas moving to newer suburbs. The rules that prevent minor parties from flourishing do not exist in Vermont, where there are extensive choices at state elections; many Vermont voters were involved in ticket splitting. The 1960 U.S. presidential election saw Vermont supporting Republican candidate Richard M. Nixon by 98,131 votes to John F. Kennedy's 69,186 votes. However, Kennedy became popular in the state and, in 1962, Philip H. Hoff was elected governor, the first Democrat to hold office since John S. Robinson in the 1850s. He campaigned actively in support of John F. Kennedy, and was re-elected in 1964 and 1966, introducing extensive social welfare reforms.

In the 1964 U.S. presidential election, Vermont broke from its Republican tradition to vote for Lyndon B. Johnson, the first time it had ever voted for a Democratic presidential candidate. It was a major upset for the Republicans, with Barry Goldwater gaining only 54,942 votes to Johnson's 108,127 votes. In 1968, Vermont returned to supporting the Republicans, with George Wallace getting only 3.2 percent, less than in any other states except Maine and Hawaii. Since Hoff's election, Vermont has alternately voted for a Democratic Party candidate and then a Republican one for governor.

In 1992, Vermont supported Bill Clinton, as the population began to develop an anti-consumerist culture reflected the 1990 election of Howard Dean as governor. Dean went on to serve five two-year terms in office, making him the second longest-serving governor in the state, the longest being the first, Thomas Chittenden. This sentiment has also dominated local city councils, with Vermont being the last state to have a Wal-Mart store. Montpelier is the only state capital in the United States that does not have a McDonalds restaurant within its city limits.

In the 2004 U.S. presidential election, Governor, Howard Dean was an early front-runner, denouncing the invasion of Iraq in 2003, and campaigning in the Democratic primaries his paying off much of the Vermont public debt, overseeing eleven balanced budgets, and lowering income tax on two occasions, while introducing universal health care for children and pregnant women. However, he lost the nomination to John Kerry who easily won Vermont for the Democrats in 2004, with the fourth largest margin of victory. Essex County in the northeast part of the state was the only county to support George W. Bush. However, in the 2006 gubernatorial elections, Republican Jim Douglas was elected, winning every county except Windham.

From about 2000, there were moves to create a Second Vermont Republic, championed by civil libertarian and anti-consumerist Thomas Naylor, a former economics professor from Duke University who wrote a book, *The Vermont Manifesto* (2003). Opinion polls showed support for secession in 2005 to be about eight percent, rising to 13 percent in 2007. There is also another movement called Vermont Canada, which wants Vermont to become the 11th province of Canada. This move has received less support.

SEE ALSO: Anti-Masonic Party; Democratic-Republican Party; Federalist Party; Slavery; Whig Party.

BIBLIOGRAPHY. F.M. Bryan, *Yankee Politics in Rural Vermont* (University of New England Press, 1974); John Buechler, "John Godfrey Saxe: The Poet as Politician, 1859," *Vermont History* (v.43/1, 1975); S.B. Hand, "Mountain Rule Revisited," *Vermont History* (v.71, 2003); Nathaniel Hendricks, "A New Look at the Ratification of the Vermont Constitution of 1777," *Vermont History* (v.34/2, 1966); R.E. Robinson, *Vermont: A Study of Independence* (Houghton Mifflin and Co., 18920; E.C. Rozwenc, *Agricultural Politics in Vermont 1860–1945* (Vermont Historical Society, 1981); D.A. Smith, *Legacy of Dissent: Religion and Politics in Revolutionary Vermont 1749–1784* (privately published, 1981).

JUSTIN CORFIELD
GEELONG GRAMMAR SCHOOL, AUSTRALIA

Veterans

SOME OF THE more recent research on electoral politics and voting behavior supports the conventional view that while voter turnout rates among Americans may be modest, in the aggregate, military veterans tend to vote at higher rates than nonveterans. For instance, according to the U.S. Census Bureau, during the 2004 presidential election, the percentage of veterans who voted was roughly 73 percent, nearly 10 percentage points higher than nonveterans. Furthermore, using longitudinal statistical analyses run on data complied by the same agency, researchers find the difference in voting behavior between veterans and nonveterans is evident as early as the 1970s. Because veterans have some of the highest turnout rates in the electorate, and because candidates campaigning for election (or re-election) seek to maximize their votes in order to win, candidates and their respective political parties often search for ways to attract veteran support. One way in which candidates accomplish this task, is by supporting and campaigning on issues that are important to veterans.

Compensation for their military service in the form of pensions is one of the more important issues facing veterans. One of the earliest elections in which this issue was raised was the 1888 presidential election. President Grover Cleveland (D) was seeking a second term and his opponent was Benjamin Harrison (R). The high tariffs during the 1880s generated a huge revenue surplus, and the political elites were debating whether to lower taxes or allocate the revenue toward efforts to liberalize the extant pension system. Cleveland and his party strongly advocated reducing the tariffs and opposed allocating the surplus revenue toward expanding the pension system. Doing so, on their view, would contribute to the already fraudulent and corrupt system. The Republicans disagreed. Harrison, a Civil War veteran, along with his fellow Republicans, fought intensely for the expansion of the pension system at the taxpayers' expense. Campaigning on liberalizing the pension system was seen by some as a gainful approach to attract members of the voting electorate, of which nearly 10 percent were Civil War veterans.

More importantly, adopting this position enabled his campaign to win the endorsement the Grand Army of the Republic (GAR), the best organized and influential veterans' organization of that time, whose membership totaled nearly 380,000. This strategy paid off for Harrison and his party at the polls, as he defeated the incumbent, winning 233 electoral votes to Cleveland's 168 electoral votes. The Republican Party also gained seats in both the House and Senate. Many attribute the Republican's victory in the 1888 election to the veterans' vote.

Due largely to the U.S. involvement in the World Wars, efforts to provide compensation for veterans remained on the national agenda, culminating in the Serviceman's Readjustment Act of 1944 (also known as the G.I. Bill). While issues important to veterans, such as health care and workers' rights, were raised in campaigns, it was not until the 1960s that veterans' issues re-asserted themselves in campaigns at the national level. This has much to do with the Vietnam War, which was the dominant issue in the 1968 presidential election between Richard Nixon (R) and Herbert Humphrey (D).

WAR PROTEST

Large numbers of the American public were becoming increasingly disgruntled about war. While veterans returning home from the war were far from united over this issue, many shared the public's concerns. Veterans' organizations, most notably the Vietnam Veterans Against the War (VVAW), of which Senator John Kerry was an active participant, formed not only to demand an end to the war, but also to raise awareness of the combat-related physical and psychological disorders, such as Post-Traumatic Stress Disorder (PRSD) to which many of American's servicemen and women have succumbed. Thus, in an effort to maximize his electoral support, Richard Nixon campaigned aggressively on ending the Vietnam War. His message appealed to many and Nixon won a landslide victory, winning 301 electoral votes.

In 1972, Nixon faced Democratic presidential nominee George McGovern for re-election. Throughout the campaign, McGovern, a veteran of the World War II, along with members of his party, strongly criticized the Nixon administration for not doing enough to end the war, and for neglecting the needs of the American soldiers who served in it. According to their platform, the Democrats proposed expanding and improving upon the facilities of the U.S. Department of Veterans Affairs (VA) and furthermore, opening the VA facilities so that the families of the veterans may receive care as well.

While McGovern's campaign and the Democratic Party emphasized veteran-related issues such as the Vietnam War and the expansion of healthcare and other opportunities for veterans, Nixon and his campaign strategists sought to depict McGovern as unpatriotic and unfit for the job of Commander in Chief. Partly as

a result of these attacks, and the remarkably high levels of political alienation among many of the Vietnam veterans, McGovern's campaign did not garner much electoral support. Nixon was re-elected by a large margin, winning 520 electoral votes.

Since the 2000 presidential election of George W. Bush and the subsequent wars in Afghanistan and Iraq, there has been a resurgence of political participation by veterans. Groups such as the Iraq and Afghanistan Veterans of America (IAVA), Iraq War Veterans Organization, and the Disabled American Veterans (DAV), are now advocating for issues such as military retirement benefits, health care, and defense just as their predecessors have done. In the 2004 presidential elections, in which John Kerry (D) campaigned against incumbent George W. Bush (R), both parties competed for the veteran vote.

The Democrats attempted to do so, moreover, by capitalizing on concerns expressed by some veterans in 2002 over the Bush administration's support for rescinding the lifetime health benefits promised to those who served in World War II and the Korean War. They argued that they would be better protectors of veterans' benefits than the Republicans. They buttressed this argument by pointing out that the Bush administration tried to restrict access to the VA hospitals, and that the Republicans in the House proposed a budget that called for a $28 billion dollar cut in veterans' programs. The Democrats presented themselves as advocates for veteran-related issues by initiating proposals to expand the benefits allotted to veterans and supporting veterans-related budget issues in Congress.

DELIVERING PROMISES

The Republicans counter-attacked, arguing that the Democratic candidates were guilty of making promises to veterans that they could not afford to deliver. However, it was the Swift Boat Veteran's for Truth (SBVT), an independent pro-Republican organization that significantly hampered the Democratic candidates' attempt to attract the veteran vote. The organization, consisting of Vietnam veterans, many of whom served alongside Kerry during the war, ran a series of television ads that sought to undermine Kerry's military service and patriotism. The ads strongly suggested that Kerry was more interested in advancing his own political agenda than protecting veterans' interests. Kerry's hesitation at responding to these attack ads, and the consequent dip in the sought-after veteran support, contributed to his defeat at the polls. President Bush was re-elected, winning 286 electoral votes to Kerry's 251.

Although the Democrats were defeated in 2004, the party's top strategists remained convinced of the potential electoral value of the veteran vote, and, as such, sought new ways to gain the support of veterans, especially those who had served in Iraq. In the 2006 elections, for example, Democratic organizations such as Band of Brothers, Iraq Veterans Against the War, and Veterans for a Secure America more aggressively appealed to the veteran population by specifically recruiting candidates with past military experience who stood against Bush's policy concerning the war, to campaign on the Democratic ticket.

Approximately 100 veterans campaigned in the 2006 congressional elections, representing the largest number since 1946. While all the veterans who campaigned were not elected, the political mobilization and participation of these veterans help contribute to the decisive victory for the Democrats, picking up 30 seats in the House and six in the Senate. Deteriorating facilities, poor military healthcare, and the mistreatment of wounded soldiers at Walter Reed Hospital and other VA facilities throughout the country are sure to be important veterans-related issues raised in future elections.

SEE ALSO: Defense; Military Hero; Military Vote; Patriotism; Vietnam.

BIBLIOGRAPHY. Bryan Bender, "Veterans Take on New Battle: Run for Office," *Boston Globe* (November 27, 2005); Linda Feldmann, "Now Running for Office: An Army of Iraq Veterans," *Christian Science Monitor* (February 22, 2006); Theda Skocpol, "America's First Social Security System: The Expansion of Benefits for Civil War Veterans," *Political Science Quarterly* (v.108/1, 1993); Niels Sorrells, "Democrats Play to Win Critical Veterans' Vote," *Congressional Quarterly Weekly* (June 21, 2003); J.M. Teigen, "Enduring Effects of the Uniform: Previous Military Experience and Voting Turnout," *Political Research Quarterly* (v.59, 2006); Wayne Washington, "Frustrated Veterans Accuse Bush of Breaking Promise," *Boston Globe* (December 22, 2002); U.S. Census Bureau, www.census.gov (cited July 2007).

OTTAWA SANDERS
BINGHAMPTON UNIVERSITY
(STATE UNIVERSITY OF NEW YORK)

Vietnam

THE WAR IN Vietnam caused domestic political division in the United States more profound than at any time since the American Civil War. Presidential candidates adopted policy positions on Vietnam in 1964, 1968, and 1972. Unhappy memories of the war would continue to echo in American politics a generation later. Reappearing in 2004, Vietnam as a campaign issue encoded anxiety about U.S. military involvement in an intractable war of counterinsurgency in Iraq and resentment of those who openly protested against war. Although U.S. involvement in the war in Vietnam began with transfers of military aid to the colonial government of French Indochina and, later, the government of South Vietnam by the Eisenhower administration, most Americans would became aware of the war only with the introduction of thousands of U.S. military advisors in 1963 by John Kennedy's administration and subsequent larger military deployments by Lyndon Johnson's administration.

Vietnam was, at best, a secondary campaign issue in the 1964 presidential election between incumbent Democratic President Lyndon Johnson, and Republican challenger Barry Goldwater. Ironically, it was Johnson who was positioned as the peace candidate against the bellicose Goldwater. Among the statements made by Goldwater that helped Johnson win a landslide were expressions of regret that the United States had not used nuclear weapons to support the French military at the decisive battle of Dien Bien Phu in 1954.

Although the peace movement gained momentum in 1967, as U.S. troop deployments in South Vietnam reached 500,000 and the U.S. bomb tonnage dropped on North Vietnam exceeded that in the Pacific theater of World War II, public opinion remained largely supportive of the war effort. The bloody Tet Offensive in early 1968, exposed the Pentagon's claims of success against the insurgency as false. Declining public support for the war was matched by declining support among Democrats for Johnson as their presidential candidate. Peace candidate Eugene McCarthy's unexpectedly strong performance in the March 12, 1968, New Hampshire Democratic Primary, receiving 42 percent of the vote to the president's 49 percent, caused a humiliated Johnson to announce on March 31 that he would no longer seek re-election.

With that decision, the 1968 Democratic nomination became a struggle between pro-war candidate Vice

Vietnam War protestors at the March on Washington in 1967. The war's political effects could be felt into the 2004 election.

President Hubert H. Humphrey, and peace candidates McCarthy and Robert F. Kennedy. The charismatic Kennedy "threw his hat into the ring" following the New Hampshire Primary, but was assassinated before the tumultuous Chicago Democratic National Convention that gave Humphrey the nomination. The Republican National Convention in Miami that gave Richard M. Nixon his party's nomination was more orderly, but protests outside the convention presented the public with print and televised images of chaotic youthful protest and police violence comparable to those captured in Chicago.

Vietnam was the dominant political issue at that historical moment, but voters were unable to treat the 1968 general election as a referendum on the war because Humphrey and Nixon's positions on the war were too similar. Both supported Vietnamization, which meant the gradual reduction in the numbers of U.S. soldiers deployed and their replacement by U.S.-trained and equipped South Vietnamese troops. The only differences were that Humphrey preferred negotiating a timetable for withdrawal of U.S. troops and Nixon believed the aerial bombardment of North Vietnam should not end without evidence of reduction of attacks by the Viet Cong. Other issues determined the outcome of the election. Nixon defeated Humphrey and third-party candidate George Wallace in a close election.

Four years later, the 1972 presidential election presented voters with a clear choice between a pro-war candidate, Republican nominee and incumbent President Nixon, and a peace candidate, Democratic nominee George McGovern. The political ground had shifted in the intervening four years. President Nixon could claim to be extricating the country, or at least its soldiers, from Vietnam. By 1972, the numbers of U.S. troops were one-fifth of their numbers in 1968, and the South Vietnamese Army was now larger and well armed though still ineffective in the field. U.S. aerial bombardment was substituted for action by troops on the ground. The Nixon administration also shifted the public debate about the war by mobilizing both sympathy for the American Prisoners of War (POWs) held in North Vietnam and antipathy toward peace activists. Nixon was re-elected in a landslide, winning every state except Massachusetts. What mattered most to a majority of voters were casualties among U.S. troops rather than the morality of the war. The withdrawal of U.S. troops meant that other issues could compete for public attention.

Without U.S. soldiers to stiffen its military, the South Vietnamese war effort abruptly collapsed in 1975 and Vietnam was re-unified. Although casualty statistics are disputed, approximately 58,000 Americans, 225,000 South Vietnamese soldiers, 500,000 North Vietnamese and Viet Cong soldiers, and two million Vietnamese civilians had died in the 12-year conflict. Despite such high cost, the lack of consensus among Americans on the lessons of Vietnam reduced discussions of the war to a minimum for a generation.

Vietnam reappeared as a secondary campaign issue in the 2004 presidential election between Republican nominee and incumbent President George W. Bush, and Democratic challenger, John Kerry. The Kerry campaign anticipated that their candidate's heroic combat record in Vietnam would win votes from military veterans because it would compare favorably with the president's poorly documented service in the Texas Air National Guard during the war. However, any possible advantage to Kerry was obviated by campaign advertisements of the 527 committee, Swift Boat Veterans for Truth, that challenged the veracity of Kerry's war record. Vietnam proved no more decisive as a campaign issue in 2004 than it had a generation earlier.

SEE ALSO: Military Hero; Military Vote; War and Peace.

BIBLIOGRAPHY. William Crotty, ed., *A Defining Moment: The Presidential Election of 2004* (M.E. Sharpe, 2005); Robert Mann, *A Grand Delusion: Americas Descent into Vietnam* (Basic Books, 2001); B.I. Page and R.A. Brody, "Policy Voting and the Electoral Process: The Vietnam War Issue," *American Political Science Review* (v.66, 1972); George Rising, *Clean for Gene: Eugene McCarthy's 1968 Presidential Campaign* (Praeger, 1997); T.H. White, *The Making of the President, 1964* (Atheneum, 1965); T.H. White, *The Making of the President, 1968* (Atheneum, 1969).

JOHN HICKMAN
BERRY COLLEGE

Virginia

VIRGINIA'S TRADITION OF democratic elections extends back to the first election of its House of Burgesses in 1619. This election was the first held in any of the American colonies, and the subsequent election of this legislature during the colonial era, and of the bicameral general assembly after 1776, mark Virginia's state legislature as the oldest continuously elected representative legislature in the world.

The 1619 election also is noteworthy because it prompted contests involving several of its newly elected burgesses. The first case was resolved when the House of Burgesses agreed to admit a pair of delegates despite their want of lawful residency within Virginia; the legislature concluded a second case by excluding two other delegates because of their refusal to recognize the binding legal authority of the body's decisions. Given the expansion of electoral democracy in America over

the next four centuries, the 1619 election in Virginia holds additional significance because it was marked by the precedent of a successful social protest against the attempted exclusion of some from participating. Prior to this particular election, several Polish craftsmen employed within the English colony of Virginia collectively pressed for voting privileges until it was determined that they, too, possessed the right to vote.

In addition to the regular election of the colonial House of Burgesses and of the Virginia House of Delegates and Senate, Virginia voters have regularly elected members of the U.S. House of Representatives and presidential electors since 1789; governors, lieutenant governors, and state attorneys general since 1851; the state Supreme Court 1852–69; and U.S. senators since 1916. Elections also have been held to select local delegates to nine state constitutional conventions between 1776 and 1956; the U.S. Constitution state ratifying convention in 1788; other statewide offices 1851–1928, as well as for ratification votes on several state constitutions and various state constitutional amendments.

Virginia's electoral tradition, moreover, includes numerous local elections. Initially, justices of the peace appointed in each county by the governor governed Virginia localities, but as early as the 1800s, the general assembly authorized towns such as Charlottesville to elect a small number of officials to enact local ordinances. Virginia's 1851 constitution established elected county magistrates throughout the state, along with elected local boards of supervisors and several other locally elected offices. Today, Virginia localities vote on local referenda issues and they regularly elect several offices, including legislative council members, Commonwealth attorneys, clerks of court, treasurers, school board members, and mayors. While Virginia's localities determine their own local electoral calendars, Virginia governors and the general assembly are elected in odd-numbered years. Congressional and presidential elections occur in even-numbered years, ensuring a robust contemporary political environment and a near-continuous cycle of campaigns, elections, and post- and pre-election analysis.

VIRGINIA'S ELECTORATE

Despite the origins and breadth of Virginia's democratic commitments, local elites and a generally conservative political culture limited popular influences on elections throughout the colonial era and for much of the 19th and 20th centuries. Voter restrictions and extended periods of low electoral competition account for the limited size and composition of Virginia's electorate. Many of these voting restrictions originated during the colonial era, but they often endured long after Virginia became a state in 1776. In 1655, for example, Virginia restricted each household to a single vote in any election regardless of the number of family dependents—a partially corrected, yet understudied legacy carried forward into the present.

In 1670, Virginia further defined the franchise to include only individuals who possessed property, an association with metrics of material wealth that persisted explicitly until 1851, and indirectly until poll taxes were prohibited in the 1960s. In 1699, Virginia denied voting rights to Catholics—a religious exclusion that persisted until at least 1785. In 1699, Virginia also became the first colony to explicitly exclude women from the pool of eligible propertied voters, a gender restriction not lifted within the state until the 1920 ratification of the Nineteenth Amendment to the U.S. Constitution. Moreover, in 1723, Virginia redefined voting rights in racialist terms to exclude free African-American and Native-American persons from those previously permitted to vote; these restrictions were formally prohibited by the Fifteenth Amendment to the U.S. Constitution (1870), although they remained effective until the enactment and enforcement of the 1965 Voting Rights Act.

RESTRICTIONS ON VOTING

In the 19th and 20th centuries, Virginia instituted additional constitutional and administrative restrictions on voting. The 1830 constitution slightly lowered the property threshold for voting, but it also decreased the size of the House of Delegates and established voter registration requirements. The 1870 and 1902 constitutions instituted voter taxes and, like the 1830 constitution, barred individuals with specified criminal convictions from voting. In 1894, the general assembly mandated the use of paper election ballots without party labels, making it nearly impossible for illiterate voters to select the candidates of their choice.

The 1902 constitution required additional pre-election literacy and understanding tests for voters, to further reduce the number of eligible African Americans on Virginia voter rolls. These tests were both effective and especially odious, not only because they accomplished

their intended objective—and with it the elimination of many semi-literate poor white voters, too—but also because they required the constant administrative complicity of state and local governmental officials, who ironically reduced the need for Democratic party members to engage in more overt forms of electoral fraud. Finally, but not surprising given past exclusionary practices, Virginia joined five other southern states to challenge the constitutionality of the 1965 Voting Rights Act; unlike its past successes, this effort ultimately failed when the U.S. Supreme Court upheld the landmark federal legislation in its 1966 *South Carolina v. Katzenbach* decision.

Although records of American elections remain incompletely compiled, several historical comparisons can be made concerning changes in the size of Virginia's electorate. During the late colonial and early national eras, elections for the House of Burgesses and the House of Delegates occurred in districts typically composed of a single county; the number of voters in contested elections in these districts varied from under 100 to approximately 600 voters. Virginia senate districts extended over several counties, but the number of voters in a contested election rarely exceeded 1,000, even into the 1820s. U.S. House elections occurred in still larger, multiple county districts; yet before 1825, these elections typically involved 1,000–2,000 voters, and only rarely more than 3,000 voters.

In addition to net district voter totals, state vote totals and their relative state population percentages offer two of the least biased historical measures of the breadth of electoral participation, especially for eras characterized by decidedly undemocratic attributes. In the 1800 presidential election, for example, 27,180 votes were cast in Virginia's 94 counties and towns; this vote total represents 3.4 percent of the state's population. The number of presidential voters declined in 1820 to under 6,000, which is less than one percent of Virginia's population. By contrast, in the 1823 congressional elections almost 25,000 votes, or 2.6 percent of the population, were recorded.

The size of Virginia's electorate steadily increased from the mid-1820s through the mid-1890s—although it is difficult to determine with certainty if increases in electoral fraud, especially after 1870, over- or underestimate the expansion of electoral participation during these decades. Nonetheless, in 1851, Virginia held its first popular vote for governor and 126,550 voters participated (or 11.2 percent of the state's population). In 1885, 289,072 voters, who represented approximately 18.2 percent of the state's population, decided the gubernatorial contest. The number of voters in congressional and presidential elections also increased during this period. By the 1880s, more than 200,000 voters were participating in U.S. House elections, with nearly 400,000 voters (or 25.8 percent of the state population) participating in the 1882 elections—a participation rate not surpassed in Virginia until the 1968 presidential election.

After 1890, the size of Virginia's electorate generally declined over the next three decades. In the 1909, 1913, and 1917 gubernatorial elections, fewer voters participated than had in Virginia's 1851 election. Remarkably, it was not until the 1953 gubernatorial contest, in which 412,457 voters participated, that the number of voters exceeded the total recorded for the 1885 gubernatorial election. After 1953, the number of voters increased significantly, with more than one million voters participating in the 1973 gubernatorial election and almost two million voters in the 2005 election. Voter participation rates in presidential elections after 1888 followed a similar, but, in several respects, more precipitous, decline.

In 1904, only 130,000 voters cast a ballot for a presidential candidate: 134,000 fewer than in the 1900 election. Moreover, in the 1908 election, only 6.6 percent of Virginia's population cast a presidential ballot: about one-third the participation rate in the 1888 presidential election.

Presidential voting increased significantly in the 1952 election, when over 600,000 voters (or 18 percent of the state population) cast ballots in Virginia. The net numbers of voters and relative participation rates have increased since 1952, with a state record of almost 3.2 million presidential voters in 2004, or 42.9 percent of Virginia's populace.

CANDIDATES AND ELECTORAL COMPETITION

The small size of Virginia's electorate throughout the colonial and early national eras—especially when compared to contemporary elections—greatly affected the candidate pool and the type of campaigns waged for local, state, and federal elected offices. Almost without exception, successful candidates were drawn from a small number of prominent local families and their election was determined by the support granted to them by a handful of local elites.

Public or extended campaigning for nomination and election was not common or particularly effective, although candidates typically accepted the social custom that they "treat" voters to liquor and food on Election Day. Although electoral competition certainly occurred, and often was magnified by the small number of votes in question, the elite and family-based determinants of Virginia's political environment defined the contours of Virginia elections until the early 1830s.

Several familiar elements of modern campaigns and elections, however, first emerged in Virginia in the 1790s. Two Virginians, Thomas Jefferson and James Madison, played critical roles in creating the first opposition national political party, the Republicans (as members identified themselves). Partisan groups and newspapers, such as the *Richmond Enquirer* established in 1804, promoted Republican party ideas throughout the state, as would future opposition groups through their newspapers or other contemporary media. Loose partisan affiliations among some of Virginia's elected officials also emerged in the 1790s, especially after the 1796 presidential election controversy.

Party affiliations, at this time, revolved primarily around national issues concerning the powers of the national government, foreign affairs, and the War of 1812. Partisanship was rarely expressed or advanced by Virginia candidates, especially in state legislative elections, as more important than local interests, personal relationships, and familial associations.

Political parties and partisanship became a permanent part of Virginia campaigns and elections with the association of Virginian Republicans with Jacksonian and Van Buren Democrats in the presidential elections of 1828, 1832, and 1836. The rise of the Whig Party in Virginia in the mid-1830s rested on disagreements with President Jackson's national policies, intra-state discontent with lagging economic conditions, and the Republican elite's disregard for particular regional or local concerns.

The Whigs won majorities in the House of Delegates in 1834, 1838–42, and again in 1844. They also were competitive in Virginia Senate and congressional elections, although Democrats won small majorities in presidential elections. In 1849, however, Virginia's interests in slavery, a malapportioned General Assembly, a relatively small swing of votes in Virginia's small electorate, a national debate over the admission of California, and the long decline of the south's representation in Congress combined to create the conditions for the Whig Party's demise and the Democratic Party's subsequent dominance over the state's elections and government until the mid-1860s.

The end of the Civil War and federal supervision of Virginia during Reconstruction opened unprecedented opportunities for voters, candidates, and party realignments. In 1867, 104,772 African-American males registered to vote, which represented 47.3 percent of the registered electorate. Almost 89 percent of these individuals turned out to cast ballots on the question of holding a state constitutional convention. The African-American vote represented 55 percent of the voter turnout and 86.2 percent of the winning majority in favor of the convention. African-American candidates were elected to approximately 22 percent of the seats in the 1867 constitutional convention, and they won smaller numbers of U.S. House and General Assembly elections until 1892, after which they were not elected to any state or federal office until 1967. Since 1967, there have been 184 African-American candidates for these offices; more than 92 percent have won. In 1989, Lawrence Douglas Wilder became the first elected African-American governor in any U.S. state. In 2000, one of Virginia's 11 U.S. Representatives, 10 of 140 General Assembly members, and nearly 240 local elected officials were African American.

The temporary expansion of the electorate during Reconstruction, along with the emergence of new economic interests, created party realignment possibilities that never fully materialized in Virginia. In 1870–1900, several new political parties—Republicans, True Republicans, Conservatives, Readjusters, Funders, and Populists—fielded candidates for the first time in Virginia. As it did when confronted by the Whigs in the 1830s and 1840s, the Democratic Party proved both resilient and dominant.

By 1884, Democrats controlled almost two-thirds of the seats in the general assembly, a level of political power that remained unchallenged for more than 100 years. With their legislative power, the Democratic Party enacted a new election law in 1884 that placed control of election boards with the Democratic-controlled General Assembly. By 1894, there were no Republicans in either the Virginia Senate or House of Delegates; and 1924–64, the Democrats (under the leadership of Governor and then U.S. Senator, Harry F. Byrd, Sr.) held Republicans to no more than 10 percent of the seats in the General Assembly. Democrat Party nominations and their all-white primary elections, thus, became tantamount to election to federal, state, and local offices in Virginia.

For the first half of the 20th century, Republicans floundered trying to break free of Democratic dominance of Virginia elections. Even repeated party declarations that they had become the "lily white" Republicans had little effect on the diminished but heavily Democratic, electorate that, in 1925, numbered less than 145,000, or 6.1 percent of Virginia's population. In 1928, almost 54 percent of Virginia voters supported the Republican presidential candidate, Herbert Hoover, but this shift in voting behavior was temporary and widely understood as a reaction against Democratic presidential candidate Al Smith, a Catholic. In 1952, and again in 1956, Virginia voted for Republican presidential candidate Dwight Eisenhower, a World War II general.

REPUBLICAN REALIGNMENT

The 1952 vote initiated a Republican realignment in Presidential elections that, except for Virginia's support for Lyndon Johnson in 1964, remains unbroken through the 2004 election. Democratic dominance of the General Assembly, however, was not immediately challenged. After the 1957 elections, Republicans held no statewide office, and only three of 40 state Senate, and six of 100 House of Delegates seats. In 1958, Republicans failed to nominate a candidate for the U.S. Senate, fielding only three candidates for the state's 10 U.S. House seats. In 1959, Republican representation in the General Assembly declined to six of 140 seats.

The activist civil rights commitments of national political leaders that culminated in the 1964 Civil Rights Act and 1965 Voting Rights Act accelerated both the detachment of Virginia Democrats from the national Democratic Party and the top-down partisan realignment of Virginia voters started in 1952. In 1969, a Republican gubernatorial candidate, Linwood Holton, won for the first time in Virginia's history, as did the next two Republican candidates, in 1973 and 1977. U.S. Senator Harry Byrd, Jr., the son of Harry F. Byrd, discarded his Democratic Party affiliation and won re-election as an Independent in 1970; since then Democrats have won only three of 13 U.S. Senate elections.

In 1971, Republicans also captured a majority of the state's U.S. House delegation, increasing their numbers to nine of 10 seats in 1980; in 2007, Republicans held eight to 11 House seats. Republicans also eventually won full control of the General Assembly, winning and retaining majorities in the Virginia senate after 1997, and the House Of Delegates after 2000. Democrats, however, have displayed a resiliency in gubernatorial elections: winning five of seven elections since 1981.

SEE ALSO: African-American Suffrage; Democratic Party; Election Laws, State and Local Elections; Fifteenth Amendment; Machine Politics and Political Bosses; Protest Voting; Realignment; Republican Party; Suffrage; Voter Turnout.

BIBLIOGRAPHY. Frank Atkinson, *Virginia in the Vanguard* (Rowman & Littlefield, 2006); Frank Atkinson, *The Dynamic Dominion* (Rowman & Littlefield, 2006); Robert Dinkin, *Voting in Provincial America* (Greenwood Press, 1977); Ronald Heinemann, et al., *Old Dominion, New Commonwealth* (University of Virginia, 2007). John Kolp, *Gentlemen and Freeholders* (Johns Hopkins University Press, 1998); Alexander Keyssar, *The Right to Vote* (Basic Books, 2000); C.A. Kromkowski, "The Virginia Elections and State Elected Officials Database Project," www.virginia.edu (University of Virginia, 2007); Philip Lampi, *A New Nation Votes American Election Returns, 1787–1825* (American Antiquarian Society, 2007); Larry Sabato, *The Democratic Party Primary in Virginia* (University of Virginia, 1977); William Shade, *Democratizing the Old Dominion* (University of Virginia, 1996).

CHARLES A. KROMKOWSKI
UNIVERSITY OF VIRGINIA

Vote by Mail

THE GENESIS OF voting by mail dates back to the 1700s when landowners whose homes were vulnerable to attack from Native Americans were allowed to vote absentee. In 1857, only Oregon made it possible for men away from home to vote. However, it was not until the Civil War when 19 of the 25 Union states and seven of the 11 Confederate states enacted legislation to provide soldiers an opportunity to vote absentee. Following the Civil War, nearly all states discontinued military absentee voting. During World War I, when three million Americans were inducted, there was renewed pressure to provide military personnel the opportunity to vote absentee. By 1917, nearly all of the 48 states pro-

vided absentee voting for the military and 24 states had enacted some form of absentee voting laws. At the close of World War II, work-related reasons were accepted by over 20 states for absentee balloting. Today all states permit absentee voting, with eight states offering voters permanent absentee-ballot status out of the 29 that allow no-excuse absentee balloting. With Vote by Mail (VBM), all registered voters receive ballots through the mail. Although VBM began as a western-state phenomenon, it is now conducted in some form in 15 states from New Jersey to Hawaii. California was the first to hold a vote-by-mail election in 1977. All states, with the exception of Oregon, provide hybrid voting, or poll voting in conjunction with absentee balloting. Oregon has no poll voting.

OREGON

In 1981, the Oregon Legislature approved a test of VBM for local elections. By 1987, VBM was made permanent for local and special elections, and a majority of counties used it. In 1993 and 1995, the first and second statewide special elections were conducted using VBM. In the summer of 1995, the Republican-controlled legislature passed a bill expanding VBM to primary and general elections. Under pressure from the Democratic minority in the legislature, who were concerned that VBM could reduce the power of the state Democratic machine, and Clinton operatives, who were concerned about the president's re-election bid in Oregon, Governor John Kitzhaber vetoed the bill, stating that more study of the issue was the prudent course. This veto came despite calls from Democratic operatives who tracked local VBM elections and determined it was party-neutral and easier for campaign organizations.

In 1995, following the resignation of Senator Bob Packwood, Democratic Secretary of State Phil Keisling exercised the option to run the December primary, and January general special elections using VBM. After Democrat Ron Wyden defeated Republican Gordon Smith, both caucuses in the legislature reconsidered their previous positions. In the 1997 legislative session, Democrats, realizing their error, supported legislation to pass VBM.

Although it passed the house, the Republican majority in the Senate allowed the bill to die. The option for statewide VBM never re-visited Governor Kitzhaber's desk, who stated he would have signed the bill into law. However, legislation passed allowing voters to register for permanent absentee status and 41 percent took advantage of this option.

In the 1998 primary election, with a record-low turnout, absentee voters accounted for nearly two-thirds of all ballots cast. This election represented the first in the nation where absentee voters, with a 53 percent turnout, cast more ballots than poll voters who turned out at 22 percent. In June of 1998, Secretary of State, Phil Keisling spearheaded an initiative to move around the Oregon Legislature and successfully garnered the number of signatures required to qualify for the November ballot using no paid signature gatherers—only volunteers. Oregon voters approved the initiative to expand VBM to primary and general elections by nearly 70 percent.

IMPLICATIONS OF VBM

VBM is credited with increasing voter turnout and saving taxpayer dollars. Indeed, the hybrid voting process (both poll voting and absentee balloting), used in every state but Oregon, requires election officials to run two elections: one for absentee voters and one for poll voters.

The savings to taxpayers of eliminating poll voting is between a third to one half the cost of running hybrid elections. Curtis Gans, Director of the Committee for the Study of the American Electorate (CSAE), contends that no-excuse absentee and early voting actually hurts voter turnout. To make his case, he uses eligible voters rather than registered voters. His arguments in a September 13, 2004 press release attributes lower turnout to diffused mobilization of voters that extends over many weeks rather than one single day.

In 2000, Michel Manmer and Michael Traugott conducted a survey of voters in Oregon before and after VBM. Their findings, outlined in "The Impact of Voting by Mail on Voter Behavior" showed only modest changes in turnout and composition of the electorate after VBM. Ultimately, VBM impacted those who generally voted, but might have difficulty participating in any given election, rather than mobilizing new voters.

This is corroborated by the 2003 study by Pricilla Southwell from University of Oregon, "Five Years Later: A re-assessment of Oregon's Vote By Mail Electoral Process", where a majority of respondents (2/3) indicated no change in their turnout. Of the one-third of the respondents who reported voting more often since the introduction of VBM, the increase came primarily from women, the disabled, homemakers, and 26–38 year olds.

As had other researchers, Manmer and Traugott as well as Southwell concluded that VBM is party-neutral.

Arguments that VBM hurts the poor and minorities who cannot afford a stamp were dispelled by another Southwell survey in 1996, following the special statewide VBM election to replace Senator Packwood. "Survey of Vote-By-Mail Senate Election" revealed that VBM voters were more likely to be minorities, single parents, younger, those who had moved within two years, students, less likely to be retired, and more likely to be paid by the hour than traditional voters and registered Independents.

FRAUD

Much of the hesitancy to implement full-scale VBM in other states centers on voter fraud with absentee balloting. However, election officials consistently site the difficulty in supervising hybrid elections where the volume of absentee-ballot requests and processing competes for time with managing poll sites and poll workers. In Project Vote, four forms of ballot fraud are associated with absentee ballots: signature forging or using factitious names; coercion; vote-buying; and siphoning absentee ballots. However, Oregon election officials who managed elections both before and after VBM underscore that managing only one type of election, vote by mail, allows closer scrutiny of the integrity of the ballot. Comparison of optically-scanned signatures on the ballot and voter-registration form has all but eliminated voter fraud. One area of concern remains with Oregon's VBM: the unregulated collection of ballots by volunteers or party operatives who then deliver them to election departments for voters. Ironically, this was the same concern of Civil War soldiers who relinquished their ballots to commanding officers who became responsible for getting the ballots to the soldiers' hometown election authorities.

CAMPAIGNING WITH VBM

Campaign managers, party operatives, candidates, and strategists insist that VBM increases the cost of running a campaign because ballots are mailed to voters between 14 and 18 days prior to the election. During this period, voters return ballots in two surges, the first week, followed by a lull, and then another surge just prior to Election Day. It is argued that both surges must be met with mail, radio, television, and other campaign activities. However, the hybrid election requires two separate campaign structures: one to communicate with and track absentee voters, and another for precinct voters. Whether a state allows no-fault absentee voting or not, absentee voters remain the most likely voters; they tend to be Republican, women, and over 65 years in age. Further, they represent a far greater percent of the voter turnout. No campaign can afford to ignore these voters. Communicating with precinct voters requires media, mail, and phoning—paid or volunteer—up to and including, Election Day. Tracking identified supporters who vote at the polls is also a massive organizational enterprise for a campaign. In the hybrid campaign, both must be done.

THE EXECUTION

The most striking difference between hybrid and VBM elections is timing. With VBM the campaign must peak when ballots are mailed, 14 to 18 days before the election, and hold a presence in the media until the elections department receives a critical mass.

That means all campaign activities are front-end loaded; a candidate and issue-based campaign must have support identified and canvassing completed the weekend after ballots leave the clerk's office. Television, to be effective, must be up and running for at least a week before the ballots leave the clerk's office. After ballots are received, many voters hold on to them, but few are undecided.

After ballots are mailed, efficient campaigns allow voters all but the last seven days to return their ballots before starting the get-out-the-vote (GOTV) effort. All media, mail, and communication should be at full tilt during that time, as the campaign re-focuses its attention to gather the critical number of volunteers for the GOTV effort that fills the final seven nights before the election. Because all ballots are returned by mail, campaigns can easily track voters by ordering activity lists (those whose ballots have been received by the county), or inactivity lists (those whose ballots are still with the voter), from the county for a small fee. Although VBM has shown only modest improvement in voter participation, the level of voter enthusiasm, dramatically reduced administrative costs compared to hybrid elections and a more manageable campaign structure suggest that this simple, low-tech approach should be considered throughout the nation.

SEE ALSO: Voter Registration; Voter Turnout; Voting, Obstacles to; Voting Methods.

BIBLIOGRAPHY. J.M. Broder, "Early Voting is Changing Campaigns," *New York Times* (October 22, 2006); Curtis Gans, "Making it Easier Doesn't Work," *Committee for the Study of the American Electorate* (September 13, 2004); Paul Gronke, "Ballot Integrity and Voting by Mail: The Oregon Experience," A Report for the Commission on Federal Election Reform, The Early Voting Information Center at Reed College (May 15, 2005); Paul Gronke, "Electing to Change How We Vote," *Los Angeles Times* (October 16, 2003); Michael Hanmer and Michael Traugott, *The Impact of Voting By Mail on Voter Behavior*, abstract (2000); Rachel Harris, "Voting-By-Mail: A Look at Modernizing the Electoral System," *California Research Bureau* (July 1999); Michael Moss, "Absentee Votes Worry Officials as Nov. 2 Nears," *New York Times* (September 13, 2004); Oregon Secretary of State, www.sos.state.or.usl (cited August 2007); Michael Rust, "Oregon Vote-by-Mail Plan is a Jeffersonian Test," *News World Communication* (1995).

CATHERINE M. SHAW
INDEPENDENT SCHOLAR

Voter Alienation

VOTER ALIENATION IS a political phenomenon occurring in electoral politics as a result of a majority of voters feeling as though the major political parties no longer represent citizens' mainstream issues and values. Consequently, voter alienation is closely linked to voter turnout. Voter alienation signals that everyday citizens no longer feel connected to politics and, therefore, decide that it is no longer in their interest to participate in politics. Alienated voters believe that their vote will not make any difference, that politics has little influence in their lives, and that the main parties do not address their concerns.

In the United States, voter alienation has occurred twice in recent history, in the 1960s and the 1990s. Voter alienation may raise serious concerns about the ability of political parties to represent and aggregate the interests of citizens'. Voter alienation is related to voter apathy and a general distrust of politics at the national level, which is indicated by voter turnout. Three schools of thought explain voter turnout: rational choice theories, sociological theories, and theories of political efficacy. Rational choice theorists argue that voters weigh the costs and benefits of their actions; voters will turn up to vote when they consider that the benefits of voting outweigh the costs of voting. Sociological theorists argue that socioeconomic class determines party identification and propensity to vote. Elites, including those with education beyond high school and voters of high socioeconomic class are more likely to vote and feel as if their vote matters. Political efficacy theorists argue that people alienated from the political process are less likely to vote. In order for citizens to turnout to vote and participate they must feel that their votes have an impact.

Voter turnout in presidential elections in the past two decades has been relatively low, averaging about 52 percent, down from a high of 63 percent in 1960. Turnout in off-year congressional elections has been much lower, hovering around 40 percent. The number of voters registered as Independents or with third parties has more than tripled during the last 30 years, to just under 13 percent, and Independent voters are the fastest-growing voter group.

Although many scholars argue that voter alienation is a signal that political parties are not performing as they should, citizens' participation in electoral politics at the local and state levels of government has increased, while participation in national-level elections has declined. Furthermore, voter alienation may have more to do with the horizontal and vertical distribution of authority in a political system, or institutional design, than anything about the general population of a country. Electoral systems, which are single-member district pluralities and produce catchall parties, may not capture the interest of citizens or represent citizens as well as proportional representation or mixed models, which foster more ideologically distinct political parties.

There is disagreement among scholars of electoral politics in the United States on the issue of voter alienation. For example, McDonald and Popkin (2001) attribute the apparent decline in turnout rate since 1972 to the increasing number of ineligible persons counted among the voting-age population, which is the denominator for the calculations by the Bureau of the Census. The causes for voter alienation, and its indicator, low voter turnout, has a number of supposed causes: economic decline, divided government, negative campaigning, the realignment of parties, and declining civic engagement are the most prominent. However, there may be alternative explanations for lower turnout in America, when compared with other industrial democracies, which have more to do with the way that U.S. political institutions are designed. Parliamentary systems that possess proportional representation or mixed electoral systems, produce strong national parties. In political systems where the national government possesses the most power and lower levels implement its decisions, responsibility for government performance is clear-cut, as is accountability. In federal systems, responsibility is divided between state and national governments, and in the United States, among two legislatures, and an executive at each level. Federalism and the separation of powers increase the costs to voters to gather and process the information about candidates and elections. Researching the proposals for a given issue and registration are neither done by the government nor are they compulsory. Moreover, the frequent primary and general elections required to fill the many elected offices increase the burden of democracy for the voter. The other two industrialized democracies with chronically low turnout rates are Switzerland and Japan, countries with diffused lines of authority and responsibility.

According to democratic theory, the most basic definition of democracy is that citizens have meaningful control of the decisions that affect their everyday lives. Increasingly, central authorities or government at the national level are making these decisions. While scholars debate the causes of voter alienation, voter alienation may signal a problem for democracies, especially those that are developing or in transition. Citizen participation is a core democratic concept.

If the public are not participating, political leaders and elites must evaluate their political programs and structures to better understand and address the issue of voter alienation.

SEE ALSO: Voter Apathy; Voter Turnout.

BIBLIOGRAPHY. R.J. Dalton, *Citizen Politics in Western Democracies: Public Opinion and Political Parties in the United States, Great Britain, West Germany, and France* (Chatham House Publishers, 1988); S.L. Popkin and Michael McDonald, "Who Votes?" *Bluebook: Ideas for a New Century* (v.1, 1998).

NICOLE FREINER
UNIVERSITY OF DAYTON

Voter Apathy

THE TERM *VOTER apathy* refers, in the narrow sense, to people abstaining from voting. In the broad sense, it includes the widespread indifference of people toward politics and governmental affairs, in general, and elections and candidates, in particular. Social scientists have identified several causes and consequences of voter apathy. The beginning of the 21st century confirmed an irony in which increasing amounts of information and effective means of communication have failed to generate increasing participation and civic engagement. Instead, an overload of information and a myriad of venues have overwhelmed the individual, generating negative or indifferent reactions toward government. In political science, this phenomenon has been named the paradox of democracy, that is, as pre-conditions for democracy prevail and democracy gains worldwide support as a social value, people become politically indifferent and electorally apathetic.

Electoral participation has consistently declined in all advanced democracies since World War II. In the United States, this is true at the federal, state, and local levels of government, both for executive and legislative elections. However, it is important to recognize that "hot" issues and head-to-head races have occasionally reversed this trend. Other indicators of traditional political participation have plummeted as well: social scientists have shown a decline in rallying, in formal petitions to authorities, and in the number of letters written from ordinary citizens to congresspeople. In turn, people are voicing their concerns on public issues through new venues such as the media, civic organizations, or through indirect participation in transnational advocacy groups.

In rational choice theory, an economic theory based on the idea that human beings are rational actors who permanently maximize the use of scarce resources, theorists argue that it is not rational for individuals to vote since because the chances of changing the electoral outcome are practically null. Because voting requires an investment of resources that do not pay off (money to get information; time to register and to go to the voting booth), the rational individual, after a cost-benefit calculation, will choose not to vote and enjoy the benefits of other's efforts to vote. A second group of theorists, grounded in social psychology, affirm that the transition from modernity to postmodernity has brought a wave of disenchantment with traditional authorities and established structures, including politicians and elections. According to these theorists, after losing the possibilities of direct participation in public decision-making, people feel detached from government and uneasy with public officials.

A third set of explanations points to the sources of voter apathy in the excessive complexity and specialization of public policies. The discussion of public issues such as the federal budget or pollution standards has become so specialized that the ordinary citizen cannot understand the terms of the debate and feels incapable of voicing his or her point of view. Other reasons, such as lack of options in the bipartisan system, vagueness of electoral proposals, and lack of depth to the ideological debate have also been pointed to as possible explanations for voters' apathy. Finally, by expanding the concept of politics to the inclusion of issues in the public agenda, Peter Bachrach and Morton Baratz have shown that in some cases, non-participation is actually a powerful way of participating.

The main consequence of voters' apathy is the steady loss of the legitimacy of the political system and the subsequent hollowing of democracy. As more citizens abstain from voting, elected officials get disconnected from the public will, which is the foundation for two pillars of democracy: electoral mandates and governmental accountability. Countries with poor citizenship (lack of involvement by ordinary people in public affairs) are prone to develop serious political pathologies such as corruption and despotism. Finally, voters' apathy is also related to social inequality; researchers have shown a correlation between voters' apathy and poverty, race, and education failure.

Attempts to curb voter apathy include information and get-out-the-vote (GOTV) campaigns. Nonpartisan civic organizations, especially, have assumed the goal of raising awareness about the importance of public engagement and voting; politicians are including GOTV messages in their electoral campaigns. Other democracies of the world, most notably in Latin America, have mandatory elections making the assumption that choosing authorities is not only a right, but also a duty of every citizen.

SEE ALSO: Get-Out-the-Vote (GOTV) Drives; Nonvoters; Political Culture; Political Cynicism; Voter Knowledge/Ignorance; Voter Turnout; Voting; Voting, Incentives for.

BIBLIOGRAPHY. Peter Bachrach and Morton Baratz, "Decisions and Non-Decisions: An Analytical Framework," *American Political Science Review* (v.56/4, 1962); S.E. Bennett, *Apathy in America: Causes and Consequences of Citizen Political Indifference, 1960–1984* (Transnational Publishers, 1986); Tom de Luca, *The Two Faces of Political Apathy* (Temple University Press, 1995).

MARTIN A. MALDONADO
UNIVERSITY OF FLORIDA

Voter Disenfranchisement

VOTER DISENFRANCHISEMENT IS the denial of the vote to a class of persons because they fail to meet a particular qualification. There have been several prevalent reasons given by election board authorities disqualifying voters throughout U.S. history. At the founding of the United States, only adult males were allowed to vote, with the exception of New Jersey, which had no requirement that voters be male.

Three of the original 13 states disenfranchised non-white voters. During this early period, states established property, taxpaying, and residency requirements as qualifications for voting. The typical property qualification required persons to own a certain amount of land in order to be eligible to vote, while taxpaying qualifications required persons to have paid taxes the year prior to the election. The rationale for the taxpaying and property qualifications was that those without money or property lacked the necessary independence to exercise the vote without influence from the more affluent. The residency requirements, which varied from a requirement of six months in the county to two years in the state, were established to ensure that voters had a stake in the community in which they were voting. According to one estimate, as a result of these voting qualifications, only 60 to 70 percent of adult white men could vote in 1790.

States joining the union in the late 18th and early 19th centuries usually instituted taxpaying qualifications rather than property qualifications for voting. The theory was that people who paid taxes, regardless of whether they owned property, should have their voices represented and their interests defended in the government that they participated in funding.

Property qualifications also became less popular as a result of increasing urbanization from industrialization, which greatly reduced the property-owning class of voters. By the middle of the 18th century, most state property qualifications had been eliminated. States also gradually eliminated taxpaying qualifications. A reason cited by one commentator for the elimination of the taxpaying requirements was the difficulty of enforcement and problems of fraud. More substantive, there was a gradual shift in ideology away from the idea that non-taxpayers and non-property-owners lacked the necessary independence to exercise the vote. Instead, the concept of universal white male suffrage gained favor, stimulated by the competition among political parties for new classes of voters. Despite the extension of the vote to an increasing number of white male voters, paupers (for example, persons receiving state economic aid), were the one remaining class of voters disenfranchised because of their economic status. The old theory concerning the independence of the voter and the view that paupers could be manipulated and influenced to vote by those with money continued to have adherents.

While the vote was extended to more white males, states in the years preceding the Civil War increasingly enacted voting qualifications that disenfranchised non-white male voters. As a result of racism and the popular belief that African Americans lacked the necessary personal qualities to vote, the number of states that disenfranchised non-white voters increased from three of 13 in 1790 to 25 of 31 in 1855.

In 1807, New Jersey became the last state to disenfranchise women. The rationales for women's disenfranchisement, like those for African American's disenfranchisement, related to their perceived capacity to vote. Women were viewed as being too delicate and too virtuous to be involved in the rough and tumble of politics. According to the prevailing ideology, women were, instead, represented through the votes of their male family counterparts. The first half of the 19th century also saw the proliferation of citizen qualifications for voting, which had the effect of disfranchising immigrant aliens. In the early 19th century, as a means of attracting immigrant settlers, new states in the midwest allowed non-citizen aliens who expressed their intention to become citizens (termed "non-citizen declarants"), to vote. By the late 19th century, the need for settlement had decreased, and states in the midwest joined states in the east and the south in establishing citizenship qualifications for voting. These qualifications were driven by concern over the dramatic increase in poor and working-class immigrants. The citizen qualifications also made it difficult for Native Americans to vote because of 18th century Supreme Court precedent that impeded the process of obtaining citizenship for Native Americans. Even for some Native Americans who navigated the process, several states established restrictions prohibiting "all Indians" from voting.

Prior to the Civil War, as a means of further circumscribing the number of eligible voters, some states enacted literacy tests and criminal disenfranchisement laws. Literacy tests required persons to demonstrate the ability to read and write in order to vote and were justified on the basis that voters needed to be educated and knowledgeable in order to effectively exercise the vote. Despite this stated rationale, literacy tests were widely seen as a means to disenfranchise poor and immigrant voters. Criminal disenfranchisement laws, which disqualified voters who had committed a certain category of crimes, were justified as a tool for retribution for the commission of crimes and as a means of general deterrence of crime. By the middle of the 19th century, all but eight states had criminal disenfranchisement laws in place.

FIFTEENTH AMENDMENT

The Fifteenth Amendment, ratified after the Civil War in 1870, was the first constitutional limitation on state discretion to enact voting qualifications. The amendment prohibited the denial of the vote on account of race. As a result of the amendment, African Americans actively participated in the voting process in the nearly 30 years after ratification. But by the beginning of the 20th century, they were disenfranchised in the south, as a result of state-sanctioned intimidation, violence, and fraud as well as the enactment of discriminatory electoral qualifications. With the goal of disfranchising African Americans, southern states enacted various qualifications. These qualifications included poll taxes that required persons to pay a fee in order to vote, and literacy tests that were sometimes accompanied by grandfather clauses that exempted persons eligible to vote prior to ratification of the Fifteenth Amendment.

After the grandfather clauses were finally declared unconstitutional in 1915, voting registrars simply used their discretion to ensure that most whites and few blacks were able to pass the tests. Finally, southern states lengthened residency requirements and broadened the reach of criminal disenfranchisement laws. The effect of intimidation, violence, fraud, and discriminatory electoral qualifications was dramatic. African-American electoral turnout in the south, which had been 60 to 85 percent of voting age African Americans in the 1880s and early 1890s, dropped to less than 10 percent in every southern state by 1900.

WOMEN'S SUFFRAGE

At the same time that African Americans were being disenfranchised in the south, the women's suffrage movement was gaining momentum. Women's participation in the labor force and economy led to challenges to the antiquated ideas regarding women's capacity to vote, and the view that women were represented by their husbands. Ultimately, the pivotal role of women in World War I served as a final repudiation of stereotypical theories supporting the disenfranchisement of women. In 1919, the women's suffrage movement culminated in the ratification of the Nineteenth Amendment, which prohibited states from denying the vote on account of sex. During the early part of the 20th century, states also began the process of enfranchising Native Americans by first granting suffrage to Native Americans deemed sufficiently assimilated. Later, prompted by the federal courts, states extended the franchise to all Native Americans.

For African Americans, particularly those in the south, the process of regaining the vote would be slow, arduous, and ultimately require federal action from Congress. With the prodding of an increasingly powerful Civil Rights Movement, Congress passed the Voting Rights Act (VRA) in 1965. The VRA suspended literacy tests in states with a history of discrimination and required those states to obtain approval from the federal government prior to enactment of new voting laws. As a result of the VRA, African Americans regained the vote in substantial numbers throughout the south. Other electoral barriers were also removed during this period. In 1964, the Twenty-Fourth Amendment banned poll taxes. By 1970, nearly all states had repealed pauper exclusion laws. The Twenty-Sixth Amendment, ratified in 1971, lowered the voting age to 18 in response to a Vietnam War movement that linked the obligation to fight in a war with the privilege of voting. Finally, the Supreme Court, in 1972, found residency requirements longer than 30 days unconstitutional, which provided transient persons with a greater opportunity to vote.

Currently, three major classes of voters remain disenfranchised: felons, immigrant aliens, and children. In a 1974 case, the Supreme Court held that states had the constitutional authority to disenfranchise felons under Section 2 of the Fourteenth Amendment. In spite of the opposition to these laws and the complaints regarding the discriminatory effect of these laws on African Americans, an overwhelming majority of states continue to maintain these laws in some form, and 5.3 million Americans are disenfranchised as a result of felon disenfranchisement laws. Arkansas was the last state to repeal alien declarant laws in 1926. Since then, immigrant aliens have only been able to secure the vote in local and municipal elections. Finally, there has been no notable movement to secure the vote for children under 18-years-old.

SEE ALSO: Fifteenth Amendment; Literacy Tests; Voting Rights Act of 1965.

BIBLIOGRAPHY. Williamson Chilton, *American Suffrage: From Property to Democracy, 1760–1860* (Princeton University Press, 1960); Alexander Keyssar, *The Right to Vote: The Contested History of Democracy in the United States* (Basic Books, 2001); J.M. Kousser, *The Shaping of Southern Politics: Suffrage Restriction and the Establishment of the One-Party South, 1880–1910* (Yale University Press, 1974).

BERTRALL ROSS
LAW CLERK, NINTH CIRCUIT COURT OF APPEALS

Voter Expectations

THE PHRASE *VOTER* expectations has several usages in studies of campaigns and elections. In dtudies from an economic perspective, the term refers to rational calculations of anticipated or future costs and benefits associated with the various candidates. In studies from a sociological perspective, the term refers to voter preferences for candidate characteristics (such as charisma, leadership, and integrity), policies (for example, supporting more or less of a government service or program), or election outcomes (for example, the chances that a certain candidate will win). In both cases, the idea is that expectations of a future outcome affect voter decisions and behavior in the short term. Expectations about the outcome of an election may affect whether or not an individual will vote. If a voter expects one candidate to win an election in a landslide, then there may be less reason to spend time and energy becoming informed about candidates or even voting on Election Day.

In terms of candidate characteristics or behavior, expectations refer to a voter's ideal, which the voter expect candidates to live up to or meet. Candidates' characteristics include personal characteristics (a candidate's appearance, style, charisma, competence, empathy, integrity, and leadership, and political role characteristics, their record as a public leader, policy positions, tendencies toward liberalism or conservatism, and position in the context of their political party). Candidates who do not meet expectations have less appeal to voters than those who meet expectations for candidate character. Voters, however, often have inconsistent or contradictory expectations. For example, voters may expect candidates to be firm in their policy positions, but also to be willing to compromise to get things done. The existence of multiple, potentially conflicting, expectations make it difficult for politicians to satisfy these expectations, and may contribute to cynicism and mistrust among voters.

Expectations are formed through an interactive process between an individual's beliefs and the information provided by candidates, the media, political parties, and advocacy groups. People have limited cognitive capacity and sensory perception and do not pay attention to the full range of information available in the environment. An individual's interpretation of political information is influenced by their unique set of beliefs, values, and attitudes formed through their socialization and other life experiences.

Expectations are formed, reinforced, or modified as people encounter new bits of information that interact with their existing information base stored in long-term memory. Voters tend to interpret fragments of information obtained through episodic attention to politics in ways that are consistent with their existing beliefs. In particular, most voters' images of candidates are affected by their party loyalties, ideological orientations, and deep-seated political attitudes relevant to the processing of information about candidates. People tend to see or invent what is favorable and they tend to distort or deny much of what is unfavorable with respect to these prior beliefs. For example, Republican and Democratic voters tend to pay attention to and incorporate information favorable to their party's candidate, while ignoring or distorting information that is unfavorable to their party's candidate. Thus, partisan voters tend to inflate expectations for their own political party's candidate, anticipating that their preferred candidate will do better in an event such as a debate or in an election than may be the case from the perspective of a neutral observer.

Expectations are also influenced by the information that voters receive from the candidates and, especially, the media. Campaigns seek to influence the impressions that voters have of the candidate by controlling the appearance and expressions of a candidate. Candidates present themselves selectively to emphasize their personal strengths and de-emphasize their weaknesses. Candidates tend to raise expectations by promising more than they may be able to deliver once in office. Candidates in high visibility campaigns, such as presidential campaigns, do not fully control the information used by voters. The news media play a critical role in setting expectations for candidates, both in terms of performance and their chances of winning a presidential nomination or election.

The news media are especially important for handicapping candidates' chances of victory. Journalists and pundits analyze fundraising records, public opinion polls, candidate endorsements and other insider commentary to produce estimates of candidates' performance in campaign events such as debates, and ultimately, the candidates' chances of victory on Election Day. The news media then judge candidates' performance relative to the pre-event expectations. Candidates whose performance in an event, such as a debate or a presidential primary election, exceeds expectations generally receive more news coverage that is also more favorable to the candidate. Candidates whose performance is judged to trail or lag behind expectations generally receive less news coverage, but that coverage is more critical of the candidate as journalists and pundits focus on why a candidate failed to meet expectations.

This kind of news coverage helps or hurts a candidate by focusing on a candidate's strengths or weaknesses, respectively. Candidates who beat expectations generally find that their fundraising efforts increase and that their standing in public opinion polls increases somewhat, while candidates who lag expectations generally find decreased fundraising success and slight declines in their standing in public opinion polls. Knowing these effects, candidates try to influence journalists' expectations for performance, often trying to lower the bar before an event and by trying to spin or frame an event after the fact so that their performance appears to be better than expectations.

SEE ALSO: Media, Role in Campaigns, Voter Alienation; Voter Apathy; Voter Knowledge/ Ignorance; Voting, Incentives for.

BIBLIOGRAPHY. H.E. Brady and Richard Johnston, *Capturing Campaign Effects* (University of Michigan Press, 2006); R.M. Hogarth and Melvin Reder, *Rational Choice* (University of Chicago Press, 1987); Samuel Popkin, *The Reasoning Voter* (University of Chicago Press, 1991).

WAYNE P. STEGER
DEPAUL UNIVERSITY

Voter Knowledge/Ignorance

THE IMPORTANCE OF citizen knowledge—or citizens' lack thereof—has been contested throughout the history of modern democratic societies. Widespread lack of political knowledge was used to justify the limitation of voting rights in the United States and Britain to male property owners into the mid-19th century. Indirect elections for institutions such as the presidency and the U.S. Senate were held, and in the wake of the Civil War, literacy and understanding tests were imposed in the southern United States to disenfranchise African Americans and uneducated whites. This pessimistic view of political knowledge among the public stands in contrast to Alexis de Tocqueville's assessment that citizens (at least white males) during this period were actively engaged in, and knowledgeable about, political issues of the day.

The advent of the scientific study of public opinion in the United States and other democratic societies dispelled the Tocquevillean notion that the public were keenly aware of the details of political life. In the concluding chapter of their path-breaking study of the politics of Elmira, New York, Bernard Berelson and his *Voting* co-authors wrote, "The democratic citizen is expected to be well informed about political affairs ...

[however] the voter falls short." This view has generally been reinforced in more recent research, in that most citizens do not appear to live up to the democratic ideal of being highly informed about politics. Voter ignorance appears to be a constant feature of politics, despite societal changes—most notably, increases in literacy rates and formal education—that would be expected to produce higher political knowledge in the electorate.

Scholars following the rational choice approach in politics explain the lack of political knowledge in the electorate as being a result of "rational ignorance": most voters derive little benefit from being better informed, and thus do not expend the effort to acquire additional knowledge about political issues or candidates. Voter knowledge appears to reflect, in part, the availability of information through the mass media; public knowledge of international political figures such as the United Nations secretary general appears to be higher in countries where print and electronic media emphasize international news, while such figures are more obscure in countries (like the United States) where regional and national news is deemed more important by media outlets. Voters also appear to respond to the demands placed on them by the political system; for example, voters' knowledge of parliamentary candidates' names in Britain dropped precipitously after party labels were added to general election ballots in the 1960s.

More recently, scholars' concerns have moved from questions about measurement to consideration of the consequences of low political knowledge in the electorate. This research has led to mixed conclusions. Some researchers, such as Larry Bartels and Scott Althaus, conclude that voter ignorance has important, systematic effects in electoral outcomes, while other researchers, such as Samuel Popkin, conclude that the differences between informed and uninformed voters are minimal, concluding that most voters' decisions are consistent with their likely "fully informed" preferences.

This debate has also entered popular political discourse, with liberal-leaning pundits and columnists attempting to understand high levels of Republican support among voters who presumably would have strong economic reasons for supporting the economic policies of the Democratic Party (less widely noticed, but also politically consequential, is widespread Democratic support among voters whose economic interests would suggest they would be Republican adherents).

Pundits advancing these arguments suggest that much of this irrational behavior is due to a lack of knowledge or understanding of the economic consequences of their voting behavior, rather than reflecting a prioritization of social issues over attitudes about economic redistribution policy. Scholars who are particularly concerned about democratic ignorance have gone so far as to suggest that the current public opinion polling and campaign processes be replaced with (either mandatory or strongly encouraged) "deliberation days" to better reflect the "true" informed preferences of the public.

SEE ALSO: Determinants of Vote Choice; Educational Level and Voting Behavior; Psychological Reasons for Voting and Nonvoting; Rational Voter Model.

BIBLIOGRAPHY. Angus Campbell, et al., *The American Voter* (Chicago University Press, 1960); P.E. Converse, "The Nature of Belief Systems in Mass Publics," reprinted in *Critical Review* (v.18/1–3, 2007); M.X.D. Carpini and Scott Keeter, *What Americans Know about Politics and Why It Matters* (Yale University Press, 1996); S.L. Althaus, "Information Effects in Collective Preferences," *American Political Science Review* (v.92, 1998); R.C. Luskin, "Measuring Political Sophistication," *American Journal of Political Science* (v.31, 1987); E.R.A.N. Smith, "The Levels of Conceptualization: False Measures of Ideological Sophistication," *American Political Science Review* (v.74, 1980); J.A. Krosnick, "Expertise and Political Psychology," *Social Cognition* (v.8, 1990); B.R. Berelson, et al., *Voting* (University of Chicago Press, 1954); S.L. Popkin, *The Reasoning Voter: Communication and Persuasion in Presidential Campaigns* (University of Chicago Press, 1991).

CHRISTOPHER NEIL LAWRENCE
TULANE UNIVERSITY

Voter Qualifications

THE CONSTITUTION OF the United States did not specify any qualification guidelines for voters, leaving the states to define the franchise for federal elections to the House of Representatives by applying the qualifications requisite in each state to vote for "the most numerous Branch of the State Legislature." Although there were no national voting qualifications, five amendments to the U.S. Constitution disallowed states from limiting suffrage in certain ways. They are: the Fifteenth (1870) and Nineteenth (1920) amendments, which prohibited discrimination based on race and sex, respectively; the Twenty-Third Amendment (1961), which allowed residents of the District of Columbia to vote in presidential elections; the Twenty-Fourth Amendment (1964), which prohibited poll or any tax requirements; and, finally, the Twenty-Sixth Amendment (1971), which ensured the right to vote for those 18 years of age or older.

The remaining suffrage provisions are still left in the hands of the states. Currently, all states require voters to be U.S. citizens and at least 18 years of age. All states have a residency requirement of some sort, while 12 states require the voter to be registered exclusively in that particular state. Only Alabama, Florida, and Vermont require voters to make an oath to defend the Constitution when registering. In Alabama, the phrase "so help me God," concludes the oath, while Vermont requires the voter to take the oath in presence of a notary public.

One possible discriminatory qualification shared by 34 states is mental competency. More controversial, however, are the felony disenfranchisement laws that most states have enacted. While most Western democratic countries allow inmates to vote, 48 American states and the District of Columbia deny incarcerated felons the franchise. Only Maine and Vermont permit inmates to vote. A total of 35 states prohibit felons on parole from voting, while 30 exclude felony probationers as well. Kentucky and Virginia deny the right to vote to all ex-offenders for life. Some other states allow certain categories of ex-offenders to apply for restoration of rights, often only after years of waiting. Due to felon disenfranchisement, it is estimated that 2.1 million Americans are denied voting rights even after completing their sentences. Given the racial skew in the felon conviction rate, African-American males are seven times more likely to be disenfranchised than the national average.

Requiring voter registration had long been criticized for posing an extra cost on electoral participation, but the National Voter Registration Act of 1993 alleviated the problem by requiring all states to offer motor-voter, agency-based, and mail-in voter registration. A new de facto qualification surfaced with the passage of the Help America Vote Act of 2002, which mandates that all states require identification from first-time voters at their polling place, if they registered to vote by mail without providing verification of their identification. Many states have gone beyond this provision by typically requiring all voters to show identification at the polls. Critics point out that the elderly, minorities, low-income constituents, and female citizens are less likely to possess photo identification and will be disproportionately deprived of the franchise on Election Day.

SEE ALSO: Election Laws, Federal Elections; Election Laws, State and Local Elections; Voting, Obstacles to.

BIBLIOGRAPHY. Alexander Keyssar, *The Right to Vote: The Contested History of Democracy in the United States* (Basic Books, 2000); Jeff Manza and Christopher Uggen, *Locked Out: Felon Disenfranchisement and American Democracy* (Oxford UniversityPress, 2006); "Citizen without Proof" *Voting Rights & Election Series* (Brennan Center for Justice at New York University School of Law, November 2006).

KAORI SHOJI
COLUMBIA UNIVERSITY

Voter Registration

VOTER REGISTRATION IS the process of formally establishing the eligibility of individuals to vote in their place of residence. The main purposes of voter registration is to ensure that only people who are entitled to vote in a jurisdiction are able to do so, and to prevent voter fraud, for example, multiple voting by the same individual or voting outside of one's jurisdiction. However, voter registration lists are also important because they can be used by election administrators in the election planning process for making budget projections and for estimating the number of polling places, poll workers, and voting materials to be assigned to a certain location. Voter registration was first adopted in 1800 and spread unevenly throughout the country. Registration practices and registration list maintenance vary by state. Registration has been found to impact turnout and a variety of reforms have been enacted to facilitate the process of registering voters and maintaining accurate and complete voter registration lists.

The first state to require voter registration was Massachusetts in 1800. In 1819, South Carolina provided registration for the city of Columbia, and Pennsylvania adopted voter registration provisions, in 1836, for the county of Philadelphia. New York City enacted a registration law in 1840, but it was repealed soon after being enacted. Until 1860, voter registration existed almost exclusively in the New England states. The extension of registration to other states came after the Civil War, the great influx of immigrants, and the growth in power and corruption of the political machines. Between 1860 and 1910, registration laws spread nationwide. They were adopted first in states with large cities and registration applied only for those cities, but the realization that voter fraud was not confined to large urban areas led to the extension of registration provisions to smaller towns and rural areas. In 2008, only North Dakota does not require voter registration.

NORTH AND SOUTH

The political movements for voter registration in the north and the south had different motivations. In the north, voter registration was instituted to prevent voter fraud and the corrupt practices of the urban political machines. It was also an important part of a larger set of progressive governmental and electoral reforms that included the civil service, direct primaries, and the secret ballot (also known as the Australian ballot, after the country where it originated). In the south, registration was racially driven and was part of a system that included the white primary, literacy tests, and the poll tax. The U.S. Constitution did not address voter eligibility requirements. Consequently, these varied from state to state, but over time uniform requirements for eligibility concerning race, sex, economic status, and age were adopted (the Fifteenth, Nineteenth, Twenty-Fourth, and Twenty-Sixth amendments). Yet, voter registration practices continued to diverge due to the administrative needs and political cultures of the individual states.

The majority of the states require voters to register from 10 to 30 days prior to an election, by mail or in person. However, seven states—Idaho, Maine, Minnesota, Montana, New Hampshire, Wisconsin, and Wyoming—have Election Day registration, also known as same-day registration, which allows eligible citizens to register and vote on Election Day. North Dakota, as the only state that does not have voter registration, relies on identification documents or sworn affidavits. The

process of keeping voter registration lists up-to-date, which is particularly important for their accuracy, is called voter registration list maintenance. This process includes correcting records with name spelling, date of birth, or address mistakes, updating addresses of voters who moved within the same jurisdiction, removing duplicate records (for example, multiple records that point to a unique voter), removing voters who moved outside of a jurisdiction, died, or are prevented from voting by state law (for example, convicted felons in some states). The process of removal of people from voter registration lists is called a purge.

States maintain voter registration lists in different ways across the states. In most states, each county was responsible for its own list, which resulted in inconsistent standards for keeping the lists updated and an inability to keep track of voters who moved across county lines. However, the Help America Vote Act of 2002 (HAVA) introduced the requirement that each state create and use a single computerized statewide voter registration database by January 1, 2006. This requirement attempts to ensure that voter registration lists are as complete and accurate as possible. The selection of a voter registration database system is a discretionary decision left to the states and they have used different systems to comply, which has resulted in top-down, bottom-up or hybrid voter registration systems. Top-down systems are those in which local election authorities provide information to a unified database maintained by the state. Bottom-up systems are those in which counties and municipalities retain their own registration lists and provide information to a state compilation of local databases at regular intervals. Hybrid databases have elements from both top-down and bottom-up systems.

VOTER TURNOUT

Registration requirements affect voter turnout. Studies show that turnout is approximately seven to 10 percent higher in states with lower registration hurdles. Hence, easing registration requirements is perceived as a way to increase turnout rates. Consequently, both Congress and state governments have adopted reforms to facilitate registration. At the federal level, Congress enacted the National Voter Registration Act (NVRA) in 1993 to ease the registration process. States have also liberalized registration requirements by allowing eligible voters to register through mail or on Election Day. In the mid-1970s, five states—Maine, Minnesota, Ohio, Oregon, and Wisconsin—adopted Election Day registration, although voters in Ohio (by constitutional amendment in 1977) and Oregon (by ballot initiative in 1975) later repealed it. Idaho, New Hampshire, and Wyoming adopted Election-Day registration in time for the 1994 election (to avoid having to implement the NVRA).

In 2006, Montana adopted same-day registration as well. However, some critics argue that interest in elections and motivation, not registration hurdles, have more impact on turnout. For example, turnout in the 1990s actually decreased for a while after the National Voter Registration Act was passed in 1993, easing registration. The fact that turnout has increased since then, pundits speculate, may be due to better organized get-out-the-vote drives or the increased competitiveness of election contests since 2000, especially presidential elections.

National election reform efforts that have directly impacted voter registration are the Uniformed and Overseas Citizens Absentee Voting Act (UOCAVA) of 1986, the National Voter Registration Act (NVRA) of 1993 (also known as "Motor Voter"), and the Help America Vote Act (HAVA) of 2002. Congress enacted UOCAVA to improve absentee registration and voting and to consolidate existing laws. The main provisions of the UOCAVA require states to permit absent uniformed services voters, their spouses and dependents, and overseas voters who no longer maintain a residence in the United States to register absentee (overseas voters are eligible to register absentee in the jurisdiction of their last residence) and to vote by absentee ballot in all elections for federal office (including general, primary, special, and runoff elections).

Congress enacted the NVRA to enhance voting opportunities for Americans and to remove the traces of discrimination that have historically resulted in lower voter registration rates for minorities and persons with disabilities. NVRA requires states to provide voter registration simultaneously with motor vehicle driver's license application or renewal, and, allows voters to apply to register to vote at other governmental offices as well. It also places limitations on the removal of voters from registration lists, and specifically prohibits purges for not voting; allowing voters to be removed from the registration rolls only at their request, because of criminal conviction, death, or

mental incapacity, or due to a change of address. The NVRA became effective on January 1, 1995, but states that as of August 1, 1994 had no voter registration or permitted same day registration at the polling place were exempt from the act. These states were Idaho, Minnesota, New Hampshire, North Dakota, Wisconsin, and Wyoming.

The HAVA addressed the need for reforms of the U.S. electoral system in the aftermath of the 2000 presidential election. Among other things, HAVA requires states to set up a single, uniform, centralized, and interactive computerized statewide voter registration list and places the primary responsibility for the development of the list at the state level. The current debate about voter registration, and possible future reforms, revolves around concerns about errors, questionable practices in the purging of voters from the lists, third-party registrations, and voter fraud, such as registration of the dead, the nonresident, and the nonhuman.

SEE ALSO: Voter Qualifications; Voter Turnout; Voting, Obstacles to.

BIBLIOGRAPHY. Stephen Ansolabehere and D.M. Konisky, "The Introduction of Voter Registration and Its Effect on Turnout," *Political Analysis* (2006); J.P. Harris, *Registration of Voters in the United States* (Brookings Institution, 1929); Justin Levitt, Wendy Welser, and Ana Munoz, *Making the list: Database Matching and Verification Processes for Voter Registration* (Brennan Center for Justice, 2006); Pippa Norris, ed., *Elections and Voting Behaviour: New Challenges, New Perspectives* (Ashgate, 1998).

VASSIA GUEORGUIEVA
AMERICAN UNIVERSITY

Voter Self-Interest

SELF-INTEREST FOR A voter comes in two types, short-term based on what the voter needs or is experiencing right then, and longer-term self-interest that might be called an ideology. A person's self-interest should be able to be used to determine whether he or she will support a given idea or not. Of equal importance to a person's self-interest is understand the ramifications of a given issue. A person who is well off is more likely to want to maintain the status quo. Those less well off are more likely to want to institute changes. A well off person tends to be conservative, while those who are not doing well under the current system are more likely to be liberal or advocate changes to the system.

While ideology and self-interest would seem to be the same, ideology tends to take a longer-term view then self-interest on a basic level (issues pertaining to an individual's immediate survival). For example, in the short run it would seem to be more advantageous for a person to be opposed to taxes. Taxes immediately take money from a person that could be used to support that person. This is especially true for those with lower income. However, the long-term view says that taxes are a good idea because they allow the government to provide services that individuals might not be able to gain access to on their own. Ideology determines how persons with similar views should consider a given topic. In this case, the policy (taxes) is in conflict with the low-income person's immediate self-interest, but in alignment with their long-term self-interest.

Sometimes the connection between the person's self-interest and the topic is not clear. Its bearing on their self-interest can be obscured by this indirect connection. For example, tax money is spent on enforcing pollution reduction standards, forcing companies to comply with pollution reduction laws. This can affect the person's environment and health, but the connection between paying taxes and the clean environment is not always obvious.

It is easy to assume people's ideologies are based on their situation (well off or not). However, there are always those who defy stereotypes. People who are well off in the system may advocate changing the system to help those less fortunate. There are also those who are not well off, yet do not want to see the system changed. These people generally perceive that the system is the reason that some people are succesful and want their chance to use the system to improve their position. However, there appears to be few people in these categories. Instead, based on data collected, it appears that individuals who support a party (or ideology) that does not seem to fit with their status in life do not follow politics. They have not taken the time to investigate and understand the policies of the party they associate with. Instead, their choice is made based on other factors, or through an incorrect application of self-interest based on an incomplete understanding of the issues.

One example of this misunderstanding of issues can be seen in cases where people do not completely understand issues and the effect they will have on them. A study done of legislation designed to reduce taxes for only the wealthiest people in the United States showed that people in lower income brackets supported a tax cut, even though it would not reduce their taxes. One reason they supported the tax cut was that they believed that their own taxes were too high. Thus, because the voters did not educate themselves fully on the issue they ended up taking a position that was actually contrary to their self-interest.

In order for a voter's self-interest to really be served, the voter must get involved with politics at some level. From there they can then start to build their understanding of that the issues and policies are. To vote in their own self-interest, that person must be concerned enough to educate themselves fully about current issues and policies. They have to progress beyond using simple titles and explanations to fully understand the impact that policies and legislation would have on them personally. Otherwise, their self-interest may be used against them.

The information voters get can come to them in many different ways. They may gain it through their own perceived self-interest in an issue. On the other hand, they may gain the information through friends, family, coworkers, or groups they associate with. The voter feels that their self-interest is the same as these other sources and therefore trusts the sources to provide them with the information they need about the issue.

Informed or not, voter self-interest is going to play a part in determining if a voter takes the time to vote. A voter who perceives that a given election is going to have little or no affect on them is not as likely to vote. On the other hand, a voter who perceives that the outcome of an elections if going to impact their life is more motivated to actually cast their vote.

SEE ALSO: Age and Voting Behavior; Cross-Pressures, Sociopolitical; Education Level and Voting Behavior; Electoral Behavior; Gender and Voting Behavior; High and Low Stimulus Elections; Income and Voting Behavior; Martial Status and Voting Behavior; Race and Voting Behavior; Religion and

Voting Behavior; Rural Vote; Social Groups and Electoral Behavior; Suburban Vote; Urban Vote.

BIBLIOGRAPHY. Larry M. Bartels, "Homer Gets a Tax Cut: Inequality and Public Policy in the American Mind" (www.princeton.edu/~bartels/ (cited September 22, 2007); Angus Campbell, Philip E. Converse, Warren E. Miller, and Donald Stokes, *The American Voter* (University of Chicago Press, 1960); Angus Campbell, Philip E. Converse, Warren E. Miller, Donald E. Stokes, *Elections and the Political Order* (John Wiley and Sons, 1966); Vincent L. Hutchings, *Public Opinion and Democratic Accountability: How Citizens Learn About Politics* (Princeton University Press, 2003); Gerald Pomper, *Voters' Choice: Varieties of American Electoral Behavior* (Dodd, Mead & Company, 1975).

DALLACE W. UNGER, JR.
INDEPENDENT SCHOLAR

Voter Turnout

VOTER TURNOUT MEASURES the percentage of votes cast by eligible voters—generally citizens over 18 years of age—at an election. Turnout rates, which are an important (but not the only) indicator of political participation, vary greatly within democracies. High turnout rates are generally a sign of the citizens' involvement in politics and give the government and the system of government legitimacy. Low turnout rates are often tied to an increase in unconventional participation methods (demonstrations, sit-ins) and reveal the peoples' dissatisfaction with the political parties and establishment. On the macro-level, institutional, structural, and socioeconomic, and cultural factors have an impact on the number of people that cast their ballot. On the micro-level, educational level, status, the age, and socialization influence an individual's decision to turn out at an election.

Important institutional factors that affect turnout rates are compulsory voting, the electoral system type, and the timing of the election. Compulsory voting, especially when non-compliance is sanctioned with fines or the loss of citizen rights, triggers higher numbers of citizens to cast their ballot at elections. In Australia, Belgium, Cyprus, Fiji, Luxembourg, Nauru, Singapore, Uruguay, where voting is compulsory, about 90 percent of the electorate votes, which is around 15 percentage points more than in those countries where voting is voluntary. With regard to the electoral system type, proportional representation (PR) commonly favors higher turnout rates than use of a plurality formula.

VOTES AND SEATS

Under PR nearly all votes are translated into seats whereas under plurality only those votes that are cast for winning candidates are converted into seats. Turnout rates where list proportional systems are used are approximately 8 percent higher under PR than under "First Past The Post" proportional systems. Under the latter category, voters generally have the least incentive to cast their ballots when a district is safe or undisputed.

Concerning the timing of the election, elections scheduled on the weekend frequently entice more people to vote than elections held on weekday. In those countries that have changed their election day from a weekday to a rest day in the past 60 years, turnout rates have increased by five or six percent.

Two secondary institutional factors, the frequency of elections and voter registration procedures, might also influence turnout rates. The frequent recurrence of elections can lead to voter fatigue, which may lead to lower voter turnout in elections. Voter registration procedures may also impact whether citizens vote or abstain in elections, as in many countries registration is a prerequisite for voting. Automatic voter registration—all citizens are automatically registered—facilitates voting for citizens and might be an indirect factor to increase turnout.

The combination of these institutional factors helps to explain higher voter turnout in some countries than in others. The low turnout rates in the United States (less than 50 percent in legislative elections) are the result of individual voter registration, frequent elections, plurality, and weekday elections. In countries such as Belgium or Australia, high turnout rates of 80 percent and above in the legislative elections are affected by compulsory voting, proportional representation, and weekend elections.

INDIVIDUAL FACTORS

Yet, these institutional characteristics are only one group of indicators, which might apply to various degrees in specific countries. Structural, socioeconomic, cultural, and individual factors add to these variables and also help to explain varying turnout rates. As a structural or political factor, the kind of election is important in determining turnout rates. As a rule, the more important the election is, the more people will turn out. Presidential and legislative elections generally have higher turnout rates than local or regional elections, because people think that more is at stake at these elections. For example, turnout rates are nearly 19 percentage points lower in the European election, which is generally considered the least important elections by European citizens, than in the respective parliamentary election.

The closeness of the race is also an influential factor in the decision to vote or not to vote. The closer the race the more rational it is for citizens to vote and the more likely it is that more voters will cast their ballots. In close races a few votes may swing the victory to one side or the other. Thus, each ballot counts more and citizens are inclined to think that their vote might be decisive. In contrast, in races in which a victory for a particular candidate or party is almost certain, citizens are less likely to vote because, as the winner is known beforehand, voting becomes less interesting or thrilling. This rule applies more so under plurality than under PR. The 2004 U.S. presidential election exemplifies this tendency. In states with turnout rates greater than 70 percent, such as Wisconsin or New Hampshire, the race between George W. Bush and John Kerry was very close—one of the two contenders won by a margin of less than two percent. In other states with turnout rates of less than 50 percent, such as Texas or Arizona, one of the two candidates won by a margin of at least 10 percent.

Socioeconomic and political variables, such as the literacy rate and the wealth of a country, further help to explain turnout rates. Although a voter's ability to read and write might not necessarily affect his or her political literacy, better cognitive skills generally correlate with higher turnout rates. In countries with literacy rates of 95 percent or higher, on average, 73 percent of the voting populations actually turns out at parliamentary elections. In countries with literacy rates of less than 95 percent, the turnout is only 68 percent. A high percentage of people who can read and write is often correlated with the material wealth of a country; in more wealthy countries, people normally have a better education.

EMBRACING VALUES

An increase in a country's socioeconomic standards often leads that society to embrace post-materialist values. Post-materialist publics should be likelier to vote than publics in traditional or industrial societies because they give relatively high priority to individual freedom and democratic values. The fact that the populaces of all Western European countries embrace post-materialist values might be one reason for the comparatively high voter turnout of 77 percent in parliamentary elections.

At the individual level, political participation should increase with one's education and status. As a rule, the upper- and middle-classes turn out at a higher degree in elections than the lower or working classes. On average, white-collar workers and people who occupy professional positions are about 10 percent more likely to vote than are people from the working class.

The voting patterns of different age cohorts reveal that political participation generally increases with age. Newly-enfranchised voters (18–29 years), in particular, have always cast their ballots in comparatively low numbers. Young people often take time to develop an interest in politics, as they lack experience with political matters and are less socially and politically integrated. Yet, the situation has exacerbated in the past 20 years, as citizens younger than 30 years of age have turned out in smaller numbers in almost all established and new democracies. In some countries, such as Great Britain or South Africa, youth participation in 21st century elections are currently 40 percent lower than the national average turnout rates. Young voters feel dissatisfied with and alienated from, the political system and the governing elites and abstain from voting. Because many young voters are not socialized into voting, it is likely that as they grow older they will continue to turn out at relatively low rates.

The first three elections generally decide if an individual will become a habitual voter or a habitual non-voter. Habitual voters regularly turn out whereas habitual non-voters may sometimes vote, but are more likely to abstain from doing so. An individual, whose political socialization period is marked by high political mobilization, is very likely to become a regular voter, as is evidenced in the late-1960s generation.

The gender variable is not well-understood and few official statistics for male and female turnout rates exist. Reserachers have some data that hint that the gender gap in the 1950s and 1960s when men participated to a greater extent than women in elections, has closed in most democracies. As of 2007, men and women participate in equal numbers in elections.

After World War II, turnout across the globe rose steadily until the 1980s: increasing from 61 percent in the 1940s to 68 percent in the 1980s. The value shift from materialist to post-materialist values and the integration of women into political processes were responsible for most of this increase. The post-1990 average dropped to 64 percent, mostly a result of younger voter apathy. Regionally, the highest turnout rates can be found in Western Europe (77 percent), and the lowest in Latin America (50 percent). However, group averages may not apply to certain countries, as Argentina has turnout rates of 80 percent, and Switzerland of merely 35 to 40 percent. Single country turnout rates have been relatively stable in the past decade. In contrast, variance in turnout within countries can be enormous, and can be explained by a mixture of all these variables.

SEE ALSO: Gender and Voting Behavior; Majority Rule; Political Culture; Political Socialization; Proportional Representation.

BIBLIOGRAPHY. M.N. Franklin, *Voter Turnout and the Dynamics of Electoral Competition in Establish Democracies Since 1945* (Cambridge University Press, 2004); International IDEA, "Voter Turnout: A Global Report," www.idea.int (cited April 2007); Pippa Norris, *Electoral Engineering: Voting Rules and Political Behavior* (Cambridge University Press, 2004); Pippa Norris, ed., *Elections and Voting Behaviour: New Challenges, New Perspectives* (Ashgate, 1998).

DANIEL STOCKEMER
UNIVERSITY OF CONNECTICUT

Voting

MANY LEARNED PERSONS have argued that the right to vote is a duty, a responsibility, and a privilege, and that it is important for all citizens to vote in every election to make sure that the democratic representative system of government is maintained. Further, they claim that those who do not vote lose their voice in the government. While the importance of voting cannot be understated, U.S. citizens are asked to vote with more frequency than in any other country. The entire structure of the government is based on citizens voting for representation, yet most presidential elections are decided by less than 70 percent of the eligible voting public.

Even fewer people vote in mid-term elections and local elections. Each citizen has a civic responsibility, which is the duty of citizens of a nation to participate in the formation of public policy and to uphold and obey the country's laws. Each citizen has an obligation to elect good, honest, wise men and women to represent them at all levels of government, to inform themselves on political issues, and to make their opinions known to their representatives. All citizens of a free society also have the duty to be actively involved in efforts to defend their freedom, improve their communities, and act responsibly toward themselves and other citizens.

Americans have often claimed that voting spreads their freedom throughout the world; yet, many citizens of the United States often take their rights for granted. According to many reports, other countries have consistently higher voter turnout than the United States. Many U.S. citizens claim that their vote does not count. In a country with a voting population of more that than 200 million in 2008, that may appear to be true, but the 2004 presidential election is a good example of why everyone who can vote should vote.

While a single vote may rarely make the difference, the more people who believe that their votes do not count, the greater the impact of their lack of participation. Many Americans have expressed frustration with America's electoral system. They ask what happens when you don't like any of the candidates. Sometimes, it is hard to make a desirable choice, but it is still the responsibility of every citizen over 18-years-old to choose. Scholars have said that if an individual cannot see the difference between candidates, it is his or her duty to become better informed, keeping alive the old adage that "knowledge is power."

To many Americans, the practice of voting has lost much of it allure. Few businesses allow employees to take Election Day off, although most states keep polls open for at least 12 hours. Some people do not have transportation to the polls. Others are confused about their rights concerning voting. After one of the largest

Citizens of a free society have the duty to be actively involved in efforts to defend their freedom, improve their communities, and act responsibly toward themselves and other citizens—a large part of this duty is turning out to vote.

voting drives in the nation's history, less than 60 percent of eligible citizens turned out in 2004 to cast their vote in the election.

Probably the most common reason people will not vote is because they feel that that one vote would not make a difference. But if everyone thought that way, then it would make a huge difference. Another reason given for not voting is that they do not have enough time. However, voting is available to every eligible person. If someone is unable to come to the polls, the government has a system to allow that person to vote absentee. There are poll booths in many public areas, schools for example.

Recently, the State of Massachusetts drafted a Bill of Responsibility to spur a greater citizen turnout on Election Day. It outlined 14 basic responsibilities voters should follow, including registering to vote before the deadline, filling out the registration form accurately, keeping their address current at their local election office, knowing where their polling place is, and reporting any violations of elections laws to the proper authorities. It attempts to create an attitude that citizens must have to attest to their rights and responsibilities. Robert Hutchins, the famous educator and former president of the University of Chicago, once wrote that people who fail to vote do not realize that their vote does not only belong to them, but also to the country. Soldiers dying in combat do not take for granted the freedom that many people fail to appreciate on a daily basis.

The most powerful demonstration of democracy in action is exercising your right to vote. Citizens need to understand that all politics is local. The concept that your vote does not count is a contention born of ignorance, apathy, and laziness. As Thomas Paine declared more than 200 years ago, "the right to vote for representatives is the primary right by which other rights are protected."

SEE ALSO: Voting, Incentives for; Voting, Obstacles to.

BIBLIOGRAPHY. C.H. Thornton and Jaeger Audrey, "Institutions, Cultures and Civic Responsibility," *Journal of College Student Development* (January/February, 2006; Sidney Verba, K.L. Scholozna, and Henry Brady, *Voice and Equality: Civic Volunteerism in American Politics* (Harvard University Press, 1995).

FRED LINDSEY
INDEPENDENT SCHOLAR

Voting, Incentives for

ACCORDING TO AN influential 1957 analysis by Anthony Downs, applying economic theory to voting, it is irrational to vote. This is true because for each individual, the odds of their vote changing the outcome of an election is extremely small. Therefore, voting makes little sense if changing the outcome of the election is the goal.

However, people continue to vote, because there are a number of incentives for voting that encourage people to go to the polls. These incentives might be social, moral, or psychological, such as misunderstanding the odds of affecting the outcome, civic duty, or a sense of being part of a collective of voters. In some cases, more concrete incentives exist, such as economic enticements, or compulsory voting.

The primary incentive to vote is that citizens want their parties and candidates to win the election. Though the true odds of one vote changing the out-

come are miniscule, some voters may not consciously or even unconsciously realize this. This is similar to the psychological mechanisms that propel people to buy lottery tickets. They overestimate their own chances of getting lucky. Misguided optimism may not be the only reason that people motivated by the desire to see their candidates win might find an incentive to vote. They also may have a sense of belonging to a collective of voters. This logic is along the lines of "if everybody did that …" If everybody refused to vote because his or her vote wouldn't be the tiebreaker, the democratic system would cease to function.

The is related to the concept of civic duty. Some people feel compelled to vote because they have been socialized into democratic norms and they believe it is their duty as good citizens to participate on Election Day. They vote because they have internalized these democratic values, or because they know it is expected within the community, and they want others to see them as good citizens. This is an especially strong incentive in smaller communities where neighbors might be more aware of each other's behavior. This tendency to vote due to social pressure has in the past been exploited by local party officials who would take note of who had voted through the day and make visits to nonvoters to encourage them. Beyond civic duty, some citizens feel compelled simply to express their opinions publicly, to have their voices heard, even if they realize they likely will not change the outcome.

More concrete incentives for voting also exist. In some times and places, financial incentives have been offered. Some crasser examples include being handed a pint of beer or a shot of whiskey for voting in early American elections, to (generally illegal) offerings of cash, or other items of value in return for votes. In 2006, a ballot measure in the state of Arizona proposed establishing a voter lottery in which each voter's name would be entered into a pool from which one lucky voter's name would be drawn. That voter would win $1 million. Incentives such as these may entice some apathetic citizens to vote, but it is unclear if they would cast informed votes, as their motivations would be monetary rather than civic.

The most compelling incentive for voting is a legal requirement to vote. This is called compulsory voting, and is practiced in dozens of democracies, including Australia, Belgium, Brazil, Egypt, Gabon, Mexico, Peru, Turkey, and Switzerland. The main argument in favor of compulsory voting is that democracy requires the consent of the governed. The only way in which the interests of all of the citizens of a country can be accurately represented is if those citizens participate, and at a minimum, cast votes. Unfortunately, turnout rates are disappointing in many countries without strong incentives like compulsory voting, making compulsory voting very appealing in low turnout countries. The sanctions imposed on nonvoters vary from country to country. Some are relatively mild, such as small fines, and not strongly enforced. In other cases, though, the sanctions can be substantial, such as being unable to withdraw a salary from the bank for a period of time in Bolivia, or disenfranchisement in Belgium (for multiple offenses).

Compulsory voting does get more voters to the polls. Countries with compulsory voting laws have higher voter turnout rates than other democracies, sometimes by wide margins. However, there is a great deal of debate about how positive this really is for representation. If citizens who would otherwise be apathetic nonvoters show up on Election Day merely because the government requires it of them, they may be essentially casting random, uninformed votes. To the extent that this is the case, those votes do not further the goal of better representing the will of the people.

One argument is that when citizens know that they will be called upon to vote, they pay more attention to politics and campaigns, so the pool of informed citizens actually increases with compulsory voting, making the meaningless vote problem less prevalent. Others argue that compulsory voting ensures the participation of segments of the population that are disadvantaged, but who tend to vote at lower rates without compulsory voting.

SEE ALSO: Psychological Reasons for Voting; Voter Apathy; Voter Self-Interest; Voter Turnout; Voting, Obstacles to.

BIBLIOGRAPHY. Angus Campbell, Philip E. Converse, Warren E. Miller, and Donald Stokes, *The American Voter* (University of Chicago Press, 1960); Anthony Downs, *An Economic Theory of Democracy* (Harper, 1957); R.C. Archibold, "Arizona Ballot Could Become Lottery Ticket," *New York Times* (July 17, 2006); Arend Lijphart, "Unequal Participation: Democracy's Unresolved Dilemma," *American Political Science Review* (v91/1, 1997); Pippa Norris, ed., *Elections and Voting Behaviour: New Challenges, New Perspectives* (Ashgate, 1998).

KIMBERLY L. NALDER
CALIFORNIA STATE UNIVERSITY, SACRAMENTO

Voting, Obstacles to

THE DEVELOPMENT OF American voting patterns and practices evolved from inherited traditions embodied in English common law and past Greek and Roman civic procedures. In light of this context, voting in America unfolded, following the precedents and circumstances of historical eras. As such, obstacles to voting varied with time and place as well as through regional practice. The obstacles encountered formed part of the nation's progress. Paramount in the American colonial heritage was the generally held belief that restrictions on the civil liberties of criminal and civil offenders were fully justified. Offenders might lose all rights, including property and the right to participate in the community as a whole. They suffered what was essentially a "civil death" and disenfranchisement was a prominent penalty if, indeed, they were qualified to vote in the first instance. Convicted felons were but one group that faced suffrage restrictions in the colonial era. Women, African Americans, those without property, and illiterates were also unable to vote.

During the long colonial period the idea of a full voting democracy was highly suspect. Society feared unleashing the rabble by allowing universal voting, would allow mob rule and produce societal breakdown. Therefore, in the 13 original colonies, voting was regulated as a right of those who had a role in society defined by their ownership of land and property or through the paying of taxes. There were also religious tests that excluded Catholics and Jews from voting, even if they met other property criteria. In practice, colonial voting was restricted to white males. However, even with the existing restrictions, participation rates could include 70–80 percent of frontier males with perhaps only 50 percent qualified to vote in the cities.

The coming of the American Revolution and eventual Independence after 1783 expanded democratic ideals and, in particular, the notion of the need for a broader-based representative government and the belief that legitimacy in public affairs could only be derived from the consent of the governed. Although general property qualifications remained common, some areas, such as Vermont, eliminated all qualifications for white males, and, by 1790, religious restrictions were ended throughout the original colonies. In six states (Maryland, Massachusetts, New York, North Carolina, Pennsylvania, and Vermont) voting rights were extended to free African-American males. There was also an extension of suffrage to those who had served in the colonial military.

STATE ROOTS

The acceptance of the U.S. Constitution after 1787 did not in itself remove obstacles to voting but instead made elections a prerogative of the states and it was here where obstacles took root. However as the 19th century unfolded the property restriction was dismantled which expanded the electorate considerably. In 1800, only three states, Kentucky, New Hampshire and Vermont had universal white male voting but over the next decades, property restrictions were slowly eliminated so that by 1860 only five states had tax restrictions, and just two preserved property qualifications. In addition many immigrants gained voting rights in this period yet the obstacles for African-American free males voting worsened with new states entering the union after 1819 denying suffrage completely, so that by 1855 only five New England states granted African-American voting rights.

Other impediments emerged during this period: women property owners in New Jersey, the only state with female suffrage, lost the vote, further manipulations excluded paupers and felons, and, in some cases, restrictions came from extending residency requirements. Such difficulties led to unrest, and the so-called 1841 "Dorr War" in Rhode Island was essentially a protest against these exclusions. The reformed 1843 Rhode Island Constitution expanded the voting base substantially, but several reservations remained. The 1848 Seneca Falls Convention produced calls for universal women's suffrage. The right of women to vote was not prohibited in the U.S. Constitution, but determining voter eligibility rested at state level; this made extending the franchise difficult and an issue that would not be finally resolved until the 20th century.

During the American Civil War of 1861 to 1865 and the Reconstruction years that immediately followed, there was further debate concerning voting obstacles that confronted newly-freed slaves in the south. However, the record of the northern states was not particularly exemplary in this regard, and the general pattern restricted African-American voting. The Civil War, though, had driven the Republican Party toward not only eliminated slavery, but also extending black suffrage. Voting was seen as necessary to the protection of newly-established rights.

The end result of this strategy was the Fifteenth Amendment of 1870, which extended male voting rights without regard to race, color, or previous conditions of servitude. After 1876, the southern states responded with a variety of means to frustrate this provision. Violence and intimidation were employed, as were qualification restrictions, fraud, and gerrymandering to undermine black voting possibilities during the late 19th century. The final withdrawal of federal troops made these tactics even more successful.

States such as Mississippi led the way in creating obstacles to African-American male voting. They employed a wide array of constraints that other Southern states soon copied for similar purposes. These included: extended residency requirements, literacy tests, property and tax qualifications, poll taxes (a head tax payment that enabled you to vote), exclusion for minor offenses, or for crimes specifically deemed to be more often committed by black males, and complicated registration procedures. When combined, these shrank the African-American voting pool to such numbers that it essentially led to exclusion. In some instances, voting was denied because of the lack of a good character endorsement and there were grandfather clauses, which gave the vote only to those who could show that their grandfathers had the vote, a clear impossibility for many African Americans in the latter 19th century. The Supreme Court eventually overturned the grandfather provision in 1915.

REVERSAL INITIATIVES

Various federal initiatives to reverse these Southern electoral obstacles were attempted, such as the Federal Elections Bill of 1890, which would have eliminated discrimination through federal election supervision, but the bill was ultimately defeated. The Twenty-Fourth Amendment to the U.S. Constitution, ratified in 1964, finally ended the poll tax as a tool for voting exclusion. More decisive action to end this level of African-American disenfranchisement in the south had to await the 1965 Voting Rights Act, subsequently extended by legislation in 1970, 1975, and 1982, to eliminate various obstacles in order to guarantee greater voting rights to all eligible citizens.

Besides southern obstruction, the late 19th century saw other states also engage in restrictions under the banner of ending voting corruption. These civic reform measures were aimed at the growing urban immigrant populations who were offered money and positions for their votes. This reform drive led to increased residency requirements, elimination of immigrant voting rights, pre-election registration, the exclusion of felons, and, by the 1920s, literacy tests in some states. Oregon, in 1924, was the last state to introduce a literacy test. In most cases, these restrictions did not end until the 1965 Voting Rights Act eliminated literacy tests as an obstacle to voting. Many western states, during this period, also excluded Asians immigrants from voting. Along with these restrictions there were further efforts to eliminate fraud and undue influence. For example one device was the Australian ballot system, which had the voter place a mark by a candidate's name on a published ballot form. In addition, the secret ballot became common practice after the 1884 presidential election, to protect voter intent.

Besides the obstacles to African-American voting, another glaring restriction was the continued exclusion of women from the right to vote. Although the call for the vote began at mid-century, success came only toward the end of the 19th century, mainly in the sparsely settled Western states. The drive became better-organized with the creation of the National American Woman Suffrage Association in the 1880s, which led to state-wide suffrage granted in the western states during the 1890s and the early decades of the 20th century. The final obstacle to national suffrage for women was eliminated following World War I when the Nineteenth Amendment was ratified in 1920. This amendment extended suffrage to American women, although southern restrictions were still in place for African-American women.

Curbs on voting rights substantially and steadily diminished throughout the 20th century. For instance the vote was extended to Native Americans in 1924, and restrictions on Asian voting were removed in the 1952 McCarran-Walter Act. In summary, American's approach to voting had dramatically expanded the franchise for white males during the nation's earliest days, but made universal voting rights difficult for many.

There are still obstacles that restrict voting rights. Voting remains a state affair and is subject to various organizational mechanisms and rules that can seem an obstacle to many. Different voting procedures, complex ballots, and voting machines can discourage people from voting. Registration and residency requirements are in use, which means that if you move frequently, lack a permanent address, or are a student, you can find local voting daunting.

In addition, there are age restrictions on voting, 18 is the normative age, nationally. Issues involving mental competency and felony convictions are still factors that can deny people the right to vote. The criminal conviction rate is a factor that has disenfranchised an estimated 13 percent of the African-American male population. Some critics interpret this situation as a voting obstacle and not a simple consequence of individual criminal behavior. Voting also remains a right of citizenship and this, in the face of a large immigrant population, can be a voting obstacle as are English language requirements. State redistricting can bring favor to one party and, thus, undercut the weight of one's vote. The general difficulty in registering in such a mobile society perhaps explains the relatively poor voter turnout in the United States as compared to other modern democracies.

SEE ALSO: Voter Alienation; Voter Disenfranchisement; Voter Knowledge/Ignorance; Voter Qualifications; Voter Registration; Voting Methods.

BIBLIOGRAPHY. Alan Abramowitz, *Voices of the People: Elections and Voting in the United States* (McGraw-Hill, 2004); Richard Braunstein, *Initiative and Referendum Voting: Governing Through Direct Democracy in the United States* (LFB Scholarly Publishing, 2004); M.M. Conway, *Political Participation in the United States* (CQ Press, 2000); N.F. Cott, ed., *No Small Courage: A History of Women in the United States* (Oxford University Press, 2000); Alexander Keyssar, *The Right to Vote: The Contested History of Democracy in the United States* (Basic Books, 2000); M.E. Rush, ed., *Voting Rights and Redistricting in the United States* (Greenwood Press, 1998).

THEODORE W. EVERSOLE, PH.D.
INDEPENDENT SCHOLAR

Voting by Regions (Sectionalism)

A RECURRING TENSION in American history is that between state, local, or regional concerns and national ones. The nation began as distinct colonies, after all, and continued to maintain distinct cultural, ethnic, and religious differences from region to region. It has often proved difficult for voters of a region to consider national interests above the interests of their region. The debate over free silver cut across not only class lines but regional ones, as western farmers sided with William Jennings Bryan and the Populists for free silver, while easterners took the side of their bankers and the gold standard. Slavery and segregation obviously raised sectionalist issues, as they involved laws that primarily affected the south (and in the case of slavery, the territories).

The admission of Missouri into the Union prompted a sectionalist divide between north and south that would recur for the next century and a half. The territory had been acquired as part of the 1803 Louisiana Purchase, and applied for statehood in 1819, seven years after the formation of the state of Louisiana. It specifically requested admission as a slave state; some American settlers in Missouri were slave-holding southerners and admission as a free state would mean giving up those slaves. With the country expanding westward, the question raised concerned more than just one state: at issue was the slave-or-free status of the western territories and future states. Northern voters wanted free states, southern voters wanted slave states: a delicate balance between the two existed in Congress, and the admission of more states would tip that balance one way or the other. The Missouri Compromise was designed to preserve that balance, designating new states as slave or free according to their latitude. Thus, Missouri entered the Union as a slave state, while Maine entered as a free state.

Not long after, the 1824 presidential election played out along lines of regional loyalties. Four favorite sons split the vote, none of them winning a majority: Secretary of State John Quincy Adams was a Bay Stater who carried the northeast, the war hero Andrew Jackson appealed to the agrarian south, and Speaker of the House Henry Clay's proposal of the Missouri Compromise won him significant support in the west. William Henry Crawford eventually dropped out of the race after suffering a stroke, but gained support in the Southeast before doing so—notably, though, Democratic-Republicans in the rest of the country ignored their party's support of Crawford and voted with their region instead. When Jackson and his supporters were dissatisfied with Adams's win and Clay's involvement in it, the 1828 election became a vicious rematch that saw mudslinging, Rachel Jackson's death by stress-induced heart attack, and a clear sectionalist bias: Adams won only the states that supported his father in 1800.

In 1832, the first national conventions for nominating party candidates were held, an innovation that was intended to focus the parties on national concerns rather than regional ones, in part to avoid indecisive elections such as that in 1824. The first party to hold a national convention, the Anti-Masonic Party, was also the first third party to operate on a national level, and perhaps had even more to lose to sectionalist disputes. The National Republican and Democratic parties followed suit. Each convention included delegates from all the states, who discussed—and argued over, and made deals regarding, and traded favors related to—the party's campaign platform and selected its candidate. Presidential primaries were instituted in a few states, but did not become de rigeur for more than a century.

CIVIL WAR

Slavery concerns remained the primary difference between voters of different regions, overshadowing other economic issues. The 1860 presidential election brought this to a head, as John Cabell Breckinridge carried the bulk of the southern states, losing to Abraham Lincoln, who won without a single southern state. The three states that Breckinridge lost went to the Constitutional Union candidate, John Bell. Stephen Douglas's candidacy had been rendered all but moot when the "Fire-Eaters"—the pro-slavery extremists pushing for secession or preparations for such—led the southern delegates out of the Democratic Convention when the party refused to support slavery in the territories, Breckinridge, the incumbent vice president, became the Southern Democrats' candidate. In most of the south, Lincoln was not even on the ballot; he won two tenths of one percent of the southern counties.

In the wake of the resulting Civil War and Reconstruction, the Democratic Party—just as the major Protestant denominations had—became the popular party of the south; the Republican Party was remembered as the party of Lincoln, and had been least forgiving during the Reconstruction years. The phrase *Solid South* is sometimes used to refer to this adoption of the Democrats as the regional party; from 1876 to 1948, every Democratic presidential candidate won the south except for Al Smith in 1928. Even then, Smith won a greater share of the south than he did the rest of the country. Thus, that election might not be read as the south's failure to support the Democratic Party, but rather a comment on Smith's electability.

That domination ended in 1948, at the Democratic National Convention. The incumbent president and nominee, Harry S. Truman, integrated the U.S. military, and the party made civil rights part of his re-election platform, causing the mass walkout of many of the southern delegates. They, and other southern supporters, formed the States' Rights Democratic Party, better known as the Dixiecrats, and had a surprising amount of success for a newly-formed third party: Governor J. Strom Thurmond of South Carolina carried four southern states and a single electoral vote in Tennessee, on a "Segregation Forever!" platform. The four states Thurmond won were the four in which the party managed to supplant the Democratic Party on the ballot. This siphoning off of Democratic votes made the fight between Truman and Thomas Dewey so close, accounting for the famous "Dewey Defeats Truman" headline based on misleading pre-election polls.

The States' Rights Democratic Party promptly dissolved, but the Dixiecrat term remained in parlance, as the south shifted its allegiances. On the local and state level, and, in general, in congressional elections, the south remained staunchly Democrat, electing pro-segregation native Democrats—even Jimmy Carter appeased the segregationist faction in his run for governor of Georgia. But in presidential elections, support moved to the Republican Party, or in 1968, to Alabama Governor George Wallace, the candidate for the American Independent Party. In 1964, having made civil rights a priority with the awareness that this would likely cost his party the South for many elections to come, Democrat Lyndon Johnson carried the south only because of the overwhelming support of African-American voters—in most southern states, white voters abandoned him.

BARRY GOLDWATER

The Democrats were not the only ones facing regional divisions that year: the moderate Republicans were based largely in the northeast, which the party's nominee, Barry Goldwater, suggested would best serve the country if it were sawed off and allowed to sink into the Atlantic. The ultraconservative Goldwater's supporters came from elsewhere in the country—the governor of New York even refused to endorse him, an unusual response from a prominent governor in a year when the party was already facing difficulty. Nevertheless, so strong was the southern opposition to Johnson and the integrationist Democrats, that Goldwater was the first Republican candidate since Reconstruction to win states such as Mississippi and Alabama. The tide had quite plainly turned.

In 1968, Richard Nixon succeeded Goldwater as the Republican nominee, but resembled him in no other respect—though more conservative than the eastern moderates, Nixon was also the former vice president to Dwight Eisenhower, whom Goldwater had belittled to a degree many close to the General found unforgivable. While Goldwater had relied on stirring up emotion and grassroots efforts, Nixon targeted the south, sensing that the time was right to bring it into the Republican fold. His campaign coined the phrase *southern strategy* for the use of this courtship to win elections, and while Nixon did not support segregation—and lost some of the south's support to Wallace—he was still able to wrest it from the vigorously integrationist Democrats, whose candidate, Hubert Humphrey, did not win a single southern state. Both Nixon and Ronald Reagan won their elections by appealing to southern conservatives, and while they did not support segregation, they spoke in favor of states' rights—which had been the justification of choice for both the pro-slavery contingent and segregationists.

Another development in 1968 was the universal adoption of primary elections. While Progressive reformers had encouraged primaries because they would indicate the popular appeal of potential candidates rather than leaving matters in the hands of the men in smoke-filled rooms, primaries remained non-binding: electors at the national conventions were free to do as they liked. After the infamous 1968 Democratic National Convention, new rules were written for the selection of the candidate; the Republican Party soon followed suit, and binding primary elections became the standard. This is notable because although the general trend in presidential elections had been to shift the power to the national level, this was in some ways a return of power to the state level. States without influential men to fill those smoke-filled rooms in a given election year would still have the chance to make their preferences known in an official capacity, and should the eventual candidates prove to be other than the ones they chose, they would know whose favor they needed to court.

SEE ALSO: Favorite Son/Favorite Daughter; Popular Sovereignty, Doctrine of; Presidential Election of 1824; Presidential Election of 1860; Presidential Election of 1948; States' Rights Party (Dixiecrats).

BIBLIOGRAPHY. William Cooper, *The South and the Politics of Slavery 1828–1856* (Louisiana State UniversityPress, 1978); Kari Frederickson, *The Dixiecrat Revolt and the End of the Solid South, 1932–1968* (University of North Carolina Press, 2000); William Freehling, *Prelude to Civil War* (Oxford University Press, 1992); Dewey Grantham, *The Life and Death of the Solid South* (University Press of Kentucky, 1992); Forrest McDonald, *States' Rights and the Union* (UniversityPress of Kansas, 2000); Merrill Peterson, *The Great Triumvirate* (Oxford University Press, 1967); Eric Walther, *The Fire-Eaters* (Louisiana State University Press, 1992); Sean Wilentz, *The Rise of American Democracy* (W.W. Norton, 2005).

BILL KTE'PI
INDEPENDENT SCHOLAR

Voting Methods

THE 2000 FLORIDA debacle has illustrated the central role played by methods of voting in the electoral process. The United States has traditionally seen a patchwork of such methods, with the administration of elections, including the choice of voting methods, left to local authorities. The methods used are largely determined by technological developments, with older methods gradually giving way to new ones, starting with the introduction of hand-counted paper ballots at the end of 19th century and shifting to electronic voting at the end of the 20th century. This process was accelerated by legislation aimed at fixing the problems of the 2000 election, with optically scanned ballots and electronic voting replacing older methods.

Until the late 19th century, voting in the United States was conducted either in public, with voters each calling out loud their choice to election officials, or by using party tickets, a list with the party's candidates for all offices contested in the election. Parties provided these ballots to voters prior to the election, and voters were encouraged to vote a straight party ticket by simply bringing the ticket to the polling place. Concerns about fraud and privacy led to the replacement of these methods with the Australian ballot. This type of paper ballot, listing all candidates and printed at the government's expense, was first used in the Australian state of Victoria in 1856. Voters marked their choice in private and then dropped their ballot in a sealed ballot box. New York was the first American state to use the Australian ballot in 1888. Currently, these hand-counted paper ballots are used by less than one percent of registered voters, primarily in small, rural areas.

Mechanical lever machines were developed and introduced in the United States at about the same time as the Australian ballot. The first use of such a machine was in Lockport, New York in 1892. By the 1930s, machines were used in all major cities, and by the 1960s they were used by well over half of American voters. These machines use a tabular ballot layout, with each row assigned to a particular office and each column assigned to a particular candidate, or vice versa. The voters pull down selected levers to indicate their choices. When the voter opens the curtain surrounding the booth and exits, levers are automatically returned to their original position.

Only the machine has a mechanism to keep the total vote count, and so an independent verification is impossible, making the machine vulnerable to tampering. Furthermore, such machines have a large number of moving parts, which makes their maintenance very difficult. The last such machine was produced in 1982, and they are gradually being replaced. In the 2006 election, only about seven percent of American voters were still using mechanical lever machines, primarily in New York State.

The 1960s brought the next generation of voting methods, represented by punch cards. Punched cards have been in use for keeping statistics since the late 19th century, and International Business Machines Corporation (IBM) developed pre-scored punched cards. Two professors at University of California-Berkeley adapted these punch cards for use in elections, and launched the company Harris Votomatic to sell their product. The system was first used in primary elections in Fulton and DeKalb counties, Georgia, in 1964. By 1986, more than one-third of registered voters in the United States were using them. The system is straightforward: voters punch holes in the card with a device. If the voter is using a Votomatic card, the only information that appears on the card itself is the number of each hole. The name of the candidate corresponding to each hole appears in a separate booklet. If the voter is using a Datavote card instead, the name of the candidate will appear next to the hole the voter must punch in order to vote for that candidate. After the vote, the ballot is either placed in a ballot box, or fed onto a computer that tabulates the total vote at the polling station.

The problems associated with this system have been well-documented since the late 1960s, and several reports published by the National Bureau of Standards during the 1980s called for the abandonment of punch cards. Studies have shown that the rate of uncounted ballots for punch card voting systems is significantly higher than is the case with any other voting system. The most problematic is the existence of chad, the waste produced by the punching of cards.

Often, the chads do not fully detach from the card, and they can work their way back into place, or they can block holes from other ballots. The events of the 2000 presidential election in Florida, where Votomatic ballots were used, was an accident waiting to happen. As a result, Congress enacted the Help America Vote Act (HAVA), which mandated the replacement of older voting technologies with modern ones. By 2006, fully 63 percent of registered voters were using new voting equipment compared to 2000, which makes these changes the largest shift in voting technology in U.S. history.

One of these new technologies is optical scanning. This method, which has its roots in standardized testing, requires voters to record their vote by filling ovals on a form with machine-readable ink or soft lead pencils. Currently, about half of registered voters in the United States use this voting technology.

Major advantages of optical scanning are the existence of individual ballots, which can be checked for errors or used for a parallel counting, if needed, and being less error-prone and more reliable than other methods. The other new technology used in U.S. elections since the 1980s is electronic voting, the electronic version of the old mechanical lever system. Instead of pulling levers, the voter uses a touch-screen, push buttons, or a similar device.

Electronic voting is more expensive than optical scanning. Furthermore, there is no paper trail, and therefore no possibility of independent verification of the results. Power outages are another serious concern, as the machine is the only place where the vote tally is stored during the results. Finally, computer experts have raised serious concerns about the security of electronic voting.

These concerns have led many localities to either replace newly-purchased electronic voting machines with optically scanned ballots, or retrofit electronic machines to add paper trails. As of 2006, 38 percent of registered voters in the United States were using electronic voting. Electronic voting is used on a large scale in a number of countries, including Belgium, Canada, France, India, and the Netherlands, but the only country where it is currently used in all elections is Brazil.

The cutting-edge voting technology is internet voting. Estonia became the first country in the world to conduct national elections using the internet (during February/March 2007). However, security-related concerns make internet voting an unlikely candidate for adoption in the United States in the foreseeable future. Another concern is that the introduction of internet voting risks to widening the gap between those who vote regularly and those who are less likely to vote, such as the poor, the less educated, and ethnic minorities, who also may have little or no access to the internet, and may not be familiar with using it.

SEE ALSO: Australian Ballot; Ballot Controversies; Ballot Issues; Help America Vote Act; Technology.

BIBLIOGRAPHY. R.M. Alvarez and T.E. Hall, *Point, Click, and Vote: The Future of Internet Voting* (Brookings Institution Press, 2004); A.N. Crigler, M.R. Just, and E.J. McCaffery, eds., *Rethinking the Vote: The Politics and Prospects of American Election Reform* (Oxford University Press, 2004); Ian Urbina and Christopher Drew, "Big Shift Seen in Voting Methods With Turn Back to a Paper Trail," *New York Times* (December 8, 2006); Voting Machines ProCon, "Historical Timeline of Electronic Voting Machines and Related Voting Technology," www.votingmachinesprocon.org (cited August 2007).

FLORIN FESNIC
UNIVERSITY OF BUCHAREST

Voting Rights Act of 1965

THE VOTING RIGHTS Act of 1965 (VRA) has been described as the most successful civil rights measure in American history. The act has two main parts. The first, in Section 2 of the act, is a permanent provision that prohibits the denial of the vote on account of a person's race or color. The second includes Sections 4 and 5, which were originally established as temporary provisions set to expire in five years, but which have been subsequently renewed four times. Under Section 4, states and political subdivisions are covered if they have a history of discrimination, which is defined as the maintenance of electoral qualifications such as literacy tests and the registration of less than 50 percent of the voting-age population in the 1964 election. Under Section 5, covered jurisdictions are required to obtain approval from the federal district court in Washington, D.C., or the U.S. attorney general prior to enacting any new electoral procedures or voting qualifications in a process called preclearance. The district court or the attorney general will only approve such electoral procedures or qualifications if there is no intent or effect of discriminating on account of race. Covered states and political subdivisions may "bail-out" or be exempted from the preclearance requirement if they demonstrate non-discrimination in voting over a certain period of time.

The purpose of the VRA was to eliminate discrimination in voting against African Americans. Partly as a result of discriminatory voting laws such as literacy tests, which were administered in an unfair manner throughout the south, the number of African Americans eligible to vote in the south was miniscule through the first half of the 20th century.

Recognizing the ineffectiveness of a litigation-based strategy to eliminating discriminatory voting laws, and as a response to continued demands from the Civil

President Lyndon Johnson signing the Voting Rights Act of 1965, with Dr. Martin Luther King, Jr. behind him. The act made progress in stopping discrimination against African Americans at the voting booth.

Rights Movement, Congress passed the far-reaching VRA in 1965. The VRA had the immediate effect of substantially increasing the number of African Americans able to vote, particularly in the south. According to the U.S. Civil Rights Commission, the number of African Americans registered to vote increased by more than 1.1 million in six of the covered southern states by 1972.

Early Supreme Court interpretation of the VRA had the effect of broadening the scope of the statute to cover a wider array of electoral procedures. Although the primary target of Congress in enacting the VRA was to do away with laws and procedures that had the purpose or effect of denying the vote to African Americans, the Supreme Court, in the 1969 case of *Allen v. State Board of Elections*, interpreted the language of Section 5 as requiring states to obtain preclearance prior to enacting laws that might dilute the vote of African Americans.

REDISTRICTING PRACTICES

Dilution usually meant procedures that reduced the opportunity of African Americans to elect their candidate of choice, such as redistricting practices that reduced the number of districts that were majority African American, the creation of multimember districts and the annexation or de-annexation of parts of a city that had the effect of decreasing the proportion of African Americans in the electoral unit. Based on the holding in *Allen*, these procedures would have to receive approval from the federal court in Washington D.C. or the attorney general. Congress renewed the temporary provisions of the VRA for another five years in 1970, adopting the interpretation of the VRA in *Allen* and banning literacy tests throughout the country for another five years.

In 1975, Congress again renewed the temporary provisions of the VRA, this time for seven years and added two additional amendments: a permanent ban on literacy tests and establishment of protections for language minorities.

In the late 1970s, the Supreme Court, in two separate decisions, interpreted the VRA in a manner that narrowed its reach. First, in *United States v. Beer*, the court determined that to obtain preclearance for changes in voting laws, a state or political subdivision needed to only demonstrate that the effect was not retrogressive. This meant that the baseline for determining whether a change in voting laws had a discriminatory effect was

the current laws. For example, if under the current law African-American voters constituted a majority, and therefore had decisive electoral influence, in two of eight electoral districts in a state, state redistricting was only discriminatory under the retrogression standard if it decreased the number of majority African-American districts to less than two. It did not matter if the percentage of majority African-American districts in the state did not correlate with the percentage of African Americans in the state.

Second, in *City of Mobile v. Bolden*, the court interpreted Section 2 of the VRA, which prohibited discrimination in voting on account of race throughout the country, as requiring the plaintiff to prove that the enacting body intended to discriminate on account of race.

Congress renewed the VRA for a third time in 1982, extending the temporary provisions for an additional 25 years. More importantly, Congress rejected the Supreme Court interpretation in *Bolden* and amended Section 2 of the VRA to allow plaintiffs to show that the law resulted in discrimination on account of race.

In the 1980s and early 1990s, the Department of Justice aggressively enforced the VRA. The result was an expansion in the number of majority-minority districts that provided racial minorities with an opportunity to elect their candidate of choice and a concomitant increase in the number of racial minority elected representatives.

In the 1993 Supreme Court case of *Shaw v. Reno*, the creation of majority-minority districts through the race-conscious enforcement of the VRA was brought into question. In *Shaw*, the court held that certain forms of race-conscious redistricting were unconstitutional. This decision was later clarified to include redistricting practices in which the legislature's predominant motivation in the location of district lines was the race of the voters. This standard has proven difficult to meet and the ability of states to create and maintain majority-minority districts has not been substantially curtailed.

In 2003, the Supreme Court interpreted the Section 5 retrogression standard to eliminate the requirement that states maintain or create majority-minority districts. In *Georgia v. Ashcroft*, the court held that influence districts in which minorities constituted less than a majority, but maintained an indeterminable amount of influence, could substitute for majority-minority districts under the retrogression standard. In 2007, Congress again renewed the temporary provisions of the VRA for another 25 years. Civil Rights opponents to the *Georgia v. Ashcroft* standard pressured Congress to amend Section 5.

The 2007 act reinstated the requirement that states maintain or increase the number of majority-minority districts in order to obtain preclearance. During the renewal process, many southern states and political subdivisions expressed their frustration with continued federal intervention in their electoral processes; a few political subdivisions subsequently challenged the 2007 act in the courts.

SEE ALSO: African-American Vote; Literacy Tests; Voter Disfranchisement.

BIBLIOGRAPHY. Bernard Grofman and Chandler Davidson, *Controversies in Minority Voting: The Voting Rights Act in Perspective* (Brookings Institution Press, 1992); J. Morgan Kousser, *Colorblind Injustice: Minority Voting Rights and the Undoing of the Second Reconstruction* (University of North Carolina Press, 1999).

BERTRALL ROSS
LAW CLERK, NINTH CIRCUIT COURT OF APPEALS

Wallace, George C. (1919–98)

ONE OF THE most controversial political figures in the United States during the second half of the 20th century, George Corley Wallace controlled the state of Alabama for decades and ran unsuccessfully for president before being seriously wounded in an attempted assassination.

Wallace was born in Clio, Alabama. He attended local public schools and, in 1942, received a law degree from the University of Alabama. Wallace served briefly in the U.S. Air Force before immersing himself in Alabama politics. He was elected to the state legislature in 1947, and as a judge in the Third Judicial District six years later. Wallace ran for governor in 1958, and the election marked a turning point in his political career. He suffered a major defeat in the Democratic primary to John Patterson, a candidate who ran on racial issues and publicly accepted the endorsement of the Alabama Ku Klux Klan.

Previously known as a moderate on racial issues, Wallace afterward became a staunch segregationist and eventually the south's most prominent political demagogue of the Civil Rights era. Using highly charged, racially divisive rhetoric designed to appeal to Alabama whites, Wallace won the governorship in 1962. The campaign set the tone for Wallace's first administration, which was marked by rising social tensions that Wallace helped generate. In 1963, following a federal court order that called for the integration of Alabama's public schools, he ordered the state police to Birmingham, Huntsville, and Mobile to keep the schools closed.

On June 11, 1963, Wallace gained national attention as he kept a campaign promise by personally "standing in the schoolhouse door" to stop two African-American students from entering the University of Alabama. Forbidden at the time by the state constitution to run for a second consecutive term, Wallace engineered the election of his wife Lurleen to the state's highest office in 1966.

Wallace had national political aspirations that culminated in his 1968 presidential campaign as the candidate of his own American Independent Party. Running a somewhat more sophisticated version of his racially divisive gubernatorial campaign, he exploited the racial concerns of some whites, spoke out against the Civil Rights movement and its leaders, attacked the federal judiciary, and chastised Vietnam War protestors. Republican Richard Nixon won the election, but Wallace carried five southern states and won 46 electoral votes and 13.5 percent of the popular vote.

Wallace was re-elected governor of Alabama in 1970 and began another ill-fated run for the presidency two years later. On May 15, 1972, while campaigning in a Laurel, Maryland shopping center, he was shot five times by a would-be assassin and permanently paralyzed. The incident effectively ended Wallace's hopes of becoming

Alabama Governor George C. Wallace (seated) applauds as President Gerald Ford (center) greets supporters during a stop in the South during the 1976 presidential campaign. Wallace by this time had undergone a remarkable political transformation.

president. Still popular in his home state, he returned to Alabama and was elected governor again in 1974, and for a final time in 1982. By his last campaign, Wallace had apparently undergone a remarkable transformation with regard to his political philosophy. Claiming to have been "born again" he publicly, and sometimes tearfully, sought forgiveness from African-American Alabamans for his past behavior.

While some were understandably skeptical, others believed Wallace, and he received significant African-American support. Wallace left office in 1987, and, his health failing, he retired from politics. He died in Montgomery, Alabama on September 13, 1998.

SEE ALSO: Alabama; Civil Rights.

BIBLIOGRAPHY. D.T. Carter, *The Politics of Rage: George Wallace, the Origins of the New Conservatism, and the Transformation of American Politics* (Louisiana State University Press, 2000); Marshall Frady, *Wallace: The Classic Portrait of Alabama Governor George Wallace* (Random House, 1996); Jeffrey Frederick, *Stand Up for Alabama: Governor George C. Wallace* (University of Alabama Press, 2007)

BEN WYNNE
GAINESVILLE STATE COLLEGE

Wallace, Henry A. (1888–1965)

HENRY AGARD WALLACE was a leftist Democrat who served at both the center and the fringe of American politics. Wallace was born in Orient, Iowa, son of Henry Cantwell Wallace and May Brodhead. He graduated from Iowa State College in 1910, and worked on his family's farm magazine until 1929. During this time, he also became known in the agribusiness community as an agronomist and agricultural scientist. He married Ilo Browne on May 20, 1914, with whom he had three children. Wallace became secretary of agriculture under Franklin D. Roosevelt, a position Wallace's father, who died in office, had held less than a decade earlier under Warren G. Harding and Calvin Coolidge. The agriculture post had often been filled with someone with left-of-center politics, or at least agrarian populism. Wallace's father had, in fact, been regarded as a liberal Republican, an important faction within that party at that time, although ignominious today. Henry Wallace's time as secretary was one of great despair in the agricultural sector, and Roosevelt's New Deal program gave Wallace the opportunity to cultivate his progressive reputation nationally.

Roosevelt had been elected president twice with John Nance Garner as his vice president. It was expected that Roosevelt would decline to seek re-election in 1940, as no president before him had run for a third term. Garner, as the two-term incumbent vice president, naturally ran for the presidency. However, Garner did not abandon his presidential campaign even after Roosevelt sought a third term. Thus, he had to be replaced. Roosevelt chose Wallace. This was also seen as a nod to the left wing of the Democratic Party. Wallace continued to serve as an ideological lightning rod while he was vice president, a time when the world was at war.

Wallace alienated Roosevelt by engaging in some personal and political squabbles with others in the Democratic Party. The party replaced him with Harry S Truman as the vice presidential candidate for the 1944 election. Presumably, if Wallace had been able to hold his tongue and endure the role of a passive vice president, then he, and not Truman, would have become president when Roosevelt died on April 12, 1945. As a face-saving measure, Roosevelt made Wallace secretary of commerce, but it was not long before Wallace's vociferousness became too much for Truman, and Wallace resigned on September 20, 1946. He briefly served as editor of the liberal magazine, *The New Republic*.

Soon afterward, Wallace led a leftist faction in the tumultuous election of 1948. Truman was challenged both on the left and the right within his own party. This was a time when fervent Anti-Communism led to expulsion of Communists and other leftists from the Democratic Party. Many gravitated to Wallace's Pro-

gressive Party. J. Strom Thurmond (then a Democrat) led a breakaway southern faction of anti-civil rights Democrats known as the Dixiecrats. Wallace received votes in all but three states, more than a million total, and kept Truman from receiving a majority of the popular vote.

However, Wallace won no electoral votes, and later came to believe he had been used as a tool by Communists in that election. He became an outspoken Anti-Communist. He spent his later years returning to his work as an agricultural scientist. Wallace died in Danbury, Connecticut on November 18, 1965 and his remains were buried at Glendale Cemetery in Des Moines, Iowa.

SEE ALSO: Presidential Campaign of 1940; Presidential Campaign of 1944; Third Parties.

BIBLIOGRAPHY. J.C. Culver and John Hyde, *American Dreamer: The Life and Times of Henry A. Wallace* (Norton, 2000); E.L. Schapsmeier and F.H. Schapsmeier, *Henry A. Wallace of Iowa: The Agrarian Years, 1910–1940* (Iowa State University Press, 1968); E.L. Schapsmeier and F.H. Schapsmeier, *Prophet in Politics: Henry A. Wallace and the War Years, 1940–1965* (Iowa State University Press, 1970); Torbjörn Sirevåg, *The Eclipse of the New Deal and the Fall of Vice President Wallace, 1944* (Garland, 1985).

TONY HILL
MASSACHUSSETTS INSTITUTE OF TECHNOLOGY

War and Peace

MANY U.S. PRESIDENTIAL elections were fought over the issue of whether or not the United States should be involved in war. The first presidential election, of George Washington in 1789, was fought after the War of Independence. All the candidates had been active in the war, mostly in the armed forces. Washington and George Clinton, another of the candidates, had served in the British forces before the War of Independence. The Tripolitan-American War of 1801–05 barely featured in the 1804 presidential election campaign, which resulted in Thomas Jefferson elected largely on the basis of public enthusiasm over the Louisiana Purchase, and the country's growing prosperity. However, by contrast, the War of 1812 was important in the 1812 presidential election campaign as it broke out just after the Democratic-Republicans had rallied around James Madison and their enemies around George DeWitt Clinton who used the war as a major election issue in his presidential campaign. Clinton promoted the war in the south and opposed it in the north, in the hope of getting support of both parts of the United States. The war surfaced again, briefly, as an election issue in 1816, even though the fighting had finished, and the peace treaty signed in 1815. This was largely because Daniel D. Tompkins, opposing Madison, had commanded the New York militia during the war.

MILITARY CREDENTIALS

The military credentials of various candidates were to prove important throughout U.S. history. The War of 1812 resulted in the rise to prominence of Andrew Jackson, who was elected president in 1828; William Henry Harrison, elected president in 1840; and Zachary Taylor, elected president in 1848. Jackson had been the hero who defeated the British at the Battle of New Orleans in 1815; Harrison had also served in the War of 1812; and Taylor was certainly a great military hero, having fought in the War of 1812, the Black Hawk War of 1832, and the defeat of the Mexicans in 1845.

In 1856 the first Republican Party candidate for the presidential election was John C. Fremont, who distinguished himself in the Mexican War, although his role as an explorer was far more important. Four years later, Abraham Lincoln, who had no war experience, was elected as president, and was to preside over the country during five years of war. The threat of war as a possible resolution to the issue of slavery was so important that John C. Bell of the Constitutional Union was able to run for election with a newly established party and managed to capture 12.6 percent of the vote, and 39 Electoral College seats. Lincoln's re-election in 1864, during the Civil War, was the first presidential election where the overriding issue of the election was war. Lincoln was able to easily defeat General George B. McClellan. The election of Ulysses S. Grant, in 1868, was largely because of his role as a Union commander in the Civil War.

During the latter part of the 19th century, the "opening up" of the United States, with the dispossession of the Native Americans, saw wars against the Indians. The creation of many new states began to affect the presidential elections, because the "frontier" states were important, electorally. The Spanish-American War of 1898 led to the choice of Theodore Roosevelt as the vice presidential candidate in 1900, and his presidency in September 1901, following the assassination of William McKinley.

In the 1916 U.S. presidential election, Woodrow Wilson was intent on maintaining neutrality on U.S. involvement in World War I, a major political issue for Wilson's opponent, Charles Evans Hughes. The nation's general dislike of the outcome of World War I, and the Treaty of Versailles, led to a reaction against U.S. interventionism, which contributed to the election of Warren Harding, an isolationist, who managed to easily defeat James Middleton Cox.

When World War II broke out in Europe in 1939, it was obvious that possible U.S. participation would become a major issue in the 1940 presidential election, with Franklin D. Roosevelt promising "Your boys are not going to be sent into any foreign wars." Roosevelt's opponent, Wendell L. Wilkie also promised that no American men would go to the "shambles of a European trench." But the attack on Pearl Harbor changed that. By the 1944 presidential election, the war, of course, had bipartisan support.

KOREAN WAR

The Korean War came in the middle of Harry Truman's second term in office, but it did, briefly, lead to a major surge of support for General Douglas MacArthur who was leading the troops from the United States and some other members of the United Nations, in the war. However, despite MacArthur's popularity, the support for him as a presidential candidate waned quickly after Truman recalled him for talks. In 1952, the election of Dwight D. Eisenhower, the Allied Commander at D-Day in 1944, and one of the most famous U.S. generals from World War II, was followed, in 1956, by his easy re-election, showing U.S. support for one of their greatest war heroes. Eisenhower's successor, John F. Kennedy, had also been a World War II war hero. He had to face major trouble during his election bid, with anger over the U.S. government failing to provide air cover for the anti-Castro Cuban insurgents during the Bay of Pigs Invasion of 1961. By contrast, the subsequent Cuban Missile Crisis managed to build Kennedy's credentials as an effective president if war arose. Owing to his assassination in November 1963, the public's views on Kennedy's actions were never tested.

The 1964 U.S. presidential election, although Lyndon B. Johnson won for his civil rights and other domestic issue stands, was partially fought over the possible use of nuclear weapons in Vietnam, something clearly contemplated by Barry Goldwater, the Republican candidate. This led to the famous Johnson television commercial, that suggested that Goldwater would lead the world into nuclear war, but that Johnson, a former lieutenant commander in the U.S. Navy, was a man of restraint.

VIETNAM WAR

Soon after the 1964 election, which Johnson won in a landslide victory over Goldwater, the Vietnam War emerges as a major political issue, and by the time of the 1968 presidential election, the draft and the war overshadowed the entire campaign, with Hubert Humphrey arguing for a gradual end to hostilities, Eugene McCarthy and Robert Kennedy (until he was assassinated during the campaign) urged an immediate end to the war, Richard Nixon offered "Peace with Honor," and General Curtis LeMay, the vice presidential running mate of George Wallace, suggested the use of nuclear weapons to bomb the Communists "back into the Stone Age." Nixon won by a significant margin, but peace in Vietnam eluded him during his first term, making his re-election bid also being contested over Vietnam. Nixon won overwhelmingly, and three months later, after the Christmas Day bombing, the North Vietnamese signed a peace agreement with the United States.

The 1976 election of Jimmy Carter, who had served in the U.S. Navy during the 1950s, was followed by the 1980 election, and then the 1984 re-election of Ronald Reagan, who had served in the U.S. Air Force during World War II. His re-election came at the height of tensions in the Cold War with many people viewing him as a strong leader in a time of crisis. His successor, elected in 1988, was George H.W. Bush, a decorated naval carrier pilot in World War II, led the United States into the Gulf War, which, in spite of an easy victory over Iraq, with few U.S. casualties, did not prevent his defeat in 1992.

The Vietnam War overshadowed the 1992 presidential election, with accusations that Bill Clinton had planned to evade the draft, if he was conscripted. There was also Dan Quayle's avoidance of combat duties, and

Al Gore's good war record in Vietnam, as well as Bush's strong record as a fighter pilot in World War II, all highlighted often during the campaign. Next were the War on Terror, and the war in Iraq playing a major role in the 2004 U.S. presidential election campaign, with John Kerry's heroism during the Vietnam War often contrasted with queries about George W. Bush's military record. The election, however, showed greater focus on the War on Terror than over events in Vietnam. The war in Iraq emerged as the major issue in the 2008 U.S. presidential election.

SEE ALSO: Civil War and Realignment; Democratic Republican Party; Vietnam.

BIBLIOGRAPHY. John Whiteclay Chambers II, ed., *The Oxford Companion to American Military History* (Oxford University Press, 1999); Irving Stone, *They Also Ran* (Doubleday, Doran & Company, 1943); T.H. White, *The Making of the President 1964* (Jonathan Cape, 1965); J.A. Woods, *Roosevelt and Modern America* (The English Universities Press, 1959).

JUSTIN CORFIELD
GEELONG GRAMMAR SCHOOL, AUSTRALIA

War on Terrorism

NINE DAYS AFTER the terrorist attacks of September 11, 2001 on the United States, President George W. Bush declared to Congress and the American people that these attacks were "acts of war." In the same speech, Bush named this war the War on Terror (also known as the War on Terrorism and the Global War on Terrorism). The scope of this war would be vast, would prominently feature military means, and would be a lengthy campaign. Bush stated: "Our war on terror begins with al Qaeda, but it does not end there. It will not end until every terrorist group of global reach has been found, stopped and defeated."

President Bush and the other architects of the War on Terror saw this campaign at its inception, as a multigenerational and era-defining struggle. They compared it to the Cold War and the 20th century fight against fascism. Since the War on Terror was first articulated by President Bush it has been a significant political issue, important in U.S. campaigns and elections.

Sea Knight helicopters maneuver the flight deck of the amphibious assault ship USS Peleliu *during flight operations, December 3, 2005. The* Peleliu *was off the coast of southern California preparing for its upcoming deployment in the global war on terrorism.*

In President Bush's speech of September 20, 2001, the War on Terror commenced with a demand on the Taliban-controlled government of Afghanistan to turn over all al-Qaeda terrorists or face repercussions. The United States invaded Afghanistan less than one month later on, October 7, 2001, in Operation Enduring Freedom (OEF). Over the following year, President Bush and various administration officials sought to make the case that confronting Iraq over its weapons of mass destruction (WMD) was central to combating terrorism. The administration argued that Saddam Hussein, the leader of Iraq, was not to be trusted and thus WMD from Iraq could end up in the hands of terrorists and be deployed against Americans. Less publicly, administration officials discussed a war against Iraq as the key to reshaping the entire region of the Middle East (or southwest Asia) because, in their estimation, military victory in such a war was overwhelmingly likely.

On March 19, 2003 the United States invaded Iraq in Operation Iraqi Freedom (OIF).

The Bush administration also established the Department of Homeland Security to coordinate the domestic security functions of various federal agencies. Congress quickly passed the Uniting and Strengthening America by Providing Appropriate Tools Required to Intercept and Obstruct Terrorism (USA PATRIOT) Act of 2001 expanding the definition of terrorism to include "domestic terrorism" and granting authority to law enforcement agencies to more easily search records, monitor communication, detain and deport immigrants, and gather intelligence domestically. The War on Terror has been criticized as primarily intended for domestic consumption, in order to boost the popularity of elected officials, and as having the effect of restricting civil liberties and freedoms beyond what is necessary or desirable.

The concept of terrorism has a history of being deployed to support political causes. In the late 20th century, anarchists used the term "terrorists" as a positive appellation to distinguish themselves from mere murderers. President Ronald Reagan also implied that terrorists were not uniformly malignant when he declared that "one man's terrorist is another man's freedom fighter" in reference to the Nicaraguan contras fighting to remove the Sandinistas from power in Nicaragua. In contrast, in the current political context, terrorism is overwhelmingly deployed by U.S. politicians and seen by U.S. citizens as uniformly pernicious and, thus, as something worth fighting. Some Americans question the conclusion that terrorism should be the lens through which foreign policy is framed, but many more question the means employed in the struggle against terrorism (especially the war in Iraq and the Bush administration's domestic security policies). While President Bush has sought to frame the War in Iraq as the "central front" in the War on Terror, most Americans now disagree, and would like to see a swift end to the war in Iraq. A vast majority of Americans disapprove of holding terrorist suspects indefinitely without legal representation, but only a minority favor closing the controversial Guantanamo Bay military detention camp. The War in Afghanistan has considerable support among the American public.

After 9/11, the first national elections were the congressional elections of 2002. Despite the strong trend of midterm losses for the president's party, in these congressional elections the Republican Party gained a small number of seats. While there are other explanations to account for such a result, a spike in presidential popularity after the attacks and the president's discursive response indicate that the War on Terror campaign may have benefited congressional Republicans in 2002. The president's approval rating experienced an unprecedented surge from 55 to 90 percent in the days following 9/11, and was still historically quite high (63 percent) at the time of the 2002 elections. The congressional elections of 2004 also resulted in small gains for Republicans in both the House of Representatives and the Senate; however, the Republican incumbent also won the presidency in 2004, which could also accont for these gains.

Most notably, the congressional elections of 2006 were proclaimed a referendum on the War in Iraq. The peace movement, military families, and veterans of the Iraq War who had been advocating for an expeditious end to the war, and many Democratic Party members mobilized for the 2006 congressional elections, supporting Democratic candidates who were critical of the administration's war and policies in Iraq. The elections resulted in large enough gains that both the House of Representatives and the Senate swung from Republican to Democratic control. However, when the Democratic leadership failed to push for binding legislation that would end the war, many criticized the Democrats for failing to fulfill the 2006 electoral mandate. In May 2007, the Democratic leadership brought to a vote a supplemental appropriations bill that lacked a binding timeline for withdrawal after President Bush vetoed a more stringent bill. However, even the vetoed bill would have allowed the administration to continue the war in Iraq for another year and half, leading a substantial number of Iraq War opponents to call on the Democrats to end the war by no longer funding it (refusing to fulfill the president's supplemental appropriations request).

The War on Terrorism is likely to continue to be a significant campaign and electoral issue. The war in Afghanistan and domestic legislation (especially the former), have been much less controversial, perhaps overshadowed by how the war in Iraq has proceeded. The political conflict will likely be highest around further congressional appropriations that allow the war to continue, but, in 2008, Democratic representatives will have to account for their voting records, and presidential candidates will be extensively questioned on their plan for Iraq.

SEE ALSO: Campaigns, Presidential; Campaigns, U.S. Representatives; Campaigns, U.S. Senators; Patriotism; Presidential Election of 2004; Presidential Election of 2008; War and Peace.

BIBLIOGRAPHY. J.E. Campbell, "The 2002 Midterm Election: A Typical or an Atypical Midterm?" *PS: Political Science and Politics* (April 2003); Stuart Croft, *Culture, Crisis and America's War on Terror* (Cambridge University Press, 2006); B.J. Gaines, "Where's the Rally? Approval and Trust of the President, Cabinet, Congress, and Government Since September 11," *PS: Political Science and Politics* (September 2002); M.J. Hetherington and Michael Nelson, "Anatomy of a Rally Effect: George W. Bush and the War on Terrorism," *PS: Political Science and Politics* (January 2003); C.K. Winkler, *In the*

Name of Terrorism: Presidents on Political Violence in the Post-World War II Era (State University of New York Press, 2006); Bob Woodward, *Plan of Attack* (Simon & Schuster, 2004); Bob Woodward, *State of Denial: Bush at War, Part III* (Simon & Schuster, 2006).

JACQUE L. AMOUREUX
BROWN UNIVERSITY

Washington

WASHINGTON, THE EVERGREEN State, is the only state named for an American. Washington's southern boundary was set by the admission of Oregon in 1859. Its eastern boundary was fixed with the creation of the Idaho Territory in 1863. Washington was admitted to the Union on November 11, 1889, at about the same time as Montana, North Dakota, and South Dakota and the year before Idaho and Wyoming. The state is often referred to as Washington State to distinguish it from the nation's capital (Washington, D.C.). The Cascade Mountains neatly separate the state into east and west, with most of the territory falling to the east of the Cascades and most of the population living in the smaller area to the west. The mountain range forms a formidable barrier, not only physical and psychological, but also political. When the state Supreme Court gave a set of redistricting instructions to a special master in 1972, they directed that the districts created cross the Cascades, if at all, only along the southern border.

In presidential politics, Washington voted Republican most of the time until 1932, voting Democratic in 1896 and 1916. In 1912, the state supported Theodore Roosevelt's third-party bid. The state was reliably Democratic 1932–48. It was Republican again 1952–84, except for 1964 and 1968. In 1976, the state supported Republican Gerald Ford, but a "faithless elector," Mike Padden of Spokane, cast his vote for Ronald Reagan, instead. In 1988, Washington went narrowly Democratic, and, since then, Democratic strength has increased in presidential contests, such that Washington is regarded as a likely, if not safe, Democratic state. A Democratic president could probably not be elected without winning Washington.

Washington appointed only Republicans to the U.S. Senate during the period of legislative election, with one exception. Since direct election was mandated by the Seventeenth Amendment, Washingtonians have been represented by Democrats more than Republicans, but this is partly due to the longevity of two Democrats, Warren G. Magnuson, who served 1944–81, and Henry M. Jackson, who served from 1953 until his death in 1983. Jackson ran for the Democratic presidential nomination in 1976. Both were replaced by Republicans, including Slade Gorton who served non-consecutive terms 1981–87 and 1989–2001. Gorton's defeat in 1986 (a bad year for Republicans) by former U.S. Secretary of Transportation Brock Adams was a due, in part, to a controversial nomination to a federal judgeship Gorton engineered. Adams declined to seek re-election in 1992 due to a sex scandal and was replaced by Democrat Patty Murray, who was re-elected in 1998 and 2004. In 2000, Gorton was defeated by Democrat Maria Cantwell, making Washington one of the few states with two women senators.

CLOSE RACES

With only two exceptions, Washington's governors were all Republicans until 1933, extending back into the territorial period. Since the 1932 election, most have been Democrats. In the 1970s, Washington was one of the first states to elect a female governor, Dixy Lee Ray. The last Republican governor, John Spellman, was elected in 1980, defeating Ray. Since Spellman's defeat by Booth Gardner in 1984, all have been Democrats. The 2004 election was extremely close, with Democrat Christine Gregoire declared the winner by 133 votes of almost three million cast. The preliminary count showed Republican Dino Rossi winning, but Gregoire prevailed in a recount that took longer than the similar non-recount in Florida in 2000.

Seattle, which rose from almost nothing to become a one of the greatest American boom cities in the late 19th century, gained status as a cutting-edge cultural center for the United States in the 1990s. Some of this impetus came from an large influx of Californians leaving that state earlier in the 1990s. Some of it came from the region's high-technology economy, led by Microsoft. Strangely enough, even as Seattle was becoming more chic for its grunge music, and the spread of then-local Starbuck's Coffee nationwide, its traditional economy was sinking. All of its large banks were taken over by out of state companies by the mid-1990s, and aircraft giant Boeing, long the mainstay of the local economy, moved its headquarters to Chicago in 2000. The political impact of these happenings has made the state more friendly to Democrats. The area across Puget Sound from Seattle, the northern part of the Olympic Peninsula, is often linked politically with Seattle and its suburbs rather than to the territory to the south along the largely unpopulated interior of the peninsula. This reflects the business and transportation patterns as well; ferries connect the two sides of the Sound, and also the many populated islands in it, and these ferries are a more typical travel mode than the land route through Tacoma.

Two parts of Washington are adjacent to large metropolitan areas based outside the state. Whatcom County, whose seat is Bellingham, is one of the more reliably Democratic rural counties of Washington. It abuts the burgeoning Vancouver, British Columbia metropolitan area. Point Roberts is a unique community, one of three exclaves of the country (Alaska and the Northwest Angle of Minnesota are the others). The only way to reach Point Roberts on land is to pass through Canada. The town's economy is boosted by being a low-tax shopping center for British Columbians. Vancouver, Washington, on the Oregon border, is just across the Columbia River from Portland, Oregon. The counties in this area are typically more Democratic than other rural parts of the state.

DEMOCRATIC STRONGHOLDS

Seattle is the most strongly Democratic part of the state. The Olympia area (the state capital) is also heavily Democratic, an influence it draws from its large population of government employees, usually a Democratic constituency. The central part of the state, east of the Cascades, is the most heavily Republican part. This area, less amenable to agriculture, is more similar politically to the range country of the rural west. The rest of eastern Washington is marginally Republican. The southeastern corner is largely agricultural, and the northeastern corner is dominated by Spokane, the state's second-largest metropolitan area.

The balance of power in elections is held in the Puget Sound suburbs. In the 2000 presidential elections, the suburban Seattle counties to the north (Snohomish, whose county seat is Everett) and to the south (Pierce, whose seat is Tacoma) went narrowly for Al Gore, but in 2004, they went narrowly for George W. Bush. With the state being slightly Democratic on a normal basis, the most usual way to produce a Republican victory is

a strong showing by Republicans in Pierce and Snohomish Counties.

SEE ALSO: Electors; Oregon; Presidential Election of 2000.

BIBLIOGRAPHY. R.L. Morrill, *Political Redistricting and Geographic Theory* (American Association of Geographers, 1981); David Nice, J.C. Pierce, and C.H. Sheldon, eds., *Government and Politics in the Evergreen State* (Washington State University Press, 1992); Thor Swanson, ed., *Political Life in Washington: Governing the Evergreen State* (Washington State University Press, 1985).

TONY L. HILL
MASSACHUSETTS INSTITUTE OF TECHNOLOGY

Watergate

WATERGATE REFERS TO the political scandal that broke in 1972, and forced Richard Nixon to resign as president of the United States two years later. The Watergate scandal began with a June 17, 1972 break-in at the Democratic National Committee headquarters at the Watergate complex in Washington, D.C. The resulting cover-up led to Nixon's resignation on August 9, 1974. Five men were arrested for breaking into the headquarters; the men were carrying electronic surveillance equipment. These five, along with two other accomplices, were tried and convicted. All seven men were either directly or indirectly employees of Nixon's Committee to Re-elect the President (CREEP).

The media played a major role in the unraveling of the Nixon administration. The *Washington Post* pursued the story and linked the burglary and burglars to CREEP. Some have stated that Watergate was nothing but a media-created issue. In fact, Watergate was not a significant factor in the outcome of the 1972 presidential campaign. Richard Nixon won re-election by a landslide. During the campaign, the media gave Watergate little coverage. Media labels, such as "Deep Throat," the "Watergate caper," "the Saturday night massacre," and "the smoking gun," helped fuel the public perception of the unraveling events of Watergate. Through the use of an informant, nicknamed "Deep Throat," Bob Woodward and Carl Bernstein uncovered information suggesting that knowledge of the break-in

After President Richard Nixon resigned following the Watergate affair, Nixon was pardoned by his successor Gerald Ford. Above, the House Judiciary Subcommittee questions Ford on pardoning Nixon on October 17, 1974.

and attempts to cover it up led directly to the White House. In his memoirs, Richard Nixon believed that public opinion was the critical factor in what he called the "overriding of my landslide mandate," referring to his 1972 landslide victory over George McGovern. The effects of the Watergate scandal did not by any means end with Nixon's resignation and the imprisonment of some of his aides. The effect on the upcoming House and Senate elections only months after his resignation was enormous. Disappointed with the Republican Party, voters across the country voted overwhelmingly for Democrats; even in districts that had been Republican strongholds for decades.

On May 16, 1973, President Nixon had asked congress to create an independent commission to propose ways of reforming the federal election process. Among the proposals, the president suggested the commis-

sion might consider were constitutional amendments changing House member's terms to four years and the president's terms to six years without the possibility of re-election. The president also suggested that a commission examine campaign financing and reporting, the length of campaigns, and methods of combating unfair campaign practices. Nixon said, "I believe that reform is essential and urgent." On April 30, 1974, Nixon discussed the Watergate affair on national television. He said he planned to ask both parties to work for new rules that would ensure clean campaigns in the future. Some suggested that Nixon's proposals stemmed from reaction against the Watergate affair.

The president's attorney suggested that Watergate presented a "unique opportunity" for bipartisan action on federal campaign practices. On January 7, 1974, the Senate Watergate investigating committee stated that it might recommend limiting presidential terms to one term if abuses in the 1972 Nixon re-election campaign proved serious enough. The committee also considered including a "radically new campaign financing system that would severely curtail the amount of private monies that could be contributed." The committee said that the possible recommendations hinged on the availability of more evidence. After Watergate, there were concerns about the scope of executive power. Congress established new programs aimed at increasing executive transparency and reducing corruption.

In 1974, the Federal Elections Commission was created as an overseer for campaign finance. The Privacy Act of 1974 established that citizens had a right to view the information that the government had collected about them. The Privacy Act not only established the legal basis for the government's transparency policy, but also required government agencies to write clear guidelines on how they would implement them, so that the transparency policy itself was transparent. In 1976, Congress passed the Government in the Sunshine Act. The law requires government meetings to be open to the public. Public agencies must give advance notice about upcoming meetings and their agendas, and they must keep public records about the meetings' results. In addition, the act carefully defines a "meeting," to prevent groups of government officials gathering to make decisions and they claimed that they were not officially meeting.

In 1978, Congress established the Inspector General Act, which created high-level officials in each federal agency to conduct independent audits and investigations. These inspectors general had broad power to explore agency operations, and authority over their own budgets and staff. Watergate demonstrated that the executive branch could not investigate itself. After considerable debate, Congress passed the Special Prosecutor Act in 1978. This law allowed the attorney general to appoint a special investigator under certain circumstances. Later legislators would name these independent counsels. Under this legislation it is up to the attorney general to determine if there is sufficient conflict of interest to warrant further investigation and prosecution.

On Sunday, September 8, 1974, President Gerald Ford announced that he had granted former President Nixon "a full, free, and absolute pardon ... for all offenses against the United States which he, Richard Nixon, has committed, or may have committed, or taken part in during the period" of his presidency. Although Watergate had little or no effect on the 1972 presidential election, months later Watergate dominated the headlines and continued to dominate the headlines long after Nixon's resignation.

SEE ALSO: Campaign Reforms; Campaign Spending; Campaign Strategies; Campaigns, Presidential; Corruption and Democratic Elections; Democratic Party; Elections Laws, Federal Elections; Republican Party.

BIBLIOGRAPHY. T.E. Cronin and M.A. Genovese, *The Paradoxes of the American Presidency* (Oxford University Press, 1998); M.A. Genovese, *The Watergate Crisis* (Greenwood Press, 1999); G.E. Lang and Kurt Lang, *The Battle for Public Opinion: The President, the Press, and the Polls during Watergate* (Columbia University Press, 1983); Michael Schudson, *Watergate in American Memory: How We Remember, Forget, and Reconstruct the Past* (Basic Books, 1993).

STEPHEN E. SUSSMAN
BARRY UNIVERSITY

Welfare and Poverty

HISTORICALLY, POVERTY AND welfare reform are not major campaign issues in the United States. Despite the fact that most people know someone who either receives government assistance or needs some form of welfare, those seeking elected office often fail to recognize the economic needs of the poor. As prevalent as poverty is in the United States, welfare reform and poverty relief should be at the top of every politician's agenda. With more than 21.1 percent of children living in poverty in the United States, those seeking elected office could use their position to create a dialogue about society addressing the needs of the poor. However, with rare exceptions, this is not the case. While most individuals running for an elected office, at the state or federal level, mention the importance of addressing the needs of the poor and the importance of addressing welfare reform, few use poverty or welfare reform as a campaign issue.

Poverty was a key issue in the presidential election of 1932. Prior to the Great Depression, the United

States enjoyed a robust economy and unprecedented job growth. In the 1928 presidential election campaign, Republican Herbert Hoover touted the slogan "a chicken in every pot and a car in every garage." This optimism disappeared with the stock market crash of 1929. The crash sent shockwaves throughout the country as businesses closed and millions found themselves out of work. Just prior to the crash, President Hoover supplied his Democratic opponents with political campaign fodder when he noted that America was closer to a triumph over poverty once and for all.

However, the United States had experienced unbelievable poverty, homelessness, and job loss as the 1932 election came into view. The Great Depression was in full swing with more than 18 million elderly, disabled, and single mothers with children already living below the poverty line. By the early 1930s, another 13 million Americans were out of work. Homeless families lived in public parks as shanty towns sprang up across the country. Most Americans did not have personal savings or retirement accounts, and those who did lost their savings when banks closed. Democratic candidate Franklin Delano Roosevelt campaigned with his New Deal, offering to develop governmental assistance programs for the poor and the homeless. Hoover responded by noting, "nobody is actually starving." Hoover was faced with hostile crowds everywhere he campaigned and Roosevelt won easily.

WAR AND POVERTY

President Lyndon B. Johnson used poverty as an issue leading up to the 1964 presidential election when he first introduced his War on Poverty during the State of the Union address on January 8, 1964. With the national poverty rate hovering at 19 percent, Johnson followed Roosevelt in attempting to address the needs of the poor. Johnson was re-elected in 1964, and legislation followed that utilized federal funds to address poverty.

In the early 1990s, Governor William Jefferson Clinton (D-AR) ran for president vowing to "end welfare as we know it." Clinton firmly believed that allowing states to experiment with welfare reform and poverty programs at the local level would ease poverty and provide greater opportunities for the poor. Clinton was elected president in 1992, vowing to help people make the transition from welfare to work. Critics, even within the Democratic Party, saw two major obstacles that would stand in the way of this

promise becoming a reality. First, welfare recipients have limited training and technological skills. Second, the jobs that many welfare recipients could receive would not pay enough to keep them off welfare and provide for their daily needs. Clinton, however, got Congress to increase the earned income tax credit, which allows low-wage workers who support a family to receive a refund from the Internal Revenue Service. Sensing that Clinton could not fulfill his promise to end welfare, the Republican Party, in 1994, used this campaign promise as an integral component of their midterm election campaign strategy. Newt Gingrich (R-GA) and Dick Armey (R-TX) campaigned under a Contract with America, promising the American electorate that within the first 100 days of the new session, they would introduce legislation to implement tougher crime laws, a balanced budget, term limits, and reformed welfare. As a result of the contract promise, Republicans gained 54 seats and took control of the House of Representatives.

POLITICAL CULTURE

Ideas about poverty and welfare affect public opinion, which in turn is woven into the fabric of the political culture in the United States. Children should not be victims of poverty and dysfunctional families; however, parents need to get jobs and work to provide for their families. Thus, two conflicting points would lead a political candidate to support programs that presently exist to help children, but at the same time they would not want to alienate potential voters who may be poor and on some type of public assistance. Similarly, the perceived social differences in structures between the poor and the rich, as well as the entrenched differentiations among race, ethnicity, and class, have resulted in a dearth of discussion of welfare reform and poverty in state and national elections. The overrepresentation of ethnic groups among welfare recipients by the media, and society as a whole results, in the discussion of welfare reform and poverty elimination as politically unacceptable, for fear of creating further racial unrest and distrust.

Political institutions also limit engagement of poverty and welfare reform issues by political candidates. Many political candidates recognize that the fragmentation of government, especially during the devolution revolution (the channeling of programs to state governments), limits possible change, and, as such, resign themselves to focus on issues that can best serve their election and re-election. Divided control of government produces policy stalemates. Political candidates need to show their constituents results, and poverty and welfare reform do not meet their political needs. Although researchers suggest that welfare reform and policies related to poverty in the United States need to be addressed, political candidates often receive policy feedback that suggests otherwise. Constituencies that benefit from an entrenched policy are likely to object to any new policy or revision that would hurt them personally, and they share these concerns with candidates.

SEE ALSO: Candidate Image; Issue Framing; Presidential Election of 1928, Presidential Election of 1932.

BIBLIOGRAPHY. D.F. Burg, *The Great Depression, An Eyewitness History* (Facts on File, 1996), J.F. Handler, *The Moral Construction of Poverty* (SAGE Publications, 1991); R.K. Weaver, *Ending Welfare As We Know It* (Brookings Institute, 2000).

RONALD ERIC MATTHEWS, JR.
MOUNT UNION COLLEGE

West Virginia

WEST VIRGINIA WAS a part of the state of Virginia until June 20, 1863, supported the Union in the American Civil War. With much of the industry in the state from logging and coal mining, it had a long labor tradition, although 14 of its 32 governors have been Republican.

The first elected governor of West Virginia was Arthur I. Boreman. Born in Pennsylvania, he had moved to the region when he was 4-years-old, and was active in the Whig Party before becoming a supporter of the Constitutional Union Party that fielded John Bell in the 1860 U.S. presidential election. After serving for six years, Boreman, in the tradition set by so many other first state governors, sought election to the U.S. Senate. His successor, Daniel D.T. Farnsworth, held the office of governor for seven days, then William E. Stevenson, a former member of the state senate, and a partner in the *Parkersburg State Journal*, was elected.

In 1870, John I. Jacob was elected governor of West Virginia, and served three two-year terms, the second after being elected as an Independent. Democrat Henry M. Matthews succeeded him, and West Virginia elected Democratic governors until 1897. In 1884, Emanuel Willis Wilson was elected as governor, and then there was a dispute over the 1888 gubernatorial election. Both Nathan Goff Jr. and Artesas Brooks Fleming claim to have won the election, and Wilson remained governor throughout the crisis, despite state Senate President Robert S. Carr wanting to hold office until the problem was resolved. On March 4, 1889, both Goff and Fleming were sworn in as governor. It was finally agreed that Fleming had won and Goff withdrew. When Fleming left office in 1893, William A. MacCorkle became the new governor, after his election in 1892. He had campaigned for improvements in transportation in the state.

The next five governors were all Republicans, each serving one term, with George W. Atkinson elected governor in 1897. In 1900, Albert B. White defeated Democrat John H. Holt, by 19,156 votes. Henry D. Hatfield campaigning for continued support of the trade union movement, and was elected in 1912. The Republican ascendancy in the the U.S. presidential elections in the 1920s saw three Republican governors of West Virginia 1921–33.

During the 1932 U.S. presidential election, the state supported Franklin D. Roosevelt, and elected Democrat Herman G. Kump as governor. He served two terms, during the height of the Great Depression. Kump's successor, Homer Adams Holt, elected in 1936, remained in office until 1940. The next governor elected was Matthew M. Neely, who had held a seat in the U.S. Senate from 1930. Neely never liked the governorship, and after only two years as governor, he tried to leave and seek re-election to the U.S. Senate.

Throughout the period beginning in the early 1930s, the Democrats held both the state's seats in the U.S. Senate, two of the three state seats in the House of Representatives, and he also dominated the state legislature and most elected state offices. The state capital of Charleston traditionally supported the Democrats, as did the area encompassing the coalfields of southern West Virginia, namely Boone, Logan, McDowell, Mingo, and Wyoming counties, with the Republicans drawing the core of their support from the counties in the Allegheny Valley, along with the mid-Ohio Valley, in particular Jackson, Mason, and Wood counties.

In 1944, Clarence W. Meadows was elected as governor, and Democrat Okey L. Patteson, who was governor 1945–49, succeeded him. The 1952 gubernatorial election involved Democrat William C. Marland defeating the Republican Rush D. Holt by 27,000 votes, after a bitter campaign during which Holt proclaimed his campaign as against corruption, and Marland launch a last-minute attack on the character of Holt, his family, and his record as a politician. In 1956, Cecil H. Underwood, a Republican, was elected governor. In 1959, Robert Byrd campaigned successfully for a place in the U.S. Senate, and was re-elected many times, making him longest serving and oldest member of the U.S. Congress.

At the start of the 1960 elections, West Virginia played an important role in the Democratic Party primaries with pollster Lou Harris advising John F. Kennedy that the people in West Virginia were worried about Kennedy's Catholicism. On the advice of Harris, Kennedy then campaigned for the primary with Franklin Roosevelt, Jr., and spoke frankly about his religious beliefs, giving him the impetus for his victory in the primary.

This showed that Kennedy could win in a largely non-Catholic state, making many Democrats begin to believe that he could win the presidential election. In 1960, West Virginia voted for Kennedy by 441,786 votes (52.7 percent) to Richard M. Nixon's 395,995 votes (47.3 percent).

This coincided with the 1960 gubernatorial election that saw Democrat William Wallace Barron elected governor. Subsequently, President-elect Kennedy tried to appoint Franklin Roosevelt, Jr. as secretary of the navy, but when the incoming Secretary of Defense, Robert McNamara, objected, Roosevelt was appointed as undersecretary of commerce. In the 1964 U.S. presidential election, the fear of a victory for Barry Goldwater was reflected in the results. Lyndon B. Johnson received 538,087 votes (67.9 percent) to Goldwater's 253,953 votes (32.1 percent). Democrat Hulett C. Smith was elected as state governor.

The 1968 U.S. presidential election saw West Virginia vote for Hubert H. Humphrey, who received 374,091 votes to Richard M. Nixon's 307,555 votes, with George Wallace receiving 2,560 votes. In the gubernatorial elections Republican, Arch Alfred Moore, Jr. was elected.

At that time, the State Constitution had a clause stating that a governor could only serve one term in office. However, the constitution was changed, and Moore was re-elected for a second term in 1972, defeating John D. Rockefeller, IV who campaigned for an end to strip mining, although in the presidential election, the state voted for Richard M. Nixon.

With John D. Rockefeller's election in 1976, a Democrat once again held the state governorship for two terms, then lost to Arch Moore who returned for his third term. Democrat Gaston Caperton then served two terms before Cecil H. Underwood managed to rally the Republicans in the 1996 gubernatorial elections. In the 1996 West Virginia gubernatorial election, the Democratic Party fielded a female candidate. In the 2000 elections, for the U.S. presidential election, the state voted for George W. Bush in a surprise upset, which led to Bush defeating Gore by 52 percent to 48 percent.

However, in the 2000 gubernatorial elections, the electorate was clearly involved in ticket splitting, voting for Bob Wise, a Democrat, as the new governor. Joe Manchin III, the incumbent governor, a Democrat, won the 2004 elections easily with 63 percent of the vote, and George W. Bush carried West Virginia in the 2004 presidential election, winning 56 percent of the vote.

SEE ALSO: Constitutional Union Party; Whig Party.

BIBLIOGRAPHY. R.A. Brisbin, et al., *West Virginia Politics and Government* (University of Nebraska Press, 1997); R.O. Curry, *A House Divided: A Study of Statehood Politics and the Copperhead Movement in West Virginia* (Pittsburgh University Press, 1964); P.F. Lutz, "The 1952 West Virginia Gubernatorial Election," *West Virginia History* (v.39/2–3, 1978); J.D. Rausch Jr., M.J. Rozell, and Harry L. Wilson, "When Women Lose: A Study of Media Coverage of Two Gubernatorial Campaigns," *Women & Politics* (v.20/4, 1999); Thomas Stafford, *Afflicting the Comfortable: Journalism and Politics in West Virginia* (West Virginia University Press, 2005); D.G. Temple and T.M. Drake, "No More Vote Buying—Maybe," *Journal of State Government* (v.59/3, 1986); W.E. Watson, "Strip Mining Wins a Victory," *New South* (v.28/1, 1973); T.H. White, *The Making of the President 1960* (Jonathan Cape, 1961); J.E. Wood, *Finance and Election Reform in West Virginia*, thesis (West Virginia University, 1976).

JUSTIN CORFIELD
GEELONG GRAMMAR SCHOOL, AUSTRALIA

Whig Party

THE WHIG PARTY, a political party from 1832 to the mid-1850s, was created out of opposition to Democrat Andrew Jackson's policies. Though the Whig Party was relatively short-lived, it was an important party that arose partially due to a close and highly controversial election and partially out of opposition to political candidates. This party's predecessor was the National Republican Party, which favored incumbent John Quincy Adams over Jackson in the election of 1828.

The dispute between the Whigs and Jackson arose primarily from Jackson's support for a strengthened presidency. Whig opponents, with the American Revolution still in mind, were concerned that a strong centralized presidency too closely resembled a kingship. The Whig Party ran presidential candidates from 1832 to the mid-1950s, but only William Harrison and Zachary Taylor were elected, both of whom were war heroes and died in office. Two other Whigs, John Tyler and Millard Fillmore, succeeded Harrison and Taylor, respectively.

The Whig Party, at least in name, paralleled the American Revolution. The name came from the Revolutionary group that supported independence from Great Britain. The name Whigs implied that the Jackson supporters were loyalists or Tories, Americans who supported the British cause in the American Revolution. The Whig Party appealed more to the business and professional class.

They favored economic development, manufacturing, financial and commercial interests, and modernization. Furthermore, they endorsed internal development such as roads, railroads, and canals, all of which would be funded by the federal government. However, there was a diversity of views within the Whig Party. What differentiated the Whigs from the Democratic Party was their strong support of congressional power over the executive branch.

The Democratic Party felt that greater centralized power should go to the president. The Whig Party had many members, including William Harrison, Henry Clay, Zachary Taylor, Winfield Scott, and Abraham Lincoln (who later defected to the Republican Party). During its existence, the Whig party only saw two of its allies elected to the presidency, Benjamin Harrison and Zachary Taylor. Harrison, who died in office, was succeeded by Whig Party President John Tyler. Millard Fillmore succeeded Zachary Taylor and was the last Whig president.

Andrew Jackson brought about many changes in his presidential term that could potentially give the president greater power than Congress. For example, the veto was as a mechanism that a president could use to strike unconstitutional bills, but Jackson changed this notion to the idea that a president could veto a bill on any grounds. Many citizens and politicians opposed this, and often Jackson was depicted as King Andrew in political cartoons. In response, many, such as Henry Clay and Vice President John Calhoun, labeled themselves National Republicans, a precursor to the Whig Party, which supported John Quincy Adams 1825–29. However, Jackson defeated Adams in 1828. In 1832, in opposition to Jackson, the Whig Party formed, but Jackson defeated Henry Clay.

In the elections of 1836, four years after the party's birth, the Whigs were not organized enough to run a national campaign. This was because the Whigs had found it difficult to find a common leader or program around which to unify, and they hoped to deny a majority of the Electoral College votes to Martin Van Buren by running several candidates across the United States. This plan failed, but only three years later, the Whigs had their first convention and nominated William Harrison as their presidential candidate. In 1840, Harrison defeated Van Buren to become the first Whig president. The Harrison victory was partially due to the Panic of 1837, a severe economic depression that hit the United States and for which Van Buren was blamed. Shortly after, Harrison died and was succeeded by John Tyler. However, Tyler was expelled from the Whig Party in 1841, because he vetoed the Whig's economic legislation.

In 1844, the Whigs nominated Henry Clay, but he was defeated by James Polk. In the election of 1848, the Whigs nominated Zachery Taylor, a general and a military war hero in the Mexican-American War. Taylor defeated Lewis Cass, but Whig enthusiasm was short-lived. The Whigs began to break up due to the Compromise of 1850, which fractionalized their supporters due to issues related to slavery and anti-slavery. In 1850, Taylor died, which further weakened the party. Taylor was succeeded by Millard Fillmore, the last Whig president.

The Democratic Party grew over time, with the Whigs losing more districts and marginal states. The Whigs ran

An 1852 Whig Party campaign banner for candidates Winfield Scott and William A. Graham.

Winfield Scott against their own incumbent President Fillmore in the 1852 election because Fillmore signed the Fugitive Slave Act. In 1854, northern and southern Whigs were divided over the Kansas-Nebraska Act, a bill devised by Illinois Senator Stephen Douglas that would repeal the Missouri Compromise of 1820 and be a major precursor to the American Civil War.

Many northern Whigs, including Abraham Lincoln, joined the Republican Party in strong opposition. In 1854, other Whigs joined the Republican Party. Over time, the remainder of the Whigs either defected or formed other parties, including the Democratic Party, the Opposition Party, the Know Nothing Party, the Constitutional Union Party, and the Native American Party. During the Reconstruction Period, in the south, Whigs

tried to reform and called themselves the Conservatives, but this resurgence was defeated by the Democrats.

SEE ALSO: Presidential Election of 1828; Presidential Election of 1852; Political Parties in American Elections.

BIBLIOGRAPHY. Thomas Brown, *Politics and Statesmanship: Essays on the American Whig Party* (Columbia University Press, 1985); D.W. Howe, *The American Whigs: An Anthology* (John Wiley & Sons, Inc., 1973).

JOSHUA MITCHELL
SOUTHERN ILLINOIS UNIVERSITY

Winner-Take-All System

IN A WINNER-TAKE-ALL system, the goal of an election is to pick a winner, and the winner takes all. This is in contrast to proportional representation, where the goal is to choose a legislature that will mirror the preferences of voters as closely as possible. There are several kinds of winner-take-all systems, and a key distinction can be made between plurality and majority formulas. Among countries using winner-take-all formulas for legislative elections, single-member district plurality is by far the most widely used (in 54 cases out of 91 studied). This system is used for legislative elections in countries such as Britain and former British colonies such as the United States or India. In this case, the candidate who receives the largest number of votes wins the election.

If a majority is needed to win an election, the requirement can be met in either of two ways. The first possibility is the system used in France for presidential elections (and, in a slightly modified form, for electing the French parliament). To be elected, a candidate must win a majority (at least 50 percent plus one of the total votes cast). If no candidate wins a majority, a runoff election is held between the top two vote getters, which ensures that the winner of the second round is elected with a majority of votes. About 30 countries, mostly former French colonies and former Soviet republics, use this system, known as the two-round system or majority-runoff, for their legislative elections. An even larger number of countries, approximately 50, hold their presidential elections under such system. This system is also used in Louisiana.

The second possibility to ensure a majority for the winner, while avoiding the need for a second round, is the alternative vote (also known as preferential voting). This system is used in Australia for legislative elections and in Ireland for presidential elections. Instead of choosing just one candidate, each voter ranks candidates: first choice, second choice, third choice, and so on. If no candidate gets a majority of first preferences, the candidate with the lowest number of first preferences is eliminated, and voters' second preferences are counted from the ballots on which that candidate was ranked first; the process continues until one candidate gets a majority of votes.

For example, in a district in which a Republican, a Democrat, and a Green candidate are running, if 100,000 voters cast a ballot, and the results (first preferences) are: 48,000 votes for the Republican candidate, 47,000 votes for the Democratic candidate, and 5,000 votes for the Green candidate, no candidate received a majority of first preferences. The Green candidate, who received the lowest number of first preferences, is eliminated. The next step is to look at the second preferences on the 5,000 ballots on which the Green candidate was marked as the first preference. If, for instance, the Democratic candidate appears as the second choice of 4,000 of Green voters, and the Republican candidate is the second preference of only 1,000 of Green voters, the total vote of the Democratic candidate becomes 51,000, and he or she is elected, despite being in the second position after the first count.

Another possible criterion for classifying winner-take-all electoral formulas is to look at the number of representatives elected in a district. The alternative vote and majority-runoff are always employed in single-member districts; for plurality, that is not always the case. The single non-transferable vote provides an example of the use of plurality in multiple member districts. The system was used 1948–93 for electing Japan's lower house, and is still used for legislative elections in Jordan and Vanuatu. Under this system, each elector has just one vote, but there are multiple seats to be filled in each district. In a three-member district, for instance, the top three vote getters are elected, and any candidate who receives 25 percent of the vote is guaranteed a seat. Another possibility is to have parties, rather than candidates, running in multimember districts, with the party winning a plurality of votes winning all seats in the districts. This is the party block vote, a system used in Sin-gapore,; this method tends to give a huge seat bonus to the largest party.

SEE ALSO: Plurality Vote; Proportional Representation.

BIBLIOGRAPHY. Pippa Norris, "Electoral Engineering: Voting Rules and Political Behavior (Cambridge University Press, 2004); Andrew Reynolds and Ben Reilly, eds., The International IDEA Handbook of Electoral System Design (International Institute for Democracy and Electoral Assistance, 1997).

FLORIN FESNIC
UNIVERSITY OF BUCHAREST

Wisconsin

NATIVE AMERICAN PEOPLE are known to have lived in Wisconsin since 10,000 B.C.E.; the first European to visit was the French explorer Jean Nicolet in 1634. A Jesuit mission was built, in 1671, at Green Bay and, gradually, a number of French traders started trading in the region. The British gained possession of the area at the Treaty of Paris in 1763, and permanent European settlement began soon afterwards. It became a part of the United States in 1783, and was a part of the Indiana Territory beginning in 1800. After the War of 1812, the Americans started organizing it, and an act of Congress on April 20, 1836 creating the Wisconsin Territory, which included not only what is now Wisconsin, but also Iowa, Minnesota, and parts of North and South Dakota.

Belmont became the capital of the territory with an elected legislature. Wisconsin voting against the introduction of its "first" constitution in April 1847. In December of that year, another constitutional convention was called and, in March 1848, another referendum was ratified; Wisconsin attained statehood on May 29, 1848. The first governor was Nelson Dewey, a Democrat from Connecticut, who had been active in politics in Wisconsin since the early 1830s. He won the 1848 election at the age of 35, getting 19,538 votes to Whig John H. Tweedy's 14,449 votes. Dewey was re-elected two years later, with a much lower turnout, winning with 16,649 votes to Whig Alexander L. Collins's 11,317 votes. However, Dewey chose not to run for a third term in 1852, instead moving to the Wisconsin senate, and becoming a state senator 1854–55. The man elected to succeed Dewey was Leonard J. Farrell from Watertown, New York. Farrell lived in Madison, where he was a prominent member of the Whig Party. The next governor was a Democrat, William A. Barstow, and in the 1855 gubernatorial elections, Barstow was declared the winner by 157 votes, with Arthur MacArthur elected lieutenant governor. However, there were many allegations of electoral fraud and on March 21, 1856, Barstow was forced to resign with MacArthur becoming the acting governor for four days. The Wisconsin Supreme Court ruled in favor of the Republican candidate, Coles Bashford, who was declared to have won the election by 1,009 votes.

REPUBLICAN GOVERNOR
Coles Bashford had been a Whig member of the Wisconsin Senate 1853–55, and when the Whig Party split over the issue of the abolition of slavery, he ran for a state assembly seat for the newly created Republican Party in 1855, before taking part in the gubernatorial elections later that year. After the state Supreme Court ruled in his favor, on March 25, 1856, he entered the state capitol with a copy of the court papers in hand, and, along with the sheriff, ordered MacArthur to vacate his office. Bashford then took up his office, becoming one of the first Republicans to be elected governor in the United States.

In 1857, he appointed William Noland, a barber and entrepreneur, as a notary public, the first African American to hold a state office in Wisconsin. He declined the re-nomination by the Republican Party. In the gubernatorial elections in 1857, fellow Republican Andrew W. Randall was elected, with Bashford leaving office on January 4, 1858. Several weeks later, there were allegations that he had been given bribes in exchange for land grants to a railroad company. Despite a cover-up, the scandal forced Bashford to flee the state. He moved to Arizona, where he held several positions. The Republican Party dominated Wisconsin politics from Bashford's election for most of the period until the 1958 gubernatorial election, with 25 of the 29 governors from the Republican Party.

For most of the 20th century, Wisconsin was the leading state in the production of dairy products, and farm policies and tariffs were major issues in the elections. During the early 20th century, the major figure on the Wisconsin political scene was Robert M. La Fol-

lette, Sr., nicknamed "Fighting Bob" La Follette. Born in Wisconsin of French ancestry, he was a member of the U.S. House of Representatives 1884–90, he supported a protective tariff, and was involved in drafting the Tariff Act of 1890. This led to a Democratic landslide, resulting in Benjamin Harrison elected as president, and George W. Peck elected as the Democratic governor of Wisconsin. On his return to Wisconsin, La Follette refused to accept a bribe offered by Philetus Sawyer, a powerful Wisconsin Republican, who wanted to influence the decision of a judge. La Follette was outraged by the offer, and soon became the leader of the progressive wing of the Wisconsin Republican Party. His Republican opponents became known as the Stalwarts; La Follette was elected as governor in 1900, with the support of Emanuel Lorenz Philipp, championing reforms including the introduction of the minimum wage, a workers' compensation scheme, open primary elections, and extending the franchise to women.

ROBERT LA FOLLETTE
Stepping down as governor in 1906, La Follette was elected to the U.S. Senate, and made a bid for the presidency in 1911, but Theodore Roosevelt defeated him. He opposed the United States going to war with Germany in 1917, and, in 1924 spoke out against the Communist-controlled Workers' Party, which stopped plans to nominate him as the presidential candidate of the Federated Farmer-Labor Party. In 1924, Robert La Follette ran for the Progressive Party in the presidential elections, and managed to win Wisconsin with 54.44 percent of the vote in his home state, heavily defeating Calvin Coolidge for the Republicans, and pushing Democrat John W. David into third place with a humiliating 8.17 percent of the vote.

Philip La Follette, the son of Robert La Follette, was elected governor of Wisconsin in 1930, served until 1933, and again 1935–39. After losing the 1938 election, he tried to launch the National Progressive Party of America as a third party, in the hopes of being able to field a candidate in the 1940 election if Franklin Roosevelt did not run for re-election. In the 1946 elections for the U.S. Senate, Robert M. La Follette, Jr., Philip's brother, lost the Republican primary election to Joseph R. McCarthy, who was to serve in the Senate for 10 years, and usher in the period known as McCarthyism. In 1951, liberal Republicans and Democrats decided to unite to try to vote out McCarthy, and were given help and support from Governor Walter Kohler, Jr. and Leonard Schmitt, a former Progressive politician who had become a maverick Republican attorney. Kohler was re-elected as governor, but this did not prevent McCarthy from winning the Republican Party primary.

The Democrats remained hopelessly divided between Henry Reuss, an attorney from Milwaukee, and Thomas E. Fairchild, a former attorney general, eventually narrowly choosing the latter. Fairchild then launched the campaign against McCarthy by attacking the incumbent senator's ethical standards and his voting record. However McCarthy had massive financial backing, and the support of newspapers ensuring his victory, as many urban blue-collar workers supported McCarthy's championing of the Taft-Hartley Act on labor management.

In 1958, Democrat Gaylord A. Nelson was elected governor of Wisconsin, and, in 1962, was succeeded by another Democratic governor, John W. Reynolds, who led a campaign for the introduction of a new state tax policy. In 1964, Republican Warren P. Knowles was elected governor in September 1964. Of the eight governors from Knowles to 2008, four have been Republican and four Democrats, showing resurgence in the two-party system. In presidential elections, Wisconsin voted for Lewis Cass, the Whig candidate in 1848, and Franklin Pierce for the Democrats in 1852. From 1856, when John Frémont was the first Republican Party candidate, Wisconsin has voted Republican in 23 of the 37 subsequent elections, only voting Democrat for Grover Cleveland in 1892; Woodrow Wilson in 1912; Franklin Roosevelt in 1932, 1936, and 1940; Lyndon B. Johnson in 1964; Jimmy Carter in 1976; and in all presidential elections from 1988 until 2004.

SEE ALSO: LaFollette, Robert M.; Presidential Election of 1924; Progressive Party; Whig Party.

BIBLIOGRAPHY. C.R. Burgchardt, *Robert M. La Follette Sr: The Voice of Conscience* (Greenwood Press, 1992); J.M. Cooper, Jr. "Why Wisconsin? the Badger State in the Progressive Era," *Wisconsin Magazine of History* (v.87/3, 2004); Michael Kades, "Incumbent without a Party: Robert M. La Follette, Jr., and the Wisconsin Republican Primary of 1946," *Wisconsin Magazine of History* (v.80/1, 1996); C.J. Svoboda, *Why and How Voters Vote in Gubernatorial Elections*, thesis (University of Wisconsin, 1995); R.C. Turner, "The Political Economy of Gubernatorial Smokestack Chasing: Bad Policy and Bad Politics?" *State Politics & Policy Quarterly* (v.3/3, 2003).

JUSTIN CORFIELD
GEELONG GRAMMAR SCHOOL, AUSTRALIA

Wyoming

THE STATE OF Wyoming was inhabited by Native American tribes long before the arrival of the first French trappers in the late 1700s. Gradually, settlers arrived, but the area was not opened up until it became a part of the Oregon Trail. By the 1850s, work had started on the Union Pacific Railroad that, in 1867, reached the town of Cheyenne, later to become the state capital. The Wyoming Territory was established in 1868, and in the following year it extended suffrage to women, becoming the first state to allow women to vote. This was, in part, to help Wyoming gain enough electors to achieve statehood. Wyoming was admitted to the Union on July 10, 1890.

Throughout its history, Wyoming has been a predominantly conservative state, and has traditionally voted Republican, with only two counties clearly Democratic. The first governor, Francis E. Warren, was a Republican. He was born in Massachusetts, and served in the American Civil War, before establishing a farm in what is now Wyoming. He was appointed governor of Wyoming Territory, in 1885, by President Chester A. Arthur, but was removed by Grover Cleveland in 1886, and reappointed by Benjamin Harrison in March 1889. In September–November 1890, he was elected as the first state governor of Wyoming. He was governor only briefly, before becoming a U.S. Senator. Dr. Amos Walker Barber succeeded him. Originally from Pennsylvania, Barber was elected as secretary of state, became acting governor, and then governor, remaining in office until 1893, whereupon he returned as secretary of state.

The third governor, John Eugene Osborne, a Democrat, defeated Barber in the 1892 gubernatorial election, with allegations of election irregularities. He remained governor until 1899, when Republican William A. Richards was elected, defeating rival candidates

William H. Holliday and Lewis C. Tidball. The next governor, DeForest Richards (no relation of William A. Richards), won the 1898 gubernatorial election, defeating Democrat Horace C. Alger by 1,394 votes. In the next gubernatorial election, in 1902, DeForest Richards defeated George T. Beck, the largest victory margin in the state thus far. However, Richards died four months into his second term, and was succeeded by Fenimore Chatterton, who became acting governor, and failed to win re-election in 1904. Part of this electoral defeat was the refusal by Chatterton to commute the death penalty imposed on Tom Horn, a murderer, was ultimately hanged for a murder that he may not have committed. John Brognard Okie, a Wyoming landowner and sheep rancher, ran for a seat in the Wyoming House of Representatives, and although he was declared the winner in a tight race, he was subsequently unseated following allegations of fraud.

ALTERNATING PARTIES

In 1905, Bryant Butler Brooks was elected governor of Wyoming, and was re-elected in 1907, the first governor of Wyoming who occupied the new governor's residence, completed in 1904. His successor was Joseph M. Carey, a Democrat, who had been in state politics since the 1870s. He had been a member of the U.S. House of Representatives 1885–90, and the U.S. Senate 1890–95. In 1912, Carey left the Republican Party and became an organizer for the Progressive Party, working to get Theodore Roosevelt re-elected. Two more Democrat governors succeeded Carey, and then Robert D. Carey, a Republican, was elected in 1919 as governor of Wyoming.

In the first part of the 20th century, Democrat and Republican governors alternated in office. Leslie A. Miller, a Democrat, became governor in 1933, and served for eight years, the first party of his term being the unexpired term of his predecessor, Frank Emerson. Miller was re-elected in 1935, but was defeated in 1939 by Nels H. Smith, a Republican. Smith held office for one term, and then lost the gubernatorial election to Lester C. Hunt, a Democrat. When Hunt was elected to the U.S. Senate, his successor, Republican Arthur G. Crane was the first of four Republican governors who controlled the state 1949–59. In the 1954 gubernatorial elections, the fourth of these governors, Milward Simpson only narrowly defeated Democrat William Jack by 56,275 votes (50.5 percent) to 55,163 votes (49.5 percent). Simpson then went on to lose the 1958 gubernatorial elections to John J. Hickey, a Democrat, who received 55,070 votes (48.9 percent) to Simpson's 52,488 votes (46.6 percent). Simpson later gained a seat in the U.S. Senate and, along with Senator Barry Goldwater of Arizona, was one of the six Republican senators who voted against the Civil Rights Bill in 1964. Simpson's son, Alan Kooi Simpson, was a moderate Republican in the Senate 1979–97.

The 1958 elections throughout the United States resulted in many Democrat victories, and John J. Hickey's victory in the Wyoming gubernatorial election was a clear example of this trend in the U.S. political scene. In the 1960 U.S. presidential election, Richard M. Nixon carried the state with 77,551 votes (55 percent) to John F. Kennedy's 63,331 votes (45 percent), with Clifford P. Hansen, a Republican, winning the 1962 gubernatorial elections by 64,970 votes (54.5 percent) to 54,298 votes (45.5 percent) for the incumbent Jack R. Gage.

In the 1964 U.S. presidential election, Lyndon B. Johnson won in a landslide, defeating Barry Goldwater by 80,718 votes (56.5 percent) to 61,998 votes (43.5 percent). The backlash against Goldwater, and also the John Birch Society, which campaigned heavily for Goldwater, saw Wyoming re-elect its Democratic senatorial incumbent, and the defeat of the Republican incumbent in the state's single House seat. The Democrats took control of the state House, and in the state Senate, they reduced Republican control to one vote.

REPUBLICAN STRONGHOLD

Since 1964, Wyoming has always voted Republican in presidential elections, but it has had Democrat governors for all but eight years since 1975. In 1966, Stanley K. Hathaway, a Republican, was elected as governor, and remained in office for eight years (two terms), later briefly serving as Gerald Ford's secretary of the interior. The 1968 U.S. presidential election resulted in victory for Richard M. Nixon who received 70,927 votes (55.8 percent), to Hubert H. Humphrey's 45,173 votes (35.5 percent), and George Wallace's 11,105 votes (8.7 percent). Although Wyoming did vote for Richard M. Nixon in 1972, in 1974 the state elected Edgar J. Herschler from Democratic Party as its governor. His term in office coincided with an energy boom, and Herschler served three terms as governor, something that was subsequently stopped with the 1992 statute on limiting gubernatorial terms. In 1982, Herschler easily defeated Warren Morton, a wealthy oil man, although the Republicans continued to hold power in both houses of the state legislature except for 1975–77. Dick Cheney represented Wyoming in the U.S. Congress 1979–89, later moving to Texas.

In 1986, Michael John "Mike" Sullivan was elected governor, defeating Pete Simpson in a surprise result. Sullivan held office for two terms. In the 1988 senatorial election, John Vinish, a Democrat, came close to defeating Republican Malcom Wallop. Sullivan's 1990 re-election was a landslide when he ran against Mary Hansen Mead, daughter of former state governor, Clifford P. Hansen. Sullivan had 104,638 votes (65.4 percent) to 55,471 votes (34.6 percent) for Mead; she only gained 4,311 more votes than she had in the Republican Party primary, indicating that her election campaign strategy failed to reach beyond her Republican supporters. In 1994, Jim Geringer, a Republican, was elected governor, serving two terms. In 2002, David Duane "Dave" Freudenthal, a Democrat, was elected as governor, and was re-elected in 2006.

Wyoming was to play a brief, but interesting, role in the early stages of the 2000 U.S. presidential election. With George W. Bush winning the Republican Party primaries, just before his announcement of Dick Cheney as his running mate, Cheney was forced to make a quick flight to Wyoming. As the president and the vice president on a presidential ticket could not be registered in the same state, Cheney, who had lived in Texas, and had registered there, was initially prevented from nomination as Bush's running mate. However, Cheney was quickly able to register as a voter in Wyoming. Their 2006 election was one of the closest in the United States, with incumbent Republican Congresswoman Barbara Cubin being re-elected with a majority of just 1,200 votes.

SEE ALSO: Progressive Party; Suffrage.

BIBLIOGRAPHY. B.B. Brooks, *Memoirs of Bryant B. Brooks: Cowboy, Trapper, Lumberman, Stockman, Oilman, Banker, and Governor of Wyoming* (Arthur H. Clark Co., 1939); Gregg Cawley and Janet Clark, *The Equality State: Government and Politics in Wyoming* (Eddie Bowers Publishing Co., 1988); Cal Clark and Janet Clark. "Wyoming Political Surprises in the Late 1980s: Deviating Elections in a Conservative Republican State," *Great Plains Quarterly* (v.11/3, 1991); J.T. Hinckley, "The 1964 Election in Wyoming," *Western Political Quarterly* (v.18/2, 1965); Loren Jost, "The Short and Controversial Political Career of Fremont County Sheepman J.B. Okie," *Wind River Mountaineer* (v.16/1, 2001); T.R. Miller, *State Government: Politics in Wyoming* (Kendall/Hunt Publishing Co., 1985); J.B. Richard, "The 1970 Election in Wyoming," *Western Political Quarterly* (v.24/2, 1971); Oliver Walter, *Equality State: Government and Politics in Wyoming* (Eddie Bowers Publishing Co., 2000).

JUSTIN CORFIELD
GEELONG GRAMMAR SCHOOL, AUSTRALIA

Zogby, John (1948–)

JOHN ZOGBY IS one of the best-known political pollsters in America, yet he is also quite controversial. Zogby's declared ambition is to become the Gallup of his generation, the brand name in polling worldwide. He had some important successes, most notably with the 1996 and 2000 presidential elections, but also some failures, as in 2004, when he called the election for Kerry. His methods are unconventional, drawing criticism from other pollsters. Zogby describes himself as a Democrat; but he describes his organization as independent and nonpartisan, doing work for both parties.

Zogby is a second generation Lebanese American, born and raised in Utica, New York. He attended Le Moyne College, a Jesuit school in Syracuse, and received a graduate degree in history from Syracuse University. He then returned to Utica where he combined teaching with consumer activism. In 1981, he made an unsuccessful attempt to get the Democratic nomination for mayor of Utica. In the early 1980s, he and his brother James were involved in Arab-American political activism, and then in 1984 they chose different careers. John started his own polling organization, Zogby International, which has 50 full-time employees and $5 million in annual sales, while James is head of the Arab-American Institute. John Zogby has polled in various places outside the United States, including Canada, Mexico, Israel, and Iran.

Zogby's first breakthrough came in 1994, when he polled the gubernatorial election in New York. He was the only pollster who indicated that the Republican challenger George Pataki would win, while all others claimed that the incumbent, Governor Mario Cuomo, would be re-elected. Pataki's victory brought Zogby in to the national spotlight. Two years later, when most polls indicated that Bill Clinton's victory over Bob Dole would be in the double-digits, Zogby was once more a lone voice, predicting a narrower margin of only 8.1 percent (the actual difference was 8.4 percent). The 2000 election was another triumph for Zogby. For the whole month of October, various polls showed George W. Bush far ahead in the lead. However, right before the election, Zogby's tracking polls showed Gore closing the gap, forecasting a tight contest. However, the 2004 election was an embarrassment for Zogby, who before the election predicted an easy victory for Kerry, with at least 311 electoral votes. On Election Day, Zogby called the election for Kerry. In his defense, Zogby argues that his final polls were on target, and his mistake was to make a prediction based on preliminary results.

Probably the most controversial of all of Zogby's methods is his weighting of the results by party. Weighting is a technique that is regularly employed in polling in order to make the sample more like the actual population from which the sample is drawn. For instance, if a pollster is interested in a representative sample of the population of the United States, but only six percent of the sample is African American, then each African American in the sample is given twice the weight of other individuals, so that the impact of African Americans in the sample becomes the same as in the population of the United States (12 percent).

According to Zogby, weighting should not be limited to race or gender, but extended to partisanship as well. The main reason is that conservatives tend to be more reluctant to answer to pollsters, and, therefore, a typical poll tends to underestimate the level of Republican support. To this, critics counter that partisanship is unlike race or gender; it is the very thing that is being studied, and it is unscientific to adjust the results based on prior assumptions about the share of Democrats and Republicans in the population.

SEE ALSO: Gallup, George; Mitofsky, Warren Jay; Polling and Election Studies Organizations.

BIBLIOGRAPHY. Larissa MacFarquhar, "The Pollster: Does John Zogby Know Who Will Win the Election?" *New Yorker* (October 18, 2004); Zogby International, www.zogby.com (cited August 2007).

FLORIN FESNIC
UNIVERSITY OF BUCHAREST

Glossary

Definitions of terms used in American campaigns and elections.

Absentee Ballot
A mailable paper ballot that is used by voters who will not be able to vote (or choose not to vote) at their home precinct on election day.

Access
The special ability of campaign contributors to meet, talk by telephone, and correspond personally with elected officials in order to "make their case" for or against a particular law, policy, regulation, appointment, and so forth.

Affiliated Committees
All political committees established, financed, or controlled by the same person, group, corporation, or labor union. Under federal law, committees affiliated with one another are considered one political committee for purposes of contribution limits.

Auction-Block Elections
Elections in which campaign giving is so dominated by vested-interest contributors as to create the impression, if not the reality, that candidates are "for sale" to the highest "bidders." These large contributors expect to "buy" access, if not actual votes, in exchange for donations.

Ballot
A piece of paper listing the candidates running for office. A ballot is used to cast a vote.

Ballot Initiative
A ballot initiative is a proposed piece of legislation that people can vote on; also called a ballot measure, referendum, or proposition.

Best Effort
A phrase taken from Federal Election Commission regulations used by candidates' campaign committees to excuse their failure to provide the FEC with complete disclosure information concerning their contributors. For example, when only the name and address, but not the employer or occupation, of a contributor is given on a campaign finance form, the words "best effort" will sometimes be written in. Some states require candidates to return checks to contributors if sufficient disclosure information is not provided.

Bicameral
Consisting of two legislative branches, such as the U.S. Congress, which consists of the House of Representatives and the Senate.

Bill of Rights

The Bill of Rights is the first 10 amendments to the U.S. Constitution. These amendments were ratified on December 15, 1791. The Bill of Rights was proposed to ensure that individuals would have civil rights and could avoid the tyranny of an overly-powerful central government.

Bipartisan

Bipartisan refers to members of the two major political parties, the Democrats and the Republicans, supporting issues according to their party's platform.

Blanket Primary

A primary election in which the names of all the candidates for all of the parties are on one ballot.

Buckley v. Valeo

A 1976 U.S. Supreme Court case in which the majority ruled that mandatory limits on campaign spending (candidates' spending of their own money), and independent expenditures are violations of the constitutional right to free speech and, thus, prohibited. The same decision upheld the constitutionality of limits on individual and committee contributions to candidates, public financing for presidential elections, and campaign contribution disclosure. The Buckley ruling applies to state and local, as well as federal, elections.

Bundling

The practice of pooling individual contributions from various people—often those employed by the same business or in the same profession—in order to maximize the political influence of the bundler. Typically, all of the checks collected in this way are sent or delivered to candidates on the same day. Political Action Committees and political party committees that have already given the maximum allowed by law often bundle individual contributions as a way of delivering even more money to candidates.

Campaign

A series of political actions (such as advertisements, public appearances, and debates) that are used to help a candidate get elected to office.

Campaign Spending Limit

A maximum amount that a candidate's campaign can spend during the election period. In its 1976 *Buckley v. Valeo* decision, the U.S. Supreme Court ruled that campaign spending limits constitute a violation of free speech unless voluntarily accepted, or accepted in exchange for public financing or other public resources. Voluntary campaign spending limits exist in 11 states and in primary and general elections for president.

Candidate

Any person who is running for an office.

Candidate Spending Limit

A maximum amount that a candidate can give or loan to his or her own campaign. According to the U.S. Supreme Court's 1976 *Buckley v. Valeo* decision, mandatory limits on candidate spending violate the Constitution's guarantee of free speech.

Cash Constituents

A politician's major campaign contributors, as distinguished from his or her ordinary constituents—the voters. The interests of cash constituents are usually linked to elected officials' committee assignments or political authority rather than to the areas they represent.

Cash Cow Committee

A legislative committee, such as banking or commerce, whose members receive higher-than-average amounts of campaign contributions from the economic interests the committee oversees.

Cashing In

Getting favorable treatment, often worth millions of dollars, from elected officials to whom one has given large campaign contributions. Such treatment can take the form of tax breaks, subsidies, regulatory exemptions, or other actions and non-actions (for example, stalling).

Caucus

An informal meeting at which potential voters and candidates or their representatives talk about the issues and their preferred candidate, and then decide which candidate they support and which delegates to send to their political party's convention.

Ceiling

An upper limit on campaign expenditures. Sometimes also refers to the upper limit on what individuals, Political Action Committees, and political parties can contribute.

Challenger

The candidate trying to unseat the person in office (incumbent).

Christmas Tree Bill

A piece of legislation that includes an assortment of special provisions—for example, tax breaks, subsidies, regulatory exemptions—often incorporated in the bill for the benefit of lawmakers' campaign contributors.

Clean Resources

Government funding and other campaign assets, such as media vouchers and free postage, that come from the public as a whole rather than from private interests.

Closed Primary

Closed primaries are elections in which only those voters who have registered with a particular political party can vote. For example, if it is a Republican primary election, only registered Republicans can vote (because that election is to choose the Republican candidate to run for office in the general election).

Compliance Funds

Money raised by major-party presidential nominees that is used for legal and accounting expenses incurred in the process of satisfying the reporting and other requirements of federal campaign finance laws. Used by candidates as a way of getting around the prohibition on fundraising during the presidential general election.

Conduit

A person, group, or organization that forwards others' contributions to candidates, a legal activity under federal law. Such contributions always count against the federal contribution limit for the donors, and sometimes against the limit for the conduit as well (in cases in which the conduit exercises contribution direction and control).

Conflict of Interest

A public official using his or her public office for private gain. For example, when a judge takes money from defendants and prosecutors, or when government officials take campaign contributions from people whose economic interests are affected by government policy-making.

Congress

The U.S. Congress is divided into the Senate and the House of Representatives. There are currently 100 Senators (2 from each state) and 435 members of the House of Representatives. Representatives are divided by population among the states, with each state having at least 1 representative.

Congressional District

An area within a state from which a member of the House of Representatives is elected. There are 435 Congressional districts. Each district has about 570,000 people. Seats in the House of Representatives are reapportioned every 10 years; since the number of Representatives is set to 435, some areas lose Representatives and others gain some.

Conservative

People who generally prefer current conditions and oppose changes. Conservatives are often referred to as the right wing.

Contribution

Money, or anything else of value (such as mailing lists, telephones, billboard space) given to a candidate's campaign committee, political party, or Political Action Committee by an individual or organization.

Contribution Limit

A maximum amount of money that an individual, Political Action Committee (PAC), or political party may contribute to a candidate's campaign committee, a PAC, or a political party. The federal government and most states impose some kind of limits on contributions to candidates from individuals and PACs.

Convention

An official meeting of the delegates of a political party at which they choose their candidates and decide upon their party platform.

Coordinated Expenditure

In federal elections, money spent by political parties on behalf of their presidential and congressional candidates in the general election. Such expenditures are limited by law, and are not direct payments to candidates, but payments by the parties to cover candidates' campaign costs.

Corruption Cost

The billions of dollars that taxpayers annually pay for unnecessary tax breaks, subsidies, regulatory exemptions, and so forth that can be at least partially, if not entirely, attributed to lawmakers' desire to gain or retain the support of big-money campaign contributors. When calculating what our current system of privately financed elections costs (and what a system of publicly financed elections would cost), the corruption cost must be factored in.

DCCC

Democratic Congressional Campaign Committee; run by Democratic members of the U.S. House of Representatives for the purpose of raising money to support Democratic candidates for the House. The DCCC raised $19.4 million during the 1993–94 election cycle.

Debate

A formal, public political discussion involving two or more candidates for office. In a debate, candidates state and defend their positions on major issues. Debates are often held in public places or are broadcast on radio, television, and/or on the internet.

Debt Retirement

The practice of raising additional campaign funds after the election is over in order to pay off the candidate's campaign debt.

Delegate

A person chosen to represent a local political party at a political convention.

Democratically Financed Elections

An electoral system in which candidates' campaigns are funded with resources that come from the people as a whole, rather than an elite few. Also, a specific legislative proposal under which eligible candidates who pledge not to accept or spend any private money whatsoever during the primary and general election periods would receive equal amounts of full public financing with which to conduct their campaigns.

Democratic Party

A major U.S. political party. The symbol of the Democratic party is the donkey. The first Democratic U.S. President was Andrew Jackson.

Disclosure

The requirement that candidates, political parties, and Political Action Committees (PACs) report the amounts and sources of their campaign contributions. Federal candidates must list each contributor's name, address, employer, and occupation. As of 1994, 23 states did not require disclosure of employer and occupation.

DNC

Democratic National Committee; the leadership, administrative, and fundraising arm of the national Democratic Party. Raises money, including "soft money," for party activities.

Dollar Politics

A political process based on money rather than votes. "If the founding fathers had wanted American democracy to use dollar bills as ballots, they would have placed cash registers where ballot boxes now stand." — Amitai Etzioni, author of *Capital Corruption*.

Double Giving

The practice of making campaign contributions to both (or all) candidates or parties during an election, as a way of "hedging one's bets" and having access to whomever wins.

DSCC

Democratic Senatorial Campaign Committee; run by Democratic members of the U.S. Senate for the purpose of raising money to support Democratic candidates for the Senate. The DSCC raised $26.4 million during the 1993–94 election cycle.

Earmarking

Occurs when a contributor writes a check to, for example, the Democratic National Committee (DNC) in response to a solicitation and designates through a notation on the check the name of a candidate for whom the contribution is intended. In this case, the DNC acts as a conduit and must identity the contribution and the contributor in federal disclosure reports.

Election Cycle

The period that extends from the day after the previous general election to the day of the next general election. The election cycles for a U.S. Representative, U.S. Senator, and the President are two years, six years, and four years, respectively. General elections are usually held the first week in November.

Electoral College

A group of people who formally elect the president of the United States. The Electoral College is composed of delegates from each state, plus the District of Columbia. The number of delegates from each state is equal to the sum of that state's Senators plus Representatives. According to the U.S. Constitution, the electors chosen by popular vote assemble in their respective state capitals on the first Monday after the second Wednesday in December and vote for president. Electors are supposed to vote for the candidate who received a plurality of votes in the state or area they represent. To become president of the United States, a candidate must receive more than half of the Electoral College votes, 270 out of 538 votes.

Equal Protection

Refers to the Equal Protection clause of the Fourteenth Amendment to the U.S. Constitution. The guarantee of "equal protection of the law" has been evoked to challenge the constitutionality of today's system of privately financed elections. It is alleged that, under such a system, citizens without access to wealth are denied their right to equal political opportunity.

Executive Branch

The part of the U.S. government that administers the laws and other affairs of the government; it includes the President, the President's staff, executive agencies (the Office of Management and Budget, the National Security Council, and so on.) and Cabinet departments (such as the State Department, the Dept. of Defense, the Dept. of Agriculture, etc.).

Exit Poll

A poll taken as people leave the voting booth. Exit polls are used to predict the outcome of the election before the polls are closed.

Express Advocacy

Paying for political advertisements and other mass communications that benefit particular candidates, a practice that is regulated by federal and state election law. Groups and individuals who pay for such communications sometimes claim that they were not engaged in express advocacy but rather issue advocacy, a constitutionally protected exercise of free speech and, therefore, not subject to contribution limits. The distinction between the two forms of advocacy is often unclear.

Fat Cat

A wealthy individual who makes large campaign contributions. Also, a member of a guerrilla theater troupe which stages actions outside political fundraisers; the actors dress like corpulent felines smoking cigars and passing out bundles of cash to politicians on behalf of vested interests.

Federal Election Campaign Act (FECA)

Congressional legislation enacted in 1971 and amended in 1974, 1976, and 1979. FECA incorporates all federal law pertaining to federal elections. Limits individual contributions to $1,000 per election to a federal candidate; $5,000 to a Political Action Committee (PAC) per calendar year; $20,000 to a national party per calendar year; and an aggregate of $25,000 per year to all federal candidates, PACs, and national parties. Also the Federal Election Campaign Act limits PAC contributions to federal candidates to $5,000 per election.

Federal Election Commission (FEC)

The U.S. government's monitoring and enforcement agency for federal elections. Created in 1974, the FEC consists of six commissioners who are appointed by the President and confirmed by the U.S. Senate and serve six-year terms. By law, no more than three commissioners may be of the same political party.

Financially Competitive

An unofficial but important phrase used by election-watchers to refer to a candidate who has at least half as much campaign money as her or his competitor.

Fingerprinting

The process of identifying contributors by determining their addresses, occupations, employers, economic interests, political and ideological affiliations, and spouses and children who may have contributed.

Floor

A minimum or set amount of public financing or other public resources (for example, free media or postage) available to all eligible candidates.

Follow the Money

Originally, the phrase is said to have been used by "Deep Throat" to tell reporters Bob Woodward and Carl Bernstein how to find out who was behind the 1972 Watergate break-in. Now, an expression indicating that one needs to look at the sources of elected officials' campaign contributions in order to understand how, and in whose interests, public policy is made.

Full Public Financing

An arrangement under which all of the campaign funds used by candidates come from the government and none comes from private sources.

General Election

The election that follows political parties' selection of their nominees (via caucus, convention, or primary election).

Gerrymandering

A process in which a voting district is broken up or the physical boundaries of a voting district are changed in order to make it easier for one political party to win future elections. The term gerrymander was coined in 1812 when a county in Massachusetts was redistricted into a salamander-like shape by Gov. Elbridge Gerry for political purposes. His last name was combined with the word salamander to get "gerrymander."

Hard Money

Federally regulated campaign contributions and other moneys spent for the purpose of influencing the outcome of a federal election.

Homemaker

Occupation often listed on campaign finance reports for wives of major contributors who give through their spouses (and other family members) as a legal way of getting around individual contribution limits.

Honest Graft

The overt, unabashed (and legal) taking of money, in the form of campaign contributions, from groups and individuals who expect and usually get privileged access and, often, various kinds of legislative and regulatory favors. "I've made a big fortune out of the game and I'm gettin' richer every day, but I've not gone in for dishonest graft ... There's honest graft and I'm an example of how it works." — George Washington Plunkett, Tammany Hall boss, circa 1905.

Honorarium

A fee for giving a speech or making a public appearance. Members of the executive branch of the federal government are prohibited from receiving honoraria, as are members of the U.S. House (since 1989) and U.S. Senate (since 1991), although they may designate a charity to which an honorarium, of up to $2,000 per speech, may be sent.

House of Representatives

The House of Representatives is part of Congress; they propose and vote on legislation (laws). There are 435 members of the House of Representatives (divided by population among the states, with each state having at least 1 representative). There are 435 Congressional districts. Each district has about 570,000 people. Seats (positions) in the House of Representatives are reapportioned every 10 years; the number of Representatives is set at 435, some areas lose Representatives and others gain some. Representatives are elected to a term of two years.

Ideological Contributor

A classification used by campaign finance analysts to denote a person or group who makes a political donation supporting a particular philosophy (for example, libertarianism) or issue (environmental protection)—as opposed to business contributors and labor contributors.

Ideological PAC

A term used by campaign finance analysts, not one defined by law, referring to a Political Action Committee (PAC) organized around an idea, philosophy, issue, or political party—as opposed to a business or labor PAC.

Incumbent

Person holding an elected office. Usually refers to an elected official running for re-election.

Independent

A person who is not associated with any political party.

Independent Expenditure

An expenditure of money for advertisements or other communications which expressly advocate the election or defeat of a candidate, which is not made in conjunction or coordination with any candidate or candidate's campaign committee. The U.S. Supreme Court has ruled that independent expenditures constitute free speech and cannot be limited by law.

Individual Contribution

Money contributed to a candidate's campaign committee, a Political Action Committee (PAC), or a political party by a single person (or more than one person on a single check), as opposed to a committee, or PAC, contribution.

In-Kind Contribution

A contribution of goods, services, or property offered free or at less than the usual charge.

In-State (In-District) Contribution

Money donated to a candidate's campaign committee by an individual residing in the state (or district) in which the election is being held.

Interested Money

Campaign contributions from individuals and groups that have a vested interest (usually economic) in a particular legislative or regulatory matter.

Issue Advocacy

A constitutionally-protected form of free speech to which contribution limits do not apply, involving the use of political advertisements and other mass communications that promote a position regarding a political issue, such as military spending or welfare reform. Groups and individuals who pay for such communications have sometimes been charged with express advocacy—that is, with advocacy that benefits particular candidates, a practice which is regulated by federal and state election law.

Joint Fundraiser

A fundraising event sponsored by more than one candidate committee, Political Action Committee (PAC), or party committee.

Judicial Branch

The part of the U.S. government that settles disputes and administers justice. The judicial branch is made up of the court system, including U.S. District Courts, many Federal courts, the U.S. Court of Appeals, and the Supreme Court.

Leadership PAC

A Political Action Committee (PAC) run by one or more elected officials. Contributions to leadership PACs are not treated as contributions to the elected officials and do not count against limits on giving to those officials.

Legislative Branch

The part of the U.S. government that makes the laws and appropriates funds. The Legislative Branch includes the U.S. House of Representative and Senate (plus congressional staffs and committees) and support agencies (such as the General Accounting Office, the Congressional Budget Office, the Library of Congress).

Legislative Favor

Something a legislator does to benefit his or her campaign contributors.

Level Playing Field

An electoral contest in which competing candidates have equal resources with which to conduct their campaigns.

Liberals

People who generally look to reform current conditions. Liberals are often referred to as the left wing.

Lobbyist

A person who tries to influence elected officials to take action, or non-action, favorable to his or her interests, beliefs, or clients.

Loophole

A way of avoiding or getting around the law, usually associated with an omission or ambiguity in the law itself.

Lowest Unit Rate

The cheapest prices for a radio or TV advertisements that broadcasters offer to their regular customers. Under various federal campaign finance reform proposals, broadcasters would have to offer the same prices, or rates, to federal candidates and their campaign committees.

Matching Funds

Public money given in a specific ratio (for example, 1:1, 2:1, or 3:1) to candidates who succeed in raising prescribed amounts of private money in individual contributions of a certain size. During presidential primaries, for example, the federal government will match up to $250 of an individual's total contributions to eligible presidential candidates. Also a provision in the Democratically Financed Elections proposal whereby candidates who choose the public financing option get additional money if independent expenditures are made against them or if privately-financed opponents spend more than the public financing amount.

Maxing Out

Making campaign contributions to candidates, Political Action Committees (PACs), and parties up to the limit allowed by law. Federal election law, for example, allows individuals to give a maximum of $1,000 per candidate per election (primaries and run-offs are counted as separate elections); $5,000 to a PAC per calendar year; $20,000 to a national political party per calendar year; and a total of $25,000 to candidates, PACs, and parties per calendar year.

McCain-Feingold Law

Also called the Bipartisan Campaign Reform Act. It is a law that attempted to reduce the influence of people giving "soft money" to politicians. The law limits the amount of "soft money" that can be given to a political party and how much can be spent on political advertising. This law was named for its sponsors, John McCain, Republican Senator from Arizona, and Russell Feingold, Democratic Senator from Wisconsin.

Midterm Election

A general election that does not coincide with a presidential election year, but occurs two years into the term of a president. In a midterm election, some members of the U.S. Senate, all members of the House of Representatives, and many state and local positions are voted on.

Money Laundering

Making a campaign contribution to an elected official (or to a campaign committee, Political Action Committee, or political party) through one or more third parties— as a device for disguising the source of a contribution and getting around contribution limits.

Money Trail

The flow of private dollars from particular vested interests into the campaign coffers, leadership Political Action Committees, foundations, and favorite causes of particular elected officials, or groups of elected officials (such as those who sit on a particular committee).

Multi-Candidate Committee

The Federal Election Committee's designation for a political committee that has made contributions to at least five federal candidates.

Non-Connected Committee

The Federal Election Committee's designation for a free-standing Political Action Committee, such as EMILY's List, that has no sponsoring or parent organization.

Non-Party Committee

Federal Election Committee term for any political committee not operated by a political party. The term makes no distinction between Political Action Committees (PACs) and other non-party committees (for example, candidate committees) even though almost all the non-party committee contributions listed on federal candidates' campaign reports are from PACs.

NRCC

National Republican Congressional Committee; run by Republican members of the U.S. House of Representatives for the purpose of raising money to support Republican candidates for the House.

NRSC

National Republican Senatorial Committee; run by Republican members of the U.S. Senate to raise money to support Republican candidates for the Senate.

Open Primary

A primary in which all registered voters can vote, regardless of in which party they are registered.

Open-Seat Election

An election in which no incumbent is running.

Out-of-State (Out-of-District) Contribution

Money donated to a candidate's campaign committee by an individual residing outside the state (or district) in which the election is being held.

Partial Public Financing

An arrangement under which a portion of the campaign funds used by candidates comes from the government, usually in the form of a grant that matches private money raised. Twenty-three states provide partial public financing to candidates, either directly or via political parties. The federal government provides partial public financing to candidates in presidential primaries.

Payoff

The return on a campaign investment made by a vested-interest contributor, for example, special appointments (such as ambassadorships), tax breaks, subsidies, regulatory exemptions, committee action to approve or block particular legislation.

Permanent Campaign

The common practice of continuous fundraising throughout one's term in office, in order to have as much money on hand as possible for the next election, thus discouraging prospective challengers.

Personal Use

Expenditure of campaign funds for such things as the candidate's wardrobe, family vacations, or mortgage payments.

Platform

A formal written document that states a political party's stances on important issues and its goals for the future.

Plurality

In most elections, the candidate who gets more votes than anyone else is the winner (even if it is not more than half of the votes). That person is said to have a plurality of the votes.

Plutocracy

The wealthy elite who dominate American politics by virtue of public officials' dependence on their campaign contributions, or by virtue of their ability to use their money to win major public office themselves.

Pockets of a Politician's Coat

An expression coined by Kent Cooper of the Federal Election Commission that refers to the various accounts for which politicians can solicit funds from contributors who may want to gain access and influence. Examples include politicians' re-election committees, soft money accounts for contributions to state and local parties, their favorite charities, their leadership Political Action

Committees, non-profit foundations they head, their legal defense funds, and politicians' own pockets for receiving personal loans, all-expenses-paid family vacations, the free use of cars, planes, accommodations, etc.

Political Action Committee (PAC)

A popular term for a political committee that is not a candidate's campaign committee or a party committee, and that is organized for the purpose of raising and spending money to elect and defeat candidates. Most PACs represent business, labor, or ideological interests.

Political Foundation

A non-profit, tax-exempt organization set up by, or on behalf of, an elected official for the stated purpose of conducting public education. In practice, such foundations are often used to advance the political careers of particular politicians; because such foundations can accept gifts of any size, moneyed interests use them to curry favor with politicians without the constraint of campaign contribution limits.

Political Party

An organized group of people with common values and goals, who try to get their candidates elected to office. The Democrats and the Republicans are the two major political parties in the United States today.

Poll Tax

Money that must be paid in order to vote. Poll taxes in some places in the United States were used to keep many poor people from voting as they could not afford to pay the tax. The Twenty-Fourth Amendment to the Constitution, ratified in 1964, made poll taxes illegal.

Popular Vote

The result of the votes of the eligible voters. The winner of the popular vote usually wins the election, but not always; sometimes the outcome of the vote of the Electoral College is different.

Precinct

The smallest geographic area in U.S. voting subdivisions, in which local party officials are elected. A precinct usually includes from 200 to 1,000 voters. Each precinct has an elected precinct captain, the neighborhood party leader. The purpose of a precinct is to vote for a candidate and to elect delegates who will go to the city or county convention, and relay the precinct's vote for that candidate.

Price of Admission
The amount of money it takes to be elected to a major public office. For example, during the 1994 congressional elections, the average winner spent $516,000, and those challengers who spent less than $150,000 lost 100 percent of the time.

Primary
An intra-party election for the purpose of determining the party's nominee in the general election.

Primary Election
An election to choose a political party's candidate for office. The winning candidates from each party will later go up against each other in the general election.

Principal Campaign Committee
The Federal Election Committee's designation for the main (or only) committee authorized by the candidate to raise and expend funds to promote his or her election or re-election.

Protest Vote
A vote for a third-party candidate (who is not likely to win) that is meant to show displeasure with the mainstream candidates or parties.

Public Financing
Campaign money supplied by the government to eligible candidates. The federal government provides presidential candidates with matching public funds in the primary and full public financing in the general election. Twenty-three states provide partial public financing to candidates for various state offices and/or to political parties.

Qualifying Contribution
A very small campaign contribution (for example, $5) to a candidate, which the candidate uses to demonstrate public support and, thus, become eligible for public financing. See "Democratically Financed Elections."

Rainmaker
A person who raises large sums of money on behalf of a candidate for public office.

Redistricting
A process in which the physical boundaries of a voting district are changed.

Referendum
Also called a ballot measure, initiative or proposition. A ballot initiative is a proposed piece of legislation that the public can vote on.

Representative Democracy
A government in which the adult citizens of the country vote to elect the country's leaders. These elected leaders make the governmental decisions.

Republican Party
A major U.S. political party also known as the G.O.P. (Grand Old Party). The symbol of the Republican party is the elephant. The Republican party was founded as an anti-slavery party in the mid-1800s. The first Republican president was Abraham Lincoln.

RNC
Republican National Committee; the leadership, administrative, and fundraising arm of the national Republican Party. Raises money, including soft money, for party activities.

Run-Off
A final, elimination election used to determine the winner among the highest vote-getters in the previous, just-held election.

Salting
A practice permitted by the Federal Election Committee whereby candidates are allowed to salt their contributor lists with up to ten pseudonyms accompanied by real addresses, as a way to catch using their lists to solicit money, which is prohibited by federal law.

Seed Money
Limited-size contributions given prior to the primary campaign period to prospective candidates who are in the process of raising qualifying contributions or exploring the feasibility of running for office.

Senate
The Senate is part of Congress. Senators propose and vote on legislation. There are 100 members of the Sen-

ate, two Senators for each state. Senators are elected to a term of 6 years.

Separate Segregated Fund
The Federal Election Committee's designation for a Political Action Committee established by a corporation or labor organization.

Soft Money
Political money raised by national and state parties that is not regulated by federal campaign finance law because, in theory, it is for generic party-building activities such as getting out the vote. In practice, it is often used to benefit specific federal candidates, and, thus, it has become a major vehicle for skirting the limitations and restrictions of federal law.

Solicitation
A request for a campaign contribution.

Stealth Campaign
The invisible campaign that the public does not see in which candidates quietly solicit campaign contributions from, and often make implicit commitments to, wealthy donors.

Straw Vote
An unofficial vote used to predict an election's outcome.

Suffrage
The right or privilege of voting.

Suffragette
A person who campaigned for the right of women to vote. The Nineteenth amendment (ratified in 1920) to the U.S. Constitution gave women the right to vote.

Super Tuesday
A day on which many primaries are held. This term originated in 1988, when many southern states decided to hold their primaries on the same day to try to boost their political importance (in relation to the importance of the New Hampshire primary and Iowa caucuses).

Surplus Funds
Campaign money left over after the election and the payment of all of the campaign's outstanding bills and debts.

Swing Voters
Voters who do not have allegiance to a particular political party.

Targeting
The practice by major campaign contributors of channeling donations to legislators and other elected officials best situated to further the contributors' agendas.

Tax Add-On
A provision in 11 states' tax laws that allows state taxpayers to add one or more additional dollars to their annual income tax bill in order to pay for the partial public financing of designated state elections. A voluntary tax surcharge.

Tax Check-Off
A provision in federal and 13 states' tax laws that allows taxpayers to earmark their income-tax dollars to pay for partial public financing of designated elections.

Tax Credits
A form of indirect public financing used in Minnesota, Oregon, and Washington, D.C., meant to encourage small individual campaign contributions and, in some cases, compliance with voluntary spending limits. For example, Oregon offers a tax credit, in the form of a refund, of up to $50 for contributions made to political parties, groups supporting or opposing ballot measures, and candidates who comply with voluntary spending limits.

Tax Deductions
A form of indirect public financing used in Arizona, California, Hawaii, North Carolina, and Oklahoma as a way of encouraging small individual contributions. For example, Oklahoma offers tax deductions of up to $100 for contributions to candidates and political parties.

Term Limits
Limits on the length of time that a politician can stay in office. For example, the President of the United States is limited to two four-year terms of office.

Third Party
Any political party other than the two major parties (currently the Democrats and Republicans).

Time Limits
State-imposed restrictions on the period of time during which candidates for state office may accept campaign contributions.

Tip of the Iceberg
That part of the money trail that is obvious from campaign disclosure reports. The unseen portion—for example, contributions from sources whose interests are hard to identify, contributions made through third parties, and contributions to entities favored by politicians, but not officially connected to their re-election campaigns.

U.S. Constitution
The official document that is the basis of government and law in the United States. It was written in 1787, and ratified in 1789. Many amendments have been added since then.

Vested Interest
A person or group that has an economic or ideological stake in the legislative and regulatory actions of government. Sometimes called a special interest, economic interest, or moneyed interest.

Viability
Usually a reference to the amount of money candidates have or can raise for their campaigns. Viable (or, sometimes, credible) candidates are those considered to have enough money to win.

Vote
A way to show your preference and choose elected leaders or decide on initiatives. People can vote by marking a piece of paper, raising their hand, or filling out a form on a computer.

Voting Booth
A small enclosure in which a person votes.

Vouchers
A proposed form of in-kind public financing by which eligible candidates and/or political parties would receive certificates entitling them to a specified amount of free campaign resources, such as postage or media time.

War Chest
Campaign money built up by incumbents well in advance of the next election to give them a financial head-start and discourage potential challengers. Often includes leftover campaign money from the last election, as well as money raised early in the term.

Watergate Reforms
A reference to the 1974, 1976, and 1979 amendments to the Federal Election Campaign Act of 1971. Motivated largely by the excesses and illegalities of President Nixon's 1972 re-election campaign, these amendments comprise the bulk of federal campaign laws today.

Wealth Primary
An unofficial, but integral (and usually decisive), part of the electoral process leading up to most primary and general elections for major public office, in which individuals and groups capable of making large campaign contributions effectively decide which candidates will have the financial wherewithal to mount winning campaigns and, thus, to govern. An exclusionary procedure in which only those with money or access to money can vote, wealth primaries have been likened to Texas's racially exclusionary white primaries of the post-World War I era, which were declared unconstitutional by the U.S. Supreme Court.

Appendix

U.S. Census Bureau
Historical Time Series Tables

Table A-1. Reported Voting and Registration by Race, Hispanic Origin, Sex and Age Groups: November 1964 to 2004

(Numbers in thousands)

Year	Total voting-age population	Total percent		White		White non-Hispanic		Black		Asian[1]		Hispanic (of any race)		Total Population	
		Total population	Citizen population	Total population	Citizen population	Total population	Citizen population	Total population	Citizen population	Total population	Citizen population	Total population	Citizen population	Male	Female
Voted															
2004[2]	215,694	58.3	63.8	60.3	65.4	65.8	67.2	56.3	60.0	29.8	44.1	28.0	47.2	56.3	60.1
2004[3]	215,694	58.3	63.8	60.3	65.3	65.7	67.1	56.2	59.9	30.7	44.6	28.0	47.2	56.3	60.1
2002	210,421	42.3	46.1	44.1	47.5	48.0	49.1	39.7	42.3	19.4	31.2	18.9	30.4	41.4	43.0
2000	202,609	54.7	59.5	56.4	60.5	60.4	61.8	53.5	56.8	25.4	43.4	27.5	45.1	53.1	56.2
1998	198,228	41.9	45.3	43.3	46.3	46.5	47.4	39.6	41.8	19.3	32.4	20.0	32.8	41.4	42.4
1996	193,651	54.2	58.4	56.0	59.6	59.6	60.7	50.6	53.0	25.7	45.0	26.8	44.0	52.8	55.5
1994	190,267	45.0	48.4	47.3	50.0	50.1	51.0	37.1	38.9	21.8	39.4	20.2	34.0	44.7	45.3
1992	185,684	61.3	67.7	63.6	69.2	66.9	70.2	54.1	59.2	27.3	53.9	28.9	51.6	60.2	62.3
1990	182,118	45.0	49.3	46.7	50.5	49.0	51.4	39.2	42.4	20.3	40.0	21.0	36.0	44.6	45.4
1988	178,098	57.4	62.2	59.1	63.4	61.8	64.2	51.5	55.0	NA	NA	28.8	48.0	56.4	58.3
1986	173,890	46.0	49.4	47.0	50.1	48.9	50.7	43.2	45.5	NA	NA	24.2	38.0	45.8	46.1
1984	169,963	59.9	64.9	61.4	65.7	63.3	66.4	55.8	60.6	NA	NA	32.7	50.0	59.0	60.8
1982	165,483	48.5	51.9	49.9	52.8	51.5	53.4	43.0	45.5	NA	NA	25.3	38.5	48.7	48.4
1980	157,085	59.3	64.0	60.9	65.4	62.8	66.2	50.5	53.9	NA	NA	29.9	46.1	59.1	59.4
1978	151,646	45.9	48.9	47.3	50.1	48.6	50.6	37.2	39.5	NA	NA	23.5	35.7	46.6	45.3
1976	146,548	59.2	NA	60.9	NA	NA	NA	48.7	NA	NA	NA	31.8	NA	59.6	58.8
1974	141,299	44.7	NA	46.3	NA	NA	NA	33.8	NA	NA	NA	22.9	NA	46.2	43.4
1972	136,203	63.0	NA	64.5	NA	NA	NA	52.1	NA	NA	NA	37.5	NA	64.1	62.0
1970	120,701	54.6	NA	56.0	NA	NA	NA	43.5	NA	NA	NA	NA	NA	56.8	52.7
1968	116,535	67.8	NA	69.1	NA	NA	NA	57.6	NA	NA	NA	NA	NA	69.8	66.0
1966	112,800	55.4	NA	57.0	NA	NA	NA	41.7	NA	NA	NA	NA	NA	58.2	53.0
1964	110,604	69.3	NA	70.7	NA	NA	NA	58.5	NA	NA	NA	NA	NA	71.9	67.0
Registered															
2004[2]	215,694	65.9	72.1	67.9	73.6	73.5	75.1	64.4	68.7	34.9	51.8	34.3	57.9	64.0	67.6
2004[3]	215,694	65.9	72.1	67.9	73.5	73.5	75.1	64.3	68.6	36.1	52.5	34.3	57.9	64.0	67.6
2002	210,421	60.9	66.5	63.1	67.9	67.9	69.4	58.5	62.4	30.7	49.2	32.6	52.5	58.9	62.8
2000	202,609	63.9	69.5	65.7	70.4	70.0	71.6	63.6	67.5	30.7	52.4	34.9	57.4	62.2	65.6
1998	198,228	62.1	67.1	63.9	68.2	67.9	69.3	60.2	63.6	29.1	48.9	33.7	55.2	60.6	63.5
1996	193,651	65.9	71.0	67.7	72.0	71.6	73.0	63.5	66.4	32.6	57.2	35.7	58.6	64.4	67.3
1994	190,267	62.5	67.1	64.6	68.4	68.1	69.4	58.5	61.3	28.7	51.9	31.3	52.9	61.2	63.7
1992	185,684	68.2	75.2	70.1	76.3	73.5	77.1	63.9	70.0	31.2	61.6	35.0	62.5	66.9	69.3
1990	182,118	62.2	68.2	63.8	69.1	66.7	69.9	58.8	63.5	28.4	56.0	32.3	55.2	61.2	63.1
1988	178,098	66.6	72.1	67.9	72.8	70.8	73.6	64.5	68.8	NA	NA	35.5	59.1	65.2	67.8
1986	173,890	64.3	69.0	65.3	69.5	67.7	70.2	64.0	67.3	NA	NA	35.9	56.4	63.4	65.0
1984	169,963	68.3	73.9	69.6	74.5	71.6	75.1	66.3	72.0	NA	NA	40.1	61.4	67.3	69.3
1982	165,483	64.1	68.5	65.6	69.4	67.5	70.1	59.1	62.6	NA	NA	35.3	53.7	63.7	64.4
1980	157,085	66.9	72.3	68.4	73.4	70.3	74.1	60.0	64.1	NA	NA	36.4	56.0	66.6	67.1
1978	151,646	62.6	66.7	63.8	67.5	65.4	68.2	57.1	60.6	NA	NA	32.9	50.1	62.6	62.5
1976	146,548	66.7	NA	68.3	NA	NA	NA	58.5	NA	NA	NA	37.8	NA	67.1	66.4
1974	141,299	62.2	NA	64.6	NA	NA	NA	54.2	NA	NA	NA	34.9	NA	62.8	61.7
1972	136,203	72.3	NA	73.4	NA	NA	NA	65.5	NA	NA	NA	44.4	NA	73.1	71.6
1970	120,701	68.1	NA	70.8	NA	NA	NA	64.5	NA	NA	NA	NA	NA	69.6	66.8
1968	116,535	74.3	NA	75.4	NA	NA	NA	66.2	NA	NA	NA	NA	NA	76.0	72.8
1966	112,800	70.3	NA	71.7	NA	NA	NA	60.2	NA	NA	NA	NA	NA	72.2	68.6
1964	110,604	NA	NA	NA	NA	NA	NA	NA	NA	NA	NA	NA	NA	NA	NA

Table A-1. Reported Voting and Registration by Race, Hispanic Origin, Sex and Age Groups: November 1964 to 2004

(Numbers in thousands)

Year	Total voting-age population	Total percent		White		White non-Hispanic		Black		Asian¹		Hispanic (of any race)		Total Population	
		Total population	Citizen population	Total population	Citizen population	Total population	Citizen population	Total population	Citizen population	Total population	Citizen population	Total population	Citizen population	Male	Female
Voted															
18 to 24 years															
2004²	27,808	41.9	46.7	42.6	47.5	48.5	49.8	44.0	47.0	23.4	34.2	20.4	33.0	38.8	44.9
2004³	27,808	41.9	46.7	42.6	47.4	48.4	49.7	44.0	47.0	24.5	34.5	20.4	33.0	38.8	44.9
2002	27,377	17.2	19.3	17.4	19.4	19.9	20.4	19.3	20.6	10.0	15.9	8.1	13.3	15.7	18.6
2000	26,712	32.3	NA	33.0	NA	37.2	NA	33.9	NA	15.9	NA	15.4	NA	30.0	34.6
1998	25,537	16.6	NA	17.2	NA	19.2	NA	15.6	NA	9.7	NA	9.0	NA	15.7	17.6
1996	24,650	32.4	NA	33.3	NA	36.9	NA	32.4	NA	19.2	NA	15.1	NA	29.8	35.0
1994	25,182	20.1	NA	21.1	NA	23.1	NA	17.4	NA	10.6	NA	10.1	NA	18.6	21.5
1992	24,371	42.8	NA	45.4	NA	NA	NA	36.6	NA	NA	NA	17.6	NA	40.5	45.1
1990	24,831	20.4	NA	20.8	NA	NA	NA	20.2	NA	NA	NA	8.7	NA	19.8	21.0
1988	25,569	36.2	NA	37.0	NA	NA	NA	35.0	NA	NA	NA	16.8	NA	34.1	38.2
1986	26,425	21.9	NA	21.6	NA	NA	NA	25.1	NA	NA	NA	11.6	NA	21.2	22.5
1984	27,976	40.8	NA	41.6	NA	NA	NA	40.6	NA	NA	NA	21.9	NA	38.7	42.8
1982	28,823	24.8	NA	25.0	NA	NA	NA	25.5	NA	NA	NA	14.2	NA	25.1	25.7
1980	28,138	39.9	NA	41.8	NA	NA	NA	30.1	NA	NA	NA	15.9	NA	38.5	41.2
1978	27,678	23.5	NA	24.2	NA	NA	NA	20.1	NA	NA	NA	11.5	NA	23.2	23.9
1976	26,953	42.2	NA	44.7	NA	NA	NA	27.9	NA	NA	NA	21.8	NA	40.9	43.4
1974	25,719	23.8	NA	25.2	NA	NA	NA	16.1	NA	NA	NA	13.3	NA	24.6	23.1
1972	24,612	49.6	NA	51.9	NA	NA	NA	34.7	NA	NA	NA	30.9	NA	48.8	50.4
1970	13,027	30.4	NA	31.5	NA	NA	NA	22.4	NA	NA	NA	NA	NA	30.6	30.0
1968	11,602	50.4	NA	52.8	NA	NA	NA	38.9	NA	NA	NA	NA	NA	50.3	50.6
1966	10,751	31.1	NA	32.6	NA	NA	NA	21.9	NA	NA	NA	NA	NA	32.3	30.3
1964	9,919	50.9	NA	52.1	NA	NA	NA	44.2	NA	NA	NA	NA	NA	51.5	50.5
Registered															
2004²	27,808	51.5	54.1	52.5	58.5	59.1	60.7	53.1	56.7	29.2	42.6	27.6	44.6	48.2	54.9
2004³	27,808	51.5	54.1	52.6	58.5	59.1	60.6	53.2	56.8	31.1	43.8	27.6	44.6	48.2	54.9
2002	27,377	38.2	43.0	39.2	43.8	44.2	45.4	39.6	41.2	21.7	34.5	20.8	34.3	34.9	41.6
2000	26,712	45.4	NA	46.3	NA	51.7	NA	48.0	NA	22.2	NA	23.2	NA	42.3	48.5
1998	25,537	39.2	NA	39.2	NA	45.0	NA	63.5	NA	17.7	NA	22.2	NA	36.4	42.0
1996	24,650	48.8	NA	49.8	NA	54.3	NA	49.4	NA	29.5	NA	27.6	NA	46.5	51.0
1994	25,182	42.3	NA	43.9	NA	48.1	NA	42.0	NA	18.3	NA	20.0	NA	40.9	43.7
1992	24,371	52.5	NA	54.6	NA	NA	NA	49.2	NA	NA	NA	24.9	NA	50.5	54.4
1990	24,831	39.9	NA	40.5	NA	NA	NA	40.2	NA	NA	NA	19.3	NA	39.5	40.2
1988	25,569	48.2	NA	48.7	NA	NA	NA	49.8	NA	NA	NA	25.3	NA	45.5	50.8
1986	26,425	42.0	NA	42.0	NA	NA	NA	46.1	NA	NA	NA	22.0	NA	41.0	43.0
1984	27,976	51.3	NA	52.0	NA	NA	NA	53.7	NA	NA	NA	29.8	NA	49.6	53.0
1982	28,823	42.4	NA	43.2	NA	NA	NA	41.8	NA	NA	NA	24.3	NA	42.4	42.5
1980	28,138	49.2	NA	51.0	NA	NA	NA	41.3	NA	NA	NA	22.5	NA	48.0	50.4
1978	27,678	40.5	NA	37.2	NA	NA	NA	37.2	NA	NA	NA	20.5	NA	39.5	41.5
1976	26,953	51.3	NA	53.7	NA	NA	NA	38.8	NA	NA	NA	29.0	NA	50.8	51.9
1974	25,719	41.3	NA	42.8	NA	NA	NA	33.6	NA	NA	NA	23.1	NA	41.8	40.8
1972	24,612	58.9	NA	60.6	NA	NA	NA	47.7	NA	NA	NA	38.9	NA	58.3	59.4
1970	13,027	40.9	NA	40.6	NA	NA	NA	33.0	NA	NA	NA	NA	NA	41.2	40.6
1968	11,602	56.0	NA	57.9	NA	NA	NA	46.4	NA	NA	NA	NA	NA	56.1	55.9
1966	10,751	44.1	NA	43.6	NA	NA	NA	34.5	NA	NA	NA	NA	NA	44.4	43.8
1964	9,919	NA	NA	NA	NA	NA	NA	NA	NA	NA	NA	NA	NA	NA	NA

Table A-1. Reported Voting and Registration by Race, Hispanic Origin, Sex and Age Groups: November 1964 to 2004

(Numbers in thousands)

25 to 44 years

Voted

Year	Total voting-age population	Total percent Total population	Total percent Citizen population	White Total population	White Citizen population	White non-Hispanic Total population	White non-Hispanic Citizen population	Black Total population	Black Citizen population	Asian[1] Total population	Asian[1] Citizen population	Hispanic (of any race) Total population	Hispanic (of any race) Citizen population	Total Population Male	Total Population Female
2004²	82,133	52.2	60.1	54.0	61.5	61.6	63.5	54.0	59.3	23.9	40.2	23.0	45.2	49.0	44.9
2004³	82,133	52.2	60.1	54.0	61.5	61.5	63.4	54.0	59.1	25.4	41.4	23.0	45.2	49.0	44.9
2002	82,228	34.1	38.9	35.3	39.5	39.7	41.0	36.1	39.4	14.0	25.9	15.3	27.6	32.7	35.4
2000	81,780	49.8	NA	51.2	NA	56.3	NA	52.1	NA	22.2	NA	23.2	NA	47.3	52.3
1998	82,993	34.8	NA	35.8	NA	39.1	NA	36.4	NA	12.9	NA	16.1	NA	33.5	36.1
1996	83,393	49.2	NA	50.8	NA	55.1	NA	47.8	NA	22.8	NA	22.9	NA	46.8	51.5
1994	83,006	39.4	NA	41.5	NA	44.6	NA	33.3	NA	17.4	NA	17.5	NA	38.6	40.2
1992	81,319	58.3	NA	60.6	NA	NA	NA	52.1	NA	NA	NA	26.4	NA	55.8	60.6
1990	80,541	40.7	NA	42.1	NA	NA	NA	37.8	NA	NA	NA	19.7	NA	39.1	42.2
1988	77,863	54.0	NA	55.9	NA	NA	NA	48.0	NA	NA	NA	27.1	NA	51.8	56.1
1986	74,927	41.4	NA	42.2	NA	NA	NA	41.2	NA	NA	NA	21.7	NA	40.3	42.4
1984	71,023	58.4	NA	60.0	NA	NA	NA	40.6	NA	NA	NA	31.1	NA	56.3	60.5
1982	66,881	45.4	NA	46.5	NA	NA	NA	43.5	NA	NA	NA	22.2	NA	44.5	46.2
1980	61,285	58.7	NA	60.3	NA	NA	NA	51.9	NA	NA	NA	30.4	NA	57.1	60.1
1978	57,536	43.1	NA	44.4	NA	NA	NA	36.7	NA	NA	NA	22.4	NA	42.5	43.6
1976	54,302	58.7	NA	60.6	NA	NA	NA	49.6	NA	NA	NA	33.2	NA	57.9	59.5
1974	51,663	42.2	NA	47.6	NA	NA	NA	36.4	NA	NA	NA	24.2	NA	42.0	42.4
1972	49,173	62.7	NA	64.0	NA	NA	NA	61.4	NA	NA	NA	39.5	NA	62.5	62.9
1970	47,056	51.9	NA	53.0	NA	NA	NA	44.1	NA	NA	NA	NA	NA	52.3	51.5
1968	46,103	66.6	NA	67.7	NA	NA	NA	60.3	NA	NA	NA	NA	NA	67.2	66.1
1966	45,061	53.1	NA	54.4	NA	NA	NA	43.9	NA	NA	NA	NA	NA	54.1	52.1
1964	45,296	69.0	NA	70.1	NA	NA	NA	61.5	NA	NA	NA	NA	NA	70.0	68.0

Registered

Year	Total voting-age population	Total percent Total population	Total percent Citizen population	White Total population	White Citizen population	White non-Hispanic Total population	White non-Hispanic Citizen population	Black Total population	Black Citizen population	Asian[1] Total population	Asian[1] Citizen population	Hispanic (of any race) Total population	Hispanic (of any race) Citizen population	Total Population Male	Total Population Female
2004²	82,133	60.1	69.3	62.0	70.6	70.2	72.4	62.2	68.2	28.9	48.7	28.8	56.7	57.6	62.5
2004³	82,133	60.1	69.3	62.1	70.6	70.1	72.3	62.2	68.2	30.7	50.1	28.8	56.7	57.6	62.5
2002	82,228	55.4	63.1	57.4	64.3	63.8	65.9	55.8	60.9	25.6	47.3	28.9	52.0	52.8	57.9
2000	81,780	59.6	NA	61.2	NA	66.8	NA	62.0	NA	26.7	NA	31.1	NA	57.3	61.8
1998	82,993	57.7	NA	59.4	NA	64.3	NA	59.5	NA	23.2	NA	29.8	NA	55.5	59.9
1996	83,393	61.9	NA	63.6	NA	68.5	NA	61.4	NA	28.5	NA	31.8	NA	59.6	64.1
1994	83,006	57.9	NA	59.9	NA	64.0	NA	55.4	NA	24.4	NA	28.4	NA	55.9	59.7
1992	81,319	64.8	NA	66.8	NA	NA	NA	62.0	NA	NA	NA	32.0	NA	62.6	67.0
1990	80,541	58.4	NA	59.9	NA	NA	NA	57.2	NA	NA	NA	30.4	NA	56.4	60.3
1988	77,863	63.0	NA	64.4	NA	NA	NA	62.1	NA	NA	NA	33.2	NA	60.6	65.4
1986	74,927	61.1	NA	61.9	NA	NA	NA	64.0	NA	NA	NA	34.5	NA	59.4	62.8
1984	71,023	66.6	NA	68.0	NA	NA	NA	53.7	NA	NA	NA	38.4	NA	64.5	68.6
1982	66,881	61.5	NA	62.9	NA	NA	NA	59.4	NA	NA	NA	30.8	NA	60.3	62.6
1980	61,285	65.6	NA	67.0	NA	NA	NA	59.5	NA	NA	NA	36.0	NA	64.3	66.8
1978	57,536	60.2	NA	61.5	NA	NA	NA	56.9	NA	NA	NA	32.7	NA	59.5	60.9
1976	54,302	65.5	NA	67.0	NA	NA	NA	59.5	NA	NA	NA	38.4	NA	64.8	66.1
1974	51,663	59.9	NA	65.0	NA	NA	NA	58.3	NA	NA	NA	37.2	NA	42.4	60.8
1972	49,173	71.3	NA	72.1	NA	NA	NA	68.7	NA	NA	NA	46.0	NA	71.2	71.4
1970	47,056	65.0	NA	65.9	NA	NA	NA	60.9	NA	NA	NA	NA	NA	65.3	64.8
1968	46,103	72.4	NA	73.3	NA	NA	NA	68.7	NA	NA	NA	NA	NA	73.0	71.9
1966	45,061	67.6	NA	68.7	NA	NA	NA	61.9	NA	NA	NA	NA	NA	68.1	67.3
1964	45,296	NA	NA	NA	NA	NA	NA	NA	NA	NA	NA	NA	NA	NA	NA

Table A-1. Reported Voting and Registration by Race, Hispanic Origin, Sex and Age Groups: November 1964 to 2004

(Numbers in thousands)

Year	Total voting-age population	Total percent		White		White non-Hispanic		Black		Asian[1]		Hispanic (of any race)		Total Population	
		Total population	Citizen population	Total population	Citizen population	Total population	Citizen population	Total population	Citizen population	Total population	Citizen population	Total population	Citizen population	Male	Female
Voted															
45 to 64 years															
2004[2]	71,014	66.6	70.4	68.6	72.0	72.0	73.2	62.6	65.3	38.3	51.1	38.5	56.2	65.3	67.9
2004[3]	71,014	66.6	70.4	68.6	71.9	72.0	73.1	62.5	65.3	38.8	51.4	38.5	56.2	65.3	67.9
2002	66,924	53.1	56.1	65.1	57.3	57.5	58.5	50.0	52.4	29.7	41.6	28.7	40.9	52.6	53.5
2000	61,352	64.1	NA	65.6	NA	68.4	NA	62.9	NA	32.0	NA	38.3	NA	62.7	65.3
1998	57,436	53.6	NA	54.7	NA	57.0	NA	52.7	NA	29.8	NA	30.7	NA	53.5	53.6
1996	53,721	64.4	NA	61.7	NA	68.6	NA	66.1	NA	32.1	NA	38.3	NA	63.7	65.1
1994	50,934	56.7	NA	58.4	NA	60.6	NA	51.6	NA	31.5	NA	29.9	NA	56.8	56.6
1992	49,147	70.0	NA	71.8	NA	NA	NA	64.9	NA	NA	NA	40.4	NA	69.8	70.2
1990	46,871	55.8	NA	57.4	NA	NA	NA	49.4	NA	NA	NA	28.7	NA	55.9	55.7
1988	45,862	67.9	NA	69.2	NA	NA	NA	64.8	NA	NA	NA	39.2	NA	68.1	67.7
1986	44,825	58.7	NA	59.7	NA	NA	NA	56.6	NA	NA	NA	38.3	NA	58.9	58.5
1984	44,307	69.8	NA	69.8	NA	NA	NA	66.2	NA	NA	NA	44.2	NA	69.8	69.8
1982	44,180	62.2	NA	63.8	NA	NA	NA	54.3	NA	NA	NA	39.9	NA	62.9	61.6
1980	43,569	69.3	NA	70.7	NA	NA	NA	61.2	NA	NA	NA	42.7	NA	69.8	68.9
1978	43,431	58.5	NA	59.9	NA	NA	NA	48.4	NA	NA	NA	38.5	NA	59.8	57.4
1976	43,293	68.7	NA	69.9	NA	NA	NA	62.3	NA	NA	NA	40.3	NA	69.7	67.9
1974	42,961	56.9	NA	58.3	NA	NA	NA	45.9	NA	NA	NA	34.2	NA	59.1	55.0
1972	42,344	70.8	NA	71.9	NA	NA	NA	61.9	NA	NA	NA	43.5	NA	72.2	69.6
1970	41,477	64.2	NA	65.4	NA	NA	NA	53.3	NA	NA	NA	NA	NA	66.3	62.3
1968	40,362	74.9	NA	76.1	NA	NA	NA	64.5	NA	NA	NA	NA	NA	75.5	73.3
1966	39,171	64.5	NA	66.2	NA	NA	NA	48.4	NA	NA	NA	NA	NA	66.9	62.2
1964	38,121	75.9	NA	77.2	NA	NA	NA	64.1	NA	NA	NA	NA	NA	78.5	73.5
Registered															
2004[2]	71,014	72.7	76.9	74.6	78.3	78.1	79.3	69.6	72.6	43.4	57.9	44.4	64.8	71.6	73.8
2004[3]	71,014	72.7	76.9	74.6	78.2	78.0	79.3	69.5	72.6	43.9	58.1	44.4	64.8	71.6	73.8
2002	66,924	69.4	73.4	71.3	74.6	74.2	75.5	66.9	70.1	41.1	57.5	43.6	62.1	68.4	70.3
2000	61,352	71.2	NA	72.7	NA	75.5	NA	70.9	NA	38.1	NA	45.1	NA	69.8	72.6
1998	57,436	71.1	NA	72.6	NA	75.3	NA	69.5	NA	40.4	NA	44.3	NA	70.4	71.8
1996	53,721	73.5	NA	71.1	NA	77.8	NA	75.1	NA	40.0	NA	45.2	NA	72.6	74.4
1994	50,934	71.7	NA	73.3	NA	75.8	NA	69.8	NA	37.9	NA	42.4	NA	70.9	72.5
1992	49,147	75.3	NA	76.9	NA	NA	NA	72.4	NA	NA	NA	45.9	NA	74.9	75.7
1990	46,871	71.4	NA	72.9	NA	NA	NA	68.9	NA	NA	NA	41.3	NA	71.2	71.6
1988	45,862	75.5	NA	76.7	NA	NA	NA	74.6	NA	NA	NA	45.6	NA	75.7	75.3
1986	44,825	74.8	NA	75.8	NA	NA	NA	74.5	NA	NA	NA	49.3	NA	74.5	75.1
1984	44,307	75.6	NA	76.6	NA	NA	NA	73.7	NA	NA	NA	51.8	NA	76.6	76.6
1982	44,180	75.8	NA	77.1	NA	NA	NA	69.8	NA	NA	NA	50.5	NA	75.8	75.5
1980	43,569	74.3	NA	77.0	NA	NA	NA	69.4	NA	NA	NA	50.6	NA	76.3	75.3
1978	43,431	75.5	NA	75.2	NA	NA	NA	69.3	NA	NA	NA	46.6	NA	75.0	73.7
1976	43,293	73.6	NA	76.4	NA	NA	NA	70.6	NA	NA	NA	46.4	NA	76.1	74.9
1974	42,961	79.7	NA	74.6	NA	NA	NA	67.2	NA	NA	NA	46.3	NA	74.7	72.7
1972	42,344	77.5	NA	80.5	NA	NA	NA	74.2	NA	NA	NA	50.3	NA	80.4	79.1
1970	41,477	81.1	NA	78.3	NA	NA	NA	71.2	NA	NA	NA	NA	NA	78.9	76.3
1968	40,362	78.9	NA	82.1	NA	NA	NA	72.1	NA	NA	NA	NA	NA	82.4	79.8
1966	39,171	NA	NA	80.2	NA	NA	NA	67.8	NA	NA	NA	NA	NA	80.9	77.1
1964	38,121	NA	NA	NA	NA	NA	NA	NA	NA	NA	NA	NA	NA	NA	NA

Table A-1. Reported Voting and Registration by Race, Hispanic Origin, Sex and Age Groups: November 1964 to 2004

(Numbers in thousands)

65 years and over

Voted

Year	Total voting-age population	Total percent		White		White non-Hispanic		Black		Asian[1]		Hispanic (of any race)		Total Population	
		Total population	Citizen population	Total population	Citizen population	Total population	Citizen population	Total population	Citizen population	Total population	Citizen population	Total population	Citizen population	Male	Female
2004²	34,738	68.9	71.0	70.5	72.2	72.2	73.1	64.1	65.9	38.2	47.7	45.9	57.0	71.9	66.7
2004³	34,738	68.9	71.0	70.5	72.2	72.2	73.1	64.1	64.9	38.4	47.9	45.9	57.0	71.9	66.7
2002	33,892	61.0	62.7	62.7	64.0	64.0	64.8	54.8	56.5	29.0	38.8	41.5	49.2	65.4	57.7
2000	32,764	67.6	NA	68.8	NA	70.0	NA	64.7	NA	37.9	NA	50.0	NA	71.4	64.8
1998	32,263	59.5	NA	60.5	NA	61.7	NA	56.2	NA	35.4	NA	41.9	NA	64.6	55.8
1996	31,888	67.0	NA	68.1	NA	69.2	NA	63.7	NA	34.3	NA	47.6	NA	70.9	64.1
1994	31,144	61.3	NA	62.8	NA	63.9	NA	51.6	NA	33.8	NA	37.6	NA	66.5	57.6
1992	30,846	70.1	NA	71.5	NA	NA	NA	64.1	NA	NA	NA	39.7	NA	74.5	67.0
1990	29,874	60.3	NA	61.7	NA	NA	NA	51.3	NA	NA	NA	40.5	NA	66.0	56.3
1988	28,804	68.8	NA	69.8	NA	NA	NA	63.5	NA	NA	NA	45.6	NA	73.3	65.6
1986	27,712	60.9	NA	61.9	NA	NA	NA	53.3	NA	NA	NA	36.5	NA	66.8	56.7
1984	26,658	67.7	NA	68.7	NA	NA	NA	61.5	NA	NA	NA	40.5	NA	71.9	64.8
1982	25,598	59.9	NA	61.1	NA	NA	NA	50.8	NA	NA	NA	29.5	NA	65.3	56.2
1980	24,094	65.1	NA	66.0	NA	NA	NA	59.4	NA	NA	NA	36.8	NA	70.4	61.3
1978	23,001	55.9	NA	57.2	NA	NA	NA	45.6	NA	NA	NA	24.9	NA	62.6	51.3
1976	22,001	62.2	NA	63.2	NA	NA	NA	54.3	NA	NA	NA	29.9	NA	68.3	58.0
1974	20,955	51.4	NA	52.8	NA	NA	NA	38.5	NA	NA	NA	28.1	NA	58.7	46.2
1972	20,074	63.5	NA	64.8	NA	NA	NA	50.6	NA	NA	NA	26.7	NA	70.7	58.4
1970	19,141	57.0	NA	58.6	NA	NA	NA	39.3	NA	NA	NA	NA	NA	65.4	50.8
1968	18,468	65.8	NA	67.4	NA	NA	NA	49.9	NA	NA	NA	NA	NA	73.1	73.3
1966	17,817	56.1	NA	57.9	NA	NA	NA	35.3	NA	NA	NA	NA	NA	64.2	49.8
1964	17,269	66.3	NA	68.1	NA	NA	NA	45.3	NA	NA	NA	NA	NA	73.7	60.4

Registered

Year	Total voting-age population	Total population	Citizen population	Total population	Citizen population	Total population	Citizen population	Total population	Citizen population	Total population	Citizen population	Total population	Citizen population	Male	Female
2004²	34,738	76.9	79.2	78.4	80.4	80.0	81.0	73.7	75.8	43.5	54.4	55.0	68.3	78.5	75.6
2004³	34,738	76.9	79.2	78.4	80.4	80.0	81.0	73.6	74.6	44.0	54.8	55.0	68.3	78.5	75.6
2002	33,892	75.8	78.0	77.3	79.0	78.7	79.7	73.5	75.7	37.2	49.8	54.8	64.9	77.3	74.7
2000	32,764	76.1	NA	77.3	NA	78.6	NA	74.3	NA	42.8	NA	56.7	NA	78.8	74.2
1998	32,263	75.4	NA	76.4	NA	77.6	NA	73.6	NA	44.1	NA	56.5	NA	78.5	73.2
1996	31,888	77.0	NA	78.1	NA	79.3	NA	75.2	NA	39.2	NA	54.2	NA	79.7	75.0
1994	31,144	76.3	NA	77.5	NA	78.7	NA	72.4	NA	40.7	NA	50.2	NA	79.2	74.3
1992	30,846	78.0	NA	79.1	NA	NA	NA	74.2	NA	NA	NA	47.9	NA	81.1	75.7
1990	29,874	76.5	NA	77.7	NA	NA	NA	71.2	NA	NA	NA	53.2	NA	79.7	74.2
1988	28,804	78.4	NA	79.9	NA	NA	NA	79.2	NA	NA	NA	51.0	NA	81.6	76.1
1986	27,712	76.9	NA	77.9	NA	NA	NA	71.4	NA	NA	NA	47.0	NA	80.6	74.3
1984	26,658	76.9	NA	77.7	NA	NA	NA	73.0	NA	NA	NA	46.7	NA	80.2	74.7
1982	25,598	75.2	NA	76.3	NA	NA	NA	68.4	NA	NA	NA	40.6	NA	78.9	72.6
1980	24,094	74.6	NA	75.4	NA	NA	NA	70.1	NA	NA	NA	44.1	NA	78.8	71.6
1978	23,001	72.8	NA	73.7	NA	NA	NA	67.6	NA	NA	NA	33.5	NA	77.6	69.5
1976	22,001	71.4	NA	72.5	NA	NA	NA	64.5	NA	NA	NA	36.5	NA	76.6	67.8
1974	20,955	70.2	NA	71.2	NA	NA	NA	62.9	NA	NA	NA	37.8	NA	75.8	66.2
1972	20,074	75.6	NA	76.5	NA	NA	NA	67.9	NA	NA	NA	34.7	NA	81.9	71.1
1970	19,141	73.7	NA	75.0	NA	NA	NA	61.5	NA	NA	NA	NA	NA	79.8	69.2
1968	18,468	75.6	NA	77.1	NA	NA	NA	62.7	NA	NA	NA	NA	NA	81.7	71.1
1966	17,817	73.5	NA	75.5	NA	NA	NA	56.2	NA	NA	NA	NA	NA	79.9	69.2
1964	17,269	NA	NA	NA	NA	NA	NA	NA	NA	NA	NA	NA	NA	NA	NA

Note: Prior to 1972, data are for people 21 to 24 years of age with the exception of those aged 18 to 24 in Georgia and Kentucky, 19 to 24 in Alaska, and 20 to 24 in Hawaii.

Note: Registration data were not collected in the 1964 Current Population Survey.

Note: NA Not available.

Note: Because of changes in the Current Population Survey race categories beginning in 2003, 2004 data on race are not directly comparable with data from earlier years.

[1] Prior to 2004, this category was 'Asian and Pacific Islanders,' therefore rates are not comparable with prior years.

Table A-2. Reported Voting and Registration by Region, Educational Attainment and Labor Force for the Population 18 and Over: November 1964 to 2004

(Percent)

Years	Region				Educational Attainment					Labor Force			
	Northeast	Midwest	South	West	Less than 9th grade	9th to 12th grade, no diploma	High school graduate or GED	Some college or Associate degree	Bachelor's degree or more	In civilian labor force	Employed	Unemployed	Not in labor force
Voted													
2004	58.6	65.0	56.4	54.4	23.6	34.6	52.4	66.1	74.2	59.3	60.0	46.4	56.2
2002	41.4	47.1	41.6	39.0	19.4	23.3	37.1	45.8	58.5	41.3	42.1	27.2	44.2
2000	55.2	60.9	53.5	49.9	26.8	33.6	49.4	60.3	72.0	54.8	55.5	35.1	63.8
1998	41.2	47.3	38.6	42.3	24.0	24.6	37.1	46.2	57.2	40.7	41.2	28.4	44.5
1996	54.5	59.3	52.2	51.8	29.9	33.8	49.1	60.5	72.6	54.3	55.2	37.2	54.1
1994	45.6	48.9	40.9	47.1	23.6	27.3	40.7	49.5	63.8	44.7	45.6	28.6	45.8
1992	61.2	67.2	59.0	58.5	35.1	41.2	57.5	68.7	81.0	62.6	63.8	46.2	58.7
1990	45.2	48.6	42.4	45.0	27.7	30.9	42.2	50.0	62.5	44.2	45.1	27.9	46.7
1988	57.4	62.9	54.5	55.6	36.7	41.3	54.7	64.5	77.6	57.5	58.4	38.6	57.3
1986	44.4	49.5	43.0	48.4	32.7	33.8	44.1	49.9	62.5	44.7	45.7	31.2	48.4
1984	59.7	65.7	56.8	58.5	42.9	44.4	58.7	67.5	79.1	60.5	61.6	44.0	58.9
1982	49.8	54.7	41.8	50.7	35.7	37.7	47.1	53.3	66.5	48.4	50.0	34.1	48.7
1980	58.5	65.8	55.6	57.2	42.6	45.6	58.9	67.2	79.9	60.4	61.8	41.2	57.0
1978	48.1	50.5	39.6	47.5	34.6	35.1	45.3	51.5	63.9	45.7	46.7	27.4	46.2
1976	59.5	65.1	54.9	57.5	44.1	47.2	59.4	68.1	79.8	60.7	62.0	43.7	56.5
1974	48.7	49.3	36.0	48.1	34.4	35.9	44.7	49.6	61.3	46.3	47.2	27.6	45.8
1972	66.4	NA	55.4	NA	47.4	52.0	65.4	74.9	83.6	65.3	66.0	49.9	59.3
1970	59.0	NA	44.7	NA	43.4	47.1	58.4	61.3	70.2	56.5	57.2	41.1	51.5
1968	71.0	NA	60.1	NA	54.5	61.3	72.5	78.4	84.1	70.6	71.1	52.1	63.2
1966	60.9	NA	43.0	NA	44.6	49.9	60.1	64.8	70.5	57.8	58.3	40.2	51.7
1964	74.4	76.2	56.7	71.9	59.0	65.4	76.1	82.1	87.5	72.4	73.0	58.0	64.6
Registered													
2004	65.3	72.8	65.5	60.1	32.5	45.7	61.5	73.7	78.1	66.5	67.1	56.3	64.4
2002	60.8	66.5	61.6	54.0	32.4	41.6	57.1	66.7	74.4	60.9	61.7	48.1	60.9
2000	63.7	70.2	64.5	56.9	36.1	45.9	60.1	70.0	77.3	64.0	64.7	46.1	54.5
1998	60.8	68.2	62.7	56.0	40.2	43.4	58.6	68.3	75.1	62.1	62.6	48.5	62.1
1996	64.7	71.6	65.9	60.8	40.7	47.9	62.2	72.9	80.4	66.3	67.0	52.5	65.1
1994	61.5	68.9	61.1	58.9	40.7	45.0	59.2	68.9	77.2	62.6	63.4	46.9	62.4
1992	67.0	74.6	67.2	63.6	43.9	50.4	64.9	75.4	84.8	68.8	69.9	53.7	66.8
1990	61.0	68.2	61.3	57.7	44.0	47.9	60.0	68.7	77.3	61.6	62.6	44.6	63.4
1988	64.8	72.5	65.6	63.0	47.5	52.8	64.6	73.5	83.1	66.3	67.1	50.4	67.2
1986	62.0	70.7	63.0	60.8	50.5	52.4	62.9	70.0	77.8	63.5	64.4	50.6	65.7
1984	66.6	74.6	66.9	64.7	53.4	54.9	67.3	75.7	83.8	68.4	69.4	54.3	68.1
1982	62.5	71.1	61.7	60.6	52.3	53.3	62.9	70.0	79.4	63.9	65.5	49.8	64.3
1980	64.8	73.8	64.8	63.3	53.0	54.6	66.4	74.4	84.3	67.4	68.7	50.3	65.8
1978	62.3	68.2	60.1	59.1	53.2	52.9	62.0	68.7	76.9	62.1	63.0	44.1	63.4
1976	65.9	72.3	64.6	63.2	54.4	55.6	66.9	75.2	83.7	67.6	68.8	52.1	65.2
1974	62.2	66.6	59.8	59.8	54.1	54.3	61.9	66.9	76.0	62.5	63.5	42.2	64.0
1972	73.9	NA	68.7	NA	61.5	63.0	74.0	81.7	87.8	73.6	74.3	58.7	70.3
1970	70.0	NA	63.8	NA	61.2	62.9	70.6	72.0	78.1	69.0	69.8	52.2	66.5
1968	76.5	NA	69.2	NA	64.6	68.5	77.7	82.9	87.0	76.1	76.6	60.3	71.3
1966	73.8	NA	62.2	NA	63.7	66.7	73.5	75.5	79.0	71.5	72.0	54.9	68.4
1964	NA	NA	NA	NA	NA	NA	NA	NA	NA	NA	NA	NA	NA

Note: Prior to 1972, data are for people 21 to 24 years of age with the exception of those aged 18 to 24 in Georgia and Kentucky, 19 to 24 in Alaska, and 20 to 24 in Hawaii.

Note: Registration data were not collected in the 1964 Current Population Survey.

Note: NA Not available.

Source: U.S. Census Bureau, Current Population Survey, November 2004 and earlier reports.

Table A-3. Reported Voting and Registration for Total and Citizen Voting-Age Population, by State for Congressional Elections: 1974-2002

(Percent, Population 18 Years and Over)

Voting rates	2002 Total	2002 Citizen	1998 Total	1998 Citizen	1994 Total	1994 Citizen	1990 Total	1990 Citizen	1986 Total	1986 Citizen	1982 Total	1982 Citizen	1978 Total	1974 Total
Alabama	48.7	49.3	51.2	51.8	45.8	46.4	51.0	52.1	53.1	54.2	49.3	50.0	46.8	N/A
Alaska	52.6	55.0	53.8	55.2	59.4	60.5	59.2	63.3	56.2	58.1	58.5	62.1	50.9	N/A
Arizona	36.8	42.4	33.8	38.2	41.9	45.7	46.2	50.4	46.2	49.1	43.1	45.6	36.9	N/A
Arkansas	45.3	46.2	42.4	42.8	41.7	42.1	46.4	48.5	47.1	47.9	53.1	54.2	41.3	N/A
California	34.2	42.5	40.5	50.4	46.0	57.5	42.4	54.3	45.3	55.1	48.6	58.6	47.9	47.5
Colorado	45.7	50.1	52.1	55.6	46.5	47.9	50.6	53.3	52.7	54.4	52.0	53.8	48.2	N/A
Connecticut	44.1	47.6	45.4	47.1	51.9	55.4	49.4	54.6	46.7	50.2	53.7	56.4	54.0	N/A
Delaware	42.9	45.3	36.5	37.7	41.4	42.3	38.4	41.5	38.0	39.2	51.2	54.8	49.1	N/A
District of Columbia	47.6	53.3	45.4	48.9	56.1	63.2	48.6	55.0	42.5	46.9	40.5	44.5	36.1	N/A
Florida	42.5	48.3	39.0	43.9	43.5	49.0	43.4	49.1	46.6	51.3	40.9	45.1	47.1	34.8
Georgia	40.0	42.3	37.4	38.6	35.7	36.5	42.3	45.2	39.4	40.7	38.6	39.5	29.0	39.6
Hawaii	41.6	45.4	48.1	53.7	46.9	52.7	51.6	57.9	53.0	58.7	54.3	59.7	49.9	N/A
Idaho	44.7	46.4	45.0	47.5	50.7	51.6	48.2	50.7	64.9	67.4	57.4	59.0	51.6	N/A
Illinois	42.9	46.8	44.5	48.2	43.0	46.2	48.3	53.1	47.3	50.6	55.0	58.3	46.9	45.4
Indiana	39.9	40.4	40.0	40.6	38.7	39.0	44.2	46.7	49.3	50.5	54.9	56.4	42.9	53.3
Iowa	48.9	50.9	51.6	52.5	52.5	53.4	50.5	51.8	48.1	49.7	56.4	58.7	46.2	N/A
Kansas	46.3	48.7	40.1	41.6	50.7	51.8	52.4	54.2	53.5	54.8	54.3	56.0	50.9	N/A
Kentucky	45.4	45.8	44.4	45.1	34.6	35.0	39.0	40.4	34.3	35.0	35.7	36.9	29.7	N/A
Louisiana	49.4	50.3	38.3	38.8	34.2	34.7	51.4	53.7	56.7	59.2	25.7	26.3	37.3	N/A
Maine	57.0	57.8	47.9	48.3	58.3	59.7	64.7	66.8	54.6	55.7	62.6	64.0	59.0	N/A
Maryland	46.6	51.0	47.3	51.3	46.9	49.3	39.4	42.4	43.1	45.8	47.3	49.9	45.4	N/A
Massachusetts	47.5	52.5	46.2	50.2	51.9	55.0	58.8	64.7	48.4	51.8	53.7	58.8	55.9	51.0
Michigan	48.3	50.3	49.7	51.1	52.3	53.5	45.4	48.9	44.5	47.2	54.0	57.1	53.6	48.8
Minnesota	64.1	67.4	64.2	65.9	58.5	58.9	62.9	64.9	59.3	61.0	66.8	68.9	64.2	N/A
Mississippi	42.5	43.1	40.2	40.2	44.3	44.5	34.7	35.5	43.7	44.0	51.9	52.9	48.5	N/A
Missouri	51.5	52.6	45.8	46.8	54.6	55.5	40.9	42.5	46.7	48.1	51.2	53.6	52.8	45.2
Montana	53.4	53.9	53.3	53.9	60.7	61.2	62.7	64.5	65.1	66.1	61.3	62.6	59.8	N/A
Nebraska	43.4	46.1	45.3	46.8	54.4	54.8	57.8	59.7	54.5	55.5	56.0	57.0	52.3	N/A
Nevada	37.0	42.7	33.1	37.0	40.4	44.4	42.5	46.1	42.5	45.1	41.6	44.5	40.7	N/A
New Hampshire	48.9	51.0	40.9	41.9	41.7	42.9	44.3	45.9	37.6	39.2	49.5	51.4	52.7	N/A
New Jersey	37.5	42.8	35.5	35.5	41.0	45.2	41.8	46.9	37.3	40.3	48.6	52.6	41.8	46.4
New Mexico	41.5	44.4	48.2	51.5	47.0	50.2	45.6	49.6	47.1	48.9	58.1	60.0	50.1	N/A
New York	38.1	43.6	41.4	48.2	45.3	51.5	41.5	48.5	43.8	50.5	48.2	54.2	46.0	48.0
North Carolina	42.4	44.7	39.4	40.4	35.8	36.4	49.3	51.0	45.2	46.1	39.0	39.7	30.9	34.1
North Dakota	56.7	57.5	57.0	57.5	61.3	61.6	60.1	61.6	72.7	74.1	64.3	65.3	59.6	N/A
Ohio	42.4	43.6	44.6	45.4	46.7	47.0	48.5	50.9	49.1	50.8	50.4	52.2	45.2	47.1
Oklahoma	47.8	49.0	40.1	40.7	46.9	47.5	49.2	51.6	48.6	50.2	46.5	47.8	50.8	N/A
Oregon	51.8	55.5	47.0	50.5	61.3	65.0	53.9	57.8	64.7	66.4	62.2	65.6	53.4	N/A
Pennsylvania	41.7	43.2	39.2	40.3	42.8	43.7	42.0	44.1	46.1	47.7	48.2	50.1	48.4	46.8
Rhode Island	46.3	50.6	48.5	52.7	51.2	54.5	53.4	60.8	47.4	52.9	55.4	58.6	56.2	N/A
South Carolina	45.6	46.6	47.1	47.5	45.4	45.9	42.8	43.9	41.3	42.4	37.4	38.2	36.0	N/A
South Dakota	65.4	66.1	50.7	50.9	64.0	64.2	57.2	59.5	65.5	66.3	62.9	63.8	62.7	N/A
Tennessee	44.3	46.5	36.2	36.5	43.1	43.5	30.5	30.9	44.0	44.9	47.2	47.9	44.6	N/A
Texas	35.2	40.7	32.9	37.0	37.8	42.4	41.4	45.7	37.4	41.3	39.7	42.6	34.3	28.3
Utah	41.5	43.8	39.9	42.1	44.2	46.5	47.1	48.8	49.4	51.4	61.1	63.2	52.3	N/A
Vermont	52.2	53.0	51.6	52.8	49.0	49.6	55.0	57.6	58.5	60.2	50.1	53.2	37.0	N/A
Virginia	34.8	37.2	30.1	31.3	46.3	48.4	37.4	39.9	37.5	39.1	45.6	47.3	42.5	33.2
Washington	47.1	50.7	45.6	48.9	46.5	49.2	43.3	46.3	48.3	51.1	50.3	54.9	40.5	N/A
West Virginia	36.8	36.9	35.9	36.0	34.0	34.2	34.7	35.6	39.2	40.2	47.4	48.1	40.6	N/A
Wisconsin	48.5	50.3	50.3	50.9	49.7	50.2	48.0	49.4	51.2	52.2	54.2	55.5	58.3	N/A
Wyoming	53.5	53.9	54.3	55.1	63.5	64.0	53.5	55.2	53.5	54.8	60.0	61.8	59.7	N/A

Note: Data for 1974 show the largest 15 states. Data are limited to the largest states in 1974 due to smaller sample sizes.

Note: Data are not available prior to 1972.

Note: N/A Not available.

Source: U.S. Census Bureau, Current Population Survey, November 2002 and earlier years.

Table A-4. Reported Voting and Registration for Total and Citizen Voting-Age Population: Congressional Elections 1982-2002

(Percent, Population 18 Years and Over)

Year	Total		White		Non-Hispanic White		Black		Asian and Pacific Islander		Hispanic (of any race)	
	Total	Citizen	Total	Citizen	Total	Citizen	Total	Citizen	Total	Citizen	Total	Citizen
2002												
Registered	60.9	66.5	63.1	67.9	67.9	69.4	58.5	62.4	30.7	49.2	32.6	52.5
Voted	42.3	46.1	44.1	47.5	48.0	49.1	39.7	42.3	19.4	31.2	18.9	30.4
1998												
Registered	62.1	67.1	63.9	68.2	67.9	69.3	60.2	63.6	29.1	48.9	33.7	55.2
Voted	41.9	45.3	43.3	46.3	46.5	47.4	39.6	41.8	19.3	32.4	20.0	32.8
1994												
Registered	62.5	67.1	64.6	68.4	68.1	69.4	58.5	61.3	28.7	51.9	31.3	52.9
Voted	45.0	48.4	47.3	50.0	50.1	51.0	37.1	38.9	21.8	39.4	20.2	34.0
1990												
Registered	62.2	68.2	63.8	69.1	66.7	69.9	58.8	63.5	28.4	56.0	32.3	55.2
Voted	45.0	49.3	46.7	50.5	49.0	51.4	39.2	42.4	20.3	40.0	21.0	36.0
1986												
Registered	64.3	69.0	65.3	69.5	67.7	70.2	64.0	67.3	N/A	N/A	35.9	56.4
Voted	46.0	49.4	47.0	50.1	48.9	50.7	43.2	45.5	N/A	N/A	24.2	38.0
1982												
Registered	64.1	68.5	65.6	69.4	67.5	70.1	59.1	62.6	N/A	N/A	35.3	53.7
Voted	48.5	51.9	49.9	52.8	51.5	53.4	43.0	45.5	N/A	N/A	25.3	38.5

Note: N/A Not available.

Source: U.S. Census Bureau, Current Population Survey, November 2002 and earlier years.

Table A-5 cont. Reported Voting and Registration for Total and Citizen Voting-Age Population, by State for Presidential Elections: 1972-2004

(Percent)

Registration Rates

State	1972 Total	1976 Total	1980 Total	1980 Citizen	1984 Total	1984 Citizen	1988 Total	1988 Citizen	1992 Total	1992 Citizen	1996 Total	1996 Citizen	2000 Total	2000 Citizen	2004 Total	2004 Citizen
Alabama	NA	67.1	70.2	71.3	75.6	77.5	73.3	74.2	77.1	78.0	73.8	74.9	73.6	74.6	72.6	74.2
Alaska	NA	NA	66.6	73.4	70.4	75.6	70.0	75.4	75.1	81.0	75.5	76.8	72.5	74.9	74.0	77.0
Arizona	NA	NA	58.7	63.4	63.0	67.7	62.5	66.9	70.5	75.9	58.5	67.2	53.3	60.1	60.3	70.8
Arkansas	NA	NA	66.4	68.1	70.4	71.4	67.4	69.1	66.5	69.4	64.4	64.9	59.4	60.8	66.1	68.4
California	71.0	59.8	60.0	72.4	61.5	75.1	59.1	76.5	57.6	76.5	56.1	70.9	52.8	65.8	55.4	68.6
Colorado	NA	NA	69.5	73.4	66.9	71.2	73.0	77.2	74.7	78.9	70.0	72.7	64.1	68.5	67.9	74.2
Connecticut	NA	72.7	72.9	78.5	72.1	77.0	73.5	79.6	76.8	84.4	69.9	74.5	62.5	67.5	65.0	70.3
Delaware	NA	NA	65.8	68.6	63.5	69.9	64.0	67.0	70.7	76.1	64.0	65.7	67.9	70.8	67.7	71.6
District of Columbia	NA	NA	56.9	62.3	60.4	70.7	64.7	71.1	73.9	81.2	73.0	77.8	72.4	79.2	67.4	75.2
Florida	68.7	62.7	63.1	69.6	62.6	69.5	63.0	71.4	62.7	71.4	61.8	68.8	60.5	69.9	62.6	71.7
Georgia	64.2	65.6	65.6	67.4	63.1	67.1	61.4	63.9	62.0	65.6	66.1	67.8	61.1	63.5	62.3	67.3
Hawaii	NA	NA	61.9	70.4	59.2	66.8	61.0	67.2	60.6	67.9	55.1	60.7	47.0	52.2	53.0	58.4
Idaho	NA	NA	73.5	78.5	73.9	78.0	69.6	73.2	71.8	76.0	68.4	70.5	61.4	63.9	66.5	69.9
Illinois	78.7	73.1	72.8	79.0	74.7	82.2	69.3	75.2	72.1	80.0	67.7	72.0	66.7	72.8	69.2	74.5
Indiana	80.9	71.3	69.3	71.9	69.7	71.6	68.4	70.8	68.0	69.5	68.5	69.3	68.5	69.7	66.8	68.3
Iowa	NA	73.8	75.7	78.2	75.7	77.4	71.9	73.4	77.9	80.2	73.0	75.3	72.2	75.9	75.7	78.4
Kansas	NA	NA	69.5	72.0	69.9	73.1	67.6	70.0	77.1	79.2	68.9	70.5	67.7	69.5	67.2	72.3
Kentucky	NA	63.1	66.3	67.9	70.0	71.8	62.2	63.7	64.9	69.2	69.4	69.7	69.7	71.5	73.3	75.1
Louisiana	NA	70.3	72.7	75.2	73.2	77.1	75.1	77.4	77.0	79.7	73.4	74.5	75.4	76.6	73.6	75.0
Maine	NA	NA	81.3	85.5	83.5	87.5	80.7	82.9	85.4	88.3	81.5	83.6	80.3	81.4	80.6	81.8
Maryland	NA	66.8	66.4	70.9	68.3	73.7	64.1	69.7	71.7	77.5	65.9	69.2	65.6	70.1	66.2	72.7
Massachusetts	77.8	76.5	72.5	78.9	69.6	76.9	71.1	76.3	72.5	81.3	66.7	71.9	70.3	76.4	72.0	77.5
Michigan	73.2	70.4	73.0	79.1	73.8	78.8	72.3	78.8	74.6	80.4	72.0	74.2	69.1	71.7	72.0	74.7
Minnesota	NA	84.3	83.7	87.2	85.8	88.5	77.6	82.8	86.1	90.9	78.3	80.7	76.7	78.9	81.8	84.5
Mississippi	NA	NA	81.1	82.5	82.6	84.9	78.2	80.0	79.3	80.9	71.6	72.1	72.2	73.2	72.5	73.7
Missouri	76.2	70.5	75.4	78.5	74.9	77.4	74.8	76.8	74.2	76.5	75.5	76.2	74.3	75.8	78.6	81.2
Montana	NA	NA	74.0	77.8	77.3	80.8	75.2	76.4	77.3	79.5	75.1	75.9	70.0	70.8	75.1	75.5
Nebraska	NA	NA	71.6	74.8	71.3	74.4	70.8	73.3	73.1	74.7	74.1	76.1	71.8	73.5	70.9	75.5
Nevada	NA	NA	53.8	59.8	50.8	57.0	54.5	58.8	63.4	70.3	59.0	65.8	52.3	58.6	56.8	65.3
New Hampshire	NA	NA	74.1	76.7	69.0	71.2	66.0	68.1	69.9	73.2	71.7	72.7	69.6	73.2	72.9	75.6
New Jersey	73.2	66.9	66.8	73.6	67.9	74.8	66.5	72.8	68.0	77.8	63.3	70.1	63.2	70.7	63.7	73.1
New Mexico	NA	NA	66.9	70.5	69.6	73.0	64.4	70.0	67.1	71.4	61.7	66.3	59.5	63.1	68.1	72.0
New York	69.1	61.0	59.5	67.9	63.5	72.4	60.4	73.9	62.0	73.9	61.0	70.2	58.6	67.8	59.5	67.5
North Carolina	63.5	58.9	60.6	63.0	65.4	66.9	63.6	65.9	68.7	71.6	68.5	70.3	66.1	69.7	68.7	72.5
North Dakota	NA	NA	91.9	94.7	91.8	94.3	94.0	95.8	90.8	93.0	90.5	91.0	100.0	92.0	88.5	89.3
Ohio	73.2	64.0	66.4	69.9	69.6	72.3	69.4	71.8	69.6	74.7	68.4	69.5	67.0	68.3	70.9	72.3
Oklahoma	NA	NA	66.2	70.1	70.5	73.9	64.6	66.8	74.3	77.5	70.1	70.9	68.3	70.0	68.4	71.9
Oregon	68.9	63.0	72.5	79.1	74.3	78.9	71.2	73.7	74.7	79.9	72.9	76.0	68.2	74.7	75.2	78.8
Pennsylvania	NA	NA	62.0	65.3	65.2	68.3	62.2	64.7	65.1	67.4	65.6	67.2	65.3	67.3	69.3	71.6
Rhode Island	NA	NA	73.0	80.2	68.6	76.0	69.1	80.5	74.0	80.5	71.7	76.0	69.7	73.7	64.2	71.3
South Carolina	NA	NA	58.2	59.6	58.4	60.6	60.4	61.9	67.0	68.6	68.2	68.4	68.0	68.8	73.1	74.6
South Dakota	NA	NA	80.7	83.4	77.5	79.4	79.9	81.9	80.1	81.9	74.8	75.4	70.9	71.6	75.5	76.8
Tennessee	NA	67.3	67.2	69.0	71.5	73.1	65.3	66.6	65.0	66.3	65.9	66.5	62.1	63.7	62.2	64.4

Table A-5 cont.   Reported Voting and Registration for Total and Citizen Voting-Age Population, by State for Presidential Elections: 1972-2004

(Percent)

| State | 2004 | | 2000 | | 1996 | | 1992 | | Registration Rates 1988 | | 1984 | | 1980 | | 1976 | 1972 |
	Total	Citizen	Total	Citizen	Total	Citizen	Total	Citizen	Total	Citizen	Total	Citizen	Total	Citizen	Total	Total
Texas	61.2	69.5	61.4	69.0	61.9	69.0	64.9	72.8	65.8	72.3	65.1	71.2	60.4	66.0	62.4	68.9
Utah	70.1	75.7	64.7	69.1	64.5	67.6	78.8	82.6	75.6	79.0	76.6	79.7	76.8	79.3	NA	NA
Vermont	73.5	75.6	72.0	73.1	72.0	73.1	76.1	81.4	77.7	80.5	74.5	78.7	73.5	76.6	NA	NA
Virginia	64.1	69.2	64.1	67.5	66.5	68.8	65.4	68.7	66.9	69.7	62.6	66.0	62.2	65.0	61.8	61.5
Washington	68.2	74.2	66.1	69.9	70.0	72.6	71.5	75.8	68.6	71.6	70.6	76.1	66.7	74.1	70.7	NA
West Virginia	67.0	67.1	63.1	63.5	64.7	65.2	64.9	66.3	64.8	66.1	69.4	71.0	69.3	71.1	NA	NA
Wisconsin	78.2	82.1	76.5	79.1	77.6	80.6	84.4	86.3	85.4	86.7	82.9	85.2	87.1	90.3	85.2	NA
Wyoming	71.0	71.6	68.6	69.1	71.2	71.8	68.1	70.6	67.7	70.0	71.7	74.4	63.8	66.7	NA	NA

Note: NA Not available.

Note: Data for 1976 show the 25 largest states and data for 1972 show the largest 15 states. Data are limited to the largest states in 1976 and 1972 due to smaller sample sizes.

Note: Data are not available prior to 1972.

Source: U.S. Census Bureau, Current Population Report, November 2004 and earlier years.

Table A-6. Reported Voting and Registration for Total and Citizen Voting-Age Population: Presidential Elections 1980-2004

(Percent, population 18 years and over)

Year	Total		White		White non-Hispanic		Black		Asian[1]		Hispanic (of any race)	
	Total	Citizen	Total	Citizen	Total	Citizen	Total	Citizen	Total	Citizen	Total	Citizen
2004[2]												
Registered	65.9	72.1	67.9	73.6	73.5	75.1	64.4	68.7	34.9	51.8	34.9	64.0
Voted	58.3	63.8	60.3	65.4	65.8	67.2	56.3	60.0	29.8	44.1	28.0	47.2
2004[3]												
Registered	65.9	72.1	67.9	73.5	73.5	75.1	64.3	68.6	36.1	52.5	34.9	64.0
Voted	58.3	63.8	60.3	65.3	65.7	67.1	56.2	59.9	30.7	44.6	28.0	47.2
2000												
Registered	63.9	69.5	65.6	70.4	70.0	71.6	63.6	67.5	30.7	52.4	34.9	57.3
Voted	54.7	59.5	56.4	60.5	60.4	61.8	53.5	56.8	25.4	43.4	27.5	45.1
1996												
Registered	65.9	70.9	67.7	72.0	71.6	73.0	63.5	66.4	32.6	57.2	35.7	58.6
Voted	54.2	58.4	56.0	59.6	59.6	60.7	50.6	53.0	25.7	45.0	26.8	44.0
1992												
Registered	68.2	75.2	70.1	76.3	73.5	77.1	63.9	70.0	31.2	61.3	35.0	62.5
Voted	61.3	67.7	63.6	69.2	66.9	70.2	54.0	59.8	27.3	53.9	28.9	51.6
1988												
Registered	66.6	72.1	67.9	72.8	70.8	73.6	64.5	68.8	NA	NA	35.5	59.1
Voted	57.4	62.2	59.1	63.4	61.8	64.2	51.5	55.0	NA	NA	28.8	48.0
1984												
Registered	68.3	73.9	69.6	74.5	71.6	75.1	66.3	72.0	NA	NA	40.1	61.4
Voted	59.9	64.9	61.4	65.7	63.3	66.4	55.8	60.6	NA	NA	32.7	50.0
1980												
Registered	66.9	72.3	68.4	73.4	70.3	84.7	60.0	64.1	NA	NA	36.3	56.0
Voted	59.3	64.0	60.9	65.4	62.8	66.2	50.5	53.9	NA	NA	29.9	46.1

Note: NA Not available.

Note: Because of changes in the Current Population Survey race categories beginning in 2003, 2004 data on race are not directly comparable with data from earlier years.

[1] Prior to 2004, this category was 'Asian and Pacific Islanders,' therefore rates are not comparable with prior years.

[2] Shows the single-race population.

[3] Shows the race alone or in-combination population.

Source: U.S. Census Bureau, Current Population Survey, November 2004 and earlier reports

Table A-7. Reported Voting Rates in Congressional Election Years by Selected Characteristics: November 1966 to 2002

(Numbers in thousands)

Characteristic	1966	1970	1974	1978	1982	1986	1990	1994	1998	2002
United States										
Total, voting age	**112,800**	**120,701**	**141,299**	**151,646**	**165,483**	**173,890**	**182,118**	**190,267**	**198,228**	**210,421**
Total voted	62,518	65,888	63,164	69,587	80,310	79,954	81,991	85,702	83,098	88,903
Percent voted	55.4	54.6	44.7	45.9	48.5	46.0	45.0	45.0	41.9	42.3
Race and Hispanic Origin										
White	57.0	56.0	46.3	47.3	49.9	47.0	46.7	47.3	43.3	44.1
White non-Hispanic	NA	NA	NA	NA	NA	NA	NA	50.1	46.5	48.0
Black	41.7	43.5	33.8	37.2	43.0	43.2	39.2	37.1	39.6	39.7
Asian and Pacific Islander	NA	NA	NA	NA	NA	NA	20.3	21.8	19.2	19.4
Hispanic (of any race)	NA	NA	22.9	23.5	25.3	24.2	21.0	20.2	20.0	18.9
Sex										
Male	58.2	56.8	46.2	46.6	48.7	45.8	44.6	44.7	41.4	41.4
Female	53.0	52.7	43.4	45.3	48.4	46.1	45.4	45.3	42.4	43.0
Age										
18 to 24 years[1]	31.1	30.4	23.8	23.5	24.8	21.9	20.4	20.1	16.7	17.2
25 to 44 years	53.1	51.9	42.2	43.1	45.4	41.4	40.7	39.4	34.8	34.1
45 to 64 years	64.5	64.2	56.9	58.5	62.2	58.7	55.8	56.7	53.6	53.1
65 years and over	56.1	57.0	51.4	55.9	59.9	60.9	60.3	61.3	59.5	61.0
Northeast, Midwest, and West										
Total, voting age	**78,355**	**83,515**	**96,505**	**102,894**	**110,126**	**114,689**	**119,740**	**123,903**	**128,104**	**136,212**
Total voted	47,712	49,264	47,058	50,305	57,171	54,487	55,558	58,574	56,058	58,046
Percent voted	60.9	59.0	48.8	48.9	51.9	47.5	46.4	47.3	43.8	42.6
Race and Hispanic Origin										
White	61.7	59.8	50.0	50.0	53.1	48.7	48.2	49.3	45.4	44.7
White non-Hispanic	NA	NA	NA	NA	NA	NA	NA	52.1	48.6	48.6
Black	52.1	51.4	37.9	41.3	48.5	44.2	38.4	40.2	40.4	39.3
Asian and Pacific Islander	NA	NA	NA	NA	NA	NA	22.1	22.5	21.1	20.0
Hispanic (of any race)	NA	NA	NA	23.9	25.8	23.8	20.5	20.8	21.4	18.2
South										
Total, voting age	**34,445**	**37,186**	**44,794**	**48,752**	**55,357**	**59,201**	**62,378**	**66,365**	**70,124**	**74,208**
Total voted	14,806	16,624	16,105	19,282	23,139	25,467	26,433	27,128	27,040	30,857
Percent voted	43.0	44.7	36.0	39.6	41.8	43.0	42.4	40.9	38.6	41.6
Race and Hispanic Origin										
White	45.1	46.4	37.4	41.1	42.9	43.5	43.5	43.0	39.2	42.9
White non-Hispanic	NA	NA	NA	NA	NA	NA	NA	45.9	42.1	46.9
Black	32.9	36.8	30.0	33.5	38.3	42.5	39.8	34.6	38.9	39.9
Asian and Pacific Islander	NA	NA	NA	NA	NA	NA	8.4	17.7	10.1	17.2
Hispanic (of any race)	NA	NA	NA	22.5	24.2	25.0	22.1	19.1	17.3	20.1

NA Not available

1/ Prior to 1972, data are for people 21 to 24 years of age with the exception of those aged 18 to 24 in Georgia and Kentucky, 19 to 24 in Alaska, and 20 to 24 in Hawaii.

Source: U.S. Census Bureau, Current Population Surveys 1966-2002.

Table A-8. Reported Registration Rates in Congressional Election Years by Selected Characteristics: November 1966 to 2002

(Numbers in thousands)

Characteristic	1966	1970	1974	1978	1982	1986	1990	1994	1998	2002
United States										
Total, voting age	**112,800**	**120,701**	**141,299**	**151,646**	**165,483**	**173,890**	**182,118**	**190,267**	**198,228**	**210,421**
Total voted	79,295	82,181	87,889	94,883	105,996	111,728	113,248	118,994	123,104	128,154
Percent voted	70.3	68.1	62.2	62.6	64.1	64.3	62.2	62.5	62.1	60.9
Race and Hispanic Origin										
White	71.6	69.1	63.5	63.8	65.6	65.3	63.8	64.6	63.9	63.1
White non-Hispanic	NA	NA	NA	NA	NA	NA	NA	68.1	67.9	67.9
Black	60.2	60.8	54.9	57.1	59.1	64.0	58.8	58.5	60.2	58.5
Asian and Pacific Islander	NA	NA	NA	NA	NA	NA	28.4	28.7	29.1	30.7
Hispanic (of any race)	NA	NA	34.9	32.9	35.3	35.9	32.3	31.3	33.7	32.6
Sex										
Male	72.2	69.6	62.8	62.6	63.7	63.4	61.2	61.2	60.6	58.9
Female	68.6	66.8	61.7	62.5	64.4	65.0	63.1	63.7	63.5	62.8
Age										
18 to 24 years[1]	44.1	40.9	41.3	40.5	42.4	42.0	39.9	42.3	39.2	38.2
25 to 44 years	67.6	65.0	59.9	60.2	61.5	61.1	58.4	57.9	57.7	55.4
45 to 64 years	78.9	77.5	73.6	74.3	75.6	74.8	71.4	71.7	71.1	69.4
65 years and over	73.5	73.7	70.2	72.8	75.2	76.9	76.5	76.3	75.4	75.8
Northeast, Midwest, and West										
Total, voting age	**78,355**	**83,515**	**96,504**	**102,894**	**110,126**	**114,689**	**119,740**	**123,903**	**128,104**	**136,212**
Total voted	57,862	58,474	61,104	65,599	71,845	74,404	74,985	78,441	79,150	82,447
Percent voted	73.8	70.0	63.3	63.8	65.2	64.9	62.6	63.3	61.8	60.5
Race and Hispanic Origin										
White	74.5	70.8	64.6	64.9	66.7	66.2	64.4	65.6	63.9	63.0
White non-Hispanic	NA	NA	NA	NA	NA	NA	NA	69.2	68.2	67.8
Black	68.8	64.5	54.2	58.0	61.7	63.1	58.4	58.3	58.5	57.0
Asian and Pacific Islander	NA	NA	NA	NA	NA	NA	30.2	29.5	30.4	31.5
Hispanic (of any race)	NA	NA	NA	32.0	33.9	33.2	30.4	29.1	31.9	30.6
South										
Total, voting age	**34,445**	**37,186**	**44,794**	**48,752**	**55,357**	**59,201**	**62,378**	**66,365**	**70,124**	**74,208**
Total voted	21,433	23,707	26,785	29,284	34,152	37,323	38,262	40,552	43,953	45,706
Percent voted	62.2	63.8	59.8	60.1	61.7	63.0	61.3	61.1	62.7	61.6
Race and Hispanic Origin										
White	64.3	65.1	61.0	61.2	63.2	63.2	62.5	62.6	63.9	63.2
White non-Hispanic	NA	NA	NA	NA	NA	NA	NA	65.9	67.4	68.0
Black	52.9	57.5	55.5	56.2	56.9	64.6	59.0	58.8	61.5	59.8
Asian and Pacific Islander	NA	NA	NA	NA	NA	NA	17.0	24.7	22.8	27.6
Hispanic (of any race)	NA	NA	NA	34.9	38.3	41.0	36.1	35.3	37.3	36.0

NA Not available

1/Prior to 1972, data are for people 21 to 24 years of age with the exception of those aged 18 to 24 in Georgia and Kentucky, 19 to 24 in Alaska, and 20 to 24 in Hawaii.

Source: U.S. Census Bureau, Current Population Surveys 1966-2002.

Table A-10. Reported Registration Rates in Presidential Election Years, by Selected Characteristics: November 1968 to 2004

(Numbers in thousands)

Characteristic	1968	1972	1976	1980	1984	1988	1992	1996	2000	2004
United States										
Total, voting age	**116,535**	**136,203**	**146,548**	**157,085**	**169,963**	**178,098**	**185,684**	**193,651**	**202,609**	**215,694**
Total voted	86,574	98,480	97,761	105,035	116,106	118,589	126,578	127,661	129,549	142070
Percent voted	74.3	72.3	66.7	66.9	68.3	66.6	68.2	65.9	63.9	65.9
Race and Hispanic Origin										
White	75.4	73.4	68.3	68.4	69.6	67.9	70.1	67.7	65.6	(X)
White non-Hispanic	(NA)	(NA)	(NA)	70.3	71.6	70.8	73.5	71.6	70.0	(X)
Black[1]	66.2	65.5	58.5	60.0	66.3	64.5	63.9	63.5	63.6	(X)
Asian and Pacific Islander	(NA)	(NA)	(NA)	(NA)	(NA)	(NA)	31.2	32.6	30.7	(X)
White alone or in combination	(X)	(X)	(X)	(X)	(X)	(X)	(X)	(X)	(X)	67.9
White alone	(X)	(X)	(X)	(X)	(X)	(X)	(X)	(X)	(X)	67.9
White alone, not Hispanic	(X)	(X)	(X)	(X)	(X)	(X)	(X)	(X)	(X)	73.5
Black alone or in combination	(X)	(X)	(X)	(X)	(X)	(X)	(X)	(X)	(X)	64.3
Black alone	(X)	(X)	(X)	(X)	(X)	(X)	(X)	(X)	(X)	64.4
Asian alone or in combination	(X)	(X)	(X)	(X)	(X)	(X)	(X)	(X)	(X)	36.1
Asian alone	(X)	(X)	(X)	(X)	(X)	(X)	(X)	(X)	(X)	34.9
Hispanic (of any race)	(NA)	44.4	37.8	36.3	40.1	35.5	35.0	35.7	34.9	34.3
Sex										
Male	76.0	73.1	67.1	66.6	67.3	65.2	66.9	64.4	62.2	64.0
Female	72.8	71.6	66.4	67.1	69.3	67.8	69.3	67.3	65.6	67.6
Age										
18 to 24 years[2]	56.0	58.9	51.3	49.2	51.3	48.2	52.5	48.8	45.4	51.5
25 to 44 years	72.4	71.3	65.5	65.6	66.6	63.0	64.8	61.9	59.6	60.1
45 to 64 years	81.1	79.7	75.5	75.8	76.6	75.5	75.3	73.5	71.2	72.7
65 years and over	75.6	75.6	71.4	74.6	76.9	78.4	78.0	77.0	76.1	76.9
Northeast, Midwest, and West										
Total, voting age	**81,594**	**93,653**	**99,403**	**106,524**	**112,376**	**117,373**	**122,025**	**125,571**	**130,774**	**138,505**
Total voted	62,409	69,256	67,306	72,290	77,584	78,769	83,816	82,770	83,228	91,513
Percent voted	76.5	73.9	67.7	67.9	69.0	67.1	68.7	65.9	63.6	66.1
Race and Hispanic Origin										
White	77.2	74.9	69.0	69.3	70.5	68.5	70.9	68.1	65.9	(X)
White non-Hispanic	(NA)	(NA)	(NA)	71.2	72.6	71.7	74.5	72.2	70.3	(X)
Black[1]	71.8	67.0	60.9	60.6	67.2	65.9	63.0	62.0	61.7	(X)
Asian and Pacific Islander	(NA)	(NA)	(NA)	(NA)	(NA)	(NA)	31.6	33.5	31.3	(X)
White alone or in combination	(X)	(X)	(X)	(X)	(X)	(X)	(X)	(X)	(X)	68.5
White alone	(X)	(X)	(X)	(X)	(X)	(X)	(X)	(X)	(X)	68.5
White alone, not Hispanic	(X)	(X)	(X)	(X)	(X)	(X)	(X)	(X)	(X)	74.3
Black alone or in combination	(X)	(X)	(X)	(X)	(X)	(X)	(X)	(X)	(X)	63.2
Black alone	(X)	(X)	(X)	(X)	(X)	(X)	(X)	(X)	(X)	63.3
Asian alone or in combination	(X)	(X)	(X)	(X)	(X)	(X)	(X)	(X)	(X)	37.1
Asian alone	(X)	(X)	(X)	(X)	(X)	(X)	(X)	(X)	(X)	36.0
Hispanic (of any race)	(NA)	(NA)	(NA)	35.5	39.0	32.4	32.9	33.8	32.7	33.4
South										
Total, voting age	**34,941**	**42,550**	**47,145**	**50,561**	**57,587**	**60,725**	**63,659**	**68,080**	**71,835**	**77,188**
Total voted	24,165	29,224	30,455	32,745	38,522	39,820	42,762	44,891	46,321	50,556
Percent voted	69.2	68.7	64.6	64.8	66.9	65.6	67.2	65.9	64.5	65.5
Race and Hispanic Origin										
White	70.8	69.8	66.7	66.2	67.8	66.6	68.5	67.0	65.2	(X)
White non-Hispanic	(NA)	(NA)	(NA)	68.1	69.5	68.8	71.3	70.5	69.3	(X)
Black[1]	61.6	64.0	56.4	59.3	65.6	63.3	64.7	64.7	65.2	(X)
Asian and Pacific Islander	(NA)	(NA)	(NA)	(NA)	(NA)	(NA)	29.3	28.1	27.6	(X)
White alone or in combination	(X)	(X)	(X)	(X)	(X)	(X)	(X)	(X)	(X)	66.7
White alone	(X)	(X)	(X)	(X)	(X)	(X)	(X)	(X)	(X)	66.7
White alone, not Hispanic	(X)	(X)	(X)	(X)	(X)	(X)	(X)	(X)	(X)	72.1
Black alone or in combination	(X)	(X)	(X)	(X)	(X)	(X)	(X)	(X)	(X)	65.2
Black alone	(X)	(X)	(X)	(X)	(X)	(X)	(X)	(X)	(X)	65.3
Asian alone or in combination	(X)	(X)	(X)	(X)	(X)	(X)	(X)	(X)	(X)	31.5
Asian alone	(X)	(X)	(X)	(X)	(X)	(X)	(X)	(X)	(X)	30.5
Hispanic (of any race)	(NA)	(NA)	(NA)	38.0	42.3	41.9	39.3	39.3	38.8	36.0

Note: NA Not available.
Note: Because of changes in the Current Population Survey race categories beginning in 2003, 2004 data on race are not directly comparable with data from earlier years.
[1] Prior to 1972, data are for people 21 to 24 years of age with the exception of those aged 18 to 24 in Georgia and Kentucky, 19 to 24 in Alaska, and 20 to 24 in Hawaii.

Source: U.S. Census Bureau, Current Population Surveys 1968 to 2004.

Resource Guide

BOOKS

Abramson, Paul R., et al. *Change and Continuity in the 2004 Elections* (CQ Press, 2006)

Ackerman, Kenneth D. *The Dark Horse: The Surprise Election and Political Murder of President James A. Garfield* (Carroll and Graf Publishers, 2003)

Ahlstrom, S. *A Religious History of the American People* (Yale University Press, 1972)

Aitken, Jonathan. *Nixon: A Life* (Regnery, 1994)

Anderson, Kristi. *The Creation of a Democratic Majority 1928-1936* (University of Chicago Press, 1979)

Andrain, Charles F. and Apter, David E. *Political Protest and Social Change* (New York University Press, 1995)

Appleby, Joyce. *Thomas Jefferson* (Henry Holt, 2003)

Aptheker, Herbert *Abolitionism: A Revolutionary Movement* (Twayne Publishers, 1989)

Aristotle. *Politics*, Jowett, Benjamin trans. (Dover, 2000)

Arnold, Scott N. *The Philosophy and Economics of Market Socialism: A Critical Study* (Oxford University Press, 1994)

Avrich, Paul. *Sacco and Vanzetti: The Anarchist Background* (Princeton University Press, 1991)

Banning, Lance. *The Jeffersonian Persuasion: Evolution of a Party Ideology* (Cornell University Press, 1978)

Banning, Lance. *Liberty and Order: The First American Party Struggle* (The Liberty Fund, 2004)

Barry, Norman P. *The New Right* (Croom Helm, 1987)

Bartels, Larry M. *Presidential Primaries and the Dynamics of Public Choice* (Princeton University Press, 1988)

Baughman, James L. *Henry R. Luce and the Rise of the American News Media* (Macmillan, 1987)

Baum, Lawrence. *The Supreme Court* (Congressional Quarterly, 1995)

Bennett, David H. *Demagogues in the Depression: American Radicals and the Union Party* (Rutgers University Press, 1969)

Berman, William C. *America's Right Turn* (Johns Hopkins University Press, 1998)

Bibby, John F. and Maisel, L. Sandy. *Two Parties— or More? The American Party System* (Westview Press, 2003)

Biles, Roger. *A New Deal for the American People* (Northern Illinois University Press, 1991)

Billington, Ray Allen. *Westward Expansion: A History of the American Frontier* (Macmillan, 1959)

Birch, Anthony H. *The British System of Government* (Routledge, 1998)

Biskupic, Joan and Witt, Elder. *The Supreme Court and Individual Rights* (Congressional Quarterly Press, 1997)

Bobbio, Norberto and Bellamy, Richard. *The Future of Democracy: a Defence of the Rules of the Game* (University of Minnesota Press, 1987)

Brands, H.W. *Woodrow Wilson* (Times Books, 2003)

Brimelow, Peter. *Alien Nation: Common Sense about America's Immigration Disaster* (Random House, 1995)

Brown, Stuart Gerry. *The First Republicans: Political Philosophy and Public Policy in the Party of Jefferson and Madison* (Syracuse University Press, 1954)

Bruchey, Stuart. *Enterprise: The Dynamic Economy of a Free People* (Harvard University Press, 1990)

Buchholz, Todd. *New Ideas From Dead Economists* (Penguin, 2003)

Bullock, Alan. *Hitler: A Study in Tyranny* (Harper and Row, 1962)

Campbell, Angus, et al. *The American Voter* (University of Chicago Press, 1960)

Caro, Robert A. *The Years of Lyndon Johnson* (Knopf, 1982–2002)

Carter, Dan T. *The Politics of Rage: George Wallace, the Origins of the New Conservatism, and the Transformation of American Politics* (Louisiana State University, 2000)

Ceaser, James W. *Reforming the Reform: a Critical Analysis of the Presidential Selection Process* (Ballinger Publishing Co., 1982)

Chalmers, David Mark. *Hooded Americanism: The History of the Ku Klux Klan* (New Viewpoints, 1981)

Chilton, Williamson. *American Suffrage: From Property to Democracy, 1760–1860* (Princeton University Press, 1960)

Clift, Eleanor. *Founding Sisters and the Nineteenth Amendment* (John Wiley and Sons, 2003)

Coakley, John, ed. *Politics in the Republic of Ireland* (Routledge, 1999)

Coicaud, Jean-Marc. *Globalization of Human Rights* (United Nations, 2003)

Collins, Rodnell. *Seventh Child: A Family Memoir of Malcolm X* (Carol Publishing Group, 1998)

Conley, Richard S. *The Presidency, Congress and Divided Government* (Texas A & M University Press, 2003)

Cook, Chris and Taylor, Ian. *The Labour Party: An Introduction to Its History, Structure and Politics* (Longman, 1980)

Cooper, John Milton. *Breaking the Heart of the World: Woodrow Wilson and the Fight for the League of Nations* (Cambridge University Press, 2001)

Cope, Kevin L. *John Locke Revisited* (Twayne, 1999)

Corrado, Anthony, et al. *The New Campaign Finance Sourcebook* (Brookings Institution Press, 2005)

Dahl, Robert Alan. *On Democracy* (Yale University Press, 2000)

Davidson, Chandler and Groffman, Bernard. *Quiet Revolution in the South: The Impact of the Voting Rights Act, 1965–1990* (Princeton University Press 1994)

Davis, David Brion. *The Fear of Conspiracy: Images of Un-American Subversion from the Revolution to the Present* (Cornell University Press, 1971)

Dearing, James W. and Rogers, Everett. *Agenda-Setting* (Sage, 1996)

Dell, Christopher. *Lincoln and the War Democrat* (Fairleigh Dickinson University Press, 1975)

Delli, Michael X. et al. *What Americans Know about Politics and Why It Matters* (Yale University Press, 1996)

Doenecke, Justus D. *Anti-Intervention: A Bibliographical Introduction to Isolationism and Pacifism from World War I to the Early Cold War* (Garland Publishing, 1987)

Douglass, Frederick. *My Bondage and My Freedom* (University of Illinois Press, 1987)

Dunkerley, James. *Power in the Isthmus: A Political History of Modern Central America* (Verso Press, 1988)

Edsall, Thomas Byrne and Edsall, Mary D. *Chain Reaction: The Impact of Race, Rights, and Taxes on American Politics* (W. W. Norton and Company, 1991)

Ehrman, John. *The Rise of Neoconservatism* (Yale University Press, 1995)

Engels, Friedrich. *The Principles of Communism* (Monthly Review Press, 1952 reprint)

Finch, Minnie. *The NAACP: Its Fight for Justice* (Scarecrow Press, 1981)

Fiorina, Morris. *Culture War?: The Myth of a Polarized America* (Pearson Longman, 2005)

Fiorina, Morris. *Retrospective Voting in American National Elections* (Yale University Press, 1981)

Flanigan, William H. and Zingale, Nancy H. *Political Behavior of the American Electorate* (CQ Press, 2006)

Fletcher, George P. *Our Secret Constitution: How Lincoln Redefined American Democracy* (Oxford University Press, 2001)

Foerstel, Herbert N. *Freedom of Information and the Right to Know* (Greenwood Press, 1999)

Franklin, Mark N. *Voter Turnout and the Dynamics of Electoral Competition in Established Democracies Since 1945* (Cambridge University Press, 2004)

Freedberg, Sydney P. *Brother Love: Murder, Money and a Messiah Ben Yahweh* (Pantheon Books, 1994)

Freidel, Frank. *The Splendid Little War* [Spanish-American War] (Dell, 1964)

Friedan, Betty. *The Feminine Mystique* (W.W. Norton, 1963)

Fromkin, David. *A Peace to End All Peace* (Avon Books, 1989)

Gillespie, David. *Politics at the Periphery: Third Parties in Two-Party America* (University of South Carolina Press, 1993)

Gorbachev, Mikhail. *Perestroika: New Thinking for Our Country and the World* (Harper and Row, 1988)

Gordon, Ann D., ed. *The Selected Papers of Elizabeth Cady Stanton and Susan B. Anthony* (Rutgers University Press, 1998)

Gould, Lewis L. *Grand Old Party: A History of the Republicans* (Random House, 2003)

Green, Donald P. and Gerber, Alan S. *Get Out the Vote: How to Increase Voter Turnout* (Brookings Institution Press, 2004)

Greenberg, Stanley B. *The Two Americas* (Thomas Dunne, 2005)

Grofman, Bernard and Davidson, Chandler. *Controversies in Minority Voting: The Voting Rights Act in Perspective* (Brookings Institution Press, 1992)

Habermas, Jürgen. *The New Conservatism: Cultural Criticism and the Historian's Debate* (MIT Press, 1989)

Hair, William Ivy. *The Kingfish and His Realm: Life and Times of Huey Long* (Louisiana State University Press, 1997)

Harding, Vincent. *Martin Luther King: The Inconvenient Hero* (Orbis, 1996)

Hart, David M. *Forged Consensus: Science, Technology and Economic Policy in the United States* (Princeton University Press, 1998)

Hatt, Christine. *Mahatma Gandhi* (World Almanac Library, 2004)

Held, David. *Models of Democracy* (Cambridge Polity Press, 2006)

Hess, Stephen and Northrup, Sandy. *Drawn and Quartered* (Elliott and Clark Publishing, 1996)

Hiro, Dilip. *Iraq: A Report From the Inside* (Granta Books, 2003)

Holsti, Ole R. *Public Opinion and American Foreign Policy* (University of Michigan Press, 2004)

Howard, Michael. *War in European History* (Oxford University Press, 2001)

Howe, Daniel Walker. *The American Whigs: An Anthology* (John Wiley, 1973)

Howe, Irving and Coser, Lewis. *The American Communist Party* (Praeger, 1957)

Huntington, Samuel P. *The Common Defense: Strategic Program in National Politics* (Columbia University Press, 1961)

Inglehart, Ronald and Welzel, Christian. *Modernization, Cultural Change, and Democracy: The Human Development Sequence* (Cambridge University Press, 2005)

Isserman, Maurice. *Which Side Were You On? The American Communist Party During the Second World War* (Wesleyan University Press, 1982)

Jacobson, Gary C. *The Politics of Congressional Elections* (Addison-Wesley, 2001)

Jacobson, Gary C. and Kernell, Samuel. *Strategy and Choice in Congressional Elections* (Yale University Press, 1981)

Johnson, Donald Bruce and Porter, Kirk H. *National Party Platforms, 1840–1972* (University of Illinois Press, 1973)

Katz, Friedrich. *The Life and Times of Pancho Villa* (Stanford University Press, 1998)

Ketcham, Ralph, ed. *The Anti-Federalist Papers and the Constitutional Convention Debates* (Mentor Books, 1986)

Key, V.O. *The Responsible Electorate: Rationality in Presidential Voting, 1936–1960* (Harvard University Press, 1966)

Keyssar, Alexander. *The Right to Vote: The Contested History of Democracy in the United States* (Basic Books, 2001)

Kousser, J. Morgan. *Colorblind Injustice: Minority Voting Rights and the Undoing of the Second Reconstruction* (University of North Carolina Press, 1999)

Kousser, J. Morgan. *The Shaping of Southern Politics* (Yale University Press, 1974)

Kyvig, David E., ed. *Unintended Consequences of Constitutional Amendments* (University of Georgia Press, 2000)

Leffler, Melvyn P. *A Preponderance of Power* (Stanford University Press, 1992)

Lichtenstein, Nelson. "Socialist Movement," *Dictionary of American History* (Thomson Gale, 2003)

Levitt, Justin, Welser, Wendy, and Munoz, Ana. *Making the List: Database Matching and Verification Processes for Voter Registration* (Brennan Center for Justice, 2006)

Lowery, David and Brasher, Holly. *Organized Interests and American Government* (McGraw Hill, 2004)

Lubell, Samuel. *The Future of American Politics* (Harper and Brothers, 1952)

Macpherson, C.B. *The Political Theory of Possessive Individualism, Hobbes to Locke* (Oxford University Press, 1962)

Maisel, Louis Sandy and Buckley, Kara Z. *Parties and Elections in America: The Electoral Process* (Rowman and Littlefield, 2004)

Mann, Robert. *A Grand Delusion: Americas Descent into Vietnam* (Basic Books, 2001)

Mark, David. *Going Dirty: The Art of Negative Campaigning* (Roman and Littlefield, 2006)

Marx, Karl. *Wage-Labour and Capital and Value, Price and Profit* (International Publishers, 1976)

Moses, Wilson J. *The Golden Age of Black Nationalism, 1850–1925* (Oxford University Press, 1988)

Nash, George H. *The Conservative Intellectual Movement in America since 1945* (Intercollegiate Studies Institute, 1998)

Nathanson, Stephen. *Should We Consent to Be Governed? A Short Introduction to Political Philosophy* (Wadsworth, 1992)

Odom, William E. *The Collapse of the Soviet Military* (Yale University Press, 1998)

Phillips, K. *The Emerging Republican Majority* (Arlington House, 1969)

Popkin, Samuel L. *The Reasoning Voter: Communication and Persuasion in Presidential Campaigns* (Chicago University Press,1991)

Powers, Richard Gid. *Not Without Honor: The History of American Anticommunism* (Yale University Press, 1998)

Reginald Horsman. *Race and Manifest Destiny* (Harvard University Press, 1981)

Remick, David. *Lenin's Tomb: The Last Days of the Soviet Empire* (Vintage, 1994)

Richardson, Darcy G. *Others: Third Party Politics From the Nation's Founding to the Rise and Fall of the Greenback-Labor Party* (iUniverse, Inc., 2004)

Rittberger, Volker, ed. *Global Governance and the United Nations System* (United Nations University Press, 2001)

Roseboom, Paolo. *A History of Presidential Elections from George Washington to Richard M. Nixon: The Definitive Account of our National Conventions, Campaigns, and Elections* (Macmillan, 1970)

Salsburg, David. *The Lady Tasting Tea: How Statistics Revolutionized Science in the Twentieth Century.* (Henry Holt, 2001)

Schrecker, Ellen. *The Age of McCarthyism* (St. Martin's Press, 1994)

Schulzinger, Robert D. *American Diplomacy in the Twentieth Century* (Oxford University Press, 1984)

Schwartz, Barry. *George Washington: The Making of an American Symbol* (Temple University Press, 1976)

Sigerman, Harriet. *Elizabeth Cady Stanton: The Right Is Ours* (Oxford University Press, 2001)

Sundquist, James L. *Dynamics of the Party System: Alignment and Realignment of Political Parties in the United States* (Brookings Institution, 1983)

Stimson, James A. *Public Opinion in America: Moods, Cycles, and Swings* (Westview Press, 1999)

Taggart, Paul. *Populism* (Maidenhead, 2000)

Thernstrom, Abigail M. *Whose Votes Count? Affirmative Action and Minority Voting Rights* (Harvard University Press, 1987)

Tibi, Bassam. *The Challenge of Fundamentalism: Political Islam and the New World Disorder* (University of California Press, 1998)

Walker, Stanley. *Dewey: An American of This Century* (Whittlesey House, 1944)

Ware, Alan. *The American Direct Primary: Party Institutionalization and Transformation in the North* (Cambridge University Press, 2002)

Wattenberg, Martin. *Is Voting for Young People?* (Pearson Longman, 2007)

Witcover, Jules. *Marathon: The Pursuit of the Presidency: 1972–1976* (Viking Press, 1977)

Wheeler, Majorie Spruill. *One Woman, One Vote* (NewSage Press, 1995)

White, John Kenneth. *The Values Divide: American Politics and Culture in Transition* (Chatham House, 2002)

White, John Kenneth and Shea, Daniel M. *New Party Politics: From Jefferson and Hamilton to the Information Age.* (Bedford/St. Martin's, 2000)

Woodward, Bob. *State of Denial: Bush at War, Part III* (Simon and Schuster, 2006)

Yarmolinsky, Avrahm. *Road to Revolution: A Century of Russian Radicalism* (Collier Books, 1962)

Zaller, John R. *The Nature and Origins of Mass Opinion* (Cambridge University Press, 1992)

JOURNALS, NEWSPAPERS, AND MAGAZINES

American Academy of Political and Social Sciences
American Journal of Political Science
American Political Quarterly
American Political Science Review
American Politics Journal
American Politics Research
British Journal of Political Science
Canadian Journal of Political Science
Chinese Political Science Review
Electoral Studies
European Journal of Political Theory
European Political Science
International Political Science Review
Journal of Democracy
Journal of Politics
Legislative Studies Quarterly
Midwest Journal of Political Science
National Political Science Review
Party Politics
Political Analysis
Political Behavior
Political Science Forum
Political Science Quarterly
Publius
Religion and American Politics
Southwestern Mass Communication Journal
The Washington Quarterly

INTERNET SOURCES

www.aipca.org – American Independent Party
www.americancentristparty.com – American Centrist Party
www.americanfascistparty.com – American Fascist Party
www.americafirstparty.org – America First Party
www.americannaziparty.com – American Nazi Party
www.americanreform.org – American Reform Party
www.communist-party.org – Communist Partyw
www.completecampaigns.com – Complete Campaigns
www.constitution-party.net – Constitution Party
www.cpgb.org – Communist Party of Great Britain
www.dsausa.org – Democratic Socialist Party
www.democrats.org – Democratic Party
www.falange.us – Christian Falangist Party of America
www.greenpart.org – Green Party
www.idu.net – Iraqi Democratic Union
www.lightparty.com – Light Party
www.lp.org – Libertarian Party
www.mnip.org – Independence Party
www.natural-law.org – Natural Law Party
www.newparty.org – New Party
www.newunionparty.org – New Union Party
www.nsm88.com – National Socialist Movement
www.peaceandfreedom.org – Peace and Freedom Party
www.politicalgraveyard.com – Political Graveyard
www.prohibition.org – Prohibition Party
www.republicans.org – Republican Party
www.socialistaction.org – Socialist Action Party
www.socialequality.com – Socialist Equality Party
www.socialistparty.org – Socialist Party
www.slp.org – Socialist Labor Party
www.spd.de – German Socialist Party
www.theamericanparty.org – American Party
www.thelaborparty.org – Labor Party
www.themilitant.com – Socialist Workers Party
www.uspacifistparty.org – U.S.A. Pacifist Party
www.veteransparty.us – Veterans Party of America
www.workersparty.org – U.S.A. Workers Party
www.workers.org – Workers World Party

Index

Note: Page numbers in **boldface** refer to volume numbers and major topics. Article titles are in **boldface**.

race and voting behavior, **2**:690
racial preferences, **1**:48
Republican Party and, **1**:47–48
Asian/Pacific-American (APA), **1**:47–48
Askew, Reubin, **1**:248
assassination
Abraham Lincoln, **2**:698, **2**:745
James A. Garfield, **2**:491
John F. Kennedy, **1**:175, **2**:640
William McKinley, **1**:34, **2**:608
Assembly of Freemen, **1**:393
Association for Public Opinion Research, **1**:425
Association of State Green Parties (ASGP), **1**:289
Atiyeh, Victor George, **2**:477
Atkinson, George W., **2**:867
Atlanta Constitution, **1**:281
Atlanta Journal Constitution, **2**:508
at-large election, 1:48–49
district elections *vs.,* **1**:48
political reform, **1**:48–49
state senates, **1**:49
Australian ballot, 1:50, 1:56
adoption of, **1**:50
Tasmanian Dodge, **1**:50
in U.S., **1**:50
AWSA. *See* American Women Suffrage Association (AWSA)
Axtell, Samuel, **2**:449
Aycock, Charles Brantley, **2**:462

B
Babbitt, Bruce, **2**:655
Babel Proclamation, **1**:328
Bacon, Gaspar, **1**:398
Badcock, Tim M., **1**:426
Baer, Max, **2**:494
Bailey, Edward F., **2**:477
Baker, Howard, **2**:650
Baker v. Carr, **1**:147
Bakke, Allan, **1**:12
Baladacci, John, **1**:389–90
balanced ticket, 1:51–52
ancestry and, **1**:52
campaign strategy, **1**:51
common qualities, **1**:51
religion and voting behavior, **1**:52
Baldwin, Raymond E., **1**:136
Baldwin, Sherman, **1**:135
ballot controversies, 1:52–55
addressing, **1**:53
direct democracy, **1**:53
finance regulation, **1**:54–55
public benefit, **1**:55
resource bias, **1**:53–54
ballot issues, 1:55–58
absentee voting, **1**:56–57
counting ballots, **1**:57–58
DREs, **1**:58
getting on ballot, **1**:55–56

paper ballots, **1**:58
punch-card system, **1**:57–58
roll-off, **1**:56
secrecy problem, **1**:56–57
straight-arm voting, **1**:56
voting machines, **1**:57
Ballot Issue Strategy Center (BISC), **1**:54
Baltimore Sun, **2**:546
Bamberger, Simon, **2**:811
bandwagon effect, 1:58–59
Bank of United States
Andrew Jackson and, **1**:157, **2**:569
opposition to, **2**:431
second, **1**:177, **2**:434
Banks, Nathaniel Prentice, **1**:397
Barber, Amos Walker, **2**:873
Barber, David, **2**:732–33
Barbour, Haley, **1**:421
Baring, Walter S., Jr., **2**:440
Barkley, Charles, **1**:73
Barlocker, William A., **2**:812
Barnes, Ben, **2**:790
Barnett, Ross, **1**:170
Barngeter, Borman Howard, **2**:813
Barone, Michael, **1**:60
Barron, William Wallace, **2**:868
Barrows, Lewis O., **1**:389
Barry, John S., **1**:406
Barstow, William A., **2**:872
Bartlett, Dewey F., **2**:475
Bashford, Coles, **2**:872
Basset, Richard, **1**:167
Bates, Curtis, **1**:328
Bates, Frederick, **1**:422
battleground states, 1:59–61
defining, **1**:59
electoral votes, **1**:60–61
Bauer, Gary, **1**:221
Baum, Elmer, **2**:790
Baumgartner, Jody, **1**:402
Bayard, James A., **2**:555
Bayard, Thomas, **2**:594
Bayh, Evan, **1**:323–24
Bay of Pigs invasion, **1**:136
BCRA. *See* Bipartisan Campaign Reform Act (BCRA)
"The Bear" ad, **1**:7
Beck, George T., **2**:873
Beckham, J. C. W., **1**:349
Beckley, John, **1**:82
Bedford, Guning, Sr., **1**:167
Begich, Nick, **1**:28
Begole, Josiah, **1**:406
Bell, Frank, **2**:439, **2**:745
Bell, John, **1**:141, **1**:348, **1**:388, **2**:584
Bellmon, Henry, **2**:475
bell-shaped curve, 1:61–62
deviations, **1**:62
mathematics, **1**:62

Nestos, Ragnvald A., 2:463
Neustadt, Richard, 2:732–33
Neutrality Acts, 1:331
Nevada, 2:439–41
  Comstock Lode, 2:439
  governors, 2:439
  Hoover Dam, 2:440
  Las Vegas, 2:439–40
  Paul Laxalt in, 2:440–41
  presidential elections, 2:440
  Purity of Elections Act (1895), 2:439
  recent elections, 2:441
  Silver-Democratic Party, 2:439
  Silver Party, 2:439
  statehood, 2:439
Newberry v. United States, 1:145
New Deal, 1:35, 1:43, 1:71, 2:624, 2:727, 2:857
  Catholic vote and, 1:112
  Franklin Roosevelt and, 1:68, 1:135, 2:866
  fundraising restrictions, 1:260
  Great Depression/realignment and, 1:286
  liberalism and, 1:368
New Democratic Club, 2:509
Newell, William A., 2:447
New England Watch and Ward Society, 1:398
New Hampshire, 2:441–43
  bellwether state, 1:63
  early party affiliations, 2:442
  governors, 2:442
  later elections, 2:442
  political role, 2:442–43
  presidential elections, 2:442, 2:443
New Hampshire Primary, 2:443–46
  Edmund Muskie in, 2:645
  eligibility, 2:445–46
  first held, 2:444
  first in nation, 2:445
  impact, 2:446
  nomination process reform, 2:444–45
  positive messages, 2:446
  winners 1952-2004, 2:445
Newhouse, Neil, 2:529
New Jersey, 2:446–49
  early U.S. history, 2:446–47
  governors, 2:447–49
  presidential elections, 2:447–48
  20th century politics, 2:447–48
New Left policies, 1:197
Newman, Edwin, 2:546
New Mexico, 2:449–51
  governors, 2:449–51
  presidential elections, 2:450–51
  recent elections, 2:450–51
  statehood/20th century, 2:449–50
New Nationalism, 1:68
New Republic, 2:857
Newsom, Gavin, 1:272
new voters, 2:694–95

New York, 2:451–54
  city and state, 2:454
  governors, 2:451–52
  multi-party system, 2:452
  presidential elections, 2:453–54
  presidents, 2:451
  senators, 2:452–53
New York Herald, 2:537
New York Times, 1:376
New York Tribune, 1:370
New Zealand, 1:428
Ney, Robert, 1:144
NFU (National Farmers Union), 1:231
Nicaragua Canal, 2:480
Nice, Harry, 1:395
Nie, Norman, 1:214
Nigh, George, 2:475
Nightline, 1:142
Nigro, Russell, 2:494
Nineteenth Amendment, 1:14, 1:201, 2:454–55, 2:539, 2:822
  eighteen-year-olds, 2:774
  ratification, 2:455, 2:677, 2:772
  women's vote, 1:203, 2:454–55
NIRA (National Industry Recovery Act), 1:356
Nixon, Richard, 1:2, 1:27, 1:30, 1:35–37, 1:43, 1:71, 1:136, 2:727, 2:859
  approval ratings, 2:543
  campaign funding, 1:77
  candidate image, 1:109
  "Checkers speech," 2:635
  debates, 2:545–46
  draft and, 1:164
  foreign policy experience, 2:638
  landslide elections, 1:361
  pardoned by Gerald Ford, 2:731, 2:865
  presidential election of 1952, 2:633–35
  presidential election of 1956, 2:637
  presidential election of 1968, 2:642–45
  resignation, 1:33, 2:647, 2:731
  scandals, 2:731
  Southern Strategy, 2:794, 2:848
  Watergate and, 2:863–65
Nixon v. Condon, 1:145
Nixon v. Herndon, 1:145
Nix, Robert, Sr., 2:494
NLRB. *See* National Labor Relations Board (NLRB)
NLU. *See* National Labor Union (NLU)
Noble Order of the Knights of Labor, 1:356
No Child Left Behind (NCLB), 1:193
Noel, Philip William, 2:721
Nolan Chart, 1:372
Nolan, David, 1:372
Noland, William, 2:872
nomination process, presidential, 2:456–57
  conventions/primaries, 2:456
  McGovern-Fraser Committee, 2:456
  reform, 2:456–57
non-affiliated voters (NAV), 1:319

Photo Credits

U.S. Library of Congress: 2, 15, 17, 35, 40, 43, 57, 66, 70, 72, 89, 109, 120, 123, 126, 132, 160, 163, 169, 176, 239, 240, 241, 249, 251, 274, 281, 286, 294, 306, 317, 329, 340, 342, 352, 357, 364, 370, 389, 400, 413, 430, 448, 449, 453, 455, 473, 481, 487, 507, 510, 517, 539, 546, 553, 554, 558, 562, 565, 567, 571, 573, 577, 580, 585, 593, 595, 599, 604, 606, 608, 614, 621, 630, 639, 648, 655, 664, 675, 677, 693, 698, 703, 719, 738, 744, 773, 776, 789, 794, 795, 799, 809, 812, 820, 851, 856, 864, 870; I-Stock: 233, 312; 440; 770; Photos.com: Front Covers, 62, 82, 153, 194, 196, 220, 291, 298, 333, 377, 423, 468, 494, 740, 768, 783; www.hillaryclinton.com 10; U.S. Census Bureau 19; Ronald Reagan Library 140; U.S. Air Force 165; Edison Media Research 213; U.S. Army 255, 731, 860; www.kansas.gov 346; www.kentucky.gov 349; www.fema.gov 420; www.mass.gov 397; www.oregon.gov 477.